Tolley's Inheritance Tax 2015-16

by

Malcolm Gunn CTA (Fellow) TEP

Tolley®

Members of the LexisNexis Group worldwide

United Kingdom	Reed Elsevier (UK) Limited trading as LexisNexis, 1-3 Strand, London WC2N 5JR
Australia	LexisNexis, Chatswood, New South Wales
Austria	LexisNexis Verlag ARD Orac GmbH & Co KG, Vienna
Benelux	LexisNexis Benelux, Amsterdam
Canada	LexisNexis Canada, Markham, Ontario
China	LexisNexis China, Beijing and Shanghai
France	LexisNexis SA, Paris
Germany	LexisNexis GmbH, Dusseldorf
Hong Kong	LexisNexis Hong Kong, Hong Kong
India	LexisNexis India, New Delhi
Italy	Giuffrè Editore, Milan
Japan	LexisNexis Japan, Tokyo
Malaysia	Malayan Law Journal Sdn Bhd, Kuala Lumpur
New Zealand	LexisNexis NZ Ltd, Wellington
Singapore	LexisNexis Singapore, Singapore
South Africa	LexisNexis, Durban
USA	LexisNexis, Dayton, Ohio

Published by LexisNexis
This is a Tolley title

A CIP Catalogue record for this book is available from the British Library.

ISBN for this volume: 9780754550693

Printed and bound by CPI Group (UK) Ltd, Croydon, CRO 4YY

Visit LexisNexis at www.lexisnexis.co.uk

Tolley's Inheritance Tax

About This Book

In 2010 we relaunched the Tolley's Tax Annuals to make them more practical and easier to use. They still contain the same trusted, valuable content but now you can find the answer you need even quicker than before.

What are the key changes?

- Key points – to direct you to matters that are of use in planning, or to areas of difficulty you may come across in practice.
- There are further practical examples – highly valued interpretation to help you understand the effects of the legislation on your day to day work. Examples are set in shaded boxes so they stand out if you need to go straight to practical interpretation.
- More contributions from practitioners using their own valuable experience.
- New, clearer text design – larger font and more white space for a more comfortable reading experience.
- Clearer contents – easier to read.
- The law and practice for the last four years is included and we have dispensed with any unnecessary historical text and statutory references.
- There are introductions for chapters – so that you can see quickly what is covered.
- We have split chapters where relevant – to break down the information into more manageable chunks and the structure of chapters has been improved.
- More headings have been introduced, with more distinct levels so that you can find the section that you want to read easily.
- Where appropriate, text has been converted to tables and lists to save you time and sentences shortened.

We hope that the new style meets your requirement for greater accessibility to the changing tax legislation and the ever increasing demands on you as a practitioner. We would be pleased to receive your feedback on the new style and any suggestions for further improvements. You can do this by emailing the Editor, Lisa Moore at lisa.moore@lexisnexis.co.uk. Technical queries will be dealt with by the author.

The text of this work has had significant editorial work to improve and clarify the text and includes full coverage of *Finance Act 2015* changes, including the new relief for estates with 10% or more in charitable gifts. Also included is a summary of current IHT planning techniques and all other relevant material to 1 July 2015 e.g. statutes, statutory instruments, court cases, Tribunal decisions, press releases, concessions, Statements of Practice, HMRC Briefs, and other publications.

Contributors

Malcolm Gunn CTA (Fellow) TEP

Malcolm Gunn is a fellow of the Chartered Institute of Taxation and a member of the Society of Trust and Estate Practitioners. He has over 40 years of experience in advising on UK tax matters. For 16 years he was editor of the weekly magazine Taxation, and in 2004 he left the magazine to concentrate on tax consultancy and advisory work, with particular focus on capital taxes and tax planning for individuals and family businesses.

Contents

Abbreviations and References

Abbreviations

A-G	Attorney-General.
AIM	Alternative Investment Market.
CA	Court of Appeal.
CCA	Court of Criminal Appeal.
CCAB	Consultative Committee of Accountancy Bodies.
CGT	Capital Gains Tax.
Ch	Chapter.
Ch D	Chancery Division.
CIR	Commissioners of HMRC ('the Board').
Commr(s)	Commissioner(s) (General or Special).
CPA	Civil Partnership Act 2004.
CTO	HMRC Capital Taxes Office.
CTT	Capital Transfer Tax.
CTTA 1984	Capital Transfer Tax Act 1984.
DTR	Double Taxation Relief.
DV	District Valuer.
ESC	HMRC Extra-Statutory Concession.
FA	Finance Act.
Fam D	Family Division (formerly Probate, Divorce and Admiralty Division).
FTT	First-tier Tax Tribunal.
HC	House of Commons.
HL	House of Lords.
HMRC	Her Majesty's Revenue and Customs.
HMRCC	Her Majesty's Revenue and Customs Commissioners.
ICTA 1970	Income and Corporation Taxes Act 1970.

ICTA 1988	Income and Corporation Taxes Act 1988.
IHT	Inheritance Tax.
IHTA 1984	Inheritance Tax Act 1984.
IHTM	Inheritance Tax Manual.
IPDI	Immediate Post-Death Interest.
ITA	Income Tax Act 2007.
ITEPA 2003	Income Tax (Earnings and Pensions) Act 2003.
ITTOIA 2005	Income Tax (Trading and Other Income) Act 2005.
NAO	National Audit Office.
NI	Northern Ireland.
PC	Privy Council.
PCm	Personal Contact (HMRC Manual).
PDA	Probate, Divorce and Admiralty Division (now Family Division).
Pt	Part.
QB	Queen's Bench Division.
R	Rex or Regina (i.e. The Crown).
RI	Republic of Ireland (Eire).
s	Section.
Sch	Schedule [4 Sch para 10 = 4th Schedule, paragraph 10].
SC	Supreme Court.
SCS	Scottish Court of Session.
SDLT	Stamp Duty Land Tax.
SI	Statutory Instrument.
SP	HMRC Statement of Practice. (SP 7/87, 15 July 1987 = 7th Statement of Practice in 1987 issued on date shown).
SVD	Shares Valuation Division.
TCGA 1992	Taxation of Chargeable Gains Act 1992.
TSI	Transitional Serial Interest.
UKFTT	UK First-tier Tax Tribunal.
USM	Unlisted Securities Market.
VOA	Valuation Office Agency.

References

(*denotes a series accredited for citation in court).

All ER	*All England Law Reports, (Butterworths, Halsbury House, 35 Chancery Lane, London WC2A 1EL).
AC	*Law Reports, Appeal Cases, (Incorporated Council of Law Reporting for England and Wales, 3 Stone Buildings, Lincoln's Inn, London WC2A 3XN).
ATC	*Annotated Tax Cases (publication discontinued).
BTC	British Tax Cases, CCH Editions Ltd, Telford Road, Bicester, Oxfordshire OX6 0XD.
Ch	*Law Reports, Chancery Division.
EG	Estates Gazette, (The Estates Gazette Ltd., 151 Wardour Street, London W1V 4BN).
ILT	Irish Law Times.
IR	*Irish Reports, (Law Reporting Council, Law Library, Four Courts, Dublin).
KB	*Law Reports, King's Bench Division (1900–1952).
LT	Decisions of the Lands Tribunal, (Lands Tribunal, 48–49 Chancery Lane, London WC2A 1JR).
[Year] QB	*Law Reports, Queen's Bench Division (1891–1901 and 1952 onwards).
QBD	Law Reports, Queen's Bench Division (1875–1890).
Sp C	Special Commissioners' decisions, (The Court Service, 15/19 Bedford Avenue, London WC1B 3AS).
SLT	Scots Law Times.
SCD	*Simon's Special Commissioners' Decisions, (Butterworths, as above).
STC	*Simon's Tax Cases, (Butterworths, as above).
STI	Simon's Tax Intelligence, (Butterworths, as above).
TC	*Official Reports of Tax Cases, (H.M. Stationery Office, as above).
TLR	Times Law Reports.
TR	*Taxation Reports (publication discontinued).
WLR	*Weekly Law Reports, (Incorporated Council of Law Reporting, as above).

The first number in the citation refers to the volume, and the second to the page, so that [1979] 2 All ER 80 means that the report is to be found on page eighty of the second volume of the All England Law Reports for 1979. Where no volume number is given, only one volume was produced in that year. Some series have continuous volume numbers.

The Tax Chamber First-tier Tax Tribunal decisions now replace the previous General Commissioners and citation references have changed to reflect this such as FTT [2009] UKFTT 141(TC), TC00109 showing the tax case year and report number followed by the hearing number in the Tax Tribunal. Earlier cases heard before the General and Special Commissioners are still shown by their original citation reference before the change.

Where legal decisions are very recent and in the lower Courts, it must be remembered that they may be reversed on appeal. But references to the official Tax Cases ('*TC*'), and to the Appeal Cases ('*AC*') may be taken as final.

In English cases, Scottish and N. Irish decisions (unless there is a difference of law between the countries) are generally followed but are not binding, and Republic of Ireland decisions are considered (and vice versa).

Acts of Parliament, Command Papers, 'Hansard' Parliamentary Reports and Statutory Instruments are obtainable from The Stationery Office, (bookshops at 12 Bridge Street, Parliament Square,, London SW1A 2JX (tel 0207 219 3890) and elsewhere at http://www.tso.co.uk/contact/bookshops/ **Hansard** (referred to as HC Official Report or HL Official Report) references are to daily issues and do not always correspond to the columns in the bound editions. **N.B.** Statements in Parliament, while useful as indicating the intention of enactments, have no legal authority if the Courts interpret the wording of the Act differently (except in the limited circumstances mentioned in **14.13** DETERMINATIONS AND APPEALS).

1

Introduction and Basic Principles

Simon's Taxes. See **I1.3, I1.4.**

Other Sources. Foster, Part A and E1.02.

Introduction

[1.1] The aim of this chapter is to provide a brief outline of the principal features and key concepts of inheritance tax. It is intended to illustrate only the basic mechanism of the tax as this is essential for an understanding of the detailed provisions covered in the following chapters. For complete details of any particular topic or area, reference should be made to the appropriate chapter.

Function and scope of tax

[1.2] Inheritance tax is a tax on chargeable transfers made by an *individual* during his life and on the value of his estate on his death. Various exemptions and reliefs are available to lessen the impact of the tax.

The tax is charged on certain events relating to settled property and there is a separate charging structure for settlements without interests in possession. See 43 SETTLEMENTS: DISCRETIONARY TRUSTS AND OTHER TRUSTS OF RELEVANT PROPERTY for new trusts arising on or after 22 March 2006. In addition, certain transfers made by close companies may be attributed to the individual participators. See 11 CLOSE COMPANIES.

Individuals domiciled in the UK are liable to inheritance tax on all chargeable transfers, whether or not the property transferred is situated in the UK. Individuals not domiciled in the UK are not liable to IHT on transfers of property situated outside the UK but are so liable, with certain exceptions, on chargeable transfers of property in the UK. In certain circumstances double tax relief may be available. See 16 DOMICILE for the extended IHT meaning of 'domicile', 20 EXCLUDED PROPERTY and 49 SITUS for full details of what property is outside the scope of the tax, and 18 DOUBLE TAXATION RELIEF for situations where DTR may be available.

Starting date and main changes to CTT

[1.3] The revised provisions relating to inheritance tax effectively replaced capital transfer tax for events occurring after 17 March 1986 although the name of the tax was not formally changed until 25 July 1986, the date of Royal Assent to the *Finance Act 1986*. The revised provisions do not affect the tax chargeable on a transfer of value occurring before 18 March 1986. [*FA 1986, Sch 19 para 40*]. However, chargeable transfers made before that date and within the lifetime cumulation period for IHT purposes may affect the tax payable on subsequent transfers.

The main amendments to the CTT provisions in the IHT legislation are:

(a) the removal of liability for tax on certain transfers of value where the transfer occurs at least seven years before the transferor's death;
(b) the reduction in the period during which the values transferred by chargeable transfers are aggregated from ten to seven years;
(c) the increase in the period before death within which tax on chargeable lifetime transfers is recomputed at the higher rates applicable on death from three to seven years (but subject to the introduction of taper relief where the transfer is more than three years before death); and
(d) the re-introduction of legislation for 22 GIFTS WITH RESERVATION similar to the old estate duty provisions.

The *Capital Transfer Tax Act 1984* may be cited as the *Inheritance Tax Act 1984*. Any reference to CTT in the *1984 Act* or any other Act passed before or in the same session as the *FA 1986* or any document executed, made, served or issued on or before the passing of *FA 1986* has effect as a reference to inheritance tax unless relating to a liability to tax arising before 25 July 1986. [*FA 1986, s 100*].

Charge to tax

[1.4] Inheritance tax is charged on the value transferred by a chargeable transfer. [*IHTA 1984, s 1*].

A chargeable transfer is any transfer of value made by an individual other than an 21 EXEMPT TRANSFER. [*IHTA 1984, s 2(1)*].

A potentially exempt transfer (PET)

A potentially exempt transfer (PET) is a transfer of value made by an individual after 17 March 1986 but before 22 March 2006 which would otherwise be a chargeable transfer and which is either a gift to another individual or a gift into an accumulation and maintenance trust or a trust for a disabled person. After 21 March 2006 a PET is a transfer of value made by an individual which would otherwise be a chargeable transfer and which is either a gift to another individual (see Example 1 below) or into a trust for a disabled person or into a trust for bereaved minors on the ending of an immediate post-death interest (IPDI). See **42** SETTLEMENTS WITH INTERESTS IN POSSESSION and **46** SETTLEMENTS: TRUSTS FOR BEREAVED MINORS.

With respect to transfers of value made, and other events occurring, after 16 March 1987 but before 22 March 2006, certain gifts by individuals into and out of settlements with interests in possession are also included. From 22 March 2006, however, there are certain transitional rules that ensure that new interest in possession which are created out existing ones before 6 October 2008 (originally 6 April 2008) i.e. TSIs ('transitional serial interests') still will qualify as PETs. See **38** POTENTIALLY EXEMPT TRANSFERS for full details. A potentially exempt transfer made seven years or more before the transferor's death is an exempt transfer and any other potentially exempt transfer is a chargeable transfer. A potentially exempt transfer is assumed to be an exempt transfer during the seven years following the transfer (or, if earlier, until immediately before the transferor's death). [*IHTA 1984, s 3A; FA 1986, Sch 19 para 1; F(No 2)A 1987, s 96; FA 2006, Sch 20 para 9; FA 2010, s 53(2)*].

In summary therefore a PET will, from 22 March 2006, comprise:

- transfers by individuals to other individuals;
- transfers by individuals to certain trusts for the disabled (see **47** SETTLEMENTS: TRUSTS FOR DISABLED PERSONS);
- transfers on or after 22 March 2006 by an individual to a bereaved minor's trust on the coming to an end of an immediate post-death interest (see **46** SETTLEMENTS: TRUSTS FOR BEREAVED MINORS);
- transfers before 22 March 2006 by an individual to an accumulation and maintenance trust (see *Marquess of Linlithgow v HMRC (and related appeals)* [2010] CSIH 19 at **44** SETTLEMENTS: ACCUMULATION AND MAINTENANCE TRUSTS);
- transfers by an individual into an interest in possession trust in which, for transfers on or after 22 March 2006, the beneficiary has a disabled person's interest (see **47** SETTLEMENTS: TRUSTS FOR DISABLED PERSONS); and
- certain transfers on the termination or disposal of an individual's beneficial interest in possession in settled property (these are in restricted circumstances following *FA 2006* and *FA 2010* below and at **31** LIFE ASSURANCE POLICIES AND ANNUITIES; **42** SETTLEMENTS WITH INTERESTS IN POSSESSION).

FA 2010 PET anti-avoidance

Following the *Finance Act 2010* it was clarified that a potential loophole whereby a person makes a settlement which confers an interest in possession on another person was to be blocked from 9 December 2009. That other person, it suggests, pays full value within *IHTA 1984, s 10* (i.e. arm's length price between two unconnected people) for the interest in settled property. In such an event neither person would have made a transfer of value because of *s 10*. The settled property then falls out of the estate of the purchaser of the interest because *IHTA 1984, s 5(1)(1A)* has the effect that an interest in possession (but this does not apply to a disabled person's interest) acquired under a new lifetime settlement made after 21 March 2006 does not for IHT purposes form part of the estate of the person entitled to the interest in possession. The new legislation has the effect of applying to a *s 5(1B)* interest the IHT charging provisions relating to the termination of an interest in possession during the life of the person entitled to it, and prevent such an event from being a potentially exempt transfer.

In summary, this anti-avoidance strategy ensures that the pre-22 March 2006 IHT treatment for settled property subject to an interest in possession also applies to settled property subject to an interest in possession to which a person domiciled in the UK became beneficially entitled on or after 9 December 2009 by virtue of a disposition not intended to confer gratuitous benefit, i.e. *s 10*. See below. [*IHTA 1984, ss 3A, 5 as amended by FA 2010, s 53(2)(3)(10)*].

Transfer of value

A transfer of value is any disposition made by a person as a result of which the value of his estate immediately after the disposition is less than it would be but for the disposition; and the amount by which it is less is the value transferred by the transfer. A person is treated as making a notional transfer of value of his whole estate immediately before his death. [*IHTA 1984, s 3(1), s 4(1)*]. A disposition is not a transfer of value if made in an arm's length (or similar) transaction. [*IHTA 1984, s 10*]. (See **51** TRANSFER OF VALUE for extended meanings of 'transfer of value' and 'disposition' and **52** TRANSFERS ON DEATH for provisions relating specifically to such transfers.)

Since the reduction in value in a person's estate includes the payment of the IHT itself where this is paid by the transferor, it is necessary in such cases to gross-up the 'net' value at the appropriate tax rate (see **1.7** below).

Person's estate

A person's estate is the combination of all the property to which *he* is beneficially entitled. However, a person's estate immediately before his death (on which inheritance tax is payable) does not include excluded property. A person beneficially entitled to an interest in possession in settled property is treated as beneficially entitled to that property excepting trust property held on statutory trusts applying at age 18 arising for minor children due to intestacy or trusts drawn in similar terms by reason of the parent's will or as a result of the Criminal Injuries Compensation Scheme. This treatment also applies where a person becomes beneficially entitled to an interest in possession after 21 March 2006 and the interest is not an immediate post-death interest or a disabled person's interest or a transitional serial interest. [*IHTA 1984, ss 5(1)(1A), 49(1), 71A; FA 2006, Sch 20 para 10*]. See *Faulkner (Adams' Trustee) v CIR* [2001] STC SCD 112 Sp C 278. See **19** ESTATE for extensions and qualifications of this basic definition.

Example 1

A wishes to pay for his grandson AA's school fees in respect of attendance at independent school and contracts with the said school (see below) for a one-off payment in the current year to be made of £74,000 in advance which will ensure that the child's education is paid for from the age of 13 to 18 without any increases in school fees over the period. Mr A has only made previous transfers to his son in 2009/10 of £318,000 which equates to a cumulation of £312,000 after using available annual exemptions as at 6 April 2010. Mr A has also agreed with the school that there will not be a refund due to Mr A of the school fees on his death.

This agreement is made between the Governors of [**Select Independent School**] by their duly authorised officer [**A. Bursar**] (hereinafter called 'the school') of the first part; and [**Mr A**].

Whereas it is proposed that [**Mr A**] does make a payment of school fees to the school until [**Mr A's**] grandson [**Master AA**] completes full time education (or as the case may be). Such said fees shall be paid to the school by [**Mr A**] in advance in the sum of £74,000 and the receipt by the school shall be sufficient discharge.

1. In consideration of the payment by [**Mr A**] of the said school fees the school agrees to keep a place open for the child [**Master AA**] until he has completed full time education or cease such education at the agreement of the contracting parties.

Etc.

This is a transfer of value within *IHTA 1984, s 3(1)* since the value of A's estate is diminished by the disposition. However, Master AA does not receive any property from A so the gift is not within *IHTA 1984, s 3A(2)(a)*. But whilst benefiting Master AA is his estate increased? Is therefore the transfer a PET?

Under *IHTA 1984, s 3A(2)(b)*, where property does not becomes comprised in the estate of another person, a transfer may still be treated as a gift to an individual provided two conditions are satisfied. These conditions are that:

(a) property does not become comprised in the estate of another person (not 'individual'), but

(b) the estate of another individual is increased.

The first condition is not satisfied because the cash given does not become directly comprised in the estate of Master AA. The second condition is not satisfied either even though the value of Master AA's estate is effectively increased by the gift. This is because the value transferred is attributable to property that has become comprised in the estate of another person. See also IHTM04058 and IHTM04060.

On the one hand tested against the definition of a PET, the gift is a transfer of value by Mr A which is chargeable but on the other hand it does not satisfy the condition that it is a transfer to an individual and cannot therefore be treated as a PET.

As IHT is based on the 'loss to the donor' principle the 'gift' of the payment to the school of the fees of the grandchild would potentially be immediately chargeable to IHT because the gift is not to an individual. Obviously if there is part (or all) of the Nil rate band available to cover the fees paid directly to the school then no actual tax would be payable. However, on death a chargeable transfer should be taken into account again when applying death rates. Whereas if the cash is given to the child or grandchild (bearing in mind the giving good receipt problem for grandchildren) then it will drop out of account after seven years. In this case though Mr A has already utilised a majority of his Nil rate band and the following calculation has to be made.

Transferor (Mr A) bears tax

		£	£
Value of gift			74,000
Deduct exempt transfers	Note (A)		
Annual exemption 2010/11		3,000	
Annual exemption 2009/10		N/A	
			3,000
			71,000
Tax on £71,000 + £312,000 (per grossing-up table **40.1** 2010.B2). See also **1.7** below.			
0–325,000 = Nil + ¼ (383,000 – 325,000)			14,500
Mr A's chargeable transfer			£85,500
Tax payable by Mr A			£14,500

Notes to the example

(A) As A has made previous transfers up to the Nil rate band threshold only part i.e. £13,000 (£325,000 – £312,000) to set against the transfer but also he will have only one year of annual exemption available to deduct from the transfer of value.

(B) The transfer of value is £88,500. A's estate is reduced by the gift of £74,000 plus the tax of £14,500 and has proved to an expensive way of funding the fees. With better planning Mr A should have made the school fees contribution before the gift of £318,000 to his son and utilised part of the nil rate band to cover the gift. The gift to the son would be a PET and drop out of account after seven years or, if Mr A died within the seven years, be covered by part of the nil rate band and possibly attract tapering relief on the balance. See **53** TRANSFERS WITHIN SEVEN YEARS OF DEATH.

Amount of tax charge

Rates

[1.5] After 14 March 1988 inheritance tax is charged at a single rate of 40%. After 17 March 1986 and before 15 March 1988 it was charged at progressively steeper rates. Only one table of rates is enacted which is applicable to transfers on death. Chargeable lifetime transfers are charged at one half of those rates, currently 20%, throughout the range of rate bands. Transfers made within seven years of death are charged at the death rates but in the case of chargeable transfers made in that period and more than three years before death, the tax charge is tapered. See **40** RATES OF TAX for tables and **53** TRANSFERS WITHIN SEVEN YEARS BEFORE DEATH for taper relief.

Cumulation

[1.6] Chargeable transfers are cumulated over a seven-year period and the rate of tax on any chargeable transfer will depend on the total value of any other chargeable transfers within the seven-year period ending with the date of the transfer (including, where applicable, chargeable transfers made before 18 March 1986 under the rules relating to Capital Transfer Tax). After seven years transfers drop out of the cumulative total. After 5 April 2009 no tax is payable on the first £325,000 of chargeable transfers as the rate is nil per cent. For the following year 2010–11 to the year 2014–15 the threshold remains at £325,000. See **40** RATES OF TAX for tables. Lower limits applied previously. References are made to the 'nil rate band maximum' which means that calculated in accordance with *IHTA 1984, s 8A(7)* and the Table depending on the date of death as stipulated in *FA 2008, Sch 4 para 10*. [*IHTA 1984, ss 7, 8, Sch 1; FA 1986, Sch 19 para 2; FA 2010, s 8*].

Grossing-up

[1.7] Although inheritance tax is essentially a tax based on the loss to the person giving rather than on the benefit to the person receiving, the tax itself may be paid either by the transferor or the transferee. Where the tax is paid by the transferor, it is part of the diminution in value of his estate and is itself included in the transfer of value. A 'net' transfer has to be grossed-up to arrive at the amount of the chargeable transfer.

Example 2

A transfers £352,000 to a discretionary trust on 1 October 2010. He has made no previous transfers.

(i) Transferor (A) bears tax

		£	£
Value of gift			352,000
Deduct exempt transfers	note (A)		
Annual exemption 2010/11		3,000	
Annual exemption 2009/10		3,000	
			6,000
			346,000
Tax on £346,000 (per grossing-up table 40.1 2010.B2)			
0–346,000 = Nil + $^1/_4$ (346,000 – 325,000)			5,250
A's chargeable transfer			£351,250
Tax payable by A			£5,250

Notes to the example

(A) As A has made no previous transfers he will have two years' annual exemptions available but in cases where *FA 1986, s 102(4)* creates a deemed PET the annual exemption is not available. See http://www.hmrc.gov.uk/manuals/ihtmanual/index.htm. **21.13** EXEMPT TRANSFERS; **22** GIFTS WITH RESERVATION.

(B) The transfer of value is £357,250. A's estate is reduced by the gift of £352,000 plus the tax of £5,250.

(ii) Transferees (trustees) bear tax

	£	£
Value of gift		352,000
Deduct exempt transfers (as in (i))		6,000
A's chargeable transfer		£346,000
Tax on £346,000 (per table 40.1 2010.B1)		
1–325,000 at 0%		
325,001–346,000 at 20%	4,200	
Tax payable by trustees		£4,200

Note

The transfer of value is £352,000. The value of the gift is the amount of the reduction in A's estate. See 7 CALCULATION OF TAX for more detailed examples.

Reduction of tax rates

[1.8] There were frequent changes in the tax rates following the introduction of capital transfer tax. For IHT purposes (and previously for CTT purposes) the rate bands are indexed in line with the retail prices index and must be increased each year unless otherwise determined by Parliament. [*IHTA 1984, s 8*]. The freezing for 2010–11 onwards of the nil rate band at £325,000 has meant that the retail prices index and the statutory indexing provisions to the RPI have been disallowed for the years to 2017–18. [*IHTA 1984, ss 7, 8, Sch; FA 2005, s 98(6); FA 2006, s 155(5); FA 2010, s 8; FA 2014, Sch 25 para* 2]. Where there has been a rate change, the new rates are used to calculate the tax on any subsequent transfer. In certain cases, because of the cumulative nature of the tax, this may mean that earlier transfers need to be 'revised' before the calculation can be made. This revision does *not* affect the amount of earlier chargeable transfers or the actual tax paid on them.

Example 3

C made a gift to a discretionary trust of £265,000 on 1 February 2004. He had made no previous transfers. He makes a further gift of £150,000 to the discretionary trust on 1 October 2010. In each case he pays any tax due.

Gift on 1 February 2004

	£	£
Value of gift		265,000
Deduct exempt transfers		
Annual exemption 2003/04	3,000	
Annual exemption 2002/03	3,000	
		6,000
		£259,000
Tax on net £254,000 per grossing-up table 40.1 2003.B2		
0–255,000 = Nil + 1/4 (255,000 – 259,000)		1,000
C's chargeable transfer		£260,000
Tax payable by C		£1,000

Gift on 1 October 2010

	£	Gross £	Tax £	Net £
Cumulative totals 1.2.2004		260,000	1,000	259,000
Revision for changes of rates (per table 40.1 2010.B1)		260,000	Nil	260,000
Value of gift	150,000			
Deduct annual exemption				
2010/11	(3,000)			
2009/10	(3,000)			
	£144,000	162,500	19,500*	143,000
		£422,500	£19,500	£403,000

*Tax on net £399,000 per grossing-up table 40.1 2010.B2		
0–399,000 = Nil + 1/4 (403,000 – 325,000)	19,500	
Deduct tax on previous transfer at rates applicable at 1.10.2010	Nil	
Tax payable by C	£19,500	

Although the cumulative totals of tax and 'net' transfers are subject to change every time there is a change of rates, it is important to note that

(a) the figures change for the purpose of calculating the amount of any tax on subsequent transfers only: there is no question of any repayment of tax; and

(b) the chargeable transfer (sometimes called the gross transfer) never alters. See 7 CALCULATION OF TAX for more detailed examples.

Death within seven years of transfer

[1.9] The tax on a chargeable lifetime transfer is initially calculated at one half of the death scale rates currently 20%. Where the transferor then dies within seven years of the transfer, the tax is recomputed at the higher death scale but the tax rates are tapered where the death is more than three years after the gift. If there is a reduction in tax rates between the chargeable lifetime transfer and the date of death, the additional tax, if any, is calculated as if the new table applicable on death had applied to the transfer. The tax payable cannot be reduced below that originally chargeable at half death rates. [*IHTA 1984, s 7, Sch 2 para 2; FA 1986, Sch 19 para 2, para 37*].

Where potentially exempt transfers are made within seven years of death, no tax would have been payable at the time of the transfer. On death, tax is calculated at the full death rates applying at the time of death, subject to the tapering relief.

Where a death occurs after 17 March 1986, the above provisions do not affect the tax chargeable on a chargeable transfer occurring before 18 March 1986. The tax on such a chargeable transfer will only be recomputed at the higher death rates if the transferor dies within three years of the transfer. [*FA 1986, Sch 19 para 40*].

See **53** TRANSFERS WITHIN SEVEN YEARS BEFORE DEATH.

Example 4

C in Example 3 in **1.8** above dies on 1 April 2011. He leaves his entire estate to his wife so no tax is payable on his estate on death (see **21.10** EXEMPT TRANSFERS). No further tax is due on the gift made on 1 February 2004 as the gift was made more than seven years previously so no tax is payable. Further tax is due on the gift to the discretionary trust made on 1 October 2010.

	£
Gift on 1 October 2010	
Chargeable transfer	£162,500
Tax at death rates applicable on 1 April 2011	
(table 40.1 2010.A1)	
325,000 – 422,500 at 40%	39,000
Deduct tax paid by C	19,500
Further tax payable by the trustees of the discretionary trust	£19,500

Interaction with other taxes

[1.10] Inheritance tax is levied separately from any other tax, so that it is possible, for example, for a transfer to suffer both inheritance tax and capital gains tax without any allowance in one for the other. For example, a lifetime gift of a property will be a disposal for capital gains tax purposes and if a benefit is reserved in the asset the value of it will be chargeable to IHT on the death of the donor but without the capital gains tax position being revisited. In general however a chargeable transfer for IHT enables capital gains tax hold over relief to apply. See **8** CAPITAL GAINS TAX.

Key points

[1.11] Points to consider are as follows.

- Where property is owned as a joint tenancy then that interest is transferred to the *surviving* joint tenant *but* it still forms part of the deceased's estate on death for IHT purposes.
- Where a lifetime gift was made within 7 years of death and IHT was charged at 20% in *lifetime* then the tax is recomputed at 40% on *death* and any additional tax is in the first instance payable by the transferee.
- Similarly where a PET becomes chargeable on the death of the transferor any extra tax will primarily become the liability of the transferee.
- Insurance cover such as diminishing term assurance may be taken out on the life of the transferor by the transferee to meet any IHT that becomes payable in the event of the transferors' death within 7 years.

2

Accounts and Returns

Cross-reference. See also 3 ADMINISTRATION AND COLLECTION.

Other Sources. Foster, Part L; IHT 400 (Notes); IHTM10000.

Simon's Taxes. See **Binder 1 Tax Office Directory, I11.2, I11.7.**

Introduction

[2.1] An account or return must be rendered in such form and containing such particulars as the Board may prescribe and an account must be supported by such books, papers and other documents, and verified (whether on oath or otherwise) in such manner as the Board may require. An account delivered to a probate registry i.e. the Probate Service (or the Probate and Matrimonial Office in Northern Ireland) is treated as delivered to the Board. [*IHTA 1984, s 257*]. See also **2.8** below. HMRC are satisfied that an accurate facsimile of an official account or other required document is within the scope of *IHTA 1984, s 257*. The most important criteria to be met are that the substitute document etc. must provide the same information as the official one; be readily recognisable as a substitute of the relevant official form; be in a form approved by HMRC and carry an agreed unique imprint; and bear the reference number of the issued official form it replaces or otherwise the taxpayer's reference. The returns for IHT on death (IHT 400, IHT 404, IHT 421, IHT 430 and IOV2) were revised in November 2012. Application for approval should be made to the Customer Service Manager at the Nottingham or Edinburgh HMRC Inheritance Tax, (see below) as appropriate. (Inland Revenue Statement of Practice SP 2/93, 13 January 1993).

Accounts and returns

[2.2] An account is a document completed by a transferor or other taxable person providing details of a transaction in respect of which inheritance tax may apply.

A return is a document normally submitted by a person other than the transferor about transactions affecting others.

The Board has power to make regulations by statutory instrument to dispense with the delivery of accounts and also to require information where accounts are not delivered. Secondary legislation provides for simplified IHT procedures in cases of minor nil-IHT paying estates and the *Finance Act 2004* extended this to bring in most non-taxpaying estates not already qualifying. This will also include estates which are substantially over the IHT threshold (currently £325,000) but are covered by the inter-spousal exemption or bequests to charitable organisations. See *Excepted estates* at **2.8** below. Under *IHTA 1984, s 256(1)(aa)* regulations will allow personal representatives to complete a short form of return which will meet the minimum requirements for both tax and probate purposes. Once such cases are dealt with under this simplified procedure they may be considered closed to further enquiry allowing the estate to be distributed and avoiding the necessity for a certificate of discharge. Further, *s 256(1A)* may require that the information and documents provided to the probate registry (England and Wales), the sheriff in Scotland and the Probate and Matrimonial Office in Northern Ireland can be passed on to HMRC and treated as if they had been passed originally to the Board of HMRC. The penalty position would be unaffected by this conduit process. See **36** PENALTIES. [*IHTA 1984, s 256 as amended by FA 2004, s 293*].

See **2.19** below for addresses to which accounts etc. should be delivered.

Forms

[2.3] The principal forms currently prescribed by the Board for IHT purposes are as follows. The forms should be used for deaths and other transfers after 17 March 1986 (chargeable events after 24 July 1986 for IHT 101). Form IHT 400 must be used where a full account is required. Completed IHT 200 forms will no longer be accepted from 9 June 2009.

IHT 100 **An account of a transfer of value** (for use for lifetime transfers by individuals or the termination (during life or on death) of an interest in possession in settled property, but not by personal representatives intending to obtain a grant of probate from a Probate Registry). Also includes an account of a chargeable event (which arises under the provisions relating to settlements without interests in possession in *IHTA 1984, Pt III, Ch III*). Instruction booklet is IHT 110. This form was updated in December 2005 and includes a worksheet IHT100WS.

IHT 205 **Return of estate information** for excepted estates.

IHT 400 **HMRC Account** (See form IHT 400 below). The latest revised version was issued on 5 November 2013 and may also be viewed below and at the HMRC website at www.hmrc.gov.uk/inheritancetax/iht400.pdf) (for use in applying for a grant of representation where the deceased died domiciled in the UK, except where the deceased died domiciled in the UK and personal application for a grant is being made by the proposed legal personal representative *and* the net estate chargeable to tax does not exceed the threshold for the imposition of tax at the date of death (taking into account any reliefs claimed) *and* the property to be covered by the grant does not include any settled land. Form IHT 37 has been drawn up by HMRC Inheritance Tax in respect of land, which is sent out with supplies of IHT 400. See below for HMRC Inheritance Tax telephone/fax orderline for stationery.

Instruction booklet is IHT 400 notes.

A grant of representation granted by the High Court in England and Wales in respect of the estate of a person dying domiciled there and noting the domicile will be recognised throughout the UK. This can be achieved by the delivery of a single HMRC Account. If such a grant is obtained when the domicile is in Scotland or NI, the grant is limited to assets in England and Wales and a further grant (requiring a further HMRC Account) may be required. The appropriate form in Scotland is also now IHT 400 (the revised version IHT 400 came into effect on 17 November 2008.

The IHT 400 must be used in all cases unless the gross value of the estate and the gifts within the previous seven years does not exceed £325,000. See **2.8** below. Where an Eik (addition) to Confirmation is required for additional assets, a Corrective Inventory C4, available from the HMRC website and updated in April 2007, should also be used. However, where an Eik to Confirmation is required because the estate has not been fully administered or none of the original executors or substitutes remains in office, then the existing Form X-1, available from the Sheriff's Court, should be used. In NI it is IHT 400. [*SI 2003/1658; SI 2004/2543 as amended*].

IHT 401 Supplementary page for use in applying for a grant of representation where the deceased died domiciled outside the UK even though the domicile is deemed to be in the UK under *IHTA 1984, s 267* (see **16.5** DOMICILE).

C4 **Corrective account** (for use where too much or too little tax has been paid on a previous account). C4–S in Scotland.

See IHT 400 notes which deals with information suggested to be provided with Accounts on Forms IHT 400 and may be obtained from HMRC Inheritance Tax. See www.hmrc.gov.uk/inheritancetax/iht400-notes.pdf.

Forms relating to other matters are mentioned under the appropriate subject headings elsewhere in this book. Orders for forms should be sent by fax to HMRC Inheritance Tax Stationery Section on 0845 234 1010 for dispatch within five working days. Telephone enquiries should be made on 0845 30 20 900.

Accounts for lifetime transfer

[2.4] Accounts for lifetime transfer are treated as follows:

(a) Every transferor who is liable for tax on the value transferred by a chargeable transfer; and
(b) every person liable for tax on the value transferred by a potentially exempt transfer (including, in relation to transfers and other events after 16 March 1987, such a transfer made under *IHTA 1984, s 52* as amended by *FA 2006, Sch 20 para 13* on the termination of an interest in possession) which proves to be a chargeable transfer; and
(c) any person within (a) or (b) above who would be so liable if tax were chargeable on that value,

must deliver to the Board an account (see **32** LIFETIME TRANSFERS for Form IHT 100) specifying all property comprised in that transfer to which tax is or would be attributable and its value, unless some other person liable for the tax (other than a joint trustee) has already delivered such an account. [*IHTA 1984, s 216(1)(4)(5); FA 1986, Sch 19 para 29; F(No 2)A 1987, Sch 7 para 4; FA 2006, Sch 22 para 7*].

Potentially exempt transfers

[2.5] There is no requirement to notify the Board on the making of such a transfer nor to deliver an account. In the case of a transfer on or after 17 March 1987 but before 22 March 2006 involving an interest in possession trust, that transfer may also become an exempt transfer if the transferor survives for seven years. In this connection, there is no immediate lifetime charge on a gift by an individual if the gift is into trust before 22 March 2006 under which another individual has a beneficial interest in possession in that gifted property, nor where the gift increases the value of trust property in which another individual has a beneficial interest in possession.

After 21 March 2006 a PET is a transfer of value made by an individual which would otherwise be a chargeable transfer and which is either a gift to another individual or into a trust for a disabled person or into a trust for bereaved minors on the ending of an immediate post-death interest (IPDI). See **38** POTENTIALLY EXEMPT TRANSFERS. There was also no immediate lifetime charge on the termination or disposal of an individual's beneficial interest in possession in trust property before 22 March 2006 where another individual becomes beneficially entitled or that trust property becomes comprised of an accumulation and maintenance settlement or the value of another individual's estate is increased. An account must be submitted where there has been a potentially exempt transfer and the transferor has not survived for seven years. The donee of a potentially exempt transfer is liable to deliver an account if the transferor dies within seven years of the transfer.

Excepted transfers

[2.6] From 6 April 2007 where property is given away, or property in which the interest subsists, is wholly attributable to cash or quoted stocks and securities, the disposal will qualify as an excepted transfer or termination — provided the cumulative total of all chargeable transfers made by the transferor in the seven years before the transfer does not exceed the IHT nil rate band. See **40** RATES OF TAX. However, where the property given away, or in which the interest subsists, is wholly or partly attributable to property other than cash or quoted stocks and securities, the disposal must pass two tests. Firstly, the value transferred by the chargeable transfer concerned together with the cumulative total of all chargeable transfers made by the transferor in the seven years before the transfer must not exceed 80% of the relevant IHT nil rate band. Secondly, the value transferred by the transfer of value giving rise to the chargeable transfer concerned must not exceed the nil rate band that is available to the transferor at the time the disposal takes place. [*Inheritance Tax (Delivery of Accounts) (Excepted Transfers and Terminations) Regulations 2008, SI 2008/605, Regs 4, 5*]. Where trustees terminate or bring to an end the life tenant's interest in settled property, the life tenant is treated as making a transfer of value. If the life tenant has not made any chargeable transfers of their own, they can give notice to the trustees that the exemptions they are entitled to are available for use against the property in which their life interest is being terminated. Where the value transferred is covered by the exemptions available, the termination is an excepted termination. [*Inheritance Tax (Delivery of Accounts) (Excepted Settlements) Regulations 2008, SI 2008/606, Reg 5*].

No account need be delivered prior to 6 April 2007 in respect of a chargeable transfer by an individual where:

(i) the value of the chargeable transfer, together with any other chargeable transfers by the same individual in the same tax year ending 5 April, does not exceed £10,000; and

(ii) the value of the chargeable transfer, together with any other chargeable transfers by the same individual in the previous ten years (presumably to be amended to seven years) does not exceed £40,000; or

(iii) an interest in possession comes to an end and the transferor gives the trustees a notice informing them of the availability of an annual or marriage or civil partnership exemption and the value transferred is wholly covered by that exemption.

The Board retain the right to call for an account by notice in writing to the individual. [*IHTA 1984, s 256(1)(a); SI 1981/1440; SI 2002/1731 revoked from 6 April 2007 and replaced by SI 2008/606*]. See **32** LIFETIME TRANSFERS for IHT 100 and www.hmrc.gov.uk/cto/forms/iht110_2.pdf.

See **2.14** below for time limits and **2.15** for submission of accounts where transfer originally treated as 'excepted'.

Gifts with reservation

[2.7] Property given but subject to a reservation where that reservation is retained until the death of the donor or where the reservation ceases within seven years of the death should be the subject of an IHT 100 account return. However, where a reservation ceases before the death of the donor then the donor is treated as having made a potentially exempt transfer of the property at the time the reservation ceases. In addition, the dismantling of pre-owned assets avoidance schemes by way of election on form IHT 500 in respect of any relevant year of assessment will ensure that the property is treated as being comprised in the original donor's estate for these purposes as a gift with reservation but will preclude the income tax charge on the annual taxable value of the pre-owned asset. See **22** GIFTS WITH RESERVATION.

Accounts for transfers on death

[2.8] The **personal representatives** of a deceased person must deliver to the Board an account of all property which formed part of the deceased's estate immediately before his death (other than property which only forms part of his estate by virtue of the provisions relating to **22** GIFTS WITH RESERVATION) and its value unless the estate is an 'excepted estate' (see below).

For deaths on or after 9 March 1999 the information provided by the personal representatives must include details of any chargeable transfers made by the deceased within seven years of his death. The personal representatives may also provide a provisional estimate of the value of an asset included in their account where, despite making all reasonable enquiries to ascertain the value, they cannot establish the exact value. In such cases, the account must contain a statement to that effect and an undertaking to deliver a further account as soon as the value is ascertained. An executor in England and Wales of settled land need only give details of the trust property comprised in the transfer (see IHT 405 below). In the case of pension scheme administrators of alternatively secured pension (ASP) funds who become liable to the payment of IHT by reason of *IHTA 1984, s 151A–D* they are responsible for delivering an account to HMRC of the property expended on dependant's benefits. [*IHTA 1984, ss 216(1)(bca), 272; FA 2006, s 160, Sch 22 paras 7, 10; FA 2008, Sch 28 para 12*]. See also **2.14** below and **37.2** PENSION SCHEMES.

The account must be presented at a probate registry, and any tax payable on delivery paid, before a grant of representation can be obtained. The cost of obtaining the grant is £215 for estates valued at more than £5,000 and cheques should be made payable to 'HM Courts and Tribunals Service'. In Scotland, such an account is called an inventory and it must be presented at a local Sheriff Court or the Commissary Office in Edinburgh. The Scottish equivalent of the grant of representation is the confirmation. See **2.19** below for addresses. The Board of HMRC may also give directions restricting assets to be included in accounts to be delivered by personal representatives. See *Robertson v CIR* [2002] STC SCD 182 Sp C 309. [*IHTA 1984, ss 216(1)(3)(3A)(3B)(4), 261; FA 1986, Sch 19 para 29; FA 1999, s 105*]. See also **36.12** PENALTIES.

Following the Senior District Judge's Direction of 27 October 2004 there are three alternative IHT certificates that may be used in varying circumstances to use in the oath to apply for a grant. These are detailed below.

In the case where the estate is not an excepted estate then the preferred oath is that applying at point 5 below:

IN THE HIGH COURT OF JUSTICE	Extracting Solicitor. . . . .
Family Division	Address. . . . . (including post code and DX number)

The District Probate Registry at Leeds

IN the Estate of AB deceased

We CD of [address]

And EF of [address]

make Oath and say

1. We believe the paper writing now produced to and marked by us to contain the true and original last will [and codicil where applicable] and testament of AB of [address in death certificate] formerly of [address in will] who died on the . . . . . . day . . . . . . 2010. . . . . born on the

. . . . day . . . . 19. . . . . . /200
. . . . aged. . . . . . years domiciled in England and Wales.

2. To the best of my/our knowledge, information and belief there was no land vested in the said deceased which was settled previously to his death and not by his will and which remained settled land notwithstanding his death.

3. We are the Executors named in the said will.

4. We will

   (i) collect, get in and administer according to the law the real and personal estate of the said deceased

   (ii) when required to do so by the Court, exhibit on oath in the Court a full inventory of the said estate

   And when so required render an account of the administration of the said estate to the Court; and when required to do so by the High Court, deliver up the grant of probate to that Court.

5. To the best of my/our knowledge, information and belief the gross estate passing under the grant amounts to £ and the net estate amounts to £ . . . .

SWORN by CD and EF the above named

Deponents)
At)
)
This day of 2010)
)
Before me,)

A Commissioner for Oaths/Solicitor.

Where there are no personal representatives because no grant of representation or confirmation has been obtained in the UK within twelve months of the end of the month in which death occurred:

(a) every person in whom *any property* of the estate vests as beneficial owner or otherwise, or who is beneficially entitled to an interest in possession in such property, on or after the deceased's death; and
(b) where property is comprised in a settlement with no person entitled to an interest in possession, every person for whose benefit any of that property, or income from it, is applied, on or after the deceased's death,

must deliver an account to the Board, specifying to the best of his knowledge and belief, the property in which he has an interest (or which is applicable for his benefit) and its value. Any property includes property which is expended on dependants' benefits arising from an alternatively secured pension (ASP) under *IHTA 1984, s 151A* or property paid to a charity within *IHTA 1984, ss 151B(4), 151C(3)(b)*. See **37.2** PENSION SCHEMES. Such an account is not required if the person concerned has satisfied the Board that an account will in due course be delivered by the personal representatives or has already been delivered by some other liable person. [*IHTA 1984, s 216(2)(4)(5)*]. See Form 409 below.

Gifts with reservation

[2.9] Any person who is liable for tax on the value of property forming part of the deceased's estate by virtue only of the provisions relating to 22 GIFTS WITH RESERVATION (or would be so liable if tax were chargeable on that value) must deliver to the Board an account specifying all property to the value of which the tax is or would be attributable and its value unless some other person liable for the tax (other than a joint trustee) has already delivered such an account. [*IHTA 1984, s 216(1)(4)(5); FA 1986, Sch 19 para 29*].

Excepted estates

[2.10] No account need be delivered for the estate of any person who has died domiciled in the UK on or after 1 September 2006 where:

(i) the estate comprises only property which has passed under the deceased's will or intestacy, or by nomination on death, or entitlement to a single interest in possession settlement, or beneficially by survivorship;

(ii) the total gross value of the estate for tax purposes (inclusive of (iii)–(v) below, as may be the case) does not exceed £325,000; (£312,000 for deaths before 6 April 2009 and after 5 April 2008; £300,000 for deaths before 6 April 2008 and after 5 April 2007; £285,000 for deaths before 6 April 2007 and after 5 April 2006; £275,000 for deaths before 6 April 2006 but after 5 April 2005) after ignoring transfers attracting APR or BPR within *IHTA 1984, ss 104, 116*;

(iii) not more than £100,000 (£75,000 for deaths before 1 September 2006 but after 5 April 2002) consists of property situated outside the UK and by reason of that person's death an ASP fund provision under *IHTA 1984, ss 151A–D* does not apply; and

(iv) the deceased died and had made no lifetime gifts chargeable to inheritance tax (including potentially exempt transfers becoming chargeable on death and gifts with reservation where the reservation subsists at death or where the property ceased to be subject to the reservation in the seven years before the donor's death) excepting lifetime transfers made within seven years of the deceased's death consisting of 'specified transfers' i.e. cash, listed shares or securities, an interest over land (and furnishings and chattels enjoyed with the land and transferred at the same time) that did not exceed £150,000 (£100,000 for deaths before 1 September but after 5 April 2000) after ignoring transfers attracting APR or BPR within *IHTA 1984, ss 104, 116* and by reason of that person's death an ASP fund provision under *IHTA 1984, ss 151A–D* does not apply. For the purposes of this condition, with effect from 1 March 2011 transfers within the normal expenditure out of income exemption and which exceed the available annual £3,000 exempt amount are treated as chargeable transfers;

(v) not more than £150,000 represents value attributable to property which, immediately before the person's death, was settled property.

No account need be delivered for the estate of any person who died on or after 6 April 2004 who was domiciled in the UK or treated as domiciled in the UK [*FA 2004, s 293*] where:

(vi) the aggregate gross value of the deceased's estate (inclusive of (iii)–(v) above, as may be the case) is £1,000,000 or less after ignoring transfers attracting APR or BPR within *IHTA 1984, ss 104, 116* and after deducting any specified exemptions (e.g. spousal, charities, etc.) so that the net chargeable estate is less than £325,000. With effect from 1 March 2011 it is also a condition that at least part of the estate passes to the surviving spouse or to charity.

(vii) with effect from 1 March 2011, an estate benefiting from the transferred unused nil rate band of a pre-deceased spouse will only have that taken into account for the purposes of the Excepted Estates Regulations where all of the pre-deceased spouse's nil band was unused. In that event the available nil band for the purposes of the Regulations is increased by 100%.

[*Inheritance Tax (Delivery of Accounts) (Excepted Estates) (Amendment) Regulations 2006, SI 2006/2141; The Inheritance Tax (Delivery of Accounts) (Excepted Estates) (Amendment) Regulations 2011, SI 2011/214)*].

For an excepted estate where the gross value does not exceed the IHT threshold (currently £325,000) the following certificate may be used in the oath to apply for a grant.

IN THE HIGH COURT OF JUSTICE Extracting Solicitor. . . . .

Family Division Address. . . . .

The District Probate Registry at Leeds

IN the Estate of AB deceased

We CD of [address]

And EF of [address]

make Oath and say

1. We believe the paper writing now produced to and marked by us to contain the true and original last will and testament of AB of [address in death certificate] formerly of [address in will] who died on the . . . . . . day . . . . . . 2010 . . . . born on the . . . . . . day . . . . . . 19. . . . . . /200 . . . . aged . . . . . . years domiciled in England and Wales.
2. To the best of my/our knowledge, information and belief there was no land vested in the said deceased which was settled previously to his death and not by his will and which remained settled land notwithstanding his death.
3. We are the Executors named in the said will.
4. We will

   (i) collect, get in and administer according to the law the real and personal estate of the said deceased

(ii) when required to do so by the Court, exhibit on oath in the Court a full inventory of the said estate

And when so required render an account of the administration of the said estate to the Court; and when required to do so by the High Court, deliver up the grant of probate to that Court.

5. To the best of my/our knowledge, information and belief the gross estate passing under the grant does not exceed £325,000 and the net estate amounts to £ and this is not a case in which a HM Revenue and Customs Account is required to be delivered.

SWORN by CD and EF the above named

Deponents)
At)
)
This day of 2010)
)
Before me,)

A Commissioner for Oaths/Solicitor.

For an excepted estate where the gross value exceeds the IHT threshold (currently £325,000) but does not exceed £1m and the chargeable estate after deducting any spouse/civil partner or charitable exemptions does not exceed the current IHT threshold the following certificate may be used in the oath to apply for a grant.

IN THE HIGH COURT OF JUSTICE Extracting Solicitor. . . . .

Family Division Address. . . . .

The District Probate Registry at Leeds

IN the Estate of AB deceased

We CD of [address]

And EF of [address]

make Oath and say

1. We believe the paper writing now produced to and marked by us to contain the true and original last will and testament of AB of [address in death certificate] formerly of [address in will] who died on the . . . . . . day . . . . 2010. . . . . . born on the . . . . . . day . . . . 19. . . . . /200 . . . . aged . . . . . . years domiciled in England and Wales.

2. To the best of my/our knowledge, information and belief there was no land vested in the said deceased which was settled previously to his death and not by his will and which remained settled land notwithstanding his death.

3. We are the Executors named in the said will.

4. We will

   (i) collect, get in and administer according to the law the real and personal estate of the said deceased

   (ii) when required to do so by the Court, exhibit on oath in the Court a full inventory of the said estate

   And when so required render an account of the administration of the said estate to the Court; and when required to do so by the High Court, deliver up the grant of probate to that Court.

5. To the best of my/our knowledge, information and belief the gross estate passing under the grant amounts to £ and the net estate amounts to £ and this is not a case in which a HM Revenue and Customs Account is required to be delivered.

SWORN by CD and EF the above named

Deponents)
At)
)
This day of 2010)
)
Before me,)

A Commissioner for Oaths/Solicitor.

No account need be delivered for the estate of any person who died on or after 6 April 2002 who was never domiciled in the UK or treated as domiciled in the UK [*FA 1986, s 267*] where

(viii) the value of such a person's estate that is situated in the UK which is attributable to cash or quoted shares or securities that pass by will, or by intestacy, or beneficially by survivorship and does not exceed £150,000. See Form IHT 400 notes at page 3.

A grant of representation will still be required but applicants will only be required to swear as to the brackets into which the value of the estate falls. Under this procedure applicants send IHT 421 to HMRC Inheritance Tax together with a set declaration that the assets of the estate did not exceed the taxable limit or threshold at the date of death. HMRC Inheritance Tax with the Court Service show that the completion of a Form IHT 421 will be required in various circumstances in flowcharts on pages 58 to 62 of the IHT 400 notes. As a result, see www.hmrc.gov.uk/inheritancetax/iht400-notes.pdf.

Once it has been worked out that there is no tax to pay, put '0' in box 6 and the form should then be signed. The form can then be sent directly to HMRC Inheritance Tax. At the same time the IHT 400 and supporting papers and a copy of the will should be sent to HMRC Inheritance Tax.

The Board retain the right to call for an account by issuing a notice to the personal representatives within 35 days of the issue of the grant of probate. In Scotland, the Board may give notice to the personal representatives within 60 days of the issue of confirmation to the estate that the Registrar, HMRC Inheritance Tax at Edinburgh has required the Commissary Clerk or Sheriff Clerk to transmit to him an inventory of the excepted estate. If no notice is issued, the personal representatives will be automatically discharged from any further tax claims (unless there is fraud or non-disclosure of material facts) and any HMRC charge (see **35.12** PAYMENT OF TAX) is extinguished without formal application. See leaflet 'What to do after a death in Scotland'.

[*IHTA 1984, s 256; SI 1981/880, SI 1981/881, SI 1981/1441; SI 1983/1039, SI 1983/1040, SI 1983/1911; SI 1987/1127, SI 1987/1128, SI 1987/1129; SI 1989/1078, SI 1989/1079, SI 1989/1080; SI 1990/1110, SI 1990/1111, SI 1990/1112; SI 1991/1248, SI 1991/1249, SI 1991/1250; SI 1996/1470, SI 1996/1472,SI 1996/1473; SI 1998/1429, SI 1998/1430, SI 1998/1431; SI 2000/965, SI 2000/966, SI 2000/967; SI 2002/1733; SI 2003/1658; SI 2004/2543*].

Estates where the deceased had an interest in settled property are not excepted estates except insofar as that property from 6 April 2002 was wholly settled property the value of which immediately before the person's death amounted to not more than £100,000. Where the value of an estate is attributable in part to property passing by survivorship in a joint tenancy or, in Scotland by survivorship, it is the deceased's beneficial interest in that property which is taken into account for the purposes of the limit in (ii) above. (Inland Revenue Press Release, 2 July 1987). [*SI 2002/1733*].

See **2.14** below for time limits and **2.15** for submission of accounts where estate originally treated as 'excepted'.

A simpler reporting regime was announced by the Chancellor of the Exchequer in the Budget speech on 17 March 2004 and is now incorporated into *FA 2004, s 293* whereby an IHT account will be required only where there is tax to pay. In most other cases contact will only be with the Probate Service in England and the Sheriff's Court in Scotland. [*Supreme Court Act 1981, s 109(1); Probate and Legacy Duties Act 1808, s 42; Administration of Estates (Northern Ireland) Order 1979, SI 1979/1575 as amended by FA 2004, s 294(3); The Finance Act 2004, Section 294 (Appointed Day) Order 2004, SI 2004/2571*]. As a result, in a vast majority of cases applying from 1 November 2004, the information on deceased's estate will be provided once to the Probate Service (or the Sheriff's Court in Scotland) who in turn will provide HMRC with information from which HMRC will determine selected cases for enquiry. This change in administration procedure ensures that only the basic information will be provided in a vast majority of cases and not the full account as in past years. The changes are now incorporated in the *Inheritance Tax (Delivery of Accounts) (Excepted Estates) Regulations 2004, SI 2004/2543 as amended by The Tax and Civil Partnership (No 2) Regulations 2005, SI 2005/3230, Reg 15* ensuring that a new category of qualifying estate where the gross value does not exceed £1 million, subject to a number of provisos, is excluded. See above at (vi). [*IHTA 1984, s 256(3A) as inserted by FA 2004, s 293(6)*]. See **2.2** above.

In order to ensure that compliance requirements are met the existing penalty rules (see **36** PENALTIES for failure to provide accounts, etc.) will apply to the delivery of incorrect information under these simplified reporting arrangements. As a result of this provision will be made to allow the information delivered to the Probate Service and then passed on to HMRC to be treated as having been delivered direct to HMRC as will be the case for the delivery of information via the Scottish Court Service. [*IHTA 1984, s 256(1A) as inserted by FA 2004, s 293(3)*]. Contact the Principal Probate Registry on 0207 947 7431/7414.

Many estates are exempt from IHT because most or all of the estate passes to a surviving spouse/civil partner, a UK charity or other exempt bodies. HMRC Inheritance Tax has identified certain circumstances where a reduced IHT 400 account may be delivered. These circumstances are as follows:

- the deceased was domiciled in the UK at the date of death, and
- most or all of the property passing by will or under intestacy passes to an 'exempt beneficiary' either:
  - (i) absolutely, or through an interest in possession trust, to the surviving spouse/civil partner, who must also be domiciled in the UK, or
  - (ii) so as to immediately become the property of a body listed in *IHTA 1984, Sch 3*, or
  - (iii) so as to immediately become the property of a charity registered in the UK, or held on trusts established in the UK for charitable purposes only, and
- the gross value of the property passing by will or under intestacy to beneficiaries other than exempt beneficiaries together with the value of 'other property chargeable on death' and the chargeable value of any gifts made in the seven years prior to death do not, in total, exceed the IHT threshold.

Other property chargeable on death mentioned above includes:

(a) joint property passing by survivorship to someone other than the deceased's surviving spouse/civil partner (assuming that he or she was domiciled in the UK);

(b) settled property in which the deceased had a life interest, other than settled property which then devolves to the deceased's spouse/civil partner, to a body listed in *IHTA 1984, Sch 3*, or to a charity registered in the UK;

(c) property that the deceased had given away but in which they reserved a benefit that either continued until death or ceased within seven years of death;

(d) property situated outside the UK which does not devolve under the UK will or intestacy.

Where the circumstances above are met, the requirement to deliver an account containing all appropriate property and the value of that property is relaxed. The account must still be delivered on Form IHT 400 and the declaration on p 13 signed.

Accounts by trustees of settlements

[2.11] The **trustees** of a settlement liable for tax on the value transferred by a transfer of value or for tax under provisions relating to **43** SETTLEMENTS: DISCRETIONARY TRUSTS AND OTHER TRUSTS OF RELEVANT PROPERTY (or who would be so liable if tax were chargeable) must deliver an account specifying all property to which tax is or would be attributable and its value, unless some other person liable for the tax (other than as joint trustee) has already delivered such an account. [*IHTA 1984, s 216(1)(4)(5)*]. An account must be rendered to the best of a taxpayer's knowledge and belief. This does not mean that he can be compelled to act as an information gatherer if he does not have information himself. (*Re Clore (decd.) (No 3), CIR v Stype Trustees (Jersey) Ltd and Others* Ch D, [1985] STC 394). (The *Stype* case also held that foreign trustees liable to pay tax are also liable to produce accounts despite difficulties of enforcement.)

Excepted terminations

[2.12] No account need be delivered on a termination of an interest in possession in settled property where:

(i) the transferor has given notice to the trustees of available exemptions under *IHTA 1984, s 57(3)* (annual exemption and gifts in consideration of marriage — see **42.9** SETTLEMENTS WITH INTERESTS IN POSSESSION), and
(ii) the value transferred does not exceed the amount of the exemption specified in the notice. See **2.4** above.

The Board retain the right to call for an account by written notice to the trustees. If no such notice is issued within six months of the termination, the trustees will automatically be discharged from any claim for tax at the expiration of that period (unless there is fraud or non-disclosure of material facts). [*SI 1981/1440; SI 2002/1731 revoked from 6 April 2007 and replaced by Inheritance Tax (Delivery of Accounts) (Excepted Transfers and Terminations) Regulations 2008, SI 2008/605, Reg 5*].

See **2.14** below for time limits and **2.15** below for submission of accounts where the termination was originally treated as 'excepted'.

Excepted settlements

[2.13] No account need be delivered in respect of an excepted settlement (i.e. one with no qualifying interest in possession) on an occasion of a chargeable event on or after 6 April 2007 where either of the following applies:

Small settlements of cash

(i) cash is the only property comprised in the settlement;
(ii) after making the settlement, the settlor provided no further property which became comprised in the settlement;
(iii) the trustees of the settlement are resident in the UK throughout the existence of the settlement;

(iv) the gross value of the settled property throughout the existence of the settlement does not exceed £1,000; and

(v) there are no related settlements.

All other settlements

- the settlor must be domiciled in the UK at the time the settlement was set up and remain so domiciled throughout the existence of the settlement until either the occasion of charge or the settlor's earlier death;
- the trustees of the settlement must be resident in the UK throughout the existence of the settlement; and
- there must be no related settlements for IHT purposes (these are other settlements created by the settlor on the same day as the RPT).
- on the relevant event (for example the ten-year anniversary of a RPT or the distribution of assets from a RPT) the value of the notional aggregate chargeable transfer does not exceed 80% of the IHT nil rate band. Similarly, where an IHT charge arises in connection with an age 18–25 trust, that trust will qualify as an excepted settlement where the value of the notional aggregate chargeable transfer under *IHTA 1984, s 71F(8)* does not exceed 80% of the nil rate band. For the purposes of calculating value for the 80% test, any possible IHT reliefs, such as business or agricultural property relief, must be ignored as well as any liabilities of the settlement. See also **43** SETTLEMENTS: DISCRETIONARY TRUSTS AND OTHER TRUSTS OF RELEVANT PROPERTY and **46** TRUSTS FOR BEREAVED MINORS.

The Board retain the right to call for an account by written notice to the trustees of the excepted settlement. If no such notice is issued within six months of the termination, the trustees will automatically be discharged from any claim for tax at the expiration of that period (unless there is fraud or non-disclosure of material facts). [*SI 2002/1732 revoked from 6 April 2007 and replaced by Inheritance Tax (Delivery of Accounts) (Excepted Settlements) Regulations 2008, SI 2008/606, Reg 5*].

[*Inheritance Tax (Delivery of Accounts) (Excepted Transfers and Terminations) Regulations 2008, SI 2008/606, Reg 4*].

Time limits for delivery of above accounts

[2.14] Table of accounts delivery dates for:

Potentially exempt transfers which prove to be chargeable	— within **twelve months** from the end of the month in which the transferor dies.
Other lifetime transfers and, for chargeable transfers on or before 5 April 2014, by trustees of settlements	— within **twelve months** from the end of the month in which a transfer is made or, if later, within the three months beginning with the date on which the person delivering the account first becomes liable for tax.
For chargeable transfers on or after 6 April 2014 by trustees of settlements	— within **six months** from the end of the month in which the event occurs.
Gifts with reservation chargeable on death	— within **twelve months** from the end of the month in which the death occurs.
Other transfers on death	— within **twelve months** from the end of the month in which death occurs or, if later, within the three months beginning with the date on which the personal representatives first act or the person liable under **2.8** (a) or (b) above first has reason to believe he is required to deliver an account.
Accounts where charge arises on ending of conditional exemption for works of art, historic buildings, etc. (whether settled property or otherwise) and for trees or underwood	— within **six months** from the end of the month in which the chargeable event occurs.
Alternatively Secured Pension (ASP) schemes on death of the scheme member	— within **twelve months** from the end of the month in which the scheme administrator makes discovery of the scheme member's death where there is a left-over pension amount at the death of the scheme member who was over the age of 75 on death and was traced after their death by the ASP scheme administrator. In such cases the left-over ASP funds are brought within the charge to IHT by *IHTA 1984, s 151A(6)*.

[*IHTA 1984, s 216(6)(6)(ac)(7); FA 1985, Sch 26 para 11; FA 1986, Sch 19 para 29; F(No 2)A 1987, Sch 7 para 4; FA 1999, s 105; FA 2006, Sch 22 para 7(5); FA 2007, Sch 19 para 24; FA 2008, Sch 28 para 12; FA 2009, Sch 56 para 1; FA 2014, Sch 21 para 4*].

See **2.15** below for position where an estate, transfer or termination originally considered 'excepted' is discovered not to be so. See also **36** PENALTIES.

Corrective and supplementary accounts

[2.15] If a person who has delivered any of the accounts under **2.4** to **2.14** above discovers a material defect, he must deliver a further account within six months to remedy the defect. If a person has not delivered an account in the mistaken belief that the transfer was an 'excepted transfer' (see **2.4** above) or the termination an 'excepted termination' (see **2.11** above), an account must be delivered within six months of the discovery. The same time limit applies where an 'excepted estate' (see **2.8** above) or an excepted settlement (see **2.11** above) is later discovered to be no longer excepted. [*IHTA 1984, s 217; SI 1981/880, SI 1981/881, SI 1981/1440, SI 1981/1441 now replaced by SI 2002/1731; SI 2002/1732; SI 2002/1733 revoked from 6 April 2007 and replaced by SI 2008/605 and SI 2008/606*].

From 1 May 2014 HMRC confirmed in their Trusts and Estates Newsletter that in certain circumstances they do not require corrective accounts to be submitted as soon as an amendment to figures previously returned is identified, but instead all corrections can be included on one account when it is believed that they are the final amendments to the value of the estate, or 18 months has passed since the date of death, whichever is earlier. Interest remains due on any additional tax in the normal way and additional payments on account can still be made in advance of submitting a corrective account. This practice is now set out at IHTM 31023.

The circumstances when this does not apply are:

- When HMRC have written to the personal representatives to notify them that a compliance check is to be made.
- The deceased's estate on death includes:
  (i) a qualifying interest in possession in settled property, or
  (ii) a gift with reservation of benefit.
- There is an overall change in the value of the estate of more than £50,000, before any exemptions or reliefs are deducted.
- The amendments relate to changes in the value of land or buildings or unlisted shares.
- The amendments relate to a claim for loss on sale of land or shares.
- Assets have been sold on which tax is being paid by instalments.

After 18 months from the date of death, all corrections should be notified as soon as they are known.

For late reporting of transfers, see **7.14** CALCULATION OF TAX.

Returns by certain persons acting for settlors

[2.16] Where a person (other than a barrister) has been concerned with the making of a settlement in the course of his trade or profession, and knows or has reason to believe (a) that the settlor was domiciled in the UK, and (b) that the trustees of the settlement are not or will not be resident in the UK, he must, within three months of the making of the settlement, make a return to the Board of the names and addresses of the settlor and the trustees of the settlement. This does not apply to any settlement made by will or where a return has already been made by another person or if any account relating to it has been delivered under **2.4** to **2.14** above. For this purpose, trustees of a settlement are not regarded as resident in the UK unless the general administration of the settlement is ordinarily carried on in the UK and the trustees or a majority of them (and where there is more than one class of trustees a majority of each class) are for the time being resident in the UK. [*IHTA 1984, s 218*].

Power to require information and call for documents

Power of the Board to require information

[2.17] The Board may by written notice (which may be combined with an income tax notice) require any person to supply any information they require for IHT purposes within not less than 30 days. Any such notice requires the consent of a Special Commissioner, which he is only to give on being satisfied that in all the circumstances the Board are justified in requiring the information.

A barrister or solicitor need not disclose, without his client's consent, any information subject to professional privilege, except that a solicitor:

(a) may be obliged to disclose the name and address of his client, and
(b) if his client is resident outside the UK and carries on a business abroad which includes the provision of services for persons in the UK relating to:
    (i) the formation of companies or settlements abroad; or
    (ii) the securing of control over, or the management or administration of, companies and settlements,

may be obliged to disclose the names and addresses of persons in the UK for whom the services are provided.

A notice can also require information for the purposes of taxes similar to IHT or chargeable on or by reference to death or gifts *inter vivos* which are contained in the law of another EC member state and to which EC Directive No 77/799/EEC of 19 December 1977 (as extended subsequently) applies and any other territory with taxed charged of a character to IHT. (Such a notice can be combined with one relating to any tax of another EC member state which is a tax on income or on capital for the purposes of the above EC Directive.) The Board may then disclose the information so obtained to the competent authorities of other EC member states and any other territory which observe rules of confidentiality no less strict than those applying in the UK.

[*FA 1978, s 77; IHTA 1984, s 219; FA 1990, ss 124, 125; FA 2000, s 147(2)*].

Power of the Board to call for documents

The Board may by written notice require any person who has delivered, or is liable to deliver, an IHT account to produce, in not less than 30 days, such documents and accounts as are reasonably required for:

(i) enquiring into the account (including and claim or election);
(ii) determining whether the account is incorrect or incomplete; and
(iii) making a determination for the purposes of a notice under *IHTA 1984, s 221* (see **14** DETERMINATIONS AND APPEALS),

except that a notice cannot oblige a person to produce documents, etc. relating to the conduct of any pending appeal by him.

Copies may be produced instead of originals but, if required in writing, the originals must be produced for inspection.

An appeal to the First Tier Tax Tribunal (FTTT) may be brought against any such requirement within 30 days of the issue of the notice. The FTTT may then confirm the notice (in which case the person has 30 days to comply) or set it aside. Neither party to the appeal can appeal against the decision of the FTTT.

[*IHTA 1984, ss 219A, 219B; FA 1999, s 106; The Transfer of Tribunal Functions and Revenue and Customs Appeals Order 2009, SI 2009/56, Sch 1, paras 112, 113*].

Power of the Special Commissioners to require particulars

On a preliminary or substantive hearing of any proceedings, the Special Commissioners may direct a party to the proceedings, other than HMRC, to deliver particulars, and to make available books, accounts and other documents, relating to the proceedings for inspection and copying by them and officers of the Board. [*SI 1994/1811, Reg 10*].

Penalties

[2.18] See **36** PENALTIES for failure to provide accounts etc. for provision of incorrect information and for failure to remedy errors in accounts etc. Also, see **36.2** PENALTIES.

Addresses

Capital Taxes Offices

[2.19]

England and Wales	Ferrers House PO Box 38 Castle Meadow Road Nottingham NG2 1BB Tel. 0115–974 3009 Fax. 0115–974 3041 DX. 701201 Nottingham 4 DX. 701202 Nottingham 4 (Pre-grant only)
Scotland	Meldrum House 15 Drumsheugh Gardens Edinburgh EH3 7UG (Shares Valuation EH3 7UH) Tel. 0131–777 4000 Fax. 0131–777 4220 DX. ED 542001 DX. ED 542002 (Shares Valuation)
Northern Ireland	Beaufort House Wellington Place Belfast BT1 6BH Tel. 028 9050 5342 Fax. 028 9050 5305 DX. 2001 NR Belfast 2

Grants of representation or confirmation

[2.20]

England and Wales	Principal Probate Registry 1st Avenue House 42–49 High Holborn London WC1V 6NP Tel 0845 3020900.
Scotland	Sheriff Clerk (Commissary Office) 27 Chamber Street Edinburgh EH1 1LB Sheriff Clerk of Glasgow and Strathkelvin 1 Carlton Place Glasgow G5 9DA

Northern Ireland	The Master Probate and Matrimonial Office Royal Courts of Justice (Northern Ireland) Chichester Street Belfast BT1 3JN

In Great Britain there are a number of local offices at which applications for grants of representation may be made. The addresses can be obtained from the Principal Probate Registry in London and the Commissary Office in Edinburgh. In the first instance Form IHT 400 is to be sent to HMRC Nottingham office (see address above) with effect from 9 January 2006. The case will then be allocated to the appropriate office. All applications for grant in an excepted estate case must continue to be sent to the appropriate Probate Registry.

In England and Wales, solicitors are now asked not to send accounts to probate registries unless they have been previously submitted to, and properly receipted by, HMRC for PAYMENT OF TAX (**35.4**) (Family Division Practice Note 30 November 1989).

Key points

[2.21] Points to consider are as follows.

- IHT400 must be sent to HMRC Inheritance Tax within twelve months of the date of death but interest will be payable after only six months following the date of death.
- IHT100 is to be completed in cases where there are chargeable lifetime transfers by individuals or where there is a termination during the lifetime of a person entitled to an interest in possession. See SETTLEMENTS WITH INTERESTS IN POSSESSION (**42.1**).
- Supplementary schedules IHT401 to IHT420 should accompany the IHT400 schedule where applicable in respect of assets the deceased was beneficially entitled to on death.
- Corrective or supplementary accounts should be submitted as soon as the personal representatives become aware of the position requiring the corrective account, except as stated at **2.15** above.
- Supporting documentary evidence is required to be submitted with the schedules e.g. IHT405 (houses, land, buildings and interests in land) it is recommended that three independent valuations are obtained with average market value being taken.

Inheritance Tax Account [Form IHT400]

HM Revenue & Customs

Inheritance Tax account

IHT400

When to use this form

Fill in this form if:

- the deceased died on or after 18 March 1986, and
- there is Inheritance Tax to pay, or
- there is no Inheritance Tax to pay, but the estate does not qualify as an excepted estate.

The IHT400 Notes, page 1, gives details about excepted estates.

Deadline

You must send this form to us within 12 months of the date of death. Interest will be payable after six months.

The Inheritance Tax (IHT) account

The account is made up of this form and separate Schedules.
You will have to fill in some of the Schedules.

To help you get started

- Gather the deceased's papers and the information you have about the deceased's estate. Make a list of the deceased's assets, liabilities, investments and other financial interests and any gifts made.
- Fill in boxes 1 to 28 then work through boxes 29 to 48 of this form to identify which Schedules you will need. If you do not have them all:
  — download them from **www.hmrc.gov.uk/ inheritancetax**
  or
  — phone the helpline to request them.
- Fill in the Schedules before moving on to complete this form.

IHT reference number

If there is any tax to pay, you will need to apply for an IHT reference number and payslip before you send this form to us. You can apply online at **hmrc.gov.uk/ inheritancetax** or fill in form IHT422 *Application for an Inheritance Tax reference* and send it to us. Apply for a reference at least two weeks before you plan to send us this form.

Filling in this form

- Use the IHT400 Notes to help you fill in this form.
- Fill in the form in black or blue ink.
- Make full enquiries so you can show that the figures you give and the statements you make are correct.
- If an instrument of variation has been signed before applying for a grant, fill in the form to show the effect of the Will/intestacy and instrument together — *see IHT400 Notes.*

Answer all the questions and fill in the boxes to help us process your form.

Help

For more information or help, or another copy of this form:

- go to **www.hmrc.gov.uk/inheritancetax**
- phone our helpline on **0300 123 1072** — if calling from outside the UK, phone **+44 300 123 1072**.

Deceased's details

1 **Deceased's name**

Title — enter MR, MRS, MISS, MS or other title

Surname

First name(s)

2 **Date of death** *DD MM YYYY*

3 **IHT reference number (if known)** *See note at the top of this form*

4 **Was the deceased male or female?**

Male ☐ Female ☐

5 **Deceased's date of birth** *DD MM YYYY*

6 **Where was the deceased domiciled at the date of death?**
See IHT400 Notes for information about domicile.

- England and Wales ☐
- Scotland ☐
- Northern Ireland ☐
- other country ☐ *specify country in box below*

If the deceased was not domiciled in the UK, fill in **IHT401** **now**, and then the rest of the form.

If the deceased was domiciled in Scotland at the date of death

7 **Has the legitim fund been discharged in full following the death?** *See IHT400 Notes*

Yes ☐ *Go to box 8*

No ☐ *Please provide a full explanation in the 'Additional information' boxes, pages 15 and 16*

Deceased's details

8 **Was the deceased:**

- married or in a civil partnership ☐
- single ☐
- widowed or a surviving civil partner ☐
- divorced or a former civil partner? ☐

9 **If the deceased was married or in a civil partnership at the time of their death, on what date did the marriage or registration of the civil partnership take place?**
DD MM YYYY

10 **Who survived the deceased?** *Tick all that apply*

- a spouse or civil partner ☐
- brothers or sisters ☐
- parents ☐
- children ☐ number
- grandchildren ☐ number

11 **Deceased's last known permanent address**

Postcode

House number

Rest of address, including house name or flat number

12 **Was the property in box 11 owned or part-owned by the deceased or did the deceased have a right to live in the property?** *Do not tick Yes to this question if the deceased was only renting the property*

Yes ☐ *Go to box 13*

No ☐ *Give details below. For example, 'deceased lived with daughter' or 'address was a nursing home'*

13 **Deceased's occupation, or former occupation if retired, for example, 'retired doctor'**

14 **Deceased's National Insurance number (if known)**

15 **Deceased's Income Tax number or Unique Taxpayer Reference (UTR) (if known)**

16 **Did anyone act under a power of attorney granted by the deceased during their lifetime? This may have been a general, enduring or lasting power of attorney.**

No ☐

Yes ☐ *Please enclose a copy of the power of attorney*

IHT400 Page 2

Contact details of the person dealing with the estate

For example, a solicitor or executor.

17 Name and address of the firm or person dealing with the estate

Name

Postcode

House or building number

Rest of address, including house name or flat number

18 Contact name *if different from box 17*

19 Phone number

20 DX number and town (if used)

21 Contact's reference

22 Fax number

23 If we have to repay any overpaid Inheritance Tax, we need to know who to make the cheque out to. Do you want any cheque we send to be made out to the firm or person shown at box 17?

Yes ☐ *Go to box 24*

No ☐ *Give the name(s) here, as you would like them to appear on the cheque*

Deceased's Will

24 Did the deceased leave a Will?

No ☐ *Go to box 29*

Yes ☐ *Go to box 25. Please enclose a copy of the Will and any codicils when sending us your account. If an instrument of variation alters the amount of Inheritance Tax payable on this estate, please also send a copy*

25 Is the address of the deceased as shown in the Will the same as the deceased's last known permanent address (at box 11)?

No ☐ *Go to box 26*

Yes ☐ *Go to box 27*

26 What happened to the property given as the deceased's residence in the Will?

If the deceased sold the property but used all the sale proceeds to buy another main residence for themselves and this happened more than once, there is no need to give details of all the events. Simply say that the 'residence was replaced by the current property'. In all other cases give details of exactly what happened to the property, and give the date of the event(s)

IHT400 Page 3

Items referred to in the Will but not included in the estate

Only fill in boxes 27 and 28 if the deceased left a Will. If they did not go to box 29.

27 Are you including on this form all assets specifically referred to in the Will?
For example, land, buildings, personal possessions, works of art or shares

No ☐ *Go to box 28*

Yes ☐ *Go to box 29*

28 Items referred to in the Will and not included on this form. *Any gifts should be shown on form IHT403*

Items given away as gifts, sold or disposed of before the deceased's death	Who was the item given or sold to, or what happened to it?	Date of gift, sale or disposal	Value of the item at the date of gift, sale or disposal £	If the item was sold, what did the deceased do with the sale proceeds?

What makes up your Inheritance Tax account – Schedules

To make a complete account of the estate you may need to complete some separate Schedules. Answer the following questions by ticking the 'No' or 'Yes' box.

29 Transfer of unused nil rate band

Do you want to transfer any unused nil rate band from the deceased's spouse or civil partner who died before them?

No ☐ Yes ☐ Use Schedule **IHT402**

30 Gifts and other transfers of value

Did the deceased make any lifetime gifts or other transfers of value on or after 18 March 1986? *See IHT400 Notes*

No ☐ Yes ☐ Use Schedule **IHT403**

31 Jointly owned assets

Did the deceased jointly own any assets (other than business or partnership assets) with any other person(s)?

No ☐ Yes ☐ Use Schedule **IHT404**

32 Houses, land, buildings and interests in land

Did the deceased own any house, land or buildings or rights over land in the UK in their sole name?

No ☐ Yes ☐ Use Schedule **IHT405**

33 Bank and building society accounts

Did the deceased hold any bank or building society accounts in their sole name, including cash ISAs, National Savings and Premium Bonds?

No ☐ Yes ☐ Use Schedule **IHT406**

34 Household and personal goods

Did the deceased own any household goods or personal possessions?

No ☐ Yes ☐ Use Schedule **IHT407**

If the deceased did not own any household goods or personal possessions or they do not have any value, please explain the circumstances in the 'Additional information' boxes on pages 15 and 16.

35 Household and personal goods donated to charity

Do the people who inherit the deceased's household goods and personal possessions want to donate some or all of them to a qualifying charity and deduct charity exemption from the value of the estate? *For example, they may wish to donate the deceased's furniture to a charity shop*

No ☐ Yes ☐ Use Schedule **IHT408**

IHT400 Page 4

What makes up your Inheritance Tax account – Schedules continued

To make a complete account of the estate you may need to complete separate Schedules. Answer the following questions by ticking the 'No' or 'Yes' box.

36 Pensions

Did the deceased have any provision for retirement other than the State Pension? *For example, a pension from an employer, a personal pension policy (or an alternatively secured pension)*

No ☐ Yes ☐ Use Schedule **IHT409**

37 Life assurance and annuities

Did the deceased pay premiums on any life assurance policies, annuities or other products which are payable either to their estate, to another person or which continue after death?

No ☐ Yes ☐ Use Schedule **IHT410**

38 Listed stocks and shares

Did the deceased own any listed stocks and shares or stocks and shares ISAs (excluding control holdings)?

No ☐ Yes ☐ Use Schedule **IHT411**

39 Unlisted stocks and shares and control holdings

Did the deceased own any unlisted stocks and shares (including AIM and OFEX), or any control holdings of any listed shares?

No ☐ Yes ☐ Use Schedule **IHT412**

40 Business relief, business and partnership interests and assets

Do you want to deduct business relief from any business interests and assets owned by the deceased or a partnership in which they were a partner?

No ☐ Yes ☐ Use Schedule **IHT413**

41 Farms, farmhouses and farmland

Do you want to deduct agricultural relief from any farmhouses, farms or farmland owned by the deceased?

No ☐ Yes ☐ Use Schedule **IHT414**

42 Interest in another estate

Was the deceased entitled to receive any legacy or assets from the estate of someone who died before them and that they had not received before they died?

No ☐ Yes ☐ Use Schedule **IHT415**

43 Debts due to the estate

Was the deceased owed any money by way of personal loans or mortgage at the date of death?

No ☐ Yes ☐ Use Schedule **IHT416**

44 Foreign assets

Did the deceased own any assets outside the UK either in their sole name or jointly with others?

No ☐ Yes ☐ Use Schedule **IHT417**

45 Assets held in trust

Did the deceased have any right to benefit from any assets held in trust (including the right to receive assets held in a trust at some future date)?

No ☐ Yes ☐ Use Schedule **IHT418**

46 Debts owed by the deceased

Do you wish to include a deduction from the estate for debts and liabilities of the following types:

- money that was spent on behalf of the deceased and which was not repaid
- loans
- liabilities related to a life assurance policy where the sum assured will not be fully reflected in the estate
- debts that the deceased guaranteed on behalf of another person?

No ☐ Yes ☐ Use Schedule **IHT419**

47 National Heritage assets

Is any asset already exempt or is exemption now being claimed, on the grounds of national, scientific, historic, artistic, scenic or architectural interest? Or does any such asset benefit from an Approved Maintenance Fund for the upkeep and preservation of National Heritage assets?

No ☐ Yes ☐ Use Schedule **IHT420**

If you answered Yes to any of questions 29 to 47, please fill in the Schedule for that asset. The Schedule number is shown at the end of each question.

48 Do you have all of the Schedules you need?

No ☐
- download the Schedules from www.hmrc.gov.uk/inheritancetax or
- phone us on 0300 123 1072 (+44 300 123 1072 from outside the UK)

When you have all the Schedules you need, fill them in before you go to box 49.

Yes ☐ Fill in the Schedules now before going to box 49

Estate in the UK

Use this section to tell us about assets owned by the deceased in the UK. You should include all assets owned outright by the deceased and the **deceased's share** of **jointly owned** assets. You will need to copy figures from the Schedules you have filled in. Any assets the deceased had outside the UK should be shown on form IHT417 *Foreign assets* and **not** in boxes 49 to 96.

Jointly owned assets

Enter '0' in the box if the deceased did not own any of the assets described.

Box	Item	Column A	Column B
49	**Jointly owned assets** *(form IHT404, box 5)*		£
50	**Jointly owned assets** *(form IHT404, box 10)*	£	

Assets owned outright by the deceased

Enter the value of the assets owned outright by the deceased in the amount boxes attached to each question. Enter '0' in the box if the deceased did not own any of the assets described.

Box	Item	Column A	Column B
51	**Deceased's residence (except farmhouses and jointly owned houses) (form IHT405, box 7). Include the value of jointly owned houses at box 49 and farmhouses at box 68 instead**		£
52	**Bank and building society accounts in the deceased's sole name (form IHT406, box 1)**	£	
53	**Cash (in coins or notes) and uncashed traveller's cheques**	£	
54	**Premium Bonds and National Savings & Investments products (form IHT406, box 5)**	£	
55	**Household and personal goods (form IHT407, box 6)**	£	
56	**Pensions (form IHT409, boxes 7 and 15). Include the value of any pensions arrears due at the date of death**	£	
57	**Life assurance and mortgage protection policies (form IHT410, box 6)**	£	
58	**Total of all the figures in column A (boxes 50 to 57)**	£	
59	**Total of all the figures in column B (boxes 49 + 51)**		£

IHT400 Page 6

Estate in the UK continued

		Column A	Column B
60	Copy the figure from box 58	£	
61	Copy the figure from box 59		£
62	UK Government and municipal securities (form IHT411, box 1), but include dividends and interest at box 64	£	
63	Listed stocks, shares and investments that did not give the deceased control of the company (form IHT411, box 2)	£	
64	Dividends or interest on stocks, shares and securities	£	
65	Traded unlisted and unlisted shares except control holdings (form IHT412, box 1 and box 2)	£	
66	Traded unlisted and unlisted shares except control holdings (see IHT412 Notes Paying tax by instalments)		£
67	Control holdings of unlisted, traded unlisted and listed shares (form IHT412, box 3, box 4 and box 5)		£
68	Farms, farmhouses and farmland (give details on forms IHT414 and IHT405)		£
69	Businesses including farm businesses, business assets and timber		£
70	Other land, buildings and rights over land (give details on form IHT405)		£
71	Interest in another estate (form IHT415, box 7)		£
72	Interest in another estate (form IHT415, box 9)	£	
73	Debts due to the estate (form IHT416, box 3 total)	£	
74	Income Tax or Capital Gains Tax repayment	£	
75	Trust income due to the deceased – *see IHT400 Notes*	£	
76	Other assets and income due to the deceased (enter details in the 'Additional information' boxes on pages 15 and 16 of this form if not given elsewhere)	£	
77	Total of all the figures in column A (boxes 60 to 65 and 72 to 76)	£	
78	Total of all the figures in column B (boxes 61 to 71)		£
79	Gross total of the estate in the UK (box 77 + box 78)	£	

IHT400 Page 7

Deductions from the estate in the UK incurred up to the date of death

80 **Mortgages, secured loans and other debts payable out of property or assets owned outright by the deceased and shown in column B on pages 6 and 7.** *For example, a mortgage secured on the deceased's house or a loan secured on a business. Enter the name of the creditor and say which property or asset the deduction relates to and describe the liability. Please provide copies of any written evidence of the debts.*

Name of creditor	Property or asset and description of liability	Amount £
	Total mortgages and secured loans £	

81 **Funeral expenses**

	Funeral costs £	
Other costs (please specify)	Headstone £	
	Total cost of funeral £	

82 **Other liabilities**
Enter any other liabilities that have not been shown in boxes 80 or 81. *For example, outstanding gas and electricity bills, credit card balances or nursing home fees.*

Creditor's name and description of the liability	Amount £
Total other liabilities £	

IHT400 Page 8

Deductions from the estate in the UK continued

Deductions summary

		Column A	Column B
83	Box 80 figure		£
84	Total of Box 81 and box 82	£	
85	Box 77 minus box 84. If the result is a minus figure enter '0' in the box and enter the deficit in box 88	£	
86	Box 78 minus box 83. If the result is a minus figure enter '0' in the box and enter the deficit in box 87		£
87	Enter the deficit figure from box 86 (if there is one)	£ 0	
88	Enter the deficit figure from box 85 (if there is one)		£ 0
89	Box 85 minus box 87	£ 0	
90	Box 86 minus box 88		£ 0
91	Total estate in the UK (box 89 plus box 90)	£ 0	

Exemptions and reliefs

92 Exemptions and reliefs deducted from the assets in the deceased's sole name shown in column A on pages 6 and 7 — *see IHT400 Notes.* **If you are deducting spouse or civil partner exemption, enter the spouse or civil partner's full name, date and country of birth and their domicile. If you are deducting charity exemption, enter the full name of the charity, country of establishment and the HMRC charities reference, if available.**
Do not include exemptions or reliefs on jointly owned assets, these should be deducted on form IHT404, at box 9. Do not deduct transferable nil rate band here or at box 93. It should be deducted at box 114 or box 2 IHT 400 calculation.

Describe the exemptions and reliefs you are deducting. For example 'cash gift to charity in the Will' and show how the amount has been calculated – please use the 'Additional information' boxes on pages 15 and 16 of this form if you need more space.	Amount deducted £
Total exemptions and reliefs from assets in **column A**	

Exemptions and reliefs continued

93 Exemptions and reliefs deducted from the assets in the deceased's sole name shown in column B on pages 6 and 7 - *see IHT400 Notes*. **If you are deducting spouse or civil partner exemption enter the spouse or civil partner's full name, date and country of birth and their domicile and/or, if you are deducting charity exemption enter the full name of the charity, the country of establishment and the HMRC charities reference, if available (unless already given at box 92). Do not include exemptions or reliefs on jointly owned assets, these should be deducted on form IHT404, at box 4.**

Describe the exemptions and reliefs you are deducting. For example, 'agricultural relief on farm' and show how the amount has been calculated – please use the 'Additional information' boxes on pages 15 and 16 if you need more space.	Amount deducted £
Total exemptions and reliefs from assets in **column B**	

	Column A	Column B
94 **Box 89 minus box 92**	£ 0	
95 **Box 90 minus box 93**		£ 0
96 **Total net estate in the UK, after exemptions and reliefs (box 94 plus box 95)**	£ 0	

Other assets taken into account to calculate the tax

	Column A	Column B
97 **Foreign houses, land, businesses and control holdings (form IHT417, box 5)**		£
98 **Other foreign assets (form IHT417, box 10)**	£	
99 **Assets held in trust on which the trustees would like to pay the tax now (form IHT418, box 12)**		£
100 **Assets held in trust on which the trustees would like to pay the tax now (form IHT418, box 17)**	£	
101 **Nominated assets. Include details of the nominated assets in the 'Additional information' boxes on pages 15 and 16 -** *see IHT400 Notes*	£	
102 **Box 98 plus box 100 plus box 101**	£	
103 **Box 97 plus box 99**		£
104 **Gifts with reservation and pre-owned assets (IHT403, box 17)**	£	
105 **Assets held in trust on which the trustees are not paying the tax now (form IHT418, box 18)**	£	
106 **Alternatively secured pension fund(s) (form IHT409, boxes 32 and 42 – only where the date of death is between 6 April 2006 and 5 April 2007 inclusive)**	£	
107 **Total other assets taken into account to calculate the tax (box 102 plus boxes 103, 104, 105 and 106)**	£	
108 **Total chargeable estate (box 96 plus box 107)**	£ 0	

IHT400 Page 10

Working out the Inheritance Tax

If there is no Inheritance Tax to pay, you do not need to fill in this page and should go to box 119 on page 12.

109 **Does any part of the estate qualify for the Reduced rate of Inheritance Tax (36%)?** *See IHT400 Notes page 52*

No ☐ *Go to box 110*

Yes ☐ *You will need to complete form IHT430 Reduced rate of Inheritance Tax*

Paying Inheritance Tax by instalments

Instead of paying all of the Inheritance Tax at once you may pay some of it in 10 annual instalments (that is, one instalment each year for 10 years). You can pay by instalments on any assets shown in **column B** on pages 6 and 7 that have not been sold.

Interest will be payable on the instalments.

The total value of the assets on which you may pay the tax by instalments is box 95 plus boxes 97 and box 99 (if any).

110 **Do you wish to pay the tax on the amounts shown in boxes 95, 97 plus 99 by instalments?**

Yes ☐ *If any of the assets in Column B have been sold, write the total value of those assets here*

£

Go to 'Simple Inheritance Tax calculation' below

Simple Inheritance Tax calculation

You can use the simple calculation in boxes 111 to 117 to work out the Inheritance Tax on the estate as long as the following apply:

- you are paying the tax on or before the last day of the sixth month after the death occurred so no interest is payable
- you want to pay all of the tax now and not pay by instalments on property in column B (see note above about paying Inheritance Tax by instalments)
- the total of any lifetime gifts is below the Inheritance Tax nil rate band
- you are not deducting double taxation relief on any foreign assets (see *note on IHT400 Calculation in IHT400 Notes*)
- you are not deducting successive charges relief on assets inherited by the deceased in the last five years from another estate on which Inheritance Tax was paid (see *note on IHT400 Calculation*)
- the estate does not qualify for the reduced rate of Inheritance Tax (36%).

If the simple calculation does not apply to you, you will need to use either form IHT400 *Calculation* or form IHT 430 *Reduced rate of Inheritance Tax* to work out the Inheritance Tax due then continue to fill in this form at box 118.

111	**Total chargeable value of gifts made by the deceased within the seven years before their death (form IHT403, box 7)**	£
112	**Aggregate chargeable transfer (box 108 plus box 111)**	£ 0
113	**Inheritance Tax nil rate band at the date of death** - *See IHT400 Rates and Tables*	£
114	**Transferable nil rate band (form IHT402, box 20)**	£
115	**Total nil rate band (box 113 plus box 114)**	£
116	**Value chargeable to tax (box 112 minus box 115)**	£ 0
117	**Inheritance Tax (box 116 multiplied by 40%)**	£ 0

IHT400 Page 11

Direct Payment Scheme

This is a scheme under which participating banks and building societies will release funds from the deceased's accounts directly to HM Revenue & Customs to pay Inheritance Tax. For National Savings & Investments, see the note on page 14.

118 Do you wish to use the Direct Payment Scheme?

No ☐

Yes ☐ *Fill in form IHT423 (you will need a separate form for each bank and building society account concerned)*

Declaration

119 I/We wish to apply for the following type of grant (see note 'Grant of representation' in IHT400 Notes to decide on the type of grant)

- Probate ☐
- Confirmation ☐
- Letters of Administration ☐
- Letters of Administration with Will annexed ☐
- Other (please specify)

To the best of my/our knowledge and belief, the information I/we have given and the statements I/we have made in this account and the Schedules attached (together called 'this account') are correct and complete. Please tick the Schedules you have filled in.

IHT401 ☐	IHT408 ☐	IHT415 ☐
IHT402 ☐	IHT409 ☐	IHT416 ☐
IHT403 ☐	IHT410 ☐	IHT417 ☐
IHT404 ☐	IHT411 ☐	IHT418 ☐
IHT405 ☐	IHT412 ☐	IHT419 ☐
IHT406 ☐	IHT413 ☐	IHT420 ☐
IHT407 ☐	IHT414 ☐	IHT430 ☐

I/We have made the fullest enquiries that are reasonably practicable in the circumstances to find out the open market value of all the items shown in this account.

The value of items in the box(es) listed below are provisional estimates which are based on all of the information available to me/us at this time.

I/We will tell HM Revenue & Customs the exact value(s) as soon as I/we know it and I/we will pay any additional tax and interest that may be due.

List the boxes in the account that are provisional here.

Where Schedule IHT402 has been filled in I/we declare that to the best of my/our knowledge and belief:

- the deceased and their spouse or civil partner were married or in a civil partnership at the date the spouse or civil partner died
- where a Deed of Variation has not been provided there has been no change to the people who inherited the estate of the spouse or civil partner.

I/We understand that I/we may be liable to prosecution if I/we deliberately conceal any information that affects the liability to Inheritance Tax arising on the deceased's death, or if I/we deliberately include information in this account which I/we know to be false.

I/We understand that I/we may have to pay financial penalties if this account is delivered late or contains false information, or if I/we fail to remedy anything in this account which is incorrect in any material respect within a reasonable time of it coming to my/our notice.

I/We understand that the issue of the grant does not mean that:

- I/we have paid all the Inheritance Tax and interest that may be due on the estate, or
- the statements made and the values included in this account are accepted by HM Revenue & Customs.

I/We understand that HM Revenue & Customs :

- will only look at this account in detail after the grant has been issued
- may need to ask further questions and discuss the value of items shown in this account
- may make further calculations of tax and interest payable to help the persons liable for the tax to make provision to meet the tax liability.

I/We understand that I/we may have to pay interest on any unpaid tax according to the law where:

- I/we have elected to pay tax by instalments
- additional tax becomes payable for any reason.

Each person delivering this account, whether as executor, intending administrator or otherwise must sign on page 13 to indicate that they have read and agreed the statements above.

IHT400 Page 12

Declaration continued

Surname

First name(s)

Postcode

House number

Rest of address, including house name or flat number

Phone number

Signature

Date *DD MM YYYY*

Surname

First name(s)

Postcode

House number

Rest of address, including house name or flat number

Phone number

Signature

Date *DD MM YYYY*

Surname

First name(s)

Postcode

House number

Rest of address, including house name or flat number

Phone number

Signature

Date *DD MM YYYY*

Surname

First name(s)

Postcode

House number

Rest of address, including house name or flat number

Phone number

Signature

Date *DD MM YYYY*

IHT400 Page 13

Checklist

For more information read the relevant page in the IHT400 Notes.

Use the checklist to remind you of:
- the actions you should take, and
- the additional information you should include when sending the Inheritance Tax forms to us.

- If the deceased died leaving a Will, provide a copy of the Will, and any codicils.

  No ☐ Yes ☐

- If the estate has been varied in any way and the variation results in either an increase or decrease in the amount of tax, provide a copy of the instrument of variation.

  No ☐ Yes ☐

- Any professional valuation of stocks and shares.

  No ☐ Yes ☐

- Any professional valuation of household effects or personal possessions.

  No ☐ Yes ☐

- Any professional valuation of houses, land and buildings.

  No ☐ Yes ☐

- A copy of any insurance policy (and annuity, if appropriate) where the deceased was paying the premiums for the benefit of someone else and any trust documents if the policy has been written in trust.

  No ☐ Yes ☐

- A copy of any trust deed(s), if the trustees are paying tax at the same time as you apply for the grant.

  No ☐ Yes ☐

- Any evidence of money owed to the deceased, including loan agreements and related trusts or policies and any evidence of the debts being released.

  No ☐ Yes ☐

- A copy of any joint life assurance policy or policy on the life of another person.

  No ☐ Yes ☐

- A copy of any structural survey and/or correspondence with the loss adjuster about any structurally damaged property.

  No ☐ Yes ☐

- If you are deducting agricultural relief, a plan of the property and a copy of the lease or agreement for letting (where appropriate).

  No ☐ Yes ☐

- If you are deducting business relief, a copy of the partnership agreement (where appropriate) and the last three years' accounts.

  No ☐ Yes ☐

- If you are deducting double taxation relief or unilateral relief, provide evidence of the foreign tax, in the form of an assessment of the foreign tax, a certificate of the foreign tax paid and (if available) the official receipt.

  No ☐ Yes ☐

- Any written evidence of debts to close friends or family.

  No ☐ Yes ☐

- Have all executors signed page 13 of this form?

  No ☐ Yes ☐

- If you have calculated your own tax, have you enclosed the calculation with this form and arranged to pay the tax?

  No ☐ Yes ☐

- If you are applying for a grant, have you enclosed form IHT421 *Probate summary?*

  No ☐ Yes ☐

Direct Payment Scheme (if used)

- If you are using the Direct Payment Scheme, have you sent a form IHT423 to each organisation from which funds will be provided? *See IHT423*

  No ☐ Yes ☐

- If you want HM Revenue & Customs to call for payment from National Savings & Investments, send us a letter detailing the investments to be used, how much of the tax is to be paid by National Savings & Investments and official letters from the relevant National Savings & Investments office stating the value of those investments.
- If you want HM Revenue & Customs to call for payment from British Government stock, send us a letter detailing the investments to be used and how much of the tax is to be paid by Government stock.

For more information on paying by National Savings or British Government stocks go to **hmrc.gov.uk** or phone the helpline for a copy of the IHT11 *Payment of Inheritance Tax from National Savings or from British Government stock.*

IHT400 Page 14

Return addresses and contact details

- If you are applying for a grant in England, Wales or Northern Ireland or confirmation in Scotland you should send the forms to: (the DX addresses are for solicitors, practitioners and banks)

  HM Revenue & Customs
  Trusts & Estates
  Inheritance Tax
  Ferrers House
  PO Box 38
  Castle Meadow Road
  NOTTINGHAM
  NG2 1BB
  DX 701201 NOTTINGHAM 4
  Phone: **0300 123 1072**
- If you want to know more about any particular aspect of Inheritance Tax or have specific questions about completing the forms:
  - go to **hmrc.gov.uk/inheritancetax**, or
  - phone the Probate and Inheritance Tax Helpline on **0300 123 1072** (**+44 300 123 1072** from outside the UK).
- If you need a copy of any of our forms or leaflets you can download them from our website or phone the Probate and Inheritance Tax Helpline to order them.

Additional information

Use this space:
- to explain the circumstances where the deceased did not own any household effects or personal possessions or they do not have any value (box 34)
- to give us any additional information we ask for, including details of:
  - any claim for discharge of legal rights (box 7)
  - other assets and income due to the deceased (box 76)
  - nominated assets (box 101)
  - successive charges relief (IHT400 Calculation, box 10).
  - why any debts that are not being repaid out of the estate are still being deducted against the estate (box 80 or 82).

Additional information continued

IHT400 Page 15

Additional information continued

IHT400 Page 16

Assets held in trust [Form IHT418]

HM Revenue & Customs

Assets held in trust

Schedule IHT418

When to use this form

Fill in this form if the deceased had the right to benefit from a trust created by a deed or under someone's Will or intestacy.

If the deceased had the right to benefit from more than one trust, you should complete a separate form for each trust.

Help

Please read the guidance notes for form IHT418 in the IHT400 Notes before filling in this form.

For more information or help or another copy of this form:

- go to **www.hmrc.gov.uk/inheritancetax**
- phone our Helpline on **0845 30 20 900**
  – if calling from outside the UK, phone **+44 115 974 3009**.

Name of deceased

Date of death *DD MM YYYY*

IHT reference number (if known)

Deceased's interest in possession

Please read the IHT400 Notes about the definitions of an 'interest in possession' and the types of interests listed below, before completing this section.

1 Did the deceased have an interest in possession which was one of the following interests?

An interest in possession that started before 22 March 2006 and remained in existence until the date of death	No ☐	Yes ☐
An immediate post-death interest	No ☐	Yes ☐
A disabled person's interest	No ☐	Yes ☐
A transitional serial interest	No ☐	Yes ☐

- If you answered Yes to any of the above questions, go to box 2.
- If you answered No to all the above questions, go to box 19.

About the trust

2 Name of the person who created the trust either during their lifetime, or by their Will or intestacy

3 Name of the trust

4 Unique Taxpayer Reference of the trust

5 Date the trust was created *DD MM YYYY*

6 Do you have details of all the assets in the trust and their values? *The trustees may only give you a 'total value' figure for the trust fund*

No ☐ Yes ☐

If you answered No to question 6, complete only the 'total' boxes at 12 and 17 on pages 2 and 3.

If you answered Yes, complete all of pages 2 and 3.

7 Name(s) and address(es) of the trustees or the solicitors acting for the trust

Continue on page 4 if necessary

Approval Ref No: L3/00

Assets in the trust

This page should only contain details of assets in trust consisting of:

- houses, land and buildings
- businesses or interests in businesses, and
- shares and securities which gave the deceased control of the company.

8 Details of the assets in the trust

Description of assets	Value at the date of death £
Total of assets	£

9 Mortgages, secured loans and other debts payable out of the assets shown in box 8

Description of liabilities	Amount £
Total of liabilities	£

10 Net assets (box 8 *minus* box 9). If a *minus* amount, write '0' £

11 Details of exemptions and reliefs to be deducted from the trust assets listed in box 8 (for example, business relief)

Description of exemptions and reliefs *If you are deducting charity exemption, enter the full name of the charity, the country of establishment and the HMRC charities reference, if available.*	Amount £
Total of exemptions and reliefs	£

12 Total (box 10 *minus* box 11) £

If the trustees want to pay the tax on these assets now, copy the amount in box 12 to form IHT400, box 99.
If not, copy the amount to box 18 of this form.

IHT418 Page 2

Interest in another estate [Form IHT415]

HM Revenue & Customs

Interest in another estate

Schedule IHT415

When to use this form

Fill in this form if the deceased had a right to a legacy or share in an estate of someone else who died before them, but which they had not received before they died.

You should fill in a separate form for each estate in which the deceased had a right to a legacy or share.

Help

For more information or help or another copy of this form:

- go to **www.hmrc.gov.uk/inheritancetax/**
- phone our Helpline on **0845 30 20 900**
  – if calling from outside the UK, phone **+44 115 974 3009**.

Name of deceased

Date of death *DD MM YYYY*

IHT reference number (if known)

Details of the person who died earlier

1 Name of the person who died earlier (the 'predecessor')

Title – enter MR, MRS, MISS, MS or other title

Surname

First names

2 Date the predecessor died *DD MM YYYY*

3 Capital Taxes or Inheritance Tax reference of the earlier estate (if known)

If you do not know the reference, give the date of grant for the earlier death (if known)

Date of grant *DD MM YYYY*

The deceased's entitlement

4 Tell us what the deceased was entitled to from the other estate. *For example, a legacy of money, a specific item, or a share of the predecessor's estate*

5 Had the deceased received any part of the entitlement before they died?

No ☐ *Go to box 7 on page 2*

Yes ☐ *Go to box 6*

6 Tell us what the deceased had already received

Deceased's entitlement

Give full details of the deceased's entitlement in boxes 7 and 9. If the deceased was entitled to a legacy of specific assets, describe the assets and give their values at the date the deceased died.

If the deceased was entitled to the remainder of the estate (the residue):

- give details of the assets and liabilities of the estate that the personal representatives of the person who died earlier held at the date the deceased died, including any legacies or other payments still to be made
- give the value of these assets at the deceased's date of death (in the same way as you value the deceased's own assets)
- deduct any legacies to other people that have still to be paid
- show how you have arrived at the net value and write it in the box provided.

If you are unable to obtain such details before you are ready to apply for a grant, give as much information as you can and include an estimate for the value.

7 The deceased's entitlement to:

- houses, land and buildings
- an interest in a business
- shares or securities that gave the deceased control of the company.

List any debts or liabilities due on these assets in this box

Details of the entitlement	Value of entitlement £

Net value 7 £ 0.00

Total of column above – *copy this amount to form IHT400, box 71*

8 Are these values estimates?

No ☐ Yes ☐

IHT415 Page 2

9 All other assets to which the deceased was entitled, whch are not shown in box 7.
List any debts or liabilities due on the other assets in this box

Details of the entitlement	Value of entitlement £

Net value 9 £ 0.00

Total of column above - *copy this amount to form IHT400, box 72*

10 Are these values estimates?

No ☐ Yes ☐

IHT415 Page 3

Probate summary [Form IHT421]

& Customs

Schedule IHT421

Name and address

Read the notes below before you fill in this box

Name

Address

Postcode

Inheritance Tax reference *if known*

Name of Probate Registry where you are sending form PA1

Leave this box blank if you are a Solicitor or are applying for a grant in Northern Ireland

Your reference (if applicable) and name of contact

Reference

Name

Your phone number (in case we have a query)

Notes

There are different procedures for applying for a grant of probate depending on who you are and where you apply for the grant.

If you are a solicitor

Either:

- enter your name and full postal address in the box above, **or**
- if you use the British Document Exchange (DX), type in or enter your DX address in capitals.

If you are filling in this form without the help of a solicitor

The action you take depends where you are taking out the grant:

- in England and Wales – leave the box above blank. Send this form with your form IHT400 Inheritance Tax account to HMRC Trusts and Estates Inheritance Tax (we will then send it to the Probate Registry where you are sending form PA1)
- in Northern Ireland – write your own name and address in the box above
- in Scotland – do not fill in this form. Please complete form C1 instead.

About this form

Fill in this form if you are applying for a grant of representation in England, Wales or Northern Ireland.

If you are in Scotland fill in form C1 to apply for a grant of confirmation instead.

Give details of the assets that became the property of the personal representatives. This will be the same property for which you are applying for a grant of representation.

Help

Please read the guidance notes *Applying for a grant* in the *IHT400 Notes* before filling in this form.

For more information or help:

- go to **www.hmrc.gov.uk/inheritancetax**
- go to **www.justice.gov.uk**
- phone our helpline on **0845 30 20 900**
- if phoning from outside the UK, phone **+44115 974 3009**.

Deceased's details *use capital letters*

Name

Title – enter Mr, Mrs, Miss, Ms or other title

Surname or family name

First name(s)

Date of death *DD MM YYYY*

Address

Postcode

House or building number

Rest of address, including house name or flat number

Where was the deceased domiciled at the date of death?

IHT421 Substitute (LexisNexis) (07/12) Page 1 HMRC Approval Reference L67/12

Summary

This is a summary for probate purposes only and will not necessarily include all the assets you have listed on the form IHT400 for Inheritance Tax purposes. It will not include:

- lifetime gifts
- foreign assets
- assets held in trust
- nominated assets
- gifts with reservation and pre-owned assets.

Estate in the UK before deductions *IHT400, box 79 + IHT404, box 13*	1	£ 0.00	
Joint assets passing by survivorship *Copy amount from IHT404, box 11, total of column A*	2	£ 0.00	
Gross value of assets for probate (box 1 minus box 2)	3	£ 0.00	*See Note below*
Liabilities *IHT400, box 83 + box 84, + IHT404, box 12*	4	£ 0.00	
Net value (box 3 *minus* box 4)	5	£ 0.00	*See Note below*
Tax and interest paid on this account Copy amount from form: • IHT400, box 117 • IHT400 Calculation, box 64, or • IHT430, box 28 as appropriate. If there is no tax to pay enter '0'.	6	£	

Signature of person or name of firm calculating the amount due

Date *DD MM YYYY*

Note

If you are a Solicitor

Copy the amounts in boxes 3 and 5 to the oath.

If you are filling in this form without the help of a solicitor

In England and Wales - copy the amounts in boxes 3 and 5 to form PA1 section E
In Northern Ireland please read instructions at **www.courtsni.gov.uk**

For HM Revenue & Customs use only

Inheritance Tax stamp

Page 2

Return of estate Information [Form IHT205]

HM Revenue
& Customs

Return of estate information

When to use this form

Fill in this version of this form only when the person died on or after 6 April 2011. Fill in this form where the person who has died ('the deceased') was domiciled (had their permanent home) in the UK at the date of death and the **gross value of the estate for Inheritance Tax is less than or equal to:**

- the excepted estate limit
- twice the excepted estate limit and form IHT217 'Claim to transfer unused nil rate band for excepted estates' is attached
- £1,000,000 and there is no Inheritance Tax to pay because of spouse, civil partner or charity exemption

Keep a copy of this form for your records as HMRC cannot provide you with a copy at a later date.

Notes

Read the notes in booklet IHT206(2011) to help you fill in this form.

Help

For more information or help:

- go to **www.hmrc.gov.uk/inheritancetax**
- phone our helpline on **0300 123 1072**

Your rights and obligations

Your Charter explains what you can expect from us and what we expect from you. For more information go to **www.gov.uk/hmrc/your-charter**

About the person who has died

1.1 **Title** enter Mr, Mrs, Miss, Ms or other title

☐

1.2 **Surname**

☐

1.3 **First name**

☐

1.4 **Date of death** DD MM YYYY

☐☐ ☐☐ ☐☐☐☐

1.5 **Marital or civil partnership status?**

Married or in civil partnership ☐

Single ☐

Divorced or former civil partner ☐

Widowed or a surviving civil partner ☐

1.6 **Occupation**

☐

1.7 **National Insurance number** if known

☐☐ ☐☐ ☐☐ ☐☐ ☐

About the estate

2 **In the 7 years before they died, did the deceased:**

make any gifts or other transfers totalling more than £3,000 per year, other than normal birthday, festive, marriage or civil partnership gifts?

No ☐ Yes ☐

or

give up the right to benefit from any assets held in trust that were treated as part of their estate for Inheritance Tax purposes?

No ☐ Yes ☐

If you answered 'Yes' to either part of this question, include the chargeable value of the gifts in box 9.1. But if this value is more than £150,000 or the assets do not qualify as 'specified transfers', **stop filling in this form. You will need to fill in form IHT400 'Inheritance Tax account' instead.**

About the estate continued

3 Did the deceased make any of the following:

a gift, on or after 18 March 1986, where they continued to benefit from, or had some right to benefit from, or use all or part of the asset?

No ☐ Yes ☐

or

a gift, on or after 18 March 1986, where the person receiving the gift did not take full possession of it?

No ☐ Yes ☐

or

an election on form IHT500 'Election for Inheritance Tax to apply to asset previously owned' that an Income Tax charge should not apply to:

- assets they previously owned, in which they retained a benefit
- the deceased's contribution to the purchase price of assets acquired by another person, but in which the deceased retained a benefit?

No ☐ Yes ☐

If you answered 'Yes' to any part of this question, **stop filling in this form. You will need to fill in form IHT400 instead.**

4 Did the deceased have the right to receive the benefit from any assets held in a trust that were treated as part of their estate for Inheritance Tax purposes?

No ☐ Yes ☐

If you answered 'Yes', and the deceased:

- was entitled to benefit from a single trust, and
- the value of the assets in that trust, treated as part of their estate, was less than or equal to £150,000

include the value of the trust assets in box 9.3.
But if the value was £150,000 or more, or there was more than 1 trust, **stop filling in this form. You will need to fill in form IHT400 instead.**

5 Did the deceased own or benefit from any assets outside the UK?

No ☐ Yes ☐

If you answered 'Yes', include the value of the overseas assets in box 9.5. But if the value of the overseas assets is more than £100,000, **stop filling in this form. You will need to fill in form IHT400 instead.**

6 Did the deceased pay premiums on any life insurance policies that were not for their own benefit or did not pay out to the estate, and did they buy an annuity at any time? Ignore any policies paid out to a surviving spouse or civil partner

No ☐ Yes ☐

If you answered Yes, **stop filling in this form. You will need to fill in form IHT400 instead.**

7 Did the deceased have any kind of pension arrangement other than the State Pension?

No ☐ Yes ☐

If you answered 'No', go to the next section 'Deceased's assets at the date of death'.

8 Did the deceased change or dispose of their pension in the 2 years before they died? Ignore any pensions paid to a surviving spouse or civil partner

No ☐ Yes ☐

If you answered Yes to this question, **stop filling in this form. You will need to fill in form IHT400 instead.**

Page 2

Deceased's assets at the date of death

Make the fullest enquiries so that you can show that the figures on this form are correct. If you cannot find the value for an item you may include your best estimate.

Assets added to the estate for Inheritance Tax for which a grant of representation is not required

9.1 **Gifts and other lifetime transfers (after deduction of allowable exemptions) made in the 7 years before they died. This does not include legacies in the will.**

Show the date and description of gifts, who they were made to and any exemptions you have deducted in the box below

Box 9.1 £

9.2 **Deceased's share of joint assets passing automatically to the surviving joint owner even if they are the husband, wife or civil partner.**

For example, a house owned as joint tenants, joint bank accounts or household goods. Describe the asset and give its whole value in the box below and say what share the deceased owned. If it is a house, give the address. Put the value of the deceased's share in box 9.2

Box 9.2 £

9.3 **Assets held in trust for the benefit of the deceased during their lifetime.**

Please tell us what assets were in the trust, the name of the person who set up the trust and the date it was set up

Box 9.3 £

9.4 **Nominated assets** Box 9.4 £

9.5 **Assets outside of the UK** Box 9.5 £

Gross value of assets for which a grant is not required (add together the figures in boxes 9.1 to 9.5) Box A £ 0

Page 3

Deceased's assets at the date of death continued

Debts payable out of assets totalled in box A

10.1	Share of mortgage on a property owned as a joint asset and shown in box 9.2	Box 10.1	£
10.2	Share of other debts payable out of joint assets	Box 10.2	£
10.3	Debts payable out of trust assets	Box 10.3	£
10.4	Debts owing to persons outside of the UK	Box 10.4	£
	Total debts payable out of assets in boxes 9.1 to 9.5 (add together boxes 10.1 to 10.4)	Box B	£ 0
	Net value of assets for which a grant is not required (box A minus box B) (this value may be nil)	Box C	£ 0

Deceased's own assets for which a grant of representation is required

Please include:

- the gross value for each item before deduction of any exemptions or reliefs
- all assets, ignoring any changes that may take place through a Deed of variation made after the death
- the deceased's share of jointly owned assets not passing automatically to the surviving joint owner.

11.1	Cash, including money in banks, building societies and National Savings	Box 11.1	£
11.2	Household and personal goods	Box 11.2	£
11.3	Stocks and shares quoted on the Stock Exchange	Box 11.3	£
11.4	Stocks and shares not quoted on the Stock Exchange	Box 11.4	£
11.5	Insurance policies, including bonuses and mortgage protection policies	Box 11.5	£
11.6	Money owed to the person who has died (outstanding loans)	Box 11.6	£
11.7	Partnership and business interests	Box 11.7	£
11.8	Value of the freehold/leasehold residence of the person who has died if owned in their sole name or as tenants-in-common	Box 11.8	£

Freehold/leasehold residence address

Postcode

Page 4

3

Administration and Collection

Simon's Taxes. See **Part I11.**

Other Sources. HMRC Customer Guide to Inheritance Tax; Mellows, Chapter 5; Foster, Part L; IHTM 30000, IHTM31000, IHTM38000, IHTM36000.

Management

[3.1] Inheritance tax is 'under the care and management of the Board' (i.e. the Commissioners for Her Majesty's Revenue and Customs, 1 Parliament Street, London SW1A 2BQ). [*IHTA 1984, s 215*]. HMRC Inheritance Tax exists to deal with the levying of inheritance tax, and accounts and correspondence should be sent to them at the addresses given at **2.19** ACCOUNTS AND RETURNS.

HMRC's care and management powers take many forms: in this work special attention is given to **23** HMRC EXTRA-STATUTORY CONCESSIONS, **24** HMRC PRESS RELEASES, and **25** HMRC STATEMENTS OF PRACTICE, which are published by the Board. Reference is also made in context to other statements made by HMRC elsewhere, e.g. in HMRC's Tax Bulletin or memoranda issued by professional bodies.

Taxpayer's Charter and Codes of Practice

[3.2] HMRC has also produced in the past, in accordance with Government initiatives generally, a Taxpayer's Charter which has set out the principles it tries to meet in its dealings with taxpayers, the standards it believes the taxpayer has a right to expect, and what people can do if they wish to appeal or complain. The current version of the charter which was published on 26 February 2013 is at https://www.gov.uk/government/publications/your-charter. It undertakes that HMRC will:

'be even-handed in the way we deal with you. We will take into account your circumstances and provide a consistent service. If you need help we will also give you the appropriate support so you can meet your obligations.

We will:

- act within the law and our published guidance
- help you understand your legal rights
- explain what you can do if you disagree with our decisions or want to make a complaint
- provide you with information in a way that meets your particular needs
- consider any financial difficulties you may be having.'

It also states that HMRC will:

'aim to take up as little of your time and money as we can.

We will:

- try to make our services straightforward and easy to access
- make it as cheap as we can for you to contact us
- explain clearly what we need from you
- do our best to give you complete, accurate and consistent advice
- do our best to get things right first time.'

Codes of Practice

A series of codes of practice, setting out the standards of service people can expect in relation to specific aspects of HMRC's work, are produced. The codes are not meant to represent any change of practice although some practices mentioned in them were not previously publicly available. Of the codes, Code of Practice 1 (COP 1), 'Putting things right when we make mistakes' issued by HMRC, is in principle applied to all HMRC functions (and thus including those relating to HMRC Inheritance Tax), although originally written mainly with tax and collection offices in mind (Inland Revenue Press Release 3 April 1996). See http://www.hmrc.gov.uk/leaflets/c11.htm. Under the most recently updated Code, the direct costs incurred by the taxpayer in dealing with HMRC will be reimbursed (this practice supersedes that contained in **25** HMRC STATEMENTS OF PRACTICE A31) and compensation paid where HMRC took an unreasonable view of the law. Other aspects of Code 1 are mentioned at **28.1** and **28.2** INTEREST ON TAX (both of which also mention reimbursement of the taxpayer's costs where there is unreasonable delay by HMRC) and **35.20** PAYMENT OF TAX.

The Adjudicator

[3.3] A taxpayer who is not satisfied with the HMRC response to a complaint has the option of putting the case to the Adjudicator. The Adjudicator, who was appointed with effect from 1 July 1993, is able to deal with complaints about HMRC's handling of a taxpayer's affairs, e.g. excessive delay, errors, discourtesy or the exercise of HMRC discretion, where the events complained of occurred after 5 April 1993. Matters subject to existing rights of appeal are excluded.

Complaints normally go to the Adjudicator only after they have been considered by the Controller of the relevant HMRC office, and where the taxpayer is still not satisfied with the response received. The alternatives of pursuing the complaint to HMRC's Head office, to an MP, or (through an MP) to the Parliamentary and Health Service Ombudsman continue to be available. See http://www.ombudsman.org.uk/.

The Adjudicator will review all the facts, consider whether the complaint is justified, and, if so, make recommendations as to what should be done.

Contact can be made with the Adjudicator's Office, 8th Floor, Euston Tower, 286 Euston Road, London NW1 3US. Tel: 020 7667 1832. Fax: 020 7667 1830. An explanatory leaflet A01 (in nine ethnic minority languages as well as English and Welsh) is available from the Adjudicator which describes the actions a taxpayer should take and how the Adjudicator will respond to complaints. See http://www.adjudicatorsoffice.gov.uk.

Accounts and information

[3.4] Transferors and other taxable persons have a duty to provide the Board with accounts containing information about transfers within a certain time after the transfers. The Board also has power to require any person to furnish them with information for IHT purposes. [*IHTA 1984, ss 216–219, 256, 257, 261*]. See **2** ACCOUNTS AND RETURNS. The Board has powers of inspection for valuation purposes. [*IHTA 1984, s 220*]. See **56.1** VALUATION.

Determinations and appeals

[3.5] When a transfer of value has been made, the Board issues a notice of determination (with a similar function to a notice of assessment for income tax, capital gains tax, etc.) showing the value of the transfer and the tax chargeable. A person who receives a notice of determination may appeal against it. The appeal will be heard by the Special Commissioners, or, in certain circumstances, by the Lands Tribunal or the High Court. [*IHTA 1984, ss 221–225*]. Special Commissioners' cases held publicly and reported may be obtained from the Special Commissioners' Office in London. See **14** DETERMINATIONS AND APPEALS.

Payment of tax

[3.6] Tax is generally due six months after the end of the month of the transfer, with an extension to the end of the following April where a chargeable lifetime transfer takes place after 5 April and before 1 October in any year. On the transfer of certain types of property, broadly land, shares and businesses, tax may be paid by instalments. Certain 'pre-eminent' types of property such as works of art, historic buildings etc. were accepted in lieu of tax (see also Capital Taxation and the IHT 420).

Where tax is not paid an HMRC charge for the unpaid tax is imposed on the property transferred. However, a person who has paid tax on a transfer or who has confirmed with HMRC that no tax is due, may obtain a certificate of discharge which serves to free the property in question from any HMRC charge. [*IHTA 1984, ss 226–232, 237–239*]. See **35** PAYMENT OF TAX and http://www.hmrc.gov.uk/cto/customerguide/page1.htm.

Interest and penalties

[3.7] Interest is charged on unpaid tax and paid on any repayment of tax overpaid (currently 3%). [*IHTA 1984, ss 233–236*]. See **28** INTEREST ON TAX. Penalties are charged for various failures to comply with the IHT legislation, for providing incorrect information and for failing to remedy errors. By reason of the *FA 2004* penalties have been increased substantially. [*IHTA 1984, ss 245–253; FA 2004, s 295*]. See **36** PENALTIES and http://www.hmrc.gov.uk/cto/customerguide/page22.htm.

Recovery of tax

[3.8] The Board may issue a notice of determination (see **3.5** above) if it appears that a transfer of value has been made, even if no account or return (see **3.4** above) of the transfer has been made. If tax or interest on tax is unpaid, the Board may take legal proceedings to recover it. If it is discovered that too little tax has been paid, the underpayment is payable with interest. However, where tax is paid and accepted on the view of the law current at the time, the amount of tax due is not affected if it appears subsequently that that view was wrong. The New Disclosure Opportunity (NDO) and Liechtenstein Disclosure Facility (LDF) follow the previous Offshore Disclosure Facility (ODF) on 2007 and can apply for IHT purposes. See **5** ANTI-AVOIDANCE. [*IHTA 1984, ss 240–244, 254, 255*]. See **35** PAYMENT OF TAX.

Limitation of liability

[3.9] The Statute of Limitations does not apply in relation IHT liabilities. Instead the position is governed by *IHTA 1984, s 240*.

Where an account has been delivered and tax paid and accepted by HMRC in full satisfaction of the liability, no further claim can be made in respect of that account more than four years after the tax was paid and accepted, or the last instalment fell due. If, however, there is a loss of tax in these circumstances brought about 'carelessly' by the taxpayer or agent for the taxpayer, the time limit for recovering any additional tax is six years.

Where no account has been delivered, and the loss of tax was not brought about deliberately by the person liable for the tax, or a person acting for them, then the time limit is 20 years. But if the loss of tax has been caused deliberately, there is no time limit at all.

Service of documents

[3.10] A notice or other document which is to be served on a person under *IHTA 1984* may be delivered to him or left at his usual or last known place of residence or served by post, addressed to him at that address or his place of business or employment. [*IHTA 1984, s 258*].

Publications

[3.11] Booklets IHT 14–18 have now been replaced by the HMRC Customer Guide to Inheritance Tax concerning inheritance tax generally which is available online at http://www.hmrc.gov.uk/cto/customerguide/page4.htm.

Those wishing to obtain booklets and pamphlets should fax their order to HMRC Inheritance Tax Probate and Inheritance Tax helpline 0300 123 1072 and those sending written application to Resources & Facilities Section, HMRC Inheritance Tax, Ferrers House, P O Box 38, Castle Meadow Road, Nottingham NG2 1BB. The Heritage leaflet 'Our Heritage' IR156 (last updated December 1996) may be obtained by telephoning the Heritage Section of HMRC Inheritance Tax on 0115 9742490 or faxing orders to 0115 9742497. Reports regarding Special Commissioners' decisions on cases held publicly and reported may be obtained at cost of £6 per copy from the Administration Office at the Tax Tribunals, 15/19 Bedford Avenue, London WC1B 3AS quoting the case number. Cheques should be made payable to 'HM Paymaster General only'. The quarterly Trusts and IHT Newsletter is available free at http://www.hmrc.gov.uk/cto/newsletter.htm.

4

Agricultural Property

Cross-references. See **6** BUSINESS PROPERTY; **7.5** CALCULATION OF TAX for application of agricultural relief where transfer partly exempt; **22.9** GIFTS WITH RESERVATION where such a gift is of agricultural property or shares in an agricultural company; **33.3** NATIONAL HERITAGE; **35** PAYMENT OF TAX and **57** WOODLANDS.

Simon's Taxes. See **I3.159, I7.2, I7.3, I8.367, I8.368, I12.6.**

Other Sources. HMRC Customer Guide to Inheritance Tax; Foster, Parts G2–3; Mellows, Parts 5.36–5.50; IHTM24000, IHTM24036.

Introduction

[4.1] Where certain conditions are satisfied, relief from inheritance tax is available on the transfer of agricultural property in the UK, the Channel Islands, the Isle of Man and within an EEA state. See **29.3** LAND for situations where qualifying agricultural land in an EEA state was subject to IHT at any time after 22 April 2003 and a refund is due. The relief is a percentage reduction in the value transferred by a transfer of value. Relief is also available on occasions on which tax is chargeable under the provisions relating to **43** SETTLEMENTS: DISCRETIONARY TRUSTS AND OTHER TRUSTS OF RELEVANT PROPERTY. [*IHTA 1984, ss 115(1)(5), 116(1) as amended by FA 2009, s 122(3); Interpretation Act 1978, Sch 1*].

The meaning of 'Agricultural Property'

Agricultural property means agricultural land or pasture and includes woodlands and any building used in connection with the intensive rearing of livestock or fish if the woodlands or building is occupied with agricultural land or pasture and the occupation is ancillary to that of the agricultural land or pasture. It also includes such cottages, farm buildings and farmhouses, together with the land occupied with them, as are of a character appropriate to the property. The definition of 'agriculture' in the *Agricultural Holdings Act 1986, s96(1)* is: '"agriculture" includes horticulture, fruit growing, seed growing, dairy farming and livestock breeding and keeping, the use of land as grazing land, meadow land, osier land, market gardens and nursery grounds, and the use of land for woodlands where that use is ancillary to the farming of land for other agricultural purposes'. Agricultural land which is taken out of production can still qualify for APR (including GAEC land) because *IHTA 1984, s 117* does not require the land to be in production either continuously or at a specific time (though there must be an intention or expectation that the land will be back in production at some time in the future). So, for example, agricultural land set aside to rotational, or even permanent, fallow can still qualify as agricultural property within the definition of *IHTA 1984, s 115(2)* and as occupied for the purposes of agriculture within the meaning of *IHTA 1984, s 117*. See June 2005 Tax Bulletin Special Edition at http://www.hmrc.gov.uk/cto/newsletter.htm. The breeding and rearing of horses on a stud farm and the grazing of horses in connection with those activities is to be taken to be agriculture and any buildings used in connection with those activities to be farm buildings. See also *Wheatley and another (Executors of Wheatley Deceased) v CIR* [1998] STC SCD 60 Sp C 149 e.g. grazing by draught horses. Livestock, deadstock and farm plant and machinery are not included but these may qualify for **6** BUSINESS PROPERTY relief, as may the value of land in excess of its agricultural value and milk quota where it is valued separately (HMRC Tax Bulletin February 1993 p 51). [*IHTA 1984, s 115(2)(4)*]. From 6 April 1995 land used for short rotation coppice (a cultivation method of producing willow, poplar and elephant grass cuttings for renewable fuel for biomass-fed power stations) will count as agricultural property and qualify for either 100% or 50% relief depending on the circumstances as will buildings used in the cultivation which will be regarded as farm buildings. Similarly, farmland and buildings used for the management of the habitat land (see (c) below) counts as agricultural property for the purposes of relief at 100% or 50%. The new provisions apply from 26 November 1996 and apply to land dedicated under the Government's Habitat Schemes. [*SI 1994/1291, SI 1994/1292, SI 1994/1293, SI 1994/2710; SI 1995/134*]. See **4.4** below and Inland Revenue Press Release 27 January 1995. [*IHTA 1984, ss 116, 124C; FA 1995, s 154(2)(3)(5); FA 1997, s 94*]. Land used for agricultural purposes may occasionally be used for other purposes (e.g. an annual point to point horse race) without the relief being jeopardised (IHTM 24061). However, careful consideration is required where land is used for other purposes such as reeds for thatching (cultivation of a crop) and pheasants for sport (food for human consumption) which are not agricultural (IHTM 24062). In addition, where derelict land has been restored to previous levels of agricultural production due to the application of manures and calcified seaweed in order to make the grasses more palatable to cattle then even though the process is not considered an 'intensive agricultural purpose' it would constitute agricultural/pasture land and not moorland.

See **2.19** ACCOUNTS AND RETURNS for Helpline numbers and now IHT 400 Notes, page 36 point 5. Also, see the end of this chapter for Form IHT 414.

Case law — 'agricultural land or pasture'

In *Starke and another (Executors of Brown) v CIR* CA, [1995] STC 689 the property in question comprised a site with an area of just over one hectare containing a farmhouse and an assortment of outbuildings, the site being used as part of a farm devoted to mixed farming, although the remainder of the farm, however, was substantially in the ownership of a farming company. The taxpayer, whilst successful in being granted leave to appeal direct to the High Court, a point of law being involved (see **14.4** DETERMINATIONS AND APPEALS), undertook in the application for leave not to contend that the land in question fell within the concluding part of *IHTA 1984, s 115(2)*, namely 'such cottages, farm buildings and farmhouses, together with the land occupied with them, as are of a character appropriate to the property'. The reason for such an undertaking being given was that the former Inland Revenue did not agree with the taxpayer that the appeal should be to the High Court and would have opposed the taxpayer's application for leave to appeal direct to the High Court if such contention had been made. In addition, because of the differing ownerships of the property in question and the remainder of the farm, such a contention may not have been possible. Consequently, because no contention was made concerning woodlands or buildings used for intensive rearing, the appeal turned on whether the land constituted 'agricultural land or pasture' within the first leg of that provision. The taxpayer contended that the *Interpretation Act 1978, Sch 1* definition of 'land' so as to include 'buildings and other structures' should apply in the expression 'agricultural land'. It was held that it did not apply because *Interpretation Act 1978, s 5* provides that definitions provided by that *Act* only apply 'unless the contrary intention appears' and by giving the expression 'agricultural land or pasture' the more limited and natural meaning for which the former Inland Revenue contended, namely that the primary meaning of 'agricultural property' was 'agricultural land or pasture' which meant 'bare land', i.e. fields or land used either for the cultivation of crops or for the grazing of animals, it was possible to give a sensible meaning to the remainder of the definition by extending the meaning of 'agricultural property' to include species of property which the expression 'agricultural land' did not cover. Because of the taxpayer's undertaking in the application for leave to appeal direct to the High Court, the decision in the case may have to be considered special to its circumstances. In a decision on 19 May 1995 the Court of Appeal dismissed the appeal by the executors.

In *Farmer v CIR* [1999] STC SCD 321 Sp C 216 it was accepted that there was a single composite business comprising of farming and letting of various farm buildings. The Special Commissioners in this case came to the decision that on the application of the 'wholly or mainly' test and taking the business as a whole it consisted mainly of farming. In support of this were the facts that the property was a business property of landed estate with a majority of the land being used for farming. The lettings element was subsidiary to the farming enterprise and was of short duration. In viewing the capital that was employed in the business amounting to about £3.5 million, £1.25 million was attributable to the letting element and the balance to farming. Also, the employees and consultants spent a greater proportion of time on the farming activities and the farm turnover exceeded the letting turnover in six years out of eight but significantly the net profit of the lettings exceeded the net profit from the farming. This last point did not sway the view that the farm was a business rather than an investment because the 'wholly or mainly' test could not be determined solely on the basis of net profits but the character of the business should be looked at as a whole. In addition, it is necessary to consider the overall position over a period of time rather than for a particular period in isolation. (See also *Millington v Secretary of State for the Environment and Another* CA, [1999] TLR 29 June 1999). See also *Harrold and others (executors of Harrold deceased) v CIR* [1996] STC SCD 195 Sp C 71 and *Dixon v CIR* [2002] STC SCD 53 Sp C 297.

In a Special Commissioners' decision in 2008, a claim for BPR was made for land let under a conacre agreement. A widow (M) inherited 33 acres of farmland on the death of her husband. She did not farm the land herself, but let it to local farmers under an agreement of this type. She died in 1999. HMRC issued a notice of determination charging IHT on her estate. Her personal representatives appealed, contending that the farmland qualified for BPR. The Special Commissioner rejected this contention and dismissed the appeal, holding that although M was carrying on a business on the land, that business consisted mainly of making or holding investments, within *IHTA 1984, s 105(3)*, so that the land was not 'relevant business property'. The Commissioner observed that 'the activities of the business consisted of the making available of its major asset to other persons for payment without the separate provision of any substantial other goods or services'. The *conacre* (derivation from 'corn acre') system is unique to Ireland and around a third of all farmland in Northern Ireland is let informally to farmers in this way, often from 20 to 30 acre farms now too small to be commercially viable. APR of 100% applies to the ordinary value of farmland and is unaffected by the Commissioners' ruling. However, where farmland has development potential but is still farmed by letting in conacre, it attracted a second relief – business property relief – also at 100% on that additional development value. Following *PN McCall & BJA Keenan (Personal Representatives of Mrs E McClean) v HMRC* [2008] STC SCD 757 Sp C 678 that business may now consist of mainly of making or holding investments, within *IHTA 1984, s 105(3)*, so that the land is not 'relevant business property'. Subsequently in *McCall (personal representatives of McClean, decd) v HMRC* 2008] STC 752, SCD the taxpayer appealed and LJ Girvan in dismissing the appeal said '*The special commissioner was fully entitled to conclude that this was not to be viewed as a business of providing grass but rather a business of holding an investment.*' *See Example below* and also **6 BUSINESS PROPERTY** and **58 TAX CASES.**

Example 1

D has owned and let 70 acres of land in Northern Ireland since 1980. This land was farmed for arable crops but under the conacre scheme he has, since 1994 let it for periods of 11 months to another local farmer for the growing of rapeseed and wheat. The 70 acres are valued at £1,200 per acre agricultural land and the value of the farmhouse is £180,000. The land is situated in a newly designated brownfield site under a Regional Development Strategy Plan to be implemented by 2016 which will be valued at £4m. On 1 July 2009, D dies and by will transfers all the land to his son, E, at a time when its agricultural value has increased to £1,500 per acre but its potential open market value is £57,000 per acre. E continues to run the farm conacre business from the farmhouse which he inherited under the terms of his father's will, the value of which has decreased to £125,000 due to the potential development encroachment.

		£
Valuations for IHT purposes		
70 acres at £1,500 per acre		105,000
Farmhouse		125,000
Development value		3,895,000
Total value		4,125,000
The transfers subject to tax on D's death:		
(i) Agricultural value of land		
70 acres × £1,500	105,000	
Less agricultural property relief at 100%	(105,000)	—
(ii) Farmhouse		125,000
(iii) Value of development land potential not attracting BPR		3,895,000
		4,020,000
Deduct Nil rate band 2009/10		325,000
Chargeable at 40% on death of D		£3,695,000
		£
IHT payable		1,478,000
Payable by ten-yearly instalments (*IHTA 1984, s 227*) of		147,800

Notes to the example

(A) Conacre (derivation from 'corn acre') is a specifically Irish tradition of letting small parcels land for a single crop. It is part and parcel of the business of small farming in particular and it is temporary by its very nature as lettings are always limited to 11 months. The rents the lets earn are very low returns and it is essentially a way of maintaining land for which a farming family has no plans in a particular season. HMRC state in the IHT Manual at IHTM24075: 'Where such arrangements are in place the availability of agricultural relief on the land, and on any 'farmhouse' where occupation for agricultural purposes is claimed by reference to the deceased's involvement with the land, is considered in exactly the same way as in the rest of the UK. That is, the availability of agricultural relief is a question of fact and degree to be decided upon the particular facts of each case.'

(B) If the whole or any part of the property concerned is sold, then the related tax still outstanding (with accrued interest if relevant) becomes payable immediately unless (i) the sale precedes the date that the first instalment is due in which case the tax does not become due until that date; or (ii) the sale is by a transferee following a 38 POTENTIALLY EXEMPT TRANSFER and the transferee dies before the transferor. Where there is a delay between the dates of contract and completion, the sale for the purposes of *IHTA 1984, s 227(4)* is deemed to take place at the completion date.

Where the prudent lotting of an agricultural estate rests on the basis of separate farm lots, the question of sporting rights should be considered as the value may be materially affected by the hypothesis of separate ownership of farms. (VOA IHT manual, section 9, para 9.3). If the whole of one or more of the lots is exempt then it is not necessary to value that lot and if it is only a part that is exempt the valuation should be done on a just and reasonable basis. (VOA IHT manual, section 9, para 9.4). See IR IHT Newsletter, April 2004 at http://www.hmrc.gov.uk/cto/newsletter.htm.

Farmhouses

[4.2] Whether a farmhouse is to be classed as agricultural property is mainly a question of the purpose of occupation rather than the actual use to which it is put by the owner/occupier. The property must also be of a 'character appropriate' to the land.

HMRC Inheritance Tax apply the following tests to determine whether a farmhouse is of a character appropriate to the land (see http://www.hmrc.gov.uk/manuals/ihtmanual/IHTM24051.htm):

- Is the farmhouse appropriate by reference to its size, layout and content with the farm buildings and the particular area of farmland being farmed?
- Is the farmhouse proportionate in size and nature to the requirements of the agricultural activities conducted on the agricultural land?
- Within the agricultural land does the land predominate so that the farmhouse is ancillary to the land?
- Would a reasonable and informed person regard the property simply as a house with land or as a farmhouse?
- Applying the 'elephant test', would you recognise this as a farmhouse if you saw it?
- How long has the farmhouse and agricultural property been associated and is there a history of agricultural production?
- Considering the relationship between the value of the house and the profitability of the land, would the house attract demand from a commercial farmer who has to earn a living from the land, or is its value significantly out of proportion to the profitability of the land?
- Considering all other relevant factors, including whether any land is let out and on what terms, is the scale of the agricultural operations in context?
- There must be some connection or nexus between 'such cottages, farm buildings and farmhouses, together with the land occupied with them' and the property to which they must be of a character appropriate.

Case law — 'Farmhouse'

In the case of *Higginson's Executors v CIR* [2002] STC SCD 483 Sp C 337 the farmhouse was originally a nineteenth-century hunting lodge with six bedrooms, 63 acres of agricultural land, three acres of formal gardens and 68 acres of woodlands. The Special Commissioner dismissed the appeal, holding that:

> 'for the purposes of *section 115(2)* the unit must be an agricultural unit: that is to say that within the unit, the land must predominate . . . (and) any qualifying cottages, farm buildings or farmhouses must be ancillary to the land.'

However, in view of the price paid for the property, it was clear that

> 'within this particular unit it is the house which predominates, and that what we have here is a house with farmland going with it (and not vice versa).'

Accordingly, the lodge was not a 'farmhouse' for the purposes of *s 115(2)*. In the case of *Lloyds TSB plc (Antrobus' Personal Representatives) v CIR* [2002] STC SCD 468 Sp C 336 however, the farmhouse, Cookhill Priory, comprised of six bedrooms and the farm was 126 acres of freehold land and six and a half acres of tenanted land. It was accepted that the Priory and the land and surrounding buildings (including a chapel) were agricultural property. The Special Commissioner allowed the appeal, finding that the property 'was in a poor state of repair and maintenance'. The result was that, even if the dwelling-house had at one time been a family home of some distinction, it had, both in appearance and in use, become a farmhouse on a working farm. On the evidence, the house was 'a farmhouse with a farm and definitely not a house with land'. It was 'of a character appropriate to the property' for the purposes of *s 115(2)*. However, having lost the case at the Special Commissioners in October 2002, HMRC Inheritance Tax issued a notice of determination on the basis that the agricultural value of the farmhouse was less than the market value. Subsequently, the case went to the Lands Tribunal where the day-to-day operations were given more focus than the management of the farm when considering the actual business of farming. When considering the operational components of the farming business for the purposes of securing APR the Tribunal stated:

> 'There is, we think, no dispute about the definition when it is expressed in this way. The question is: who is the farmer of the land for the purposes of s 115(2)? In our view it is the person who lives in the farmhouse in order to farm the land on a day-to-day basis. It is likely, although it may not necessarily always be the case, that his principal occupation will consist of farming the land comprised in the farm. We do not think that a house occupied with a farm is a farmhouse simply because the person living there is in overall control of the agricultural business conducted on the land; and in particular we think that the lifestyle of the farmer, the person whose bid for the land is treated as establishing the agricultural value of the land, is not the farmer for the purposes of these provisions.'

It may be a matter of dispute whether the above *dictum* is persuasive enough to influence other cases where the farmhouse under scrutiny for APR incorporates this 'lifestyle buyers' application. The result did secure discount of 30% in the value for APR purposes. See *Lloyds TSB plc (Antrobus' Personal Representatives) v Twiddy (Inland Revenue Capital Taxes)*

[2006] 1 EGLR 157, [2006] RVR 138, Land Trib, **56** VALUATION and IHTM24036 at http://www.hmrc.gov.uk/manuals/ihtmanual/IHTM24036.htm.

In *Rosser v CIR* [2003] STC 311, SCD a former farmhouse was ostensibly treated as a 'retirement' home and did not qualify as agricultural property whereas a barn within the same curtilage was treated as such due to the fact that is was in general use for farming. The effect of *s 115(2)* was that 'broiler houses' on a farm could only qualify for relief if they had been 'a subsidiary part of the purpose of an overall agricultural activity carried out on the land'. Since they had been let to a separate company, this was not the case. Accordingly, the broiler houses were not 'ancillary' to the farm, within *s 115(2)*, and did not qualify for relief. See *Williams (Williams' Personal Representatives) v HMRC* [2005] STC 782, SCD.

In *Arnander, Lloyd & Villiers (McKenna's Executors)*, a small country estate comprising a large house with six acres of gardens and some domestic outbuildings, and 187 acres of land, most of which was farmland, the Special Commissioner reviewed the evidence in detail and held that three of the outbuildings qualified for relief but that the main house and eight of the outbuildings did not. The house which the couple lived in was not 'the main dwelling from which the agricultural operations over the land were conducted and managed'. See *Arnander (executors of McKenna, decd) v HMRC*, [2006] STC 800, [2007] RVR 208, SCD.

In *HMRC v Atkinson and Smith* [2011] UKUT 506 (TCC), [2012] STC 289 decision date 31 October 2011, relief was held not to be available for a bungalow let to a family farming partnership of which the deceased was a member. He had lived in a bungalow on the farm until 2002, when he became ill and moved to a care home where he died in 2006. His bungalow remained uninhabited during his illness, although he occasionally visited it and his possessions remained there. His executors claimed that the bungalow qualified for agricultural property relief as being occupied by the partnership for agricultural purposes up to the date of death. HMRC rejected the claim and the Upper Tax Tribunal upheld HMRC's case on the basis that as the partnership had made no use of the bungalow after the deceased moved into care. Accordingly it was not correct to say that it was occupied for the purposes of agriculture after the deceased moved out. See **58** TAX CASES.

In *Hanson v HMRC* [2012] UKFTT 95 a farmhouse owned by a settlement in which the deceased had an interest in possession had been jointly occupied by him and his son up to the date of his death. The son ran his own farming business from the property on land which he owned personally. Originally the business was conducted in partnership with the deceased but on dissolution of the partnership the son continued the business as a sole trader. The trustee of the settlement claimed agricultural property relief in respect of the farmhouse as it was occupied for agricultural purposes. HMRC refused the claim, citing the decision in *Rosser v CIR* (see above) as authority for the proposition that the house and applicable farmland must be in both common occupation and common ownership ownership. The First Tier Tax Tribunal allowed the trustee's appeal on the basis that a test of common occupation of farmhouse and farmland fits the scheme of the IHT legislation best. Relief was therefore due.

In *Golding and Middleton (executors of Golding dec'd) v Revenue and Customs Comrs* [2011] UKFTT 351 (TC) a modest three-bedroom detached property was held to be of a character appropriate to the 16.29 acres of land held with it. HMRC did not argue that the property was outside the definition of farmhouse and the First-tier Tax Tribunal said that they were right to concede this point. The dispute centred on the limited farming activity conducted by the deceased (egg production from approximately 70 free range hens) and the paucity of profit from the sale of eggs, which never exceeded £1,600 in the fours years up to the date of death. However, the Tribunal considered that the level of profit was not of particular interest in deciding the point at issue and that the question was this: was the deceased farming? The Tribunal noted that the deceased was 80 years of age at the time of his death and accordingly it would not be reasonable to expect an extensive farming activity from someone of that age. Otherwise very few farms would qualify for relief. It was held that he was farming as a vocational activity, as is common amongst farmers who may be prepared to forgo luxuries. See now IHTM 24053 where HMRC state that 'you should advise taxpayers relying on this case that each case is judged on its own particular facts' and it is unlikely that similar facts will found in many other cases. HMRC remain of the view that the profit of a farmer is a useful indicator of the activities undertaken in considering whether or not a property is a 'farmhouse'.

Farming companies

[4.3] Relief extends to shares and securities if agricultural property forms part of the company's assets and part of the value of the shares or securities can be attributed to the agricultural value of the agricultural property. [*IHTA 1984, s 122*]. See **4.15** below.

In normal circumstances if the tenant of an agricultural holding is a company then there is less likelihood of the landlord eventually obtaining vacant possession than if the tenant is an individual because a company does not die. (VOA IHT manual, section 9, para 9.8).

Agricultural value applies to that part of the value of shares in or debentures of a company which is attributable to the agricultural value of qualifying agricultural property, provided that the particular conditions set out in *IHTA 1984, s 122* are satisfied. This will be determined by Shares Valuation Division (SVD). Also SVD will notify the DV of any agricultural property owned by a company which qualifies for relief (Form VAL 63 or 63A) when referring the case to the DV. (VOA IHT manual, section 16, para 16.21).

Nature of relief

[4.4] The relief is a percentage reduction of the value transferred by a transfer of value (including an occasion on which tax is chargeable under the rules on **43** SETTLEMENTS WITHOUT INTERESTS IN POSSESSION). The percentage reduction is made before deduction of the annual exemption and other **21** EXEMPT TRANSFERS and before grossing-up where the transferor pays the tax.

Subject to the conditions in **4.5** below, the percentage is:

(a) **100%** in relation to transfers of value made, and other events occurring, after 9 March 1992 (previously 50%) of the agricultural value of the property transferred if either:
- (i) the transferor immediately before the transfer enjoyed either the right to vacant possession or the right to obtain it within the next twelve months; or
- (ii) the transferor has been beneficially entitled to his interest since before 10 March 1981; and
  - (1) if he had disposed of it by a transfer of value immediately before that date, he would have been entitled to claim the 50% relief available after 6 April 1976 and before 10 March 1981; and
  - (2) that relief would not have been restricted by reference to the limits of £250,000 or 1,000 acres (whichever was the more favourable to the taxpayer) applying between those dates (see also Note (A) below); and
  - (3) the interest did not in the period from 10 March 1981 to the date of transfer, give him the vacant possession rights in (a)(i) above and did not fail to give him those rights because of any act or deliberate omission by him during that period.

(b) **100%** in relation to transfers of value of farmland let for periods exceeding twelve months which is let on or after 1 September 1995 (the commencement date of the *Agricultural Tenancies Act 1995* and *Agricultural Holdings (Scotland) Act 1991, s 12* by right of succession in Scotland). [*IHTA 1984, s 116(2)(c) as inserted by FA 1995, s 155(1)*]. Previously the relief was 50% where let farmland which did not or still does not, under an existing pre-1 September 1995 agreement, entitle the transferor to vacant possession or the right to obtain vacant possession within the next twelve months. A tenancy starting on or after 1 September 1995 by reason of statutory succession to an existing tenancy is not excluded from the full relief but there is doubt regarding the adding of land to an existing tenancy (HMRC Tax Bulletin, August 1995 p 241). However, *FA 1996, s 185* enables a tenancy acquired by succession by way of death of the existing tenant to be treated as commencing on the date of death where this is on or after 1 September 1995. A statutory succession would normally take effect from the grant of succession to the new tenancy but this is overridden for the purposes of *IHTA 1984* and the commencement is taken as the date of death of the tenant being succeeded. In the case of a tenant's retirement in favour of a new tenant on or after 1 September

1995 but there is the landowner's death in between the notice of retirement and the succession by the new tenant, the date of the tenancy is deemed to have commenced for these purposes as just before the landowner's death. This has the effect of allowing 100% relief from the date of the death of the landowner whereas under normal rules the relief would only be available from the grant of the new tenancy. [*IHTA 1984, s 116(5A)–(5D)* as inserted by *FA 1996, s 185*].

The *Agricultural Holdings Act 1986*
The *Agricultural Tenancies Act 1995, s 4(1)(g)* affords the opportunity to grant a new tenancy, on or after 1 September 1995, thereby permitting the landlord 100% agricultural property relief and allowing the tenant to remain under the protection of *AHA 1986* (see **4.19** at the conclusion of this chapter).

(c) **100%** in relation to chargeable transfers of value of farmland and related buildings that have been dedicated to wildlife habitats on or after 26 November 1996 which meet the usual ownership criteria. [*FA 1997, s 94* inserting new *IHTA 1984, s 124C*]. Land and any related buildings will be treated as agricultural land and associated farm buildings where the land and buildings are dedicated to the Government's Habitat Schemes under any of the following:

- *Habitat (Water Fringe) Regulations 1994, SI 1994/1291, Reg 3(1)* as amended by *SI 1996/1480* and *SI 1996/3106.*
- *Habitat (Former Set-Aside Land) Regulations 1994, SI 1994/1292* as amended by *SI 1996/1478* and *SI 1996/3107.*
- *Habitat (Salt-Marsh) Regulations 1994, SI 1994/1293* as amended by *SI 1995/2871* and *SI 1995/2891; SI 1996/1479* and *SI 1996/3108.*
- *Habitats (Scotland) Regulations 1994, SI 1994/2710, Reg 3(2)(a)* as amended by *SI 1996/3035.*
- *Habitat Improvement Regulations (Northern Ireland) 1995, SR(NI) 1995/134, Reg 3(1)(a).*

Habitat schemes
Previously these habitat schemes, which protect the environment and maintain the countryside by taking land out of agriculture for 20 years, could not satisfy the occupation test in **4.5**(a) below. It was considered that this would put farmers at a disadvantage over those not engaging in such environmentally friendly schemes. The change in legislation was therefore introduced to rectify this. However, the legislation makes no specific reference to any relief for a farmhouse where the land is in a habitat scheme and HMRC will deny relief for the house where the occupier is not engaged in any farming work. The legislation does not affect in any way the situation where land is farmed in an ecologically benign i.e. organic way because this land, although dedicated in this way for ten years, attracts agricultural property relief in any case. Where land is let on or before 31 August 1995 and it qualifies as part of a Habitat Scheme as above the result will be that relief is available at the reduced rate of 50%. See example below.

Example 2

D has owned and farmed 700 acres of land since 1970. This land has been farmed for arable crops but under the set-aside scheme he has, since 1994 under the *Habitat (Former Set-Aside Land) Regulations 1994*, taken out 200 acres for a period of 20 years to be used for rare nesting owls in accordance with the Government's Habitat Scheme. Also two former grain storage warehouses, valued at £34,000, have been converted to a hide and an information centre. These have both been let to the Conservation Volunteer Development Society since 1994. The remaining 500 acres continue to be farmed as crops for human consumption. The value of the farmland is £1,500 per acre and the set-aside land is valued at £950 per acre. D dies on 30 September 2009 and leaves all the farmland including set-aside to his son E. The value of the farmhouse is £125,000.

	£
500 acres at £1,500 per acre	750,000
Farmhouse	125,000
200 acres of Habitat land at £950 per acre	190,000
Value of agricultural property	1,065,000
Less amount of agricultural relief @ 100%	(1,065,000)
Chargeable	Nil
	£
Former grain storage warehouse	34,000
Less amount of agricultural relief @ 50%	(17,000)
Total value of farm on which tax is chargeable	17,000

Notes to the example

(A) As the former grain storage warehouses are associated farm buildings within the Habitat Scheme, the owner is entitled to agricultural property relief but because the buildings were rented out on or before 31 August 1995 only 50% relief is due.

(B) The normal conditions for relief in **4.5** above apply to the land in the Habitat Scheme.

(C) 50% in relation to transfers of value made, and other events occurring, after 9 March 1992 (previously 30%) in cases not covered by (a), (b) or (c) above.

[*IHTA 1984, s 116(1)–(3) (5A)–(5E) (7); F(No 2)A 1992, s 73, Sch 14 paras 4, 8; FA 1995, ss 154(2), 155; FA 1996, s 185*]. See Tolley's Capital Transfer Tax 1986/87 and earlier editions for the agricultural property relief available for CTT purposes after 6 April 1976 and before 10 March 1981.

Example 3

A and B, who are brothers, farm 1,500 acres of arable land under a tenancy in common agreement with the landowner X. B dies on 26 July 2007 and leaves his share of the tenancy to A's son C. At the beginning of October 2007 A decides to retire and let his son C have his share of the tenancy as from 1 November 2007 and advises X by notice in writing. Landowner X dies on 16 November 2008. The tenancy agreement and the provisions of B's will are not resolved until 18 January and 28 August 2009 respectively.

In the case of C's succession to B's tenancy, this will be treated as having commenced on B's death notwithstanding X's death later on 16 November 2008. In the case of A's decision to retire in favour of his son C the tenancy will be treated as having commenced on 16 November 2008 for the purposes of the rate of any agricultural relief on the death of X. In this latter case of retirement the succession by C to the tenancy of the land let to A can take effect up to 30 months from November 2007. Therefore 100% agricultural property relief applies to the let land on gift or transfer subject to the other qualifying conditions.

Notes to the example

(A) *IHTA 1984, s 116(5A)*, inserted by *FA 1996, s 185*, relates to successions to tenancies in Scotland whereas *s 116(5B)* relates to tenancies other than in Scotland. See also *Agricultural Holdings (Scotland) Act 2003, ss 20, 22* where a short limited duration tenancy or a limited duration tenancy may be bequeathed or transferred by reason of intestacy to a person entitled to succeed to the deceased's intestate estate and the executor shall be entitled so to transfer the interest without the consent of the landlord. This may well have been preceded by a Notice of Interest in Acquiring Land signed by a tenant under *The Agricultural Holdings (Forms)(Scotland) Regulations 2004* but still 100% APR should be available to the landlord in these cases.

(B) *Section 116(5D)* relates to the situation above where X dies on or after 1 September 1995 following a notice of retirement but before the new tenancy has taken effect and takes place within 30 months of the notice being given (which also includes an assignment or assignation in Scotland).

(C) The notice of retirement must be a notice or other written intimation given by the tenant (joint tenants or tenants in common) to the landowner indicating, under whatever terms, that the person or persons in the notice should become the tenant of the property. This may arise from, say, a three-generation tenancy renewable every five years.

The increases in the relief from 30% to 50%, and from 50% to 100%, mentioned above will be interpreted as applying not only to transfers of value made after 9 March 1992 but also to charges or further charges to IHT arising on a death after that date in respect of a transfer of value made before 10 March 1992 (Inland Revenue Press Release, 10 March 1992 and correspondence with the publisher).

Example 4

X has owned since 1983 1,000 acres of land. In June 1992 he began to farm the land, utilising 800 acres for that purpose. The remaining 200 acres are not used for any business purposes. On 1 July 2009 X transfers all the land to his son, Y, at a time when its agricultural value was £1,000 per acre and its open market value £1,500 per acre. He had not used his annual exemptions for 2008/09 and 2009/10. X dies on 6 September 2011. Y has continued to run the farm business since the date of the gift.

The value of the gift for inheritance tax purposes before relief is

		£	£
1,000 acres at £1,500 per acre			£1,500,000
The transfer subject to tax is			
(i)	Agricultural value of land		
	800 acres × £1,000	800,000	
	Less agricultural property relief at 100%	(800,000)	—
(ii)	Non-agricultural value of land		
	800 acres × £500		400,000
(iii)	Value of land not used in business		
	200 acres at £1,500 per acre		300,000
			700,000
Deduct annual exemptions (2008/09 and 2009/10)			6,000
Value transferred by PET becoming chargeable on death			£694,000

Notes to the example

(A) Business property relief may be available in respect of the £400,000 excess of the open market value over the agricultural value.

(B) IHT will be charged at 80% of full rates as X died more than three but not more than four years after the gift.

(C) The 100% relief applies in relation to transfers of value made, and other events occurring, after 9 March 1992, and replaced a 50% relief.

(D) Extra-Statutory Concession F17 (see **23** HMRC EXTRA-STATUTORY CONCESSIONS) extends to 100% from 50% the agricultural property relief where the transferor's interest in the property either:
   (i) carries the right to vacant possession within 24 months of the date of transfer; or
   (ii) is, notwithstanding the terms of the tenancy, valued at an amount broadly equivalent to the vacant possession value.

In the case of (a) above the landlord may have a contractual right to serve notice to the tenant to vacate the property within twelve months of the date of transfer but because of the *Agricultural Holdings Act 1986* (and similar legislation in Scotland and Northern Ireland) vacant possession cannot be obtained for a further twelve months after the tenancy agreement is terminated. It also arises where there is a tenancy which lasts for more than one and less than two years (*Gladstone v Bower* [1960] 2 QB 384, [1960] 3 All ER 353, CA type of arrangement).

In the case of (b) above the transferor and the tenant are so closely connected that in practice the value of the property on the open market is broadly the same as with vacant possession e.g. land let to a company by the transferor who also controls that company. The above concession is to apply from the date of the press release but also in respect of earlier chargeable transfers where liability has not yet been agreed.

APR summary — land and buildings

A summary of the above may be detailed as follows:

Summary of situations where 100% relief is due in respect of agricultural property

Circumstance	Qualifying requirements	Relevant legislation applicable
Vacant possession.	Vacant possession of the agricultural property must be held by the transferor including land farmed subject to a licence. See (a) above.	*IHTA 1984, s 116(2)(a).*
Land let subject to a tenancy beginning on or after 1 September 1995.	Applies in respect of all land that is subject to a farm business tenancy. It applies to land let that is subject to a succession tenancy granted on or after 1 September 1995. An extension of the relief applies where either (i) a valid retirement notice for succession has been made after 1 September 1995, or (ii) the tenant has died after that date and the tenancy has become vested or obtained by another person. See (b) above.	*IHTA 1984, s 116(2)(c), (5A)–(5D)* as extended by *FA 1996, s 185(2); Agricultural Holdings Act 1986, s 25.*
Near vacant possession value or short-term loss of vacant possession.	Applies where the transferor's interest in the property does not carry vacant possession but is valued near vacant possession value e.g. land let to a company where the company is controlled by the transferor. See (e) above and **4.14** below. Alternatively, the transferor must have the right to obtain vacant possession within 24 months. See (e) above.	Extra-Statutory Concession F17. See **23** HMRC EXTRA-STATUTORY CONCESSIONS. *IHTA 1984, s 116(2)(a).*
Pre-1981 'full-time working farmer' provision.	Applies where land has been continuously let to a partnership or company since prior to 10 March 1981 which the transferor has previously farmed in some capacity. See (a) above.	*IHTA 1984, s 116(2)(b).*
Post-5 April 1995.	Applies where land and buildings used in the cultivation of short-rotation coppice.	*FA 1995, s 154.*
Post-25 November 1996 'dedicated wildlife habitats'.	Applies where land is being used or has been let on or after 26 November 1996 dedicated to wildlife habitats. See (c) above.	*IHTA 1984, s 124C.*

'Agricultural value'

Agricultural value is the value of agricultural property on the assumption that it is subject to perpetual covenant prohibiting its use otherwise than as agricultural property. Therefore any development value cannot benefit from agricultural property relief, although it may qualify for business property relief if it is farmed in hand.

Farm cottages occupied by persons employed solely for agricultural purposes in connection with the agricultural property are valued without taking any account of the fact that the cottages are suitable for the residential purposes of persons not so employed. *IHTA 1984, s 115(3)* does not require 'exclusive occupation' for agricultural purposes as evidenced in the case of, say, a country manor house which is purchased at a premium (because of the tax shelter relief obtained) where agricultural land adjoining the manor house is also acquired notwithstanding the fact that it is farmed under a contracting agreement. See Taxation Magazine, 3 April 2003 p 14. [*IHTA 1984, ss 115(3), 169*]. Extra-Statutory Concession F16 gives relief to certain farm cottages that would not normally be relieved from IHT on a lifetime or death transfer. The condition that a farm cottage is occupied by persons employed solely for agricultural purposes is also satisfied in respect of chargeable transfers from 13 February 1995 where the cottage is occupied by a retired farm worker or his/her surviving spouse or civil partner if the occupation is either:

(a) protected under the *Rent (Agriculture) Act 1976* or *Housing Act 1988* (or similar legislation in Scotland and Northern Ireland); or
(b) under a lease granted as part of the worker's contract of employment in agriculture which has a similar effect to that of a protected tenancy or licence (e.g. lease granted as terms of employment).

Where the valuation of the land reflects the benefit of milk quota, agricultural relief is given on that value (HMRC Tax Bulletin February 1993 p 51).

The value of a farm cottage may be restricted, sometimes to its agricultural value, where the property is both agricultural and occupied as such. If the cottage is not occupied as such the value should reflect the use to which it may be legally put. (VOA IHT manual, section 9, para 9.18).

If at the date of transfer there are crops growing on the land these are legally part of the land until severed. However, the DV should exclude the value of growing crops from their report unless the CTO specifically requests otherwise and if the DV is aware that the value includes growing crops without a separate figure then the case should be returned to the CTO. (VOA IHT manual, section 9, paras 9.40 and 9.41). The value of permanent or temporary pasture and the value of cultivations or unexhausted manures should be included and where the value of growing crops have been included with the value of the land then the CTO will ask them to state their separate values. (VOA IHT manual, section 9, para 9.41).

Example 5

A has owned and occupied land for the purposes of agriculture for the last three years and transfers it to a discretionary trust in May 2010. He has not used his annual exemption for either the year 2009/10 or 2010/11. The value of the gift for inheritance tax purposes is £100,000 and the agricultural value is agreed at £70,000.

		£	£
Value transferred			100,000
Less relief of 100% on £70,000			70,000
			30,000
Less	Annual exemption 2010/11	3,000	
	Annual exemption 2009/10	3,000	6,000
Net value transferred (subject to grossing-up if tax paid by donor)			£24,000

Conditions of relief

Occupation and ownership

[4.5] The agricultural property must have been either:

(a) **occupied** by the transferor for the purposes of agriculture throughout the period of two years ending with the date of transfer, or

(b) **owned** by the transferor for the period of seven years ending with the date of transfer and have been occupied throughout that period (by him or another person) for the purposes of agriculture. [*IHTA 1984, s 117*]. See *Wheatley's Executors v CIR* [1998] STC SCD 60 Sp C 149.

See also IHT 17, p 14.

Interest in possession in settled agricultural property

[4.6] A person with such an interest is regarded as the beneficial owner of the settled property where it arose before 22 March 2006, or where it is an immediate post-death interest, a transitional serial interest or a disabled person's interest. In such circumstances a change of beneficial interest may causes a new qualifying period to commence for the purposes of the relief. [*IHTA 1984, s 49(1)*].

Replacements

[4.7] Where agricultural property *occupied* by the transferor on the date of transfer replaced other agricultural property, condition (a) above is satisfied if both properties together with any earlier agricultural property directly or indirectly replaced were occupied by that person for the purposes of agriculture for periods comprising at least two years within the five years ending with the date of the transfer. Where agricultural property *owned* by the transferor on the date of the transfer replaced other agricultural property, condition (b) is satisfied if the respective properties were both owned by the transferor and occupied (by him or another person) for the purposes of agriculture for at least seven years within the ten years ending with the date of the transfer.

In both cases relief is limited to what it would have been if any one or more of the replacements in the respective periods had not taken place. For this purpose, changes resulting from the formation, alteration or dissolution of a partnership are disregarded. [*IHTA 1984, s 118*].

Occupation by company or partnership

[4.8] Occupation by a company controlled by the transferor is treated as occupation by the transferor. 'Control' is defined by *IHTA 1984, s 269*, see 35.8 PAYMENT OF TAX. Occupation by a Scottish partnership is treated as occupation by the partners. [*IHTA 1984, s 119*].

Binding contract for sale

[4.9] Relief will not be given if at the time of the transfer, the transferor has entered into a binding contract for sale of (i) agricultural property (unless the sale is to a company in return for an issue of shares which will give the transferor control of that company); or (ii) shares or securities in agricultural companies (see **4.15** below) except where the sale is made for the purpose of reconstruction or amalgamation. [*IHTA 1984, s 124*].

Further conditions for lifetime transfers

[4.10] Agricultural property relief is only available where any part of the value transferred by a 38 POTENTIALLY EXEMPT TRANSFER proves to be a chargeable transfer if, in addition to the conditions in **4.5** above, the conditions listed below are also satisfied. Similarly, where a chargeable lifetime transfer, other than a potentially exempt transfer, made within seven years of the transferor's death is reduced under the agricultural property relief provisions, the additional tax chargeable by reason of death must be calculated as if the relief had not been received unless the following additional conditions are satisfied.

Subject to the provisions below for replacement property, the additional conditions are:

(a) that the original property was owned by the 'transferee' throughout the period beginning with the date of the chargeable transfer and ending with the transferor's death or, if earlier, the transferee's death (the 'relevant period') and is not at the time of death subject to a binding contract for sale; and

(b) except in a case falling within (c) below, the original property is agricultural property immediately before the death and has been occupied (by the transferee or another) for the purposes of agriculture throughout the relevant period; and

(c) where the original property consists of shares or securities of a company, that throughout the relevant period the agricultural property in question was owned by the company and occupied (by the company or another) for the purposes of agriculture.

'*Transferee*' means the person whose property the original property became on that chargeable transfer or, where on the transfer the original property became or remained settled property in which no qualifying interest in possession subsists, the trustees of the settlement.

Where any shares owned by the transferee immediately before the death would either be identified with the original property under the provisions of *TCGA 1992, ss 126–136* (reorganisations of share capital, conversion of securities and company reconstructions and amalgamations) *or* were issued to him in consideration of the transfer of agricultural property consisting of the original property (or part), his period of ownership of the original property is treated as including his period of ownership of the shares (in relation to transfers of value made, and other events occurring, before 17 March 1987 the shares were treated as if they were the original property (or part)).

Where part only of the original property satisfies the conditions in (a) to (c) above, proportionate agricultural property relief is given.

Example 6

A is the freehold owner of agricultural land which at current vacant possession value is estimated to be valued at £850,000. On 29 September 1989, he enters into an agricultural tenancy (with more than two years to run) with a farming partnership comprising his two sons and his grandson for a full market rental of £25,000 p.a. The tenanted value is estimated at £500,000.

In July 2010 his grandson is killed in a farming accident and a new letting agreement is made between the two sons and A for a full market rent of £35,000 p.a. on 15 September 2010.

A dies on 1 October 2010 when the tenanted value of the land has risen to £600,000.

	£
Transfer at death (tenanted valuation)	600,000
Deduct agricultural property relief	600,000
IHT payable	Nil

Notes to the example

(A) As the land is let under an agreement on or after 1 September 1995 relief of 100% is available. Only 50% relief would have been available if the existing tenancy had continued. [*IHTA 1984, s 116; FA 1995, s 155; FA 1996, s 185*].

(B) The addition of land to an *AHA 1986* tenancy will have the effect of a surrender and re-grant on or after 1 September 1995 thereby ensuring the landlord receives 100% relief.

Replacement property

[4.11] Where the transferee has disposed of all or part of the original property before the death of the transferor and applied the whole of the consideration received in acquiring a replacement property within the 'allowed period' after the disposal of the original property or part (or has entered into a binding contract to acquire replacement property within that time), then, provided the disposal and acquisition are both made in transactions at arm's length or on terms such as might be expected to be included in such a transaction, the conditions in (a) to (c) above are taken as satisfied if:

(i) the replacement property is owned by the transferee immediately before the transferor's death (or immediately before the transferee's death if earlier) and is not at that time subject to a binding contract; and
(ii) throughout the period beginning with the date of the chargeable transfer and ending with the disposal, the original property was owned by the transferee and occupied (by him or another) for the purposes of agriculture; and
(iii) throughout the period beginning with the date when the transferee acquired the replacement property and ending with the death, the replacement property was owned by the transferee and occupied (by him or another) for the purposes of agriculture; and
(iv) the replacement property is agricultural property immediately before the death.

If the transferor dies before the transferee and all or part of the original property has been disposed of before the transferor's death (or is subject to a binding contract for sale at that time) then if the replacement property is acquired (or a binding contract entered into) after the transferor's death but within the 'allowed period' after the disposal of the original property, or part, conditions (i) and (iii) above do not apply and any reference to a time immediately before the transferor's death is taken as a reference to the time when the replacement property is acquired.

Where any shares owned by the transferee immediately before the death would either be identified with the replacement property under the provisions of *TCGA 1992, ss 126–136* (as above) *or* were issued to him in consideration of the transfer of agricultural property consisting of the replacement property (or part), his period of ownership of the original property is treated as including his period of ownership of the shares (in relation to transfers of value made, and other events occurring, before 17 March 1987 the shares were treated as if they were the original property (or part)).

Where a binding contract for the disposal is entered into at any time before the disposal of the property, the disposal is regarded as taking place at that time.

'Allowed period' means the period of three years or such longer period as the Board may allow. In relation to transfers of value made, and other events occurring, before 30 November 1993, the legislation effectively provided for the allowed period to be twelve months. [*IHTA 1984, ss 124A, 124B; FA 1986, Sch 19 para 22; FA 1987, s 58, Sch 8 para 9; FA 1994, s 247(2)(3)*]. The three-year (or longer) allowed period will apply not only to transfers of value

made after 29 November 1993 but also to charges or further charges to IHT arising on a death after that date in respect of a transfer of value made before 30 November 1993 (HMRC response in ICAEW Faculty of Taxation Memorandum TAX 9/94).

Where agricultural property which is a farming business is replaced shortly before the owner's death by non-agricultural business property the period of ownership of the original property will be relevant for applying the minimum ownership condition to the replacement property. If all the conditions for business property relief (see **6** BUSINESS PROPERTY) are satisfied relief will be available on the replacement business property. (HMRC Tax Bulletin December 1994 p 183).

In order to remove doubt that has arisen in the past in determining whether there is a PET or a chargeable transfer, the availability of APR is ignored for the purposes of the further conditions for lifetime transfers. This new subsection applies to any transfer of value on or after 28 November 1995. [*IHTA 1984, s 124A(7A); FA 1996, s 185(4)*].

Gifts with reservation of benefit

Where a person makes a lifetime gift of property which qualifies for agricultural property relief, and reserves a benefit in it, the amount of relief available on the death of the donor is determined by treating ownership and any occupation by the donor prior to the gift as ownership and occupation of the donee. So the donee thereby acquires the donor's history of ownership and occupation.

In the case of a gift of shares in a farming company, three conditions apply for agricultural property relief to be available on the death of the donor who reserves a benefit in them:

- at the time of the gift the shares must qualify for either business or agricultural relief;
- the donee must retain ownership of the shares throughout the period between the date of gift and the date of charge; and
- at the time of the charge the shares must remain eligible for relief if the donee were to make a gift of them at that time.

Successions and successive transfers

[4.12] Where property transferred had been inherited on a death, for the purposes of **4.5**(a) and (b) above the transferor is deemed to have owned it (and, if he subsequently occupies it, to have occupied it) from the date of death. If the deceased was the transferor's spouse or civil partner the periods are extended to include any period of occupation or ownership of the spouse or civil partner. [*IHTA 1984, s 120(1); The Tax and Civil Partnership Regulations 2005, SI 2005/3229, Reg 22*]. See also **4.4** Note C above.

Agricultural property which does not satisfy the conditions in **4.5**(a) or (b) above can qualify for relief if all the following conditions are satisfied.

(a) All or part of the value transferred by an earlier transfer was eligible for the relief in **4.4** above (or would have been if such relief had been capable of being given at the time of that transfer).
(b) All or part of that property became the property of the subsequent transferor or his spouse or civil partner because of the earlier transfer, and at the time of the subsequent transfer it was occupied for the purposes of agriculture by that person or the personal representative of the earlier transferor.
(c) That property, or any directly or indirectly replacing it, would otherwise have been eligible for relief were it not for **4.5**(a) or (b) above. If the value transferred by the earlier transfer only partly relates to the property or any replacing it, only the same proportion of the value on the later transfer qualifies for relief.
(d) Either the earlier or the subsequent transfer is a transfer on the death of the transferor.

Where the property eligible for relief above replaced the property or part referred to in (c) above, relief is limited to what it would have been if any one or more of the replacements had not taken place. For this purpose, changes resulting from the formation, alteration or dissolution of a partnership are disregarded. [*IHTA 1984, s 121; The Tax and Civil Partnership Regulations 2005, SI 2005/3229, Reg 23*].

Shares etc. in agricultural companies

[4.13] The transfer of shares or securities in a company may attract relief if:

(a) agricultural property forms part of the company's assets and part of the value of the shares or securities can be attributable to the agricultural value of the property; and
(b) the shares or securities gave control of the company to the transferor immediately before the transfer. For 'control' see **35.8** PAYMENT OF TAX. If their value is reduced under the rules relating to sales of related property within three years after death (see **56.22** VALUATION) the shares or securities must be sufficient, without any other property, to give control; and
(c) either:
    (i) the agricultural property was occupied by the company for the purposes of agriculture throughout the period of two years ending with the date of the transfer and the shares or securities were owned by the transferor throughout that period; or
    (ii) the agricultural property was owned by the company throughout the period of seven years ending with that date and was throughout that period occupied (by the company or another) for the purposes of agriculture *and* the shares or securities were owned by the transferor throughout that period.

Example 7

AC Ltd is an unquoted agricultural company of which A owns 60% of the shares.

The company owns	£
4,000 acres of land – agricultural value	4M
Other trading assets (net)	2M
Total value of company	£6M
A's shareholding is valued at	£4.5M

All necessary conditions for relief are satisfied.

If A were to die in, say, November 2010 the position as regards his shareholding would be as follows

	Total Value	Land	Other Assets
	£	£	£
Value of assets of company	£6M	£4M	£2M
Value of shares, split in same proportions	£4.5M	£3M	£1.5M
Agricultural property relief (100% of £3M)	(3.0M)		
Business property relief (100% of £1.5M)	(1.5M)		
Chargeable to IHT	Nil		

Note to the example

(A) The legislation appears to require that both agricultural property relief and business property relief be given, each against its appropriate part of the value. [*IHTA 1984, s 114*]. When some of the land owned by the company is tenanted and attracts only 50% agricultural property relief, the total relief given will be less than would be the case if business property relief at 100% were given on the whole value.

Where the transferred shares etc. replaced other eligible property (i.e. either agricultural property, or shares etc. the value of which is wholly or partly attributable to agricultural property), the conditions regarding the transferor's period of ownership of the shares etc. are treated as satisfied if the transferor owned the shares etc. and the other eligible property which preceded it for at least two of the last five years in the case of (i) above and at least seven of the last ten years in the case of (ii) above.

The provisions relating to replacements of agricultural property at **4.5** above also apply to agricultural shares etc.

Notes

(A) For the purposes of **4.4**(a)(i) and **4.4**(a)(ii)(3) above the transferor's interest in agricultural property means the company's interest.

(B) For the purposes of (c) above the company is treated as occupying land at any time when it was occupied by a person who subsequently controls the company.

[*IHTA 1984, ss 122, 123*].

Liabilities to acquire agricultural property

[4.14] For transfers of value made or treated as made on or after 17 July 2013, it is no longer possible to reduce the value of an asset for IHT purposes by securing a loan on it where the loan is used to acquire or maintain (directly or indirectly) another asset which qualifies for certain IHT reliefs, including agricultural property relief. Instead the loan will be primarily deductible from the asset qualifying for relief. These rules have equal effect for charges on settlements holding relevant property within *IHTA 1984, s 58*.

This rule applies to any liability incurred on or after 6 April 2013. In the case of any such liability incurred in respect of agricultural property, the loan is to be primarily deducted from the value of that property before any applicable reliefs for such property are given. If the liability exceeds the value of the asset concerned, the excess may be deducted from other chargeable assets, first those qualifying for agricultural or business reliefs and thereafter other assets without relief. If the agricultural property is gifted during lifetime, the loan is to be deducted only from the value of that property if the lifetime gift is or becomes a chargeable transfer, so that the liability cannot also be deducted from the estate on death. But if the lifetime gift is a PET and the donor survives for seven years, retaining liability for the loan, it may then be deducted from the estate on death.

A loan is considered by HMRC to indirectly finance an asset where it is initially used to buy asset 1 which is later sold and the proceeds reinvested in asset 2. The loan then indirectly finances asset 2 (see HMRC IHT Manual para IHTM 28018). On this view it is not possible to circumvent the disallowance by first acquiring non-agricultural property with a loan, subsequently selling that property and then acquiring agricultural property with the proceeds.

Where a liability is incurred partly for relievable property, as described above, and partly for other assets not qualifying for the reliefs, any part repayments of a liability are to be attributed first to the proportion of it incurred for the non-relievable property. If a loan is incurred partly in relation to assets within any of (ii), (iii) or (iv) above and partly in relation to assets within (i) above, part repayments are to be attributed primarily to the part relating to the assets within (ii), (iii) or (iv). For HMRC's view on apportionments of liabilities between relievable and non-relievable property, see IHT Manual para 28021. [*IHTA 1984, ss 162A and 162B*].

Grants of agricultural tenancies

[4.15] The grant of a tenancy of agricultural property in the United Kingdom, Channel Islands or Isle of Man for use for agricultural purposes is not a transfer of value if made for full consideration in money or money's worth. [*IHTA 1984, s 16*]. See also **56.4** VALUATION.

Scottish agricultural leases

Scottish agricultural leases — fixed terms

[4.16] Where on a person's death any part of the value of his estate is attributable to the interest of a tenant in *an unexpired portion of a lease* for a fixed term of agricultural property in Scotland, any value associated with any prospect of renewal of the lease by tacit relocation is left out of account, provided either he had been tenant of that property for at least two years immediately preceding his death or he had become tenant of that property by succession. [*IHTA 1984, s 177(1)(3)*].

Scottish agricultural leases — tacit relocation

[4.17] Where on a person's death any part of the value of his estate is attributable to the value of the interest of a tenant of agricultural property in Scotland *held by virtue of tacit relocation* (i.e. on a year to year basis), and the interest is acquired at his death by a new tenant, the value of that interest is left out of account, provided either he had been tenant of that property for at least two years immediately preceding his death or he had become tenant of that property by succession. The value to be left out of account does not include the value of any rights to compensation in respect of tenant's improvements. [*IHTA 1984, s 177(2)–(4)*]. See also **56.4** VALUATION.

Foot and mouth

[4.18] The incidence of foot and mouth disease throughout the United Kingdom in the earlier part of 2001 and 2007 had an impact on the farming community resulting in the deferment of payment of tax and interest. See **28.4** INTEREST ON TAX. In a number of situations the deferral of tax as a result of the foot and mouth outbreak resulted in the late payment of inheritance tax and the consequent interest charge was not payable. Now where there is a disaster or emergency interest on unpaid tax it may be deferred where the Commissioners agree such a case warrants it. [*FA 2008, s 135*]. See also **33.3** NATIONAL HERITAGE.

Will planning for agricultural property

[4.19] Where a farming business is to be left on death to beneficiaries there will be certain periods when the farm will be under the management of the executors or trustees. There are a number of factors that should be borne in mind for such circumstances. It must be remembered that the agricultural property (and business property) must be specifically gifted to the person concerned to qualify for the APR (and BPR where relevant). A legacy payable out of the property is not a specific gift and does not qualify. It should be incumbent on the will drafter to ensure that the executors or trustees have full power to run and manage the farm or have the powers to engage a manager to run the business. The Society of Trust and Estate Practitioners standard provisions do not include these powers. Therefore when drafting the will the executors or trustees, where a will trust is involved, should include powers to trade, delegate, manage etc. This might be on the following basis with regard to a will trust for a farming enterprise:

IN WITNESS etc

FIRST SCHEDULE

The Property

[Here identify the Property]

SECOND SCHEDULE

The Initial Settled Property

[Here specify the property that has been transferred to the Original Trustees.]

THIRD SCHEDULE

Additional administrative powers

The Trustees have the following additional powers:

1. *Investment.* The Trustees may invest Trust Property in any manner as if they were beneficial owners. In particular the Trustees may invest in property in any part of the world and in unsecured loans. The Trustees are under no obligation to diversify the Trust Fund. The Trustees may invest in speculative or hazardous investments.

2. *Joint Property.* The Trustees may acquire property jointly with any Person and may blend Trust Property with other property.

3. *General Power of Management and Disposition:* The Trustees may effect any transaction relating to the management or disposition of Trust Property as if they were beneficial owners. The Trustees shall have power to employ servants and independent contractors and to purchase plant and equipment in connection with any trade or business or the management of any property.

4. *Delegation;* A Trustee may delegate in writing any of his functions to any Person. A Trustee shall not be responsible for the default of that Person (even if the delegation was not strictly necessary or expedient) provided that he took reasonable care in his selection and supervision.

5. *Trade:* The Trustees may carry on a trade, in any part of the world, alone or in partnership.

6. *Nominees:* The Trustees may vest Trust Property in any Person as nominee, and may place Trust Property in the possession or control of any Person. The Trustees may have the power to employ and remunerate a nominee or nominees in any part of the world to hold any property subject to the trusts hereof.

The Schedule continues with other administrative powers.

A situation may arise where the farmer wishes to leave the farm and agricultural land to the wife to manage and then pass on to the children but by doing so would not benefit from the 100% APR as the gift/willed assets would in any case be exempt due to the inter spouse or civil partner exemption. If there are other non-agricultural/business assets that do not attract any relief an option may be to leave the farm and agricultural land to the children and the other assets to the wife as in the example below.

Example 8

Farmer A, who is married to W and has a daughter D, is the freehold owner of a farm and agricultural land which at current vacant possession value is estimated to be valued at £850,000. On 29 September 2010 A dies and leaves by his will the farm and agricultural property and his other assets including investments valued at £1.25 million into a two-year discretionary trust. There are specific powers in the will to appoint out before grant. Within the two-year period but not before the first three months have expired the Trustees appoint out of the trust £325,000 in cash and the farm to the daughter D. W is appointed £950,000 in cash and investments. After a period D sells the farm to W who pays for it out of part of the assets inherited from her late husband A as follows:

STEP 1	
Daughter (D)	£
Transfer of farm by appointment from trust	850,000
Deduct agricultural property relief	850,000
IHT payable	Nil
Transfer of cash by appointment from trust	325,000
Deduct nil rate band	325,000
IHT payable	Nil
Wife (W)	£
Transfer of cash/investments by appointment from trust	950,000
Deduct inter-spouse/civil partner exemption	950,000
IHT payable	Nil

STEP 2	Assets
D	£
Cash for farm	850,000
Original nil rate band transfer	325,000
IHT payable	Nil
W	£
Farm	850,000
Balance of original inter-spouse/civil partner transfer	100,000
IHT payable	Nil

Notes to the example

(A) The Stamp Duty Land Tax implications have not been addressed here and this potential charge must be weighed up with the potential saving in IHT, i.e. £320,000 (£1,125,000 – 325,000 × 40%) if the cash and investments to the value of the farm and the Nil rate band had initially been left to D instead and the farm to the wife together with the balance of cash of £100,000. [*FA 2003, s 55(2)*].

(B) A transfer on death by W, assuming she will die first and has been farming the land for two years, to D of the farm and the assets of £100,000 of cash and investments will be covered by APR and part of the Nil rate band.

(C) There may be a concern that the daughter may not wish to sell the farm to W but it must be in the daughter's own interests as any subsequent gift by W to D during lifetime or on death could incur IHT of up to £250,000 (£950,000 – 325,000 × 40%) if this does not happen.

(D) In a case where, for example, a deceased's estate has a farm that would qualify for APR which is left to the wife and a share portfolio that would be taxable and is left to the daughter, a deed of variation may be entered into whereby there is an exchange of assets under *IHTA 1984, s 142(1)* i.e. '. . . the making, in respect of another of the dispositions, of a variation . . . ' so that the wife receives the share portfolio and the daughter receives the farm, each being exempt. In any other case a transfer, such as the one in the example above, by deed of variation might constitute transfers for any consideration, including consideration less than full consideration, which would be ineffective under *IHTA 1984, s 142(1)(3)*. See also **13.2** and **13.3** DEEDS OF VARIATION AND DISCLAIMER.

Key points

[4.20] Points to consider are as follows.

- The majority of farming activities are undertaken as a sole trader or in partnership. In the case of a partnership, any assets held outside the partnership by the partners individually but used in the business may be entitled to only 50% BPR. Other business structures are available, such as Limited Liability Partnerships and private limited companies, which offer limited liability and flexibility in terms of keeping assets outside of creditor entitlement in cases of business failure. However, those assets would be entitled to BPR at only 50% if held by the business owners outside such limited liability vehicles, although 100% APR may nevertheless be available so long as a farm business tenancy is in place or, in the case of occupation by a company, the landowner has control of the company.
  Landlords whose tenants enjoy security of tenure under the *Agricultural Holdings Act 1986* provisions, should consider taking advantage of an amendment to the *Agricultural Tenancies Act 1995* which came into effect from 19 October 2006. *Agricultural Tenancies Act 1995, s 4(1)(g)* (inserted by *Regulatory Reform (Agricultural Tenancies) (England and Wales) Order 2006, SI 2006/2805*) permits a new tenancy to be granted from 19 October 2006 to an existing *Agricultural Holdings Act 1986* tenant over the same (or substantially the same) land and allows the tenant to enjoy the same security of tenure as before even though a new

tenancy is expressly granted. 100% APR relief is available for the new lease in such circumstances, in place of 50% APR for the previous lease. ESC D39 may enable this to be free of capital gains tax liability for the tenant's deemed disposal of the old lease so long as the new lease or tenancy is on identical terms to the previous one except as regards duration and rent payable. There is however no similar concession for stamp duty land tax purposes and a surrender a re-grant will normally incur liability to that tax.

- APR applies to assets within the definition of agricultural property and occupation of such property and is given in priority to BPR, which is given generally where there is an interest in a business. BPR is only given if it is claimed and therefore where APR is not available with regard to a farming activity for live stock, deadstock, farm equipment, milk quota, single farm payments and bank balances (within reasonable case law boundaries) then as long as they are within a qualifying trading activity BPR will be available to be claimed. See 7 CALCULATION OF TAX.
- Certain areas of diversification a farmer may undertake will not attract entitlement to APR, such as land rented for caravan and tent pitches, car boot sales, etc. as these constitute income from land or property. Sporting rights such as shooting and fishing on the farmer's land would not entitle the farmer to APR. See *Earl of Normanton v Giles* where occupation by livestock otherwise than to produce food for human consumption, for example, the keeping of birds such as pheasants for sport was held not to be agricultural for the purposes of *Rent (Agriculture) Act 1976, s 1* [1980] 1 WLR 28.
- Certain aspects of a working farm do not attract APR such as farm equipment e.g. combines, tractors, derelict buildings/redundant buildings, harvested crops or livestock as stated in the point above, but growing crops transferred with the land being transferred does qualify, as does a milk quota attached to the land being transferred.
- Farm cottages occupied by someone not connected with the farming do not qualify for APR unless the person is:
  - (i) a retired farm employee;
  - (ii) a spouse/civil partner of a deceased farm worker;
  - (iii) living in the cottage under a lease granted by reason of their former farming employment contract; and
  - (iv) a protected tenant with statutory rights vis *Rent (Agriculture) Act 1976.*

Agricultural relief [Form IHT 414]

HM Revenue & Customs

Agricultural relief

Schedule IHT414

When to use this form

Fill in this form if you are deducting agricultural relief on form IHT400. Use a separate form for each agricultural holding and send in a plan showing the location and extent of the holding.

Help

Please read the guidance notes for form IHT414 in the IHT400 Notes before filling in this form. For more information or help or another copy of this form:

- go to **www.hmrc.gov.uk/inheritancetax/**
- phone our Helpline on **0845 30 20 900**
  – if calling from outside the UK, phone **+44 115 974 3009**.

Name of deceased

Date of death *DD MM YYYY*

IHT reference number (if known)

Agricultural property

1 Give the address and a full description of the agricultural holding on which you are deducting agricultural relief.
You must also fill in form IHT405 Houses, land, buildings and interests in land to give details of the property concerned

Address

Description

2 When and how did the deceased acquire the holding?
For example, the deceased may have inherited the property, received it as a gift, or bought it themselves

3 Was the holding, or any part of it, subject to a binding contract for sale at the date of transfer?

No ☐ *Go to box 4*

Yes ☐ *Give full details of the contract and clearly identify the part of the property that was sold on the plan you supply*

4 Are there any outstanding planning consents on the holding which have not been implemented?

No ☐ *Go to box 5*

Yes ☐ *Give brief details of the planning consents*

IHT414 **(Substitute)(LexisNexis)** Page 1 HMRC Approval ref: L11/08

Use of agricultural land

Please read the guidance notes for form IHT414 in the IHT400 Notes for information on the amount of detail required in this section.

5 Give a detailed description of the day-to-day farming activities carried out on the land throughout the seven years prior to the date of transfer (or the period of ownership, if less than seven years)

6 Give details of the extent of the deceased's involvement in the activities described in box 5 throughout the two years prior to the date of transfer. *For example, what actual tasks did the deceased carry out and how many hours did the deceased spend on these tasks each week*

Let land

7 Was the land subject to any lease, licence or tenancy immediately before the transfer?

No ☐ *Go to box 11*

Yes ☐ *Go to box 8*

8 To whom was the land let?

Title - *enter MR, MRS, MISS, MS or other title*

Name

Relationship to the deceased, if any

9 When did the letting start? *DD MM YYYY*

10 What was the original duration or term of the letting?

11 Are you deducting agricultural relief at 50% or 100%?

50% ☐ 100% ☐

Send in a copy of the tenancy agreement if there is one.

IHT414 Page 2

Farmhouses and cottages

Only fill in this section if you are deducting agricultural relief on farmhouses and cottages. Agricultural relief is only available for farmhouses and cottages that are occupied for the purposes of agriculture. Whether each property will qualify for relief depends on who lived there and whether it is regarded as 'of a character appropriate' to the property.

Please answer the following questions for each property. *Continue on an additional sheet if necessary.*

Property 1

12 Address and/or description of the property, for example, 'Farmhouse at Ashdown Farm, Hay Lane, Hoxton'

13 Was the property unoccupied (even temporarily) during the seven years prior to the date of transfer?

No ☐ *Go to box 14*

Yes ☐ *Give the date(s) the property was empty*

14 Did the deceased live at the property?

Yes ☐ *Go to box 16*

No ☐ *Give details of the person(s) who lived at the property, the date(s) they lived there and explain the extent of their involvement in the farming activities described at box 5*

15 If the property was let, describe the type of tenancy (for example, agricultural tenancy, assured shorthold) and say how much rent was paid

Property 2

Address and/or description of the property, for example, 'Farmhouse at Ashdown Farm, Hay Lane, Hoxton'

Was the property unoccupied (even temporarily) during the seven years prior to the date of transfer?

No ☐ *Go to box 14*

Yes ☐ *Give the date(s) the property was empty*

Did the deceased live at the property?

Yes ☐ *Go to box 16*

No ☐ *Give details of the person(s) who lived at the property, the date(s) they lived there and explain the extent of their involvement in the farming activities described at box 5*

If the property was let, describe the type of tenancy (for example, agricultural tenancy, assured shorthold) and say how much rent was paid

IHT414 Page 3

Farm buildings

16 Give a full description of any farm buildings from which agricultural relief is deducted stating who was using them and for what purpose. Please do not use phrases such as 'general storage' or 'agricultural purposes' as these are insufficient.

Agricultural relief and lifetime transfers

If you are deducting agricultural relief on a gift there are additional conditions that must be met before the relief is due. Please answer these additional questions to help us to decide if the relief is due.

'Relevant period' means the period between the date of the gift and the date of death of the deceased (or death of the person who received the gift, if they died first).

17 Was the holding agricultural property immediately before the end of the relevant period?

No ☐ Yes ☐

18 Was the holding owned by the person who received the gift throughout the relevant period?

No ☐ Yes ☐

19 Was the holding occupied (by the person who received the gift or by someone else) for agricultural purposes throughout the relevant period?

No ☐ Yes ☐

20 Was the holding subject to a binding contract for sale immediately before the end of the relevant period?

No ☐ Yes ☐

Any other information

Please use this box if you have any further details you would like to give us or if you do not have enough space in any of the boxes on pages 1 to 4.

IHT414 Page 4

5

Anti-Avoidance

Cross-references. See **11.8** CLOSE COMPANIES; **21.23** EXEMPT TRANSFERS; **22** GIFTS WITH RESERVATION; **30.2** LIABILITY FOR TAX; **31.9** LIFE ASSURANCE POLICIES AND ANNUITIES; **45** SETTLEMENTS: INTERESTS HELD ON PROTECTIVE TRUSTS; **42.11** SETTLEMENTS WITH INTERESTS IN POSSESSION; **43.13** and **43.22** SETTLEMENTS: DISCRETIONARY TRUSTS AND OTHER TRUSTS OF RELEVANT PROPERTY; **56.21** VALUATION.

Simon's Taxes. See **A2.122, A6.1212, I2.104, I2.2, I3.115, I3.116, I3.7.**

Other Sources. Tolley's Income Tax 2010–11; IHTM09151 et seq.

Approach of the courts

The *Duke of Westminster* case and Ramsay approach

[5.1] The classical interpretation of the constraints upon the Courts in deciding cases involving tax avoidance schemes is summed up in Lord Tomlin's statement in the *Duke of Westminster v CIR* HL 1935, 19 TC 490 that 'every man is entitled if he can to order his affairs so that the tax attaching . . . is less than it otherwise would be'. The judgment was concerned with the tax consequences of a single transaction, but in *Ramsay*, and subsequently in *Furniss v Dawson*, the House of Lords has set bounds on the ambit within which this principle can be applied in relation to modern sophisticated and increasingly artificial arrangements to avoid tax. With the introduction of the general anti-abuse rule in *FA 2013*, HMRC now consider that the decision in the *Duke of Westminster* case is no longer relevant and it seems likely that the focus of all future counteraction of avoidance schemes will be under this new statutory rule.

Cases on past IHT avoidance arrangements

Countess Fitzwilliam and others v CIR is the first case in which the question of the application of the *Ramsay* principle to transactions entered into with a view to the avoidance of inheritance tax (or, more strictly, its predecessor, capital transfer tax) has arisen. The trustees of a will trust (who included the deceased's widow F and her daughter H) were empowered to appoint within 23 months of the death of the deceased (which occurred in September 1979) the residue of the estate amongst a class of beneficiaries which included F (then aged 81) and H. In order to avoid a heavy charge to tax on an appointment directly to H or, should an appointment be made to F, on her death when it was envisaged she would make H the beneficiary of her own will, a complex five-step scheme was entered into by F, H and the trustees ('the taxpayers'). It was claimed by the taxpayers that the five steps, the first of which took place on 20 December 1979 and the last on 7 February 1980, should be viewed separately with the result that by reason of a number of available reliefs (some of which still have application to inheritance tax) no liability to capital transfer tax arose. The former Inland Revenue issued notices of determination claiming that the five steps constituted a preordained single composite transaction effected to avoid tax and that *Ramsay* applied to permit a charge to tax on the deceased's estate on the basis of appointments directly to F and H.

The Special Commissioners found for the Revenue, but this was rejected in both the Chancery Division and the Court of Appeal on the grounds that the only true and reasonable conclusion from the facts found by the Commissioners was contrary to their conclusion that the five steps formed a preordained series of transactions. In the House of Lords the Revenue accepted that step 1 did not form part of such a series but argued that the steps 2 to 5 did. The leading judgment in the House of Lords stated that the correct approach to a consideration of steps 2 to 5 was to ask whether realistically they constituted a single and indivisible whole in which one or more of the steps was simply an element without independent effect and whether it was intellectually possible so to treat them. It was held that both questions should be answered in the negative. The case put by the Revenue did not depend on disregarding for fiscal purposes any one or more of steps 2 to 5 as having been introduced for fiscal purposes only and as having no independent effect, nor on treating the whole of steps 2 to 5 as having no such effect. Each of the four steps had a fiscal effect of giving rise to an income tax charge on F or H for a period of time, and there was a potential capital transfer tax charge should either have died whilst in enjoyment of the income. Although steps 2 to 5 were 'preordained', in the sense that they formed part of a pre-planned tax avoidance scheme and that there was no reasonable possibility that they would not all be carried out, the fact of preordainment in that sense was not sufficient in itself to negative the application of an exemption from liability to tax which the series of transactions was intended to create, unless the series was capable of being construed in a manner inconsistent with the application of the exemption. In the particular circumstances of the case, the series of transactions could not be so construed. Two or more transactions in the series could not be run together, as in *Furniss v Dawson*, nor could any one or more of them be disregarded. There was no rational basis on which the four separate steps could be treated as effective for the purposes of one provision which created a charge to tax on a termination of an interest in possession but ineffective for the purposes of two other provisions which gave exemptions from that charge where the interest was disposed of for a consideration and where the interest reverted to the settlor. Accordingly, the case was one to which the *Ramsay* principle, as extended by *Furniss v Dawson*, did not apply.

In *Hatton*, a scheme to avoid tax, which bore some similarity to that in *Fitzwilliam*, was found by the Special Commissioners and Chancery Division to be preordained and one to which the *Ramsay* principle applied (although it should be noted that the Chancery Division judgment in the case was given prior to the judgments of the Court of Appeal and House of Lords in *Fitzwilliam*).

In the decision by the House of Lords in the *Ingram* case concerning a scheme whereby a lease over a property was retained and the freehold was given away, Lord Hoffmann stated: 'The scope of the Ramsay principle does not arise and I therefore prefer to say nothing about it'. The legislation at *FA 1986, ss102A, 102B and 102C* was introduced to counteract the arrangement.

In another case *Melville v CIR* [2000] STC 628; Ch D [2000] All ER(D) 832; CA [2001] STC 1271 the Court of Appeal held that powers over trusts are potential 'property' for inheritance tax purposes. This had the effect of creating an avoidance of IHT liability when used as part of an avoidance scheme because the holder of the power had effective dominion over the settled property, if he chose to exercise it. A power was different in character from a reversionary interest.

Nevertheless, the holder of a general power of appointment had a valuable right, the value of which had to be taken into account in the holder's estate under *IHTA 1984, s 5(1)* unless excluded by some other provision. See now *IHTA 1984, s 272*, which states that property does not include a settlement power, and *IHTA 1984, s 47A* inserted by *FA 2002, s 119*, which defines a settlement power as any power over, or exercisable (whether directly or indirectly) in relation to, settled property or a settlement. However, for deaths on or before 16 April 2002, *FA 2002, s 119* disapplies charges on those earlier deaths which might have otherwise arisen from the stated side effects of the decision arising out of the *Melville* case.

Targeted legislation

[5.2] Anti-avoidance legislation is intended to counteract transactions designed to avoid taxation but *bona fide* transactions may sometimes be caught also.

In *CIR v Eversden and another (executors of Greenstock deceased)* CA, [2003] STC 822, the strategy was effected by the husband making a gift into trust under which the wife took an initial interest in possession for life or six months, whichever was the shorter. Alternatively, the trustees of the settlement can be given wide powers to terminate the life interest and appoint on varied trusts. Husband and wife are capable of benefiting in a reversionary interest by being added as potential beneficiaries and without the gifts with reservation rules applying. Although the settlor will in these circumstances almost certainly have made a gift, the gifts with reservation rules in *FA 1986, s 102* did not apply as it was excluded by *FA 1986, s 102(5A)* with respect to the inter-spouse/civil partner exemption i.e. *IHTA 1984, s 18*. The settlor and wife were able therefore to reserve whatever benefits over the settled property as required. The exemption by *FA 1986, s 102(5A)* came into play only if the gift in settlement constituted a transfer of value and one which was exempt by virtue of the spousal exemption. The strategy was blocked by *FA 2003, s 185* with effect from 20 June 2003.

IHTA 1984, s 81A counters the use of '*Melville*' type schemes, after *Melville* above, a case on an aspect of an earlier version of the scheme which was superseded by anti-avoidance legislation. See above. The strategy was that the settlor of a settlement retains a valuable reversionary beneficial interest which was taken into account in determining the amount by which the value of his 'estate' is diminished when he makes the settlement, so that the value transferred under *IHTA 1984, s 3* is within the IHT nil rate band even though the actual value of the settled property exceeded it. These schemes originated as a means of obtaining CGT hold-over relief under *TCGA 1992, s 260* (disposals which were IHT immediately chargeable transfers) for lifetime dispositions whilst minimising IHT liability. That use of these schemes for this purpose was finally rendered ineffective with effect from 9 December 2003 by excluding hold-over relief for settlor-interested settlements. [*TCGA 1992, ss 169B–169F*]. However, Melville type schemes were adapted as a means of avoiding an immediate IHT charge on settling property by lifetime disposition under the post-21 March 2006 IHT rules. They remain possible planning vehicles for short term trusts designed to bring about a disposal for capital gains tax purposes.

In order to counteract the use of similar schemes to avoid IHT liability *IHTA 1984, s 81A* was introduced which makes two provisions in relation to any reversionary interest in 'relevant property' which is owned by someone who has acquired that interest for a consideration in money or money's worth, or which is owned by the settlor, the settlor's wife, or the settlor's civil partner. The first is that the falling in of the reversion by reason of the reversioner becoming entitled to an interest in possession in the settled property, is treated as a disposition of a reversionary interest at that time i.e. *IHTA 1984, s 81A(1)*. The second is that a transfer of value of such a reversionary interest, whether before it falls in or at the time when a reversionary interest in possession falls in, is not now a PET, i.e. *IHTA 1984, s 81A(2)*. See **42.11** SETTLEMENTS WITH INTERESTS IN POSSESSION and example below. This anti-avoidance applies on or after 9 December 2009. [*FA 2010, s 52(2)*.]

> ***Example 1***
>
> Melvin settles property on trusts under which after a period of trusts for other persons (discretionary or interest in possession) Melvin has a life interest then the retained future life interest is not initially an interest in possession. However, it is a reversionary interest. Therefore for these purposes it would be part of Melvin's estate for IHT and the value of it as a retained interest is taken into account in assessing the value transferred by the transfer of value, which is thus

a low value. When the initial period of trusts for other persons come to an end, Melvin's interest becomes an interest in possession, the falling into possession of the reversionary interest would not normally cause an IHT charge because it happens automatically. There would in these circumstances be neither a disposal nor any operation effected by any person which might be classed as an associated operation. On becoming an interest in possession the interest ceases to form part of Melvin's estate under the terms of *IHTA 1984, s 5(1)(1A)*, as amended and inserted by *FA 2006*. Therefore once it is an interest in possession Melvin could assign it onto trusts for other beneficiaries without it becoming an occasion of charge. Also, if Melvin decides to give away his reversionary interest while it is still a reversionary interest by making an absolute assignment of it to another individual, it would be a PET. Alternatively, a similar result arises where a person pays someone else full or substantial consideration for making a settlement under which the purchaser has a reversionary interest.

The anti-avoidance consequence is that Melvin is now deemed to have given away his reversionary interest at the earlier date rather than at the later date when it falls in. It will therefore now be an immediately chargeable lifetime transfer and not a PET as above. At that stage then, unless there is another exemption for Melvin to call on, or it does not exceed Melvin's available nil rate band, there is immediately a charge to IHT at 20% of the value of the reversionary interest. Alternatively, if Melvin retains the reversionary interest until it falls in and he becomes entitled to an interest in possession then there is a deemed disposition of the reversionary interest by Melvin and the transfer of value is no longer a PET i.e. new *IHTA 1984, s 81A(2)*. In most cases the value transferred is likely to be the value of the reversionary interest at the time of gift by Melvin and this is likely to be the same as the value of the succeeding interest in possession.

The wide-ranging anti-avoidance provisions of *FA 2010, s 53* ensure that the pre-22 March 2006 IHT regime for settled property subject to an interest in possession now applies to settled property subject to an interest in possession to which a person domiciled in the UK became beneficially entitled on or after 9 December 2009 which is within *IHTA 1984, s 10* (not conferring gratuitous benefit). This new category of interest in possession is now caught within *IHTA 1984, s 5(1B)* inserted by *FA 2010, s 53(3)(b)*. The anti-avoidance relating to interests in possession acquired in transactions not conferring any gratuitous benefit on or after 9 December 2009 is in encapsulated in *FA 2010, s 53* as in the example below. The various IHT charging provisions are applied to *IHTA 1984* throughout by reference to *FA 2010, s 5(1B)* and cross-referenced to this chapter section and the example below and throughout this work. See **42.11** SETTLEMENTS WITH INTERESTS IN POSSESSION. This anti-avoidance applies on or after 9 December 2009. [*FA 2010, s 53(10)*].

Example 2

Whereas the type of scheme at Example 1 above counteracts an avoidance scheme which took advantage of a shortcoming in the *FA 2006* changes to trusts, the *IHTA 1984, s 53* anti-avoidance appears to be proactive legislation. For instance, say Patricia makes a settlement which confers an interest in possession on Bertie for life, and he is well off financially compared to Patricia so pays full value for the interest and therefore it is a commercial transaction to which *IHTA 1984, s 10* applies. Therefore neither of them, because of *IHTA 1984, s 10*, makes a transfer of value. Bertie then ensures that on his death the remainder is passed on to his relative Charlie who also pays a commercial rate for his future interest. When Bertie dies the settlement passes to Charlie and there is no IHT charge because all transactions were to date ordinary commercial transactions per se. Because of this the settled property has fallen out of the estate of Bertie. Patricia's estate did of course increase in value by the amount paid but this could well have been within the nil rate band. This has the subsidiary effect of ensuring that Bertie's estate on death is not encumbered by the life interest and the nil rate band to the extent it has not been depleted and any transferable nil rate band is available to set against the chargeable estate on death whereas it would have been 'apportioned' between the free estate and life interest. However, *FA 2010, s 53* now has the effect that an interest in possession (other than a disabled person's interest which is different) acquired under a new lifetime settlement made after 21 March 2006 now notwithstanding *IHTA 1984, s 10* exclusion does now form part of the estate of the person entitled to the interest in possession. In consequence the pre-22 March 2006 IHT regime for settled property subject to an interest in possession applies to settled property subject to an interest in possession to which a person domiciled in the UK became beneficially entitled on or after 9 December 2009 by virtue of a disposition falling within *FA 2010, s 53(10)*. See **41.2** SETTLEMENTS — GENERAL.

The following anti-avoidance provisions relating to inheritance tax include some which have not been formally so designated but have been selected from the legislation as being broadly of an anti-avoidance nature.

(a) **Associated operations.** See 5.5 below.
(b) **Close companies.** See **11.2** and **11.8** CLOSE COMPANIES.
(c) **Exempt transfers.** See **21.10** for transfers between spouses/civil partners and **21.23** EXEMPT TRANSFERS for abatement of certain exemptions on death.
(d) **Gifts with reservation.** See **22** GIFTS WITH RESERVATION.
(e) **Liability for tax of transferor's spouse/civil partner.** See **30.2** LIABILITY FOR TAX.
(f) **Annuity purchased in conjunction with life policy.** See **31.9** LIFE ASSURANCE POLICIES AND ANNUITIES.
(g) **Protective trusts.** See **45** SETTLEMENTS: INTERESTS HELD ON PROTECTIVE TRUSTS.
(h) **Termination of an interest in possession.** See **42.9–42.11** SETTLEMENTS WITH INTERESTS IN POSSESSION.
(i) **Initial interest of settlor or spouse/civil partner and property moving between settlements.** See **43.19** and **43.22** SETTLEMENTS: DISCRETIONARY TRUSTS AND OTHER TRUSTS OF RELEVANT PROPERTY.
(j) **Related property.** See **56.21** VALUATION.
(k) **Excluded property settlements.** See **20.2** and **20.12** EXCLUDED PROPERTY.
(l) **Funds in alternatively secured pensions.** See **37.2** PENSION SCHEMES.
(m) **Reversionary interests of purchasers or settlors in relevant property.** **42.11** SETTLEMENTS WITH INTERESTS IN POSSESSION.

General anti-avoidance rule

[5.3] With effect from Royal Assent to the *Finance Act 2013*, 17 July 2013, a general anti-abuse rule applies for most tax purposes, including inheritance tax. The rule is designed to counteract tax advantages arising from tax arrangements that are abusive. For these purposes, 'tax arrangements' are widely defined to include any arrangements where it would be reasonable to conclude that the obtaining of a tax advantage was the main purpose or one of the main purposes of the arrangements.

Arrangements are 'abusive' if they 'cannot reasonably be regarded as a reasonable course of action in relation to the relevant tax provisions'. This test requires having regard to all the circumstances, including whether the arrangements are consistent with any principles on which the tax provisions are based, including their policy objectives, whether the arrangements include one or more contrived or abnormal steps, and whether they are intended to exploit any shortcomings in the relevant tax provisions. If however the tax arrangements accord with established practice, and HMRC have indicated its acceptance of that practice, this is an example of something which might indicate that the arrangements are not abusive.

Tax arrangements which are caught by the new rule may be counteracted by an adjustment on a 'just and reasonable' basis.

Where HMRC consider that the general anti-abuse rule applies, the 'designated HMRC officer' must follow the procedural requirements set out in *FA 2013, Sch 41*. This involves giving written notice to the taxpayer specifying the arrangements and the tax advantage which the officer considers to be caught by the general anti-abuse rule, and the counteraction which the officer considers ought to be taken. The taxpayer then has 45 days beginning with the day on which the notice is given (not the day on which it is received) to send written representations in response to the notice. If no representations are made, or if they are made but the officer still considers that the tax advantage should be counteracted, the matter must then be referred to the 'GAAR Advisory Panel'. At the same time as referring the matter to the Panel, the designated HMRC officer must give the taxpayer notice that this reference has been made and the taxpayer then has 21 days from the date on which notice is given to send to the Panel written representations on the latter. These representations must be copied to the HMRC officer. The decision of the Panel is not binding on HMRC, although it will be taken into account in any subsequent appeal to the Tax Tribunals.

Provision is made for consequential relieving adjustments to be made after a counteraction of a tax advantage has become final. A person has 12 months from that date to make a claim for one or more consequential adjustments to be made in respect of any tax to which the general anti-abuse rule applies. Upon receipt of the claim, HMRC must make such of the consequential adjustments claimed as are just and reasonable. For inheritance tax purposes, the claim must be made in writing and the provisions of *IHTA 1984, s 221* apply as if the claim were a claim under that Act.

Guidance from the GAAR Panel

[5.4] HMRC has published guidance on the new general anti-abuse rule which has been approved by the Advisory Panel. See www.hmrc.gov.uk/avoidance/gaar-part-abc.pdf. The guidance states that the new rule amounts to a rejection of the approach taken by the Courts in cases such as *Duke of Westminster v CIR* (1936) 19 TC 490 to the effect that taxpayers are free to use their ingenuity to reduce their tax bills by any lawful means, however contrived those means might be and however much the tax consequences might diverge from the real economic position. The guidance goes on to state that 'in many circumstances there are different courses of action that a taxpayer can quite properly choose between. The GAAR is carefully constructed to include a number of safeguards that ensure that any reasonable choice of a course of action is kept outside the target area of the GAAR'.

Part D of the guidance was updated on 30 January 2015 and discusses specific tax planning arrangements. Part VI of Part D considers six inheritance tax arrangements and sets out views on whether or not they would be liable to counteraction. The 6 examples are as follows.

Pilot trusts

C wishes to leave his estate in trust for his seven grandchildren. He wants to ensure that the settlements are not subject to IHT after his death. C establishes one settlement per day over a period of seven days, settling £100 on each. He revises his Will so that he leaves a specific legacy of £250,000 free of tax to each settlement.

The GAAR analysis of this arrangement is explained as follows. Because the settlements were created on consecutive days, they are not related settlements and so the rate of tax is calculated without reference to the other settlements, notwithstanding that the substantial addition of funds came about as a result of a single event – C's death.

Do the means of achieving the substantive tax results involve one or more contrived or abnormal steps? Had C's Will established a single settlement for the benefit of all of his grandchildren that trust would have been subject to IHT. And if seven separate settlements had been established by his Will, they would have been related settlements so each would have been taken into account with the other to establish the rate of tax. Establishing the 'pilot' trusts on separate days before death had no purpose other than to put the trusts in a tax-advantaged position. Arguably therefore these are contrived steps.

Do the tax arrangements accord with established practice and has HMRC indicated its acceptance of that practice? The practice was litigated in the case of *Rysaffe Trustee v IRC* [2003] STC 536. HMRC lost the case and did nothing to change the legislation prior to 2013, and so must be taken to have accepted the practice.

The conclusion is therefore that the arrangements accord with established practice accepted by HMRC and are accordingly not regarded as abusive.

Discounted gift schemes

The settlor makes a gift into settlement but retains certain rights in the insurance bond. Typically the rights retained may be in a series of single premium policies maturing on successive anniversaries of the creation of the settlement or to future capital payments if the settlor is alive at the prospective payment date. The arrangement is viewed as a 'carve-out' or 'shearing arrangement' so that provided the rights in the bond retained by the settlor are sufficiently clearly defined he is not taxed on the value of the gifted property. The rights are therefore split into a retained fund for the settlor which is effectively held on a bare trust and a settled fund from which he is excluded and which is held for other beneficiaries such as his children. The retained fund comprises the right of the settlor to withdraw a certain fixed amount – usually 5% from capital each year for the next 20 years if alive. The transfer of value he is treated as making for inheritance tax purposes is the value of the settled fund that he gives away and is substantially discounted as a result of his retained rights.

The GAAR analysis of this arrangement is explained as follows. In *Ingram v CIR* [1999] STC 37, the House of Lords held that there is nothing in principle behind the gifts with reservation provisions that stops the donor carefully dividing up his cake, giving away a slice and retaining the remaining cake. Continued enjoyment of the latter does not amount to a reservation in the former. Arrangements of the type adopted are known as 'shearing' operations. *FA 1986, s 102A–C* were introduced to stop shearing arrangements in relation to certain carve out schemes over land, but no legislative action has been taken in relation to other types of assets to stop such arrangements. The discounted gift scheme can be seen as a classic shearing operation on property other than land.

Are there contrived or abnormal steps? Creating two distinct funds or a carve out may be considered contrived.

Do arrangements accord with established practice? These arrangements accord with established practice as is indicated by a number of technical publications.

Accordingly the arrangements are not within the scope of the GAAR.

Excluded property trust and debt

The trustees of a settlement made by a person not domiciled in the United Kingdom buy a property in the UK. At the ten-year anniversary of the settlement, it will be liable to inheritance tax at a maximum of 6%. Shortly before that time, the trustees borrow funds from a bank and secure the debt on the property. The borrowed money is paid out to the settlor on the understanding that the money will be returned. Shortly after the ten-year anniversary, the settlor adds the funds back to the trust and the trustees use it to repay the loan.

The GAAR analysis of this arrangement is explained as follows. By charging the UK property with debt and paying the cash out to the settlor abroad, the trustees have tried to avoid the ten-year charge. Even if the taxpayer has found a way to circumvent the specific provisions of FA 2013, Sch 36 it is clear (according to the Guidance) that the policy intent expressed there is to prevent a deduction against UK property except where the loan was taken out to acquire the UK property.

Are there contrived or abnormal steps? Borrowing with the intention of removing the cash from charge and then repaying the loan shortly thereafter is not a normal transaction. Borrowing taken out simply to avoid tax may in this context be regarded as a contrived step.

Are the arrangements intended to exploit any shortcomings in the relevant tax provisions? FA 2013 makes it clear that the general intention of the legislation is to grant inheritance tax deductions only in respect of borrowing taken out to acquire the particular property, with only limited exceptions, for example, where the value of the property acquired with the borrowings at the relevant time of charge is less than the amount borrowed (and not artificially devalued) in which case the excess may be set against other property. If the UK property was sold just before the ten-year anniversary, HMRC accepts that the sale proceeds (if retained abroad) would not be subject to inheritance tax. Similarly, if the trustees had borrowed and lost the money on a poor investment the liability could be deducted against the house. However in this case the UK property continues to be owned before and after the ten-year anniversary and one would therefore expect inheritance tax to be due on all its value. The real economic value of the UK property has not been reduced; it is always intended to use the cash borrowed to repay the debt as soon as the anniversary has passed and the cash has been paid out of the trust in an attempt to circumvent the provisions but with the parties agreeing in advance that the moneys will be resettled shortly thereafter. In looking at the application of the GAAR it is appropriate to look at the wider context of the transaction before and after the ten-year anniversary and in the light of *FA 2013* to consider the context in which liabilities have been incurred.

Do the tax arrangements accord with established practice which has been accepted by HMRC? HMRC has not indicated its acceptance of this practice and HMRC considers that in the light of *FA 2013* it is clear that liabilities may be deducted only if certain principles are satisfied.

On the facts given, the conclusion is that the arrangements are abusive arrangements to which HMRC would seek to apply the GAAR. Under the proposed counteraction, the liabilities would be ignored in calculating the tax due on the house and the transaction counteracted on this basis.

Use of employee benefit trust

The taxpayer arranges for a private company to be incorporated with substantial share capital. The taxpayer and her advisers are the only employees of the company. The company does not trade but holds the money on deposit. The company establishes an employee benefit trust for the benefit of the employees of the company and their families with existing participators being excluded from benefit under the trust except in relation to distributions taxable as income. The funds in the trust are claimed to be exempt from inheritance tax as being within *IHTA 1984, s 86*.

Although the taxpayer established the employee trust prior to her death, the same result could have been achieved by including the terms of the trust in her Will, or the beneficiaries of her estate could have executed a Deed of Variation to establish the trust. Following her death, the family are no longer connected to a former participator, so they can now benefit from the trust by way of capital distributions.

Are the arrangements consistent with any principles on which the relevant tax provisions are based and the policy objectives of those provisions? The intention of the exemption in the legislation is to provide an incentive to diversify share ownership or at least the benefits of share ownership among a wider group of people who are then incentivised to run the company profitably. The company has not traded and the only three employees of the company are the taxpayer and her advisers. While the taxpayer is alive, therefore, the trust serves little purpose, other than to provide an income. However, on her death, her children are no longer connected to a former participator in the company. Provided that they are employees or otherwise within the permitted class of beneficiaries set out in *s 86*, there is then nothing to prevent the trustees from distributing the trust assets to them with only minimal IHT under *IHTA 1984, s 72*. The arrangement is plainly contrary to the principles behind the legislation which is to give favoured treatment to trusts for employees of a genuine business. In this case, there is no genuine business that is set to continue and no genuine employees.

Are there contrived or abnormal steps? The scheme as a whole is contrived, serving no real purpose other than to allow wealth to pass from S to her children without an IHT charge on her death.

Are the arrangements intended to exploit any shortcomings in the relevant tax provisions? Although the definition of 'connected persons' is extended for IHT purposes by *s 270*, the normal interpretation, which breaks a connection with someone who has died, continues to apply. *Section 28* does not limit the exemption to employee trusts with a minimum number of unrelated employees.

Do the tax arrangements accord with established practice? HMRC has not indicated its acceptance of this practice.

The conclusion is that the arrangements are abusive arrangements to which HMRC would seek to apply the GAAR. The proposed counteraction would be to ignore the fact that the trust qualified as an employee trust and impose an immediate entry charge on the taxpayer in respect of the settlement of the shares on the basis that it is a relevant property settlement and a further charge if she died within seven years.

Acquisition of excluded property settlement interest

A non-UK domiciled settlor settles funds upon trust and the trustees have power to nominate another person who can become entitled to the reversionary interest in it. A UK domiciled individual (D) who wishes to avoid inheritance tax, is nominated as the reversionary beneficiary, this nomination becoming irrevocable after a given period of time. The existing income beneficiary of the trust grants D the option to purchase its income interest for

£1 million, exercisable on the payment of a further nominal sum. D transfers his newly acquired reversionary interest to a UK trust for his intended beneficiaries and then exercises the option to acquire the income interest. That interest is now part of D's estate but separate from the reversionary interest and has little or no value for IHT. It therefore escapes inheritance tax on his death.

It is argued that the value of D's estate has been reduced by the £1 million used to purchase the trust interests. At the time of the purchase, D exchanged £1 million for rights that would enable him to access the £1 million in the trust, so there is little or no loss to his estate. As D did not purchase the reversionary interest in the offshore trust, it is not prevented from being excluded property, so no account is taken of the value of the interest when it is transferred into trust, and no charge to IHT arises. The purchased income interest is not an interest in possession for IHT purposes, so the underlying trust assets do not form part of the taxpayer's estate. The provisions of *IHTA 1984, s 48(3B)* apply only to purchases of interests in possession in excluded property trusts not to the purchase of other types of interest in such trusts. The nature of the reversionary interest is that alone, it has little or no value, so the charges that normally apply when assets leave a trust will not apply either.

Are the substantive results of the arrangements consistent with any principles on which the relevant tax provisions are based? This scheme is designed to allow a UK domiciled individual to transfer assets into trust for the ultimate benefit of his family avoiding the risk of failing to survive seven years and the immediate entry. This is contrary to the long-standing basic principles and policy objectives of IHT. In 2005, Parliament legislated to stop UK domiciliaries from buying interests in possession in excluded property trusts and thereby avoiding inheritance tax in a way similar to that outlined above. Further legislation stopping similar schemes was passed in 2010 and 2012. Therefore even if the taxpayer devises a scheme that is not caught by the specific terms of existing anti-avoidance legislation or he purchases slightly different types of interest or acquires similar interests in a slightly different way this is clearly contrary to the policy and intent of Parliament.

Are contrived or abnormal steps involved? If D had transferred £1 million directly to his heirs, there would have been no immediate charge to tax; but had he failed to survive seven years, it would have been subject to IHT. He would not have been able to benefit from the income. If D had transferred £1 million into trust, there would have been an immediate charge to tax at up to 20% of the value transferred. These could be described as the 'normal steps' that D might take. The steps taken by D are significantly different to these normal steps and can therefore be called abnormal. The scheme is contrived in that it involves a number of steps that must be executed in a particular order and to a specific time frame to gain the tax advantage.

Are the arrangements intended to exploit any shortcomings in the relevant tax provisions? Although it is considered by HMRC that the above arrangement is caught by the *FA 2012* legislation the taxpayer may devise even more complex and contrived variants whereby he acquires a slightly different type of interest in the trust without falling foul of the existing anti-avoidance provisions and thereby exploits shortcomings in the provisions.

Do the tax arrangements accord with established practice? HMRC has not indicated that these arrangements give rise to the claimed tax result. Parliament has repeatedly indicated by passing further anti-avoidance legislation that it is not an acceptable practice.

Accordingly on the facts given, the arrangements are abusive arrangements to which HMRC would seek to apply the GAAR. The likely counteraction would be to adopt the policy approach taken in the legislation and impose an immediate entry charge on D in respect of the purchase of the trust interest and a further charge if he died within seven years.

Mortgage on UK real estate by foreign domiciliary

R is domiciled abroad and wishes to buy a valuable house in the UK for his occupation. He has a number of options:

1. R buys the house in his own name, using his own cash resources to fund the purchase.
2. R settles cash from his own resources into a trust that purchases the house. R is a beneficiary of the trust.
3. R, even if he could have funded the purchase from his existing resources, chooses to borrow from a bank to fund a large part, say 70%, of the purchase price.
4. R (as in 2. above) partially funds the trust. The trustees (as in 3. above) then borrow the remainder of the purchase price from a bank.
5. R deposits foreign investments with a bank thereby enabling the bank to lend a greater amount (say 95%) to fund the purchase of the property. The borrowing is again secured on the property.
6. R having funded a trust to the value of, say, 5%, of the purchase price of the house, agrees to guarantee the trustees' borrowing. This enables R's trust to borrow the remainder of the purchase price from a bank. The borrowing is again secured on the property.
7. R has an existing substantive discretionary trust which he settled many years ago. R is one of the beneficiaries. The trustees have been looking to buy UK property suitable for R and his children to use as each of them visit the UK for a few weeks a year. The trustees could afford to buy the new house using existing resources but instead they accept an offer from R to lend them the purchase price via an offshore company that is wholly owned by R. The loan is interest free and repayable on demand. The company owned by R secures the loan on the house.
8. R settles cash from his overseas resources into a newly established trust which then lends it back to him via an underlying company for the purchase of the house in his own name.
9. R adds cash from his overseas resources to a trust, known as the Loan Trust, where he is settlor and beneficiary. His spouse or other relative sets up another trust, known as the Property Trust, which is funded with, say, £1,000 cash. R adds no funds to the Property Trust. The Loan Trust forms an overseas company into which the cash is transferred and the company lends the cash to the Property Trustees who acquire the UK property that R wishes to occupy. The loan is repayable on demand and may be interest-free, interest-bearing or index-linked. The Property Trustees incur no personal liability as the lender may have recourse to the house only.

The Guidance notes that in options 3 and 4 the borrowing provides a clear inheritance tax advantage compared to options 1 and 2. As R is not domiciled in the UK the cash he retains personally abroad is not subject to inheritance tax and the UK property is devalued by commercial borrowing. The same tax advantage, albeit to a greater extent, is claimed to apply in options 5 to 9. The reservation of benefit rules do not apply to options 1, 3, 5 and 8 because R owns the property. There is a reservation of benefit in options 2, 4, 6 and 7, but the taxpayer argues that this is only on the net value of the property. In option 8, the liability is not, it is claimed, caught by *FA 1986, s 103* as a self-generated liability due to it being funded with excluded property (see *FA 1986, s 103(4)*).

In option 9, there is no charge on the death of R because he has not gifted any property to the Property Trust (so the reservation of benefit provisions do not apply) and he is a beneficiary only of the Loan Trust that holds excluded property. As he has made no gift to the Property Trust, *FA 1986, s 102, Sch 20 para 5(4)* are not in point. If he has made such a gift then it is argued that the UK property is devalued by the loan taken out to acquire it.

The pre-owned assets charge does not apply to any of the options. In 1, 3, 5 and 8 R has made no disposal of the property and does not satisfy the contribution condition since the property has been acquired by him and not a third person. It does not apply to the other options on the basis that even if the contribution condition is satisfied, the loan in which R reserves a benefit (or in the case of option 2 the house itself) derives its value from the house and therefore protection under *Sch 15 para 11(3)* is available.

HMRC does not accept R's analysis of the legislation and in particular the deductibility of loans against UK property in which he reserves a benefit under options 2, 4, 6 and 7. The GAAR analysis below should be read with this point in mind.

Are the substantive results of the arrangements consistent with any principles on which the relevant tax provisions are based? It is reasonable to conclude that the obtaining of a tax advantage was the main purpose or one of the main purposes of options 7 to 9. This may not be so in relation to options 3 to 6. R might prefer to borrow from a bank to allow him more flexibility to make other investments with his cash or to preserve his liquidity. The intention behind the inheritance tax legislation is to tax UK assets and UK domiciliaries. Options 3 and 4 are an application of the rules whereby IHT is chargeable on the net value of UK assets. The fact that R or his trustees could have funded the purchase using foreign investments is irrelevant: R is not compelled to turn assets which are outside the territorial scope of the tax into assets which are subject to tax, whatever his motivation for the borrowing. R's or the trustees' borrowing is a normal commercial transaction and is not contrived or abnormal. While reservation of benefit may be in point in relation to option 4, the GAAR is not thought to apply to option 3 or option 4.

Options 5 and 6, similarly, represent a commercial decision by R or his trustees. Choosing to borrow a higher amount is similarly neither contrived nor abnormal. R takes the economic consequences of borrowing commercially. It can reasonably be regarded as a reasonable course of action.

In option 7, loans to trusts do occur for all sorts of non-tax reasons and therefore cannot be considered in themselves to be necessarily abnormal or contrived. Even though the loan is tax-motivated and (in some senses) self-generated, it involves a single straightforward step. The position might well be different, however, if the trust were not established for some time already or substantive: for instance if R were the sole or principal beneficiary or able to direct the trustees or revoke the trust. A loan to such a newly created trust might be considered a contrivance. In the above example the loan may not be mainly tax motivated anyway e.g. the trustees may wish to preserve cash for liquidity purposes, but even if it were the arrangement is still not necessarily abusive.

In option 8, the cash goes in a circle back to the settlor via a trust and loan arrangement. The position might be different under the GAAR if the trust had been in existence for some time so the gift was not made in contemplation of a loan back. The settlor sets up a trust as a vehicle to lend to himself. The setting up of the trust and company is done simply to enable a loan to be made back to the settlor and this is a contrived step. *FA 1986, s 103* was designed to stop assets being given away that are then lent back by the donee and it may be thought that option 8 is using a possible loophole in *s 103* to circumvent the intended policy.

In option 9, the combination of a nominal-value settlement specifically set up to own the property coupled with the establishment of a separate loan trust and a corporate vehicle underlying it which is then used to make a loan which is on a non-recourse basis is on these facts set up only to achieve an artificial tax deduction. And, while taken individually, the steps may be considered normal, when taken in combination they may be considered abnormal. However, each case would be taken on its own facts and a situation where, for instance, both trusts were substantial and existing trusts or where the loan was on fully commercial terms or where the property trust was established for a different beneficiary apart from the settlor might be considered differently (see option 7 above).

Do the tax arrangements accord with established practice? Neither of the last two options accord with established practice and HMRC has not indicated acceptance of the interpretation that foreign domiciliaries are not caught by *s 103* as a matter of principle.

The conclusion reached is that options 3 and 4 are straightforward applications of the legislation and would not be caught by the GAAR. Similarly, options 5 and 6 involve commercial arrangements which are neither contrived nor abnormal and HMRC would not seek to invoke the GAAR against them. With option 7, while economically the liability appears to be self-generated, the trust is of substance and the arrangements are not necessarily contrived or abnormal. Thus, although some observers might consider this to be unreasonable, it is possible to see that other reasonable observers might reach a different view. As such these particular facts may well not be caught by the GAAR but it is important to realise that this is a borderline case and each such case would have to be considered on its own facts. Options 8 and 9, on these particular facts, would be caught by GAAR. The liabilities would be ignored in calculating the tax due on the house and the transaction counteracted on this basis. However, as with option 7, each case would have to be considered on its full facts and it is not impossible that different scenarios might potentially be saved from the GAAR by the double-reasonableness test.

Reversionary Lease scheme in relation to a residence

Not included in Part D of the guidance are *Ingram* type arrangements. As an example, the taxpayer grants a long lease over his home to his son for no consideration, to take effect in 20 years' time. Under the lease, the son covenants to pay the cost of maintaining the property. The taxpayer is able to continue to occupy the property for the next 20 years as he continues to own the freehold. *FA 1986, s 102A* is considered not to apply where the taxpayer has held the freehold for at least seven years. The result of the scheme is that the taxpayer has divided his home into two different interests: the lease and the freehold. He has gifted the lease of his home to his son, retaining the freehold, which diminishes in value over the following 20 years.

HMRC's 11 December 2012 draft guidance document gave the view that the failure of the reservation of benefit rules to cover a situation where an individual creates two different interests in a property is a shortcoming that the scheme is intended to exploit. On the facts given, the arrangements are abusive arrangements to which HMRC would seek to apply the GAAR. However this draft guidance does not appear in the guidance approved by the GAAR Advisory Panel with effect from 15 April 2013 and so it would appear that the panel did not agree HMRC's view. Instead the April 2013 guidance contains a reference to the House of Lords decision in *Ingram v IRC* [2000] 1 AC 293; [1999] 1 All ER 297 in which it was held that there is nothing in principle behind the gifts with reservation provisions that stops the donor carefully dividing up his cake, giving away a slice and retaining the remaining cake.

Associated operations

[5.5] If inheritance tax applied only to each separate transaction, it would be possible to split some transfers of value into several parts, the sum of which was less than the total value actually transferred. To counter this, the separate transactions are treated as 'associated operations' which together comprise one transfer of value. But see *Rysaffe Trustee Co (CI) Ltd v CIR* [2001] STC SCD 225 Sp C 290; [2002] STC 872; CA [2003] EWCA Civ 356.

Definitions

'*Associated operations*' are any two or more operations of any kind by the same person or different persons and whether simultaneous or not:

(a) which affect the same property, or one of which affects some property while the other or others affect property which represents, whether directly or indirectly, that property, or income arising from that property, or any property representing accumulations of any such income, or

(b) where one operation is effected with reference to a second or with a view to enabling the other to be effected or facilitating its being effected, and any further operation having a like relation to any of those two, and so on.

'*Operation*' includes an omission.

Where a transfer of value is made by associated operations carried out at different times it shall be treated as made at the time of the last of them. The transfer of value is reduced by the value transferred by any earlier operations which were also transfers of value by the same transferor, except to the extent that the transfer made by earlier operations, but not the operations as a whole, was covered by the exemption for transfers between spouses/civil partners (see **21.10** EXEMPT TRANSFERS). [*IHTA 1984, s 268(1)(3)*].

In *Reynaud v CIR* [1999] STC (SCD) 185 it was held that there was no associated operation where shares qualifying for business property relief were sold to trustees, after which the shares were subject a buy back by the company.

In *Rysaffe Trustee Co (CI) Ltd* [2003] STC 536 it was held that there were no associated operations where five identical settlements were set up within about one month. The decision in the High Court reported at [2002] STC 872 provides a detailed analysis of when the associated operations might apply and when they will not be in point. Examples given of when these provisions may apply are (i) where a disposition which is effectively by A to C is channelled through B with a view to picking up a saving of inheritance tax in the process, and (ii) where an asset, instead of being transferred to a transferee by a single transfer of the whole asset, is fragmented and transferred in stages, with a view to achieving an overall reduction in the value transferred.

Example 3

H owns a set of four Chippendale chairs valued, as a set, at £6,000. Individually they would be valued at only £1,000, although a pair would be worth £2,500 and three £4,000.

He gives one chair to his son each year over four years, during which time all values increase at 10% p.a. (simple). In the fifth year H dies.

	£	£
Year 1		
Value of four chairs	6,000	
Deduct value of three	4,000	
Value transferred		2,000
Year 2		
Basic computation ignoring the associated operations rule		
Current value of three chairs	4,400	
Deduct value of two	2,750	
Value transferred	£1,650	
Revised to take account of associated operations rule		
Current value of four chairs	6,600	
Deduct value of two	2,750	

	3,850	
Deduct value transferred in Year 1	2,000	
		1,850
Year 3		
Current value of four chairs	7,200	
Deduct value of one	1,200	
	6,000	
Deduct value transferred in Years 1 and 2	3,850	
		2,150
Year 4		
Current value of four chairs	7,800	
Deduct value transferred in Years 1, 2 and 3	6,000	
Value transferred		1,800
Total values transferred		£7,800

The following are *not* associated operations.

(i) The granting of a lease for full consideration with any operation effected more than three years later.

(ii) An operation effected on or after 27 March 1974 with any operation before that date.

[*IHTA 1984, s 268(2)*].

See *CIR v Macpherson and Another*, HL 1988 [1988] STC 362 where, by a majority decision, on the special facts of the case a commercial agreement (involving custody of paintings), which both facilitated an appointment made the following day and reduced the value of the property so appointed, was regarded as an operation associated with the appointment. See also *Reynaud & Others v CIR* [1999] STC SCD 185 Sp C 196 where the transfer of shares in a company into a discretionary trust and the subsequent purchase by that company of its own shares was not a disposition affected by the associated operations rules.

In practice, HMRC will not use the associated operation provisions where a husband shares capital with his wife who 'chooses to make gifts out of the money she has received from her husband', unless it is a blatant case of a husband's gift to his wife made on condition that she should at once use the money to make gifts to others. (Official Report, Standing Committee A 13 February 1975 Col 1596). See also IHTM11091.

Example 4

If in the example above H had wished to give away the chairs over two years instead of four, he might first have given two chairs to his wife (exempt), so that each could give the son one chair each year.

Year 1	£	£
(i) Value transferred by husband to son		
Value of two chairs (as half of a set of four linked by the related property rule)	3,000	
Deduct value of one chair (as half of a pair)	1,250	
		1,750
(ii) Value transferred by wife (similar calculation)		1,750
Year 2		
Value transferred by husband, applying the associated operations rule		
Current value of four chairs	6,600	
Deduct value transferred in Year 1 by H and W	3,500	
Value transferred		3,100
Total values transferred		£6,600

Notes to the example

(A) In this case, the total of the values transferred can exceed the value of the assets, although it must be doubtful whether the HMRC would seek to apply the full rigours of the section unless the transfer by the wife in Year 1 had fallen within her annual exemptions, or she had survived seven years so that the gift was exempt.

(B) See *IHTA 1984, s 161* for the related property rule, and see also **56.21** VALUATION.

(C) The result above could have been achieved in another way. The first transfer by the husband to his spouse is quantified at £3,000 – the second to the son is quantified at £1,750 as in the example. If through *section 268* one looks at the position as if the transfer of value was made on the last of the operations, the calculation would be:

Value in H's estate before any transfer (i.e. value of 4 chairs at the date of last transfer	£6,600
Value in husband's estate after all transfers	Nil
Value transferred	£6,600
Deduct value of earlier operations:	
Transfer to wife disregarded *s 268(3)*	Nil
Transfer to son	£1,750
Value transferred	£4,850

So the value transferred is £1,750 + £4,850 = £6,600. HMRC Inheritance Tax would not seek to raise a charge to tax on the actual transfers by the wife to the son.

The CTO may ask the DV for the value effectively transferred by one transfer being the last of a series of associated operations. If any of the earlier operations were themselves transfers of value, other than transfers between spouses/civil partners [*IHTA 1984, s 18*], then the adjustment will be dealt with by the CTO.

Pre-owned assets

[5.6] Further anti-avoidance measures apply from 6 April 2005 which were introduced following a short consultation period (consultation document 'The Tax Treatment of Pre-Owned Assets') to counteract the free continuing use of assets that have been ostensibly gifted. It appears that this anti-avoidance was instigated because of the large amount of tax that has been, and is likely to be, lost through for example the 'double trust' home loan schemes, successful *Eversden* structures (see above) and chattels that are gifted and then rented back under *FA 1986, Sch 20 para 6(1)(a)*. The income tax charge is to be applied in respect of any benefit received in chargeable circumstances in the initial year of assessment or thereafter, but donor(s) will not be chargeable if the scheme is dismantled, or the donor(s) decides to pay a full market rent. This anti-avoidance legislation institutes latent retrospective taxation and applies to existing arrangements that have been in place for many years as well as future arrangements. The income tax charge can apply to assets in circumstances where the user of the asset does not own it but it was purchased with funds provided by him. Tangible assets e.g. a house or land or chattels, and intangible assets such as life assurance policies will come within the income tax charge. In the case of realty the 'appropriate rental value' is the annual rent equal to the annual value. For chattels the chargeable amount is the interest that would be payable for the taxable period at a prescribed rate on an amount equal to the value of the chattel at the valuation date. In the case of intangible assets the chargeable amount is the interest that would be payable for the taxable period at a prescribed rate on an amount equal to the value of the intangible asset at the valuation date. The prescribed rate is currently 3.25% and is related to the official rate of interest as defined in *ITEPA 2003, s 181*. In all three cases apportionment applies where the asset is not wholly within the charge due to retained ownership of part of the asset or in relation to part of the year of assessment by reference to the valuation date. [*FA 2004, Sch 15 paras 4, 7, 9; Charge to Income Tax by Reference to Enjoyment of Property Previously Owned Regulations 2005, SI 2005/724, Regs 2–4*]. See also **56.1** VALUATION. Regulations provide that land and chattels will be valued every five years. In the initial year *FA 2004, Sch 15; Charge to Income Tax by Reference to Enjoyment of Property Previously Owned Regulations 2005, SI 2005/724, Reg 4* applies a valuation will be made and this will apply to the following four succeeding years. In the fifth year *after* the first chargeable year a new valuation will be made on 6 April and this will then apply for that year and the four succeeding years and so on. The actual valuation date for these purposes will be 6 April in the year or if later the commencement of the 'taxable period' when the asset first becomes chargeable. Initially, therefore, the first valuation date may be any date in the tax year from 6 April but subsequent valuation dates after five years have expired will normally be on 6 April. However, no income tax charge will apply where the appropriate amount for any given tax year is not more than £5,000.

In order to provide an escape route from incurring the income tax charge detailed above, taxpayers who have existing schemes that come within the charge may elect for special transitional relief that allows them to avoid the charge to income tax by dismantling the original gift scheme. The timing of the election is not tied to a particular date as it is related to the point at which the individual first came within the charge but the latest date for existing schemes was to be 31 January 2007 for 2005/06. [*FA 2004, Sch 15 paras 21, 22 and 23*]. However, *FA 2007* inserted an amendment to the 2004 legislation so that HMRC may allow a later time limit in particular cases that are deemed appropriate. [*FA 2004, Sch 15 para 23(3); FA 2007, s 66*]. This election (see IHT500 below) will then ensure that the asset is treated as part of the individual's taxable estate for IHT purposes while he continues to enjoy the property in accordance with the gifts with reservation rules. Under the gifts with reservation rules the property would be potentially eligible for IHT reliefs and exemptions providing the necessary requirements for those reliefs and exemptions were met. In the case of a couple who are married or in a civil partnership who jointly own a property and who are both caught by the provisions of *Sch 15*, if they both wish to have it treated as property subject to a reservation, they must both make an election. However, it may still, in certain circumstances, be appropriate for the taxpayer to suffer the income tax charge under existing schemes and avoid the IHT charge. See **22** GIFTS WITH RESERVATION.

In the Pre-Budget Report Statement on 5 December 2005 further anti-avoidance measures regarding the pre-owned assets regime were highlighted for reverter to settlor trusts; it suggested that there is a gap in the legislation so that an owner of an asset can transfer it into a trust but still enjoy the use of the asset. In order to prevent avoidance the pre-owned assets income tax charge will apply from 5 December 2005 to such situations so that where the former owner of an asset (or a person who contributed to its acquisition) enjoys the asset under the terms of the trust, and the trust property may in due course revert to the settlor (or to the spouse, civil partner or the widow, widower or surviving civil partner of the settlor) where an exemption is applicable under *IHTA 1984, ss 53(3)(4), 54(1)(2)* the income tax charge will apply subject to an election for the property to fall back into their estate for IHT purposes. It will apply to all trusts, whenever created, where the property will or could qualify for the reverter to settlor or settlor's spouse/civil partner exemption. [*IHTA 1984, ss 53(3)(4), 54; FA 2004, Sch 15; FA 2006, s 80*].

The method of election recommended by HMRC is that prescribed in the form IHT 500 as follows:

HM Revenue & Customs

Election for Inheritance Tax to apply to asset previously owned

Fill in this form if you are chargeable to Income Tax on the benefit you receive from property you previously owned but want to elect for the property to be treated as part of your estate for Inheritance Tax purposes.

You should read the notes IHT501 as you fill in this form. Please provide information for all sections, inserting 'not applicable' where appropriate.

About the person making the election

Title

Unique Taxpayer Reference (UTR)

Surname

National Insurance number

First name(s)

Address

Date of birth *DD MM YYYY*

Postcode

HMRC Income Tax office

HMRC Income Tax office reference

About the property subject to the election

The property is:

an interest in land ☐ a chattel ☐ intangible property ☐

Description of the property

 Approval Ref No: L13/07

Name(s) of the legal owners of the property

What is the nature and extent of your interest in the property?

Name(s) of anyone else who receives a benefit from the property

Details of disposal(s) or contribution(s)

Is the property conditionally exempt from Inheritance Tax or Capital Gains Tax on an earlier event?

Yes ☐ No ☐

If 'Yes', please provide details

The election

I elect that the property specified above is to form part of my estate for Inheritance Tax purposes under the provisions of paragraphs 21 to 23, Schedule 15 to the Finance Act 2004.

Signature of person making the election

Capacity

Date *DD MM YYYY*

The election applies from the year of Assessment beginning on

6 April

When you have completed this form send it to:

Pre-owned Assets Section
HMRC Inheritance Tax
PO Box 38
Castle Meadow Road
Nottingham
NG2 1BB

Document Exchange: **DX 701201 Nottingham 4.**

Probate and Inheritance Tax helpline:
0845 30 20 900.

For further guidance go to:
www.hmrc.gov.uk/poa/index.htm

Page 2

The Liechtenstein Disclosure Facility (LDF)

[5.7] The Liechtenstein Disclosure Facility (LDF) offers opportunity for taxpayers with undisclosed offshore liabilities to regularise their tax affairs up to the end of the last filed tax year. It is now set to close on 31 December 2015. It can be available where a person has inherited offshore assets that were not originally declared in a deceased's estate. Full details are available in a guidance booklet: www.gov.uk/government/publications/offshore-disclosure-facilites-liechtenstein.

The facility offers the benefit of restricting assessable years back to 1999 only, and limiting penalties to 10% up for tax years up to 2008/09. Higher penalties, normally 20%, will apply thereafter. There is also the assurance that criminal tax proceedings will not be pursued in cases where full disclosure is given and the source of funds do not relate to wider criminal activity.

The facility requires provision of certificate of confirmation of relevance, issued by a Liechtenstein financial intermediary, when submitting the application. The intermediary therefore needs to be involved at the outset and this normally means transferring funds into the management of the intermediary on a medium term basis.

The Liechtenstein Disclosure Facility (LDF) followed the previous Offshore Disclosure Facility (ODF) and New Disclosure Opportunity (NDO) and can apply for IHT purposes. See example below. The NDO facility notification period was extended to 31 January 2010 for all paper and before 12 March 2010 for online notifications.

Example 5

Bob's UK domiciled mother died in June 2005 and left him £1 million which was originally invested in Jersey but not through a UK bank or agency. On receiving advice Bob moved the money to Liechtenstein in early 2007 but by that time he had moved the money to Liechtenstein in early 2007 when it was evident that the NDO was to be introduced. The NDO and LDF have relevance for IHT purposes so there are a number of implications. The inheritance of £1 million should have been included in the IHT400 completed after his mother's death and, if not included, the Personal Representatives/Executors will have to rectify the omission. At this stage there is unlikely to be any nil rate band and transferable nil rate band (if applicable) available to the PRs/Executors and therefore the IHT charge will be at 40%. If his mother was still alive then as a gift it would have been a potentially exempt transfer and provided she had survived 7 years from the date of the gift it would have been exempt. Where there has been an omission from an account that has already been made then the NDO 20% penalty regime has expired as above will apply. Where there has been no IHT account made then the penalty will be limited to £1 million × 10% = £100,000. However, there is no time limit of 10 years for which HMRC can go back for an omission regarding IHT as opposed to the case of income tax.

If the investment in Jersey had been through a UK branch or agency then the following scenario would have applied: A letter would have been received by Bob which was dated 14 June 2007 and related to the original Offshore Disclosure Facility (ODF) but by that time he had moved the money to Liechtenstein in early 2007 when it was evident that the NDO was to be introduced. If Bob did not advise his accountant at the time then there would have been an NDO penalty of

20% of the tax due as he failed to respond to the ODF. Assuming Bob paid income tax at a marginal rate of 40% and a gross accrued interest rate received of 2.5% (total £134,375) his tax and penalty will be £53,750 (tax) and £10,750 (penalty) plus interest on unpaid tax of £9,621 making a total of £74,121 payable 31 January 2010 if he had notified HMRC. Interest runs from 31 January following the tax year of assessment i.e. 31 January 2007 for 2005/06 the earliest year. If he failed to notify by 31 January 2010 then the penalty would rise to between 30% and 100% depending on any mitigating circumstances that the accountant can put successfully to the HMRC. However as he had transferred the account to Liechtenstein in early 2007 the LDF will now apply with a penalty of 10%.

Similarly, the PRs/Executors have a responsibility to ensure a corrective IHT account is submitted and a penalty on the tax omission of £400,000 i.e. £1 million × 40% will amount to £400,000 as above for income tax purposes. Interest will also run from six months after the date of death i.e. from 1 January 2006 to 31 March 2010. This is calculated to be in the region of £53,530 and the PRs/Executors would now be looking at a potential offer of £400,000 (tax) and say £40,000 (10% penalty) plus interest on unpaid tax of £53,530 making a total of £493,530. There may of course be further liabilities relating to the years prior to the 2005 inheritance when omissions were applicable from Bob's mother's tax returns which at this stage are unquantifiable.

Bob will declare personal liabilities from 2005 under the LDF and give sufficient details of the source of the funds to enable HMRC to consider the completeness of the disclosure. His mother's estate and PRs/Executors may have liabilities prior to 2005. HMRC may seek to recover the earlier liabilities. If Bob elects for the Composite Rate Option (i.e. 40% tax + 10% penalty + interest) he will be responsible for all liabilities for the period commencing April 1999 and HMRC will not take any further action against the estate or PRs/Executors regarding this source as it is now covered by the LDF terms. See www.hmrc.gov.uk/disclosure/liechtenstein-faq.htm#28

Disclosure of Tax Avoidance Schemes

[5.8] *FA 2004, ss 306–319* impose obligations on promoters of certain tax avoidance schemes, and in some cases on persons entering into transactions under such schemes, to disclose those schemes to HMRC. See **5.9** below. The primary legislation provides the framework for these disclosure rules, with the detail provided by regulations made by statutory instrument.

HMRC have published detailed guidance notes on the disclosure rules which may be accessed via the search facility on its website ('DOTAS Guidance'). The legislation is policed by the HMRC's Anti-Avoidance Group (Intelligence) unit; see www.hmrc.gov.uk/avoidance/index.htm, which includes links to the legislation and the official guidance plus various forms to be used for making disclosures. The address of the unit is HM Revenue & Customs, Anti-Avoidance Group (Intelligence), 1st Floor South, 22 Kingsway, London, WC2B 6NR.

Simon's Taxes. See A7.2.

Arrangements covered by the rules

[5.9] Initially, the *Tax Avoidance Schemes (Prescribed Descriptions of Arrangements) Regulations 2004* (*SI 2004/1863* as amended by *SI 2004/2429* and revoked by *SI 2006 No 1543*) applied the disclosure rules only to certain arrangements related to financial products and certain arrangements connected with employment and limited the scope of the rules to income tax, corporation tax and capital gains tax advantages. The rules have been progressively extended and with effect from 6 April 2011 apply to certain inheritance tax arrangements by virtue of the *Tax Inheritance Tax Avoidance Schemes (Prescribed Descriptions of Arrangements) Regulations 2011* (*SI 2011 No 170*) and *The Inheritance Tax Avoidance Schemes (Information) (Amendment) Regulations 2011 (SI 2011 No 171)*.

Under the 2011 Regulations arrangements fall with the scope of the disclosure rules if:

(a) as a result of any element of them property becomes relevant property within the meaning of *IHTA 1984, s 58(1)*; and
(b) a main benefit of the arrangements is that an advantage is obtained in respect of the lifetime IHT entry charge on the transfer of value by which the property becomes relevant property.

The regulations contain three exceptions from the new disclosure requirements. These cover arrangements which are the same, or substantially the same as those:

(i) which were first made available for implementation before 6 April 2011; or
(ii) in relation to which the date of any transaction forming part them falls before 6 April 2011: or
(iii) in relation to which a promoter first made a firm approach to another person before 6 April 2011.

In broad terms therefore only schemes to avoid the lifetime IHT entry charge on a transfer into trust are caught and if the scheme itself pre-dates 6 April 2011 it need not be disclosed. The IHT advantage must also relate to a transfer of value into trust and therefore dispositions which are not transfers of value (for example, a disposition for maintenance of family *IHTA 1984, s 11*) are considered to be outside the scope of the Regulations. Note also that the hallmarks of tax avoidance schemes in the 2004 Regulations are not applied for IHT purposes, so disclosure must be made even though the scheme concerned could not be regarded as commanding a premium fee.

Grandfathering

[5.10] HMRC has published a list of schemes which it does not require to be disclosed under these provisions because it is already aware of them. However a scheme may nevertheless have to be disclosed if it is part of wider arrangements which are outside those which are grandfathered.

The list of schemes not requiring disclosure is:

(1) **Arrangements that qualify for reliefs/exemptions:** this includes a single step that qualifies for a relief/exemption, where this does not depend on the inclusion of other steps, and also arrangements which qualify for multiple reliefs/exemptions or more than one application of the same relief, or a single relief/exemption plus further steps in each case where they are covered by the grandfathering rule.

(2) **The purchase of business assets with a view to transferring them into a relevant property trust after 2 years.**

(3) **The purchase of agricultural assets with a view to transferring them into a relevant property trust after the qualify for relief.**

(4) **Pilot trusts:** these do not require disclosure if there is no advantage in relation to the IHT entry charge on creation. Note that an advantage in relation to 10 yearly or exit charges is not disclosable under the Regulations.

(5) **Discounted gift trusts:** most of these are not disclosable because all the trusts are bare trusts but where this is not the case disclosure is not required where the grandfathering provisions apply.

(6) **Excluded property trusts, disabled trusts, employee benefit trusts within *IHTA 1984, s 86* and qualifying interest in possession trusts:** these are not disclosable unless there is an advantage in relation to the relevant property entry charge.

(7) **Transfers on death into relevant property trusts.**

(8) **Changes in the distribution of deceased's estates:** variations, disclaimers etc. of interests in a deceased's estate which are not transfers of value by virtue of *IHTA 1984, s 17* are not disclosable, nor are distributions from property settled by will within *s 144*.

(9) **Transfers within the nil band every seven years.**

(10) **Loan into relevant property trust: this is not disclosable where it is made a single step.**

(11) **Insurance property trusts:** the transfer of death benefits into trust and the payment of premiums on a trust policy are not disclosable, except where part of other arrangements giving an advantage in relation the relevant property entry charge.

(12) **Chargeable transfer followed by potentially exempt transfer:** this is within the grandfathering exemption, except where there are further arrangements giving an advantage with respect to the relevant property entry charge.

(13) **Deferred share schemes:** normally non disclosable unless part of scheme outside the grandfathering provisions.

(14) **Retention of reversionary interest by settler:** not disclosable if grandfathering rule applies.

(15) **Gifts to companies:** these are chargeable transfers but do no involve relevant property in trust and so are outside the scope of the Regulations.

Returns

[5.11] The promoter of arrangements within these Regulations must make disclosure to HMRC under the provisions of the 2004 Regulations and the applicable time limit is the same as for other direct tax schemes, usually being within 5 days of making the scheme available for implementation. The Scheme Reference Number will then be allocated by HMRC and any person who is a party to arrangements which are notifiable under the Regulations, and who is also required to make a return under *IHTA 1984, s 216* (Delivery of accounts) in respect of them, must disclose the scheme reference number in that return. Where no return under *s 216* is required, disclosure to HMRC must be made on form AAG4 within 12 months of the end of the month in which the first of the relevant transactions is entered into.

Penalties

[5.12] Penalties are chargeable for failures to comply with the duties summarised at **5.11** above and detailed in the primary legislation noted below contained in *FA 2004*:

(a) duty of promoter to notify HMRC of notifiable proposals or arrangements (*FA 2004, s 308(1)(3)*);
(b) duty of taxpayer to notify where the promoter is not UK-resident (*FA 2004, s 309(1)*);
(c) duty of parties to arrangements to notify where there is no promoter (*FA 2004, s 310*);
(d) duty of promoter to notify parties of the scheme reference number (*FA 2004, s 312(2)*);
(e) duty of client to notify other parties to the arrangements concerned and who might be expected gain a tax advantage from them of the reference number (*FA 2004, s 312A(2)*);
(f) (from 1 January 2011) duty of promoter to provide details of clients (*FA 2004, s 313ZA*);
(g) duty of promoter to respond to inquiry (*FA 2004, ss 313A, 313B*);
(h) duty of introducer to give details of persons who have provided information (*FA 2004, s 313C*);

There is an initial penalty of up to £5,000 for any failure to comply with any one of the above duties. However, with effect from 1 January 2011, where the failure relates to (a), (b) or (c) above, the initial penalty is up to £600 for each day during the 'initial period'. The 'initial period' begins with the day after that on which the time limit for complying with the requirement expires and ends with the earlier of the day on which the penalty is determined and the last day before the failure ceases. The actual amount of the daily penalty should be arrived at after taking account of all relevant considerations, including the desirability of providing a deterrent and the amount of fees likely to be received by a promoter or the tax saving sought by the taxpayer. If, after taking account of those considerations, the maximum daily penalty seems inappropriately low, it can be increased to any amount up to £1 million.

Penalties are determined by the First-tier Tribunal. Where HMRC consider that a daily penalty has been determined to run from a date later than it should, they can commence proceedings for a redetermination of the penalty.

A further penalty or penalties of up to £600 applies for each day on which the failure continues after the initial penalty is imposed.

HMRC may appeal to the Tribunal for an order that a specified proposal or arrangements shall be treated as notifiable. There is also a separate power for HMRC to apply to the Tribunal, specifying the promoter, for an order that a specified proposal or arrangements is notifiable. Wherever daily penalties apply, the maximum is increased to £5,000 per day where, in relation to the proposal or arrangements in question, an order has been made by the Tribunal. Where the order is made, the increased maximum only applies to days falling after the period of ten days beginning with the date of the order.

Where an order is made by the Tribunal, doubt as to notifiability is not a reasonable excuse for the purposes of *TMA 1970, s 118(2)* after the expiry of ten days beginning with the date of the order.

Parties to notifiable arrangements who fail to notify HMRC of the scheme reference number etc. are liable to a penalty of £100 in respect of each scheme to which the failure relates. The penalty is increased for a second failure, occurring within three years from the date on which the first failure began, to £500 in respect of each scheme to which the failure relates (whether or not the same as the scheme to which the first failure relates). Any further such failures occurring within three years from the date on which the previous failure began, result in a penalty of £1,000 in respect of each scheme to which the failure relates (whether or not the same as the schemes to which any of the previous failures relates).

The Treasury has the power to amend the above maxima of £600, £5,000, and £1 million by statutory instrument.

A party to notifiable arrangements who fails to give the reference number (for example, by including it in a return) is liable to a penalty of £100 for each scheme (i.e. each set of notifiable arrangements) to which the failure relates. A second such failure within a period of 36 months gives rise to a penalty of £500 per scheme. A third or subsequent failure within 36 months gives rise to a penalty of £1,000 per scheme. The normal penalty regime for incorrect tax returns does not, however, apply in relation to any such failure.

[*TMA 1970, s 98C; FA 2004, ss 315, 319; FA 2007, s 108(9); FA 2008, s 116, Sch 38 para 7; FA 2010, Sch 17 paras 10, 11; SI 2004 No 1864, Reg 8B; SI 2007 Nos 3103, 3104; SI 2008 No 1935; SI 2010 No 2743; SI 2010 No 2928, Regs 1, 4; SI 2010 No 3019; SI 2011 No 170; SI 2011 No 171*].

6

Business Property

Cross-references. See **4** AGRICULTURAL PROPERTY; **5.1** ANTI-AVOIDANCE; **7.5** CALCULATION OF TAX for application of business relief where transfers partly exempt; and **22.9** GIFTS WITH RESERVATION where such a gift is of relevant business property.

Simon's Taxes. See **I5.455, I7.1.**

Other Sources. Tolley's Capital Gains Tax 2010/11; Foster, Part G1; Mellows, Parts 5.24–5.34; HMRC Inheritance Tax Manual; IHTM25000, IHTM18331.

Introduction

[6.1] Where the qualifying conditions are satisfied, relief from inheritance tax is available on a transfer of value which is attributable to the value 'relevant business property'. It is a fallacy therefore to state that the relief only applies to transfers of business property, since the requirement is that the value of the transfer must be attributable to such property. The significance of this distinction was highlighted in the *Nelson Dance case* (see **6.4** RELEVANT BUSINESS PROPERTY) where it was held that relief applied to a gift of an asset used for a business, whilst the business itself was not transferred. The relief is a percentage reduction in the value transferred by the transfer of value (see Table below) and applies to transfers in life and on death and to occasions on which tax is chargeable under the provisions relating to SETTLEMENTS: DISCRETIONARY TRUSTS AND OTHER TRUSTS OF RELEVANT PROPERTY (43). The percentage reduction is made before deduction of the annual exemption and other EXEMPT TRANSFERS (21) and before grossing-up where the transferor pays the tax. It should be noted that unlike agricultural property relief there is no territorial limitation on undertakings entitled to business property relief and therefore can include business situated worldwide. See also Foster on inheritance tax at section G1.11.

Relevant business property after 5 April 1996

In relation to transfers of value made, and other events occurring, **after 5 April 1996** the categories of 'relevant business property' qualifying for business property relief (BPR) are as follows:

(a)	Unincorporated business (**6.4**(a) below)	100%
(b)	Unquoted securities which either by themselves or with other such securities or unquoted shares gave the transferor control (**6.4**(b) below)	100%
(c)	Any unquoted shares in a company not listed on a recognised stock exchange but including those traded in the USM or the AIM or OFFEX markets (**6.4**(b), (d) below)	100%
(d)	Shares or securities giving control of a 'quoted' company (**6.4**(b) below)	50%
(e)	Land, buildings, machinery or plant held either (a) by a partner and used for the purposes of a business conducted by the partnership or (b) by a controlling shareholder and used by that company for the purposes of its business or (c) by the trustees of a settlement and used for the purposes of a business carried on by a life tenant of the settlement (but see (**6.4**) and (**6.4**(c) below — HMRC consider that this heading applies only to lifetime transfers)	50%

Conditions for business property relief

[6.2] The conditions to be satisfied are:

(a) the business, whether unincorporated or incorporated into a company in respect of the value of which relief is claimed, is a qualifying business, see **6.3** below; and

(b) the asset must be relevant business property, see above and **6.4** below; and

(c) the asset must have been owned for a minimum period, see **6.8** below.

There are further conditions to be satisfied by lifetime transfers, see **6.11** below.

Definition of qualifying business

[6.3] '*Business*' includes a business carried on in the exercise of a profession or vocation but does not include a business carried on otherwise than for gain which will exclude many 'hobby' businesses and loss-making businesses from the relief. [*IHTA 1984, s 103(3)*]. See *C & E Commissioners v Lord Fisher* [1981] STC 238 for Ralph Gibson J's six tests on the factors to be considered in respect of a business carried on for gain. See HMRC Tax Bulletin October 1999, p 699.

Example 1

Bill 'the bet' Hill, an Authorised Bookmaker, is an on-course bookmaker with a 'pitch' at Sandown Park racecourse as well as his own independent bookmakers in Wallington, Surrey. He had originally obtained the bookmaking business by inheritance from his father many years previously. The 'pitch' is valued at £98,000 (see point (C) below) and the business in Wallington where he conducts his business other than on race days at Sandown Park is valued at £210,000. Bill also provides a deposit to the National Joint Pitch Council of £25,000, being the security required for a rails bookmaker. Bill dies on 25 December 2010 and leaves the business to his son Alan.

	£
Value of Wallington bookmakers	210,000
Pitch at Sandown Park racecourse	98,000
Deposit held by National Joint Pitch Council	25,000
Total	333,000
Deduct business property relief 100%	(333,000)
IHT payable	Nil

Notes to the example

(A) The business including pitch must meet the statutory requirements of *IHTA 1984, ss 103–114* in order to qualify for 100% BPR.

(B) Rule 17.1.3 of the National Pitch Rules (Fourth Edition) deals with the transfer of Seniority Positions and states that ' . . . subject to no consideration in money or money's worth being paid, by transfer on retirement or Will, to a member of the Authorised Bookmaker's immediate family, being defined for the purposes of this Rule 17 as the Authorised Bookmaker's spouse, parents, children or sibling'. In this case a transfer of the 'pitch' to Bill's son is allowable under the Rules. See www.njpc-ltd.co.uk/index.htm.

(C) Under *TCGA 1992, s 274* where the market value of an asset has been 'ascertained' for IHT purposes then that value is also used for CGT purposes to be the market value. In the case of a bookmaker's pitch see HMRC Interpretation RI 210.

Exclusions

A business or interest in a business, or shares or securities of a company, do not qualify if the business (or the business of the company) *consists wholly or mainly* (see below) of dealing in securities, stock or shares, land or buildings or making or holding investments, unless the business is:

(a) wholly that of a 'market maker' (before the Stock Exchange reform, a jobber) or that of a discount house and, in either case, is carried on in the UK; or
(b) that of a holding company of one or more companies whose business does qualify.

Land holding or dealing businesses

A land holding or dealing business, however, can qualify, provided it includes building construction or land development, and the housing stock of a building business can qualify if regarded as stock in trade.

> '*Mr Lawson:* "As with many, if not all building companies their stock of houses would be regarded as stock in trade—I know that in some cases the houses may rapidly be transferred to a holding company in the Group, but in the company which does the building they will be regarded as stock in trade—will the Chief Secretary assure us that that type of company is not comprised in the category of company that is described as that dealing in land or buildings."'
>
> '*Mr Barnett:* "I can give the hon and learned Gentleman that assurance."'

HC Official Report, 30 June 1976, cols 1268, 1269.

In *DWC Piercy's Executors v HMRC* [2008] STC SCD 858 Sp C 687 a property development company (T) owned some land in Islington on which it had erected some workshops, which it let out. T's major shareholder died in 1999. His executors claimed business property relief. HMRC rejected the claim on the grounds that because T received significant rental income, its business consisted mainly of 'making or holding investments', within *IHTA 1984, s 105(3)*. The executors appealed, contending that it still wished to develop the land in Islington for residential purposes but had been unable to do so because of uncertainty about proposals for a new railway line. The Special Commissioner accepted this evidence and allowed the appeal, finding that the company continued to hold its land as trading stock, and holding that it was not an 'investment company' for the purposes of *s 105*. The Commissioner also held that 'the only type of land-dealing company whose shares fail to qualify for the relief is . . . some sort of dealing or speculative trader that does not actively develop or actually build on land'.

Definition — 'wholly or mainly'

The term '**consists wholly or mainly**' is not simply a quantitative test of 50% or more, but it is a qualitative test determined by 'not the degree or level of activity, but rather the nature of the activities which are carried on' (*HMRC v Personal Representatives of Pawson deceased* [2013] UKUT 50 (TCC)). See *Powell and Halfhide (executor of G E Pearce deceased) v CIR* [1997] STC SCD 181 Sp C 120; *Furness v CIR* [1999] STC SCD 232 Sp C 202. The leading decision is now *Carnwath J in George & Loochin (Stedman's Executors) v CIR* CA [2003] EWCA Civ 1763 [2004] STC 147, where staff time, turnover, gross and net profit on each activity were all taken into account. See **58 TAX CASES**.

Case law

In the case of *Hall & Hall (Hall's Executors) v CIR* [1997] STC SCD 126 Sp C 114; the letting of caravans on 45-year leases which comprised 84% of the deceased's income in the form of rent and standing charges resulted in the determination that the business had consisted 'mainly of making or holding investments'.

In contrast, the net profitability of lettings on a farm when compared with that of the less profitable farming business could not be the sole yardstick as to whether the business consisted 'mainly' of holding investments in *Farmer and another (Executors of Farmer deceased) v CIR* [1999] STC SCD 321 Sp C 216. Although the lettings were more profitable than the farm, the overall context of the business, the capital employed, the time spent by the employees and consultants and the levels of turnover supported the conclusion that the business consisted mainly of farming.

In *Weston (Weston's Executor) v CIR* [2000] STC SCD 30 Sp C 222, the business of a company included the purchase and sale of caravans, the sale of caravans for commission on behalf of owners, and the grant of the right to pitch caravans on the caravan park run by the company. The business also included the maintenance and administration of the park, and the supply for a consideration of electricity and bottled gas used by the pitch holders at the park. However looked at in the round, the business was mainly an investment business with ancillary sales, and business property relief was therefore denied.

In *Burkinyoung (executor of Burkinyoung deceased) v CIR* [1995] STC SCD 29 Sp C 3 a business of letting furnished flats on assured shorthold tenancies was held to be wholly one of making and holding investments and so is excluded from relief. Also, in the similar case of *Martin and Horsfall (executors of Moore deceased) v CIR* [1995] STC SCD 5 Sp C 2 the letting of properties as small industrial units was not a business as the units consisted wholly or mainly of the 'making or holding of investments'. In determining these cases, Stephen Oliver QC referred to an income tax decision and suggested that the provision of security services or heating/cleaning services, independent of the lease requirements, for specific charge would not be an activity of holding investments. As it was where services are provided under the lease then that may be deemed to be connected with and incidental to holding investments. [*IHTA 1984, s 105(3)*]. In a more recent case a woman owned a number of shares in a company which owned more than 100 different properties. Her executors claimed business property relief. HMRC rejected the claim on the basis that the shares were not 'relevant business property', because the company's business consisted mainly of 'making or holding investments', within *IHTA 1984, s 105(3)*. The executors appealed, contending that because the company carried out maintenance work on the properties, it should not be treated as falling within *s 105(3)*. The Special Commissioner rejected this contention and dismissed the executors' appeal, holding that 'the company's maintenance activity is not the separate provision of services; it is inherent in property ownership'. On the evidence, the company's business consisted 'mainly of holding investments'. See *Clark (executors of Clark deceased) v HMRC* [2005] STC SCD 823 Sp C 502. However, in a more recent case the activities of a money lender which encompassed lending to various family companies 'was in the business of making loans and not in the business of investing in loans . . . the loans were not investments for their own sake but the provision of a finance facility to the other companies'. Accordingly, the shares in the money lending company qualified for business property relief. *Phillips and Others (Phillips' Executors) v HMRC*, [2006] STC SCD 639 Sp C 555.

In contrast, the decision of the Commissioners in *Stedman's Executors v CIR* [2002] STC SCD 358 Sp C 323 determined that, as '72% of the site fees goes in overheads (*sic*) . . . most of which relate to the provision of upkeep of the common parts', this was 'the provision of services and not the business of holding investments'. The Court of Appeal upheld this decision with Carnwath LJ stating that, on the evidence, the holding of property as an investment was only one component of the business, and did not prevent the company from qualifying for business property relief (*George & Loochin (Stedman's Executors) v CIR* CA [2003] EWCA Civ 1763; [2004] STC 147). As this was only the second time the Court of Appeal had considered BPR, the previous case being *Fetherstonaugh and others v CIR* [1984] STC 261, it is interesting to note Carnwath LJ's comment in conclusion:

> 'I find it difficult to see any reason why an active family business of this kind should be excluded from business property relief, merely because a necessary component of its profit making activity is the use of land.'

In a change to the HMRC Manual, it is now stated at IHTM25278 in relation to caravan and furnished holiday lettings that are the subject of a BPR claim:

> 'Recent advice from Solicitor's Office has caused us to reconsider our approach and it may well be that some cases that might have previously qualified should not have done so. In particular we will be looking more closely at the level and type of services, rather than who provided them.'

The decision in the *Pawson* case referred to above related to seaside bungalow let on a weekly basis as holiday accommodation. It was a standard holiday let business, in that the property was fully furnished and equipped, and it was cleaned between lets and freshly laundered bedding provided on each occasion. The appeal was allowed by the First-tier Tax Tribunal on the basis that significant services were provided, such that 'an intelligent businessman would not regard the ownership of a holiday letting property as an investment and would regard it as involving far too active an operation for it to come under that heading'. That decision was reversed on appeal by HMRC. The Upper Tribunal stated that the First-tier did not explain how an intelligent businessman could conclude that the services elements in the business outweighed the investments elements and the only conclusion reasonably open to the Tribunal on the facts was that the property was mainly held as an investment. *Personal Representatives of Pawson deceased v HMRC* [2013] UKUT 50.

A further attempt to secure business property relief for furnished holiday lets was made in *Green v HMRC* [2015] UKFTT 0236 (TC). The *Pawson* case was distinguished on the basis that the business comprised a number of let units so that the average annual income was far higher at £87,000 as opposed to around £6,100 in the *Pawson* case. Furthermore, if the properties had been let on assured shorthold tenancies, the income produced would be around £35,000, so that the additional £52,000 of annual income must be produced by the services provided. However the Tribunal upheld HMRC's argument that the size of the business is irrelevant and the services did not produce the level of income suggested since the investment element in the business was predominant. Relief was therefore denied.

In *Trustees of David Zetland Settlement v HMRC* TC/2010/05387, trustees held a commercial building divided into small office units let to tenants for periods normally ranging between one and five years, although these terms were operated on a flexible basis so that they might be terminated earlier. The senior trustee had an office on site and was engaged for much of his time on the management of the premises. There was also a team of staff, including a receptionist, cleaner, handyman and porters, each employed by the trustees. On the premises were a café, operated with the support of the trustees, and other facilities such as bicycle park and meeting rooms available for hire on a daily or hourly basis. The trustees also carried out conversion work to suit the tenants and dilapidations work on termination of each tenancy, some of which produced profits for the trust. It was contended that the business was eligible for business property relief in view of the fact that the trustee and the staff were mostly engaged on providing their services to the tenants. The First Tier Tribunal held that the business in the round was one of holding an investment and was not eligible for business property relief.

In *Best (Exor of Buller deceased) v HMRC* [2014] UKFTT 077 (TC) a company held and managed a business centre comprising approximately 10% offices, and the balance being two thirds warehousing used by retailers or wholesalers and one third light industrial use. In total there were approximately 400 people in or around the Centre on a typical working day. The deceased spent considerable time each week at the Business Centre dealing with the everyday matters that might arise with occupiers. On his death the company employed a full-time replacement as a site administrator. Units were occupied under licence agreements not conferring exclusive possession of a unit. Twenty-four hour security was provided along with a receptionist, forklift driver, maintenance person, office facilities, meeting rooms, central telephone switchboard and various other business facilities. Nevertheless it was held that the investment activity of letting the units was the predominant activity and the company was therefore mainly an investment company. The claim to business property relief on the shares was therefore refused.

Holding of 'investments'

Where relatively substantial amounts of surplus cash have been accumulated in a business, it must first be determined whether or not the business has become mainly one of holding investments, and if not whether all or part of the cash reserves are 'excepted assets'. In the Special Commissioner's decision in *Brown's Executors v CIR* [1996] STC SCD 277 Sp C 83 it was held that the sale of a night club, an asset of the proprietor's unquoted UK company Gaslight, resulting in capital being held on deposit interest account pending the further investment in a future premises was not a change in the nature of the business carried on by the company. HMRC had contended that at the time of the proprietor's death the company's business consisted wholly or mainly in the making and holding of investments and therefore excluded the shares from being qualifying business property. However, the Commissioner found in favour of the taxpayer because the proprietor intended to purchase suitable alternative premises and the deposit account holding the proceeds was of necessity short term to conclude a purchase. In the case of *Beckman v CIR* [2000] STC SCD 59 Sp C 226 monies in a business remaining a capital account on retirement of a partner was held on death to be 'simply those of a creditor of the business' and would therefore not qualify for BPR. The retention of large sums of money in the business after retirement should be avoided because there is no reason *per se* for such a retention which might be expected to be paid out as dividend or capital distribution.

Claims for relief for livery businesses may currently be subjected to particular scrutiny by HMRC. These businesses range from those where full care and provision of the horses is undertaken by the owner of the business to those where little more than stabling is provided with the owners of the horses being required to provide the care of them. The latter, commonly known as DIY liveries, will not benefit from business property relief since they are akin to a property rental business. The former should qualify for relief. Many liveries have elements of both types of business and these may experience reluctance by HMRC to allow relief.

Market maker

A '**market maker**' is a person who holds himself out at all normal times in compliance with the rules of either The Stock Exchange or, after 22 March 1992, traders on the London Financial Futures and Options Exchange (LIFFE) who are recognised by LIFFE (Administration and Management) as willing to buy and sell securities etc. With effect from 31 December 2012 the business of traders on any regulated market elsewhere in the EEA, which has been notified to the European Commission and who are recognised by that market, is also within the meaning of 'market maker'. [*IHTA 1984, s 105(4)(7); FA 1986, s 106; SI 1992/3181; SI 2012/2903*].

Relevant business property

[6.4] Business property qualifying for relief is in the following classes. See IHT 17, p 3.

(a) Unincorporated businesses

An unincorporated business is a property consisting of a qualifying business (see **6.3** above) or interest in such a business (e.g. sole trade, profession, share in partnership). [*IHTA 1984, s 105(1)(a)*]. The value of a business or of an interest in a business is the net value of the business or interest therein, i.e. the value of the assets used in the business including goodwill, less the business liabilities but not, according to IHT 17, p 5, money loaned to a business. In valuing an interest in a business, regard must only be had to assets and liabilities by reference to which the net value of the entire business would fall to be ascertained.

In *Ninth Marquess of Hertford and others (Executors of eighth Marquess of Hertford deceased) v CIR*, [2005] STC SCD 177 Sp C 444 part of a historic house was open to the public, while part was used as a private residence and not open to the public. The freeholder died in 1997. HMRC issued a notice of determination charging IHT on 22% of the value of the house, on the basis that only 78% of the house was open to the public and thus only 78% of the house qualified for business property relief. The freeholder's executors appealed, contending that the house was a single asset and that the effect of *IHTA 1984, s 110(b)* was that the whole of the house qualified for business property relief even though 22% of the house was not open to the public. The Special Commissioner accepted this contention and allowed the appeal, observing that *s 110* made no provision for apportionment.

See also 33 NATIONAL HERITAGE. Also, HMRC states 'If the business owed any money to the deceased, often through a loan account, you must **not** add that value to the value of the capital and current accounts. A loan does not qualify for business relief.' [*IHTA 1984, s 110*]. See also *Hardcastle & Hardcastle (Vernede's Executors) v CIR*, [2000] STC SCD 532 Sp C 259 and *Mallender & Others (Drury-Lowe's Executors) v CIR*, Ch D [2001] STC 514 below.

In *Brander (Representative of the fourth Earl of Balfour) v HMRC* (2009) FTT 101 the appellant succeeded in integrating a property business within the overall estate and the whole qualified for BPR. The Scottish estate in question, Whittingehame, was owned by a trust founded by the first Earl. The Fourth Earl had the liferent (i.e. under Scottish trust law giving a right to the income of the estate and the power, within limits, to manage it). The estate was a typical one for Scotland, including farms (both managed by the estate and leased), woodland, shooting and 28 leased cottages. In late 2002 the Earl succeeded in having the trust wound up, the property becoming his absolutely. He then put it into a partnership that he managed jointly with his heir, his nephew. In June 2003 the Earl died. His executors claimed BPR on the Earl's share in the partnership, to reduce the taxable value of the Estate. HMRC sought to deny the relief but the Judgment stated 'Most estates of the type under discussion are heavily based on farming and to some extent on forestry and woodland management and related shooting interests. The letting side was ancillary to the farming, forestry, woodland and sporting activities. The farming activities, albeit they include agricultural tenancies, occupied by far the greater area of the estate' (see, for example, *Farmer v IRC* 1999 STC (SCD) 321).

The Nelson Dance case

In the more recent case *Nelson Dance Family Settlement Trustees*, Ch D [2009] STC 802 Sp C 682, a farmer in 2002 transferred some farmland, which had development value, to the trustees of a family settlement. HMRC issued a ruling that 'none of the value transferred was attributable to the value of relevant business property'. The trustees appealed. The Special Commissioner allowed the appeal and held that:

> 'everything turns on the loss in value to the donor's estate, rather than what is given or how the loss to the estate arises, except where the identity of the recipient is crucial to a particular exemption.'

But that the business property relief was

> 'much more concerned with values than property. Although the attribution is to the net value of the business as a whole, this does not imply that the value transferred must relate to the whole business. Indeed the exclusion for value attributed to excepted assets in *s 112* shows that the value transferred may need to be attributed to the value of particular business assets (although that would equally be the case if the relief were restricted to transfers of the whole business). Presumably the attribution to the net value of the business is to put a ceiling on the relief to prevent a transferor giving away the total assets of the business, claiming business relief for them, while retaining the liabilities and paying them out of other assets (although that seems to be possible for agricultural relief as the relief is given in terms of attribution to the agricultural value of agricultural property).'

IHTA 1984, s 104 should be construed as meaning that 'all that is required is that the value transferred by the transfer of value is attributable to the net value of the business'. Accordingly, the transfer of the farmland qualified for 100% business property relief. HMRC's appeal was dismissed. *See* also **4.1** AGRICULTURAL PROPERTY and **58** TAX CASES.

Example 2

D has owned and farmed 700 acres of land in Northern England since 1980. This land was farmed for arable crops but due to D's age he transfers the farm land into a family trust for his children. The 700 acres are valued at £1,200 per acre agricultural land. D will continue to live in the farmhouse. The land is situated close to a newly designated brownfield site under a Regional Development Strategy Plan to be implemented by the end of 2010 which will be accessed by a one-acre ransom strip of the farmland which is valued at £2 million.

		£
Valuations for IHT purposes		
700 acres at £1,500 per acre		1,050,000
Development value of 1-acre ransom strip		1,998,800
Total value of transfer into trust		3,050,000
The transfers subject to tax:		
(i) Agricultural value of land		
700 acres × £1,500	1,050,000	
Less agricultural property relief at 100%	(1,050,000)	—
(ii) Value of development land		
1 acre less agricultural value		1,998,800
		1,998,000
Deduct development land attracting 100% BPR		(1,998,000)
Chargeable at 20%		£Nil

Notes to the example

(A) In *Nelson Dance Family Settlement Trustees*, [2008] STC SCD 792 Sp C 682 the Special Commissioner found in favour of the taxpayer who had claimed 100% BPR in respect of the land transferred into the settlement. In examining *IHTA 1984, s 104(1)* the Special Commissioner stated that the assets comprised in the declarations of trust were attributable to the net value of the business as they were a component part of the assets used in the business contributing to the net value. Accordingly, the transfer of the farmland qualified for 100% business property relief.

(B) The Special Commissioner stated that certain inheritance tax text books, which HMRC had quoted as authority were erroneous in concluding that the meaning of *IHTA 1984, s 104(1)* should mean that the whole of a business had to be transferred in order to attract BPR. Therefore when considering BPR and 'relevant business property' the question is

> '. . . much more concerned with values than property. Although the attribution is to the net value of the business as a whole, this does not imply that the value transferred must relate to the whole business.'

(C) In the Court of Appeal the Special Commissioner's decision was upheld and Sales J stated 'the general principle governing the operation of the *IHTA* is the loss to donor principle, which directs attention to changes in the value of the transferor's estate rather than in that of the transferee', and that 'any charge to tax does not turn upon what happens to property transferred when it is in the hands of the transferee.' *HMRC v Nelson Dance Family Settlement Trustees (re the)*, Ch D [2009] STC 802.

Settled property with interest in possession

In *Fetherstonhaugh and Others v CIR* CA, [1984] STC 261 it was decided that relief at what was then 50% in 1977 (now 100%) was available in relation to land of which a sole trader was life tenant and on which he had carried on a farming business prior to his death. HMRC's interpretation of this decision is that, where there is a transfer of value of a life tenant's business or interest in a business (including assets of which he was life tenant which were used in that business) the case falls within **6.4**(a) above and 100% relief is available. Where, by contrast, the transfer of value is only of any land, building, machinery or plant, used wholly or mainly for the purposes of a business carried on by the life tenant and in which he has an interest in possession under a settlement, the relief is available only at 50% under **6.4**(d)(iii) below if the transfer takes place without the business itself being disposed of. Thus relief under *IHTA 1984, s105(3)(e)* applies only to lifetime transfers of such assets. Note that there is no limitation on the type of interest in possession relevant for these purposes, as there is no tie-in with the *FA 2006* changes to the treatment of interests in possession for IHT.

Lloyd's Underwriters

In the case of **Lloyd's Underwriters** who converted to a NameCo, HMRC will by concession allow business property relief on the value of the underlying assets, subject to certain limitations, up to and including 31 December 2006. Previously, before Names converted to limited company status, it is understood that the CTO did restrict BPR treatment if assets so deposited were excessive compared with the underwriting undertaken. From 1 January 2007 regard must be had to the degree of likelihood that such assets that are put up as security will be drawn to meet the NameCo's losses. These may be met directly if they are third part Funds at Lloyd's (FAL) or indirectly if they are in the form of bank guarantee(s). The valuation of the assets needs to take into account the diminution in their value arising from the fact that the individual or his estate does not have unfettered use of the assets during the period the FAL requirements are in place or the guarantee(s) are available to be called upon. See Lloyd's Market Bulletin 86/411, 6 December 2003 and 31 May 2006. Also, the right to a share of the Lloyd's syndicate profit/loss is an asset/liability of the business and HMRC regards that the loss should be a liability incurred for the purpose of the business and is not left out of account for BPR purposes. Restrictions on claiming BPR apply from 1 January 2007. See www.lloyds.com/Lloyds_Market/Taxation/Taxation_bulletins/. In *Hardcastle v CIR* [2000] STC SCD 532 Sp C 259 this underwriting case concerned trading profits and losses. However, HMRC also claims that land (or the interest in the reversion) which is 'not used' in the underwriting business but supported a guarantee should be left out of account for BPR purposes. See *Hardcastle & Hardcastle (Vernede's Executors) v CIR* [2000] STC SCD 532 Sp C 259 and *CIR v Mallender and Others (Executors of Drury–Lowe deceased)*, Ch D [2001] STC 514. (See Lloyd's Market Bulletin, 8 May 2001). The business of corporate Lloyd's members may qualify for relief. The address of the CTO dealing with Lloyd's Underwriters' inheritance tax is Shares Valuation Division, Fitz Roy House, PO Box 46, Castle Meadow Road, Nottingham NG2 1BD. Tel 0115 974 2222, fax 0115 974 2197, DX 701203 Nottingham 4. See below for the position regarding settled property used in the business of a person with an interest in possession in that property.

(b) Partnership interests

The interest of a partner in the partnership business may qualify for business property relief if a qualifying business is carried on by the partnership (see **6.3**). The interest of the partner must be valued either by reference to the terms of the partnership agreement, if applicable, or if not by reference to the market value of the partner's interest in the partnership business at the relevant time. It will normally be necessary for the partnership accounts to be made up to the date concerned although HMRC may not require this if the normal accounting date is only a few weeks removed. See further **34 PARTNERSHIPS**.

Land owned by a partner and used by the partnership for a qualifying business is eligible for 50% relief only whereas if the land is transferred into the partnership to become partnership property, 100% relief will be available. However, if all the value in an asset is declared to be held as partnership property but allocated to one partner alone, it is uncertain whether this is effective to allow 100% relief; it is advisable for all partners to have some share in each asset.

Business property relief is accepted as being available for partnership interests in the circumstances detailed in the table below:

	Event	IHT payable on	BPR available
1.	Partnership determines on death. Partnership assets realised and estate entitled to deceased's share of proceeds.	Value of partnership interest.	Yes
2.	Partnership continues with estate entitled to represent the deceased.	Value of partnership interest.	Yes
3.	Partnership continues with partnership share falling into the deceased's estate but with the option for other partners to acquire either on valuation or formula.	Value of partnership interest (valuation or formula).	Yes
4.	Partnership continues with the share of the deceased partner accruing to the surviving partners with the estate entitled to payment on valuation or formula.	Value of partnership interest (valuation or formula).	Yes
5.	A double option agreement is entered into under which the surviving partners have an option to buy and the PRs an option to sell, such options to be exercised within a stated period after the partner's death.	Value of partnership interest (valuation or formula).	Yes

Notes to the table

(A) It is normal for the Testator to make provision in the partnership agreement rather than by testamentary disposition.

(B) Concern has arisen in the past that the decision in *Spiro v Glencrown* [1991] 1 All ER 680 provided authority for an option to be a contract for sale (see items 3 and 5 in Table above) thereby resulting in no BPR being available. Early in 1996 the CTO confirmed that there had been no change in their opinion regarding SP 12/80 (see above) and that the case would not be cited as an authority for an option constituting a binding contract for sale. See also Key Points below.

Interests in Limited Liability Partnerships

HMRC's published view is that in the case of an LLP investing in unquoted shares in trading companies, it would be inappropriate to allow relief on the basis that the underlying assets constitute business property: the true position is that the nature of the business conducted by the LLP falls within *IHTA 1984, s105(3)* (business wholly or mainly one of making or holding investments) so that relief is not available. See IHTM25094. HMRC's view has been further clarified in an ICAEW Technical release which confirms that an LLP cannot have the treatment as a holding company, for which special provision applies (*IHTA 1984, s101(4)*), and so business property relief depends on whether or not the LLP itself carries on a qualifying business. If it does, then if any shares held are used in the business (rather than being held as investments), it is possible that the interest in the LLP may qualify for relief, provided that it does not fail the 'wholly or mainly' test of *s105(3)*.The question of whether an asset is used in the business or held as an investment will be highly fact specific. For example, a professional farming partnership might be required to hold a minimum stake within a genetics company in order to get specific semen for their bovine herds, or in a crop company to get the best seed at the best price. If this stake is not held as an investment, but with the intention of ensuring that the trade continues and succeeds, then holding such a stake is unlikely to cause any restriction or removal of relief.

An LLP which only holds the shares in a company or in companies will have no relief, even if one of those companies is a trading company and the other companies hold the assets relevant to the trade (ICAEW Technical Release Tech 01/14 tax).

See further on this topic article by James Kessler QC in which he gives his opinion that HMRC's analysis above is fundamentally wrong. Relief is available to the members of the LLP on the basis that a transfer of an interest in the partnership is attributable to any relevant business property, that is any shares in unquoted trading companies, held by it. [*IHTA 1984 s104(1)*]. (Taxation 20 March 2014 p 8).

Settled property used for partnership business

A deceased with a beneficial interest in possession of settled assets is treated as the beneficial owner of those assets for IHT purposes. They cannot therefore be contributed to a partnership as partnership assets and gain 100% relief under *IHTA 1984, s 105(1)(a)*. Instead, where they are used in a partnership in which the deceased was a partner, they can only obtain 50% business property relief under *s 105(1)(d)*.

(c) Shares and securities

From 6 April 1996, the relief for shares or securities of a company carrying on a qualifying business (see **6.3** above) is as follows:

(i) if they are quoted and (either with or without other such shares or securities owned by the transferor) gave the transferor *control* of the company immediately before the transfer, they qualify for 50% relief;

(ii) in the case of unquoted shares the relief is at 100%;

(iii) in the case of unquoted securities which (either by themselves or with other such securities or unquoted shares owned by the transferor) gave the transferor control of the company immediately before the transfer, relief is at 100%. [*IHTA 1984, s 105(1)(b)(bb) and (cc); F(No 2)A 1992, s 73, Sch 14 paras 2(1)–(3), 8; FA 1996, s 184(2), Sch 41 Pt VI*].

Where a control test applies, it is not necessary for either the transferor or the transferee to have control after the transfer. Loan stock not carrying rights which contribute to control will not qualify for relief (see IHTM25171). Note that, in relation to transfers of value made, and other events occurring before 6 April 1996, different rates of relief apply as in **6.16** below.

For the purposes of inheritance tax 'quoted' means listed on a recognised stock exchange and 'unquoted' means not so listed. The words 'recognised stock exchange' include those exchanges defined as such for the purposes of *ITA*

2007, s 1005 previously *ICTA 1988, s 841* as amended by *Financial Services and Markets Act 2000, s 287*. See also EU Directive 22001/34/EC and www.hmrc.gov.uk/fid/rse.htm. In addition there are a number of other stock exchanges which have not yet have been designated by the Board for the purposes of *ITA 2007, s 1005* previously *ICTA 1988, s 841*. In practice, however, recognition for IHT purposes depends on whether the law of the country where it is situated recognises the exchange or market in question and whether it provides an adequate trading floor (this last requirement is now becoming obsolete). Both tiers of the NASDAQ stock market have recognised stock exchange status and securities traded thereon are quoted for IHT purposes but with effect from 28 November 2001 shares admitted to EU junior markets and to NASDAQ Europe are regarded as unquoted (see IHTM25192).

Holding companies

For the purposes of the relief a company and all its subsidiaries are members of a group [*IHTA 1984, s 111*] and 'holding company' and 'subsidiary' have the same meanings as in the *Companies Act 2006, s 1159, Sch 6*. [*IHTA 1984, ss 103(1)(2), 104*]. Under *s 1159(1)*, a company is a 'subsidiary' of another company, its 'holding company', if that other company:

(a) holds a majority of the voting rights in it; or
(b) is a member of it and has the right to appoint or remove a majority of its board of directors; or
(c) is a member of it and controls alone, pursuant to an agreement with other members, a majority of the voting rights in it,

or if it is a subsidiary of a company that is itself a subsidiary of that other company.

A holding company is not excluded from relief so long as its business consists wholly or mainly in holding one or more companies whose businesses themselves are within the relief. [*IHTA 1984, s 105(4)(b)*]. But the value of any subsidiary which does not carry on a qualifying business must be excluded, unless its business is wholly or mainly holding land or buildings occupied by other group members who are carrying on a business which qualifies for relief. [*IHTA 1984, s 111*].

Therefore shares in holding companies which own shares in trading subsidiaries benefit from the relief. However, there are categories of excepted assets that are left out of account when calculating whether there is an entitlement to business property relief and reference should be made to these circumstances below. [*IHTA 1984, s 112(2)*].

Definition — 'control'

'*Control*' is defined by *IHTA 1984, s 269* and means control of powers of voting on all questions affecting the company as a whole which if exercised would yield a majority of the votes capable of being exercised on them. See *Walding and Others (Executors of Walding, deceased) v CIR* [1996] STC 13 and **35.8** PAYMENT OF TAX. In determining whether the transferor has control, any shares or securities which are related property (see **56.20** LIFE ASSURANCE

POLICIES AND ANNUITIES) must be added. However in the *Walding* case shares in the name of the deceased's grandson, aged 4 years, were *not* to be excluded from the overall calculations of votes, notwithstanding the fact that due to his age he lacked capacity to exercise his voting rights. The Judge held that *s 269(1)* allowed relief where the deceased controlled the powers of voting on all matters affecting the entire company. In this connection, the capabilities of persons in whose name the shares were registered was not an issue. The relief was denied. See **58** TAX CASES. See also IHT 400 Notes and *Walker's Executors v CIR* [2001] STC SCD 86 Sp C 275 where the casting vote gave control and entitlement to BPR.

There is no relief if the company is being wound up or otherwise in the process of liquidation at the time of the transfer unless the business of the company is to continue after a reconstruction or amalgamation which is either the purpose of the winding up etc. or takes place not later than one year after the transfer. [*IHTA 1984, s 105(5)*].

Alex, Bernard, Charlie and David own 25% each of the shares in ABCD Ltd. Alex has land in the company which is being used by the company for business purposes but he wants to transfer the land out of the company to his daughter. He does not have control for these purposes. However, the shares are divided into four separate classes in December 2010 which will carry control in January for Alex, February for Bernard, March for Charlie and April for David. In January 2011 Alex transfers his land out of the company as at that time he has 'control' and is therefore entitled to 50% BPR. The use of a *Bushell v Faith* [1970] AC 1099 clause can be beneficial in these circumstances. See **58** TAX CASES.

Example 3

A has owned for many years 60,000 shares in X Ltd, a trading company now listed on the Alternative Investment Market (AIM), whose issued share capital is 100,000 shares of £1 each. All shares carry full voting rights. A gifts to his son 20,000 shares in June 2003, a further 20,000 in June 2005 and the remaining 20,000 in June 2007. The son agrees to pay any IHT on all gifts. A dies in May 2010, at which time his son still owns the shares. Each gift qualifies for 100% business property relief. The same would apply if A had made a single gift of all his shares and that event the following further advantages could be obtained:

- the option to pay tax by instalments. [*IHTA 1984, ss 227(1)(b), 228(1)(a)*];
- the transfer of any buildings or plant and machinery where the transferor controlled the company immediately before the transfer would attract 100% relief under *IHTA 1984, ss 104(1)(a), 105(1)(b)*.

Example 4

A owns 85% of the share capital of H Ltd, an unquoted company which has two wholly-owned subsidiary companies S Ltd and P Ltd. H Ltd and S Ltd are trading companies and P Ltd is a property investment company. The issued share capital of H Ltd is 100,000 ordinary shares of £1 each valued at £8 per share. The values of the issued shares in S Ltd and P Ltd are £250,000 and £300,000 respectively.

A gave 10,000 shares in H Ltd to his son in August 2008. He had already made chargeable transfers using up his basic exemptions. His son agreed to pay any IHT. A dies in January 2011, at which time his son still owns the shares.

	£	£
Value of gift		80,000
Deduct business property relief 100% × £80,000	80,000	
Less 100% × 80,000 × $\frac{£300,000}{£800,000}$	30,000	
		50,000
PET becoming chargeable transfer on death		£30,000

Note to the example

(A) The value of H Ltd shares at £8 each is for a holding of 75% or more therefore the transfer of 10% of his holding does not give rise to the 'Loss to donor' provisions. [*IHTA 1984, s 269*].

(d) Land, building, machinery or plant

Land, building, machinery or plant which, immediately before the transfer, was used wholly or mainly for the purposes of a qualifying business (see **6.3** above) carried on by:

(i) a company controlled by the transferor; or
(ii) a partnership of which he then was a partner; or
(iii) the transferor and was settled property in which he was then beneficially entitled to an interest in possession (but see below). [*IHTA 1984, s 105(1)(d)(e)*].

Any assets under this heading *owned by the transferor* and used wholly or mainly for the purposes of a business under (i) to (iii) above, only qualify for relief if that business, or the transferor's interest in it, or the shares or securities in the company are also relevant business property. For example, in cases where an asset is owned personally by a partner and used in his partnership (which would qualify for 50% BPR) the inheritance tax position would be improved if the asset brought into the partnership and held as a partnership asset where it will attract 100% BPR. [*IHTA 1984, s 105(6)*].

HMRC consider that (iii) above applies only to lifetime transfers as in the case of transfers on death 100% relief will normally apply to the whole of the business interest including the settled assets used in the business.

See below for binding contracts for sale and excepted assets. Also, HMRC states ' . . . you will need to obtain open market values for land and any other assets included at "book value" such as stock and goodwill.'

Example 5

M has for many years owned a factory used in the business of Q Ltd, of which he has control. In September 2010, M gives the factory to his son S when its value is £700,000. He has made no previous chargeable transfer, but made a gift of £3,000 in 2009/10. M dies in October 2011, when the factory is being used for business purposes by the partnership of which S is a member. S agreed to pay any IHT on the gift.

	£
Value of gift	700,000
Deduct business property relief (50%)	350,000
	350,000
Deduct annual exemption (2010/11)	(3,000)
PET becoming chargeable transfer on death	£347,000
IHT payable at full rates* (death within 3 years)	£8,800

* 6 April 2011 nil rate band of £325,000 (table 40.1 2011.A1)

Notes to the example

(A) If M wishes also to dispose of shares in Q Ltd by sale or gift after which he would no longer have control, he should give the factory to his son *before* disposing of the shares, otherwise business property relief would not be available on the gift of the factory.

(B) If the factory had been used by Q Ltd at the date of M's death, no business property relief would be available on the gift since the factory would not be relevant business property in S's hands at the date of death.

HMRC clearances

[6.5] Non-statutory clearance applications will be accepted from business owners and their advisers where there is demonstrable material uncertainty about the IHT-BPR consequences of a transfer of value that follows a transaction affecting their business on areas of material uncertainty arising within four Finance Acts of the introduction of any new legislation. Alternatively, clearance applications will be accepted where legislation preceding the last four Finance Acts and there is material uncertainty around the tax outcome of a real issue of commercial significance to the business itself, determined by reference to the scale of the business and the impact of the issue upon it. For a clearance to be binding on HMRC the taxpayer must provide IHT-BPR Clearances Team, at the time the clearance is sought, with the full facts and context of the transaction, and set out the legislative uncertainty in question. If the taxpayer has applied for a non-statutory clearance, but has not received it by the time that an IHT account is due to be submitted, then the account must still be sent in before the time limit. If this occurs the taxpayer should complete the account according to their own view of the correct tax treatment of the particular transaction. The normal interest and penalty rules will apply if an account is incorrect, whether or not the transactions have been the subject of a clearance.

HMRC aim to provide clearances within 28 calendar days that will give certainty to business owners as to the IHT-BPR consequences of their transactions. HMRC consider the taxpayer is able to rely on any clearance, however for a clearance to be considered binding on HMRC, all the relevant facts should be set out and attention drawn to all the issues in the application. HMRC expect businesses to interpret this relatively broadly, for example, by providing information on related transactions where relevant. IHT does not arise as a consequence of the commercial transaction itself but of a later event if that event is a transfer of value. In these circumstances, HMRC's view of the application of inheritance tax law to the availability of business property relief for a business, an interest in a business, certain shares and securities or certain business assets applies to the facts and circumstances existing at the date of the commercial transaction. HMRC will not be bound by a clearance given if there is a change in circumstances between the date of the commercial transaction and a later transfer of value. A change of circumstances includes a change in the nature of the business or the structure of the business, a change in the nature of the interest held by the person to whom the application applies, or a change in the legislation relating to business property relief.

Example 6

Lin Wong holds all the shares in an unquoted trading company which trades oriental and Chinese rugs from Hong Kong. Rather than tie up money in working capital or premises, Lin Wong placed liquid funds on call at the bank amounting to £250,000 in comparison with a turnover of £600,000. The funds are earmarked for the purchase and import of granite Chinese garden statues and pagodas, a new business. At the time of the proposed purchase of the stock for the new enterprise business the Chinese currency increases in value relative to the pound sterling and the funds are kept on deposit and she switches her exploration of suppliers of granite statues and pagodas to Japan. Lin Wong, the proprietor, wishes to pass on both businesses to her son and evidence is put forward that there had been consideration given to acquiring a new enterprise associated with imports from Japan some eight months ago. A question arises whether the £250,000 cash on deposit was required for the purposes of the business and is consequently relevant business property. In considering also *IHTA 1984, s 112(2)(b),* i.e. whether the cash is a category of *excepted* assets that is left out of account when calculating whether there is an entitlement to business property relief, surplus cash, notwithstanding it is held by a limited company, is an excepted asset but those monies should be earmarked or used for 'some palpable business purpose'.

Lin Wong, with advice from her advisers makes a non-statutory clearance application for 100% BPR in respect of the new business as well as the existing one, citing the Special Commissioner's case *Brown's Executors v CIR* [1996] STC SCD 277 Sp C 83 where it was held that the sale of a night club resulting in capital being held on deposit interest account pending the further investment in a future premises was not a change in the nature of the business carried on by the company. Any contention that at the time of the proprietor's death the company's business consisted wholly or mainly in the making and holding of investments, and therefore excluded from being qualifying business property, would be erroneous. However, the Commissioner found in favour of the taxpayer because the proprietor intended to purchase suitable alternative premises and the deposit account holding the proceeds was of necessity short term to conclude a purchase. Also, distinguishing these circumstances from *Barclays Bank Trust Co Ltd v CIR* [1998] STC SCD 125 Sp C 158 where the Commissioner held that, for the purposes of *s 112*, 'required' did not include 'the possibility that the money might be required should an opportunity arise to make use of the money in two, three or seven years' time . . . The word "required" implies some imperative that the money will fall to be used upon a given project or for some palpable business purpose' and that indeed is the case with regard to the current application. See 58 TAX CASES. With regard to the IHTM25303 instruction that:

> 'If the deceased acquired the shares in the new company within two years of death, they will not satisfy IHTA84/S106. However we need to consider whether they can satisfy the requirements of IHTA84/S107.'

Binding contracts for sale

[6.6] If at the time of the transfer a binding contract for sale has been entered into, the property will not qualify as relevant business property unless:

(i) it is a business or an interest in a business and the sale is to a company which is to carry on the business and is in consideration wholly or mainly for shares or securities in the company; or
(ii) it is shares or securities in a company and the sale is for the purpose of reconstruction or amalgamation. [*IHTA 1984, s 113*].

HMRC consider there is a binding contract for sale where partners or shareholder directors of companies enter into an agreement (known as a 'buy and sell' agreement) whereby, in the event of the death before retirement of one of them, the deceased's personal representatives are obliged to sell and the survivors are obliged to purchase the deceased's business interest or shares. Funds for the purchase are frequently provided by means of life assurance policies. (HMRC Statement of Practice SP 12/80, 13 October 1980). In order to circumvent the 'buy and sell' agreements constituting binding contracts, the use of an option to purchase that does not constitute a binding contract for sale should be considered as an alternative to protect the BPR. HMRC's attitude to several possible wordings of a partnership deed was subsequently discussed in correspondence between HMRC and the accountancy bodies. See ICAEW Memorandum TR 557, 19 September 1984 and Law Society Gazette, 4 September 1996.

Excepted assets

[6.7] The value of any relevant business property which is attributable to 'excepted assets' does not qualify for relief.

Apart from business property relief qualifying under (c)(i) or (c)(ii) above only, '*excepted assets*' are those neither:

(i) used wholly or mainly for the purposes of the business concerned throughout the last two years before the transfer (or since acquisition if more recent); nor
(ii) required at the time of the transfer for the future use of the business.

[*IHTA 1984, s 112(2)(a), (b)*].

Where the business concerned is carried on by a group company, the use of an asset for the purposes of a business carried on by another company which at the time of use and immediately before the transfer was also a group member is treated as use for the purpose of the business concerned unless that other company's membership of the group is disregarded under *IHTA 1984, s 111*.

An asset is not relevant business property by virtue only of **6.4** (c)(i) or (c)(ii) above unless:

(A) it was used for the purpose of the business carried on by the company or partnership throughout the two years immediately preceding the transfer; or

(B) it replaced another asset so used and it and the other asset and any asset directly or indirectly replaced by that other asset were so used for periods comprising at least two years within the five years immediately before the transfer.

The qualifying period under (A) or (B) above is reduced in the case of successive transfers in a similar manner to the minimum period of ownership (see **6.8** below) provided the asset (or it and the assets replaced by it) was or were so used throughout the period between the earlier and subsequent transfer (or throughout the part of that period during which it or they were owned by the transferor or his spouse or civil partner). [*IHTA 1984, s 112(3); FA 2005, s 103; The Tax and Civil Partnership Regulations 2005, SI 2005/3229, Reg 21*].

An asset which is wholly or mainly used for the business cannot be an excepted asset even though there may be substantial, albeit less than 50%, non-business use of it. But where a property is not used wholly or mainly for the business, although a part of it is so used exclusively, that part qualifies for relief [*IHTA 1984, s 112(4)*]. See IHTM25354:

> 'Land or building which is only partly used for the business must be separated into qualifying and non-qualifying parts for the purposes of relief. Qualifying parts would include a room or rooms in a doctor's house used as his waiting room and surgery, or the ground floor of a three-storey building used by its owner as a shop, provided they were exclusively used for business purposes.'

For the above purposes, an asset is deemed not to have been used wholly or mainly for the purposes of the business concerned at any time when it was wholly or mainly for the personal benefit of the transferor or a person connected with him. [*IHTA 1984, s 112(6)*]. See *Barclays Bank Trust Co Ltd v CIR* [1998] STC SCD 125 Sp C 158 where the deceased held half the shares in an unquoted trading company which traded in bathroom and kitchen fittings. It had substantial liquid funds on call at the bank amounting to £450,000 in comparison with a turnover of £600,000. The proprietor died and evidence was put forward that there had been consideration given to acquiring a new enterprise some eight months before her death. The target company was later liquidated with no further progress. Ultimately, seven years later the company spent £350,000 purchasing goods from China. The question arose whether all the cash on deposit at the time of death was required for the purposes of the business. The Special Commissioners held that the £300,000 was not required for the purpose of the business. This case is considered by HMRC to be authority for the proposition that in considering *IHTA 1984, s 112(2)(b)*, i.e. (ii) above, surplus cash is an excepted asset unless it is earmarked or used for 'some palpable business purpose'. However, it may be arguable that the bank account is one indivisible asset and either the whole of it is an excepted asset, or none of it (the apportionment rule applying only to land or buildings).

See also HMRC's published view that additional surplus cash held by a company as an additional reserve in a time of recession remains an excepted asset unless it is held for an identifiable future business purpose. (ICAEW Technical Release Tech 01/14 tax).

Where a company is entitled to BPR because it is mainly engaged in trading activities but is also involved in holding investments, it may be that there are no excepted assets. See SVM111220: 'If a company does carry on an investment business ancillary to its trading business, it cannot be said that the investments made have not been used for the purposes of the hybrid (mainly trading, partly investment) business. Thus those investments cannot be regarded as excepted assets'.

Minimum period of ownership

[6.8] The property described in **6.4** above will not qualify for relief unless:

(i) it was owned by the transferor for a minimum period of two years immediately preceding the transfer; or

(ii) it replaced other property which qualified (apart from the two year period) immediately before the replacement and both properties together (or all properties if other qualifying property had been previously replaced directly or indirectly) were owned by the transferor for at least two years out of the five years immediately preceding the transfer. See also *AM Brander (Earl of Balfour's Personal Representative) v HMRC* [2010] UKUT 300 (TC), TC00069. [*IHTA 1984, ss 106, 107(1)*].

It should be noted that the period of ownership relates to the 'relevant business property' and not the particular assets used in the business concerned. Hence if a sole trader, who has owned the business for over two years, uses personal cash resources to buy new assets used in the trade, those assets immediately benefit from 100% business property relief.

Minority shareholdings under **6.4**(c)(ii) above and **6.16** below do not qualify as replacement property but where such shares owned by the transferor immediately before the transfer would be identified with other shares previously owned by him for capital gains tax purposes under *TCGA 1992, ss 126–136* (reorganisations of share capital, conversions, amalgamations and reconstructions), the combined period of ownership may be taken for the purposes of (i) above or the additional requirement for substantial minority shareholdings below. [*IHTA 1984, s 107(4); FA 1996, s 184(3), Sch 41 Pt VI*]. A technical defect in the drafting of the Finance Bill clause meant that the replacement facility available to controlling shareholdings ((i) and (ii) above) would have been withdrawn. As this was not intended, amendments were made to allow both the existing replacement facilities for majority and minority holdings to be available to all unquoted holdings regardless of size. (See Inland Revenue Press Release 26 March 1996). [*IHTA 1984, s 107(4); FA 1996, s 184(3)*]. See also *Mrs MA Vinton & Mrs JJ Green (Mrs M Dugan-Chapman's Executors) v HMRC* [2008] STC SCD 592 Sp C 666; Ch D [2010] EWHC 904.

Example 7

From January 2004, A owns 85% of the share capital of Glum Ltd, i.e. 85,000 shares, an unquoted company valued at £150,000 until January 2008 when he exchanges his shares for AIM Happy Ltd shares. AIM Happy Ltd is an AIM-listed company. These replacement shares comprise one ordinary share in AIM Happy Ltd for each share in Glum Ltd. The AIM Happy Ltd shares are sold on the Stock Exchange when they become listed in December 2008. A holds the proceeds in cash and in July 2009 the whole of the cash is reinvested in buying further AIM-listed shares in Despondent Ltd, which is a trading company. The cash was held in a specific reinvestment account prior to the purchase of the Despondent Ltd shares. See *Barclays Bank Trust Co Ltd v CIR* [1998] STC SCD 125 Sp C 158 above. A dies in January 2010 when the shares are valued at £150,000 and his other worldly assets at £850,000. By the terms of his will he leaves the AIM shares to his son and also £325,000 to his son and the balance of assets to his widow.

Over the last five years (see (ii) above) A has owned unquoted shares, AIM listed shares, quoted shares, cash and then AIM-listed shares in that order. Working backwards, the shares currently held in Despondent Ltd have only been held for seven months and do not come within the two-year period of ownership within *s 106*. Prior to that, cash was held for six months and this is not relevant business property within *s 105* and neither were the quoted shares that were sold by A within the month of their becoming quoted. The original unquoted shares in Glum Ltd were transferred to AIM Happy Ltd shares and were both held for a total period of five years to qualify under (ii) above. However, when looking at the requirement in *IHTA 1984, s 107(1)(a)*

> '. . . it replaced other property and it, that other property and any property directly or indirectly replaced by that other property were owned by the transferor for periods which together comprised at least two years falling within the five years immediately preceding the transfer of value . . . '

the Glum Ltd shares do qualify for the two-year period within the last five years. Under *IHTA 1984, s 107(1)(b)* requires that 'any other property concerned . . . would have been relevant business property in relation to the transfer' and in this respect the cash and quoted securities do not comply. As Glum Ltd shares were exchanged for AIM-listed shares but then for AIM Happy Ltd quoted shares, the eventual replacement property, i.e. the quoted shares, are not relevant business property. See also Key Points below.

Therefore, under this strict interpretation the inheritance by the son of the shares in the Despondent Ltd shares do not qualify under the two-year rule within the last five years under *s 107(1)*. Had A, on receiving notice of the quotation of the AIM-listed shares liquidated the investment prior to quotation on the stock exchange, and had not invested in cash subsequently, the criteria for *s 107(1)(b)* would have been met and BPR relief on the currently held AIM shares in Despondent Ltd would have attracted 100% BPR.

Notes to the example

(A) Where such shares owned by the transferor immediately before the transfer would be identified with other shares previously owned by him for capital gains tax purposes under *TCGA 1992, ss 126–136* (reorganisations of share capital, conversions, amalgamations and reconstructions), the combined period of ownership may be taken for the purposes of (i) and (ii) above.

(B) The Shares Valuation Division manual at para 111060 states that the nature of the business carried on by or on the *s 105(1)* business property need not be the same throughout the two-year period. But there must have been a business throughout that period e.g. if a company carried on a farming business until one year before a transfer and then changed its activity to providing recreational facilities for families, the shares in it would be relevant business property if the transferor had owned them for the two years before the transfer. For companies, the manual states: 'If the company's business had changed from a non-qualifying business such as investment to a non-investment business within two years of the date of transfer, you should refer the case to the Appeals Team.' However, it is arguable that the two year test applies only to the holding of the shares and not to the conduct of trading activities by the company.

(C) A should have perhaps looked at reinvestment of the cash in, say, woodlands, which attract both CGT exemption and qualify for 100% BPR. [*TCGA 1992, s 250(1)*]. Currently, small parcels of commercial woodlands can be bought and sold through specialist agents which qualify the purchaser for 100% BPR. An election may be made within two years (or such longer time as the Board allow *IHTA 1984, s 125(3)*) for the value of any trees or underwood on any land in the UK not being AGRICULTURAL PROPERTY (4) for the purposes of agricultural property relief to be left out of account in determining the value transferred on death. The value of the land cannot be excluded. The claim must be made by a person liable for the whole or part of the tax. The tax is deferred and becomes chargeable on a later disposal. [*IHTA 1984, s 125*]. In this way, A would have had relevant business property throughout the two-year qualification period and, in the unexpected case of his demise, the relief under *s 125* would have been available to his son as well as the 100% BPR.

Relief cannot be more than what it would have been had the replacement (or any one or more of the replacements) not taken place (i.e. increases in value by replacement are ignored). For this purpose, changes resulting from formation, alteration or dissolution of a partnership, or from the acquisition of a business by a company controlled by the former owner of a business, are disregarded. [*IHTA 1984, s 107(2)(3)*].

Inherited property is treated as being owned from the date of death. If the spouse or civil partner inherits then ownership includes the period owned by the deceased spouse or civil partner. [*IHTA 1984, s 108; FA 2005, s 103; The Tax and Civil Partnership Regulations 2005, SI 2005/3229, Reg 19*].

Successive transfers

[6.9] Relief is given on relevant business property not owned for the minimum period under (i) or (ii) above by the transferor if:

(a) he or his spouse or civil partner acquired property (or part) by an earlier transfer on which business property relief was, or would have been, due; and
(b) that property, or any property directly or indirectly replacing it, would (apart from the two-year qualifying period) have been relevant business property in relation to the subsequent transfer; and
(c) either the earlier transfer or the subsequent transfer took place on death.

Relief cannot be more than what it would have been had the replacement (or any one or more of the replacements) not taken place (i.e. increases in value by replacement are ignored). For this purpose, changes resulting from formation, alteration or dissolution of a partnership, or from the acquisition of a business by a company controlled by the former owner of a business, are disregarded. [*IHTA 1984, s 109*]. See IHT 17, p 7.

Example 8

In January 2008 A owns 85% of the share capital of Glum Ltd i.e. 85,000 shares, an unquoted company valued at £150,000. A transfers his business to Happy Ltd in exchange for shares. The replacement shares are comprised of one ordinary share in Happy and one share in its wholly-owned subsidiary company Sad Ltd for each share in Glum Ltd. Happy Ltd and Sad Ltd are trading companies. The issued share capital of Happy Ltd is 100,000 ordinary shares of £1 each valued at £1.50 per share. The value of the 100,000 issued shares in Sad Ltd is £30,000.

A gives half his new shares to his son in August 2008. He had already made chargeable transfers using up his basic exemptions. His son agreed to pay any IHT. A dies in January 2011, at which time his son still owns the shares.

	£	£
Value of gift to son		90,000
Deduct business property relief 100% × £90,000	90,000	
Less $100\% \times 90{,}000 \times \frac{£30{,}000}{£180{,}000}$	15,000	
		75,000
PET becoming chargeable transfer on death		£15,000

Note to the example

(A) The value of Happy Ltd shares at A's death will attract business property relief on their value but under *IHTA 1984, s 107(2)* the business property relief is not to exceed what it would have been had the replacement shares or any one or *more* of the replacements not taken place. Therefore on the death of A HMRC will require evidence of the prior value of Glum Ltd and a similar computation will apply in respect of the value of the shares not attracting BPR as shown in the example above. Under *IHTA 1984, s 109* operates to extend BPR where *s 106* would deny relief (i.e. minimum period of ownership not met), however, *s 109(3)* similarly operates so as not to increase the amount of BPR available.

Liabilities to acquire business property

[6.10] For transfers of value made or treated as made on or after 17 July 2013, it is no longer possible to reduce the value of an asset for IHT purposes by securing a loan on it where the loan is used to acquire or maintain (directly or indirectly) another asset which qualifies for certain IHT reliefs, including business property relief. Instead the loan will be primarily deductible from the asset qualifying for relief. These rules have equal effect for charges on settlements holding relevant property within *IHTA 1984, s 58*. But they apply only to the transferor of the IHT transfer of value, and so do not apply to a liability within an investment company taken on in order to use the loan proceeds to buy trading assets.

This rule applies to any liability incurred on or after 6 April 2013. In the case of any such liability incurred in respect of business property, the loan is to be primarily deducted from the value of that property before any applicable reliefs for such property are given. If the business property is gifted during lifetime, the loan is to be deducted only from the value of that property if the lifetime gift is or becomes a chargeable transfer, so that the liability cannot also be deducted from the estate on death. But if the lifetime gift is a PET and the donor survives for seven years, retaining liability for the loan, it may then be deducted from the estate on death.

A loan is considered by HMRC to indirectly finance an asset where it is initially used to buy asset 1 which is later sold and the proceeds reinvested in asset 2. The loan then indirectly finances asset 2 (see HMRC IHT Manual para IHTM28018). On this view it is not possible to circumvent the disallowance by first acquiring non-business property with a loan, subsequently selling that property and then acquiring agricultural property with the proceeds.

Where a liability is incurred partly for relievable property, as described above, and partly for other assets not qualifying for the reliefs, any part repayments of a liability are to be attributed first to the proportion of it incurred for the non-relievable property. For HMRC's view on apportionments of liabilities between relievable and non-relievable property, see IHT Manual para 28021. See also **56.19** for further analysis. [*IHTA 1984, ss 162A and 162B*].

Further conditions for lifetime transfers

[6.11] Business property relief is only available where any part of the value transferred by a POTENTIALLY EXEMPT TRANSFER (**38**) proves to be a chargeable transfer if, in addition to the conditions in **6.3** to **6.8** above, the conditions listed below are also satisfied. Similarly, where a chargeable lifetime transfer, other than a potentially exempt transfer, made within seven years of the transferor's death is reduced under the business property relief provisions, the additional tax chargeable by reason of death must be calculated as if the relief had not been received unless the following conditions are satisfied.

Subject to the provisions below for replacement property, the additional conditions are:

(a) that the original property was owned by the 'transferee' throughout the period beginning with the date of the chargeable transfer and ending with the transferor's death or, if earlier, the transferee's death; and
(b) in relation to a notional transfer of value made by the transferee immediately before the death in (a) above, the original property would, ignoring the minimum period of ownership requirement in *IHTA 1984, s 106* (see **6.8** above), be relevant business property unless, for transfers made, and other events occurring, after 16 March 1987, the original property consists of shares or securities:

(i) which were 'quoted' at the time of the chargeable transfer; or
(ii) fell within **6.16** below in relation to the transfer and were 'unquoted' throughout the period referred to in (a) above.

Thus for shares in an unquoted trading company, it does not matter if, after a lifetime gift of the shares, the company ceases to trade and becomes an investment company. On the death of the donor within seven years of the gift the only requirement to prevent clawback of relief on the gift is that the company continues to be unquoted (*IHTA 1984 s 113A(3)(a)*).

'*Transferee*' means the person whose property the original property became on that chargeable transfer or, where on the transfer the original property became or remained settled property in which no qualifying interest in possession subsists, the trustees of the settlement.

Example 9

X transfers the share of his 25% interest in Amalgam Ltd (an AIM company) to his son Y and also transfers land and buildings in his partnership to his other son Z on 16 June 2007. X has already used up his annual exemptions for the current year and the previous one. The shares are valued at £640,000 and the land and buildings at £676,000. In February 2009 Amalgam Ltd is quoted on the London Stock Exchange and Y's share value increases to £1 million.

Z sells the land and property to one of the partners in May 2009 and invests the whole proceeds in an unquoted company receiving shares to the value of £800,000. X dies on 6 June 2010.

Theoretical computation on death if shares in Amalgam Ltd had remained unquoted.

	£	Gross	Tax
Value of shares to Y	640,000		
Deduct BPR 100%	640,000	Nil	Nil
Partnership assets to Z	676,000		
Deduct BPR 50%	338,000		
	338,000		
PET becoming chargeable transfer on death	£338,000	13,000	5,200

The tax payable on failed BPR and PETs that have become chargeable because of X's death within 7 years:

Computation on death.

X's early death within 3 years of the gift of a non-controlling shareholding in Amalgam Ltd results in the loss of relief. Although Y did not own the shares for a minimum period of two years, i.e. June 2007 to February 2009 before they became quoted, this does not matter for the purposes of *IHTA 1984, s 113A* provided the shares were owned throughout the period by Y, which they were.

	£	£
Value of shares to Y	640,000	
Deduct annual exemption	Nil	
		640,000

Value of property to Z after BPR	338,000		
Deduct annual exemption	Nil	338,000	
		978,000	
Less nil rate band		(325,000)	
		640,000 × 40% = £256,000	

Apportionment of tax

Gift to Y

$$\frac{£640,000}{£978,000} \times £256,000 = \quad £167,526$$

Gift to Z

$$\frac{£338,000}{£978,000} \times £256,000 = \quad £88,474$$

Z has sold the business assets in the partnership and reinvested the proceeds in other relevant business property which attracts 100% BPR (i.e. unquoted shares) as opposed to 50% for the original assets (i.e. land and buildings) in the partnership. Z's replacement of the partnership assets with unquoted shares qualifies for replacement property relief *IHTA 1984, s 113B*. However, Z's position is affected by Y's loss of 100% BPR in respect of the transfer of shares to Y by X.

Notes to the example

(A) In light of these circumstances Y and Z have tax liabilities on X's death that arise from a quotation on the London Stock Exchange of Amalgam Ltd shares. However, Y's interest (taken at book value) in Amalgam shares of £360,000 (£1 million – £640,000) is reduced immediately by the tax due of £173,231.

(B) Z could have taken the view that his position was vulnerable to Y's decision to accept quoted shares (with no control) and X's death within seven years of the gifts. Insurance on a reducing basis could have been taken out by Z to protect his position and cover the liability of £83,274 (i.e. £88,474 – £5,200).

Where any shares owned by the transferee immediately before the death would either be identified with the original property under the provisions of *TCGA 1992, ss 126–136* (reorganisations of share capital, conversion of securities and company reconstructions and amalgamations) *or* were issued to him in consideration of the transfer of a business or an interest in a business consisting of the original property (or part), the shares are treated as if they were the original property (or part).

Where part only of the original property satisfies the conditions in (a) and (b) above, proportionate relief is given.

Replacement property

[6.12] Where the transferee has disposed of all or part of the original property before the death of the transferor and applied the whole of the consideration received in acquiring a replacement property within the 'allowed period' after the disposal of the original property or part (or has entered into a binding contract to acquire replacement property within that time), then, provided the disposal and acquisition are both made at arm's length or on terms such as might be expected to be included in such a transaction, the conditions in (a) and (b) above are taken as satisfied if:

(i) the replacement property is owned by the transferee immediately before the transferor's death (or immediately before the transferee's death if earlier); and
(ii) throughout the period beginning with the date of the chargeable transfer and ending with the death (disregarding any period between the disposal and acquisition) either the original property or the replacement property was owned by the transferee; and
(iii) in relation to a notional transfer of value made by the transferee immediately before the death, the replacement property would, ignoring the minimum period of ownership requirement, be relevant business property.

If the transferor dies before the transferee and all or part of the original property has been disposed of before the transferor's death (or is excluded by the provisions relating to binding contracts for sale under **6.4** above from being relevant business property in relation to the notional transfer under (iii) above) then if the replacement property is acquired (or a binding contract entered into) after the transferor's death but within the 'allowed period' after the disposal of the original property, or part, condition (i) above does not apply and any reference to a time immediately before the death is taken as a reference to the time when the replacement property is acquired.

Where any shares owned by the transferee immediately before the death would either be identified with the replacement property under the provisions of *TCGA 1992, ss 126–136* (above) *or* were issued to him in consideration of the transfer of a business or an interest in a business consisting of the original property (or part), the shares are treated as if they were the replacement property (or part).

Where a binding contract for the disposal of any property is entered into at any time before the disposal of the property, the disposal is regarded as taking place at that time.

'*Allowed period*' means the period of three years or such longer period as the Board may allow. In relation to transfers of value made, and other events occurring, before 30 November 1993, the legislation effectively provided for the allowed period to be twelve months. [*IHTA 1984, ss 113A, 113B; FA 1986, Sch 19 para 21; FA 1987, s 58(1)(2), Sch 8 para 8; F(No 2)A 1992, s 73, Sch 14 paras 3, 8; FA 1994, s 247(1)(3)*]. The three-year (or longer) allowed period will apply not only to transfers of value made after 29 November 1993 but also to charges or further charges to IHT arising on a death after that date in respect of a transfer of value made before 30 November 1993 (HMRC response in ICAEW Faculty of Taxation Memorandum TAX 9/94).

Where business property which is relevant business property is replaced shortly before the owner's death by agricultural property, the period of ownership of the original property will be relevant for applying the minimum ownership condition to the replacement agricultural property. If all the conditions for agricultural property relief (see **4** AGRICULTURAL PROPERTY) are satisfied relief will be available on the replacement agricultural property. (HMRC Tax Bulletin December 1994 p 183).

Transitional provisions

[6.13] The amendments made to *IHTA 1984* by *FA 1987, Sch 8* (broadly amendments to the status of Unlisted Securities Market shares and securities, business property, agricultural property and payments by instalments with effect in relation to transfers of value made, and other events occurring, after 16 March 1987) are disregarded in determining under (a) and (b) and (i)–(iii) above whether any property acquired by the transferee before 17 March 1987 would be relevant business property in relation to a notional transfer of value made after 16 March 1987. [*FA 1987, s 58(3)*]. In broad terms, this protects the position of shares and securities dealt in on the Unlisted Securities Market which were the subject of a transfer before 17 March 1987 in circumstances where the transferor died after 16 March 1987 and within seven years of the transfer.

Further provisions, which are to be read as one with the business property provisions of *IHTA 1984*, apply where by reason of a death occurring after 9 March 1992:

(1) a potentially exempt transfer made before 10 March 1992 proves to be a chargeable transfer, or
(2) additional tax falls to be calculated in respect of a chargeable transfer (other than a potentially exempt transfer) made before 10 March 1992 and within seven years of the death.

In these circumstances, then, for the purposes of the replacement property provisions of *IHTA 1984, ss 113A, 113B* above, it is to be assumed that the amendments made by *F(No 2)A 1992, Sch 14* (broadly amendments to business property relief (including the status of Unlisted Securities Market shares and securities and increased relief in certain cases), agricultural property relief, payment by instalments and gifts with reservation with effect in relation to transfers of value made, and other events occurring, after 9 March 1992) came into effect at the time the transfer was made, and, in a case within (2) above, that so much of the value transferred as would have been reduced in accordance with the business property relief provisions as amended by *F(No 2)A 1992, Sch 14* was so reduced. Where disregarding the amendments made by *F(No 2)A 1992, Sch 14*, any shares or securities transferred fell within *IHTA 1984, s 105(1)(b)* (see **6.4**(b) above) in relation to the transfer, those amendments are disregarded in determining whether (b) (i) and (ii) above apply to the shares or securities. [*F(No 2)A 1992, s 73, Sch 14 para 9*]. In broad terms, this protects the position of a transferee who receives Unlisted

Securities Market shares and securities before 10 March 1992 out of a majority holding where the company acquires a recognised stock exchange listing, and the transferor dies, after 9 March 1992 and within seven years of the transfer.

In order to remove doubt that has arisen in the past a new *IHTA 1984, s 113A(7A)*, is inserted by *FA 1996, s 184(5)*, so that the availability of business relief is to be disregarded in determining whether a transfer falls within the rules in *s 113A*. The clawback rules will apply in respect of any potentially exempt or chargeable transfer to which *s 113A* applies and is effective after 27 November 1995. [*IHTA 1984, s 113A; FA 1986, Sch 19 para 21; FA 1996, s 184(5)*].

Business property — payment of tax by instalments

[6.14] Where IHT payable is attributable to the value of either:

(a) a business or interest in a business carried on for gain; or
(b) shares or securities in certain circumstances; or
(c) land of any description, wherever situated,

the person paying the tax may elect to pay it in ten equal yearly instalments if the transfer is made on death, *or* if it is one on which tax is charged on settled property under *IHTA 1984, Pt III* and the property concerned remains in the settlement, *or* if the tax is borne by the person benefiting from the transfer. [*IHTA 1984, ss 227, 228*]. See **35.5** PAYMENT OF TAX for full details.

Interest on tax payable by instalments

[6.15] With certain exceptions, interest on tax payable by instalments which is attributable to any shares or securities, business or interest in a business runs from the date of each instalment [*IHTA 1984, s 234*]. See **35.9** PAYMENT OF TAX.

Historical rates and conditions

Conditions prior to 6 April 1996

[6.16] The percentage rates appropriate to the different classes of relevant property detailed in **6.4** above are as followsin relation to transfers of value made, and other events occurring, after 9 March 1992 and before 6 April 1996:

(a)	Unincorporated business (**6.4**(a) above)	100%
(b)	Shares or securities giving control of an 'unquoted' company (**6.4**(b) above)	100%

(c)	Shares giving more than 25% voting control of an 'unquoted' company not within (b) above (see (i) below)	**100%**
(d)	Shares or securities giving control of a 'quoted' company (**6.4**(b) above)	50%
(e)	Shares in an 'unquoted' company not within (b) or (c) above (**6.4**(d)(ii))	50%
(f)	Land, buildings, machinery or plant in a partnership or in a controlled company or in a settlement (but see **6.4** and **6.4**(c) above)	50%

In relation to transfers of value made, and other events occurring, after 16 March 1987 and before 6 April 1996, minority holdings are classified as follows.

(i) Substantial minority holdings, i.e. holdings not falling within (b) above which (either with or without other such shares or securities owned by the transferor) gave the transferor control of over 25% of the powers of voting on all questions affecting the company as a whole and for this purpose there was included any shares or securities which were related property, see **56.21** VALUATION. Where shares or securities were comprised in a settlement, any voting powers which they can give to the trustees were deemed to be given to the individual (if any) beneficially entitled in possession to those shares or securities. Where there were shares or securities of any class with voting powers only on the winding up of the company and/or on any question primarily affecting that class, the reference above to 'all questions affecting the company as a whole' was to be read as referring to all such questions except those to which the powers of the particular class applied. [*IHTA 1984, s 105(1)(bb), (1A), (1B); FA 1987, s 58, Sch 8 para 5* as repealed by *FA 1996, Sch 41 Pt VI*].

(ii) Shares were excluded from the relief if they were insufficient by themselves, without other property, to satisfy the 25% test above immediately before the transfer *and* their value was reduced because of a qualifying sale within three years of death, see **56.22** VALUATION. [*IHTA 1984, s 105(2A); FA 1987, s 58, Sch 8 para 5* as repealed by *FA 1996, Sch 41 Pt VI*].

(iii) Other minority holdings not falling within **6.4**(b) or (i) above. [*IHTA 1984, s 105(c); FA 1987, s 58, Sch 8 para 5 as repealed by FA 1996, Sch 41 Pt VI*].

In relation to transfers of value made, and other events occurring, after 9 March 1992 and before 31 March 1996, then, in relation to any shares or securities within **6.4**(b) above or shares within this paragraph, 'unquoted' meant not so quoted and for these purposes the Alternative Investment Market (AIM) was treated as unquoted. [*IHTA 1984, s 105(1ZA); F(No 2)A 1992, s 73, Sch 14 paras 2(4), 8 (see HMRC Press Release, 20 February 1995)*]. This definition only applied for the purposes of defining relevant business property above and payment by instalments (see **35.5** PAYMENT OF TAX). Prior to 6 April 1996 shares or securities were excluded from relief if they were insufficient by themselves, without other property, to give control immediately before the transfer *and* their value is reduced because of a qualifying sale within three years of death, see **56.22** VALUATION. [*IHTA 1984, s 105(2); F(No 2)A 1992, s 73, Sch 14 paras 2(5), 8*]. (The shares by themselves may qualify for relief under as minority holdings of '*unquoted*' shares.) From 6 April 1996 onwards quoted shareholdings and unquoted securities are only subject to the 'control' test and value reduction method. [*IHTA 1984, s 105(2); FA 1996, Sch 14 Pt VI*].

See **6.11** above for certain transitional reliefs where shares or securities have changed their status in relation to transfers of value made, and other events occurring after 9 March 1992 and before 6 April 1996.

Additional requirement for substantial minority shareholdings prior to 6 April 1996

To qualify for relief in relation to transfers of value made, and other events occurring, after 16 March 1987 and before 6 April 1996 as a substantial minority shareholding under 6.16 below, the 25% control test must have been satisfied throughout the two years immediately before the transfer or, where the rules relating to inherited property or successive transfers above apply and the transferor owned the shares for a period of less than two years immediately before the transfer, throughout that lesser period. [*IHTA 1984, s 109A; FA 1987, s 58, Sch 8 para 7* now repealed by *FA 1996, Sch 41 Pt VI*].

'Ownership' is not defined but would have its meaning in normal usage and includes both beneficial and legal ownership so that the two year rule must be satisfied by the life tenant in a settlement and by the trustees in a discretionary trust (Official Report Standing Committee E, 24 June 1976 cols 1275/1276).

Conditions after 16 March 1987 and before 10 March 1992

In relation to transfers of value made, and other events occurring, **after 16 March 1987 and before 10 March 1992:**

(A)	Unincorporated business (**6.4**(a) above)	**50%**
(B)	Shares or securities giving control of a company (**6.4**(b) above)	**50%**
(C)	Shares giving more than 25% voting control of an 'unquoted' company not within (B) above	**50%**
(D)	Shares in an 'unquoted' company not within (B) or (C) above	**30%**
(E)	Land, buildings, machinery or plant in a partnership or in a controlled company or in a settlement (but see **6.4** and **6.4**(c) above)	**30%**

Meaning of 'quoted' and 'unquoted'

In relation to any shares or securities within the Table above '*quoted*' means quoted on a recognised stock exchange or dealt in on the Unlisted Securities Market and '*unquoted*' means neither so quoted nor so dealt in. [*IHTA 1984, s 272; FA 1987, s 58(2), 8 Sch 17*]. This definition applied for all IHT purposes, and *still* continues to do so, in relation to transfers of value made, and other events occurring, after 9 March 1992 for purposes *other* than defining relevant business property above and payment by instalments.

See **6.11** above for certain transitional reliefs where shares or securities have changed their status in relation to transfers of value made, and other events occurring after 16 March 1987 and before 10 March 1992.

Conditions before 17 March 1987

In relation to transfers of value made, and other events occurring, **before 17 March 1987**:

(1)	Unincorporated business (**6.4**(a) above)	50%
(2)	Shares or securities giving control of a company (**6.4**(b) above)	50%
(3)	Shares in a company not within (2) above and not 'quoted' on a recognised stock exchange (**6.4**(d) above)	30%
(4)	Land, buildings, machinery or plant in a partnership or in a controlled company or in a settlement (but see **6.4** and **6.4**(c) above)	30%

In relation to transfers of value made, and other events occurring, before 17 March 1987, the classification of minority holdings was simply to shares in a company which were not within the Table at (2) above and which were not quoted on a recognised stock exchange. Shares in companies dealt in on the Unlisted Securities Market were *not* treated as quoted securities for this purpose and qualified for relief under this category. (HMRC Statement of Practice SP 18/80, 23 December 1980).

'*Quoted*' and '*unquoted*' have the same meanings as in **6.4**(d) above subject to *FA 1996, Sch 38 para 2(1)(2)*. [*IHTA 1984, ss 104, 105; FA 1987, s 58, Sch 8 para 4; F(No 2)A 1992, s 73, Sch 14 paras 1, 2, 8*].

The increases in the relief from 30% to 50%, and from 50% to 100%, mentioned above will be interpreted as applying not only to transfers of value made after 9 March 1992 but also to charges or further charges to IHT arising on a death after that date in respect of a transfer of value made before 10 March 1992 (HMRC Press Release, 10 March 1992 and correspondence with the publisher).

Business property relief applies only to the part of a transfer represented by relevant business property (see **6.4** above). It is given without claim. It is not given on the agricultural value of land where AGRICULTURAL PROPERTY (**4**) relief is given. [*IHTA 1984, s 114(1)*].

Where woodlands are transferred and capital transfer tax or inheritance tax previously deferred (see **57** WOODLANDS) becomes chargeable, that tax is deducted from the later transfer before business property relief is applied. [*IHTA 1984, s 114(2)*].

Key points

[6.17] Points to consider are as follows.

- There is often a risk of actively sheltering too many non-qualifying business assets within a qualifying business and the whole enterprise failing the BPR test because it becomes wholly or mainly an investment holding business. The facts of each individual case should be carefully considered, as should the relevant case law. However in *Brander (Representative of the fourth Earl of Balfour v HMRC* (2009) FTT 101 the appellant succeeded in integrating a property business within the overall estate such that the whole qualified for BPR (see **6.4**(A) above).
- Normally where a director shareholder or a partner in a business enters into a 'buy and sell' agreement so that surviving directors and partners within the business have to buy the shares or partnership interest from the deceased's personal representatives then if this is a mutual *requirement* to sell the interest or shares or the surviving shareholders or partners are *obliged* to buy the shares or interest then this would constitute a 'binding contract for sale' and no BPR would be available. [*IHTA 1984, s 113*]. However, HMRC have stated that certain circumstances where there is an *option* then in their view it would not constitute a 'binding contract for sale'. *IHTA 1984, s 113* would not apply where:
  (i) the deceased's interest passes to the surviving partners, who are required to pay the personal representatives a particular price; or
  (ii) the deceased's interest falls into the estate, but with an option for the surviving partners to purchase it.
  Also, statement of practice SP12/80 states that an *option* conferring an option for personal representatives to sell the deceased's interest to the survivors is not to constitute a binding contract for sale. BPR would in such circumstances be available providing the terms of the agreement stipulate a *requirement* i.e. a two-way option, to sell or buy is clearly evident. See IHTM25292 and SP12/80 at 25.2.
- Care should be taken when giving advice in relation to BPR claims where an individual shareholder acquires under a rights issue and an offer for subscription. Business property must be retained for two years before it qualifies for relief but only if the new shares so acquired can be identified with other shares previously owned, and those previously owned shares had been held for two years, then all of the shares qualify. In *Vinton and Others v Fladgate Fielder (a firm)* Fladgate LLP in the Chancery Division this condition was satisfied in relation to the 300,000 shares which a widow had acquired immediately before her death under the rights issue (because she acquired them in the right of her

ownership of a holding of 750,000 shares). However, the shares that the widow acquired on the renunciation by a fellow director and relative (Mrs Vinton) of her rights, and the shares which the widow acquired under the offer for subscription, were not acquired by her in the right of any existing holding of hers: they were acquired by her for reasons entirely unconnected with her existing holding. They were simply bought. Therefore by reason of *IHTA 1984, s 107(1)(a)* meant that her estate have suffered a charge of inheritance tax (to the extent of the unavailability of BPR) and that the estate has therefore been denuded to that extent (to the ultimate detriment of the residuary beneficiaries). See *Vinton and Others v Fladgate Fielder (a firm)*, Ch D [2010] EWHC 904.

The *Nelson Dance* case at **6.4** above permits relief to be given for assets used within a business which are the subject of a gift, i.e. it is not necessary for part of the business itself to be the subject of the gift.

Business and partnership interests and assets [Form IHT 413]

HM Revenue & Customs

Business and partnership interests and assets

Schedule IHT413

When to use this form

Fill in this form if the deceased had any assets or an interest in a business or business partnership and you are deducting business relief on form IHT400. Answer the following questions and give the further details we ask for. If you need more space, use box 25 on page 4.

If necessary, fill in a separate form for each business or business asset concerned.

If the deceased's interest in a business consisted of a control holding of shares, do not include that interest here, put it on form IHT412 instead.

Name of deceased

Date of death *DD MM YYYY*

IHT reference number (if known)

Help

Please read the guidance notes for form IHT413 in form IHT400 Notes before filling in this form. For more information or help or another copy of this form:

- go to **www.hmrc.gov.uk/inheritancetax/**
- phone our Helpline on **0845 30 20 900**
  – if calling from outside the UK, phone **+44 115 974 3009**.

Ownership, contract for sale and business interests

Ownership

1 Did the deceased own the business interest throughout the two years up to the date of death?

No *Go to box 2*

Yes *Go to box 3*

2 Business relief is not normally due if the shares or business interest was not owned throughout the two years up to the date of death. If you feel that business relief is still due, say why.

Contract for sale

3 Was the whole or any part of the business, interest in a business, or were any of the business assets, subject to a binding contract for sale at the date of death?

No *Go to box 7 on page 2*

Yes *Go to box 4*

4 Date of contract *DD MM YYYY*

5 Enter details of the assets sold under the contract

Description	Value (£)

6 Business relief cannot be deducted on businesses, business interests, business assets or any part of them that were subject to a binding contract for sale at the date of death unless they were a business or an interest in a business and the sale is to a company which is to carry on the business, and is made wholly or mainly in consideration of shares in or securities of that company. If this applies, please enter the details.

IHT413 **(Substitute)(LexisNexis)** Page 1 HMRC Approval ref: L11/08

Business or interest in a partnership

7 What was the value of the deceased's business or interest in a partnership at the date of death?

£

Include this value in form IHT400, box 69

8 What is the name and main activity of the business or partnership?

9 How has the value for the business or partnership been calculated? Enter details of the assets and liabilities included in the calculation. *If a professional valuation has been obtained, please enclose a copy*

Please provide copies of the latest three years' accounts

10 Is the business an interest in a partnership?

No ☐ *Go to box 16*

Yes ☐ *Fill in boxes 11 to 15 and enclose a copy of the partnership agreement. If there is no written agreement, describe the informal terms in box 25*

11 Date on which the partnership began *DD MM YYYY*

12 Unique Taxpayer Reference of the partnership

13 Name(s) of the people who provided the capital

14 What contribution did each person make to the capital?

15 How are the profits from the partnership shared?

16 Is the business or interest in a partnership to be sold as a result of the death?

No ☐ Yes ☐

17 Total amount of business relief you are deducting from the business or interest in a business (for transfers after 9 March 1992 this will always qualify for relief at a rate of 100%, if eligible)

£

Include the business relief in form IHT400, box 93

IHT413 Page 2

Asset(s) owned by the deceased and used by a company controlled by the deceased or a partnership of which they were a member

Include any shares the deceased owned in the company on form IHT412 *Unlisted shares and control holdings.*

18

Describe the assets owned by the deceased and used by the business or a company	Value of asset(s) £
Total value of assets	£ 0.00

Include this total in form IHT400, box 69

19 What is the main activity of the business or company shown above?

20 What was the deceased's interest in the partnership or company shown above? Tick one box only

☐ Member of a partnership

☐ Control of the company

21 Total amount of business relief you are deducting on the assets used by the business or company (for transfers after 9 March 1992 this will always qualify for relief at a rate of 50%, if eligible)

£

Include the business relief in form IHT400, box 93

Business relief on lifetime gifts

Only answer the following questions if you are deducting business relief in connection with a lifetime transfer.

22 Was the business, interest in a business or asset concerned owned by the person who received the gift throughout the relevant period (see IHT400 Notes)?

No ☐ Yes ☐

23 Would the business, interest in a business or asset concerned have qualified for business relief if the person who received the gift had made a transfer of the property at the date of death?

No ☐ Yes ☐

24 Was the business, interest in a business or asset concerned subject to a binding contract for sale immediately before the end of the relevant period (see IHT400 Notes)?

No ☐ Yes ☐

IHT413 Page 3

Additional information

Please use this page to enter any additional information that you have not been able to fit into boxes 1 to 24.

25

IHT413 Page 4

7

Calculation of Tax

Cross-references. See 1 INTRODUCTION AND BASIC PRINCIPLES; 4 AGRICULTURAL PROPERTY; 6 BUSINESS PROPERTY; 21 EXEMPT TRANSFERS; 22 GIFTS WITH RESERVATION; 38 POTENTIALLY EXEMPT TRANSFERS; 39 QUICK SUCCESSION RELIEF; 40 RATES OF TAX; 51 TRANSFERS OF VALUE; 52 TRANSFERS ON DEATH; 53 TRANSFERS WITHIN SEVEN YEARS BEFORE DEATH; 57 WOODLANDS.

Simon's Taxes. See I3.256, I3.5, I4.1, I4.231–I4.243.

Other Sources. Tolley's Tax Computations 2010–11; IHTM26000.

Introduction

[7.1] Inheritance tax is levied on the value transferred by a 9 CHARGEABLE TRANSFER at the rate or rates applicable at the time of the transfer. The transfer is treated as the highest part of the aggregate of the chargeable amount plus the values transferred by any previous chargeable transfers made by the transferor in the period of seven years ending with the date of transfer. [*IHTA 1984, ss 1, 7*].

Rates of tax

Only one table of rates is set out in the legislation and this is applicable to transfers on death. These are charged at a flat rate of 40% on the excess of the transfer over the available nil rate band or bands. Chargeable lifetime transfers are charged at one-half of the death rates (i.e. 20%). Transfers made within seven years of death are charged at the death rates but in the case of chargeable transfers made in that period and more than three years before death, the tax charge (note, *not* the value of the gift) is tapered. [*IHTA 1984, s 7*]. See **40** RATES OF TAX and **53** TRANSFERS WITHIN SEVEN YEARS OF DEATH. There is no subsequent credit or repayment for tax paid on a transfer *before* a reduction in the scale rates even if less tax would have been payable if the transfer had been made after the reduction in rates. In certain cases, where tax is chargeable by reference to an event before a reduction of tax by the substitution of new rate tables, *IHTA 1984, Sch 2* provides that the new rates are to be used. See **33.14** and **33.27** NATIONAL HERITAGE, **43.17** SETTLEMENTS: DISCRETIONARY TRUSTS AND OTHER TRUSTS OF RELEVANT PROPERTY, **53.1** TRANSFERS WITHIN SEVEN YEARS BEFORE DEATH and **57.4** WOODLANDS.

The value transferred is the loss in value to the transferor's estate, that is, the amount by which the value of the transferor's estate immediately after the disposition in question is less than it would be but for that disposition. [*IHTA 1984, s 3(1)*].

Chargeable transfer

A chargeable transfer is any transfer of value made by an individual, other than an EXEMPT TRANSFER (**21**). [*IHTA 1984, s 2(1)*]. Certain lifetime transfers are designated potentially exempt transfers. A potentially exempt transfer is a transfer of value made by an individual after 17 March 1986 which would otherwise be a chargeable transfer and which is either a gift to another individual or a trust for a disabled person, or prior to 22 March 2006 a gift into an accumulation and maintenance trust. From 22 March 2006 a gift into a bereaved minor's trust on termination of an immediate post-death interest is also potentially exempt. In relation to transfers of value made, and other events occurring, after 16 March 1987, certain gifts by individuals into and out of settlements with interests in possession are also included. See **38.1** POTENTIALLY EXEMPT TRANSFERS for full details. A potentially exempt transfer made seven years or more before the transferor's death is an exempt transfer and any other potentially exempt transfer is a chargeable transfer. A potentially exempt transfer is assumed to be an exempt transfer during the seven years following the transfer (or, if earlier, until immediately before the transferor's death). [*IHTA 1984, s 3A; FA 1986, Sch 19 para 1; F(No 2)A 1987, s 96*].

Transferor bearing tax

Where the transferor bears the tax on a lifetime transfer, the inheritance tax liability is taken into account in calculating the reduction in the value of his estate. [*IHTA 1984, ss 3(1), 162(3)*]. The 'net' transfer is grossed up at the appropriate rate(s) in order to arrive at the amount of the chargeable transfer. The chargeable transfer is always the gross, not the net, figure. See **40** RATES OF TAX for grossing-up tables. Where the transferee bears the tax on lifetime transfers, no grossing-up is required as the tax liability is not part of the reduction in value of the transferor's estate.

On death the tax is charged on the value of the deceased's estate immediately before his death and grossing-up is not required.

There are special rules for allocating the tax where the transfer is partly chargeable and partly exempt, see 7.5 below.

As the tax is charged on a cumulative basis, a careful record must be kept of all chargeable transfers made and the tax thereon.

Lifetime transfers — examples

[7.2]

(i) With transferor bearing the tax.

A transfers £69,000 to a discretionary trust on 1 May 2010, £265,000 on 31 December 2010 and a further £43,000 on 1 February 2011. He bears the tax and he has made no other chargeable transfers. His inheritance tax position is as follows.

	£	£
Gift on 1 May 2010		69,000
Deduct Annual exemption 2010/11	3,000	
Annual exemption 2009/10	3,000	6,000
		63,000
Covered by nil rate band of £325,000		
Gift on 31 December 2010		265,000
(*Note.* Annual exemption already used for 2010/11)		
Cumulative net transfers		£328,000
Tax thereon (see grossing-up table at 40.1 2010.B2)		
0 – 325,000		
325,001 – 328,000 (£3,000 × 1/4)		750
Tax on gift		£750

Gift on 1 February 2011

	Gross	Tax	Net
Cumulative totals	328,750	750	328,000
Add Latest net transfer of £43,000	53,750	10,750*	43,000
	£382,500	£11,500	£371,000
*Tax on £371,000 per table 40.1 2010.B2			
0 – 325,000			
325,001 – 371,000 (£46,000 × 1/4)		11,500	
		11,500	
Deduct Tax on previous transfers		750	
Tax on latest gift		£10,750	

(ii) With transferee bearing the tax on the latest gift.

If, in example (i) above, the trustees agree to pay the tax on the latest gift, the tax will be calculated on that transfer (without grossing-up) using the table at 40.1 2010.B1 RATES OF TAX as follows.

	£
Previous chargeable transfers	328,750
Chargeable transfer on 1 February 2011	43,000
	£371,750
Tax on £43,000 is	
328,750 – 371,750 (£43,000 × 20%)	£8,600

(iii) For transfers under the CTT provisions and more than 7 years before latest transfer, see previous editions.

Transfers on death — example

[7.3]

A dies on 5 September 2010 leaving an estate valued at £338,000, of which he bequeaths £103,000 to his wife and the balance elsewhere. His lifetime chargeable transfers in the seven years before death totalled £97,265. Tax due from his estate (using the table at **40.1** 2010.A1) is as follows.

	£	£
Previous chargeable transfers		97,265
Value of estate at death	338,000	
Deduct exempt bequest to wife	103,000	
Chargeable residue		235,000
Total cumulative chargeable transfers		£332,265
Tax due from estate on £235,000		
97,265 – 325,000 (£227,735 at nil%)		
325,001 – 332,265 (£7,265 at 40%)		2,906
		£2,906

Potentially exempt transfers and additional tax liability on death — example

[7.4]

A made the following lifetime transfers on which he paid any tax as appropriate

January 1979	Gift to individual C	£50,000
December 1985	Gift to individual D	£65,000
May 1992	Gift to individual C	£96,000
November 1992	Gift to discretionary trustees	£117,000

He died in November 1994 leaving his estate valued at £320,000 to his sons C and D.

Tax payable following lifetime transfers

			£	£
Gift to C in January 1979				50,000
Deduct	Annual exemption	1978/79	2,000	
		1977/78	2,000	
	Small gifts exemption		100	4,100
Cumulative net transfers				£45,900
Tax thereon				£2,128
Gross transfer				£48,028
Gift to D in December 1985				65,000
Deduct annual exemption 1985/86			3,000	
1984/85			3,000	6,000
				£59,000

Tax on latest gift of £59,000 (*Note.* There has been a change in tax rates)

	Gross	Tax	Net
Gross transfers in previous ten years adjusted for change in rates applicable after 5 April 1985	48,028		48,028
Add latest net transfer of £59,000	66,824	7,824*	59,000
	£114,852	£7,824	£107,028

*Tax on £107,028 at grossing-up rates applicable after 5 April 1985	
0 – 85,700	3,300
85,701 – 107,028 (£21,328 × 7/33)	4,524
	7,824
Deduct tax on transfers in previous ten years at rates applicable after 5 April 1985	
Tax on latest gift	£7,824

Gift to C in May 1992

The gift of £96,000 is a potentially exempt transfer to the extent it exceeds the available annual exemption (£3,000 for 1992/93 and £3,000 for 1991/92 brought forward), i.e. £90,000 (see **38.2** POTENTIALLY EXEMPT TRANSFERS), but incurs no immediate liability to tax

Gift to discretionary trustees in November 1992

Tax on gift of £117,000

(*Note.* There has been a change in tax rates and the gift in January 1979 is more than seven years before the latest gift)

	Gross	Tax	Net
Gross transfers in previous seven years adjusted for change in rates applicable after 9 March 1992	66,824		66,824
Add latest net transfer of £117,000	125,456	8,456*	117,000
	£192,280	£8,456	£183,824

*Tax on £183,824 at grossing-up rates applicable after 9 March 1992 (see table at **40.1** 1992.B2 RATES OF TAX)

0 – 150,000	
150,000 – 183,824 (£33,824 × 1/4)	8,456
	8,456

Deduct tax on transfers in previous seven years at rates applicable after 9 March 1992			
Tax on latest gift		£8,456*	

Tax payable following death in November 1994

Gift to C in January 1979

Gift to D in December 1985

These gifts are before 18 March 1986 and more than three years before death. No additional tax is payable (see **54.7** TRANSITIONAL PROVISIONS).

Gift to C in May 1992

The potentially exempt transfer of £90,000 (see above) becomes a chargeable transfer following A's death within seven years. Since it is made not more than three years before death, there is no reduction in tax rate (see **53.1** TRANSFERS WITHIN SEVEN YEARS BEFORE DEATH). The gift to D in December 1985 is within seven years of the gift and must be aggregated.

There has been a change in tax rates at death.

	Gross	Tax	Net
Gross transfers in previous seven years adjusted for the change in rates applicable after 5 April 1992	66,824		66,824
Add latest gross transfer	90,000	2,730*	87,270
	£156,824	£2,730	£154,094

*Tax on £156,824 at rates applicable on death after 9 March 1992

0 – 150,000	
150,001 – 156,824 (£6,824 × 40%)	2,730
Tax payable by C	£2,730

Gift to discretionary trustees in November 1992

Additional tax is due following A's death within seven years. However, the gift is made not more than three years before death, so there is no reduction in tax rate. The gifts in December 1985 and May 1992 are within seven years of the gift of £117,000 and must be aggregated.

	Gross	Tax	Net
Gross transfers in previous seven years	156,824	2,730	154,094
Add latest gross transfer of £125,456	125,456	50,182*	75,274
	£282,280	£52,912	£229,368

*Tax on £282,280 at rates applicable on death after 9 March 1992

0 – 150,000	
150,001 – 282,280 (£132,280 × 40%)	52,912
	52,912
Deduct tax on transfers in previous seven years at rates applicable after 9 March 1992	2,730
	50,182
Deduct tax already paid	8,456
Additional tax payable by trustees	£41,726

Transfer on death in November 1994

The gift to D in December 1985 is made more than seven years before death. The gifts made in May 1992 and November 1992 must be aggregated with the death estate as they are both made within seven years of death. These gifts entail gross transfers of £90,000 and £125,456 respectively resulting in cumulative chargeable transfers of £215,456 immediately prior to death.

Cumulative chargeable transfers in previous seven years	215,456
Value of estate	320,000
Total cumulative chargeable transfers	£535,456
Tax due from estate of £320,000	
215,457 – 535,456 (£320,000 × 40%)	£128,000

Partly exempt transfers

[7.5] Where a transfer is partly exempt and partly chargeable, special provisions apply to allocate the tax chargeable and the benefit of the exemption. The circumstances will arise mainly with transfers on death but may also apply where, for example, property is distributed out of a 'relevant property' settlement (see **43** SETTLEMENTS: DISCRETIONARY TRUSTS AND OTHER TRUSTS OF RELEVANT PROPERTY) between exempt and non-exempt beneficiaries. On death, a common situation is where, after specific chargeable gifts, the residue of the estate is left to the widow and is therefore exempt. The provisions are contained in *IHTA 1984, ss 36–42*. '*Specific gift*' means any gift other than a gift of residue or any share in residue, and therefore rather confusingly includes both specific legacies and general cash legacies. [*IHTA 1984, s 42(1)*]. In Scotland legal rights claimed by a person entitled to claim such rights are treated as a specific gift which bears its own tax. In determining the value of such legal rights, any tax payable on the estate of the deceased is left out of account. [*IHTA 1984, s 42(4)*]. Any liability of the transferor which is not taken into account in arriving at the value of his estate (including liabilities non-deductible or abated under *FA 1986, s 103*, see **52.9** TRANSFERS ON DEATH) is treated as a specific gift. [*IHTA 1984, s 38(6); FA 1986, Sch 19 para 13*]. Any value transferred which is not a specific gift is made out of residue. [*IHTA 1984, s 39*].

See below for the application of business and agricultural property reliefs.

Attribution of value to specific gifts

[7.6] If a specific gift is fully exempt (e.g. gift of specified property or a cash legacy to spouse) then that gift will not bear any tax. The legislation achieves this by stating that the value of that gift is to correspond to that same amount ('such part') of the total value transferred. By contrast an exempt residuary gift (e.g. gift of residue to spouse) may suffer the tax on a specific gift which does not bear its own tax (a tax-free gift). Where residue is part exempt and part chargeable (e.g. part to spouse and part to son) the exempt part will not bear any tax attributable to the chargeable part. [*IHTA 1984, ss 38(1), 41*]. See *Re Benham's Will Trusts; Lockhart v Harker, Read and the National Lifeboat Institution* Ch D, [1995] STC 210 in which the testatrix listed A and B beneficiaries and those in List A were to benefit 3.2 times the size of the fund compared to List B beneficiaries. The Court's view of the testatrix's intention was that each beneficiary of the respective lists, whether charitable or not, should receive the same amount from the express terms of the will as the other beneficiaries within the same list. In view of this the beneficiaries who were not charities received grossed up shares so that they achieved equality with the charitable beneficiaries. (See also Taxation magazine 20 April 1995 p 53.) The case is now final and until the matter is re-examined in the courts those drafting wills should pay particular attention to the wording and executors are advised to review their interpretation of the terms of the will when *s 41* is to apply.

Case law — Benham

The effect of *Re Benham's Will Trusts* (see above) is that where there is exempt and non-exempt residue and the will is worded such that if the Testator/Testatrix has not ensured that the non-exempt residue bears its tax then the inheritance tax is likely to be borne out of the estate rather than by the non-exempt beneficiaries wholly out of their portion of the residue. Seemingly, following *Benham's* this will have the effect of increasing the size of the inheritance tax bill. This may not be a problem where the beneficiaries are husband/wife and sons/daughters who would wish to limit the inheritance tax liability in the first instance and amicably redefine the will to take advantage of the redefinition of gifts between themselves. However, as happened in the *Benham's* case, the beneficiaries were not family and the view of one of the exempt residuary beneficiaries that their charity should have the benefit of their exempt status and this therefore meant that the estate should pay as little inheritance tax as possible, did not hold sway. The Court's view that the intention of the Testatrix was that each beneficiary should receive the same amounts as the other beneficiaries (in each list) consequently the non-exempt residue had to be grossed up. It was clause 3 of the late Jane Mary Benham's will that centred around the problems and was drawn up as follows:

> 'As to the residue after such payment aforesaid to pay the same to those beneficiaries as are living at my death and who are listed in List A and List B hereunder written in such proportions as will bring about the result that the aforesaid beneficiaries named in List A shall receive 3.2 times as much as the beneficiaries in list B, and in each case for their own absolute and beneficial use and disposal.'

To avoid this the will should state that the non-exempt residue is to bear its own tax or the result following *Benham's* will be a greater incidence of tax (see bullet point three below and Precedent). However, the CTO has stated:

> 'Generally speaking the Court is concerned in such cases to establish the intention of the testator or testatrix from the wording of the will and admissible extrinsic evidence. If the will is drafted in common form with a direction to ascertain residue after payment of funeral and testamentary expenses and debts followed by a bequest of that residue then it is focusing on the ascertainment and division of disposable residue rather than on what each residuary beneficiary is to receive. Accordingly wills so drafted would not appear to involve *Benham* style grossing up computations.'

See The Tax Journal, 5 September 1996, p 3. However, *Holmes & Another v McMullen & Others* Ch D [1999] STC 262 in the Chancery Division did not follow *Benham,* and Blackburne J held that an equal division of disposable residue between relatives and charities meant that the IHT attributable to the relatives' shares had to be borne by those shares, since to subject the charities . . . share to any part of that burden was prohibited.

Will drafting post Benham

(1) As to one share absolutely for my wife (husband) [*or give name already defined as such*] if she(he) survives me for 28 days

(2) As to another share (or as to the whole if the preceding gift fails) for all of my children as are alive at my death [and reach the age of 18] and if more than one in equal shares PROVIDED that if any child of mine [is already dead or] dies before me [or before reaching that age] but leaves a child or children alive at the death of the survivor of my child and me who reach the age of [*18*] or marry under that age then such equal shares so much of the Trust Fund as that child of mine would have taken on attaining a vested interest

AND the shares given by (1) and (2) above shall be such shares as before [after] the deduction of any inheritance tax attributable to them respectively are of equal value [or are of equal values bearing to one another in the proportions (2:1) the larger share being given by (1)(2)].

Example

Assume that the net residue of £200,000 is to be divided equally between a charity and the surviving son. The estate rate is 40% (i.e. the nil rate band has been utilised).

The options:

- Divide the residue equally so that the charity gets £100,000 and the son gets £100,000 and he then bears the tax of £40,000 out of the share he receives. This is the Charity's beneficial option: the *Holmes* option above which is now preferred by the courts following the decision in that case. See Tolley's Practical Tax Service Newsletter dated 10 March and 28 July 1999.

	£
Charity	100,000
Son	60,000
HMRC	40,000
Total	£200,000

- Calculate the tax on the £100,000 (son's share) and the tax of £40,000 is then deducted from the £200,000 and the balance of £160,000 divided equally between the Charity and the son who each get £80,000. The son's beneficial option but precluded by *IHTA 1984, s 41(b)*.

	£
Charity	80,000
Son	80,000
HMRC	40,000
Total	£200,000

- Gross up the son's share so that the charity and the son end up with the same net amount after the son's share has suffered tax i.e. the £200,000 divided in the proportions 60:60:40 as follows:

	£
Charity	75,000
Son	75,000
HMRC	50,000
Total	£200,000

The above is HMRC's preferred option and that arrived at in the *Benham's* case.

Where two or more specific gifts are in excess of an exemption limit, relief for the exemption is given to gifts bearing their own tax before other gifts. Any excess relief is allocated to the other gifts in proportion to their values. [*IHTA 1984, s 38(2)*].

Where specific gifts which do not bear their own tax are the only chargeable part of a transfer the tax on them (found by grossing-up) is borne by the residuary estate. [*IHTA 1984, s 38(3)*].

Example 1

A dies in July 2010 leaving estate valued at £386,000. He leaves a tax-free legacy to his daughter of £331,000 and the residue to his widow. He has made no previous chargeable transfers.

	£
Tax-free legacy	331,000
Tax thereon (see table at 40.1 2010.A2) is (6,000 × $^2/_3$)	4,000
Grossed-up legacy	£335,000
Value of estate	386,000
Deduct chargeable estate	335,000
Exempt residue to widow	£51,000

Where tax-free specific gifts are not the only chargeable gifts very complex rules must be followed. An assumed rate of tax must be calculated on a hypothetical chargeable estate for the purpose of allocating values to the chargeable and exempt parts of an estate. [*IHTA 1984, s 38(4)(5)*].

Example 2

A dies in July 2010 leaving an estate valued at £535,000. He leaves a tax-free legacy to his daughter of £341,000, a property worth £10,000 bearing its own tax to a nephew, and the residue of his estate equally between his widow and his son. He has made no previous chargeable transfers.

	£	£
Hypothetical chargeable estate:		
Tax-free specific gift to daughter		341,000
Tax thereon (as if legacy was the only chargeable gift – £16,000 × ²/₃)		10,666
Grossed-up specific gift to daughter		351,666
Specific gift bearing own tax to nephew		10,000
Total of specific gifts		361,666
Chargeable residue		
Gross estate	535,000	
Deduct total of specific gifts	361,666	
Residue	£173,334	
Half-share of residue to son		86,667
Hypothetical chargeable estate		£448,333
Calculation of assumed tax rate		
Tax on £448,333 would be (see table at **40.1** 2010.A1 RATES OF TAX)	£49,333	
Assumed rate is		

$$\frac{£49{,}333}{£448{,}333} \times 100 = 11.00365\%$$

Re-gross tax-free legacy to daughter using assumed rate

$$£341{,}000 \times \frac{100}{100 - 11.00365} = £383{,}162$$

	£	£
Calculate chargeable estate and tax thereon		
Grossed-up value of tax-free legacy		383,162
Specific gift bearing own tax		10,000
Total of specific gifts		393,162
Chargeable residue:	535,000	
Deduct total of specific gifts	393,162	
Residue	£141,838	
Half-share of residue to son		70,919
Hypothetical chargeable estate		£464,081
Tax on chargeable estate of £464,081 (see table at **40.1** 2010.A1 RATES OF TAX) is		£55,632

$$\text{Estate rate is } \frac{55{,}632}{464{,}081} \times 100 = 11.98756\%$$

Distribution of estate		
Specific gifts payable:	to daughter	341,000
	to nephew	10,000

	£	£
		351,000
Tax on gift to daughter		
Gift grossed at assumed rate on £393,162 (see above)		
Tax thereon at estate rate of 11.98756%		47,131
Note. The nephew pays the tax on his gift of £10,000 at the estate rate of 11.98756% which is £1,198		
Total specific gifts plus tax		£398,131
Gross estate		535,000
Deduct total specific gifts plus tax		398,131
Residue		£136,869
Allocation of estate		
Widow (one half residue)		68,434
Son (one half residue)	68,435	
Tax on son's share at estate rate		
£68,435 at 11.98756%	8,203	
Payable to son		60,232
Legacies to daughter and nephew		351,000
Tax borne by residue (£47,131 + £8,203)		55,334
		£535,000

Application of business and agricultural property relief where transfers partly exempt

[7.7] With respect to transfers of value made after 17 March 1986, the rules for apportioning the value of an estate between specific gifts and residue (in order to determine the exempt and chargeable parts) are modified for transfers including property qualifying for business and agricultural property reliefs.

(a) Specific gifts of business or agricultural property are to be taken at their value as reduced by the business or agricultural property relief attributable to such property.

(b) Any other specific gifts not within (a) above are to be taken to be the fraction of their value given by the formula:

$$\frac{V - S}{E - P}$$

where:

V = Total value transferred (i.e. as reduced by business and agricultural property reliefs)

S = Specific gifts within (a) above as reduced by the attributable relief

E = Total value transferred *before* deduction of business and agricultural property reliefs

P = Specific gifts within (a) above *before* deduction of the attributable relief

For the purposes of the above provisions, the value of a specific gift of relevant business or agricultural property does not include the value of any other gift payable out of that property (e.g. a pecuniary legacy charged on the relevant property) and that other gift is not itself treated as a specific gift of relevant business or agricultural property.

IHTA 1984, ss 38 and *39* (see above) have effect subject to the above provisions. [*IHTA 1984, s 39A; FA 1986, s 105*].

Example 3

A dies in July 2010 leaving an estate valued at £405,000. The estate includes a sweet shop business valued at £30,000 (for which 100% business property relief is available) and a small tenanted farm valued at £10,000 (for which only 50% agricultural property relief is available as the tenancy commenced before 1 September 1995). He leaves a tax-free legacy to his daughter of £350,000, the tenanted farm bearing its own tax to his nephew and the residue of his estate equally between his widow and his son. He has made no previous chargeable transfers.

Application of business and agricultural property reliefs: Under (a) above, the value of the specific gift of the tenanted farm is taken as the value of it as reduced by the applicable agricultural property relief, i.e. £10,000 – £5,000 = £5,000.

Under (b) above

V = £405,000 – £30,000 – £5,000	=	£370,000
S = £10,000 – £5,000	=	£5,000
E	=	£405,000
P	=	£10,000

The value of the tax-free specific gift to the daughter is reduced to:

$$\frac{£370{,}000 - £5{,}000}{£405{,}000 - £10{,}000} \times £350{,}000 = £323{,}418$$

£26,582 (£350,000 – £323,418) of business property relief has therefore been allocated to the tax-free specific gift to the daughter, leaving £3,418 (£30,000 – £26,582) of business property relief to be allocated to residue.

	£	£
Hypothetical chargeable estate:		
Tax-free specific gift to daughter		323,418
Tax thereon (as if legacy was the only chargeable gift – £3,418 × $^{2}/_{3}$)		2,279
Grossed-up specific gift to daughter		325,697
Specific gift bearing own tax to nephew		5,000
Total of specific gifts		330,697
Chargeable residue		
Gross estate	405,000	
Deduct total of agricultural and		

	£	£
Business property reliefs	35,000	
Value transferred after reliefs	370,000	
Deduct total of specific gifts	330,697	
Residue	£39,303	
Half-share of residue to son		19,651
Hypothetical chargeable estate		£350,348

The calculation of the assumed tax rate, chargeable estate and tax thereon, distribution of the estate and allocation of the estate then proceed in the same manner (but with different amounts) as in *Example 2* above. Agricultural and business property reliefs will be apportioned as above in the distribution of the estate.

Note to the examples

The above example shows that business property relief will be apportioned to the exempt half-share of residue transferred to the widow and thereby effectively wasting some of the relief otherwise available. In this and similar situations the wastage can be avoided by ensuring that all agricultural and business property are subject of specific gifts to non-exempt beneficiaries if part of the estate is destined to go to an exempt beneficiary such as the widow/widower or a charity, as it is understood that HMRC Inheritance Tax insist on the strict application of *IHTA 1984, s 39A*. Also see Example at **4.18** AGRICULTURAL PROPERTY.

Abatement

Abatement not attributable to tax

[7.8] Where a gift would be abated because of an insufficiency of assets under the normal rules for the administration of estates, the abated value will be taken for the purposes of inheritance tax. [*IHTA 1984, s 37(1)*].

Abatement for tax — specific gifts

[7.9] Where the grossed-up value attributable to specific gifts (see 7.5 above) exceeds the value transferred, they are treated as reduced to the extent necessary to reduce their value to that of the value transferred in the order in which, under the terms of the relevant disposition or any rule of law, the reduction would fall to be made on a distribution of assets. [*IHTA 1984, s 37(2)*].

Gifts made separately out of different funds

[7.10] Where there are gifts taking effect on a death both out of the deceased's own estate and out of a settled fund, the provisions in 7.5 and 7.8 above are applied separately to each fund. [*IHTA 1984, s 40*]. Subject to the application of the *Ramsay* principle or the associated operations provisions, the Board consider that the rate of tax to be used for grossing up should be found by looking at each fund separately and in isolation. See **5.1** ANTI-AVOIDANCE. Previously they thought that the rate applicable to the total value of all property chargeable on the death should be used (letter from Capital and Valuation Division reproduced at 1990 STI 446).

Example

A dies in June 2010 with a nil cumulative total. Of his free estate of £1,000,000, the sum of £330,000 free of tax is left to his son and the residue is left to his widow. A was the life tenant of a settlement the funds of which were worth £500,000 at the date of his death. His interest under the settlement passed to his grandchildren. Under the Board's revised practice the chargeable estate and tax thereon would be calculated as follows.

	£
Hypothetical chargeable estate	
Tax-free specific gift to son	330,000
Tax thereon (see table at **40.1** 2010.A2) is (£5,000 × $^2/_3$)	3,333
Grossed-up specific gift to son	333,333
Life interest in settlement bearing own tax and passing to grandchildren	500,000
Hypothetical chargeable estate	£833,333
Calculation of assumed tax rate	
Tax on £833,333 would be (see table at **40.1** 2010.A1)	£203,333
Assumed rate is	

$$\frac{203{,}333}{833{,}333} \times 100 = 24.39996\%$$

No further re-grossing is required and the assumed rate becomes the estate rate

Distribution of estate	
Tax-free gift to son	333,333
Grossed-up gift to son is £333,333 and tax on this at the estate rate of 24.39996% is	81,333
Life interest bearing its own tax (so that trustees will be liable for tax on it at the estate rate, i.e. £122,000)	500,000
Widow's exempt residue	585,334
	£1,500,000

Tax chargeable in certain cases of future payments

[7.11] Special provisions apply where a disposition made for a consideration in money or money's worth is a transfer of value and any payments made or assets transferred *by the transferor* in pursuance of the disposition are made more than one year after the disposition i.e. the provisions apply where the transferor acquires property at an overvalue.

Tax is charged as if any payment made etc. was made in pursuance of a separate disposition made, without consideration, at that time and the amount of the payment etc. was the 'chargeable portion' of the full payment.

The '*chargeable portion*' of any payment etc. is such proportion of its value at that time as is found by multiplying it by the fraction

$$\frac{A}{B}$$

where

A = the value actually transferred by the disposition as a whole; and
B = the value, at the time of that disposition, of the aggregate of the payments etc. made or to be made by the transferor.

[*IHTA 1984, s 262*].

Example

M acquires property from P on 1 January 2010 which is worth £30,000 but for which he agrees to pay £20,000 immediately and two further instalments of £10,000 each on 1 January 2011 and 1 January 2012. The discounted value of the two future instalments on 1 January 2010 at, say, 10% interest, is £17,355 (£9,091 + £8,264).

The value transferred by the disposition as at 1 January 2010 is

	£
Immediate payment	20,000
Present value of future instalments	17,355
	37,355
Value of property received from P	30,000
Value transferred by disposition	£7,355

The chargeable portion of each of M's payments is

$$\frac{7,355}{37,355} = 19.69\%$$

i.e. the potentially exempt transfers are (ignoring annual exemptions)

On 1 January 2009 £20,000 × 19.69%	= 3,938
On 1 January 2010 £10,000 × 19.69%	= 1,969
On 1 January 2011 £10,000 × 19.69%	= 1,969
	£7,876

Note to the example

'The element of the bounty is ascertained by examining the entire position at the moment of the original disposition . . . ' see previous CTO Advanced Instruction Manual, para C58.

Chargeable transfers affecting more than one property

[7.12] Where more than one property is comprised in a chargeable transfer, the tax which is attributable to each separate property is in the proportions which the separate values bear to the whole (subject to any provisions reducing the amount of tax attributable to the value of any particular property). [*IHTA 1984, s 265*].

More than one chargeable transfer on one day

[7.13] Where more than one lifetime chargeable transfer is made on the same day by the same person, the transfers are treated as made in the order which results in the lowest value chargeable and the rate of tax charged on each transfer is the effective rate (total tax divided by total transfers) which would apply if there has been one transfer of the total amount. The same rules regarding transfers on the same day apply to chargeable transfers from settlements without interests in possession if they are made out of property comprised in the same settlement. [*IHTA 1984, s 266*]. The previous CTO Advanced Instruction Manual stated that:

> 'It is important to bear in mind that a gift by cheque is not complete until the cheque itself is cashed . . . and thus where transfers are made by way of several cheques *IHTA 1984, s 266(1)/IHTA 1984, s 43(2)* will operate only if the cheques are **cleared** on the same day. The date on which the cheque is **drawn** is immaterial.'

See also *Curnock (Curnock's Personal Representative) v CIR* [2003] STC SCD 283 Sp C 365 where a cheque issued before the date but not cleared until after death still formed part of the deceased's estate on death. See **58** TAX CASES.

Transfers reported late

[7.14] Provisions are made to deal with the situation which arises where a transfer ('the earlier transfer') is not notified to the Board by an account or other information within the required period (see **2.14** ACCOUNTS AND RETURNS) and is not discovered until after the tax on a later transfer has been paid and accepted by the Board (or if no tax was payable, when the later transfer was notified in an account).

The provisions are as follows.

(a) Where the transfer which is reported late ('the earlier transfer') is made within the seven years preceding the later transfer, the tax payable on the earlier transfer is the amount which would have been payable on that transfer if it had been reported at the correct time (i.e. using the table of rates applicable at that time) plus the additional tax that would have been charged on the later transfer if the earlier transfer had been taken into account. Where a later transfer (A) is itself an earlier transfer in relation to a subsequent later transfer (B), the additional tax chargeable on (A) by virtue of its being an earlier transfer in relation to (B) is left out of account in the calculation required when (A) itself is a later transfer.

(b) Where two or more transfers in the seven-year period are reported late, the additional tax on a later transfer is apportioned between them on a pro rata basis; but if one of these unreported transfers is discovered after the liability on another has been settled, any further tax is payable on the latest transfer to be reported.

(c) Where the earlier transfer is made more than seven years before the later transfer, the tax payable on the earlier transfer is still the amount which would have been payable on that transfer if it had been reported at the correct time. The tax payable on the later transfer is not affected because of the seven-year cumulation rule.

(d) Where no account of a person's excepted estate is required by the Board, an account of that estate shall, be treated as having been delivered on the last day of the prescribed period in relation to that person. See **2.14** ACCOUNTS AND RETURNS.

[*IHTA 1984, s 264*].

Note. The legislation still refers to a ten-year period in (a) and (b) above but this should presumably be amended due to the reduction in the cumulation period from ten to seven years. The principle is, however, unaffected.

A transfer is discovered (i) if notified by an account etc. after the required period, on the date so notified or (ii) in any other case, on the date when the Board give notice of a determination (see **14.1** DETERMINATIONS AND APPEALS). [*IHTA 1984, s 264(9)*].

Interest on tax overdue will run from the due date of payment (see **35** PAYMENT OF TAX), but from that date to six months after the date of discovery the interest will be on the amount of tax which would have been payable if the transfer had been reported at the proper time. Thereafter, the interest will be on the actual tax payable. [*IHTA 1984, s 264(6)*].

Exemption limits

[7.15] If the earlier transfer would have been wholly or partly exempt because it was within the limits of an exemption and the later transfer actually received the benefit of the same exemption, the later transfer is not disturbed and the exemption which would have applied to the earlier transfer is reduced accordingly. [*IHTA 1984, s 264(7)*].

Settled property

[7.16] The provisions of *IHTA 1984, s 240(3)* apply to cases where any fraud, wilful default or neglect by the settlor of a **43** SETTLEMENTS: DISCRETIONARY TRUSTS AND OTHER TRUSTS OF RELEVANT PROPERTY comes to the knowledge of the Board. For the position regarding penalties in respect of return periods starting on or after 1 April 2009 where the return is due on or after 1 April 2010 see **35.20** PAYMENT OF TAX and **36.2** PENALTIES. In consequence, the provisions relating to transfers reported late do not apply to such settled property for IHT purposes.

Inheritance tax account [Form IHT 400 Calculation]

HM Revenue & Customs

Inheritance Tax account

IHT400 Calculation

When to use this form

Fill in this form if you have already filled in the form IHT400 up to and including box 109, the simple calculation is not suitable and you now wish to work out the Inheritance Tax yourself.

Help

For more information or help:

- go to **www.hmrc.gov.uk/inheritancetax/**
- phone our Helpline on **0845 30 20 900**
  – if calling from outside the UK, phone **+44 115 974 3009**.

Gifts and other transfers of value

If the deceased made any gifts or other transfers of value in the seven years before they died, the chargeable value of these gifts and transfers will reduce the amount of the Inheritance Tax nil rate band available to the estate on death.
Fill in the boxes below to find out the amount of the nil rate band available on death.

1	Inheritance Tax nil rate band at the date of death See *IHT400 Rates and tables*	£
2	Transferable nil rate band (form IHT402, box 20)	£
3	Total nil rate band at the date of death (box 1 + box 2)	£ 0.00
4	Total chargeable value of gifts and other transfers of value made by the deceased within the seven years before their death (form IHT403, box 7). *Do not include gifts with reservation here, include them on the IHT400, box 104 instead.*	£
5	Balance of Inheritance Tax nil rate band available (box 3 *minus* box 4) (if this figure is a minus, enter '0' in box 5)	£ 0.00

Calculation of Inheritance Tax

6	Total chargeable estate (copy from form IHT400, box 108)	£
7	Inheritance Tax nil rate band available (copy from box 5)	£ 0.00
8	Value chargeable to tax (box 6 *minus* box 7). If the result is a minus amount enter '0'. If the figure is '0' do not fill in any more of this form, go to form IHT400, box 119.	£ 0.00
9	Inheritance Tax (box 8 x 40%)	£ 00000000 . 0 0

Successive charges relief

If in the the five years before they died, the deceased inherited money or assets from another person's estate on which Inheritance Tax was paid, you may deduct successive charges relief to stop that legacy being taxed twice in a short period of time.

10 Is successive charges relief due?

No ☐ *Enter '0' in box 17 and go to box 18*

Yes ☐ *Follow the instructions below for working out successive charges relief*

- You will need to find out the value of the estate of the first person to die and the amount of Inheritance Tax paid in order to work out the relief due.
- You will also need to know what the deceased was entitled to receive from the estate. You can find this out by asking the executor of the estate of the first person to die for this information.
- If you are deducting successive charges relief enter:
  - the IHT reference of the first person to die
  - their full name, and
  - date of death

  in the 'Additional information' boxes on pages 15 and 16 of form IHT400.

IHT400 Calculation **(Substitute)(LexisNexis)** Page 1 HMRC Approval ref: L11/08

11	How much Inheritance Tax was paid on the estate of the first person to die?	£ .
12	What was the net value of the estate of the first person to die, after deducting liabilities and exemptions?	£ .
13	Box 11 ÷ box 12	.
14	What was the deceased's entitlement from the estate of the first person to die?	£ .
15	Box 13 x box 14	£ 00000000 . 0 0

The amount of relief available depends on the number of years between the first and second deaths and is shown in the table.

Years between the two deaths	Percentage reduction
One year or less	100%
One to two years	80%
Two to three years	60%
Three to four years	40%
Four to five years	20%
Over five years	0%

For example, if the second death was on 3 March 2007 and the first death was on 17 August 2005, there is more than one year between the two deaths, but less than two years, so the percentage reduction would be 80%.

16	Enter the percentage reduction	%
17	The amount of successive charges relief due: box 15 x box 16.	£ 00000000 . 0 0
18	Inheritance Tax on the chargeable estate (box 9 *minus* box 17)	£ 00000000 . 0 0

Successive charges relief - Example 1

11	How much Inheritance Tax was paid on the estate of the first person to die?	£10,000 . 0 0
12	What was the net value of the estate of the first person to die, after deducting liabilities and exemptions?	£340,000 . 0 0
13	Box 11 ÷ box 12	0 . 0 2 9 4
14	What was the deceased's entitlement from the estate of the first person to die?	£200,000 . 0 0
15	Box 13 x box 14	£5880 . 0 0

£10,000 ÷ £340,000 = 0.0294

£200,000 x 0.0294 = £5880
This is the amount of Inheritance Tax paid on the deceased's share of the estate of the first person to die.
You now need to look at how much relief is due on that amount of tax.

The amount of relief available depends on the number of years between the first and second deaths and is shown in the table.

Years between the two deaths	Percentage reduction
One year or less	100%
One to two years	80%
Two to three years	60%
Three to four years	40%
Four to five years	20%
Over five years	0%

For example, if the second death was on 3 March 2007 and the first death was on 17 August 2005, there is more than one year between the two deaths, but less than two years, so the percentage reduction would be 80%.

If there were between one and two years between the two deaths, then the table shows that the percentage reduction would be 80%

16	Enter the percentage reduction	80 %
17	The amount of successive charges relief due: box 15 x box 16.	£4,704 . 0 0

£5,880 x 80 ÷ 100 = £4,704.
This amount of successive changes relief that is due.

IHT400 Calculation Page 2

Tax that may be paid by instalments

The tax on some types of unsold property and assets may be paid in 10 annual instalments, that is, one instalment per year for ten years. The property and assets on which tax may be paid in this way are unsold houses, land, buildings, some types of shares and the net value of a business or an interest in a business after deduction of business relief.
These assets and properties are listed on pages 6 and 7 on form IHT400 in ***column B***. The total value of the assets on which you may pay the tax by instalments is on form IHT400, box 95, plus box 97 + box 99 (if any).
As soon as any of the property or assets are sold you will have to pay all the remaining tax. If you choose to pay tax by instalments on these assets you will have to pay interest on the outstanding tax.

19 Property and assets on which instalments of tax may be available (form IHT400, box 95 + box 103). £

20 Value of property and assets shown in **column B** of form IHT400 which have been sold or on which you wish to pay the tax now and not pay by instalments (these may be assets at boxes 49, 51, 66, 67, 68, 69, 70 or 71). Enter the total of these assets which may have been sold and which you wish to pay the tax on now. £

21 Value of property and assets shown in **column B** of form IHT400 on which the tax is being paid by instalments (box 19 *minus* box 20). If the answer is '0', enter '0' in box 26 and go to box 39) £

Instalments due now

You only need to work out the tax that is being paid by instalments if the due date for the first instalment has passed or is less than 30 days away. Otherwise you can miss out boxes 22 to 38 and go straight to box 39. The first instalment of tax is due on the last day of the sixth month after the date of death. For example, the deceased died on 17 July 2007, the due date for the payment of the first instalment is 31 January 2008. The table of due dates below will help you to work out the due date.

Month of death	*Due date*
January	31 July
February	31 August
March	30 September
April	31 October
May	30 November
June	31 December
July	31 January
August	28/29 February
September	31 March
October	30 April
November	31 May
December	30 June

22 What is the instalment due date? *DD MM YYYY*

23 Has the instalment due date passed or is it less than 30 days away?

No *Write '0' in box 24 and then go to box 39*

Yes *Go to box 24*

24 How many of the 10 instalments are due now?

25 Box 21 ÷ box 6

26 Box 25 x box 18. This is the tax that may be paid by instalments before any double taxation relief is deducted. £ 00000000 . 0 0

27 Did the form IHT400 include any unsold foreign houses, land, businesses or control holdings? (form IHT400, box 97)

No *Copy the figure from box 26 into box 36. Continue from box 37*

Yes *Read the information about double taxation relief on the next page*

IHT400 Calculation Page 3

Double taxation relief

If foreign tax equivalent to Inheritance Tax was paid on the value of foreign assets, double taxation relief may be due if there is a double taxation convention between the UK and the other country. If there is no convention, we may still be able to give 'unilateral relief'. You can find out more in our customer guide at: **www.hmrc.gov.uk/inheritancetax/**

If you wish to claim double taxation or unilateral relief, enclose with form IHT400 a 'certificate of tax paid' from the overseas tax authority, showing the amount of foreign tax paid. We may ask further questions about the claim after the Grant is issued. You must also fill in schedule IHT417 *Foreign assets* detailing the assets outside the UK.

28 Is double taxation relief due on the unsold foreign houses, land, businesses and control holdings of shares?

No ☐ *Copy the figure from box 26 into box 36. Continue from box 37*

Yes ☐ *Go to box 29*

29	Value of **unsold** foreign houses, land, businesses and control holdings on which foreign tax has been paid (form IHT400, box 97, £ sterling)	£
30	Inheritance Tax on the chargeable estate (copy from box 18)	£ .
31	Total chargeable estate (copy from box 6)	£
32	Box 30 ÷ Box 31	.
33	Box 29 x box 32	£ 00000000 . 0 0
34	Foreign tax paid on the unsold foreign houses, land, businesses and control holdings (£ sterling)	£ .
35	The relief is the **lower** of boxes 33 and 34. Write the lower amount in here.	£ .
36	Net tax to be paid by instalments (box 26 *minus* box 35). If no double taxation relief is being deducted, copy the value from box 26 into here	£ 00000000 . 0 0
37	Divide the amount in box 36 by 10 to work out how much each of the 10 instalments of tax should be. Enter the answer here.	£ 00000000 . 0 0
38	Tax that may be paid by instalments that is being paid now Multiply the amount in box 37 by the number of instalments that are due now (box 24). Enter the answer here. Go to box 39.	£ 00000000 . 0 0

Double taxation relief - Example 2

29	Value of **unsold** foreign houses, land, businesses and control holdings on which foreign tax has been paid (form IHT400, box 97, £ sterling)	£ 20,000
30	Inheritance Tax on the chargeable estate (copy from box 18)	£ 12,000 . 0 0
31	Total chargeable estate (copy from box 6)	£ 330,000
32	Box 30 ÷ Box 31	0 . 0 3 6 4
33	Box 29 x box 32	£ 728 . 0 0
34	Foreign tax paid on the unsold foreign houses, land, businesses and control holdings (£ sterling)	£ 2,000 . 0 0
35	The relief is the **lower** of boxes 33 and 34. Write the lower of those two boxes in here.	£ 728 . 0 0

£12,000 ÷ £330,000 = 0.0364

0.364 x £20,000 = £728

The foreign tax paid was £2,000, so put that figure in box 34.

Compare the two figures in boxes 33 and 34. The double taxation relief due is the lower of the figures in boxes 33 and 34. £728 is lower than £2,000 so £728 is the double taxation relief on the unsold foreign houses, land and buildings. Enter that figure in box 35.

IHT400 Calculation Page 4

Tax that is not being paid by instalments

Inheritance Tax may only be paid by instalments on unsold houses, land, businesses and on certain types of shares. The Inheritance Tax on all sold houses, land, businesses, shares and all other types of assets, such as bank accounts and household and personal goods must be paid when you send in this form. You can also choose to pay all of the tax now.

39 Property and assets on which instalments are not available (IHT400, box 94 + IHT400, box 102 + IHT400 Calculation, box 20) If the answer is 0, write '0' in box 41 and go to box 53. £

40 Box 39 ÷ box 6 [ ] . [ ][ ][ ][ ]

41 Box 40 x box 18. This is the tax that may not be paid by instalments before any double taxation relief is deducted. £ 00000000 . 0 0

42 Did the form IHT400 include any sold foreign houses, land, businesses and control holdings? (form IHT400, box 97) or other foreign assets (form IHT400, box 98)

No [ ] *Copy the figure from box 41 into box 53, then continue from box 54*

Yes [ ] *Read the information about double taxation relief on page 4 then go to box 43*

Double taxation relief

See the note about double taxation relief at the top of page 4.

43 Is double taxation relief due on the sold foreign houses, land, businesses and control holdings, and other foreign assets?

No [ ] *Copy the figure from box 41 into box 53. Continue from box 54.*

Yes [ ] *Go to box 44.*

For an example of how to work out double taxation relief, see Example 2 on page 4

44 Value of any **sold** foreign houses, land, businesses and control holdings (IHT400, box 97) on which foreign tax has been paid. (£ sterling) £

45 Value of other foreign assets on which foreign tax has been paid (IHT400, box 98, £ sterling) £

46 Total foreign property on which the tax is not being paid by instalments (box 44 + box 45, £ sterling) £ 0.00

47 Inheritance Tax on the chargeable estate (copy from box 18) £ 00000000 . 0 0

48 Total chargeable estate (copy from box 6) £

49 Box 47 ÷ box 48 [ ] . [ ][ ][ ][ ]

50 Box 49 x box 46 £ 00000000 . 0 0

51 Foreign tax paid on the foreign property and assets on which the tax is **not** being paid by instalments (£ sterling) £ . [ ][ ]

52 The relief is the **lower** of boxes 50 and 51. Write the lower amount in here. £ 00000000 . 0 0

53 Net tax that is not being paid by instalments
- Box 41 minus box 52
- If no double taxation relief is being deducted, copy the value from box 41 into box 53. (If box 41 was 0, enter '0' in here) £ 00000000 . 0 0

Page 5

Interest

Inheritance Tax is due to be paid on the last day of the sixth month after the date of death. Interest will be due even if you have not got a grant by then. Interest will also be due even if we have not contacted you or anybody else (for example, the trustees of a trust or someone who received a gift from the deceased). The law says that interest will be added to any unpaid tax after this date. Interest is not a penalty, it compensates the Exchequer for the delay in receiving the money due to it. If you pay too much tax, we pay interest on the repayment to you at the same rate as we would charge interest if tax was overdue.

Interest starts on the first day of the seventh month after the date of death. For example, the deceased died on 17 July 2007, interest will be due from 1 February 2008 on all unpaid tax whatever the reason the tax has not been paid. The table below will tell you the date that interest starts.

Month of death	Interest starts from
January	1 August
February	1 September
March	1 October
April	1 November
May	1 December
June	1 January
July	1 February
August	1 March
September	1 April
October	1 May
November	1 June
December	1 July

54 What is the date interest starts? *01 MM YYYY*

0 1

If the tax is being paid after this date you must add interest to the tax being paid.

55 Has the date at box 54 passed, or is it likely to pass before you pay the tax?

No *Enter '0' in boxes 57, 58, 60 and 61 then go to box 62*

Yes *Go to box 56 to work out the interest due*

Working out interest using the online interest calculator

56 The easiest way to work out the interest due is to use the interest calculator which you can find on our website at: **www.hmrc.gov.uk/tools/inheritancetax/interest-rate-calculator.htm**

If you use the interest calculator you should work out the interest on the tax that is being paid by instalments (box 38) and the tax that is not being paid by instalments (box 53).

Do you wish to use the interest calculator to work out the interest due?

No *Go to the helpsheet 'Working out interest on Inheritance Tax payments' and follow the instructions there*

Yes *Go to box 57*

57 **Interest on tax that is *not* being paid by instalments**

You only need to do this calculation if the figure in box 53 is greater than 0.

- Go to the interest calculator at: **www.hmrc.gov.uk/tools/inheritancetax/interest-rate-calculator.htm**
- In the 'start date' box on the calculator enter the date from box 54.
- In the 'end date' box on the calculator enter the date you expect to be sending in the IHT400.
- In the 'amount of tax' box enter the amount of tax not being paid by instalments from box 53.
- Use the 'calculate' button to find out how much interest is due.
- Enter the amount of interest in here. £ ☐ • ☐☐

58 **Interest on tax that is being paid by instalments**

You only need to do this calculation if the figure in box 38 is greater than 0.

- Go to the interest calculator at: **www.hmrc.gov.uk/tools/inheritancetax/interest-rate-calculator.htm**
- In the 'start date' box on the calculator enter the day after the date the most recent instalment fell due. If there is only one instalment due (the figure in box 24 is '1'), this date will be the date in box 54. If two instalments are due, the start date will be one year on from the date in box 54 and so on.
- In the 'end date' box on the calculator enter the date you expect to be sending in the IHT400.
- In the 'amount of tax' box enter the amount of tax being paid by instalments from box 38.
- Use the 'calculate' button to find out how much interest is due.
- Enter the amount of interest in here. £ ☐ • ☐☐

59 Is '1' the number in box 24?

No ☐ *Go to box 60*

Yes ☐ *Enter '0' in box 60 and go to box 61*

60 **Additional interest on tax that is being paid by instalments when more than one instalment is due**

When more than one instalment of tax is due, you will have to work out an additional amount of interest unless the instalments of tax are interest free.

Interest free instalments

Instalments of tax are interest free for certain types of assets as long as the instalments are paid on time. The assets on which the instalments are interest free are:

- shares or securities, except shares in an investment or property company, which will only qualify if the company is
  - a holding company of companies, which are not investment or property companies
  - a market maker or discount house in the UK
- a business or interest in a business carried on for gain
- land which qualifies for agricultural relief
- timber

It would be a very unusual situation if you need to work out the interest on these types of assets where the instalments are being paid late. The helpsheet 'Working out interest on Inheritance Tax payments' will explain what to do.

- If the instalments are not interest free (and most will not be), go to the interest calculator at: **www.hmrc.gov.uk/tools/inheritancetax/interest-rate-calculator.htm**
- In the 'start date' box on the calculator enter the date from box 54.
- In the 'end date' box on the calculator enter the date the most recent instalment became due.
- In the amount box enter the total amount of tax being paid by instalments from box 36.

Use the 'calculate' button to find out how much interest is due.

Enter the amount of interest here. (This is the figure for box 60.) £ ☐ • ☐☐

IHT400 Calculation Page 7

For example, the deceased died on 6 July 2005. The date tax is due is 31 January 2006. The tax being paid by instalments is £10,000. The first instalment of £1,000 is due on 31 January 2006, the second instalment on 31 January 2007 and so on. The application for a Grant was made on 18 June 2007, so that two instalments had to be paid at that time. The 'end' date in this example would be 31 January 2007.

In the 'amount of tax' box enter the total amount of tax being paid by instalments (from box 36). In this example this will be £10,000.

61	Total interest on tax being paid by instalments (box 58 + box 60)	£ 00000000 . 0 0
62	Total tax and interest payable now where the tax is being paid by instalments (box 38 + box 61)	£ 00000000 . 0 0
63	Total tax and interest which is not being paid by instalments, (box 53 + box 57)	£ 00000000 . 0 0
64	**Total Inheritance Tax and interest on the estate being paid now** (box 62 + box 63)	£ 00000000 . 0 0

Tax payable on gifts and lifetime transfers

The tax and interest shown at box 64 is the tax and interest which is payable now in order for you to be able to obtain a grant of representation. Depending on the circumstances of the estate, there may be more tax and interest to pay by the person(s) who received lifetime gifts from the deceased. We may also ask the person(s) who received the gifts for more details of the gifts on a separate account.

If the deceased made lifetime gifts which were over the Inheritance Tax nil rate band or gifts with reservation, further tax will be payable and we will send calculations of the tax when you have sent this form to us. If you want to work this out for yourself, you can find out how lifetime gifts are taxed on death in our customer guide at: **www.hmrc.gov.uk/inheritancetax/**

Taper relief

If there is additional tax to pay on lifetime gifts, taper relief may be available. This will apply in the following circumstances:

- the total value of gifts must be more than the Inheritance Tax nil rate band
- the gifts must have been made between three and seven years before the deceased died

The relief reduces the amount of tax payable on a gift, not the value of the gift itself.

You can find more information on taper relief in our customer guide at: **www.hmrc.gov.uk/inheritancetax/**

Trusts

If the deceased benefited from any assets held in trust shown on form IHT418 and the trustees have not paid the tax with this account, further tax will be due. We will send a calculation of the tax to the trustees named on the form IHT418.

If there are amendments made to the value of the trust assets or the value of the deceased's estate this will affect both the tax due on the trust assets and the tax due on the deceased's estate. If this is the case, we will send you further calculations of tax.

What to do when you have filled in this form

If you are filling in this form without the help of a solicitor or other adviser, send the form in with your form IHT400 so that we can see how you have worked out the tax. Continue filling in the IHT400 from box 118.

If you are a solicitor or other professional adviser, you do not need to send in this form if you do not want to, but if you have included an amount of successive charges relief in box 17 or double taxation relief in boxes 35 or 52, send this form to us with the form IHT400 so that we can see how these reliefs were worked out.

IHT400 Calculation Page 8

8

Capital Gains Tax

Cross-reference. See **56.6** VALUATION for valuation at death for capital gains tax purposes.

Simon's Taxes. See **C3.501–C3.505, I3.611–I3.615, I5.911–I5.916.**

Other Sources. Tolley's Capital Gains Tax 2010–11.

Introduction

[8.1] A *lifetime* disposition may give rise to a chargeable gain subject to capital gains tax. There is no capital gains tax on property passing on death. For the purposes of inheritance tax no account is taken of any capital gains tax borne by the transferor in determining the reduction in value in his estate. *Section 5(4)* makes it clear that the value of a transferor's estate immediately after the transfer of value 'do not include his liability (if any) for any other tax or duty resulting from the transfer.' [*IHTA 1984, s 5(4)*].

Example 1

A makes a gift of land worth £100,000 to the trustees of a discretionary settlement in which he retains an interest. The gift incurs capital gains tax liability of £15,000. The transfer of value for inheritance tax purposes (subject to grossing-up for the IHT payable) is £100,000 (i.e. the same as if A had sold the land and given the £100,000 proceeds to the trustees).

Relief for CGT against IHT

[8.2] Capital gains tax paid is taken into account for IHT purposes in the following circumstances.

(a) If the transferor fails to pay all or part of the capital gains tax within twelve months of the due date, an assessment may be made on the donee [*TCGA 1992, s 282 as amended by FA 2004, s 116*] and the amount of such tax borne by the donee is treated as reducing the value transferred. There is a similar effect when the transfer is from a settlement but this only applies if the capital gains tax is borne by a person who becomes absolutely entitled to the settled property concerned. [*IHTA 1984, s 165(1)(2)*].

Example 2

In the Example in **8.1** above, if A fails to pay the £15,000 capital gains tax and it is borne by the trustees, the value transferred by A is £85,000 for the purposes of inheritance tax.

(b) Where a person sells, or is treated as having sold, national heritage property on the breach or termination of an undertaking (see **33.10** NATIONAL HERITAGE) any capital gains tax payable is deductible in determining the value of the asset for IHT purposes. [*TCGA 1992, s 258(8)*].

(c) Where the transferee pays the CGT rather than the transferor then the CGT paid by the transferee may be deducted from the value transferred in determining the loss to the *transferor's* estate for IHT purposes. [*IHTA 1984, s 165(1)*].

If IHT becomes payable in circumstances [other than the above], there is no relief for any of the CGT payable on the transfers.

Relief for IHT against CGT

[8.3] Where capital gains tax on a disposal not at arm's length has been held over under *TCGA 1992, s 165* (relief for gifts etc. of business assets), or *TCGA 1992, s 260* (relief for gifts on which inheritance tax is chargeable), the transferee may deduct in the capital gains tax calculation on subsequent disposal the lesser of the IHT paid in respect of the gift and the amount of the chargeable gain on the disposal. A similar relief applies to hold over under the provisions of *FA 1980, s 79* as extended by *FA 1981, s 78* and *FA 1982, s 82* (general relief for gifts etc. before 14 March 1989). The IHT deductible may be that arising on a potentially exempt transfer becomes a chargeable transfer on the transferor's death within seven years and where the inheritance tax is re-determined in consequence of the transferor's death within seven years of the chargeable transfer or is otherwise varied, all necessary adjustments are to be made whether by assessment, discharge or repayment. [*TCGA 1992, ss 67(2)(3), 165(10)(11); FA 2004, s 116*].

The foregoing relief is subject to the anti-avoidance provisions regarding private residence relief which is subject to a hold-over election under *TCGA 1992, s 260*. [*TCGA 1992, s 260(7)(8); FA 2004, s 116, Schs 21, 22*].

[8.4] For full details of capital gains tax, see Tolley's Capital Gains Tax.

Key points

[8.5] Points to consider are as follows.

- With CGT at up to 28% the incentives for lifetime gifts for estate planning purposes are much reduced. A particular trap to be avoided is a lifetime gift where the donor fails to survive for seven years in which event the tax free uplift in base cost on death does not apply, capital gains tax on the gift remains in place and IHT liability on the death is incurred. Where no CGT hold over relief applies, there is no relief against capital gains tax for IHT on the gift.
- For shares in private investment companies, the capital gains tax liability on a gift can be reduced by making a gift of a minority interest in the company. Unlike the IHT rules, the value for capital gains tax purposes of the holding gifted takes no account of the size of the shareholding from which the gift is made. If the gift is to a relevant property trust for the benefit of children or grandchildren the transferor could retain control as a trustee if need be and he would also be able to make payments of any IHT by ten yearly instalments in the case of certain gifted assets.
- Where gifts are made now where there is a capital gain at 28% but the prospect of an IHT charge at 40% later on the PET then insurance cover such as diminishing term assurance may be taken out on the life of the transferor by the transferees to meet any IHT that becomes payable in the circumstances above in the event of the transferors' death within 7 years.

9

Chargeable Transfer

Simon's Taxes. See **I3.101–I3.113, I3.311, I3.312, I3.511, I3.521, I3.531, I4.101.**

Definition

[9.1] A chargeable transfer is any **51** TRANSFER OF VALUE made by an individual other than an **21** EXEMPT TRANSFER. [*IHTA 1984, s 2(1)*]. *Note.* A transfer of value can be made by a person but a chargeable transfer can be made only by an individual, although individual participators in a close company may be charged in respect of certain transfers made by the company (see **11** CLOSE COMPANIES). Inheritance tax is charged on the value transferred by a chargeable transfer. [*IHTA 1984, s 1*].

Certain lifetime transfers are designated potentially exempt transfers. A potentially exempt transfer is a transfer of value made by an individual after 17 March 1986 which would otherwise be a chargeable transfer and which is either a gift to another individual or a gift into an accumulation and maintenance trust or a trust for a disabled person. In relation to transfers of value made, and other events occurring, after 16 March 1987, certain gifts by individuals into and out of settlements with interests in possession are also included. See **38** POTENTIALLY EXEMPT TRANSFERS for full details. A potentially exempt transfer made seven years or more before the transferor's death is an exempt transfer and any other potentially exempt transfer is a chargeable transfer. A potentially exempt transfer is assumed to be an exempt transfer during the seven years following the transfer (or, if earlier, until immediately before the transferor's death). [*IHTA 1984, s 3A; FA 1986, Sch 19 para 1; FA 2010, s 53(2)*].

The estate of a deceased person is treated as a transfer of value equal to the value of his estate made immediately before his death and is chargeable to inheritance tax. See **52** TRANSFERS ON DEATH for detailed provisions.

Seven-year cumulation period

[9.2] Chargeable transfers are cumulated over a seven-year period. After seven years transfers drop out of the cumulative total. The rate of tax on any chargeable transfer is determined from the tables at **40** RATES OF TAX by reference to the transferor's cumulative total of chargeable transfers within the previous seven years (including, where appropriate, potentially exempt transfers previously made becoming chargeable and chargeable transfers made before 18 March 1986 under the rules relating to CTT). [*IHTA 1984, s 7; FA 1986, Sch 19 para 2*].

Nil rate tax band

[9.3] The first £325,000 of chargeable transfers in the seven-year cumulation period are taxable at nil per cent for the period 6 April 2009 onwards. See **40** RATES OF TAX. The total of chargeable transfers is calculated after making any allowance for the annual exemptions but see **22** GIFTS WITH RESERVATION for circumstances where the annual exemption cannot be utilised although it may be available. No tax is payable but such transfers do have to be included in the transferor's cumulative total. [*IHTA 1984, ss 7, 8, Sch 1; FA 1986, Sch 19 para 36; FA 2010, s 8*]. Various factors affect the application of the nil rate band, including the effect of the annual exemption, previous chargeable transfers becoming 'out-of-time', potentially exempt transfers becoming chargeable and a reduction of tax rates where there are previous taxable chargeable transfers within the seven-year cumulation period. See examples at **1.8** and **1.9** INTRODUCTION AND BASIC PRINCIPLES, **7.4** CALCULATION OF TAX and also **40** RATES OF TAX. An account may still need to be submitted in respect of a chargeable transfer even if no tax is payable because it falls within the nil rate band. See **2.4–2.11** ACCOUNTS AND RETURNS.

Time of gift

[9.4] As a basic rule no chargeable transfer can take place until there has been a disposition resulting in a shift of value from one estate to another.

Voidable transfers

[9.5] Where it can be shown that the whole or part of a chargeable transfer has been set aside by virtue of any enactment or rule of law as voidable or otherwise defeasible, a claim may be made for the transfer to be treated as void initially and for any tax paid to be repaid (with interest free of tax from the date of the claim). The tax rate applied to later chargeable transfers must be recalculated.

Repayment cases

[9.6] A similar claim may also be made for the repayment of inheritance tax in respect of any other chargeable transfer made before the claim that would not have been payable if the transfer that has been set aside had been void initially. Again, the liability is extinguished if the tax has not been paid. In the case of an amount which is repayable on a claim under *IHTA 1984, s 150*, the repayment interest start date is the date on which the claim is made. A claim under this section must be made not more than four years after the claimant knew, or ought reasonably to have known, that the relevant transfer has been set aside. [*IHTA 1984, ss 150, 236(3); FA 1989, s 179(1); FA 2009, Sch 51 para 8, Sch 54 para 11*].

Pools syndicates and other similar arrangements

[9.7] There is no chargeable transfer where football winnings, National Lottery (now Lotto) etc., are shared among the members of the syndicate in accordance with the terms of an agreement drawn up before the win. (**25.E14** HMRC STATEMENTS OF PRACTICE). The prior agreement can be verbal or written and it is recommended that a written record is made but it is not necessary to lodge this with HMRC Inheritance Tax. Providing an agreement is in existence any winnings by the syndicate leader which are passed on to the members of the syndicate are not chargeable to IHT.

However, in the event of a big win by a syndicate then HMRC Inheritance Tax may wish to see something similar to the following:

Agreement between the members of the [XYZ] Lottery* Syndicate

We, the parties hereunder, contributing [equal] amounts on a **weekly**/monthly/yearly* basis to the syndicate hereby confirm that the winnings from such game of chance will be distributed in **equal**/proportionate* shares to the stake contributed by each individual member as shown **below**/in the accompanying schedule*. Such stakes/contributions applied in the purchase of such tickets or the winnings arising therefrom and distributed by the appointed manager in accordance with the agreed shares shall not be a gift within *IHTA 1984, ss 2, 3A* but shall be treated as having no liability to inheritance tax in accordance with Inland Revenue Statement of Practice E14. The above shall apply to the members of this syndicate including the appointed manager being the first named member below.

Syndicate member.	Stake/contribution.	% share of prize	Date
1) X. Signed Mill Cottage, Netherington, Wilts SP4 8QS	£3 per week/month/year	33.3%	23 April 2010

Address			
2) Y *Etc.*	£3 per week/month/year	33.3%	26 April 2010

* deleted as appropriate.

10

Charities

Cross-references. See **21.2** and **21.4** EXEMPT TRANSFERS for gifts to charities; and **23.F2** HMRC EXTRA-STATUTORY CONCESSIONS for Roman Catholic religious communities.

Simon's Taxes. See **I3.333, I4.215, I5.641, I5.642, I5.644.**

Other Sources. Tolley's Income Tax 2010–11; Tolley's Capital Gains Tax 2010–11; Foster, Parts C3.33, D2.15; IHTM11101.

Introduction

[10.1] Under *Recreational Charities Act 1958, s 1* amended by *Charities Act 2006, s 5*, the provision, in the interest of social welfare, of facilities for recreation or other leisure time occupation, is deemed to be charitable (subject to the principle that a trust or institution to be charitable must be for the public benefit). See in this connection *Guild v CIR* HL, [1992] STC 162, a CTT case where it was initially held in the SC that the phrase or for 'some similar purpose in connection with sport' in a bequest made to a sports centre might include non-charitable purposes and thus would not be 'for charitable purposes only' within *FA 1975, Sch 6 para 10* (now *IHTA 1984, s 23*). However, this was overturned in the HL, Lord Keith stating that, on a 'benignant construction', where the first part of the bequest (i.e. to the sports centre) was charitable, the phrase in the second part (i.e. 'or some similar purpose'), meaning the provision of facilities for the public at large, must also be charitable. For examples of purposes held to be charitable, see Tolley's Income Tax 2010–11. See Tolley's Capital Gains Tax 2010–11 for tax relief for gifts of qualifying investments and interests in land to a charity by an individual. Also gifts to Community Amateur Sports Clubs are exempt for inheritance tax purposes as well as capital gains tax. [*ICTA 1988, s 587B inserted by FA 2002, s 43 and ICTA 1988, s 587C inserted by FA 2002, s 97; ITA 2007, ss 23, 24(1), 431(1), 445(1), Sch 1 paras 328, 536*].

Definitions

'*Charity*' means a body of persons or trust that is established for charitable purposes only meets the jurisdiction condition (i.e. EU, etc.), meets the registration condition (i.e. *Charities Act 1993, s 3*) and meets the management condition (i.e. its managers are fit and proper). [*Charities Act 2006, s 1; ICTA 1988, ss 505, 506(1); IHTA 1984, s 272 now repealed; ITTOIA 2005, s 878(1); FA 2006, ss 55, 56; ITA 2007, ss 519, 543(1); CTA 2009, s 1319; FA 2010, s 30, Sch 6*].

'*Charitable purposes*' comprise a purpose which is for the public benefit or falls within any of the following descriptions of purposes the prevention or relief of poverty, the advancement of education, the advancement of religion and a many other charitable purposes within *Charities Act 2006, s 2(2)*. A purpose falling within *s 2(2)* must be for the public benefit if it is to be a charitable purpose and in any reference to the public benefit is a reference to the public benefit as that term is understood for the purposes of the law relating to charities in England and Wales but it is not to be presumed that a purpose of a particular description is for the public benefit. The Charity Commission for England and Wales must issue guidance in pursuance of its public benefit objective within *Charities Act 2006, s 6*.

UK charity tax reliefs were extended, with effect from 6 April 2010, by *FA 2010, Sch 6* to certain organisations which are equivalent to charities and Community Amateur Sports Clubs in the EU and in the European Economic Area countries of Norway and Iceland, following a judgment in the European Court of Justice in January 2009; see *Persche v Finanzamt* [2009] STC 586. These charities must be registered with any regulators in their home country which the law requires the organisation to register with, such as the Charity Commission in England and Wales, and have managers that are fit and proper persons. On application for UK tax reliefs, HMRC will make checks to ensure that the charity concerned satisfies the UK definition of charity and conforms with the requirements set out in *FA 2010, Sch 6*. Claims to charitable tax reliefs in respect of organisations equivalent to UK charities in the EU, Norway or Iceland on or after the date of the ECJ judgment on 27 January 2009 and before 6 April 2010 will be considered on a case by case basis, but HMRC refuse all claims for gifts to EU charities prior to that date.

Gifts

[10.2] Gifts to charities are generally exempt from inheritance tax including the gifts of qualifying investments introduced by the *Finance Act 2000* for capital gains tax purposes (see above). From 6 April 2012 where 10% or more of any component of an estate has been given to charity, a reduced rate of inheritance tax (36%) will apply to that component. There is no charge to tax when certain settled property becomes held for charitable purposes only without limit of time. See details at **21.2** and **21.4** EXEMPT TRANSFERS. See CTO Newsletter, July 1997 at http://www.hmrc.gov.uk/cto/newsletter.htm.

Example 1

Betty is very wealthy and wishes to benefit her village to a great extent and has discussions with the leader of the Parish Council and they agree the following:

- to provide £250,000 in a Trust Fund for the education and benefit of local children;

- to build a church annex for Sunday school worship costing £75,000;
- to provide £500,000 for a centre for the training and welfare of the community;
- a gift of £250 to every individual in the village.

In order to ensure that Betty falls within the requirements of *IHTA 1984, s 23* so that her gifts are for charitable purposes only she must not take any benefit. This is likely to be the case as even though she is resident in the village she will not be likely to benefit from the subject of her gifts e.g. the educational trust, Sunday school and the training/welfare centre. Whilst this is not a matter that is going to cause a problem for IHT purposes with regard to *s 23(4)* it might have done for income tax purposes under *FA 1990, s 25(2)*.

THIS DECLARATION OF TRUST is made on *30 September 2010* by THE TRUSTEES of the [. . . . .] EDUCATIONAL FOUNDATION

The object of the Charity shall be to further the education (including social and physical training) of children attending [. . . . .] in the County of . . .

The Trustees shall apply the net income of the Trust Fund in one or more of the following ways:

in awarding scholarships, exhibitions, bursaries or maintenance allowances tenable at any school, university or other educational establishment approved by the Trustees to persons under 25 years of age who, or whose parents or guardians, are resident in [. . . . .] or who are attending or have attended an educational establishment in that area for not less than 7 years and who are in need of financial assistance;

in providing financial assistance, outfits, clothing, tools, instruments or books to such persons on leaving school, university or other educational establishment to prepare them for or assist their entry into a trade, profession or service;

in awarding to such persons grants or maintenance allowances to enable them to travel whether in the United Kingdom or abroad in furtherance of their education;

in otherwise furthering the education of such persons.

The Trust Deed continues with Powers of Investment, etc.

To educate, relieve and rehabilitate persons resident in [. . . . .] who by reason of their social and economic circumstances are unable to gain employment or to further their formal education by providing for such persons for a period not exceeding. . . . . . years for any one individual, workshops and such other training facilities as will enable them to obtain work experience and acquire and develop vocational skills.

To advance religious education in accordance with the doctrines and principles of the [*Name*] faith by means of Sunday schools and otherwise.

Note that in the case of the training/welfare charitable donation above it may be too widely drawn so as to preclude relief. A trust for the relief of unemployment is not charitable whereas the relief of poverty is charitable as is the furtherance of education. Again, care needs to be taken when setting up the necessary trust deed. However, with the introduction of gifts to Community Amateur Sports Clubs (CASCs) being exempt for inheritance tax purposes as well as capital gains tax she might consider this option as an answer to bullet point three above. CASCs must be open to the whole community and provide facilities for, and promote participation in, one or more eligible sports. These clubs must be registered with HMRC.

In addition, the Charities Commission has a narrower 'healthy recreation' condition which bars certain sports from charitable status and exclusion will also apply to professional boxing, polo clubs etc. See http://www.charity-commission.gov.uk/. HMRC's registration procedure is by way of forms CASC3 and CASC4 which should be sent together with the club's governing document, latest accounts and rule book, etc to HMRC Sports Clubs Unit. See http://www.hmrc.gov.uk/charities.

Trusts

[10.3] Where a charity takes the usual form of a trust in which there is no interest in possession i.e. a discretionary trust, special rules apply. Where the trusts on which property is held require part of the income to be applied for charitable purposes, a corresponding part of the settled property is regarded as held for charitable purposes, for the purposes of the rules in *IHTA 1984, Part III, Ch III* relating to **43** SETTLEMENTS: DISCRETIONARY TRUSTS AND OTHER TRUSTS OF RELEVANT PROPERTY (other than the provisions of *ss 78, 79* relating to conditionally exempt occasions and exemption from ten-yearly charge for National Heritage property). [*IHTA 1984, s 84*]. Provided the property is held for charitable purposes only, whether for a limited time or otherwise, it is not 'relevant property' and there is no ten-year anniversary charge under *IHTA 1984, s 64* (see **43.3** and **43.6** SETTLEMENTS: DISCRETIONARY TRUSTS AND OTHER TRUSTS OF RELEVANT PROPERTY). In addition, if the property becomes held for charitable purposes without any time limit, there is no charge to tax at other times (proportionate charge to tax) on distributions. See **10.4** below for property leaving temporary charitable trusts.

Case law — St Dunstan's charity

In the case of *St Dunstan's v Major* [1997] STC SCD 212 Sp C 127 the gift to the Charity by way of Deed of Variation and the claiming of gift aid relief by the personal representative was precluded. But where a bequest is part of a will or the assets are left to someone to make the gift to the charity then the charity exemption is in point under *IHTA 1984, s 23* and where the beneficiary makes a subsequent transfer to the charity gift aid relief will also be available; the charity being able to claim the basic rate relief in respect of the gift aid and the higher rate relief being claimed by donor who has been a beneficiary under the will and benefited the charity. Alternatively, providing the above procedures are adhered to the opportunity to claim gift aid relief and exemption under *s 23* will be available. A form of Trust document that utilises the Charities Aid Foundation documentation and flexible donation options is shown below but refer to CAF Trust Department regarding conditions applying before use. Tel. 03000 1230280.

Trust document

1 Definitions

(a) The 'Donor' is the person whose name appears below under Donor Details.

(b) The 'Trustees' are the trustees for the time being of the Charities Aid Foundation.

(c) The 'Foundation' is the Charities Aid Foundation.

(d) The 'Trust Fund' is the amount of cash, or stocks and shares, given to the Charities Aid Foundation by the Donor and entered in the Schedule below together with any further sums or securities which may be given to the Foundation to be held upon the same terms and shall also be interpreted as the money, investments or property which may from time to time represent the original cash, stocks and shares or securities given to the Foundation.

[(e) The 'Conditions' are those conditions printed on the reverse of this Trust Document or any future amendment thereof.]

(f) The 'Successor' (or successors) is the person (or persons) duly appointed by way of a Successor Election Form who, following the death of the Donor, has the power to distribute the Trust Fund for charitable purposes.

2 *Donor Details*

Full Name . . . .

Title Mr/Mrs/Miss/Ms/Other . . . .

Address . . . .

. . . .

Postcode . . . . Tel: . . . .

3 *Schedule*

Amount of cash £ . . . .

Or

Share details:-

Nominal	Holding
. . . .	. . . .
. . . .	. . . .

4 The Trust Fund, together with the income arising thereon, is to be held by the Trustees upon trust under the name of .to the intent that it shall be distributed for charitable purposes as may from time to time be determined by the Donor during his/her lifetime and thereafter as may be determined by any Successors for their respective lives.

5 It is the wish of the Donor (without in any way seeking to fetter the investment powers of the Trustees) that initially the Trust Fund be invested as follows:-

	% (approx)
CAF UK Equity Growth Fund	. . . .
CAF Bond Income Fund	. . . .
CAF Equitrack Fund	. . . .
CAF Socially Responsible Fund	. . . .
Cash Deposit Fund	. . . .
Other	. . . .

6 The Donor shall, during his/her lifetime, have power to appoint a successor (or Successors) who upon the death of the Donor, will have all the rights and powers attributed to the donor including the power to appoint his/her own Successor (or Successors) subject to the Trustees having the discretion to limit the number of Successors to two in number at any one time.

7 The trust will terminate when the Trust Fund has been completely distributed or when the Trust Fund has been transferred to the Foundation Fund of the Charities Aid Foundation under condition (d) overleaf.

8 The management and operation of the Trust Fund shall be subject to the conditions and any future amendment thereof.

9 This document shall be governed by and construed in accordance with the Laws of England.

. . . .

Donor's Signature

. . . .

Date

. . . .

Trust Manager (Countersigned on behalf of the Charities Aid Foundation).

. . . .

Date

* Conditions apply to the Trust Document which are not reproduced here other than in (A) below.

Notes to the Trust Document

(A) In 7 above the reference to the condition is 'If and so far as the purposes of the Trust fund are, in the opinion of the Trustees, no longer possible or practical or should the trust upon which the Trust Fund is held fail for any reason then the Trust Fund together with any undistributed income arising therefrom shall be transferred to and held as part of the Foundation Fund of the Charities Aid Foundation'.

(B) For chargeable periods commencing after 21 March 2006, tax relief will be available for charities where only or part of a trade is carried on for a primary charitable purpose or where a trade is partly carried on by the beneficiaries of a charity. The trade must be split into two separate parts, a primary charitable purpose part, with tax relief under *ICTA 1988, s 505* given on the primary charitable purpose part or on the profits of the part carried on by the beneficiaries of the charity in respect of the non-primary purpose part. [*ICTA 1988, ss 505, 506 as amended by FA 2006, ss 55, 56; ITA 2007, ss 525(2)–(4),*

539(2), 540(1)–(3), 541(2)–(6), 562(4)–(5), 563(2)–(6), Sch 1 paras 326, 327, Sch 2 para 107]. See Tolley's Income Tax 2010–11 and Tolley's Capital Gains Tax 2010–11 for tax relief for gifts of qualifying investments and interests in land to a charity by an individual.

Property leaving temporary charitable trusts

[10.4] Property which is held on charitable trusts only until the end of a specific period (whether defined by date or in some other way) is subject to a charge when either:

(a) it ceases to be held for charitable purposes otherwise than by being applied for charitable purposes (but see also **21.4** EXEMPT TRANSFERS for certain situations where there is no charge when property becomes that of a qualifying political party or a national body mentioned in *IHTA 1984, Sch 3* or, under certain conditions, a body not established or conducted for profit), or

(b) the trustees make a 'disposition' (otherwise than for charitable purposes) which reduces the value of the settled property. '*Disposition*' includes an omission to exercise a right, unless not deliberate, which is treated as made at the latest time that the right could be exercised. [*IHTA 1984, ss 70(1)(2)(10), 76*].

No charge arises

(i) if, under (b) above, the trustees do not intend to confer gratuitous benefit and either the transaction is at arm's length between persons not connected with each other (see **12** CONNECTED PERSONS) or is such as might be expected in such a transaction; or

(ii) if, under (b) above, the disposition is a grant of a tenancy of agricultural property in the UK, Channel Islands or Isle of Man, for use for agricultural purposes and made for full consideration in money or money's worth; or

(iii) on the payment of costs or expenses attributable to the property; or

(iv) where any payment is, or will be, income for income tax purposes of any person (or, in the case of a non-resident, would be if he were so resident); or

(v) in respect of a liability to make a payment under (iii) or (iv) above.

'*Payment*' includes a transfer of assets other than money.

[*IHTA 1984, ss 63, 70(3)(4)*].

Tax is charged on the amount by which the trust property is less immediately after the event giving rise to the charge than it would have been but for the event (i.e. the loss to the donor principle), grossed-up where the settlement pays the tax.

The rate at which tax is charged is the aggregate of the following percentages for each complete successive quarter in 'the relevant period'.

	Cumulative Total
0.25% for each of the first 40 quarters	10%
0.20% for each of the next 40 quarters	8%
0.15% for each of the next 40 quarters	6%
0.10% for each of the next 40 quarters	4%
0.05% for each of the next 40 quarters	2%
Maximum rate chargeable after 50 years	30%

The rate charged may be reduced if any of the property is, or was, **20** EXCLUDED PROPERTY, see **10.5** below.

Definitions

'*Relevant period*' is the period beginning with the day on which the property became (or last became) held on charitable trusts, or 13 March 1975 if later, and ending on the day before the chargeable event. Where property in respect of which tax is chargeable was relevant property (see **43.3** SETTLEMENTS: DISCRETIONARY TRUSTS AND OTHER TRUSTS OF RELEVANT PROPERTY) immediately before 10 December 1981 (e.g. in a discretionary trust) and became (or last became) comprised in a temporary charitable trust after 9 December 1981 and before 9 March 1982, the relevant period begins with the day on which the property became (or last became) relevant property before 10 December 1981 or 13 March 1975 if later. [*IHTA 1984, s 70(5)(6)(8)(9)*].

'*Quarter*' means a period of three months. [*IHTA 1984, s 63*].

See also **43.19** and **43.22** SETTLEMENTS: DISCRETIONARY TRUSTS AND OTHER TRUSTS OF RELEVANT PROPERTY which also apply to temporary charitable trusts.

Example 2

On 1 January 1972 A settled £100,000 on temporary charitable trusts. The income and capital were to be applied for charitable purposes only for a period of 25 years from the date of settlement, and thereafter could be applied for charitable purposes or to or for the settlor's grandchildren. On 1 January 2011 the trustees paid £50,000 to charity and the balance of the settlement, valued at £75,000, to the three grandchildren.

The relevant period is the period from settlement of the funds or, if later, 13 March 1975 to 1 January 2011, i.e. 143 complete quarters, and the amount on which tax is charged is £75,000 gross.

The rate of tax is:

	%
0.25% for 40 quarters	10.00
0.20% for 40 quarters	8.00
0.15% for 40 quarters	6.00
0.10% for 23 quarters	2.30
	26.30%

IHT payable is 26.30% × £75,000 = £19,725

Example 3

Assume the same facts as in the above Example 2 except that the trustees apply £75,000 net for the settlor's three grandchildren, and the balance to charity. The rate of tax is, as before, 26.30%

IHT payable is $\frac{26.30}{100-26.30} \times £75{,}000 =$ £26,764

The gross payment to the beneficiaries is £75,000 + £26,764 = £101,764.

Excluded property

[10.5] Where the whole or part of the amount on which tax is charged as in 10.4 above is attributable to property which was 20 EXCLUDED PROPERTY at any time during the relevant period, then, in determining the rate at which tax is charged in respect of that amount or part, no quarter throughout which the property was excluded property is to be counted. [*IHTA 1984, s 70(7)*].

Key points

[10.6] Points to consider are as follows.

- In some appropriate cases it is possible to obtain both income tax and IHT relief and for the charity or collecting agency such as the Charities Aid Foundation (CAF) to obtain increased funds. Say, a testator makes a pecuniary legacy to a beneficiary and expresses in his will that he/she wishes the beneficiary to benefit a charity but this is a non-binding request and then the beneficiary in turn makes a gift to the charity or CAF within two years both IHT and income tax reliefs will be due. The beneficiary receives an extension in the basic rate band of tax and if a higher rate tax payer (40% or 50%) will receive tax relief on the amount over and above the basic rate band under gift aid relief. The charity reclaims the basic rate tax relief and benefits from the gift which was treated as donated net of basic rate. Provided this is done within two years of death of the testator *IHTA 1984, s 143* comes into play whereby the legacy is treated as if the testator had bequeathed the amount to the charity (i.e. transferee in the legislation) and consequently receives the appropriate IHT relief. Such a procedure does to a great extent rely on the beneficiary carrying out the testator's wishes but where there is a mutual philanthropic interest there should be no worry.

- The *Charities Act 2006* changed the original definition to one of charitable objects of which there were thirteen. Care needs to be taken when drawing up a will that benefits a charity that the charity does in fact comply so that IHT relief is obtained. *Section 2(1)* states the charitable descriptions and some of these (i.e. d to l) are new and not tested. The objects clause should be scrutinised by the Charity Commission so that all new charities are within that definition. If it turns out that a charity is in default because of a shortcoming in its clause there may be problems regarding any specific charitable gift and consequently the IHT relief. The use of a body like the CAF does therefore avoid the problem.
- Following the litigious case of *RSPCA v Sharp and Ors* [2010] STC 975 (Ch) care should be taken with regard to residuary legacies to charities. The RSPCA was the residuary legatee under the will of George Mason dated 19 January 2005. George Mason died on 18 June 2007. *Clause 6* stated '[6.] *MY TRUSTEES shall stand possessed of my residuary estate upon trust for the Royal Society for the Prevention of Cruelty to Animals of Causeway Horsham West Sussex RH12 1HG for its general purposes and I direct that the receipt of the secretary treasurer or other proper officer shall be a sufficient discharge to my trustees.*' The RSPCA did not agree with the Executors' construction of the provisions of the will on the basis it was not the most tax efficient way to administer the will. This means that although the case was lost by the RSPCA care should be taken when drafting a will that leaves bequests to a charity so that it is clear whom amongst the beneficiaries will bear the burden of the tax as and when it arises.
- One way around the above problem may be for the beneficiary(ies) to inherit the residuary estate and then effect the deceased's wishes to benefit a particular charity or the CAF from the residuary estate. The assets may be investments, interests in land, etc. which are suitable for Qualifying Investment Donation Relief (QIDR) within *ITA 2007, ss 431, 432*. The beneficiary undertakes to donate, say £100,000 in capital from a building society investment within the two years following the date of death. [*IHTA 1984, s 142*]. The beneficiary obtains tax relief at their marginal rate, so a 50% tax rate would give the beneficiary an extension of the basic rate band of £100,000 giving tax relief at 50%. The instrument of variation within two years gives the estate relief at 40%. Any increase in the chargeable gains within the two year period could be minimal in the case of the beneficiary. If the beneficiary's income is mainly comprised of dividends then the saving will be slightly less because of the lower dividend rate. In this way the situation faced in the RSPCA case is avoided with the benefit accruing to the charity, estate and beneficiary.
- UK charity tax reliefs including IHT are now available for gifts to certain organisations which are equivalent to charities and Community Amateur Sports Clubs (CASCs) in the EU and in the European Economic Area (EEA) countries of Norway and Iceland. Wills may now be drawn up to include such charities and

the appropriate relief will be due provided HMRC accepts that the 'fit and proper persons' test is met. A list of EU charities accepted as qualifying for relief is to be published by HMRC. Relief can be accessed through the new variations form, which will be available to download HMRC website. Until this form is available please follow the usual process which can be found at www.hmrc.gov.uk/charities/gift_aid/reclaim.htm. Claims for exemption may also be made for gifts to EU charities made by the will of a person who died on or after 27 January 2009.

11

Close Companies

Cross-references. See **4.14** AGRICULTURAL PROPERTY for agricultural companies; **6** BUSINESS PROPERTY; and **20.5** EXCLUDED PROPERTY for Government securities held by close companies.

Simon's Taxes. See **I6.1**.

Other Sources. Tolley's Corporation Tax 2010–11, Chapter 13; Foster, Part F1; IHTM14851.

Introduction

[11.1] A company can make a **51** TRANSFER OF VALUE as a *person* but only an individual can make a **9** CHARGEABLE TRANSFER. However, where a close company makes a transfer of value that value is apportioned among its participators and treated as if each had made a transfer of the apportioned part (except to the extent that the transfer is to that participator). [*IHTA 1984, s 94(1)*]. Also, where unquoted share or loan capital (or any rights attached thereto) is altered, the participators are treated as having made a disposition, see **11.8** below.

Definitions

'*Close company*' is as defined by *ICTA 1988, s 414* for the purposes of corporation tax with the addition that companies resident outside the UK are treated as close companies if they would otherwise be within the definition. Broadly, a company is close if it is under the control of five or fewer participators or participators who are directors. [*IHTA 1984, s 102(1)*].

'*Participator*' in a company (whether resident in the UK or not) is as defined by *ICTA 1988, s 417* for the purposes of corporation tax but with the exclusion of a person who is a participator by reason only of being a loan creditor. [*IHTA 1984, s 102(1)*]. The definition includes any person

(i) possessing, or entitled to acquire, share capital or voting rights; or
(ii) possessing, or entitled to acquire, a right to receive, or to participate in, distributions; or
(iii) entitled to ensure that present or future income or assets of the company will be applied; directly or indirectly, for his benefit.

See Tolley's Corporation Tax 2010–11 for full definitions of '*close company*' and '*participator*'.

Apportionment

[11.2] The value transferred (see **11.4** below) by the company is apportioned among the participators according to their respective 'rights and interests' in the company *immediately before the transfer* and any amount so apportioned to a close company is further apportioned among its participators, and so on.

Exceptions

[11.3] The following are not apportioned.

(a) Any value attributable to any payment or transfer of assets to any person who brings it into account for the purposes of his income tax or corporation tax computations (including UK company dividends and other distributions not chargeable to income tax or corporation tax under *ICTA 1988, s 208*).
(b) Any amount apportionable to an individual domiciled outside the UK which is attributable to any property outside the UK.

[*IHTA 1984, s 94(2)*].

Definitions

'*Rights and interests*' in a company include those in the assets of the company available for distribution among the participators in a winding-up or in any other circumstances. They do not include:

(i) preference shares (as defined by *ICTA 1988, s 210(4)*) where any transfer of value by the company or any other close company has only a small effect on their value compared with the effect on the value of other parts of the company's share capital; or
(ii) the rights and interests of 'minority participators' of a subsidiary company which disposes of an asset, as a transfer of value, to another 'group' company (within the terms of *TCGA 1992, ss 171(1), 171A(2)*) and that transfer has only a small effect on the value of the rights and interests of the minority participators compared with those of other participators.

A '*minority participator*' is a participator of the transferor company which is not, and is not a person connected with, a participator of the 'principal company' (before 14 March 1989, 'principal member') of the group or of any of the principal company's (before 14 March 1989, principal member's) participators.

'*Principal company*' and '*group*' are as defined in *TCGA 1992, s 170 as amended by FA 2000, Sch 29 para 14*. Before 14 March 1989, the '*principal member*' of a group is the member of which all the other members are '*75% subsidiaries*' (within *ICTA 1988, s 413(3)*).

[*IHTA 1984, ss 96, 97, 102(2); FA 1989, s 138(6); FA 2000, Sch 29 para 14; FA 2001, s 106; FA 2002, s 42(3)*].

Value transferred

[11.4] A transfer of value made by a close company is the amount by which the value of its assets immediately after a disposition is less than it would be but for the disposition, and this reduction (ignoring dispositions of **20** EXCLUDED PROPERTY) is the value transferred for apportionment among its participators. See **51** TRANSFER OF VALUE generally and **51.2** in particular for dispositions which are not transfers of value. The surrender by a close company of surplus advance corporation tax or losses within a group under *ICTA 1988, ss 240 (now repealed), 402* is not treated as a transfer of value. [*IHTA 1984, ss 3(1), 10, 94(3), 98(1)*]. A bonus issue of shares will not be a transfer of value nor will a genuine commercial transaction. In *Postlethwaite's Executors v HMRC* where a FURBS payment was not within *IHTA 1984, s 94* and that the payment was a disposition not intended to confer gratuitous benefit, within *IHTA 1984, s 10*. See **58** TAX CASES.

A dividend paid by a subsidiary to its parent is not a transfer of value nor is a transfer of assets between a wholly-owned subsidiary and its parent or between wholly-owned subsidiaries. (**25.E15** HMRC STATEMENTS OF PRACTICE).

Example 1

The ordinary shares of companies A and B are held as follows (in January 2011)

		A	B
Individuals	X	80%	
	Y	20%	
	Z		10%
Company A			90%

Company B is non-resident and Z is domiciled in the UK. Company A sells a property valued at £220,000 to a mutual friend of X and Y for £20,000. The following month, company B sells a foreign property worth £100,000 to X for £90,000.

Company A

	£
The transfer of value is £220,000 – £20,000	200,000
Apportioned to X 80% × £200,000	160,000
Y 20% × £200,000	40,000
	£200,000

Company B

The transfer of value of £10,000 is apportioned

To X 80% × 90% × £10,000	7,200
Deduct increase in X's estate	10,000
	—
To Y 20% × 90% × £10,000	1,800
To Z 10% × £10,000 note (C)	1,000
	£2,800

Notes to the example

(A) If the sale by company A were to X (or Y), there would be no apportionment because the undervalue would be treated as a net distribution, thus attracting income tax.

(B) On the sale by company B, X would not be liable to income tax.

(C) If Z were not domiciled in the UK, his share of the transfer of value would not be apportioned to him. [*IHTA 1984, s 94(2)(b)*].

Charge on participators

[11.5] Where a close company makes a transfer of value which is apportioned among its participators as above, inheritance tax becomes chargeable as if each such participator who is an individual had made a transfer of value after deduction of tax (if any) equal to the amount apportioned to him, less the amount (if any) by which his estate is more than it would be but for the company's transfer. For this purpose his estate is treated as not including any rights or interests (see **11.2** above) in the company. [*IHTA 1984, s 94(1)*].

Example 2

Assume the values transferred by X, Y and Z above in **11.4** and that X and Y have each made previous chargeable transfers in excess of £325,000 since January 2004 and have used up their annual exemptions for 2009/10.

	X	Y	Z
Company A	£	£	£
Value transferred	160,000	40,000	
Annual exemptions 2010/11	(3,000)	(3,000)	
	157,000	37,000	
Tax (25% of net)	39,250	9,250	
Gross transfer	£196,250	£46,250	
IHT	£39,250	£9,250	
Company B			
Value transferred	7,200	1,800	1,000
Deduct increase in X's estate	(10,000)	—	—
		1,800	1,000
Deduct annual exemption		—	1,000

	1,800	—
Tax (25% of net)	450	
Gross transfer	£2,250	
IHT	£450	

Note to the example

(A) Although it is understood that HMRC would follow this method of calculation in the above example, there is an alternative view which follows the exact wording of *IHTA 1984, s 94(1)*. This view is that the grossing-up should take place before the increase in X's estate is deducted. In the above example, it makes no difference as the gross transfer would still be less than the increase in X's estate. But suppose that X held 90% of the ordinary shares in Company A. His value transferred would then be £8,100 (90% × 90% × £10,000) and this alternative method would proceed as follows.

	£
Value transferred	8,100
Tax (25% of net)	2,025
	10,125
Deduct increase in X's estate	(10,000)
	£125
IHT thereon at 20%	£25

Where a close company makes a transfer of value to another company and an individual is a participator in both companies, any amount apportioned to him of the transferor company's transfer may be reduced by his apportioned part of the increase, due to the transfer, in the estate of the transferee company. [*IHTA 1984, s 95*].

Trustees

[11.6] Where a person is a participator in his capacity as trustee of a settlement, any amount apportioned to him less the amount (if any) by which the value of the settled property is more than it would be apart from the company's transfer (leaving out of account the value of any rights or interests in the company) is treated as follows.

(a) If a qualifying interest in possession subsists in the settled property, a part of that interest corresponding to the amount apportioned (as reduced) is treated as having come to an end on the making of the transfer.

(b) If no qualifying interest in possession subsists in the settled property, the trustees are treated for the purposes of the rules relating to 43 SETTLEMENTS: DISCRETIONARY TRUSTS AND OTHER TRUSTS OF RELEVANT PROPERTY as having made, at the time of the transfer, a disposition as a result of which the value of the settled property is reduced by a corresponding amount.

[*IHTA 1984, s 99*].

Note. For transfers within (b) above the amount is grossed-up under *IHTA 1984, s 65(2)* (see **43.12** SETTLEMENTS: DISCRETIONARY TRUSTS AND OTHER TRUSTS OF RELEVANT PROPERTY) where the trustees pay the tax.

Where the amount apportioned to a person is not more than 5% of the value transferred, it is to be disregarded in determining the rate of tax on any later transfers made by him. [*IHTA 1984, s 94(4)*].

Exemptions

[11.7] A participator can set his annual exemption against any amount apportioned to him but not the exemptions for small gifts, normal expenditure gifts, or gifts in consideration of marriage. The exemptions for gifts to charities and political parties and for national purposes or public benefit are available. [*IHTA 1984, ss 3(4), 19(5), 20(3), 21(5), 22(6), 94(5)*].

Alteration of share capital, etc.

[11.8] Where there is an alteration in the share or loan capital of a close company not consisting of quoted shares or securities (for transfers and other events occurring before 17 March 1987, shares or securities quoted on a recognised stock exchange) or in any rights attaching to its unquoted shares or debentures (for transfers and other events occurring before 17 March 1987, shares or debentures not quoted on a recognised stock exchange), the alteration is treated as having been made by a disposition by the participators whether or not it would otherwise fall to be so treated. Such a disposition is not a 38 POTENTIALLY EXEMPT TRANSFER, and is therefore in all cases a chargeable transfer, subject to the application of any available exemptions. Alterations are not to be taken to have affected the value of the unquoted shares etc. immediately before the alteration. '*Alteration*' includes extinguishment. [*IHTA 1984, s 98; FA 1986, Sch 19 para 20; FA 1987, s 58, Sch 8 para* 2]. Any decrease in value arising from an alteration brought about by a death is to be disregarded in arriving at the value of the estate on death. [*IHTA 1984, s 171(2)*].

Example 3

In January 2011 the share capital of company H, an investment company, is owned by P and Q as follows:

P	600	
Q	400	
	1,000	ordinary £1 shares

The shares are valued at £10 per share for P's majority holding and £4 per share for Q's minority holding.

The company issues 2,000 shares at par to Q and the shares are then worth £3.50 per share for Q's majority holding and £1.50 per share for P's minority holding. P has previously made chargeable transfers in excess of £325,000 since January 2004 and has utilised his 2010/11 and 2009/10 annual exemptions.

The transfer of value for P is

	£
Value of holding previously	6,000
Value of holding now	900
Decrease in value	5,100
Tax (25% of net)	1,275
Gross transfer	£6,375
IHT thereon at 20%	£1,275

Notes to the example

(A) P's transfer of value is *not* a potentially exempt transfer. [*IHTA 1984, s 98(3)*].

(B) An alternative charge may arise under *IHTA 1984, s 3(3)* (omission to exercise a right) but the transfer would then be potentially exempt and only chargeable if P died within seven years.

For the above purposes, and in relation to transfers and other events after 16 March 1987, '*quoted*', in relation to any shares or securities, means quoted ('*listed*' from 1 April 1996) on a recognised stock exchange or dealt in on the Unlisted Securities Market, and '*unquoted*', in relation to any shares or securities, means neither so quoted nor so dealt in. [*IHTA 1984, s 272; FA 1987, s 58(2), Sch 8 para 17; FA 1996, Sch 38 para 2*]. In relation to transfers and other events after 9 March 1992, Unlisted Securities Market shares and securities are only treated as unquoted for the purposes of defining relevant business property (see **6.4** BUSINESS PROPERTY), loss on sale of unquoted shares (see **56.24** VALUATION), and payment of tax by instalments (see **35.5** PAYMENT OF TAX). For all IHT purposes, and in relation to transfers and other events before 17 March 1987, Unlisted Securities Market shares and securities were not regarded as quoted on a recognised stock exchange (Inland Revenue Statement of Practice SP 18/80, 23 December 1980).

It is understood (see Law Society's Gazette 11 September 1991) that HMRC treat deferred shares issued after 5 August 1991 which subsequently come to rank equally, or become merged with, another class of shares as an alteration of rights within *IHTA 1984, s 98(1)(b)* (alteration in rights attaching to unquoted shares or debentures, etc.). Previously such an issue 'could' (the original statement by the former Inland Revenue said 'would' but it is understood they accepted 'could' as appropriate) have been treated as within *IHTA 1984, s 98(1)(a)* (alteration in unquoted share or loan capital).

HMRC have refused to confirm that either a purchase, redemption or repayment of a company's own shares or the alteration to any Articles of Association to enable it to make such a purchase etc. will not give rise to a transfer of value under *IHTA 1984, s 94*. (CCAB Memorandum, 22 June 1982). See **48.9** SHARES AND SECURITIES.

Trustees

[11.9] Where a person is a participator in his capacity as trustee and the disposition would, if he were beneficially entitled to the settled property, be a transfer of value made by him, the following consequences arise.

(a) *If an individual is beneficially entitled to an interest in possession* (e.g. a life interest) in the whole or part of so much of the settled property as consists of unquoted shares or securities of the close company (before 17 March 1987 shares or securities of the close company not listed on a recognised stock exchange), part of the individual's interest (equal to the amount of the decrease in value of the shares etc. in which the interest subsists) is treated as coming to an end. The amount of the decrease in value is the decrease caused by the alteration and is not grossed-up. [*IHTA 1984, s 100; FA 1987, s 58, Sch 8 para 3*].

(b) *If no individual is beneficially entitled to an interest in possession* in the whole of so much of the settled property as consists of the unquoted shares etc. then a charge to tax automatically arises under *IHTA 1984, s 65(1)(b)* (see **43.12** SETTLEMENTS: DISCRETIONARY TRUSTS AND OTHER TRUSTS OF RELEVANT PROPERTY).

Liability for tax

[11.10] Liability for tax is treated as follows:

(a) **On a transfer of value by the company apportioned to participators** (see **11.2** above). The company is primarily liable for the tax chargeable on amounts apportioned but, if it is unpaid by the time it ought to have been paid (see **35** PAYMENT OF TAX), the persons to whom any amounts have been apportioned and any individuals benefiting from the transfer become liable subject to the following limitations.
   (i) A person to whom not more than 5% of the value transferred is apportioned is not liable for any of the tax.
   (ii) Each of the other persons to whom any part of that value has been apportioned is liable only for the corresponding proportion of the tax.
   (iii) A person benefiting from the transfer by an increase in value of his estate is liable only to the extent of that increase. [*IHTA 1984, s 202*].

Note. Whoever pays the tax, it is the participators (except those within (i) above) whose cumulative totals of transfers are increased. [*IHTA 1984, ss 3(4), 94(4)*].

A taxation warranty may be in order where transfers in shares in a close company are involved. In spite of the heading to *IHTA 1984, s 94* which states 'charge on participators' *s 202(1)(a)* makes it clear that tax is payable by the company. However, if the tax remains unpaid it can be collected from the participators by reason of *s 202(1)(b)*. In order to counteract the possibility of such a charge the following warranty may be inserted:

Taxation Warranty

1. General

All returns computations and payments which should or should have been made by the Company for any fiscal purpose have been prepared on a proper basis and submitted within the prescribed time limits and are up to date and correct and none of them is now the subject or likely to be the subject of any dispute with HMRC and will not give rise to any disallowance . . .

8. Inheritance Tax

The Company has made no transfer of value within the IHTA 1984, sections 94 or 99 in respect of close companies and charges on participators respectively.

No person has the power under IHTA 1984, section 212 to raise any capital transfer tax or inheritance tax by the sale of or charge over any of the Company's assets.

There is no unsatisfied liability to capital transfer tax or inheritance tax attached to or attributable to the assets of the Company or the shares of the Company and neither the assets nor the shares are subject to HMRC/Capital Taxes charge as is mentioned in IHTA 1984, section 237.

Note: *Further conditions apply to the Taxation Warranty that are not relevant to this work.*

(b) **On an alteration of share capital or rights** (see **11.8** above). The participators who own the shares or debentures are liable for the tax on the disposition made by them. [*IHTA 1984, s 98(1)*].

Interest in possession owned by close company

[11.11] Where a close company is entitled to an interest in possession in settled property, the participators of that company are treated, for the purposes of inheritance tax (except for the provisions of *IHTA 1984, s 55* relating to the acquisition by a person of a reversionary interest expectant on an interest to which he is already entitled), as being entitled to that interest according to their respective rights and interests in the company.

If such participators include the trustees of a settlement and a person is beneficially entitled to an interest in possession in the whole or part of the settled property, that beneficiary is treated as entitled to the whole or a corresponding part of the interest to which the trustees would otherwise be treated as entitled. For consideration of this provision, see *Powell-Cotton v CIR* Ch D, [1992] STC 625 where an interest in possession for the life of P in part of settled property was held by a close company shares in which were gifted to a charity by P who held a life interest in the remaining part of the settled property. It was held that there had been a termination of P's interest (which he was deemed to hold by virtue of *IHTA 1984, s 101*). [*IHTA 1984, s 101 as amended by FA 2006, Sch 20 para 26*].

From 22 March 2006 where a close company is entitled to an interest in possession in settled property, that interest in possession will also include an immediate post-death interest (IPDI) or a transitional serial interest (TSI). Where there is a disposal of rights and interests in the close company to 'a later participator' then for these purposes the later participator will be entitled to that interest in possession according to their respective rights and interests in the company. See **42** SETTLEMENTS WITH INTERESTS IN POSSESSION for full details. [*IHTA 1984, s 101 as amended by FA 2006, Sch 20 para 26*].

Note: In cases where property is held on **42** SETTLEMENTS WITH INTEREST IN POSSESSION which are settled on or after 22 March 2006, not being an IPDI or a TSI, whereby the close company acquired the interest for full consideration in money or money's worth from an individual who was beneficially entitled to it then it is not relevant property for the purposes of *IHTA 1984, s 58(1C)*. [*FA 2006, Sch 20 para 19(3)*].

Employee benefit trusts (EBT)

Property held in TRUSTS FOR EMPLOYEES (**55**) is not relevant property including property held on SETTLEMENTS WITH INTERESTS IN POSSESSION (**42**) which is settled on or after 22 March 2006 which is not an IPDI, a TSI or a disabled person's interest.

The transfer of the shares into an EBT is an exempt transfer if the value transferred is attributable to shares or securities in the company provided:

- the beneficiaries of the trust include all or most of the person's employed by holding office with the company;
- within one year the trustees hold more than half of the ordinary shares of the company having majority voting powers (there being no provision or agreement affecting this without the trustees consent);
- the trust does not permit any of the settled property to be applied for the benefit of a participator in the company or a participator in another close company that has benefited the same trust or any person connected with the previously mentioned.

[*IHTA 1984, s 28*].

The settled property is held on trusts for the benefit of the persons employed in the company and spouses or civil partners or relatives of the employees using a settlement along these lines:

THIS SETTLEMENT is made the . . . . day of . . . . BETWEEN (1) [Settlor] of [address] ('the Settlor') and (2) [trustees] of [addresses] ('the Original Trustees')

WHEREAS

The Settlor wishes to make provision for the employees of [.........] and companies in the same group (if applicable) and has transferred into the names of the Original Trustees the investments specified in the first schedule ('the Investments') to be held by the Original Trustees and their successors as trustees for the time being of this settlement on and with and subject to the following trust powers and provisions

NOW THIS DEED WITNESSES as follows:

1. Definitions and interpretation

1.1 In this settlement unless the context otherwise requires the following expressions shall have the following meanings

1.1.1 'the Trustees' means the Original Trustees . . . *continues*

1.1.2 'the Trust Fund' means the Investments . . . *continues*

1.1.3 'the Beneficiaries' means such of the following persons (not being an Excepted Person) as shall for the time being during such period of 80 years be in existence namely:

1.1.3.1 persons for the time being and from time to time employed by or holding office with a Group Company and any wife husband widow widower or child or other issue or dependant of any such employee or officer or of any deceased employee or officer

1.1.3.2 any person who at any time has been or shall have been employed by or has held or shall have held office with a Group Company and any wife husband widow widower or child or other issue or dependant of any such past employee or officer

and 'Beneficiary' means any one of the 'Beneficiaries

The Precedent continues

There are a number of important uses of an employee trust; the trust offers a non-quoted company the opportunity of creating a market for the sale and purchase of shares. These trusts can also be used to build up large shareholdings in sympathetic control so that the company will be protected against unwanted takeovers and outside interference. The employee trust will also build up good relations between staff and the employer. The trust provides for protection of workers and ex-workers in times of hardship or ill health. [*IHTA 1984, s 13*]. Sums paid to the employee benefit trust will also be deductible for corporation tax purposes when 'qualifying benefits' are provided from the scheme to employees i.e. a payment or transfer of cash or assets that attracts tax and NICs or on termination of an employee's termination of employment. [*CTA 2009, ss 1290–1296*]. Therefore special care should be taken in the wording of the deed so that the funds are 'for the sole purpose' or 'with the dominant intention of' their being potential emoluments. See *Dextra Accessories Ltd and Others v MacDonald* CA [2004] STC 339; HL [2005] UKHL 47 and *Sempra Metals Ltd v HMRC* CA [2008] STC SCD 1062. See also the disguised remuneration provisions of *FA 2011, Sch 2*.

In order to qualify for favoured treatment an employee trust must satisfy the conditions set out in *IHTA 1984, s 86* and the necessity that all or most of the employees must be within a class of potential beneficiaries (see above). If the trust falls outside *IHTA 1984, s 28* (or *ss 13, 86*) then contributions to the trust may be a transfer of value. If *IHTA 1984, s 86* does not apply then the trust will be subject to a ten-year anniversary charge and an exit charge when capital is distributed. An exit charge will in certain circumstances arise under *IHTA 1984, s 72*.

Sometimes the EBT does not hold more than 50% of the shares in the employing company and therefore the exemption will not apply. [*IHTA 1984, s 28(2)*]. However, there are a number of options in that within the year the trustees may be able to purchase the sufficient quantity of shares from a third party but whether the other party is going to agree to this is probably dependent on a number of factors.

Inheritance tax charges in relation to employee trusts

Revenue and Customs Brief 18/11 issued on 4 April 2011 confirmed views previously expressed by HMRC in its Brief 61/09 concerning inheritance tax charges in respect of employee benefit trusts. Where a close company makes a transfer of value (*IHTA 1984, s 3*) to an employee benefit trust an inheritance tax charge arises under *IHTA 1984, s 94* unless, broadly, the disposition:

- is not a transfer of value under *IHTA 1984, ss 10* (dispositions not intended to confer gratuitous benefit), *12* (dispositions allowable in computing profits for corporation tax) or *13* (dispositions by close companies for benefit of employees);
- is eligible for other relief.

Where there is a transfer of value it is apportioned between the individual participators according to their respective rights and interest in the company immediately before the contribution to the Employee benefit trust is made. There is an immediate charge of 20% on the value transferred (the contribution) in excess of the participator's unused nil rate band.The liability for the charge to inheritance tax that arises under *IHTA 1984, s 94* is the company's or, so far as the tax remains unpaid, the participator's (*IHTA 1984, s 202*).

In relation to the possible application of *IHTA 1984, s 10*, HMRC considers that it will not apply if there is the slightest possibility of gratuitous intent at the date the contribution is made. Furthermore, To meet the terms of *s 10* the transaction must either:

- have been made at arm's length between persons not connected with each other (as defined in *IHTA 1984, s 270*);
- was such as might be expected to be made in a transaction at arm's length between persons not connected with each other.

An employee benefit trust is a discretionary trust and to satisfy the conditions of *IHTA 1984, s 86* the trustees' discretion must remain unfettered. Given that the potential beneficiaries under an employee benefit trust normally include the participators themselves; the employees or former employees; and/or the wives, husbands, civil partners, widows, widowers, surviving civil partners and children and step-children under the age of 18 of such employees and former employees HMRC is of the view that it will normally be difficult to show that the conditions of *IHTA 1984, s 10* are met. See however the decision in *Postlethwaite's Executors v HMRC* [2007] STC (SCD) 83 in which, contrary to the foregoing view of HMRC, it was held that a transfer by a small company set up by an engineer to an employer financed retirement benefit scheme for his benefit was within *IHTA 1984, s 10* as dispositions not intended to confer gratuitous benefit.

In relation to the possible application of *IHTA 1984, s 12*, HMRC considers that relief under this section cannot be given provisionally while waiting to see whether the contribution will become allowable for corporation tax purposes; and is only available to the extent that a deduction is allowable to the company for the tax year in which the contribution is made.

In relation to the possible application of *IHTA 1984, s 13*, this exclusion does not apply where (amongst other things) the contributions by the Close Company are made to an employee benefit trust that does not satisfy *s 86*, and the participators in the company and any person connected with them are not excluded from benefit under the terms of the Employee Benefit Trust and so *s 13(2)* applies.

Relief from inheritance tax may, however, be available where the value transferred is attributable to relevant business property. The relevant requirements must however be satisfied, so that the business must not be an excluded one, for example a company the business of which consists wholly or mainly of making or holding investments and the value of the relevant business property transferred must not be attributable to any excepted assets.

12

Connected Persons

Simon's Taxes. See **C2.110, I3.142.**

Other Sources. Foster, Parts C1.42 and F2; HMRC Customer Guide to Inheritance Tax; IHTM04442.

[*IHTA 1984, s 270; TCGA 1992, s 286; FA 2005, s 103; ITA 2007, ss 993, 994, Sch 1 para 411*]

Introduction

[12.1] For many tax purposes, certain persons are treated as being so closely involved with each other that either they must be viewed as the same person or transactions between them must be treated differently from transactions 'at arm's length'. Any question of whether a person is connected with another is determined for the purposes of *IHTA 1984*, as it is for the purposes of capital gains tax, by *TCGA 1992, s 286 as amended by The Tax and Civil Partnership Regs 2005, SI 2005/3229, Reg 121* but with modification to the meaning of 'relative', 'settlement', 'settlor' and 'trustee'. [*ITA 2007, ss 993, 994*].

Relatives for the purposes of the IHT definition of connected persons include uncles, aunts, nephews and nieces, unlike the equivalent definition for capital gains tax purposes.

The meanings of 'settlement', 'settlor', and 'trustee' have the same meanings as in the IHT legislation, although in practical terms this meaning will normally coincide with that applicable for capital gains tax purposes.

Individuals

[12.2] An individual is connected with his spouse or civil partner, or with relatives (including their spouses) of his or of his spouse or civil partner. It appears that a widow or widower is no longer a spouse (*Vestey's Exors and Vestey v CIR* HL 1949, 31 TC 1). Spouses divorced by decree nisi remain connected persons until the decree is made absolute (*Aspden v Hildesley* Ch D 1981, 55 TC 609). See definition of relative in **12.6** below. [*ITA 2007, s 993(2)*].

Settlements

[12.3] **A trustee of a settlement**, in his capacity as such, is connected with:

(a) the settlor (see **12.8** below) if an individual; and
(b) any person connected with the settlor; and
(c) a body corporate connected with the settlement (see **12.8** below).

HMRC has confirmed (a) above applies as regards the time when a settlement is created and property first transferred to it. On the death of the settlor, neither (a) nor (b) apply (former Inland Revenue Tax Bulletin February 1993 p 56). [*ITA 2007, s 993(3)*].

Partner

[12.4] **A partner** is connected with any person with whom he is in partnership and with the spouse/civil partner or a relative of that person, except in relation to acquisitions and disposals of partnership assets pursuant to bona fide commercial arrangements. In the case of a civil partnership recognised under the *Civil Partnership Act 2004* from 5 December 2005 the individuals in such a union will be treated as 'connected persons' as they will be close relatives of each other.

Company

[12.5] **A company is connected with another company** if:

(a) the same person controls both, or
(b) one is controlled by a person [A] who has control of the other in conjunction with persons connected with him [A], or
(c) a person [A] controls one company and persons connected with him [A] control the other, or
(d) the same group of two or more persons control both, or
(e) a group of two or more persons has control of each company and the groups can be regarded as the same by treating one or more members of either group as replaced by a person with whom he is connected.

[*ITA 2007, s 993(5)*].

A company is connected with another person if that person (either alone or with persons connected with him) has control of it.

[*ITA 2007, s 993(6)*].

Control

[12.6] **Persons acting together to secure or exercise control of a company** are treated in relation to that company as connected with one another and with any person acting on the directions of any of them to secure or exercise such control. Control may be 'exercised' passively, see *Floor v Davis* HL 1979, 52 TC 609.

[*ITA 2007, s 993(7)*].

'*Relative*' means brother, sister, ancestor or lineal descendant, uncle, aunt, nephew and niece. In the circumstances regarding the taxation of 'pre-owned' assets within *FA 2004, s 84, Sch 15* 'relative' shall, as well as the definition of 'relative' in *ITA 2007, s 993(2), Sch 1 para 411* (formerly *ICTA 1988, s 839*), be extended to include uncle, aunt, nephew and niece. See **22.1** GIFTS WITH RESERVATION. [*ICTA 1988, s 839; TCGA 1992, s 286(8); IHTA 1984, s 270; FA 2004, Sch 15 para 2; The Tax and Civil Partnership Regs 2005, SI 2005/3229, Reg 121; ITA 2007, s 993(2), Sch 1 para 411*].

'*Company*' includes any body corporate or unincorporated association but does not include a partnership. [*TCGA 1992, s 288(1); ITA 2007, s 994(1)*].

'*Settlement*' and '*settlor*' are defined in *IHTA 1984, ss 43, 44* (see **41.6** SETTLEMENTS — GENERAL).

'*A body corporate connected with the settlement*' is a close company (or one which would be close if resident in the UK), the participators in which include the trustees of the settlement, or a company controlled by such a close company etc. 'Control' is as defined in *ITA 2007, s 995(1)–(3)* (formerly *ICTA 1988, s 840*), i.e. the power of a person by shareholding or voting power (whether directly or through another company), or under Articles of Association or other regulating documents, to secure that the company's affairs are conducted according to his wishes. See also *Walding and Others (Executors of Walding, deceased) v CIR* [1996] STC 13 and **6.4** BUSINESS PROPERTY; TAX CASES (**58**). [*ICTA 1988, s 682A(2)*].

Application

[12.7] Persons acting together to secure or exercise control of a company are treated in relation to that company as connected with one another and with any person acting on the directions of any of them to secure or exercise such control. Control may be 'exercised' passively, see *Floor v Davis* HL 1979, 52 TC 609.

Circumstances where the connected persons rules apply for IHT are relatively limited compared to the wider significance of the rules for capital gains tax purposes.

For the purposes of the exclusion for dispositions which are not intended to confer gratuitous benefit, it must be shown that the transaction concerned was at arm's length between persons not connected with each other, or such as might be expected between such persons. [*IHTA 1984, s 10*]. See **51.2**.

The relief for dispositions by close companies for the benefit of employees contains a condition that the trusts must not permit the settled property to be applied for the benefit of a person who is connected with a participator in the company, past or present [*IHTA 1984, s 13*]. A similar exclusion applies for the purposes of the relief for gifts by individuals on employee trusts. [*IHTA 1984, s 28*]. See **55.4** and **55.5**.

There is a charge where a transaction between trustees of an interest in possession settlement and a person who is, or is connected with, persons having certain interests under the settlement. [*IHTA 1984, s 52(3)*]. See **42.10**.

For the purposes of the excepted assets rules for business property relief, an asset is not to be treated as used wholly or mainly for the purposes of a business at any time when it was used wholly or mainly for the personal benefit of the transferor or of a person connected with him. [*IHTA 1984, s 112(6)*]. See 6.7.

13

Deeds of Variation and Disclaimers

Cross-reference. See **52.15** TRANSFERS ON DEATH.

Simon's Taxes. See **I4.411–I4.423, I5.254, I12.412.**

Other Sources. Foster, Part D4; HMRC IHT Newsletter, August 2002, April 2004, August 2004 and April 2006; HMRC Customer Guide to Inheritance Tax; IHTM35011.

Disclaimers and Variations

[13.1] A disposition by a deceased person (by will, on an intestacy or otherwise) may be disclaimed or varied after the death by a deed executed by the person who benefits under the disposition. The deed is effectively a lifetime gift by the legatee but, if the following conditions are met, the disclaimer or variation is treated for inheritance tax purposes as if made by the deceased, and any disclaimed benefit is treated as if never conferred, nor is the disclaimer or variation treated as a transfer of value. [*IHTA 1984, ss 17(a), 142(1)*].

Example 1

A dies in December 2010 leaving his estate of £354,000 to his wife absolutely. His wife, having an index-linked widow's pension and other assets of her own, agreed with her sons, B and C, that they could benefit from the estate to the extent of the nil rate band in the sum of £325,000 in equal shares, i.e. £162,500 each. As this is a variation after 31 July 2002 a separate election/statement is not required and instead it is sufficient for the instrument itself to state that a variation is to have effect for inheritance tax purposes only where additional tax is due. For variations before 1 August 2002 a deed of variation should be duly executed, and an election made under *IHTA 1984, s 142(2)*.

A had made no chargeable transfers before his death.

	£
Exempt transfer to widow	29,000
Transfer to B	162,500
Transfer to C	162,500

	£325,000
IHT payable	Nil

Notes to the example

(A) If A's widow died five years later when her estate was valued at, say, £354,000, IHT payable would be £11,600 (assuming the £325,000 nil rate band is in force). If no instrument including a variation had been made on A's death and his widow's estate was, as a result, £679,000 (i.e. £325,000 going to the sons now added to £354,000 in her estate in five years), the IHT payable on her death would have been £141,600. However, the introduction of the transferability of the nil rate band now results in the personal representatives of the widow's estate being entitled to claim the late husband's nil rate band which would be up to £325,000 ensuring that the total estate of the widow is covered by the two nil rate bands. The instrument has in this case increased the IHT liability by £11,600 but has ensured that the sons received their £162,500 five years earlier than would have been the case if the widow had retained her late husband's property until her death. See Note (B) below. [*IHTA 1984, s 8A; FA 2006, s 155; FA 2008, s 10, Sch 4 para* 2].

(B) In a case as above where no instrument is effected A's estate would have been added to that of his wife and, say through judicious investment, had increased to £340,000 making a total estate on the wife's death of £694,000, then A's transferable nil rate band with that of his wife would have resulted in IHT of £17,600. The nil rate band utilised by effecting the variation in favour of the sons utilised the whole of the £325,000 at the date of A's death. If no variation had been made and the nil rate band was £325,000 at the date of death of the wife, then this is the potential claimable amount. [*IHTA 1984, s 8A(3); FA 2008, s 10, Sch 4 para* 2].

(C) It may be appropriate in a case where the widow or widower might remarry to use the nil rate band discretionary trust by the use of a deed of variation so that the assets subject to the deed are secured outside of the survivor's estate. In this case, both the sons benefit from the father's estate subject to their mother not having a depleted income.

Disclaimers

[13.2] A disclaimer of an interest in the estate of a deceased person must:

(a) be made in writing within two years of the death.

(b) not be made for any consideration in money or money's worth, except the making, in respect of another of the deceased's dispositions, of another disclaimer or variation which is treated as made by the deceased. See IHTM35100. Therefore costs in drawing up and effecting the disclaimer should not be met by the recipient out of non-estate assets.

[*IHTA 1984, s 142(1)(3)*].

A similar provision relating to a disclaimer of an interest in settled property is not subject to the two year time limit, even though the settlement may be created by will, however it remains the case for both this provision and for disclaimers of an interest in an estate that any disclaimer must be valid as a matter of general law. This requires that no benefit should have been taken from the interest.

[*IHTA 1984, s 93*].

THIS DEED OF DISCLAIMER is made by. . . . . of. . . . .
("Mr A")

WHEREAS

(A) [. . . . .] died on . . . . ("the Testator")

(B) The Testator left a will dated . . . . ("the Will")

By clause 3(1) of the Will the Testator left Mr A a pecuniary legacy of ten thousand pounds (£10,000) ("the Legacy")

Mr A. wishes to disclaim the Legacy

NOW THIS DEED WITNESSES as follows:

Mr A disclaims the Legacy

Mr A confirms that he has accepted or received no benefit from the Legacy

EXECUTED AS A DEED on . . . . 2010.

SIGNED as a deed and delivered)
by [Mr A] in the presence)
of:)

Notes to the Precedent

(A) The deed should be unilateral. The personal representative should not be a party.
(B) There is no need (or reason) to recite details of the grant of probate if it has already been obtained, or to endorse a memorandum on the disclaimer subsequently if it has not.
(C) A minor cannot make a disclaimer without a court order. The disclaimer may also have adverse consequences such as grossing up in cases of a residuary estate being partially exempt or where BPR or APR is adversely affected.
(D) The precedent assumes that Mr A is not a residuary beneficiary, as the disclaimed legacy will fall into residue.
(E) No elections are required; *ss 62(6)* and *142(1)* have automatic effect.
(F) No stamp is required.

Variations

[13.3] Variations are treated as follows:

(a) The variation must be made in writing, by any of the persons who benefit or would benefit from the dispositions, within two years of the death.

(b) For variations where the death of the deceased occurred on or after 6 April 2012, and where the variation is to any extent in favour of a charity or charitable trust, it is a requirement that the charity or charitable trustees must be notified of the existence of the variation.

(c) For instruments dated after 31 July 2002 it is no longer necessary for an election to be made and notified to HMRC. Instead the instrument itself should contain a statement as to the variation. Where the variation results in additional tax being payable, any of the persons in (b)(i) or (ii) above shall, within six months after the day on which the instrument is made, deliver a copy of it to the Board of HM Revenue and Customs and notify them of the additional tax that is due. [*IHTA 1984, s 218A; FA 2002, s 120(2)*]. The penalty for not complying with *s 245A(1A)* is an amount not exceeding £100 and a further penalty of £60 for every day after the day on which the failure was declared by the court or Special Commissioners and up until the day before the day on which the requirements are complied with. In addition to the preceding penalty under *s 245A(1A)* a further penalty can arise where a disposition on death is varied by the beneficiaries and gives rise to an additional tax IHT liability. In these circumstances where there is a continuing failure to deliver an instrument varying a disposition and notification of additional tax payable within 18 months after the day on which the instrument is made, a penalty of up to £3,000 may be charged. No penalty arises under any of the above provisions where there is 'reasonable excuse' for the failure unless the failure is not remedied without unreasonable delay after the excuse has ceased. Also see **36.12** PENALTIES. [*IHTA 1984, s 245A(1A)(1B)(5); FA 2002, s 120(3); FA 2004, s 295(3)*].

(d) The variation must not be made for any consideration in money or money's worth, except the making, in respect of another of the deceased's dispositions, of another variation or disclaimer which is treated as made by the deceased. See, however, IHTM35100 which states: 'The bar against consideration relates only to extraneous consideration and will not prevent a rearrangement of assets within the will'. In a recent case the residue of a will was left to the surviving spouse but subject to a substantial legacy to a son from a previous marriage. The stepson renounced his legacy. Had the renunciation been tax-effective, it would have increased the spouse-exempt portion of the estate, and reduced the overall IHT borne by the estate. The proceeds of the estate were paid to the widow in cash. Three days later she made a cash gift to her stepson of £1 million. HMRC reviewed documents and considered that the variation of the estate and the subsequent payment to the stepson were related. The widow and the stepson contended that the cash payment was made as a separate gift — to set him up in business. The Commissioners decided that the disclaimer was made for consideration, and therefore *IHTA 1984, s 142(1)* did not apply. See *Mrs M Lau (W Lau's executor) v HMRC* [2009] STC SCD 352 Sp C 740. See also Note (D) in Example in **4.18** AGRICULTURAL PROPERTY.

[*IHTA 1984, s 142(1)–(3) as amended by FA 2002, s 120(1)*].

General conditions

[13.4] Although *IHTA 1984, s 142* does not require the execution of a deed for the alteration of dispositions taking effect on death, but simply an instrument in writing, the use of a deed is considered prudent. (Law Society's Gazette 18 December 1991) (See IHTM35021.)

HMRC have also specified certain conditions which they consider must be satisfied before an instrument of variation can come within *IHTA 1984, s 142.*

(i) The instrument must clearly indicate the dispositions that are the subject of it, and vary their destinations as laid down in the will, or the law of intestacy, or otherwise. It is not necessary that the instrument should purport to vary the will or intestacy provisions themselves: it is sufficient if the instrument identifies the disposition to be varied and varies its destination.

Deed of Variation in intestacy

THIS DEED OF VARIATION dated . . . . 2010 . . . . is made between:

(1) 'the Administrators' . . . . [Names]. . . . . [Addresses]. . . . .

(2) 'the Personal Representatives' [of, say, the widow/widower (*see note (A) below in **Notes to the Deed***)]

(3) 'the substituted Beneficiary' . . . . [Name]. . . . . [Address]. . . . .

WHEREAS

1.1 XY ('the Deceased') died intestate on . . . . [Date] . . . . and Letters of Administration of his estate were granted to the Administrators by the Principal . . . . [Name]. . . . . District Probate Registry on . . . . [Date]. . . . .

1.2 AB (the widow/widower of the deceased) was entitled to the whole of the deceased's estate.

1.3 AB died on . . . . (2009). . . . . and a grant of representation was made to the Personal Representatives by the Principal . . . . [Name]. . . . . District Probate Registry on . . . . [date].

(4) The Personal Representatives and the substituted Beneficiary:

2.1 agree that the provisions of the Schedule shall be construed as if they constituted the deceased's will and his/her estate shall be administered accordingly;

2.2 direct the Administrators to distribute the estate of the deceased in accordance with the provisions of the Schedule.

(5) The parties elect for [section 142 of the Inheritance Tax Act 1984] and [section 62 of the Taxation of Chargeable Gains Act 1992] as amended by Finance Act 2002, section 120 and/or section 52 to apply to this deed.

(6) It is certified that this instrument falls within category M in the schedule to the Stamp Duty (Exempt Instruments) Regulations 1987.

SCHEDULE

Signed as a Deed by the Administrators in the presence of . . . . [Name] . . . .

. . . . [Address] . . . .

Signed as a Deed by the Personal Representatives in the presence of. . . . . [Name] . . . .

. . . . [Address] . . . .

Signed as a Deed by the substituted Beneficiary in the presence of . . . . [Name] . . . .

. . . . [Address] . . . .

Notes to the Deed

(i) It will not necessarily be the case that the widow/widower will be entitled to the whole estate (see **52.21** TRANSFERS ON DEATH) and therefore references to widow/ widower of the deceased would be replaced by the 'original beneficiary' and the 'substituted beneficiary'.

(ii) If a residuary beneficiary benefits under an intestacy but wishes to make a complete disclaimer then he/she needs clearly to disclaim both the residuary gift and the resulting entitlement under intestacy.

(ii) Where there is more than one variation in relation to the same will or intestacy, HMRC consider that an election validly made is irrevocable and that an instrument will not fall within *IHTA 1984, s 142* if it *further* redirects any item (or part of any item) that has already been redirected by an earlier instrument. (Law Society's Gazette 22 May 1985). This has been confirmed by the decision in the case of *Russell and Another v CIR* Ch D, [1988] STC 195. However, in *Lake v Lake and others* Ch D, [1989] STC 865 an originating summons was sought for rectification of an original deed of variation where HMRC had claimed that a later deed entered into was inoperative following *Russell* above. The order for rectification was granted as it was shown that the original deed did not carry out the intentions of the parties concerned. See also in this connection *Matthews v Martin and others* Ch D 1990, [1991] BTC 8048 where an order for rectification was granted as the original deed did not reflect the agreement reached between the parties because of errors in the preparation of the draft for execution. See also *Wills v Gibbs and Others* [2007] unreported but summarised at **58** TAX CASES.

HMRC Inheritance Tax have confirmed that they do not regard a deed as having been made for a consideration in money's worth where it is entered into solely to avoid or compromise a claim under the *Inheritance (Provision for Family and Dependants) Act 1975* (Tolley's Practical Tax 1984, p 112). See also Note (D) in Example in **4.18** AGRICULTURAL PROPERTY.

HMRC Inheritance Tax have also made it clear that under *s 142(1)(a)* the words 'or otherwise' can apply to the automatic inheritance of a deceased owner's interest in jointly held assets by the surviving joint owner(s) (Inland Revenue Tax Bulletin, October 1995, p 254). HMRC Inheritance Tax have stated that there has been confusion in this area suggesting that the surviving joint owner could not vary the inheritance in such circumstances and HMRC give the example below.

Example 2

A family home is owned by mother and son as beneficial joint tenants and, on the mother's death, her interest is passed by survivorship to the son who then becomes the sole owner of the property. The son could vary his inheritance of his mother's interest by redirecting it to his children and this would enable the half share of the property to skip one generation on transfer.

Where a variation to which the above provisions apply results in property being held in trust for a person for a period of not more than two years after the death, the disposition which takes place at the end of that period is treated as if it had taken place at the beginning of that period, but any distribution or application of property occurring in that period is unaffected (i.e. will be chargeable to inheritance tax under the provisions relating to settled property). In Scotland, property which is subject to a proper liferent is deemed to be held in trust for the liferenter. [*IHTA 1984, s 142(4)(7)*]. See also *Soutter's Executry v CIR* [2002] STC SCD 385 Sp C 325 where a woman (S) died in November 1999 and the value of her estate was less than the IHT threshold. She owned a house, in which she lived with a friend (G). Under her will, she gave G the right to live in the house, rent free. G died in November 2000. In an attempt to reduce the IHT due on G's death, S's executors and G's executors purported to execute a deed of variation of S's estate, under *IHTA 1984, s 142*, removing the provision whereby G could live in the house rent free. The former Inland Revenue issued a notice of determination that the purported deed of variation was ineffective because the deed of variation was not a disposition of property and had no effect. S's executors appealed. The Special Commissioner dismissed the appeal, observing that 'the executors of a liferentrix have nothing they can vary'. G's executors 'had neither right, title or interest to any liferent'. They 'could not have continued to receive the liferent so they had nothing to give up or vary. The liferent was not and could not be assigned to them . . . a purported assignation of an expired liferent has no reality'. Some commentators suggest that the view that there was nothing to vary is incorrect and there is conceptually no difference between the position where a beneficiary has spent a gift or sold a gifted asset before the execution of a variation, which would be allowed, and the case in point. See Taxation Magazine, 22 May 2003, p 197. See also HMRC IHT Newsletter, December 2001 at http://www.hmrc.gov.uk/cto/newsletter.htm.

The above provisions regarding disclaimers and variations apply whether or not the administration of the estate is complete or the property concerned has been distributed in accordance with the original dispositions. They apply to 'property comprised in a person's estate' immediately before his death which term includes 20 EXCLUDED PROPERTY but not any settled property in which the deceased had only an interest in possession nor property to which he was treated as entitled under the provisions relating to 22 GIFTS WITH RESERVATION. [*IHTA 1984, s 142(5)(6); FA 1986, Sch 19 para 24*].

Example 3

Assume H dies in June 2011, leaving £300,000 all to his wife W, whose estate is valued at £250,000. H had already made PETs a few years previously to his two children amounting to £175,000. W marries J, a widower with no children, in December 2010. J dies in July 2011 leaving his estate of £325,000 to W. J has not made any previous transfers. W then dies in May 2012 leaving her entire estate among her children. W's personal representatives are entitled to claim half H's nil rate band as he had used up half in respect of the PETs within the seven years prior to his death. This would entitle W's personal representatives to claim £162,500 (i.e. 50% × £325,000) as well as her own full nil rate band of £325,000. W's personal representatives also may claim the transferable nil rate band of J in an amount of 100% resulting in an amount of £325,000. However, the personal representatives can only claim a maximum of £325,000 from either or both previous deceased spouses. Therefore it is more beneficial to claim the transferable nil rate band of J of £325,000 and effect a deed of variation benefiting the two children within the two-year time limit in respect of H's assets transferred to his wife on his death in June 2011. The variation must be made in writing, by any of the persons who benefit or would benefit from the dispositions, within two years of the death, i.e. by June 2013. The variation results in additional tax being payable, the personal representatives shall, within six months after the day on which the instrument is made, deliver a copy of it to the Board of HM Revenue and Customs and notify them of the additional tax that is due. [*IHTA 1984, s 8A(5)(6); FA 2008, s 10, Sch 4 para 2*]. Without the deed of variation the estate of W would have had an IHT liability of £90,000 (i.e. £250,000 + £300,000 (H's portion) + £325,000 (J's portion) = £875,000 – 650,000 × 40%) whereas if the variation was made in respect of H's assets the position would be as follows:

	£
W's estate	250,000
J's estate portion	325,000
Total	575,000
Less assumed Nil rate bands 2011/12	(575,000)
Chargeable	£Nil
IHT payable	Nil

	£
H's estate	300,000
PETs failed	175,000
Total	475,000
Less Nil rate band 2011/12	(325,000)
Chargeable	£150,000
IHT payable	£60,000

THIS DEED OF VARIATION is made. . . . . 2010.

BETWEEN

1.	"the Wife's Executors"	Namely. . . . . and . . . . both. . . . . solicitors of . . . .
2.	"the Husband's Executors"	Namely. . . . . and . . . . both. . . . . solicitors of . . . .
3.	"the Children"	Namely: (1). . . . . of . . . . (2). . . . . of . . . . (3). . . . . of . . . .

WHEREAS

(A) H ("the Husband") late of. . . . . died on. . . . .

(B) The Husband's Executors are the executors appointed under his will ("the Will") probate to which was granted by the Leeds District Probate Registry on. . . . .

(C) In his will the Husband left his entire estate to the Wife

(D) W ("the Wife") late of. . . . . died on. . . . .

(E) The Wife's Executors are the executors appointed under her will dated . . . . and who will be applying for Probate a memorandum of which will be endorsed on this deed

(F) The Children are the residuary beneficiaries entitled between them to the entire estate of the Wife.

(G) The parties wish to vary the dispositions of the Husband's estate as follows

(H) Such variation will leave the estate of the Wife solvent and capable of answering all debts taxes liabilities and testamentary expenses

NOW THIS DEED WITNESSES

(1) The Will shall be deemed to read and always to have read as if in it the Husband had left (subject to tax) a pecuniary legacy of one hundred and fifty thousand pounds (£150,000) to each of the Children

(2) It is certified that this instrument falls within category L in the schedule to the Stamp Duty (Exempt Instruments) Regulations 1987.

(3) The parties elect for [section 142 of the Inheritance Tax Act 1984] and [section 62 of the Taxation of Chargeable Gains Act 1992] as amended by section 120 and/or section 52 of the Finance Act 2002 to apply to this deed.

EXECUTED AS A DEED on the day and year first above written

SIGNED etc.

Notes to the example

(A) The recital that the second estate will still be left solvent is considered extremely important.

(B) Often the executors of H and W will be identical. They should be listed as two separate parties. There is no difficulty in the executors being parties twice to the deed in distinct capacities (see *Rowley, Holmes & Co v Barber* [1977] 1 All ER 801). This would probably be the case here and as the children may be the executors even though they will have a liability in respect of the variation of H's estate, they will benefit from the fact that there is no IHT liability in respect of W's estate (which includes J's assets).

(C) In the past a Stamp Duty certificate would have been included. It was not necessarily required as invariably there was no element of gift. The fact that category M originally mentioned deeds of variation did not mean that category M actually applied to all deeds of variation. The bulk of deeds of variation had an underlying element of gift and therefore were ordinarily stamped at category L. Prior to 1 December 2003 all instruments of variation were either liable to Stamp Duty, or certified as exempt from Stamp Duty under the categories L or M in *Stamp Duty (Exempt Instruments) Regulations 1987, SI 1987/597*. From 1 December 2003, any instrument involving a land transaction falls within the new Stamp Duty Land Tax (SDLT) regime and does not need stamping. [*FA 2003, s 125*]. An instrument of variation that varies the devolution of land only, requires no certificate of exemption to be attached from 1 December 2003 onwards. Category M exemption certificate is only attached where an instrument of variation alters the destination of stocks and shares or marketable securities, e.g. where stocks and shares are left by the deceased in his will to the spouse and there is a variation of the will to take advantage of the nil rate band so as to benefit chargeable beneficiaries.

(D) The two tax elections would have been needed to be made if the death occurred before 1 August 2002, see **13.3**. However, it may not be applicable for both elections to be made as in the case of capital gains, for example, there may be assets with CGT losses to take into account or gains which may be covered by the annual CGT exemption, currently £10,100. And also from 1 August 2002 notification to the Board will be required only if additional tax is payable as a result of the variation.

(E) Where it is not practicable for all the beneficiaries of W's estate whose entitlements in practical terms are being varied, to join in the deed, perhaps because they are numerous and geographically diverse, it ought to suffice for the executors in the second estate to get clear authorities from each beneficiary to enter into the deed and then simply to recite that they are duly authorised and directed by all of those relevantly entitled to benefit under the will to enter into the variation.

No specific provision has been included to deal with the income position.

(F) Income tax has not been addressed in this precedent.

(G) The question arises whether the variation may be ineffective with regard to H's assets within W's estate, but this will only be the case where, say, W was the life tenant in settled property under H's will and whilst she would be capable of disposing of her life interest during her lifetime that life interest is deemed incapable of being disposed of after her death. HMRC Inheritance Tax suggest that 'in the real world' the interest ceases to exist on death and therefore there is nothing to vary with regard to W's estate. Clearly, a variation in these circumstances on the terms of J's will becoming immediately known should have been made during

W's lifetime. However, as this is not a case of settled property with a life interest being redirected then the problem does not arise. See http://www.hmrc.gov.uk/cto/newsletter.htm for issues of December 2001 and April/May 2002. See also *Soutter's Executry v CIR* [2002] STC SCD 385 Sp C 325.

Case law

The case of *Marshall v Kerr* HL, [1994] STC 638 concerned the effects on what is now *TCGA 1992, s 87* (overseas resident trusts) on what is now *TCGA 1992, s 62(6)* (see Tolley's Capital Gains Tax 2010–11 under Death). Under this last provision, it is possible to vary or disclaim dispositions of the deceased so that, for capital gains tax purposes, a variation or disclaimer is ignored as a disposal and a variation is treated as made by the deceased and a disclaimed benefit is treated as never having been conferred. It was held that the person executing the variation was the settlor of the chose in action which comprised the property disposed of under the variation and there was nothing in the deeming provisions of *TCGA 1992, s 62(6)* which required any assumption to the contrary; see now the provisions of *TCGA 1992, s 68C*. The decision that the person making the variation was the settlor of the property varied is of no application to inheritance tax since the deeming provisions of *IHTA 1984, s 142* are by reference to 'this Act' (i.e. *IHTA 1984*) whereas the relevant deeming provisions of *TCGA 1992, s 62* are by reference to 'this section'. On this view, confirmed by the former Inland Revenue Tax Bulletin February 1995, p 195, a variation or disclaimer would therefore for all inheritance tax purposes be deemed to be made by the deceased (e.g. for deciding whether settled property is **20.2** EXCLUDED PROPERTY).

Under Scots law there are certain circumstances in which a residuary legatee can make a partial disclaimer. Where this is possible HMRC accepts that *IHTA 1984, s 142* applies (see also E18 at **25** HMRC STATEMENTS OF PRACTICE). The same treatment may apply to partial disclaimers made under English law since they are thought to be valid where the part disclaimed is not onerous and either the legacy concerned is a pecuniary one or the will states expressly or by implication that partial disclaimers can be made (Tolley's Practical Tax 1994, pp 31 and 56).

See **52.15** TRANSFERS ON DEATH for other alterations of dispositions on death which are not transfers of value. For waiver of loans to be effected by deed, see **19.1** ESTATE.

Planning

[13.5] Under *FA 2004, s 84, Sch 15 para 16* relating to 'Pre-owned assets' provides that under *IHTA 1984, s 17* where beneficiaries of a deceased's estate agree between themselves to vary the will or the intestacy provisions then any party to the variation is not to be taxed as a former owner by reason of having had an interest under the original will or intestacy provisions. There was some doubt expressed whether the wording of *FA 2004, s 84, Sch 15 para 16* protected a widow/widower from a charge where an interest in possession in a house is taken but subsequently that interest in possession is terminated and occupation still continues. HMRC have confirmed in an exchange of correspondence with the CIOT that such situations will be excluded from charge:

> . . . all instruments of variation to which section 142(1) IHTA 1984 applies will come within the protection afforded by paragraph 16 of Schedule 15.

As an election may be made within two years of the death under *IHTA 1984, s 17* this gives a period of grace with no charge arising in respect of rental value of the property or chattels in question where these are enjoyed by a 'relative' within *ITA 2007, ss 993, 994, Sch 1 para 411* (formerly *ICTA 1988, s 839*) including uncle, aunt, nephew, niece, settlement, settlor and trustee. This applies from 6 April 2005 and consequently the two-year period of grace mentioned above would only fully apply from deaths on or after that date. [*FA 2004, Sch 15 para* 2].

IHT/CGT charge on share transfers

The situation may arise where one spouse/civil partner may transfer shares to another spouse/civil partner on a nil gain/nil loss basis and the transferee spouse/civil partner dies sometime later leaving those same shares to the surviving spouse/civil partner with the attaching increased probate value unencumbered by the burden of an historic acquisition price, saving a substantial CGT charge and enjoying the benefit of the inter-spousal/civil partnership transfer exemption under *IHTA 1984, s 18*. However, if the transferee spouse/civil partner dies within days/weeks of the gift and the shares pass back by survivorship to the original donor then for transfer purposes the date of acquisition is the date of death and the surviving spouse's/civil partner's acquisition falls within the 30 days matching period for share disposals. [*TCGA 1992, s 106A(5)*]. This may give rise to a substantial CGT liability in the donor spouse's disposal computation. See example below.

Example 4

Wife W acquired 1,000 shares in Dido Ltd in June 1987 for £90,000. W gives H 1,000 shares on 1 August 2010. H then dies on 30 August 2010 leaving his estate to W. The shares are valued at that time to be £342,000 and are left to his wife along with all his other assets. The inter spouse exemption rules out any charge under the excluded property provisions of *IHTA 1984, s 18* but under the matching CGT rules for shares the disposal on 1 August must be matched with the acquisition at the date of death on 30 August thereby negating any probate value uplift. Had H died one day later the shares would have been uplifted from the original cost of £90,000 (indexation no longer applying) to £342,000 with the opportunity for W to sell at that uplifted base value with little or no CGT.

In order to rectify this problem a deed of variation might be entered into by the parties; the deed of variation alters the late spouse's (H) will to create an interest in possession trust for the surviving spouse (W) enabling the trustees to pay capital to the surviving spouse. The deed of variation must be made before the shares are sold and within two years of the date of death. The result is that, even if the shares have been transferred to the surviving spouse, they will be treated as being acquired by the trustees at the value on death of the transferee spouse (H). [*TCGA 1992, s 62(1)*]. Subsequently the trustees make a capital appointment of the transfer of the shares to the surviving spouse (W) who acquires the shares at market value at the date of appointment and will not have reacquired them within 30 days of having given them to the late spouse thereby avoiding the matching rules. If the value of the shares has increased in the period between the date of death and appointment this may be covered by the annual CGT exemption or unused personal losses or there may be a loss to carry forward arising out of the appointment from the trust depending on the rise or fall in the market for those shares.

Rearrangement in contradiction of Testator's wishes

The beneficiaries of a will may decide amongst themselves to rearrange the distribution of the estate to effect different inheritance tax consequences by the use of a deed of variation or a disclaimer or by application to the Court either under the *Inheritance (Provision for Family and Dependants) Act 1975* or if they are *sui juris* under the *Variation of Trusts Act 1958*. See also Note (A) in the Example below. In this latter case the Court's consent which is embodied in a Court Order must be made within two years. In the case of *Goulding and Another v James and Another* [1997] 2 All ER 239 the rearrangement of the beneficial interests to take advantage of tax planning schemes was successful despite the testatrix's previous intentions that the assets should devolve to the beneficiaries in another way. Such was the rearrangement that not only did it rearrange the division of the assets in contradiction of the testatrix's wishes but that there was also the subsidiary insertion of a tax planning scheme for the management of the funds. Note that in *Glowacki's Personal Representatives v HMRC* [2008] STC SCD 188 Sp C 631 the Commissioner held that *IHTA 1984, s 142* 'cannot operate to remove property from a person's estate so that it is no longer part of the estate subject to the deemed transfer of value on death under *s 4*. What *s 142* must vary is the destination of the estate on its deemed transfer under *s 4*'.

Legacy to charity

In a Special Commissioners case a deed of variation redirecting a legacy to a charity was claimed as a gift by the original beneficiary eligible for gift aid relief for income tax purposes because the *FA 1990, s 25(2)(a)(e)* provisions for relief were met—this was disputed by the Inspector of Taxes. Also the transfer of value arising from the deed of variation was exempt from inheritance tax to the extent that the value transferred was attributable to property which is given to charities. [*IHTA 1984, s 23(1)*]. In this particular case the legacy of £20,000 to the charity, who had renounced probate and the deceased's son had applied for a Grant of Letters of Administration, was payable out of the property bequeathed to the son, W. The terms of the will were that the residue was to be held in trust for the son, W. By effecting the deed of variation and reducing the inheritance tax by £8,000 (i.e. £20,000 @ 40%) the residue of the estate was £8,000 more than it would have been had the gift to the charity been made without taking advantage of *IHTA 1984, s 142*. As sole residuary beneficiary W ultimately benefited from the inheritance tax saving notwithstanding that the residue available to W had been reduced by £12,000. The charity's position remained unaffected in that it claimed repayment of tax from HMRC of £6,666.67 being the tax withheld at basic rate on the gift although the charity's appeal against the former Inland Revenue's assessment to recover this amount was dismissed. W therefore was by the timeous election under *s 142* able to redirect a legacy to the charity claiming gift aid relief for income tax purposes and relief for charitable donations under *IHTA 1984, s 23*. It is thought that if it can be arranged for the inheritance tax to accrue to a third party, or to be added to the gift to the charity, the scheme should succeed. See *St Dunstans v Major* [1997] STC SCD 212 Sp C 127 and **10.3** CHARITIES.

Breach of duty

On another matter, the fact that a solicitor failed to advise a testatrix of the possibility of executing a deed of arrangement under *s 142* and, on the testatrix's death, advising her residuary beneficiaries of the contents of the will in time for them to effect an election under that section; it was held by the court not to be a breach of duty in not advising the testatrix about the tax avoidance schemes of another estate and also the executor owed no duty to inform a legatee that there was a prospective legacy. Accordingly in this case there was no obligation on the executor to advise of the possibility of tax mitigation by way of *IHTA 1984, s 142*. However, a duty of care to an intended beneficiary is clear from Lord Nolan's dictum in *White v Jones* [1995] 1 All ER 691 and this might extend to advising a beneficiary of circumstances that might jeopardise a claim being submitted under *s 142* (see *Cancer Research Campaign v Ernest Brown & Co*, Ch D [1997] STC 1425).

In drawing up an Instrument of Variation it should be distinguished whether the interest is an absolute one or a life interest only. In the case of an absolute interest passed on to the survivor who in turn dies the property passed on subsists in the donee's estate and it is possible for those inheriting on the second death to redirect the estate of the first person to die provided the second death is within two years of the first death. See http://www.hmrc.gov.uk/cto/newsletter.htm, April 2006, p 2. Contrast this with the position where the survivor is given a life interest in property on the first death; that interest expires on the death of the life tenant and there is no property capable of disposition. Therefore where there is a life tenancy comprising part of an estate and that person dies, then as the variation is made after the death of the life tenant, at that time there is no interest in existence and hence no opportunity to redirect. In such a case a variation to assign a life interest might be considered. See *Soutter's Executry v CIR* [2002] STC SCD 385 Sp C 325 above and example below.

Example 5

H dies on 31 August 2009 leaving an estate comprising farmland to his widow for life and thereafter to his two adult sons if they survive her, with substitution provisions in favour of grandchildren (those in existence being minors). The estate is non-chargeable because of the inter-spousal exemption but there is a potential problem that if the widow dies in excess of two years after the death of the husband there can be no variation of the husband's estate. The widow can vary her life interest in favour of her sons to ensure that they benefit from any available APR. The widow's personal representatives will in due course be able to claim some or the entire transferable nil rate band of H which is unutilised.

THIS DEED OF VARIATION is made. . . . . 2010.
BETWEEN

1.	"the Mother"	Namely. . . . . . . of. . . . .
2.	"the Sons"	Namely. . . . . of. . . . . . .
		Namely. . . . . of. . . . . . .
3.	"the Executors"	Namely:
		(1). . . . . of . . . .
		(2). . . . . of . . . .
		(3). . . . . of . . . .

WHEREAS

(A) . . . . of. . . . . ('the father') died on . . . . [2009]

(B) The Father's will dated . . . . ('the Will') appointed Executors to be executors and trustees of his estate.

(C) The Executors obtained probate of the Will from the [. . . . .] District Probate Registry on . . . . [2009]

(D) Under the Will the Mother is by Clause 3 entitled to the net income of the residuary estate for the remainder of her life ('her Life Interest')

(E) The property detailed in the schedule ('the Property') is comprised of the residuary estate of the Testator

(F) The Mother wishes to vary the dispositions of the Will as follows:

NOW THIS DEED WITNESSES

(1) The Will shall be deemed to read and always to have read (so far as on account of the contingent remainders such is possible) as if the Property has been left (subject to tax) to the sons as tenants in common in equal shares absolutely

(2) In furtherance of clause 1 the Mother assigns to the Sons her Life Interest to the extent of the Property (and no more) to hold the same unto themselves as tenants in common in equal shares absolutely

(3) The parties elect for [section 142 of the Inheritance Tax Act 1984] and [section 62 of the Taxation of Chargeable Gains Act 1992] as amended by Finance Act 2002, section 120 and/or section 52 to apply to this deed.

EXECUTED AS A DEED on the day and year first above written

the Schedule

. . . . and . . . . being

end of the Schedule

SIGNED etc.

Notes to the example

(A) On account of the substitutional provisions a full *Saunders v Vautier* 4 Beav 115 variation to deem the land direct to the sons is not possible as the consents of the minors and unborns are unavailable. It should be remembered that where any potential beneficiaries are minors, or are otherwise *sui juris*, it will be necessary for any variation to be approved on their behalf by the courts. This could include unborn children if the wording of the will is wide-ranging. Even though HMRC will normally accept that a woman who is aged over 55 is past child-bearing age this is not necessarily true in practice. [*Variation of Trusts Act 1958; Trusts (Scotland) Act 1961*].

(B) Pending the mother's death title to the land would remain in the trustees unless some arrangement were reached between the trustees and the sons to transfer title on a protected basis.

14

Determinations and Appeals

Cross-reference. See 3 ADMINISTRATION AND COLLECTION.

Simon's Taxes. See **A3.7, A5.3, A5.6, I11.301–I11.315, I11.373.**

Other Sources. Foster, Part L3; IHTM37000.

Introduction

[14.1] From 1 April 2009 appeals reforms came into effect covering both direct and indirect taxes of which IHT is categorised as direct are conceived by the Ministry of Justice under the auspices of the *Tribunals, Courts and Enforcement Act 2007*. The General Commissioners and Special Commissioners were abolished with effect from 1 April 2009 — *Tribunals, Courts and Enforcement Act 2007, Sch 23, Pt 1; Tribunals, Courts and Enforcement Act 2007 (Commencement No 6 and Transitional Provisions) Order 2008, SI 2008/2696*. Time limits which had already started will continue to run and all appeals made on and after 1 April 2009 will be to the Tribunals Service (see below). Cases remitted by a court on or after 1 April 2009 will also be remitted to the Tribunals Service.

First-tier Tax Tribunal

In June 2012 Sir Jeremy Sullivan was appointed Senior President of Tribunals which includes the Tax Chamber of the Tribunals Service and has its own judiciary, Rules of Procedure and a new location for processing direct tax appeals. It is independent of HMRC, who previously controlled listing and other aspects of case management in the former General Commissioners system, which many outside observers have always doubted was sufficiently distanced from HMRC. This new Central Processing Centre (CPC) for direct tax appeals is located at Tribunals Service, Tax, 2nd Floor, 54 Hagley Road, Birmingham B16 8PE in the Tribunals Service Pathfinder Administrative Support Centre, where specialist tax appeals work will be dealt with by dedicated tax appeals staff. There will be a network of 130 hearing centres across the country and the facility for additional hired venues. In cases of Complex hearings there will be limited locations for hearings.

It is expected that the main differences that users will see will be that appeal notices will be sent directly to the Tribunals Service by the appellant rather than to HMRC, there will be four procedural tracks depending on the complexity of the appeal and there will be a new costs regime.

Upper Tribunal

Members of the judiciary will work at the CPC in order to give judicial direction where required and manage cases appropriately. There will also be two full-time, tax-dedicated registrars at the CPC, who will carry out quasi-judicial functions, e.g. categorise cases received at the CPC into tracks, identify tax cases which are complex (and therefore eligible to enter the costs regime) and bring these to the attention of the judiciary for a decision; liaise with the Upper Tribunal regarding those rare cases which start at that court, or which appeal to it from the First-tier Tribunal.

The route of appeal from the First-tier will be to the Upper Tribunal, which is a superior court of record similar to the High Court. Appeal to the Upper Tribunal will be on a point of law only, and with permission of the First-tier or the Upper Tribunal. The exception to this will be those extremely rare cases which start in the Upper Tribunal, where onward appeals will be to the Court of Appeal or the Court of Sessions in Scotland.

Tribunal Procedure Committee (TPC)

The Tribunal Procedure Committee (TPC) have set out a number of rules that govern the operation of the Tribunal system as well as specific rules for the area of taxation. Invariably many appeals including most IHT appeals against HMRC decisions will be, in the first instance, to the First-tier Tribunal. The initial appeal against a decision by HMRC will have been to them within 30 days of their decision and then failed to agree or asked for a review (*The Tribunal Procedure (First-tier Tribunal)(Tax Chamber) Rules 2009, SI 2009/273, rules 25 and 26*). The review will be made by someone else in the HMRC's Business Unit apart from the initial caseworker. A decision will normally be made, after considering representations, within 45 days or some longer period as agreed between the parties. In cases where the appeal was made before 1 April 2009 and the review option is exercised before 1 April 2010 then the review period is 90 days and not 45 days subject to a longer period by agreement. Having exhausted these options an appeal is being made against the decision by the HMRC it will be made in writing to the Tax Tribunal situated in Birmingham within 30 days of receiving the reviewing officer's decision letter. The Tax Tribunal will then manage the case by liaising with the parties to the dispute. See Appeal to First-tier Tribunal form below. [*IHTA 1984, s 223A–I; Transfer of Tribunal Functions and Revenue and Customs Appeals Order 2009, SI 2009/56, paras 116, 117*].

Tribunals Service
Tax

Notice of Appeal

Appeal Reference Number - For Tribunals Service use only:

This form should be used to make or notify an appeal to the Tax Chamber of the First-tier Tribunal against decisions made by Her Majesty's Revenue and Customs (HMRC).

Please read the guidance attached to this form before completing the Notice of Appeal. Further Information on appealing is contained in our leaflets "Making an appeal" and "At your hearing". These leaflets can be downloaded from our website www.tribunals.gov.uk and are also available in hard copy upon request by telephoning 0845 223 8080.

1. Appellant's details

Title or company or organisation	
First Name	
Surname	
Address (including postcode)	
Daytime Telephone Number	
Email Address	
National Insurance Number	
Tax Reference Number e.g. VAT registration number, corporation tax reference (if applicable)	
Nature of Appellant's Business (indirect tax only)	

2. Appellant's representative's details (if applicable)

Name of organisation or business (if applicable)	
Contact name	
Address (including postcode)	
Telephone Number	
Email Address	
Reference	

Tribunals Service, Tax - Notice of Appeal - Ref TS-TaxAp1 (02.09) 1

3. Details of the decision(s) you are appealing

HMRC Reference Number	
Date of Decision(s)	
The amount of tax or penalty (if applicable)	

4. Applications for Hardship (Indirect Tax Appeals Only)

Applications not to pay disputed amounts pending the outcome of the appeal on grounds of hardship must be made to HMRC in the first instance.

- Have you paid the disputed tax?

  ☐ Yes ☐ No ☐ No requirement to pay

- If you are required to pay the tax but have not done so, have you applied to HMRC for their agreement that the appeal may proceed without payment?

  ☐ Yes ☐ No

- If you applied to HMRC, please tell us the status of the application:

  ☐ Granted ☐ Refused ☐ Pending HMRC decision

Please note that you will have to send us some documents – see box 10

Reasons why you think the hardship should be allowed (if applicable)

2 Tribunals Service, Tax – Notice of Appeal – Ref TS-TaxAp1 (02.09)

5. Time limit for making an appeal

Your completed appeal form should reach the Tribunals Service within the time set out in the decision(s) letter you received from HMRC. If your appeal is likely to reach us after that period, you must ask the tribunal to extend the time limit for making the appeal giving full reasons why it is late.

I request that the time for making the appeal be extended: ☐ Yes

Reasons why the appeal is made late (if applicable)

6. Grounds for appeal

Please use this box to say why you think HMRC's decision(s) is wrong giving reasons. If you are appealing against more than one decision, you must explain why you think each one is wrong.

Tribunals Service, Tax – Notice of Appeal – Form Ref (02.09) 3

7. Result

Please say below what you think the decision(s) should have been if you do not already make that clear in box 6:

8. About your requirements

If you or anyone coming to a tribunal has a disability or a particular need, please set out the details below:

9. Signature

☐ I am the Appellant ☐ I am the representative of the Appellant

Name

Signature (not required for Appeals sent by email)

Date

10. Document checklist

A copy of the HMRC decision(s) you are appealing against is enclosed with this form. ☐

A copy of any statement of reasons for that decision(s) is enclosed with this form. ☐

A copy of any hardship decision or letter to HMRC about hardship is enclosed with this form. If you are asking the Tribunal to consider hardship because HMRC have refused, tick this box to confirm that you have sent the list of supporting documents (see box 4). ☐

11. Additional information

Please email or post this completed form and any other supporting documents to:-

Email: taxappeals@tribunals.gsi.gov.uk

Address: **Tribunals Service**
Tax
2nd Floor
54 Hagley Road
Birmingham
B16 8PE

We have a series of leaflets which provide guidance on the appeals process. These leaflets are available by request or by downloading from our website at **www.tribunals.gov.uk.** If you need this form in an alternative format e.g. large font, Braille or in Welsh Language, or require hard copies of our leaflets, please telephone **0845 223 8080**. Textphone users can contact us through **Typetalk** on **18001084522380800**.

12. What will happen next?

Once we have received your completed Notice of Appeal form and associated documents, we will contact you with information on how your appeal will proceed. For further information about the next steps, please refer to our leaflets "Making an Appeal" and "At your hearing".

Tribunals Service, Tax – Notice of Appeal – Form Ref (02.09) 5

Manner of making an appeal

Once the appeal has been received by the Tax Tribunal it will be allocated to one of four case categories (*The Tribunal Procedure (First-tier Tribunal)(Tax Chamber) Rules 2009, SI 2009/273, rule 23*) i.e. default paper, basic, standard and complex. The category of default will be decided on written evidence submitted and HMRC's Statement of case and an oral hearing may be requested and any decision may be listed for hearing if the decision is not agreed. Detailed information on the default paper process is issued on form ARTG8370.

A basic appeal will involve amongst other things penalties for incorrect returns. The new penalty procedure in these circumstances is the same as for existing assessments to tax. The right of appeal to the First-tier Tribunal or Upper Tribunal against decisions by HMRC to impose a penalty or the amount of that penalty. The taxpayer who appeals against the imposition of a penalty is not required to pay any penalty before a penalty appeal has been determined. The Tribunal may substitute its own decision for that of HMRC and if it does so it may rely on the use of the special reduction for certain circumstances to which the HMRC has recourse. If the Tribunal considers the decision by HMRC on the special reduction is flawed then the Tribunal may substitute its own decision. [*FA 2009, Sch 56 paras 13–15*]. See also **36.2** PENALTIES.

Case law — Tribunal's decision

HMRC imposed penalties totalling £560 on an individual (F), for failing to submit his income tax returns for 2004/05 and 2005/06 until 2009. F appealed, contending that he had previously submitted the returns in question, and that the returns which he had filed online in 2009 had been duplicates. The tribunal observed that HMRC's records showed that they had received F's 2004/05 return in January 2006, but had returned it to F on the grounds that it was incomplete. HMRC had written to F at a farm although F had written to HMRC from a flat in a town. HMRC had failed to explain why they had continued writing to F at an address which differed from the one which he had given them in correspondence. F's evidence had 'a ring of truth about it' and HMRC had not proved that he had failed to submit the returns by the due date. See *P Frossell v HMRC* [2010] UKFTT 80, TC00392.

Hearings procedure

There is a limited exchange of papers in this category and the notification will be made at the hearing and notified in writing. Detailed information on the basic process is issued on form ARTG8350. Basic cases are listed for a relatively informal hearing within the broader Tribunals Service. The Tribunals Service will be able to arrange hearings in local hired venues, in the courts estate or arrange video conferencing on the basis of post code as given on the notice of appeal. The hearings will normally be listed for a morning (10.00am) or an afternoon session (2.00pm) in a Tribunals hearing centre, with other tax cases (Basic or default paper).

A standard appeal will cover most contentious appeal cases that do not come within the default and basic categories. It is likely that a majority of IHT appeals will come into this category. HMRC will provide a statement of case within 60 days of being notified by the Tax Tribunal. At this stage the parties then have 42 days to provide a list of papers which will be relied upon at the hearing. Decisions will normally be made in writing to the parties but may be made on the day of the hearing. Standard and Complex cases will normally require a bespoke hearing and will normally be listed for a day's hearing at least. Many will be listed within the network of hearing centres based around London (Bedford Square), Manchester and Edinburgh, though suitable venues are also available in the broader Tribunals Service. The choice of venue may be more complex in these cases, as factors such as the requirement for specialist representation have to be taken into account.

Complex cases usually involve lengthy and involved issues or large amounts of tax and are likely to be heard in the first instance by the Upper Tribunal. HMRC will provide a Statement of case within 60 days of being notified by the Tax Tribunal. At this stage the parties then have 42 days to provide a list of papers which will be relied upon at the hearing (*The Tribunal Procedure (First-tier Tribunal)(Tax Chamber) Rules 2009, SI 2009/273, rules 25 and 27*). Decisions will normally be made in writing to the parties but may be made on the day of the hearing.

As regards costs, there will be no awards in the First-tier Tribunal except where either side has acted unreasonably or the case is a complex one. Costs can be awarded in complex cases though the appellant (not HMRC) can opt out of this before the hearing. In contrast the Upper Tribunal will have a full costs regime. In a recent case an individual (H) had failed to submit tax returns, and HMRC had issued estimated assessments. Subsequently H submitted late returns showing very low income, and HMRC agreed to withdraw the assessments. H applied for costs. The First-Tier Tribunal rejected his application, holding that HMRC had not acted unreasonably. See *J Hannigan v HMRC* [2010] UKFTT 141, TC00447.

Point of law appeal

If HMRC, the appellant or another party to the proceedings think that the Tribunal's decision is wrong on a point of law, then an appeal may be made to the Upper Tribunal. At this stage, the contributions in dispute must, if that is not already the case, be paid. If the appellant is successful, the amount will be repaid. The First-tier Tribunal may initially review its own decision on receipt of an application of appeal to the Upper Tribunal (*The Tribunal Procedure (First-tier Tribunal)(Tax Chamber) Rules 2009, SI 2009/273, rule 41*) and the *Tribunals, Courts and Enforcement Act 2007, s 9*). See First-tier Application for Permission to Appeal to Upper Tribunal form below. A refusal of appeal by the First-tier tribunal must be accompanied by an explanation why and an option to have the rejection reviewed by the Upper Tribunal. Further, appeals against the Upper Tribunal decisions will be heard the Court of Appeal, the Court of Appeal in Northern Ireland or Court of Sessions in Scotland. Complex cases follow the same procedures as those for standard cases but with more directions for the appeal and ending with a special directions hearing (*The Tribunal Procedure (First-tier Tribunal)(Tax Chamber) Rules 2009, SI 2009/273, rule 27*). Costs may be awarded to the other party to the appeal where it was considered that one party had acted 'unreasonably' or the case was within the complex (*The Tribunal Procedure (First-tier Tribunal)(Tax*

Chamber) Rules 2009, SI 2009/273, rule 10). A party may opt out of the costs within 28 days of the case being categorised (*The Tribunal Procedure (First-tier Tribunal)(Tax Chamber) Rules 2009, SI 2009/273, rule 10 para 1*). Therefore in most cases that are Default paper, Basic or Standard will have no costs rule attaching.

Place of hearing appeal

There will be a network of 130 hearing centres across the country and the facility for additional private hearings. See also *TMA 1970, ss 49A–49I* inserted by *Transfer of Tribunal Functions and Revenue and Customs Appeals Order 2009, SI 2009/56, Sch 1, para 30*. Standard and Complex cases will normally require a bespoke hearing and will normally be listed for a whole day's hearing at least. Many will be listed within the network of hearing centres based around London (Bedford Square), Manchester and Edinburgh, though suitable venues are also available in the broader Tribunals Service. Telephone contact numbers are: Birmingham Tax Unit 0845 223 8080, the Upper Tribunal 020 7612 9700. The address of the Finance and Tax Chamber is the Upper Tribunal Office, Finance and Tax Chamber, 45 Bedford Square, London, WC1B 3DN.

FIRST-TIER TRIBUNAL
TAX

FIRST-TIER TRIBUNAL APPLICATION
FOR
PERMISSION TO APPEAL TO UPPER TRIBUNAL

Office stamp (date received)

This form should be used when making an application to the First-tier Tribunal for permission to appeal to the Upper Tribunal. You **must** apply to the First-tier Tribunal for permission to appeal before you make an application/appeal to the Upper Tribunal.

Please Read the guidance notes before completing the application for permission to appeal. Use black ink and complete the form in **CAPITALS** or in typewriting.
Use another sheet of paper if there is not enough space for you to say everything.
(Please put your name at the top of any additional sheets)

A Applicant's details

Appeal reference number	
Title or company or organisation	
First name	
Surname	
Address	
Telephone number	
Email address	
Do you have a representative?	☐ Yes ☐ No If yes please give your representative's details below
Name of organisation or business (if applicable)	
Contact name	
Address	
Telephone number	
Email address.	
Reference number (if any)	

Tribunals Service, Tax - Appn for Permission to Appeal First-tier Tribunal –TC April 2009

B About the First-tier Tribunal decision

Please tick the document which gives the decision against which you would like to appeal:

☐ Full written statement of reasons

☐ Notification that the statement of reasons has been amended or corrected following a review

☐ Notification that an application for the decision to be set aside has been unsuccessful

C Time limit for making a First-tier application for permission to appeal.

Your completed application for permission to appeal should reach the Tribunal Service within 56 days of the First-tier Tribunal sending you notice of the decision you would like to appeal against. If it is likely to reach us after this time you must ask the tribunal to extend the time limit for making the application giving full reasons why it is late.

I request that the time limit for making the application be extended: ☐ Yes

Reasons why the application is made late (if applicable).

Tribunals Service, Tax - Appn for Permission to Appeal First-tier Tribunal –TC April 2009

D Reasons for applying and outcome requested

Please state what **error (s) of law** you consider the tribunal has made and the result you are seeking.

If you want to say more, please use another sheet of paper

E Application for Permission to Appeal to the Upper Tribunal

I apply for permission to appeal to the Upper Tribunal

I authorise my representative named in **Part A** above to act on my behalf in all proceedings before the First-tier Tribunal.*

(* Delete if you have no representative or you are a solicitor filling in this form on behalf of a client)

Applicant's/Solicitor's signature

Date / /

After you have filled in the form please send to the tribunal office dealing with your appeal

If you need this form in an alternative format e.g. large font, Braille or in Welsh Language please telephone **0845 223 8080.** Text-phone users can contact us through **Type-talk** on **1800108452238080**

Once the Tribunals Service has received your applications it will be considered by the Tribunal Judge and you will be informed of the outcome and the next steps you have to take.

You can find out more on our web site **www.tribunals.gov.uk**

Tribunals Service, Tax - Appn for Permission to Appeal First-tier Tribunal –TC April 2009

Notice of determination

[14.2] Where it appears to the Board that a transfer of value has been made (or a claim received in respect of such a transfer) it may issue a notice in writing to any person who appears to be the transferor, the claimant or to be liable for any of the tax chargeable stating that they have determined the matters specified in the notice. The matters are all or any of:

(a) the date of the transfer;
(b) the value transferred and the value of any property to which the value transferred is wholly or partly attributable;
(c) the transferor;
(d) the tax chargeable and the persons who are liable to pay it;
(e) the amount of any payment made in excess of the tax for which a person is liable and the date from which, and the rate at which, tax or any repayment of tax overpaid carries interest; and
(f) any other matter that appears to the Board to be relevant.

This also applies to occasions on which tax is chargeable under the rules in *IHTA 1984, Pt III, Ch III* relating to **43** SETTLEMENTS: DISCRETIONARY TRUSTS AND OTHER TRUSTS OF RELEVANT PROPERTY, to events or occasions on which tax is chargeable under *IHTA 1984, s 32* or *s 32A* on conditionally exempt **33** NATIONAL HERITAGE property and to disposals of growing timber (see **57** WOODLANDS) left out of account on a previous death which gives rise to a charge under *IHTA 1984, s 126*.

The notice of determination [now review] will be based on any account or return which the Board are satisfied is correct or, otherwise, will be made according to the Board's best judgment. The notice must state the time and manner in which an appeal may be made. See *Two Settlors v CIR* [2004] STC SCD 45 Sp C 385; *Thomson (Thomson's Executor) v CIR* [2004] STC SCD 520 Sp C 429.

[*IHTA 1984, s 221(1)–(4)(6); FA 1985, Sch 26 para 5; The Transfer of Tribunal Functions and Revenue and Customs Appeals Order 2009, SI 2009/56, paras 120, 121*].

Conclusive nature of determination

[14.3] Subject to any variation agreed in writing or on appeal or later adjustments for underpaid or overpaid tax, a notice of determination is conclusive against the person on whom it is served. If it is served on the transferor and specifies the value of the transfer, or earlier transfers, it is also conclusive in respect of later transfers of value (whether or not made by the transferor) against any other person. [*IHTA 1984, s 221(5)*].

For all matters relating to the administration and collection of IHT, a notice of determination which can no longer be varied or quashed on appeal is sufficient evidence of the matters so determined. [*IHTA 1984, s 254(1)*].

Appeals against determinations

Appeal to Special Commissioners

[14.4] An appeal may be made against a notice of determination within 30 days of its service. The appeal must be in writing to the Board and must state the grounds of the appeal. See *Jacques v HMRC* [2006] STC SCD 40 Sp C 513. The Special Commissioners [now substitute Tribunal] will generally hear appeals (but see **14.5** and **14.6** below for exceptions) and their decision is final except on a point of law (but see *Edwards v Bairstow and Harrison* HL 1955, 36 TC 207 as a leading case on jurisdiction of Court on questions of fact) and they may confirm, vary or quash the determination appealed against. [*IHTA 1984, ss 222(1)(2), 224(5)*; *Transfer of Tribunal Functions and Revenue and Customs Appeals Order 2009, SI 2009/56, para 115*].

On an appeal before the Special Commissioners (see **14.8** below), they may allow the appellant to put forward any ground of appeal not specified in the notice of appeal and may take it into consideration if satisfied that the omission was not wilful or unreasonable. From 1 April 2009 if an appeal is notified to the Tribunal it must confirm the determination appealed against (or that determination as varied on a review under *s 223E*) unless the Tribunal is satisfied that it ought to be varied (or further varied) or quashed. [*IHTA 1984, s 224(4)*; *Transfer of Tribunal Functions and Revenue and Customs Appeals Order 2009, SI 2009/56, para 118*]. See IHT 14, p 21.

Appeal direct to High Court

[14.5] An appeal may be made direct to the High Court (or Court of Session in Scotland and Court of Appeal in Northern Ireland) if the appellant and the Board agree. If the Board does not agree, the High Court may, on application by the appellant, give leave for appeal direct to that Court if it is satisfied the matters to be decided are likely to be substantially confined to questions of law. [*IHTA 1984, s 222(3)(5)*]. In these circumstances, the High Court has the same powers to confirm, vary or quash a determination of the Board as the Special Commissioners would have had if the appeal had gone first to them. (*Von Ernst & Cie SA and Others v CIR* Ch D 1979, [1979] STC 478).

In *Bennett and Others v CIR* Ch D 1994, [1995] STC 54 it was stated that whilst a precondition of the grant of leave is that the appeal is substantially confined to questions of law there will be instances where the case's 'novelty or importance or otherwise' is such that it can and should proceed to the High Court in the interests of justice.

Appeal to Lands Tribunal [now part of the Upper Tribunal]

[14.6] Land valuation appeals (re land in the UK only) were determined by the Lands Tribunal and not by the Special Commissioners or the High Court. Any dispute on the value of land in an appeal to the Special Commissioners or High Court which was made on or after 27 July 1993, or had not begun to be heard before then, is referred to the Lands Tribunal. From 1 June 2009 the

Lands Tribunal has transferred to the Upper Tribunal, it is now the Lands Chamber of the Upper Tribunal but rules changes for the Lands Chamber are minimal. If and so far as the question in dispute on any appeal under this section which has been notified to the Upper Tribunal or the High Court is a question as to the value of land in the United Kingdom, the question shall be determined on a reference to the appropriate Lands Chamber. Appeal may be [notified] to the High Court, on an application made by the appellant, where the Board is satisfied that the matters to be decided on the appeal are likely to be substantially confined to questions of law and gives leave for that purpose. See *Prosser (personal representatives of Jempson deceased) v CIR* [2003] STC SCD 250 Sp C 362. Guidance on property valuations for IHT purposes may be obtained from the Royal Institution of Chartered Surveyors (RICS) in the form of their leaflet GN21. See also HMRC Tax Bulletin Issue 63 'Guidance on Property Valuations'. [*IHTA 1984, s 222(4)–(4B); FA 1993, s 200(1)(3); Transfer of Tribunal Functions and Revenue and Customs Appeals Order 2009, SI 2009/56, para 115; Transfer of Tribunal Functions (Lands Tribunal and Miscellaneous Amendment) Order 2009, SI 2009/1307, Sch 1 para 167*]. The Tribunal may be required to state a case for the Court of Appeal or the Court of Session in Scotland. [*Lands Tribunal Rules SI 1963/483*].

Prior to 27 July 1993, the question as to the value of an interest in UK land, taking into account the liability to repay a discount allowed to a purchaser under the 'right to buy' provisions of *Housing Act 1980*, was a question as to the value of land within the exclusive jurisdiction of the Lands Tribunal (*Alexander v CIR* CA, [1991] STC 112).

The address of the Lands Tribunal is at Procession House, 55 Ludgate Hill, London EC4M 7JW. DX 149065 Ludgate Hill 2.

Late appeals

[14.7] **A late appeal** may be accepted by the Board or the Special Commissioners. The Board must consent to the appeal if satisfied there was reasonable excuse for the delay and that the application was made thereafter without unreasonable delay. Otherwise it must refer the application to the Commissioners for their decision. [*IHTA 1984, s 223*].

Special Commissioners — jurisdiction and procedure

[14.8] From 1 April 2009 the original appeal proceedings from the Special Commissioners detailed within *IHTA 1984, ss 225, 225A* are abolished but detailed below are the previous rules for historical purposes. [*IHTA 1984, ss 225, 225A; Transfer of Tribunal Functions and Revenue and Customs Appeals Order 2009, SI 2009/56, para 119*].

For appeal proceedings where the notice of the hearing of the appeal is given after 31 August 1994, formal rules of procedure and jurisdiction for the Special Commissioners are introduced by statutory instrument under wide regulatory powers granted to the Lord Chancellor. These wide regulatory powers have been used to include appeals under the *Proceeds of Crime Act 2002, s 320(1)*. [*TMA 1970, ss 46A, 56B–56D; IHTA 1984, s 225A; F(No 2)A 1992, s 76, Sch 16 para 8; FA 1994, s 254; SI 1994/1811 as amended by Special Commissioners (Jurisdiction and Procedure) (Amendment) Regulations 2003, SI 2003/968*].

In preparation for a hearing rules are set down as regards the following: the listing of proceedings for hearing on the application of any party by notice served on the Clerk to the Special Commissioners (15/19 Bedford Avenue, London WC1B 3AS) Tel: 020 7612 970. [*Reg 3*]; the power of the Special Commissioner to give directions to assist in the determination of any procedural issue [*Reg 4*]; the summoning of witnesses [*Reg 5*]; the agreement of documents [*Reg 6*]; the power of the Presiding Special Commissioner to order that appeal proceedings be heard together or in succession where a common issue is involved [*Reg 7*]; the power of the Special Commissioners to direct that another party should be joined as a party in the proceedings, a preliminary hearing should be held and any proceedings should be postponed or adjourned [*Regs 8, 9, 11*]; the power of the Special Commissioners on a preliminary hearing or substantive appeal hearing to direct the delivery of relevant particulars and documents from any party to the appeal and the powers of those Commissioners or inspecting party to inspect and copy the particulars and documents so delivered [*Reg 10*]; and the adduction of expert evidence or report prepared by an assessor nominated under the *Proceeds of Crime Act 2000, s 320(2)*. [*Reg 12*].

As regards the hearing and determination of proceedings, rules are provided to cover the following matters: the constitution and sittings of a Tribunal formed by any one, two or three of the Special Commissioners [*Reg 13*]; the representation of the respondent by a barrister, advocate, solicitor or any officer of the Board and any other party to the appeal by a legally qualified person, a member of an incorporated society of accountants or, unless the Tribunal directs otherwise, any other person [*Reg 14*]; the hearing of an appeal before the Tribunal to be in public unless a party to the appeal is able to satisfy the Tribunal that the hearing should be in private and the Special Commissioner so directs [*Reg 15*]; the power of the Tribunal to decide to hear and determine proceedings if a party fails to attend or to be represented at a hearing for which notice has been given unless there is good cause, or to postpone or adjourn the hearing in the light of representations made in writing or otherwise [*Reg 16*]; and the procedure and evidence at the hearing of the appeal as regards such matters as the assessment of the truth and weight of any evidence and the appearance of witnesses [*Reg 17*]. The respondent in an appeal under *Proceeds of Crime Act 2002, s 320(2)* will be the Director of the assets Recovery Agency. See *Rose v Director of Assets Recovery Agency* [2006] STC SCD 472 Sp C 543.

A decision of the Tribunal is given by a majority of votes where it comprises two or three Special Commissioners, the Special Commissioner presiding in a Tribunal of two being entitled to a second or casting vote. A final determination of the Tribunal, whether given orally at the end of the hearing or reserved, must be recorded in a dated and signed document which must contain a statement of facts found and the reasons for the determination. A copy of the document must then be sent to each party, the date of sending it being treated as the date on which the final determination is made in the case of a reserved final determination, and must be accompanied by a notification of the provisions of *TMA 1970, SI 1994/1811* and the rules of court relating to appeals from the Special Commissioners, and of the time within which, and the manner in which, such appeals have to be made. After reserving final determination, the Tribunal can give a written decision in principle on one or more issues arising and this must contain a statement of facts and the reasons for the decision and a copy of it must be sent to each party. The making of the final determination is then adjourned until the parties agree any further questions or, failing agreement, the Tribunal decides those questions. The final determination need then only state facts and reasons insofar as these have not been dealt with already in any decision in principle given already. [*Reg 18*]. The Tribunal may review and set aside or vary the decision in principle or final determination (or both) where any party or the Clerk or any of the staff of the Special Commissioners makes an administrative error, a party failed to appear or be represented at the hearing but had good cause for such failure, or accounts or other information had been sent to the Clerk or the HMRC prior to the hearing but had not been received by the Tribunal until after the hearing. A written application for such a review stating grounds in full must be made within 14 days of the date on which the document recording the decision in principle or, as the case may be, the final determination was sent. A Tribunal proposing to review of its own motion must send notice of such a proposal to the parties within the same 14-day period. The Tribunal can determine the review by upholding the decision in principle or final determination, by substituting a new decision or determination in the same manner as in *Reg 18* above, or by ordering a rehearing. [*Reg 19*].

There are further rules relating to: the publication of reports of decisions in principle and final determinations where appropriate, but so that any report relating to an appeal heard in private is published so far as possible in a form which does not identify any of the persons whose affairs are dealt with therein [*Reg 20*]; the ordering of costs incurred by the Tribunal and, if required, the other parties against a party (including a party who has withdrawn his appeal or application) to the proceedings who has acted wholly unreasonably [*Reg 21*]; the referring of questions of values relating to land to the Lands Tribunal (see **14.6** above) by the Tribunal or, if the hearing of the appeal has not begun, by an officer of the Board [*Reg 23*]; the award of penalties (see **36** PENALTIES) against any party or person for failure to comply with Tribunal directions [*Reg 24*]; the treatment of clerical mistakes in documents recording a Tribunal direction or decision and of irregularities resulting from any failure to comply with any provision of *SI 1994/1811* itself or with any direction given by a Tribunal before a decision is reached [*Reg 25*]; the requiring of a notice under *SI 1994/1811* to be given in writing unless the Tribunal authorises the giving of an oral notice [*Reg 26*]; and the service and substituted service of documents [*Regs 27, 28*].

Case law — penalties

A former tax inspector (E) was appointed as Clerk to three divisions of the General Commissioners. In his returns, he claimed significant deductions for travelling and secretarial assistance (provided by his wife). In 2005 HMRC began an investigation into his returns, and formed the opinion that E had significantly overstated his expenses. They issued discovery assessments under *TMA, s 29* and imposed penalties under *TMA, s 95*, at the rate of 35% of the evaded tax. E appealed. the First Tier Tribunal reviewed the evidence in detail and observed that E had failed to produce documentary records and 'surprisingly, given his background, did not co-operate fully with the enquiry'. The Tribunal held that, despite E's failure to discharge 'the burden of proof on him in relation to the figures', he should be allowed a deduction of £500 p.a. for travel expenses and of £11,000 p.a. for secretarial assistance (both figures being slightly higher than those conceded by HMRC). With regard to the penalty, the Tribunal held that E had been negligent and that 'the abatement given in relation to co-operation is generous'. Accordingly the Tribunal directed that the penalty should be increased to 40% of the evaded tax. See *J Evans v HMRC* [2010] UKFTT 140, TC00446.

Reports regarding Special Commissioners' decisions

Prior to the commencement of *SI 1994/1811 as amended by Special Commissioners (Jurisdiction and Procedure) (Amendment) Regulations 2003, SI 2003/968* above, similar rules to those contained in *Regs 5, 10*, and *14* above applied. [*IHTA 1984, s 224(1)–(3); SI 1994/1813, Sch 1 para 20, Sch 2 Pt I*]. For reports obtainable regarding Special Commissioners' decisions see **3.11** ADMINISTRATION AND COLLECTION.

Appeal from determination of Special Commissioners

[14.9] Any party to an appeal, if dissatisfied in point of law with the determination of that appeal by the Special Commissioners, may appeal against that determination to the High Court (in Scotland, the Court of Session, and in NI, the Court of Appeal). See *Thorogood v CIR* Ch D [2005] All ER (D) 201; STI 920 and **58** TAX CASES. As mentioned in **14.8** above, the final determination will be accompanied by a notification of the rules of court relating to such appeals, time limits and the manner in which appeals must be made.

The High Court etc. hears and determines any question of law arising on the appeal and may reverse, affirm or amend the determination appealed against, or remit the matter to the Special Commissioners with the Court's opinion on it, or make such other order in relation to the matter as the Court thinks fit. [*IHTA 1984, s 225; SI 1994/1813, Sch 1 para 21*].

Where notice of the appeal hearing was given before 1 September 1994, similar provisions applied save that an appellant had to make a written request to the Special Commissioners within 30 days of their determination for a case to be stated and signed and pay a fee of £25. Within 30 days of the case being received, the appellant had to send it to the High Court and, no later than the time of sending it, a copy of it to every other party. [*IHTA 1984, s 225*].

Cases may be continued up to the Court of Appeal and Supreme Court under normal procedures.

Case law — stated case

An individual (J) appealed against assessments for 1995/96 and 1996/97. In February 2009 the General Commissioners dismissed his appeals, and J requested a 'stated case'. The Commissioners asked J to identify 'the question of law on which he required a case to be stated', observing that the effect of

General Commissioners (Jurisdiction and Procedure) Regulations 1994, SI 1994/1812, Reg 20(4) was that 'if the Commissioners are not satisfied that the question identified is a question of law the Commissioners may refuse to state a case'. J refused to comply with this request, contending that *Reg 20(4)* contravened the *Human Rights Act 1998*. The Commissioners therefore refused to state a case, and J applied for judicial review. The CS dismissed his application. Lord Bracadale observed that J had failed to provide any 'sensible explanation' for refusing to identify a question of law, and that 'relatively general questions of law could easily have been focused'. He specifically distinguished the 2006 decision in *Rouf (t/a The New Balaka Restaurant) v Dundee Commrs*. See *Jesner v Renfrew Commrs* [2010] CSOH 23.

'Leapfrog' procedures

[14.10] See 14.5 above for appeal direct to the High Court. It is also possible to bypass the Court of Appeal and to appeal direct from the High Court to the House of Lords in certain cases where the appeal concerns a point of law of general public importance. [*Administration of Justice Act 1969, Pt II*].

Judicial review

[14.11] A taxpayer who is dissatisfied with the exercise of administrative powers may in certain circumstances (e.g. where HMRC have exceeded or abused their powers or acted contrary to the rules of natural justice or where the Special Commissioners have acted unfairly or improperly) seek a remedy in one of the prerogative orders of mandamus, prohibition or certiorari. This is now done by way of application for judicial review under *Supreme Court Act 1981, s 31* and *Order 53* of the *Rules of the Supreme Court*. See also *Arkwright and Another (Williams' Personal Representatives) v CIR* Ch D [2004] STC 1323. The issue on an application for leave to apply for judicial review is whether there is an arguable case (*R v CIR (ex p Howmet Corporation and another)* QB, [1994] STC 413). The procedure is generally used where no other, adequate, remedy, such as a right of appeal, is available. See *R v Special Commrs (ex p Stipplechoice Ltd) (No 1)* CA 1985, [1985] STC 248 and *(No 3)* QB 1988, [1989] STC 93, *R v HMIT (ex p Kissane and Another)* QB, [1986] STC 152 and *R v CIR (ex p Goldberg)* QB 1988, 61 TC 403. There is a very long line of cases in which the courts have consistently refused applications where a matter should have been pursued through the ordinary channels as described above. See, for example, *R v Special Commrs (ex p Morey)* CA 1972, 49 TC 71; *R v Special Commrs (ex p Emery)* QB 1980, 53 TC 555; *R v Walton General Commrs (ex p Wilson)* CA, [1983] STC 464; *R v Special Commrs (ex p Esslemont)* CA, 1984 STI 312; *R v Brentford Commrs (ex p Chan)* QB 1985, 57 TC 651. See also, however, *R v HMIT and Others (ex p Lansing Bagnall Ltd)* CA 1986, 61 TC 112 for a successful application where the inspector issued a notice under a discretionary power on the footing that there was a mandatory obligation to do so, and *R v CIR (ex p J Rothschild Holdings plc)* CA 1987, 61 TC 178 where the former Inland Revenue was required to produce internal documents of a general character relating to their practice in applying a statutory provision. See, however, *R v CIR (ex p Taylor)* CA, [1988] STC 832 where an application for discovery of a document was held to be premature. In *R v Inspector of Taxes, Hull (ex p Brumfield and others)* QB 1988, 61 TC 589 the court was held to have jurisdiction to entertain an application for judicial review of a failure by the former Inland Revenue to apply an established practice not embodied in a published extra-statutory concession but this should be compared with *R v CIR (ex p Fulford-Dobson)* QB 1987, 60 TC 168 where it was held that there had been no unfair treatment by the former Inland Revenue when it failed to apply a published extra-statutory concession because it was clear from the facts of the case that it was one of tax avoidance and this was a clearly stated general circumstance (see HMRC Pamphlet IR 131 mentioned in **23** HMRC EXTRA-STATUTORY CONCESSIONS) in which concessions would not be applied. It was held that there had been no unfairness by the former Inland Revenue when it refused to assess on the basis of transactions that the applicants claimed they would have entered into had an Inland Revenue statement of practice been published earlier (*R v CIR (ex p Kaye)* QB, [1992] STC 581). A similar view was taken in *R v CIR (ex p S G Warburg & Co Ltd)* where the Revenue declined to apply a previously published practice because not only was it not clear that the taxpayer's circumstances fell within its terms but also the normal appeal procedures were available.

There was held to have been no unfairness in two cases where the former Inland Revenue resiled from assurances given by its officers as to its course of action to be taken in regard to intended transactions put to it in 'advance clearance' form by the taxpayer where the latter, having received the assurances, subsequently entered into actual transactions similar to those envisaged in the request for clearance. In order to bind HMRC to any such assurances, it would seem necessary not only to make complete, clear, correct and unqualified representations of the circumstances in a written request and subsequently enter into actual transactions on all fours with those envisaged in the request but to ensure that request is sent to the appropriate HMRC officer or office (*R v CIR (ex p MFK Underwriting Agencies Ltd & Others)* QB 1989, 62 TC 607; *Matrix-Securities Ltd v CIR* HL, [1994] STC 272). See further Revenue Tax Bulletin August 1994, p 137.

The first step is to obtain leave to apply for judicial review from the High Court. Application for leave is made ex parte to a single judge who will usually determine the application without a hearing. The Court will not grant leave unless the applicant has a sufficient interest in the matter to which the application relates. See *CIR v National Federation of Self-employed and Small Businesses Ltd* HL 1981, 55 TC 133 for what is meant by 'sufficient interest' and for discussion of availability of judicial review generally.

Time limit

[14.12] Applications must be made within three months of the date when the grounds for application arose. The Court has discretion to extend this time limit where there is good reason, subject to conditions, but is generally very reluctant to do so. Grant of leave to apply for review does not amount to a ruling that application was made in good time (*R v Tavistock Commrs (ex p Worth)* QB 1985, 59 TC 116).

Parliamentary history of legislation

[14.13] Following the decision in *Pepper v Hart* HL, [1992] STC 898, the Courts are prepared to consider the parliamentary history of legislation, or the official report of debates in Hansard, where all of the following conditions are met.

(i) Legislation is ambiguous or obscure, or leads to an absurdity.
(ii) The material relied upon consists of one or more statements by a Minister or other promoter of the Bill together if necessary with such other parliamentary material as is necessary to understand such statements and their effect.
(iii) The statements relied upon are clear.

Unfortunately the consideration of the parliamentary legislation is dependent on the legislative programme at the time of discussion and was aptly alluded to by Lord Higgins in Hansard debates, 10 May 2001, Col 2232 as follows:

> 'As I pointed out on Second Reading, the debates in another place were very heavily programmed and the discussion on this issue was rather limited.
>
> There is a particular disadvantage in this context, in view of the extent to which the courts can, as a result of *Pepper v Hart*, take into account the *travaux préparatoires* of any Bill.'

15

Diplomatic Immunity

Simon's Taxes. See I9.327.

Introduction

[15.1] Diplomatic agents (i.e. heads of mission or members of diplomatic staff) of foreign states are exempt from all duties and tax except, *inter alia*, taxes on:

(a) private immovable property situated in the UK;
(b) capital taxes on investments made in commercial undertakings in the UK; and
(c) 'estate, succession or inheritance duties' on property in the UK except on movable property which is in the UK solely due to the presence of the deceased as a member of the mission or as a member of the family of a member of the mission. [*Diplomatic Privileges Act 1964, s 2*].

Head of mission

The head of a diplomatic mission will normally supply the Foreign and Commonwealth Office with a list of the staff of the mission etc. and, once such persons have been accepted as *persona grata*, exemption from liability will apply where appropriate. See The London Diplomatic List, December 2009. Any question which arises as to whether a person is entitled to privilege or immunity is to be settled conclusively by a certificate issued by or under the authority of the Secretary of State. [*DPA 1964, s 4; ITA 2007, s 841*]. See also IHTM11270.

Diplomatic family members

Relief is extended to members of the families of diplomatic agents (provided they are not UK nationals) and members of the administrative and technical staff of the mission, together with their families (provided they are not nationals or permanent residents in the UK).

OECD treaty models

In interpreting inheritance tax and estate treaties between the UK and any other country consideration should be given as to whether the treaty was based on the OECD 1966 Estate Tax Draft Model or the OECD 1982 Estate Tax

Model. This is because when interpreting certain terms in a treaty, either based on the 1966 Model or the 1982 Model, the 1982 version had a close relationship in application terms to the 1977 OECD Income Tax Model. Commentaries on the articles will vary significantly depending on the original model that was used. In the case of diplomatic and consular officials the 1982 Model refers to them in *Art 13*, whereas the 1966 Model refers to them in *Art 14*. *Article 13* of the 1982 Model convention provides that the convention does not affect the fiscal privileges of diplomatic agents or consular officials under the general rules of international law or under *special agreements*.

Consular officers, their families and staff

[15.2] Similar provisions apply as to diplomatic agents except that the *Consular Relations Act 1968, Arts 49, 51* expressly exclude from exemption 'duties on transfers' unless on movable property belonging to a deceased and in the UK solely because of his presence as a member of the consular post etc.

A *member of a consular post* means a consular officer, a consular employee or a member of the service staff. A *consular officer* means the person charged with the duty of acting as head of a consular post and any other person entrusted with the exercise of consular functions. A *consular employee* means any person employed in the administrative or technical service of a consular post; and a *member of the service staff* means any person employed in the domestic service of the consular post. [*CRA 1968, Sch 1 para 1*].

Officials of international organisations

Officials of international organisations including representatives, members of committees or missions etc. may be specified by Order in Council as exempt from certain taxes. [*International Organisations Act 1968; Arms Control and Disarmament (Privileges and Immunities) Act 1988, s 1(2)*]. The position of **officials etc. of the European Communities** is covered by the *Protocol on the Privileges and Immunities of the European Communities 1965*. [*European Communities Act 1972*].

16

Domicile

Cross-reference. See **18** DOUBLE TAXATION RELIEF.

Simon's Taxes. See **I9.201–I9.206**.

Other Sources. Tolley's Tax Planning 2010–11; Foster, Part J2; HMRC publication HMRC6 and 17 April 2002 Treasury Budget Report; HMRC Customer Guide to Inheritance Tax; IHTM13000.

Introduction

[16.1] Chargeability to UK inheritance tax depends on where a person is domiciled or 'deemed' to be domiciled. If a person is domiciled or deemed domicile in the UK that person is liable to IHT on their worldwide assets wherever situated. Also, those individuals who are *not* domiciled in the UK are nonetheless liable to IHT on assets situated in the UK. Therefore it is important to that UK domicile status is considered as a priority. Domicile is uniquely specific to the UK whereas other countries abroad refer to residency, source and nationality or citizenship. See **16.6** below. A person must be domiciled in a single legal jurisdiction, for example either England, Scotland or Northern Ireland, or one of the states comprising the United States of America. There are a number of specific classes of UK domicile as follows:

(i) domicile of origin;
(ii) domicile of dependency;
(iii) domicile of choice; and
(iv) deemed domicile.

Every person receives at birth a *domicile of origin*. A legitimate child born in the lifetime of his or her father has the father's domicile at the time of their birth and that is determined by the father's permanent homeland; in other cases the domicile of origin is that of the mother at the time of the child's birth. A child may in certain circumstances take the domicile of the mother up until the age the age of sixteen. See **16.3** below. *Domicile of dependency* occurs where, say, a father (or mother in circumstances in **16.3** below) changes their domicile before the child has attained the age of sixteen and consequently the child's domicile changes with that of the father (or mother). *Domicile of choice* can arise where a person is sixteen or over takes up residence in a new jurisdiction with the intention of fixing his sole or chief residence there permanently or indefinitely. Strong evidence is required for a change of a person's domicile of origin to that of choice and convincing steps must be taken to show a different country has become their homeland and all ties with the UK have been severed. See *Gaines Cooper v HMRC* [2008] STC 1665 (Ch D) and the Supreme Court refused Gaines Cooper's application for leave to appeal, so the CA decision is now final. Where a domicile of choice is abandoned, the domicile of origin automatically revives.

Deemed domicile applies for UK IHT purposes where a person has been resident in the UK for 17 out of the last 20 tax years but see Key Points at **16.7** below, or, a person has been UK domiciled within the preceding three *calendar* years. This latter case is likely to apply where a person has changed their UK domicile status to one of choice but will still be within the IHT net for that period. See below and **18.1**.

In future HMRC will consider opening an enquiry where domicile could be an issue, or making a determination of Inheritance Tax in such cases, only where there is a significant risk of loss of UK tax. See Revenue & Customs Brief 34/10 at 25.1 HMRC STATEMENTS OF PRACTICE.

General case law

[16.2] A person may have only one place of domicile at any given time denoting the country or state considered his permanent home. He acquires a *domicile of origin* at birth (normally that of his father). It may be changed to a *domicile of choice*, but this must be proved by subsequent conduct. See *Re Clore (deceased) (No 2), Official Solicitor v Clore and Others* Ch D, [1984] STC 609 for a case where English domicile of origin was retained as a result of failure to establish a settled intention to reside permanently in Monaco. Actual settlement abroad is necessary as well as intention; see *Plummer v CIR* Ch D, [1987] STC 698. If a domicile of choice is established but later abandoned (by actual action, not by intention or declaration only, see *Faye v CIR* Ch D 1961, 40 TC 103) reversion to domicile of origin is automatic as recently confirmed in *Barlow Clowes International Ltd (in liquidation) and Others v Henwood* [2008] EWCA Civ 577. A case of this was *Civil Engineer v CIR* [2002] STC SCD 72 where the abandonment of a Hong Kong domicile of choice, thereby reviving a UK domicile, resulted in a chargeable transfer in respect of the setting up of a discretionary trust in the interim that relied on the taxpayer's perception that he was non–UK domiciled. See also *Anderson (Anderson's Executor) v CIR* [1997] 1998 STC SCD 43 Sp C 147 in which a domicile of choice of England in place of Scotland (origin) suggested by HMRC failed due to the insufficient persuasive elements of the abandonment of Mr Anderson's roots in Scotland. See *Allen & Hateley (executors of Johnson) v HMRC*, [2005] STC SCD 614 Sp C 481 where the Special Commissioners determined whether a person of UK origin had lost her domicile of choice in Spain by coming to reside in England in order to be cared for by a relative (domicile held not to have been lost).

Domicile is a concept of private international law and does not correspond with either residence or nationality. See *Earl of Iveagh v Revenue Commissioners* SC (RI), [1930] IR 431; *Fielden v CIR* Ch D 1965, 42 TC 501 and *CIR v Cohen* KB 1937, 21 TC 301. This last case shows how difficult it is to displace a *domicile of origin* by a *domicile of choice* but contrast *In re Lawton* Ch D 1958, 37 ATC 216. See also *In re Wallach* PDA 1949, 28 ATC 486, *Buswell v CIR* CA 1974, 49 TC 334, *Steiner v CIR* CA 1973, 49 TC 13, *CIR v Bullock* CA 1976, 51 TC 522 and *In re Furse decd., Furse v CIR* Ch D, [1980] STC 597; *A Beneficiary v CIR* [1999] STC SCD 134 Sp C 190; *Moore's Executors v CIR* [2002] Sp C 335.

Minors

[16.3] The domicile of a minor normally follows that of the person on whom he is legally dependent. Under *Domicile and Matrimonial Proceedings Act 1973, s 3* (which does not extend to Scotland), a person first becomes capable of having an independent domicile when he attains 16 or marries under that age. Under *s 4* thereof, where a child's father and mother are alive but living apart, his domicile is that of his mother if he has his home with her and has no home with his father. For Scotland, see *Family Law (Scotland) Act 2006, s 22* by which where the parents of a child are domiciled in the same country and the child has a home with a parent or a home with both of them, up to the age of 16 the child's domicile is the same as that of the parents. Otherwise the child is domiciled in the country with which he or she has the closest connection.

Married women

[16.4] Up to 31 December 1973, a woman automatically acquired the domicile of her husband on marriage. From 1 January 1974 onwards, the domicile of a married woman is to be ascertained 'by reference to the same factors as in the case of any other individual capable of having an independent domicile' except that a woman already married on that date will retain her husband's domicile until it is changed by acquisition or revival of another domicile. [*Domicile and Matrimonial Proceedings Act 1973, ss 1, 17(5)*]. A woman married before 1974 does not reacquire her domicile of origin and retains her husband's domicile unless she subsequently establishes her own domicile of choice. See *CIR v Duchess of Portland* Ch D 1981, 54 TC 648 and Form D31 of IHT 100. In the recent House of Lords decision involving a matrimonial case *Mark v Mark* HL, [2005] UKHL 42 it was decided that the legality of a wife's presence in the UK was irrelevant when considering her domicile of choice within *Domicile and Matrimonial Proceedings Act 1973, s 5(2)* and therefore it was held that it is possible for someone who is present in the UK illegally to have a domicile of choice in the UK.

Deemed domicile for IHT

[16.5] For the purposes of IHT only, an individual may be treated as domiciled in the UK at a time (the 'relevant time') when he is domiciled abroad under general law. This applies where:

(a) he was domiciled (under general law) in the UK at any time during the three years immediately preceding the relevant time; or
(b) he was resident (see below) in the UK in not less than 17 of the 20 years of assessment (i.e. years ending on 5 April) ending with the year of assessment in which the relevant time falls. See also IHT 401 question 6 on page 1; and
(c) the terms of a double tax treaty do not operate to override this rule (see below).

[*IHTA 1984, s 267(1)*].

In the circumstances regarding the taxation of 'pre-owned' assets within *FA 2004, s 84, Sch 15* 'domicile' for the purposes of the scope of the charge, includes deemed domicile within *IHTA 1984, s 267*, so that such treatment will include UK and, in some circumstances, overseas property. [*FA 2004, Sch 15 para 12*].

Example

David leaves the UK on 1 January 2008 and becomes a Dutch citizen. David moves to Brussels in Belgium during the later part of 2009 in order to avoid Dutch wealth tax. He owns a property in the Dordogne, France and owned a property in Cornwall which was given to his aged Aunt. He occupies it rent free for three months in the summer when she goes to reside in his Dordogne residence rent free for the same period, i.e. a reserved right. Neither of them pays the household bills when staying in the respective properties. He dies in a car crash in Belgium on 24 December 2010 and leaves all his assets to his brother who is resident in Spain.

The Netherlands levies estate duty on assets that pass on the death of an individual who was a Dutch resident at the moment of death, *or* who died a Dutch citizen within ten years of leaving the Netherlands i.e. 'trailing tax'. Dutch forced succession rules (legitieme portie) must also be taken into account.

Belgium levies estate duty taxes on non-resident donors if they die owning real estate situated in that jurisdiction. Belgium is party to treaties with only France and Sweden which allow Belgium to subject real property to estate duty.

France levies estate duties on immovable assets of non-residents such as real estate that pass on death. There are also forced heirship implications relevant to immovable property owned in France by non-residents.

Spain levies estate duty on a resident recipient, i.e. the beneficiary of a will if the person is resident in Spain.

United Kingdom levies inheritance tax on worldwide assets of *deemed* domiciliaries.

Summary: Although David is non-resident in France at the time of his death, France will tax the real estate i.e. the realty situated there, on the market value at the date of death. Similarly, although David is non-resident in the Netherlands the effect of the Dutch 'trailing taxes' regime which applies for a ten-year period, as detailed above, is to subject both the French and UK properties to Netherlands estate duty tax. There are no double tax treaties providing for exemption from estate duties levied on real estate. Spain will tax on the basis that the recipient i.e. David's brother is resident in Spain and not take into account the fact that David was non-resident and non-domiciled. The UK will tax David's worldwide assets (see above) and this will include the French and UK properties because he was domiciled (under general law) in the UK at any time during the three years immediately preceding the relevant time, i.e. 1 January 2008 to 24 December 2010, but this is less than three years. There is no statutory definition of 'year' and therefore in the absence of such a definition 'year' will mean a period of twelve calendar months. See *CIR v Hobhouse* [1956] 1 WLR 1393. In addition, from 6 April 2009 David will have a liability to IHT on the Cornwall property occupied by his Aunt because it was a gift of property which he now uses. David will also have a potential income tax liability under *FA 2004, Sch 15* for his use of the property for the three months in the summer of 2010 prior to his death. The property in the UK will be treated as part of his estate under *IHTA 1984, s 102* and by reason of his deemed UK domicile.

The result of the combined estate duty taxes in the UK, Netherlands, France and Spain and the possible income tax liability under former Schedule D Case VI in the UK could be that very little of the estate passes to the brother. The estate duty taxes exigible will be subject to unilateral double taxation relief where this is relevant. See *Heirs of Van-Hilten Van der Heijden v Inspecteur van der Belastingdienst/Partculieren/Ondernemingen buitenland te Heerlen* [2006] WTLR 919 (C-513/03) and **18.3** DOUBLE TAXATION RELIEF.

Exclusions

The above provisions do not apply:

(i) in determining whether exempt government securities which are in the beneficial ownership of a non-domiciled person (or are settled property to which such a person is entitled to a qualifying interest in possession) are excluded property, see **20.5** EXCLUDED PROPERTY;

(ii) in determining whether certain savings to which persons domiciled in the Channel Islands or Isle of Man are beneficially entitled are excluded property, see **20.8** EXCLUDED PROPERTY;

(iii) where the domicile of a person is determined under the terms of a double taxation agreement which related to estate duty (and CTT) and still applies for IHT purposes. The agreements concerned are currently those with France, Italy, India and Pakistan and in general the treaty override applies only in respect of the charge on death — see further **16.6** below;

(iv) in determining whether settled property which became comprised in a settlement before 10 December 1974 is excluded property, see **20.2** EXCLUDED PROPERTY; and

(v) in determining the settlor's domicile for the purposes of *IHTA 1984, s 65(8)* in relation to property which became comprised in the settlement before 10 December 1974, see **43.13** SETTLEMENTS: DISCRETIONARY TRUSTS AND OTHER TRUSTS OF RELEVANT PROPERTY.

Election to be treated as UK domiciled for IHT

An individual who is not, or has not been, domiciled in the UK, but whose spouse or civil partner is so domiciled, may, from 6 April 2013, elect to be treated as UK domiciled for IHT purposes. The purpose of making such an election is to enable the full spouse exemption to apply to transfers of value from the domiciled to the non-domiciled party.

The election may be either a '*lifetime election*' or a '*death election*'. A lifetime election is one made by a non-domiciliary who at any time on or after 6 April 2013 and during the period of seven years ending with the date of the election had a spouse or civil partner who was UK domiciled. A 'death election' is one made within two years, or such longer time as HMRC may allow, of the death on or after 6 April 2013 of a person who at any time after that date and within the seven year period ending with the death was UK domiciled but whose spouse or civil partner was not so domiciled. Both elections are irrevocable, although they cease to have effect if the person who made the election becomes non-UK resident for income tax purposes for four successive tax years after the time that the election was effective. A death election may be made by the personal representatives of a non-domiciled individual whose spouse or civil partner predeceased.

An election will not impact on the exemptions for Government securities and foreign currency bank accounts in relation to non-UK domiciled owners or trust beneficiaries (see **20.5** EXCLUDED PROPERTY), nor will it affect relief available under double tax treaties which were in force prior to 17 July 2013. An election is also ignored for the purposes of the deemed domicile provisions of *IHTA 1984, s 267* so as to prevent adverse interaction between the two sets of provisions.

There is no specified format for an election but HMRC require it to include the full name and address of the person making it, their date of birth, the date from which the election is to take effect and the full name and date of birth of the UK domiciled spouse or partner. Elections should be sent to Trusts and Estates Risk Team (Elections), Inheritance Tax, Ferrers House, Castle Meadow Road, Nottingham NG2 1BB.

Where an election has effect from a previous date, it may result in gifts made by that person since the effective date becoming chargeable transfers. In such cases the due dates for submitting an account of the transfer and for payment of tax are modified so that the date of the election is substituted for the date of the transfer.

[*IHTA 1984, ss 267ZA, 267ZB*].

UK residence before 1993/94

Residence in the UK for years of assessment before 1993/94 was determined as for income tax purposes, but without regard to any dwelling-house available in the UK for the person's use. After 1992/93, residence in the UK is determined simply as for income tax purposes, but in practice the position may be unchanged because of the amendments for 1993/94 and subsequent years made by *FA 1993, s 208(1)(4)* to *ICTA 1988, s 336* (now *ITA 2007, s 831*) for income tax purposes so as to provide that the residence status of temporary residents in the UK be decided without regard being had to the availability of the use of living accommodation in the UK. Registration and voting as an overseas elector are removed from determination of domicile for tax purposes under *IHTA 1984, s 267(1)(a)*. [*IHTA 1984, s 267; FA 1993, s 208(3)(5), Sch 23 Pt V; FA 1996, s 200; ITEPA 2003, s 722, Sch 6 paras 1, 48*].

IHT 100

An account on Form IHT 100 (old Forms IHT 100 and IHT 101 were replaced as from April 2003) is required and also when there is a transferor who is non-UK domiciled and has transferred property that is not excluded property (i.e. asset held outside the UK) then supplementary form D31 should be completed as part of the IHT 100. This form asks for details of chargeable events if the transferor is domiciled in a foreign country or if the transferor is treated as domiciled in the UK. The form does not require details of foreign assets or foreign currency bank accounts held with the main UK banks or ANZ Grindlays Bank Plc, Banque Nationale de Paris Plc, Italian International Bank Plc or Wesleyan savings Bank Plc. In addition, if the transferor was not ordinarily resident in the UK at the date of the chargeable event UK government securities that are authorised as being exempt from tax is also treated as excluded property for these purposes. Even though the Channel Islands and Isle of Man are treated as not being included in the UK, if a transferor was domiciled in one of those jurisdictions at the date of the chargeable event, War Savings Certificates, National Savings Certificates, Ulster Savings Certificates, Premium Bonds, Save As You Earn schemes and deposits with the National Savings & Investments (NS & I) are treated as excluded property.

Definition — United Kingdom

The United Kingdom comprises England, Scotland, Wales and Northern Ireland. The Channel Islands (Jersey, Guernsey, Herm, Brecqou, Jethou, Lithou (which is not inhabited), Alderney and Sark) and the Isle of Man are not included. Great Britain comprises England, Scotland and Wales only.

Foreign aspects

[16.6] The concept of *domicile* in relation to inheritance tax and estate duties is particular to the UK but other jurisdictions depend on residency, source and nationality or citizenship. For instance the UK, Ireland and Malta tax only if the non-resident is domiciled in that jurisdiction. Particularly, the UK applies inheritance tax to all dispositions by an individual domiciled in the UK but only to assets situated in the UK if he is domiciled abroad. This may be at odds with other jurisdictions that tax solely on a residency basis. Some jurisdictions tax assets located in the jurisdiction, commonly known as 'source' taxation. Invariably this includes immovable property such as realty and will also include movable property such as share certificates in companies based in that jurisdiction. Where registration of an asset is required by notarial deed in the jurisdiction this fact may also require that the asset be included as a taxable source where the non-resident owner dies. However, even though registration is a practical means of enforcement by some jurisdictions moveables may be exempt where held by non-domiciles.

Nationality and/or citizenship is an important factor in a number of jurisdictions. In jurisdictions where this is a dominant requirement tax can be applied on the basis that the deceased is a national even though that individual was non-resident at the time of death.

Double tax agreements

The concept of domicile when considered with other countries with which the UK has agreements (see **18.2** DOUBLE TAXATION RELIEF) can give rise to some disparate domicile treatment.

(a) **Ireland** (1978/1107), the definition of domicile includes the deemed domicile rules of *IHTA 1984, s 267* but introduction of the Irish capital acquisitions tax (CAT) should be referred to in terms of residence superseding domicile. [*Irish Finance Act 2000*].

(b) **India** (1956/998), the UK deemed domicile rules of *IHTA 1984, s 267* cannot be applied to the worldwide assets of someone who dies with an Indian domicile under local law.

(c) **Pakistan** (1957/1522), the UK deemed domicile rules of *IHTA 1984, s 267* cannot be applied to the worldwide assets of someone who dies domiciled in Pakistan under local law. However, the foregoing does not apply to Bangladesh.

(d) **USA** (1979/1454), where an individual does not have a permanent home in the UK or USA he is deemed to be domiciled in the country in which he has his centre of vital interests rather than the country of habitual abode.

(e) **France** (1963/1319), under *Article V(2)* where the deceased was domiciled in Great Britain the French succession duty is not applied to property situated outside of France.

(f) **Italy** (1968/304), domicile is determined under the provisions of *Article II*.

Key points

[16.7] Points to consider are as follows.

- The location of assets is key after establishing non-UK domicile status. Only UK situated assets come within chargeability and overseas assets are excluded. Table of asset locations:

Asset	**Location/situs**
Land, buildings and leases including any share in land or a building.	Where the land is physically situated.
Registered shares and securities (but see Government stocks above).	Where the shares or securities are registered or traded.
An interest in an unincorporated business or an interest in a partnership.	Where the business is carried out.
Chattels and personal possessions.	Where the item is situated at the time of the transfer or at the date of death.
Debts owed to the deceased.	Where the debtor lives at the time of transfer or on death.
Bank accounts.	Where the bank or branch holding the account is situated.

- Under *IHTA 1984, s 267(b)* the 17 year rule (see above) relates to tax years (not calendar years as in *s 267(a)*) and as a result of this an individual can become resident for these purposes before the seventeen years has expired. This will happen in cases such as where individual X came to work in the UK on 4 April 1995 (i.e. tax year 1994/95, the first year to be counted) but intends to return abroad. On 6 April 2010 (i.e. 2010/11 the seventeenth tax year by one day) he will become deemed domicile in the UK even though he has only been resident for 15 calendar years and three days. This is because the person has actually entered his seventeenth *tax* year and that is what distinguishes the rule for deemed domicile status. Clearly a file note should be made on all non-UK domiciled individuals to review the case by at least the fourteenth year of residence depending on their original date of arrival so that future residence intentions and the implications thereof can be discussed. Note, however, that pre-1975 agreements with France, Italy, India and Pakistan (see **18.2**) may preclude such adverse treatment on death although it is important to distinguish the situation from general domicile law in those countries.

- Domicile may in certain circumstances change many times during a persons life. For instance, Sven was born in Norway and takes his father's domicile of origin until his father comes to work in the UK when he is fourteen. His father changes his domicile to that of 'choice' deciding to stay permanently in the UK and therefore Sven's domicile changes to the UK because of dependency. Sven's domicile of dependency changes at 16 to a domicile of choice of the UK. When Sven gives up his domicile of choice of the UK at 18 to go abroad his original domicile of origin will revert to Norway. He will not be deemed domicile in the UK within *IHTA 1984, s 267* as he has not been within the requirement of either *s 267(1)(a)* or *(b)*.
- If a person intends to change their domicile of origin of the UK to that of a domicile of choice elsewhere there are a number of core rules regarding changes to their personal circumstances that must be adhered to as an absolute requirement. These include:
  (i) cut all ties with the UK e.g. sell UK property, close bank accounts, cancel club subscriptions, liquidate or transfer investments out of UK jurisdiction, etc;
  (ii) reinstate items at (1) above in new country;
  (iii) ensure that all friends and relatives appreciate the new choice of domicile;
  (iv) change passport to take up new citizenship in the country of choice;
  (v) make sure that visits to the UK are limited or fleeting after giving up UK domicile;
  (vi) ensure that everyday actions indicate a permanent attachment for the country of choice;
  (vii) ensure that a foreign will is drawn up and burial/cremation wishes show an attachment to the country of choice; and
  (viii) business interests in the UK are concluded.

The above matters will not be conclusive and each case will be treated on its own merits but the points above will go a long way to proving a domicile of choice. In the case of (vii) above, much is made of the burial in Switzerland of the actor Richard Burton for tax reasons rather than his beloved Wales. However, on giving up a domicile of origin in the UK there will still be a potential liability to IHT on worldwide assets for a period of three years under *IHTA 1984, s 267(1)(a)*. Also, any assets that are situated in the UK at the time of death will still be subject to IHT and therefore to avoid this point (i) above should be adhered to as a priority.

An area often overlooked is gifts to a non-domiciled spouse or civil partner. Under *IHTA 1984, s 18(2)* the spouse or civil partner gift exemption is restricted, following *FA 2013*, to the nil band amount of £325,000. Therefore where a UK domiciled spouse transfers over £325,000 to their non-UK domiciled partner or spouse on death all or part of their nil rate band of £325,000 will have to be utilised. Unfortunately, such gifts in lifetime up to the £325,000 limit do not come within the PETs regime under *IHTA 1984, s 3A* since they are fully exempt, not potentially exempt and once the £325,000 has been fully utilised it is never again reinstated as it is a lifetime allowance. However, the PETs regime will apply to lifetime gifts in excess of £325,000 and if the UK domiciled spouse survives seven years following the gift to the spouse then the gift will fall out of account within *s 3A*. Where spouses are UK domiciled and gifts are made between them and then one becomes non-UK domiciled those previous gifts will be set against the £325,000 limit and any excess will be a PET but with the possibility that there may be a charge to IHT on death if seven years have not elapsed since the original transfer. This follows from *IHTA 1984, s 18(2)* 'shall not exceed the exemption limit at the time of the transfer *less any amount* previously taken into account for the purposes of the exemption conferred by this section'. Emphasis added.

Domicile outside the United Kingdom [Form IHT 401]

HM Revenue & Customs

Domicile outside the United Kingdom

Schedule IHT401

When to use this form

Fill in this form if you have claimed that the deceased was not domiciled in the United Kingdom (UK).

Help

Please read the guidance notes on domicile in the IHT400 Notes before filling in this form. For more information or help or another copy of this form:

- go to **www.hmrc.gov.uk/inheritancetax/**
- phone our Helpline on **0845 30 20 900**
  – if calling from outside the UK, phone **+44 115 974 3009**.

Name of deceased

Date of death *DD MM YYYY*

IHT reference number (if known)

Deceased's domicile

1 Was the deceased domiciled in the UK at any time during the three years up to the date of death?

No ☐ Yes ☐

If Yes, do not complete this form, as we will regard the deceased as domiciled in the UK. You must include their entire estate in form IHT400.

2 Has the deceased's domicile been agreed for other HM Revenue & Customs purposes?

No ☐ *Go to box 6*

Yes ☐ *Go to box 3*

3 Date of the agreement *DD MM YYYY*

4 Name and address of the HM Revenue & Customs office that agreed the deceased's domicile

Postcode

5 HM Revenue & Customs reference number

Deceased's residency for tax purposes

6 Was the deceased resident in the UK for Income Tax purposes during the four tax years up to the date of death?

No ☐ Yes ☐ *If Yes, give date(s) when the deceased was treated as resident in the UK during the last 20 tax years.*

From	To	From	To

IHT401 **(Substitute)(LexisNexis)** Page 1 HMRC Approval ref: L11/08

Deceased's history

We need this information to get a full picture of the deceased's life. This will help us decide their domicile.

7 Where was the deceased born?

Town

Country

8 What was the deceased's nationality at birth?

9 What was the deceased's nationality at death?

10 On what date(s) did the deceased leave the UK to set up their main home abroad?

11 Tell us about the deceased's education and employment history

12 Give details of the deceased's visits to the UK, how long they stayed and the purpose of those visits

13 Tell us why you believe the deceased did not intend to remain in or return to the UK and provide any evidence you may have to support this

Continue on the 'Additional information' boxes on pages 15 and 16 of form IHT400 or a separate sheet, if necessary.

IHT401 Page 2

If the deceased was male, go to box 21
If the deceased was female, go to box 14

14 Was the deceased married on or before 1 January 1974?

No ☐ *Go to box 21*

Yes ☐ *Answer the following questions*

We need this information because a married woman's domicile was affected by her husband's domicile, if they were married before 1 January 1974.

15 Where was the deceased's husband born?

Town

Country

16 What was the deceased's husband's nationality at birth?

17 What is the husband's nationality? If he is deceased, what was his nationality when he died?

18 Tell us about the deceased's husband's education and employment history while she was married to him, up to and including 1 January 1974.
If she had more than one husband before this date, tell us about each husband up to and including 1 January 1974

IHT401 Page 3

Deceased's estate

19 Who will benefit from the deceased's estate under the law or Will that applies in the claimed country of domicile?

20 Are you deducting surviving spouse or civil partner exemption?

No ☐ *Go to box 24*

Yes ☐ *Give brief details of the assets the surviving spouse or civil partner will receive following the death*

21 Explain how the estate is to be distributed and how you have established this. *If you have had professional advice from someone in the deceased's country of domicile, attach a copy of this*

22 Did the deceased leave any assets outside the UK?

No ☐

Yes ☐ *Give approximate value*

£

23 Do you expect the terms of a Double Taxation Convention or Agreement to apply to any of the assets owned by the deceased?

No ☐ Yes ☐

24 Is any foreign tax to be paid on assets in the UK as a result of the deceased's death?

No ☐ Yes ☐

IHT401 Page 4

17

Double charges Reliefs

Simon's Taxes. See **I3.502, I3.513, I3.534, I3.543, I3.545, I4.163.**

Other Sources. HMRC Customer Guide to Inheritance Tax; Foster, Part C5.13.

Introduction

[17.1] Without specific relief, a double charge to IHT could arise in various circumstances, for example where a donor makes a gift to a donee who subsequently makes a gift back to the donor, and the donor dies within seven years of making the initial gift. Regulations made in 1987 (see *SI 1987/1130*) contain provisions to eliminate the potential double charge in the main circumstances which arise in practice. They work by a process of calculating the IHT chargeable on alternative bases, each one disregarding the other potentially chargeable amount, and then preserving the higher of the tax charges under the two calculations.

The circumstances covered by the Regulations

Relief from double charge is provided for in four specified cases.

(a) Where property given by a potentially exempt transfer is subsequently returned (otherwise than for full consideration) by the donee to the transferor and, as a result of the transferor's death, both that property and the potentially exempt transfer become chargeable to tax. See **17.2** below.

(b) Where property given by a transfer of value which is chargeable when made is returned (otherwise than for full consideration) by the donee to the transferor and that property is also chargeable as part of the transferor's estate on his death. See **17.3** below.

(c) Where a transfer of value is or subsequently becomes a chargeable transfer and, at the transferor's death, his estate owes to the transferee a debt which under the rules relating to such liabilities falls to be abated or disallowed in determining the value of the estate chargeable on the death. This relief is detailed at **52.11** TRANSFERS ON DEATH.

(d) Where there is a transfer by way of gift which is, or subsequently becomes, a chargeable transfer, but the gift is also caught by the reservation of benefit provisions on the death of the donor so that it is taxable twice, once as a chargeable transfer and secondly as part of the estate on death by reason of the reservation of benefit. This relief is detailed at **22.13** GIFTS WITH RESERVATION.

A fifth category of relief from double charges was introduced as part of the pre-owned assets provisions: see **17.4** below.

Potentially exempt transfers and death

[17.2] Relief from double charge to tax is given where, after 17 March 1986, an individual ('the deceased') makes a transfer of value to a person ('the transferee') which is a potentially exempt transfer that proves to be a chargeable transfer and where immediately before his death the deceased was beneficially entitled to property:

(a) which he acquired from the transferee otherwise than for full consideration in money or money's worth after making the potentially exempt transfer; *and*
(b) which was transferred to the transferee by the potentially exempt transfer or which is property directly or indirectly representing that property; *and*
(c) value attributable to which is a chargeable part of his estate on death.

Where the above conditions are fulfilled, there must be separately calculated the total tax chargeable as a consequence of the death of the deceased:

(i) disregarding so much of the value transferred by the potentially exempt transfer as is attributable to the value of property within (c) above which is included in the chargeable transfer on death; and
(ii) disregarding so much of the value of the property within (c) above which is included in the chargeable transfer on death as is attributable to property value of which is transferred by the potentially exempt transfer.

If charging the relevant property as part of the death estate under (i) above produces a higher amount of tax than would be payable if the charge on the potentially exempt transfer under (ii) was taken instead, the value transferred by the potentially exempt transfer is reduced by reference to the amount of the value of that property which is included in the chargeable transfer on death. Conversely, the potentially exempt transfer is charged if it produces the higher amount of tax with a corresponding reduction in the value of that property which is included in the chargeable estate on death. Where the amount calculated under (i) above is higher, to avoid the value of the same property entering twice into the tax calculations, this reduction applies for all IHT purposes.

Where the total tax chargeable under (i) and (ii) above is identical, calculation (i) is treated as producing a higher amount. [*FA 1986, s 104(1)(a); SI 1987/1130, Regs 4, 8*].

Example

A makes a potentially exempt transfer of £60,000 (annual exemptions having been used) to B in July 2004. In March 2006 A makes a gift of £281,000 (after annual exemptions of £3,000 × 2) into a discretionary trust and the trustees pay IHT of £1,200. He makes a further gift of £55,000 (before annual exemption for the year) to the same trust in August 2006, the trustees paying IHT of £10,400.

B dies in January 2007 and the 2004 potentially exempt transfer returns to A. A dies in May 2010. His death estate of £310,000 includes the 2004 potentially exempt transfer, returned to him in 2006, which at the time of A's death is worth £216,000. It is assumed for the purposes of this computation that tax rates and bands remain as those pertaining from 6 April 2010.

First calculation: charge the returned potentially exempt transfer in A's death estate and ignore the potentially exempt transfer made in 2004

	IHT payable
	£
July 2004	
Potentially exempt transfer £60,000 ignored	—
March 2006	
Gift £281,000	
Tax £NIL less £1,200 already paid (see note)	—
August 2006	
Gift £52,000 as top slice of £333,000	
Tax £NIL less £10,400 already paid	—
May 2010	
Death estate £310,000 as top slice of £643,000	127,200
Total tax due as a result of A's death	£127,200

Second calculation: charge the potentially exempt transfer made in 2004 and ignore the value of the returned potentially exempt transfer in A's death estate

	IHT payable
	£
July 2004	
Potentially exempt transfer £60,000	
Tax £NIL	—
March 2006	
Gift £281,000 as top slice of £341,000	
Tax £1,600 less £1,200 already paid	400
August 2006	
Gift £52,000 as top slice of £393,000	
Tax £20,800 less £10,400 already paid	10,400

May 2010	
Death estate £94,000 as top slice of £487,000	37,600
Total tax due as a result of A's death	£48,400

The first calculation gives the higher amount of tax. The potentially exempt transfer made in 2004 will be ignored, and tax on other transfers will be as in the first calculation.

Note

In the first calculation, the tax of £127,200 on death does not allow for any 39 QUICK SUCCESSION RELIEF that might be due by reference to any tax charged in connection with B's death. Such relief could reduce the tax given by the first calculation. Credit for the tax already paid on the March 2006 and August 2006 gifts is restricted to the lower of the tax already paid and the tax payable as a result of death i.e. Nil. There is no repayment of the excess.

Chargeable transfers and death

[17.3] Relief from double charge to tax is given where, after 17 March 1986 and within seven years before his death, an individual ('the deceased') makes a transfer of value to a person ('the transferee') which is a chargeable transfer and where immediately before his death the deceased was beneficially entitled to property:

(a) which he acquired from the transferee otherwise than for full consideration in money or money's worth after making the chargeable transfer; *and*

(b) which was transferred to the transferee by the chargeable transfer or which is property directly or indirectly representing that property; *and*

(c) value attributable to which is a chargeable part of his estate on death.

Where the above conditions are fulfilled, there must be separately calculated the total tax chargeable as a consequence of the death of the deceased

(i) disregarding so much of the value transferred by the lifetime chargeable transfer as is attributable to the value of property within (c) above which is included in the chargeable transfer on death; *and*

(ii) disregarding so much of the value of the property within (c) above which is included in the chargeable transfer on death as is attributable to property, value of which is transferred by the lifetime chargeable transfer.

If charging the relevant property as part of the death estate under (i) above produces a higher amount of tax than would be payable if the charge on the lifetime chargeable transfer under (ii) was taken instead, the value transferred by the lifetime chargeable transfer is reduced by reference to the amount of the value of that property which is included in the chargeable transfer on death. Conversely, the lifetime chargeable transfer is charged if it produces the higher amount of tax with a corresponding reduction in the value of that property which is included in the chargeable estate on death.

Where the higher amount is calculated under (i) above

(A) credit is available for tax already paid on the lifetime chargeable transfer which is attributable to the value disregarded under that calculation (but not exceeding the amount of tax due on death attributable to the value of the property in question); and

(B) to avoid the value of the same property entering twice into the tax calculations, the reduction applies for all IHT purposes other than a ten-year anniversary charge or a proportionate charge to tax on a discretionary settlement arising before the death of the deceased.

Where the total tax chargeable under (i) and (ii) above is identical, calculation (i) is treated as producing the higher amount. [*FA 1986, s 104(1)(d); SI 1987/1130, Regs 7, 8*].

Double charges following election into IHT under the pre-owned assets provisions

[17.4] The pre-owned assets regulations relating to income tax now include provisions to avoid a double charge to IHT where a chargeable person elects that the gift with reservation provisions apply to the relevant property. [*FA 1986, s 104(1); Charge to Income Tax by Reference to Enjoyment of Property Previously Owned Regulations 2005, SI 2005/724, Reg 6; Inheritance Tax (Double Charges Relief) Regulations 2005, SI 2005/3441, Reg 3*]. A double charge can arise where the chargeable person makes a gift of property or a debt that is a potentially exempt transfer for IHT purposes. If that same property is then liable to the income tax charge the person may decide to make an election on Form IHT500 that the property is subject to the IHT reservation of benefits rules. If that person then dies within seven years of the original gift a double charge to IHT may arise, firstly, by reason of the original transfer and secondly when the property is added back into the death estate for the purposes of the gift with reservation rules. The new provision avoids the double charge by opting for the IHT on transfer that produces the highest overall amount of IHT and thereby reduces the other transfer to nil.

Relief is given where a double charge to IHT arises in situations where arrangements are caught by the pre-owned assets income tax provisions in *FA 2004, Sch 15* which are subsequently dismantled by the individual but he/she dies within seven years. The conditions for double charge relief in these circumstances are as follows:

(a) the disposal condition or the contribution condition is met as respects the relevant property; and

(b) the deceased makes a transfer the result of which a third party becomes entitled to the benefit of a debt owed to the deceased; and

(c) before the deceased's death, any outstanding part of the debt is wholly written off, waived or released, and the write off, waiver or release is made otherwise than for full consideration in money or money's worth;

(d) further conditions apply so that:

(i) the deceased dies on or after 6 April 2005; and

(ii) on the deceased's death, the transfer of value treated as made immediately before the deceased's death included the relevant property, or any property representing that relevant property; and

(iii) as a result of the deceased's death, the transfer of value referred to in (b) above has become a chargeable transfer.

See HMRC's IHT Manual at 14701–14 for HMRC examples of how the double charge reliefs work in practice. [*Inheritance Tax (Double Charges Relief) Regulations 2005, SI 2005/3441*].

18

Double Taxation Relief

Cross-references. See **16** DOMICILE; **49.5** SITUS.

Simon's Taxes. See **I9.123, F4.1.**

Other Sources. Tolley's Tax Planning 2010–11; Foster, Part J5; IR Leaflet IHT 18; HMRC Customer Guide to Inheritance Tax; IHTM27000.

Introduction

[18.1] Where inheritance tax is chargeable in the UK, and tax of a similar character or which is chargeable on or by reference to death or gifts inter vivos is also charged by another country (an 'overseas territory') on the same property, relief may be available:

(a) under the specific terms of a double tax agreement between the UK and that other country, or
(b) under the unilateral double tax relief provisions contained in the UK legislation. [*IHTA 1984, ss 158(1), 159(1)*].

A Green Paper was issued regarding the proposed EU Succession Directive entitled 'Wills and Succession in Europe' which required responses by September 2005. The European Parliament was still debating the 'Green Paper on Succession and Wills', COM (2005) 65 published in March 2005 and further clarifications were debated from the beginning of June 2006. In October 2007 the House of Lords (European Union Committee) debated (HL Paper 12, published 4 December 2007) the Green Paper with a view to addressing some of the concerns that had arisen and this was published on 24 March 2010. Much debate concerned the phrase 'habitual residence' in terms of domicile and also forced heirship implications of many European countries.

European Union Committee Sixth Report on European Succession in March 2010 stated:

> 'The concepts of habitual residence and domicile are less certain than nationality but impose a more consistent connection between the succession and the law to be applied to it. They are not only different from each other but can have a different meaning depending on the jurisdiction in which they are being used. In broad terms habitual residence connotes the place, based on past experience, where an individual usually resides. Domicile is a more stringent test and takes into account, to a greater

extent than the test of habitual residence, the intention of the person concerned as to his or her permanent home. The concept of domicile as it applies in England and Wales is outlined in Box 2. The distinction can become critical where a person is seconded to another Member State to work. In those circumstances the domicile is more likely to remain that of the home Member State whilst the habitual residence is more likely to be that of the Member State of secondment.'

See *Heirs of Van-Hilten Van der Heijden v Inspecteur van der Belastingdienst/Partculieren/Ondernemingen buitenland te Heerlen* [2006] WTLR 919 (Case: C-513/03) and example at **16.5** DOMICILE.

Double tax agreements

[18.2] An agreement with another country is made by Order in Council after a draft has been approved by resolution by the House of Commons and may give retrospective relief.

The Board is authorised to exchange with the other government any information required provided the Board or its authorised officer is satisfied as regards confidentiality. This authority has been further enhanced by changes in the *FA 2003* which relax the obligations of secrecy and insert changes to the wording governing the exchange of information by changing the wording *in IHTA 1984, ss 158(1A), 220A* from 'necessary for the carrying out of' to 'foreseeably relevant to the administration or enforcement of'. [*IHTA 1984, ss 158(1A), 220A inserted by FA 2000, s 147(1) and as amended by FA 2003, ss 197, 198*].

Domicile not affected by *IHTA 1984, s 267*

Any provisions relating to estate duty in an existing agreement are extended to capital transfer tax and inheritance tax payable on a death (but not on lifetime transfers). Provisions in such agreements relating to the determination of domicile are not affected by *IHTA 1984, s 267* which treats certain persons as domiciled in the UK when they are domiciled abroad under the general law, see **16.5** DOMICILE. [*IHTA 1984, s 158*].

The existing estate duty agreements which now apply to inheritance tax on death are (country and statutory instrument year and number).

France (1963/1319), **India** (1956/998), **Italy** (1968/304), **Pakistan** (1957/1522) and **Switzerland** (1957/426) (see also 1994/3214 below).

The existing capital transfer tax agreements which now apply to inheritance tax on chargeable lifetime transfers and death are (country and statutory instrument year and number).

Ireland (1978/1107), **South Africa** (1979/576), **Sweden** (1981/840 with amending protocol 1989/986) and **USA** (1979/1454).

Inheritance tax agreements entered into in respect of chargeable transfers on death are (country and statutory instrument year and number).

Switzerland (1994/3214), **Netherlands** (1980/706 with amending protocol 1996/730).

The specific provisions of the particular agreement concerned must be studied carefully. For instance, the agreement with France does not extend to Northern Ireland, the Pakistan convention remains in force despite the abolition of the death duties law in 1978 and the agreement with India remains in force despite the abolition of Indian estate duty law in 1985, see **16.6** DOMICILE. See HMRC Tax Bulletin, June 2001.

UK and Netherlands Protocol

See also UK and Netherlands Protocol which entered into force on 3 June 1996 amending the Convention signed in The Hague on 11 December 1979. (*Treaty Series No 73 (1996) Cmnd 3336*).

HMRC have stated:

> 'As both countries may have the right to tax the assets, these agreements usually have rules that say which country may tax the different assets. We will not give up our right to tax any assets until we have evidence from the foreign authority that the assets have been included for tax in the foreign country and tax has been paid. If you feel that certain assets should not be taxed in the UK because an agreement says so, you should let us have evidence that foreign tax has been paid on the assets as soon as you can.'

Unilateral relief by UK

[18.3] Where relief is not available under a double tax agreement, relief may be obtained by means of a credit for the overseas tax against the UK inheritance tax. This unilateral relief is also applied if greater relief is obtained than under an agreement. The relief is as follows.

(a) Where the property is situated in the overseas territory and not in the UK, the credit is the whole amount of the overseas tax.

Example 1

Where property is situated in an overseas territory only

A, domiciled in the UK, owns a holiday home abroad valued at £396,000 which he gives to his son in July 2010. He is liable to local gifts tax of, say, £8,830. He has made no previous transfers and does not use the home again at any time before his death in February 2015. Assumes that nil rate band in force at that time is £325,000. See **40** RATES OF TAX.

	£	£
Market value of holiday home		396,000
Annual exemption 2010/11	(3,000)	
Annual exemption 2009/10	(3,000)	
		(6,000)
Chargeable transfer		£390,000

IHT payable at 60% of full rates by son (death between 4 and 5 years after gift) £65,000 × 40% × 60%	15,600
Unilateral relief for foreign tax	(8,830)
IHT borne	£6,770

Note to the example

(A) If the overseas tax suffered exceeded the UK liability before relief, there would be no IHT payable but the excess would not be repayable.

Example 2

Where property is situated in both the UK and an overseas territory

M, domiciled in the UK, owns company shares which are regarded as situated both in the UK and country X under the rules of the respective countries. On M's death in June 2010 the shares pass to M's son S. The UK IHT amounts to £5,000 before unilateral relief. The equivalent tax liability arising in country X amounts to £2,000.

Apply the formula

$$\frac{A}{A+B} \times C$$

shown below

The unilateral relief available is

$$\frac{5{,}000}{5{,}000+2{,}000} \times £2{,}000 = £1{,}429$$

IHT payable = £5,000 – £1,429 = £3,571

(b) Where the property is:
(i) situated neither in the UK nor the overseas territory; or
(ii) situated both in the UK and the overseas territory,
the credit is in accordance with the following formula.

$$\frac{A}{A+B} \times C$$

where:
A = the amount of inheritance tax;
B = the overseas tax; and
C = whichever of A or B is the smaller.

(c) Where tax is imposed in two or more overseas territories in respect of property which is:
(i) situated neither in the UK nor in any of those territories; or
(ii) is situated in the UK and in each of those territories,
the formula above applies but:
A = the amount of inheritance tax;
B = the aggregate of the overseas tax imposed in each of those territories; and

C = the aggregate of all, except the largest, of A and the overseas tax imposed in each of them.

Where credit is allowed under (a) above or under the terms of a double tax agreement in respect of overseas tax imposed in one overseas territory, any credit under (b) above in respect of overseas tax imposed in another is calculated as if the inheritance tax at A in the formula were reduced by that credit. Similarly, where in the case of an overseas territory within (b) or (c) above, credit is allowed against the overseas tax for tax charged in a territory in which the property is situated, the overseas tax at B in the formula is treated as reduced by the credit.

References to tax imposed in an overseas territory are references to tax chargeable under the laws of that territory and paid by the person liable to pay the tax. [*IHTA 1984, s 159*].

Example 3

Where tax is imposed in two or more overseas territories on property situated in the UK and each of those territories

Assume the facts in the example in 2 above except that a third country imposes a tax liability on the death as the shares are regarded as also situated in that country.

UK IHT before unilateral relief	£5,000
Tax in country X	£2,000
Tax in country Y	£400

Apply the formula

$$\frac{A}{A+B} \times C$$

shown above

The unilateral relief available is

$$\frac{5{,}000}{5{,}000+2{,}000+400} \times (2{,}000+400) = £1{,}622$$

IHT payable £5,000 – £1,622 = £3,378

19

Estate

Cross-references. See **29** LAND for estates of land; **41** SETTLEMENTS — GENERAL, **42** SETTLEMENTS WITH INTERESTS IN POSSESSION, **46** SETTLEMENTS: TRUSTS FOR BEREAVED MINORS and **56** VALUATION.

Simon's Taxes. See **I3.211, I3.212, I5.201, I5.202, I5.214, I5.256, I5.713.**

Introduction

[19.1] 'Estate' is one of the key concepts of IHT because of the loss to donor principle which underlies the tax. (See **1** INTRODUCTION AND BASIC PRINCIPLES for general exposition). During life, the value transferred by a transfer of value is the amount by which the transferor's estate is reduced by that transfer. On death, a person is treated as having made a transfer of value equal to the value of his estate immediately before his death. [*IHTA 1984, ss 3(1), 4(1)*].

Loans as part of estate

Where a loan is made between individuals, HMRC Inheritance Tax will not accept that the loan has been waived and the estate of the lender reduced unless the waiver was effected by deed. (Law Society's Gazette, 18 December 1991). See also *Moggs (Moggs' Executor) v CIR* [2005] STC SCD 394 Sp C 464.

THIS DEED is made by:

(1) "Father" namely [ ] of [ ]

In favour of

(2) "Son" namely [ ] of [ ]

RECITALS

A. Son is indebted to Father for the loan brief details of which are set out in the schedule below ("the Loan")

B. By this waiver Father intends to utilise the annual exemption available to him under section 19 of the Inheritance Tax Act 1984

WAIVER

1. Father waives and releases in favour of Son Three Thousand pounds (£3,000.00) of the Loan
2. The continuing balance of the indebtedness due under the Loan following this waiver is set out in part 2 of the schedule

The Schedule

Part 1 – [details of "the Loan"]

Part 2 – balance now [ ]

EXECUTED AS A DEED)
and DELIVERED on)
2010)
FATHER in the presence of)

Note to the waiver

It is imperative that waivers of loan are made by Deed. Estoppels apart (which should not be relied on) waivers under hand, by letter etc. are simply ineffective due to a lack of consideration.

Definition — person's estate

A person's estate, for IHT purposes, is the aggregate of all the 'property' to which he is *beneficially entitled*, except that the estate of a person immediately before his death does not include 20 EXCLUDED PROPERTY or property to which *IHTA 1984, ss 71A, 71D* (i.e. bereaved minor's trust and an 'aged 18–25 trust') apply and does not include, from 22 March 2006, certain interests in possession other than an IPDI, a TSI, a disabled person's trust. These trusts will be charged to IHT under the trusts taxing regimes applicable depending on whichever trust is in point. See *Anand v CIR* [1997] STC SCD 58 Sp C 107 and *O'Neill and others v IRC* [1998] STC SCD 110 Sp C 154. '*Property*' includes rights and interests of any description but does not include property to which he is entitled as a corporation sole (e.g. as Archbishop of Canterbury). His liabilities, including his liability for IHT (but not any other tax or duty) on the value transferred, are taken into account in determining the value of his estate. However, a liability not incurred for a consideration in money or money's worth is left out of account unless it is a liability imposed by law. [*IHTA 1984, ss 5(1)(3)–(5), 271, 272; FA 2006, Sch 20 para 10, 28*].

Estate on death

[19.2] There are additional rules for the valuation of a person's estate immediately before his death. See 52.2 TRANSFERS ON DEATH.

General powers

[19.3] A person who has a 'general power' (or would have if he were *sui juris*) to dispose of, or to charge money on, any property other than settled property is treated as beneficially entitled to the money or property. '*General power*' means a power or authority enabling a person by whom it is exercisable to appoint or dispose of property as he thinks fit. [*IHTA 1984, s 5(2)*]. See *Kempe and Roberts (personal representatives of Lyon, deceased) v CIR* [2004] STC SCD 467 Sp C 424. In the case of a Power of Attorney [now Lasting Power of Attorney] care should be exercised as applying *dicta* of Russell J in *Re Reckitt*, CA [1928] 2 KB 244, 'the primary object of a power of attorney is to enable the attorney to act in the management of his principal's affairs. An attorney cannot, in the absence of a clear power to do so, make presents to himself or to others of his principal's property.' See *McDowall & Others (McDowall's Executors) v CIR* [2004] STC SCD 22 Sp C 382. As settled property is specifically excluded, the existence of a general power of appointment in a trust deed does not result in the settled property being deemed to be included in the estate of the trustee. It has been held that a right reserved by the settlor to require his trustees to revest in him settled property was property forming part of his estate immediately after the settlement. This could have resulted in 'double counting' because the person entitled to an interest in possession in the settled property would have been treated as beneficially entitled and the general power of appointment would be property of the appointor's estate. *Melville v CIR*, [2000] STC 628; CA [2001] STC 1271. In this case the position has now been rectified by legislation in *FA 2002, s 119(4)*. The section reverses the effects of the *Melville* case from 17 April 2002 by providing expressly that powers over trusts are not to be treated as property. Powers which have been acquired for money or money's worth will not be disregarded for IHT purposes by reason of *FA 2002, s 119(3)* inserting new *IHTA 1984, s 55A*. Interestingly, in *Sillars and Another v CIR* [2004] STC SCD 180 Sp C 401 the deceased transferred her building society account into the names of herself and her two daughters. In putting the account into their joint names the deceased had intended to make an immediate gift. The daughters did regard a one-third share of the balance in the account as being theirs. Withdrawals from the account were made either to or for the benefit of the mother until her death. On the mother's death the whole of the account formed part of her estate. Although the deceased's power over the account was not a *general power* in the ordinary sense it did fit the definition. The deceased was able to dispose of the balance as she thought fit and there was no accounting to see whether more than one-third was being extracted from the account. The daughters did not therefore have a general power over the account 'enabling the person by whom it is exercisable to dispose of or appoint property as he thinks fit'. See also **5.1** ANTI-AVOIDANCE.

Settled property

[19.4] Persons beneficially entitled to an interest in possession in settled property is treated as beneficially entitled to the property in which the interest subsists, i.e. his estate for IHT purposes includes the value of any settled property in which he has such an interest (and not the actuarial value of the interest itself). [*IHTA 1984, s 49(1)*].

Example 1

X, a widower, who has a life interest in a settlement since 1995, dies in June 2010 with his nil rate band of £325,000 available but having used the available annual exemptions. On his death X has a free estate of £302,000. The value of his trust fund is £263,000 making a total value of £565,000. By the terms of his will he leaves the trust fund to his nephew and leaves the personal estate of £302,000 to his daughter.

Although the nil rate band available of £325,000 would have meant that his daughter received the whole of the personal estate of X free of IHT, the trust fund has to be taken into account as well. The result is that both the trustees of the settlement and the executors will have a liability to account for IHT as follows:

Calculation on death of X	
Value of X's estate at June 2010 *IHTA 1984, s 49(1)(1A)* (see above).	£
Value net free estate	302,000
Add Trust fund	263,000
	£565,000

IHT on chargeable gift of £565,000 is charged in the nil rate band up to £325,000.

	£
£0–325,000 at Nil%	Nil
Estate chargeable @ 40%	240,000
Tax due on death of X	£96,000
Calculate estate rate: £96,000/565,000 × 100 = 16.99115	
Executors' portion £302,000 × 16.99115% =	£51,313
Trustees' portion £263,000 × 16.99115% =	£44,687
IHT payable	£96,000

Notes to the example

(A) A person beneficially entitled to an interest in possession in settled property in existence prior to 22 March 2006 is treated as beneficially entitled to the property in which the interest subsists, i.e. he is treated as owning it absolutely. There is an IHT charge based on the value of the settled property in which his interest subsists when a beneficiary disposes of his interest or it otherwise comes to an end, i.e. either as a transfer on death or as a PET where the termination of the interest occurs during the lifetime of the tenant, e.g. where there is an exercise of a power of appointment. [*IHTA 1984, ss 49(1), 51(1), 52(1); FA 2006, Sch 20 paras 4, 7, 12–13*].

(B) Under *IHTA 1984, s 49A* the niece has an IPDI which arises under the will of X and she is treated as beneficially entitled to an interest in possession in settled property in which the interest subsists. See **42** SETTLEMENTS WITH INTERESTS IN POSSESSION. If an IIP in favour of the niece is created out of an existing IIP before 6 October 2008 it cannot be either a transitional serial interest (TSI) or an IPDI. [*IHTA 1984, ss 49C, 49D, 49E as amended by FA 2008, s 141*].

See **52.2** TRANSFERS ON DEATH for exceptions to the above where settled property reverts to the settlor, or in certain circumstances to the settlor's spouse, on the death of a person entitled to an interest in possession in that property. For the position from 22 March 2006 see **41** SETTLEMENTS — GENERAL and **42** SETTLEMENTS WITH INTERESTS IN POSSESSION.

A reversionary interest

A reversionary interest in settled property is generally **20** EXCLUDED PROPERTY, i.e. it forms part of the estate of the person entitled to the reversionary interest, except immediately before his death (see **19.1** above, so it is not liable to tax as part of the estate on death). For lifetime transfers, the interest is not taken into account in determining the value transferred by any transfer of value. The exceptions to this rule are (i) where the reversionary interest has been retained by a settlor, spouse or civil partner; (ii) where it has been acquired for consideration in money or money's worth; and (iii) where certain anti-avoidance provisions apply (*IHTA 1984, s74A*). Where a person entitled to an interest (whether in possession or not) in any settled property acquires a reversionary interest expectant (whether immediately or not) on that interest, the reversionary interest is not part of his estate. See also **5** ANTI-AVOIDANCE. [*IHTA 1984, ss 3(1)(2), 5(1), 48, 55(1); FA 2006, Sch 20 para 10*].

A trustee of settled property

A trustee of settled property is the legal, not the beneficial, owner of the property so the property does not form part of his estate. See **19.3** above for the position where a trustee has general powers of appointment etc. Where a trustee is remunerated for his services by an interest in possession in settlement property (e.g. an annuity) the interest is not part of his estate except to the extent that it represents more than reasonable remuneration. [*IHTA 1984, s 90*].

HMRC Inheritance Tax normally expects to deal with the reversionary interest but the DV may be asked by HMRC whether or not consideration paid by the lessee represented the full consideration for the grant of the lease for life. It is only these cases that the DV will be involved in the use of Life Tables in order to arrive at the required value. HMRC Inheritance Tax will inform the DV of the age and sex of the person by reference to whose death the lease will determine. (VOA IHT manual, section 8, para 8.22).

Key points

[19.5] Points to consider are as follows.

- Powers of appointment are usually either a special power or a general power. In addition, there is also recourse to hybrid powers which may be categorised as coming within a general power or special power. Under the new *Perpetuities and Accumulations Act 2009, s 11* a 'general power' and 'special power' are defined as follows:

(i) a *general power* of appointment is one which is exercisable by one person alone, and under which that person could exercise the power to appoint the entire trust to themselves, without the consent of anyone else or compliance with any other condition; and

(ii) a *special power* is any power of appointment which is not a general power of appointment (i.e. it entitles the holder to appoint the trust to whomever they like).

The new *Perpetuities and Accumulations Act 2009, s 11* extends the perpetuity period for trusts created after 5 April 2010 to 125 years and means it is no longer necessary to have a life in being as the basis of the perpetuity period and consequently drafting a Royal life clause is not relevant.

- Whilst the new *Perpetuities and Accumulations Act 2009, s 11* extends the perpetuity period for trusts created after 5 April 2010 up to 125 years, this does not apply to trusts created before that date. There may be IHT consequences if assets are resettled to take advantage of the longer accumulation period.
- It should be remembered that a general power (see Key Point above) under which the donee has a power to appoint over settled property is not beneficially entitled to that property for IHT purposes. This results from *IHTA 1984, s 5(2)* which states 'other than settled property'.
- In certain cases an order may be sought under the *Variation of Trusts Act 1958, s 1(1)* to insert a new perpetuity period of 125 years and therefore extend the life of the trust so postponing any exit charge and CGT under *TCGA 1992, s 71*. This would apply to trusts created by settlement, will trust, etc. before 6 April 2010.

20

Excluded Property

Cross-references. See **49** SITUS; **51** TRANSFER OF VALUE.

Simon's Taxes. See **I5.702, I5.711, I5.712, I5.714, I9.3.**

Other Sources. Foster, Parts C2.17, C4.43, D1.21, E7.02, J3; HMRC Customer Guide to Inheritance Tax; IHTM04251.

Introduction

[20.1] Excluded property is property which is outside the scope of charge to inheritance tax. The value transferred by a transfer of value does not take account of the value of any excluded property ceasing to form part of a person's estate as a result of a disposition [*IHTA 1984, s 3(1)(2)*] and a person's estate immediately before his death (on which inheritance tax is payable) does not include excluded property. [*IHTA 1984, s 5(1)*]. Similarly, if the excluded property is settled property, the termination of an interest in possession in it is not taxable (see **42** SETTLEMENTS WITH INTERESTS IN POSSESSION) and nor is it relevant property for the purposes of the rules for **43** SETTLEMENTS: DISCRETIONARY TRUSTS AND OTHER TRUSTS OF RELEVANT PROPERTY. [*IHTA 1984, ss 53(1), 58(1)*]. The types of excluded property are described below.

Property abroad

Assets held by non-domiciliaries

[20.2] Property which is not comprised in a settlement (but including a reversionary interest in settled property, see **20.4** below) and which is situated outside the UK is excluded property if the person beneficially entitled to it is an individual domiciled outside the UK and not deemed domiciled in the UK (see **16.5**). [*IHTA 1984, ss 6(1)(1A), 48(3), (3A) as inserted by FA 2003, s 186(2)(3)*]. A double tax treaty may specify where property is situated. [*IHTA 1984, s 158(1)*]. See **16.5** DOMICILE for special provisions and **49** SITUS for situation of property generally.

Settlements made by non-domiciliaries

Settled property (including a reversionary interest which is itself settled property) situated outside the UK is excluded property if the settlor was domiciled outside the UK when the settlement was made. It follows therefore that the domicile status of beneficiaries of the trust, or the residence of the trustees, is irrelevant in determining whether any of the settled property is excluded property. But if the settlor adds funds to the trust at a time when he is UK domiciled, or has become deemed domiciled, the added funds cannot be excluded property according to HMRC's interpretation of the legislation; this interpretation is open to question although it has not so far been challenged in any appeal. Authorised units trusts and shares in open-ended investment companies are also excluded property in trusts created by a foreign domiciled settlor. See *A Beneficiary v CIR* [1999] STC SCD 134 Sp C 190. For property in a settlement before 10 December 1974, the special provisions relating to domicile in *IHTA 1984, s 267* (see **16.5** DOMICILE) do not apply. The status of excluded property is determined immediately before vesting (*Von Ernst and Cie SA v CIR* IRC [1980] 1 All ER 677, CA 1979, [1980] STC 111, CA).

Where UK assets in a settlement made by a non-domiciled settlor are sold and the proceeds reinvested in overseas assets, no IHT exit charge arises (see *IHTA 1984, s 65(7)*). Defective drafting of *s 65(7)* did not originally prevent an exit charge where funds not qualifying as excluded property were reinvested in authorised unit trusts or shares in open-ended investment companies, but this defect was corrected with full retrospective effect to 15 October 2002 by *FA 2013, s 175*.

Where the settlor's spouse has an initial interest in possession in a settlement created after 26 March 1974, not being one arising on or after 22 March 2006 in a lifetime settlement, two conditions must be satisfied if any of the trust assets are to continue to be excluded property in any continuing relevant property trust after the life interest ends. The first condition is that the settlor must be non-domiciled and not deemed-domiciled when the settlement was made. The second condition is that the settlor' spouse must be non-domiciled and not deemed-domiciled when the life interest terminates.

Provisions to block avoidance schemes

Because the domicile status of trust beneficiaries is irrelevant for the purposes of determining whether trust assets are excluded property, it was possible to avoid IHT liability by purchasing an interest in an excluded property trust. To prevent such schemes, an initial draft of anti-avoidance measures were introduced with effect from 5 December 2005 to prevent UK domiciled individuals who become entitled to interests in pre-existing foreign trusts originally settled by non-UK domiciliaries which are treated as excluded property within *IHTA 1984, s 48(3)* from being treated as excluded property if it is acquired for money or money's worth. It is immaterial whether the consideration is given by the person acquiring the interest in possession in the settlement or someone else or whether the entitlement arises by way of will or intestacy. Any IHT arising as a result of this avoidance provision applying from 5 December 2005 to the day before enactment of the *FA 2006* on 19 July 2006 will be due 14 days after enactment. If the acquired interest is subsequently resettled by someone who is domiciled outside the UK relief may still be available under *IHTA 1984, s 48(3)* in respect of the new settlement.

In summary therefore *FA 2006* anti-avoidance has provided that property is not excluded property if:

(a) an individual is, or has been, beneficially entitled to an interest in possession in the property at any time;
(b) the individual is, or was, domiciled in the UK at the time; and
(c) their entitlement arose directly or *indirectly* as a result of a disposition for consideration in money or money's worth made on or after 5 December 2005. It does not matter whether the consideration was given by the individual with the interest in possession or by someone else (this also includes cases in which an entitlement arose indirectly include entitlements arising under a will or the law relating to intestacy).

[*IHTA 1984, s 48(3B)(3C)*].

This anti-avoidance legislation is extended by *FA 2012, s 208*, with effect from 20 June 2012 for arrangements entered into on or after that date, to cover cases where a UK domiciled individual, or a close company in relation to which the individual is a participator, acquires an interest in excluded property (or property which was foreign situs property at any time during the arrangements), other than an interest in possession which forms part of the individual's estate. For this purpose there is an interest in settled property if the property, or any derived property, is, will or may become payable to, or applicable for the benefit of, the individual or the individual's spouse or civil partner in any circumstances, or if the individual or the individual's spouse or civil partner enjoys a benefit deriving (directly or indirectly) from the property or any derived property. There must also be a 'relevant reduction' in the individual's estate, broadly a reduction in value by virtue of entering into the arrangements to acquire the interest. Where *s 208* applies to arrangements, not only is the excluded property status of foreign trust assets withdrawn, but in addition the individual purchasing the trust interest makes a chargeable transfer equal to the amount by which the scheme reduces his estate for IHT purposes. If the scheme relates to the individual's interest in possession in settled property within *IHTA 1984, s 49(1)*, and it reduces the value of the settled property, a corresponding chargeable transfer is treated as made by the beneficiary and he is liable for any tax due as a result together with the trustees.

[*IHTA 1984, ss 48(3D–F), 74A–C*].

Liabilities to finance excluded property

For transfers of value made or treated as made on or after 17 July 2013, it is no longer possible to reduce the value of an asset for IHT purposes by securing a loan on it where the loan is used to acquire or maintain (directly or indirectly) excluded property. Instead the loan the loan is not to be taken into account for IHT purposes. This rule has equal effect for charges on settlements holding relevant property within *IHTA 1984, s 58*.

The rule applies to liabilities whenever incurred. If the excluded property is subsequently disposed of for full consideration, the liability may then be deductible for IHT purposes to the extent that the proceeds of the disposal are not used to acquire or maintain other excluded property, or to pay off another loan which cannot be taken into account by virtue of this provision. A liability may be taken into account to the extent that it exceeds the value of any of the excluded property not disposed of, but not where this excess is attributable to arrangements to secure a tax advantage, an increase in the amount of the liability, or a disposal of any of the excluded property. For example, if a loan is taken out to buy shares in a foreign incorporated company, and arrangements are then made for tax reasons to reduce the value of those shares, the loan will remain non-deductible.

A loan is considered by HMRC to indirectly finance an asset where it is initially used to buy asset 1 which is later sold and the proceeds reinvested in asset 2. The loan then indirectly finances asset 2 (see HMRC IHT Manual para IHTM 28018). On this view it is not possible to circumvent the disallowance by first acquiring UK property with a loan, subsequently selling that property and then acquiring excluded property with the proceeds. Equally where a loan is taken out to buy a UK asset, say a painting, and that asset becomes excluded property, for example by being removed from the UK, the loan is deductible only to the extent that it exceeds the value of that asset and subject also to there being no arrangements to secure a tax advantage.

See further commentary at **56.19**.

Situs

[20.3] See **49** SITUS for the rules determining where property is situated.

Table of asset locations:

Asset	Location/situs
Land, buildings and leases including any share in land or a building.	Where the land is physically situated.
Registered shares and securities (but see Government stocks above).	Where the register is kept on which the shares or securities are registered.
An interest in an unincorporated business or an interest in a partnership.	Where the business is carried out.
Chattels and personal possessions.	Where the item is situated at the time of the transfer or at the date of death.
Debts owed to the deceased (other than specialty debts).	Where the debtor lives at the time of transfer or on death.

Bank accounts.	Where the bank or branch holding the account is situated.

See also below for form IHT417.

Reversionary interest

[20.4] A reversionary interest is excluded property unless:

(a) it has at any time been acquired (whether by the person entitled to it or by a person previously entitled) for a consideration in money or money's worth; or

(b) it is the interest expectant on the determination of a lease which is treated as a settlement because the lease is for life or lives, or for a period ascertainable only by reference to death, or which is terminable on, or at a date ascertainable only by reference to, a death, and was not granted for full consideration in money or money's worth. Where a lease, not granted at a rack rent, is at any time to become a lease at an increased rent, it shall be treated as terminable at that time; or

(c) for a settlement made after 15 April 1976, it is one to which either the settlor or his spouse or civil partner is (or, for a reversionary interest acquired after 9 March 1981, has been) beneficially entitled.

(d) where the anti-avoidance provisions of *IHTA 1984, s 74A(1)* apply (that is, in relation to avoidance schemes involving the purchase of an interest in an excluded property trust), the interest acquired is a reversionary interest in the trust concerned but another interest in that trust is or can be acquired.

If a reversionary interest falls into one of the exceptions in (a)–(c) it may still be excluded property in certain circumstances if it is situated outside the UK. See **20.2** above. Additionally, a reversionary interest is to be treated as excluded property where the reversioner to that property is non-UK domiciled. This assists non-UK domiciled individuals who have a reversionary interest but die before that interest falls in and will no longer have the threat of an IHT charge in those particular circumstances for instance. [*IHTA 1984, s 48(3A)(b) as inserted by FA 2003, s 186(3)*].

Where more than one person is the settlor in relation to a settlement and the circumstances so require, the above provisions apply as if the settled property were comprised in separate settlements. HMRC normally apply this general rule, that is the circumstances are normally regarded as requiring it.

[*IHTA 1984, ss 43(3), 44(2), 48(1)(2)(3A)(b); FA 2003, s 186(3)*]. See also **41.6** SETTLEMENTS — GENERAL for meaning of reversionary interest.

Government securities

[20.5] The inheritance tax exemption for Government securities is summarised as follows by HMRC at IHTM27241:

- FOTRA securities (that is, those free of tax to persons resident abroad) issued before 29 April 1996 and acquired before 6 April 2013 will be exempt provided the beneficial owner is both domiciled and ordinarily resident outside the UK.
- 3½% War Loan 1952 or after acquired before 6 April 2013 will only be exempt if the beneficial owner is both domiciled and ordinarily resident outside the UK, even if the chargeable event is after 6 April 1998.
- All other government securities issued before 6 April 1998 without FOTRA conditions will be exempt from that date if acquired before 6 April 2013 provided the beneficial owner is ordinarily resident outside the UK. Domicile is no longer relevant.
- All other government securities issued after 29 April 1996 and acquired before 6 April 2013 will be exempt provided the beneficial owner is ordinarily resident outside the UK. Domicile is no longer relevant.
- In relation to all categories listed above, for securities acquired after 6 April 2013 the requirement as to ordinary residence is removed and replaced with a condition that the beneficial owner is resident outside the United Kingdom.

Thus in the circumstances set out above the securities are excluded property if:

(a) they are beneficially owned by such a person and are not settled property; or

(b) they are settled property and such a person is entitled to a qualifying interest in possession in them. If a close company is the person entitled, the participators in the company are treated as being entitled to the interest according to their respective rights and interests in the company; or

(c) they are settled property in which there is no qualifying interest in possession (see **43.1** SETTLEMENTS: DISCRETIONARY TRUSTS AND OTHER TRUSTS OF RELEVANT PROPERTY) and all known persons for whose benefit the settled property or income from it has been or might be applied or who are or might become beneficially entitled to an interest in possession in it are of a description specified in the condition in question. See *Montague Trust Co (Jersey) Ltd and Others v CIR* Ch D [1989] STC 477.

Where:

(i) after 19 April 1978 and before 10 December 1981 property ceased to be comprised in one settlement and, by the same disposition, became comprised in another settlement; or

(ii) after 9 December 1981 property ceased to be comprised in one settlement and became comprised in another without any person in the meantime having become entitled to the property (and not merely to an interest in possession in it),

the property in the second settlement will only be excluded property if these requirements are satisfied by both settlements. However, this does not apply where a reversionary interest in the property expectant on the termination of a qualifying interest in possession subsisting under the first settlement was settled on the trusts of the second settlement before 10 December 1981.

A charity cannot be a 'known person for whose benefit the settled property . . . might be applied' (*Von Ernst & Cie SA and Others v CIR* CA 1979, [1980] STC 111).

Note that in the few cases where domicile remains relevant for the purposes of this exemption (FOTRA securities issued before 29 April 1996), the deemed domicile provisions of *IHTA 1984, s 267* are disapplied [*IHTA 1984, s 267(2)*].

[*IHTA 1984, ss 6(2), 48(4)–(7), 101(1), 267(2); FA 1996, s 154, Sch 28 paras 7, 8*].

Overseas pensions

Transfers on death only

[20.6] Any pension receivable from a fund set up under the *Government of India Act 1935, s 273* (or a corresponding fund under *Overseas Pensions Act 1973, s 2*) is to be left out of account in determining the value of a person's estate immediately before his death.

Transfers generally

[20.7] Any pension, gratuity, sum payable on or in respect of death or a return of contributions (including interest thereon) paid from certain pension funds relating to service in overseas territories is to be treated as paid by the government of the territory concerned. It will thus constitute property situated outside the UK (see **49** SITUS) and will be excluded property if the pensioner is domiciled overseas (see **20.2** above). The pensions are those:

(a) paid out of any fund established in the UK by the government of any country which at the time the fund was established was, or formed part of, a colony, protectorate, protected state or 'UK trust territory' for the sole purpose of paying pensions etc. in respect of service under that government e.g. DFID Overseas Pensions Department;
(b) paid out of the Central African Pension Fund established by *Federation of Rhodesia and Nyasaland (Dissolution) Order in Council 1963, s 24*;
(c) paid under a scheme made under *Overseas Pensions Act 1973, s 2* which is constituted by the *Pensions (India, Pakistan and Burma) Act 1955* (or similar);
(d) paid under the scheme constituted under *Overseas Pensions Act 1973, s 2* by *Overseas Service Act 1958, ss 2, 4(2)* (or similar); and
(e) for which the UK has assumed responsibility within the meaning of *Overseas Pensions Act 1973, s 1* exclusive of any increase in the pension under *Pensions (Increase) Act 1971* or any enactment repealed by that Act.

'*UK trust territory*' means a territory administered by the UK government under the trusteeship system of the United Nations.

[*IHTA 1984, s 153*].

Persons domiciled in Channel Islands or Isle of Man

Savings

[20.8] The following savings to which persons domiciled in the above Islands are beneficially entitled are excluded property.

(a) War savings certificates.
(b) NS&I National savings certificates (including Ulster savings certificates).
(c) NS&I Premium bonds.
(d) NS&I Deposits with the National Savings Bank or with a trustee savings bank.
(e) Any certified contractual savings scheme (e.g. SAYE schemes with qualification in the prospectus) within the meaning of *ICTA 1988, s 326(2)(6)* and *ITEPA 2003, Sch 3 para 48(1) as replaced by ITTOIA 2005, ss 702(1), 703(2)(3), 704(2), 705(1), 707(1)*.

For the above purposes, the special provisions relating to domicile in *IHTA 1984, s 267* (see **16.5** DOMICILE) does not apply.

[*IHTA 1984, ss 6(3), 267(2)*].

Visiting forces

[20.9] Emoluments paid by the Government of a country designated by Order in Council to a member of a visiting force of that country (including the member of a civilian component) are excluded property provided that member is not a British citizen, a British Dependent Territories citizen or a British Overseas citizen. Any tangible movable property in the UK solely because of the presence of that member is also excluded. [*Visiting Forces (Inheritance Tax) (Designation) Order 1998, Art 1; ITA 2007, s 833*].

A period during which any such member is in the UK by reason solely of his being such a member is not treated for inheritance tax purposes as a period of residence in the UK or as creating a change of residence or domicile. [*IHTA 1984, ss 6(4), 155*].

The *Visiting Forces (Inheritance Tax) (Designation) Order 1998, SI 1998/1516* comes into effect in respect of the following countries on the later of the date the country becomes party to the agreement or the day after the date on which the Order was made (i.e. 25 June 1998).

Designated countries:

- Armenia
- Austria

- Azerbaijan
- Belarus
- Finland
- Georgia
- Kazakhstan
- Kyrgyzstan
- The Former Yugoslav Republic of Macedonia
- Moldova
- Russia
- Switzerland
- Turkmenistan
- Ukraine
- Uzbekistan

Special discretionary trusts

[20.10] Where tax is charged when property leaves certain trusts, no account is taken of any quarter throughout which the property was excluded property when determining the appropriate rate of tax. [*IHTA 1984, ss 70(7), 71(5), 72(5), 73(3), 74(3)*]. See **10.5** CHARITIES; **44.9** SETTLEMENTS: ACCUMULATION AND MAINTENANCE TRUSTS; **45.3** SETTLEMENTS: INTERESTS HELD ON PROTECTIVE TRUSTS; **47.5** SETTLEMENTS: TRUSTS FOR DISABLED PERSONS; and **55.8** TRUSTS FOR EMPLOYEES.

Chevening Estate and Apsley House

[20.11] Inheritance tax does not apply to property held on trusts under the *Schedule* to the *Chevening Estate Act 1959* or rights conferred by the *Wellington Museum Act 1947*. [*IHTA 1984, s 156*].

Non-UK domiciles (AUT and OEIC investments)

[20.12] Investments in authorised unit trusts (AUTs) or open-ended investment companies (OEICs) are excluded property whilst held by non-domiciled individuals or trusts of which the settlor was non-UK domiciled at the time the settlement was made. These provisions were introduced to boost the competitiveness of UK-authorised funds in the international market place. The treatment of such investments as excluded property applies to IHT occasions of charge on or after 16 October 2002.

The IHT anti-avoidance measures mentioned in **20.2** above apply from 5 December 2005 to prevent UK domiciled individuals who purchase interests in pre-existing foreign trusts originally settled by non-UK domiciliaries which benefit from the exemption attaching to such property or under *IHTA 1984,* *s 48(3A)* relating to holdings in AUTs and OEICs from obtaining the benefit of excluded property. It is immaterial whether the consideration is given by the person with the interest in possession in the settlement or someone else arising by way of will or intestacy. Any IHT arising as a result of this avoidance provision applying from 5 December 2005 to the day before enactment of the *FA 2006* on 19 July 2006 will be due 14 days of enactment. If the acquired interest is subsequently resettled by someone who is domiciled outside the UK relief may still be available under *IHTA 1984, s 48(3A)* in respect of the new settlement. See **20.2** above. [*IHTA 1984, ss 6(1A), 48(3A)(a) as inserted by FA 2003, s 186(3) and amended by FA 2006, s 157(3)–(6)*].

Non-residents' bank accounts

[20.13] On the death prior to 6 April 2013 of a person not domiciled, resident or ordinarily resident in the UK immediately before his death, the balance on any 'qualifying foreign currency account' is not included in the value of his estate immediately before his death. This also applies to such an account held by trustees of settled property in which the deceased held a beneficial interest in possession unless the settlor was domiciled in the UK at the time he made the settlement or the trustees are domiciled, resident and ordinarily resident there at the time of the beneficiary's death.

With effect for deaths on or after 6 April 2013, this exemption continues to apply but is modified to delete the requirements relating to ordinary residence outside the UK. The conditions for exemption of a foreign currency bank account held by a person at the time of death are therefore that he is not domiciled and not resident in the UK immediately before his death.

For Transfers of value on or after 17 July 2014, a liability which is attributable to financing an account within this exclusion from IHT is not deductible from the value of the account holder's estate on death. If the liability exceeds the balance on the account, the excess is deductible so long as it does not arise from arrangements made either to secure a tax advantage or to increase the liability for example by rolling up interest on the loan. [*FA 2014, Sch 25 para 3*].

See **56.20** for further details.

Awards for gallantry

[20.14] A decoration or other award is excluded property if it was awarded for valour or gallant conduct and no interest in it has ever changed hands for money or money's worth. This was previously the subject of HMRC extra-statutory concession F19, which was enacted with effect from 6 April 2009. With effect from 3 December 2014 the exclusion was extended to include a decoration or other similar award:

(a) that is designed to be worn to denote membership of (i) an Order that is, or has been, specified in the Order of Wear published in the London Gazette, or (ii) an Order of a country or territory outside the United Kingdom;
(b) that is, or has been, specified in the Order of Wear;

(c) that was awarded for, or in connection with, a person being, or having been, a member of, or employed or engaged in connection with, the armed forces of any country or territory;

(d) that was awarded for, or in connection with, a person being, or having been, an emergency responder within the meaning of *IHTA 1984, s 153A* (death of emergency service personnel, see **59.3**); or

(e) that was awarded by the Crown or a country or territory outside the United Kingdom for, or in connection with, public service or achievement in public life.

[*IHTA, s 6(1B), (1C); FA 2015, s 74*].

Foreign assets [Form IHT 417]

HM Revenue & Customs

Foreign assets

Schedule IHT417

When to use this form

Fill in this form if the deceased was domiciled in the United Kingdom (UK) when they died and owned assets abroad. For Inheritance Tax purposes, the Channel Islands and the Isle of Man are not in the UK. You should give details of all the assets situated outside the UK that the deceased owned.

Help

The guidance notes to help you fill in this form are on page 4. For more information or help or another copy of this form:

- go to **www.hmrc.gov.uk/inheritancetax/**
- phone our Helpline on **0845 30 20 900**
  – if calling from outside the UK, phone **+44 115 974 3009**.

Name of deceased

Date of death *DD MM YYYY*

IHT reference number (if known)

Assets outside the UK

Enter details of assets consisting of:

- houses, land and buildings
- businesses or interests in businesses
- shares and securities which gave the deceased control of the company.

1	Description of assets - see note on page 4	Value in foreign currency at the date of death	Exchange rate at the date of death	Value of assets at the date of death £ sterling
			Total 1	£

(Substitute)(LexisNexis)

IHT417 Page 1 Approval Ref No: L3/00

2 Details of liabilities to be deducted from the foreign assets shown in box 1
If a loan charged on a property shown in box 1 arose in the UK, include the amount on form IHT400, box 80, and not here

Description of liabilities	Value in foreign currency at the date of death	Exchange rate at the date of death	Amount of liability £ sterling
		Total liabilities **2**	£

3 Net assets (box 1 *minus* box 2). If a *minus* amount, write '0' and read IHT400 Notes on how to deal with a deficit

3 £

4 Details of exemptions and reliefs being deducted against foreign assets shown in box 1

Description of exemptions and reliefs *If you are deducting charity exemption, enter the full name of the charity, the country of establishment and the HMRC charities reference, if available.*	Amount of exemption or relief £
Total exemptions and reliefs **4**	£

5 Net total of foreign houses, land, businesses and control holdings of shares (box 3 *minus* box 4). If box 3 is '0' write '0' in box 5

5 £

Copy this amount to form IHT400, box 97

IHT417 Page 2

Other assets outside the UK

Enter details of the other assets owned by the deceased outside the UK which were not shown in box 1.
For example, bank accounts.

6

Description of assets	Value in foreign currency at the date of death	Exchange rate at the date of death	Value of assets at the date of death £ sterling
		Total 6	£

7 Details of liabilities to be deducted from the foreign assets shown in box 6

Description of liabilities	Value in foreign currency at the date of death	Exchange rate at the date of death	Amount of liability £ sterling
		Total liabilities 7	£

8 Net assets (box 6 *minus* box 7). If a *minus* amount, write '0' and read IHT400 Notes on how to deal with a deficit — 8 £

IHT417 Page 3

9 Details of exemptions and reliefs being deducted against foreign assets shown in box 6

Description of exemptions and reliefs *If you are deducting charity exemption, enter the full name of the charity, the country of establishment and the HMRC charities reference, if available.*	Amount of exemption or relief £
Total exemptions and reliefs	9 £

10 Net total of other foreign assets (box 8 *minus* box 9). If box 8 is '0', write '0' in box 10 — 10 £

Copy this amount to form IHT400, box 98

Notes

Domicile

If the deceased was domiciled in the UK when they died, use this form to tell us about assets owned abroad. In some circumstances, you may find it easier to fill in more than one form. For example, if the deceased left a separate Will to deal with all or part of their foreign estate they may have appointed different personal representatives. These assets will still form part of the deceased's estate.

For more information about domicile, see IHT400 Notes.

Description of assets

Houses, land and buildings

You should give a full description of the property and enclose any professional valuations obtained, a plan and photographs of the property if you have any.

You should also comment on the following:

- the condition the property was in
- whether it is in a remote or urban location
- what additional facilities the property has, such as a swimming pool
- whether there was any planning permission
- whether a sale of the property is imminent.

Businesses and control holdings

Please enclose copies of the latest accounts and provide a calculation of how the valuation has been arrived at.

Currency conversions

You should show the value of the asset in the foreign currency as at the date of death. Then show how you have converted that value to pound sterling. Major currencies should generally be converted at the closing mid-point figure given in the 'Pound Spot Forward against the Pound' table shown in the financial pages of daily newspapers or on the Internet.

Less common currencies may be converted at the rates shown in the 'FT Guide to World Currencies', published weekly in the Financial Times on Mondays and also by searching on the Internet.

Jointly owned foreign assets

If the deceased owned any foreign assets jointly, you should include those assets on this form and not on form IHT404 *Jointly owned assets*. Use the 'Additional information' boxes on pages 15 and 16 of form IHT400, to give full details of the joint ownership of foreign assets.

Double taxation relief

If tax that is similar to Inheritance Tax has been paid on an asset in another country, you may be able to deduct double taxation relief. The form IHT400 *Calculation* will show you how to work out the double taxation relief.

IHT417 Page 4

21

Exempt Transfers

Cross-references. See **4** AGRICULTURAL PROPERTY; **6** BUSINESS PROPERTY; **10** CHARITIES; **13** DEEDS VARYING DISPOSITIONS ON DEATH; **15** DIPLOMATIC IMMUNITY; **33** NATIONAL HERITAGE; **38** POTENTIALLY EXEMPT TRANSFERS; **55** TRUSTS FOR EMPLOYEES.

Simon's Taxes. See **I3.154, I3.155, I3.3, I4.2, I4.445, I4.446, I5.336.**

Other Sources. Form P11(Notes); Foster, Parts C and D; IHT 110; IHT 400 Notes; IHTM11000; HMRC Customer Guide to Inheritance Tax; IHTM43001–IHTM43035.

General exemptions

Nil rate tax band

[21.1] Currently, the first £325,000 of chargeable transfers in any seven-year period are taxable at nil%. See **9.3** CHARGEABLE TRANSFER and **40** RATES OF TAX.

Gifts to charities

[21.2] Gifts to charities are exempt from inheritance tax. [*IHTA 1984, s 23(1)*]. [**Case Study 9**]. See also **21.4** below for transfer of property from certain trusts to charities. See IHTM11101.

Property is given to a charity if it becomes the property of the charity or is held on trust for charitable purposes only. [*IHTA 1984, s 23(6)*]. Where the value transferred (i.e. the loss to the transferor's estate as a result of the disposition) exceeds the value of the gift in the hands of the charity (or political party), the exemption extends to the whole value transferred. (See E13 at **25** HMRC STATEMENTS OF PRACTICE).

'*Charity*' has the meaning given by *ITA 2007, ss 519, 543(1)* for income tax purposes, i.e. 'any body of persons or trust established for charitable purposes only' and up to 27 January 2009 was considered by HMRC to exclude all foreign charities. With effect from 6 April 2010 UK charity tax reliefs were extended by *FA 2010, Sch 6* to certain organisations which are equivalent to charities and Community Amateur Sports Clubs in the EU and in the European Economic Area countries of Norway and Iceland, following a judgment in the European Court of Justice on that date. Claims to this extended relief for gifts on or after the date of the ECJ judgment on 27 January 2009 and before 6 April 2010 will be considered on a case by case basis. A community amateur sports club, if it is a registered club, will be treated as a charity for inheritance tax purposes. Following *Finance Act 2002* the '*charity*' exemption is also extended to include a club that is registered as a community amateur sports club, and is required by its constitution to be, and is a club that (a) is open to the whole community; (b) is organised on an amateur basis; and (c) has as its main purpose the provision of facilities for, and the promotion of participation in, one or more eligible sports. [*FA 2002, Sch 18 paras 1–3, 9(2); ITA 2007, s 430(1)(d)*]. See *Dreyfus (Camille & Henry) Foundation Inc v CIR* HL 1955, 36 TC 126. [*IHTA 1984, s 272*]. See also **10** CHARITIES.

Reduced rate for certain estates with 10% gifts to charities

For deaths on or after 6 April 2012 Inheritance tax is charged on the net chargeable value of an estate at a rate of 36% where 10% or more of that estate has been left to charity.

Where the estate comprises only the deceased's 'free estate', the value of the estate on which the 10% threshold is based, (the 'baseline') is the value of the net estate charged to IHT after deducting all available reliefs, exemptions and available nil rate band, but excluding the charitable legacy itself. The total amount of charitable legacies is compared with the baseline amount to see if the estate qualifies for the reduced IHT rate (the '10%').

In cases in which the estate for IHT purposes includes assets additional to those in the 'free estate', the 10% test is applied to each category of assets, described as a 'component', that makes up the aggregate estate. The components are:

(a) the 'general component' being the free estate passing under the terms of the will. This excludes other components listed below and also gifts with reservation of benefit chargeable on the death;
(b) the 'survivorship component' being jointly owned assets passing by survivorship (in England, Wales and Northern Ireland), or under a special destination in Scotland, or under corresponding provisions of any applicable foreign law;
(c) the 'settled property component', being settled property comprised in the estate by virtue of an interest in possession to which the deceased was beneficially entitled.

If the assets passing to charity from one component exceed 10% of the baseline, other components may be merged with it to give an aggregate baseline. This merging of components requires an election to be made by all those who are 'appropriate persons' for each of the components involved; the appropriate persons are the personal representatives in relation to the general component, the settlement trustees in relation to the settled component and the surviving joint owner or owners in relation to the survivorship component.

The value of the assets passing to charity from a particular component are compared to the baseline amount for that component. The baseline amount is calculated after deducting from that component all available reliefs, exemptions and the appropriate proportion of the available nil rate band, as increased by the transfer of nil rate band provisions. If the 10% test for a component is passed, IHT is charged on that particular component at 36%.

The reduced rate of IHT will apply automatically if the estate or component passes the 10% test. If it does not, IHT is charged at the full rate. However, personal representatives and other relevant persons may elect for the reduced rate not to apply if, for example, the benefit obtained from applying the reduced rate is likely to be minimal and they do not wish to incur additional costs of valuing items left to charity.

These provisions apply equally to charitable legacies made by will or by an Instrument of Variation. The conditions for an Instrument of Variation to be taken into account for IHT purposes are amended so that the reduced rate applies only if it is shown that the charity has been notified that the devolution of the estate has been varied in its favour. [*FA 2012, s 209; IHTA 1984 Sch 1A*].

Example 1

The estate of Percival who dies after 6 April 2012 is valued at £425,000, comprising quoted investments and cash. He leaves a legacy of £10,000 to the National Trust and the residue of £415,000 less IHT passes to his children. The IHT payable will be £90,000 at 36% – £32,400 because 10%of the estate after deduction of the nil-band is left to charity. So the gift to the charity reduces the residue by only £2,400 (£10,000 gift less IHT reduction £40,000 – £32,400). If Percival died on 5 April 2012 the IHT payable would be £36,000.

Exceptions

[21.3] The exemption above does not apply under any of the following circumstances.

(a) If the testamentary or other disposition giving the property:
- (i) takes effect on the termination of any interest or period after the transfer is made (e.g. a gift to a person for life and then to the charity); or
- (ii) depends on a condition which is not satisfied within twelve months after the transfer; or
- (iii) is defeasible. (For this purpose, any disposition which has not been defeated within twelve months of the transfer and is not defeasible after that time is treated as not being defeasible (whether or not it was capable of being defeated before that time).)

(b) If the property is:
- (i) an interest in other property and that interest is less than the donor's; or
- (ii) an interest in other property and that property is given for a limited period; or
- (iii) an interest in possession in settled property and the settlement does not come to an end in relation to that settled property on the making of the transfer (unless the transfer is a disposition whereby the use of money or other property is allowed by one person to another) (see *Powell-Cotton v CIR* Ch D, [1992] STC 625); or
- (iv) land or a building given subject to an interest reserved or created by the donor entitling him, his spouse or civil partner or a person connected with him to possess or occupy the whole or part of the property rent-free or at a rent less than obtainable in an arm's length transaction between unconnected persons; or
- (v) not land or a building and is given subject to an interest reserved or created by the donor other than an interest created by him for full consideration in money or money's worth or an interest which does not substantially affect the enjoyment of the property by the person or body to whom it is given; or
- (vi) property of which any part may become applicable for purposes other than charitable purposes or those of a body within **21.5** to **21.8** below; or
- (vii) given in consideration of the transfer of a reversionary interest which under *IHTA 1984, s 55(1)* (see **19.4** ESTATE) does not form part of the estate of the person acquiring that interest.

(c) If immediately before the time when it becomes the property of the charity, the property is comprised in a settlement and, at or before that time but after 11 April 1978, an interest under the settlement is or has been acquired for a consideration in money or money's worth by that or another charity or body within **21.5** to **21.8** below (otherwise than *from* another charity or body within **21.5** to **21.7** below). For these purposes, a person is treated as acquiring an interest for a consideration in money or money's worth if he becomes entitled to it as a result of transactions which include a disposition for such consideration (whether to him or another) of that interest or other property. The exception does not apply if the transfer is a disposition whereby the use of money or other property is allowed by one person to another.

In (b)(i) above any question whether any interest is less than the donor's and in (b)(iv) and (v) above whether property is given subject to an interest, is decided at a time twelve months after the transfer.

See **51.3** TRANSFER OF VALUE for modification of the above where the transfer of value is an uncommercial loan. See also **21.23** below.

[*IHTA 1984, ss 23(2)–(5), 56(1)(3)–(6)(8); F(No 2)A 1987, Sch 7 para 2; FA 1998, s 143(2)(a); FA 2002, Sch 18 para 9(2)*]. See *Bailhache Labesse Trustees Ltd & Others v HMRC*, [2008] STC SCD 869 Sp C 688.

Settled property becoming held for charitable purposes

[21.4] No charge to tax arises when property ceases to be relevant property in a **43** SETTLEMENTS: DISCRETIONARY TRUSTS AND OTHER TRUSTS OF RELEVANT PROPERTY or ceases to be comprised in a temporary charitable trust (see **10.4** CHARITIES), a maintenance fund for historic buildings (see **33.23** NATIONAL HERITAGE, **44** SETTLEMENTS: ACCUMULATION AND MAINTENANCE TRUST, **45** SETTLEMENTS: INTERESTS HELD ON PROTECTIVE TRUST, **47** SETTLEMENTS: TRUST FOR DISABLED PERSONS, or **55** TRUST FOR EMPLOYEES) and becomes property held for charitable purposes only without limit of time (defined by date or otherwise). Also exempt is the settlement on discretionary trusts by a person's will of property which then becomes held, within two years of death, for charitable purposes only without limit of time. See **52.15** TRANSFERS ON DEATH. See also Tolley's Income Tax 2010–11 for information on gifts to charity from certain settlements. [*FA 2000, s 44*].

The exemption does not apply under the following circumstances.

(a) The disposition is defeasible. (For this purpose any disposition which has not been defeated within twelve months of the transfer and is not defeasible after that time is treated as not being defeasible (whether or not it was capable of being defeated before that time).)
(b) The property or any part of it can be applied otherwise than for charitable purposes or the purposes of a body within **21.6** to **21.8** below (but see *FA 1998, s 143(4)*).
(c) At or before the time of the disposition, an interest in the settlement is, or has been, acquired for a consideration in money or money's worth (or as a result of transactions which include a disposition for such consideration, whether to that body or another person, of that interest or other property) by a charity or body within **21.6** to **21.8** below otherwise than *from* a charity or body within **21.6** or **21.7** below.

If the amount on which tax would otherwise be charged (before grossing-up if applicable and before **6** BUSINESS PROPERTY relief or **4** AGRICULTURAL PROPERTY relief) exceeds the value of the property immediately after it becomes the property of the recipient body (less any consideration for the transfer received by the trustees), the amount on which tax is charged is restricted to the excess. [*IHTA 1984, ss 76(1)(3)–(8), 144; FA 1998, s 143*].

These provisions also apply where the settled property mentioned above becomes that of the bodies within **21.6** to **21.8** below. See also **43.22** SETTLEMENTS: DISCRETIONARY TRUSTS AND OTHER TRUSTS OF RELEVANT PROPERTY.

Gifts to housing associations

[21.5] Transfers of value after 13 March 1989 to registered social landlords (within the meaning of *Housing Associations Act 1985* or *Housing (Northern Ireland) Order 1981, Part VII (SI 1981/156)* and *Housing Act 1996, Part I*) are exempt to the extent that the value transferred is attributable to land in the United Kingdom. [*IHTA 1984, s 24A(1)(2); FA 1989, s 171*]. See IHTM11211.

Exceptions are the same as those applying to gifts to charities, see **21.2** above [*IHTA 1984, ss 23(2)–(5), 24(3), 56(1)(3)–(6)(8); FA 1998, s 143(3)*].

Gifts for national purposes

[21.6] Gifts to certain national bodies (see list under **33.29** NATIONAL HERITAGE) are exempt from inheritance tax. [*IHTA 1984, s 25(1), Sch 3*]. See IHTM11221.

Exceptions are the same as those applying to gifts to charities, see **21.2** above, but **21.3**(b)(i) and (ii) do not prevent the exemption from applying in relation to property consisting of the benefit of an agreement restricting the use of land. [*IHTA 1984, ss 23(2)–(5), 25(2), 56(1)(3)–(6)(8)*].

See also **21.4** above which applies equally to settled property becoming the property of a national body under *IHTA 1984, s 25(1)*. [*IHTA 1984, ss 76(1)(3)–(8), 144; FA 1998, s 143(4)*].

Gifts to political parties

[21.7] All gifts made to qualifying political parties after 14 March 1988 are exempt from inheritance tax. For gifts made before 15 March 1988 exemption was limited to £100,000 if made on or within one year of death. Certain uncommercial loans which were transfers of value were not subject to the £100,000 limit. See **51.3** TRANSFER OF VALUE. A political party qualifies for exemption if, at the last general election (i.e. by-elections are ignored) preceding the transfer of value:

(a) two members of that party were elected to the House of Commons, or
(b) one member of that party was elected to the House of Commons and not less than 150,000 votes were given to candidates who were members of that party.

[*IHTA 1984, s 24(1)(2); FA 1988, s 137*].

Qualifying parties are listed in HMRC's Inheritance Tax Manual at para 11197. It should be noted that if a gift is made to a party not qualifying for exemption of any sort it will be a chargeable transfer, not a potentially exempt transfer as it does not increase the estate of another individual. Exceptions are the same as those applying to gifts to charities, see **21.2** above. [*IHTA 1984, ss 23(2)–(5), 24(3), 56(1)(3)–(6)(8)*].

See also **21.4** above which applies equally to settled property becoming the property of a qualifying political party. [*IHTA 1984, ss 76(1)(3)–(8), 144; FA 1998, s 143(4)*].

Gifts for public benefit

Disposals before 17 March 1998

[21.8] Gifts of eligible property to bodies not established or conducted for profit were, if the Board so directed (whether before or after the transfer), exempt from inheritance tax. [*IHTA 1984, s 26(1); FA 1985, s 95*].

Exceptions were the same as those applying to gifts to charities, see **21.2** above. [*IHTA 1984, ss 23(2)–(5), 26(7), 56(1)(3)–(6)(8)*].

Eligible property

Eligible property was:

(a) land which in the opinion of the Board was of outstanding scenic, historic or scientific interest;
(b) a building for the preservation of which special steps should in the opinion of the Board be taken by reason of its outstanding historic, architectural or aesthetic interest and the cost of preserving it;
(c) land used as the grounds of a building within (b) above;
(d) an object which at the time of the transfer was ordinarily kept in, and was given with, a building within (b) above;
(e) property given as a source of income for the upkeep of property within these sub-paragraphs;
(f) a picture, print, book, manuscript, work of art or scientific collection which in the opinion of the Board was of national, scientific, historic or artistic interest. ('*National interest*' included interest within any part of the UK.)

[*IHTA 1984, s 26(2)(9); FA 1985, s 95*].

The Board did not give a direction (i) unless in their opinion, the body who received the property was an appropriate one to be responsible for its preservation or the preservation of the character of the land with (a); or (ii) in relation to property within (e) above, if or to the extent that the property would, in their opinion, produce more income than was needed (with a reasonable margin) for the upkeep of the other property in question.

Before giving a direction, the Board could require undertakings (which could be varied by agreement) concerning the use, disposal, and preservation of the property and reasonable access to it for the public. Any obligation imposed by an undertaking was enforceable by injunction (in Scotland by petition under *Court of Session Act 1988, s 45* (before 29 September 1988, *Court of Session Act 1868, s 91*)), and any purported disposition in contravention of an undertaking was void. [*IHTA 1984, s 26(3)–(6); FA 1985, s 95*].

See also **21.4** above which applied equally to settled property becoming the property of a body not established or conducted for profit. The restrictions on eligible property and Board requirements was as above. [*IHTA 1984, ss 76, 144; FA 1985, s 95*].

Disposals after 16 March 1998

[21.9] The above provisions are repealed due in main to the unrestricted exemption on transfers to charitable bodies existing elsewhere in the legislation. [*FA 1998, s 143(4)*].

Transfers between spouses or civil partners

[21.10] Transfers of value between spouses or civil partners are exempt from inheritance tax:

(a) where property becomes comprised in the transferee's estate, by the amount by which the transferor's estate is diminished; or
(b) in any other case (e.g. payment by the transferor of his spouse's or civil partner's debt), by the amount by which the transferee's estate is increased.

For these purposes, property is given to a person if it becomes his property or is held in trust for him.

[*IHTA 1984, s 18(1)(4); The Tax and Civil Partnership Regulations 2005, SI 2005/3229, Reg 7*].

£325,000 domiciliary gift limit

If, immediately before the transfer, the transferor, but not the transferor's spouse or civil partner, is domiciled in the UK the spouse exemption is subject to an upper limit . [*IHTA 1984, s 18(2)*]. This is a lifetime limit and once fully absorbed by lifetime gifts it cannot thereafter be restored. Any such lifetime gift, if not within some other exemption, will be primarily allocated to the limited exempt amount and only when that limit is exceeded will the gift be a potentially exempt transfer. Equally, gifts in excess of the exemption have no protection from the IHT reservation of benefit rules (see **22** GIFTS WITH RESERVATION). On the death of a UK domiciled spouse or civil partner, exemption for assets passing to a non-UK domiciled surviving spouse or civil partner will therefore be subject to the applicable limit, less the amount of lifetime gifts which have already been allocated to this exempt amount. From 1982 to 5 April 2013 the limit was £55,000, and with effect for deaths and transfers on or after 6 April 2013, the limit is equal to the IHT nil band and is therefore £325,000. Therefore if there were lifetime gifts before 5 April 2013 which absorbed the £55,000 allowance, on death of the transferor after that date the balance of the higher allowance from that date will be available, currently £270,000. If the entire estate who dies after 5 April 2013 passes to the surviving spouse or civil partner and there have been no lifetime gifts, anything in excess of £325,000 is a chargeable legacy. In such cases where the net estate is above the nil rate band plus £325,000 there will be no nil rate band to transfer. Where the net estate is less than the nil rate band plus £325,000, there will still be an amount of nil rate band available to transfer. See also IHTM11011, IHTM11033. [*FA 2013, s 178*].

From 6 April 2013 an individual who is not domiciled in the UK (disregarding the IHT deemed domicile provisions of *IHTA 1984, s 267*, but whose spouse or civil partner is so domiciled, may elect to be treated as UK domiciled. The election may be either:

(a) a 'lifetime election' made at any time when the person making the election is non-UK domiciled but the person's spouse or civil partner is UK domiciled, or
(b) a 'death election' made within two years of the death on or after 6 April 2013 of the person's UK domiciled spouse or civil partner. This election may be made by the personal representatives of the non-UK domiciled spouse, in the event of that person's death.

Both elections are irrevocable, and apply only for IHT purposes so that they will have no application to the remittance basis rules for other tax purposes. An election has effect on the date specified in it, which must be on or after 6 April 2013. Subject to this, a lifetime election may specify a date which is within the period of seven years ending with the date on which it is made, and a death election may specify a date which is within seven years of the death of the UK domiciled spouse. In both cases the parties must have been married or civil partners throughout the period covered by the election.

The effect, on the death of a domiciled spouse leaving his or her estate to a surviving non-domiciled spouse, will be to allow full spouse exemption on that death, but on the death of the surviving spouse foreign assets of that spouse will not be excluded property for IHT purposes. However an election will cease to have effect if the person who made it becomes non-UK resident for income tax purposes for four successive tax years after the time that the election was effective. It will also not have any effect on the excluded property status of assets transferred into trust by the non-domiciled spouse before an election takes effect, nor on excluded property within *IHTA 1984, ss 6(3)* or *48(4)* (FOTRA gilts) and s *6(3)* (certain National Savings products). HMRC states that elections will need to be made in writing to them but there will be no prescribed form.

Example 2

George is UK domiciled and owns a house in the UK worth £3 million. His wife Monique is not domiciled in the UK for inheritance tax purposes and has only foreign assets worth £2 million. George dies on 1 August 2013 leaving his estate to Monique.

The IHT on the death of George is:

£3,000,000 less the spouse exemption £325,000 less the nil band £325,000, chargeable amount therefore £2,350,000. IHT liability is £940,000.

On death of Monique on 1 September 2018 when her domicile status for IHT remains unchanged, IHT will once again be due on the UK house. Assuming that its value has not changed, and that the IHT on George's death was paid from her overseas assets, the IHT on Monique's estate will be £3 million less £325,000, chargeable amount £2,675,000. IHT liability on that amount is £1,070,000, giving total liability on both deaths of £2,010,000.

If Monique had elected within two years of the death of George to be treated as domiciled in the UK with effect from 1 August 2013, no IHT would be payable on George's death. On Monique's death, IHT would then be due on both her UK and foreign assets. If they remain unchanged from George's death and having the same values, the IHT liability would be on £5,000,000 less her nil band and less George's nil band transferred to her estate, chargeable amount £4,350,000. The IHT liability on her estate would then be £1,740,000.

An election has no impact on the relief available under double tax treaties were in force prior to the introduction of this new provision.

Where an election has effect from an earlier date, it may cause dispositions already made by that person to become chargeable transfers. In that event the time limit for delivery of an account to HMRC for those chargeable transfers is extended to twelve months from the end of the month in which the election is made.

Exceptions

[21.11] Unless the transfer of value is a loan of money or property (see **51.3** TRANSFER OF VALUE) the spouse above exemption does not apply:

(i) if the testamentary or other disposition giving the property takes effect on the termination of any interest (e.g. a life interest in settled property) or period after the transfer is made, but this does not exclude a gift which is dependent on the spouse/civil partner surviving the donor spouse/civil partner by a specified period; or

(ii) if it depends on a condition which is not satisfied within twelve months after the transfer is made; or

(iii) if property is given in consideration of the transfer of a reversionary interest which under *IHTA 1984, s 55(1)* (see **19.4** ESTATE) does not form part of the estate of the person acquiring that interest. [*IHTA 1984, ss 18(3), 56(1)*].

Where a spouse purchased a reversionary interest in settled property after 15 April 1976 for a consideration in money or money's worth, the exemption does not apply on the falling in of the reversion by the termination of the interest on which the reversionary interest is expectant unless a loan of money or property is involved, see **51.3** TRANSFER OF VALUE. For these purposes, a person is treated as acquiring an interest for a consideration in money or money's worth if he becomes entitled to it as a result of transactions which include a disposition for such consideration (whether to him or another) of that interest or other property. [*IHTA 1984, s 56(2)(5)–(7); F(No 2)A 1987, Sch 7 para 2*].

See also **21.23** below.

Gifts on trusts for employees

Subject to detailed conditions, a gift of shares or securities into trust for employees is an exempt transfer. With effect from 6 April 2014, the exemption extends to certain gifts into an employee ownership trust. See **55** TRUSTS FOR EMPLOYEES.

Sums Paid under the Equitable Life (Payments) Act 2010

[21.12] The value of any right to a payment under the *Equitable Life (Payments) Act 2010* is to be left out of account in determining (a) the value of a person's estate on death, and (b) the value of relevant property on a ten-year anniversary, in each case where the payment is made after the date of the chargeable event.

Lifetime transfers only

Annual gifts

[21.13] Annual gifts are treated as follows:

(a) **Annual exemption.** Transfers of value during the lifetime of a person up to a total of £3,000 per fiscal year are exempt from inheritance tax. See IHTM14141, IHT110 and 210. [*IHTA 1984, s 19(1)(4)*].
Where the gifts (if any) fall short of the above limit, the shortfall is carried forward to the next following year and added to the allowance *for that year only*.
Where the gifts exceed the limit, the excess must:
  (i) if the gifts were made on different days, be attributed, so far as possible, to a later rather than an earlier transfer; and
  (ii) if the gifts were made on the same day, be attributed to them in proportion to the values transferred by them.
[*IHTA 1984, s 19(2)(3)*].

(b) Where a transfer of value is a **38** POTENTIALLY EXEMPT TRANSFER, in the first instance it is left out of account for the above purposes. However, if it proves to be a chargeable transfer, it is taken to have been made in the year in which it was made later than any transfer of value which is not a potentially exempt transfer. [*IHTA 1984, s 19(3A); FA 1986, Sch 19 para 5*]. The relevance of this provision is discussed at **38.2** POTENTIALLY EXEMPT TRANSFERS. See also **19.1** ESTATE for loan waiver using annual exemption.
For the purposes of the pre-owned assets anti-avoidance legislation within *FA 2004, Sch 15,* the disposal of any property which is an outright gift to an individual and is for the purposes of *IHTA 1984* a transfer of value that is *wholly* exempt by reason of *s 19* will be an excluded transaction. [*FA 2004, Sch 15 para 10(1)(e), (2)(e)*].

Example 3

S, who has made no other transfers of value, made gifts to his sister of £5,000 on 1 June 2008 and £4,000 on 1 May 2009. S dies on 1 September 2010 with an estate valued at £325,000. See **40** RATES OF TAX.

Annual exemptions are available as follows

2008/09	£	£
1 June 2008 Gift		5,000
Deduct 2008/09 annual exemption	3,000	
2007/08 annual exemption (part)	2,000	
		5,000
		Nil

2009/10	£
1 May 2009 Gift	4,000
Deduct 2009/10 annual exemption	3,000
PET becoming chargeable on death	£1,000

The PET, having become a chargeable transfer as a result of death within seven years, is covered by the nil rate band but is aggregated with the death estate in computing the IHT payable on death and therefore £1,000 is chargeable at 40%.

(c) **Small gifts to same person.** Transfers of value during the lifetime of a person up to a total of £250 per fiscal year *to any one person* are exempt from inheritance tax. The gifts must be outright (i.e. not settled) but include free use of property (see **51.3** TRANSFER OF VALUE). This exemption is in addition to the annual exemption under (a) above and applies to any number of gifts up to £250 to separate persons but it cannot be used to cover part of a larger gift i.e. the exemption will only apply where the value of all gifts in a year *to any individual* does not exceed £250. Form P11(Notes) states that 'This exemption covers gifts at birthdays and Christmas' but is not actually solely restricted to such gifts. [*IHTA 1984, s 20*]. See IHTM14180.

Notes to (a) and (b) above.

(i) The exemptions apply separately to husband, wife or civil partners.

(ii) The value of gifts is calculated without tax (i.e. they are not grossed-up). [*IHTA 1984, ss 19(1), 20(1)*]. The exemptions apply only to transfers actually made (i.e. during lifetime) and not where deemed to have been made (such as on death or on a transfer by a settlement), but (a) does apply to transfers of value by a close company which are apportioned among its participators (see **11.5** CLOSE COMPANIES) and to the value chargeable on the termination of an interest in possession in settled property (see **42.9** SETTLEMENTS WITH INTERESTS IN POSSESSION). [*IHTA 1984, ss 3(4), 19(5), 20(3), 57, 94(5)*].

(iii) For the purposes of the pre-owned assets anti-avoidance legislation within *FA 2004, Sch 15,* the disposal of any property which is an outright gift to an individual and is for the purposes of *IHTA 1984* a transfer of value that is *wholly* exempt by reason of *s 20* will be an excluded transaction. [*FA 2004, Sch 15 para 10(1)(e), (2)(e)*].

Gifts in consideration of marriage or civil partnership

[21.14] Gifts in consideration of any one marriage or civil partnership by any one transferor (e.g. husband and wife are treated separately) are exempt from inheritance tax on the value transferred without tax (i.e. there is no grossing-up) up to the following limits:

(a) £5,000 by a parent of either party to the marriage or civil partnership.
(b) £2,500 by one party to the marriage or civil partnership to the other or by a grandparent or remoter ancestor.
(c) £1,000 in any other case.

Any excess of gifts over the above limits is attributed in proportion to the values transferred. Form P11(Notes) prior to the civil partnership legislation being introduced stated that the gift should be made 'on or shortly before the marriage' and 'to be fully effective on the marriage taking place'. The common usage form of '...on the occasion of the marriage . . . ' is also acceptable. See IHTM14201 where HMRC state:

> 'Gifts or settlements made **after** marriage or civil partnership do not qualify for the exemption unless made in the fulfilment of a binding promise **before** marriage or civil partnership. You may assume that there is a binding promise for this purpose whenever the transferor has definitely told the donee that they were going to make the gift if the marriage or civil partnership takes place'.

Gifts must be outright to a party to the marriage or civil partnership, or settled gifts exclusively for the following persons who are or may become entitled to any benefit under the settlement (using Form 222).

(i) The parties to the marriage or civil partnership, issue of the marriage or civil partnership, or a wife or husband or civil partner of any such issue.
(ii) A subsequent spouse or civil partner of a party to the marriage or civil partnership, or any child of the family, or the spouse or civil partner of any such child, of a subsequent marriage or civil partnership of either party.
(iii) As respects a reasonable amount of remuneration, the trustees of the settlement.

'*Child of the family*' above includes in relation to parties to a marriage or civil partnership, a child of one or both of them. [*The Tax and Civil Partnership Regulations 2005, SI 2005/3229, Reg 8(6)*].

'*Issue*' includes any person legitimated by a marriage, or adopted by husband and wife jointly. [*IHTA 1984, s 22(1)–(5)*].

The exemptions apply only to actual lifetime gifts, not to transfers deemed to have been made (but include a loan of money or property, see **51.3** TRANSFER OF VALUE) and to the value chargeable on the termination of an interest in possession in settled property (see **42.9** SETTLEMENTS WITH INTERESTS IN POSSESSION). [*IHTA 1984, ss 3(4), 22(6), 57*]. See IHTM14201 for examples of non-qualification vis:

> 'Where before the marriage or civil partnership the donor has taken steps towards making the gift, for example, by instructing their solicitors or brokers, but the gift is not completed until after the marriage or civil partnership, it does not qualify.'

Note

The exemption will not be lost:

(A) if some other person can benefit from the settlement only in the event of any child to the marriage or civil partnership dying without attaining a specified age; or

(B) on the operation of a protective trust to which a person within (i) or (ii) above is the principal beneficiary.

Dispositions for maintenance of family

[21.15] A disposition is not a transfer of value if it is made during lifetime:

(a) by one party to a marriage or civil partnership for the maintenance of the other party; or

(b) by one party to a marriage or civil partnership for the maintenance, education or training of a child of either party for a period up to 5 April after attaining the age of eighteen or, if later, after ceasing full-time education or training. '*Child*' includes step-child and adopted child; or

(c) by any person for the maintenance, education or training of a child not in the care of a parent of his for a period up to 5 April after attaining the age of eighteen or, if the child has been in the care of the disponer for substantial periods before that age, after ceasing full-time education or training; or

(d) in favour of an illegitimate child of the person making the disposition and is for the maintenance, education or training of the child for a period up to 5 April after attaining the age of eighteen or, if later, after ceasing full-time education or training; or

(e) as a reasonable provision for the care or maintenance of a dependent relative (i.e. a relative of self, spouse or civil partner who is incapacitated by old age or infirmity from maintaining himself or his mother or father or his spouse's or civil partner's mother or father). By concession, such a disposition is also exempt if made by a child in favour of his unmarried mother if she (although not so incapacitated) is genuinely financially dependent on that child. See *R McKelvey (personal representative of DV McKelvey) v HMRC* [2008] STC SCD 944 Sp C 694. (See F12 at **23** HMRC EXTRA-STATUTORY CONCESSIONS).

'*Marriage*' or '*civil partnership*' includes a former marriage or civil partnership where a disposition has been made on its dissolution or varied later.

'*Step-child*' in relation to a civil partner is the meaning given within *Civil Partnership Act 2004, s 246.*

For the purposes of the pre-owned assets anti-avoidance legislation within *FA 2004, Sch 15*, the disposal of any property which is a disposition falling within the requirements of this paragraph will be an excluded transaction. [*FA 2004, Sch 15 para 10(1)(d), (2)(d)*].

If a disposition as above only partially satisfies the conditions, it will be separated into exempt and non-exempt parts. An exempt disposition which is a disposal of an interest in possession in settled property is not treated as terminating that interest so as to make it chargeable to tax under *IHTA 1984, s 51(1)* (see **42.9** SETTLEMENTS WITH INTERESTS IN POSSESSION). [*IHTA 1984, ss 11, 51(2); The Tax and Civil Partnership Regulations 2005, SI 2005/3229, Reg 4*]. The non-exempt part may qualify as a **38** POTENTIALLY EXEMPT TRANSFER.

Normal expenditure out of income

[21.16] A transfer of value during lifetime is exempt if, or to the extent that, it is shown:

(a) that it was made as part of the normal (i.e. typical or habitual) expenditure of the transferor; and
(b) that (taking one year with another) it was made out of his income; and
(c) that, after allowing for all transfers of value forming part of his normal expenditure, the transferor was left with sufficient income to maintain his usual standard of living.

[*IHTA 1984, s 21(1)*].

For these purposes 'normal' is not defined but in reply to questions raised by the Committee of the Association of Corporate Trustees the HMRC Capital Taxes have stated 'There is no rule of thumb. We basically judge each case on its merits. We do look very closely at the standard of living of the transferor. The test of normality requires patterns of giving to be established. That is why it is not always possible to say that, at the time it is made, a particular gift is or is not exempt as normal.' STEP Newsletter, May 1998, p 17. However, see note (C) to the example below. Note that from November 2008 Form IHT 403 at page 6 has been revised to include a Table asking whether the deceased made any regular gifts out of income. HMRC Inheritance Tax now requires these details of the income and expenditure on Form IHT 403 to support the claim under *IHTA 1984, s 21*.

The exemption applies only to transfers actually made and not where deemed to have been made. [*IHTA 1984, ss 3(4), 21(5)*]. The first gift in a series can qualify as 'normal' provided there is clear evidence that further gifts are intended. 'Income' for the purposes of exemption, means net income after income tax and is determined in accordance with normal accountancy rules rather than income tax rules (HMRC Pamphlet IHT 1 paras 5.13 and 5.14 originally stated the above but this explanation was absent from the replacement IHT 15, p 7). In the IHT 110 (Notes) it additionally states 'A one-off payment, even if it was out of income, will not be exempt'.

In the case *Bennett and Others v CIR* Ch D 1994, [1995] STC 54 Lightman J stated that a pattern of gifts is intended to remain in place for more than a nominal period and for a sufficient period (barring unforeseen circumstances).

Also, the amount of the expenditure need not be fixed nor the individual recipient be the same but a pattern established by proof of the existence of a prior commitment or resolution or by reference only to a sequence of events. In this particular case the deceased had adopted a pattern of expenditure in respect of the surplus income which was part of her normal expenditure despite her death just over one year after executing a form of authority to distribute her surplus income (see also Taxline March 1995 Item 40). See also *Nadin v CIR* [1997] STC SCD 107 Sp C 112 at **58** TAX CASES.

To the trustees of [   ] trust ('the Trust')

1 I request and direct you to pay fifty per cent of the net after tax income due to me from the Trust to my son [   ]

2 My son's receipt shall be a complete discharge to you for my strict entitlement under the terms of the Trust

3 This authority shall be revocable by me at will but

3.1 I confirm that I have no current intention of revoking it

3.2 May be acted on by you unless and until you have notice of such revocation]

4 I confirm that I have taken such legal or other professional advice as I see fit

5 For the avoidance of doubt this authority is given to you under seal

SIGNED AS A DEED and	)
DELIVERED on	)
2010	)
By	)
in the presence of:—	)

Note to deed

(A) Clause 3 is thought to be consistent with *Bennett*.

Example 4

A wife pays annual life assurance premiums on a policy in favour of her son. The income of her husband and herself for 2010/11 is

	£
Husband's salary	25,000
Wife's salary	6,600
	£31,600

Income levels are not expected to fluctuate wildly from year to year.

The wife's disposable income is

	£
Salary	6,600
Tax thereon (personal allowance £6,475)	25
Personal income	£6,575

Notes to the example

(A) Depending on her lifestyle, the wife is probably able to show that she has sufficient income to justify a 'normal expenditure' gift of, say, a £1,000 premium paid annually (and therefore habitual). In Form P11(Notes) HMRC state that 'Examples of usual expenditure are where the deceased was paying a regular premium on an insurance policy for the benefit of another person, or perhaps they were making a monthly or other regular payment'.

(B) If the wife was also accustomed to pay personally for an annual holiday costing, say, £2,500, it might be difficult to show that the life assurance premium was paid out of income.

(C) It has been suggested that HMRC Inheritance Tax do not, as a general guide, review cases where the gift out of income is not greater than one third of net income i.e. £2,191 in the above case.

A premium on a life insurance policy

[21.17] **A premium on a life insurance policy** on his own life paid directly or indirectly by the transferor is not part of his normal expenditure if at any time an annuity was purchased on his life, unless it is shown that the purchase of the annuity and the making or varying of the insurance (or any prior insurance for which the first-mentioned insurance was directly or indirectly substituted) were not associated operations (see **5.5** ANTI-AVOIDANCE) (i.e. were not 'back to back'). [*IHTA 1984, s 21(2)*]. The practice 'is to regard policies and annuities as not being affected by the associated operations rule if, first, the policy was issued on full medical evidence of the assured's health, and, secondly, it would have been issued on the same terms if the annuity had not been bought'. (Official Report, Standing Committee A, 5 February 1975 Col 872). See also **31.9** LIFE ASSURANCE POLICIES.

Income does not include the capital element of a life annuity purchased after 12 November 1974. [*IHTA 1984, s 21(3)(4)*].

Loans of property etc.

[21.18] **Loans of property etc.** will be exempt from inheritance tax if instead of (a) and (b) above there were substituted the condition that the transfer was a normal one by the transferor. See **51.3** TRANSFER OF VALUE. [*IHTA 1984, s 29(1)(4)*].

Transfers allowable for income tax or conferring retirement benefits

[21.19] A disposition is not a transfer of value if:

(a) it is allowable in computing profits or gains for income tax or corporation tax; or

(b) it is a contribution to an approved retirement benefit scheme (occupational pension scheme); or

(c) it is to provide:

(i) benefits on or after retirement for a person not connected with the transferor who is or has been in his employ; or

(ii) benefits on or after the death of such a person for his widow or dependants or surviving civil partner; or

(d) it is a contribution after 22 July 1987 under approved personal pension arrangements entered into by an employee of the person making the disposition.

Where benefits under (c) are greater than could be provided under (b), the excess is a transfer of value. Dispositions under more than one of the kinds described in (b), (c) and (d) in respect of service by the same person, are exempt only to the extent that the benefits do not exceed what could be provided by a disposition of the kind described in any one of those subparagraphs. For the purposes of (c) above, the right to occupy a dwelling at a rent less than would be expected in a transaction at arm's length between persons not connected with each other is regarded as equivalent to a pension equal to the additional rent that might be so expected.

If a disposition as above only partially satisfies the conditions, it will be separated into exempt and non-exempt parts. From 6 April 2006 a person's contributions to an employees' registered pension scheme or scheme within *ICTA 1988, s 615(3)* will also not be a transfer of value as above. Contributions by an employer to a registered pension scheme or *ICTA 1988, s 615* scheme in respect of an employee are not treated as transfers of value. Also, contributions to a qualifying non-UK pension scheme by an employer for an employee will not be chargeable to IHT. [*IHTA 1984, s 12; F(No 2)A 1987, s 98(2)(3); FA 2004, s 203(2); The Tax and Civil Partnership Regulations 2005, SI 2005/3229, Reg 5; FA 2006, Sch 22 para 2; FA 2008, Sch 29 para 18*].

The above exemptions apply to lifetime dispositions only. (Official Report Standing Committee E, 29 June 1976 Col 1435).

Transfers on death only

Death on active service, etc.

[21.20] No inheritance tax is payable on the death of a person from wound, accident or disease contracted whilst on active service against an enemy (or on service of a similar nature) during that time or from aggravation during that time of a previously contracted disease. See IHTM11281. For deaths on or after 19 March 2014, the relief is extended to provide exemption from charge on the death for lifetime potentially exempt transfers and chargeable transfers. This exemption only applies when the HMRC Inheritance Tax receives a valid certificate issued by the Ministry of Defence. These types of certificate are detailed at IHTM11301 and IHTM11302 and may be obtained from:

Defence Business Services
Joint Casualty and Compassionate Centre (Attn SO3 Deceased Estates)
Imjin Barracks

Innsworth
Gloucester
GL3 1HW
(Tel 01452 712 612 Extension 5680/8174)

The following information should be provided:

- the deceased's service number;
- a copy of the death certificate;
- any relevant supporting medical evidence such as a post-mortem report.

Exemption applies to a person certified by the Defence Council or the Secretary of State as dying from the above causes inflicted or incurred whilst in the armed forces, or if not a member of those forces, whilst subject to the law governing any of those forces by reason of association with or accompanying them. [*Armed Forces Act 1981; IHTA 1984, s 154*]. The wound does not have to be the only or direct cause of death, provided it is a cause (*Executors of 4th Duke of Westminster (otherwise Barty-King) v Ministry of Defence* QB 1978, [1978] STC 218). The exemption applies to the estates of those killed on active service in the Falklands conflict (HMRC Press Release 23 June 1982) and, with effect for deaths on or after 19 March 2014, to those responding to emergency circumstances in the course of the person's duties as a member of the armed forces or as a civilian subject to service discipline. Where a common seaman, marine or soldier died before 12 March 1952 in the service of the Crown and his estate was wholly exempt from estate duty and under his will he left a limited life interest, no inheritance tax is charged on such exempted property which passes under the terms of the will on the termination of the limited interest. (See F13 at **23** HMRC EXTRA-STATUTORY CONCESSIONS.)

Transferable nil rate band

Since the introduction of the transferable nil rate band (TNRB) the opportunity to claim the relief on the second death has required a clarification of the above rules. For deaths before 12 March 1952, two separate schemes of relief from Estate Duty for those killed or missing in action were in force. One was a *complete exemption* relief and the another *conditional remission*. The service rank of the person killed or missing determined which scheme applied. Complete exemption applied to all ranks up to and including Corporal (Army and Royal Air Force: a Lance Sergeant was treated as a corporal), Chief Petty Officer (Royal Navy) and Sergeant in the Royal Marines, as well as Fleet Air Arm ratings. The conditional remission applied to all service ranks not eligible for complete exemption. Remission also applied on the death of any person who was drowned or killed, within a period of twelve months, by reason of injuries received as a result of operations of war in the period from 3 September 1939 to 31 March 1948. The aim of the extension was to provide relief to the estates of civilians killed in the blitz, or drowned following the torpedoing of a ship. Where complete exemption applies, the whole of the nil rate band is transferred for use on the death of the surviving spouse. In these cases, the application for TNRB need contain only the killed or missing person's rank and proof that he or she died in service. The remission was limited to the first £5,000 of property comprised in the estate for Estate Duty purposes. Where the value of the property passing to specified relatives and/or property passing to other people exceeded £5,000, Estate Duty was charged on the balance at a reduced rate. For estates in England or Wales, the Grant will show the amount of any Estate Duty paid when the Grant was taken out. If any duty was paid, no TNRB will be available. See also April 2009 HMRC Inheritance Tax and Trusts Newsletter at http://www.hmrc.gov.uk/cto/newsletter.htm.

Death of emergency service, police or armed forces personnel

[21.21] Certain exemptions are provided for deaths on or after 19 March 2014 of emergency personnel and those in the police or armed forces where, in broad terms, the death arose by virtue of their status as such persons.

The reliefs are:

(a) that no potentially exempt transfer made by the person becomes a chargeable transfer because of the death;
(b) that the estate on death is not chargeable to IHT; and
(c) that no additional IHT becomes due because of a chargeable transfer made by the person within seven years of the death, although tax already paid is not refundable.

The reliefs for *emergency personnel* apply where he or she:

(a) dies from an injury sustained, accident occurring or disease contracted at a time when that person was responding to emergency circumstances; or
(b) dies from a disease contracted at some previous time, the death being due to, or hastened by, the aggravation of the disease during a period when that person was responding to emergency circumstances.

'*Emergency circumstances*' means circumstances which are present or imminent and are causing or likely to cause (a) the death of a person or animal, (b) serious injury to, or the serious illness of, a person or animal, (c) serious harm to the environment or to any property, or (d) a worsening of any such injury, illness or harm.

A person is 'responding to emergency circumstances' if the person (a) is going anywhere for the purpose of dealing with emergency circumstances occurring there, or (b) is dealing with emergency circumstances, preparing to do so imminently or dealing with the immediate aftermath of emergency circumstances.

Emergency personnel within the reliefs are:

(a) those in the fire services or fire and rescue services;
(b) those in search services or rescue services (or both);
(c) those providing medical, ambulance or paramedic services;
(d) those in police service;
(e) those providing services for the transportation of organs, blood, medical equipment or medical personnel; or
(f) a person engaged by the government of a state or territory, an international organisation or a charity in connection with the provision of humanitarian assistance.

The reliefs for *constables, former constables and those in the armed forces* apply where he or she:

(a) dies from an injury sustained or disease contracted in circumstances where the person was deliberately targeted by reason of his or her status as a constable or armed service person, or former constable or armed service person; or

(b) dies from a disease contracted at some previous time, the death being due to, or hastened by, the aggravation of the disease by an injury sustained or disease contracted in circumstances mentioned above.

The relief for armed service personnel requires a certificate by the Defence Council or the Secretary of State.

[*IHTA 1984, ss 153A, 155A; FA 2015, s 75*].

Non-residents' bank accounts

[21.22] See **52.6** TRANSFERS ON DEATH for the exemption of certain foreign currency bank or Post Office accounts held by persons not domiciled, resident or ordinarily resident in the UK at death. For deaths on or after 6 April 2013 the requirement as to ordinary residence was removed by *FA 2013, Sch 46 para 118*.

'Bank' for this purpose takes the same meaning as *ITA 2007, s 991* (formerly *ICTA 1988, s 840A*) and includes the Bank of England and any institution authorised by the *Financial Services and Markets Act 2000, Part 4*.

Abatement of exemptions

[21.23] Where a transfer on a death after 26 July 1989 is wholly or partly exempt under any of **21.2** or **21.5–21.10** above or under **33.23**, **33.24** NATIONAL HERITAGE or **55.4** TRUSTS FOR EMPLOYEES, and the recipient of the property (the trustees where applicable) disposes of property not derived from the transfer on death in settlement of all or part of a claim against the deceased's estate, the exemption for the transfer on death is abated. The (otherwise exempt) gift on death is treated instead as a chargeable specific gift not bearing its own tax, up to the lower of:

(i) the value of the property transferred in that gift;

(ii) the amount by which the estate of the recipient of the property immediately after the disposition settling the claim is less than it would be but for the disposition.

In determining the value of the recipient's estate for the purposes of (ii), no deduction is made for the claim, no account is taken of any liability of the recipient for any tax on the disposition, and the provisions giving relief for AGRICULTURAL PROPERTY (**4.1**) and BUSINESS PROPERTY (**6.1**) are disregarded.

The abatement does not apply to the extent that the claim against the deceased's estate is in respect of a liability to be taken into account in determining the value of that estate for inheritance tax purposes. See **52.9** TRANSFERS ON DEATH for liabilities to be taken into account.

[*IHTA 1984, s 29A; FA 1989, s 172*].

Key points

[21.24] Points to consider are as follows.

- Where on a death normal expenditure out of income under *IHTA 1984, s 21* is claimed the Personal Representatives will usually have to provide full details on form IHT 403 detailing all income and outgoings for the previous six years. This includes such expenditure as holiday costs, occasional presents (e.g. birthday and Christmas gifts, etc.). Other items of household expenditure such as council tax, water rates, etc. may be obtained from utility suppliers but inevitably there will be other items of regular household expenditure which is not easily obtained and estimates should be avoided. Income details may in most cases be obtained from previously submitted tax returns but non-taxable income such as ISAs should also be taken into account even though such income will not of course have been included on the tax returns previously.
- Gifts in consideration of marriage are treated as jointly owned by the two parties to the marriage whereas other gifts and legacies by way of will are treated as the ownership of the transferee or the legatee. In such cases where there is joint ownership those assets jointly owned on a death then where one party has contributed wholly to a joint bank account then their share will be treated as 100% by HMRC despite the account being held in joint names. IHT404 does not make a distinction between jointly owned assets or those assets held as tenants in common. At the end of IHT404 a list of assets passing on by reason of survivorship is deducted at the end of IHT404 in the summary probate form IHT421 to take into account this fact. Care should be taken in distinguishing ownership of assets in this connection for IHT400 completion purposes and the *Law of Property Act 1925*.
- Exemption under *IHTA 1984, s 154(1)(b)* (Death on active service) should be considered as in **21.20** above. In this connection, a person may die many years after the conflict in which they sustained their injuries but if a link exists then it may well be worth making a claim. HMRC manual states 'the exemption applies only if the Defence Council or the Secretary of State certifies that the deceased was within one of the exempted categories of service when he or she received the injury, contracted the disease or suffered the aggravation of the disease which caused the death'. At first sight there may appear only a tenuous link between the death and the original injury but for instance the case of mustard gas attacks on the trenches in the first world war led to deaths from respiratory diseases. Recent wars have a high

incidence of post-war syndrome and similar to the *Executors of 4th Duke of Westminster (otherwise Barty-King) v Ministry of Defence* QB 1978, [1978] STC 218 it may be possible to show a link as was the case in Westminster when the Duke died of cancer in 1967 after sustaining a wound whilst on active service in 1944.

- Where one spouse is UK domiciled and the other is not, and the UK domiciled spouse is the first to die, a decision must be taken about whether the survivor should elect to be treated as UK domiciled for IHT purposes, thereby allowing the full spouse exemption to apply at that time. In principle, if the main asset in their estates is a UK home and that is likely to remain the case, then the election will normally be worthwhile. If however this is not the case, it is unlikely that the election will be beneficial unless either the non-domiciled spouse expects to become deemed domiciled in due course or else the two have failed to take any advice about potential inheritance tax liabilities. If the survivor is expected to become deemed domiciled, then all that person's worldwide assets can equally be expected to be liable to IHT on death, including those inherited from the deceased spouse (subject to the availability of quick succession relief); in such circumstances the spouse exemption on the first death is likely to be an important relief. If however the survivor can preserve non-domiciled status for IHT purposes, and tax advice is taken in good time, it will not normally be worth making the election and thereby forgoing all the potential advantages for IHT purposes through holding excluded property, even if it means that liability to IHT arises on the death of the domiciled spouse leaving all assets to the survivor.

22

Gifts with Reservation

Cross-references. See **2.8** ACCOUNTS AND RETURNS; **5.5** ANTI-AVOIDANCE for associated operations; **30.5** LIABILITY FOR TAX; **37.2** PENSION SCHEMES.

Simon's Taxes. See I3.4, I7.198, I7.382.

Other Sources. Form P11(Notes); IHT 110; Foster, Parts C4 and C5; HMRC Customer Guide to Inheritance Tax; IHTM14301.

Introduction

[22.1] Before 17 March 1986 it was possible to make a gift of an asset and the IHT position in relation to the gift was unaffected by any continuing benefits to the donor from the gift. A typical example was a gift into a discretionary trust where the settlor was one of the potential beneficiaries. To prevent the effectiveness of such arrangements for IHT purposes, legislation was introduced to ensure that the gifted assets remain within the donor's estate on death if the reservation of benefit continues up to that time. If it ceases before then, a potentially exempt transfer is treated as occurring. Pre-17 March 1986 arrangements continue to be outside the reservation of benefit provisions, but, subject to exclusions, the legislation applies to all gifts after that date.

The rule is that, subject to the exceptions in **22.2** below, where, after 17 March 1986, an individual disposes of any property (by way of gift or otherwise) and either:

(a) possession and enjoyment of the property is not *bona fide* assumed by the donee at or before the beginning of the 'relevant period'; or

(b) *at any time* in the relevant period the property is not enjoyed to the entire exclusion, or 'virtually' to the entire exclusion, of the donor; or

(c) *at any time* in the relevant period the property is not enjoyed to the entire exclusion, or virtually to the entire exclusion, of any benefit to the donor by contract or otherwise (and for this purpose a benefit which the donor obtained by virtue of any associated operations (see **5.5** ANTI-AVOIDANCE), of which the gift is one, is treated as a benefit to him by contract or otherwise);

then, if and so long as any of the conditions in (a) to (c) above apply, the property is referred to (in relation to the gift and the donor) as '*property subject to a reservation*'. See *HD Lyon's Personal Representatives v HMRC; Trustees of the Alloro Trust v HMRC* [2007] Sp C 616 where the manner in which a trust, set up by the settlor, had been operated meant that the 'possession and enjoyment of the property' within (a) above had not been 'bona fide assumed by the donee at the beginning of the relevant period', within *s 102(1)(a)*. HMRC have set out examples of 'virtually the entire exclusion' which come within the *de minimis* occupation criteria in Revenue Interpretation 55.

Any question where property falls within (b) or (c) above is, so far as that question depends on the identity of the property, determined by reference to the property which is at that time treated as comprised in the gift. See **22.3** to **22.6** below for special rules where the property changes after the gift or the donee predeceases the donor.

The effect of the above is that:

(i) if, immediately before the donor's death, there is any property which, in relation to him, is property subject to a reservation then, to the extent that the property would not otherwise form part of his estate immediately before death, it is treated as property to which he was beneficially entitled at that time; and

(ii) if at any time before the end of the relevant period, any property ceases to be property subject to a reservation, the donor is treated as having at that time made a disposition of the property by a disposition which is a POTENTIALLY EXEMPT TRANSFER (**38**).

Definitions

'*Relevant period*' is the period ending on the date of the donor's death and beginning seven years before that date or, if later, on the date of the gift.

'*Virtually*' is not defined but it is intended to prevent the rules applying where the benefit enjoyed by the donor is small. HMRC have published the following examples of situations which they consider a benefit to the donor may be disregarded:

(a) a house which becomes the donee's residence but where the donor subsequently stays, in the absence of the donee, for not more than 2 weeks each year, or stays with the donee for less than one month each year;

(b) social visits, excluding overnight stays made by a donor as a guest of the donee, to a house which they had given away, such visits being no more than would have taken place without the gift;

(c) a temporary stay for some short term purpose in a house the donor had previously given away, such as while the donor convalesces after medical treatment; while the donor looks after a donee convalescing after medical treatment; while the donor's own home is being redecorated;

(d) a house together with a library of books which the donor visits less than five times in any year to consult or borrow a book, but not where the books are used regularly, for example in connection with work.

Life policies. Any property comprised in a gift made after 17 March 1986 falls within the reservation of benefit provisions if the gift consists of or includes, or is made in connection with, a policy of insurance on the life of the donor or his spouse/civil partner or their joint lives *and* the benefits which will or may accrue to the donee as a result of the gift vary by reference to benefits accruing to the donor or his spouse/civil partner (or both) under that or another policy. Policies on joint lives include those on joint lives and the life of the survivor. Benefits accruing to the donor or his spouse/civil partner (or both of them) include benefits accruing by virtue of the exercise of rights conferred on either or both of them. For the HMRC's understanding of when an insurance is made, see **32.2** TIME OF DISPOSITION.

Exceptions to the GWR rule

[22.2] The above provisions do not apply in the following circumstances.

(a) To the extent that the disposal by way of gift is an exempt transfer by virtue of:

   (i) *IHTA 1984, s 18 as amended by FA 2003, s 185(2)* (transfers between spouses/civil partners except where provided by *FA 1986, s 102(5A)(5B)*, see **21.10** EXEMPT TRANSFERS);

   (ii) *IHTA 1984, s 20* (small gifts, see point (b) at **21.13** EXEMPT TRANSFERS);

   (iii) *IHTA 1984, s 22* (gifts in consideration of marriage, see **21.14** EXEMPT TRANSFERS);

   (iv) *IHTA 1984, s 23* (gifts to charities, see **21.2** EXEMPT TRANSFERS);

   (v) *IHTA 1984, s 24* (gifts to political parties, see **21.7** EXEMPT TRANSFERS);

   (vi) *IHTA 1984, s 24A* (gifts to housing associations, see **21.5** EXEMPT TRANSFERS);

   (vii) *IHTA 1984, s 25* (gifts for national purposes, see **21.6** EXEMPT TRANSFERS);

   (viii) *IHTA 1984, s 27 as amended by FA 1998, s 144* (maintenance funds for historic buildings, see **33.23** NATIONAL HERITAGE); or

   (ix) *IHTA 1984, ss 28 and 28A* (employee trusts, see **55** TRUSTS FOR EMPLOYEES).

   [*FA 1986, s 102(5); The Tax and Civil Partnership Regulations 2005, SI 2005/3229, Reg 44*]. *Note.* The annual exemption (see further **38.2** POTENTIALLY EXEMPT TRANSFERS) and the normal expenditure out of income exemption are not included.

(b) If the disposal by way of gift is made under the terms of a policy issued in respect of an insurance made before 18 March 1986 *unless* the policy is varied on or after that date so as to increase the benefits secured or extend the term of the insurance. Any change in the terms of the policy made in pursuance of an option or other power conferred by the policy is deemed to be a variation of the policy except for the exercise of an indexation option with respect to benefits or premiums before 1 August 1986 if the option or power could only be exercised before that date. [*FA 1986, s 102(6)(7)*].

(c) In the case of property which is an interest in land or a chattel (corporeal movable in Scotland), retention or assumption by the donor of actual occupation of, or actual enjoyment of an incorporeal right over, the land or actual possession of the chattel (corporeal movable in Scotland) is disregarded for the purposes of **22.1**(B) and (C) above if it is for full consideration in money or money's worth. [*FA 1986, Sch 20 para 6(1)(a),(3)*]. HMRC considers that for this provision to apply full consideration should be provided throughout the relevant period (see **22.1** above), so that any rent passing should be reviewed at appropriate intervals to reflect market changes. Any consideration passing will be treated as full if it lies within a range of values reflecting normal valuation tolerances (Inland Revenue Tax Bulletin November 1993 p 98).

CHATTEL LEASE

PARTIES:

1. 'The Parents' namely, ...

2. 'The Children' namely . . . .

BACKGROUND

A. The Children are the beneficial owners of the chattels set out in the Schedule below ('the Chattels')

B. The Children wish to allow the Parents the use and enjoyment of the Chattels on the basis of full consideration payable by the Parents

AGREEMENT

1. Bailment

The Children grant a lease of the Chattels to the Parents for the following term and generally on the terms and conditions following:

2. The Term

The term of the lease shall be equal to the joint lives and life of the survivor of the Parents, terminable earlier:

2.1 Upon six months written notice given by either party

2.2 Immediately upon default of any obligations contained in clause 9

2.3 Immediately upon both the Parents or the survivor of them becoming mentally incapable within the meaning of section 94 (2) of the Mental Health Act 1983.

3. Ownership

3.1 The Children retain the ownership of the Chattels

3.2 The Children reserve the right to fix any plating or other means of identification to the Chattels or any of them

3.3 The Parents covenant not (nor take steps) to sell, deal, charge or part with the Chattels in any other way contrary to the ownership of the Children

3.4 The Parents will immediately pay any sum required to remove any lien which may arise over the Chattels.

4. Enjoyment and Housing

4.1 The Children covenant with the Parents (provided the Parents pay the rent and perform the Parents' covenants) that the parents shall peaceably hold and enjoy the Chattels during the term without any interruption by the Children or any person rightfully claiming under or in trust for any of them

4.2 The Chattels shall be housed at . . . . [Name of property] . . . . or at other locations from time to time agreed between the Parents and the Children

5. Rental

5.1 The initial annual rental for the Chattels shall be £. . . . . per annum (which is agreed by the Children and the Parents to reflect . . . . . . % of the current open market value of the Chattels)

5.2 The rental shall be paid annually; the first year's rental is due on the signing of this agreement (and the Children acknowledge receipt of it); further annual rental payments shall be due on the anniversaries of this agreement. Such adjustment as is necessary on the termination of the agreement by the death of the survivor of the Parents shall be made as is required; otherwise there shall be no adjustment

5.3 The rental shall be reviewable by agreement at three yearly intervals from the date of this Agreement to ensure that the Parents give full consideration for the use and enjoyment of the Chattels. In default of agreement the reviewed rent shall be determined by a valuer appointed by the President for the time being of the Incorporated Society of Valuers and Auctioneers acting as expert and not an arbitrator; either party shall be at liberty to request the President to make such an appointment.

6. Insurance

6.1 The Parents will insure the Chattels for their full replacement cost comprehensively against all risk with the interest of the Children noted on the Policy and will duly and punctually pay all premiums and on request will promptly produce the insurance policy and proof of payment of premiums to the Children. All claims under such insurance policy will be dealt with in accordance with the written direction of the Children. All claims and moneys received by the Parents under such insurance policy shall be held by the parents in trust for the Children

7. Preservation and Repair

7.1 The Parents undertake to preserve the Chattels

7.2 The Parents undertake to keep the Chattels clean and in good and substantial repair and will bear the cost of any repairs not covered by insurance

7.3 The Parents will permit the Children and any person authorised by them at any reasonable hour to view or survey the state and condition of the Chattels

7.4 The Parents will forthwith after being required to do so by the Children make good any want of repair in the Chattels

PROVIDED that nothing in this clause shall require the Parents to maintain the Chattels in anything other than their current condition or require the Parents to improve or put the Chattels into first rate condition

8. Security

8.1 The Parents undertake to put in place, maintain and bear the cost of such security arrangements as are from time to time agreed between the Parents and Children or as are reasonably stipulated by the Children to reflect the requirements of any relevant insurance company, advice from the Police or advice otherwise specifically received from a specialist security company engaged for the purpose

9. Default

If the Parents default in the punctual payment of any of the instalments of rent provided for, or default in the payment of the insurance premiums as provided for, or default in the performance of any of the terms and conditions of this agreement, the Children may immediately retake possession of the Chattels, without notice to the Parents, with or without legal process, and the parents by this agreement authorise and empower the Children to enter the premises or other places where the Chattels may be found and to take and carry away the Chattels. All moneys due under this agreement shall become immediately due and payable plus all reasonable costs of repossession

EXECUTED on 2010

Signed by . . . .

Note to the Precedent

(A) The initial rent should be arrived at preferably by written negotiation between two competent valuers aware of the terms of the lease, the value and condition of the chattels, cost of insurance and security, etc.

(B) The agreement is said to be a chattel lease as that is the common understanding. Strictly it is a bailment agreement though nothing turns on that.

(d) In the case of property which is an interest in land, any occupation by the donor of the whole or any part of the land is disregarded for the purposes of **22.1**(b) and (c) above if

(i) it results from a change in circumstances of the donor since the time of the gift, being a change which was unforeseen at that time and was not brought about by the donor to receive the benefit of this provision; *and*

(ii) it occurs at a time when the donor has become unable to maintain himself through old age, infirmity or otherwise; *and*

(iii) it represents a reasonable provision by the donee for the care and maintenance of the donor; *and*

(iv) the donee is a relative of the donor or his spouse/civil partner. [*FA 1986, Sch 20 para 6(1)(b); The Tax and Civil Partnership Regulations 2005, SI 2005/3229, Reg 46*].

Case law — *Ingram* Schemes

In the case of *Ingram v IRC*, [2000] 1 AC 293,[1999] STC 37, HL; the case revolved around the transfer of property on 29 March 1987 by Lady Ingram to her Solicitor who then, as nominee, granted Lady Ingram 20-year leasehold interests and then transferred the land subject to the leases to Trustees to hold on trust for specified beneficiaries. The widow continued to live at the property until her death in 1989. HMRC treated the transfer as a gift with reservation and issued a notice of determination accordingly. The House of Lords allowed the executors' appeal. Lord Hoffmann held that:

> 'although (*s 102*) does not allow a donor to have his cake and eat it, there is nothing to stop him from carefully dividing up the cake, eating part and having the rest. If the benefits which the donor continues to enjoy are by virtue of property which was never comprised in the gift, he has not reserved any benefit out of the property of which he disposed.'

For these purposes, 'property' was 'not something which has physical existence like a house but a specific interest in that property, a legal construct, which can co-exist with other interests in the same physical object. *Section 102* does not therefore prevent people from deriving benefit from the object in which they have given away an interest. It applies only when they derive the benefit from that interest'. The policy of *s 102* was to require people to 'define precisely the interests which they are giving away and the interests, if any, which they are retaining'. The interest, which the widow retained, was 'a proprietary interest, defined with the necessary precision'. The gift was 'a gift of the capital value in the land after deduction of her leasehold interest in the same way as a gift of the capital value of the fund after deduction of an annuity'.

The *Ingram* case therefore laid down an important principle for the purposes of the legislation, commonly described as the 'carve out principle'. If an interest in asset to be given away is carved out and retained by the donor, with there being no benefit retained in the remaining interest in that asset, the reservation of benefit provisions do not apply to the interest given away.

Buzzoni and Others v IRC [2013] EWCA Civ 1684, involved a leasehold property rather than a freehold. An individual held a lease for 100 years less one day in respect of a residential property and on 21 November 1997 she granted an underlease commencing on future date to a nominee company. The underlease was then transferred to a trust for her sons. The superior landland consented to the grant of the underlease on condition that the underlease contained the usual covenants on the part of the underlessee. The covenants which were contained in the underlease mirrored many of those contained in the headlease, e.g. payment of the service charges and an undertaking to keep the property in good repair, these all taking effect on the date when the underlease fell into possession. Both the First Tier Tax Tribunal and the Upper Tribunal held that the covenants were a clear benefit reserved to the headlessee out of the gift of the underlease and so there was a reservation of benefit.

However, the Court of Appeal reversed those decisions. The central point is whether or not the donee's enjoyment of the property gifted is to the exclusion of any benefit to the donor. The focus is not primarily on the question whether the donor has obtained a benefit from the gifted property but whether the donee's enjoyment of that property remains exclusive. In this case any benefit to the donor did not have any impact on the donee's enjoyment of the property and therefore the reservation of benefit rules were not in point.

See **5.** for HMRC's views on reversionary lease schemes under the general anti-avoidance rule enacted in the Finance Act 2013.

Post-8 March 1999 anti-avoidance

From 9 March 1999 the scheme in the *Ingram* case, as described above was blocked by new counter avoidance measures. These apply where there is a disposal of land by way of gift on or after that date and the donor or his spouse/civil partner enjoys a significant right or interest, or is a party to a significant arrangement, in relation to the land. A right, interest or arrangement in relation to the land is significant only if it entitles the donor to occupy all or part of the land, or enjoy a right in relation to it, otherwise than for full consideration in money or money's worth. However an interest retained is not significant, and thus these anti-avoidance provisions do not apply, if:

- it does not and cannot prevent the enjoyment of the land to the entire exclusion (or virtually the entire exclusion) of the donor;
- it does not entitle the donor to occupy all or part of the land immediately after the gift, but would do so were it not for the interest gifted; or
- it was granted or acquired more than seven years before date of the gift.

The first of these exclusions appears to deal with retained interests which are de minimis. The second of the above deals with the case where a person gives another an immediate lease over land by way of gift; this is not an arrangement to which the legislation was intended to apply and hence the second exclusion takes it out of the scope of the provisions. The third exclusion is considered to permit most deferred lease schemes to escape the reservation of benefit provisions. For example a deferred lease of a property, commonly for 999 years, to commence in say 20 years' time should be outside the scope of the 1999 legislation if the donor's retained freehold interest was acquired more than seven years prior to the gift. It is understood that these reversionary lease schemes are accepted by HMRC as being outside the 1999 legislation where the donor's freehold interest was acquired more than seven years previously, but as a result they fall within the pre-owned assets charge (see **5.6**).

In addition, the gift of an undivided share in land on or after 9 March 1999 will be treated as a gift with reservation unless either:

- the donor does not occupy the property, for example where it is let;
- the donor occupies the land to the exclusion of the donee for full consideration in money or money's worth; or
- the donor and donee occupy the land and the donor receives no material benefit, other than a negligible one, by or at the donee's expense in connection with the gift.

[*FA 1986, s 102B(4)*].

Post-19 June 2003 anti-avoidance: Eversden schemes

In *CIR v Eversden and another (executors of Greenstock deceased)* [2003] STC 822 the Court of Appeal held that the reservation of benefit provisions did not apply where there was a gift on (pre-22 March 2006) interest in possession trusts for the spouse which later terminated in favour of discretionary trusts from which the settlor could benefit. This was because the reservation of benefit provisions contain a complete exclusion from their scope for gifts by which the estate of the spouse is increased. See TAX CASES (58).

Accordingly a targeted anti-avoidance now applies to bring such 'Eversden trusts' within the scope of the reservation of benefit provisions. From20 June 2003 this anti-avoidance provision ensures that the reservation of benefit provisions will apply where a gift is made on or after that date and:

(a) the property becomes settled property by virtue of the gift; and
(b) the trusts of the settlement give an interest in possession to the donor's spouse/civil partner, so that the gift is exempt from IHT because the exemption for transfers between spouses/civil partners and the rule that treats an interest in possession as equivalent to outright ownership; and
(c) between the date of the gift and the donor's death the interest in possession comes to an end; and
(d) when that interest in possession comes to an end, the beneficiary does not become beneficially entitled either to the settled property, or another interest in possession in it.

The anti-avoidance provisions also apply to ensure that *FA 1986, s 102(5B)* is to apply as if the gift had been made immediately after the relevant beneficiary's interest in possession has ended so that it is only the circumstances after that date which determine whether the property is subject to reservation even in the case where the donor dies within seven years. In addition, *FA 1986, s 102(5C)* duplicates the rule in *FA 1986, s 51(b)* which treats an interest in possession as coming to an end when it is disposed of and reinforces the fact that a reference to property or an interest in property includes part of any property or interest. [*FA 1986, s 102(5)(A), (B), (C); FA 2003, s 185(3); The Tax and Civil Partnership Regulations 2005, SI 2005/3229, Reg 44*].

The above provisions do not make the gift of land a gift with reservation where:

- the gift was itself an exempt transfer covered by the main exemptions from inheritance tax in *FA 1986, s 102(5)* (including transfers between spouses) until 19 June 2003. See *Essex and another (executors of Somerset deceased) v CIR* [2002] STC SCD 39 and *Eversden*; or
- due to unforeseen circumstances, the donor occupies the land because he/she becomes unable to maintain himself/herself through old age, infirmity or otherwise, and, the interest in land represents reasonable care and maintenance provided by the donee, who is a relative.

Example 1

Alistair, aged 79 years, owns a property that is valued at £340,000. He gives the property to his daughter on 31 March 2008 at the time he enters a nursing home as an infirm resident. However, on 31 December 2010 the nursing home closes due to the imposition of onerous Local Authority regulations imposed on the nursing home. *Care Standards Act 2000, ss 22, 23.* In view of the fact that there is a shortage of nursing home beds available in the vicinity Alistair returns to the former family home to live with his daughter who gives up her job to care for him full time. Under *FA 1986, Sch 20 para 6(1)(b)* Alistair's occupation of the property, now owned by his daughter, will not be treated as a gift with reservation because:

(a) the change resulting in the reoccupation of the property arose out of 'unforeseen' circumstances which were not brought about by the donor; and

(b) it occurs at a time when the donor is unable to maintain himself because of old age, infirmity or otherwise; and

(c) the gift represents reasonable care and maintenance provided by the donee which in this case can be equated with the loss of earnings by the daughter; and

(d) the daughter is a relative.

Alistair dies on 16 June 2013. Providing that within (c) above it can be determined that the care and maintenance was 'reasonable' and the other factors within (a), (b) and (d) are in point, the donor's occupation and enjoyment of the gifted land will be disregarded concerning the provisions on gifts with reservation. HMRC does not state what 'reasonable' equates to but states in a letter dated 19 February 1987 'What is *reasonable* will of course depend on the facts of the case'. However, in Tax Bulletin, Issue 9 November 1993 within *FA 1986, Sch 20 para 6(1)(b)* a definition is made by comparison with the shorter Oxford English Dictionary and the corollary of this when defining 'reasonable' would be that the care and maintenance is 'as much as is appropriate or fair; moderate'. In these circumstances the care and maintenance which is full time might be argued to be appropriate and fair for an infirm person commensurate with nursing home standards.

[*FA 1986, ss 102(1)–(5)(5A)–(5C), 102A–B, Sch 20 para 6(1)(c)(2), 7; FA 1999, s 104; FA 2003, s 185(2)(3); The Tax and Civil Partnership Regulations 2005, SI 2005/3229, Regs 44, 45*].

Notes

(1) The disposition by which the property becomes subject to a reservation may itself be a chargeable transfer (e.g. a gift to a discretionary trust with the settlor among the class of beneficiaries). Provided certain conditions are met, regulations provide for the avoidance of a double charge to tax in these circumstances. See **22.13** below.

(2) The amount of the benefit or enjoyment retained by the donor is not important. If a gift falls within the provisions the value of all the property subject to the reservation is taken into account.

(3) Any property which the donor's spouse/civil partner enjoys or benefits from does not automatically fall within the above provisions.

(4) See **38.2** POTENTIALLY EXEMPT TRANSFERS for HMRC treatment of the annual exemption in relation to the potentially exempt transfer deemed to be made as in (ii) above.

Example 2

On 19 June 1992 D gave his house and contents to his grandson G, but continued to live in it alone paying no rent. The agreement between D and G read as follows:

> I give to . . . . [Grandson G]. . . . . my house known as . . . . [Postal address]. . . . . that constitutes my principal private residence but subject to his bearing any inheritance tax attributable to its value. I also give to . . . . [Grandson G]. . . . . those of my personal chattels, specified in the schedule annexed hereto, in my house known as . . . . [Postal address] . . . . which constitute furniture or articles of household use or ornament; jewellery or articles of personal use or adornment; books photographs and articles relating to any sport hobby or other pastime also subject to his bearing any inheritance tax attributable to their value.

The house and contents were valued at £130,000. On 5 May 2006 D remarried, and went to live with his new wife F. G immediately moved into the house, which was then valued at £333,000.

On 3 January 2011 D died, leaving his estate of £200,000 equally to his granddaughter H and his wife F.

Gift 19 June 1992

As the gift was made more than seven years before death, it is a PET which has become exempt.

5 May 2006 release of reservation

The release of D's reservation is a PET which becomes chargeable by reason of D's death between 4 and 5 years later. IHT is charged, at 60% of full rates on the basis of the Table of rates in force at the time of death, on the value of the house at the date of release of reservation.

		£	£
Gift			333,000
Deduct annual exemptions	2006/07*	Nil	
	2005/06*	Nil	
* see note (C) below			
			Nil
Chargeable transfer			£333,000
Tax thereon (assuming no change in rates)			
0–325,000 at nil%		—	
325,001–333,000 at 40%		3,200	
		£3,200	
IHT payable at 60% of full rates, 60% × £3,200 =			£1,920

Death 3 January 2011

IHT is charged at full rates on the chargeable estate of £100,000 (£100,000 passing to the wife is exempt) in the bracket £333,000 to £433,000.

Tax thereon
£333,001–433,000 at 40% £40,000

Notes to the example

(A) The reference to principal private residence is designed to secure exemption under *TCGA 1992, s 222* but an election should exist where there are two or more properties (inclusive of those abroad).

(B) The agreement between the D and his grandson G above is not ideal as there are likely to be a number of factors that might be open to dispute, particularly the schedule if it does not have, say, an insurance valuation and photographs attaching.

(C) It would appear that under *FA 1986, s 102(4)* HMRC practice is not to reduce a PET by the available annual exemption. This is detailed in the Tax Bulletin, issue 9, November 1993 which stated ' . . . but the value of the PET cannot be reduced by any available annual exemption under section 19 IHTA 1984. The statement in paragraph 3.4 IHT 1 booklet, which indicates that the annual exemption may apply if the reservation ceases to exist in the donor's lifetime and a PET is treated as made at that time, is incorrect'. The new version of IHT 110 definitively states 'The law states that the exemption for gifts out of income and the annual exemption do not apply to a gift with reservation'.

Post-5 April 2005 anti-avoidance

Further anti-avoidance measures apply from 6 April 2005 have been introduced following a short consultation period on the consultation document 'The Tax Treatment of Pre-Owned Assets' to counteract the free continuing use of assets that have been ostensibly gifted. Subsequently, a Technical Guidance note was issued on 17 March 2005. Further Technical Guidance Notes were subsequently issued, the latest being on 2 November 2007 at http://www.hmrc.gov.uk/poa/poa_news.htm. See also **5.6** ANTI-AVOIDANCE. HMRC's consultative document concentrated mainly on a charge to income tax, under *Sch D Case VI* [now see *ITTOIA 2005*], on former owners of assets on the benefit of using the asset(s) unless the asset has been sold to an unconnected party at arm's length. [*FA 2004, Sch 15 paras 4, 7, 9; Charge to Income Tax by Reference to Enjoyment of Property Previously Owned Regulations 2005, SI 2005/724, Regs 2–4*]. Taxpayers who have existing schemes that come within the charge may, by the relevant filing date i.e. 31 January in the year of assessment immediately following the initial year or such later date as HMRC may allow, elect for special transitional relief that allows them to avoid the charge to income tax by dismantling the original gift scheme. [*FA 2004, Sch 15 para 23(3)* as amended by *FA 2007, s 66*]. For IHT 500 election form see below. This will then ensure that the asset is treated as part of the individual's taxable estate for IHT purposes in accordance with the gifts with reservation rules while the individual continues to enjoy the property. Under those rules the property would be potentially eligible for IHT reliefs and exemptions (e.g. APR and BPR) providing the necessary requirements for those reliefs and exemptions were met. However, it may still in certain circumstances be appropriate to suffer the income tax charge under existing schemes and avoid the IHT charge. In addition, the charging provisions do not apply to property within an 'exemption from charge' or to the extent that it comes within an 'excluded transaction' category.

Substitutions and accretions of unsettled property

[22.3] Special rules are required to cover cases where the property changes hands after the gift or the donee predeceases the donor.

Basic rule

Where the donor makes a gift, other than a sum of money in sterling or any other currency then if at any time before the 'material date' the donee ceased to have the possession and enjoyment of any of the gifted property, the property, if any, received by him in substitution for that property is treated as if it had been comprised in the original gift instead of the property of which the donee ceased to have possession and enjoyment. This includes, in particular:

(a) in relation to any property disposed of by the donee, any benefit received by him by way of consideration for the sale, exchange or other disposition; and
(b) in relation to a debt or security, any benefit received by the donee in or towards the satisfaction or redemption thereof; and
(c) in relation to any right to acquire property, any property acquired in pursuance of that right. Any consideration given by the donee, in money or money's worth, is allowed as a deduction in valuing the original gift at any time after the consideration is given. This does not apply to any part (not being a sum of money) of that consideration which is property comprised in the same or another gift from the donor and is treated either as forming part of his estate immediately before death or as being attributable to the value transferred by a potentially exempt transfer made by him.

The '*material date*' is the date of the donor's death, or, if earlier the date on which the property ceases to be property subject to a reservation.

Gift by donee

Where, before the material date, the donee makes a gift of the property comprised in the gift to him or otherwise voluntarily divests himself of it (except under compulsory purchase) for less than the value of the property at that time, then, unless he does so in favour of the donor, he is treated as continuing to have possession and enjoyment of that property. For these purposes, the donee is treated as divesting himself, voluntarily and without consideration, of any interest in property which merges or is extinguished in another interest held or acquired by him in the same property. [*FA 1986, Sch 20 paras 1, 2(1)–(5), 3(1)*].

The effect of the above is as follows:

(i) If the original gift subject to a reservation is of money in sterling or other currency it appears that the reservation ceases when the money is spent on acquiring any property.

(ii) If the disposal by the donee is for full consideration, the property received in substitution is treated as the original gift. As drafted, one interpretation is that this provision only applies to the first substitution and that on a second substitution (e.g. the application of the proceeds of sale of the original property for full consideration) the reservation ceases. It is understood that HMRC Inheritance Tax do not agree with this interpretation, and their view is that the property received on second and subsequent substitutions is also treated as the original gift. This point is unlikely to be resolved until the matter is tested in the courts.

(iii) If the disposal by the donee is for less than full consideration, the donee is treated as continuing to have possession and enjoyment of the original property.

Shares and debentures

[22.4] Where any shares in or debentures of a body corporate are comprised in the original gift and the donee is issued with, or granted rights to acquire, further shares or debentures (in the same or any other body corporate) otherwise than by way of exchange, the further issue or rights granted are treated as having been comprised in the gift in addition to the original property. (Where the shares etc. are issued by way of exchange, the *basic rule* above applies.)

This applies where the issue or grant of rights is:

(a) made to the donee as holder or as having been the holder; or
(b) made to him in pursuance of an offer or invitation made to him as being or having been the holder; or
(c) an offer or invitation in connection with which any preference is given to him as being or having been the holder. [*FA 1986, Sch 20 para 2(6)(7)*].

Consideration by donee

Any consideration given by the donee, in money or money's worth, for the issue or grant of rights is allowed as a deduction in valuing the original gift at any time after the consideration is given. This does not apply to any part of that consideration:

(i) which, not being a sum of money, is property comprised in the same or another gift from the donor and is treated either as forming part of his estate immediately before death or as being attributable to the value transferred by a potentially exempt transfer made by him; or
(ii) as consists in the capitalisation of reserves or in the retention of any property distributable by the body corporate; or
(iii) is otherwise provided (directly or indirectly) out of the assets or at the expense of the body corporate or any associated body corporate. For this purpose, two bodies are deemed to be associated if one has control of the other or if another person has control of both. [*FA 1986, Sch 20 para 3*].

Early death of donee

[22.5] Where there is a gift and the donee dies before the material date (see 22.3 above) the provisions of 22.3 and 22.4 above apply to any property comprised in the gift as if:

(a) the donee had not died and the acts of his personal representative were his acts; and
(b) property taken by any person under his testamentary dispositions or his intestacy (or partial intestacy) were taken under a gift made by him at the time of his death. [*FA 1986, Sch 20 para 4*].

Application to settlements

Settlement by donor

[22.6] Where there is a disposal by way of gift and the property becomes settled property by virtue of the gift, the provisions relating to gifts with reservation apply as if the property comprised in the gift consisted of the property in the settlement on the 'material date' except insofar as that property neither is, nor represents, nor is derived from, property in the original gift. In practical effect this means that there is automatic tracing of reservation of benefit through all the changes which may later take place in the underlying assets in the trust. For these purposes:

(a) any property comprised in the settlement on the material date which is derived, directly or indirectly, from a loan made by the donor to the trustees is treated as derived from property originally comprised in the gift; and
(b) where, under any trust or power relating to settled property, income arising from that property after the material date is accumulated, the accumulations are not treated as derived from the property.

The '*material date*' is the date of the donor's death or, if earlier, the date at which the property ceased to be property subject to a reservation.

If the settlement comes to an end before the material date as respects all or any part of the property which, if the donor had died immediately before that time, would be treated as comprised in the gift, then

(i) the property in question (other than property to which the donor then becomes absolutely and beneficially entitled in possession); and
(ii) any consideration (not consisting of rights under the settlement) given by the donor for any of the property to which he so becomes entitled,

is treated as comprised in the original gift in addition to any other property so comprised. [*FA 1986, Sch 20 para 5(1)(2)(4)(5)*].

It is understood that HMRC Inheritance Tax accepts that the interaction of *FA 1986, s 102(3)* in **22.1**(i) above and *IHTA 1984, s 48(3) as amended by FA 2006, s 157* (see **20.2** EXCLUDED PROPERTY) is such that if a non-UK domiciled settlor creates a discretionary settlement of assets situated outside the UK and is included as a possible beneficiary, the gifts with reservation rules do not apply because the excluded property provisions are paramount. The fact that the settlor becomes domiciled in the UK after creating the settlement would also not give rise to the operation of *FA 1986, s 102(3)* should he die while so domiciled but should the settlor become so domiciled and then cease to be a beneficiary, such cesser is deemed to be a potentially exempt transfer of the settled assets (notwithstanding that they are excluded property) by reason of *FA 1986, s 102(4)* in **22.1**(ii) above and will be liable to tax in accordance with 53 TRANSFERS WITHIN SEVEN YEARS OF DEATH (Tolley's Practical Tax 1989 p 176).

Settlement by donee

[22.7] Where the donor's gift is not settled property but the property is settled by the donee before the material date, the above provisions for settlements by the donor apply as if the settlement had been made by the original gift. For this purpose, property which becomes settled property under any testamentary disposition of the donee or his intestacy (or partial intestacy) is treated as settled by him. [*FA 1986, Sch 20 para 5(3)*].

Continuing benefit after termination of life interest

[22.8] Up to 21 March 2006 there was no reservation of benefit where a life interest was terminated and following that termination discretionary trusts followed under which the former life tenant could benefit. This was because the termination was not treated as a gift by the life tenant.

Accordingly new provisions were introduced to bring such arrangements within the scope of the reservation of benefit provisions. From 22 March 2006, where an interest in possession is in one of the categories which result in the life tenant being treated as beneficially entitled to settled property for IHT purposes (for example, a life interest which commenced before that date) and that interest comes to an end during that person's lifetime then the termination is to be treated as if it was a gift for the purposes of the gifts with reservation rules. Therefore where the interest in the property has terminated and the individual with the former interest in possession either receives or may receive benefits thereafter from the assets concerned then the gifts with reservation rules may apply in the same way as if the life tenant had made a gift of those assets personally. This is subject to the application of the exclusions from charge noted above. [*FA 1986, s 102ZA*].

Agricultural property and business property

[22.9] Where there is a gift of an asset which at the time of gift qualifies for agricultural property relief or business property relief, and the gift is caught by the reservation of benefit provisions, a special rule applies to determine whether either of those reliefs may apply to any potentially exempt transfer treated as taking place when the reservation ceases, or alternatively to the charge in respect of those assets on the death of the donor. In very broad terms either of these reliefs will only apply at the later time if the asset concerned continues to be within the relief in the hands of the donee. Thus relief will be available for a business asset if it continues to be used for a qualifying business by the donee, but if it is used by him for non-business purposes, any reservation of benefit charge on the donor will not be reduced by business property relief. The donor's and the donee's periods of ownership are aggregated for the purposes of establishing whether the applicable period of ownership test is satisfied.

In more detail, where there is a disposal by way of gift which, in relation to the donor, is at that time:

(a) relevant business property (see **6.4** BUSINESS PROPERTY); or
(b) agricultural property to which *IHTA 1984, s 116* applies (see **4.4** AGRICULTURAL PROPERTY); or
(c) shares or securities in agricultural companies to which *IHTA 1984, s 122(1)* applies (see **4.14** AGRICULTURAL PROPERTY),

and that property is subject to a reservation, then, subject to the exception below, any question as to the availability and appropriate percentage of agricultural or business property relief on the 'material transfer of value' is determined as if, so far as it is attributable to the gifted property, the transfer was made by the donee. For these purposes only, in determining whether the requirements as to minimum period of ownership and/or occupation are fulfilled (see **4.5** AGRICULTURAL PROPERTY and **6.8** BUSINESS PROPERTY) the donor's ownership prior to the gift is treated as the donee's and any occupation by the donor (before or after the gift) is treated as occupation by the donee.

The exception is that any question as to whether, on the material transfer of value, any shares or securities qualify for business property relief where control or 25% voting control is an issue is determined as if the shares or securities were owned by the donor and had been owned by him since the gift.

Where the gift falls within (c) above, agricultural property relief is not available (for transfers and other events occurring before 17 March 1987 the above provisions did not apply) unless *IHTA 1984, s 116* (see **4.4** AGRICULTURAL PROPERTY) applied in relation to the value transferred by the disposal *and* throughout the period from the gift to the 'material date' the shares and securities are owned by the donee. For this purpose only, in determining whether the requirements of **4.13**(c) AGRICULTURAL PROPERTY are fulfilled the requirements as to the ownership of the shares or securities there mentioned are assumed to be fulfilled.

The '*material transfer of value*' is, as the case requires, the transfer of value on the donor's death or on the property concerned ceasing to be subject to a reservation and '*material date*' is construed accordingly.

Early death of donee

[22.10] If the donee dies before the material transfer of value, then, as respects any time after his death, references to the donee include references to his personal representatives or, if appropriate, the person by whom the property or shares etc. concerned were taken under a testamentary disposition made by the donee or under his intestacy (or partial intestacy). [*FA 1986, Sch 20 para 8; FA 1987, s 58, Sch 8 para 18; F(No 2)A 1992, s 73, Sch 14 para 7*].

Estate duty cases

[22.11] The estate duty legislation contained similar, but not identical, provisions relating to gifts with reservation. It is, therefore, currently uncertain to what extent the estate duty cases are relevant for IHT purposes. In *Pearson and Others v CIR* HL, [1980] STC 318 it was held that the meaning of 'interest in possession' for estate duty purposes was not relevant for CTT purposes but this does not necessarily mean that similar decisions will be applied with respect to gifts with reservation.

The following decisions in estate duty cases must, therefore, be considered subject to this background.

(a) *Exclusion of the donor from enjoyment under* **22.1**(B) *above*. This condition is not fulfilled if at some later date after the gift the property or income therefrom is voluntarily applied by the donee to the donor, even if the latter is under an obligation to repay sums used by him (*New South Wales Commissioners of Stamp Duties v Permanent Trustee Co. of New South Wales Ltd PC*, [1956] AC 512). The deceased may remain as a guest in a house he has given without tax being attracted provided that there was no agreement to this effect and it was a *bona fide* gift (*A-G v Seccombe* KB, [1911] 2 KB 688—contrast *Revenue Commissioners v O'Donohoe* SC (RI), [1936] IR 342) but this proposition is open to question following *Chick v New South Wales Commissioners of Stamp Duties* PC, [1958] AC 435.

(b) *Exclusion of the donor from any benefit under* **22.1**(C) *above*. Arrangements between the donee and a third party to give the donor benefit is within this provision, but retention of rights under a contract made prior to the gift and quite separate from it, is not. The gift of land already subject to a lease to the donor is not a gift with reservation as the lease is not part of the gift (*Munro v New South Wales Commissioners of Stamp Duties* PC 1933, [1934] AC 61). But compare *Nicholas v CIR* CA, [1975] STC 278 where the donor's lease was acquired at the same time as the gift. (*Note*. The question of whether the owner of property (in particular, land) can grant a lease to himself or a nominee for himself may need to be answered by reference to the legal jurisdiction concerned. In the Scottish stamp duty case of *Kildrummy (Jersey) Ltd v CIR* CS, [1990] STC 657 the grant of a lease of land by the owners of the freehold interest to a nominee for themselves prior to the transfer of the freehold reversion to a third party was declared a nullity on the ground that a person cannot contract with himself. In the English law of property case of *Rye v Rye* HL 1961, [1962] AC 496 it was held that *Law of Property Act 1925, s 72(3)* does not enable a person or persons who are the freeholders of land to grant a lease to himself or themselves but, although not at issue, the judgment

of Radcliffe LJ suggests the use of a nominee in such circumstances would be valid. These cases may be pertinent when considering the *Munro* decision in the context of IHT and gifts with reservation.)
Examples of 'benefit' include a covenant by the donee to pay the donor's debts and funeral expenses (*Grey (Earl) v A-G* HL, [1900] AC 124); a power reserved to the donor to charge a capital sum on the subject matter of the gift (*Re Clark*, (1906) 40 ILT 117); a collateral annuity to the donor secured by personal covenant (*A-G v Worrall* QB 1894, [1891–94] All ER 861); remuneration paid to the settlor as trustee, but *not* money spent on maintenance and education of the donor's children (*Oakes v New South Wales Commissioners of Stamp Duties* PC 1953, [1954] AC 57).

(c) *Settlements*. A reservation of benefit arises where a settlor is included as a potential beneficiary under a discretionary trust (see *A-G v Heywood* QB, [1887] 19 QBD 326; *A-G v Farrell* CA, [1931] 1 KB 81; and *Gartside v CIR* HL, [1968] AC 553) but not necessarily where a spouse is included. The inclusion of the spouse may have income tax disadvantages (unless the trust contains non-income producing assets) but the inclusion of a widow or widower will not do so (*Lord Vestey's Executors and Vestey v CIR* HL 1949, 31 TC 1). Trustees are treated as having possession on behalf of the beneficiaries (*Oakes v New South Wales Commissioners of Stamp Duties* PC 1953, [1954] AC 57). A settlement of shares in favour of an infant child with absolute gift provided he reached the age of 21 but with a resulting trust to the donor if the child failed to reach that age is not a gift with reservation as the property comprised in the gift is the equitable interest which the donor had created in the shares (*New South Wales Commissioners of Stamp Duties v Perpetual Trustee Co. Ltd* PC, [1943] AC 425).

Variations and disclaimers

[22.12] The provisions relating to variations and disclaimers in *IHTA 1984, s 142* (see **13.1** DEEDS OF VARIATION AND DISCLAIMERS) do not apply to property to which the deceased was treated as entitled under the gifts with reservation rules. [*IHTA 1984, s 142(5); FA 1986, Sch 19 para 24*].

Double charges — gifts with reservation and death

[22.13] Without specific relief, a double charge to tax could arise where there is a transfer by way of gift of property which is or subsequently becomes a chargeable transfer and the property is, by virtue of the rules relating to gifts with reservation, subject to a further transfer which is chargeable as a result of the transferor's death. The pre-owned assets regulations relating to income tax now include provisions to avoid a double charge to IHT where a chargeable person elects that the gift with reservation provisions apply to the relevant property. [*FA 1986, s 104(1); Charge to Income Tax by Reference to Enjoyment of Property Previously Owned Regulations 2005, SI 2005/724, Reg 6; Inheritance Tax (Double Charges Relief) Regulations 2005, SI 2005/3441, Reg 3*]. A double charge can arise where the chargeable person makes a gift of property or a debt that is a potentially exempt transfer for IHT purposes. If that same property is then liable to the income tax charge the person may decide to make an election on form IHT500 under *FA 2004, Sch 15 para 21* that the property is subject to the IHT reservation of benefits rules. If that person then dies within seven years of the original gift a double charge to IHT may arise, firstly, by reason of the original transfer and secondly when the property is added back into the death estate for the purposes of the gift with reservation rules. The new provision avoids the double charge by opting for the IHT on transfer that produces the highest overall amount of IHT and thereby reduces the other transfer to nil. See example 1 below.

Relief from double charge to tax is given where the following conditions are fulfilled.

(a) An individual ('the deceased') makes a transfer of value by way of gift of property after 17 March 1986 which transfer is or proves to be a chargeable transfer.

(b) The property in relation to the gift and the deceased is property subject to a reservation.

(c) *Either*:
   (i) the property is treated as property to which the deceased was beneficially entitled immediately before his death (as the property is then subject to a reservation); *or*
   (ii) the property ceases to be property subject to a reservation and is the subject of a potentially exempt transfer at that time.

(d) *Either*:
   (i) the property is comprised in the estate of the deceased immediately before his death and value attributable to it is a chargeable part of this estate on death; *or*
   (ii) the property is property transferred by the potentially exempt transfer in (c)(ii) above, value attributable to which is transferred by a chargeable transfer.

Where the above conditions are fulfilled, there must be separately calculated the total tax chargeable as a consequence of the death of the deceased:

(A) disregarding so much of the value transferred by the transfer of value under (a) above as is attributable to property to which (d) above refers; and

(B) disregarding so much of the value of property to which (d) above refers as is attributable to property to which (a) above refers.

Whichever of the two calculations produces the higher amount of IHT as a result of the death remains chargeable and the value of the other transfer is reduced by reference to the value of the transfer which produced that amount.

Where the higher amount is calculated under (A) above:

(I) credit is available for tax already paid on the lifetime chargeable transfer which is attributable to the value disregarded under that calculation (but not exceeding the amount of tax due on death attributable to the value of the property in question); and

(II) to avoid the value of the same property entering twice into the tax calculations, the reduction in value applies to all IHT purposes except a ten-year anniversary charge or proportionate charge to tax on a discretionary trust arising before the transferor's death if the transfer by way of gift was chargeable to tax when made.

Where the total tax chargeable under (A) and (B) above is identical, calculation (A) is treated as producing the higher amount. [*FA 1986, s 104(1)(c); SI 1987/1130, Regs 5, 8*].

Relief is given where a double charge to IHT arises in situations where arrangements are caught by the pre-owned assets income tax provisions in *FA 2004, Sch 15* which are subsequently dismantled by the individual but he/she dies within seven years. The conditions for double charge relief in these circumstances are as follows:

(a) the disposal condition or the contribution condition is met as respects the relevant property; and

(b) the deceased makes a transfer the result of which a third party becomes entitled to the benefit of a debt owed to the deceased; and

(c) before the deceased's death, any outstanding part of the debt is wholly written off, waived or released, and the write off, waiver or release is made otherwise than for full consideration in money or money's worth, and

(d) the following conditions must be fulfilled:
    (i) the deceased dies on or after 6 April 2005; and
    (ii) on the deceased's death, the transfer of value treated as made immediately before the deceased's death included the relevant property, or any property representing that relevant property; and
    (iii) as a result of the deceased's death, the transfer of value referred to in (b) above has become a chargeable transfer.

See HMRC's IHT Mamual at IHTM14711–14 for HMRC examples of how the double charge relief works in practice. [*Inheritance Tax (Double Charges Relief) Regulations 2005, SI 2005/3441*].

Example 3

A entered into a lifetime loan scheme, commonly known as a 'double trust' scheme, in June 2006. He then sold his house to a trust fund for £500,000 and he is a life tenant of that trust fund. The trustees do not pay the purchase price but give A an IOU instead. A then gifts the IOU to a second trust for the benefit of his children B and C. A remains in occupation of the property but the outstanding debt will reduce A's estate on death under *IHTA 1984, s 162* by the amount of the loan. Under *FA 2004, Sch 15* A makes an election under *ibid* paragraph 21 so that the value of the house becomes subject to the gifts with reservation rules. A dies in July 2010 and the house at that date is valued at

£750,000 and A's estate is worth £500,000. See 53 TRANSFERS WITHIN SEVEN YEARS OF DEATH. However, the house is also chargeable within the estate because it constitutes a gift with reservation following the election under *FA 2004, Sch 15, para 21*.

As a double charge would now arise each calculation should be considered in isolation.

First calculation: charge to tax using the original gift in the death estate.

	£	£
Transfer in June 2006		
Taxable gift	500,000	
Less Nil rate band using the table at 40.1 2010.A1	(325,000)	
Taxable balance	175,000	
Tax payable @ 40%	70,000	
Less Taper relief @ 40% (i.e. between 4 and 5 years)	(28,000)	42,000
Taxable estate	500,000	
Tax payable @ 40%	200,000	200,000
Total IHT payable		242,000

Second calculation: charge to tax using the gifts with reservation rules in the death estate (ignoring PET in June 2006).

	£	£
Estate	500,000	
Add Gift with reservation	750,000	
Taxable balance	1,250,000	
Less Nil rate band using the table at 40.1 2010.A1	(325,000)	
	925,000	
Tax payable @ 40%	370,000	
Total IHT payable		370,000

Notes to the example

(A) The charge to tax using the gift with reservation will be used by HMRC Inheritance Tax and the charge using the original gift will be reduced to nil by using the double charge relief. [*Inheritance Tax (Double Charges Relief) Regulations 2005, SI 2005/3441, Reg 4(4)*].

(B) It should be noted that the double charge relief provisions will not always apply when a perceived double charge arises. This will happen where an election is made in respect of the property subject to an '*Eversden*' type scheme (see 5.2 ANTI-AVOIDANCE) with the result that one spouse/civil partner has made a potentially exempt transfer and the other spouse's/civil partner's estate includes property subject to a reservation so that both charges are unaffected by the double charge relief provisions. The provisions only apply where there is a double charge in respect of one individual.

Example 4

A made a potentially exempt transfer of £150,000 to B in January 1998. In March 2005, A made a gift of land worth £336,000 into a discretionary trust of which he is a potential beneficiary. The gift was a gift with reservation but also a chargeable lifetime transfer on which IHT of £14,600 would have been paid at rates current at the time assuming there were no other previous transfers; the trustees paid the tax; no annual exemptions were available.

A dies in February 2010 without having released his interest in the trust. His estate is valued at £440,000 including the land in the discretionary trust currently worth £360,000.

First calculation: charge the land subject to the gift with reservation in A's death estate and ignore the gift with reservation.

	IHT payable £
January 1998	
Potentially exempt transfer (now exempt)	—
March 2005	
Gift with reservation (ignored)	—
February 2010	
Death estate £440,000	
Tax £46,000 less £14,600 already paid on the gift with reservation*	31,400
Total tax due as result of A's death	£31,400

* Credit for the tax already paid cannot exceed the amount of the death tax attributable to the value of the gift with reservation property i.e.

$$\frac{360{,}000}{440{,}000} \times £31,400 = £25,691.$$

Credit is therefore given for the full amount of tax paid £14,600.

Second calculation — charge the gift with reservation and ignore the land in the death estate

	IHT payable £
January 1998	
Potentially exempt transfer (now exempt)	—
March 2005	
Gift with reservation £336,000	
Tax £2,640 less £14,600 already paid (see note (A))	Nil
February 2010	
Death estate £80,000 (ignoring gift with reservation land) as top slice of £416,000	32,000
Total tax due as result of A's death	£32,000

Notes to the example

(A) 60% of the full rate for the date of death for a transfer more than 4 years but not more than 5 years before death i.e. 60% × 40% × (£336,000 – £325,000).

(B) The second calculation gives the higher amount of tax. In the first calculation the value of the gift with reservation transfer is reduced to nil and tax on death is charged with credit for the tax already paid. However, the credit provisions do *not* affect the choice of calculation, even if they operate to turn what was the higher amount of tax into the lower amount. See IHTM14571.

Key points

[22.14] Points to consider are as follows.

- Gifts to family members are quite often not formalised by deed of gift and this can cause problems later. For instance, many family arrangements are such that on the death of the individual family members have informal arrangements whereby they take possession of chattels of the deceased on a prior understanding that these have been passed to the beneficiaries under a prior verbal agreement. Whilst verbal agreements are common place the gift of a chattel should be by deed or delivery. Therefore in the absence of both the gift cannot be perfected because there is no deed and the chattel still remains in possession of the donor and lacks delivery. These circumstances mean that there is not a gift with reservation of benefit under *FA 1986, s 102(1)* and the chattel still remains in the estate of the deceased and as such should be included in IHT407. It would be better for a gift either to be perfected by delivery or by deed of gift as follows:
THIS MEMORANDUM records that on the . . . . day of . . . . 2010 the undersigned [*Donor*] of [*Address*] ('the Donor') gave and by word of mouth expressed himself/herself to give to the undersigned [*Donee*]of [*Address*] ('the Donee) [all the furniture effects and moveable property] which [are] specified in the Schedule attached hereto ('the Chattel(s)) for the absolute sole use of the/and benefit of the Donee and at the same time the Donor delivered the Chattel(s) to the Donee and placed the Donee in possession and unrestricted control of the Chattel(s) and at the same time the Donee accepted the gift.
- In a similar case to the above Key Point, the donor may keep the chattel in their home despite the signing of the deed of gift. This may be for a number of reasons including security, insurance or for personal enjoyment. This creates a GWR problem and the market value of the chattel will be included in the estate of the donor on death and valued at that date. This has the added problem in that the donee will not be able to claim the uplifted CGT value on death under *TCGA 1992, s 62* as the donee effectively took possession on the signing of the deed of gift. Therefore there will not only be a GWR charge but the CGT uplift

is not available. In any case it is important to get a receipted memorandum of gift as in the Key Point above so that the date of the gift is noted for future reference with regard to the seven year rule.

- Under *FA 2004, s 84, Sch 15 para 16* relating to 'Pre-owned assets' provides that under *IHTA 1984, s 17* where beneficiaries of a deceased's estate agree between themselves to vary the will or the intestacy provisions then any party to the variation shall not be taxed as a former owner by reason of having had an interest under the original will or intestacy provisions. As an election may be made within two years of the death under *IHTA 1984, ss 142, 147* and *Administration of Estates Act 1925, s 47A* this gives a period of grace with no charge arising in respect of rental value of the property or chattels in question where these are enjoyed by a 'relative' within *ITA 2007, s 993 formerly ICTA 1988, s 839* including uncle, aunt, nephew and niece.

23

HMRC Extra-Statutory Concessions

[23.1] This chapter has been expanded to include the full text of HMRC extra-statutory concessions relevant to IHT. Note *FA 2008, s 160* enables the Treasury to make an order by statutory instrument giving effect to an existing HMRC concession. This may include a concession, statement of practice, press release or in any other way.

The following is the full text of the concessions published (or to be published) in HMRC Pamphlet IR 1. Any concessions announced but not yet designated by a formal prefix are listed at the end of the chapter in date order. In the pamphlet it is stated: 'The concessions described within are of general application, but it must be borne in mind that in a particular case there may be special circumstances which will require to be taken into account in considering the application of the concession. A concession will not be granted in any case where an attempt is made to use it for tax avoidance'. See **14.10** DETERMINATIONS AND APPEALS.

[23.2]

F. INHERITANCE TAX

F6 **Blocked foreign assets.** Where, because of restrictions imposed by the foreign government, executors who intend to transfer to this country sufficient of the deceased's foreign assets for the payment of the inheritance tax attributable to them cannot do so immediately, they are given the option of deferring payment until the transfer can be effected. If the amount in sterling that the executors finally succeed in bringing to this country is less than this tax, the balance is waived.
See **35.24** PAYMENT OF TAX.

F10 **Partnership assurance policies.** A partnership assurance scheme under which each partner effects a policy on his own life in trust for the other partners is not regarded as a settlement for inheritance tax purposes if the following conditions are fulfilled.

(a) The premiums paid on the policy fall within *IHTA 1984, s 10* (*FA 1975, s 20(4)*) (exemption for dispositions not intended to confer a gratuitous benefit on any person);

(b) the policy was effected prior to 15 September 1976 and has not been varied on or after that date (but the exercise of a power of appointment under a 'discretionary' trust policy would not be regarded as a variation for this purpose); and

(c) the trusts of the policy are governed by English law or by Scottish law, provided that in the latter case the policy does not directly or indirectly involve a partnership itself as a separate persona.

See **34.1** PARTNERSHIPS.

F13 Subsequent devolutions of property under the wills of persons dying before 12 March 1952 whose estates were wholly exempted from estate duty under *FA 1894, s 8(1)*. Where a person died before 12 March 1952 and his estate was wholly exempted from estate duty as the property of a common seaman, marine or soldier who died in the service of the Crown and under his will he left a limited interest to someone who dies on or after 12 March 1975, inheritance tax is not charged on any property exempted on the original death which passes under the terms of the will on the termination of the limited interest. Note that withdrawal of this concession was proposed by HMRC in a Technical Note dated 31 January 2014.

See **21.20** EXEMPT TRANSFERS.

F15 Woodlands. *FA 1986, 19 Sch 46* denies potentially exempt transfer treatment for Inheritance tax purposes to all property comprised in a single transfer any part of which, however small, is woodlands subject to a deferred Estate Duty charge. By concession the scope of this paragraph will henceforth be restricted solely to that part of the value transferred which is attributable to the woodlands which are the subject of the deferred charge.

See **38.4** POTENTIALLY EXEMPT TRANSFERS and **57.5** WOODLANDS.

F16 Agricultural property and farm cottages. On a transfer of agricultural property which includes a cottage occupied by a retired farm employee or their widow(er), the condition in *IHTA 1984, s 117* and *IHTA 1984, s 169* concerning occupation for agricultural purposes is regarded as satisfied with respect to the cottage if either:

- the occupier is a statutorily protected tenant; or
- the occupation is under a lease granted to the farm employee for his/her life and that of any surviving spouse as part of the employee's contract of employment by the landlord for agricultural purposes.

See **4.4** AGRICULTURAL PROPERTY.

F17 Relief for agricultural property. On a transfer of tenanted agricultural land, the condition in *IHTA 1984, s 116(2)(a)* is regarded as satisfied where the transferor's interest in the property either:

- carries a right to vacant possession within 24 months of the date of the transfer; or
- is, notwithstanding the terms of the tenancy, valued at an amount broadly equivalent to the vacant possession value of the property.

See **4.4** AGRICULTURAL PROPERTY.

F20 Late compensation for World War II claims.

Schemes continue to be established in the UK and abroad which provide compensation for wrongs suffered during the Second World War era. When this is received by the original victim or their surviving spouse, this almost inevitably comes late in life when their plans for the disposal of their wealth have already been made. Ministers have agreed that the cash value of these claims may be excluded from inheritance tax in the following cases where compensation is paid in modest round-sum, or otherwise cash-limited, amounts:

- single ex-gratia lump sums of £10,000 payable to each surviving member of British groups interned or imprisoned by the Japanese during the Second World War or their surviving spouse as announced by the Government on 7 November 2000;
- financial compensation of fixed amounts payable from the German foundation 'Remembrance, Responsibility and Future' to claimants – or their surviving spouse – who were slave or forced labourers or other victims of the National Socialist regime during the Second World War;
- financial compensation of $1,000 payable from the Holocaust Victim Assets Litigation (Swiss Bank Settlement) to each of the slave or forced labourers qualifying under the aforementioned German foundation scheme;
- financial compensation by way of fixed amounts to the victim or their surviving spouse from the Swiss Refugee Programme;
- financial compensation by way of fixed amounts to the victim or their surviving spouse from Stichting Maror-Gelden Overheid (Dutch Maror); and
- financial compensation by way of a one-time payment to the victim or their surviving spouse from the following:
- monies allocated by the Federal German Government (the Hardship Fund);
- the Austrian National Fund for Victims of Nazi Persecution;
- the French Orphan Scheme.

Payments of this kind would normally increase the value of a deceased person's chargeable estate at death, either because a claim paid in their lifetime has increased their total assets, or because the right to a claim not yet paid is itself an asset of their estate.

By concession, where such a payment has been received at any time, either by the deceased or his or her personal representatives under the arrangements, the amount of the payment may be left out of account in determining the chargeable value of his or her estate for the purposes of inheritance tax on death. Similarly, where a person qualifies for more than one payment then each amount may be left out of account.

All enquiries about this extra-statutory concession in particular cases (quoting the full name and date of death of the deceased plus the Inland Revenue Capital Taxes reference number if known) should be directed to:

Inland Revenue Capital Taxes – IHT, Ferrers House, PO Box 38, Castle Meadow Road, Nottingham NG2 1BB.

For members of the DX system:

Inland Revenue Capital Taxes, DX 701201, Nottingham 4.

B. Other tax concessions applied to inheritance tax

B41 Claims to repayment of tax. Under *TMA 1970* unless a longer or shorter period is prescribed, no statutory claim for relief is allowed unless it is made within six years from the end of the tax year to which it relates.

However, repayments of tax will be made in respect of claims made outside the statutory time limit where an over-payment of tax has arisen because of an error by the Inland Revenue or another Government Department, and where there is no dispute or doubt as to the facts. See 35.20 PAYMENT OF TAX.

24

HMRC Press Releases

[24.1] The following is a summary in date order of Press Releases referred to in this book (other than those containing Extra-Statutory Concessions and Statements of Practice, as to which see 23 HMRC EXTRA-STATUTORY CONCESSIONS and 25 HMRC STATEMENTS OF PRACTICE). Certain pre-18 July 1978 Press Releases were reissued as Statements of Practice on 18 June 1979. Note *FA 2008, s 160* enables the Treasury to make an order by statutory instrument giving effect to an existing HMRC concession. This may include a concession, statement of practice, press release or in any other way.

HMRC also publish an online only version of its IHT Newsletter at http://www.hmrc.gov.uk/cto/newsletter.htm.

12.2.76	**Interests in possession — inheritance tax: settled property.** The Board do not consider that a mere power of revocation or appointment, in certain conditions, will prevent an interest being an 'interest in possession'. See 27.2 INTEREST IN POSSESSION.
17.1.79	**Life assurance premiums — measure of value for purposes of IHT.** See 31.5 LIFE ASSURANCE POLICIES AND ANNUITIES.
23.6.82	**Killed in war exemption — Falkland Islands.** The estates of those killed on active service in the Falklands conflict will be exempt from CTT and IHT. See 21.20 EXEMPT TRANSFERS.
18.3.86	**Gifts with reservation and insurance policies.** The Revenue's understanding of when an insurance is made is given. See 32.2 LIFETIME TRANSFERS.
2.7.87	**Inheritance tax—reductions in requirements for delivery of accounts on death.** Advice is given. See 2.8 ACCOUNTS AND RETURNS.
10.3.92	**Increases in agricultural and business property relief.** The effective commencement of the increases is explained by the Revenue. See 4.4 AGRICULTURAL PROPERTY and 6.16 BUSINESS PROPERTY.
17.12.92	**Public access to conditionally exempt works of art.** See 33.3 NATIONAL HERITAGE.
17.2.93	**Revenue Adjudicator and Codes of Practice.** The appointment of an independent adjudicator and the publication of codes of practice are announced. See 3.1 ADMINISTRATION AND COLLECTION.
10.5.93	**Public access to conditionally exempt works of art.** See 33.3 NATIONAL HERITAGE.
2.8.93	**Inheritance tax — The Register of conditionally exempt works of art.** See 33.3 NATIONAL HERITAGE.
8.9.94	**Individuals coming to the United Kingdom to take up employment: Administrative measures.** See 16.5 DOMICILE.
6.3.95	**Double taxation agreement: Switzerland.** See 18.2 DOUBLE TAXATION RELIEF.

16.1.96	**The Register of conditionally exempt works of art.** See **33.3** NATIONAL HERITAGE.
16.1.96	**Law of domicile.** See **16.5** DOMICILE.
25.1.2000	**Inland Revenue account — reduced account for exempt estates.** See **2.8** ACCOUNTS AND RETURNS.

25

HMRC Statements of Practice

[25.1] This chapter has been expanded to include the full text of HMRC Statements of Practice relevant to IHT. Note *FA 2008, s 160* enables the Treasury to make an order by statutory instrument giving effect to an existing HMRC concession. This may include a concession, statement of practice, press release or in any other way.

The following is the full text of those Statements of Practice published in HMRC Pamphlet IR 131 (November 1996), or subsequently announced for inclusion therein, which are referred to in this book.

Statements are divided into those originally published before 18 July 1978 (which are given a reference letter (according to the subject matter) and consecutive number, e.g. E11) and later Statements (which are numbered consecutively in each year, e.g. SP 10/86).

Certain statements marked in IR 131 as obsolete will continue to be referred to in the text (having been relevant in the last six years), and the original source is quoted in such cases, as it is where the Statement awaits inclusion in IR 131.

ACCUMULATION AND MAINTENANCE SETTLEMENTS: IHTA 1984, s 71

E1 **Powers of appointment**

1. It is not necessary for the interests of individual beneficiaries to be defined. They can for instance be subject to powers of appointment. In any particular case the exemption will depend on the precise terms of the trust and power concerned, and on the facts to which they apply. In general, however, the official view is that the conditions do not restrict the application of *IHTA 1984, s 71* to settlements where the interests of individual beneficiaries are defined and indefeasible.
2. The requirement of *IHTA 1984, s 71(1)(a)* (formerly *FA 1982, s 114(1)(a)*) is that one or more persons will, on or before attaining a specified age not exceeding twenty five, become beneficially entitled to, or to an interest in possession in, the settled property or part of it. It is considered that settled property would meet this condition if at the relevant time it must vest for an interest in possession in some member of an existing class of potential beneficiaries on or before that member attains 25. The existence of a special power of appointment would not of itself exclude *s 71* if neither the exercise nor the release of the power could break the condition. To achieve this effect might, however, require careful drafting.

3. The inclusion of issue as possible objects of a special power of appointment would exclude a settlement from the benefit of *s 71* if the power would allow the trustees to prevent any interest in possession in the settled property from commencing before the beneficiary concerned attained the age specified. It would depend on the precise words of the settlement and the facts to which they had to be applied whether a particular settlement satisfied the conditions of *s 71(1)*. In many cases the rules against perpetuity and accumulations would operate to prevent an effective appointment outside those conditions. However the application of *s 71* is not a matter for a once-for-all decision. It is a question that needs to be kept in mind at all times when there is settled property in which no interest in possession subsists.
4. Also, a trust which otherwise satisfies the requirement of *s 71(1)(a)* would not be disqualified by the existence of a power to vary or determine the respective shares of members of the class (even to the extent of excluding some members altogether) provided the power is exercisable only in favour of a person under 25 who is a member of the class.

SUPERANNUATION, LIFE INSURANCE AND ACCIDENT SCHEMES

E3 **Superannuation schemes**

1. This Statement clarifies the IHT liability of benefits payable under pension schemes.
2. No liability to IHT arises in respect of benefits payable on a person's death under a normal pension scheme except in the circumstances explained immediately below. Nor does a charge to IHT arise on payments made by the trustees of a superannuation scheme within *IHTA 1984, s 151* (formerly *FA 1975, 5 Sch 16*) in direct exercise of a discretion to pay a lump sum death benefit to any one or more of a member's dependants. It is not considered that pending the exercise of the discretion the benefit should normally be regarded as property comprised in a settlement so as to bring it within the scope of *IHTA 1984, Pt III* (formerly *FA 1975, 5 Sch*). The protection of *IHTA 1984, s 151* would not of course extend further if the trustees themselves then settled the property so paid.
3. Benefits are liable to IHT if:
   (a) they form part of the freely disposable property passing under the will or intestacy of a deceased person. This applies only if the executors or administrators have a legally enforceable claim to the benefits; if they were payable to them only at the discretion of the trustees of the pension fund or some similar persons they are not liable to IHT; or

(b) the deceased had the power, immediately before his death, to nominate or appoint the benefits to any person including his dependants.

4. In these cases the benefits should be included in the personal representatives' account (schedule of the deceased's assets) which has to be completed when applying for a grant of probate or letters of administration. The IHT (if any) which is assessed on the personal representatives' account has to be paid before the grant can be obtained.
5. On some events other than the death of a member information should be given to the appropriate Capital Taxes Office [now HMRC Inheritance Tax]. These are:
   (i) the payment of contributions to a scheme which has not been approved for income tax purposes;
   (ii) the making of an irrevocable nomination or the disposal of a benefit by a member in his or her lifetime (otherwise than in favour of a spouse) which reduces the value of his or her estate (e.g. the surrender of part of the pension or lump sum benefit in exchange for a pension for the life of another);
   (iii) the decision by a member to postpone the realisation of any of his or her retirement benefits.
6. If IHT proves to be payable the Capital Taxes Office [now HMRC Inheritance Tax] will communicate with the persons liable to pay the tax.
7. See also Statement of Practice 10/86. Tax Bulletin No 2 of February 1992; the article inheritance tax — Retirement Benefits, etc.

See **37.2** PENSION SCHEMES.

E4 **Associated operations.** Life assurance policies and annuities are regarded as not being affected by the associated operations rule if, first, the policy was issued on full medical evidence and, secondly, it would have been issued on the same terms if the annuity had not been bought.

See **31.9** LIFE ASSURANCE POLICIES AND ANNUITIES.

INTERESTS IN POSSESSION SETTLEMENTS

E5 **Close companies.** The Board consider that the general intention of *IHTA 1984, s 101* is to treat the participators as beneficial owners for all the purposes of that Act. Consequently, the conditions of *IHTA 1984, s 52(2),* and *53(2)*, are regarded as satisfied where it is the company that in fact becomes entitled to the property or disposes of the interest.

See **42.9** SETTLEMENTS WITH INTERESTS IN POSSESSION.

E6 **Power to augment income.** This statement sets out the effect for IHT of the exercise by trustees of a power to augment a beneficiary's income out of capital.

In the normal case, where the beneficiary concerned is life tenant of the settled property this will have no immediate consequences for IHT. The life tenant already has an interest in possession and under the provisions of *IHTA 1984, s 49(1)* (formerly *FA 1975, 5 Sch 3(1)*) is treated as beneficially entitled to the property. The enlargement of that interest to an absolute interest does not change this position (*IHTA 1984, s 53(2)*; formerly *FA 1975, 5 Sch 4(3)*) and it is not affected by the relationship of the beneficiary to the testator.

In the exceptional case, where the beneficiary is not the life tenant, or in which there is no subsisting interest in possession, the exercise of the power would give rise to a charge to tax under *IHTA 1984, s 52(1)*, although on or after 17 March 1987 this may be a potentially exempt transfer, or a charge under *IHTA 1984, s 65(1)(a)* (formerly *FA 1975, 5 Sch 4(2) or 6(1)*). But if the life tenant is the surviving spouse of a testator who died before 13 November 1974, exemption might be available under *IHTA 1984, 6 Sch 2* (formerly *FA 1975, 5 Sch 4(7)*).

The exercise of the power would be regarded as distributing the settled property rather than as reducing its value, so that *IHTA 1984, s 52(3)* and *IHTA 1984, s 65(1)(b)* (formerly *FA 1975, 5 Sch 4(9)* and *6(3)*) would not be in point.

See **27.7** INTEREST IN POSSESSION.

E7 **Protective trusts.** In the Board's view, the reference to trusts 'to the like effect as those specified in *s 33(1)* of the *Trustee Act 1925*' – contained in *IHTA 1984, ss 73* and *88* (both derived from *FA 1975, 5 Sch 18*) – is a reference to trusts which are not materially different in their tax consequences.

The Board would not wish to distinguish a trust by reason of a minor variation or additional administrative duties or powers. The extension of the list of potential beneficiaries to brothers and sisters is not regarded as a minor variation.

See **45.1** PROTECTIVE TRUSTS.

SETTLED PROPERTY — MISCELLANEOUS

E9 **Excluded property.** Property is regarded, for the purposes of *IHTA 1984, s 48(3)* (formerly *FA 1975, 5 Sch 2(1)*) as becoming comprised in a settlement when it, or other property which it represents, is introduced by the settlor.

See **20.2** EXCLUDED PROPERTY.

E11 **Employee trusts.**

This statement clarifies the application of *IHTA 1984, s 13(1)* (formerly *FA 1976, s 90(1)*) where employees of a subsidiary company are included in the trust.

The Board regard *IHTA 1984, s 13(1)* (formerly *FA 1976, s 90(1)*) as requiring that where the trust is to benefit employees of a subsidiary of the company making the provision those eligible to benefit must include all or most of the employees and officers of the subsidiary and the employees and officers of the holding company taken as a single class. So it would be possible to exclude all of the officers and employees of the holding company without losing the exemption if they comprised only a minority of the combined class. But the exemption would not be available for a contribution to a fund for the sole benefit of the employees of a small subsidiary. This is because it would otherwise have been easy to create such a situation artificially in order to benefit a favoured group of a company's officeholders or employees. But even where the participators outnumber the other employees the exemption is not irretrievably lost. The requirement to exclude participators and those connected with them from benefit is modified by *IHTA 1984, s 13(3)* (formerly *FA 1976, s 90(4)*). This limits the meaning of 'a participator' for this purpose to those having a substantial stake in the assets being transferred and makes an exception in favour of income benefits. So even where most of the employees are also major participators or their relatives an exempt transfer could be made if the trust provided only for income benefits and the eventual disposal of the capital away from the participators and their families.

This restriction does not affect the exemptions offered by *IHTA 1984, s 86* (formerly *FA 1975, 5 Sch 17*) from tax charges during the continuance of a trust for employees which meets the conditions of that paragraph.

See **55.5**(a) TRUSTS FOR EMPLOYEES.

NON-SETTLED PROPERTY — MISCELLANEOUS

E13 **Charities.**

1. *IHTA 1984, ss 23* and *24* (formerly *FA 1975, 6 Sch 10* and *11*) exempt from IHT certain gifts to charities and political parties to the extent that the value transferred is attributable to property given to a charity etc. *IHTA 1984, ss 25* and *26* (formerly *FA 1975, 6 Sch 12* and *13*) exempt certain gifts for national purposes and for the public benefit.
2. Where the value transferred (i.e. the loss to transferor's estate as a result of the disposition) exceeds the value of the gift in the hands of a charity, etc., the Board take the view that the exemption extends to the whole value transferred.

See **21.2** EXEMPT TRANSFERS.

E14 **Pools etc. syndicates.** No liability to IHT arises on winnings by a football pool or similar syndicates provided that the winnings are paid out in accordance with the terms of an agreement drawn up before the win.

Where for example football pool winnings are paid out, in accordance with a pre-existing enforceable arrangement, among the members of a syndicate in proportion to the share of the stake money each has provided, each member of the syndicate receives what already belongs to him or her. There is therefore no 'gift' or 'chargeable transfer' by the person who, on behalf of the members, receives the winnings from the pools promoter.

Members of a pool syndicate may think it wise to record in a written, signed and dated statement, the existence and terms of the agreement between them. But the Inland Revenue cannot advise on the wording or legal effect of such a statement, nor do they wish copies of such statements to be sent to them for approval or registration. Where following a pools win the terms of the agreement are varied or part of the winnings are distributed to persons who are not members of the syndicate, an IHT liability may be incurred. The same principles apply to premium bonds syndicates and other similar arrangements.

See **9.7** CHARGEABLE TRANSFER.

E15 **Close companies — group transfers.** This statement clarifies the position concerning dividend payments and transfers of assets from a subsidiary company to a parent or sister company as appropriate. The statement refers to capital transfer tax (CTT), but applies equally to IHT.

Whether or not a disposition is a transfer of value for CTT purposes has to be determined by reference to *IHTA 1984, s 3(1), (2)*, and *s 10* which provides that a disposition is not a transfer of value if it was not intended to confer any gratuitous benefit on any person, subject to the other provisions of that subsection.

In the Board's view, the effect is that a dividend paid by a subsidiary company to its parent is not a transfer of value and so *IHTA 1984, s 94* does not start to operate in relation to such dividends. Nor do the Board feel that they can justifiably treat a transfer of assets between a wholly-owned subsidiary and its parent or between two wholly-owned subsidiaries as a transfer of value.

See **11.4** CLOSE COMPANIES.

SCOTS LAW

E18 **Partial disclaimers of residue.** Under Scots law there are certain circumstances in which a residuary legatee can make a partial disclaimer. Where this is possible the Inland Revenue accepts that the provisions of *IHTA 1984, s 142*, which deal with disclaimers, apply.

See **13.2, 13.4** DEEDS OF VARIATION AND DISCLAIMERS.

STATEMENTS AFTER JULY 1978

SP 10/79 **Power for trustees to allow a beneficiary to occupy a dwelling house.** Many wills and settlements contain a clause empowering the trustees to permit a beneficiary to occupy a dwelling house which forms part of trust property as they think fit. The Board do not regard the existence of such a power as excluding any interest in possession in the property.

Where there is no interest in possession in the property in question the Board do not regard the exercise of power as creating one if the effect is merely to allow non-exclusive occupation or to create a contractual tenancy for full consideration. The Board also take the view that no interest in possession arises on the creation of a lease for a term or a periodic tenancy for less than full consideration, though this will normally give rise to a charge for tax under *IHTA 1984, s 65(1)(b)* (formerly *FA 1982, s 108(1)(b)*). On the other hand if the power is drawn in terms wide enough to cover the creation of an exclusive or joint right of residence, albeit revocable, for a definite or indefinite period, and is exercised with the intention of providing a particular beneficiary with a permanent home, the Revenue will normally regard the exercise of the power as creating an interest in possession. And if the trustees in exercise of their powers grant a lease for life for less than full consideration, this will also be regarded as creating an interest in possession in view of *IHTA 1984, ss 43(3)* and *50(6)* (formerly *FA 1975, 5 Sch 1(3)* and *3(6)*).

A similar view will be taken where the power is exercised over property in which another beneficiary had an interest in possession up to the time of exercise.

See **27.6** INTEREST IN POSSESSION.

SP 12/80 **Business relief — 'Buy and Sell' agreements.** The Board understand that it is sometimes the practice for partners or shareholder directors of companies to enter into an agreement (known as a 'Buy & Sell' agreement) whereby, in the event of the death before retirement of one of them, the deceased's personal representatives are obliged to sell and the survivors are obliged to purchase the deceased's business interest or shares, funds for the purchase being frequently provided by means of appropriate life assurance policies.

In the Board's view such an agreement, requiring as it does a sale and purchase and not merely conferring an option to sell or buy, is a binding contract for sale within *IHTA 1984, s 113*. As a result the Inheritance Tax business relief will not be due on the business interest or shares. (*IHTA 1984, s 113* provides that where any property would be relevant business property for the purpose of business relief in relation to a transfer of value but a binding contract for its sale has been entered into at the time of the transfer, it is not relevant business property in relation to that transfer.)

See **6.4** BUSINESS PROPERTY at *Binding contracts for sale.*

SP 1/82 **The interaction of income tax and inheritance tax on assets put into settlements.**

1. For many years the tax code has contained legislation to prevent a person avoiding higher rate income tax by making a settlement, while still retaining some rights to enjoy the income or capital of the settlement. This legislation, which is embodied in *ICTA 1988, Pt XV*, [now *ITTOIA 2005 Pt 5, Ch 5*] provides in general terms that the income of a settlement shall, for income tax purposes, be treated as that of the settlor in all circumstances where the settlor might benefit directly or indirectly from the settlement.
2. If the trustees have power to pay or do in fact pay inheritance tax due on assets which the settlor puts into the settlement the Inland Revenue have taken the view that the settlor has thereby an interest in the income or property of the settlement, and that the income of the settlement should be treated as his for income tax purposes under *ICTA 1988, Pt XV*. [now *ITTOIA 2005, Pt 5 Ch 5*]
3. The inheritance tax legislation ([*IHTA 1984, s 199*]) however provides that both the settlor and the trustees are liable for any [inheritance tax] payable when a settlor puts assets into a settlement. The Board of Inland Revenue have therefore decided that they will no longer, in these circumstances, treat the income of the settlement as that of the settlor for income tax purposes solely because the trustees have power to pay or do in fact pay inheritance tax on assets put into settlements.
4. This change of practice applies to settlement income for 1981–82 *et seq*.

See **30.2** LIABILITY FOR TAX.

SP 8/86 **Treatment of income of discretionary trusts.** This statement sets out the Board's existing practice concerning the inheritance tax/capital transfer tax treatment of income of discretionary trusts.

The Board of Inland Revenue take the view that:

- Undistributed and unaccumulated income should not be treated as a taxable trust asset; and
- For the purposes of determining the rate of charge on accumulated income, the income should be treated as becoming a taxable asset of the trust on the date when the accumulation is made.

This practice applies from 10 November 1986 to all new cases and to existing cases where the tax liability has not been settled. However see now *IHTA 1984 s64 (1A)* introduced by *FA 2014* with effect for occasions on which tax falls to be charged on or after 6 April 2014. This provides that, for 10 year anniversary charges, undistributed income which arose more than five years before the anniversary date is to be treated as accumulated.

See **43.3** SETTLEMENTS: DISCRETIONARY TRUSTS AND OTHER TRUSTS OF RELEVANT PROPERTY.

SP 10/86 **Death benefits under superannuation arrangements.** The Board confirm that their previous practice of not charging capital transfer tax on death benefits that are payable from tax-approved occupational pension and retirement annuity schemes under discretionary trusts also applies to inheritance tax.

The practice extends to tax under the gifts with reservation rules as well as to tax under the ordinary inheritance tax rules. See **37.2** PENSION SCHEMES.

SP 6/87 **Acceptance of property in lieu of Inheritance Tax, Capital Gains Tax and Estate Duty**

1. The Revenue may, with the agreement of the Secretary of State for National Heritage (and, where appropriate, other departmental ministers), accept heritage property in whole or part satisfaction of an inheritance tax, capital transfer tax or estate duty debt. Property can be accepted in satisfaction of interest accrued on the tax as well as the tax itself.
2. No capital tax is payable on property that is accepted in lieu of tax. The amount of tax satisfied is determined by agreeing a special price at which the departmental ministers reimburse the Revenue. This price is found by establishing an agreed value for the item and deducting a proportion of the tax given up on the item itself, using an arrangement known as the 'douceur'. The terms on which property is accepted are a matter for negotiation.
3. *FA 1987, s 60* and *F(No 2)A 1987, s 97* provide that, where the special price is based on the value of the item at a date earlier than the date on which it is accepted, interest on the tax which is being satisfied may cease to accrue from that earlier date.
4. The persons liable for the tax which is to be satisfied by an acceptance in lieu can choose between having the special price calculated from the value of the item when they offer it or when the Revenue accept it. Since most offers are made initially on the basis of the current value of the item, the Revenue considers them on the basis of the value at the 'offer date', unless the offeror notifies them that he wishes to adopt the 'acceptance date' basis of valuation. The offeror's option will normally remain open until the item is formally accepted. But this will be subject to review if more than two years elapse from the date of the offer without the terms being settled. The Revenue may then give six months notice that they will no longer be prepared to accept the item on the 'offer date' basis.
5. Where the 'offer date' option remains open and is chosen, interest on the tax to be satisfied by the item will cease to accrue from that date.

See **35.10** PAYMENT OF TAX.

SP 7/87 **IHT — deduction of reasonable funeral expenses.** The Board take the view that the term 'funeral expenses' in *IHTA 1984, s 172* allows a deduction from the value of a deceased's estate for the cost of a tombstone or gravestone.

See **52.9** TRANSFERS ON DEATH.

SP 2/93 **Inheritance tax — the use of substitute forms**

Introduction

1. This Statement explains the Board of Inland Revenue's approach towards the acceptance of facsimiles of inheritance tax forms as substitutes for officially produced printed forms.

Legislative context

2. *IHTA 1984, s 257(1)* says that all accounts and other documents required for the purposes of the Act shall be in such form and shall contain such particulars as the Board may prescribe. The Board of Inland Revenue are satisfied that an accurate facsimile of an official Account or other required document will satisfy the requirements of the Section.

What will be considered an accurate facsimile?

3. For any substitute inheritance tax form to be acceptable, it must show clearly to the taxpayer the information which the Board have determined shall be before him or her when he or she signs the declaration that the form is correct and complete to the best of his or her knowledge. In other words, the facsimile must accurately reproduce the words and layout of the official form. It need not, however, be colour printed.
4. The facsimile must also be readily recognisable as an inheritance tax form when it is received in the Capital Taxes Offices [now HMRC Inheritance Tax], and the entries must be distinguishable from the background text. Where a facsimile is submitted instead of a previously supplied official form it is important that it bears the same reference as appeared on the official form. It is equally important that if no official form was supplied the taxpayer's reference should be inserted on the facsimile.
5. Advances in printing technology now mean that accurate facsimile forms can be produced. The Board will accept such forms if approval by the Capital Taxes Offices [now HMRC Inheritance Tax] of their wording and design has been obtained before they are used. Any substitute which is produced with approval will need to bear an agreed unique imprint so that its source can be readily identified at all times.

Applications for approval

6. Applications for approval should be made to in England, Wales and Northern Ireland

   The Customer Service Manager
   Inland Revenue
   Capital Taxes Office [now HMRC Inheritance Tax]
   Ferrers House
   PO Box 38
   Castle Meadow Road
   NOTTINGHAM NG2 1BB
   or
   DX 701201 Nottingham 4

or in Scotland
The Customer Service Manager
Inland Revenue
[Meldrum House
15 Drumsheugh Gradens
EDINBURGH EH3 7UG]
or
DX 542001 EDINBURGH 14
All applications will be considered as quickly as possible.
Further information available

7. A set of guidelines giving further details on the production of substitute forms is available on application to the appropriate office at the above address.

See **2.2** ACCOUNTS AND RETURNS.

SP 6/95 **Legal entitlement and administrative practices.** Where an assessment has been made and this shows a repayment due to the taxpayer, repayment is invariably made of the full amount. But where the end of the year check applied to Schedule E taxpayers shows an overpayment of £10 or less, an assessment is not normally made and the repayment is not made automatically.

As regards payment of tax assessed, where a payment to the Collector exceeds the amount due and the discrepancy is not noted before the payment has been processed, the excess is not repaid automatically unless it is greater than £1.

For inheritance tax (and capital transfer tax), assessments that lead to repayments of sums overpaid are not initiated automatically by the Capital Taxes Offices [now HMRC Inheritance Tax] if the amount involved is £25 or less.

The aim of these tolerances is to minimise work which is highly cost-ineffective; they cannot operate to deny repayment to a taxpayer who claims it.

See **35.20** PAYMENT OF TAX.

Domicile and Inheritance Tax

This Revenue & Customs Brief details changes to the circumstances in which HM Revenue & Customs (HMRC) will consider an individual's domicile and decide whether to make a determination of Inheritance Tax based on that. These changes are being made because in HMRC experience the existing guidelines were not working well for the customer and HMRC. In future, by adopting a wider risk-based approach HMRC will ensure that resources are deployed in the most cost effective way.

Revenue & Customs Brief 17/09 issued on 25 March 2009 described changes to procedures following the changes to the remittance basis rules and the residence rules made by the Finance Act 2008. The relevant sections are in Appendix A below and these are superseded by the revised guidance below.

Revised guidance. The revised guidance applies to dispositions made after the issue of this Revenue & Customs Brief. In future HMRC will consider opening an enquiry where domicile could be an issue, or making a determination of Inheritance Tax in such cases, only where there is a significant risk of loss of UK tax. The significance of the risk will be assessed by HMRC using a wide range of factors. The factors will depend very much on the individual case but will include, for example:

- a review of the information available to HMRC about the individual on HMRC databases;
- whether there is a significant amount of tax (all taxes and duties not just Inheritance Tax) at risk.

HMRC does not consider it appropriate to state an amount of tax that would be considered significant, as the amount of tax at stake is only one factor. It should be borne in mind that HMRC will take into account the potential costs involved in pursuing an enquiry, and also those of potential litigation should the enquiry not result in agreement between HMRC and the individual; clearly such costs can be substantial. Where HMRC does open an Inheritance Tax enquiry in any of these cases, it will keep the factors in view and may stop the enquiry at any stage if it considers the continuation of the enquiry is not cost effective. The outcome of such an enquiry may be that HMRC does not consider it appropriate to make a determination of the Inheritance Tax. Individuals should also bear in mind that enquiries into domicile involve a detailed inquiry into all of the relevant facts and HMRC is likely to require considerable personal information and extensive documentary evidence about the taxpayer and the taxpayer's close family.

Appendix A: Extract from Revenue & Customs Brief 17/09 superseded by Revenue & Customs Brief 34/2010 issued on 24 August 2010. 'Where an individual who is not domiciled in the UK settles non-UK assets into a non-UK resident trust then assets in that trust will not be subject to Inheritance Tax. Following the release of the new HMRC guidance on domicile most settlors should now be able to decide for themselves whether or not they are UK domiciled.' 'An individual setting up a non-resident trust who, having taken account of the new HMRC guidance, considers they are non-UK domiciled is not obliged to submit an Inheritance Tax account to HMRC. If the settlor is non-UK domiciled then no Inheritance Tax is due. But if an Inheritance Tax account is submitted in these circumstances, HMRC will continue its existing practice and only open an enquiry into that return if the amounts of Inheritance Tax at stake make such an enquiry cost effective to carry out. At present that limit is £10,000'.

26

Inheritance Tax Planning

Introduction

[26.1] This chapter contains a summary of the more common arrangements currently used in Estate Planning. It should be borne in mind that the arrangements are described in outline only, focusing primarily on inheritance tax issues, although other relevant tax consequences are mentioned where appropriate. However all estate planning requires professional advice specific for the client and there may be other tax issues not mentioned here which will be relevant in the particular case concerned. This chapter is therefore intended as an initial guide only so that possible planning techniques appropriate to the client may be investigated further. Arrangements relevant to clients not domiciled in the UK are not included as this is a more complex area, particularly having regard to the proposals for annual charges on UK property interests held by non-natural persons.

The Main Residence

[26.2] Reversionary lease arrangements may, in appropriate circumstances, be outside the scope of the legislation introduced in the wake of the House of Lords decision in favour of the taxpayer in *Ingram v CIR* [2000] 1 AC 293, [1999] STC 37, HL, and appearing at *FA 1986, s 102A*. As an example, the arrangement works by parents granting a lease of the home to their children to come into effect on the expiry of 21 years at the latest, or on the death of the surviving parent whichever is the earlier. The lease will commonly be for at least 99 years, and may be for a longer period. So long as the parents originally purchased a freehold interest in the property more than 7 years prior to the grant of the reversionary lease, it is not considered that *FA 1986, s 102A* applies and hence there is no gift with reservation of benefit. It is understood that HMRC now accept this interpretation of the legislation. See however *Buzzoni (executor of the estate of Mrs Lia Kamhi, deceased) v CIR* [2011] UKFTTT 267(TC), [2011] SFTD 771, [2011] SWTI 1946 for a case involving a leasehold property, rather than a freehold, and as a result it was caught as a reservation of benefit owing to the covenants in the sublease.

If it is correct that the scheme with a freehold does not involve any gift with reservation, then there will be a liability under the pre-owned asset legislation at *FA 2004, Sch 15*. However the value of the reversionary lease will initially be very low and should be within the de-minimis exception for at least the first five years.

The main downside is that the capital gains tax base cost of the reversionary lease will be very low so that as the years pass and the reversionary lease acquires value, thereby depressing the value of the freehold interest, the reduction in inheritance tax is counter-balanced by a capital gains tax liability on the holders of the reversionary lease should they ever dispose of the property. Unless they are living at the property (in which event an alternative scheme may be better) the gain in their hands cannot be within the main residence exemption. Because of this, the scheme is best suited for a residence which it is intended will remain in the ownership of the family indefinitely.

More sophisticated versions of the arrangement use a trust to hold part of the freehold interest, with the reversionary lease being granted to a separate fund within the trust. This provides full capital gains tax exemption for the reversionary lease. However such arrangements require very careful drafting of the documentation.

Equity Release

[26.3] An alternative arrangement in relation to the family home would be to take out a commercially available equity release arrangement and to make a gift of the cash to the next generation as a lifetime potentially exempt transfer. A commercial equity release is an excluded transaction for the purposes of the pre-owned assets legislation, and there are no capital gains tax issues with this arrangement. Nevertheless it must be acknowledged that people who have spent their lifetimes paying off a mortgage on their own home will not readily relish taking out a new mortgage in their later years for inheritance tax planning purposes.

Joint Ownership

[26.4] Where children continue to be resident with their parents and this is likely to remain the case, the parents could put the property into the joint ownership of themselves and the children resident with them. Although there is a gift involved with this arrangement and therefore a potentially exempt transfer, it would be outside the reservation of benefit provisions so long as the conditions in *FA 1986, s 102B(4)* are satisfied, these being that the donors do not receive any benefit, other than a negligible one, which is provided by or at the expense of the donees for some reason connected with the gift. In practical terms, this means that the donees must not bear more than a fair proportion of the running expenses of the home. Ideally, this issue can be avoided entirely if the parents continue to pay all outgoings.

It should be noted that the legislation does not deal with the question of what fractional shares in the property may be held in order to be within the exclusion from reservation of benefit. Equal ownership by all parties is undoubtedly acceptable, but one can expect a challenge from HMRC if children are given substantially greater shares in the property than the parents retain. Such a challenge can only be on the basis that there is an implied condition in the legislation and that seems to be rather a weak proposition.

The Family Debt Scheme

[26.5] If the home is owned by, say, the husband, he could sell it to his wife for full market value with the proceeds remaining outstanding as a debt. He then gives away the debt to his children as a lifetime gift. This arrangement is simply a variation on the widely marketed home loan arrangements which ultimately culminated in the introduction of the pre-owned assets legislation. However that legislation contains an exemption for situations where the property concerned is transferred to the spouse and hence this scheme does not give rise to an annual income tax charge.

There is however no exemption from the stamp duty land tax provisions for a sale between married persons and so there can be liability to that tax.

The arrangement can be adapted for other properties in the ownership of one of the spouses because there can be no capital gains tax payable where the disposal is to the spouse.

The terms of the debt need careful consideration as if it is payable on demand, but in fact is never called in by the children to whom it is given, it would seem easier to allege that a benefit has been reserved out of the gift by associated operations. As an alternative the loan could have a fixed repayment date, or in some cases it may be structured as a relevant discounted security. However it is understood that HMRC currently take the view that all varieties of the scheme involve a reservation of benefit and a case on this point, involving the pre-2004 home loan schemes, was expected to surface at the Tax Tribunals. So far however it has not materialised.

Let Properties

[26.6] A share in a let property may be given away to a settlor interested trust with the result that the share in the trust is outside the settlor's estate for inheritance tax purposes by virtue of *FA 1986, s 102B(3)*. As the trust is settlor-interested, capital gains tax holdover relief will not be applicable and accordingly the capital gains tax position on the transfer into the trust will require review. Also the income will be treated as that of the settlor for income tax purposes, and it may therefore be sensible to give the settlor an entitlement to income.

Although the gift into the trust is not within the reservation of benefit rules, it is nevertheless a chargeable transfer for inheritance tax purposes, and should therefore be confined to the settlor's available nil rate band if an initial inheritance tax liability is to be avoided.

Other Lifetime Trusts

[26.7] It may be appropriate to use up the available inheritance tax nil rate band by making a gift into a trust that is not settlor-interested. The advantage of this is that it enables assets which have accrued but unrealised capital gains to be held over into the trust, and equally on distribution out of the trust at some later time hold over can once again apply.

Assets which do not currently have any capital gain but which are expected to appreciate in value in the future may be sold to a family trust with the proceeds left outstanding as a debt due to the vendor. There will be no significant inheritance tax transfer of value with this arrangement, but there will be a disposal for capital gains tax purposes, and equally a sale for the purposes of stamp duty land tax if the asset is a property interest. Assuming that the debt is not given away, this arrangement amounts to an estate freezing operation so that only the growth in value is outside the vendor's estate, and for that reason he or she must not be a beneficiary of the trust.

Even so, if the loan is interest-free, there are various cases, such as *Jenkins v IRC* 26 TC265, which indicate that the settlement will be settlor-interested for income tax and capital gains tax purposes whilst the debt remains outstanding. This could equally have ramifications for inheritance tax purposes as regards gift with reservation of benefits, and if that view is correct, it would be appropriate to ring fence repayment of the debt away from growth in value of the trust assets so as to confine any reservation of benefit strictly to the amount of the outstanding debt.

Chattels and Works of Art

[26.8] These may be given away to the next generation with custody of the items retained by the donor on payment of a commercial 'rent' to the donees. The capital gains tax position on the gift will need to be reviewed. The main advantage of these arrangements is that the payments due to the donees may be quite low owing to the onerous obligations on the person retaining the use of the chattels in relation to safe keeping and insurance. At one time it was thought that HMRC would accept approximately 1% of the value of the items per annum as being full consideration, although more recently there have been reports that HMRC no longer accept that payments at this level are sufficient. It has always been advised that level of rent should be determined by donor and donees appointing valuers to negotiate the amount payable on behalf of their clients. If full consideration is given on an annual basis, there will be no reservation of benefit issues for inheritance tax purposes, although of course the initial gift will be a transfer of value. Also, full consideration takes the arrangement out of the charge to pre-owned assets tax.

A key point is ensuring that ownership of the chattels passes to the donees, and this normally requires a declaration of gift together with delivery of the items to them. If they remain in the possession of the donor, there will be no delivery and no effective gift. This issue may be dealt with either by following the formalities under the *Bills of Sale Act 1878*, which are fairly convoluted and many will find them off-putting. An alternative is for there to be a sale under the *Sale of Goods Act 1979*, with payment of nominal consideration to the vendor.

Exempt Assets

[26.9] Investment of cash funds in exempt assets such as agricultural property or shares in unquoted trading companies may be considered. There are commercially available schemes by which cash funds are invested in a managed portfolio of shares listed on the Alternative Investment Market. These will benefit from inheritance tax business property relief after two years of ownership, whereas investment in agricultural property requires seven years of ownership if the land is let under a farm business tenancy, the two year test for agricultural land applying only if it is farmed by the owner.

Another commercially marketed arrangement designed to secure business property relief within two years works by setting up a wholly owned company which enters into property development partnerships with other investors. The developments are managed so as to minimise risks, whilst providing an income return which can be drawn out of the company by way of dividend.

It should be noted that following the new rules on deductibility of debts in *FA 2013*, any borrowings taken out after 5 April 2013 to finance the acquisition of agricultural or business property are to be deducted primarily from the value of that property for IHT purposes, notwithstanding the fact that they may be secured on other assets.

Exempt Gilts

[26.10] All UK Government securities issued after 29 April 1996 are exempt from inheritance tax if the beneficial owner is ordinarily resident outside the United Kingdom. There is no two year ownership test for the securities. Accordingly if surplus cash is invested in such securities by an individual who is not ordinarily resident in the UK, they may then be given to a family trust from which the settlor should be excluded, or given directly to the next generation. This will not involve any transfer of value for inheritance tax purposes.

Divorce Settlements

[26.11] So long as a settlement agreed between parties on divorce is within the exemption in *IHTA 1984, s 10* (dispositions not intended to confer gratuitous benefit), the funds concerned may be transferred directly into a trust for the recipient, rather than being paid to that person outright. The transfer into trust will not be a chargeable transfer nor will the funds within the trust be within the estate of any person for inheritance tax purposes. The reservation of benefit provisions will not apply because neither of the parties has made any gift.

Share Freezing Arrangements

[26.12] If the business of a family company does not qualify for inheritance tax business property relief (for example if it is a property investment company) it is possible to freeze the value of the existing ordinary share capital by issuing a new class of shares which takes the rights to (a) all annual profits above a stated level, being approximately the current level of profit, and (b) all growth in assets values above the current asset value of the company. This requires extensive rewriting of the Articles of Association of the company and it must also be borne in mind that the alteration in the share or loan capital of a close company can result in a chargeable transfer being made by the existing shareholders by virtue of *IHTA 1984, s 98*. The relevant thresholds for the share freezing operation therefore need to be carefully set. The new class of shares is likely to have a nil base cost for capital gains tax purposes.

Insurance Based Schemes

[26.13] The main insurance based estate planning schemes fall into two categories, these being gift and loan trusts and discounted gift schemes.

Under a gift and loan trust, a discretionary trust is created with a nominal sum and the client then makes a loan to the trustees with the funds being invested in a single premium life insurance bond. The trustees take the 5% annual withdrawals which are available from the bond and use this to repay the loan owing to the client over the next 20 year period. The remaining funds within the bond grow free of inheritance tax outside the estate of the client.

It will normally be preferable for the client not to be the person who forms the discretionary trust with the nominal sum. This is to prevent the arrangement involving any gift by the client with the loan repayments being a benefit reserved out of it.

Discounted gift schemes involve the contribution of a lump sum payment to a trust set up the benefit of the next generation and under the terms of the trust the settlor retains an entitlement to a predetermined level of cash withdrawals during his or her lifetime. Because the settlor has carved out a fixed entitlement and given away the balance of the funds to the other beneficiaries the scheme is outside the inheritance tax gift with reservation of benefit provisions. The settlor's entitlement to the payments for the rest of his life discounts the value of the gift to the next generation for inheritance tax purposes. The other beneficiaries may have absolute entitlements, in which case the gift to them counts as a potentially exempt transfer, or alternatively they may take their benefits under a discretionary trust, in which case the value of the gift into the trust will be a chargeable transfer and should be structured so as to fall within the available nil rate band. These schemes are very popular because they effectively enable a gift of capital to be made with retained rights to income but outside the reservation of benefit regime. HMRC accept the validity of the arrangements, although they have challenged the discount figure in relation to the value of the potentially exempt transfer in some cases at the tax Tribunals. Revenue and Customs Brief 22/13 and the HMRC Trusts and Estates Newsletter December 2013 contain further guidance on HMRC's views. As a general rule, the scheme is most suitable for retired persons in their 70s. It should be borne in mind that it is inflexible and may be difficult to unwind if the settlor should later wish to do so.

Short Term Trust for Surviving Spouse

[26.14] One of the complications of estate planning is often the capital gains tax liability which arises on gifts of assets during lifetime to the next generation. This problem can be quite acute under the current capital gains tax regime where the rate of tax on a gain may be 28%, not far short of the inheritance tax rate of 40% so that substantial tax liability can arise on a gift of an asset with a low base cost. If one spouse is in poor health whereas the other remains in good health, or alternatively where one spouse is considerably older than the other, it may be appropriate for the spouse with the shorter life expectancy to leave assets on trust for the surviving spouse for a short period of time, say one year. This secures the spouse exemption on the death and also a tax free uplift in base costs for capital gains tax purposes. On termination of the trust for the spouse, so long as the assets pass absolutely to other beneficiaries there will be a potentially exempt transfer by the surviving spouse. It is preferable for this arrangement to be set up by Will rather than by deed of variation since for the latter, the trust for the surviving spouse must remain in place for more than two years because of the provisions of *IHTA 1984, s 142(4)*.

27

Interest in Possession

Cross-references. See **41** SETTLEMENTS — GENERAL; **42** SETTLEMENTS WITH INTERESTS IN POSSESSION; **43** SETTLEMENTS: DISCRETIONARY TRUSTS AND OTHER TRUSTS OF RELEVANT PROPERTY.

Simon's Taxes. See **I5.141–I5.152, I5.201.**

Other Sources. Foster, Part E2; HMRC Customer Guide to Inheritance Tax; IHTM16000.

Introduction

[27.1] Up to 21 March 2006, a person with an interest in possession in all or part of settled property was treated as beneficially entitled to the property or part in which his interest subsisted. Alternatively, if there was no interest in possession the special charging rules relating to settlements of 'relevant property' apply (see **43.1** SETTLEMENTS: DISCRETIONARY TRUSTS AND OTHER TRUSTS OF RELEVANT PROPERTY). [*IHTA 1984, ss 49, 50, 58, 59*]. For IHT purposes it was therefore important to establish into which category a settlement fell.

From 22 March 2006 an interest in possession to which a person becomes beneficially entitled on or after that date will result in that person being treated as beneficially entitled to the property concerned only if it is either (i) an immediate post death interest (see **42.2** SETTLEMENTS WITH INTERESTS IN POSSESSION), (ii) a disabled person's interest (see Chapter **47** SETTLEMENTS: TRUSTS FOR DISABLED PERSONS), or (iii) a transitional serial interest (see **42.2**). [*IHTA 1984, s 49 as amended by FA 2006, Sch 20 para 4*].These are described as qualifying interests in possession [*IHTA 1984, s 59*]. From 9 December 2009, this treatment was also extended to trust interests in possession for which full consideration was paid by the beneficiary to the settlor, this being intended to block an avoidance scheme [*IHTA 1984, s 5(1B)*].

Interests in possession which arose before 22 March 2006 and which continued thereafter were unaffected by the above changes introduced in *FA 2006* and therefore the beneficiary continues to be treated as beneficially entitled to the settled property in which the interest subsists for so long as that same interest endures.

The IHT treatment of settlements with interests in possession is detailed further at **42** SETTLEMENTS WITH INTERESTS IN POSSESSION.

Meaning of 'interest in possession'

[27.2] There is no statutory definition of 'interest in possession' in the IHT legislation (except see **27.3** below for Scotland). The explanation of the expression 'qualifying interest in possession' (see **43.1** SETTLEMENTS: DISCRETIONARY TRUSTS AND OTHER TRUSTS OF RELEVANT PROPERTY) merely clarifies what is meant by 'qualifying'. What is meant by an interest in possession is therefore a matter of general law as interpreted by the courts in the light of the specific IHT legislation.

The authoritative statement on the meaning of the term for CTT (and therefore IHT) purposes is to be found in the majority opinions in the House of Lords in *Pearson and Others v CIR* HL, [1980] STC 318. The salient facts to be derived from this case are as follows.

(a) There must be a **present right to the present enjoyment** of certain settled property for there to be an interest in possession in that property. So a person with an interest in possession must have an immediate right to trust income as it arises. It should be noted that it is of no consequence that no income actually arises so it is not necessary to ensure that a life tenant actually receives income in order to establish the interest in possession. See *Oakley & Hutson (Jossaume's Personal Representatives v CIR* [2005] STC SCD 343 Sp C 460 at **58** TAX CASES.

(b) If the trustees have **any power to withhold income** as it arises there is no interest in possession. There is a distinction between a power to terminate a present right to present enjoyment and a power which prevents a present right of present enjoyment arising. It follows that:

   (i) *a power to accumulate income* is sufficient to prevent a beneficiary from having an interest in possession. (*Note*. per Inland Revenue Press Release 12 February 1976, if any accumulations must be held solely for the person having the interest or his personal representatives, this does not amount to a power to withhold income.) The position is the same if there is a trust to accumulate. Whether or not income is in fact accumulated is irrelevant.

   (ii) *an overriding power of appointment* which could be used to defeat the interest of a beneficiary does not prevent that interest from being in possession if it does not affect the right of the beneficiary to the income which has already arisen.

   (iii) *the possibility of future defeasance* of an interest does not prevent it from being in possession until the occurrence of the relevant event.

(iv) *a power of revocation* does not prevent an interest from being in possession until it is exercised.

(c) There is a distinction between trustees' **administrative powers**, such as those to pay duties, taxes etc. and their **dispositive powers** to dispose of the net income of the trust. The existence of the former does not prevent an interest from being in possession. Any interest in possession will be in the net income of the trust after deduction of administrative expenses.

The HMRC view was previously expressed in their Press Release of 12 February 1976 which they regard as not inconsistent with the majority HL opinions in *Pearson*.

Scotland

[27.3] In Scotland, any reference to an interest in possession in settled property is a reference to an interest of any kind under a settlement by virtue of which the person in right of that interest is entitled to the enjoyment of that property, or would be so entitled if the property were capable of enjoyment, (including an interest of an assignee under an assignation of an interest of any kind in property subject to a proper liferent, other than a reversionary interest) and that person is deemed to be entitled to a corresponding interest in the whole or any part of the property comprised in the settlement. [*IHTA 1984, s 46*]. For further background on Scottish Trusts see HMRC Trust Manual at http://www.hmrc.gov.uk/manuals/tsemmanual/tsem6520.htm.

In a Scottish case, an individual (D) transferred certain securities and investments to trustees in 1962. The income arising from the trust was treated for tax purposes as income of the settlor under *FA 1958, s 22* (now *ITTOIA 2005, ss 624–628*). D died in 1981 and then his wife died in 2002. HMRC issued a notice of determination on the basis that she had enjoyed an interest in possession in the settled property. The trustees appealed. The Special Commissioner dismissed the appeal, finding that D's widow had effectively enjoyed 'a power of veto: the whole of the free annual income of the trust fund had to be paid or applied to her or for her benefit from year to year unless or until she should concur with a consideration by the trustees that it was proper and expedient for a lesser amount to be so paid or applied'. Accordingly the trust deed had conferred an interest in possession. See *Trustees of the Douglas Trust (for Mrs I Fairbairn) v HMRC* [2007] STC SCD 338 Sp C 593.

Trustee Act 1925

[27.4] *Trustee Act 1925, s 31* can affect a beneficiary's right to trust income with a corresponding effect on whether or not he has an interest in possession. In *Swales and Others v CIR* Ch D, [1984] STC 413, an appointment of income contingent upon the occurrence of a vesting event was intended to carry the right to the intermediate income of the fund, and *Trustee Act 1925, s 31(1)(ii)* applied to that intermediate income with the effect that the beneficiary was entitled to an interest in possession in the trust fund. In *Re Delamere's Settlement Trusts, Kenny and Others v Cunningham-Reid and Others* CA 1983,

[1984] 1 All ER 584, the point at issue was whether, on the facts, *Trustee Act 1925, s 31(2)* applied, as this determined whether or not the beneficiaries had interests in possession. It was held not to apply, with the result that the beneficiaries did have interests in possession.

Sole object of discretionary trust

[27.5] The fact that income from trust funds is to be held upon 'protective trusts' to be paid to or applied for a class of beneficiaries at the trustees' absolute discretion has been held not to give the sole existing beneficiary a protected life interest. Nor does that beneficiary have an interest in possession by virtue of being the sole current existing object of a discretionary trust if the trusts are for a class of beneficiaries which has not closed and there is a reasonable possibility of other members of the class coming into existence. The possibility, however remote, that another discretionary object could come into existence is sufficient to prevent him from having the necessary immediate entitlement to trust income as it arises. (*Moore and Osborne v CIR* Ch D, [1984] STC 236.)

Occupation of dwelling-house by beneficiary

[27.6] Trustees under a will or settlement may have power to allow a beneficiary to occupy a dwelling-house comprised in the trust on such terms as they think fit. Where there is no interest in possession in the dwelling house HMRC do not regard the exercise of the power as creating one if the effect is merely to allow non-exclusive occupation, or to create a contractual tenancy for full consideration. The creation of a lease for a term or a periodic tenancy for less than full consideration does not create an interest in possession, though it may give rise to a charge under *IHTA 1984, s 65*. (See **43.12** SETTLEMENTS: DISCRETIONARY TRUSTS AND OTHER TRUSTS OF RELEVANT PROPERTY.) On the other hand, if the power is drawn in terms wide enough to cover the creation of an exclusive or joint right of residence, albeit revocable, for a definite or indefinite period, and is exercised with the intention of providing a particular beneficiary with a permanent home, HMRC will normally regard the exercise of the power as creating an interest in possession; see HMRC Statement of Practice SP10/79. A lease for life for less than full consideration will also be regarded as an interest in possession. (In another context see *Harrison and Another v Gibson and Others* Ch D [2005] TLR 24 January 2006 where the testator's intentions as to occupancy of his bungalow 'in trust to my wife' did not give an absolute interest to his wife under *Administration of Justice Act 1982, s 22*.) (See also **41.6**(e) SETTLEMENTS — GENERAL.) A similar view will be taken where the power is exercised over property in which another beneficiary had an interest in possession up to the time of the exercise.

Case law

In the case of *Judge and another (personal representatives of Walden deceased) v HMRC* [2005] STC SCD 863 Sp C 506 a deceased husband's will gave his house to trustees, with a declaration that they should allow his widow (W) to occupy the house 'for such period or periods as they shall in their absolute discretion think fit'. W previously had no interest in the property and continued to occupy the house until her death in 2003. HMRC issued a notice of determination on the basis that her husband's will had given her an interest in possession in the house (see also Inland Revenue Statement of Practice SP 10/79, 15 August 1979). Her personal representatives appealed. The Special Commissioner allowed their appeal, holding that the effect of W's husband's will was that she 'had no right to occupy the property but the trustees were given a discretion (but not a duty) to allow her to occupy'. In the summary the Commissioner stated:

> 'With the exclusion of the words "with the consent in writing of my wife during her lifetime" this asset creates a trust for the sale of Perrymead Street and provides that the proceeds of sale are to be held as for the residuary (discretionary) fund. However, the words "with the consent in writing of my wife during her lifetime" prevents the sale taking place during the life of Mrs Walden unless she consents in writing. In the absence of such consent, the sale cannot take place, but any net rents and profits until sale are to be held on the (discretionary) trusts of the residuary fund. In my view, this part of clause 3 manifests the intention of Mr Walden that Mrs Walden, during her lifetime, could unilaterally postpone the sale of Perrymead Street but that, if she did, then the rents and profits were to be held on the discretionary trusts of the residuary fund. This part of the clause makes it clear that Mrs Walden had no right to the income of Perrymead Street pending sale.'

Accordingly therefore, Mrs Walden did not have the right to occupy Perrymead Street and did not have an interest in possession in the property. Despite the case being found in favour of the taxpayer and the husband's will being held to create discretionary trusts with no tax being payable by the estate, it has not dealt with all uncertainties in this area, partly because it is a decision of the Special Commissioner which is not a binding precedent, and partly because all similar cases will depend on the particular wording of the trusts concerned. Further issues will arise where the trust relates to a share in the property where the surviving spouse holds the remaining interest. In order to reduce any inference that an interest, trustees should perhaps regularly reconsider their discretionary powers documenting such deliberations in writing for record. Another possibility is to grant the surviving spouse a shorthold lease for minimal rent, which SP10/79 acknowledges prevents an interest in possession from applying; alternatively consider creating a formal licence to occupy. (Inland Revenue Statement of Practice SP 10/79, 15 August 1979 at **25** HMRC STATEMENTS OF PRACTICE.) See also Taxation Magazine, 20 May 2004 p 183.

See also *CIR v Lloyds Private Banking Ltd* [1998] STC 559 in which a will included a clause stating that 'while my Husband ... remains alive and desires to reside in the [matrimonial home] and keeps the same in good repair and insured comprehensively to its full value with Insurers approved by my Trustee and pays and indemnifies my Trustee against all rates taxes and other outgoings in respect of the property my Trustee shall not make any objection to such residence and shall not disturb or restrict it in any way'. This was held to create an interest in possession in the property.

Precedent for occupation of trust property

Where two or more beneficiaries have interests in possession in a property held in trust and it is agreed that one shall have exclusive occupation of it, making a compensatory payment to the other beneficiary or beneficiaries, the agreement set out below may be adapted to suit the case.

Agreement between the Trustees and Beneficiary for the occupation of trust property [pursuant to *Trusts of Land and Appointment of Trustees Act 1996, section 13*]

THIS AGREEMENT is made the . . . . . . day of . . . . . . 2010. . . . . . . between

. . . . [Trustee]. . . . . of . . . . [Address] . . . . and . . . . [Trustee]. . . . . of . . . . [Address]. . . . . hereinafter known as 'the Trustees' and . . . . [Beneficiary]. . . . . of . . . . [Address]. . . . . hereinafter known as 'the Beneficiary'.

WHEREAS

(1) The Trustees are the present Trustees of:

(a) a conveyance ('the Conveyance') dated . . . . [date] . . . . . . and made between the parties and

(b) a settlement ('the Settlement') of even date with and made between the same parties in the same order as the Conveyance.

(2) The freehold property (the 'Property') described in the schedule is vested in the Trustees and is held on trusts under which the Beneficiary is entitled to an interest in possession.

(3) The Trustees have determined in accordance with the provisions of the Trusts of Land and Appointment of Trustees Act 1996, section 13 that the Beneficiary may occupy the Property on the following terms and conditions including the payment by the Beneficiary to . . . . [Name of second Beneficiary]. . . . . of . . . . [Address]. . . . . hereinafter known as . . . . [Name]. . . . . (who is also entitled to an interest in possession under the trusts affecting the Property) of such annual sums as are stated in this agreement.

NOW IT IS AGREED as follows:

1 *Licence*

The Trustees permit the Beneficiary to reside in and occupy the Property until the agreement is determined in accordance with the provisions below.

2 *Tenant not to assign*

This licence is personal to the Beneficiary and he/she shall not assign it or allow any other person or persons to occupy the whole or any other part of the property.

3 *Payment*

The Beneficiary undertakes to pay to . . . . [Name] . . . . the annual sum of £. . . . . by equal half yearly instalments payable in arrears throughout the currency of this licence so long as

. . . . [Name]. . . . . is entitled to an interest in possession under the Trusts affecting the property, the first such instalment to be paid on . . . . [Date]. . . . . and the subsequent instalments to be paid on . . . . [Date]. . . . . and . . . . [Date]. . . . . in each year and the last payment to be made on the termination of the licence or on such earlier date as . . . . [Name]. . . . . ceases to be entitled to an interest in possession under the trusts affecting the property (whether due to the death of . . . . [Name]. . . . . or for any other reason) and to be a proportionate payment.

Notes to the Agreement

(A) Further provisions on powers, proper law, etc. and full administrative provisions are required to effect this agreement.

(B) Note that in the above agreement the second Beneficiary is excluded from occupying land under the *Trusts of Land and Appointment of Trustees Act 1996, s 13(1)* but he/she still retains an interest in possession in that land. On the death of the occupying Beneficiary and upon the second Beneficiary becoming sole life tenant of the trust fund he/she can no longer be excluded from occupation under *s 13(1)* nor will he/she be required to pay compensation (see point 3 'Payment' in Agreement above) under *s 13(6)*.

Power to augment income out of capital

[27.7] Where a trustee exercises a power to augment the income of a beneficiary out of capital, this will have no immediate IHT effect if the beneficiary is a life tenant who has an interest in possession, as by virtue of *IHTA 1984, s 49(1)* he is already treated as beneficially entitled to the property. In other circumstances the exercise of the power is likely to give rise to a tax charge. (**25.E6** HMRC STATEMENTS OF PRACTICE).

Time of creation of interest in possession

Age of majority

[27.8] Under *Family Law Reform Act 1969, s 1*, the age of majority is reduced from 21 to 18 although for settlements created before 1 January 1970, the relevant age of majority remains 21. Where an interest is created by a special power of appointment made after 31 December 1969 under a settlement made before 1 January 1970, HMRC regard the beneficiary's interest in possession as arising at 18. (**25.E8** HMRC STATEMENTS OF PRACTICE but now withdrawn — IR Press Release 30 September 1996).

Administration period

[27.9] Where a person would have been entitled to any interest in possession in the whole or part of the residue of the estate of a deceased person had the administration of the estate been completed, he is regarded for inheritance tax purposes as becoming entitled to an interest in possession in the unadministered estate and in the property (if any) representing ascertained residue, or a corresponding part of it, on the date as from which the whole or part of the income of the residue would have been attributable to his interest had the residue been ascertained immediately after the date of death. [*IHTA 1984, s 91*].

Survivorship clauses

[27.10] Where under the terms of a will or otherwise property is held for any person on condition that he survives another for a specified period not exceeding six months, the disposition taking effect at the end of the period (or on death if the person does not survive until then) is treated as having had effect from the beginning of the period. This has no effect on distributions etc. occurring before the disposition. [*IHTA 1984, s 92*].

28

Interest on Tax

Cross-references. See 7.14 CALCULATION OF TAX for transfers reported late and 35 PAYMENT OF TAX.

Simon's Taxes. See **I11.405, I11.411, I11.541.**

Other Sources. Foster, Part L5.31–2; IHTM36000.

Interest on tax overdue

[28.1] Interest is chargeable on unpaid inheritance tax from the due date (see 35.1 PAYMENT OF TAX) to the date of payment at the following rates. Computations below show the position where there is an interest charge in excess of the current rates in force. See http://www.hmrc.gov.uk/rates/interest.htm.

After 28 September 2009	3% p.a.
After 23 March 2009 and before 29 September 2009	0% p.a.
After 26 January 2009 and before 24 March 2009	1% p.a.
After 5 January 2009 and before 27 January 2009	2% p.a.
After 5 November 2008 and before 6 January 2009	3% p.a.
After 5 January 2008 and before 6 November 2008	4% p.a.
After 5 August 2007 and before 6 January 2008	5% p.a.
After 5 September 2006 and before 6 August 2007	4% p.a.
After 5 September 2005 and before 6 September 2006	3% p.a.
After 5 September 2004 and before 6 September 2005	4% p.a.
After 5 December 2003 and before 6 September 2004	3% p.a.
After 5 August 2003 and before 6 December 2003	2% p.a.
After 5 November 2001 and before 6 August 2003	3% p.a.
After 5 May 2001 and before 6 November 2001	4% p.a.
After 5 February 2000 and before 6 May 2001	5% p.a.
After 5 March 1999 and before 6 February 2000	4% p.a.
After 5 October 1994 and before 6 March 1999	5% p.a.
After 5 January 1994 and before 6 October 1994	4% p.a.
After 5 December 1992 and before 6 January 1994	5% p.a.
After 5 November 1992 and before 6 December 1992	6% p.a.
After 5 July 1991 and before 6 November 1992	8% p.a.

After 5 May 1991 and before 6 July 1991	9% p.a.
After 5 March 1991 and before 6 May 1991	10% p.a.
After 5 July 1989 and before 6 March 1991	11% p.a.
After 5 October 1988 and before 6 July 1989	9% p.a.
After 5 August 1988 and before 6 October 1988	8% p.a.
After 5 June 1987 and before 6 August 1988	6% p.a.
After 15 December 1986 and before 6 June 1987	8% p.a.
After 17 March 1986 and before 16 December 1986	
— transfers on death and potentially exempt transfers	9% p.a.
— all other transfers	11% p.a.

From 18 August 1989 the Treasury may, in an order in the form of a statutory instrument, prescribe formulae for computing interest rates so that if circumstances change so as to change the rate of interest prescribed, the Board must by order specify the new rate and the day from which it has effect. Prior to 18 August 1989 the Treasury had to prescribe each change of rate in an order in the form of a statutory instrument.

Any interest accruing on or after 6 April 1997 is calculated as if every year is a leap year (i.e. 366 days). This will give a small advantage to the taxpayer in three out of every four years.

Interest is payable gross and it is not deductible in computing income, profits or losses for tax purposes. It is refundable to the extent that the tax concerned is subsequently cancelled.

For the above purposes, where:

(a) additional tax becomes chargeable as a result of the transferor's death within seven years of a chargeable transfer (including tax payable under the provisions relating to **43** SETTLEMENTS: DISCRETIONARY TRUSTS AND OTHER TRUSTS OF RELEVANT PROPERTY because of the settlor's death within that period), and

(b) a political party is liable for tax on the death of the transferor within one year after a gift in excess of £100,000 made before 15 March 1988,

the chargeable transfer is deemed to have been made on death.

Acceptance of property in satisfaction of tax

Where after 16 March 1987, the Board agree to accept property (acceptance by the AIL Panel of Resource) in satisfaction of any IHT, CTT or estate duty (see **35.10** PAYMENT OF TAX) on terms that the value to be attributed to the property for the purposes of the acceptance is determined at a date earlier than that on which the property is actually accepted, the terms of the agreement may provide that the amount of tax which is satisfied by the acceptance of the property does not carry interest from that earlier date. [*IHTA 1984, ss 233, 236(1)(1A); FA 1986, Sch 19 paras 32, 33; FA 1987, s 60; F(No 2)A 1987, s 97; FA 1988, Sch 14; FA 1989, ss 178, 179; SI 1985/560; SI 1986/1944; SI 1987/887; SI 1988/1280; SI 1988/1623; SI 1989/1002; SI 1989/1297; SI 1989/1298*].

Example 1

B died on 10 February 2010. The executors made a payment on account of IHT of £70,000 on 30 June 2010 on delivery of the account. The final notice of determination was raised by HMRC Inheritance Tax on 19 June 2011 in the sum of £102,500. The rate of interest for these purposes is assumed to be 5% for the purpose of this example.

Date of chargeable event (death) — 10 February 2010
Date on which interest starts to accrue — 1 September 2010

	£
IHT payable	102,500
Payment made on account 30 June 2010	70,000
Balance due	£32,500
Assessment raised by HMRC Inheritance Tax 19 June 2011	
Interest payable (1.9.2010 to 19.6.2011)	
£32,500 at 5% for 292 days	£1,300

Example 2

F gave his holiday home in Cornwall to his granddaughter G on 7 August 2006. On 23 May 2010 F died. He had made no use of the property at any time after 7 August 2006. G made a payment of £15,000, on account of the IHT due, on 1 January 2011. The liability was agreed at £27,000, and the balance paid, on 17 February 2011. The rate of interest for these purposes is assumed to be 5%.

Date of PET — 7 August 2006
Date on which PET becomes chargeable — 23 May 2010
Date on which IHT is due — 1 December 2010

	£
IHT payable	27,000
Payment made on account 1 January 2011	15,000
Balance due	£12,000
Interest payable	
On £27,000 from 1.12.2010 to 1.1.2011	
£27,000 at 5% for 31 days	115
On £12,000 from 1.1.2011 to 17.2.2011	
£12,000 at 5% for 47 days	77
Total interest payable	£192

Where HMRC delay their reply to a letter or other enquiry for no good reason, and the delay in total exceeds by more than six months its 28-day target for replies, then no interest will be charged on tax that was unpaid during the period of the delay, and any reasonable costs incurred directly because of the delay will be reimbursed (HMRC Code of Practice 1).

Interest on tax repaid

[28.2] Currently the interest repayable in respect of IHT overpaid is 0.5%, this rate being effective from 29 September 2009. Any repayment of tax or interest paid will carry interest from the date of payment until the order for repayment is issued at the above rates and such interest will be tax-free. [*IHTA 1984, s 235*]. Where inheritance tax is repaid as a result of an order that is made under the *Inheritance (Provision for Family and Dependants) Act 1975, ss 2, 19* as amended by the *Family Law Act 1996, s 66* special treatment applies, see **28.4** below.

Where HMRC delay their reply to a letter or other enquiry for no good reason, and the delay in total exceeds by more than six months its 28-day target for replies, then interest will be paid on repayments of tax due but not repaid during the period of the delay, and any reasonable costs incurred directly because of the delay will be reimbursed as well as consolatory payments in serious cases (revised HMRC Code of Practice 1 issued in April 1996). (*IHTA 1984, s 235* above would normally cover *by statute* all circumstances involving interest on repayments of tax including those of HMRC delay.) See http://www.hmrc.gov.uk/rates/interest-repayments.htm.

Interest on payment by instalments

[28.3] See **35.9** PAYMENT OF TAX.

Special cases

[28.4] Tax overpaid or underpaid in consequence of the *Inheritance (Provisions for Family and Dependants) Act 1975* (or NI equivalent) (see **52.17** TRANSFERS ON DEATH) does not carry interest before the date of the order. [*IHTA 1984, ss 146(1), 236(2) to be amended from a date to be specified by FA 2009, ss 101, 102, Sch 53 para 8, Sch 54 paras 10–12*].

In 2001 and 2007 HMRC introduced a cancellation of interest in respect of deferred tax resulting from financial difficulty brought about by the outbreak of foot and mouth disease. The circumstances where this may apply to inheritance tax is detailed in **33** NATIONAL HERITAGE.

Interest will normally become payable on the unpaid inheritance tax six months after the end of the month in which the chargeable event occurred (see **35.1** PAYMENT OF TAX). In the case of foot and mouth disease which affected farming businesses both these interest payments arising on the IHT and CGT tax liabilities payable but deferred will be cancelled. [*FA 2001, s 107(1)*]. The Government declared the United Kingdom free of the disease at midnight on 14 January 2002 but HMRC were aware that for some time after that the financial and economic effect would remain and they continued to help those affected. See IR Press Release 18 March 2002. Now where there is a disaster or emergency interest on unpaid tax it may be deferred where the Commissioners agree such a case warrants it. [*FA 2008, s 135*].

29

Land

Cross-reference. See **14.5** DETERMINATION AND APPEALS re land valuation.

Simon's Taxes. See **I4.311, I7.302, I7.401, I8.361**.

Introduction

[29.1] Land includes (unless the contrary intention appears) buildings and other structures, land covered with water, and any estate, interest, easement, servitude or right in or over land, but does not include any estate, interest or right by way of mortgage or other security. In *Chelsea Yacht and Boat Co Ltd v Pope*, CA [2001] 2 All ER 409 where a houseboat moored to a pontoon and embankment wall by ropes constituted a chattel and not part of the land which consequently would affect the option to pay by instalments. In contrast in *Cinderella Rockerfellas Ltd v Rudd* [2003] All ER 219 a floating nightclub permanently attached to the land by ropes and hains would constitute part of the land which consequently would affect the option to pay by instalments. See 35.5 PAYMENT OF TAX. In any Act passed before 1 January 1979, 'land' includes messuages, tenements and heraditaments, houses and buildings of any tenure. [*Interpretation Act 1978, s 5, Sch 1, Sch 2 para 5(b); IHTA 1984, s 272*]. See also IHTM23001. The Land Registry Office is the preferred source of information for HMRC. See http://www.landregistry.gov.uk/.

Chargeable transfers of land

[29.2] Inheritance tax applies to chargeable transfers of land situated in the UK and to land situated abroad but in which an interest is held by a person domiciled in the UK. Certain special provisions apply as below.

Agricultural land and business land

[29.3] Where property in the UK, Channel Islands, Isle of Man or EEA state is transferred, and that property was used for agricultural purposes or was held as an asset of a business or used for the purposes of a business, a reduction in value for the purposes of inheritance tax may be claimed. See 4 AGRICULTURAL PROPERTY and 6 BUSINESS PROPERTY for details. Also, the *Finance Act 2009* introduced legislation to retrospectively extend inheritance tax agricultural property relief and woodlands relief from 22 April 2009 onwards to property in the European Economic Area (EEA). In cases where tax is due or has been paid on or after 23 April 2003 in respect of EEA agricultural property or woodlands under the old rules then, by way of claim, a deferral or cancellation of the tax will apply. Where the claim results in a refund of tax this will be repaid with repayment supplement. For 2003/04 the claim had to be made by 31 January 2010. This extended APR and woodlands relief also applies where property placed into trust which then suffers periodic or exit charges and to such charges where IHT was paid or due on or after 22 April 2009. Similarly, where property was gifted and has become a PET within *IHTA 1984, s 3A* and the tax was due or paid because it 'failed' then the relief will apply retrospectively. [*Interpretation Act 1978, s 5, Sch 1; IHTA 1984, ss 115, 116, 125; FA 2009, s 121*].

In the case of agricultural or business property that may qualify for 100% relief HMRC Inheritance Tax state that the open market value should still be used. Personal representatives may consider using their own estimate of the value of the property in the expectation that the business will in any case be covered by the 100% agricultural or business relief. A reason for using a nominal value may be the cost of a professional valuer's fees to the estate. However, nominal or ill considered values should be avoided because if relief is not due for some reason and there is an uplift in the nominal value put on the business by the personal representatives, then the consequent uplift to the correct value may incur a penalty. Also, for the purposes of *TCGA 1992, s 274* the value for CGT purposes should be 'ascertained' and not a nominal estimated value. See example in **6.3** BUSINESS PROPERTY and also at http://www.hmrc.gov.uk/cto/newsletter.htm, April 2004.

Case law

In *Tapp v HMRC* [2008] EW Lands TMA/284/2008 a Lands Tribunal case shows the necessity of documentation, including photographs, regarding the state of repair of property at the time of death but a subsequent visit by the District Valuer at a later date may indicate a higher value which was not reflected at the time of death. See IHTM23203. This may also apply to land which, say, adjoins a potential gravel extraction site which is subject of planning consent at the time of the death valuation. At the time of the District Valuer's visit a public enquiry has recommended to the Secretary of State that the appeal by the gravel extraction company should be dismissed hence resulting in a higher market valuation at the time of the inspection visit. For special valuation matters concerning minerals see IHTM23197.

The *conacre* (derivation from 'corn acre') system is unique to Ireland and around a third of all farmland in Northern Ireland is let informally to farmers in this way, often from 20 to 30-acre farms now too small to be commercially viable. APR of 100% applies to the ordinary value of farmland however, where farmland has development potential but is still farmed by letting in conacre, it attracted a second relief – business property relief – also at 100% on that additional development value. Following the Northern Ireland Court of Appeal hearing in *McCall (Personal Representatives of Mrs E McClean (deceased)) v HMRC*, CA (NI) [2008] STC 990 Sp C 678 that business may now consist of mainly of making or holding investments, within *IHTA 1984, s 105(3)*, so that the land is not 'relevant business property'. *See* **4.1** AGRICULTURAL PROPERTY and **58** TAX CASES.

Free use of land

[29.4] A charge to inheritance tax may arise where an owner allows the use of land to another person for a fixed or minimum period for inadequate consideration. See **51.3** TRANSFER OF VALUE for details.

Housing associations

[29.5] Gifts of land in the UK to registered housing associations after 13 March 1989 are exempt. See **21.5** EXEMPT TRANSFERS.

National heritage land

[29.6] Land and buildings which are of outstanding historic or other interest may be exempt from inheritance tax under certain conditions, see **33** NATIONAL HERITAGE.

Payment of tax by instalments

[29.7] Under certain conditions, where a liability to inheritance tax arises on the transfer of land and buildings of any description, wherever situated, an election to pay the tax by ten annual instalments may be made. See **35.5** PAYMENTS OF TAX for details and HMRC Customer Guide to Inheritance Tax.

Sales within three (or four) years after death

[29.8] Special provisions apply, see **56.9** VALUATION.

Transfers within seven years before death

[29.9] See 53 TRANSFERS WITHIN SEVEN YEARS BEFORE DEATH for special provisions.

Woodlands

[29.10] See 57 WOODLANDS for special provisions.

Key points

[29.11] Points to consider are as follows.

- The open market value of agricultural property may exceed its agricultural value where the land has planning permission or there is development or amenity value, or mineral value (such as gravel or sand extraction potential). A difference between the open market value and the agricultural value often occurs on farms where there are ranges of traditional buildings suitable for conversion into residential or commercial use; in many areas these can have significant excess value. Agricultural relief will not be available in respect of the excess value but business relief may be available as an alternative. Care should be taken to confirm that the parts of the farm with excess value for non-agricultural use are actually used as an asset of a qualifying business if business relief is to be claimed. Problems frequently arise with traditional buildings suitable for development that are obsolete for modern farming methods and have not been used for the business for some considerable time and do not qualify for 100% BPR or APR.
- Where land is situated in the United Kingdom HMRC rely on professional advice from the Valuation Office Agency (VOA), or the Valuation and Lands Agency (VLA) in Northern Ireland, in arriving at a valuation unless specifically stated otherwise. Although most land in the UK which is chargeable to tax on the death is referred to the VOA there are some exceptions such as land subject to a binding contract for sale at the date of death. The role of the District Valuer (DV) is to agree the agricultural value and in cases where, the property has value for development or value for other non-agricultural uses or there is an imposing farmhouse in a location that would appeal to non-farming purchasers e.g. 'lifestyle farmers' the DV will also agree an open market value for the property. The DV bases his valuation at inspection on local knowledge, or on the basis of information provided by the parties and the inspection itself. If the DV has doubts as to whether or not part, or the whole, of the property

was occupied for the purposes of agriculture he will let HMRC know and await further instructions from HMRC. This often occurs in the context of barns and other farm buildings, where the information provided by the parties suggests that there has been an agricultural element to the occupation but inspection suggests no recent such use.

- It would be advantageous to receive the development land at a high value for CGT purposes for any future disposal but this is only of benefit where the land is covered by the APR or BPR 100% exemptions. Hope value arising out of development potential or change of use then such excess value will not attract agricultural relief. As the excess value may attract business relief but a claim for business relief on the value of agricultural property on the excess over its agricultural value — e.g. farmland with planning permission, development value or mineral value (such as gravel and sand) is dependent on it being 'relevant business property'.

Houses, land, buildings and interests in land [Form IHT 405]

HM Revenue & Customs

Houses, land, buildings and interests in land
Schedule IHT405

When to use this form

You do not need to fill in this form if the only items of property were jointly owned. You should fill in form IHT404 *Jointly owned assets* instead.

Fill in this form to give details of all the land and buildings or rights over land (such as fishing rights) owned by the deceased in their sole name.

We tell you how to value these assets in form IHT400 Notes

If you have a professional valuation, please enclose a copy with the completed form.

Name of deceased

Date of death *DD MM YYYY*

IHT reference number (if known)

Help

For information or help or another copy of this form:
- go to **www.hmrc.gov.uk/inheritancetax/**
- phone our Helpline on **0845 30 20 900**
- – if calling from outside the UK, phone **+44 115 974 3009**.

Details of the person we should contact about the valuation of houses or land

Only fill in this section if the person we should contact is different from the one named on form IHT400, box 17.

1 Name and address of the firm or person dealing with the valuation of the houses or land.

Title – enter MR, MRS, MISS, MS or other title

Name

Postcode

House or building number

Rest of address, including house name or flat number

2 Contact name, if different from box 1

3 Phone number

4 DX number and town (if used)

5 Contact's reference

6 Fax number

IHT405 **(Substitute)(LexisNexis)** Page 1 HMRC Approval ref: L11/08

Property details

Give details of each item of property. You should only include property in the deceased's own name. Jointly owned property should be included on form IHT404 and not here.
If the deceased owned a large number of properties use more than one form.

Item number - Number each item of property.

Full address or description of property - Give the address or full description of the property. If the property has no street number or it is farmland or other land without an address, enclose a plan that clearly shows the boundaries of the property.

Tenure - State whether the deceased owned the property outright (freehold) or had a lease (leasehold). For leasehold property enter the number of years left on the lease and the annual ground rent.

Details of lettings/leases - If the property was let out by the deceased, you must provide a copy of the lease, sublease, business or agricultural tenancy agreement. If the following information is not contained in the lease, sublease and so on, or if there is no written agreement, please enter in this column:

date the tenancy/lease began
date the tenancy is due to end
what rent is payable and whether the rent can be reviewed
who is responsible for the outgoings on the property
name of the tenant.

If the property was unoccupied at the date of death, write 'vacant'.

Value of agricultural, business or woodlands relief or heritage exemption - If you are deducting agricultural relief, woodlands relief, business relief or claiming heritage exemption, enter the value of the property that you say qualifies for relief or exemption.
You cannot deduct business relief on businesses that deal in properties or investments.

Deceased's residence

7

A Item number	B Full address or description of property	C Postcode of property	D Tenure *(For example, freehold or leasehold. If leasehold, tell us the length of the lease and the annual ground rent, if applicable.)*	E Details of lettings/leases	F Value of agricultural, business or woodlands relief or heritage exemption deducted £	G Open market value at the date of death £
				Totals 7	£ 0.00	£ 0.00

Total of column above - *copy this amount to form IHT400, box 51*

IHT405 Page 2

Other land, buildings and rights over land

For rights over land (such as fishing or mineral rights) give details of those rights, as well as details of the land

8

A Item number	B Full address or description of property	C Postcode of property	D Tenure *For example, freehold or leasehold. If leasehold, tell us the length of the lease and the annual ground rent, if applicable*	E Details of lettings/leases	F Value of agricultural, business or woodlands relief or heritage exemption deducted £	G Open market value at the date of death £
				Totals 8	£ 0.00	£ 0.00
						Total of column above - *include this amount in form IHT400, boxes 68 to 70*

Please make sure the total value of the properties on this form is reflected in form IHT400. Include the value of agricultural, business or woodlands relief on form IHT400, box 93.
You will also need to fill in form IHT413 if you have deducted business relief or IHT414 if you have deducted agricultural relief.

IHT405 Page 3

Special factors that may affect the value

9 Were any of the properties listed on this form subject to any special factors, such as major damage or development potential, that may affect their value?
If the property is damaged in a way that is covered by building insurance, it may affect the way we value it.

No ☐ *Go to box 12* Yes ☐ *Give details using the same item number(s) used in the first column starting on page 2*

Item number	Details of the special factors. *Enclose a copy of the survey or structural engineer's report, or planning approval notice if appropriate*

If the property was damaged, please go to box 10, otherwise go to box 12.

10 Did the deceased's insurance cover all or part of the repairs?

No ☐ Yes ☐

11 Do you intend to make a claim under the deceased's insurance policy?

No ☐ Yes ☐ *If Yes, attach copies of any correspondence you have had with the insurers or loss adjusters*

Property sale

12 Have any of the properties been sold or do you intend to sell any of them within 12 months of the date of death?

No ☐ *You have finished this form* Yes ☐ *Give details using the same item number(s) used on pages 2 and 3.*

A Item number	B Say whether the property has 'already been sold' 'is on the market now' or 'will be sold later'. If the property has been sold, give the date contracts were exchanged (or missives concluded for property in Scotland)	C Asking price (or agreed sale price). Do not deduct the costs of the sale £	D Say whether the sale was/is to a relative, friend or business colleague of the deceased	E Price for fixtures, carpets and curtains, if included in the sale price £	F Do you want to use the sale price as the value at the date of death?

IHT405 Page 4

30

Liability for Tax

Cross-references. See **11.10** CLOSE COMPANIES for liability of participators; **33.10** NATIONAL HERITAGE for persons liable on a chargeable event; **35** PAYMENT OF TAX; **37.2** PENSION SCHEMES; **52.19** TRANSFERS ON DEATH for liability where legitim is claimed in Scotland; **57.3** WOODLANDS for person liable on a disposal.

Simon's Taxes. See **Part I10, I11.211**.

Other Sources. Foster, Part K; HMRC Customer Guide to Inheritance Tax; IHTM28000.

More than one person liable

[30.1] According to the nature of a chargeable transfer, one or more persons may be liable for the tax and if they do not pay then other persons may be liable up to certain limits and with a right of recovery. Except as provided otherwise, where two or more persons are liable for the same tax each of them is liable for the whole of it. [*IHTA 1984, s 205*].

Lifetime transfers

[30.2] Subject to the rules in 30.7 below for lifetime transfers within seven years of death, the primary person liable is the transferor. If the tax remains unpaid after it ought to have been paid, the following persons are also liable.

(a) Any person the value of whose estate is increased by the transfer.
(b) Any 'person in whom the property is vested' (whether beneficially or otherwise) or who is beneficially entitled to an interest in possession in it at any time after the transfer (e.g. a nominee, trustee, life tenant, but

see **30.10** below) to the extent that the tax is attributable to the value of that property. See **30.5** below for the extension of the meaning of 'person in whom property is vested' which also applies to lifetime transfers.

(c) Where by the chargeable transfer any property becomes comprised in a settlement, any person for whose benefit any of the property or income from it is applied.

References to property include any property directly or indirectly representing it.

Limitation of liability

[30.3] The liability of persons within (a) to (c) above is limited to the tax which would be payable on the value transferred as reduced by the tax remaining unpaid (i.e. the liability cannot be for a greater amount than tax on the property transferred without grossing-up). Liability is further limited as follows.

(i) In the case of a trustee, it is limited to the value of the property he has received, disposed of or has become liable to account for to the beneficiaries and any other property as is for the time being available in his hands for the payment of tax (or might have been so available but for his own neglect or default).
Note. For income tax purposes, the income of a settlement is treated as that of the settlor where he might benefit directly or indirectly from the settlement. HMRC do not take the view that, solely because the trustees have power to pay, or do in fact pay, inheritance tax due on assets which the settlor puts into the settlement, the settlor has an interest in the income or property of the trust and any income should be treated as the settlor's. (former Inland Revenue Statement of Practice SP 1/82 6 April 1982 see **25** HMRC STATEMENTS OF PRACTICE).

(ii) A person within (b) above, other than a trustee, is only liable to the extent of the property concerned.

(iii) A person within (c) above is liable only to the extent of the property or income (as reduced by income tax borne by him in respect of that income) applied for his benefit by the trustees. [*IHTA 1984, ss 199(1)(4)–(5), 204(2)(3)(5)(6)*].

Example 1

A settled £78,000 on discretionary trusts in December 2010, having previously made chargeable transfers on 31 March 2010 totalling £325,000.

A's liability is as follows	£
Gift	78,000
Deduct 2010/11 annual exemption	3,000
	£75,000
Grossed at 20%	£93,750
IHT thereon at 20%	£18,750

Example 2

Transferee

In the example above A pays only £10,000 of IHT and defaults on the balance of £8,750, so that the trustees become liable as transferee.

The trustees' liability is not, however, £8,750 but is as follows	£
Original gross	93,750
Deduct IHT unpaid	8,750
Revised gross	£85,000
IHT thereon at 20%	17,000
Deduct IHT paid by A	10,000
Now due from trustees	£7,000

Example 3

Person in whom property is vested

In January 2011 C transferred to trustees of a discretionary trust shares in an unquoted property company worth, as a minority holding, £50,000. However, the transfer deprives C of control of the company with the result that the value of his estate is reduced by £210,000. He has already used his nil rate band and annual exemptions.

C's liability is as follows	£
Net loss to him	210,000
Grossed at 20%	262,500
IHT thereon at 20%	52,500
C fails to pay so that the trustees become liable, as follows	
	£
Original gross	262,500
Deduct unpaid IHT	52,500
	£210,000
IHT thereon at 20%	£42,000

Notes to the example

(A) The trustees' liability cannot exceed the value of the assets which they hold, namely the proceeds of sale of the shares, less any CGT and costs incurred since acquisition, plus any undistributed income in their hands.

(B) Prior to 2004/05 when there was a differential between the marginal income tax rate (40%) and the rate applicable to trusts (34%) a further liability on the beneficiary could arise. If the trustees had already distributed net income of £2,000 to beneficiary D who is liable to pay additional higher rate income tax of £182 thereon (i.e. £3,030 × 6%), D could have been made to pay IHT of £1,818, being the net benefit received by him. From 6 April 2004 this will not arise as the rate applicable to trusts was increased to 40%. From April 2010 the rate applicable to trusts increased to 50% and the dividend rate is now 42.5%. [*ICTA 1988*, *s 686(1A)* as amended by *FA 2004, s 29(2)* and *ITA 2007, s 9(1)(2); FA 2009, s 6*].

Transferor's spouse or civil partner

[30.4] Where a transferor is liable for tax on a chargeable transfer and has made another, separate transfer to his spouse or civil partner and both transfers took place while they were married to each other, the spouse or civil partner is also liable for the tax on the chargeable transfer. The liability of the spouse or civil partner is limited to the market value of the gift to the spouse or civil partner at the time of the spouse/civil partner transfer. In addition, where the transfer to the spouse or civil partner is *before* the chargeable transfer and the property transferred to the spouse or civil partner is not tangible movable property, the liability of the spouse or civil partner is limited to the market value of the gift received *at the time of the chargeable transfer* (or if the gift has been sold, its market value at the time of the sale) if this is lower than the market value at the time of the spouse/civil partner transfer. [*IHTA 1984, s 203; The Tax and Civil Partnership Regulations 2005, SI 2005/3229, Reg 36*]. This is an anti-avoidance provision to enable tax to be recovered from the spouse or civil partner where it cannot be recovered from the transferor or other person as above.

Transfers on death

[30.5] The persons liable are as follows.

(a) *The deceased's 'personal representatives'* in respect of property not comprised in a settlement immediately before death and settled land in the UK which devolves upon or vests in them. The liability is a personal rather than a representative liability of the personal representatives (see also Personal Contact manual, para 3.19 issue 12/94), and their non-UK residence does not prevent either liability or the UK courts' jurisdiction to deal with IHT claims (*CIR v Stype Investments (Jersey) Ltd*; *Re Clore (deceased)* CA, [1982] STC 625 and *CIR v Stannard* Ch D, [1984] STC 245). However, the liability is limited to the unsettled assets received and the UK land settled immediately before the death and available at any time in their hands for the payment of tax (or such assets and land which might have been available but for their own neglect or default). In Scotland, an executor is not liable under this provision for tax on any heritable property vested in him under *Succession (Scotland) Act 1964, s 18*. The European Convention on Human Rights and *Human Rights Act 1998* which came into effect on 2 October 2000 has now confirmed that HMRC cannot seek penalties from the personal representatives of a deceased person who was liable for a penalty. In addition any such penalties already collected must now be repaid and these repayments should include repayment interest at the rate applicable under *IHTA 1984, s 233*. Such interest would run from the date the penalties are paid to the date of repayment by HMRC.

Under certain wills, the deceased may not have given any indication of how the burden of inheritance tax is to be allocated among the items of property in the estate. Where personal representatives are liable for tax on chargeable transfers on death, then, subject to any contrary intention in the will, any tax payable on the value of unsettled UK property which vests in them is to be treated as part of the general testamentary and administration expenses of the estate. Where any tax paid by the personal representatives does not fall to be treated in this way, the tax must, where necessary, be repaid to them by the person in whom the property is vested. References to tax include interest on tax.

(b) *The trustees of a settlement* which immediately before death comprised property passing on the death. The liability is limited to the value of the property the trustees have received, disposed of or have become liable to account for to the beneficiaries and any other property for the time being as is in their hands for the payment of tax (or might have been so available but for their own neglect or default).

(c) *Any person in whom property is vested* (whether beneficially or otherwise) *or who is beneficially entitled to an interest in possession in it* at any time after the death (but see **30.10** below) to the extent that tax is attributable to the value of the property. The liability is limited to the extent of the property.

(d) *Any person for whose benefit any of the property or income comprised in a settlement immediately before death was applied after death*. The liability is limited to the property or income (as reduced by income tax borne by him on that income) applied for his benefit by the trustees.

(e) *The administrator of any registered pension scheme in respect of funds which are chargeable under IHTA 1984, ss 151A, 151C or 151D*. The liability is intended to apply in the case where individuals use alternatively secured pension (ASP) to pass on tax-privileged retirement savings to their dependants rather than to provide a pension in retirement. See **37.2** PENSION SCHEMES.

References to property include any property directly or indirectly representing it. See also *MB Smith v HMRC (and related appeals)* [2009] STC SCD 132 Sp C 742.

[*IHTA 1984, ss 200(1), 204(1)–(3)(5), 209(1), 210, 211; FA 2006, s 160, Sch 22 para 5; FA 2008, Sch 28 para 11*].

For the above purposes, entitlement to part only of the income of any property is deemed to be entitlement to an interest in the whole property. The whole tax attributable to the property can therefore be recovered from any beneficiary. [*IHTA 1984, s 200(3)*].

Example 4

Personal representatives of E, who died on 30 September 2010, received the following assets.

	£
Free personal property	155,265
Land bequeathed to F (which, under the terms of the will, bears its own IHT)	29,735
Private residence, bequeathed to spouse/civil partner	51,000

A trust in which E had a life interest was valued at £154,000. Under the will of E, legacies of £15,000, each free of IHT, were given to F and G and the residue was left to H. E had made no chargeable transfers during his lifetime.

	Persons liable	£	IHT £
IHT is borne as to			
Chargeable transfer			
Free personal property	PRs	155,265	2,565
Land bequeathed to F	F	29,735	491
Private residence to spouse/civil partner	—	Exempt	Nil
Trust fund	Trustees	154,000	2,544
		£339,000	£5,600

	£	£
The residue left to H is as follows		
Free personal property		155,265
Deduct IHT	2,565	
Legacies to F and G	30,000	32,565
		£122,700

Note to the example

(A) If the will had not directed that the IHT on the land bequeathed to F be borne by F, the IHT would be payable out of residue. [*IHTA 1984, s 211*].

Definitions

'*Personal representative*' includes any person by whom or on whose behalf an application for a grant of administration or for the resealing of a grant made outside the UK is made; and also includes persons within (i) below. [*IHTA 1984, s 272*].

'*Persons in whom the property is vested*' includes (i) any person who becomes liable as executor or trustee by taking possession of or intermeddling with property (or in Scotland, intromits with property or has become liable as a vitious intromitter) and (ii) any person to whom the management of property is entrusted on behalf of a person not of full legal capacity. [*IHTA 1984, ss 199(4), 200(4)*].

A person who transfers the sale proceeds of English property belonging to the estate of a deceased person out of English jurisdiction has been held to have intermeddled with the estate and to be liable for IHT as *executor de son tort* (*CIR v Stype Investments (Jersey) Ltd Re Clore (deceased)* CA, [1982] STC 625).

Gifts with reservation

[30.6] Where property is treated as forming part of a deceased person's estate under the rules relating to **22** GIFTS WITH RESERVATION, a personal representative is only liable for the tax on that property if it remains unpaid for twelve months after the end of the month in which death occurs and, subject to that, only to the extent mentioned in (a) above. [*IHTA 1984, s 204(9); FA 1986, Sch 19 para 28*].

Lifetime transfers with additional liability arising through death

[30.7] For transfers of value before 15 March 1988, if death occurred within one year of a gift to a political party (see **21.7** EXEMPT TRANSFERS) in excess of £100,000, the tax due on death was the liability of the political party only. [*IHTA 1984, s 206; FA 1988, Sch 14*].

Death within seven years

[30.8] Where a transferor dies within seven years of making a **38** POTENTIALLY EXEMPT TRANSFER or a chargeable lifetime transfer, the persons liable for the tax on the value transferred by the potentially exempt transfer or the additional tax on the chargeable transfer are as follows.

(a) The personal representatives but only to the extent that
    - (i) no other person within (b) below is liable for the tax because of their limitation of liability as detailed below; or
    - (ii) tax remains unpaid twelve months after the end of the month in which death occurs.

    Subject to the above, the personal representatives are only liable to the extent of the unsettled assets received and the UK land settled immediately before death and available at any time in their hands for the payment of tax (or such assets and land which might have been available but for their own neglect or default).

    Without prejudice to the application of *IHTA 1984, s 199(2)*, HMRC will not usually pursue personal representatives who, having obtained a certificate of discharge (see **35.15** PAYMENT OF TAX) and distributed the estate before a chargeable lifetime transfer comes to light, have made the fullest enquiries that are reasonably practicable in the circumstances to discover lifetime transfers and done all in their power to make a full disclosure of them to HMRC (letter from Capital and Valuation Division reproduced at [1991] STI 238).

The previous CTO Advanced Investigation Manual stated at paragraph U.27:

> 'The liability of the transferor's personal representatives is a sensitive area of the legislation.'

However, the current manual at IHTM10811 now states:

> 'The general rule is that the personal representatives (IHTM05012) are accountable. They have to complete and return an IHT 200 [now IHT 400] for the deceased's estate. The only exception to this rule is where the estate is an 'excepted estate' (IHTM06011).'

(b) Any person within **30.2**(a) to (c) above subject to the limitation of liability as in **30.3**(i) to (iii) above (but *not* the preambles thereto). In broad terms this means that the recipient of the lifetime potentially exempt transfer has primary liability for the IHT payable in respect of it, but limited to the value of the gift.

[*IHTA 1984, ss 199(1)(2)(5), 204(1)–(3)(5)(7)(8); FA 1986, Sch 19 paras 26, 28*].

Example 5

On 31 December 2010, H, who had made no earlier chargeable transfers other than to utilise his annual exemptions for 2010/11 and earlier years, transferred £368,000 into a discretionary trust and, a month later, settled an asset worth £20,000 into the same trust. H paid the appropriate IHT. On 30 June 2013 H died.

The trustees become liable to further IHT as follows

	£	£
Original net gift	£368,000	£20,000
Grossed-up at half of full rates	£378,750	£25,000
IHT (paid by H) See **40.1** rates 2010.B2	£10,750	£5,000
IHT at 80% of death rates applicable in June 2013 on original gross (death between 3 and 4 years after gifts)	5,040	8,000
Deduct IHT paid originally by H	10,750	5,000
Now due from trustees	Nil	£3,000

Note to the example

(A) The additional IHT on death is calculated using the rates in force at the date of death. See **40.1** rates 2010.A1. If the IHT at the new death rates, as tapered, was less than the IHT paid on the original chargeable transfer, there would be no repayment as in this case.

Example 6

The second gift in the example above had fallen in value to £18,000 by the time of H's death.

The trustees may claim to reduce the IHT payable as follows

	£
Original gross gift	25,000
Deduct drop in value (£20,000 – £18,000)	2,000
Revised gross	£23,000
IHT thereon at 80% of death rate applicable in June 2013	7,360
Deduct IHT paid by H	5,000
	£2,360

Note to the example

(A) If the asset had fallen in value to £10,625 or less, so that the revised gross became £15,625 or less and the IHT at 80% of death rates £5,000 or less, the trustees would have no liability because H had already paid IHT of £5,000.

Settled property

[30.9] Where a chargeable transfer is made, or is deemed to be made, out of settled property, the persons liable for the tax are:

(a) the trustees of the settlement (to the extent shown in 30.5(b) above), or, if they do not pay;

(b) any person entitled (whether beneficially or not) to an interest in possession in the settled property (but liability of a person entitled to a beneficial interest is limited to the extent of the property); and

(c) any person for whose benefit any of the settled property or income from it is applied at or after the time of transfer (but liability is limited to the extent of the property or income (as reduced by income tax borne by him in respect of that income) applied for his benefit by the trustees); and

(d) the settlor, where the chargeable transfer is made during his lifetime and the trustees are not for the time being resident in the UK except that:
   - (i) where the chargeable transfer is made within seven years of the death of the transferor but, after 16 March 1987, is not a potentially exempt transfer, the settlor is not liable for the extra tax due because of the death within seven years; and
   - (ii) there is no liability where the settlement was made before 11 December 1974 if the trustees were resident in the UK when the settlement was made but have not been resident in the UK at any time between that date and the time of the transfer; and
   - (iii) after 16 March 1987, there is no liability if a potentially exempt transfer proves to be a chargeable transfer where the settlement was made before 17 March 1987 if the trustees were resident in the UK when the settlement was made but have not been resident in the UK at any time between 16 March 1987 and the death of the transferor.

> For these purposes, the trustees of a settlement are regarded as not resident in the UK unless the general administration of the settlement is ordinarily carried on in the UK and the trustees or a majority of them (including a majority of each class where there is more than one class of trustees) are for the time being resident in the UK. Where more than one person is a settlor in relation to a settlement, for these purposes the property is treated as comprised in separate settlements.

References to property include any property directly or indirectly representing it. [*IHTA 1984, ss 201, 204(2)(3)(5)(6); FA 1986, Sch 19 para 27; F(No 2)A 1987, Sch 7 para 3*].

Retiring trustees' indemnity

Retiring UK trustees need to ensure that they have in place an indemnity which they can rely on, or they will have to retain sufficient cash to meet tax liabilities when they retire in favour of non-resident trustees. Whilst these tax liabilities will normally be in respect of capital gains there may be an IHT liability. Therefore the trustees' indemnity should be effected in similar terms to the following.

Recitals

The retiring Trustee(s) having made full enquiries of the Appointer and the continuing Trustee(s) and the new Trustees and in reliance on the answers to these enquiries is satisfied that (as the Appointer and the continuing Trustee(s) and the new Trustees hereby confirm) there is no proposal that the Trustees of the Settlement may become neither resident nor ordinarily resident in the United Kingdom.

In consideration of the retiring Trustee(s) retiring and being discharged from the trusts of the Settlement the continuing Trustees and the new Trustee(s) have agreed to give indemnity which appears below.

Operative Part

The continuing Trustee(s) and the new Trustee(s) hereby jointly and severally COVENANT with the retiring Trustee(s) at all times fully and effectually to indemnify [him/her/them] and [his/her/their] personal representatives and estates from and in respect of all United Kingdom tax liabilities (e.g. Inheritance Tax, Income Tax, etc.), fiscal and other outgoings, claims, costs, expenses, and liabilities whatsoever to be incurred following the appointment of the new Trustee(s) as Trustee(s) in place of the retiring Trustee(s) including (but without limitation) any Capital Gains Tax which may at any future time or times become payable in the event of the Trustees of the Settlement becoming neither resident nor ordinarily resident in the United Kingdom at any time or times.

Note to the Recital

(A) If a tax liability does subsequently arise then the retiring trustees may have recourse to the *Misrepresentation Act 1967*. *Section 2(1)* of the *Misrepresentation Act 1967* provides:

> 'Where a person has entered into a contract after a misrepresentation has been made to him by another party thereto and as a result thereof he has suffered loss, then, if the person making the misrepresentation would be liable to damages in respect thereof had the misrepresentation been made fraudulently, that person shall be so liable notwithstanding that the misrepresentation was not made fraudulently, unless he proves that he had reasonable ground to believe and did believe up to the time the contract was made that the facts represented were true.'

A purchaser of property

[30.10] A 'purchaser' of 'property' and a person deriving title from or under such a purchaser, is not liable for any tax attributable to the property unless the property is subject to an HMRC charge (see **35.12** PAYMENT OF TAX). [*IHTA 1984, ss 199(3), 200(2)*].

'*Purchaser*' means a purchaser in good faith for consideration in money or money's worth other than a nominal consideration and includes a lessee, mortgagee or other person who for such a consideration acquires an interest in the property in question.

'*Property*' includes rights and interests of any description. [*IHTA 1984, s 272*].

Deed of inheritance tax indemnity

[30.11] PARTIES

1. "Father" namely

2. "Son" namely

RECITAL

Immediately after the execution of this deed Father intends to give Son a cheque for £ . as a gift subject to inheritance tax ("the Gift")

IHT INDEMNITY

1. The Liability

   "The Liability" means any [additional] liability to inheritance tax probably chargeable in respect of the Gift arising or crystallising on or by reason of the death of Father

2. Incidence

   Son acknowledges that the burden of inheritance tax (if any) on the Gift shall be borne by Son

3. Covenant and Indemnity

Son covenants with Father and his personal representatives to pay the Liability (whether by direct discharge to HMRC or by reimbursement to Father's estate or otherwise) immediately upon demand following an assessment on Father's estate and generally to keep Father and his personal representatives indemnified against the liability

4. Effluxion

The indemnity given by this deed shall lapse and be extinguished on the seventh anniversary of the date of the Gift if Father is still then living

5. Limitation

The indemnity given by this deed shall be limited to £ . . . .

EXECUTED as a deed on 2010

SIGNED AS A DEED AND)
DELIVERED by
FATHER in the presence of:—)

Witness' signature

Address

Occupation

SIGNED AS A DEED AND)
DELIVERED by
SON in the presence of:—)

Witness' signature

Address

Occupation

Note to the deed

An indemnity of this nature will be sufficient to ensure there is no grossing up and to mark for family purposes who carries the burden in the event of premature death. If there is any serious prospect of it having to be relied on through enforcement then further provisions may be needed e.g. dealing with interest after the due date, reporting, costs, etc.

31

Life Assurance Policies and Annuities

Cross-references. See **44.4** SETTLEMENTS: ACCUMULATION AND MAINTENANCE TRUSTS; **34.1** PARTNERSHIPS for partnership assurance policies.

Application

[31.1] Where a life assurance policy matures on the death of the person who took out the policy and remained the beneficial owner, the policy monies are included in his estate for the purposes of inheritance tax. [*IHTA 1984, s 171(1)*]. See IHTM20000 at http://www.hmrc.gov.uk/manuals/ihtmanual/index.htm.

Where the policy is expressed to be for the benefit of the spouse, civil partner or children under the *Married Women's Property Act 1882*, a trust is created in their favour so that the person whose life is assured never has an interest in the policy and the proceeds will not be included in his estate on his death. [*Married Women's Property Act 1882, s 11 as amended by Civil Partnership Act 2004, s 70*].

To [   ] Life Assurance Company

MWPA TRUST

This request is an integral part of the attached application and I declare that such application is made by me as settlor ("the Settlor") and request that the policy(ies) issued pursuant thereto shall be issued under the provisions of [Married Women's Property Act 1882] or [Married Women's Policies of Assurance (Scotland) Act 1880] or [Law Reform (Husband and Wife) Act (Northern Ireland) 1964] and subject to the powers and provisions in the Schedule below upon trust and for the benefit of:

I wish to appoint as trustees additional to myself the following persons whose concurrence is evidenced by execution hereto (and "the Trustees" shall be a reference to the trustees for the time being) of these trusts.

The receipt of the Trustees shall be a complete discharge to [. . .] for moneys payable under the policy.

Schedule of Further Trust Provisions

1. The Trustees shall have power to invest any moneys in their hands in or upon any investment of any nature and wherever situated and whether income producing or not and whether an investment strictly so called (including the effecting of policies of life assurance or annuities for the life of any beneficiary or other person and further including the purchase of freehold or leasehold land as an investment or the residence of a beneficiary) free from all duties of diversification as if the Trustees were the absolute beneficial owners

2. The Trustees shall have full power to surrender/convert/sell/auction or otherwise deal with any policy subject to these trusts notwithstanding that the sum assured may be increased or decreased

3. Section 31 of the Trustee Act 1925 shall apply as if:

   3.1 the words "may in all the circumstances be reasonable" had been omitted from paragraph (i) of subsection (1) and in substitution there had been inserted the words "the Trustees may in their absolute discretion think fit" and as if the proviso at the end of subsection (1) had been omitted

   3.2 in subsection (2) the words "as follows:—" and the paragraphs (i) and (ii) thereof had been omitted and replaced by "upon trust for that person absolutely"

4. Section 32 of the Trustee Act 1925 shall apply as if the words "one half" were omitted from proviso (a) to subsection (1)

5. The Trustees shall have power as they in their absolute discretion think fit to pay or apply any moneys for the time being subject to the trusts hereof (or borrowed hereunder) in or towards the discharge of any Inheritance Tax or other fiscal imposition the liability for which would otherwise fall either directly or indirectly on any beneficiary whether or not the interest or such beneficiary under the trusts hereof is absolute or contingent or vested in possession or in remainder or reversion PROVIDED that no such payment shall exceed the value of such beneficiary's interest at the time of such payment

6. The power of appointing new or additional trustees shall be exercisable by the Settlor during his lifetime

7. The receipt of a parent or guardian in respect of any benefit payable or transferable to a minor beneficiary shall be a sufficient discharge to the Trustees who shall be under no obligation to see to its application

8. Neither the Settlor nor the Trustees shall be under any obligation whatsoever to keep up any policy subject to these trusts or to reinstate the same if it becomes void and the Settlor shall have no right by way of lien or otherwise to reimbursement of any premiums paid or subsequently paid in respect of any policy subject to these trusts

9. These trusts shall be governed by and construed in accordance with the Law of England

Dated ______________ 2010 ______________

(The Settlor) Signed

(The further Trustees) Signed

Dated ______________ 2010 ______________

Where an annuity under an approved trust scheme or contract or, after 22 July 1987, under approved personal pension arrangements or, from 6 April 2006, a registered pension scheme (or *ICTA 1988, s 615(3)* scheme) is payable on a person's death to the widow, widower, surviving civil partner or dependant and the terms of the scheme etc. gave the deceased the option to have a sum of money i.e. cash payable to his personal representatives, he is not treated as having been beneficially entitled to that sum which is therefore not included in his estate. [*IHTA 1984, s 152; F(No 2)A 1987, s 98(5); FA 2004, s 203(5); The Tax and Civil Partnership Regulations 2005, SI 2005/3229, Reg 33*]. For the valuation of an annuity which is an interest in possession (IIP) chargeable on property, see **42.5** SETTLEMENTS WITH INTERESTS IN POSSESSION.

Compensation fund payments arising out the 11 September 2001 terrorist attacks that comprise part of the UK victims' estates are not subject to IHT. The Victim's Compensation Fund of 2001 was established by the US government as an alternative to any legal proceedings that the victims' estates could take under the law as it stood on 11 September. The legislation was actually passed after 11 September 2001 but claims under the compensation fund have no value at that date for IHT purposes. Payments made after that date are not chargeable to IHT in any case so that part of a victim's estate comprising of the compensation fund payment is not subject to IHT. See also April/May 2002 issue at http://www.hmrc.gov.uk/cto/newsletter.htm.

Transitional serial interest (TSI)

[31.2] Where a person (stipulated as being 'C' in the legislation) is beneficially entitled to a present interest in settled property with regard to a life insurance policy entered into before 22 March 2006, those rights under the contract or in property in the settlement directly or indirectly representing rights under the contract are, for the purposes of *IHTA 1984, Pt III, Ch III,* a transitional serial interest only if a number of conditions are satisfied:

- The first condition is that the settlement must have commenced before 22 March 2006 and the property comprised in the settlement was property which consisted of or included rights under the insurance contract to which 'C', or some other person, was beneficially entitled an interest in possession which for these purposes is designated 'the earlier interest';
- The second condition is either:
  that 'the earlier interest' in the insurance contract came to an end on or after 6 October 2008 on the death of the person beneficially entitled to it and 'C' became beneficially entitled to the present interest at one of the following times:
  (i) at the time of the ending of the earlier interest; or
  (ii) on the death of the person beneficially entitled to an interest in possession at the time of the ending of the earlier interest (i.e. (i) above); or

(iii) on the ending of a second or last in a series of unbroken consecutive sequences of interests in possession to the first where a person becomes beneficially entitled at the time of the ending of the earlier interest (i.e. (i) above) each of which has ended on the death of the person with beneficial entitlement;

or that 'C' became beneficially entitled to the present interest:

(i) on the coming to an end of an interest in possession that is a TSI under *s 49C* on the death of the person who is beneficially entitled to it. See **42.1** SETTLEMENTS WITH INTERESTS IN POSSESSION; or

(ii) on the ending of a second or last in a series of unbroken consecutive sequences of interest in possession the first of which is a TSI under *s 49C* each of which has ended on the death of the person with beneficial entitlement.

- The third condition is that rights under the contract of insurance were comprised in the settlement from 22 March 2006 to the date when 'C' became beneficially entitled;
- The fourth condition is that neither *IHTA 1984, s 71A* (bereaved minor's trust) applies to the property in which the interest subsists nor is the interest a disabled person's interest.

This TSI category relating to life assurance policies is more limited than the other two categories at **42.1** SETTLEMENTS WITH INTERESTS IN POSSESSION in that it does not apply to any property settled before 22 March 2006, but only to property settled which comprises rights under a contract of life insurance entered into before 22 March 2006. The benefit of this TSI category is that it can apply to more than one of a chain of successive interests in possession, provided each one qualifies as a TSI. Similarly to the category 2 spouse/civil partner TSI at **42.1** SETTLEMENTS WITH INTERESTS IN POSSESSION it only applies to TSIs falling into possession on the death of a person previously entitled to an interest in possession.

The legislation in *IHTA 1984, s 49E* above provides for TSI treatment to apply to contracts of insurance after 5 October 2008 for contracts set up before 22 March 2006 and pre-22 March 2006 settlements. The main purpose being to allow TSI relief on premiums that continue to be paid after 22 March 2006 on a policy settled on IIP or accumulation and maintenance trusts before that date. However, if after 5 October 2008 a power of appointment is exercised to appoint any new beneficiary who is not absolutely entitled this will result in the trust coming within the new regime. See Example 1 below.

[*IHTA 1984, s 49E; FA 2006, Sch 20 para 5; FA 2008, s 141*].

Pre-22 March 2006 life insurance within an IIP trust

[31.3] Where a life policy has been settled on an interest in possession (IIP) trust before 22 March 2006 but that premiums continue to be paid on that policy the whole of the value of the policy itself still qualifies for transitional protection as an asset of a trust in existence before 22 March 2006. This transitional treatment will continue to apply as long as the original terms of the policy continue. Also, where someone succeeds to the policy on the death of the policy holder then transitional protection will continue. [*IHTA 1984, s 46A; FA 2006, Sch 20 para 11*]. See Fosters Inheritance Tax, para E1.56.

Pre-22 March 2006 life insurance within an A & M trust

[31.4] Similar to above where a life policy has been settled on accumulation and maintenance (A&M) trust before 22 March 2006 but that premiums continue to be paid on that policy the whole of the value of the policy itself still qualifies for transitional protection as an asset of a trust in existence before 22 March 2006. This transitional treatment will continue to apply as long as the original terms of the policy continue. Also, where someone succeeds to the policy on the death of the policy holder then transitional protection will continue. See Fosters Inheritance Tax, para E5.26 and also **44** SETTLEMENTS: ACCUMULATION AND MAINTENANCE TRUSTS. [*IHTA 1984, s 46B; FA 2006, Sch 20 para 11*].

Care needs to be taken regarding the payment of further premiums as detailed in IHTM20331:

> 'If a transferor puts a policy into an accumulation and maintenance trust or a disabled trust and then pays the renewal premiums direct to the insurance company, PET treatment will therefore not be available. This is because the premiums as such do not become settled property. However, if the transferor makes payments to the trustees and they use those payments to pay the renewal premiums PET treatment is available – even if payment by the transferor is by a cheque which the trustees endorse in favour of the insurance company. Neither the associated operations provisions nor the principle in Ramsey/Furniss should be invoked to deny PET treatment in these cases.'

Example 1

A is to pay premiums of £4,000 p.a. on a policy on his own life (policy 1) which commenced on 1 January 2006. He assigns the policy into trust in favour of a number of potential beneficiaries including his wife (see Deed of Assignment below). The market value of the policy at the date of gift is £3,000. A also pays annual premiums of £2,000 on a policy (policy 2) on his life which commenced on 2 January 2006 written in favour of his son S. The original policy terms permit a variation of beneficiaries and the policy is assigned on discretionary trust in favour of his grandson GS on 6 October 2008. The cumulative premiums paid to that date are £6,000 and the value of the policy is £4,000. In July 2014 A becomes gravely ill and the value of the policy at 2 January 2016 is £155,000. A has utilised his £275,000 of his nil rate band in the previous seven years to 2 January 2016. The nil rate band at that stage is assumed to be £350,000. See **40** RATES OF TAX.

THIS DEED OF ASSIGNMENT AND DECLARATION OF TRUST is made the *first* day of *January* 2006

BETWEEN:

"the Settlor" namely [. . . . .].

and

"The Trustees" namely the Settlor and [. . . . .] and [. . . . .].

which expression shall include other trustees or trustee for the time being of these trusts

WHEREAS:

(A) The Settlor is the beneficial owner of the policy(ies) of life assurance detailed in the Second Schedule below ("the Policy")

(B) The Settlor wishes to settle the Policy upon the following trusts

NOW THIS DEED WITNESSES

(1) The Settlor ASSIGNS the Policy and all its benefits and all moneys payable under it and any other property representing the same from time to time to the Trustees UPON TRUST (and subject to the powers and provisions of the Schedule of Further Trust Provisions) for the benefit of such one or more exclusively of the other or others of:

   (A) Any spouse, widow or widower of the Settlor
   (B) Any children of the Settlor whenever born
   (C) Any grandchildren of the Settlor whenever born
   (D) Any spouse, widow or widower or anyone falling within B or C
   (E) Any one or more individual(s) benefiting from the estate of the Settlor under Will or under intestacy
   (F) Any other individual nominated by the Settlor during lifetime in writing to the Trustees other than the Settlor in such shares and upon such trusts (and subject to such powers and provisions) as the Trustees being at least two in number or a trust corporation shall appoint by Deed or Deeds revocable or irrevocable executed not later than two years following the death of the Settlor and in default of any such appointment

UPON TRUST for Scope and Red Cross in equal shares absolutely

EXECUTED as a deed on *first January 2006*.

Assignment of policy (policy 1)

The gift is valued either at

(i) market value (£3,000), or

(ii) the accumulated gross premiums paid (£4,000) if greater i.e. £4,000.

Continued premiums paid into a policy effected in trust before the Budget (22 March 2006) will not cause the policy to be subject to the new IHT trust provisions that apply to post-21 March 2006 trusts. Provided that the original policy terms permit, the terms of a policy can be varied post-21 March 2006 without causing the policy to be subject to the new IHT provisions. This means that the benefits can be increased or the term of the policy extended without changing the inheritance tax treatment of the policy. If one of the policy named (see extract above) becomes entitled to an interest in possession via an appointment to him before 6 October 2008 (a TSI), this will not cause the policy to be subject to the new IHT rules. If one of the named in A to F in the policy document becomes entitled to an interest in possession following the death of the previous holder of the interest in possession, this will not cause the policy to be subject to the new IHT rules provided the previous holder of the interest:

- held that interest on Budget day (22 March 2006); or
- held that interest as a TSI (so that it had been made via an appointment to him before 6 October 2008).

Annual premiums (policy 2)

The payment of an annual premium is regarded as an annual gift, the amount of the transfer being the net premium after deduction of any tax relief at source or the gross premium where paid without deduction. In this case no tax relief is due so £2,000 is the figure that is taken for these purposes. Continuing payment of premiums paid into a policy effected in trust before the Budget (22 March 2006) will not result in the policy becoming subject to the new IHT trust provisions that apply to post-21 March 2006 trusts. Premiums paid after Budget day to these trusts will continue to be treated as PETs and will not be chargeable lifetime transfers. Also, providing the original policy terms permit, the terms of a policy can be varied post-21 March 2006 without resulting in the policy becoming subject to the new IHT provisions. The result is that, in those circumstances, the benefits can be increased or the term of the policy extended without changing the inheritance tax treatment of the policy. Whilst the gifts of the premiums after 21 March 2006 where there has been a subsequent appointment of a new beneficiary will no longer be treated as PETs within *s 46A(4)* transfers should still be exempt under the annual exemption or gifts out of normal expenditure. See **21** EXEMPT TRANSFERS.

Re-assignment of policy (policy 2)

Where there is the possibility of a change in the named/default beneficiaries after 5 October 2008 it should be avoided unless the appointment is absolute. In this particular case the power to appoint a new beneficiary within the terms of the policy has been exercised in favour of GS after 5 October 2008 but on discretionary trusts and therefore brings the policy into the new regime of charge (see below) and triggers a chargeable lifetime transfer by the son S. Providing S's transfer was less than £10,000 per annum or £40,000 cumulative over the past ten years prior to 6 April 2007 it would not need to have been reported on Forms IHT100 and IHT100a but now see **2.4** ACCOUNTS AND RETURNS. This will depend on previous cumulative total of gifts to date and adding the accumulated premiums or the market value of the policy at that point.

Ten-yearly charge

Initial ten-yearly charge for period 6 October 2008 to 2 January 2016	£
Value of relevant property on 2.1.2016	155,000
Value of property in related settlements	—
	155,000
Assumed cumulative total	275,000
	£430,000
IHT at lifetime rates after assumed nil rate band of £350,000	£16,000
Effective rate $\frac{16,000}{430,000} = 3.72093\%$	
Rate of ten-year anniversary charge: 3/10 × 3.72093% = 1.116279%	
Ten-year anniversary charge: 28*/40 × 1.116279% × £155,000	£1,211

* i.e. 28 complete quarters from 6 October 2008 to first ten-year anniversary.

Notes to the example

(A) Pre-22 March 2006 life policy trusts will not be subject to the new IHT taxing rules provided the original terms of the policy continue and where someone succeeds to the policy on the death of the policy holder then transitional protection will continue. The payment of ongoing premiums for life policies owned by trusts will not constitute additions to the trust thereby bringing them into the new IHT charging provisions. On the premature death of the wife prior to A the life policy trust above would still qualify as subsequent beneficiaries would be entitled and therefore the terms of the trust would not have altered since it was set up pre-22 March 2006 within the stipulations of *IHTA 1984, s 46A inserted by FA 2006, Sch 20 para 11*.

(B) In the case of the life policy trust assigned for the benefit of the grandson GS after 5 October 2008 as this is not an absolute appointment then the new taxing regime within *IHTA 1984, s 43(2)* will apply with the prospect of 20% life time charge (where gifts to the trust exceed the nil rate band) ten yearly charge on the value of the trust fund on the tenth anniversary of the policy and potential exit charge when the policy proceeds are paid out to the beneficiary. In this case the ill health of A prior to the first ten-yearly charge has resulted in a substantial revaluation of the policy.

(C) Existing accumulation and maintenance settlements that hold life policies needed to be reviewed before 6 April 2008.

Assignment of policy

[31.5] Where the benefits of a life policy (or contract for an annuity payable on a person's death) are assigned as a gift or for less than full value, there is a transfer of value and inheritance tax is chargeable (unless any reliefs may be claimed, see **21** EXEMPT TRANSFERS).

The value of a life policy or contract *transferred before death* is to be taken as not less than:

(a) the total premiums or other consideration paid at any time (under the policy or contract or any policy or contract for which it was substituted) before the transfer of value; *less*

(b) any sum received, at any time before the transfer of value, for a surrender of any right conferred by the policy or contract (or a policy or contract for which it was substituted).

This provision does not apply unless the policy or contract ceases to be part of the transferor's estate as the result of the transfer of value. [*IHTA 1984, s 167(1)(2); FA 1986, Sch 23 Pt X*].

The special rules for valuing a policy above do not apply where the policy is one under which the sum assured becomes payable only if the person whose life is insured dies (i) before the expiry of a specified term, or (ii) both before the expiry of a specified term and during the life of a specified person. Where under the policy the term ends, or can be extended to end, more than three years after the making of the insurance, if neither the person whose life is insured nor the specified person dies before the expiry of the specified term, the rules do not apply if the policy satisfies the conditions that the premiums are payable during at least two-thirds of that term and at yearly or shorter intervals, *and* the premiums payable in any one period of twelve months are not more than twice the premiums payable in any other twelve months. [*IHTA 1984, s 167(3)*].

Unit linked policies

[31.6] Where the benefit secured under a policy is expressed in units the value of which is published and subject to fluctuation and the payment of each premium secures the allocation to the policy of a specified number of such units, then the value to be taken as above will take into account any investment loss on those units. This is done by deducting from the total premiums etc. paid, the difference between the value of the units when they were first allocated and their value at the time of the transfer of value. [*IHTA 1984, s 167(4)*].

Settlements

[31.7] References above to a transfer of value include an event on which there is a charge to tax under the provisions relating to **43** SETTLEMENTS: DISCRETIONARY TRUSTS AND OTHER TRUSTS OF RELEVANT PROPERTY in *IHTA 1984, Pt III, Ch III* (except *s 79*, see **33.22** NATIONAL HERITAGE), other than an event on which tax is chargeable in respect of the policy or contract by reason only that its value is reduced otherwise than by these provisions. [*IHTA 1984, s 167(5)*].

Premiums continued by donor

[31.8] Where a policy is transferred and the donor continues to pay the premiums, or provides the money for this purpose, then a transfer of value occurs on each occasion, based on the decrease in value of the donor's estate (i.e. the special rules above for valuing the policy on its assignment do not apply to later payments of premiums). These payments may be exempt, see **21** EXEMPT TRANSFERS. HMRC take the view that where the payment of a premium on a life assurance policy is a transfer of value, the amount of the transfer is the net amount of the premium after deduction under *ICTA 1988, s 266(5)* (tax relief at source) or the gross premium where paid without deduction. (HMRC Press Release 17 January 1979.)

Example 2

A has paid premiums of £2,000 p.a. for six years on a policy on his own life. He gives the policy to his son B. The market value of the policy at the date of gift is £11,000 but due to a demutualisation policy enhancement is uplifted to £12,500 (see HMRC Tax Bulletin, April 1998, p 520). A also pays annual premiums of £2,000 on a policy on his life written in favour of his son.

Assignment of policy

The gift is valued either at:

(i) market value (£12,500); or

(ii) the accumulated gross premiums paid (£12,000) if greater (but they are not).

Annual premiums

The payment of an annual premium is regarded as an annual gift, the amount of the transfer being the net premium after deduction of any tax relief at source or the gross premium where paid without deduction.

Notes to the example

(A) The gifts are PETs. The assignment of the policy will only become chargeable if A dies within seven years, and only the annual premiums paid within seven years of A's death will be chargeable.

(B) Exemptions available for reduction of the chargeable transfer on assignment include the annual exemption and the marriage exemption.

(C) The normal expenditure exemption may be available to A for premiums paid and the annual exemption may also be claimed to exempt the gift in whole or in part.

(D) Normal expenditure relief is not available when a policy and annuity have been effected on a back-to-back basis (with certain exceptions).

Annuity purchased in conjunction with life policy

[31.9] The use of annuities in conjunction with life policies is known as 'back to back' arrangements.

Example 3

The purchase of an immediate annuity for a lump sum would reduce the purchaser's estate and provide him with an income for life. If he arranged an insurance on his own life but for the benefit of another person whom he wished to benefit at his death, the proceeds would be free of tax because they are not part of his estate. There would be further advantages if he paid the premiums on the policy and could obtain exemption from inheritance tax on them, e.g. as normal expenditure out of income (see **21.16** EXEMPT TRANSFERS).

The following provisions reduce the effectiveness of 'back to back' arrangements.

Where a life insurance is made, varied or substituted and an annuity on the life of the insured is purchased at any time before or after that date and the benefit of the insurance policy is vested in a person other than the purchaser of the annuity, the purchaser of the annuity is treated as making a transfer of value at the time the benefit of the policy became vested in the other person. The value transferred is the lesser of:

(a) the aggregate of (i) the value of the consideration given for the annuity and (ii) any premium paid or other consideration given under the policy on or before the transfer; and

(b) the value of the greatest benefit capable of being conferred at any time by the policy, calculated as if that time were the date of the transfer.

The above provisions also apply where an annuity payable on a person's death is substituted for 'life insurance policy'.

The above provisions do *not* apply if it can be shown that the purchaser of the annuity and the making, variation or substitution of the insurance were not associated operations (see **5.5** ANTI-AVOIDANCE). [*IHTA 1984, s 263*].

In practice, such policies and annuities are not regarded as being affected by the associated operations rule if the policy was issued on full medical evidence of the insured's health and it would have been issued on the same terms if the annuity had not been bought. (See at **25** HMRC STATEMENTS OF PRACTICE). See also *AC Smith v HMRC (and related appeals)* Ch D [2007] EWHC 2304, Sp C 605 at **58** TAX CASES.

If the transferor pays, either directly or indirectly, a premium on a life insurance on his life and an annuity on his life is purchased at any time, the premium will not be treated as part of his normal expenditure out of income unless it can be shown that the associated operations rule (see above) does not apply. [*IHTA 1984, s 21(2)*].

See **21.16** EXEMPT TRANSFERS for normal expenditure out of income and that chapter generally for exemptions which might be applied to the transfers of value mentioned above.

Key points

[31.10] Points to consider are as follows.

- Schedule IHT410 of IHT400 requests details of life assurance policies the deceased was paying regular instalments on or lump sum payments whether on the life of the deceased or another life. If the policy was in connection with mortgage protection the details should be included on IHT410 but if it is a joint mortgage protection policy the details are to be included on form IHT404 *Jointly owned assets*.
- A great number of life assurance policies are written in trust for the benefit or potential benefit of third parties. Where an individual is nominated as the beneficiary so that the benefits are payable to that person or persons indicates there is a general power over benefits and consequently the proceeds of the policy will form part of their estate within *IHTA 1984, s 5(2)*. However, an irrevocable nomination might be made during lifetime but provided the individual was in good health the policy would have little value and might be easily covered by the annual exemption. Clearly, an irrevocable nomination would not be something to be undertaken lightly as personal circumstances might change later but one could foresee such a nomination taking place for children or grandchildrens' benefit in the event of the individual policy holder's death.
- In certain circumstances Trustees may wish to protect the trust from a charge to IHT on the premature death after a termination of an interest which is a PET or in the case of an individual a gift that comes within a PET. In such cases level term assurance for at least seven years would be appropriate with the maturity value

decreasing as the tapering provisions apply after the first three years following the PET eventually reducing to zero after the expiry of the seventh year with a consequent diminishing of premiums.

- Where property in an estate is the right to claim a lump sum and an annuity and such a right is not assignable it will nonetheless still be valued on an assumption that it could be sold on the open market. On that basis a policy has a value appropriate to what it could be sold for on the open market with a discount so for instance in *DM Fryer & Others (Personal Representatives of Ms P Arnold) v HMRC* (see **58** TAX CASES) the Commissioner upheld HMRC's contention that 'the concept of a 'disposition' was widened by *s 3(3)* to include passive dispositions, meaning omissions which resulted in the enhancement of another person's estate or of settled property in which no interest in possession subsisted'. The Commissioner held that the disposition should be treated as having taken place on the date of her death. The omission to exercise the right to take annuity benefits from the age of 50 (now this would be 55) had increased the value of the settled property, and the evidence showed that this had been intentional and *s 3(3)* applied.

32

Lifetime Transfers

Cross-references. See **1** INTRODUCTION AND BASIC PRINCIPLES; **2.4** ACCOUNTS AND RETURNS and 7 CALCULATION OF TAX.

Simon's Taxes. See **Part I3.**

Other Sources. HMRC Customer Guide to Inheritance Tax.

Introduction

[32.1] An individual is subject to inheritance tax on every **9** CHARGEABLE TRANSFER made by him after 17 March 1986. Chargeable transfers are any transfers of value made by an individual other than **21** EXEMPT TRANSFERS. For inheritance tax purposes, certain lifetime transfers are designated **38** POTENTIALLY EXEMPT TRANSFERS. Such a transfer made seven years or more before the death of the transferor is an exempt transfer and any other such transfer is a chargeable transfer. The tax is normally levied on the value of the reduction in the transferor's **19** ESTATE caused by the chargeable transfer which includes the inheritance tax on the value of the gift where the transferor pays that tax (i.e. the value of the gift, after taking account of any exempt transfers, is grossed-up). If the transferee bears the tax, the transferor's estate is reduced only by the value of the gift itself (after exemptions). See **32.3** below. Dispositions not intended to confer gratuitous benefit are not transfers of value. See point (a) at **51.2** TRANSFER OF VALUE. For definition of estate, see **19** ESTATE. The chargeable transfers are aggregated during a seven-year period to arrive at the scale rate of tax applicable (see 7 CALCULATION OF TAX). [*IHTA 1984, ss 2(1)(2), 3, 3A, 7, 10; FA 1986, Sch 19 para 1; F(No 2)A 1987, s 96; FA 2006, Sch 20 para 9*].

See also IHTM14000 at www.hmrc.gov.uk/manuals/ihtmanual/index.htm.

Time of disposition

[32.2] As a basic rule no CHARGEABLE TRANSFER (chapter 9) can take place until there has been a disposition resulting in a shift of value from one estate to another. The legal requirements that must be fulfilled to ensure such a shift vary depending on the subject matter of the gift. Usually all the requirements relating to the species of gift must be satisfied by the donor before the gift becomes effective. One common exception is where the donor has done all in his power to transfer the property e.g. signed a stock transfer form and delivered the scrip. See **32.3** LIFETIME TRANSFERS.

A gift of moveable property must have words of gift and a delivery of the subject matter of that gift to be effective. See Key Points at gifts with reservation (**22** GIFTS WITH RESERVATION) for an example where a words of the gift were conclusive but the actual delivery was not completed satisfactorily and therefore the GWR rules applied. See also *Irons v Smallpiece* [1819] 2 B & Ald 551.

Freehold or leasehold land

Freehold or leasehold land is gifted on the conveyance or assignment under seal or declaration of trust evidenced in writing.

Choses in possession

Choses in possession (e.g. motor cars, furniture) are gifted when the appropriate formalities are completed. This could be the execution of a deed, declaration of trust or actual or constructive delivery. In the case of chattels that are capable of being physically handed over by a donor then constructive delivery may be the preferred option in a formal presentation in, say, domestic surroundings. Where an item is large and not portable then it may still be the subject of a constructive delivery if the donor expresses to the donee that he is making the gift of the item to the donee and places his hands on the item in question (see *Rawlinson v Mort* (1905) 21 TLR 774). Alternatively, the donor may hand over the physical means of making the item the ownership of the donee by surrendering the keys to, say, a locked bureau (see *Dublin City Distillery Limited v Doherty* [1914] AC 823, 843). In the case of leases relating to chattels the anti-avoidance provisions introduced by *FA 1999, s 104* only apply to land and not chattels. Therefore leases of chattels are possible but the law of bailment should be taken into account as there is a suggestion that this counters such a lease arrangement. See also **22.1** GIFTS WITH RESERVATION for a standard Memorandum of Gift. See also *Torts (Interference with Goods) Act 1977, s 10(1)* and *Law of Property Act 1925, s 188.*

In cases where delivery of the chattels to the donee is not to take place, for example where the donee wishes to retain possession of them paying a market rent for the enjoyment of them, there should be either: (a) a document of transfer under Bills of *Sale Act 1878, s 4*, for which detailed conditions and formalities under that Act apply, as well as a requirement to register it at the Central Office of the Royal Courts of Justice, or (b) a sale under the *Sale of Goods Acts* for which documentation is not required for an effective transfer of title although payment of the purchase price is required, even though in the present case the transaction may be at substantial undervalue.

Choses in action

Choses in action (e.g. shares, insurance policies) are normally gifted on the completion of the appropriate transfer or assignment although negotiable instruments are transferable by delivery. A transfer of shares is not complete until all the requirements of the company's articles have been complied with or the individual has complied with them to the best of his powers (*Re Rose, Rose and Others v CIR* CA, [1952] 1 All ER 1217). See also *Companies Act 2006, s 544*.

Short form memorandum evidencing a gift of shares subject to tax

[32.3] MEMORANDUM OF GIFT OF

Father:	Of
Son	Of

MEMORANDUM that on Father transferred by way of gift to Son (subject to the payment of any Inheritance Tax) the shares listed in the schedule below to the intent that they have become and are the absolute property of Son and IN CONSIDERATION of such transfer Son undertook to pay any Inheritance Tax in respect of such gift assessed upon Father or his personal representatives and indemnifies Father and his personal representatives accordingly.

SCHEDULE

Dated:
Signed by Father:
Signed by Son:

Note to the Precedent

(A) Stocks and shares can be owned both at law and in equity as tenants in common or as joint tenants, but shares in a company are only assignable in law in the books of the company subject to the articles of association. From 6 April 2008, *Companies Act 2006, s 544* provides that shares or stocks are transferable subject to the *Stock Transfer Act 1963* and regulations within *Companies Act 2006, Part 21, Chapter 2*.

Short form memorandum evidencing a gift of chattel(s)

[32.4] The gift of a chattel(s) during lifetime should normally be evidenced so that when the gift is called into question there is proof on both sides, the donor and the donee, that such a gift was effected at the time stated. The chattels may be in co-ownership either as joint tenants or as tenants in common and therefore it is important to attach a Schedule (see below) detailing the chattels and their ownership division. This may be useful not only for the purposes of determining future IHT liabilities but also in connection with bankruptcy, winding-up and divorce, for example. It is important that there is no reservation of benefit in the gift once it has been disposed for IHT purposes and a short form memorandum is detailed below:

MEMORANDUM OF GIFT OF CHATTEL(S)

THIS MEMORANDUM records that on the . . . . day of . . . . 2010 the undersigned [*Donor*] of [*Address*] ('the Donor') gave and by word of mouth expressed himself/herself to give to the undersigned [*Donee*] of [*Address*] ('the Donee') [all the furniture effects and moveable property] which [are] specified in the Schedule attached hereto ('the Chattel(s)') for the absolute sole use of the and benefit of the Donee and at the same time the Donor delivered the Chattel(s) to the Donee and placed the Donee in possession and unrestricted control of the Chattel(s) and at the same time the Donee accepted the gift.

Dated:

SCHEDULE

[Identification is made here of all chattels which have been given by the Donor]

Signed by [*Donor*]:

Signed by [*Donee*]:

Interests under trusts

[32.5] Interests under trusts are gifted when the necessary formalities have been completed. A disposition of an equitable interest must be in writing (*Grey and Another v CIR* [1960] AC 1, [1959] 3 All ER 603, HL and *Oughtred v CIR* HL, [1960] AC 206, [1959] 3 All ER 623, HL). See *Stenhouse's Trustees v Lord Advocate* CS 1983, [1984] STC 195, 1984 SC 12, Ct of Sess for position when trustees make an appointment which is in part in breach of trust until a later date.

Cheques

Cheques are gifted on payment (not when the cheque is received) i.e. the gift remains incomplete until the cheque is cleared by the paying bank (*Owen, Re, Owen v CIR* Ch D, [1949] 1 All ER 901, [1949] TR 189). See *Curnock (Personal Representative of Curnock, dec'd) v CIR* [2003] STC 283, SCD where monies represented by a cheque issued before the date but not cleared until after death still formed part of the deceased's estate on death. See TAX CASES (58).

Insurance policies

Insurance policies (e.g. where written to benefit a person other than the person insured or paying the premiums) are treated by HMRC as made when one party has unconditionally accepted an offer (or counter-offer) from the other party and has notified the other party accordingly (see Inland Revenue Press Release 18 March 1986).

Omission to exercise a right

[32.6] The omission to exercise a right (unless not deliberate) is treated as a disposition if it decreases the value of one person's estate and increases the estate of another person or the value of a settlement without an interest in possession. The disposition is treated as made at the time, or latest time, the right could have been exercised. [*IHTA 1984, s 3(3)*]. See *Macauley & Another v Premium Life Assurance Co Ltd*, Ch D 29 April 1999 unreported where a scheme failed to take account of *s 3(3)* so that the whole of the free estate became liable to IHT on death. A claim that the six-year time limit laid down by the *Limitation Act 1980* precluded liability was rejected by the court.

Voidable transfers

[32.7] Where it can be shown that the whole or part of a chargeable transfer has been set aside by virtue of any enactment or rule of law as voidable or otherwise defeasible, a claim may be made for the transfer to be treated as void initially and for any tax paid to be repaid: see 9 CHARGEABLE TRANSFER.

Lifetime transfers and IHT100

[32.8] An account on Form IHT 100 is required when there is a chargeable event described below.

- Lifetime transfers made by an individual that are chargeable to inheritance tax at the time they are made (supplementary event form IHT 100a) subject to the exclusion mentioned in paragraph **32.9** below.
- A potentially exempt transfer where the transferor has died within seven years bearing in mind that there is no requirement to tell HMRC Inheritance Tax regarding the transfer while the transferor is still alive.
- A termination of an interest in possession in settled property (supplementary event form IHT 100b) e.g. the ending of a life interest, which occurs during the life of the life tenant and is chargeable to inheritance tax at the time of the event. If the interest in possession is not chargeable at the time it is made then there is no requirement to advise HMRC Inheritance Tax unless the life tenant dies within seven years of the event.
- A termination of an interest in possession in settled property within seven years of the death of the life tenant.
- A termination of an interest in possession in settled property *arising* as a result of the life tenant's death.
- Property is given subject to a reservation where the reservation is retained until the death of the transferor.
- Property ceases to be held on discretionary trusts and there is a proportionate charge or exit charge (supplementary event form IHT 100c).

- A ten-year anniversary charge on a discretionary trust (supplementary event form IHT 100d).
- Assets are no longer held on special trusts (supplementary event form IHT 100e) e.g. the flat rate charge.
- Recapture charges are exigible e.g. the ceasing of an entitlement to conditional exemption (supplementary event form IHT 100f).
- Assets ceasing to benefit from conditional exemption and being subject to a recapture charge (supplementary event form IHT 100f) e.g. sale of trees, timber or underwood.

Initially IHT 100 is completed together with supplementary Forms D31 to D40 which provide for information on the assets where required. In addition, there is the Form IHT 100WS which can be used to calculate the tax that will be due regarding the chargeable event.

Exclusion from IHT100 submission

[32.9] There are exceptions to the above cases where an IHT100 does not have to be submitted and these apply in the following circumstances:

(a) where a gift or other transfer of value by an individual is wholly exempt;

(b) where a gift or other transfer of value prior to 6 April 2007 by an individual in circumstances where the amount of the gift and any other chargeable transfer made by the individual in the same tax year does not exceed £10,000 and the amount of the gift and any other chargeable transfer made by the individual in the ten years previously ending on the date of the gift does not exceed £40,000; see **2.4** ACCOUNTS AND RETURNS;

(c) where there is a termination of an interest in possession where the life tenant has given the trustees notice advising them of the availability of the annual exemption and/or marriage exemption and that/those exemptions cover the whole of the value transferred.

HMRC retain the right to call for an account by notice in writing to the individual. [*IHTA 1984, s 256(1)(a); SI 1981/1440; SI 2002/1731*]. See also **2.4** ACCOUNTS AND RETURNS and www.hmrc.gov.uk/cto/forms/iht110_2.pdf.

Inheritance Tax Account [Form IHT100]

HM Revenue & Customs

Inheritance Tax Account

Fill in this account to tell us about any of the events listed below. You should read the guidance notes before filling in any box on this or the accompanying forms. Complete all names and addresses in capital letters.

A About the chargeable event

Tick one of the following boxes.

		Tick box	Event form
A1	Gifts and other transfers of value including failed potentially exempt transfers.		IHT100a
A2	Ending of an interest in possession in settled property.		IHT100b
A3	Assets in a discretionary trust ceasing to be relevant property (proportionate charge), or a charge to tax arising on an age 18-25 trust.		IHT100c
A4	Discretionary trust ten-year anniversary (principal charge).		IHT100d
A5	Assets ceasing to be held on special trusts (flat rate charge). *See form IHT110 'How to fill in form IHT100'.*		IHT100e
A6	Cessation of conditional exemption and disposal of trees or underwood (recapture charge).		IHT100f
A7	Chargeable event in respect of an alternatively secured pension fund on death of scheme member, death of a dependant or relevant dependant, or relevant dependant ceasing to be a relevant dependant.		IHT100g

This account must be accompanied by the event form shown against the box you have ticked.

B About the transferor/settlement

Title of transferor/settlor

B1

Surname of the transferor/settlor

B2

Forename(s) of the transferor/settlor

B3

Address, or last usual address of the transferor/settlor

B4

Post Code

Date of birth of the transferor/settlor

B5 / /

Date of death of the transferor/settlor (where appropriate)

B6 / /

IHT reference for the transferor/settlor (where appropriate)

B7

Date of the chargeable event

B8

Income Tax or Self Assessment reference of the transferor/settlor

B9

National Insurance number of the transferor/settlor

B10

Domicile of the:
- settlor when the settlement was made, or
- testator at the date of death, or
- transferor at the date of transfer

B11

Name of the settlement (where appropriate)

B12

IHT reference for the settlement (if known)

B13

Income Tax reference for the settlement

B14

Enter a, b, c or d as appropriate in box B15:
a married or in civil partnership
b single
c divorced or former civil partner
d widowed or surviving civil partner B15

(Substitute)(LexisNexis)

IHT100 www.hmrc.gov.uk/inheritancetax/ Helpline 0845 30 20 900 Approval Ref No: L25/11

C **Person to whom communication should be sent**

Name and address of the person to whom communications should be sent

C1

Post code

Contact name

C2

DX number and exchange (if used)

C3

Phone number

C4

Reference

C5

Capacity

C6

***Important**. Read the following notes and the more detailed instructions in IHT110 'How to fill in form IHT100' before filling in the rest of this form. One of the event forms IHT100a, IHT100b, IHT100c, IHT100d, IHT100e, IHT100f or IHT100g must be filled in and returned with this form.*

Fill in section **D**, **E** and **F** to tell us about ***the assets included in the chargeable event as follows:***

If you have ticked box

- **A1**, tell us about the assets that were given or transferred.
- **A2**, tell us about the assets in respect of which this interest in possession ceased.
- **A3**, tell us about the assets that ceased to be relevant property (proportionate charge).
- **A4**, tell us about the relevant property in the settlement (principal charge).
- **A5**, tell us about the assets which ceased to be held on special trusts (flat rate charge).
- **A6**, tell us about the assets on which a charge to Inheritance Tax arises (recapture charge).
- **A7**, tell us about the assets in the alternatively secured or unsecured pension fund.

D Supplementary pages - **Do not complete section D if you are telling us about the assets in an alternatively secured or unsecured pension fund - go to section E.**

You must answer **all** the questions in this section. You should read the notes starting at page 12 of IHT110. If you answer yes to a question you will need to fill in the supplementary pages shown. If you do not have all of the supplementary pages, phone our helpline on **0845 30 20 900**.

		Yes	No	
• **Domicile outside the United Kingdom**	Was the transferor domiciled outside the UK at the date of the transfer or the date of the settlement?	☐	☐	D31
• **Stocks and shares**	Do the assets about which you are telling us include stocks and shares?	☐	☐	D32
• **Debts due to the settlement**	Was there any money on loan from the settlement either on mortgage or by personal loan, that had not been repaid at the date of the chargeable event?	☐	☐	▶ D33
• **Insurance**	Were any insurance policies included in the transfer?	☐	☐	▶ D34
• **Household and personal goods**	Do the assets being reported include household and personal goods?	☐	☐	▶ D35
• **Land, buildings, trees or underwood**	Do the assets being reported include any land, buildings, trees or underwood in the UK?	☐	☐	D36
• **Agricultural relief**	Are you deducting agricultural relief?	☐	☐	D37
• **Business relief**	Are you claiming business relief?	☐	☐	▶ D38
• **Foreign assets**	Do the assets being reported include any assets outside the UK?	☐	☐	D39
• **Other information**	Use this form to provide any additional information	☐	☐	▶ D40

2

E Assets in the UK where tax may not be paid by instalments

• Listed stocks, shares and investments *(box SS1 form D32)*	E1	
• UK Government and municipal securities *(box SS2 form D32)*	E2	
• Unlisted stocks and shares *(details from form D32)*	E3	
• Traded unlisted stocks and shares *(details from form D32)*	E4	
• Dividends or interest *(details from form D32)*	E5	
• National Savings investments *(show details on form D40)*	E6	
• Bank and building society accounts *(show details on form D40)*	E7	
• Cash	E8	
• Debts due to the settlement, trust or fund and secured on mortgage *(box DD1 form D33)*	E9	
• Other debts due to the settlement or fund *(box DD1 form D33)*	E10	
• Life assurance policies *(box IP1 form D34)*	E11	
• Capital Gains Tax repayment	E12	
• Household and personal goods *(box HG1 form D35)*	E13	
• Other assets *(show details on form D40)*	E14	
Total assets *(sum of boxes E1 to E14)*	E15	

• **Liabilities**

Name of creditor	Description of liability	Amount £

Total liabilities	E16	
Net total of assets less liabilities *(box E15 less box E16)*	E17	

• Exemption and reliefs *(Do not include any annual exemption here, enter it at box F18)*
If you are deducting charity exemption, enter the full name of the charity, the country of establishment and the HMRC charities reference, if available.

Total Exemptions and reliefs	E18	
Chargeable value of assets in the UK where tax may **not** be paid by instalments *(box E17 less box E18)*	E19	

3

F

Assets in the UK where tax may be paid by instalments

Do you wish to pay the tax on these assets by instalments?

Yes ☐ No ☐ Number of instalments being paid now ☐

• Residential property			F1
• Farms			F2
• Business property			F3
• Woodlands, trees or underwood			F4
• Other land and buildings			F5
	Interest in a business	Interest in a partnership	
• Farming business	F6.1	F6.2	F6
	Interest in a business	Interest in a partnership	
• Other business interests	F7.1	F7.2	F7
	Farm trade assets	Other business assets	
• Business assets	F8.1	F8.2	F8
• Listed shares and securities *(control holding only)*			F9
	Control holding	Non-control holding	
• Unlisted shares	F10.1	F10.2	F10
	Control holding	Non-control holding	
• Traded unlisted shares	F11.1	F11.2	F11
		Total assets *(sum of boxes F1 to F11)*	F12

Liabilities, exemptions and reliefs

- Name of mortgagee — Property on which the mortgage is secured — Amount outstanding £ — F13
- Other liabilities — F14

Net total of assets less liabilities *(box F12 less boxes F13 and F14)* F15

- Exemptions and reliefs *(do not include any annual exemption here, enter it at box F18)*
  If you are deducting charity exemption, enter the full name of the charity, the country of establishment and the HMRC charities reference, if available. F16

Chargeable value of assets in the UK where tax may be paid by instalments *(box F15 less box F16)* F17

- Annual exemption being deducted F18

4

G Summary of the chargeable event

If you wish to work out the tax yourself you should fill in form IHT100WS so that you can copy the figures to this section and to section H. *You do not have to work out the tax. If you do not wish to do so, leave this section and section H blank and go straight to section J.*
Guidance on how to fill in parts G and H are given on page 25 of the guide - 'How to fill in form IHT100'. The box number WSA1 etc. refer to the boxes in the worksheet from which the figures come.

Lifetime transfers (event forms IHT100a and IHT100b)

Previous transfers made by the transferor which need to be taken into account *(box WSA1)*	G1	
Threshold at date of transfer *(box TX2)*	G2	
Balance of threshold available *(box TX3)*	G3	
Assets where the tax may not be paid by instalments:		
• Assets in the UK *(box WSA2)*	G4	
• Foreign assets *(box WSA3)*	G5	
Value of assets where tax may not be paid by instalments *(box WSA4)*	G6	
Assets where the tax may be paid by instalments:		
• Assets in the UK *(box WSA5)*	G7	
• Foreign assets *(box WSA6)*	G8	
Total assets where tax may be paid by instalments *(box WSA7)*	G9	
Total value of transfer *(box WSA8)*	G10	
Annual exemption *(box WSA9)*	G11	
Chargeable transfer *(box WSA10)*	G12	

Go to box H1 on page 6 to work out the tax.

Non-interest in possession settlements (event forms IHT100c and IHT100d)

Assets where the tax may not be paid by instalments:		
• Assets in the UK *(box WSB1)*	G13	
• Foreign assets *(box WSB2)*	G14	
Value of assets where tax may not be paid by instalments *(box WSB3)*	G15	
Assets where the tax may be paid by instalments:		
• Assets in the UK *(box WSB4)*	G16	
• Foreign assets *(box WSB5)*	G17	
• Value of assets where tax may be paid by instalments *(box WSB6)*	G18	
• **Total value on which tax is chargeable** *(box WSB7)*	G19	

Go to box H7 on page 6 to work out the tax

5

Flat rate charge and recapture charge (event forms IHT100e and IHT100f)

- Value of assets where tax may not be paid by instalments *(flat rate charge box WSC3: recapture charge box WSD3)* — G20
- Value of assets where tax may be paid by instalments *(flat rate charge box WSC6: recapture charge box WSD4)* — G21
- Total value of assets on which tax arises *(flat rate charge box WSC7: recapture charge box WSD5)* — G22

H Working out the tax

Lifetime transfers (event forms IHT100a and IHT100b)

- Value chargeable to tax *(box WSA10)* — H1
- Tax *(box TX9)* — H2
- Relief on successive charges *(box TX10)* — H3
- Double taxation relief *(box TX11)* — H4
- Tax previously paid on this transfer, if any *(box TX12)* — H5
- Tax due on this transfer *(box TX13)* ***Go to box H13*** — H6

Principal and proportionate charges (event forms IHT100c and IHT100d)

- Value on which tax is chargeable *(box WSB7)* — H7
- Rate *(box R24)* — H8 %
- Tax *(principal charge box TX39 plus box TX46: proportionate charge box TX59 plus box TX67)* — H9
- Reduction against tax *(principal charge only box TX40 plus box TX47)* — H10
- Double taxation relief *(principal charge box TX42 plus box TX49: proportionate charge box TX60 plus box TX68)* — H11
- **Tax payable on this transfer *(principal charge box TX43 plus box TX50: proportionate charge box TX61 plus box TX69)*** — H12

Working out the tax that is payable on this account

Lifetime transfers / Principal charge / Proportionate charge

- Tax which may not be paid by instalments *(lifetime: box TX18, principal: box TX41, proportionate: box TX59)* — H13
- Successive charges relief *(lifetime: box TX19)* — H14
- Double taxation relief *(lifetime: box TX20, principal: box TX42, proportionate: box TX60)* — H15
- Tax previously paid, if any *(box TX21)* — H16
- Interest *(lifetime: box TX23, principal: box TX44, proportionate: box TX62)* — H17
- **Tax and interest which may not be paid by instalments** *(lifetime: box TX24, principal: box TX45, proportionate: box TX63)* — H18

6

- Tax which may be paid by instalments *(lifetime box TX29: principal box TX48: proportionate box TX67)* — H19
- Successive charges relief *(lifetime box TX30)* — H20
- Double taxation relief *(lifetime box TX31: principal box TX49: proportionate box TX68)* — H21
- Tax previously paid *(lifetime box TX32)* — H22
- Number of instalments being paid now *(lifetime box TX34: principal box TX51: proportionate box TX70)* — H23 / 10
- Tax now payable *(lifetime box TX35: principal box TX52: proportionate box TX71)* — H24
- Interest on instalments to be added *(lifetime box TX36: principal box TX53: proportionate box TX72)* — H25
- **Tax and interest being paid now which may be paid by instalments** *(lifetime box TX37: principal box TX54: proportionate box TX73)* — H26
- **Total tax and interest payable on this account** *(lifetime box TX38: principal box TX55: proportionate box TX74)* — H27

Working out the tax: • Flat rate charge (event form IHT100e) • Recapture charge (event form IHT100f)

- Tax which may not be paid by instalments *(flat rate charge box TX75: recapture charge box TX104 or box TX117)* — H28
- Double taxation relief on the tax which may not be paid by instalments *(flat rate charge box TX76)* — H29
- Tax not payable by instalments *(flat rate charge box TX77)* — H30
- Interest *(flat rate charge box TX78: recapture charge box TX105 or box TX118)* — H31
- Tax which may not be paid by instalments and interest now payable *(flat rate charge box TX79: recapture charge box TX106 or box TX119)* — H32
- Tax which may be paid by instalments *(flat rate charge box TX80: recapture charge box TX110 or box TX120)* — H33
- Double taxation relief on the tax which may be paid by instalments *(flat rate charge box TX81)* — H34
- Tax which may be paid by instalments *(flat rate charge box TX82)* — H35
- Number of instalments due *(flat rate charge box TX83: recapture charge box TX111 or box TX121)* — H36 / 10
- Tax now payable *(flat rate charge box TX84: recapture charge box TX112 or box TX122)* — H37
- Interest *(flat rate charge box TX85: recapture charge box TX113 or box TX123)* — H38
- **Tax which may be paid by instalments and interest now payable** *(flat rate charge box TX86: recapture charge box TX114 or box TX124)* — H39
- **Tax and interest now payable on this account** *(flat rate charge box TX87: recapture charge box TX115 or box TX125)* — H40

7

J Authority for repayment of Inheritance Tax

In the event of any Inheritance Tax being overpaid the payable order for the overpaid tax and interest in connection with this chargeable event should be made out to:

K Disclosure of tax avoidance scheme

If any party to this account is submitting the account in respect of a transaction forming part of notifiable arrangements then:

- give the scheme reference number in box K1; and,
- enter the last day of the tax year in which, or the date on which, a tax advantage is expected to be obtained in respect of the notifiable arrangements in box K2.

Tax avoidance scheme reference number (SRN)

K1

Tax year or date when tax advantage is expected

K2

L Declaration

I/we have filled in and am/are sending back to you the following event form

L1

and the supplementary pages listed below (together called 'this account').

L2

If you give false information or conceal any information that affects the liability to Inheritance Tax arising on the chargeable event, or you fail to remedy anything in this account which is incorrect within a reasonable time, or this account is delivered late, you may be liable to financial penalties and/or you may face prosecution. Where you have elected to pay tax by instalments you may have to pay interest on any unpaid tax according to the law.

I/we declare to the best of my/our knowledge and belief the information I/we have given in this account is correct and complete.

Each person delivering this account whether as transferor, transferee or trustee, must sign below to indicate that they have read and agree the statements above.

Full name and address *Signature* *Date* *Capacity: Transferee, transferor, trustee, other(specify)*	*Full name and address* *Signature* *Date* *Capacity: Transferee, transferor, trustee, other(specify)*
Full name and address *Signature* *Date* *Capacity: Transferee, transferor, trustee, other(specify)*	*Full name and address* *Signature* *Date* *Capacity: Transferee, transferor, trustee, other(specify)*

Remember to fill in and return the correct event form

8

Inheritance tax worksheet [Form IHT100 (WS)]

HM Revenue & Customs

Inheritance tax worksheet

Working out the taxable transfer and inheritance tax.

Section A: **Use this section to work out the tax on lifetime transfers and the ending of interests in possession.**

Section B: **Use this section to work out the tax on principal and proportionate charges.**

Section C: **Use this section to work out the tax on a flat rate charge.**

Section D: **Use this section to work out the tax on a recapture charge.**

A Lifetime transfers (event forms IHT100a or IHT100b).

Other transfers of value to be taken into account to calculate the total tax.

Total value of lifetime transfers made during the 7 years ending on the date of this transfer to be taken into account.
(Take this figure from the following: IHT100a box 2.4 or IHT100b box 2.4).

WSA1 £ — *Copy to box G1 on IHT100*

Assets where the tax may not be paid by instalments.

- Assets in the UK *(box E19 on form IHT100).* — WSA2 £ — *Copy to box G4 on IHT100*
- Foreign assets *(box FP7 form D39).* — WSA3 £ — *Copy to box G5 on IHT100*
- Total value of assets where the tax may not be paid by instalments *(box WSA2 plus box WSA3).* — WSA4 £ — *Copy to box G6 on IHT100*

Assets where the tax may be paid by instalments.

- Assets in the UK *(box F17 form IHT100).* — WSA5 £ — *Copy to box G7 on IHT100*
- Foreign assets *(box FP12 form D39).* — WSA6 £ — *Copy to box G8 on IHT100*
- Total assets where the tax may be paid by instalments *(box WSA5 plus box WSA6).* — WSA7 £ — *Copy to box G9 on IHT100*
- Total value of transfer *(box WSA4 plus box WSA7).* — WSA8 £ — *Copy to box G10 on IHT100*
- Annual exemption *(box F18 IHT100).* — WSA9 £ — *Copy to box G11 on IHT100*
- **Chargeable transfer** *(box WSA8 minus box WSA9).* — WSA10 £ — *Copy to box G12 on IHT100*

IHT100 WS **(Substitute)(LexisNexisButterworths)**

1

HMRC CT 12/05

- Annual exemption applicable to the property on which the tax may **not** be paid by instalments.

£ (box WSA9) X (box WSA4) £ / (box WSA8) £ = WSA11 £

- Annual exemption applicable to the property on which the tax may be paid by instalments.

£ (box WSA9) X (box WSA7) £ / (box WSA8) £ = WSA12 £

Working out the total tax that is payable.

- Other transfers of value to be taken into account *(box WSA1).* — TX1 £
- Threshold at the date of transfer *(box IHT100a 2.6 or IHT100b 2.6).* — TX2 £ *Copy to box G2 on IHT100*
- Balance of tax threshold available *(box TX2 minus box TX1). If the result is a negative amount enter nil at box TX3.* — TX3 £ *Copy to box G3 on IHT100*
- Amount chargeable to tax *(box WSA10).* — TX4 £
- Amount on which tax is payable *(box TX4 minus box TX3).* — TX5 £

Is the transferee paying the tax or does the transfer consist of the ending of an interest in possession in settled property?

Yes ☐ *Copy the amount in box TX5 to box TX6.*

No ☐ *Use the calculation below to work out the amount to write in box TX6.*

Grossing-up *(For boxes TX6 and TX7 the rate of tax is 40% if the charge arose because of the transferors death otherwise it is 20%).*

(TX5) £ X $\frac{100}{100-40}$ or $\frac{100}{100-20}$ — TX6 £

Tax on TX6 £ @ 40% or 20% — TX7 £

Taper relief. Taper relief is allowable on a transfer of value made more than three years and not more than seven years before the date of the transferor 's death. *(If you wish to claim taper relief work out the relief using the table on page 16 copy the amount from TR2).* — TX8 £

- Tax *(box TX7 minus box TX8).* — TX9 £ *Copy to box H2 on IHT100*
- Relief on successive charges. *(Work out the relief using the calculation on page 17 and copy the result from box SC8).* — TX10 £ *Copy to box H3 on IHT100*
- Double taxation relief. *(Work out the relief using the calculation on page 17. Copy the lower of boxes DT2 and DT5 to this box).* — TX11 £ *Copy to box H4 on IHT100*
- Tax previously paid on this transfer (if any). *(From box 7.3 on form IHT100a or box 7.3 on form IHT100b).* — TX12 £ *Copy to box H5 on IHT100*
- **Tax due on this transfer** *(box TX9 minus box TX10, box TX11 and box TX12).* — TX13 £ *Copy to box H6 on IHT100*

2

Tax which may not be paid by instalments.

- Chargeable value of the assets on which tax may **not** be paid by instalments *(box WSA4 minus box WSA11).* — TX14 £

Tax TX15 £ *(Copy from box TX9)* X TX16 £ *(Copy from box TX14)* / TX17 £ *(Copy from box WSA10)* = TX18 £ *Copy to box H13 on IHT100*

- Successive charges relief attributable to the assets on which tax may **not** be paid by instalments. *(Work out the relief using the calculation on page 17. Copy the results from SC6 to this box).* — TX19 £ *Copy to box H14 on IHT100*

- Double taxation relief attributable to the property on which tax may not be paid by instalments. *(Work out the relief using the calculation on page 17 and the value of the foreign assets on which the tax may not be paid by instalments. Copy the lower of DT2 and DT5 to this box).* — TX20 £ *Copy to box H15 on IHT100*

- Tax previously paid on this transfer which may not be paid by instalments. *(From box 7.1 form IHT100a or box 7.1 form IHT100b).* — TX21 £ *Copy to box H16 on IHT100*

- **Tax which may not be paid by instalments** *(box TX18 minus box TX19, box TX20 and box TX21).* — TX22 £

- Interest - You may use the tables on page 15 to work out any interest due *(Copy the figure from box IT4).* — TX23 £ *Copy to box H17 on IHT100*

Tax which may not be paid by instalments and interest now being paid *(box TX22 plus box TX23).* — TX24 £ *Copy to box H18 on IHT100*

Tax which may be paid by instalments.

- Chargeable value of the property on which tax may be paid by instalments *(box WSA7 minus box WSA12).* — TX25 £

Tax TX26 £ *(Copy from box TX9)* X TX27 £ *(Copy from box TX25)* / TX28 £ *(Copy from box WSA10)* = TX29 £ *Copy to box H19 on IHT100*

- Successive charges relief attributable to the assets on which tax may be paid by instalments. *(Work out the relief using the calculation on page 17. Use the amounts that relate to assets on which the tax may not be paid by instalments. Copy the results from SC7 to this box).* — TX30 £ *Copy to box H20 on IHT100*

- Double taxation relief attributable to property on which tax may be paid by instalments. *(Work out the relief using the calculation on page 17 and the value of the foreign assets on which the tax may be paid by instalments. Copy the lower of DT2 and DT5 to this box).* — TX31 £ *Copy to box H21 on IHT100*

3

• Tax previously paid on this transfer *(from box 7.2 form IHT100a or box 7.2 form IHT100b).*	TX32	£ *Copy to box H22 on IHT100*
• Tax which may be paid by instalments *(box TX29 minus box TX30, box TX31 and box TX32).*	TX33	£
• Number of instalments being paid now *(section F page 4 IHT100).*	TX34	/10 *Copy to box H23 on IHT100*
• **Tax payable now** *(box TX33 multiplied by box TX34).*	TX35	£ *Copy to box H24 on IHT100*
• Interest - You may use the tables on page 15 to work out any interest due *(copy the figure from box IT9).*	TX36	£ *Copy to box H25 on IHT100*
Tax which may be paid by instalments and interest now being paid *(box TX35 plus box TX36).*	TX37	£ *Copy to box H26 on IHT100*
Total tax and interest now being paid in this account *(box TX24 plus box TX37).*	TX38	£ *Copy to box H27 on IHT100*

B **Settlements (event forms IHT100c and IHT100d).**

Assets where the tax may not be paid by instalments.

• Assets in the UK *(box E19 form IHT100).*	WSB1	£ *Copy to box G13 on IHT100*
• Foreign assets *(box FP7 form D39).*	WSB2	£ *Copy to box G14 on IHT100*
• Value of assets where tax may **not** be paid by instalments *(box WSB1 plus box WSB2).*	WSB3	£ *Copy to box G15 on IHT100*

Assets where tax may be paid by instalments.

• Assets in the UK *(box F17 form IHT100).*	WSB4	£ *Copy to box G16 on IHT100*
• Foreign assets *(box FP12 form D39).*	WSB5	£ *Copy to box G17 on IHT100*
• Value of assets where tax may be paid by instalments *(box WSB4 plus box WSB5).*	WSB6	£ *Copy to box G18 on IHT100*
• Total value on which tax is chargeable *(box WSB3 plus box WSB6).*	WSB7	£ *Copy to box G19 on IHT100*
• Value of the settlement at the date of the last ten-year anniversary to be taken into account *(box 3.5 on form IHT100c).*	WSB8	£
• Value of settlement at the date of commencement *(box 2.1 on form IHT100c).*	WSB9	£
• Value of related settlements *(box 2.6 on form IHT100c or box 1.14 on form IHT100d).*	WSB10	£

4

• Value of non-relevant property *(box 1.12 on form IHT100d).*	WSB11	£
• Additions to the settlement *(box 2.3 or 3.7 form IHT100c).*	WSB12	£
• Value of assets which became relevant property since the last ten-year anniversary *(box 3.9 column E on form IHT100c).*	WSB13	£
• Aggregable previous chargeable transfers *(box 2.8 or 3.4 on form IHT100c or box 1.10 on form IHT100d).*	WSB14	£
• Value on which proportionate charges have arisen *(box 3.3 on form IHT100c or box 1.5 on form IHT100d).*	WSB15	£

Working out the rate.

Value of assumed chargeable transfer.

Box R1, complete in respect of principal charge only.

Value of relevant property *(box WSB7).*	R1	£
Value of the transfer at the last ten-year anniversary *(box WSB8).*	R2	£
Value of settlement at date of commencement *(box WSB9).*	R3	£
Value of related settlements *(box WSB10).*	R4	£
Value of non-relevant property *(box WSB11).*	R5	£
Value of additions *(box WSB12).*	R6	£
Value of the assets which became relevant property since the last ten-year anniversary *(box WSB13).*	R7	£
Total value of assumed chargeable transfer *(Sum of boxes R1 to R7).*	R8	£

Aggregate value of assumed previous chargeable transfers.

Previous cumulative total *(box WSB14).*	R9	£
Value on which proportionate charges have arisen *(box WSB15).*	R10	£
Total *(box R9 plus box R10)*	R11	£
Aggregable chargeable transfers *(box R8 plus box R11)*	R12	£

Tax on the aggregable chargeable transfers *(box R12) =*

Tax on the first	R13	£		R14	£ 0.00

(Write the inheritance tax threshold at the date of the chargeable event in box R13).

Tax on the balance	R15	£	@ 20%	R16	£

(box R12 minus box R13. If the result is a negative amount write '0' in box R15).

Total *(box R14 plus box R16).*	R17	£

Tax on the aggregate value of assumed previous transfers *(R11).*

Tax on the first	R18	£		R19	£ 0.00

Write the inheritance tax threshold at date of the chargeable event in box R18).

Tax on the balance	R20	£	@ 20%	R21	£

(box R11 minus box R18. If the result is a negative amount write '0' in box R20).

5

Total tax on assumed previous transfers *(box R19 plus box R21).* R22 £

Total tax *(R17 minus R22).* R23 £

Effective rate = $\frac{(R23)}{(R8)}$ x 30 = R24 %

Copy to box H8 on IHT100

Calculating the tax.

To calculate the inheritance tax on a principal charge continue below from box TX39.
To calculate the inheritance tax on a proportionate charge go to page 8 and continue from box TX56.

Principal Charge (Ten-Year Anniversary).

Tax which may not be paid by instalments.

• Tax on £ *(box WSB3)* x % *(box R24)* = TX39 £

Reduction against tax which may **not** be paid by instalments.

If the relevant property included in box WSB3 was not relevant property during the whole of the ten years ending on this anniversary the tax at TX39 may be reduced for each successive complete quarter during which it was not relevant property. Use the table to calculate the reduction where applicable (see guidance notes IHT113 "How to fill in IHT100WS").

Value of relevant property at the ten-year anniversary. *(From question 1.3 form IHT100d).*		Rate % *(box R24).*		Complete quarters between the last ten-year anniversary and the date on which the asset last became relevant property.		40		Reduction in tax.
A		B		C		D		E
						40		
	x		x		÷	40	=	
						40		
						40		
						40		

Total reduction TX40 £

• Tax *(box TX39 minus box TX40).* TX41 £

Copy to box H13 on IHT100

Double taxation relief attributable to property on which tax may **not** be paid by instalments. *(Work out the relief using the calculation on page 17 and the value of the foreign assets on which the tax may be paid by instalments. Copy the lower of DT2 and DT5 to this box).* TX42 £

Copy to box H15 on IHT100

Tax which may not be paid by instalments *(box TX41minus box TX42).* TX43 £

• Interest - *You may use the tables on page 15 to calculate any interest due. (Copy the figure from box IT4).* TX44 £

Copy to box H17 on IHT100

6

Tax which may not be paid by instalments and interest now being paid
(box TX43 plus box TX44).

TX45 £
Copy to box H18 on IHT100

Tax which may be paid by instalments.

- Tax on £ ______ *(box WSB6)* x ______ % *(box R24)* = TX46 £

Reduction against the tax which may be paid by instalments.

If the relevant property included in box WSB6 which may be paid by instalments was not relevant property during the whole of the ten years ending on this anniversary the tax at TX46 may be reduced for each successive complete quarter during which it was not relevant property. Use the table to calculate the reduction where applicable (see guidance notes IHT113 "How to fill in IHT100WS").

Value of relevant property at the ten-year anniversary. *(From question 1.3 form IHT100d).*	x	Rate % *(box R24).*	x	Complete successive quarters between the last ten-year anniversary and the date on which the asset last became relevant property.	÷	40	=	Reduction in tax.
A		B		C		D		E
						40		
	x		x		÷	40	=	
						40		
						40		
						40		

Total reduction TX47 £ 0.00

- Tax *(box TX46 minus box TX47).* TX48 £
  Copy to box H19 on IHT100

- Double taxation relief attributable to assets on which the tax may be paid by instalments. *(Work out the relief using the calculation on page 17 and the value of the foreign assets on which the tax may be paid by instalments. Copy the lower of DT2 and DT5 to this box).* TX49 £
  Copy to box H21 on IHT100

- Tax which may be paid by instalments *(box TX48 minus box TX49).* TX50 £

- Number of instalments being paid now *(section F page 4 form IHT100).* TX51 /10
  Copy to box H23 on IHT100

- Tax which may be paid by instalments payable now *(box TX50 x box TX51).* TX52 £
  Copy to box H24 on IHT100

- Interest - *You may use the tables on page 15 to calculate any interest due. (Copy the figure from box IT9).* TX53 £
  Copy to box H25 on IHT100

Tax which may be paid by instalments and interest now being paid
(box TX52 plus box TX53).

TX54 £
Copy to box H26 on IHT100

Total tax and interest now being paid on this account
(box TX45 plus box TX54).

TX55 £
Copy to box H27 on IHT100

7

Calculating the tax.

Proportionate Charge.

Tax which may not be paid by instalments.

Value on which tax may not be paid by instalments *(box WSB3).* TX56 £

*The amount of tax depends on when the assets which are subject to this chargeable event became comprised in this settlement. Use the table below to calculate the tax which may **not** be paid by instalments. (See notes on "How to fill in IHT100WS").*

Complete the following table for assets on which tax may **not** be paid by instalments.

Line1. Enter the value of the assets comprised in this chargeable event that were relevant property at the date on which the settlement commenced or the date of the last ten-year anniversary if later.

Remaining lines. Write in the figures from box 2.11 or box 3.11 on form IHT100c.

	Date on which the asset last became relevant property or the date of the last ten-year anniversary if later.	Value of the assets at the date of this chargeable event. £		Rate % *(box R24).*		Number of quarters between the date in column **A** and the date of this chargeable event.		40		Tax. £
	A	B	x	C	x	D	÷	E	=	F
1								40		£
2								40		£
3								40		£
4			x		x		÷	40	=	£
5								40		£
6								40		£

Total * £ Total tax TX57 £ 0.00

**This amount should be equal to the amount in box TX56.*

Grossing. *If the tax is **not** being paid out of relevant property in this settlement copy the amount in box TX56 to box TX58 and the amount in box TX57 to box TX59.*
If the tax is being paid out of relevant property in this settlement the value of the assets which cease to be relevant property must be grossed-up to find the true value of the transfer. Go to the grossing calculation on pages 15 to 16 to work out the revised value of the transfer and bring the figures back to boxes TX58 and TX59.

Revised value on which tax may not be paid by instalments *(from box GC4 page 16).* TX58 £

Revised tax which may not be paid by instalments *(from box GC6 page 16).* TX59 £ *Copy to box H13 on IHT100*

- Double taxation relief applicable to assets on which the tax may **not** be paid by instalments. *(Work out the relief using the calculation on page 17 and the value of the foreign assets on which the tax may not be paid by instalments. Copy the lower of DT2 and DT5 to this box).* TX60 £ *Copy to box H15 on IHT100*

- **Tax which may not be paid by instalments** *(box TX59 minus box TX60).* TX61 £

- Interest - *You may use the tables on page 15 to calculate any interest due. (Copy the figure from box IT4).* TX62 £ *Copy to box H17 on IHT100*

8

Tax which may not be paid by instalments and interest now being paid
(box TX61plus box TX62).

TX63 £
Copy to box H18 on IHT100

Tax which may be paid by instalments.

Value on which tax may be paid by instalments is chargeable *(box WSB6).*

TX64 £

Complete the following table for assets on which the tax may be paid by instalments.

Line 1. Enter the value of the assets that were relevant property at the date on which the settlement commenced or the date of the last ten-year anniversary if later.

Remaining lines. Write in the figures from box 2.11 or box 3.11 on form IHT100c.

	Date on which the asset last became relevant property or the date of the last ten-year anniversary if later.	Value of the assets at the date of this chargeable event. £		Rate % *(box R24).*		Number of quarters between the date in column A and the date of this chargeable event.		40		Tax. £
	A	B	x	C	x	D	÷	E	=	F
1								40		£
2								40		£
3								40		£
4			x		x		÷	40	=	£
5								40		£
6								40		£

Total * £ Total tax TX65 £ 0.00

**This amount should be equal to the amount in box TX64.*

Grossing. *If the tax is **not** being paid out of the relevant property in this settlement, copy the amount in box TX64 to box TX66 and the amount in box TX65 to box TX67.*
If the tax is being paid out of relevant property in this settlement the value of the assets which ceased to be relevant property must be grossed up to find the true value of the transfer. Go to the grossing calculation on pages 15 to 16 to work out the revised value of the transfer and the tax and bring the figures back to boxes TX66 and TX67.

Revised value on which tax may be paid by instalments *(from box GC5).*

TX66 £

Revised tax which may be paid by instalments *(from box GC7).*

TX67 £
Copy to box H19 on IHT100

- Double taxation relief applicable to assets on which the tax may be paid by instalments. *(Work out the relief using the calculation on page 17 and the amounts relating to assets on which the tax may be paid by instalments. Copy the lower of DT2 and DT5 to this box).*

TX68 £
Copy to box H21 on IHT100

- **Tax which may be paid by instalments**
(box TX67 minus box TX68).

TX69 £

- Number of instalments being paid now *(section F page 4 IHT100).*

TX70 /10
Copy to box H23 on IHT100

- Tax which may be paid by instalments payable now *(box TX69 x box TX70).*

TX71 £
Copy to box H24 on IHT100

9

- Interest - *You may use the tables on page 15 to calculate any interest due. (Copy the figure from box IT9).*

TX72 — *Copy to box H25 on IHT100*

Tax which may be paid by instalments and interest now being paid *(box TX71 plus box TX72).*

TX73 — *Copy to box H26 on IHT100*

Total tax and interest now being paid on this account *(box TX63 plus box TX73).*

TX74 — *Copy to box H27 on IHT100*

C **Flat Rate Charge.**

Assets on which tax may not be paid by instalments.

- Assets in the UK *(box E19 IHT100).* — WSC1
- Foreign assets *(box FP7 form D39).* — WSC2
- Value on which tax may not be paid by instalments *(box WSC1 plus box WSC2).* — WSC3 *Copy to box G20 on IHT100*

Assets on which the tax may be paid by instalments.

- Assets in the UK *(box F17 form IHT100).* — WSC4
- Foreign assets *(box FP12 form D39).* — WSC5
- Value on which tax may be paid by instalments *(box WSC4 plus box WSC5).* — WSC6 *Copy to box G21 on IHT100*
- Assets on which the charge arises *(WSC3 plus WSC6).* — WSC7 *Copy to box G22 on IHT100*

Calculating the tax.

Tax which may not be paid by instalments.
(Copy the information from box 1.6 on from IHT100e).

Use the table below to work out the tax which may not be paid by instalments.
To work out the tax to put in column D use the table R25 on page 12 below.

No.	Date asset last became subject to special trusts.	Value of assets at the date of this chargeable event. £	Number of complete quarters between the date in column **A** and the chargeable event.	Tax *(see table R25).* £
	A	B	C	D
1				
2				
3				
4				
5				
6				

Total value* £   Total tax TX75 £ 0.00 *Copy to box H28 on IHT100*

** This amount should equal the amount in box WSC3.*

10

- Double taxation relief attributable to the assets on which tax may not be paid by instalments. *(Work out the relief using the calculation on page 17 and the amounts relating to assets on which the tax may not be paid by instalments. Copy the lower of DT2 and DT5 to this box).*

TX76 £ — *Copy to box H29 on IHT100*

- Tax which may not be paid by instalments *(box TX75 minus box TX76).*

TX77 £ — *Copy to box H30 on IHT100*

Interest - You may use the tables on page 15 to calculate any interest due *(copy the figure from box IT4).*

TX78 £ — *Copy to box H31 on IHT100*

Tax which may not be paid by instalments and interest now payable *(box TX77 plus box TX78).*

TX79 £ — *Copy to box H32 on IHT100*

Tax which may be paid by instalments.
(Copy the information from box 1.6 on form IHT100e).

Use the table below to work out the tax which may be paid by instalments.
To work out the tax to put in column D use the table R25 on page 12 below.

No.	Date asset last became subject to special trusts.	Value of assets at the date of this chargeable event. £	Number of complete quarters between the date in column **A** and the chargeable event.	Tax *(see table R25).* £
	A	B	C	D
1				
2				
3				
4				
5				
6				

Total value* £ Total tax TX80 £ 0.00 — *Copy to box H33 on IHT100*

* *This amount shound equal the amount in box WSC6.*

- Double taxation relief attributable to assets on which the tax may be paid by instalments. *(Work out the relief using the calculation on page 17 and the amounts relating to assets on which the tax may be paid by instalments. Copy the lower of DT2 and DT5 to this box).*

TX81 £ — *Copy to box H34 on IHT100*

- Tax which may be paid by instalments *(box TX80 minus box TX81).*

TX82 £ — *Copy to box H35 on IHT100*

- Number of instalments being paid now *(section F page 4 IHT100).*

TX83 /10 — *Copy to box H36 on IHT100*

- Tax which may be paid by instalments payable now *(box TX82 x box TX83).*

TX84 £ — *Copy to box H37 on IHT100*

- Interest - *You may use the tables on page 15 to calculate any interest due. (Copy the figure from box IT9).*

TX85 £ — *Copy to box H38 on IHT100*

- **Tax which may be paid by instalments and interest now payable** *(box TX84 plus box TX85).*

TX86 £ — *Copy to box H39 on IHT100*

Total tax and interest now being paid on this account *(box TX79 plus box TX86).*

TX87 £ — *Copy to box H40 on IHT100*

11

Tax payable Table R25

Use this table to work out the tax on each asset or group of assets that last became held on special trusts on the same date. If more than one asset or more than one group of assets is listed on the tables at TX75 or TX80 separate calculations will be needed for each asset or group of assets.

No.	Capital value *(from col B).* £	X	Number of quarters *(from col C).*		X	Rate.	=	Tax. £
	A		B			C		D
1			1- 40			0.25%		
2			41- 80			0.20%		
3			81-120			0.15%		
4			121-160			0.10%		
5			161-200			0.05%		

Total R25 £ 0.00

Copy the result back to column "D" on the table at TX75 or TX80 on page 10 or 11 above.

D Recapture Charges.

Calculating the tax.

Previous cumulative total to be taken into account *(box 5.3 form IHT100f).* WSD1 £

Value of the transferors/settlors estate at the date of death for inheritance tax purposes *(box 5.1 form IHT100f).* WSD2 £

Assets on which the tax may **not** be paid by instalments *(box E19 form IHT100).* WSD3 £ *Copy to box G20 on IHT100*

Assets on which the tax may be paid by instalments *(box F17 form IHT100).* WSD4 £ *Copy to box G21 on IHT100*

Value on which tax is now chargeable *(box WSD3 plus box WSD4).* WSD5 £ *Copy to box G22 on IHT100*

Tax threshold *(box 5.4 form IHT100f).* WSD6 £

Calculation of tax 1.

Use this calculation unless the asset was relevant property in a discretionary trust between the date on which it became conditionally exempt and the date of this chargeable event.

Previous lifetime transfers *(box WSD1).* TX88 £

Value of the transferors/settlors estate at the date of death for inheritance tax purposes *(box WSD2).* TX89 £

Total *(box TX88 plus box TX89).* TX90 £

Threshold at the date of the chargeable event *(box WSD6).* TX91 £

Balance of the threshold available *(box TX91 minus box TX90. If box TX91 minus box TX90 is a negative amount write "0" in this box).* TX92 £

Amount on which tax is now chargeable *(box WSD5).* TX93 £

Value on which tax is payable *(box TX93 minus box TX92).* TX94 £

12

Rate of tax *(20% or 40%. Use the flowchart R26 on page 18 to find out the rate to use).* — TX95 %

Tax *(box TX94 X box TX95).* — TX96 £

Proportion of tax charged *(30%, 40%, 100%. Use the flowchart R26 on page18 to find out the proportion to use).* — TX97 %

Tax = *(box TX96 X box TX97).* — TX98 £

Tax previously paid *(disposals of timber or underwood from box 4.1 form IHT100f).* — TX99 £

Tax on this chargeable event *(box TX98 minus box TX99).* — TX100 £

Tax which may not be paid by instalments.

(Copy from box TX100) TX101 £ X *(Copy from box WSD3)* TX102 £ / TX103 £ *(Copy from box WSD5)* = TX104 £ *Copy to box H28 on IHT100*

Interest - *You may use the tables on page 15 to calculate any interest due. (Copy the figure from IT4).* — TX105 £ *Copy to box H31 on IHT100*

Tax which may not be paid by instalments and interest now payable *(box TX104 plus box TX105).* — TX106 £ *Copy to box H32 on IHT100*

Tax which may be paid by instalments

(Copy from box TX100) TX107 £ X *(Copy from box WSD4)* TX108 £ / TX109 £ *(Copy from box WSD5)* = TX110 £ *Copy to box H33 on IHT100*

Number of instalments being paid now *(section F page 4 IHT100).* — TX111 /10 *Copy to box H36 on IHT100*

Tax which may be paid by instalments payable now *(box TX110 box TX111).* — TX112 £ *Copy to box H37 on IHT100*

Interest - *You may use the tables on page 15 to calculate any interest due. (Copy the figure from IT9).* — TX113 £ *Copy to box H38 on IHT100*

Tax which may be paid by instalments and interest now payable *(box TX112 plus box TX113).* — TX114 £ *Copy to box H39 on IHT100*

Tax and interest now payable *(box TX106 plus box TX114).* — TX115 £ *Copy to box H40 on IHT100*

Calculation 2. Use this calculation if the asset became conditionally exempt when held in a discretionary trust and at that time it was and since then continued to be relevant property.

Value of assets on which the tax may not be paid by instalments *(box WSD3).* — TX116 £

13

Use the table below to work out the tax which may not be paid by instalments.
To work out the tax to put in column D use the table R25 on page 12 above.
Take the information from box 5.5 form IHT100f.

No.	Date on which settlement commenced or of last ten-year anniversary before asset became settled property if later.	Value of asset at the date of the chargeable event. £	Number of complete quarters between the date in column A and the chargeable event.	Tax *(See table R25).* £
	A	B	C	D
1				
2				
3				
4				
5				
6				

Total value £ Total tax TX117 £ *Copy to box H28 on IHT100*

Interest - *You may use the tables on page 15 to work out any interest due. (Copy the figure from box IT4).* TX118 £ *Copy to box H31 on IHT100*

Tax which may not be paid by instalments and interest now due *(box TX117 plus box TX118).* TX119 £ *Copy to box H32 on IHT100*

Use the table below to work out the tax which may be paid by instalments.
To work out the tax to put in column D use the table R25 on page 12 above.
Take the information from box 5.5 form IHT100f.

No.	Date on which settlement commenced or of last ten-year anniversary before asset became settled property if later.	Value of asset at the date of the chargeable event. £	Number of complete quarters between the date in column A and the chargeable event.	Tax *(See table R25).* £
	A	B	C	D
1				
2				
3				
4				
5				
6				

Total value £ Total tax TX120 £ *Copy to box H33 on IHT100*

Number of instalments being paid. TX121 /10 *Copy to box H36 on IHT100*

Tax now payable *(box TX120 x box TX121).* TX122 £ *Copy to box H37on IHT100*

Interest - *You may use the tables on page 15 to work out any interest due. (Copy the figure from box IT9).* TX123 £ *Copy to box H38 on IHT100*

Tax and interest that may be paid by instalments payable now *(box TX122 plus box TX123).* TX124 £ *Copy to box H39 on IHT100*

Total tax and interest payable now *(box TX119 plus box TX124).* TX125 £ *Copy to box H40 on IHT100*

14

Working out the interest.

Assets on which the tax may not be paid by instalments.

Date interest starts. IT1 / /

Date interest ends. IT2 / /

IT3 Start and end dates for interest.	No of days.	Daily rate.*	Interest payable.

(Page 33 IHT113, "How to fill in IHT100WS").

Total IT4 £

Assets where the tax may be paid by instalments.

IT5 Start and end dates for interest.	No of days.	Daily rate.*	Interest payable.

Total IT6 £

Additional interest.

IT7 Start and end dates for interest.	No of days.	Daily rate.*	Interest payable.

Total IT8 £

• **Total interest** *(IT6 plus IT8).* IT9 £ 0.00

Grossing.

If the tax is being paid out of the relevant property in this settlement, the amounts shown in column F of the tables at TX57 and TX65 must be grossed up to take account of the tax being paid.

Because the rate of tax is different for each of the assets or groups of assets shown in the tables, separate calculations must be done for each.

Use the formula below to gross the value transferred and work out the revised tax.

Box TX57/65 (column F) / *Box TX57/65 (column B)* X 100 = GC1 £

Box TX57/65 (column B) / *100 - Box GC1* X 100 = GC2 £

Revised tax payable *(box GC2)* £ X *(box GC1)* % = GC3 £

15

- Repeat the calculation for each entry in rows 1-6 in the tables at boxes TX57 and TX65.
- Add up the grossed-up values (taken from box GC2) on which tax may not be paid by instalments. (You may use the table below) and copy the total back to box TX58.
- Add up the grossed-up values (taken from box GC2) on which tax may be paid by instalments and copy the total back to box TX66.
- Add up the tax which may not be paid by instalments taking the results from box GC3 and copy the total back to box TX59.
- Add up the tax which may be paid by instalments taking the results from box GC3 and copy the total back to box TX67.

Calculation							Total
Revised value on which tax may not be paid by instalments.	1	2	3	4	5	6	GC4 £ 0.00 *Copy to box TX58*
Revised value on which tax may be paid by instalments.	1	2	3	4	5	6	GC5 £ 0.00 *Copy to box TX66*
Revised tax which may not be paid by instalments.	1	2	3	4	5	6	GC6 £ 0.00 *Copy to box TX59*
Revised tax which may be paid by instalments.	1	2	3	4	5	6	GC7 £ 0.00 *Copy to box TX67*

Taper relief

Use the table below to work out the taper relief.

Tax.	Time of transfer before the date of death.	Rate of relief.	Amount.
TR1			TR2
	Not more than three years	Nil	
	More than 3 but not more than 4 years	20%	
	More than 4 but not more than 5 years	40%	
	More than 5 but not more than 6 years	60%	
	More than 6 but not more than 7 years	80%	
	More than 7 years	Nil	

Take the figure for TR1 from box TX7.

16

Working out successive charges relief.

First transfer.

Net Value of first transfer for inheritance tax *(box 5.2 form IHT100a or 5.2 form IHT100b).* SC1 £

Inheritance tax paid on the first transfer *(box 5.3 form IHT100a or box 5.3 form IHT100b).* SC2 £

Assets in the first transfer included in this transfer

Assets on which tax may not be paid by instalments *(box 5.4 form IHT100a or box 5.4 form IHT100b).* SC3 £

Assets on which tax may be paid by instalments *(box 5.5 form IHT100a or box 5.5 form IHT100b).* SC4 £

Rate of relief *(box 5.6 form IHT100a or box 5.6 form IHT100b).* SC5 %

Relief on assets on which tax may not be paid by instalments

SC2 £ / SC1 £ X SC3 £ SC5 % = SC6 £

Relief on assets on which tax may be paid by instalments

SC2 £ / SC1 £ X SC4 £ SC5 % = SC7 £

Total relief *(SC6 plus SC7).* SC8 £

Working out double taxation relief.

Value of the foreign property included in form D39 on which foreign tax has been paid (in sterling). DT1 £

Foreign tax paid on the assets included in DT1 (in sterling). DT2 £

Formula for relief.

Tax on this transfer DT3 £ / DT4 £ *Value of this transfer* X *Value of foreign property* DT1 £ = DT5 £

The relief is the **lower** of boxes DT2 and DT5.

17

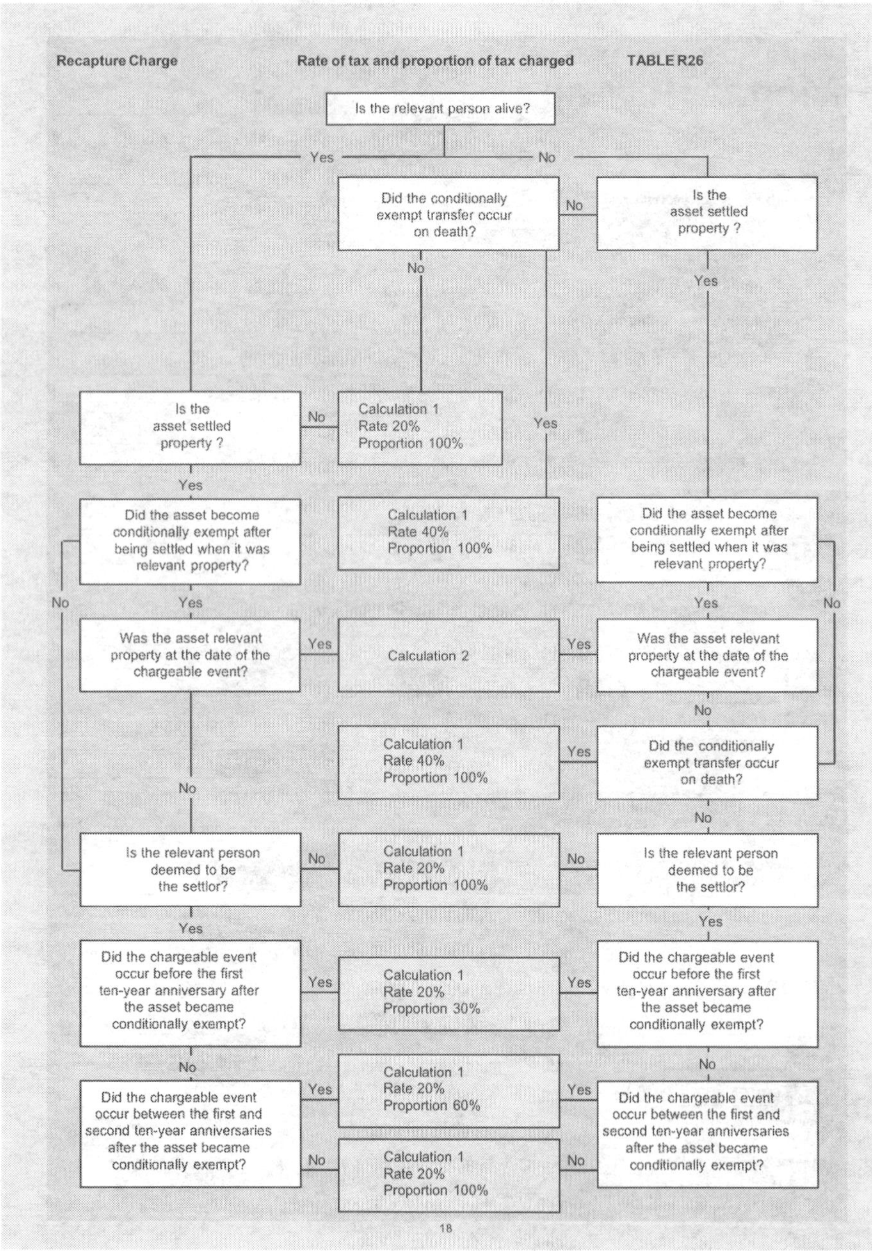
Recapture Charge
Rate of tax and proportion of tax charged
TABLE R26
Is the relevant person alive?
Yes
No
Did the conditionally exempt transfer occur on death?
No
Is the asset settled property ?
No
Yes
Is the asset settled property ?
No
Calculation 1 Rate 20% Proportion 100%
Yes
Yes
Did the asset become conditionally exempt after being settled when it was relevant property?
Calculation 1 Rate 40% Proportion 100%
Did the asset become conditionally exempt after being settled when it was relevant property?
No
Yes
Yes
No
Was the asset relevant property at the date of the chargeable event?
Yes
Calculation 2
Yes
Was the asset relevant property at the date of the chargeable event?
No
Calculation 1 Rate 40% Proportion 100%
Yes
Did the conditionally exempt transfer occur on death?
No
No
Is the relevant person deemed to be the settlor?
No
Calculation 1 Rate 20% Proportion 100%
No
Is the relevant person deemed to be the settlor?
Yes
Yes
Did the chargeable event occur before the first ten-year anniversary after the asset became conditionally exempt?
Yes
Calculation 1 Rate 20% Proportion 30%
Yes
Did the chargeable event occur before the first ten-year anniversary after the asset became conditionally exempt?
No
No
Did the chargeable event occur between the first and second ten-year anniversaries after the asset became conditionally exempt?
Yes
Calculation 1 Rate 20% Proportion 60%
Yes
Did the chargeable event occur between the first and second ten-year anniversaries after the asset became conditionally exempt?
No
Calculation 1 Rate 20% Proportion 100%
No
18

33

National Heritage

Cross-references. See **2.14** ACCOUNTS AND RETURNS for rendering an account on ending of conditional exemption; **21.6** EXEMPT TRANSFERS for gifts for national purposes; **21.8** EXEMPT TRANSFERS for gifts for public benefit.

Simon's Taxes. See **A4.620**, **I7.501–508**, **I4.161A**, **I4.218**, **I5.337**, **I7.5**, **I11.541**.

Other Sources. VOA IHT manual, section 1, http://www.hmrc.gov.uk/heritage/.

Introduction

[33.1] On certain conditions, transfers of national heritage property can be exempted from inheritance tax. In March 2005, following the Goodison Report, the Museum, Libraries and Archive's Acceptance in Lieu Panel which advises on items that are acceptable in lieu of tax was given more power under the Contracting Out (Functions in Relation to Cultural Objects) Order 2005 to act on behalf of the Secretary of State of the Department for Culture, Media and Sport (or the appropriate Minister outside England) to approve offers under *IHTA 1984, s 230* and allocation under the *National Heritage Act 1980, s 9*.

National heritage property may also be given or sold by private treaty without tax liability to specified national bodies or may be transferred to individuals or settlements with conditional exemption. The detailed provisions are stated below. See also Form IHT 420 at the end of this chapter.

National heritage property

[33.2] The following types of property are within the term 'national heritage property' provided they are so designated by the Board.

(a) Any:
- (i) picture, print, book, manuscript, work of art or scientific object, or any other thing not yielding income, which appears to the Board to be pre-eminent for its national, scientific, historic or artistic interest (introduced by *FA 1965*);
- (ii) any collections or groups of objects within (i) above which, taken as a whole, appears to the Board to be so pre-eminent (introduced by *FA 1973, s 46*); and
- (iii) any objects where they are associated with a particular building and where the Secretary of State believes it is desirable for that object to remain associated with a particular building or where objects have a significant association with a particular place.

Definitions

'*National interest*' includes interest within any part of the UK.

'*Pre-eminence*'-in determining whether an object or collection is pre-eminent, any significant association with a particular place is to be taken into account ie the 'Waverley criteria'. The object or collection should be central, rather than of merely marginal significance, in the context of display in a public collection or important historic building and should satisfy one or more of the following tests which follow those laid down by the AIL Panel:

- Does the object have an especially close association with our history and national life? This category includes foreign as well as British works, e.g. gifts from foreign sovereigns or governments and objects that have been acquired abroad in circumstances associated with our history. It also includes objects closely associated with some part of the United Kingdom, or with the development of its institutions and industries. Some objects that fall under this category will be of such national importance that they deserve to enter a national museum or gallery. Others may well be of a lesser degree of national importance although they will be significant in a local context. This category will also include works which derive their significance from a local connection and which may therefore qualify as 'pre-eminent' to a local authority or independent museum or gallery.
- Is the object of especial artistic or art-historical interest? This category includes objects deserving of entering a national museum or gallery as well as other objects that may not be pre-eminent in a national museum or gallery but will be pre-eminent in local authority, university or independent museums or galleries which do not already possess items of a similar genre or quality. For example, outstanding items of decorative or applied art would come within this category for consideration.
- Is the object of especial importance for the study of some particular form of art, learning or history? This category includes a wide variety of objects, not restricted to works of art such as engineering plans or models, which are of especial importance for the study of, say, a particular scientific development. The category also includes objects forming part of an historical unity series or collection either in one place or in the country as a whole. Without a particular object or group of objects, both a unity and a series may be impaired.
- Does the object have an especially close association with a particular historic setting? This category will include primary works of art, manuscripts, furniture or other items that have an especially close association with an important historic building. The category may include paintings, furniture especially commissioned for a particular house or a group of paintings having an association with a particular location including those being returned to their original setting.

(See also Inland Revenue Press Release 17/99, 11 February 1999.)

Pre-eminent and associated objects

Now HMRC Inheritance Tax refers offers of 'pre-eminent' or 'associated' objects (see (iii) above) to the Acceptance in Lieu (AIL) panel, which is comprised of 10 people and is currently under the chairmanship of Jonathan Scott. This panel, the council for museums, archives and libraries, takes into account the views of independent experts and advises the Secretary of State whether the property offered is suitable for acceptance in lieu by the Commissioners of HMRC in terms of the objects' pre-eminence. The AIL Panel meets once a month and also advises the Secretary of State on questions of allocation of objects (either temporary or permanent). Where land and buildings are offered HMRC Inheritance Tax refers to the Department of Culture Media and Sports (DCMS) who in turn consult advisers such as the Countryside Commission, the Forestry Authority and English Heritage. The Historic Manuscripts Commission advises the Secretary of State on the permanent allocation of records, archives and manuscripts. The Accounting Standards Board (ASB) published an exposure draft, FRED 42 in June 2008 on valuation of heritage assets but dropped a view that such assets would have to be valued.

For claims made before 31 July 1998, objects or collections within (i) and (ii) above could be designated if they appeared to the Board to be of national, scientific, historic or artistic interest. There was no requirement to satisfy the standard of 'pre-eminence' but only a lower standard of 'museum quality'.

(b) Land which in the opinion of the Board is of outstanding scenic or historic or scientific interest.

(c) A building for the preservation of which special steps should in the opinion of the Board be taken by reason of its outstanding historic or architectural interest.

(d) Land which in the opinion of the Board is essential for the protection of the character and amenities of such a building as is mentioned in (c) above.

(e) An object which in the opinion of the Board is historically associated with such a building mentioned in (c) above.

[*IHTA 1984, s 31(1)(5); FA 1985, Sch 26 para 2(2); FA 1998, Sch 25 para 4*].

The introduction of the pre-eminence test under (a) above may have the effect, in certain circumstances, of rendering previously exempted objects chargeable to a latent estate duty previously deferred but now exigible. Also, in the Finance Bill Committee Stage Debates the Financial Secretary's answer to questions on the definition of 'pre-eminent' exacted the following reply:

> 'An object must be pre-eminent or associated with a historical building; it does not have to be both. If the collection is pre-eminent in its own right, it should qualify. If it is not, its connection with a building may allow it to qualify as pre-eminent.'

(Hansard, 16 June 1998, Col 896).

Conditionally exempt transfers

[33.3] The Board may, on a claim (see below), designate property as eligible under **33.2** above and a transfer of such property is exempt from inheritance tax if certain conditions are met and undertakings given. Such a transfer is called a 'conditionally exempt transfer'. The failure to observe an undertaking is a 'chargeable event' and tax will become chargeable (see **33.10** and **33.14** below). It is understood that HMRC review all conditionally exempt transfers of land under **33.2**(b) at five-yearly intervals to ensure that undertakings are observed (HC Written answer, Hansard 18 June 1992, Vol 209, Cols 629, 630). A gift cannot be conditionally exempt if it is entirely exempt as a gift to a spouse/civil partner or to a charity. See **21.2** and **21.10** EXEMPT TRANSFERS. [*IHTA 1984, ss 30(1)(2)(4), 31, 32(1)(2); FA 1985, s 95, Sch 26 para 1; FA 1998, Sch 25 para 7*].

Conditions

[33.4] Exemptions may be given for transfers on death and lifetime gifts but the latter are eligible only if:

(a) the transferor or his spouse or civil partner has been beneficially entitled to the property throughout the six years ending with the transfer; or
(b) the transferor acquired the property on a death and the acquisition was itself a conditionally exempt transfer.

[*IHTA 1984, s 30(3); The Tax and Civil Partnership Regulations 2005, SI 2005/3229, Reg 11*].

Interaction with potentially exempt transfers

[33.5] The above provisions are disregarded in determining whether a transfer is a POTENTIALLY EXEMPT TRANSFER (**38**). Where the transfer in question is a potentially exempt transfer, no claim under the above provisions can be made until the transferor has died. [*IHTA 1984, s 30(3A)(3B); FA 1986, Sch 19 para 7*]. If the transferor survives for seven years after the transfer, the potentially exempt transfer becomes an exempt transfer and there is no need to make a claim for conditional exemption. If the transferor dies within the seven-year period, a claim for conditional exemption may be made and the question whether any property is appropriate for designation is determined by reference to circumstances existing after the transferor's death. [*IHTA 1984, s 31(1A); FA 1986, Sch 19 para 8*]. There is no conditional exemption if the property has been disposed of by sale before the transferor's death [*IHTA 1984, s 30(3C); FA 1986, Sch 19 para 7*] but a potentially exempt transfer which would have proved to be a chargeable transfer is an exempt transfer to the extent that the property has or could be designated under **33.2** above and, after the transfer in question and before the transferor's death, has been disposed of by way of sale by private treaty or otherwise to one of the bodies listed in **33.29** below or has been accepted by the Board in satisfaction of tax (see **35.10** PAYMENT OF TAX). [*IHTA 1984, s 26A; FA 1986, Sch 19 para 6*].

Where only part of a property is granted conditional exemption it is the actual transfer of value which is exempted rather than the property itself. Accordingly, the District Valuer should value the entire property and then apportion this figure on a just and reasonable approach between the value attributable to the heritage property and that attributable to the taxable non-heritage property. (VOA IHT manual, section 20, para 20.13).

Undertakings

[33.6] An undertaking must be given, by such a person as the Board think appropriate in the circumstances of the case, that, until the person beneficially entitled to the property dies or the property is disposed of:

(i) in the case of property under **33.2**(a) above, the property will be kept permanently in the UK and will not leave it temporarily except for a purpose and a period approved by the Board; and such steps as are agreed with the Board will be taken for the preservation of the property and for securing reasonable access to the public (but confidential documents may be excluded altogether or to a limited extent from the public access requirement), and

(ii) in the case of land under **33.2**(b), such steps as are agreed with the Board will be taken for its maintenance and the preservation of its character, and for securing reasonable access to the public, and

(iii) in the case of buildings, amenity land or objects within **33.2**(c)–(e), such steps as are agreed with the Board will be taken for its maintenance, repair and preservation and for securing reasonable access to the public and, if it is an object within **33.2**(e) above, for keeping it associated with the building concerned.

[*IHTA 1984, ss 30(1), 31(2)–(4); FA 1985, s 95, Sch 26 paras 1, 2(3)*].

Where the transfer in question is a POTENTIALLY EXEMPT TRANSFER (**38**) which has proved to be a chargeable lifetime transfer and at the time of the transferor's death an undertaking has been given by the appropriate person under *IHTA 1984, Sch 4 para 3(3)* (maintenance funds for historic buildings, see **33.23** below) or *TCGA 1992, s 258* with respect to any of the property to which the value transferred by the transfer is attributable, that undertaking is treated as having been given under the above provisions. [*IHTA 1984, s 31(4G); FA 1986, Sch 19 para 8*].

Public access

Reasonable access to the public. For undertakings given on or after 31 July 1998, public access cannot be confined to access by prior appointment only. [*IHTA 1984, s 31(4FA); FA 1998, Sch 25 para 5*]. As a result, in the case of objects within **33.2**(a) above, the 'V & A list' procedure described below ceases to apply. Where an undertaking whether original or a replacement undertaking is given on or after 31 July 1998 then:

- public access to the tax-exempt assets cannot be restricted to 'appointment' access through the owner or his/her agent (see former Inland Revenue letter sent to owners of conditionally exempt chattels on 31 March 1999 below);
- the owner may be required to publicise the terms of the undertaking and any other information relating to exempt assets which will otherwise be considered confidential.

[*FA 1998, Sch 25 paras 5, 6*].

'*Public access*', above, means that all owners of exempt assets will have to provide a measure of 'open' access to those assets, but this will only be in accordance with the terms agreed with HMRC set out in the undertaking. The law requires 'public access' to be reasonable and this will depend upon the nature and type of the asset as well as the preservation and maintenance needs of that asset. See *Re Applications to Vary the Undertakings of 'A' and 'B'* [2005] STC SCD 103 Sp C 439 below. For example, the measure of access for a large building may not be reasonable in the case of a smaller building or, say, a delicate object. In this latter case it may be appropriate to mix 'open' access with 'appointment' access if the preservation of the object requires it. In certain circumstances it may be appropriate to suspend or exclude public access. This occurred during 2001 when the foot and mouth outbreak resulted in the restriction of access to land and buildings which was exempted from IHT on condition that the appointed land and buildings were open to access by the general public. Provided the risk assessment at the time warranted the suspension of access to the land or building then it was not be necessary to make up the lost days of access later in that year. The then CTO stated that a typical case for suspension of access by the public would be where a historic building is bounded by farm land that was subject to foot and mouth restrictions. See IR Tax Bulletin Special Edition — Foot and Mouth Disease, May 2001, IR Press Release 18 March 2002. Now where there is a disaster or emergency interest on unpaid tax it may be deferred where the Commissioners agree such a case warrants it. [*FA 2008, s 135*].

Chattels exemption

For chattels exempt in their own right 'open' access may be provided by displaying the objects at:

- the residence of the individual or at the place the object(s) is kept (restricted to the area in which the object is displayed, unless the building itself is tax exempt in which case this facility will not apply);
- a museum or gallery to which the public have access (see Revised DCMS model loan agreement for AIL in-situ offer revised at 30 December 2002);
- any other building open to the public, e.g. a local Record office;
- the appropriate European Heritage Open Days event free of charge (i.e. Heritage Open Days (England), Doors Open Days (Scotland), London Open House, European Open Days in Wales and Northern Ireland); and
- local, regional or touring exhibitions.

Objects may be loaned for display in the public collection of a national institution, local authority, university or independent museum and this period will count as 'open'. Historically associated objects will normally be displayed in the building concerned.

If a chattel is located in a building which is itself tax exempt the period of access will be the same as that for the building, i.e. 25 to 156 days each year. In other situations the minimum period will be 5 to 100 days a year and the Museums, Archives and Libraries Council will advise HMRC where this applies. HMRC may be prepared to consider a two-year accounting period rather than a one-year period in certain circumstances.

In the case of exempt buildings and their amenity land the minimum period of 'open' access will be 25 to 156 days each year. In the case of land the access will, in general, be during daylight hours and on defined routes but with agreed closure periods for sporting activities, land management, nature conservation, etc. In most circumstances it will be open to the individual to charge a fee to view the exempt building but this must be reasonable from the point of view of the public at large.

Access disclosure

Publicising access and undertakings is a requirement of conditional exemption for heritage assets. The *Finance Act 1998* tightened up on the rules and individuals will now be required to disclose more information. HMRC Inheritance Tax will expect the individual to make such an undertaking available to any member of the public who asks to view it. The undertaking in relation to the building or exempt chattel may be displayed at the premises and HMRC may also enter the details on their internet website. HMRC issued a letter on 31 March 1999 to all owners of conditionally exempt chattels stating that they should reply in writing detailing the 25 days the property would be open to the public without prior appointment. Subsequently, HMRC indicated a degree of flexibility on the time limit for replies. HMRC issued a form titled 'Proposal' with the letter for signature by owners in connection with publicising their undertakings as follows:

> 'I/We shall give appropriate publicity to the public access arrangements, namely by agreeing that the Inland Revenue may:
>
> - publicise the availability of this access via the internet or other appropriate means, and
> - provide anyone who requests it with a copy of the undertaking.
>
> I/We further agree to make public my/our undertakings in relation to conditionally exempt property and to disclose and/or copy them as appropriate to any third party who asks.'

The information required for the website will be a description of each object, full address of the building and opening times, and name, address and telephone number of the contact person (i.e. owner, agent, etc.). In the case of land HMRC may also require a copy of the undertaking together with any related management plan to be given free of charge to any local authority in which the land is situated. The authority and HMRC's advisers (e.g. Countryside Commission) will be free to make this information available to members of the public. The owner of amenity land must show the location of the land including the National Grid references for all points of entry onto that land. HMRC also require the name, address and telephone number of the person who can give further details of the amenity land on request. In the case of scenic land the owner may be required to advertise the details in the local tourist office and/or town hall, display map boards at each point of entry to the land and waymark the permitted paths, bridleways, etc.

A further letter was issued from the Capital Taxes Office [now HMRC Inheritance Tax] accepting that no obligation exists for owners to make proposals regarding the variation of existing undertakings. Also, HMRC have conceded that it is dependent on them to review existing undertakings and then make proposals for variations as well as leaving some existing arrangements in place under the old 'V & A List Arrangements'. See below. In addition the personal circumstances of those dictated by existing undertakings are relevant in deciding whether it is 'just and reasonable, in all the circumstances' for the terms of the current undertakings to be altered. [*IHTA 1984, s 35A(2)(c) as inserted by FA 1998, Sch 25 para 10(1)*]. See http://www.hmrc.gov.uk/cto/newsletter.htm, April 2001.

Owners of buildings open to the public may be required to publicise the public access arrangements by:

(1) advertising details in the local paper, tourist office and/or town hall;
(2) advertising details in one of the annual national guides to historic houses, i.e. *Hudson's Historic Houses and Gardens* and *Johansens Historic Houses Castles & Gardens*;
(3) placing a sign at the main entrance of the property with details of opening times; or
(4) informing appropriate local council and education authorities.

For undertakings given before 31 July 1998, the HMRC issued guidelines on what was considered to be reasonable public access as regards works of art etc. within **33.2**(a) above. One option for securing access is for the owner to allow viewing by appointment and, subject to conditions, to lend it for special exhibitions on request to directors or curators of public collections for up to six months in any two-year period. A register ('the V & A list') of objects granted conditional exemption, computerised with database search, is available for public consultation at the Victoria and Albert Museum (London), National Library of Scotland (Edinburgh), National Museum of Wales (Cardiff) and Ulster Museum (Belfast). Access may be obtained through the internet on www.hmrc.gov.uk/heritage/lbsearch.htm Publicity is given to the register in a number of ways and it is updated quarterly to ensure that the individual (who, for security reasons, does not have to be the owner concerned) shown as a contact point can be consulted. If a prospective viewer is unable to make viewing arrangements HMRC Inheritance Tax should be contacted. Previously a selective audit of the register ensured that undertakings on public access and preservation of objects in the UK were being observed. However, as from 1 April 2000 the Heritage Section took over the responsibility and now deals with owners and their agents directly. The reports are expected to be completed and returned to the Heritage Section within two months of request. (Inland Revenue Press Releases 17 December 1992, 10 May 1993, 2 August 1993 and subsequent Press Releases issued quarterly). See also former Inland Revenue Tax Bulletin August 1993 p 89. See CTO Newsletter December 1996 in Chapter 61 and IHT Newsletter October 2001.

Publicity requirements regarding public access to land within **33.2**(b) above were given in HC Written Answer 9 February 1987, Hansard Vol 110, Col 35. Undertakings regarding such land were reviewed every five years to ensure they are being observed (HC Written Answer 18 June 1992, Hansard Vol 209, Cols 629, 630). See also former Inland Revenue Tax Bulletin August 1993 p 89.

Additional undertaking for amenity land

[33.7] An *additional* undertaking is required for amenity land within **33.2**(d) above, called the '*relevant land*', which is over and above the requirement for an undertaking at (iii) above. The person seeking conditional exemption for the relevant land must provide (or secure, if necessary, from another person) undertaking(s) that until the death of the person beneficially entitled to the building for which the relevant land is an amenity or any other amenity land of that building which is either between it and the relevant land or physically closely connected with one of them, or until that property is disposed of, such steps as are agreed with the Board will be taken for the maintenance, repair, preservation and securing of reasonable public access to the building or other amenity land. Where different persons are entitled (either beneficially or otherwise) to the building and the other amenity land, separate undertakings are required in respect of each by whomever the Board think appropriate. These undertakings are required notwithstanding the fact that another undertaking is already effective for that building or other amenity land. Such undertakings will have been given with respect to the building etc., whereas the additional undertaking, although relating to the maintenance etc. of the building etc., is given with respect to the relevant amenity land. [*IHTA 1984, s 31(4A)–(4F); FA 1985, ss 94, 95, Sch 26 para 2(4)*].

Variations of undertakings

[33.8] Undertakings may be varied by agreement between the Board and the person bound by the undertaking. Failing such agreement, a Commissioner may approve a proposed variation by the Board:

- for any undertaking given on or after 31 July 1998; or
- for any undertaking given before 31 July 1998 (unless there has been a chargeable event after the giving of the undertaking and before that date) but only so as to impose wider requirements for:
  - (i) public access where existing undertakings are confined to access by prior appointment only; and/or
  - (ii) publication of details of the exemption.

For replacement undertakings sought on or after 31 July 1998 to preserve an existing exemption (IHT or CTT) the person will need to comply with the rules on undertakings in force on the date the undertaking is given. [*FA 1998, Sch 25 para 7*]. This does not affect any replacement undertakings given under the rules relating to estate duty. If the conditionally exempt item is sold there will normally be a charge to tax but a replacement undertaking may be given for another item. However, the Heritage Section of HMRC Inheritance Tax should be advised promptly of the change in such circumstances or they will be in breach of the undertaking. Form IHT100 (event form IHT 100f) should be completed where there is an ending of a conditional exemption and this should be delivered within six months from the end of month in which the event giving rise to the tax charge occurs. Form Cap100 is appropriate for the ending of a CTT conditional exemption. There is no prescribed form of account for the ending of an Estate Duty conditional exemption. In order to avoid interest and penalties an early submission of Form IHT 100 is recommended.

HMRC had stated that about 1,000 cases needed review arising from the undertakings given before 31 July 1998 but this would take some time. Originally, suggestions for access on terms not limited to access by prior appointment were sought by the end of June 1999 but this was extended to the end of the following month July. HMRC will accept advance proposals with regard to public access without prior appointment and if they consider that changes should be made to the undertaking and these cannot be mutually agreed then a right of appeal to the Special Commissioners exists. Up to the end of a six-month period the matter can be referred to the Special Commissioners who may either confirm the HMRC's proposals or reject them according to whether they consider the proposals just and reasonable. The Special Commissioners will only consider the reasonableness of HMRC proposals, not those of the person bound. There is no statutory right of appeal against the Special Commissioners' ruling but either side may be able to appeal to the Court for a review on a point of law. In *Re Applications to Vary the Undertakings of 'A' and 'B'* [2005] STC SCD 103 Sp C 439 HMRC had agreed that the owners of certain valuable works of art should have the benefit of 'conditional exemption' from IHT. Subsequently, HMRC made applications, under *IHTA 1984, s 35A*, to vary the undertakings so as to give wider publicity to the existence of the items, and wider access to them. The Special Commissioner dismissed HMRC's applications, holding that 'the accumulated burdens placed on the particular owner' would 'so outweigh the benefit to the public as to make it neither just nor reasonable for me to direct that the proposals take effect'. There would be 'a serious intrusion into the family lives of the owners', and 'the increased risks of theft and damage to the owners' possessions' would go 'beyond what Parliament had in mind when empowering the inclusion of extended access requirements and publication requirements'. [*IHTA 1984, s 35A (2)(c)*]. This has now been acknowledged by HMRC Inheritance Tax in their letter to owners and advisers and it is thought that HMRC will now make their requests for greater access less burdensome following the above case.

HMRC will consider changes to their proposals by the person bound but the law:

- requires the undertaking to be appropriate to the asset concerned, so when they consider the changes they have regard to any change in the personal circumstances of the person bound; and
- does not provide for any appeal if the proposals put forward cannot be accepted.

[*IHTA 1984, s 35A; FA 1998, Sch 25 para 8*].

Claims

[33.9] A claim should be made on Form IHT 420. Copies are available from HMRC Inheritance Tax, Nottingham at the address shown in **2.19** ACCOUNTS AND RETURNS. In relation to transfers of property after 16 March 1998, the claim must be made no more than two years after the transfer of value or, in the case of potentially exempt transfers, the date of death. In either case the Board may allow a longer period. [*IHTA 1984, s 30(3BA); FA 1998, Sch 25 para 2*]. The Board will consider each application to extend the two-year period on its own merits but have stated that any oversight or mistake on the applicant's part or their adviser's, or the making of a post-death variation, will not normally by itself be an acceptable reason to allow a late claim. A primary claim for agricultural or business property relief may delay matters beyond the two-year claim period in which case a protective claim may be advisable. Normally a claim may not be made in advance except in the cases of:

- any claim for exemption from the IHT ten-yearly charge on discretionary trusts, as such claims must be made, and assets designated, before the date of the charge, but note that this rule will cease to apply with effect from Royal Assent to the Finance (No 2) Act 2015 following which a claim will be admissible within two years after the date of charge or such longer time as HMRC may allow; and
- approval of a proposed heritage maintenance fund.

[*IHTA 1984, s 79(3), Sch 4 para 1(2)*].

HMRC expect applicants to make their claims without undue delay.

Chargeable event

[33.10] Where there has been a conditionally exempt transfer of any property, tax is charged on the first occurrence after the transfer (or, if the transfer was a POTENTIALLY EXEMPT TRANSFER (38) after the transferor's death) of a chargeable event. Where properties are '*associated properties*' (i.e. a building within 33.2(c) above and any amenity land or objects within 33.2(d) or (e) related to that building), tax is chargeable on the first event after a conditionally exempt transfer (or, if the transfer was a potentially exempt transfer, after the transferor's death) of *any* of the associated properties (or part) on the *whole* of each of the associated properties (or part) for which the event is a chargeable event. Subject to exceptions below, there is a '*chargeable event*' on a material failure to observe an undertaking within 33.3 above, on the death of any person beneficially entitled to any property and on any disposal of any property. [*IHTA 1984, ss 32(1)–(3), 32A(1)–(4); FA 1985, Sch 26 para 4; FA 1986, Sch 19 paras 9, 10; FA 1998, Sch 25 para 7*].

Where a chargeable event arises in respect of heritage property which was allowed conditional exemption on the death of the owner, the lower 36% rate of IHT cannot be claimed on that event even if the remaining estate had satisfied the conditions for that rate (see 52.13).

Exceptions

[33.11] There is no chargeable event in the following situations.

(a) If a failure to observe an undertaking or a disposal relates to one only of the associated properties or part of it, and the associated properties as a whole have not been materially affected, the Board may, if so satisfied, direct that the chargeable event be limited to the property or part actually affected by the failure of undertaking, etc. [*IHTA 1984, s 32A(10); FA 1985, s 95, Sch 25 para 4*].

(b) There is no chargeable event on death if within three years the personal representatives (or trustees or person next entitled if settled property, see 33.18 *et seq.* below) make a disposal of property by way of sale by private treaty or gift to one of the national bodies listed in *IHTA 1984, Sch 3*, or where the property is accepted in lieu of tax. A disposal is likewise not a chargeable event where it is one of this nature. Where there is then a subsequent death or disposal there is no chargeable event with respect to the property (or part) concerned unless there has been another, intervening, conditionally exempt transfer. The disposal of one or part of a group of 'associated properties' to a national body or in lieu of tax does not mean that the remaining associated properties are not chargeable. Conditional exemption only continues for the property retained if the necessary undertaking is given by such person or persons as the Board thinks appropriate. [*IHTA 1984, ss 32(4), 32A(5)–(7); FA 1985, Sch 26 para 4; FA 1998, Sch 25 para 7*].

(c) Death, or disposal otherwise than by sale, is not a chargeable event if the transfer of value thereby made is itself a conditionally exempt transfer or if the necessary undertaking is given by such person or persons as the Board think appropriate. [*IHTA 1984, ss 32(5)(5AA), 32A(8)(8A); FA 1985, Sch 26 para 4; FA 1998, Sch 25 para 7*].

(d) A disposal by sale of one or part of a group of associated properties gives rise to a chargeable event limited to that part of the associated properties actually disposed of (if it is not otherwise exempt) if the necessary undertaking is given by such person or persons as the Board think appropriate. [*IHTA 1984, s 32A(9); FA 1985, Sch 26 para 4; FA 1998, Sch 25 para 7*].

The person liable

The person liable to pay the tax chargeable is

(i) in the case of breach of undertaking or death, the person who, if the property were sold at that time, would be entitled to receive (whether for his benefit or not) the proceeds of sale or any income arising from them; or

(ii) in the case of disposal, the person by whom or for whose benefit the property is disposed of.

[*IHTA 1984, s 207(1)–(2B); FA 1985, Sch 26 para 10*].

Transferability of nil rate bands and the deferred charge, etc.

[33.12] From 9 October 2007 married couples and those in civil partnerships will be allowed to transfer any unused nil rate band on their death to the surviving spouse or civil partner (referred to in the legislation respectively as the 'deceased' and the 'survivor'). In addition, the transferable unused nil rate band will be available to the widow, widower or surviving civil partner irrespective of when the original spouse or civil partner died. [*IHTA 1984, s 8A* as inserted by *FA 2008, s 10, Sch 4 para 2*]. This may have been during the period when Capital Transfer Tax operated or when Estate Duty applied in which, rare, cases the new provisions are adapted to those situations. The personal nil rate band maximum of the deceased is the amount shown in the appropriate Table depending on the date of death as stipulated in *FA 2008, Sch 4 para 11*. [*IHTA 1984, s 8C(1)–(5)* as adapted by *FA 2008, Sch 4 para 11*].

See Example 2 in **21.10** EXEMPT TRANSFERS. In cases where there has been a deferred charge on, say, heritage property such as in *IHTA 1984, ss 32(1)–(3), 32A(1)–(4)* and there is subsequently unused nil rate band available to the surviving spouse or civil partner, then that charge is taken into account before calculating the unused nil rate band of the surviving spouse or civil partner. See Example 1 below. If there is more than one deferred charge before the transfer of the nil rate band to the spouse or civil partner these deferred charges similarly reduce the nil rate band that may be claimed. See Example 2. Further, if there is a deferred charge after the nil rate band of the deceased has been claimed by the surviving spouse's personal representatives then any available nil rate band to be claimed against the deferred charge will be reduced by the amount claimed by the survivor's personal representatives. See Example 3 below. [*IHTA 1984, ss 8A, 8C as inserted by FA 2008, Sch 4 para 2*]. See HMRC Inheritance Tax manual IHTM43044–IHTM43046.

Example 1

Chargeable event during lifetime of surviving spouse or civil partner

C died in August 2002 having made chargeable transfers of £125,000 and previously, a conditionally exempt gift of heritage property to his brother, B. C had left the balance of his estate to his wife, D. In October 2008, the heritage property conditional exemption is breached when it is valued at £104,000. D dies in February 2010.

The claim for the unused nil rate band by D's personal representatives must be calculated after taking into account the proportion of C's nil rate band used to cover previous chargeable transfers and the heritage property conditional exemption breach. C had used ½ of his nil rate band on his death (i.e. (£250,000 – £125,000) ÷ £250,000 × 100%) so at the time of the chargeable event in October 2008 the current nil rate band is £312,000. As the amount on which tax is chargeable is £104,000 (see below) this is the amount referred to as TA below and the nil rate band at the date of breach is NRBME below. This is calculated to be one-third (i.e. £104,000 ÷ £312,000) and this is deducted from the amount of the available nil rate band on C's death i.e. ½ – ⅓ = 16.667%. At the time of D's death when the nil rate band has increased to £325,000 the remaining portion of C's nil rate band available to D's personal representatives at that time is £54,168 (i.e. £325,000 × 16.667%). [*IHTA 1984, s 8C* as inserted by *FA 2008, Sch 4 para 2*].

Notes to the example

(A) The transferable amount of the unused nil rate band of the predeceased C to D in this example is calculated by applying the unused nil rate band under *IHTA 1984, s 8A(2)(4)* as follows:

$$\text{Percentage} = \left(\frac{\text{E}}{\text{NRBMD}} - \frac{\text{TA}}{\text{NRBME}}\right) \times 100$$

where:

M = maximum amount that could be transferred on the predeceased person's death where it is chargeable at the nil rate band at that time, i.e. £250,000;

VT = value actually transferred by the chargeable transfer or nil if applicable, i.e. £125,000;
E = the amount by which M above is greater than VT above, i.e. £125,000 (£250,000 – £125,000);
NRBMD = the nil rate band maximum applying at the time of the deceased spouse's or civil partner's death, i.e. £250,000;
TA = the amount on which tax is charged i.e £104,000;
NRBME = the nil rate band maximum at the time of the event giving rise to the deferred charge, i.e. £312,000.

(B) C's estate at death will be increased to take account of the chargeable event to determine the rates applicable to any later chargeable event as in Example 2 below. [*IHTA 1984, s 34(1)(2); FA 1985, Sch 26 para 5*].

	£
Cumulative total of previous chargeable transfers of relevant person C	125,000
Valuation of conditionally exempt property	104,000
Revised cumulative total for relevant person C	£229,000

Example 2

Two or more chargeable events during lifetime of surviving spouse or civil partner

C died in August 2002 having made chargeable transfers of £125,000 and previously, a conditionally exempt gift of heritage property to his brother, B. C had left the balance of his estate to his wife, D. In October 2008 and December 2008, the two items of conditionally exempt property are sold by B for £63,415 each and capital gains tax of £11,415 is payable. D dies in February 2011.

The claim for the unused nil rate band by D's personal representatives must be calculated after taking into account the proportion of C's nil rate band used to cover previous chargeable transfers and the heritage property conditional exemption breach. C had used ½ of his nil rate band on his death (i.e. (£250,000 – £125,000) ÷ £250,000 × 100%). At the time of the chargeable events in October and December 2008 the nil rate band is £312,000. As the amounts on which tax is chargeable after CGT is £52,000 on each chargeable event these amounts are referred to as TA below and the nil rate band at the date of sale is NRBME below. These amounts are each calculated to be one-sixth (i.e. £52,000 ÷ £312,000) and are deducted from the amount of the available nil rate band on C's death (i.e. ½ – (1/6 + 1/6) = 16.667%). At the time of D's death, when the nil rate band has increased to £325,000, the portion of C's nil rate band still available to the personal representatives at that time is therefore £54,168 (i.e. £325,000 × 16.667%). [*IHTA 1984, s 8C(2)(3)* as inserted by *FA 2008, Sch 4 para 2*].

Notes to the example

(A) The transferable amount of the unused nil rate band of the predeceased C to D in this example is calculated by applying the unused nil rate band under *IHTA 1984, s 8A(2)(4)* as follows:

$$\text{Percentage} = \frac{E}{NRBMD} - \left(\frac{TA}{NRBME} + \frac{TA}{NRBME}\right) \times 100$$

where:

M = maximum amount that could be transferred on the predeceased person's death where it is chargeable at the nil rate band at that time, i.e. £250,000;

VT = value actually transferred by the chargeable transfer or nil if applicable, i.e. £125,000;

E = the amount by which M above is greater than VT above, i.e. £125,000 (£250,000 – £125,000);

NRBMD = the nil rate band maximum applying at the time of the deceased spouse's or civil partner's death, i.e. £250,000;

TA = the amount on which tax is charged, i.e. £52,000;

NRBME = the nil rate band maximum at the time of the event giving rise to the deferred charge, i.e. £312,000 but if the second sale had been in December 2009 this figure would have been £325,000 not £312,000.

		£
Cumulative total of previous chargeable transfers of relevant person C		125,000
Net sale proceeds of conditionally exempt property October 2008	63,415	
Deduct capital gains tax payable	(11,415)	52,000
Net sale proceeds of conditionally exempt property December 2008	63,415	
Deduct capital gains tax payable	(11,415)	
Chargeable transfer		52,000
Revised cumulative total for relevant person C		£229,000

Example 3

Chargeable event after the death of the surviving spouse or civil partner

C died in August 2002 having made chargeable transfers of £125,000 and previously, a conditionally exempt gift of heritage property to his brother, B. C had left the balance of his estate to his wife, D. D dies in February 2011 with an estate valued at £350,000. In October 2011, the conditionally exempt property is sold for £300,000 and capital gains tax of £54,000 is payable.

The claim for the unused nil rate band by D's personal representatives on form IHT402 (previously IHT216) has already been made by the time the conditionally exempt property is sold and becomes chargeable. C had used half of his nil rate band on his death (i.e. (£250,000 – £125,000) ÷ £250,000 × 100%) so D's personal representatives are entitled to claim ½ × £325,000. D's nil rate band of £325,000 added to the predeceased C's available nil rate band of £162,500 (i.e. (£250,000 – £125,000) ÷ £250,000 = ½ × £325,000) makes a total of £487,500. Of this amount, £350,000 is used to cover the estate of D of which £25,000 is part of C's original nil rate band. In October 2011, the property is sold by the brother B for £300,000 and capital gains tax of £52,000 is payable, making net proceeds of £248,000. Therefore, the unused proportion of C's nil rate band of £200,000 (i.e. (£125,000 + £25,000) – £350,000) is available to set against the net sale proceeds of the conditionally exempt property as below. [*IHTA 1984, s 8C(4)(5)* as inserted by *FA 2008, Sch 4 para 2*].

Notes to the example

(A) In a case of breach of undertaking or death the person who is liable to pay the tax is the person who, if the property were sold at that time, would be entitled to receive (whether for his benefit or not) the proceeds of sale or any income arising from them, i.e. B. The tax is due six months after the end of the month in which the disposal took place. [*IHTA 1984, s 226(4)*].

(B) If the relevant person is dead, the rate of tax will be the rate applicable to the property if it were added to the value of C's estate on death and formed the highest part of that value.

		£
Cumulative total of previous chargeable transfers of relevant person C		125,000
Value of property at date of sale in October 2011	300,000	
Deduct capital gains tax	(52,000)	
Chargeable transfer		248,000
Revised cumulative total for relevant person C		£373,000
Inheritance tax payable after deducting the available nil rate band (by reference to death rates in February 2010), i.e. £350,000 – £150,000 (£125,000 + £25,000) = £200,000 – £248,000 £48,000 at 40% = £19,200 payable by B		

Conditional exemption on death before 7 April 1976

[33.13] Similar rules apply in respect of conditional exemption granted under previous legislation on deaths before 7 April 1976. [*FA 1975, ss 32, 34(3)–(6); IHTA 1984, ss 35(2), 207(4)(5), Sch 5 paras 1, 3(1)–(4), Sch 6 para 4(2); FA 1985, Sch 26 paras 7, 13; FA 1986, Sch 19 para 12*].

Charge to tax

[33.14] Different provisions apply according to the date of the conditionally exempt transfer or occasion (see **33.18** below) on which the chargeable event arises. In each case the tax is due six months after the end of the month in which the chargeable event occurs. [*IHTA 1984, s 226(4); FA 1985, Sch 26 para 11*]. See **33.10** above for person liable to pay the tax.

A conditionally exempt transfer can arise during lifetime or on death. The tax on a subsequent chargeable event is on the value of the property at the time of the event (i.e. there is no 'grossing-up') and where the event is a disposal on a sale not intended to confer any gratuitous benefit on any person and at arm's length between unconnected persons (or on similar terms), the value is equal to the sale proceeds (with proportionate reduction where the conditional exemption applied only to part of the property) [*IHTA 1984, s 33(1)(a)(3)(4)*] less any capital gains tax chargeable. [*TCGA 1992, s 258(8)*].

The rate at which tax on a subsequent chargeable event is charged is determined by reference to the relevant person. [*IHTA 1984, s 33(1)(b)*].

Relevant person

The 'relevant person' is:

(i) if there has been only one conditionally exempt transfer or one conditionally exempt occasion (see **33.18** below) before the event, the person who made that transfer or the person who is the settlor in relation to the settlement in respect of which the occasion occurred;

(ii) if there have been two or more such transfers or occasions, and the last was before, or only one of them was within, the period of thirty years ending with the event, the person who made the last transfer or the person who is the settlor in relation to the settlement in respect of which the last occasion occurred;

(iii) if there have been two or more such transfers or occasions within that period, whichever person or settlor the Board may select. [*IHTA 1984, ss 33(5), 78(3)*].

The rate of tax will be, subject to the exceptions below,

(a) if the relevant person is alive, the rate applicable to the property if it were added to the cumulative total of his chargeable transfers at the date of the chargeable event and tax calculated using rates applicable to lifetime transfer. The amount is only notionally added for this purpose and does not affect the rate of tax on later transfers made by the relevant person unless he is also the person who made the last conditionally exempt transfer (see **33.16** below). The rates are not affected by the death of the relevant person after the chargeable event. [*IHTA 1984, ss 33(1)(b)(i)(2A), 34(1); FA 1986, Sch 19 para 11*].

(b) if the relevant person is dead, the rate applicable to the property if it were added to the value of his estate on death and formed the highest part of that value. If the relevant person made the conditionally exempt transfer on death (but the property was not treated as forming part of his estate under the rules relating to GIFTS WITH RESERVATION (**22**)) the death rates are used. In any other case, tax is calculated using the rates applicable to lifetime transfers. If the relevant person is the settlor and the settlement was created on his death, the death rates are used, if not tax is calculated using the rates applicable to lifetime transfers. If the chargeable event occurs after tax is reduced by the substitution of a new table of rates, the new rates are used. Where the relevant person died before 18 March 1986, nevertheless, the amount of tax payable is calculated as if the amendments to *IHTA 1984, s 7* in *FA 1986, 19 Sch 2* (rates of tax for transfers within seven years of death and tapering relief) had applied at the time of death. [*IHTA 1984, ss 9, 33(1)(b)(ii)(2), 78(4), Sch 2 para 5; FA 1985, Sch 26 para 5; FA 1986, Sch 19 paras 11, 19, 41*].

Exceptions

If the relevant person is determined as in (i) to (iii) above by reference to a conditionally exempt occasion (see **33.18** below)

(A) the rates under (a) and (b) above will be reduced to **30%** of the full charge if the occasion occurred before the first ten-year anniversary (see **43.6** SETTLEMENTS: DISCRETIONARY TRUSTS AND OTHER TRUSTS OF RELEVANT

PROPERTY) to fall after the property became comprised in the settlement concerned and **60%** of the full charge if the event occurred after the first and before the second ten-year anniversary.

(B) the rate under (b) above is, where the relevant person died before 13 March 1975, and subject to (A) above, the rate applicable to the property as if the relevant person died when the chargeable event occurred and the chargeable amount were added to, and formed the highest part of, the value on which estate duty was chargeable when he in fact died. [*IHTA 1984, s 78(4)(5)*].

Conditionally exempt transfers or occasions in (i) to (iii) above do not include those made before any previous chargeable event on the same property or before any event mentioned in **33.10**(b) above. [*IHTA 1984, s 33(6); FA 1985, Sch 26 para 6*].

Tax credit

[33.15] Subject to below, where there is a chargeable transfer after a conditionally exempt transfer of the same property (wholly or in part), any tax charged is allowed as a credit:

(a) if the chargeable transfer is also a chargeable event (see **33.10** above), against the tax chargeable on that chargeable event;

(b) if the chargeable transfer is not also a chargeable event, against the tax chargeable on the next chargeable event on the property.

Where after a conditionally exempt transfer of any property there is a potentially exempt transfer of all or part of that property, and *either* the potentially exempt transfer is a chargeable event with respect to the property *or* after the potentially exempt transfer but before the transferor's death a chargeable event occurs with respect to the property, the tax charged under the above provisions on the chargeable event is allowed as a credit against any tax which may become chargeable by reason of the potentially exempt transfer proving to be a chargeable transfer. No relief is due under (a) or (b) above. [*IHTA 1984, s 33(7)(8); FA 1986, Sch 19 para 11*].

Example 4

Chargeable event during lifetime of relevant person

C, who has made previous chargeable transfers during August 2003 of £230,000, makes a conditionally exempt gift of property in February 2004. In October 2010, the property is sold for £500,000 and capital gains tax of £90,000 is payable.

		£
Cumulative total of previous chargeable transfers of relevant person		230,000
Net sale proceeds of conditionally exempt property	500,000	
Deduct capital gains tax payable	(90,000)	
Chargeable transfer		410,000

Revised cumulative total for relevant person	£640,000
Inheritance tax payable (by reference to lifetime rates in October 2010)	
£315,000 at 20% = £63,000	

Example 5

Chargeable event after relevant person is dead

D died in April 1995 leaving a taxable estate of £325,000 together with conditionally exempt property valued at £600,000 at the breach in October 2010.

	£
Value of relevant person's estate at death	350,000
Value of conditionally exempt property at date of breach	600,000
	£950,000

Inheritance tax payable (by reference to full rates applicable in October 2010)
£600,000 at 40% = £240,000

Example 6

Property inherited in 1984 from A's estate by B, who gave the necessary undertakings so that the property is conditionally exempt, is given in December 2009 by B to C. C agrees to pay any inheritance tax arising from the transfer but does not wish to give the necessary undertakings, so a chargeable event arises. B dies in March 2011.

		£
A's estate at date of death in 1984		180,000
B's cumulative chargeable transfers at date of chargeable event in December 2009 (all in 2009/10)		86,000
Value of property at date of chargeable event		266,000
Inheritance tax on chargeable event (subject to tax credit)		
		£
Value of A's estate at date of death		180,000
Value of property at date of chargeable event		266,000
		£446,000
Inheritance tax payable		
£121,000 (£446,000 – 325,000) at 40% =		£48,400
Inheritance tax on B's gift		
Cumulative total of previous transfers		86,000
Value of property gifted	266,000	
Deduct annual exemption 2010/11	3,000	263,000
		£349,000
Inheritance tax arising on gift of £263,000		£9,600
Tax credit		
IHT on B's gift		9,600
IHT on chargeable event	48,400	

Deduct tax credit	(9,600)	
		38,800
Total inheritance tax borne		£48,400

Effect of chargeable event on subsequent transfers

[33.16] The person who made the last conditionally exempt transfer before the chargeable event (not necessarily the relevant person) will have his cumulative total of chargeable transfers increased by the amount of the property on which tax is paid on the chargeable event and, consequently, the rate of tax applicable to all his subsequent chargeable transfers is increased. Where that person is dead, but he is the relevant person in relation to a later chargeable event, the value of his estate at death will be increased by the amount on which tax is paid on the first chargeable event to determine the rates applicable to the later chargeable event. [*IHTA 1984, s 34(1)(2); FA 1985, Sch 26 para 5*].

Settlor

[33.17] If the 'relevant person' is not the person who made the last conditionally exempt transfer of the property and at the time of the chargeable event, or at any time within the preceding five years, the property is or has been comprised in a settlement made within 30 years before that event and a person who is a settlor of that settlement has made a conditionally exempt transfer of the property within those 30 years (excluding any made before any previous chargeable event on the same property or before any event mentioned in **33.10**(b) above), then the amount of the property chargeable at the time of the chargeable event is added to the cumulative total of the settlor (and not to that of the person who made the last conditionally exempt transfer). [*IHTA 1984, s 34(3)(4); FA 1985, Sch 26 para 6*].

Where the last conditionally exempt transaction before a chargeable event was a conditionally exempt occasion (see **33.18** below) as opposed to a conditionally exempt transfer, the above does not apply. [*IHTA 1984, s 78(6)*].

Example 7

Multiple conditionally exempt transfers

D died in December 1983 leaving a conditionally exempt property to his son E. D's taxable estate at death was £230,000. In 1992 E gave the property to his daughter F. F gave the necessary undertakings so this transfer was also conditionally exempt. In December 2010 F sold the property for its market value of £500,000 and paid capital gains tax of £80,000. During 1992 E had made chargeable transfers of £20,000 and he has made no other transfers.

	£	£
Value of relevant person's estate at death		230,000
Net sale proceeds of conditionally exempt property	500,000	
Deduct capital gains tax	80,000	
Chargeable transfer		420,000
		£650,000
Inheritance tax payable by F		
£325,000 at 40% =		£130,000
Previous cumulative total of E		20,000
Add chargeable transfer		420,000
E's revised cumulative total		£440,000

Notes to the example

(A) There have been two conditionally exempt transfers within the period of 30 years ending with the chargeable event in December 2010. HMRC may select either D or E as the 'relevant person' for the purpose of calculating the tax due. The IHT liability will be higher if D is selected. [*IHTA 1984, ss 33(5), 78(3)*].

(B) As F receives the proceeds of sale, she is the person liable to pay the IHT. [*IHTA 1984, s 207(1)*].

(C) Although the IHT is calculated by reference to D's cumulative total, it is E whose cumulative total is adjusted as he made the last conditionally exempt transfer of the property. [*IHTA 1984, s 34(1)*].

(D) As the chargeable event occurs after a reduction in the rates of tax, the new rates are used to calculate the tax payable. [*IHTA 1984, Sch 2 para 5*].

Settlements

Conditionally exempt occasions

[33.18] A national heritage property (see **33.2** above) comprised in a settlement without interests in possession (**43** SETTLEMENTS: DISCRETIONARY TRUSTS AND OTHER TRUSTS OF RELEVANT PROPERTY) may be transferred with exemption from inheritance tax provided:

(a) the property has been comprised in the settlement throughout the six years ending with the transfer, and
(b) on a claim being made, the property is designated by the Board as being within **33.2** above, and
(c) the requisite undertaking (or undertakings) in **33.3** above are given by such person as the Board thinks appropriate.

Any event, other than a transfer, which would otherwise give rise to a charge under the provisions relating to SETTLEMENTS WITHOUT INTERESTS IN POSSESSION **44**, is also exempt if the above conditions are satisfied. An exempt transfer or event as above, is a '*conditionally exempt occasion*'. [*IHTA 1984, s 78(1)(2); FA 1985, s 95, Sch 26 para 8*].

In relation to transfers of property or other events occurring after 16 March 1998, the claim under (b) above must be made no more than two years after the date of the transfer or other event in question, although the Board may allow a longer period. [*IHTA 1984, s 78(1A); FA 1998, Sch 25 para 3*].

Chargeable events

[33.19] Chargeable events giving rise to a tax liability are as in **33.10** above with appropriate modification so that references to a conditionally exempt transfer include references to a conditionally exempt occasion; references to a disposal otherwise than by sale include references to any occasion on which tax is chargeable under the provisions relating to settlements without qualifying interests in possession (other than the ten-year anniversary charge for which see **33.22** below); and references to an undertaking in **33.3** above include the undertaking in **33.18** above. [*IHTA 1984, s 78(3); FA 1985, Sch 26 para 8*].

Example 8

A, who is still alive, settled property and investments on discretionary trusts in September 1988, conditional exemption being granted in respect of designated property. In April 2002, the designated property was appointed absolutely to beneficiary C who gave the necessary undertakings for exemption to continue. However, in February 2011, C sold the property for £135,000 net of costs, suffering a capital gains tax liability of £20,000. At the time of C's sale, A had cumulative chargeable transfers of £40,000.

			£
Cumulative total of previous chargeable transfers of relevant person			40,000
Net sale proceeds of conditionally exempt property			115,000
			£155,000
		Inheritance tax payable by C	
£110,000	At Nil	—	
£5,000	At 20%	1,000	
£115,000		£1,000	£1,000

Notes to the example

(a) A is the relevant person in relation to the chargeable event as he is the person to effect the only conditionally exempt transfer *and* the person who is settlor in relation to the settlement in respect of which the only conditionally exempt occasion arose. [*IHTA 1984, ss 33(5), 78(3)*].

(b) HMRC have discretion to select either the conditionally exempt transfer (by A to the trustees) in 1988 or the conditionally exempt occasion (from the trustees to C) in 2002 as the 'last transaction' for the purposes of determining who is the relevant person. A is the relevant person regardless of which is selected but the HMRC are more likely to choose the earlier transfer as this will result in a greater amount of tax being collected. [*IHTA 1984, ss 33(5), 78(3)(4)*].

(c) The chargeable amount of £115,000 does not increase either A's cumulative total or that of the trustees for the purpose of calculating the IHT liability on any subsequent transfers. As the last conditionally exempt transaction before the chargeable event was a conditionally exempt occasion rather than a conditionally exempt transfer, the provisions of *IHTA 1984, s 34* (which allow for an increase in the cumulative total) do not apply. [*IHTA 1984, s 78(6)*].

Charge to tax

[33.20] The tax on a chargeable event is on the value of the property at the time of the event (i.e. there is no grossing-up) and where the event is a disposal on a sale not intended to confer any gratuitous benefit on any person and at arm's length between unconnected persons (or on similar terms), the value is equal to the sale proceeds (with proportionate reduction where the conditional exemption applied only to part of the property) [*IHTA 1984, ss 33(1)(a)(3)(4), 78(3)*] less any capital gains tax chargeable. [*TCGA 1992, s 258(8)*].

The rate of tax will be as in **33.14** above.

Where a chargeable event arises in respect of settled property which was allowed conditional exemption on an earlier death, the lower 36% rate of IHT cannot be claimed on that event even if the remaining estate had satisfied the conditions for that rate: see **52.13** TRANSFER ON DEATH. Tax is due six months after the end of the month in which the chargeable event occurs. [*IHTA 1984, s 226(4); FA 1985, Sch 26 para 11*].

Tax credit

[33.21] The same credit applies as in **33.14** above with the substitution of 'conditionally exempt occasion' for 'conditionally exempt transfer'.

Exemption from the ten-year anniversary charge

[33.22] Where, on or before the occasion on which property became comprised in the settlement, there has been:

(a) a conditionally exempt transfer of the property, or
(b) a disposal to which *TCGA 1992, s 258(4)* applies (capital gains tax relief for works of art etc.)

there is no liability to the ten-year anniversary charge (see **43.6** SETTLEMENTS: DISCRETIONARY TRUSTS AND OTHER TRUSTS OF RELEVANT PROPERTY) on any such anniversary that falls before such a time as where (a) applies a chargeable event occurs, or where (b) applies, property is treated as sold under *TCGA 1992, s 258(5)*.

Where (a) or (b) above do not apply but the Board have, on a claim, designated under **33.2** above relevant settled property (see **43.3** SETTLEMENTS: DISCRETIONARY TRUSTS AND OTHER TRUSTS OF RELEVANT PROPERTY) and the requisite undertaking or undertakings have been given, the ten-year charge will not apply but a charge will arise on the first occurrence of any event that would be a chargeable event under **33.10** above. Thereafter charges to tax under *IHTA 1984, s 64* will apply. No charge will arise, however, if after the property becomes settled property and before the occurrence of a chargeable event, there has been a conditionally exempt occasion (see **33.18** above) in respect of the property.

Tax is charged on the value of the property at the time of the event. The rate at which tax is charged is the aggregate of the following percentages for each complete successive quarter in 'the relevant period'.

	Cumulative Total
0.25% for each of the first 40 quarters	10%
0.20% for each of the next 40 quarters	8%
0.15% for each of the next 40 quarters	6%
0.10% for each of the next 40 quarters	4%
0.05% for each of the next 40 quarters	2%
Maximum rate chargeable after 50 years	30%

'*Relevant period*' is the period beginning with the latest of

(i) the day on which the settlement commenced; and
(ii) the date of the last ten-year anniversary of the settlement to fall before the day on which the property became comprised in the settlement; and
(iii) 13 March 1975

and ending with the day before the event giving rise to the charge.

'*Quarter*' means a period of three months.

Where National Heritage property became comprised in the settlement in the previous ten years and exemption from the ten-year anniversary charge on qualifying property has been obtained as above, the value of the consideration given for that property is nevertheless taken into account when calculating the rate at which tax is charged on the other (non-national heritage) property in the settlement. The amount is included under *IHTA 1984, s 66(5)(b)* as a previous chargeable transfer by the notional transferor (see **43.8** and **43.10** SSETTLEMENTS: DISCRETIONARY TRUSTS AND OTHER TRUSTS OF RELEVANT PROPERTY).

[*IHTA 1984, ss 61(1), 63, 79(1)–(9); FA 1985, s 95, Sch 26 para 9*].

An account must be delivered within six months from the end of the month in which the chargeable event occurs and any tax payable is due at the expiration of that period. Interest on overdue tax runs from the due date (see **28** INTEREST ON TAX). [*IHTA 1984, ss 216(7), 226(4), 233(1)(c); FA 1985, Sch 26 para 11; FA 1989, s 179(1)*].

The persons liable for the tax are the trustees of the settlement and any person for whose benefit any of the property or income from it is applied at or after the time of the event occasioning the charge. [*IHTA 1984, s 207(3)*].

Example 9

Trustees own National Heritage property for which the necessary undertakings have been given and the property has been designated by the Treasury. The property was settled in July 1974 and is the sole asset of the trust. No appointments or advances of capital have been made. On 30 October 2010, there is a breach of the undertakings. At this date the property is valued at £150,000.

Ten-year anniversary charge

There is no liability in 1984, 1994 or 2004.

Breach in October 2010

Value of property at time of event	£150,000

The relevant period is the period from the date of settlement or, if later, 13 March 1975 to 29 October 2010, i.e. 142 complete quarters.

The rate of tax is

	%
0.25% for 40 quarters	10.00
0.20% for 40 quarters	8.00
0.15% for 40 quarters	6.00
0.10% for 22 quarters	2.20
	26.20%
IHT payable is 26.20% × £150,000 =	£39,300

Maintenance funds for historic buildings

[33.23] The capital transfer tax provisions detailing the conditions to be met to exempt transfers into maintenance funds for historic buildings were introduced, with effect from 2 May 1976, by *FA 1976, s 84* and amended in 1980 and 1981. These provisions were replaced in 1982 by legislation subsequently consolidated as *IHTA 1984, ss 27, 57(5), Sch 4 paras 1–7* in relation to events after 8 March 1982 although much of the previous legislation was reproduced. Previously existing exempt funds are treated as approved under the revised provisions relating to CTT and the provisions relating to IHT, and designations, undertakings and acceptances are likewise treated as having been made under *CTTA 1984, Sch 4 para 3(3)* or *IHTA 1984, Sch 4 para 3(3)*. [*IHTA 1984, Sch 4 paras 1(3), 3(5)*].

Provided the necessary conditions are met, there is no charge to inheritance tax either when the property is settled (but see **21.23** EXEMPT TRANSFERS for abatement of this exemption) or applied for approved purposes.

Qualifying conditions

[33.24] A transfer of value is an exempt transfer to the extent that the value transferred by it is attributable to property which by virtue of a transfer becomes, or immediately after the transfer remains, comprised in a settlement and in respect of which a Board direction has effect at or after the time of the transfer. The Board may give a direction in respect of property proposed to be comprised in the settlement. [*IHTA 1984, ss 27(1), 57(5), Sch 4 para 1(2)*]. Exemption will not apply to a transfer which falls within certain situations in *IHTA 1984, ss 23, 56*. See **21.2**(a), (b)(i)(ii)(iii)(vii) and point (c) at **21.2** EXEMPT TRANSFERS. [*IHTA 1984, ss 27(2), 56(1)(3)(4)*].

The Board *must* so direct (on a claim being made, see below) if they are satisfied:

(a) that its property during the six years from the date on which it became comprised in the settlement can only be applied:
  (i) for the maintenance, repair or preservation of, or making provision for public access to, property which is for the time being qualifying property as defined in **33.2**(b) above in relation to which the requisite undertaking has been given under **33.3** above and no tax has become chargeable since the last undertaking given, or for defraying the expenses of the trustees or for reasonable improvement of property so held; or
  (ii) as respects income not so applied or accumulated, for the benefit of a body mentioned in **33.29** below or a charity which exists wholly or mainly for maintaining, repairing or preserving for the public benefit, buildings of historic or architectural interest, land of scenic, historic or scientific interest or objects of national, scientific, historic or artistic interest; and

(b) that any property ceasing at any time in that period (or before the death of the settlor if earlier) to be comprised in the settlement can only devolve on a body or charity as mentioned in (ii) above; and

(c) that income arising from property in the settlement can at any time after the end of that period only be applied as mentioned in (i) and (ii) above; and

(d) that the property is of a character and amount appropriate for the purposes of the settlement.

The provisions as to variations of undertakings in **33.3** above also apply to undertakings under (a)(i) above. [*IHTA 1984, Sch 4 para (3A); FA 1998, Sch 25 para 8*].

Meaning of 'repair'

In (a)(i) above structural 'repair' to the heritage property will normally qualify but alterations will not unless they are 'necessary to preserve the existing property' such as a new roof but not the conversion of a new wing of a house. Running repairs and maintenance costs will normally qualify e.g. preservation of stonework and fabric, internal redecorations and general maintenance. Heating costs will qualify where they are necessary either to maintain or preserve the building or its qualifying contents or as a consequence of public access. Where land is concerned, clearance, provision of fences and firebreaks, upkeep of ditches and fences and provision of sluices are allowable. In the gardens, seeds, plants, materials, implements, greenhouse heating costs and gardeners' wages are allowed. (VOA IHT manual, section 20, para 20.24).

Claims, etc.

FA 1998, s 144 introduces *IHTA 1984, s 27(1A)* which imposes the need to make a claim no more than two years after the date of the transfer or such longer period as the Board may allow for transfers of value made on or after 17 March 1998. The requirement of *IHTA 1984, s 27(1A)* does not apply where property enters a maintenance fund from an interest in possession trust already in existence following the death of a person entitled to that interest — see **33.26** below.

Where the transfer into the maintenance fund was an exempt transfer made by a person entitled to a beneficial interest in possession in the property (the 'beneficiary') or the transfer fell within **33.26** below, for directions given after 16 March 1987 for the reference to the settlor in (b) above there is substituted a reference to either the settlor or the beneficiary.

If a trust has been, or is to be, set up for the maintenance etc. of a property within **33.2**(b)–(e) above but the property has not been subject to a conditionally exempt transfer, the Board can, on a claim, designate the property and accept the necessary undertakings and it will then be treated as qualifying property.

[*IHTA 1984, Sch 4 para 1(1), 2(1)(a), 3; FA 1985, s 95, Sch 26 para 12; FA 1987, s 59, Sch 9 paras 2, 5*].

Where property is transferred from one settlement to another and a tax charge is excluded under *IHTA 1984, Sch 4 para 9* (see **33.27**(iii) below) or would have been excluded but for *IHTA 1984, Sch 4 para 9(4)* (see **33.27**(iii)(b) below) then (a) and (b) above do not apply and (c) applies with the omission of 'at any time after the end of that period'. The full restrictions do, however, continue to apply until the qualifying conditions have been satisfied for a period of six years from the date on which the property became comprised in the earlier maintenance settlement. [*IHTA 1984, Sch 4 para 4*].

Where more than one person is the settlor in relation to a settlement and the circumstances so require *IHTA 1984, Sch 4 paras 1–7* apply as if the settled property was comprised in separate settlements. [*IHTA 1984, s 44(2)*].

The Board may, by notice in writing, withdraw the direction from a specified date if the facts cease to warrant its continuance. [*IHTA 1984, Sch 4 para 5; FA 1985, s 95*].

The trustees must:

(i) be approved by the Board;
(ii) include either a trust corporation (i.e. a person so constituted for the purposes of the *Law of Property Act 1925* or the *Administration of Estates (Northern Ireland) Order 1979, Article 9*), or a solicitor, or a member of an incorporated society of accountants or a member of such other professional body as the Board allow; and

(iii) at the time the direction is given, be resident in the UK. For this purpose, trustees are regarded as resident in the UK if the general administration is ordinarily carried on there and the trustees or a majority of them (including a majority of each class where there is more than one class of trustees) are resident there. Where a trust corporation is a trustee, residence is determined as for corporation tax.

The trustees must furnish the Board with such accounts and other information as it reasonably requires. The trusts on which the property is held are enforceable at the suit of the Board which has the rights and powers of a beneficiary regarding the appointment, removal and retirement of trustees.

[*IHTA 1984, Sch 4 paras 2(1)(b)(2)(3), 6, 7; FA 1985, s 95*].

Transfers from discretionary settlements etc

[33.25] A charge to tax under *IHTA 1984, s 65* does not arise where property comprised in a settlement without interests in possession (**43** SETTLEMENTS: DISCRETIONARY TRUSTS AND OTHER TRUSTS OF RELEVANT PROPERTY) (the original settlement) ceases to be relevant property and either:

(a) becomes comprised in a settlement in respect of which a direction under **33.24** above then has effect (the maintenance fund), or
(b) is transferred to an individual who in turn makes an exempt transfer to such a fund within the permitted period and the value of the exempt transfer is attributable to that property. The '*permitted period*' is 30 days from the date the property ceases to be relevant property or two years if that occasion was on the death of any person.

The exemption will not apply if:

(i) the amount on which tax would otherwise be charged (before grossing-up if applicable and before BUSINESS PROPERTY (**6**) relief or AGRICULTURAL PROPERTY (**4**) relief) exceeds the value of the property immediately after it becomes, in (a) above, property in respect of which the direction has effect or, in (b) above, comprised in the maintenance settlement (less any consideration received by the original trustees under (a) or the individual under (b)). In these cases, the amount on which tax is charged is restricted to the excess without grossing-up and ignoring business property relief and agricultural property relief, or
(ii) the trustees of the maintenance fund under (a) above acquired an interest under the original settlement, at or before the time when the property in question is transferred, for a consideration in money or money's worth or as a result of transactions which include a disposition for such consideration (whether to them or another) of that interest or of other property, or
(iii) the individual under (b) above has acquired the property for a consideration in money or money's worth or as the result of transactions which include a disposition for such consideration (whether to him or another) of that or other property.

[*IHTA 1984, Sch 4 paras 16–18*].

See also the provisions of **43.19** and **43.22** SETTLEMENTS: DISCRETIONARY TRUSTS AND OTHER TRUSTS OF RELEVANT PROPERTY which also apply to property settled or appointed on maintenance funds.

Transfers from interest in possession settlements following the death of the beneficiary

[33.26] Where a person dies after 16 March 1987 but before 22 March 2006 and immediately before his death he was entitled to an interest in possession in settled property, then, subject to the exceptions below, if, within two years after his death, the property becomes held on qualifying trusts within **33.24** above (whether in the same or a different settlement) the disposition is treated as having been made by the deceased. Accordingly, no disposition or other event occurring after his death and before the property becomes subject to those trusts is, so far as it relates to the property, a transfer of value or an occasion for a charge to tax.

Where a person dies on or after 22 March 2006 and immediately before his death he was entitled to an interest in possession in settled property, then, subject to the exceptions below, if, within two years after his death, the property becomes held on qualifying trusts within **33.24** above (whether in the same or a different settlement) the disposition is treated as having been made by the deceased but only if the interest in the settlement was:

(1) an immediate post-death interest (see SETTLEMENTS WITH INTERESTS IN POSSESSION (**42**)),
(2) a disabled person's interest (see SETTLEMENTS: TRUSTS FOR DISABLED PERSONS (**47**)), or
(3) a transitional serial interest or falls within *s 5(1B)* (see below and SETTLEMENTS WITH INTERESTS IN POSSESSION (**42**)).

Where the property becomes held on the qualifying trusts as a result of court proceedings (and could only have done so) the two year period is extended to three years. An amendment to *IHTA 1984, s 57A(1A)* was made by *FA 2010, s 53(5)* which allows relief for property passing into a maintenance fund to apply in relation to settled property but this is subject to the new *IHTA 1984, s 5(1B)* interest. This new *s 5(1B)* interest is an anti-avoidance section applying to exclude relief so that the pre-22 March 2006 rules (see (1)–(3) above) applying to settled property in which there is an interest in possession applies to settled property subject to an interest in possession to which a person domiciled in the UK became beneficially entitled on or after 9 December 2009 by virtue of a disposal falling within *IHTA 1984, s 10* (not conferring gratuitous intent) are disapplied. The *Finance Act 2010* changes contain no exclusion of the periodic and exit charges on relevant property from applying to settled property subject to a *s 5(1B)* interest in possession and therefore IHT charges under the relevant property rules will be imposed in addition to any IHT charges arising as a result of this section. See ANTI-AVOIDANCE (**5**).

The provisions do not apply if:

(a) the disposition by which the property becomes held on qualifying trusts depends on a condition or is defeasible;

(b) the property which becomes held on those trusts is itself an interest in settled property;

(c) the trustees who hold the property on those trusts have, for a consideration in money or money's worth, acquired an interest under a settlement in which the property was comprised immediately before the death of the beneficiary or at any time thereafter; or

(d) the property which became held on those trusts does so for a consideration in money or money's worth, or is acquired by the trustees for such a consideration, or has at any time since the death of the beneficiary been acquired by any other person for such consideration.

If the value of the property when it becomes held on the qualifying trusts is lower than that part of the value transferred on the death which is attributable to the property, the provisions apply to the property only to the extent of the lower value.

For the purposes of (c) and (d) above a person is treated as acquiring property for a consideration in money or money's worth if he becomes entitled to it as a result of transactions which include a disposition for such consideration (whether to him or another) of that or other property. [*IHTA 1984, s 57A; FA 1987, s 59, Sch 9 paras 1, 4; FA 2006, Sch 20 para 17; FA 2010, s 53*].

Property leaving a maintenance fund

[33.27] A charge to tax arises on property in an approved maintenance fund:

(a) which is applied otherwise than for the purposes in **33.24**(a)(i) or (ii); or

(b) which devolves otherwise than on a body or charity as mentioned under **33.24**(a)(ii); or

(c) which devolves on a qualifying body or charity under **33.24**(a)(ii) above but, at or before the time of devolution, an interest under the settlement in which the property was comprised immediately before the devolution is or has been acquired for a consideration in money or money's worth (or as the result of transactions which include a disposition for such consideration, whether to that body, etc. or to another person) by that or another such body, etc. For this purpose, any acquisition from another such body, etc. is disregarded; or

(d) where, if (a) or (b) above do not apply, the trustees make a disposition which reduces the value of the settled property. '*Disposition*' includes an omission to exercise a right, unless not deliberate, which is treated as made at the latest time the right could be exercised.

[*IHTA 1984, Sch 4 para 8(1)–(3)(5)(6)*].

No charge arises under the following circumstances

(i) If, under (d) above, the trustees do not intend to confer a gratuitous benefit and either the transaction is at arm's length between persons not connected with each other (see **12** CONNECTED PERSONS) or is such as might be expected in such a transaction.

(ii) If, under (d) above, the disposition is a grant of tenancy of agricultural property in the UK, Channel Islands or Isle of Man, for use for agricultural purposes made for full consideration in money or money's worth.

(iii) If the property becomes comprised in another approved maintenance fund as a result of an exempt transfer under **33.24** above within the permitted period i.e. 30 days from the date on which tax would otherwise be chargeable *or* two years if that occasion was the death of the settlor. Where the transfer into the maintenance fund was an exempt transfer made by a person entitled to a beneficial interest in possession in the property (the 'beneficiary') or the transfer fell within **33.26** above, for occasions of charge or potential charge after 16 March 1987 for the reference to the death of the settlor there is substituted a reference to either the death of the settlor or the beneficiary.

This exemption is not available.

(a) if the person making the exempt transfer acquired the property for money or money's worth or as a result of transactions which include a disposition for such consideration (whether to him or another) of that or other property, or

(b) if the amount on which tax would otherwise be charged (before grossing-up, if applicable, and before BUSINESS PROPERTY (**6**) relief or AGRICULTURAL PROPERTY (**4**) relief) exceeds the value of the property immediately after it becomes comprised in the settlement (less any consideration for the transfer received by the person who makes the transfer). The amount on which tax is charged is, however, limited to the excess, without grossing-up or taking into account business property relief or agricultural property relief.

(iv) If the settlor or his spouse or civil partner become beneficially entitled to the property, or, if the settlor has died in the preceding two years, the settlor's widow or widower or surviving civil partner become beneficially entitled to it. This exemption is not available:

(a) if, at or before the time when the settlor, etc. becomes beneficially entitled to the property, he acquires or has acquired an interest under the approved maintenance fund for a consideration in money or money's worth or as the result of transactions which include a disposition for such consideration (whether to him or another) of that or of other property, or

(b) if the amount on which tax would otherwise be charged (before grossing-up, if applicable, and before BUSINESS PROPERTY (**6**) relief or AGRICULTURAL PROPERTY (**4**) relief) exceeds the value of the property immediately after it becomes the property of the settlor, etc. (less any consideration for its transfer received by the trustees). The amount on which tax is charged is, however, limited to the excess, without grossing-up or taking into account business property relief or agricultural property relief, or

(c) if the property was relevant property before it became, or last became held in the approved maintenance fund and, by virtue of **33.25**(a) or (b) above, no proportionate charge to tax arose (or no such charge would have arisen apart from **33.25**(i)) on its ceasing to be relevant property. See **43.3** and **43.12** SETTLEMENTS: DISCRETIONARY TRUSTS AND OTHER TRUSTS OF RELEVANT PROPERTY for '*relevant property*' and '*proportionate charge to tax*' respectively, or

(d) if, before the property last became comprised in an approved maintenance fund (the second fund) it was comprised in another such fund (the first fund) and it ceased to be comprised in the first fund and last became comprised in the second fund in circumstances such that by virtue of (iii) above no charge to tax arose (or no charge would have arisen but for (iii)(b) above), or

(e) unless the person who becomes beneficially entitled to the property is domiciled in the UK at the time when he becomes so entitled.

Where the transfer into the maintenance fund was an exempt transfer made by a person entitled to a beneficial interest in possession in the property (the 'beneficiary') or the transfer fell within **33.26** above, for occasions of charge or potential charge after 16 March 1987 the above provisions do not apply if the beneficiary had died at or before the time when the property became property subject to the charge to tax. Otherwise, the above provisions apply with the substitution of 'beneficiary' for 'settlor' wherever occurring. Where, however, the property becomes property to which the beneficiary's spouse, civil partner, widow or widower or surviving civil partner is beneficially entitled, the charge to tax is only avoided where the spouse etc. would have become beneficially entitled to the property on the termination of the interest in possession (but see **33.26** above) if the property had not then become held on maintenance trusts.

(v) Where the property becomes held for charitable purposes only without limit of time or the property of a political party qualifying for exemption under *IHTA 1984, s 24*, a national body mentioned in *IHTA 1984, Sch 3*, or, under certain conditions, a body not established or conducted for profit (see **21.4, 21.6–21.8** EXEMPT TRANSFERS).

[*IHTA 1984, s 76, Sch 4 paras 8(3), 9, 10, 15A; FA 1987, s 59, Sch 9 paras 3, 6; The Tax and Civil Partnership Regulations 2005, SI 2005/3229, Reg 39*].

Loss to the donor principle

Tax is charged on the amount by which the trust property is less immediately after the event giving rise to the charge than it would have been but for the event (i.e. the loss to the donor principle), grossed-up where the settlement pays the tax. [*IHTA 1984, Sch 4 para 8(3)*].

Note that for the purposes of the capital gains tax counter avoidance legislation within *FA 2004, s 117, Sch 22* where trustees acquire property with the benefit of *TCGA 1992, s 260* holdover relief and are denied the relief on disposal of the property, if it is property within the meaning of *IHTA 1984 Sch 4* the main residence relief is preserved on a subsequent disposal by them. [*TCGA 1992, s 226B as inserted by FA 2004, Sch 22 para 6*]. See Note C to the Precedent in **33.24** above.

Rates of tax

[33.28] The rate at which tax is charged depends upon whether or not the chargeable property has previously been relevant property comprised in a settlement without interests in possession (43 SETTLEMENTS: DISCRETIONARY TRUSTS AND OTHER TRUSTS OF RELEVANT PROPERTY).

(A) Where the property chargeable was relevant property before it became (or last became) held in the approved maintenance fund and, by virtue of 33.25(a) or (b) above, no proportionate charge to tax arose (or no such charge would have arisen apart from 33.25(i)) on its ceasing to be relevant property, the rate at which tax is charged is the aggregate of the following percentages for each complete successive quarter in 'the relevant period'

	Cumulative Total
0.25% for each of the first 40 quarters	10%
0.20% for each of the next 40 quarters	8%
0.15% for each of the next 40 quarters	6%
0.10% for each of the next 40 quarters	4%
0.05% for each of the next 40 quarters	2%
Maximum rate chargeable after 50 years	30%

'*Relevant period*' is the period *beginning* with the latest of the date of the last ten-year anniversary of the settlement in which the property was comprised before it ceased (or last ceased) to be relevant property *or* the day on which the property became (or last became) relevant property before it ceased (or last ceased) to be such property *or* 13 March 1975 and *ending* on the day before the chargeable event. Where property in respect of which tax is chargeable has at any time ceased to be and again become property in an approved maintenance fund such that by virtue of (iii) above no charge to tax arose (or no charge would have arisen but for (iii)(b) above) it is treated for these purposes as having been the property of an approved maintenance fund throughout the permitted period in (iii) above.

'*Quarter*' means a period of three months.

[*IHTA 1984, Sch 4 paras 8(4), 11*].

(B) In all other cases, the rate at which tax is charged is the higher of:

(1) the aggregate of the percentages for each successive quarter in the relevant period as in the table in (A) above (but see below for the meaning of relevant period in this context), and

(2) if the settlor is alive, the effective rate applicable to the property if it were added to the cumulative total of his chargeable transfers at the date of the chargeable event and tax calculated using the rates applicable to lifetime transfers. The rate or rates determined in respect of any occasion are not affected by the death of the settlor after that occasion, and

(3) if the settlor has died since 12 March 1975, the effective rate applicable to the property if it were added to the value of his estate on death and formed the highest part of that value. If the settlement was made on death, the death rates are used, if not, the rates applicable to lifetime transfers are used, and

(4) if the settlor died before 13 March 1975, the effective rate that would be applicable to the property if the settlor dies when the chargeable event occurred and the chargeable amount were added to and formed the highest part of the value on which estate duty was chargeable when in fact he died. If the settlement was made on death, the death rates are used, if not, the rates applicable to lifetime transfers are used.

Where the transfer into the maintenance fund was an exempt transfer made by a person entitled to a beneficial interest in possession in the property (the 'beneficiary') or the transfer fell within **33.26** above, for occasions of charge or potential charge after 16 March 1987 for the reference in (1) to (4) above to the settlor there are substituted references to the beneficiary. Under (3) and (4) if the beneficiary had died at or before the time when the property became property subject to the charge, the death rates are used, if not the rates applicable to lifetime transfers are used.

Where (4) above applies or where under (3) above the settlor died before 18 March 1986, nevertheless, the amount of tax payable is calculated as if the amendments to *IHTA 1984, s 7* in *FA 1986, Sch 19 para 2* (rates of tax for transfers within seven years of death and tapering relief) had applied at the time of death.

'*Relevant period*' under (1) above means the period beginning with the day on which the chargeable property became (or *first* became) comprised in an approved maintenance fund and ending with the day before the event giving rise to the charge. For this purpose, any occasion on which the property became comprised in an approved maintenance fund and which occurred before an occasion of charge to tax under (a) to (d) above (other than the event currently giving rise to the charge or an occasion which would not be an occasion of charge but for (iii)(b) above) is disregarded.

'*Effective rate*' in (2) to (4) is the rate found by expressing the tax chargeable as a percentage of the amount on which it is charged.

For the purposes of (2) to (4) above, where tax is chargeable on property which has previously been comprised in another settlement and ceased to be comprised in that first settlement in circumstances such that, by virtue of (iii) above no charge to tax arose (or no charge would have arisen but for (iii)(b) above), '*settlor*' is construed as a reference to the person who was settlor of the first settlement, or, if the Board so determine, the current settlement. Where property has previously been comprised in more than one settlement and ceased to be comprised in each of them and became comprised in another or the current settlement in similar circumstances, '*settlor*' is construed as a reference to the person who was settlor of the first of the previous settlements, or, if the Board so determine, any other of the previous settlements or the current settlement. Similarly, for occasions of charge after 16 March 1987 where the transfer into the maintenance fund was an exempt transfer made by a person entitled to a beneficial interest in possession in the property (the 'beneficiary') or the transfer fell within **33.26** above, '*beneficiary*' may be, if the Board so determine, construed as a reference to the person who was settlor of the current settlement or, where the property has previously been comprised in more than one settlement, any of the previous settlements or the current settlement.

Where, in the period of seven years preceding the current charge, there has been a previous charge where the tax was calculated at the rate under (2) to (4) above and the person who is the settlor for the purposes of the current charge was the settlor for the purposes of the previous charge, the amount on which tax was charged on the previous charge (or if there have been more than one, the aggregate of the amounts on which tax was charged on each) is taken for the purposes of calculating the rate of the current charge:

(i) under (2) above, to be the value transferred by a chargeable transfer made by the settlor immediately before the occasion of the current charge; and

(ii) under (3) or (4) above, to increase the value there mentioned by an amount equal to the amount or aggregate on which tax was previously charged.

This applies whether or not the settlements are the same and, if the settlor is dead, whether or not he has died since the other charge. Where the transfer into the maintenance fund was an exempt transfer made by a person entitled to a beneficial interest in possession in the property (the 'beneficiary') or the transfer fell within **33.26** above, for occasions of charge or potential charge after 16 March 1987 for the references to the settlor there are substituted references to the beneficiary.

[*IHTA 1984, Sch 4 paras 12–14, 15A; FA 1986, Sch 19 paras 38, 42; FA 1987, s 59, Sch 9 paras 3, 6*].

In (3) and (4) above, where tax is reduced by the substitution of a new Table of rates between the date of death and the chargeable event, the new rates are used. [*IHTA 1984, Sch 2 para 6*].

Property in pre-*FA 1982* maintenance funds which are treated as approved under the current provisions by *IHTA 1984, Sch 4 para 1(3)* (see **33.23** above) is for the purposes of calculation of the rates of charge treated as having become property in an approved maintenance fund at the time of the original transfer of value. [*IHTA 1984, Sch 4 para 15*].

Example 10

On 1 January 1989 P settled £500,000 in an approved maintenance fund for his historic mansion during the lives of himself and his wife, W. P died in February 1994, his taxable estate and lifetime transfers chargeable on death amounting to £175,000. On 1 January 2010, the date of death of W, the fund, which has been depleted by extensive repairs to the mansion, is valued at £300,000. £80,000 is transferred to the National Trust, which also accepts the gift of the mansion, and the balance is paid to P's grandson G.

No IHT is payable on the £80,000 paid to the National Trust, but the balance passing to G is liable to IHT at the higher of a tapered scale rate (the 'first rate') and an effective rate calculated by reference to P's estate (the 'second rate'). [*IHTA 1984, Sch 4 paras 12–14*].

First rate

The property was comprised in the maintenance fund for 20 years, i.e. 80 quarters.

The scale rate is

	%
0.25% for each of the first 40 quarters	10.0
0.20% for each of the next 40 quarters	8.0
0.15% for each of the next 4 quarters	0.6
	18.6%

Second rate

The effective rate is calculated, using half Table rates applying on 1 January 2010 (taken as those rates applying on 6 April 2009), as if the chargeable amount transferred (£220,000) had been added to the value transferred by P on his death (£175,000) and had formed the highest part of the total. Half Table rates at **40.1 2009.A1** RATES OF TAX are used because the fund was set up in P's lifetime.

		£
£137,000	at nil	—
£83,000	at 20%	16,600
£220,000		£16,600

The effective rate is

$$\frac{16{,}600}{220{,}000} \times 100\% = 7.55\%$$

IHT payable is £220,000 at 18.6% = £40,920

Gifts, etc. to national bodies

[33.29] Gifts to the following bodies (i.e. *Schedule 3* bodies) whether or not national heritage property are exempt from inheritance tax. For exceptions, see **21** EXEMPT TRANSFERS.

- The National Gallery.
- The British Museum.
- The National Museums of Scotland.
- The National Museum of Wales.

- The Ulster Museum.
- Any other similar national institution which exists wholly or mainly for the purpose of preserving for the public benefit a collection of scientific, historic or artistic interest and which is approved for this purpose by the Treasury.
- Any museum or art gallery in the UK which exists wholly or mainly for that purpose and is maintained by a local authority or university in the UK.
- Any library the main function of which is to serve the needs of teaching and research at a university in the UK.
- The Historic Buildings and Monuments Commission for England.
- The National Trust for Places of Historic Interest or Natural Beauty.
- The National Trust for Scotland for Places of Historic Interest or Natural Beauty.
- The National Art Collections Fund.
- The National Endowment for Science, Technology and the Arts.
- The Trustees of the National Heritage Memorial Fund.
- The Friends of the National Libraries.
- English Nature.
- The Historic Churches Preservation Trust.
- Scottish National Heritage.
- Countryside Council for Wales.
- Any local authority within *ITA 2007, s 838.*
- Any Government department (including the National Debt Commissioners).
- Any university or university college in the UK.
- A health service body within *ICTA 1988, s 519A* and *FA 2004, s 148.*

Since the 1984 Act similar national institutions are, with Treasury approval or the Board of HMRC, also included in the list of bodies within *IHTA 1984, Sch 3.*

[*National Heritage Act 1980; IHTA 1984, s 25(1), Sch 3; FA 1985, s 95; National Heritage (Scotland) Act 1985, Sch 2 para 4; National Health Service and Community Care Act 1990, s 61(5); Environmental Protection Act 1990, Sch 6 para 25; National Heritage (Scotland) Act 1991, Sch 2 para 9*].

See also **21.4** EXEMPT TRANSFERS which equally applies to settled property becoming the property of bodies listed above. [*IHTA 1984, s 76*].

Sales by private treaty to national bodies

[33.30] To encourage *sales* to approved bodies as above, the conditional exemption from IHT will not be lost on such a transaction (but see **33.10**(b) above for exception where there are associated properties). [*IHTA 1984, ss 32(4), 32A(5); FA 1985, Sch 26 para 4*]. Even if the work of art has not been formally exempted from IHT, a sale of this character by concession will not normally attract CGT. The price paid by the museum etc. in a private treaty sale is based on an agreed valuation of the picture or object in the open market or at auction. The amount the buyer offers to pay takes into account the tax exemption and divides the benefit of the exemption between both parties. The government has advised museums etc. that, in general, the seller should receive 25% (10% in the case of real property) of the benefit of tax exemption, subject to negotiations above or below this figure where flexibility is appropriate. It has been suggested that this amount of 25% should be increased to 50% by Resource's *Acceptance in Lieu: A Review* in January 2001, para 3.21. The final sum received will therefore be more than the net sum on an open market sale (i.e. gross value less tax) because the seller shares in the amount of tax saved. The addition is sometimes known as 'the douceur' (see also HMRC Capital Gains Tax Manual, para 73370) and the arrangement is an administrative not a statutory one.

A claim for exemption from inheritance tax on the transfer of a heritage object, whether in life or on death, is normally made on or shortly after the transfer. Where an estate includes an object in respect of which a claim might be made, and the executors or administrators wish to sell the object by private treaty while the estate is in the course of administration and before a claim has been made, nothing in the legislation prevents designation of the object as exempt before or on such sale. The price is a matter for free negotiation between the parties but there is no capital gains tax exemption where no undertaking has been given regarding maintenance, preservation and access unless allowed concessionally. (Hansard Vol 9 No 153 Col 697, Written Answer for 31 July 1981).

No CGT is charged if property is accepted in lieu of IHT although it is usually necessary for HMRC Inheritance Tax to calculate a notional charge in arriving at the approximate tax credit. (See also VOA IHT manual, section 20, para 20.60).

Acceptance in satisfaction of tax

[33.31] If IHT has to be paid on any assets, it may be possible to offer a work of art, chattel, etc. in satisfaction of the liability. This is known as acceptance in lieu and the work of art accepted is exempt from IHT, whether or not it has been formally exempted. If the Secretary of State agrees with advice received from the AIL panel then a particular item(s) may be accepted in lieu of tax. Each Secretary of State (England, Wales, Scotland and Northern Ireland) will be ultimately responsible for the decision. The standard of objects which can be so accepted is very much higher than that applicable for conditional exemption. They have to satisfy a test of 'pre-eminence' either in the context of a national, local authority, or university collection, or through association with a particular building. A further administration requirement has been introduced to ensure that due diligence procedure with respect to the provenance and title to the chattel offered in lieu of tax. This is a result of the claims for restitution of chattels by descendants of Holocaust victims.

The benefit of the tax exemption is taken into account by adding 25% (the douceur) of the value of that exemption to the estimated value of the object after payment of notional tax. The amount thus calculated is offset against the tax liability of the estate on other property. However, see Taxation, 10 November 1994 page 123 regarding the Capital Taxes Office [now HMRC Inheritance Tax] refusal in some cases to accept assets of national importance in lieu of tax chargeable on the estate where those assets are inheritance tax exempt for any other reason e.g. business property relief.

Example 11

Trustees of deceased Lord Charles offer to the AIL Panel a chattel estimated to be worth £1 million at auction and seven acres of land with an arboretum designed by Capability Brown valued at £500,000. The IHT liability at 40% would be £400,000 on the chattel and £200,000 on the land. The douceur in the case of the chattel is 25% of the IHT due and in the case of the land is 10%. Therefore, the amount accepted in lieu of tax with douceur in these two circumstances would be as follows:

Chattel (auction value)	£1,000,000
Less: IHT @ 40%	£(400,000)
	£600,000
Add: Douceur at 25% × £400,000	£100,000
Sub-total	£700,000
Land (Valuation by the RICS)	£500,000
Less: IHT @ 40%	£(200,000)
	£300,000
Add: Douceur at 10% × £200,000	£20,000
	£320,000
Total acceptance in lieu (AIL) for chattel and land	£1,020,000

Persons wishing to offer a work of art in lieu of tax should send details to HMRC Inheritance Tax, London at the address in **2.19** ACCOUNTS AND RETURNS. See also **35.10** PAYMENT OF TAX. When HMRC receives an offer in lieu of tax it normally seeks the following details relating to the taxable occasion for which the offer in lieu of tax relates.

(1) A full description of the items being offered, giving, where appropriate, the artist, the medium (oil on canvas, watercolour, porcelain, bronze, etc.) and dimensions. Any exhibition history, literature and provenance should also be supplied. For archival offers, a full calendar, if available, should be supplied. Where a calendar is not on hand, a detailed description should be provided with the number of pieces in each section of the archive.

(2) Three good quality photographs, preferably in colour, of each item being offered. This is not required for archival offers.

(3) The valuation at which each item is being offered and a justification of the value by reference to previous sales of that artist or the dale of similar works. Unless HMRC has agreed to the alternative, the valuation should be that for the date the offer is made to them.

(4) A statement explaining why the items are being proposed as pre-eminent or, where appropriate, the association with an historic property.

(5) A statement of any allocation wishes or conditions that are part of the offer.

Such evidence might best also be provided to the AIL panel at the same time as when sent to HMRC.

Property may also be accepted in satisfaction of interest accrued on CTT, IHT or ED as well as in lieu of the tax itself. When an offer is made in lieu of tax the amount of that tax which is satisfied by the acceptance of the property at the *valuation* date does not carry late payment interest after that date under AIL. In the case where tax has been paid in advance to obtain Grant of Probate a successful completion of the offer will result in a repayment of tax and any interest. Where the AIL panel require an item on offer for AIL to be replaced by another item the 'interest holiday' will still apply from the original offer and not the requested revised offer. Where property is accepted neither CGT, Stamp Duty nor VAT is charged. (VOA IHT manual, section 20, para 20.30). [*IHTA 1984, s 230*; *FA 2009, Sch 53 para 14*].

Estate duty

[33.32] On the occurrence of a chargeable event, estate duty may still be payable on heritage objects granted conditional exemption under the estate duty provisions. Where the object was conditionally exempt on an inter vivos gift the 'taper' relief of *FA 1960, s 64* is only given for clawback assessments made before 3 May 1984. (HMRC Press Release 3 May 1984). See also **54** TRANSITIONAL PROVISIONS.

Key points

[33.33] Points to consider are as follows.

- *Enactment of Extra Statutory Concessions Order 2009, SI 2009/730* has been given statutory effect in *TCGA 1992, s 258(2)* to provide that private treaty sales to *IHTA 1984, Sch 3* bodies of pre-eminent works of art or heritage property of companies or other bodies are not subject to CGT or CT charge from 6 April 2009. The 'douceur' (see above at **33.30**) is also now available to companies and other bodies whose chargeable gains are assessed to corporation tax.
- Single items or collections can form the subject of an acceptance in lieu claim. The usual standard items might include pictures, archives, sculptures as well as scientific and historical items. However, modes of transport such as boats, classic cars, planes, etc. can be offered as well as others. For instance, Captain Swift, an ex-Queen's Messenger, dies leaving a collection of silver greyhound medals (the symbol of the Messenger Service originally broken off a silver chalice owned by Charles II which showed tacit connection to Royal authority) accumulated over the years from auctions and personal connection. These are considered as a pre-eminent collection together and are valued at £150,000. This gives the estate a IHT liability of £60,000 which it can ill afford

along with the insurance costs of the collection. Providing the collection is in the ownership or at the disposal of the persons liable for the tax, and HMRC and the relevant Culture Minister accept that the collection is 'pre-eminent' within *IHTA 1984, s 230(4)* and the various provenances detailed in the point below are secured its acceptance in lieu of tax with a douceur of 25% could satisfy IHT of up to £105,000! Conditional exemption might also be due in which case no IHT liability would necessarily be due (see above at 33.3).

- The Museums Libraries and Archives Council (MLA) requires considerable amount of provenance of the item being offered and a due diligence form will be required to be signed. This form is obtainable from the MLA or their website www.mla.gov.uk. Any application should ideally be made in good time e.g. shortly after death by the executors/PRs/beneficiaries so that IHT due on the estate i.e. 6 months after the end of the month in which death occurs, so that it may be taken into account in the tax calculation. See IHT Newsletter, May 2003 edition where it states 'In other words, if people have already paid their IHT bill in full, we will not entertain a subsequent offer to transfer assets.' This exclusion will not necessarily apply if at the time the IHT is paid on obtaining the grant or confirmation the offer in lieu is notified to HMRC or money is held by HMRC to pay IHT on order of the payer as that is still classed as belonging to the payer not HMRC.
- There are difficulties when the person hoping to make the offer is not the person liable to pay the IHT. To avoid this a claim under deed of variation may be made re *IHTA 1984, ss 142, 144* or pre-death the will states such items are to be left in residue.

National Heritage assets – Conditional Exemption and offers in lieu of tax [Form IHT 420]

HM Revenue & Customs

National Heritage assets
Conditional exemption and maintenance funds
Schedule IHT420

When to use this form

Fill in this form:

- to claim heritage conditional exemption for any assets in the estate
- if conditional exemption was allowed on any of the assets in the estate in the past
- if any of these or any other assets in the estate are maintained from a maintenance fund.
- to claim exemption for any assets passing under the deceased's will to the trustees of a maintenance fund

If there is not enough room on this form for all the information, please continue on the Additional information pages 15 and 16 on form IHT400.

Conditional exemption is available for objects, land and buildings if they are important to the national heritage. In return, new owners must agree to look after the assets and provide public access to them without a prior appointment.

Outright transfers into maintenance funds (settlements for HMRC approved national heritage purposes which meet certain statutory requirements) are exempt from Inheritance Tax.

Name of deceased

Date of death *DD MM YYYY*

IHT reference number (if known)

Help

Please read the guidance notes for form IHT420 in the IHT400 Notes before filling in this form.

For more information or help :

- go to **www.hmrc.gov.uk/inheritancetax/**
- phone our Helpline on **0845 30 20 900**
  – if calling from outside the UK, phone **+44 115 974 3009**.

For another copy of this form go to **www.hmrc.gov.uk/inheritancetax/**

Assets on which conditional or maintenance fund exemption is being claimed

1 Enter details of the assets in the deceased's estate for which you are claiming conditional or maintenance fund exemption

Describe the asset and enter the box number where this asset is shown on form IHT400	Value at the date of death £

IHT420 (Substitute) (LexisNexis) (Version 02/2011) Page 1 L11/08

Assets previously benefiting from heritage exemption

Use this section to tell us about assets in the estate that have previously benefited from heritage exemption.

2 In the past were any assets in the estate granted exemption from Inheritance Tax, Capital Transfer Tax, Estate Duty or Capital Gains Tax, on the grounds that they were heritage assets?

No ☐ If No, please go to **box 4**

Yes ☐ If Yes, please enter the details below

Describe the asset and enter the box number where this asset is shown on form IHT400	Date the asset was given to or inherited by the deceased	Name of person to whom asset now passes	Current open market value £

3 Give any reference numbers used by us when the earlier exemption was agreed. Please give the name of the person(s) who gave the asset(s) to the deceased and if they are now dead, their date of death.

Maintenance funds

4 Are any assets in the estate maintained by a maintenance fund?

No ☐ If No, you have finished this form

Yes ☐ If Yes, please enter the details below

Describe the asset and enter the box number where this asset is shown on form IHT400	Date the maintenance fund was established and our IHT reference	Name of person to whom the asset now passes

IHT420 Page 2

34

Partnerships

Cross-references. See 4 AGRICULTURAL PROPERTY and 6 BUSINESS PROPERTY for relief applicable to disposal of partnership assets; 12 CONNECTED PERSONS; 35.5 PAYMENT OF TAX for payment by instalments.

Simon's Taxes. See I6.2.

Other Sources. VOA IHT manual, sections 7, 19; Foster, Part F2.

Introduction

[34.1] A partnership is the relationship which subsists between persons carrying on a business in common with a view of profit. [*Partnership Act 1890, s 1*]. It is a question of fact whether a particular person is truly a party to such a relationship or is merely a senior employee who is being held out as a partner. The usual tests must, therefore, be applied in order to establish the truth of the relationship. The absence of a formal partnership agreement under *Partnership Act 1890* is not definitive of the existence or non-existence of a partnership. See *Burrell* [1997] STC 1413. An English partnership is not a legal entity in the same way as a company, but a *collection of separate individuals*. This being so, the provisions of inheritance tax apply to each partner as an individual and to his interest in the firm's assets. (See also VOA IHT manual, section 19, para 19.8.) Also, Limited Liability Partnerships (LLP) and Family Limited Partnerships (FLP) are also available to be set up under the *Limited Partnerships Act 1907* and *Limited Liability Partnerships Act 2000* which offer an alternative to ordinary partnerships. These types of partnership have to be registered at Companies House and provide limited liability in respect of the respective parties contribution but are treated for IHT purposes as 'see-through'. See Key Points below and *IHTA 1984, s 267A*; *LLPA 2000, s 11*.

'Buy and sell' agreements

[34.2] See 6.4 BUSINESS PROPERTY for the effect of a partnership 'buy and sell' agreement on the availability of business property relief on the transfer of a partner's interest in the partnership.

Goodwill

[34.3] Where goodwill is ignored for incoming and outgoing partners then *IHTA 1984, s 10* would probably apply so that there is no transfer of value. It would also apply where consideration passes which is equal to the market value or the value which would pass between persons at arm's length. See also *A-G v Boden and Another* KB 1911, [1912] 1 KB 539; *A-G v Ralli* 1936, 15 ATC 523 and *Re White (deceased) White v Minnis and Another*, Ch D [1999] 2 All ER 663.

Other partnership transactions

[34.4] Many transactions between partners will be on the basis of arm's length values with consideration passing in some form or other. Otherwise the normal rules apply for inheritance tax purposes.

In the case of partnership property the starting point is the valuation of the whole, but it is recognised that because of the fragmented ownership, a purchaser would expect to pay a lower price than if the whole of the property had been available as a single entity. Note the discount should not exceed 10%. (VOA IHT manual, section 19, para 19.8 but also see **56.8** VALUATION).

Partnership assurance policies

Partnership assurance policies taken out before 15 September 1976 (and not varied since that date) on normal business terms on trusts under English law (or Scots law provided the policy does not directly or indirectly involve a partnership itself as a separate persona) will not be regarded as settlements for inheritance tax purposes if the premiums paid fall within *IHTA 1984, s 10* (see above). The exercise of a power of appointment under a 'discretionary' trust policy would not be regarded as a variation. (See F10 at **23** HMRC EXTRA-STATUTORY CONCESSIONS).

Scottish partnerships

Scottish partnerships are legal entities, so that provisions relating to individuals might not strictly apply, but in practice it is thought that the provisions would be applied as for the rest of the UK. In this connection, a Scottish Limited Liability Partnership which forms the basis of a Lloyd's member's underwriting vehicle might form the claim for a 'fast track' application to distribute and in this connection apply for leave to distribute the estate on the basis that no further provision need be made for Lloyd's creditors. The claim form is supported by an affidavit (or witness statement) in the form of a Chancery Master's Practice Form adapted as necessary. It should also be accompanied by draft minutes (see Chancery Master's Practice Forms) and a statement of costs (see Costs Practice Direction). (VOA IHT manual, section 19, para 19.11).

HMRC Inheritance Tax will decide when a property in the occupation of a partnership is to be regarded as a partnership asset and advise the DV accordingly as well as all the partner's beneficial interests in the assets, or if not known, state the number of partners and the way in which the profits are divisible between them. (VOA IHT manual, section 7, para 7.34).

Under English law, unlike Scottish law, a partnership cannot of itself hold an interest in land and the grant of a tenancy is to one or more of the individual partners. (VOA IHT manual, section 9, para 9.9).

Foreign partnerships

The situs of a partnership controlled and managed abroad is outside the UK and accordingly the interest in it of a partner not domiciled and not deemed domiciled in the UK is excluded property for IHT purposes. This remains so even though some assets of the partnership may be in the UK, for example a UK property. There is no provision which treats a partnership as transparent for IHT purposes and thus the existence of UK assets within the partnership does not affect the excluded property status of the partnership interest for non-domiciliaries.

Limited Liability Partnership (LLP)

Limited Liability Partnership (LLP) members are treated as if they are partners in a partnership. This ensures that inheritance tax will be charged in respect of members' interests in a LLP as it relates to partners' interests in a partnership and that business property relief will be available on the same basis. The structure of a family limited partnership in contrast to a LLP is that the injected family wealth is set out in a partnership deed and that deed regulates the rights which the partnership interest provides. For more detail on the IHT advantages of such a partnership see Key Points below. See also **6.4** BUSINESS PROPERTY. These provisions have come into effect from 6 April 2001. [*IHTA 1984, s 267A as inserted by Limited Liability Partnerships Act 2000, s 11; SI 2001/3316*].

Although a limited liability partnership is in law a body corporate, the trade carried on is treated as if carried on in partnership by the members and not by the LLP as such. However, since a partnership does not have treatment as a transparent entity for inheritance tax purposes, the interests of the partners on death or lifetime transfer are in the partnership itself and not in the underlying assets. Accordingly, HMRC consider that if the main business of a LLP is to hold shares in unquoted trading companies, the partners' interests are not in those companies but in the partnership itself whose business is 'wholly or mainly holding investments' and therefore not eligible for business property relief (ICAEW Technical Release Tech 01/14 tax). This view is disputed by leading tax counsel; the partners' interests are attributable to the value of relevant business property, that is, the shares in unquoted trading companies [*IHTA 1984, s 104*]and so should qualify for relief (see article by James Kessler QC and Oliver Marre, Taxation, 20 March 2014, p 80).

Under the terms of ICAEW Technical Release Tech 01/14 tax, HMRC allow full business property relief if the main business of the LLP is to conduct a trade and shares in companies are held as part of the business operations. If they are not so held, HMRC will consider whether they fall to be treated as excepted assets within *IHTA 1984 s 112*.

Although property to which an LLP is entitled, or which it occupies or uses, is treated for inheritance tax purposes as property to which its members are entitled this provision has the crucial qualification that this is 'as partners'

(*IHTA 1984, s 267A*), so that the partners cannot claim personal entitlement to the underlying assets. Transfers of value are similarly treated made by the individual members and not by the LLP itself. [*LLPA 2000, s 11*].

Civil partnerships

[34.5] With the introduction of the *Civil Partnership Act 2004* (CPA 2004), which received Royal Assent on 18 November 2004, it is possible for same sex couples to have their relationship legally recognised following a registration process which will then entitle them to acquire legal rights similar to heterosexual married couples. There are certain restrictions and the individuals who must be of the same sex must be unmarried and not party to another civil partnership whilst also not being related to each other. [*CPA 2004, s 3, Sch 1*]. Once they have their registration certificate they will be treated similarly to married couples with regard to both legal and taxation matters including IHT. [*FA 2005, s 103; The Tax and Civil Partnership Regulations 2005, SI 2005/3229*]. In *Burden & Burden v United Kingdom* [2006] ECHR Case 13378/05; [2007] STC 252 two elderly sisters lived together in a jointly-owned house on land which they had inherited from their parents. They lodged a complaint with the ECHR, contending that the provisions of *IHTA 1984, s 18* (as amended by the *Tax and Civil Partnership Regulations 2005*) were a breach of *Article 14* of the *European Convention on Human Rights*, because when one of them died, the survivor would be required to pay IHT on her sister's share of their home, whereas no IHT would have been charged if they had lived together as a registered lesbian civil partnership. The ECHR rejected their application holding that

> 'the inheritance tax exemption for married and civil partnership couples . . . pursues a legitimate aim, namely to promote stable, committed heterosexual and homosexual relationships by providing the survivor with a measure of financial security after the death of the spouse or partner.'

See 58 TAX CASES.

The *CPA 2004* created a new legal status of civil partner in respect of their relationship and applies from 5 December 2005 when the *CPA 2004* came into force. One effect of this is that where one civil partner has been living in another's property and/or being supported then they can make application under *Inheritance (Provision for Family and Dependants) Act 1975* for reasonable financial provision. [*CPA 2004, Sch 4 paras 15–27*]. See paragraph 24.5 of the Chancery Guide at http://www.hmcourts-service.gov.uk/cms/publications.htm. For tax purposes civil partners will be treated the same way as married couples and tax charges and anti-avoidance rules apply in equal measures. For IHT purposes transfers between the two of them will be exempt from tax during lifetime and on death. The same treatment applies for CGT purposes so that in the situation where two properties are owned by them one will have to be treated as the main residence as with married couples. An election should be made within two years of the certificate being issued. [*TCGA 1992, s 222(5)(6)*]. Where only one property is owned, whether jointly or solely by one partner or both, then it will be treated as the main residence for principal private residence exemption purposes.

Key points

[34.6] Points to consider are as follows.

- IHT400 Schedule IHT413 should be completed in respect of any partnership interest and where there are separate partnership interests or assets in partnerships then a separate IHT413 must be completed.
- Where there is a transfer of assets into a FLP then it is treated as a PET and providing the donor survives seven years the gift will drop out of account. The gift is not treated as a settlement within the relevant property regime and consequently does not attract up to a 6% charge for these purposes. Under *IHTA 1984, s 272A* it means that the partners are entitled to the assets vis 'property to which a limited liability partnership is entitled, or which it occupies or uses, shall be treated as property to which its members are entitled, or which they occupy or use, as partners' and therefore comprises as part of their chargeable estate for IHT purposes. Also, for income tax and CGT purposes a FLP is transparent and IT and CGT allowances maybe set against income arising and capital gains on sale of interests in the FLP. The FLP is therefore a good method for family members to convert chargeable assets for IHT purposes into assets for family members attracting BPR which also has the attraction of limited liability. Consideration should be made regarding the *Financial Services and Markets Act 2000* which is beyond the scope of this work.
- Whilst APR was restricted to UK situated businesses BPR has never been subject to that geographical restriction. Therefore partnership interests held abroad will qualify for 100% BPR where the qualification requirements are met. The overseas situation of the partnership would be ideally in a country where there is no death/estate tax or the equivalent BPR exemption applies to avoid unreclaimable unilateral tax deduction on the incidence of a transfer of the partnership interest. Although this is not an IHT case see *Swift v HMRC* [2010] UKFTT 88, TC00039 where the Tribunal found as fact that the members' interests in the particular US Limited Liability Company under consideration were 'not similar to share capital but something more similar to partnership capital of an English partnership'.
- In the case of spouses/civil partners who die in *commorientes* circumstances then the situation is complicated further by the potential effect of the anomaly regarding inter-spouse exemption under *IHTA 1984, s 18* which will apply to civil partnership situations; as there is an exempt transfer on the death under

s 18(1) then the transfer to the younger spouse/partner is not a chargeable transfer. However, the younger of the spouses/civil partners is deemed to have inherited the elder's estate under the *Law of Property Act 1925, s 184* but for the purposes of IHT under *IHTA 1984, s 4(2)* eliminates mutual gifts between individuals in such circumstances and there is no transfer of value to the younger spouse or civil partner on which inheritance tax can be charged. There is a view therefore that the elder's estate escapes inheritance tax completely and therefore a survivorship condition, which is normally desirable, is deliberately excluded in the event of the spouses and civil partners dying simultaneously. This also means that the unused nil rate band claimed by the personal representatives of the younger could benefit from the whole or part of the deceased elder civil partner's nil rate band making a current maximum amount of £650,000. See IHTM12197 for text and a useful example.

- Under the provisions of *CPA 2004, Sch 4 para 13* amendment is made to *Intestates' Estate Act 1952, s 5, Sch 2* to ensure that the surviving civil partner acquires the home shared with the deceased in priority to other family members of the deceased.
- An individual partner's share in a partnership (subject to meeting the necessary requirements) will obtain 100% BPR on the death of that partner, whereas an individual partner's property that is used by the partnership attracts BPR at only 50%. Care should be taken to determine the exact ownership of such assets in order to secure the appropriate relief.

35

Payment of Tax

Cross-references. See 3 ADMINISTRATION AND COLLECTION; 28 INTEREST ON TAX; 30 LIABILITY FOR TAX.

Simon's Taxes. See **I11.4, I11.5, I11.6.**

Other Sources. Foster, Part K; IHTM30000.

Due date of tax

Lifetime transfers

[35.1] Subject to the exceptions listed below, inheritance tax is due six months after the end of the month in which the chargeable transfer is made unless made after 5 April and before 1 October in any year when tax is due on 30 April in the following year.

Exceptions

Tax chargeable on the ending of conditional exemption for works of art, historic buildings etc. on woodlands and on maintenance funds for historic buildings is always payable six months after the end of the month in which the chargeable event occurs. With effect for charges arising on or after 6 April 2014 under *IHTA 1984, Part 3, Chapter 3* (relevant property trusts etc.), the same due date for payment applies. [*IHTA 1984, s 226 (3C)* inserted by *FA 2014, Sch 25, para 5(2)*].

It should be noted that tax will often become payable before accounts (see 2 ACCOUNTS AND RETURNS) are due to be rendered.

Transfers on death

[35.2] Inheritance tax is due six months after the end of the month in which death occurs but personal representatives must pay the tax for which they are liable *on delivery of their account* (even if before the due date) and may also at the same time pay any other tax on the death at the request of the persons liable. The *FA 2007* changes make provision for situations where there is a left-over pension pot at the death of an ASP scheme member who was over the age of 75 on death and was traced after their death by the scheme administrator. In such cases the left-over ASP funds are brought within the charge to IHT by *IHTA 1984, s 151A(6)* but the scheme administrator has six months from the end of the month in which they discovered the scheme member's death to pay any IHT due. [*IHTA 1984, s 226(4) inserted by FA 2007, Sch 19 para 25*].

Lifetime transfers with additional liability on death

[35.3] Where tax or additional tax is due at death because:

(a) a 38 POTENTIALLY EXEMPT TRANSFER proves to be a chargeable transfer; or
(b) the transferor dies within seven years of making a chargeable lifetime transfer; or
(c) gifts have been made before 15 March 1988 and within one year of death to a political party in excess of £100,000; or
(d) the settlor dies within seven years of the transfer and a further liability arises under the rules relating to 43 SETTLEMENTS: DISCRETIONARY TRUSTS AND OTHER TRUSTS OF RELEVANT PROPERTY,

the additional tax is due six months after the end of the month in which death occurs.

[*IHTA 1984, s 226(1)–(4); FA 1986, Sch 19 para 30; FA 1988, Sch 14*].

Without prejudice to the recovery of the remainder of any tax due, the Board may, in the first instance, accept or demand payment by reference to the value stated in an account delivered to them. [*IHTA 1984, s 226(5)*].

Addresses for payment of tax

[35.4]

England and Wales	HMRC Banking Team, St Mungo's Road, Cumbernauld, Glasgow G70 5WY Tel. 0845 3020900 Fax. 0115 974 2432 DX 550100 Cumbernauld 2 Note: Electronic transfer payments are made to Citi bank Sort code 08-32-10, Account 12001136 when using BACS or CHAPS.
Scotland	HMRC, Meldrum House, 15 Drumsheugh Gardens, Edinburgh EH3 7UG. Tel. 0131–777 4050 Fax. 0131–777 4220 DX 542001 Edinburgh 14 Note: Electronic transfer payments regarding the Edinburgh office are now made to Bank of England, Sort code 10-00-00, Account 23430303 when using BACS or CHAPS. When using Bank Giro Credit use the Sort code 10-53-92 but the same Account number. Note: Any payments sent by post should be marked for the attention of the Cashier.
Northern Ireland	HMRC, HMRC Inheritance Tax, Dorchester House, 52–58 Great Victoria Street, Belfast BT2 7QL. Tel. 028 9050 5353 Fax. 028 9050 5305 DX 2001 NR Belfast 2 Note: Electronic transfer payments regarding the Belfast office are now made to Bank of England, Sort code 10-00-00, Account 23430303 when using BACS or CHAPS. When using Bank Giro Credit use the Sort code 10-53-92 but the same Account number.

Where personal representatives apply personally for a grant of representation (see **2.19** ACCOUNTS AND RETURNS for addresses) they will be told how much tax should be paid before the grant can be obtained and the address at which the tax should be paid. In a change to the system and following discussions between the British Bankers' Association and the Building Societies' Association HMRC have agreed that personal representatives can draw on funds held in the deceased's bank or building society account (NS&I (formerly National Savings) are not within the scheme yet) solely for the purpose of paying inheritance tax prior to the grant.

In this connection a revised Form IHT 423 has been added to the existing IHT 400 for this use.

There is one problem with electronic lodgement payment that impacts on the speed of obtaining probate; the result of electronic lodgement is that it takes at least three working days for the paperwork to reach HMRC Inheritance Tax from the Citi bank and therefore if speed is essential sending a cheque is the recommended alternative. Also, a HMRC Inheritance Tax reference number should only be applied for prior to using the direct payment scheme where tax is due on the estate. To obtain a HMRC Inheritance Tax reference for use with this scheme, the HMRC Inheritance Tax recommend telephoning their Helpline on 0845 30 20 900. See www.hmrc.gov.uk/cto/newsletter.htm, December 1995, July 1997, August 2003, April 2006, December 2006, April 2007 and April 2009.

Payment by instalments

[35.5] An election in writing to the Board may be made to pay the tax due by ten equal yearly instalments in respect of property listed below. The first instalment is payable on the due date on which the whole tax would otherwise be due if it were not payable by instalments, see **35.1** above. Where the transfer is on death, the first instalment is due six months after the end of the month in which death occurs even if the personal representatives must otherwise pay tax before that date.

The tax outstanding (with interest to the time of payment, see **35.9** below) may be paid at any time. If the whole or any part of the property concerned is sold or ceases to be comprised in a settlement, then the related tax still outstanding (with accrued interest) becomes payable forthwith unless (i) the sale precedes the date that the first instalment is due in which case the tax does not become due until that date; or (ii) the sale is by the transferee following a **38** POTENTIALLY EXEMPT TRANSFER and the transferee dies before the transferor. For these purposes, the sale of an interest in a business is treated as a sale of part of the business and payment of a sum in satisfaction of the whole or part of an interest in a business otherwise than on sale is treated as a sale of the interest or part at the time of payment. Where there is a delay between the dates of contract and completion, the sale for the purposes of *IHTA 1984, s 227(4)* is deemed to take place at the completion date (Tolley's Practical Tax 1991 p 200). *Note.* Where *IHTA 1984, s 107* (see **6.8** BUSINESS PROPERTY) allows for the extension of business relief to property which replaces relevant business property in a situation where a business is acquired by a company controlled by the former owner of the business, the right to pay by instalments is in practice not lost because of the 'sale' of the business to the company (Tolley's Practical Tax 1989 p 191).

Transfers on death

[35.6] The eligible property is:

(a) land and buildings of any description, wherever situated;

(b) listed or unquoted shares or securities which gave control of the company (see **35.8** below) to the deceased;

(c) unquoted shares or securities (in relation to transfers made, and other events occurring, before 17 March 1987, shares or securities not listed on a recognised stock exchange) not within (b) above:
   (i) which attract (together with tax on any other transfer under (a) to (e) on which the same person is liable) not less than 20% of the tax liable by that person in the same capacity; or
   (ii) if the Board are satisfied that the tax attributable to the shares or securities cannot be paid in one sum without undue hardship;

(d) unquoted shares (not securities) (in relation to transfers made, and other events occurring, before 17 March 1987, shares not quoted on a recognised stock exchange) not within (b) with a value exceeding £20,000 where either:
   (i) their nominal value is not less than 10% of the total nominal value of all the shares of the company at the time of death; or
   (ii) they are ordinary shares (see **35.8** below) with nominal value not less than 10% of all ordinary shares of the company at the time of the death;

(e) the net value of a business (see **35.8** below) or an interest in a business carried on for gain, including a profession or vocation.

Lifetime transfers

[35.7] The right to elect to pay tax on lifetime transfers by instalments in respect of the property listed below is restricted to cases:

(i) where the tax is borne by the person benefiting from the transfer (understood to be taken by HMRC Inheritance Tax to mean the transferee) (but see (F) below); or

(ii) where the transfer is made under the settled property provisions in *IHTA 1984, Pt III* in respect of settled property which remains in the settlement.

In relation to transfers of value made, and other events occurring, after 16 March 1987, tax cannot be payable by instalments where a **38** POTENTIALLY EXEMPT TRANSFER proves to be a chargeable transfer or additional tax becomes payable due to the death of the transferor within seven years of the transfer unless *either* the property was owned by the 'transferee' throughout the period from the date of the transfer to the transferor's death (or, if earlier, his own death) *or*, for the purposes of determining the tax (or additional tax) due, the value of the property is reduced by agricultural or business property relief by virtue of the replacement property provisions. See **4.5** AGRICULTURAL PROPERTY and **6.11** BUSINESS PROPERTY. If the property consists of unquoted shares or securities, there is an additional condition that the shares or securities remained unquoted throughout the period from the date of the transfer to the transferor's death (or, if earlier, the transferee's death).

In relation to transfers of value made, and other events occurring, before 17 March 1987, where a **38** POTENTIALLY EXEMPT TRANSFER proved to be a chargeable transfer, the tax payable could not be paid by instalments unless the property transferred was owned by the 'transferee' immediately before the transferor's death (or, if earlier, his own death).

'*Transferee*' means the person whose property the qualifying property became on the transfer or, where on the transfer the property became comprised in a settlement in which no qualifying interest in possession subsists, the trustees of the settlement.

The eligible property is:

(A) land and buildings of any description, wherever situated;
(B) listed or unquoted shares or securities which gave control (see **35.8** below) of the company to the transferor or to the trustees of the settlement;
(C) unquoted shares or securities (before 17 March 1987 and after 9 March 1992, shares or securities not listed on a recognised stock exchange) not within (B) where the Board are satisfied (on the assumption that the shares etc. are retained by the person liable to pay the tax) that the tax attributable to the shares or securities cannot be paid in one sum without undue hardship;
(D) unquoted shares etc. — as for transfers on death under (d) above;
(E) the net value of a business (see **35.8** below) or an interest in a business carried on for gain, including a profession or vocation;
(F) trees or underwood left out of account on death (see **57** WOODLANDS) and later disposed of in a lifetime transfer. In this case the right to pay by instalments is available to both the transferor and transferee and does not cease if the timber is later sold.

[*IHTA 1984, ss 227–229; FA 1986, Sch 19 para 31; FA 1987, s 58, Sch 8 paras 15–17; F(No 2)A 1992, s 73, Sch 14 paras 5, 6, 8; FA 1996, Sch 38 para 5; FA 2009, Sch 53 para 7(2)*].

Example 1

F died on 17 December 2010 leaving a free estate of £395,000, including £75,000 (after business property relief at 50%) in respect of plant and machinery in a partnership. An election is made to pay inheritance tax on the plant and machinery by 10 equal yearly instalments.

Inheritance tax on free estate			£
On first	£325,000		Nil
On next	£70,000	at 40%	28,000
	£395,000		£28,000

IHT applicable to business property

$$\frac{75{,}000}{395{,}000} \times £28{,}000 \qquad £5{,}316$$

1st instalment due 1.7.2011	£531
2nd instalment due 1.7.2012	£531

And so on

Example 2

On 1 December 2010 G gave his land in a partnership of which G was a partner to his son S who agreed to pay any IHT on the transfer. The land was valued at £600,000. G had made prior chargeable transfers of £140,000, had already used his 2009/10 and 2010/11 annual exemptions, and he died on 31 December 2014.

Selected to pay the IHT by ten yearly instalments and paid the first on 1 August 2015, and the second on 1 September 2016. On 1 December 2016 he sold the land, and paid the balance of the IHT outstanding on 1 February 2017. It is assumed that the rate of interest on unpaid inheritance tax for this purpose is 3% p.a. throughout.

Inheritance tax on gift

		£
Value of land		600,000
Deduct business property relief at 50%		300,000
PET becoming chargeable on death		£300,000
IHT payable in the band £140,001–£440,000		
	£	
£140,001–325,000	Nil	
£325,001–440,000 at 40%	46,000	
	£46,000	
Total IHT payable at 60% of full rates (death between 4 and 5 years after gift)		£27,600
1st instalment due 1.7.2015	2,760	
Interest at 3% from 1.7.2015 to 1.8.2015		
$^{31}/_{366}$ × £2,760 × 3%	7	
		2,767
2nd instalment due 1.7.2016	2,760	
Interest at 3% from 1.7.2016 to 1.9.2016		
$^{62}/_{366}$ × £2,760 × 3%	14	
		2,774
Balance due on sale on 1.12.2016	22,080	
Interest at 3% from 1.12.2016 to 1.2.2017		
$^{62}/_{366}$ × £22,080 × 3%	112	
		22,192
Total IHT and interest		£27,733

Note to the example

(A) Interest on unpaid tax after 5 April 1998 is calculated using 366 days as the denominator rather than 365 days. See CTO Newsletter Extract, March 1997 at www.hmrc.gov.uk/cto/newsletter.htm. See **28.1** INTEREST ON TAX.

Definitions

[35.8] Definitions relating to 35.5 above are as follows.

'*Control of company*' by a person is when he can exercise control of a majority of votes on all questions affecting the company as a whole, and for this purpose there will be included any shares or securities which are related property (see **56.21** VALUATION) and where shares or securities are comprised in a settlement, any voting powers which they give to the trustees of the settlement are deemed to be given to the individual beneficially entitled in possession to those shares or securities (or to the trustees if there is no such individual). See *Walker's Executors v CIR* [2001] STC SCD 86 Sp C 275. Where there are shares or securities of any class with voting powers only on the winding-up of the company and/or on any question primarily affecting that class, then the reference above to 'all questions affecting the company as a whole' are to be read as referring to all such questions except those to which the powers of the particular class apply. In the case of *Walding and Others (Executors of Walding deceased) v IRC* Ch D [1996] STC 13 where the point at issue was whether the deceased had 'the control of powers of voting on all questions affecting the company as a whole'. [*IHTA 1984, s 269(1)*]. The deceased's holding of 45 shares out of 100 gave control, in the view of the Executors, because 24 shares held by a four year old grandson of the deceased could not realistically be exercised in the voting rights of the company due to the minor's mental or physical incapacity. The judge held that *s 269(1)* allowed relief where the deceased controlled the powers of voting on all matters affecting the company. However, even though the grandson was too young to exercise his voting rights, *s 269(1)* required his company at the date of death. The court dismissed the Executors' appeal and no BPR relief was due; *IHTA 1984, s 269(1)* deals with the ambit of the powers of voting, not the capabilities of the shareholders in whose names the shares were registered. [*IHTA 1984, s 269; ITA 2007, s 995*].

'*Ordinary shares*' are shares which carry either (i) a right to dividends not restricted to dividends at a fixed rate or (ii) a right to conversion into shares carrying such a right as in (i). [*IHTA 1984, s 228(4); ITA 2007, s 989*].

In relation to transfers of value made, and other events occurring, after 9 March 1992, then, in relation to any shares or securities, '*quoted*' means quoted on a recognised stock exchange, and '*unquoted*' means not so quoted. [*IHTA 1984, ss 227(1AA), 228(5); F(No 2)A 1992, s 73, Sch 14 paras 5, 6, 8*]. This definition applies additionally for defining relevant business property (see **6.4** BUSINESS PROPERTY) but otherwise, for transfers of value made, and other events occurring, after 9 March 1992 does not apply generally for IHT purposes. In relation to transfers of value made, and other events occurring, after 16 March 1987 but before 10 March 1992, '*quoted*', in relation to any shares or securities, means quoted on a recognised stock exchange or dealt in on the Unlisted Securities Market, and '*unquoted*', in relation to any shares or securities, means neither so quoted nor so dealt in. [*IHTA 1984, s 272; FA 1987, s 58(2), Sch 8 para 17*]. This applied for all IHT purposes and *still*, in relation to transfers of value made, and other events occurring, after 9 March 1992, does so for purposes other than defining relevant business property and the above provisions. It should also be noted that as from 1 April 1996 the word '*quoted*' on a recognised stock exchange is substituted by the word '*listed*'. [*FA 1996, Sch 38 paras 2, 5*]. In relation to transfers of value made, and other events occurring, before 17 March 1987, shares and securities in companies dealt in on the Unlisted Securities Market were not treated as quoted on a recognised stock exchange for all IHT purposes (Inland Revenue Statement of Practice SP 18/80, 23 December 1980). See IR Press Release, 25 April 2001 for the proposed revised listing arrangements and its effect on the term 'recognised stock exchange'. The Alternative Investment Market (AIM) opened for business on 19 June 1995 with transitional arrangements until 29 September 1995 (see also IRPR 20 February 1995). This market will ostensibly replace the USM which was wound up at the end of 1996. (See also Company Secretary's Review, Vol 18 No 12, 19 October 1994).

Whilst *FA 2007* inserted new definitions of 'recognised stock exchange' for the purposes of income tax and capital gains tax, the change did not include inheritance tax. HMRC have in the past confirmed that AIM shares and PLUS quoted market were to be unlisted for the purposes of, for example, CGT taper relief (as they were not included on the UK official list, required by new *ITA 2007, s 1005(3)*). However, the new definition for IHT will not in itself mean that the treatment of such shares will change for IHT purposes as they continue to be treated as unquoted. [*ITA 2007, s 1005; FA 2007, s 109, Sch 26*].

'*Net value of a business*' is the value of the assets used in the business (including goodwill) reduced by the total amount of any liabilities incurred for the purposes of the business; and in ascertaining the net value of an interest in a business, (e.g. a partnership share), regard is to be had only to those assets and liabilities which would have been used in calculating the net value of the entire business. [*IHTA 1984, s 227(7)*].

Interest

[35.9] Interest on unpaid portion of tax payable by instalments is added to each instalment where applicable and paid accordingly. See **28.1** INTEREST ON TAX above for rates of interest. [*IHTA 1984, ss 227(2), 233, 234(1); FA 1989, s 179(1); FA 2009, Sch 53 para 7(3)*]. They apply as follows.

On the balance outstanding at each instalment date commencing with the date the instalment is due to be paid in respect of:

(i) land under **35.5**(a) and **35.5**(A) above (unless it is a business asset under **35.5**(e) or **35.7**(E) above or agricultural property reduced by **4** AGRICULTURAL PROPERTY relief); and
(ii) shares and securities under **35.5**(b)(c) and (d) and **35.5**(b)(c) and (d) in companies whose business is wholly or mainly dealing in securities, stocks or shares or making or holding investments *unless* the business

consists of being a holding company for subsidiaries whose business does not fall within those categories or the business is wholly that of a 'market maker' (before the Stock Exchange reform, a jobber) or a discount house and, in either case, is carried on in the UK or with effect from 31 December 2012 within the European Economic Area.

A '*market maker*' is a person who holds himself out at all normal times in compliance with the rules of either The Stock Exchange or, after 23 March 1992, LIFFE (Administration and Management) as willing to buy and sell securities etc. and is recognised as doing so by the Council of the Stock Exchange. [*IHTA 1984, s 234(2)–(4); FA 1986, s 107; SI 1992/3181; Companies Act 2006, s 1159*].

No interest (except for late payment of an instalment) is payable apart from those cases in (i) and (ii) above.

Acceptance of property in satisfaction of tax

[35.10] The Board may, if they think fit and the Ministers agree, on application of any person liable to pay tax, accept property within the following categories in whole or part payment of tax and interest (see VOA IHT manual, section 20, para 20.31 and also www.culture.gov.uk/cultural_property/acceptance_lieu.htm.)

(a) Land. In practice only land with a particular amenity value will normally be accepted. Agricultural land as such will not normally be accepted unless it is associated with an historic building. Buildings will normally only be accepted if they are of architectural or historic interest and can be put to amenity use such as display as part of the national heritage.

(b) Any objects which are or have been kept in any building (i) accepted in satisfaction of IHT, CTT or estate duty or (ii) belonging to the Crown or Duchies of Lancaster or Cornwall or (iii) belonging to, or used for the purposes of, a government department or (iv) protected under the *Ancient Monuments and Archaeological Areas Act 1979* or the *Historic Monuments Act (Northern Ireland) 1971* or (v) belonging to certain museums and other bodies specified in *IHTA 1984, Sch 3* (see list under **33.29** NATIONAL HERITAGE). It must appear desirable to 'the Ministers' for the objects to remain associated with the building.

(c) Any picture, print, book, manuscript, work of art, scientific object or other thing which the Ministers are satisfied is pre-eminent for its national, scientific, historic or artistic interest. This includes a collection or group of such objects. (The test of 'pre-eminence' is 'would the object be a pre-eminent addition to a public collection, whether national, local authority or university?'. The object must be something which stands out for its particular qualities and will attract special attention when displayed, and is not merely a normal addition to a public collection.) However, see Taxation, 10 November 1994, p 123 regarding restrictions on the acceptance of assets of national importance in lieu of tax where those assets are exempt for other reasons e.g. BPR.

[*National Heritage Act 1980, ss 12, 13; IHTA 1984, s 230;* Capital Taxation and the National Heritage (IR67) not now in print].

HMRC and DCMS requirements

HMRC have confirmed that if a claim is made under *IHTA 1984, s 230* for acceptance in lieu of tax but the offeror has already paid the IHT they will not accept a subsequent offer to transfer assets in lieu. However, HMRC will entertain an offer where:

- all the tax has been paid in advance in order to obtain the grant or confirmation, provided that at or around the time of payment HMRC are notified of the possibility that an offer in lieu of the tax will be made; or
- HMRC are holding money on account of a liability to pay interest and tax where the money is held to the taxpayer's order but remains unpaid.

See www.hmrc.gov.uk/cto/newsletter.htm, May Special Edition 2003 p 2.

Where HMRC agree under *IHTA 1984, s 230* to accept property in satisfaction of the amount, and under those terms the valuation of the property is determined at an earlier date then the amount of tax which is satisfied by the acceptance of the property does not carry late payment interest after that date. [*National Heritage Act 1980, ss 12, 13; IHTA 1984, s 230; FA 2009, Sch 53 para 14*].

The Department for Culture, Media and Sport has drawn up a model *in situ* loan agreement for use when drawing up a loan agreement covering Chattel(s) accepted in whole or part satisfaction of capital taxes and any other liabilities under the provisions of *IHTA 1984, s 230* but which are to be displayed to the public *in situ* at the Borrower's premises.

For acceptances after 16 March 1987, the special price at which the item is accepted is calculated from the value of the item on the date the property is offered unless the person liable for the tax which is to be satisfied by an acceptance in lieu notifies HMRC that he wishes them to adopt the value of the property on the date of acceptance. See Inland Revenue Statement of Practice SP 6/87, April 1987. Before 17 March 1987, only the 'acceptance date' arrangements were available. Where the 'offer date' arrangements are chosen, interest on the tax satisfied by the item ceases to accrue on that date, see **28.1** INTEREST ON TAX.

A person having power to sell property in order to raise money for payment of tax may agree with the Board for the property to be accepted under the above conditions and such agreement shall be treated as a sale made under the said power. [*IHTA 1984, ss 231, 233(1A); FA 1987, s 60; F(No 2)A 1987, s 97*]. Before 1 April 1998 an amount equal to the Estate Duty, CTT or IHT had to be paid over by the Department of Culture, Media and Sport (DCMS) to the Board under the *National Heritage Act 1980, s 8*. From 1 April 1998 this reimbursement system is abolished. In order to facilitate the above the *Exchequer Audit Department Act 1866, s 10* will be required to contain information about property accepted in lieu of tax on or after 1 April 1998. [*FA 1998, s 145*]. The appointed day for the purposes of this section is 4 November 1998. [*Finance Act 1998, s 145, (Appointed Day) Order 1998, SI 1998/2703*].

'*The Ministers*' means the Secretary of State and the Lord President of the Council. [*National Heritage Act 1980, s 12(1); IHTA 1984, s 230(5); SI 1986/600*].

APPLICATION FOR ACCEPTANCE OF LAND IN SATISFACTION OF TAX

I/We* . . . . of . . . . apply for acceptance by the Board of HMRC of the property herein detailed in the accompanying Schedule in satisfaction of tax and accrued interest by way of sections 230 and 233 of the Inheritance Tax Act 1984. In support of this application I/we* the offeror(s) supply the following:

(a) Four copies of a valuation of the land at the date of 'offer' for acceptance in satisfaction of tax;

(b) Full colour photographs of the land;

(c) Valuation and full description of the land;

(d) Application for inspection of the land may be addressed to:

Name: . . . .

Address: . . . .

. . . .

Telephone: . . . . . .

(e) Certain wishes/conditions apply to the said land and these are attached to the enclosed documents.

I/We* look forward to receiving your reply concerning the above application under sections 230 and 233, IHTA 1984.

Signed . . . .

Capacity: . . . .

Dated: . . . .

* Delete as appropriate

Note to the claim

(A) In preparing the 'full description' attaching to the claim in (c) above the following particulars, which are considered by the VOA when they present a report to the CTO, are likely to be of importance where relevant:

(1) the situation of the property;

(2) its general amenities;

(3) any known matters of historical interest;

(4) any accepted features of architectural merit;

(5) elevations (e.g. Georgian), constructions, accommodation and condition of all buildings;

(6) public services available;

(7) any sporting rights with the property;

(8) total areas of the land;

(9) the tenure of the property;

(10) particulars of growing timber;

(11) any restrictions, rights or covenants affecting the property;

(12) whether any of the property is situated in a Special Site of Scientific Interest under the *Wildlife and Countryside Act 1981*;

(13) mention should be made of any easements and reservations necessitated by a division of the land previously;

(14) the nature and condition of any private roads and access drives;

(15) the nature and condition of any boundary fences shown on the map and which of these are provided or maintained with the property;

(16) tenancies attaching to the property with a note of any portions of the property where vacant possession can be offered;

(17) rents and outgoings;

(18) any valuable fixtures (e.g. chandeliers, panelling, tapestries, etc.) and whether these are to pass with the property;

(19) the existing use of the property and any proposals, applications and decisions under the *Town and Country Planning Acts and Regulations* which may affect it;

(20) whether any part of the property is scheduled as an ancient monument or a building of special architectural or historical interest;

(21) if the property is situated in a National Park;

(22) any prospective acquisition by a public body;

(23) any published material on the property e.g. brochures, press articles, etc. should be attached.

(See VOA IHT manual, section 20, para 20.33 and Appendix 29 and see also SP 6/87 at 25 HMRC STATEMENTS OF PRACTICE.)

Certificates of tax deposit

[35.11] Certificates of tax deposit Series 7, which enable money to be set aside for payment of future tax liability, may be used in payment of inheritance tax. Interest from 6 March 2009 (maximum rates are currently between 0.25% and 0.75% for deposits of £100,000 or more) is received on these certificates from the date of purchase until the date on which the tax in respect of which they are surrendered falls due. Certificates may also be encashed but the rate of interest is currently also 0% (for less than one month) – 0.75% for deposits of £100,000 or more (for more than 12 months). Deposits of less than £100,000 attract interest rates of 0% (if applied against tax) and the interest is 0% if withdrawn for cash. Purchase of certificates of tax deposit for under £100,000 may be made by cheque to HMRC DMB Banking Shipley, Victoria Street, Shipley BD98 8AA. See also IHTM10253.

HMRC charge

[35.12] Where any tax or interest is unpaid, an HMRC charge is imposed for that amount on:

(a) any property to which the tax is attributable by its transfer;
(b) any property comprised in a settlement where the chargeable transfer arises on the creation of the settlement or is made under *IHTA 1984, Pt III* in respect of settled property; and
(c) any property relating to heritage assets charged under the existing provisions of *IHTA 1984, ss 32, 32A, 79, Sch 4 para 8* or *Sch 5 para 1* or *3*. Where the event giving rise to the charge is a disposal to a purchaser of the property or object in question, no charge may be imposed on that property or object or any property for the time being representing it.

The charge may be imposed on any property directly or indirectly representing the above.

[*IHTA 1984, s 237(1)(2)(3B)(3C); FA 1999, s 107*].

HMRC charge not applying

No charge may be imposed on:

(i) personal or movable property in the UK (excluding leaseholds in relation to deaths after 8 March 1999) treated as transferred on the death of the beneficial owner (other than settled property in which the deceased was beneficially entitled to an interest in possession) and which vests in his personal representatives;
(ii) heritable property situated in Scotland (but where this is disposed of, any property representing it is subject to the charge).

[*IHTA 1984, s 237(3)(4); Trusts of Land and Appointment of Trustees Act 1996, Sch 14; FA 1999, s 107*].

Priority of charge

[35.13] An HMRC charge on any property is effective after any incumbrance thereon which is allowable as a deduction in valuing that property for the purposes of IHT e.g. a mortgage. [*IHTA 1984, s 237(5)*].

Validity of charge on disposition

[35.14] A disposition of property subject to an HMRC charge takes effect subject to that charge. However, property disposed of to a purchaser will not be subject to any HMRC charge if at the 'time of disposition'

(A) in the case of land in England and Wales, the charge was not registered as a land charge or, in the case of registered land, was not protected by notice on the register; or
(B) in the case of land in Northern Ireland the title to which is registered under the *Land Registration Act (Northern Ireland) 1970*, the charge was not entered as a burden on the appropriate register maintained

under that *Act* or was not protected by a caution or inhibition or, in the case of other land in NI, the purchaser of the property had no notice of the facts giving rise to the charge; or

(C) in the case of personal property situated in the UK other than in (A) and (B) above, and of any property situated outside the UK, the purchaser had no notice of the facts giving rise to the charge; or

(D) in the case of any property, a certificate of discharge (now 'closure letter', see **35.15** below) had been given by the Board and the purchaser had no notice of any fact invalidating the certificate.

In the above circumstances, the charge ceases to apply to the property but then applies to the property representing it. (Note that the above does not apply to a donee who would receive property subject to any charge whether or not it was registered or he had notice of it.) [*IHTA 1984, ss 237(6), 238(1)*].

'*Time of disposition*' means (i) in relation to registered land, the time of registration of the disposition; and (ii) in relation to other property, the time of completion. [*IHTA 1984, s 238(3)*].

Where a **38** POTENTIALLY EXEMPT TRANSFER proves to be a chargeable transfer, property concerned which has been disposed of to a purchaser before the transferor's death is not subject to an HMRC charge but property concerned which has been otherwise disposed of before the death and property which at the death represents any property disposed of to a purchaser is subject to the charge. [*IHTA 1984, s 237(3A); FA 1986, Sch 19 para 34*].

Where property is disposed of to a purchaser subject to an HMRC charge, such charge ceases to apply after six years from the later of the date on which the tax became due and the date on which a full and proper account of the property was first delivered to the Board in connection with the chargeable transfer concerned. [*IHTA 1984, s 238(2)*].

A closure letter (previously a certificate of discharge, see **35.15** below) cancels any HMRC charge applying to the property specified. [*IHTA 1984, s 239(3)*]. Applications for the cancellation of an HMRC charge entered on property under the *Land Registration Acts 1925–1971* should be made on Form Cap 37. See **2.8** ACCOUNTS AND RETURNS for automatic discharge of 'excepted estates' and **2.11** for 'excepted terminations' of settled property.

Closure letters

[35.15] On the application of the person liable for tax on the transfer of specified property, the Board may give (must give if the property is transferred on death or the transferor has died), if satisfied that the tax has been or will be paid, a closure letter to that effect. An application with respect to the tax which is or may become chargeable by a **38** POTENTIALLY EXEMPT TRANSFER may not be made earlier than two years after the transferor's death (except as allowed by the Board at any earlier time after death). Such a closure letter will discharge the property from HMRC charge (see **35.12** above) on its acquisition by a purchaser. [*IHTA 1984, s 239(1)(2A)(3)(5); FA 1986, Sch 19 para 35*].

On the application of the person who is, or might be liable for the whole or part of the tax on a transfer of value, the Board may determine the amount of the tax or determine that no tax is chargeable and, subject to the payment of any tax, may give (must give if the transfer of value is made on death or the transferor has died) a closure letter of their determination. The application must be after two years from the transfer (or earlier if the Board allow) and delivery made of a full account (see 2 ACCOUNTS AND RETURNS). An application with respect to the tax which is or may become chargeable by a 38 POTENTIALLY EXEMPT TRANSFER may not be made earlier than two years after the transferor's death (except as allowed by the Board at an earlier time after the death). Such a closure letter discharges all persons from any further tax on the transfer and extinguishes any HMRC charge for that tax. [*IHTA 1984, s 239(2)(2A)(3)(5); FA 1986, Sch 19 para 35*]. 'Closure letters' replaced the previous certificate of discharge and apply from 30 April 2007. The closure letter will confirm either that no tax is due or that all the tax due has been paid or, in the case of deferred/instalment property e.g. timber/land that the tax has, but for those items, been paid. Application for clearance should not be made until the applicants are reasonably certain that all aspects of the estate have been settled. This means that executors should have checked with the trustees that the value of all settled property has been notified and agreed with HMRC Inheritance Tax. Trustees should have made similar enquiries of executors before lodging their application (CTO Practice Note published in Taxation Practitioner August 1994, p 6).

Case law — Closure notice

In *HH Collinson v HMRC* an individual (C) claimed that he had made a tax loss of more than £400,000 in 1998/99 as a result of certain transactions in securities. In January 2001 the Revenue began an enquiry into C's return. In September 2009 C applied to the First-Tier Tribunal for a closure notice. The tribunal granted his application, and directed that HMRC should issue a closure notice within 30 days. Judge Shipwright observed that 'nine years is a considerable time to wait to know whether a Government Department will or will not allow your claim. If the claim is denied it is not until a closure notice has been issued that an appeal can be lodged. It could be some time then before the case is heard and a decision reached. The longer the period from the time the actual transactions took place the harder it is to find documents and reliable evidence. Witnesses cease to be available and memories fade. This makes it harder for there to be a fair trial in a reasonable time.' [2010] UKFTT 165, TC00470.

Effect of fraud or failure to disclose material facts etc

[35.16] The above closure letters are invalid in a case of fraud or failure to disclose material facts and do not affect any further tax on further property afterwards shown to be included in a deceased's estate immediately before his death or arising from an alteration of dispositions under a deed of family arrangement or similar document. They are valid in favour of a purchaser of property who had no notice of any invalidation. [*IHTA 1984, s 239(4)*]. A closure letter will also be invalid where a claim under *IHTA 1984, s 8A(3)* has been overstated. See also 5.7 ANTI-AVOIDANCE

For HMRC's practice regarding the liability of personal representatives previously issued with a closure letter who discover a further chargeable lifetime transfer, see 30.7 LIABILITY FOR TAX.

Excepted estates

[35.17] Subject to the same rules regarding fraud etc. (see above), where an estate is an excepted estate (see 2.8 ACCOUNTS AND RETURNS), if the Board do not issue a notice calling for an account, the personal representatives will automatically be discharged from any further claim for tax or charge on property at the end of the prescribed period. In these cases, there is no need to apply for a closure letter. If the Board issue a notice calling for details of the estate, automatic discharge does not apply and the normal course must be followed. [*SI 2002/1733*; Inland Revenue Press Release 2 July 1987].

Excepted terminations

[35.18] Where the termination of an interest in possession is an 'excepted termination' (see 2.11 ACCOUNTS AND RETURNS), unless within the period of six months from the termination the Board issue a notice requiring an account, the trustees will be discharged from any claim for tax on the value of that property. This provision does not discharge any person in a case of fraud or failure to disclose material facts. [*SI 1981/1440; SI 2002/1731*].

Recovery of tax

[35.19] No legal proceedings to recover tax or interest can be taken by the Board unless the amount has been agreed in writing or specified in an undisputed notice of determination (see 14 DETERMINATIONS AND APPEALS). Tax and interest may, without prejudice to any other remedy, be sued for and recovered in a Scottish sheriff court if the amount sought does not exceed the sum for the time being specified in the *Sheriff Courts (Scotland) Act 1971, s 35(1)(a)*.

Where proceedings to recover tax or interest are taken in a county court or sheriff court, the court may be addressed by any authorised officer of the Board, and a certificate by an officer of the Board that the tax or interest is due or that, to the best of his knowledge and belief, it is unpaid is sufficient evidence of that fact in any proceedings for its recovery.

If an appeal to the Special Commissioners (now Upper Tribunal), or direct to the High Court, is pending, only agreed undisputed tax is recoverable. Where an appeal is taken a stage further, the disputed tax is payable (and adjusted after that appeal has been determined). [*IHTA 1984, ss 242–244, 254(2); FA 1993, s 200(2)(3)*].

Adjustment of tax

Underpayments

[35.20] Where too little tax has been paid, the deficiency is payable with interest whether or not the original payment was stated in a notice of determination; but where the payment was made and accepted in full satisfaction of tax in accordance with an account duly delivered to the Board no proceedings for any additional tax may be brought after six years from the later of:

(a) the date on which the payment (or last instalment) was made and accepted; and
(b) the date on which the tax (or last instalment) became due.

At the end of that period any liability for additional tax and any HMRC charge for that tax is extinguished. See also **35.15** above.

If there is fraud, wilful default or neglect by a person liable for tax, the six years begin when the Board first has knowledge of these circumstances. For periods starting on or after 1 April 2009 where the return is due on or after 1 April 2010 the six year period is reduced to four years. In certain cases the six year time limit remains in place in a case where there is a loss of tax brought about by 'careless' action by a person liable for the tax (or a person acting on behalf of such a person). Proceedings in such a case of 'careless' action may be brought at any time not more than six years after the later of the date on which the payment of tax was made (and accepted by HMRC) or the date tax was due and this includes payments made by the instalment option. Further, in a case involving a loss of tax brought about by 'deliberate' action by a person liable for the tax (or a person acting on behalf of such a person) may be brought at any time not more than 20 years after the later of those dates. [*Finance Act 2008, Schedule 40 (Appointed Day, Transitional Provisions and Consequential Amendments) Order 2009, SI 2009/571*].

This also applies to fraud by the settlor of a settlement in the case of tax chargeable under the rules relating to **43** SETTLEMENTS: DISCRETIONARY TRUSTS AND OTHER TRUSTS OF RELEVANT PROPERTY. In the case of a settlement the new provisions above apply to a person liable for the tax and are to be treated as including references to a person who is the settlor in relation to the settlement. [*IHTA 1984, s 240; FA 2009, Sch 51 paras 11, 12*].

Where the fraud etc. is by a settlor, HMRC have confirmed that they would not seek to recover the full amount of the additional tax due from the trustees of the settlement personally where the trustees had acted in good faith and had insufficient trust funds left with which to pay the tax. (Law Society's Gazette 12 December 1984).

It is understood from HMRC's Press Office that the concession A19 (revised on 11 March 1996) in the HMRC Pamphlet IR1 (Arrears of tax arising through official error) is unavailable where an inheritance tax liability is in point. HMRC's statement that the principles of Code of Practice 1 (wherein the concession is mentioned) are applied 'to all parts of the Inland Revenue' (Inland Revenue Press Release 17 February 1993) should be read in the light of this.

Overpayments

[35.21] Where an overpayment of tax or interest is proved to the satisfaction of the Board, repayment will be made provided the claim is made within six years from the payment (or last payment). For periods starting on or after 1 April 2009 where the return is due on or after 1 April 2010 the six year period is reduced to four years. Where the sum overpaid is £25 or less, the assessment leading to repayment is not automatically initiated by HMRC Inheritance Tax and must be requested by the taxpayer. [*IHTA 1984, s 241; FA 2009, Sch 51 para 13* and see SP 6/95 at **25** HMRC STATEMENTS OF PRACTICE].

If too much tax was paid because of a mistake by HMRC or any other Government department, repayment can be claimed within twenty years of the original overpayment (see B41 at **23** HMRC EXTRA-STATUTORY CONCESSIONS and Code of Practice 1). The European Convention on Human Rights and *Human Rights Act 1998* which came into effect on 2 October 2000 has now confirmed that HMRC cannot seek penalties from the personal representatives of a deceased person who was liable for a penalty. In addition any such penalties already collected must now be repaid and these repayments should include repayment interest at the rate applicable under *IHTA 1984, s 233*. Such interest would run from the date the penalties are paid to the date of repayment by HMRC.

For Scotland only, the time limits above of six years do not apply to adjustments of tax arising due to a person claiming or renouncing his right to legitim. See **52.19** TRANSFERS ON DEATH. [*IHTA 1984, s 147(8)(9)*].

Payment by court

[35.22] Where IHT is attributable to any property in the possession or control of a court pending proceedings for its administration, the court must provide any unpaid tax, or interest, out of such property. [*IHTA 1984, s 232*].

Payment on previous view of law

[35.23] Any payment made and accepted in satisfaction of any liability for tax and on a view of the law then generally adopted, will only be disturbed on the same view of the law, notwithstanding that it appears from a subsequent legal decision or otherwise that the view was or may have been wrong. [*IHTA 1984, s 255*].

Foreign assets

Payment out of foreign assets

[35.24] Where, because of restrictions imposed by the foreign government, executors cannot immediately transfer to this country sufficient of the deceased's foreign assets for payment of the inheritance tax liability attributable to them, they are given the option of deferring payment until the transfer can be effected. If the amount in sterling that the executors finally succeed in bringing to this country is less than this tax, the balance is waived. (See F6 at 23 HMRC EXTRA-STATUTORY CONCESSIONS).

Foreign-owned works of art

[35.25] Where a work of art normally kept overseas becomes liable to inheritance tax on the owner's death solely because it is physically situated in the UK at the relevant date, the liability will be waived if the work was brought into the UK solely for public exhibition, cleaning or restoration. Despite the flexibility of concession F7 it is perhaps wise to ensure that HMRC Inheritance Tax is approached in these circumstances to ensure that no IHT liability will be attached if the foreign domiciliary dies with an artwork in the United Kingdom and a chargeable event arises. If the work of art is held by a discretionary trust (or is otherwise comprised in settled property in which there is no interest in possession) the charge to tax under *IHTA 1984, s 64* (ten-year anniversary charge) will similarly be waived. (See written ministerial statement by Dawn Primarolo MP, Hansard Col 11 WS, 25 February 2003 and F7 which has been now amended to include this provision at 23 HMRC EXTRA-STATUTORY CONCESSIONS.)

Powers to raise tax etc

[35.26] Any transferee or devisee who is liable to tax (including interest) on the value of any property may raise the money by sale or mortgage of, or a terminable charge on, that property whether or not the property is vested in him. A person with limited interest in the property who pays the tax is entitled to a similar charge on the property as if raised by a mortgage to him. [*IHTA 1984, s 212*].

Refund by instalments

[35.27] Where a person has paid tax which is or might at his option have been payable by instalments and he is entitled to recover part or the whole of it from another person, that other person (unless otherwise agreed between them) is entitled to refund the tax by the same instalments (and with the same interest thereon) as might have been paid to the Board. [*IHTA 1984, s 213*].

A clause regarding *IHTA 1984, s 213* such as that detailed below might be appropriate where, for instance, a company is a close company where it paid IHT by a lump sum where it could have paid by instalments. These circumstances are likely to arise where there may have been gifts or settlement of the company's shares or gifts to the company prior to the sale to the purchaser. Where the close company paid the IHT by a lump sum in circumstances where it could have paid by instalments, 'the Covenantors' must reimburse 'the Purchaser' by lump sum and may not pay by instalments unless it is agreed otherwise as seen below.

Taxation Indemnity

THIS TAX DEED is made the . . . . . . day of . . . . BETWEEN

(1) The persons whose names and addresses are set out in Part I of the Schedule ('the Covenantors');

(2) The companies whose names and registered offices are set out in Part II of the Schedule ('the Companies');

(3) . . . . [Name of Company]. . . . . registration number . . . . [reg. number]. . . . . whose registered office is at . . . . [address]. . . . . ('the Purchaser' which expression shall where the context so admits include its successors and assigns).

WHEREAS pursuant to an agreement ('the Agreement') dated . . . . [date]. . . . . the Purchaser has today completed the purchase from the Covenantors of the whole of the issued share capital of . . . . [Name of company]. . . . . in reliance *inter alia* upon the indemnities contained in this deed.

NOW IT IS AGREED as follows:

1 **General** . . . *etc.*

2 **The indemnities**

The Covenantors jointly and severally covenant with the Company and the Purchaser to indemnify them and hold them harmless against any liability:

2.1 The Inheritance Tax Act 1984, section 213 shall not apply in relation to any payments to be made by the Covenantors under this deed.

2.2 *etc.*

Note: Further conditions apply to the Tax Indemnity that are not relevant to this book

Certificates of tax paid

[35.28] A person who has paid tax not ultimately due from him may apply to the Board for a certificate specifying the tax paid and the debts and incumbrances allowed in valuing the property and any certificate is conclusive evidence of payment as between the payer and the person by whom the tax specified falls to be borne. [*IHTA 1984, s 214*].

Direct payment scheme – Bank or building society account [Form IHT 423]

HM Revenue & Customs

Direct payment scheme bank or building society account

Schedule IHT423

When to use this form

Fill in this form if you want to pay the Inheritance Tax that is due, by transferring money from the deceased's bank or building society account(s).
Please fill in a separate form for each account.

Help

Please read the guidance notes on the direct payment scheme in the IHT400 Notes before filling in this form.
For more information or help or another copy of this form:

- go to **www.hmrc.gov.uk/inheritancetax/**
- phone our Helpline on **0845 30 20 900**
  – if calling from outside the UK, phone **+44 115 974 3009**.

Where to send this form

The form should be sent to the bank or building society concerned and not to HM Revenue & Customs Inheritance Tax.

Name of deceased

Date of death *DD MM YYYY*

IHT reference number

Transfer details

I/We have applied for a grant of representation or Confirmation for the estate of the deceased and request that the amount shown below is transferred from the deceased's account to HM Revenue & Customs to pay the Inheritance Tax due.

Deceased's account details

Name of bank or building society

Sort code

Account number

Building society account roll or reference number

Amount to be transferred

In words

In figures

£

Transfer to HM Revenue & Customs

Name of bank

Bank of England

Sort code

10 – 53 – 92

Account number

23430303

Please turn to page 2 to sign the Declaration. It is important that everyone who is applying for the grant of representation or Confirmation to the estate of the deceased signs this form.

Declaration

The amount shown on page 1 is required to pay all or part of the Inheritance Tax due. If HM Revenue & Customs needs to repay the tax paid before the grant or Confirmation is issued they are authorised to return the money to the account shown on page 1.

First representative

Surname

First name(s)

Postcode

Rest of address, including house number/flat number

Signature

Date *DD MM YYYY*

Second representative

Surname

First name(s)

Postcode

Rest of address, including house number/flat number

Signature

Date *DD MM YYYY*

Third representative

Surname

First name(s)

Postcode

Rest of address, including house number/flat number

Signature

Date *DD MM YYYY*

Fourth representative

Surname

First name(s)

Postcode

Rest of address, including house number/flat number

Signature

Date *DD MM YYYY*

IHT423 Page 2

Application for an Inheritance Tax reference [Form IHT 422]

HM Revenue & Customs

Application for an Inheritance Tax reference

Schedule IHT422

When to use this form

Fill in this form if there is any Inheritance Tax (IHT) to pay on the estate. You will need an IHT reference number before you can make a payment. If you intend to pay by cheque, you will also need an IHT payslip.

You can apply for an IHT reference and payslip online. Go to our website at **www.hmrc.gov.uk/inheritancetax/**

If you do not have access to the Internet you can get an IHT reference and a payslip by filling in this form and posting it to the address to which you intend to send the form IHT400. We will send the reference and payslip (if required) to you by post.

You must fill in all the details we request or we may not be able to allocate a reference.

Where to send this form

Use the following address if you intend to apply for a grant of representation in England & Wales or Northern Ireland:

HM Revenue & Customs Inheritance Tax
PO Box 38
Castle Meadow Road
Nottingham — DX: 701201
NG2 1BB — Nottingham 4

Use the following address if you intend to apply for Confirmation in Scotland:

HM Revenue & Customs Inheritance Tax
15 Drumsheugh Gardens
Edinburgh — DX: ED 542001
EH3 7UG — Edinburgh 14

Deceased's details

Surname *in capital letters*

Forename(s)

Any other names the deceased was known by

Date of birth *DD MM YYYY*

National Insurance number (if known)

Date of death *DD MM YYYY*

Country in which you will be applying for probate/Confirmation

England or Wales ☐ Scotland ☐

Northern Ireland ☐

Your details

I wish to pay Inheritance Tax by transferring money from the deceased's bank or building society account(s) and am applying for a reference number only ☐

I wish to pay Inheritance Tax and am applying for both a reference and a payslip ☐

I am an agent acting for the executors/administrators of this estate ☐

I am the executor/administrator of this estate ☐

Enter your name and address

Your reference, if any

The reference and any payslip will be sent to this address

2. Deceased's details

Please fill in this section if you are paying tax on an estate and filling in form IHT400 or IHT 100b.

Surname *in capital letters*

First name(s)

Any other names the deceased was known by

Date of birth *DD MM YYYY*

National Insurance number (if known)

Date of death *DD MM YYYY*

Country in which you will be applying for probate/confirmation *(tick one box)*

England or Wales ☐ Scotland ☐

Northern Ireland ☐

3. Name of settlor or transferor

Please fill in this section if you are filling in form IHT100 and paying tax on:
- a trust
- a gift to a trust or
- any other immediately chargeable transfer.

Surname *in capital letters*

First name(s)

Name of settlement

Date of settlement *DD MM YYYY*

Date of event you are reporting *DD MM YYYY*

Tell us what type of event you are reporting *(tick one box)*

Immediately chargeable transfer ☐

Exit charge ☐

Ten year anniversary ☐

Charge on an Alternatively Secured Pension ☐

Other *please give details below* ☐

Expected date the IHT100 Inheritance Tax account will be submitted *DD MM YYYY*

36

Penalties

Simon's Taxes. See **I11.7.**

Other Sources. Foster, Part L7; Adjudicator's Leaflet AO 1; IHTM36000.

Introduction — IHT Penalties

[36.1] A uniform penalty regime to apply across all taxes administered by HMRC is in the process of being introduced. Penalties will fall under three main headings:

(1) failure to deliver an account;
(2) inaccuracies in returns delivered;
(3) late payment of IHT due.

Other penalties apply to those who give false information to another person for the purposes of an account to be delivered by that person and failure to notify HMRC of an under-assessment issued by it. There is in addition a penalty for failure to make a return under *IHTA 1984, s 218* (formation of non-resident trusts).

The uniform penalty regime is to be brought into effect by Statutory Instruments. At present only the penalties for inaccuracies in returns, giving of false information and failure to notify under-assessments have been brought into effect; see *Finance Act 2008, Sch 40 (Appointed Day, Transitional Provisions and Consequential Amendments) Order 2009, SI 2009/571*. These provisions are extended by *FA 2015* to introduce higher penalties for failures in relation to offshore matters but from a date yet to be announced, expected to be April 2016. The existing IHT penalty regime in *IHTA 1984, Pt VIII* continues to apply to other compliance failures, until such time as the remaining aspects of the uniform penalty regime are brought into effect for IHT.

This chapter details the penalty regime as currently in force. The final part at Chapter **36** summarises aspects of the uniform penalty regime which have yet to be brought into effect.

Errors in accounts; the Post-31 March 2009 penalty regime

[36.2] Where documents are to be filed with HMRC for inheritance tax purposes the penalty regime under *FA 2007, Sch 24* applies with effect for documents where the liability to pay IHT arises on or after 1 April 2010, or in the case of documents produced under the excepted estates regulations (see **2.10** ACCOUNTS AND RETURNS) where the death is on or after 1 April 2009. These penalties apply to errors in documents or information supplied for the purposes of an IHT return and where is either careless or deliberate. The previous IHT penalty regime will apply to events occurring before those dates. [*IHTA 1984, s 247(1), (2); FA 2007, s 97, Sch 249; FA 2008, Sch 40 para 21(c); FA 2009, s 106, Sch 55; Finance Act 2008, Sch 40 (Appointed Day, Transitional Provisions and Consequential Amendments) Order 2009, SI 2009/571*].

Definitions — Reasonable care, careless, deliberate and concealed

An inaccuracy is 'careless' if it is due to a failure to take reasonable care. References to negligence in the preparation of accounts only apply prior to the introduction of the uniform penalty regime. The reasonable care will be satisfied where personal representatives have followed HMRC Inheritance Tax written guidance, made suitable enquiries of asset holders, ensured valuations followed correct instructions and generally sought advice where necessary and cleared up inconsistencies in information received. HMRC consider the personal representatives should obtain at least one professional valuation of assets such as properties although there is no requirement to do so if the value can be clearly established by some other method. Where an agent is appointed by the personal representatives to do the work then on receiving the completed IHT400 or IHT205/207/C5 forms from the agent the personal representatives should check the forms to ensure that all relevant material details required have been included. Where IHT is payable other than in connection with a death by, say, a transferor or trustee then similarly they should ensure that all relevant material details required have been included even where completed. For instance, where an agent has been appointed to complete the necessary documentation this fact will not excuse the personal representatives, transferor or trustees from their responsibility to ensure that the documents supplied to HMRC are accurate and could result in a charge of carelessness and attract the appropriate penalty charge as shown in the table below.

If an inaccurate return is now submitted to HMRC Inheritance Tax then the inaccuracy may be reviewed to determine whether it can be categorised as *careless*, *deliberate but not concealed* or *deliberate and concealed*. HMRC consider reasonable care has been taken where accurate records have been kept to ensure returns are correct, checking what the correct position is when it is unclear and then advising HMRC Inheritance Tax promptly of any error. In defining 'reasonable care' HMRC state that 'it is simply a question of examining what the person did or failed to do and asking whether a prudent and reasonable person would have done that or failed to do that in those circumstances'. However, there will be different interpretations in certain unique circumstances and it will be a case which is in dispute that proceeds to the tribunals and courts. See *Cairns (personal representatives of Webb deceased) v R & C Commissioners* [2009] STI 1801 TC00008 where a summons alleging fraud and negligence was dismissed because *'Something more than the bare words of the relevant statute were required to ensure that fair notice was given'*. Also, the inaccuracy penalty percentage will depend on whether the nature of the disclosure was prompted or unprompted and the penalty adjudged depending on that circumstance. [See *FA 2007, Sch 24 para 3(1)(a)*]. See also Taxation Magazine 19 February 2009, page 172.

Level of penalty

As stated above, in considering the penalty position with regard to *careless*, *deliberate* or *deliberate and concealed* HMRC will consider whether the disclosure of an inaccuracy was *prompted* or *unprompted*. In the table below 'unprompted disclosure' means that the person has no reason to believe that HMRC Inheritance Tax have discovered or are about to discover the failure to pay the required contributions. 'Prompted disclosure' is likely to apply in all other cases. Where the person has made a prompted disclosure in a 'careless' case this attracts a maximum 30% penalty of potential lost revenue but this may be reduced as in the table where the person liable then assists in determining the quantity of unpaid IHT and allowing HMRC Inheritance Tax access to records to check the amount unpaid tax that has been quantified. See at http://www.hmrc.gov.uk/cto/newsletter.htm, April 2009. There are examples of how the reduction for disclosure will be calculated in the Compliance Handbook at CH82440 onwards.

The *Finance Act 2015* introduces amendments to the level of penalties but these provisions have yet to be brought into force. They are expected to apply from April 2016. The amendments will restrict the table below to inaccuracies relating to 'domestic matters'. Where the inaccuracy relates to an 'offshore transfer' or an 'offshore matter' higher penalties will apply, depending on the overseas territory concerned. 'Offshore matters' relate to assets situated in a territory outside the UK for inheritance tax purposes immediately after the relevant chargeable transfer. 'Offshore transfers' are those where the chargeable disposition involves a transfer of assets and after it is made, but before the filing date for the IHT return, the assets or part of them are transferred outside the UK with deliberate intent.

The three categories of overseas territories which currently apply under *FA 2004, Sch 24* for income tax and capital gains tax purposes, will also apply for inheritance tax purposes. The categories are designed to take account of the degree to which information exchange takes place with the territory concerned. The levels of penalty will be 37.5% for category 1 territories, 87.5% for category 2 territories and 125% for category 3 territories, reduced by up to one-half for prompted disclosure, and minimums for unprompted disclosures of 0%, 25% and 40% respectively.

There are provisions for reduction of penalties because of special circumstances, suspension of penalties where this will help to avoid further penalties for careless inaccuracies, and a right of appeal to the Tribunal. However the power to mitigate under TMA, s102 is disapplied. [*FA 2008, Sch 40 (Appointed Day, Transitional Provisions and Consequential Amendments) Order 2009, SI 2009/571; TMA, s 103ZA*].

Since the only possibility for reducing a penalty for careless error to nil is where unprompted disclosure is made to HMRC, it follows that all such errors should be notified to HMRC as soon as they come to light. To reduce the need to make separate disclosure each time an amendment to an IHT account becomes necessary HMRC have stated that 'in future there will be no need to notify HMRC every time there's an amendment to the initial calculation. Provided the changes do not:

- total, individually or collectively, more than £50,000;
- comprise items of land/realty or unquoted shares;
- comprise loss on sale of land or shares claims;
- relate to a case that is subject to a compliance check,

you will only need to tell us 18 months from the date of death or at the point the estate is finalised, whichever is earlier.

Penalties are not charged for inaccuracies on returns where a taxpayer has taken reasonable care to get it right. If an inaccuracy was due to reasonable care not being taken, we will not charge a penalty provided:

- you give us full details about the inaccuracy and why it happened by the dates specified above; and
- you had no reason to think we were about to discover the inaccuracy.

Penalties may be charged if applicable if the notification is incomplete or the original inaccuracy was deliberate or deliberate and concealed.'

[HMRC Trusts and Estates Newsletter April 2012].

Factor	Disclosure	Minimum Penalty	Maximum Penalty
Careless	Unprompted	0%	30%
Careless	Prompted	15%	30%
Deliberate, not concealed	Unprompted	20%	70%
Deliberate, not concealed	Prompted	35%	70%
Deliberate & Concealed	Unprompted	30%	100%
Deliberate & Concealed	Prompted	50%	100%

Other penalties for errors

A penalty of 100% of potential lost revenue applies where a person deliberately supplies false information to, or deliberately withholds information from, another person for the purposes of an IHT account to be submitted by that other person. The penalty may be reduced to 30% for unprompted disclosure, and 50% for prompted disclosure. See *T C Hutchings v HMRC* TC04221 in which a 50% penalty, amounting to £87,533, was upheld where the son of the deceased had received a substantial gift of cash offshore a few months before the death but failed to mention it to the executors in response to their enquiries about lifetime gifts. [*FA 2007, Sch 24 para 1A*].

A penalty of 30% of potential lost revenue applies where a person fails to take reasonable steps to notify HMRC of an under-assessment, or determination showing too little tax, issued by HMRC. HMRC must consider whether the person knew, or should have known, about the under-assessment. The penalty may reduced to 15% for prompted disclosure. [*FA 2007, Sch 24 para* 2].

The wide-ranging powers given to HMRC to give notice in writing requiring a person to provide information or to produce documents apply to inheritance tax from 1 April 2009. These can give rise to a tax-related penalty after fixed penalties have been issued but the failure by the taxpayer continues. This tax-related penalty can be a very substantial sum in the context of inheritance tax; see *HMRC v Tager* [2015] UKUT 0040 (TCC) in which a tax related penalty of £1,171,020 was imposed for failure to deal with HMRC enquiries in relation to a death in March 2005, with return submitted late in January 2009, and information notices issued in September 2011 not attended to. [*FA 2008, Sch 36 para 39*].

Failure to make a return penalty

[36.3] Where a person liable to deliver an account fails to do so within the prescribed period he is liable to a penalty of £100. If no proceedings for declaration of the failure are commenced within six months of the date by which the account should have been delivered, and the accountable person has not delivered the account by the end of that six-month period, there is a further liability to a penalty of £100. These penalties are restricted, in total, to the amount of the taxpayer's IHT liability. There is a further penalty not exceeding £60 for every day after the day on which the failure has been declared by a court or the Tax Tribunal and before the day on which the account is delivered. This latter liability is avoided if the account is delivered before proceedings in which the failure could be declared are commenced. In addition to the foregoing penalties, if the failure to deliver an account continues after one year from the latest date by which it should have been delivered, and there would have been liability to tax shown in the account, a penalty not exceeding £3000 may be imposed. HMRC's standard calculation of penalties payable for late submission of accounts is set out at IHTM 36023.

Where a person has a reasonable excuse for the failure, he is not liable to a penalty unless he fails to remedy it without unreasonable delay after the excuse has ceased [*IHTA, s 245*].

Penalties under this heading are to be brought within the scope of the scheme already existing for income tax and capital gains tax under *FA 2009*, *Sch 55* from a date yet to be announced but expected to be April 2016. This will introduce higher penalties involving 'offshore matters' and 'offshore transfers' at the same levels as described above for inaccuracies in returns.

Penalty for offshore asset moves

With effect from 27 March 2015 a new penalty applies where assets are moved on or after that date from a 'specified territory' to a 'non-specified territory' and the main, or one of the main purposes, of the movement is to prevent the discovery of a loss of revenue by HMRC. It is intended that territories will be 'specified' by Statutory Instrument once they have committed to exchanging information under the new Common Reporting Standard.

Where an asset move has been made (see below), an additional penalty may be imposed where a person has been liable for an earlier penalty for a deliberate failure to make a return or for deliberate error in documents submitted. The additional penalty is 50% of the earlier penalty.

The asset moves giving rise to the additional penalty can be of various types: firstly, where the taxpayer remains beneficial owner of the asset even though the asset has moved from a specified territory to a non-specified territory; secondly, where the person holding the asset made a corresponding change of residence; and thirdly, where there has been a change in ownership arrangements of the asset. In applying the tests, any second or later asset purchased with all or part of the proceeds of sale of the original asset will be regarded as the original asset.

There is a right of appeal to the Tax Tribunals against the penalty. Also in two situations a person will not be liable to the additional penalty, these being where:

- the tax unpaid as a result of a deliberate error in a document giving rise to the original penalty has been assessed or determined before 27 March 2015; and
- the tax unpaid as a result of a failure to make a return giving rise to the original penalty has been assessed or determined before 27 March 2015 and the failure relating to it has been remedied by that date.

The reason for the introduction of this additional penalty is that as more overseas territories enter into agreements to provide greater automatic exchange of information with the UK under the new Common Reporting Standard, with first information exchanges to be made in 2017, HMRC considers that there is a risk that money and investments will be moved from those territories to others that have not entered into such agreements in order to continue to hide past failures to pay tax lawfully payable.

[*FA 2015, s 121, Sch 21*].

Penalty assessment procedure

Penalty assessment procedure — where a penalty has been assessed as payable, notified to the taxpayer as well as the period for which the penalty is assessed then the penalty must be paid within 30 days of the date on which the notice of penalty is issued. The procedure in these circumstances is the same as for existing assessments to tax. Supplementary assessments may be issued where an earlier penalty assessment was underestimated. The assessment must be made on or before the later of two stipulated dates: the first date is the last day of the period of two years beginning with the date in column 4 of the table at *FA 2009, Sch 56 para 1(4)* i.e. the last date on which payment may be made without incurring a penalty. See also **35.1** PAYMENT OF TAX. The second date is the last date of the period of twelve months beginning with the end of the appeal period of the assessment of tax to which the penalty applies, or if there is no assessment made the date on which the amount of tax is ascertained. A right of appeal is open to the taxpayer. See **14.1** DETERMINATIONS AND APPEALS.

Example

X dies on 26 November 2009 and the personal representatives (PRs) to the estate made the necessary return on Form IHT400 and paid the tax due within the six month period. Prior to his death X had been contacted by HMRC regarding omissions from his tax returns in connection with an offshore account (IHT421 Probate summary). X had ignored the enquiry letter and subsequent reminders prior to his death. The personal representatives have now received notification of the enquiry and after making investigations they produce a letter from an offshore account that although the address is the same as the deceased the name on the account is different to that of the deceased. Enquiries of the agent acting for the deceased unearth the fact that X sent the letter to him and asked what he should do. The agent stated that in his view the wrong address had been entered incorrectly by the offshore bank and unless X knew any differently the bank should be notified that they had sent the letter to the wrong address. X died before the agent could receive a reply from him as to the action he had taken.

Further enquiries and full documentation provided to HMRC by the PRs and agent regarding the deceased reveal that X was also known by an alternate name and the alias was included in the will when it was drawn up but was overlooked when the death certificate was drawn up and when the oath was sworn. The letter from the offshore bank states that the capital in the account amounts to £120,000. The outstanding IHT due on this is charged at 40% on the whole sum as the nil rate bands have been utilised and no exemptions exist in respect of the offshore account.

HMRC Inheritance Tax, apart from the ongoing income tax obligations, review the penalty situation

The PRs have made a *prompted disclosure* of a *careless* inaccuracy.	£
The Potential Lost Revenue (PLR) is £48,000*.	48,000
The percentage for the quality of the disclosure has been calculated as 60%. See Note C below.	
The maximum penalty is 30% and the minimum penalty is 15%. So the maximum disclosure reduction is 30% – 15% = 15%	
The actual reduction percentage for disclosure is 15% x 60% = 9%	
Penalty percentage to be charged is 30% – 9% = 21%	
The penalty to be charged is £48,000 × 21% =	10,080
Total IHT and penalty due	58,080
*IHT (PLR) on an omitted estate of £120,000 = £48,000	

Note to the example

(A) HMRC state that in example 4 at CH82161 'Elizabeth submitted an IHT account in respect of her late father's estate. The estate exceeds the amount of the IHT "nil rate band" and is wholly non-exempt. At a later date, Elizabeth uncovers a further bank account containing £50,000. The potential lost revenue (PLR) is £20,000 (£50,000 × 40%).' Similarly, in this case the personal representatives were careless in not ensuring the alias on the deceased's will was duplicated on the death certificate or oath. It is common practice in check list notes to the oath form to state '*Insert the deceased's full name, true name. Where the deceased was known by another name and such name is required to appear in the grant, confirm the true name and state the reason for the alias, if necessary in a separate paragraph at the end.*'

(B) HMRC indicate in example 4 at CH82422 what a prompted disclosure is considered to be: 'During an enquiry into an inheritance tax account, we referred the value of a the deceased's house to the Valuation Office Agency and tell the personal representatives that we have done so. The personal representatives subsequently correct the value upwards saying that they sold the property for the higher value shortly before submitting the account. This is a prompted disclosure.' Similarly, in this example the omission would come into the category of prompted disclosure.

(C) The disclosure reduction is obtained by assessing the quality of each of the three elements of the disclosure i.e. timing, nature and extent of the disclosure. In this case HMRC have concluded that there was no initial disclosure so no discount applies but there was full assistance by the PRs (and agent) uncovering why the document was inaccurate and why HMRC were not told about the under-assessment with a positive approach to explaining the omission (30% discount). Finally, the extent of the disclosure was full and unreserved by the PRs (30% discount). See also CH82440, CH82450 and CH82460.

(D) Note that in the case of the omission from the yearly tax returns of interest earned on the offshore account deposit and not reported to HMRC under the Offshore Disclosure Facility (ODF) and Liechtenstein Disclosure Facility (LDF) there will be additional penalties and interest. See Tolley's Income Tax 2010/11 and 5.7 ANTI-AVOIDANCE.

(E) HMRC may charge another person(s) such as an agent a penalty where a person(s) (the personal representatives in this case) submits a return that contains an inaccuracy, and the inaccuracy is attributable to that agent deliberately supplying false information or deliberately withholding information. The agent must also intend for the personal representatives IHT400 return submission to contain an inaccuracy that (1) leads to an understatement of tax liability, (2) a false or inflated statement of a loss, or (3) a false or inflated claim to repayment of tax. In this case it is (1) that is an issue and not (2) or (3). However, on the facts it appears that the agent had no knowledge of the deceased's alias and from correspondence sent before X died did not deliberately choose to supply false information or deliberately withhold information from X or the personal representatives. See CH81166 and CH84545.

(F) It may be that X would, had he been living, have been prosecuted for a criminal offence of evading tax. If so the double jeopardy principle applies so that a person whose conduct makes them liable to a penalty as a result of an inaccuracy or an under-assessment as well as a prosecution for a criminal offence, will not suffer both effects. [*FA 2009, Sch 55 para 26*].

Penalties under IHTA 1984; summary and history

[36.4] Failure to deliver an IHT account under *IHTA 1984, s 216* or a corrective supplementary account under *IHTA 1984, s 217*. See **2.4** to **2.15** ACCOUNTS AND RETURNS.

Penalty of £100 (£50 for accounts to be delivered before 27 July 1999) unless the tax payable is less than £100 or there is a reasonable excuse (see below). For accounts due to be delivered on or after 27 July 1999, a further penalty of £100 where proceedings in which the failure could be declared are not commenced within the period of six months from the date that the account was due to be delivered and where the account has not been delivered at the end of that six-month period. The total of these penalties cannot exceed the amount of tax payable.

A daily penalty of up to £60 (£10 for accounts due to be delivered before 27 July 1999) from the date the failure is declared by a court or the Special Commissioners (now see **14.1** DETERMINATIONS AND APPEALS) until the account is delivered.

These provisions came into effect where the period within which the person is required to deliver the account expires after six months from the date of Royal Assent to the *FA 2004* i.e. from 22 January 2005 onwards. [*FA 2004, s 295(5)*].

From 1 April 2009 existing appeals against HMRC decisions which would previously have been heard by the General or Special Commissioners are heard by the Tax Chamber of the First-tier Tribunal and Upper Tribunal. The General Commissioners continued to hear appeals until 31 March 2009 but any that they were unable to hear by that date were sent to the Tribunal Service for them to arrange a hearing. Any part-heard appeals in the system on 1 April 2009 had to be re-heard by the First-tier Tribunal. Appeals made on or after 1 April 2009 against decisions by the General Commissioners made before 1 April 2009 will go to the High Court. [*The Transfer of Tribunal Functions and Revenue and Customs Appeals Order 2009, SI 2009/56, paras 120, 121, Sch 3, para 11(3)*].

Failure to make a return under *IHTA 1984, s 218* (non-resident trustees) and failure to comply with a notice under *IHTA 1984, s 219 as amended by FA 2000, s 147(2)* (power to require information). See **2.16** and **2.17** ACCOUNTS AND RETURNS.

Penalty up to £300 (£50 for returns/notices required to be delivered before 27 July 1999) plus a daily penalty of up to £60 (£10 for returns/notices required to be delivered before 27 July 1999) from the date the failure is declared by a court or the Tax Tribunal until the return is made.

Failure to comply with a notice under *IHTA 1984, s 219A* (power to call for documents, etc.). See **2.17** ACCOUNTS AND RETURNS.

Penalty up to £50 plus daily penalty of up to £30 from the date the failure is declared by a court or the Special Commissioners [now substitute Tribunal] until the notice is complied with.

Continued failure to deliver an IHT account under *IHTA 1984, s 216(6), (7)*. See **2.14** ACCOUNTS AND RETURNS.

A penalty charge of up to £3,000 applies if the failure to deliver an account continues after the anniversary of the filing dates within *IHTA 1984, s 216(6), (7)* unless there is a reasonable excuse for the late delivery. These penalty provisions apply from the end of the period of twelve months beginning with the date on which the *FA 2004* received Royal Assent i.e. 22 July 2004 where the failure to deliver an account under this section is on or before that date. Where failure to deliver an account under this section is on or before that date then the anniversary for delivery is twelve months from the expiry date given within *IHTA 1984, s 216(6), (7)*.

Failure to comply with requirements of *IHTA 1984, s 218(A)*. See **13.3** DEEDS VARYING DISPOSITIONS ON DEATH.

A penalty can arise where a disposition on death is varied by the beneficiaries and gives rise to an additional tax liability. In these circumstances where there is a failure to deliver instrument varying a disposition and notification of additional tax payable within eighteen months after the day on which the instrument of variation is made, a penalty of up to £3,000 may be charged. Where the due date for notification expired before Royal Assent i.e. 22 July 2004 the penalty charge does not apply until 12 months after that date. No penalty arises where there is 'reasonable excuse' for the failure and that failure continues after the anniversary of the six-month period. See IHTM36023.

Definition — reasonable excuse

No penalty arises under the IHT penalty regime (but not the uniform penalty regime under *FA 2007, Sch 24*) where there is *reasonable excuse* for the failure unless the failure is not remedied without unreasonable delay after the excuse has ceased. From 1 April 2003 HMRC Inheritance Tax changed the process by which they deal with potential penalties on tax paying accounts sent to them outside the normal 12-month period allowed under *IHTA 1984, s 216*. A standard letter will now automatically be issued by them, as part of their initial processing of the new account, which explains that the account is late and a penalty arises. At the bottom of the letter is a payment slip to accompany the payment of any penalty.

Attached to the letter is a form that allows the personal representatives or their agent to provide an explanation if they believe a reasonable excuse exists (IHT 13, pp 3 and 4 detail what HMRC Inheritance Tax constitute 'reasonable excuse') so that the penalty does not have to be paid.

Note that unlike penalties under *s 245(2)(a),(3)*, penalties under *s 245(4A)* are not capped by the amount of tax on the account.

[*IHTA 1984, ss 245, 245A as amended by FA 1999, s 108; FA 2004, s 295(2), (3) and (5)–(8) and Transfer of Tribunal Functions and Revenue and Customs Appeals Order 2009, SI 2009/56, paras 120, 121*].

Special Commissioners

[36.5] Failure to comply with direction of Special Commissioners (see **36.2** above and **14.1** DETERMINATIONS AND APPEALS) under *SI 1994/1811* (see **14.9** DETERMINATIONS AND APPEALS) including *Reg 10* thereof (**power of Special Commissioners to obtain information;** see **2.17** ACCOUNTS AND RETURNS), or **failure to attend in obedience to witness summons of Special Commissioners;** refusal to be sworn, answer questions or provide documents under *Reg 5* thereof (subject to certain exceptions including those relating to legal privilege and documents of tax advisers), where the appeal hearing is notified after 31 August 1994. Penalty up to £10,000. [*SI 1994/1811, Reg 24*].

Failure to answer summons of Special Commissioners or refusal to be sworn or to answer questions where the appeal hearing was notified before 1 September 1994. Penalty up to £50. [*IHTA 1984, s 246; SI 1994/1813, Sch 1 para 20, Sch 2 Pt I*].

Fraud and neglect

[36.6] Fraudulent or negligent supply of information or documents to the Board under the provisions of *FA 2004*. Following *FA 2004* the distinction between 'fraud' and 'negligence' is redundant and there is no *per se* actual fixed monetary amount of penalty. The penalty is now limited to the difference between the true tax payable, the additional tax, and the tax based on the incorrect information supplied. The result of this is that if there is no additional tax due there is no penalty notwithstanding the incorrect information being supplied. [*IHTA 1984, s 247(1) as amended by FA 2004, s 295(4)*]. Under *IHTA 1984, s 247(3)* the distinction between 'fraud' and 'negligence' is also redundant as the new amending provisions in *FA 2004* charge a penalty for providing incorrect information, whatever the reason, at a maximum of £3,000 in all cases excepting under *s 245(2)(a),(3)*, penalties under *s 245(4A)* are not capped by the amount of tax on the account. This could mean, oddly, that someone not liable for the tax but furnishes incorrect information or documents could suffer a penalty of up to £3,000 where there is no increase in the amount of the tax payable, whereas the person liable for the tax would not! This has been further extended by including circumstances where an incorrect claim has been made under *IHTA 1984, s 8A* so that where 'any other person is liable' a tax geared penalty may be suffered. It remains to be seen how this disparity will work in practice. The effective date of these changes is in respect of incorrect information supplied following the date of Royal Assent to *FA 2004* i.e. 23 July 2004. See http://www.hmrc.gov.uk/cto/newsletter.htm, August 2004. [*IHTA 1984, s 247(3) as amended by FA 2004, s 295(9)*].

Fraudulent or negligent supply of information

Fraud or negligent supply of information or documents to the Board up to and including Royal Assent to *FA 2004* i.e. 22 July 2004:

(a) by any person liable for the tax:
  (i) **if fraud** — penalty up to £3,000 plus an amount equal to the difference between the true tax and the tax based on the fraudulent information etc. (before 27 July 1999, £50 plus twice that amount).

- (ii) **if negligence** — penalty up to £1,500 (before 27 July 1999, £50) plus the difference between the true tax and the tax based on the negligent information etc.

(b) by any person not liable for the tax:
- (i) **if fraud** — penalty up to £3,000 (before 27 July 1999, £500).
- (ii) **if negligence** — penalty up to £1,500 (before 27 July 1999, £250).

Fraud or negligent supply of information or documents regarding the transferability of the nil rate band. Under *IHTA 1984, s 247(2)* a penalty is calculated which can include the liability of another person, but only where *IHTA 1984, s 8A* applies in establishing that person's liability. This means that if an incorrect account is delivered on the first death, as a result of which there is an overstatement of transferable nil rate band on the second death, the tax underpaid on the second death as a result of the incorrect account is in point in calculating the penalty that is due in connection with that incorrect account. This change takes effect from 21 July 2008, so it can only apply where an incorrect account in relation to the first death is delivered after that date.

[*IHTA 1984, s 247(1)–(3); FA 1999, s 108; FA 2008, Sch 4 para 6*].

Assistance

[36.7] Assisting in, or inducing, the supply of any information or document known to be incorrect. Penalty up to £3,000. [*IHTA 1984, s 247(4); FA 1999, s 108*].

Discovery

[36.8] Errors discovered of a material respect in any information or document supplied by a person without fraud or negligence shall be treated as negligence under **36.6** parts (a)(ii) or (b)(ii) above unless remedied without unreasonable delay. 'Unreasonable delay' is not a fixed defined period but within HMRC's Compliance Handbook in relation to direct tax matters it refers to more than 30 days from the date of issue of the assessment. See CH81090. If any other person notices an error in a return etc. not submitted by him whereby tax for which that other person is liable has been or might be underpaid, he must inform the Board without unreasonable delay, otherwise he will be subject to the penalty for negligence under **36.6**(b)(ii) above. [*IHTA 1984, s 248*].

Procedure

[36.9] Penalty proceedings are by the Board (in Scotland, by the Board or the Lord Advocate) and may be commenced before the Special Commissioners [now Upper Tribunal] or in the High Court (or the Court of Session as the Court of Exchequer in Scotland) as civil proceedings by the Crown. An appeal may be lodged by either party against decisions by the Special Commissioners (see **36.2** above and **14.1** DETERMINATIONS AND APPEALS) on a question of law and by the defendant (or, in Scotland, the defender) against the amount of penalty awarded which may be confirmed, reduced or increased by the Court. Any penalty awarded by the Special Commissioners [now Upper Tribunal] is recoverable by the Board as a debt due to the Crown. [*IHTA 1984, ss 249, 252; Transfer of Tribunal Functions and Revenue and Customs Appeals Order 2009, SI 2009/56, para 122*]. *Summary penalties* may be awarded by the Special Commissioners in respect of **36.4**(d) and **36.5** above with appeal available to the High Court (or Court of Session in Scotland). [*IHTA 1984, s 251; SI 1994/1813, Sch 1 para 22*]. The Board may mitigate penalties before or after judgment. [*IHTA 1984, s 253*].

Time limits

[36.10] No proceedings for penalties may be brought more than three years after notification by the Board of the tax properly payable in respect of the chargeable transfer concerned. The European Convention on Human Rights and *Human Rights Act 1998* which came into effect on 2 0ctober 2000 has now confirmed that HMRC cannot seek penalties from the personal representatives of a deceased person who was liable for a penalty. In addition any such penalties already collected must now be repaid and these repayments should include repayment interest at the rate applicable under *IHTA 1984, s 233*. Such interest would run from the date the penalties are paid to the date of repayment by HMRC. [*IHTA 1984, s 250*].

False statements

[36.11] 'False statements to prejudice of Crown and public revenue' are indictable as a criminal offence (*R v Hudson* CCA 1956, 36 TC 561). In the case of *R v Fogon* [2003] STC 461 a question arose as to whether the appellant fell within *Criminal Justice Act 1988, s 71(4)* 'a person benefits from an offence' or *s 71(5)* 'a person derives a pecuniary advantage'. The Judge held that the prosecution's approach was correct and that the case was covered by *s 71(4)* as:

> 'He diverted the money to a concealed account for his own purposes and failed to declare it to the Inland Revenue.'

Therefore it was concluded that 'money transferred to the account [Company] was property obtained in connection with the commission of the offence' and came within *s 71(4)*.

Mitigation

[36.12] The *Finance Act 2007, Sch 24* introduced a new framework of penalty impositions from 1 April 2008 relating to direct tax matters including 'careless', 'deliberate' and 'concealed' actions which result in loss of tax; however, inheritance tax was initially excluded and had its own framework for penalty sanctions but now see above for the position from 1 April 2009 where documents (IHT400 or IHT205/207/C5) containing inaccuracies are to be filed with HMRC Inheritance Tax from 1 April 2010. [*IHTA 1984, s 253*].

In relation to the IHT penalty rergime HMRC Inheritance Tax will normally exercise their statutory power under *IHTA, s 253* to charge a lower penalty in a negotiated settlement. Starting with the maximum figure of penalty HMRC

Inheritance Tax will reduce it depending on how much is disclosed to them, how co-operative the parties are and how grave the offence. The rule of thumb that HMRC Inheritance Tax use in their negotiations will be as follows:

Disclosure — a reduction in the penalty of up to 20% (or even up to 30% with full and voluntary disclosure). However, if there is denial that anything is wrong until the last possible moment then there will be little or no reduction. Full and voluntary disclosure without prompting from HMRC Inheritance Tax will attract the maximum reduction or thereabouts. HMRC Inheritance Tax indicated that in between these two extremes a wide variety of circumstances are possible and consideration will be given to the amount of information given, how soon it was given and how that information contributed to the settling of the enquiries by HMRC Inheritance Tax.

Co-operation — a reduction in the penalty of up to 40%. If information is supplied to HMRC Inheritance Tax promptly after discovery and questions are answered honestly and accurately then the maximum reduction will apply. In addition, the maximum reduction is dependent on the relevant facts being supplied and the tax, once it is calculated, being paid promptly. Delays, untrue or evasive answers, or nothing was done until HMRC Inheritance Tax took formal action will not attract a reduction at all.

Gravity — a reduction of 40%. HMRC Inheritance Tax takes into account the reasons for failing to deliver an account and the amount of money involved. The less serious the matter the bigger the reduction in the penalty.

Penalties yet to be brought into effect

[36.13] Failure to make return penalties under *FA 2009, Sch 55* have yet to be brought into force for IHT by Statutory Instrument. It is understood that HMRC are continuing to work on the introduction of these penalties in conjunction with counsel. Explanatory Notes to FA 2015 indicate a possible start date of April 2016. When brought into force the uniform penalty applying across virtually all taxes administered by HMRC will apply to IHT. In summary, these provide that where a penalty has been assessed as payable, and failure continues after the end of the period of three months beginning with the penalty date a penalty of £10 for each day is charged whilst the failure continues during the period of 90 days beginning with the date specified in the notice of penalty given by HMRC. [*FA 2009, Sch 55 paras 2, 3 and 4*]. If the failure to pay the penalty continues after the end of the period of six months beginning with the penalty date then a further loading penalty of 5% of any liability to tax which would have been shown in the return in question or £300 whichever is the greater. [*FA 2009, Sch 55 para 5*]. Where the failure to pay the penalty continues after the end of the period of twelve months beginning with the penalty date then there is a further loading penalty. However, the penalty will depend on whether the original inaccuracy was deliberate but not concealed or deliberate and concealed. In the case of the former the further loading penalty is 70% of any liability to tax which would have been shown in the return in question or £300 whichever is the greater. In the case of the latter the further loading penalty is 100% of any liability to tax which would have been shown in the return in question or £300 whichever is the greater. In all other cases there is a further loading penalty of 5% of any liability to tax which would have been shown in the return in question or £300 whichever is the greater.

Higher penalties are expected to be brought into effect from April 2016 where 'offshore matters' and 'offshore transfers' are involved and at the same levels as described at **36.2** for inaccuracies in returns.

[*FA 2009, Sch 55 para 6*].

Late payment of tax penalty

A new penalty regime is to be introduced for the late payment of inheritance tax. The regime was set up by *FA 2009, Sch 56* to apply across virtually all taxes administered by HMRC but has yet to be brought into force for IHT by Statutory Instrument. A right of appeal will be included and if it is determined that a reasonable excuse applies for the failure then the penalty may be discharged or mitigated. Also, if the taxpayer enters into a payment agreement with HMRC to pay the inheritance tax then any late payment penalty will be removed if the taxpayer meets the terms of the agreement. See also **35.1** PAYMENT OF TAX.

Under the forthcoming regime, a taxpayer will be liable to pay a penalty of 5% of the unpaid tax. If the amount of this tax remains unpaid after the end of 5 months beginning with penalty date then the taxpayer is liable to a penalty of 5% of that amount. Further, if any amount of that tax is still unpaid after the end of the period of 11 months beginning with the penalty date a further 5% penalty is payable. [*FA 2009, Sch 56 para 3*]. In certain cases where there are penalty provisions HMRC Inheritance Tax may stay the penalty or agree a compromise but this will not apply where the taxpayer is unable to pay the penalty or there is a potential loss of revenue which is balanced by a potential overpayment by another taxpayer. [*FA 2009, Sch 56 para 9*].

In a case where a taxpayer is subject to a tax charge makes a request of HMRC to defer the payment before the penalty date and HMRC agree to defer that charge before (or after) the date then the taxpayer is not liable to the penalty at that time. If the taxpayer breaks the agreement then the penalty will be due by reference to the date of issue of the original notice. Such an agreement between the taxpayer and HMRC is broken if the tax is not paid by the end of the deferral period or there is non-compliance by the taxpayer of a condition of the agreement. [*FA 2009, Sch 56 para 10*].

Key points

The introduction of the uniform tax penalty regime in 2008 can give rise to eye-watering penalties in the context of inheritance tax and any suggestion that the Tribunals would mitigate them substantially, given that inheritance tax liabilities are commonly significant amounts as compared to other taxes, is a serious misapprehension. The case of *Tager v HMRC* (see **36.2** other penalties for errors) demonstrates that the Tax Tribunal will see nothing wrong with imposing a 100% penalty for failure to respond adequately to a notice to supply information where the tax liability is over £1,000,000 and the failure to supply information and make returns has persisted for some years.

We have yet to see the penalties for late payment of tax brought into effect for inheritance tax purposes, but rest assured, the time is coming when that will take place. HMRC say that they are currently working on the practical issues involved. When these are brought into effect, the old regime under which interest only is charged will be replaced and the standard late payment of tax penalties applicable to self-assessment will apply to inheritance tax. Practitioners dealing with inheritance tax returns will need to take the utmost care in order to avoid such penalties being claimed from them personally by their clients.

37

Pension Schemes

Cross-references. See **20.6** EXCLUDED PROPERTY for overseas pensions; **21.19** EXEMPT TRANSFERS for dispositions conferring retirement benefits; **31** LIFE ASSURANCE POLICIES AND ANNUITIES.

Simon's Taxes. See E7.509, I4.125, I5.633–I5.635.

Other Sources. Foster, Parts C1.55, D1.25, E6.36–37, K1.25.

Introduction

[37.1] Property held as part of a superannuation scheme or fund (including retirement annuity contracts) approved by HMRC for income tax purposes or, after 22 July 1987, held under approved personal pension arrangements and, from 6 April 2006, registered pension schemes (or *ICTA 1988, s 615(3)* schemes) or a qualifying non-UK pension scheme are not subject to inheritance tax under the provisions relating to settlements without interests in possession (43 SETTLEMENTS: DISCRETIONARY TRUSTS AND OTHER TRUSTS OF RELEVANT PROPERTY).

Benefits becoming payable

However, where a benefit has become payable under such a scheme etc. and subsequently becomes comprised in a settlement made by a person other than the person entitled to the benefit, the person entitled to the benefit is treated as the settlor and the usual provisions relating to such settlements apply. In addition, the Treasury may make provision for or in connection with the application of IHT in relation to the Pension Protection Fund, Fraud Compensation Fund and the Board of the Pension Protection Fund so that regulations may include provision for and in connection with the taxation of compensation payments made under the *Pensions Act 2004, s 162*. The regulations may apply from any time after 5 April 2005. Unregistered pension schemes with no contributions on or after 6 April 2006 will benefit from that relief in place at 5 April 2006 and those pension schemes with post 5 April 2006 contributions which are protected will attract limited relief from IHT inclusive of an indexation factor. In order to ensure that lump sum rights cannot fall below the value of the fund as at 6 April 2006 for IHT purposes minor amendments have been made to ensure that the formula in *FA 2004, Sch 36 para 57* for calculating the value is not compromised, [*IHTA 1984, ss 58, 151(1)(1A)(5), s 271A; F(No 2)A 1987, s 98(4); FA 2004, s 203(3), (4), Sch 36 paras 56–58; FA 2005, s 102, Sch 10 para 58; FA 2008, Sch 29 para 18*]. See **43.3** SETTLEMENTS: DISCRETIONARY TRUSTS AND OTHER TRUSTS OF RELEVANT PROPERTY and Fosters Inheritance Tax, para E6.33 and E6.34.

For these purposes a 'qualifying non-UK pension scheme' is a pension scheme (other than a registered pension scheme) which is established in a country or territory outside the United Kingdom and satisfies the requirements that are set out in regulations. Such regulations have now been made and retrospectively to schemes from 6 April 2006. [*IHTA 1984, s 271A as inserted by FA 2008, Sch 29 para 18; Inheritance Tax (Qualifying Non-UK Pension Schemes) Regulations 2010, SI 2010/51*].

Application

[37.2] Where a person is entitled to an interest in or under a scheme etc. which ends on his death, the interest will not be included in his estate if it:

(a) is, or is a right to, a pension or annuity, and
(b) is not an interest resulting from the application of any benefit provided under the fund or scheme otherwise than by way of a pension or annuity.

Other rights (e.g. rights to repayment of contributions on death before retirement age) are chargeable to IHT.

[*IHTA 1984, s 151*].

A person entitled to a pension or annuity satisfying the conditions of (a) and (b) above is not treated as being beneficially entitled to the property in which the interest subsists. The fund is not, therefore, liable to IHT on his death. In the case of Guaranteed Annuities if the deceased was receiving payments under an annuity and died before the end of the annuity period, the right to receive the remainder of the payments is an asset of the estate and the value should be included on Form IHT 406 at page 1. See below. HMRC Inheritance Tax has prepared an annuity calculator on its website which calculates the open market value of remaining period.

Where a person has a general power to dispose of his benefits as he thinks fit, he is treated as beneficially entitled to the interest. If a benefit passes only at the discretion of the trustees of the scheme and is not a legally enforceable claim by the personal representatives (PRs), there is no liability to inheritance tax. See *Kempe and Roberts (personal representatives of Lyon, deceased) v CIR* [2004] STC SCD 467 Sp C 424.

Where there is a tax liability, it is due from the pensioner or his personal representatives but not from the trustees of the scheme etc.

Changes arising from *FA 2004, s 203* ensure that IHT relief is applicable to contributions to registered pension schemes and for pension schemes for non-residents within *ICTA 1988, s 615(3)* or a qualifying non-UK pension scheme such that transfers of value are not treated as chargeable transfers for IHT purposes.

Benefits under pension schemes from 6 April 2011

On 22 June 2010, the Government announced it was to end the existing rules that create an effective obligation to purchase an annuity by age 75 from April 2011 to enable individuals to make more flexible use of their pension savings. As an interim measure, provision was made in *Finance (No 2) Act 2010, s 6, Sch 3* so that the tax rules will not make members of registered pension schemes who reach the age of 75 on or after 22 June 2010 buy an annuity or otherwise secure a pension income until they reach the age of 77.

FA 2011, Sch 16 removed the requirement to buy an annuity by the age of 75 and the alternatively secured pension rules were repealed, both with effect from 6 April 2011. Individuals are able to leave their pension funds invested in a drawdown arrangement and to make withdrawals throughout their retirement, subject to an annual cap. The maximum withdrawal of income that an individual was able to make from most drawdown funds on reaching minimum pension age was capped at 100% of the equivalent annuity that could have been bought with the fund value. Most of the rules preventing registered pension schemes from paying lump sum benefits after the member has reached the age of 75 were removed.

From April 2015 there are in principle no restrictions on the amount of funds which can be taken after retirement, although existing pension schemes will require an amendment to their rules to allow this. An income tax charge applies for the funds taken as a lump sum the rate being 45% (55% prior to April 2015), apart from death benefits from the funds held for those who die before age 75, which will remain tax free. Following the death of the scheme member, nominated beneficiaries can alternatively take periodic benefits from the pension scheme which will be taxed at their marginal rate of income tax. Pension funds which fall under these flexible provisions can be nominated to a beneficiary post death, and the use of previous pension bypass trusts is no longer necessary.

Because of these changes with effect from 6 April 2011, inheritance tax ceased to apply to drawdown pension funds remaining under a registered pension scheme, including when the individual dies after reaching the age of 75. Also with effect from 6 April 2011, inheritance tax charges under *IHTA 1984, s 3(3)* that apply to registered pension schemes and qualifying non-UK resident pension (QNUP) schemes where the scheme member omits to take their retirement entitlements (e.g. a failure to buy an annuity) were removed. Thus *IHTA 1984, s 12 (2A)–(2E)* and *ss 151A, 151B, 151BA, 151C, 151D, 151E* are all repealed with effect from 6 April 2011. These changes will also apply to superannuation funds that are occupational pension schemes by virtue of *TA 1988, s 615(3)*. [*FA 2011, s 65 and Sch 16*].

Anti-avoidance applying prior to 6 April 2011

Anti-avoidance measures applied from 6 April 2006 to 5 April 2011 to charge IHT on the death of a registered scheme member on or after the age of 75 where funds are held in an alternatively secured pension (ASP) within *FA 2004, s 165*. The charge was intended to apply in the case where individuals use ASPs to pass on tax-privileged retirement savings to their dependants within six months of death by reason of Rules 5 and 6 of *FA 2004, s 167* rather than to provide a pension in retirement. Broadly, an IHT charge will be made on the left-over ASP funds on death of the scheme member passed on to a 'relevant dependant' including:

- a dependant's scheme pension;
- a dependant's annuity;
- a dependant's unsecured pension; or
- a dependant's ASP

but funds paid to charity within a specified period will be exempt. A 'relevant dependant' for these purposes is includes spouse, civil partner or person financially dependant on the scheme member before their death. [*FA 2004, Schs 28, 29; FA 2007, s 69, Sch 19 paras 19–23*]. The charge will be based on the value of the taxable property at the time the charge arises and will be calculated by reference to the tax-free threshold and rate of tax in place at that time by way of *IHTA 1984, Sch 1*. See **40.1** RATES OF TAX. In the case of the 'relevant dependant's' benefits the charge will be deferred until entitlement to such benefits ceases.

The above provisions had effect on the death of a scheme member after 5 April 2006 but are repealed with effect from 6 April 2011. The pension scheme administrator is the person who is liable for tax chargeable under *IHTA 1984, s 151B*. [*IHTA 1984, ss 151(2)–(4), 151A–C, 210; FA 2004, s 203(4); FA 2006, s 161, Sch 22 paras 3, 4, 6; Inheritance Tax (Delivery of Accounts)(Excepted Estates)(Amendment) Regulations 2006, SI 2006/2141; FA 2008, Sch 29 para 18*].

Example 1

Fredrick, a widower – who is a member of the Allied plc Pension Scheme which is registered – is aged 75 on 18 July 2006 and sets up an alternatively secured pension (ASP) within Rule 6 of *FA 2004, s 165*. Fred dies on 31 December 2006. The fund in the undrawn ASP is valued at £160,000 which is subjected to IHT under *IHTA 1984, s 151A*, as shown in the computation below. Alternatively, in the second part of the example, if the ASP is passed along with his estate valued £610,000 to his sister, Alexandra, who has been financially dependent upon him for many years, within six months of his death and she receives a dependant's unsecured pension then a calculation will be made on her death. See Letter of Wishes below. Alexandra dies three years later on 26 November 2010 when remaining funds in the ASP are valued at £100,000. Fred has previous chargeable transfers of £97,265. Frederick's deceased wife's assets were all transferred on her death into a nil rate band discretionary trust for the grandchildren.

***IHTA 1984, s 151A* calculation when Frederick dies**	£	£
Previous chargeable transfers		97,265

Value of estate at death excluding ASP	450,000	
Add Value of ASP at 31 December 2006	160,000	
Chargeable residue		610,000
Total cumulative chargeable transfers		£707,265
Tax due from estate on £707,265		
97,265 – 285,000 (£187,735 at nil%)		—
285,001 – 707,265 (£422,265 at 40%)		168,906
		£168,906

IHT due on ASP = £160,000/£707,265 × 168,906 = £38,210

IHTA 1984, s 151B **calculation when Alexandra dies**

Previous chargeable transfers		97,265
Value of estate at death excluding ASP	450,000	
Add Value of ASP at 26 November 2010	100,000	
Chargeable residue		550,000
Total cumulative chargeable transfers		£647,265
Tax due from estate on £647,265		
97,265 – 325,000 (£227,735 at nil%)		—
325,001 – 647,265 (£322,265 at 40%)		128,906
		£128,906

IHT payable by the ASP fund administrator:
Revised IHT due on ASP = £100,000 × 40% = £40,000.

Notes to the example

(A) Frederick will have had the option to draw alternatively secured income (ASI) which can be between the lower limit of nil up to 70% of the notional annuity that could be purchased under annuity assumptions set by the Government Actuary's Department (GAD) using the member's available drawdown fund. This reduced upper limit and the required annual revaluation of the drawdown fund should result in the fund not being depleted to nil over the period. When the ASP member dies where the scheme rules allow the dependants of the deceased member may benefit from the residual (see letter of wishes below). However, no lump sum may be paid but pension income can continue to be paid to the chosen dependant(s). Alternatively, where there are no dependants the residual lump sum may be paid to a charity or it may be paid back to the original sponsoring company i.e. Allied plc Pension Scheme in this case or used to augment the fund for existing scheme members.

(B) The IHT payable by the ASP fund administrator under *IHTA 1984, s 151A(3)(4)* in the first computation applies if the ASP is not applied to provide dependant's benefits within six months of death whereas if Frederick passes the fund in the undrawn ASP to Alexandra within the six-month period *s 151B* will apply as in the second computation. The calculations are mutually exclusive and the ASP administrator would have a IHT liability of £38,210 on Frederick's demise or £40,000 if the undrawn ASP is passed on to Alexandra and she dies later so that the liability is recalculated. This latter liability is because *IHTA 1984, s 151B(5)* inserted by *FA 2006, s 160(2), Sch 22 paras 1, 4* to ensure that tax is charged at the rate, or rates, at which it would have been charged on the death of the scheme member if the aggregate amounts (reduced by any charitable payment) had been included in the value transferred and the amount on which the tax is charged had formed the *highest* part of that value. Note that the position for IHT purposes changed from 6 April 2007. See examples below. [*IHTA 1984, ss 151A, 151B, Sch 2 para 6A inserted by FA 2006, Sch 22 paras 4–6, 9, 10*].

(C) In the case where a scheme member who died before the age of 75 years and, for example, a dependant of theirs takes the pension benefits in a dependant's unsecured scheme only later, on reaching 75 years themselves, for it to become an ASP the dependant's chargeable estate will then include the value of the ASP on their death. Any payments made to charity within six months beginning with the end of the month in which the death occurs will be deducted before the charge to IHT. [*IHTA 1984, s 151C inserted by FA 2006, Sch 22 para 4*].

For the guidance of the Management Committee, I nominate the person(s) named above to be the beneficiary/beneficiaries in the event of my death. I request the Management Committee to consider paying a pension to the above person under Rules 5 and 6 of *FA 2004, s 167*. I understand that my wishes cannot be binding on the Management Committee but that they will be considered when benefits become payable. . . . .

Please read these notes carefully before completing the form.

On your death, certain benefits will be paid from the . . . . Pension Scheme.

So that these benefits can be paid free of inheritance tax, the Rules of the . . . . Pension Scheme give the Management Committee absolute discretion regarding the people to whom pensions and cash are paid.

In reaching its decision, however, the Management Committee will take account of your wishes and you can complete this nomination form with details of the person(s) you would like to receive a benefit on your death.

Income tax charge on unauthorised payment

The *Finance Act 2007, Sch 19 paras 19–23* changed the inheritance tax rules to take into account an income tax charge arising because of an unauthorised payment under *FA 2004, Part 4* when calculating the IHT liability arising after such an income tax charge has been imposed. In addition, any liabilities on an alternatively secured pension (ASP) scheme arising under *IHTA 1984, s 151A* are 'top-sliced' for deaths arising from 6 April 2007 to ensure that the nil rate band, if available, is used against the non-ASP part of the estate in priority to the ASP. See Example 2 below for the post-5 April 2007 position. If there is part of the nil rate band remaining after setting it against the non-ASP estate of the scheme member then this may be available to set against ASP funds, and any IHT liability arising thereon is settled by the ASP scheme administrator. Where a scheme member dies with funds in a pension scheme that would have been an ASP had the scheme administrator been able to trace the member before he/she reached the age of 75 years then the date that the scheme administrator becomes aware of the scheme member's death will be the date for the purposes of *s 151A(a)(b)* in calculating the 'relevant amount' to be subject to tax.

Top-slicing relief

Any of the above liabilities on an alternatively secured pension (ASP) scheme arising under *IHTA 1984, s 151B* are 'top-sliced' to ensure that the nil rate band, if available, is used against the non-ASP part of the estate of the original scheme member in priority to the ASP. See Examples 3–6 below that show the treatment where there is an IHT charge before an unauthorised payment charge and where there is an IHT charge after an unauthorised payment charge where part of the nil rate band is available. Where a relevant dependant entitled to a pension fund inherited from a scheme member dies with funds in a pension scheme that would have been an ASP had the scheme administrator been able to trace the scheme member before their reaching the age of 75 years, the date that the scheme administrator becomes aware of the scheme member's death will be the date for the purposes of *s 151B(a)(b)* in calculating the amount to be subject to tax. New taxing rules in such circumstances follow those within *s 151A* allowing, on the cessation of the relevant dependant's pension, for unused nil rate band of the original scheme member to be grossed up under *s 151A(4C)* and set against the balance of the ASP funds remaining on the cessation of the dependant's pension. The nil rate band to be taken into account for these purposes is that applying at the time of the cessation of the relevant dependant's pension. If there has been a reduction in the tax rates since the scheme member's death then for these purposes the tax rate to be applied will be the latest as if it had been in force at the time of the scheme member's death.

Where a relevant dependant dies with another pension fund within *s 151C*, any ASP arising under *IHTA 1984, s 151C* is 'top-sliced' from 6 April 2007 to ensure that the nil rate band, if available, is used against the non-ASP part of the estate of the original scheme member in priority to the ASP. Any income tax charge arising because of an unauthorised payment under *FA 2004, Part 4* is taken into account in calculating the IHT tax liability. The income tax relieved within *s 151C(3)(a)* in this way is that which arose before IHT was charged in relation to any unauthorised member payments and reduces the subsequent IHT charge.

Where there is an ASP and any unused nil rate band of the original scheme member has not been fully utilised against the non-ASP funds the balance may be grossed up under *s 151C(3C)* and set against the balance of the ASP funds not previously assessed under *s 151A*. This 'previously untaxed dependant's alternatively secured pension fund amount' is that part of an individual's ASP that has not given rise to an unauthorised payment charge before IHT arose on the ASP. In addition, under *s 151C(3D)* where an amount of ASP charged under *s 151C* has previously been charged under *s 151A* then this amount shall be excluded from the IHT charge on the later event. *[IHTA 1984, ss 151A–C as amended by FA 2007, Sch 19 paras 19–23]*. See ACCOUNTS AND RETURNS (**2**), PAYMENT OF TAX (**35**), http://www.hmrc.gov.uk/cto/newsletter.htm, April 2007.

Example 2

Frederick, a widower (as in Example 1 above but reflecting the IHT situation after 5 April 2007) – who is a member of the Allied plc Pension Scheme which is registered – is aged 75 on 18 July 2007 and sets up an alternatively secured pension (ASP) within Rule 6 of *FA 2004, s 165*. Frederick dies on 31 December 2007. The fund in the undrawn ASP is valued at £160,000 which is subjected to IHT under *IHTA 1984, s 151A(2) as amended by FA 2007, Sch 19 para 20(2)*, as shown in the computation below. Frederick has previous chargeable transfers of £97,265.

IHTA 1984, s 151A **calculation when Frederick dies**	**£**	**£**
Previous chargeable transfers		97,265
Value of estate at death including ASP	610,000	
Deduct value of ASP at 31 December 2007	160,000	
Chargeable residue		450,000
Total cumulative chargeable transfers		£547,265
Tax due from estate on £547,265		
97,265 – 300,000 (£202,735 at nil%)		—
300,001– 547,265 (£247,265 at 40%)		98,906
IHT due on estate excluding ASP settled by PRs.		£98,906
IHT due on ASP = £160,000 × 40% = £64,000 i.e. top slice.		£64,000
IHT liability of £64,000 is settled by the ASP scheme administrator.		

Notes to the example

(A) If Frederick died in 2007/08 then under the *FA 2007, Sch 19* changes the ASP fund in his estate would be treated as the top slice in contrast to 2006/07 when the rules ensured that IHT payable by the ASP fund administrator under *IHTA 1984, s 151A(3)(4)* in Example 1 above attracted a proportion of the nil rate band. This only applies if the ASP is not applied to provide dependant's benefits within six months of death. The ASP administrator would have an IHT liability of £64,000, a substantial increase on the 2006/07 amount even taking into account the increase of £15,000 in the nil rate band. [*IHTA 1984, ss 151A(2) as inserted by FA 2007, Sch 19 paras 20(2)*].

(B) As the value of the estate excluding ASP funds is in excess of the nil rate band, any top-slicing relief that might have been available, *s 151A*, is not available and the ASP administrator suffers an IHT charge of 40% without any 'top-slicing'. Whereas if Frederick passes the fund in the undrawn ASP to Alexandra within the six-month period *s 151B* will apply and there would be no IHT charge at that time.

Example 3

Fred, a widower – who is a member of the Allied plc Pension Scheme which is registered – is aged 75 on 18 July 2007 and sets up an alternatively secured pension (ASP) within Rule 6 of *FA 2004, s 165*. Fred dies on 31 December 2007.

The fund in the undrawn ASP is valued at £200,000 and there is an IHT charge *before* an unauthorised payment charge. The ASP is valued at £200,000. Fred has no previous chargeable transfers prior to his death.

Calculation when Fred dies	£	£
Previous chargeable transfers		Nil
Value of estate at death excluding ASP	200,000	
Deduct Proportion of nil rate band used at 31 December 2007	200,000	
Chargeable residue		Nil
Tax due from estate		£Nil
Calculation *IHTA 1984, s 151A*		
Balance of nil rate band available £100,000 (£300,000 – £200,000)		
Value of ASP funds becoming chargeable = £200,000	200,000	
Unused nil rate band available grossed up £100,000 × (100/100 – 70)% =	333,333	
IHT due on ASP funds		£Nil

Notes to the example

(A) Fred dies with an ASP that has not previously been subject to an unauthorised payment charge and he leaves an estate (excluding the ASP value) that does not exceed his available nil rate band. [*IHTA 1984, s 151A(4B)*]. In these circumstances the balance of the nil rate band is set against the ASP value and under *s 151A(4C)* the balance of the nil rate band i.e. £100,000 in this example is grossed up and set against the ASP value of £200,000.

(B) The *FA 2007, Sch 19 para 20* insertion of *s 151A(4C)* where the previously untaxed ASP is grossed up as follows in accordance with the following formula:

$$\frac{\text{UNRB} \times 100}{100 - \text{MUPR}}$$

where:

UNRB = unused nil rate band in excess the chargeable transfers less any previously untaxed ASP fund; and

MUPR = the maximum unauthorised payment rate i.e. the maximum aggregate rate chargeable by *FA 2004, Part 4* i.e. 70% in this example by reason of *FA 2004, ss 208, 209(6), 240*.

Example continued

Fred, as above, dies on 31 December 2007. The fund in the undrawn ASP is valued at £200,000 and there is an IHT charge unauthorised payment charge *before* the IHT is due when the ASP is valued at £200,000. Fred has no previous chargeable transfers prior to his death.

Calculation when Fred dies	£	£
Previous chargeable transfers		Nil

Calculation when Fred dies	£	£
Value of estate at death excluding ASP	200,000	
Deduct Proportion of £300,000 nil rate band used at 31 December 2007	200,000	
Chargeable residue		Nil
Tax due from estate		£Nil
Calculation *IHTA 1984, s 151A*		
Unauthorised payment charge = £200,000 × 70% = 140,000		
ASP funds chargeable to IHT will therefore be £200,000 – £140,000 unauthorised payment charge =	£60,000	
Balance of nil rate band available (£300,000 – £200,000 above) =	£100,000	
IHT due on ASP funds		£Nil

Note to the example

(A) The amount of the ASP funds charged to IHT differs depending on whether or not the unauthorised payment charges have arisen before or after the IHT due date. Where the unauthorised payment charges have been deducted before IHT is due then IHT is calculated by reference to the net value of the ASP funds as in this example. And conversely, as in the previous example, where IHT is due before the unauthorised payment charges are made then IHT is calculated by reference to the gross value of the ASP funds with an adjustment to the unused nil rate band to set against the ASP funds.

Example 4

Bert, a bachelor – who is a member of the Allied plc Pension Scheme which is registered – is aged 77 and has an alternatively secured pension (ASP) within Rule 6 of *FA 2004, s 165*. The fund in the undrawn ASP is valued at £200,000 which is subjected to IHT as shown in the computation below. The ASP is passed along with Bert's estate valued at £280,000 to his sister, Adriana, who has been financially dependent upon him for many years, within six months of his death and she receives a dependant's unsecured pension; a calculation then will be made on her death. Adriana dies three years later on 26 November 2010 when remaining funds in the ASP are valued at £200,000. Bert has no previous chargeable transfers prior to his death.

Calculation when Bert dies	£	£
Previous chargeable transfers		Nil
Value of estate at death excluding ASP	280,000	
Deduct Proportion of nil rate band of £300,000	280,000	
Chargeable residue		Nil
Tax due from estate		£Nil
***IHTA 1984, s 151B* calculation when Adriana dies**		
Balance of nil rate band available in 2010/11 is £325,000 – £280,000 = £45,000		
Unused nil rate band available grossed up £45,000 × (100/100 – 70)% =	150,000	
Balance of ASP funds remaining on Adriana's death i.e. cessation of dependant's pension =	200,000	

Calculation when Bert dies	£	£
IHT on ASP funds		£Nil

Notes to the example

(A) Bert dies with an ASP that has not previously been subject to an income tax charge under *FA 2004, Part 4* before IHT was charged. In these circumstances the balance of the nil rate band in 2010/11, i.e. £45,000 in this example, is grossed up and set against the ASP fund. [*IHTA 1984, s 151BA*].

(B) The unused nil rate band is grossed up by application of the formula in *IHTA 1984, s 151A(4C)*. Had the ASP fund been subject to income tax, the relief provision as inserted by *FA 2007, Sch 19 para 20* would have applied where the income tax resulting from unauthorised pension payment charges would have been applied and would reduce the amount chargeable to IHT 'by the amount previously charged to income tax', i.e. 70% in the example above.

Example 5

Alan, a bachelor – who is a member of the Allied plc Pension Scheme which is registered – is aged 78 and has an alternatively secured pension (ASP) within Rule 6 of *FA 2004, s 165*. Alan dies on 31 December 2007. The fund in the undrawn ASP is valued at £200,000. The ASP is passed along with Alan's estate valued at £320,000 to his sister, Amanda, who has been financially dependent upon him for many years, within six months of his death and she receives a dependant's unsecured pension; a calculation then will be made on her death. Amanda dies three years later on 26 November 2010 when remaining funds in the ASP are then valued at £100,000. Alan had no previous chargeable transfers prior to his death.

Calculation when Alan dies	£	£
Previous chargeable transfers		Nil
Value of estate at death excluding ASP	320,000	
Deduct nil rate band of £300,000	300,000	
Chargeable residue		Nil
Tax due from estate £20,000 × 40%		£8,000
***IHTA 1984, s 151B* calculation when Amanda dies**		
Balance of nil rate band available in 2009/10 = £5,000 (£325,000 – £320,000)		
Unused nil rate band then grossed up by reference to *IHTA 1984, s 151A(4C)* i.e. £5,000 × (100/100 – 70)% =	16,666	
Balance of ASP fund on cessation of Amanda's entitlement	100,000	
IHT on ASP funds		£Nil

Note to the example

(A) Alan dies with an ASP that has not previously been subject to a tax charge and he leaves an estate (excluding the ASP value) that exceeds his available nil rate band in 2007/08. In these circumstances the nil rate band which has increased on Amanda's death in 2010/11 is deducted from the chargeable estate in 2007/08 and grossed up under *s 151A(4C)* and set against the ASP value at that time.

Example 6

Alan, as in Example 5 above, who is a member of the Allied plc Pension Scheme which is registered – is aged 78 and has an alternatively secured pension (ASP) within Rule 6 of *FA 2004, s 165*. Alan dies on 31 December 2007. The fund in the undrawn ASP is valued at £200,000. The ASP is passed along with Alan's estate valued £320,000 to his sister, Amanda, who has been financially dependent upon him for many years, within six months of his death and she receives a dependant's unsecured pension; a calculation then will be made on her death. Amanda dies some years later on 26 November 2012 when remaining funds in the ASP are then valued at £100,000 but there is an unauthorised payment charge *before* any IHT is due. Alan had previous chargeable transfers prior to his death of £97,265.

Calculation when Alan dies	£	£
Previous chargeable transfers		97,265
Value of estate at death including ASP	422,735	
Deduct Value of ASP at 31 December 2007	200,000	
Chargeable residue		222,735
Total cumulative chargeable transfers		£320,000
Tax due from estate on £320,000		
97,265 – 300,000 (£202,735 at nil%)		—
300,001– 320,000 (£20,000 at 40%)		8,000
IHT due on estate excluding ASP		£8,000
No IHT due on ASP at this stage as it is used to provide pension benefits for a relevant dependant.		
***IHTA 1984, s 151B* calculation when Amanda dies**		
Balance of nil rate band available in 2012/13 (£325,000 – £320,000) =	5,000	
Balance of ASP fund chargeable to IHT on cessation of Amanda's entitlement = £100,000 – £70,000 unauthorised payment charge =	30,000	
IHT on ASP funds		£Nil

Notes to the example

(A) When Alan dies with an ASP that has not previously been subject to an unauthorised payment charge and he leaves an estate (excluding the ASP value) that exceeds his available nil rate band then a charge to IHT will arise on his estate at that time. In these circumstances the whole of the nil rate band in 2007/08 is utilised against the non-ASP estate. However, when Amanda dies in 2012/13 (assuming there has been no change in the nil rate band of £325,000) the ASP value at that time forms the highest part of the estate i.e. ASP of £100,000 is added to £320,000. The nil rate band at that stage is £325,000 and under *s 151A(4B)(4C)* the remaining unused balance of the nil rate band i.e. £5,000 (see Note B below) in this example is set against the ASP value after the unauthorised payment charge on Amanda's death. [*IHTA 1984, s 151A(4B) as inserted by FA 2007, Sch 19 para 20(4)*].

(B) Note in the above calculation that the balance of available nil rate band in 2012/13 of £5,000 is calculated by reference to the original non-ASP estate of £320,000 as this is 'the value actually transferred by that chargeable transfer (or nil if there is no such chargeable transfer) . . . ' less the current nil rate band of £325,000 in 2012/13. [*IHTA 1984, s 151A(4B)(a) as inserted by FA 2007, Sch 19 para 20(4)*].

Members of pension schemes and who were married or in a civil partnership may pass on any unused nil rate band on their death to the surviving spouse or civil partner where there is a subsequent charge under *IHTA 1984, s 151B*. [*IHTA 1984, s 151BA(8)*]. These changes apply from 6 April 2008. The availability of the nil rate band arising on the death of the member is calculated as a proportion of the unused nil rate band compared with the used proportion to make up 100% as shown in Example 7 below and *IHTA 1984, s 151BA(9)–(12)*. Once this proportion of unused nil rate band is calculated this is applied to the nil rate band applying at the date of death of the surviving spouse or civil partner to give the amount of unused nil rate band to be added to that available of the surviving spouse or civil partner on their death to set against the *s 151B* charge after taking into account any used proportion utilised in the intervening period. However, for 2009/10 it cannot exceed currently £650,000. [*IHTA 1984, s 8A*].

Where a member or a dependant of a member has died after reaching the age of 75 years having pension/annuity rights and there is a tax charge under *FA 2004, Part 4*, e.g. an unauthorised payment charge, then the tax is to be calculated in accordance with *s 151E*. The calculation of the charge by reason of *s 151D* is to be the top slice of the scheme member or dependant. The availability of the nil rate band arising on the death of the member is calculated as a proportion of the unused nil rate band compared with the used proportion to make up 100% as shown in Example 7 and *IHTA 1984, s 151E(11)*. [*IHTA 1984, ss 151D, 151E as inserted by FA 2008, Sch 28 para 10*].

Example 7

Jack – who is a member of the Allied plc Pension Scheme which is registered – is aged 78 and has a pension within Rule 6 of *FA 2004, s 165*. Jack dies on 31 December 2008. The fund in the undrawn pension is valued at £200,000. The pension is passed along with Jack's estate to his wife, Jill, and together are valued at £320,000 after a legacy to his son of £100,000. With regard to the lump sum received by Jill a calculation then will be made on her death. Jill dies some years later on 26 November 2012 when remaining funds in the pension are then valued at £360,000 but there is an unauthorised payment charge *before* any IHT is due. Jack had no previous chargeable transfers prior to his death.

Calculation when Jack dies	£	£
Previous chargeable transfers		Nil
Value of estate at death including pension	420,000	
Deduct Value of the pension at 31 December 2008	200,000	

Calculation when Jack dies	£	£
Balance of potentially chargeable residue		220,000
Total		£220,000
£0 – £100,000 at nil%		—
£120,000 exempt under *IHTA 1984, s 18.*		—
IHT due on estate excluding pension		£Nil
No IHT due on pension at this stage as it is used to provide pension benefits for a relevant dependant.		
***IHTA 1984, s 151E* calculation when Jill dies**		
Balance of nil rate band available in 2012/13 (£300,000 – £100,000) ÷ £300,000 × 100%) = 66.6666% × £325,000		216,666
Balance of pension fund chargeable to IHT on cessation of Jill's entitlement = £360,000 – £252,000 unauthorised payment charge		108,000
IHT on pension funds		£Nil

Notes to the example

(A) When a person dies after reaching the age of 75 with a pension that has not previously been subject to an unauthorised payment charge and he leaves an estate (excluding the pension value) that does not exceed his available nil rate band then that proportion expressed as a percentage will be available for the surviving spouse or civil partner on their subsequent death to set against any pension value after taking into account any unauthorised payment charge. The deduction on the survivor's death is the calculation that deducts the *nil rate band maximum* from the 'used up percentage' calculated as follows:

$$100 - \left\langle \frac{E}{NRBM} \times 100 \right\rangle$$

where:

E = the amount by which M is greater than VT in the case of the member (see Note A in Example 1 at **21.10** EXEMPT TRANSFERS);

M = maximum amount that could be transferred on the predeceased person's death where it is chargeable at the nil rate band at that time;

VT = value actually transferred by the chargeable transfer or nil if applicable;

NRBM = the nil rate band maximum applying at the time of the deceased member's death.

The *nil rate band maximum* above is the amount shown in the appropriate Table depending on the date of death as stipulated in *FA 2008, Sch 4 para 10*. [*IHTA 1984, s 151BA(6)–(7)*].

(B) Where the survivor spouse or civil partner dies *before* the event giving rise to the charge then the personal nil rate band maximum of the member is reduced appropriately. [*IHTA 1984, s 151BA(8)–(10)*]. The personal nil rate band maximum of the member is the amount shown in the appropriate Table depending on the date of death as stipulated in *FA 2008, Sch 4 para 10*. The appropriate deduction is reduced by any amount at which tax was charged at nil per cent on the death of the survivor which was increased by reason of *IHTA 1984, s 8A*.

(C) Where the survivor spouse or civil partner did *not* die before the event giving rise to the charge then the tax charged on the death of the survivor is the percentage in *IHTA 1984, s 8A(3)* as adjusted by

$$\frac{AE}{ANRBM} \times 100$$

where:

AE = the adjusted excess i.e. the amount by which M would be greater than VT in the case of the member (see Note A above) if the taxable amount were included in the value transferred by the chargeable transfer made on the member's death, and

ANRBM = the adjusted nil rate band maximum applying at the time of the deceased member's death. [*IHTA 1984, s 151BA(10)(11)*].

(D) Where an unauthorised payment is made by a pension scheme and a member or a dependant of a registered scheme dies after the age of 75 years then a charge to IHT will be made based on that unauthorised payment less any unauthorised payment charges arising under *FA 2004, Part 4*. [*IHTA 1984, s 151D(1)–(4)*]. The rate of charge under *s 151D* is calculated as if the amount chargeable is the top slice of the member's or dependant's estate at the time of the relevant unauthorised payment. The personal nil rate band maximum of the member is the amount shown in the appropriate Table depending on the date of death as stipulated in *FA 2008, Sch 4 para 10*. The *nil rate band maximum* for these purposes is the nil rate band in the Table reduced by the 'used up percentage' calculated as follows:

$$100 - \left\langle \frac{E}{NRBM} \times 100 \right\rangle$$

where:

E = the amount by which M is greater than VT in the case of the member (see Note A in Example 1 at **21.10** EXEMPT TRANSFERS);

M = maximum amount that could be transferred on the predeceased person's death where it is chargeable at the nil rate band at that time;

VT = value actually transferred by the chargeable transfer or nil if applicable;

NRBM = the nil rate band maximum applying at the time of the deceased member's death.

[*IHTA 1984, s 151E(3)–(6) as inserted by FA 2008, Sch 28 para 10*].

(E) Where in circumstances that *s 151D* applies and the survivor spouse or civil partner dies *before* the unauthorised payment event giving rise to the charge then the personal nil rate band maximum of the member is reduced appropriately. The personal nil rate band maximum of the member is the amount shown in the appropriate Table depending on the date of death as stipulated in the *FA 2008, Sch 4 para 10*. The appropriate deduction is reduced by any amount at which tax was charged at nil per cent on the death of the survivor which was increased by reason of *IHTA 1984, s 8A*. [*IHTA 1984, s 151E(7)–(9) as inserted by FA 2008, Sch 28 para 10*].

(F) Where the survivor spouse or civil partner did not die before the event giving rise to the charge then the tax charged on the death of the survivor is the percentage in *IHTA 1984, s 8A(3)* as adjusted by

$$\frac{AE}{ANRBM} \times 100$$

where:

AE = the adjusted excess i.e. the amount by which M would be greater than VT in the case of the member (see Note A above) if the taxable amount were included in the value transferred by the chargeable transfer made on the member's death, and

ANRBM = the adjusted nil rate band maximum applying at the time of the deceased member's death. [*IHTA 1984, s 151E(10)(11) as inserted by FA 2008, Sch 28 para 10*].

IHTA 1984, s 3(3) two year exception

IHT concessionary practice dating from 1992 applies up to 5 April 2011 in relation to pension choices by scheme members who die under the age of 75. Under the concession, IHT is not charged under *IHTA 1984, s 3(3)* if a scheme member does not exercise their right to take pension benefits, for example, when an enhanced death benefit is paid to a beneficiary who is a spouse, civil partner or a financial dependant of the scheme member, at the time of their death, as a result of the member not taking their pension when their life expectancy was seriously impaired. If the scheme member makes a disposition of their pension benefit within two years of their death and even though the scheme member was in good health at that time but their life expectancy was seriously impaired then up to 5 April 2011 a *section 3(3)* charge will apply in respect of the deferral of the pension. See also HMRC Statement of Practice SP E3 regarding CTT, and HMRC Statement of Practice SP 10/86, 9 July 1986, see **25** HMRC STATEMENTS OF PRACTICE, confirming that their existing CTT practice is extended to IHT (including the gifts with reservation rules). [*IHTA 1984, ss 3(3), 12(2A)–(2G) inserted by FA 2006, s 160, Sch 22 para 2*]. Legislation has now been introduced so that lump sum payments in respect of registered pension schemes and *ICTA 1988, s 615(3)* schemes with effect from 6 April 2006 will not attract charges under the relevant property regime if they are paid within the stipulated time frame by the pension scheme trustees or persons having control of the scheme. The time allowed for the payment of lump sum by the scheme will run from the date on which the pension scheme is notified of the scheme member's death or, if earlier, when the scheme trustees or persons having control of the scheme could reasonably have been aware of that member's death. Prior to 6 April 2006 and the A-day pension rules being implemented, HMRC did consider relevant property rules applied in the cases of death benefits held on trusts for distribution amongst relatives or dependants. This HMRC concessionary practice only applies now to distributions within two years of the scheme member's death. [*IHTA 1984, s 58(2A)(a)(b); FA 2007, Sch 20 paras 20, 24(9)*].

Cash options

[37.3] When a person dies and his widow or other dependant becomes entitled to an annuity under the terms of a superannuation scheme or fund (including annuity contracts) or, after 22 July 1987, the terms of approved personal pension arrangements or, after 5 April 2006, registered pension schemes (or *ICTA 1988, s 615(3)* schemes), or a qualifying non-UK pension scheme the fact that the deceased could have chosen instead that a cash sum be paid to his personal representatives is not to be regarded as giving him the type of 'general power' within *IHTA 1984, s 5(2)* (see **19.3** ESTATE) which would result in that sum being included in his estate on death. [*IHTA 1984, s 152; F(No 2)A 1987, s 98(5); FA 2004, s 203(5); FA 2008, Sch 29 para 18*].

Death benefits

[37.4] Where a trust of the death benefit payable under a pension policy is created, a charge under *IHTA 1984, s 3(3)* may arise up to 5 April 2011. HMRC Inheritance Tax has stated, in a letter to the Association of British Insurers, that a charge in this connection will be raised in very limited circumstances only. For example, where a policyholder is aware that he is terminally ill and at or after that time either takes out a new policy and assigns the death benefit, or assigns on trust the death benefit of an existing policy, or pays further contributions to a single premium policy or enhanced contributions to a regular premium policy, the death benefit of which has previously been assigned on trust, a charge under *s 3(3)* may be contemplated as the arrangements were not intended to make provision for the policyholder's own retirement, given the prospect of an early death. However, HMRC Inheritance Tax have indicated that they would not pursue a claim in these circumstances where the death benefit was paid to the policyholder's spouse and/or dependants (See ICAEW TR 854, 1991 STI 1118, HMRC Tax Bulletin, February 1992, p 11, The Tax Journal, 19 June 2000 and CTO guidance note 'The Inheritance Tax Treatment of Deferral of Annuity Purchase and Income Withdrawal under Personal Pensions'.)

Case law

In *DM Fryer & Others (Personal Representatives of Ms P Arnold) v HMRC* [2010] UKFTT 87 (TC), TC00398 a woman was born in 1942 and in 1995 she set up a discretionary trust. Later that year she took out a pension plan. It was agreed that if she died before taking her retirement benefits, then the value of those benefits would pass to her discretionary trust. In 2002, shortly before her 60th birthday, she was diagnosed as suffering with terminal cancer. She died in 2003 without having taken the available benefits. HMRC issued a determination charging IHT on the basis that, by failing to take her retirement benefits when she reached the age of 60 in 2002, she had made a disposition of value for the purposes of *IHTA 1984, s 3(3)*. Her personal representatives appealed, contending firstly that she should not be treated as having made any such disposition, and alternatively that if she had made such a disposition, it was not 'intended to confer a gratuitous benefit', so that *IHTA 1984, s 10(3)* applied. The First-Tier Tribunal rejected these contentions and dismissed the appeal in principle, subject to a reduction in HMRC's valuation of the disposition. Clark J upheld HMRC's contention that 'the concept of a "disposition" was widened by *s 3(3)* to include passive dispositions, meaning omissions which resulted in the enhancement of another person's estate or of settled property in which no interest in possession subsisted'. He rejected HMRC's contention that the deemed disposition should be treated as having taken place on her 60th birthday (which was her normal retirement date under her pension policy), holding that the disposition should be treated as having taken place on the date of her death. Her omission to exercise her rights had increased the value of the settled property, and the evidence showed that this had been intentional. Accordingly *IHTA 1984, s 10* did not apply. With regard to the appropriate valuation, Clark J reviewed the evidence in detail and found that the total benefits amounted to £119,800. He directed that this should be discounted by 25%, resulting in a chargeable consideration of £89,950.

In *Parry and others as Personal representatives of R F Staveley deceased* [2014] UKFTT 419 (TC) the deceased was diagnosed with terminal cancer early in 2006. Subsequent to that she transferred the funds in a section 32 pension plan into a personal pension plan, the terms of which would allow the entire fund to be paid to her estate or to other beneficiaries. She was keen to ensure that her ex-husband could not benefit from the fund. She took no benefits from the policy prior to her death in December 2006 and nominated her two sons as the beneficiaries to receive the death benefits from the fund.

HMRC considered that the transfer of funds from the section 32 policy was a transfer of value for IHT purposes but the executors argued that it was exempt as being made without gratuitous intent – the purpose was to ensure the fund could not benefit the ex-husband. The Tribunal accepted that the exemption applied in relation to the transfer of the funds.

HMRC also considered that the failure to take pension benefits was an omission to exercise a right which caused an increase in the sons' estates. The decision on this point involved extensive analysis of *IHTA 1984, s 12* as it stood before the repeal of *subsections 2A-2E* by *FA 2011*. The Tribunal found for HMRC on this issue.

Key points

[37.5] Points to consider are as follows.

- The *Finance Act 2011* transformed the tax treatment of registered pension schemes and the *Finance Act 2015* has now introduced total flexibility. Hence funds in a SIPP are, for many pensioners, no longer locked in the scheme and inaccessible (apart from the longstanding 25% lump sum withdrawal facility). Furthermore the fund remaining on the death of the pensioner, the whole of his or her pension fund can be used to provide a pension income to dependants. As an alternative the trustees of the pension scheme may pay the fund as a lump sum to beneficiaries and, assuming that they are payable at the discretion of the pension trustees, the taxation of these lump sum payments is:

(a) if the taxpayer dies before the age of 75 and before drawing benefits the pension fund can be paid to beneficiaries as a lump sum free of tax;

(b) if the taxpayer dies after the age of 75 but before drawing benefits the pension fund can be paid as a lump sum to beneficiaries less a tax charge of 45% or may be used to provide income benefits taxed at their marginal rates.

This makes private pension funds much more attractive in overall financial planning. For higher rate taxpayers the effective cost of providing a pension fund of £1,000 is now either £600, or £550 for those on the highest tax rate, and that fund can provide an income in retirement by means of indefinite drawdown plus lump sum benefits to heirs on death of £550. £600 invested outside a pension scheme and left to the next generation might incur 40% inheritance tax on death, leaving only £360 available after tax. Lifetime inheritance tax planning and use of exemptions can of course have impact on this analysis, but the new pensions regime is certainly offers more encouragement to pension savings than previously.

Qualifying non-resident pension schemes also have their attractions since they have equal IHT exemption on death of the pensioner, but without the 45% tax charge applying, and they are free of the investment restrictions which apply to SIPPS. On the other hand there are of course no tax reliefs for contributions. These schemes are available to both UK residents and non-residents and although in theory there is no limit on the amount which can be contributed, it is necessary to operate the QNUP as a pension scheme and not a family trust. Hence the amount contributed should be suitable in terms of what it will provide as a pension income for the contributor. It is also essential that sums are not contributed by an employer as in that event other anti-avoidance legislation applies. There are no particular reliefs from capital gains tax and income tax anti-avoidance rules. Perhaps the reason why QNUPS are not more widely used is the uncertainty of the continuing tax treatment of them. In the associated QROP marketplace, HMRC made a surprise announcement in December 2011 setting out a number of changes to the way qualifying recognised overseas pension schemes must be set up and run. It further shocked the market in QROP provision in April 2012 when it published an updated list of recognised schemes that saw hundreds summarily deleted, including 310 out of 313 Guernsey schemes.

- There are incentives for deferring the state retirement pension and such a deferral attracts a taxable lump sum after 12 months. However, whilst the lump sum is taxable as income when received the fact that if the person dies before receipt they do not receive the accrued benefit means that there can be no IHT charge on that lump sum on premature death.

Pensions [Form IHT409] over page.

HM Revenue & Customs

Pensions

Schedule IHT409

When to use this form

Fill in this form if the deceased received, or had made provision for, a pension or benefit from an employer or under a personal pension policy other than the State Pension.

If the deceased had more than one pension or benefit for any one section of this form, you will need to complete a separate form for each pension and benefit.

Help

Please read the guidance notes for form IHT409 in the IHT400 Notes before filling in this form. For more information or help or another copy of this form:

- go to **www.hmrc.gov.uk/inheritancetax/**
- phone our Helpline on **0845 30 20 900**
  – if calling from outside the UK, phone **+44 115 974 3009**.

Name of deceased

Date of death *DD MM YYYY*

IHT reference number (if known)

Continuing pension payments

1 Did any payments under a pension scheme or personal pension policy continue after the deceased's death?
Answer No if the only payments made were:

- *small arrears of pension from the last monthly payment in the deceased's lifetime to the date of death*
- *continuing payments of a reduced widow's, widower's or surviving civil partner's pension, or*
- *only paid because the pension provider did not know about the death.*

No ☐ *Go to box 8*

Yes ☐ *Go to box 2*

Pension scheme or policy details

2 Name of the pension scheme or title of the personal pension policy

3 Is the scheme or policy registered by HMRC for Income Tax purposes?

No ☐ Yes ☐

4 How often were the payments made and in what amounts?

5 Date of the final guaranteed payment *DD MM YYYY*

6 Give details of any increase in the payments between the date of death and date of final guaranteed payment

7 Value of the right to receive the remainder of the payments

£

Include this amount in form IHT400, box 56

IHT409 **(Substitute)(LexisNexis)** Page 1 HMRC Approval ref: L11/08

Lump sum benefit

8 Was a lump sum payable under a pension scheme or a personal pension policy as a result of the deceased's death?

No ☐ *Go to box 16*

Yes ☐ *Go to box 9*

9 Was the lump sum payable to the deceased's personal representatives, either by right, because there was no-one else who qualified to receive the payment or because it contained an element of protected rights?

No ☐ *Go to box 10*

Yes ☐ *Go to box 12*

10 Could the deceased, right up to their death, have signed a 'nomination' which bound the trustees' of the pension scheme to make a payment to a person nominated by the deceased?

No ☐ *Go to box 11*

Yes ☐ *Go to box 12*

11 Was it at the trustees' discretion to choose who should receive the lump sum, even if the deceased had signed a 'letter of wishes'?

No ☐ *Go to box 12*

Yes ☐ *Go to box 16*

12 Name of the pension scheme or title of the personal pension policy from which the lump sum was paid

13 Is the scheme or policy registered by HMRC for Income Tax purposes?

No ☐ Yes ☐

14 Name of the person who received the lump sum payment and their relationship to the deceased

15 Amount of the lump sum payment
Do not enter an amount if the payment was made at the discretion of the trustees

£

Include this amount in form IHT400, box 56

Changes to pension benefits

16 Did the deceased, within the two years before they died, dispose of any of the benefits payable, or make any changes to the benefits to which they were entitled, under a pension scheme or personal pension policy?

No ☐ *Go to box 22*

Yes ☐ *Go to box 17*

17 Name of the pension scheme or title of the personal pension policy

18 Is the scheme or policy registered by HMRC for Income Tax purposes?

No ☐ Yes ☐

19 Date the benefit was nominated, appointed, assigned, or changed *DD MM YYYY*

20 Name of the person who received the benefit and their relationship to the deceased

21 If changes were made to the benefits, please explain what those changes were

IHT409 Page 2

Contributions to a pension scheme within two years of death

22 Did the deceased or the deceased's employer make any contributions to a pension scheme within the two years before the date of death?

No ☐ *Go to box 25*

Yes ☐ *Go to box 23*

23 Who made the payments?

24 When were the payments made and how much were they for?

Alternatively secured pension funds

- If the date of death was before 6 April 2006 do not fill in this section.
- If the date of death was between 6 April 2006 and 5 April 2007 inclusive, fill in all of this section.
- If the date of death was after 5 April 2007 fill in boxes 25 to 27 only.

25 Did the deceased benefit from an alternatively secured pension (ASP) fund as the original scheme member?

No ☐ *Go to box 33*

Yes ☐ *Go to box 26*

26 Scheme administrator's name and address details

Title - *enter MR, MRS, MISS, MS or other title*

Name

Postcode

House or building number

Rest of address, including house name or flat number

27 Scheme reference number

28 Value of the fund at the date of death

£

29 Value of the fund being used to provide benefits for the deceased's relevant dependants

£

30 Is the fund being used to purchase an annuity for the deceased's relevant dependant which will come to an end on or before the death of the relevant dependant?

No ☐ Yes ☐

31 Amount of the fund now passing to charity

£

32 Net value chargeable to tax
(Box 28 *minus* box 29 *minus* box 31)

£

Include this amount in form IHT400, box 106

Dependant's pension fund

- If the date of death was before 6 April 2006 do not fill in this section.
- If the date of death was between 6 April 2006 and 5 April 2007 inclusive, fill in all of this section.
- If the date of death was after 5 April 2007 fill in boxes 33 to 37 only.

33 Did the deceased benefit from:

- a dependant's ASP fund or dependant's unsecured pension fund to which they became entitled as the 'relevant dependant' of a scheme member who died with an ASP?

  No ☐ Yes ☐

- a dependant's ASP fund derived from the pension lump sum death benefit of a scheme member who died before the age of 75?

  No ☐ Yes ☐

If you answered No to both questions, you have finished this form.

If you answered Yes to either question, go to box 34.

34 Name of the scheme member referred to in question 33

35 Original scheme member's date of birth *DD MM YYYY*

36 Original scheme member's date of death *DD MM YYYY*

37 Original scheme member's IHT reference (if known)

38 Scheme administrator's name and address details

Title - *enter MR, MRS, MISS, MS or other title*

Name

Postcode

House or building number

Rest of address, including house name or flat number

39 Scheme reference number

40 Value of the fund at the date of death

£

41 Amount of the fund now passing to charity

£

42 Net value of the chargeable estate
(Box 40 *minus* box 41)

£

Include this amount in form IHT400, box 106

38

Potentially Exempt Transfers

Cross-references. See **2.4** and **2.11** ACCOUNTS AND RETURNS; **4.5** AGRICULTURAL PROPERTY; **6.11** BUSINESS PROPERTY; **7** CALCULATION OF TAX; **28.1** INTEREST ON TAX; **30.7** LIABILITY FOR TAX; **33.3** NATIONAL HERITAGE; **35.1** PAYMENT OF TAX for due date of payment; **35.5** for payment by instalments; **35.12** for HMRC charges; **35.15** for certificates of discharge; **51.5** TRANSFER OF VALUE for the repayment of certain debts during lifetime being treated as potentially exempt transfers.

Simon's Taxes. See I3.311–I3.319, I3.322.

Other Sources. HMRC Customer Guide to Inheritance Tax; Foster, Parts C3, C4 and C5.

Introduction

[38.1] Except as provided to the contrary under **38.4** below, a potentially exempt transfer is a transfer of value made by an individual which would otherwise be a chargeable transfer and which falls into one of the following categories.

(a) A gift to another individual of property which:
  (i) becomes comprised in his estate; or
  (ii) if not falling within (i) above, increases the value of his estate.

  Included is a gift made by an individual into a settlement or which increases the value of settled property, and, in either case, another individual has a beneficial interest in possession in that settlement.

(b) A gift into an accumulation and maintenance trust before 22 March 2006 which gift, by virtue of the transfer, becomes *property* to which *IHTA 1984, s 71* applies, see **44.4** SETTLEMENTS: ACCUMULATION AND MAINTENANCE TRUSTS.

(c) A gift to a disabled trust which gift, by virtue of the transfer, becomes *property* to which *IHTA 1984, s 89* applies, see **47.1** SETTLEMENTS: TRUSTS FOR THE DISABLED.

(d) The disposal or termination by an individual of his beneficial interest in possession in settled property by gift before 22 March 2006 on which event:

(i) another individual becomes beneficially entitled to the property in which the interest subsisted or an interest in possession in that property; or

(ii) that property is settled on accumulation and maintenance trusts or trusts for the disabled; or

(iii) the value of another individual's estate is increased.

(e) A gift to a trust for a bereaved minor on or after 22 March 2006 which gift, on the ending of an immediate post-death interest (IPDI) which, by virtue of the transfer, becomes property to which *IHTA 1984, s 71A* applies but whereby the beneficial entitlement is passed on to the trust and was effected during the beneficiary's lifetime. [*IHTA 1984, s 3B inserted by FA 2006, Sch 20 para 9(5)*].

Proviso re 'identifiable property'

For the purposes of (b) and (c) above some identifiable property must become subject to the trusts, otherwise the gift remains a chargeable transfer. For example, the payment by the settlor of an insurance premium on a policy written for the beneficiaries of an accumulation and maintenance trust would be a chargeable transfer. If, however, the settlor provides the trust with the funds from which to pay the premiums, the gift would be a potentially exempt transfer. For the purposes of (d), however, there are certain transitional rules that ensure that new interests in possession which are created out existing ones before 6 October 2008 ('transitional serial interests') still will qualify as PETs. See **42** SETTLEMENTS WITH INTERESTS IN POSSESSION.

Summary of qualifying PETs

In summary therefore a PET will, from 22 March 2006, comprise:

- transfers by individuals to other individuals;
- transfers by individuals to certain trusts for the disabled (see **47** SETTLEMENTS: TRUSTS FOR DISABLED PERSONS);
- transfers on or after 22 March 2006 by an individual to a bereaved minor's trust on the coming to an end of an immediate post-death interest (see **46** SETTLEMENTS: TRUSTS FOR BEREAVED MINORS);
- transfers before 22 March 2006 by an individual to an accumulation and maintenance trust (see **44** SETTLEMENTS: ACCUMULATION AND MAINTENANCE TRUSTS);
- transfers by an individual into an interest in possession trust in which, for transfers on or after 22 March 2006, the beneficiary has a disabled person's interest (see **47.1** SETTLEMENTS: TRUSTS FOR DISABLED PERSONS); and
- certain transfers on the termination or disposal of an individual's beneficial interest in possession in settled property (these are in restricted circumstances following *FA 2006* at **31.1** LIFE ASSURANCE POLICIES AND ANNUITIES; **42.1** SETTLEMENTS WITH INTERESTS IN POSSESSION).

With regard to the last point above the anti-avoidance amendments to *IHTA 1984, s 3A* have the effect of applying to a *s 5(1B)* interest (i.e. an interest in possession to which a person domiciled in the UK became beneficially entitled on or after 9 December 2009 by virtue of a disposition falling within *IHTA 1984, s 10* vis an interest in settled property without gratuitous benefit to some other person) the IHT charging provisions relating to the termination of an interest in possession during the life of the person entitled to it. Such an interest is not a PET and in the absence of an available nil rate band or exemptions a chargeable occasion arises. This applies to interest in possession of a person to which a person is entitled to if that entitlement arises on or after 9 December 2009.

[*IHTA 1984, ss 3A(1)–(3)(6)(6A)(7), 3B, 5(1B); FA 1986, Sch 19 para 1; F(No 2)A 1987, s 96(1)–(3); FA 2006, Sch 20 para 9, Sch 26 Pt 6; FA 2010, s 53(2)(3)*].

Consequences of treatment as potentially exempt transfer

[38.2] A potentially exempt transfer made seven years or more before the death of the transferor is an exempt transfer and any other potentially exempt transfer is a chargeable transfer. [*IHTA 1984, s 3A(4); FA 1986, Sch 19 para 1*]. A potentially exempt transfer is assumed to be an exempt transfer during the seven years following the transfer or, if earlier, until immediately before the transferor's death. [*IHTA 1984, s 3(A)(5); FA 1986, Sch 19 para 1*].

As potentially exempt transfers are assumed to be exempt at the time of the transfer, no IHT is payable at that time. If the transferor makes a subsequent chargeable lifetime transfer (e.g. a gift to a discretionary trust) the earlier potentially exempt transfer does not enter into the transferor's cumulative total at that time. Where, however, the transferor dies within seven years of the potentially exempt transfer, it becomes a chargeable transfer at the actual date of the gift. Tax is calculated at the full death rates applying at the time of death, subject to taper relief, see **53.1** TRANSFERS WITHIN SEVEN YEARS BEFORE DEATH. Tax on subsequent chargeable lifetime transfers may, therefore, not only need to be revised under the rules for TRANSFERS WITHIN SEVEN YEARS BEFORE DEATH (53) but will also be affected by the revision of the transferor's cumulative total.

Example

X makes a potentially exempt transfer to Y of £338,000 on 1 January 2004 and then on 1 August 2009 makes a chargeable transfer of £150,000 of an existing life interest within *s 59* in favour of his son into discretionary trust. X dies on 31 December 2010 with an estate valued at £500,000.

On the initial gift of the £338,000 to Y this will be a PET and no charge arises and no cumulation either. The subsequent gift to Z Trust is chargeable but at the time of the gift the nil rate band is greater than the gift of his life interest into the Trust and therefore there is no charge to lifetime rates. However, with the death of X the PET now becomes chargeable because the gift was within seven years of X's death and this will be a charge to tax at death rates after the reallocation of the nil rate band to the gift. This has a knock-on effect in that the chargeable gift into the Trust which was made later and was not subject to tax because of the nil rate band now becomes chargeable to inheritance tax at death rates.

		£		
Y's liability becomes:		338,000		
	Less 2003/04, 2002/03	6,000		
		332,000		
	Less nil rate band	325,000		
		£7,000	@ 40% =	£2,800
	Less taper relief (80% for surviving six years)			2,240
	Tax payable by Y			£560
Z Trust liability becomes:		150,000		
	Less 2009/10, 2008/09	6,000		
		144,000	@ 40% =	£57,600
X's death estate liability becomes:		£500,000	@ 40% =	£200,000

As the gift into the Trust was within three years of the death there is no taper relief. The liability arising on Y and the Z Trustees and X's personal representatives will probably not be planned for and therefore either or both may be unable to pay the additional liability thereby shifting the burden of tax onto X's personal representatives. Situations such as this should ideally be planned for by both Y and Z Trustees and X's personal representatives taking out insurance cover for the period of seven years after the gifts. As personal representatives do not have an implied power to take out such insurance cover it makes sense for the original will to be drawn up with the empowering clause. Also, X should have planned his gifts in a better way by transferring the gift to the Trust firstly and the gift to Y second. This would have had the effect of providing the nil rate band for the Trust which would have an impact in reducing future rates of charge on the discretionary trust.

Treatment of annual exemption in relation to a potentially exempt transfer

[38.3] Where a transfer of value is a potentially exempt transfer, in the first instance it is left out of account for the purposes of allocating the £3,000 annual exemption. However, if the transfer subsequently proves to be a chargeable transfer, it is taken to have been made in the tax year in which it was actually made but later than any transfer of value in the same year which is not a potentially exempt transfer. The insertion of *subsection 3A* into *IHTA 1984, s 19* by *FA 1986* created a problem in that if a transfer of value qualified as a PET, the annual exemption if not already used would not be used against the PET but would be carried forward. However, *s 19(3A)(b)* provides that if the PET becomes chargeable within seven years then the annual exemption will be set against the PET first. This means that when considering the order of dispositions where there are annual exemptions available then the order of those gifts is important. See Key Points below. [*IHTA 1984, s 19(3A); FA 1986, Sch 19 para 5*].

HMRC historical view

Prior to the publication of the January 1991 edition of their booklet IHT 1, HMRC had indicated that the effect of *IHTA 1984, s 19(3A)* was that where the annual exemption had been used in determining the amount of a chargeable lifetime transfer in the same tax year, it was not necessary to revise that amount by reallocating the annual exemption to an earlier potentially exempt transfer made in the same year which proved to be chargeable. However, on this analysis, where an unused annual exemption was carried forward to the following year and set against a chargeable transfer in that year, a potentially exempt transfer in the earlier year which became chargeable received the benefit of that exemption, rather than the chargeable transfer in the later year.

The HMRC view, whilst giving sense to *IHTA 1984, s 19(3A)*, appeared to conflict with the words of *IHTA 1984, s 3A(1)(b)*, namely 'Any reference in this Act to a potentially exempt transfer is a reference to a transfer of value . . . which, apart from this section, would be a chargeable transfer (or to the extent to which, apart from this section, it would be such a transfer)' (see **38.1** above and **38.4**(a) below). In this context it should be noted that *IHTA 1984, s 2(1)* defines chargeable transfer as a transfer of value which is made by an individual but which is not an exempt transfer. In the January 1991 edition of IHT 1, HMRC stated (at paragraph 5.16) that 'If a gift to an individual [or, presumably, one of the other qualifying categories in **38.1** above] is entitled to the annual exemption it is an exempt transfer and not a potentially exempt transfer'. At paragraph 5.17 it provided the following example:

> 'A makes a gift of £10,000 in May 1987. In October 1987 she makes a gift into a discretionary trust (so it is a gift chargeable when made). The annual exemption for 1987/88 is set against the first £3,000 of the May gift, leaving a potentially exempt transfer of £7,000. The whole of the October gift into discretionary trust is immediately chargeable. Any relief carried forward from 1986/87 is also set against the May gift. So if A has made no transfers in 1986/87 there will be a total of £6,000 to be set against the May gift, leaving a potentially exempt transfer of £4,000.'

Unfortunately IHT 15 which replaced IHT 1 did not duplicate the example but under this previous treatment it would appear HMRC currently ignore *IHTA 1984, s 19(3A)*. Its treatment would also mean that it is to the taxpayer's benefit to arrange transfers that have to be made in the same year so that a chargeable transfer (against which the annual exemption is set) precedes a potentially exempt transfer which may never become chargeable (in which case, any set-off of annual exemption would have been wasted). See Key Points below.

On similar arguments to the above, HMRC have stated that where a potentially exempt transfer is treated as made under *FA 1986, s 102(4)* as a result of a reservation of benefit ceasing to exist in the donor's lifetime (see example at **22.1** GIFTS WITH RESERVATION), no deduction of annual exemption can be made if the potentially exempt transfer proves to be a chargeable transfer (HMRC Tax Bulletin November 1993 p 98).

Exceptions

[38.4] The following transfers are not to be regarded as potentially exempt transfers.

(a) A transfer to the extent to which it would in any case be an EXEMPT TRANSFER (**21**). [*IHTA 1984, ss 2, 3A(1)(b); FA 1986, Sch 19 para 1; FA 2006, Sch 20 para 9*].

(b) A transfer on which tax is in any circumstances to be charged *as if* a transfer of value has been made other than, after 16 March 1987, a transfer made under *IHTA 1984, s 52* (charge on the termination of an interest in possession). [*IHTA 1984, s 3A(6); FA 1986, Sch 19 para 1; F(No 2)A 1987, s 96(1)(2)*]. This excludes from treatment as a potentially exempt transfer the charge on:
   (i) participators where a close company makes a transfer of value, see **11.1** CLOSE COMPANIES; and
   (ii) the termination of an interest in possession in settled property before 17 March 1987, see **42.9** SETTLEMENTS WITH INTERESTS IN POSSESSION.

(c) Before 17 March 1987 a transfer of value resulting from the giving of consideration in money or money's worth where a person became entitled to an interest in possession in settled property as a result of the disposition. [*IHTA 1984, s 49(3); FA 1986, Sch 19 para 14; F(No 2)A 1987, s 96(4)*].

(d) Before 17 March 1987 a disposition by which a reversionary interest (whether immediate or not) is acquired by a person entitled to an interest (whether in possession or not) in the settled property. [*IHTA 1984, s 55(2); FA 1986, Sch 19 para 15; F(No 2)A 1987, s 96(5)*].

(e) A disposition treated as having been made by the participators of a close company where there is an alteration in the share or loan capital of a close company not consisting of quoted shares or securities (in relation to transfers of value made, and other events occurring, before 17 March 1987, shares or securities quoted on a recognised stock exchange) or in any rights attaching to its unquoted shares or debentures (in relation to transfers of value made, and other events occurring, before 17 March 1987, shares or debentures not quoted on a recognised stock exchange). [*IHTA 1984, s 98(3); FA 1986, Sch 19 para 20; FA 1987, s 58, Sch 8 para 2*]. See **11.8** CLOSE COMPANIES.

(f) If made after 1 July 1986, the first transfer of value including woodlands on which estate duty was deferred on a death before 13 March 1975. [*FA 1986, Sch 19 para 46*]. Although this provision denies treatment as a potentially exempt transfer to all property comprised in a single transfer of value any part of which, however small, is woodlands subject to a deferred estate duty charge, by concession after 4 December 1990 it will be restricted in its scope to that part of a transfer of value which is attributable to such woodlands (see F15 at **23** HMRC EXTRA-STATUTORY CONCESSIONS).

Key points

[38.5] Points to consider are as follows.

- When advising on the use of annual exemptions to cover gifts in a particular year where there is are PETs and chargeable transfers, careful consideration should be made as to the order of the gifts/PETs and chargeable transfers if they are made in the same tax year. Normally, it should be made clear that gifts that are likely to be PETs (i.e. providing the donor survives seven years from the date of the gift) should be made after any chargeable gift *within the same tax year*. This applies even where there are a number of gifts made in a tax year and the annual unutilised exemption from the previous year is also available. For instance, John makes three gifts on three consecutive days; the first two are PETs of £5,000 and £5,000 and the third is a gift into discretionary trust £16,000 which is an immediately chargeable transfer. The annual exemption of £3,000 from the previous year along with £2,000 of the current year's annual exemption will be set against the first gift leaving £1,000 to set against the second gift and the balance becoming potentially chargeable only on John's death within the seven years. Therefore if the donor survives the PETs by seven years they will become exempt transfers but the third gift will have been chargeable; in effect in this scenario the annual exemptions have been 'wasted'. It is of course the case that if John dies within seven years *IHTA 1984, s 19(3A)(b)* comes into play and the annual exemptions against the PETs on days one and two and have not been wasted. In general it is probably best to consider this with regard to the donor's expected life expectancy because if the gift into the discretionary trust was made first then the position would be that the £6,000 would be set against the discretionary trust gift chargeable as before but both gifts of £5,000 would become chargeable with the transferees paying the tax and this may not be what the donor wished.
- The potential problem above would not happen in a case where the chargeable transfer is in a later or earlier year. For instance, in the case above if John makes the £16,000 gift in a later year the annual exemption(s) would be available to offset against the chargeable gift and the two gifts of £5,000 both in the prior year would, if he dies within seven years of those PETs, be allocated the annual exemptions chronologically and the result would be as shown. The chargeable transfer in the later year attracting its own annual exemption(s).
- Another matter to consider in both the above examples is if the donor's nil rate band is still unutilised. For instance, the second gift by John is only covered to a certain extent by the annual exemption and the balance (i.e. £4,000) would be chargeable on death as a failed PET because the nil rate band had been fully utilised at that point. However, if John has not used his nil rate band at that stage then on death £4,000 of the nil rate band would be used to cover the failed PET of £4,000 and £16,000 would have already been used to cover the gift of £16,000 into discretionary trust. This would mean that the estate and the beneficia-

ries would be utilising £20,000 less of the nil rate band than if John had survived the seven year period immediately after each gift. However, the additional tax due as a result of John's death i.e. 20% would be payable by the donee and trustees not the estate personal representatives but the estate has lost the benefit of £20,000 @ 40% = £8,000.

- Many gifts made by an individual to, say, another individual do not have income tax, CGT or stamp duty implications. For instance, a classic car given by one individual to another has value but does not produce income subject to income tax *per se* and is a wasting asset for the purposes of CGT. No stamp duty payable because it is a gift. However, there is value attaching for IHT purposes and therefore the gift may well become relevant for IHT purposes if the gift is a PET and the donor does not survive seven years from the date of the gift. The gift should be enjoyed by the transferee to the entire exclusion of the donor otherwise anti-avoidance gifts with reservation of benefit provisions may apply. [*FA 1986, s 102(1)(a), (1)(b)*]. Just as important is the delivery of the gift. In other words, has the gift been correctly transferred by memorandum of gift (see example below) that the transferee signs as receipt or has the chattel been gifted by delivery i.e. the donee has actually taken delivery into his/her possession of the chattel. See Key Points at **22.14** GIFTS WITH RESERVATION.
- In the case above where a gift is made of a chattel some form of documented transfer is helpful especially if HMRC question the gift at a later date. In the case of the example of the classic car above the DVLA transfer form (V5C) would be sufficient as this requires details of the transferee and the purchase price, if any. However, in the case of a transfer of a chattel a memorandum of gift witness being present *at the time of the gift* is incontrovertible evidence of the gift vis:

THIS MEMORANDUM records that on the . . . . day of . . . . 2010 the undersigned [*Transferor*] of [*Address*] ('the Transferor') gave and by word of mouth expressed himself/herself to give to the undersigned [*Transferee*]of [*Address*] ('the Transferee) [all the furniture effects and moveable property] which [are] specified in the Schedule attached hereto ('the Chattel(s)) for the absolute sole use of the/and benefit of the Transferee and at the same time the Transferor delivered the Chattel(s) to the Transferee and placed the Transferee in possession and unrestricted control of the Chattel(s) and at the same time the Transferee accepted the gift.

Dated:

SCHEDULE

[*Identification is made here of all chattels which have been given by the Transferor*]

Signed by [*Transferor*]: ....

Signed by [*Transferee*]: ....

STATUTORY DECLARATION

I/We [..........](Declarant). . . . . of [..........]. . . . . do solemnly and sincerely DECLARE as follows;

1. I am [a Solicitor of the Supreme Court]/[over the age of 18 years] and competent to make this declaration.

2. On the . . . . day of . . . . 2010 at .... in the morning/afternoon I was present at . . . . [..........] . . . . where:

   (i) I saw [..........]. . . . . standing in the [hall of ....] and adjacent to a George III mahogany Serpentine sideboard on which he placed his hand at the same time [..........*(i.e. Transferor)*]. . . . . stated to [..........*(i.e. Transferee)*] . . . . "I give you this George III Mahogany sideboard and you may remove it to your home in London". Immediately thereafter I saw [..........*(i.e. Transferor)*]. . . . . lock the sideboard by its key and hand the key to [..........*(i.e. Transferee)*]. . . . . who then took it from him.

SECOND SCHEDULE.

Declaration of gifted items continues . . .

AND I make this solemn declaration conscientiously believing the same to be true and by virtue of the *Statutory Declarations Act 1835*

DECLARED at . . . .

this . . . . day of . . . .

(signature of declarant) ....

2010. . . . . . .

Before me

(signature of person before whom declaration is made)

[A solicitor or A Commissioner for Oaths or as appropriate].

FIRST SCHEDULE

SECOND SCHEDULE

39

Quick Succession Relief

Cross-reference. See also **52** TRANSFERS ON DEATH.

Simon's Taxes. See **I4.165, I5.283.**

Other Sources. HMRC Customer Guide to Inheritance Tax; Foster, Part D1.65, D1.65, E2.83; IHTM22000.

Application

[39.1] Where there is a later transfer of any property within five years of an earlier transfer ('the first transfer') which increased the transferor's estate and the later transfer:

(a) arises on death; or
(b) is of settled property and (i) the transferor was entitled to an interest in possession in the property, (ii) the first transfer was of the same property, and (iii) the first transfer either was or included the making of the settlement or was made after the making of the settlement,

the tax payable on the later transfer is reduced by:

$$\text{Percentage} \times \frac{(G-T)}{G} \times T$$

where:

G = gross (chargeable first transfer);

T = tax on first transfer.

The percentages are as follows:

Period between transfers	*Percentage*
One year or less	100%
More than 1 year but not more than 2 years	80%
More than 2 years but not more than 3 years	60%
More than 3 years but not more than 4 years	40%
More than 4 years but not more than 5 years	20%

Where in relation to the first transfer there is more than one later transfer, if full relief cannot be given because the tax charge on the earliest of them is insufficient, credit may be given on later transfers in chronological order until credits representing the whole of (G – T) × T/G have been given. Credit of (for example) £1,200 on a later transfer after 2½ years represents £1,200/60% = £2,000, and the maximum relief on any later transfer would be limited to the appropriate percentage (60%, 40% or 20%) of ((G – T) × T/G – £2,000).

In calculating whether or to what extent the first transfer increased the value of the transferor's estate (i.e. (G – T)/G), any excluded property consisting of a reversionary interest to which he became entitled either on the occasion of, or before, that transfer is left out of account. [*IHTA 1984, s 141*].

Where the earlier occasion was a lifetime transfer and the transferee dies before the transferor, relief may still be available even though it cannot be determined whether any tax is in fact payable on the potentially exempt transfer (or further tax in respect of a lifetime transfer chargeable when made) until seven years have elapsed from the date of the gift or the transferor dies before the expiry of that period. Provided the transferee dies within five years of the gift, quick succession relief will be given in the transferee's estate in the normal way once the amount of the tax on the gift is quantified.

Where the later transfer qualifies to any extent for the lower 36% rate of IHT (see **52.13**: estates where 10% or more of any component is given to charity), any quick succession relief given to the estate as a whole must be divided between the relevant components by reference to the tax that is payable by each component, and not the capital value of those components. [*IHTA s 141A*].

Example

On 1 January 2011 A died with a net estate valued at £400,000. In December 2006 he had received a gift from B of £20,000. B died in November 2008 and A paid the IHT (amounting to £8,000) due as a result of B's potentially exempt transfer becoming chargeable within the three years before the death.

A was also entitled to an interest in possession in the whole of his father's estate. His father had died in February 2007 with a net estate of £306,000 on which the IHT paid was £2,400. On A's death, the property passed to A's sister and was valued at £145,000. A had made no previous transfers and left his estate to his brother.

	£
Free estate	400,000
Settled property	145,000
Taxable estate	£545,000

IHT on an estate of £545,000 = £88,000

Quick succession relief

The gift from B was made more than four but not more than five years before A's death so quick succession relief at 20% is available.

QSR =	$20\% \times £8{,}000 \times \frac{12{,}000}{20{,}000}$	£960

Interest in possession in father's will trust	£
Net estate before tax	306,000
Tax	2,400
Net estate after tax	£303,600

A's death was more than two but not more than three years after his father's so relief is given at 60%.

QSR =	$60\% \times £2{,}400 \times \frac{303{,}600}{306{,}000}$	£1,428

Tax payable on death of A		£	£
IHT on an estate of £545,000			88,000
Deduct QSR			
On gift from B		960	
On father's estate		1,428	
			2,388
IHT payable			£85,612
On free estate	$\frac{400{,}000}{545{,}000} \times £85{,}612$		£62,834
On settled property	$\frac{145{,}000}{545{,}000} \times £85{,}612$		£22,778

Note to the example

(A) The relief is given only by reference to the tax charged on the part of the value received by the donee. Therefore, the tax paid must be apportioned by applying the fraction 'net transfer received divided by gross transfer made'.

Key points

[39.2] Points to consider are as follows.

- If there are two successive charges on the settled property within a period of five years the tax payable on the second charge is reduced, and the reduction is a percentage of the tax payable on the earlier transfer. The second settled property charge must arise on the termination of an interest in possession, and the first such charge must have increased the estate of the life tenant who was the holder of that interest and be determined by reference to the same settled property. This latter condition means in effect that, where the life tenant's interest arose on or after 22 March 2006, it must be an IPDI, a disabled person's interest or a TSI and as a result increased the beneficiary's estate for IHT purposes.
- Form IHT415 should be used to claim quick succession relief if the administration of the earlier estate has not been completed and the deceased had not received their share of that estate before they died. If the deceased had already received their gift and relief is being deducted then you must enter:
- the IHT reference of the first person to die;
- their full name, and
- their date of death,

  in the Additional Information boxes on pages 15 and 16 of Form IHT400.
- Under *IHTA 1984, s 159* unilateral credit for overseas tax can be allowed not only on death but also in respect of lifetime dispositions where some type of gift tax is charged in that foreign country. The basic conditions to be satisfied in connection with a lifetime or death transfer are that both UK IHT and overseas tax must be chargeable by reference to the same event and attributable to the value of the same property, and that the foreign tax is similar in character to IHT. See **18** DOUBLE TAXATION RELIEF. Where QSR is allowed, the amount of IHT attributed to the property is the net amount after allowing the relief. Some countries such as Australia, Canada and New Zealand do not have estate taxes and the USA has federal and state estate taxes so examination of the prior gift and estate duty tax attaching to it is required.

40

Rates of Tax

Rates	**40.1**

Cross-references. See 7 CALCULATION OF TAX and 53 TRANSFERS WITHIN SEVEN YEARS BEFORE DEATH.

Simon's Taxes. See I3.5, I4.1.

Rates

[40.1] *Inheritance tax is levied on the value transferred by a* CHARGEABLE TRANSFER (9) at the rate or rates applicable to the highest part of the aggregate of that value and the values transferred by any chargeable transfers made by the transferor in the period of seven years ending with the date of the transfer. [*IHTA 1984, ss 1, 7(1)*].

Only one table of rates is enacted which is applicable to transfers on death. Chargeable lifetime transfers are charged at one half of those death rates throughout the range of rate bands. Transfers made within seven years of death are charged at the death rates but in the case of chargeable transfers made in that period but more than three years before death (including potentially exempt transfers which become chargeable transfers), the tax charged is tapered, see **53.1** TRANSFERS WITHIN SEVEN YEARS BEFORE DEATH. [*IHTA 1984, s 7(2)–(4), Sch 1; FA 1986, Sch 19 paras 2, 36*].

Indexation of rate bands

The rate bands are subject to a provision for annual indexation annually unless Parliament determines otherwise. If the Retail Prices Index as published by the Office of National Statistics for September in any year is higher than that for the previous September, then from the following 6 April the lower and upper limits of the rate bands in the tables applying in the previous year are increased by the same percentage as the percentage increase in the index. [*Transfer of Functions (Registration and Statistics) Order 1996, SI 1996/273*]. The figures are rounded up, if necessary, to the nearest £1,000. The Treasury specifies the new rate bands by statutory instrument before the start of the tax year in question. There is no provision for a reduction in the bands on a fall in the Index. For years before 1994/95 the calculation was made by reference to the change in the Index during the year to the previous December. The indexing provisions are not applied for 1987/88, 1988/89, 1992/93, 1993/94, 1994/95, 1996/97 and 2002/03 but were relevant for 1995/96, 1997/98, 1998/99,

1999/2000, 2000/01, 2001/02, 2003/04, 2004/05, 2005/06 and the rates of the nil rate band for 2013/14 onwards have been fixed until 2017/18 (see Tables below). [*IHTA 1984, s 8; FA 1986, Sch 19 para 3; FA 2010, s 8; FA 2014, Sch 21 para 2*].

Transferable nil rate band

Although only one table of rates is enacted, a table for chargeable lifetime transfers is also given below. Grossing-up tables are included to simplify calculations which involve net transfers. From 9 October 2007 married couples and those in civil partnerships may transfer any unused nil rate band on their death to the surviving spouse or civil partner. This may have been during the period when Capital Transfer Tax operated or when Estate Duty applied. See further details at **52.14**. [*IHTA 1984, ss 8A, 8C; FA 2008, Sch 4, paras 10, 11*].

TRANSFERS ON DEATH AFTER 5 APRIL 2009

2010.A1 Tax on transfers

	Gross taxable transfers £	Gross cumulative totals £	Rate
First	325,000	0–325,000	Nil
Above	325,000		40% for each £ over 325,000

2010.A2 Grossing-up of specific transfers on death which do not bear their own tax

	Net transfers £	Tax payable thereon £
0–	325,000	Nil
Above	325,000	Nil + ⅔ (66.666%) for each £ over 325,000

CHARGEABLE LIFETIME TRANSFERS AFTER 5 APRIL 2009 AND BEFORE 6 APRIL 2015

2010.B1 Tax on gross transfers

	Gross taxable transfers £	Gross cumulative totals £	Rate
First	325,000	0–325,000	Nil
Above	325,000		20% for each £ over 325,000

2010.B2 Grossing-up of net lifetime transfers

	Net transfers £	Tax payable thereon £
0–	325,000	Nil
Above	325,000	Nil + ¼ (25%) for each £ over 325,000

TRANSFERS ON DEATH AFTER 5 APRIL 2008 AND BEFORE 6 APRIL 2009

2008.A1 Tax on transfers

	Gross taxable transfers £	Gross cumulative totals £	Rate
First	312,000	0–312,000	Nil
Above	312,000		40% for each £ over 312,000

2008.A2 Grossing-up of specific transfers on death which do not bear their own tax

	Net transfers £	Tax payable thereon £
0–	312,000	Nil
Above	312,000	Nil + 2/3 (66.666%) for each £ over 312,000

CHARGEABLE LIFETIME TRANSFERS AFTER 5 APRIL 2008 AND BEFORE 6 APRIL 2009

2008.B1 Tax on gross transfers

	Gross taxable transfers £	Gross cumulative totals £	Rate
First	312,000	0–312,000	Nil
Above	312,000		20% for each £ over 312,000

2008.B2 Grossing-up of net lifetime transfers

	Net transfers £	Tax payable thereon £
0–	312,000	Nil
Above	312,000	Nil + 1/4 (25%) for each £ over 312,000

TRANSFERS ON DEATH AFTER 5 APRIL 2007 AND BEFORE 6 APRIL 2008

2007.A1 Tax on transfers

	Gross taxable transfers £	Gross cumulative totals £	Rate
First	300,000	0–300,000	Nil
Above	300,000		40% for each £ over 300,000

2007.A2 Grossing-up of specific transfers on death which do not bear their own tax

	Net transfers £	Tax payable thereon £
0–	300,000	Nil

Above	300,000	Nil + 2/3 (66.666%) for each £ over 300,000

CHARGEABLE LIFETIME TRANSFERS AFTER 5 APRIL 2007 AND BEFORE 6 APRIL 2008

2007.B1 Tax on gross transfers

	Gross taxable transfers £	Gross cumulative totals £	Rate
First	300,000	0–300,000	Nil
Above	300,000		20% for each £ over 300,000

2007.B2 Grossing-up of net lifetime transfers

	Net transfers £	Tax payable thereon £
0–	300,000	Nil
Above	300,000	Nil + 1/4 (25%) for each £ over 300,000

TRANSFERS ON DEATH AFTER 5 APRIL 2006 AND BEFORE 6 APRIL 2007

2006.A1 Tax on transfers

	Gross taxable transfers £	Gross cumulative totals £	Rate
First	285,000	0–285,000	Nil
Above	285,000		40% for each £ over 285,000

2006.A2 Grossing-up of specific transfers on death which do not bear their own tax

	Net transfers £	Tax payable thereon £
0–	285,000	Nil
Above	285,000	Nil + 2/3 (66.666%) for each £ over 285,000

CHARGEABLE LIFETIME TRANSFERS AFTER 5 APRIL 2006 AND BEFORE 6 APRIL 2007

2006.B1 Tax on gross transfers

	Gross taxable transfers £	Gross cumulative totals £	Rate
First	285,000	0–285,000	Nil
Above	285,000		20% for each £ over 285,000

2006.B2 Grossing-up of net lifetime transfers

	Net transfers £	Tax payable thereon £
0–	285,000	Nil
Above	285,000	Nil + 1/4 (25%) for each £ over 285,000

TRANSFERS ON DEATH AFTER 5 APRIL 2005 AND BEFORE 6 APRIL 2006

2005.A1 Tax on transfers

	Gross taxable transfers £	Gross cumulative totals £	Rate
First	275,000	0–275,000	Nil
Above	275,000		40% for each £ over 275,000

2005.A2 Grossing-up of specific transfers on death which do not bear their own tax

	Net transfers £	Tax payable thereon £
0–	275,000	Nil
Above	275,000	Nil + 2/3 (66.666%) for each £ over 275,000

CHARGEABLE LIFETIME TRANSFERS AFTER 5 APRIL 2005 AND BEFORE 6 APRIL 2006

2005.B1 Tax on gross transfers

	Gross taxable transfers £	Gross cumulative totals £	Rate
First	275,000	0–275,000	Nil
Above	275,000		20% for each £ over 275,000

2005.B2 Grossing-up of net lifetime transfers

	Net transfers £	Tax payable thereon £
0–	275,000	Nil
Above	275,000	Nil + 1/4 (25%) for each £ over 275,000

TRANSFERS ON DEATH AFTER 5 APRIL 2004 AND BEFORE 6 APRIL 2005

2004.A1 Tax on transfers

	Gross taxable transfers £	Gross cumulative totals £	Rate
First	263,000	0–263,000	Nil
Above	263,000		40% for each £ over 263,000

2004.A2 Grossing-up of specific transfers on death which do not bear their own tax

	Net transfers £	Tax payable thereon £
0–	263,000	Nil
Above	263,000	Nil + 2/3 (66.666%) for each £ over 263,000

CHARGEABLE LIFETIME TRANSFERS AFTER 5 APRIL 2004 AND BEFORE 6 APRIL 2005

2004.B1 Tax on gross transfers

	Gross taxable transfers £	Gross cumulative totals £	Rate
First	263,000	0–263,000	Nil
Above	263,000		20% for each £ over 263,000

2004.B2 Grossing-up of net lifetime transfers

	Net transfers £	Tax payable thereon £
0–	263,000	Nil
Above	263,000	Nil + 1/4 (25%) for each £ over 263,000

TRANSFERS ON DEATH AFTER 5 APRIL 2003 AND BEFORE 6 APRIL 2004

2003.A1 Tax on transfers

	Gross taxable transfers £	Gross cumulative totals £	Rate
First	255,000	0–255,000	Nil
Above	255,000		40% for each £ over 255,000

2003.A2 Grossing-up of specific transfers on death which do not bear their own tax

	Net transfers £	Tax payable thereon £
0–	255,000	Nil
Above	255,000	Nil + $^2/_3$ (66.666%) for each £ over 255,000

CHARGEABLE LIFETIME TRANSFERS AFTER 5 APRIL 2003 AND BEFORE 6 APRIL 2004

2003.B1 Tax on gross transfers

	Gross taxable transfers £	Gross cumulative totals £	Rate
First	255,000	0–255,000	Nil
Above	255,000		20% for each £ over 255,000

2003.B2 Grossing-up of net lifetime transfers

	Net transfers £	Tax payable thereon £
0–	255,000	Nil
Above	255,000	Nil + $^1/_4$ (25%) for each £ over 255,000

TRANSFERS ON DEATH AFTER 5 APRIL 2002 AND BEFORE 6 APRIL 2003

2002.A1 Tax on transfers

	Gross taxable transfers £	Gross cumulative totals £	Rate
First	250,000	0–250,000	Nil
Above	250,000		40% for each £ over 250,000

2002.A2 Grossing-up of specific transfers on death which do not bear their own tax

	Net transfers £	Tax payable thereon £
0–	250,000	Nil
Above	250,000	Nil + 2/3 (66.666%) for each £ over 250,000

CHARGEABLE LIFETIME TRANSFERS AFTER 5 APRIL 2002 AND BEFORE 6 APRIL 2003

2002.B1 Tax on gross transfers

	Gross taxable transfers £	Gross cumulative totals £	Rate
First	250,000	0–250,000	Nil
Above	250,000		20% for each £ over 250,000

2002.B2 Grossing-up of net lifetime transfers

	Net transfers £	Tax payable thereon £
0–	250,000	Nil
Above	250,000	Nil + 1/4 (25%) for each £ over 250,000

TRANSFERS ON DEATH AFTER 5 APRIL 2001 AND BEFORE 6 APRIL 2002

2001.A1 Tax on transfers

	Gross taxable transfers £	Gross cumulative totals £	Rate
First	242,000	0–242,000	Nil
Above	242,000		40% for each £ over 242,000

2001.A2 Grossing-up of specific transfers on death which do not bear their own tax

	Net transfers £	Tax payable thereon £
0–	242,000	Nil
		Nil + 2/3 (66.666%) for each £ over 242,000
Above	242,000	

CHARGEABLE LIFETIME TRANSFERS AFTER 5 APRIL 2001 AND BEFORE 6 APRIL 2002

2001.B1 Tax on gross transfers

	Gross taxable transfers £	Gross cumulative totals £	Rate
First	242,000	0–242,000	Nil
Above	242,000		20% for each £ over 242,000

2001.B2 Grossing-up of net lifetime transfers

	Net transfers £	Tax payable thereon £
0–	242,000	Nil
Above	242,000	Nil + 1/4 (25%) for each £ over 242,000

TRANSFERS ON DEATH AFTER 5 APRIL 2000 AND BEFORE 6 APRIL 2001

2000.A1 Tax on transfers

	Gross taxable transfers £	Gross cumulative totals £	Rate
First	234,000	0–234,000	Nil
Above	234,000		40% for each £ over 234,000

2000.A2 Grossing-up of specific transfers on death which do not bear their own tax

	Net transfers £	Tax payable thereon £
0–	234,000	Nil
Above	234,000	Nil + 2/3 (66.666%) for each £ over 234,000

CHARGEABLE LIFETIME TRANSFERS AFTER 5 APRIL 2000 AND BEFORE 6 APRIL 2001

2000.B1 Tax on gross transfers

	Gross taxable transfers £	Gross cumulative totals £	Rate
First	234,000	0–234,000	Nil
Above	234,000		20% for each £ over 234,000

2000.B2 Grossing-up of net lifetime transfers

	Net transfers £	Tax payable thereon £
0–	234,000	Nil
Above	234,000	Nil + 1/4 (25%) for each £ over 234,000

41

Settlements — General

Cross-references. See also 27 INTEREST IN POSSESSION; 42 SETTLEMENTS WITH INTERESTS IN POSSESSION; 43 SETTLEMENTS WITHOUT INTERESTS IN POSSESSION.

Simon's Taxes. See **Part I5**.

Other Sources. Foster, Parts E and M8; HMRC Customer Guide to Inheritance Tax; IHTM16000.

Introduction

[41.1] Inheritance tax applies to certain transactions and events relating to settlements. For this purpose settlements are divided into two main categories.

(a) Settlements with qualifying interests in possession.
(b) Settlements without qualifying interests in possession.

The charging provisions for the two types of settlement are completely different and are detailed at 42 SETTLEMENTS WITH INTERESTS IN POSSESSION; 43 SETTLEMENTS WITHOUT INTERESTS IN POSSESSION. See 27 INTEREST IN POSSESSION for meaning of '*interest in possession*'. A '*qualifying*' interest in possession is an interest in possession to which an individual (or a company in the business of acquiring such interests on commercial terms) is beneficially entitled. From 22 March 2006 a '*qualifying*' interest in possession will also include an immediate post-death interest (IPDI), a disabled person's interest, a transitional serial interest (TSI) or an interest in possession to which a company is beneficially entitled. [*IHTA 1984, s 59 as amended by FA 2006, Sch 20 para 20*].

Tax on settlements with interests in possession

[41.2] The normal charging provisions for ordinary transfers of value (see 1 INTRODUCTION AND BASIC PRINCIPLES) apply with some modification to settlements with interests in possession. For interests created prior to 22 March 2006 a person beneficially entitled to an interest in possession in settled property is treated as beneficially entitled to that property, and on the termination or disposal of that interest tax is charged as if he had made a transfer of value of the property in which his interest subsisted. For interests created on or after that date, this treatment applies only in the case of

(i) an immediate post-death interest;
(ii) a disabled person's interest; or
(iii) a transitional serial interest.

It follows that any post-22 March 2006 interest in possession not within any of those three categories will fall within the relevant property regime – see **43** SETTLEMENTS WITHOUT INTEREST IN POSSESSION, and as a result any change in entitlements to income will have no consequences for IHT. From 22 March 2006 a person beneficially entitled to an interest in possession in settled property which is terminated is charged to tax as if he had made a transfer of value of the property in which his interest subsisted only if his interest first arose prior to that date, or is an IPDI or a TSI. See **38.1** POTENTIALLY EXEMPT TRANSFERS. See **42** SETTLEMENTS WITH INTERESTS IN POSSESSION for full details regarding IPDIs and TSIs. [*IHTA 1984, ss 49, 49A–49D, 51, 51A, 52; FA 2006, Sch 20 paras 11–13*].

Tax on settlements without interests in possession

[41.3] There is a separate charging regime for settlements without interests in possession. There are also special rules for certain types of settlements without interests in possession. See **10** CHARITIES; **33** NATIONAL HERITAGE; **37** PENSION SCHEMES; **44** SETTLEMENTS: ACCUMULATION AND MAINTENANCE TRUSTS; **45** SETTLEMENTS: INTERESTS HELD IN PROTECTIVE TRUSTS; **46** SETTLEMENTS: TRUSTS FOR BEREAVED MINORS; **47** SETTLEMENTS: TRUSTS FOR DISABLED PERSONS; **55** TRUSTS FOR EMPLOYEES.

Property entering settlement

[41.4] Tax is charged on the settlor in the normal way when he transfers property into a settlement. A transfer made by an individual after 17 March 1986 and before 22 March 2006 is a potentially exempt transfer (PET) to the extent that it constitutes a gift into an accumulation and maintenance trust or a trust for the disabled. In relation to transfers of value made, and other events occurring, after 16 March 1987 and before 6 October 2008, certain gifts by individuals into settlements with interests in possession are also included. In this latter case certain transitional rules apply to ensure that new interests in possession which are created out of existing ones before 6 October 2008 ('transitional serial interests') still will qualify as PETs. See **38.1** POTENTIALLY EXEMPT TRANSFERS for full details. Such transfers made seven years or more before the transferor's death are exempt transfers. Any other potentially exempt transfer is a chargeable transfer. [*IHTA 1984, ss 49, 49C–49E as* *amended by FA 2008, s 141*]. See 42 SETTLEMENTS WITH INTERESTS IN POSSESSION; 43.22 SETTLEMENTS: DISCRETIONARY TRUSTS AND OTHER TRUSTS OF RELEVANT PROPERTY for property moving between such settlements.

Settlements not liable to IHT

[41.5] Broadly, settled property situated outside the UK escapes IHT if the settlor did not have a UK DOMICILE (16) at the time the settlement was made but see *Civil Engineer v CIR* [2002] STC SCD 72. A reversionary interest in settled property is also normally outside the scope of IHT. From 5 December 2005 anti-avoidance measures apply to prevent UK domiciled individuals who become entitled directly or indirectly to interests in pre-existing foreign trusts which were originally settled by non-UK domiciliaries and would be treated as excluded property within *IHTA 1984, s 48(3)* from benefiting from such treatment if that interest is acquired for money or money's worth. This also applies to the excluded property provisions regarding such property under *IHTA 1984, s 48(3A)* relating to holdings in AUTs and OEICs, [*IHTA 1984, s 48(3), (3A), (3B), (3C); FA 2006, s 157*]. See 20 EXCLUDED PROPERTY, 49 SITUS and former IR Tax Bulletin, February 1997, pp 398 and 399.

Definitions

[41.6] **'Settlement'** means any disposition or dispositions of property, whether effected by instrument, by parol (i.e. verbal or oral) or by operation of law, or partly in one way and partly in another whereby the property is for the time being:

(a) held in trust for persons in succession or for any person subject to a contingency; or
(b) held by trustees on trust to accumulate the whole or any part of any income of the property or with power to make payments out of that income at the discretion of the trustees or some other person, with or without power to accumulate surplus income; or
(c) charged or burdened (otherwise than for full consideration in money or money's worth paid for his own use or benefit to the person making the disposition), with the payment of any annuity or other periodical payment payable for a life or any other limited or terminable period. [*IHTA 1984, s 43(1)(2)*].

'Settlor' includes any person by whom the settlement was made directly or indirectly and any person who has provided funds directly or indirectly for the purpose of or in connection with the settlement or has made with any other person a reciprocal arrangement for that other person to make the settlement. Where more than one person is a settlor in relation to a settlement, and the circumstances so require, the settled property is treated as if comprised in separate settlements for the purposes of the provisions relating to inheritance tax on settled property other than *IHTA 1984, s 48(4)–(6)* (exempt gilts, see 20.5 EXCLUDED PROPERTY). [*IHTA 1984, s 44*].

The words 'for the purpose or in connection with' contained in *IHTA 1984, s 44* imply there must at least be a conscious association of the provider of funds with the settlement in question. It is insufficient that the settled funds should historically have been derived from the provider of them. If it were otherwise, anyone who gave funds unconditionally to another person which that other person later settled would fall to be treated as the settlor or as a settlor of the funds (*Countess Fitzwilliam and others v CIR (and related appeals)* HL, [1993] STC 502).

Case law

In the case of *CIR v Lloyds Private Banking Ltd* [1998] STC 559 Sp C 133 the following clause in the will created a settlement pursuant to *IHTA 1984, s 43(2)* viz.

> '(1) While my Husband . . . remains alive and desires to reside in the property and keeps the same in good repair and insured comprehensively to its full value with Insurers approved by my Trustee and pays and indemnifies my Trustee against all rates taxes and other outgoings in respect of the property my Trustee shall not make any objection to such residence and shall not disturb or restrict it in any way and shall not take any steps to enforce the trust for sale on which the property is held or to realise my share therein or to obtain any rent or profit from the property.
>
> On the death of my said Husband . . . I devise and bequeath the said property . . . to my Daughter . . . absolutely.'

The Commissioner accepted the Trustee's contention that the words 'on the death of' might simply be read as 'subject to the foregoing'. The facts of this appeal showed an instance where the rule stated by Wood V C in *Maddison v Chapman* (1859) 4 K & J 709 might be approved and it was held that there was an absolute gift of the separate share to the daughter, subject only to a direction to the Trustee to postpone sale. See also *Rysaffe Trustee Co (CI) Ltd v CIR* [2003] STC 536 where in the Court of Appeal the Judges upheld Park J in the original case: A settlor had executed five settlements within a period of 35 days, and transferred shares of equal value to each settlement. HMRC had issued a notice of determination that the five holdings should be treated as a single settlement for the purposes of the charge to tax under *IHTA 1984, s 64*. The company which acted as the trustee of the settlements appealed. The Ch D allowed the appeal, holding that there were five separate settlements for the purposes of *s 64*. Park J held that 'it is up to the settlor who places property in trust to determine whether he wishes to create one trust or several trusts, or for that matter merely to add more property to a settlement which had already been created in the past'. Each settlement was created by a 'disposition' within *IHTA 1984, s 43*. The 'associated operations' provisions of *IHTA 1984, s 268* did not apply, since their 'practical operation' was 'comparatively limited'. *IHTA 1984, s 268* was 'not an operative provision which of itself imposes inheritance tax liabilities. It is a definition of an expression (associated operations) which is used elsewhere. The definition only comes into effect in so far as the expression "associated operations" is used elsewhere, and then only if the expression in another provision is relevant to the way in which that other provision applies to the facts of the particular case.'

Other types of settlement

The following are also treated as settlements.

(d) *A foreign settlement*. Any disposition which would fall within (a) to (c) above if it were regulated by the law of any part of the UK, or if under foreign law the administration of the property is governed by provisions equivalent in effect. [*IHTA 1984, s 43(2)*]. See also **20.2** EXCLUDED PROPERTY.

(e) A lease of property for life or lives, or for a period ascertainable only by reference to a death, or which is terminable on, or at a date ascertainable only by reference to, a death, *unless* the lease was granted for full consideration in money or money's worth.
For this purpose a lease not granted at a rack rent which is at any time to become a lease at an increased rent is to be treated as terminable at that time.
In Northern Ireland, this does not apply to a lease in perpetuity within the meaning of the *Renewable Leasehold Conversion Act 1849, s 1* or a lease to which *s 37* of that Act applies. [*IHTA 1984, s 43(3)(5)*].

(f) *In Scotland*, (i) an entail; (ii) any deed by virtue of which an annuity is charged on, or on rents of, any property (the property being treated as the property comprised in the settlement); and (iii) any 'deed' creating or reserving a proper liferent of any property whether inheritable or movable (the property from time to time subject to the proper liferent being treated as the property comprised in the settlement). '*Deed*' includes any disposition, arrangement, contract, resolution, instrument or writing. [*IHTA 1984, s 43(4)*].

(g) *In Northern Ireland*, references to property held in trust for persons include references to property standing limited to persons. [*IHTA 1984, s 43(5)*].

(h) *Usufruct*: in the April 2013 HMRC *Trusts & Estates Newsletter*, it was stated that HMRC have always been of the view that a usufruct will 'more than likely fall to be treated as a settlement for IHT purposes, although HMRC recognises that the arrangements differ between jurisdictions and the circumstances of each need to be considered'. This means that, for a usufruct created on or after 22 March 2006, the property concerned may be considered to be held in a relevant property settlement, with consequent entry charge on creation and subsequent 10-yearly charges arising. Comments on the *Trusts Discussion Forum* concerning this statement have indicated that it is considered to be open to challenge.

Life interest settlement

[41.7] There are now, following the post-21 March 2006 trusts regime, different IHT consequences with regard to the termination of life interests in a settlement. Following the changes made in 2006 regarding the tax treatment of settlements (see above) an existing life interest will be treated in certain ways depending on whether it is:

(a) a qualifying interest in possession created before 22 March 2006, including an interest in possession that is an immediate post-death interest, a transitional serial interest or a disabled person's interest, in each case where the life tenant is entitled to the income of the settled property as it arises, or

(b) is a life interest not falling within any of the categories in (a) above and therefore falls within the relevant property regime, for example an interest in possession arising on or after 22 March 2006 under a lifetime settlement. [*IHTA 1984, Pt III, Ch III*].

In (a) above the termination of an income interest in an interest in possession settlement will be a PET if the funds are thereupon distributable absolutely to a beneficiary and providing the life tenant survives seven years from the termination in favour of another it will become an exempt transfer. Otherwise it will normally be a chargeable transfer to the extent that it is not covered by exemptions or the nil rate band. In (b) however, the termination of a life interest which is within the relevant property regime is not a PET as the life tenant is not treated as having a beneficial interest in the trust fund and consequently the settlement funds do not leave the relevant property regime. No exit charge is therefore applicable under the relevant property regime either.

(A) John has a life interest in a family settlement set up many years ago (i.e. prior to 22 March 2006). In 2010 the trustees decided to terminate his life interest in favour of a life interest for his son, Percy. On this event John will make a chargeable transfer of the value of the settled property and the interest that now subsists for Percy comes within the relevant property regime 43 SETTLEMENTS: DISCRETIONARY TRUSTS AND OTHER TRUSTS OF RELEVANT PROPERTY. In 2014 John died and the trustees then terminated Percy's life interest in order to assist John's wife, Janet, by giving her an interest in the settlement income. The termination of Percy's interest has no relevance for IHT purposes and the settlement remains within the relevant property regime. Had the trustees not made the appointment in favour of Percy, but instead had arranged for Janet's interest to arise on John's death Janet's interest would have been a TSI and would not at that stage come within the relevant property regime. At some stage in the future Janet's life interest will be terminated and at that stage the settlement will enter the relevant property regime.

(B) A family settlement is set up in 2008 and Angela is the life tenant. This settlement comes within the relevant property regime. See SETTLEMENTS: DISCRETIONARY TRUSTS AND OTHER TRUSTS OF RELEVANT PROPERTY (43). In 2010 Angela marries well and is not in need of income and therefore the trustees decide to terminate her life interest in favour of her younger sister who is about to go to university. This termination of Angela's life interest is not a PET because Angela has no beneficial entitlement to the capital that underlines that interest. There is no exit charge when Angela's life interest ceases in favour of her sister unless the interest is an absolute interest in which case there will be an exit charge unless there are IHT reliefs available. Even if Angela's sister's revocable interest is wholly or partly terminated in the future because, say, Angela has become divorced and needs income, then there will be no charge under the relevant property regime unless this coincides with a periodic charge or there is a termination in favour of Angela in which case there will be an exit charge.

Key points

[41.8] Points to consider are as follows.

- As the trust income tax rate is the highest marginal rate (45%) it may be advantageous to make a revocable settlement in favour of a beneficiary who has a lower marginal rate than that of the trust.
- The date when a settlement is made is in most cases when property first becomes comprised in it under *IHTA 1984, s 60*. This date of commencement is particularly important under the relevant property regime as this determines the when the ten year periodic charge is applied. The commencement of various settlements can be summarised as follows:
  (i) the settlement of the *initial capital* notwithstanding later larger additions of capital sets the commencement date so if the settlement is within the relevant property regime the periodic ten-year anniversary charge will be by reference to the date the initial capital was introduced to the settlement;
  (ii) a settlement created by will commences at the date of death under *IHTA 1984, s 83* but if a small pilot trust was set up before death and the will merely adds capital to that trust then the original pilot trust set up date will apply.
  (iii) where a settlement is created by deed of variation the date of commencement will be the date of death and not the date of the variation which may be up to two years later. However, for income tax and CGT purposes the date will not necessarily be the same as IHT i.e. date of death, because income will have already been paid out for that interim period and a CGT election may not actually be made under *TCGA 1992, s 62*.
  (iv) an interest in possession settlement arising before 22 March 2006, or an IPDI or disabled person's interest arising after 21 March 2006 commences on the date the settlor's or their spouse's/civil partner's beneficial interest in possession comes to an end. See **42** SETTLEMENTS WITH INTERESTS IN POSSESSION and *IHTA 1984, s 80*. However, the date of the ten-yearly anniversary charge is not affected as this is related to the original settlement commencement date under *IHTA 1984, s 61(2)*. See **43** SETTLEMENTS:

DISCRETIONARY TRUSTS AND OTHER TRUSTS OF RELEVANT PROPERTY.

42

Settlements with Interests in Possession

Cross-references. See also **27** INTEREST IN POSSESSION; **31** LIFE ASSURANCE POLICIES AND ANNUITIES; **41** SETTLEMENTS — GENERAL; **43** SETTLEMENTS: DISCRETIONARY TRUSTS AND OTHER TRUSTS OF RELEVANT PROPERTY.

Simon's Taxes. See **I3.524–I3.527, I5.201–241, I5.2.**

Other Sources. Foster, Parts E1–4; HMRC Customer Guide to Inheritance Tax; IHTM16000.

Introduction — Interest in possession (IIP)

[42.1] A person beneficially entitled to an interest in possession in settled property in existence prior to 22 March 2006 is treated as beneficially entitled to the property in which the interest subsists, i.e. he is treated as owning it absolutely. There is an IHT charge based on the value of the settled property in which his interest subsists when a beneficiary disposes of his interest or it otherwise comes to an end i.e. either as a transfer on death or as a PET where the termination of the interest occurs during the lifetime of the tenant for example where there is an exercise of a power of appointment. [*IHTA 1984, ss 49(1), 51(1), 51A, 52(1); FA 2006, Sch 20 paras 11–13*]. See **38.1** POTENTIALLY EXEMPT TRANSFERS. See **27** INTEREST IN POSSESSION for meaning of 'interest in possession'. *Note* that the actual actuarial value of the interest is irrelevant except in the limited cases where an interest is acquired for money or money's worth. See **42.10** below.

Post-21 March 2006 interest in possession

From 22 March 2006 newly created IIP settlements will be treated under the relevant property taxing regime unless the interest is an immediate post-death interest (IPDI) or a transitional serial interest (TSI) or a disabled person's interest. See below and 31 LIFE ASSURANCE POLICIES AND ANNUITIES; 43 SETTLEMENTS: DISCRETIONARY TRUSTS AND OTHER TRUSTS OF RELEVANT PROPERTY. [*IHTA 1984, ss 49(1A), 51(1A); FA 2006, Sch 20 paras 4, 11; FA 2010, s 53(4)*]. Any new trusts created from 22 March 2006 which are not IPDI or TSI trusts will be subject to certain requirements before they qualify for exclusion from the relevant property regime. See SETTLEMENTS WITHOUT INTEREST IN POSSESSION (43) and SETTLEMENTS: DISCRETIONARY TRUSTS AND OTHER TRUSTS OF RELEVANT PROPERTY (47).

Immediate post-death interest (IPDI)

[42.2] An IPDI arises for IHT purposes where a person (stipulated as being 'L' in the legislation) is beneficially entitled on or after 22 March 2006 to an interest in possession in settled property and a number of conditions are satisfied. For such trusts set up by will or intestacy the following conditions must apply:

- the first condition is the requirement that the interest in settled property arises *immediately* on the death of the settlor by reason of will or intestacy;
- the second condition is that 'L' becomes beneficially entitled to an interest in possession on the death of the testator or intestate;
- the third condition is that rules regarding bereaved minor's trusts under *IHTA 1984, s 71A* do not apply in these circumstances to property in which the interest subsists and the interest is not a disabled person's interest-see SETTLEMENTS: TRUSTS FOR BEREAVED MINORS (46);
- the fourth condition is that at all times since 'L' became beneficially entitled to the interest in possession that neither *IHTA 1984, s 71A* (bereaved minor's trust) applies to the property in which the interest subsists nor is the interest a disabled person's interest.

[*IHTA 1984, ss 49(1), 49A, 51A, 52(2A), 53(2A); FA 2006, Sch 20 paras 5, 11–13; FA 2010, s 53(4)*].

Example 1

X, who is married to L (his second wife), dies on 12 January 2010 having already made gifts on 21 May 2008 of £318,000 utilising his available annual exemptions and nil rate band. By his will he leaves his assets to his second wife L in trust for life and then on her death on trusts to his son S now aged 30. See extract below. His estate is valued at £760,000 including the value of the house in which they live of £340,000. X had made no gifts in the year to 5 April 2008 but had used his annual exemptions prior to 2007/08.

L dies on 8 January 2012 when the trust assets are valued at £800,000. The terms of the trust are that the assets are to be held on trusts with overriding powers to apply capital and accumulated income to the beneficiary son S.

TRUST INCOME

Subject to the Overriding Powers below I leave my residuary estate on trust:

(1) My Trustees shall pay the income of the Trust Fund to my widow during her life and my Trustees shall have power to pay or apply capital for her benefit;

(2) Subject thereto, my Trustees shall have power to accumulate the whole or any part of the Residuary Fund and that income shall be added to the Trust Fund;

(3) Subject to that, the Trust Fund shall be held on trust for . . . . [Name]. . . . . absolutely.

Calculation on death of X

	£	£
Value transferred on 21 May 2008		318,000
Deduct annual exemption 2008/09	3,000	
annual exemption 2007/08	3,000	6,000
		£312,000

IHT on chargeable gift of £312,000 is charged in the nil rate band up to £312,000.

	£
£0–300,000 at Nil%	Nil
Estate chargeable i.e. balance of estate is exempt under *IHTA 1984, s 18*	Nil

Calculation on death of L

Value of L's estate at 8 January 2012 by reason of *IHTA 1984, s 49(1)(1A)*. See above.	£800,000
See table at **40.1** 2010.A1 RATES OF TAX.	
£0–325,000	Nil
£325,001–£800,000 at 40%	£190,000
IHT payable	£190,000

See Note (B).

Notes to the example

(A) Most married couples and those in civil partnerships would want to defer the IHT burden until the last death especially where there is a property of substantial value in the estate which may have to be sold. In this particular case it is a second marriage and X wishes to benefit his spouse with a life interest but that his son S ultimately benefits on the death of his step-mother. Under *IHTA 1984, s 49A* L has an IPDI which arises under the will of X and L is treated as beneficially entitled to an interest in possession in settled property in which the interest subsists, i.e. see (1) in extract above where L is treated as owning it absolutely and certain disposals of interests in possession by individuals (e.g. renouncing by L of L's life interest or the Trustees defeating L's interest) may be potentially exempt transfers. However, as L did not survive seven years but dies within three years of her husband's death, and as part of her estate is an IIP, that interest is chargeable potentially at 40% after the deduction of her nil rate band. Note that an IPDI does not necessarily have to be in favour of a surviving spouse/civil partner and could be an alternative source of providing funds for the next generation or younger individuals.

(B) The settlement of the trust assets in favour of the son would have been treated as an IIP settlement but following *FA 2006, Sch 20 para 4* it will not now be treated as such. See SETTLEMENTS: DISCRETIONARY TRUSTS AND

OTHER TRUSTS OF RELEVANT PROPERTY (43). Therefore, as this IIP in favour of the son is created out of an existing IIP on or after 6 October 2008 it cannot be either a transitional serial interest (TSI see below) or an IPDI. An immediate charge of 40% has been levied as above and there will be further charges incurred under the relevant property taxing rules for discretionary trusts to the extent that the assets are held on continuing trusts. See SETTLEMENTS: DISCRETIONARY TRUSTS AND OTHER TRUSTS OF RELEVANT PROPERTY (43) for a continuation of this example.

Example 2

Frank wishes to leave his estate on trust for his son Robert for life, then to Robert's wife Sylvia if she survives him for life, and then to his grandchildren absolutely. Before the changes made by *FA 2006 Sch 20*, the IHT position would be a chargeable transfer on the death of Frank, an exempt transfer on the death of Robert if Sylvia survives, and a further chargeable transfer on the death of Sylvia. However, the position is now that there is no spouse exemption on the death of Robert, assuming Sylvia survives him because Sylvia's interest is not an IPDI; it does not arise on the death of the testator whose will created the settlement (Frank).

To resolve this problem Frank's will could give Robert a power to appoint the settled funds by his own will on trust to Sylvia for life, following which the trusts for the grandchildren will take effect. If Robert exercises this power, the trusts for Sylvia will then be effected by Robert's will, not Frank's, and the trusts for Sylvia will arise on the death of Robert, thus satisfying the requirements for an IPDI. The spouse exemption will then be available on the death of Robert.

Transitional serial interest (TSI)

1. On or after 22 March 2006 and before 6 October 2008 (Category 1)

[42.3] Where a person (stipulated as being 'B' in the legislation) is beneficially entitled on or after 22 March 2006 but before 6 October 2008 to an interest in possession in settled property then for the purposes of *IHTA 1984, Pt III, Ch II* that interest is a transitional serial interest only if a number of conditions are satisfied:

- the settlement must have commenced before 22 March 2006 and the property comprised in the settlement was property to which 'B' (the beneficiary of the current interest), or some other person, was beneficially entitled an interest in possession which for these purposes is designated 'the prior interest';
- the prior interest came to an end on or after 22 March 2006 but before 6 October 2008;
- 'B' becomes beneficially entitled to the current interest on or after 22 March 2006 and before 6 October 2008;
- neither *IHTA 1984, s 71A* (bereaved minor's trust) applies to the property in which the interest subsists nor is the interest a disabled person's interest.

2. On death of spouse or civil partner on or after 6 October 2008 (Category 2)

[42.4] Alternatively, a TSI arises where a person (stipulated as being 'E' in the legislation) is beneficially entitled to an interest in possession in settled property then for the purposes of *IHTA 1984, Pt III, Ch II* that interest is a transitional serial interest only if a number of conditions are satisfied:

- the settlement must have commenced before 22 March 2006 and the property comprised in the settlement was property to which a person other than 'E' was beneficially entitled an interest in possession which for these purposes is designated 'the previous interest';
- the previous interest came to an end on or after 6 October 2008 on the death of the other person who for these purposes is designated as 'F';
- immediately before 'F' died, F was the spouse or civil partner of 'E';
- E became beneficially entitled to the successor interest on F's death;
- neither *IHTA 1984, s 71A* (bereaved minor's trust) nor a disabled person's interest applies to the property in which the successor interest subsists.

[*IHTA 1984, ss 49B–D, 51(1A), 52(2A), 54A(1A); FA 2006, Sch 20 paras 5, 12, 13, 16; FA 2008, s 141; FA 2010, s 53(4)*].

In circumstances where there is a settled life insurance contract under *IHTA 1984, s 49E* that is to be treated as a TSI see **31.1** LIFE ASSURANCE POLICIES AND ANNUITIES.

Example 3

A transferred £260,000 on 1 October 2004 into an interest in possession trust of which his brother C is the life tenant. On 31 August 2008, C released his life interest i.e. 'the prior interest' in the first condition above, then valued at £320,000, to an IIP settlement in favour of his child 'B'. A's cumulative chargeable transfers in the last seven years amounted to £230,000. A was still alive on 31 August 2008, at which date C's cumulative chargeable transfers in the last seven years amounted to £130,000 and he (C) had not used his annual exemptions for 2008/09 and 2007/08. See table at **40.1** 2010.A1 RATES OF TAX.

The transfer by A on 1 October 2004 is a potentially exempt transfer which will not become chargeable unless A dies before 1 October 2011.

The transfer by C meets the four conditions at 1. above and B's interest is therefore a TSI. The transfer is therefore a potentially exempt transfer and is not charged at lifetime rates, i.e. one-half of death rates 20%, after taking into account cumulative transfers of £130,000.

If, however, C released his life interest i.e. 'the prior interest' on 5 May 2010 when valued at £350,000 then the second condition above would not be met and the IHT relevant property regime would apply going forward with the following results.

Normal calculation

	£	£
Value transferred by C on 5 May 2010		350,000
Deduct annual exemption 2010/11	3,000	
Annual exemption 2009/10	3,000	6,000

	£344,000
IHT on £344,000 is charged in the band £130,001 to £474,000.	
See table at **40.1** 2010.A1 RATES OF TAX.	£
£130,001–325,000	Nil
£325,001–474,000 at 20%	29,800
IHT payable	£29,800

Notes to the example

(A) C's cumulative chargeable transfers following the gift on 5 May 2010 will incur an immediate 20% IHT charge due to his having made other chargeable transfers prior to that date but within seven years of the gift. In addition, if C dies within seven years of the gift then his estate will be subject to a further 20% charge. A report of the transfer on 5 May 2010 should be made to HMRC Inheritance Tax on Form IHT100 and 100a with C paying the tax due. See ACCOUNTS AND RETURNS (**2**).

(B) The funds of £350,000 in the trust for B will be held under the discretionary trust taxing regime so that a charge on the trust fund assets will occur every 10th anniversary of up to 6%. See SETTLEMENTS: DISCRETIONARY TRUSTS AND OTHER TRUSTS OF RELEVANT PROPERTY (**43**) for a continuation of this example including exit charges. [*IHTA 1984, ss 51, 51A; FA 2006, Sch 20 para 12*].

(C) Had C died on or after 6 October 2008 and chosen to leave his interest in possession to his wife so that she succeeded his interest and the five Category 2 conditions mentioned above are met then a succeeding interest will arise to the wife. This is potentially very useful in the context of a trust that is an IIP for one spouse with a succeeding IIP for the survivor which under normal rules applying under *IHTA 1984, s 49C* would not have applied after 5 April 2008.

Close company entitled to IIP

Where a *close company* is entitled to an interest in possession, this is treated for IHT purposes as being owned by the participators. From 22 March 2006 where a close company is entitled to an interest in possession in settled property, that interest in possession will also include an immediate post-death interest (IPDI) and a transitional serial interest (TSI). See below and **11.11** CLOSE COMPANIES.

Value of property in which interest subsists

Entitlement to all income or property

[42.5] If the interest is in all the income arising from the settled property, the beneficiary is treated as owning the whole property. The position is the same where there is no income but the beneficiary is entitled to the use or enjoyment of the property.

Entitlement to part of the income only

Entitlement to part of the income only (if any) of the property is treated as giving an interest in possession in the same proportion of the property as his income entitlement bears to the whole income. Where a person is entitled to a specified amount of income i.e. an annuity (or the whole income less a specified amount) in any period, his interest in the settled property is such part (or the whole less such part) of the property as produces that amount in that period. Where there is a chargeable transfer of such an interest, the Treasury prescribe higher and lower income yields (to prevent manipulation of the value transferred by altering the income). Where it is the property supporting an annuity which is to be charged, the minimum value is the 'actual' dividend yield compiled for the FT Actuaries Share Indices in place of the previous method which took the 'gross' yield. Where the remainder of the settled property is to be charged, the maximum value of the property supporting the annuity is the annuity grossed up at the gross dividend yield for British Government Stocks ('Irredeemables') at the date the property has to be valued (the balance of the settled property being the value of the property to be charged). The Treasury has power to alter the higher and lower values by statutory instrument and the most recent change was on 28 January 2000. [*IHTA 1984, s 50(1)–(4); SI 1980/1000; SI 2000/174*].

Cessation of annuity

[42.6] Where an annuitant dies or disposes of his interest in possession, and the annuity is charged wholly or in part on real or leasehold property and the Board is satisfied that a capital valuation of the property at the relevant date restricted to its existing use reflects an anticipated increase in rents obtainable for that use after that date, appropriate relief will be given in calculating the 'slice', i.e. proportion of the property on which tax is payable (see F11 at **23** HMRC EXTRA-STATUTORY CONCESSIONS).

Entitlement to shared use of property

[42.7] Where a person entitled to an interest in possession is not entitled to any income of the property but is entitled, jointly or in common with one or more other persons, to its use and enjoyment, his interest is taken to subsist in such part of the property as the proportion which the annual value of his interest bears to the aggregate annual value of his and the other interest(s). See *Woodhall (Woodhall's Personal Representatives) v CIR* [2000] STC SCD 558 regarding the right to occupy a house jointly. [*IHTA 1984, s 50(5)*].

Leases

[42.8] Where a lease is treated as a settlement (see point (e) at **41.6** SETTLEMENTS — GENERAL), the lessee's interest in the property is in the whole of the property less the value of the lessor's interest, see **56.14** VALUATION. [*IHTA 1984, s 50(6)*].

Termination of an interest in possession

[42.9] Inheritance tax is chargeable (but see exceptions below) when a beneficial interest in possession in settled property comes to an end because of (i) the death of the person entitled to the interest or (ii) the actual or deemed termination of that person's interest during his life (including disposal to a third party). That person is treated as if he had made a transfer of value and the value chargeable is the value of the property in which his interest subsisted, as if he were the transferor of that property, so that tax is charged at his personal cumulative rate of tax (but see also **42.11** below). References to property or to an interest in property include references to part of any property or interest. [*IHTA 1984, ss 51(1)(3), 52(1)*]. In *Mrs Patch's Executors v HMRC* [2007] STC SCD 453 Sp C 600 a deed of partition had resulted in a transfer of value under *IHTA 1984, s 52(1)*. See *Miller and Others v CIR* CS 1986, [1987] STC 108 where, on the death of the life tenant, it was held that the trustees' powers regarding disposition of the trust fund were administrative and not dispositive and CTT on the whole fund was chargeable. From 22 March 2006 where the interest disposed of is IPDI or a TSI (see **42.1** above) and is not an interest to which *IHTA 1984, s 71A* (bereaved minor's trust) applies then that person is treated as if he had made a transfer of value and the value chargeable is the value of the property in which his interest subsisted, as if he were the transferor of that property. In such circumstances tax is charged at his personal cumulative rate of tax. References to property or to an interest in property include references to part of any property or interest. [*IHTA 1984, ss 51(1), 52(1) as amended by FA 2006, Sch 20 paras 12, 13*].

Close company entitlement

From 22 March 2006 where a close company is entitled to an interest in possession in settled property, that interest in possession will also include an immediate post-death interest (IPDI) and a transitional serial interest (TSI) as an interest in possession to which a company is beneficially entitled. Where there is a disposal of rights and interests in the close company to 'a later participator' then for these purposes the later participator will be entitled to that interest in possession according to their respective rights and interests in the company. See **11** CLOSE COMPANIES for full details. [*IHTA 1984, s 101 as amended by FA 2006, Sch 20 para 26*].

Subject to the application of the *Ramsay* principle or the associated operations provisions, the Board consider that, where an interest in possession comes to an end during the lifetime of the person entitled to it, the settled property in which the interest subsisted should be valued in isolation without reference to any similar property in the estate of the beneficiary. Previously HMRC thought that the value should be determined as a rateable proportion of the aggregate value of that settled property and other property of a similar kind in the person's estate (letter from Capital and Valuation Division reproduced at 1990 STI 446). The value of settled property continues to be determined by the Board in this latter manner where the interest in possession is terminated through the death of the person entitled to it. The construction of the legislation supports this view. See also (c) below where the settled property is excluded property. See also **42.5** above for the value of property in which the interest subsists.

Annual and marriage gifts exemption set-off

Although termination of an interest in possession during a person's life is generally treated as if he were the transferor, the exemption for small gifts and for normal expenditure out of income (see **21** EXEMPT TRANSFERS) do not apply. The annual exemption and the exemption for gifts in consideration of marriage apply subject to the transferor giving notice in such form as the Board may prescribe (currently Form 222) to the trustees, within six months of the transfer, informing them of the availability and extent of the exemption. For the purposes of gifts in consideration of marriage (see **21.14** EXEMPT TRANSFERS) references to outright gifts and settled gifts include cases where property respectively ceases or remains settled property after the termination of the interest in possession.

SETTLED PROPERTY—ANNUAL AND MARRIAGE GIFTS EXEMPTION

Notice under Inheritance Tax Act 1984, sections 57(2) and/or (3) to. . . . . [Trustees full names]. . . . . the Trustees of the. . . . . [Name and title of settlement]. . . . .

I . . . . [Full name]. . . . . in the knowledge that my beneficial interest in possession in property in the sum of £. . . . . comprised in the above Trust was terminated on . . . . [Date]. . . . . hereby give notice that the amounts of

(a) £. . . . . of the annual exemption*

(b) £. . . . . of the exemption for gifts in consideration of marriage*

was/were then available to me and is/are to be applied against the transfer value deemed to be made by the termination.

Signed. . . . . Dated. . . . .

* Delete as appropriate

Notes to the Claim

(A) The Trustees should retain the completed form in case it is subsequently required for presentation to HMRC Inheritance Tax.

(B) If the person signing the form later becomes aware that any correction is required he/she should inform the Trustees immediately.

(C) Notice has to be given within six months of the release.

It is also possible to incorporate the notice into the deed of release so that the releasor signs the notice at one and the same time. This may be worded as below:

DEED OF RELEASE

The Releasor . . . . [Name]. . . . . gives notice to the Trustees of . . . . [Name]. . . . . Settlement that pursuant to Inheritance Tax Act 1984, sections 57(2) and/or (3)* that the £3,000 annual exemption and/or the [£1,000/£2,500/£5,000*] gift in consideration of marriage exemption for 2010/11 are available to him/her and are to be applied against the transfer of value deemed to be made by this deed. The Releasor undertakes to notify the Trustees if he/she becomes aware that a correction is necessary to the notice contained in this clause.

Signed. . . . . Dated. . . . .

Releasor [Name]

Notes to the Release

(A) The annual exemption for the previous year may also be used by the Releasor if it is available.

(B) *Asterisks denote where deletion of non-applicable exemptions should be made by the Releasor.

If the interest is disposed of for a consideration in money or money's worth, the amount of the value transferred is reduced by that consideration (but excluding from the consideration the value of any reversionary interest in the property or any interest in other property in the same settlement). Where the property consists of an interest in a pre-owned asset which is disposed of by an individual in an arm's length transaction to a person not connected with him then that property will be treated as excluded for the purposes of *FA 2004, Sch 15*. [*IHTA 1984, s 52(2); FA 2004, Sch 15 para 10(1)*]. A reduction also applies where a close company disposes of the interest (**25.E5** HMRC STATEMENTS OF PRACTICE). See **42.10** part (b) below for position of person acquiring the interest.

Tax not chargeable on disposal of IIP

Tax is not chargeable in the following circumstances.

(a) Where, after 16 March 1987, the disposal of a beneficial interest in possession by a beneficiary is a POTENTIALLY EXEMPT TRANSFER (**38**) which is made seven years or more before death (and is consequently an exempt transfer). [*IHTA 1984, s 3A(2)(4); FA 1986, s 101(3), Sch 19 para 1; F(No 2)A 1987, s 96(1)(2), Sch 9 Pt III*].

(b) On a *disposal* of an interest in possession for maintenance of family, see **21.15** EXEMPT TRANSFERS. [*IHTA 1984, s 51(2)*].

(c) Where the settled property is EXCLUDED PROPERTY (**20**). [*IHTA 1984, s 53(1)*]. For consideration of the position where settled property is excluded property in relation to a person who holds similar property in his free estate (e.g. shares in a company) in the light of the Board's statement mentioned above regarding principles of valuation, see Taxation, 9 July 1992, p 371.

(d) Where the person whose interest comes to an end becomes on the same occasion beneficially entitled to the property or, prior to 12 March 2008, to another interest in possession in the property (but if the value of the new interest is less than the old, tax is chargeable on the difference); from 12 March 2008 it is a requirement that the replacement interest qualifies as a disabled person's interest or a transitional serial interest. [*IHTA 1984, ss 52(4)(b), 53(2)*]. This also applies where a close company becomes entitled to an absolute interest, etc. (**25.E5** HMRC STATEMENTS OF PRACTICE).

(e) Where the interest comes to an end and reverts to the settlor in his lifetime, unless the settlor (or his spouse after 11 April 1978) had purchased the reversion for money or money's worth but see **5** ANTI-AVOIDANCE. This relief does not apply where its application depends on a reversionary interest having been transferred into a settlement after 9 March 1981. [*IHTA 1984, ss 53(3)(5)(7), 54(1)(3)*]. (See Notes (i) and (ii) below, **5.5** ANTI-AVOIDANCE and also **52.2** TRANSFERS ON DEATH.)

(f) Where the interest comes to an end and the settlor's spouse or civil partner becomes beneficially entitled to the settled property either absolutely or on qualifying interest in possession trusts, provided the settlor's spouse or civil partner is then domiciled in the UK and neither the settlor nor the spouse or civil partner had acquired a reversionary interest in the property for money or money's worth. This exemption also applies where the property reverts to the settlor's widow or widower or surviving civil partner if the settlor died less than two years before the interest comes to an end. This relief does not apply where its application depends on a reversionary interest having been transferred into a settlement after 9 March 1981. [*IHTA 1984, ss 53(4)(5), 54(2)(3)*]. (See Notes (i) and (ii) below, **5.5** ANTI-AVOIDANCE and also **52.2** TRANSFERS ON DEATH.)

(g) On the coming to an end of an interest held by a surviving spouse (or surviving former spouse) of a person who died before 13 November 1974 where estate duty was paid on that death on the property in which the interest subsists (or would have been paid but for any exemption). [*IHTA 1984, Sch 6 para 2*]. (See also **52.2** TRANSFERS ON DEATH.)

(h) Where the principal beneficiary's interest in a protective trust is determined, see **45** SETTLEMENTS: INTERESTS HELD ON PROTECTIVE TRUSTS.

(i) Where a trustee is remunerated for his services as a trustee by an interest in possession in settlement property (e.g. an annuity) except to the extent that it represents more than reasonable remuneration. [*IHTA 1984, s 90*].

(j) Where a person disclaims an interest in settled property to which he has become entitled. This does not apply if the disclaimer is made for a consideration in money or money's worth. [*IHTA 1984, s 93*].

(k) Where property comprised in a settlement (but not a reversionary interest in settled property, see **43.13**) is a holding in an authorised unit trust or a share in an open-ended investment company unless the settlor was domiciled in the UK at the time the settlement was made. [*IHTA 1984, s 48(3A)(a) as inserted by FA 2003, s 186*].

(l) Where a person's beneficial interest entitlement before 22 March 2006 comes to an end on or after that date but the interest was one to which *IHTA 1984, s 71A* (bereaved minor's trust) applies. See **46.1** SETTLEMENTS: TRUSTS FOR BEREAVED MINORS. [*IHTA 1984, s 53(1A) inserted by FA 2006, Sch 20 para 14*].

(m) Where an immediate post-death interest comes to an end in the lifetime of the beneficiary and on that occasion the settled property becomes held on a bereaved minor's trust, in which case the transfer of value is potentially exempt. [*IHTA 1984, s 3A (1A)*].

Notes

(i) For the purposes of (e) and (f) above, a person is treated as acquiring an interest for a consideration in money or money's worth if he becomes entitled to it as a result of transactions which include a disposition for such consideration (whether to him or another) of that interest or of other property. [*IHTA 1984, s 53(6)(8)*].

(ii) For the purposes of (e) and (f) above as they apply on the termination by death of an interest in possession, where it cannot be known which of two or more persons died first, they are assumed to have died at the same instant. [*IHTA 1984, s 54(4)*]. See also **52.13** TRANSFERS ON DEATH.

(iii) For relief for successive charges on an interest in possession, see **39.1** QUICK SUCCESSION RELIEF.

Example 4

A had an interest in possession in a settlement valued at £265,000 with remainder to his son S. On 1 July 2008, A released his life interest to S in consideration of S's marriage on 2 July 2008. A had made no gifts since 5 April 2008 but had used his annual exemptions prior to that date. His cumulative total of chargeable transfers at 5 April 2008 was £88,000, and these had all been made since 1 July 2002. A died on 30 June 2010.

The release of A's life interest is a potentially exempt transfer which becomes chargeable by reason of A's death within seven years. The charge is at full rates with no tapering relief as the transfer took place within three years before death. See table at **40.1** 2010.A2 RATES OF TAX.

	£	£
Value of property		265,000
Exemptions		
Annual 2008–9	3,000	
In consideration of marriage	5,000	
		8,000
Chargeable transfer		£257,000

	Gross	Tax	Net
	£	£	£
Cumulative total b/f	88,000	—	88,000
Chargeable transfer	265,000	8,000.00	257,000
See table at **40.1** 2010.A2	£353,000	£8,000.00	£345,000
Tax payable by trustees as a consequence of A's death			£8,000

Notes to the example

(A) The annual gifts exemption and the exemption of gifts in consideration of marriage apply if notice is given to the trustees by the donor within six months of the gift — see Deed of Release form earlier. This requirement seems to apply even though the gift is potentially exempt when made.

(B) The tax payable is computed by reference to the transferor's cumulative total of chargeable transfers within the previous seven years, and the chargeable transfer forms part of his cumulative total carried forward.

(C) The release of A's life interest to S in consideration of S's marriage is a PET because S's interest becomes a transitional serial interest (TSI) because a new settlement is created on or after 22 March 2006 but out of an old IIP which commenced before 22 March 2006 and the original interest came to an end prior to 6 October 2008 i.e. 1 July 2008 when S (stipulated as being 'B' in the legislation) became beneficially entitled to the interest in possession on 1 July 2008. S will benefit from the transitional rules as detailed in Example 5 below.

Example 5

A typical case to which both category 1 and category 2 TSIs will apply is where property is settled before 22 March 2006 upon trust for S for life, with remainder to S's spouse (or civil partner) for life. Say S died before 6 October 2008 leaving a widow, her successor life interest will be a category 1 TSI within **42.1** above. But if S died on or after 6 October 2008, that life interest will be a spouse/civil partner category 2 TSI within **42.1** above. It should be noted that had S surrendered his life interest before 6 October 2008 so that his wife's life interest then fell into possession, her life interest would have been a category 1 TSI, whereas if S surrenders his life interest on or after 6 October 2008, his wife's successor life interest would not be a TSI since an interest in possession will only be a category 1 TSI when it falls into possession before 6 October 2008, and will only be a spouse/civil partner category 2 TSI when it falls into possession on the death of the holder of the previous interest.

Notes to the example

(A) It is not a requirement of a category 2 spouse/civil partner TSI at **42.1** above (or indeed a category 1 TSI) that the trust of the successor (or current) interest is declared or appointed before 22 March 2006. Therefore, where property is settled before 22 March 2006 upon trust for S for life remainder to S's children, and on or after 22 March 2006 but during S's lifetime and in exercise of a special power of appointment in the settlement deed, a life interest is appointed to S's widow, S's widow's life interest should be a category 1 or 2 TSI if and when it falls into possession following S's death.

(B) One important consequence of a surviving spouse's or civil partner's interest in possession being a TSI is that the spouse/civil partner exemption from inheritance tax should apply on the death of the first spouse/civil partner to die to the extent of the settled property in which both interests in possession subsist.

Anti-avoidance

[42.10] Anti-avoidance provisions apply as follows.

(a) Where there is a transaction between the trustees of a settlement and a person who is, or is connected with:
  (i) the person beneficially entitled to an interest in the property, or
  (ii) a person beneficially entitled to any other interest in that property or to any interest in any other property comprised in the settlement, or

(iii) a person for whose benefit any of the settled property may be applied,

and, as a result of the transaction, the value of the first-mentioned property is reduced, a corresponding part of the interest is deemed to come to an end (with consequent tax liability). An exception to this provision is where there would be no TRANSFER OF VALUE (51) if the trustees themselves were beneficially entitled to the property (e.g. an arm's length transaction with no gratuitous benefit intended). [*IHTA 1984, s 52(3)*].

(b) Where the person acquires an interest in possession in settled property as a result of a disposition for a consideration in money or money's worth, the actuarial value of the interest acquired and not the value of the underlying assets supporting the interest, must be looked at to determine whether the consideration given equals the market value of the interest. [*IHTA 1984, s 49(2)*]. The difference between the consideration given and the actuarial value of the interest acquired is a transfer of value. In relation to transfers of value made, and other events occurring, before 17 March 1987, no transfer of value resulting from the giving of consideration so mentioned could be a POTENTIALLY EXEMPT TRANSFER (38). [*IHTA 1984, s 49(3); FA 1986, Sch 19 para 14; F(No 2)A 1987, s 96(4)*].

(c) New wide-ranging anti-avoidance provisions of *FA 2010, s 53* ensure that the pre-22 March 2006 IHT regime for settled property subject to an interest in possession now applies to settled property subject to an interest in possession to which a person domiciled in the UK became beneficially entitled (on or after 9 December 2009) which is within *IHTA 1984, s 10* (not conferring gratuitous benefit) is not to be treated as a PET. See 5 ANTI-AVOIDANCE.

Chargeable transfer on termination of interest in possession where funds settled by a potentially exempt transfer

[42.11] Where the circumstances below apply, special anti-avoidance provisions apply to a chargeable transfer of a '*relevant interest*' i.e. a chargeable transfer made on the coming to an end of an interest in possession in settled property during the lifetime of a person beneficially entitled to it or on the death of a person beneficially entitled to an interest in possession in settled property. From 22 March 2006, in this latter case where special anti-avoidance provisions apply to a chargeable transfer of a '*relevant interest*' on the death of a person beneficially entitled to an interest in possession in settled property that interest is either a disabled person's interest or a transitional serial interest. See above and SETTLEMENTS: TRUSTS FOR DISABLED PERSONS (47).

Special anti-avoidance provisions

The circumstances are as follows.

(a) The whole or part of the value transferred by the chargeable transfer is attributable to property in which the relevant interest subsisted and which became settled property in which there subsisted an interest in possession (whether the relevant interest or an earlier one) on the making by the settlor of a potentially exempt transfer after 16 March 1987 and within seven years of the chargeable transfer.

(b) The settlor is alive at the time when the relevant interest comes to an end.

(c) On the coming to an end of the relevant interest, any of the property in which the interest subsisted becomes settled property in which no 'qualifying interest in possession' subsists other than property to which *IHTA 1984, s 71* applies (accumulation and maintenance trusts). From 22 March 2006 references to *IHTA 1984, s 71* (accumulation and maintenance settlements) are omitted. For '*qualifying interests in possession*' see **43.1** SETTLEMENTS: DISCRETIONARY TRUSTS AND OTHER TRUSTS OF RELEVANT PROPERTY.

(d) Within six months of the coming to the end of the relevant interest, any of the property in which that interest subsisted has neither become settled property in which a qualifying interest in possession subsists nor the subject of an accumulation and maintenance trust, but only in this latter case up until 21 March 2006, nor become property to which an individual is beneficially entitled.

The IHT chargeable in such circumstances is the greater of the tax calculated under the *special rate of charge* below and the tax calculated under the normal rules (i.e. as if the person entitled to the interest in possession has made a transfer of the trust property).

Special rate of charge

The special rate of charge is the aggregate of:

(i) IHT at lifetime rates on an *assumed chargeable transfer* equal to the value transferred by the relevant transfer (or where only part of the value is attributable to 'special rate property' that part of the value) and which is made at the time of the relevant transfer by an *assumed transferor* who has made aggregate chargeable transfers in the preceding seven years equal to the aggregate of the values of chargeable transfers made by the settlor in the seven years ending with the date of the settlor's potentially exempt transfer; and

(ii) IHT, if any, that would otherwise have been chargeable on the value transferred by the relevant transfer and which is attributable to the value of the property other than the special rate property.

The tax under (i) above is treated as tax attributable to the value of the settled property in which the relevant interest subsisted.

'*Special rate property*' means the property in which the relevant interest subsisted or, where any part of that property does not fall within (a) above or does not become settled property of the kind mentioned in (c) above, so much of that property as appears to the Board (or, on appeal, the Special Commissioners) to be just and reasonable.

The death of the settlor after the chargeable transfer cannot increase the tax chargeable unless, at the time of the transfer, the tax under the special rule is greater than the tax under the normal rules.

The death of the person beneficially entitled to the relevant interest in possession after the chargeable transfer cannot increase the tax chargeable unless, at the time of the transfer, the tax under the normal rules is greater than the tax under the special rules.

Where two or more previous chargeable transfers within these provisions have been made during the period of seven years ending on the date of the current transfer and the settlor is the same in each case, on calculating the tax on the current transfer, the value relating to the previous transfer or transfers attributable to the value of property which was special rate property in relation to those transfers is deemed to be the value of a chargeable transfer of equivalent value made by the settlor immediately before the potentially exempt transfer. This applies whether or not the transfers relate to the same settlement. [*IHTA 1984, ss 54A, 54B; F(No 2)A 1987, s 96, Sch 7 para 1; FA 2006, Sch 20 para 16; Sch 26 Pt 6*].

Example 6

B transferred £100,000 on 1 October 2005 into an interest in possession trust of which his brother C is the life tenant. On 31 August 2010, C released his life interest, then valued at £182,000, to a discretionary settlement in favour of his children. B's cumulative chargeable transfers in the last seven years amounted to £230,000. B was still alive on 31 August 2010, at which date C's cumulative chargeable transfers in the last seven years amounted to £155,000 and he (C) had not used his annual exemptions for 2010/11 and 2009/10. See table at **40.1 2010.A1** RATES OF TAX.

The transfer by B on 1 October 2005 is a potentially exempt transfer which will not become chargeable unless B dies before 1 October 2012.

The transfer by C is a chargeable lifetime transfer, which is charged at lifetime rates, i.e. one half of death rates, taking into account cumulative transfers of £155,000. If, however, a higher tax liability would be produced by substituting B's cumulative transfers at the time of his PET for those of C at the time of his transfer, this takes precedence over the normal calculation.

Normal calculation

	£	£
Value transferred by C on 31 August 2010		182,000
Deduct annual exemption 2010/11	3,000	
annual exemption 2009/10	3,000	6,000
		£176,000

IHT on £176,000 is charged in the band £155,001 to £331,000.

	£
£155,001–325,000	Nil
£325,001–331,000 at 20%	1,200
	£1,200

Calculation under Section 54A

Value transferred by C on 31 August 2010, after exemptions as above	£163,000

IHT on £176,000 is charged in the band £230,001 to £406,000.

£230,001–325,000	Nil
£325,001–406,000 at 20%	£16,200

IHT payable is therefore £16,200.

Notes to the example

(A) C's cumulative chargeable transfers following the gift in August 2010 will be £331,000 (*not* £406,000).

(B) If B dies after 31 August 2010 and before 1 October 2012, the IHT liability of £16,200 may increase. For example, B's cumulative chargeable transfers at 1 October 2005 may increase due to his having made other PETs prior to that date but within seven years of death. If the IHT liability had been determined under normal rules because this produced a liability greater than that produced by a calculation under *IHTA 1984, s 54A*, such liability could not be affected by the death of B. [*IHTA 1984, s 54B(1)*].

Key points

[42.12] Points to consider are as follows.

- When completing IHT400 and there is a beneficial interest in possession held by the testator then accompanying schedule IHT418 should be completed but care should be taken by the PRs to distinguish that the interest is in fact an IIP at point 1. Also, where exemptions and reliefs are available these should be claimed at point 8 *et seq*.
- Following on from the *FA 2006, Sch 20* changes to the trusts regime, property that has been in a settlement for two years that attracts BPR (or APR) and where subsequent changes are made to the constitution of the settlement vis trustees appointing an IIP, then the two year qualification periods under *IHTA 1984, ss 106, 117* will not require a further two-year qualification period unlike previously in *Burrell & Anor v Burrell & Ors* [2005] STC 569 (Ch D) where a deed of appointment on a beneficiary's nineteenth birthday would not have had the benefit of BPR as it was within the two-year period within *s 106*.
- For the purposes of establishing if there has been a transfer on death, where it cannot be known which of two or more persons died first they are assumed to have died at the same instant (i.e. the rule in the *Law of Property Act 1925, s 184* that the elder is deemed to have died first does not apply for these purposes). [*IHTA 1984, s 4(2)*]. In the case of married couples (and now civil partnerships) this may require a survivorship condition to be imposed in their respective wills but that the survivorship condition should not apply in the will of the elder in the situation where there are simultaneous deaths. The survivor condition inserted into the will of the elder, would be worded along the lines of:

  '. . . if . . . [spouse/civil partner] survives me by 30 days, or he/she is deemed to survive me under *section 184* under the *Law of Property Act 1925*, I give the residue of my estate to him/her absolutely.'

However, where a testator ensures there is an IPDI for the first beneficiary which is then followed by a successive life interest for another beneficiary then the latter successive interest would not be an IPDI because the second beneficiary's life interest does not arise on the testator's death but that of the life tenant. In these cases a survivorship such as that above in the testator's will regarding the first beneficary's survivorship would ensure that the interest for the second beneficiary would qualify as an IPDI under *IHTA 1984, s 92*. See also IHTM16110.

- The commencement date of a settlement is important for a number of reasons e.g. in the case of a discretionary settlement the ten-yearly anniversary charge, but the date will vary depending on a number of factors as follows:
  - (i) the settlement of the *initial capital* notwithstanding later larger additions of capital sets the commencement date so if the settlement is within the relevant property regime the periodic ten-year anniversary charge will be by reference to the date the initial capital was introduced to the settlement;
  - (ii) a settlement created by will commences at the date of death under *IHTA 1984, s 83* but if a small pilot trust was set up before death and the will merely adds capital to that trust then the date of the pilot trust will apply.
  - (iii) where a settlement is created by deed of variation the date of commencement will be the date of death and not the date of the variation which may be up to two years later. However, for income tax and CGT purposes the date will not necessarily be the same as IHT i.e. date of death, because income will have already been paid out for that interim period and a CGT election may not actually be made under *TCGA 1992, s 62*.
  - (iv) Where an interest in possession arising before 22 March 2006, an IPDI or disabled person's interest arising after 21 March 2006 a settlement commences on the date the settlor's or their spouse/civil partner's beneficial interest in possession comes to an end. See **42** SETTLEMENTS WITH INTERESTS IN POSSESSION. However, the date of the ten-yearly anniversary charge is not affected as this is related to the original settlement commencement date under *IHTA 1984, s 61(2)*. See **43** SETTLEMENTS: DISCRETIONARY TRUSTS AND OTHER TRUSTS OF RELEVANT PROPERTY.

43

Settlements: Discretionary Trusts and other Trusts of Relevant Property

Cross-references. See **10** CHARITIES; **27** INTEREST IN POSSESSION for meaning of interest in possession; **33.16** NATIONAL HERITAGE for settlements of such property and **33.23** for maintenance funds for historic buildings; **41** SETTLEMENTS — GENERAL for definitions of settlement and settlor; **44** SETTLEMENTS: ACCUMULATION AND MAINTENANCE TRUSTS; **45** PROTECTIVE TRUSTS; **46** SETTLEMENTS: TRUSTS FOR BEREAVED MINORS; **47** SETTLEMENTS: TRUSTS FOR DISABLED PERSONS and **55** TRUSTS FOR EMPLOYEES.

Simon's Taxes. See **I5.3, I5.4.**

Other Sources. HMRC Customer Guide to Inheritance Tax; Foster, Part E3–4.

Introduction

[43.1] Separate charging rules apply to settlements containing 'relevant property'. Before 22 March 2006, these were primarily discretionary trusts, being those where no beneficiary had interests in possession. From 22 March 2006, the scope of the provisions was widened considerably.

For transfers and events occurring after 17 March 1986, amendments are made to the rules governing the calculation of tax to incorporate the reduction in the cumulation period for the settlor's chargeable transfers before the commencement of the settlement to seven from ten years.

Note that charges under these provisions are not affected in any way by gift with reservation of benefit charges on the settlor where he or she retains an interest in the trust. Therefore a settlor-interested trust may be within the yearly charging regime described in this chapter and the settlor will potentially be liable to IHT in respect of the trust funds in the event of death whilst still having an interest in the settlement, or having had such an interest within seven years prior to death. This is subject to very limited exceptions.

A consultative document entitled 'Inheritance Tax: A fairer way of calculating trust charges' was published on 6 June 2014 and this contained a number of proposals for changes to the IHT relevant property regime, said to have negligible tax impact. It was announced in the Autumn Statement on 3 December 2014 that not all the proposals in the document are to be implemented and draft legislation was published for the following changes. These have been included in the Summer 2015 Finance Bill and are due to take effect from the date of Royal Assent to it:

(a) that non-relevant property in the trust will not be brought into the IHT calculations;

(b) that where there are additions on the same day to two or more settlements which have the same settlor, ten year charges on each settlement will take into account the initial value and the same-day additions in the other settlement or settlements. This will commonly impact on the use of multiple lifetime pilot trusts to which funds are added by will. There are equivalent changes to the calculation of exit charges between anniversaries; and

(c) that the special IHT provision for settlements with initial interest in possession to settlor or spouse (*IHTA 1984, s80*) will be amended to correct a defect in the amendments made in 2006. Changes were made at that time to the section applying to settlements made on or after 22 March 2006, but earlier settlements were unaffected with the result that if the initial interest to one spouse was followed by an interest to the other, the settlement continued to be outside the relevant property regime. This defect was to be corrected with effect from Royal Assent to the *Finance Act 2015* but the relevant legislation did not appear in the Act passed before Parliament was dissolved.

Post 21 March 2006 rules

From 22 March 2006 any new trusts that are set up *inter vivos* will be trusts of relevant property, subject to limited exceptions (see **43.3** below). In broad terms relevant property trusts are subject to an IHT charge of up to 6% on the value of the assets in the trust every tenth anniversary. In addition, there will also be an exit charge of up to 6% on the value of capital distributions to beneficiaries in line with **43.3** and **43.9–43.12** below.

Similarly relevant property trusts which arise on death are subject to this charging regime. These are trusts other than:

- trusts created by will or intestacy under which a beneficiary became entitled to an interest in possession on the death of the testator i.e. IPDI (see **42.1** SETTLEMENTS WITH INTERESTS IN POSSESSION);
- trusts set up for a bereaved minor whose full entitlement vests at the age of 18 years, similar trusts set up for a child upon attaining the age of 25 or earlier and certain existing A & M trusts up until 6 April 2008 (see **44.4** SETTLEMENTS: ACCUMULATION AND MAINTENANCE TRUSTS); or
- trusts set up for disabled persons (see **47** SETTLEMENTS: TRUSTS FOR DISABLED PERSONS)

Charitable trusts and certain other special purpose trusts

There is a charge to IHT (under the ordinary rules, see INTRODUCTION AND BASIC PRINCIPLES (**1**)) when property enters a settlement without an interest in possession with the exception of certain lifetime transfers into accumulation and maintenance trusts prior to 22 March 2006 and trusts for the disabled which are POTENTIALLY EXEMPT TRANSFERS (**38**). There is also a ten-yearly charge on property remaining in the settlement and a proportionate charge to tax, based on the time that has elapsed since the date of settlement or the last full ten-year charge, on property leaving the settlement. For this treatment of existing trusts without interest in possession existing before 22 March 2006 and those created after that date see below.

The legislation refers to a 'principal charge to tax at the ten-year anniversary' and a 'principal charge to tax at other times'. In this chapter, the terms 'ten-year anniversary charge' and 'proportionate charge' have been adopted.

Certain special trusts are singled out for favourable treatment, principally charitable trusts, maintenance funds for historic buildings, employee trusts, protective trusts, trusts for bereaved minors and trusts for the disabled. This is achieved by excluding property held on such trusts from the definition of 'relevant property'. (See **43.3** below.) These trusts are dealt with in other chapters. See the cross-references at the beginning of this Chapter.

Qualifying interest in possession

[43.2] The special charging rules apply to relevant property which is settled property in which there is no qualifying interest in possession. 'Interest in possession' is not defined in the IHT legislation and its interpretation is a matter of general law as applicable in the context of IHT. See **27** INTEREST IN POSSESSION. A '*qualifying interest in possession*', for the purposes of the special charging rules, means an interest in possession to which:

(a) an *individual* is beneficially entitled; or
(b) a *company* is beneficially entitled provided:

(i) that the business of the company consists wholly or mainly in the acquisition of interests in settled property; and
(ii) that the company has acquired the interest for full consideration in money or money's worth from an individual who was beneficially entitled to the interest.

'*Individual*' includes participators of a close company which is entitled to an interest in possession. See **11.11** CLOSE COMPANIES for full details.

Where the acquisition under (b)(ii) was before 14 March 1975, the condition in (b)(i) above is satisfied if the business of the company was as described at the time of the acquisition or the company has permission to carry on contracts of long-term insurance under the *Financial Services and Markets Act 2000, Pt 4*. 'Contracts of long-term' means contracts which fall within *Financial Services and Markets Act 2000 (Regulated Activities) Order 2001, SI 2001/544, Sch 1, Pt II*. Also, if it carries on, through a branch or agency in the United Kingdom, the whole or any part of any long-term business which it is authorised to carry on by an authorisation granted outside the UK for the purposes of the first long-term insurance Directive. [*IHTA 1984, s 59; FA 1995, s 52(4)(5)*].

Key concepts

Relevant property

[43.3] The provisions impose a charge to tax on relevant property i.e. settled property in which there is no qualifying interest in possession, other than:

(a) property held for charitable purposes only, whether for a limited time or otherwise (see **10** CHARITIES);
(b) property held in TRUSTS FOR BEREAVED MINORS (**46**) 'age 18–25 trusts' and up to 6 April 2008 at the latest accumulation and maintenance trusts;
(c) property held on discretionary trusts arising on the forfeiture of a protective life interest before 12 April 1978 (see **45** SETTLEMENTS: INTERESTS HELD ON PROTECTIVE TRUSTS);
(d) property held on TRUSTS FOR DISABLED PERSONS (**47**) including such trusts settled before 10 March 1981 in which there is no interest in possession;
(e) property held in TRUSTS FOR EMPLOYEES (**55**), including employee trusts in which there is an INTEREST IN POSSESSION (**42**) to which the employee became entitled on or after 22 March 2006 which is not an IPDI, a TSI or a disabled person's interest;
(f) property held in approved maintenance funds for historic buildings (see **33.23** NATIONAL HERITAGE);
(g) property held in PENSION SCHEMES (**37**) (but not benefits which, having become payable under a fund or scheme, become comprised in a settlement);
(h) property comprised in a trade or professional compensation fund i.e. any fund, maintained or administered by a representative association of persons carrying on a trade or profession, the only or main objects of

which are compensation for, or relief of, losses or hardship that, through the default (or alleged default) of persons carrying on the trade or profession or their agents or servants, are incurred or likely to be incurred by others;

(i) EXCLUDED PROPERTY (20);

(j) a sum received in respect of and assets representing (but not income or gains arising from them) a payment made in lieu of pool betting duty for football ground improvements or to support games etc. and;

(k) property forming part of a premiums trust fund or ancillary trust fund of a corporate member of Lloyd's;

(l) property held on SETTLEMENTS WITH INTERESTS IN POSSESSION (42) which are settled on or after 22 March 2006 which are an IPDI or a TSI;

(m) property held on SETTLEMENTS WITH INTERESTS IN POSSESSION (42) which are settled on or after 22 March 2006 whereby CLOSE COMPANIES (11) acquired the interest for full consideration in money or money's worth from and individual who was beneficially entitled to it and that acquired entitlement was not an IPDI or a TSI;

(n) property applied to pay a lump sum death benefit within *FA 2004, s 168(1)* (registered pension scheme lump sum death benefits) from the date of death of the scheme member to the date when the payment is made by the pension scheme;

(o) property held in an *ICTA 1988, s 615(3)* scheme or a qualifying non-UK pension scheme where the lump sum benefit is paid out within two years beginning with the earlier of the:
   (a) date of notification to the scheme trustees, or persons having control of the scheme, of the scheme member's death; or
   (b) day on which the trustees, or persons having control of the scheme, could reasonably be expected to know of the scheme member's death.

(p) property held in an oil and gas decommissioning trust. This is effective from 20 March 1993.

(q) Works of art held in trust and situated in the United Kingdom for one or more of the purposes of public display (but not with a view to sale), cleaning and restoration (and for no other purpose) where the settlor of the trust was non domiciled in the UK at the time when the settlement was made. This applies in relation to the charge on ten year anniversaries only. [*IHTA 1984, s 64(2)* inserted by *Enactment of Extra-Statutory Concessions Order 2009, Article 13*].

[*IHTA 1984, s 58(1)(1A)(1B)(1C),(2),(2A); FA 1990, s 126(1)(5); FA 1991, s 121(1)(4); FA 1994, s 248; FA 2006, Sch 20 para 19; FA 2007, Sch 20 paras 20, 24(9); FA 2008, Sch 29 para 18*].

See the appropriate chapters for events giving rise to a charge to tax.

Treatment of income

[43.4] HMRC takes the view that:

(a) *undistributed* and *unaccumulated* income should not be treated as a taxable trust asset; and

(b) for the purposes of determining the rate of charge on *accumulated income*, the income should be treated as becoming a taxable asset of the trust on the date when the accumulation is made.

See SP 8/86 at **25** HMRC STATEMENTS OF PRACTICE.

Where income is left undistributed without any specific decision to accumulate it, HMRC has in the past argued that there has been de facto accumulation after a period of a few years, but there is no such presumption under trust law except where *Trustee Act 1925, s 31* applies. For ten year charges arising on or after 6 April 2014 the position is governed by legislation. Where the income arose more than five years before that date of charge from relevant property in which there was no interest in possession (of any type) it is to be treated as relevant property within the settlement, and as having been such throughout the ten year period. Exceptions from this rule are:

(a) where the settlor was non-UK domiciled when the settlement was made and the income is either held outside the UK or is invested at the date of charge in an authorised unit trust or open-ended investment company; or
(b) where the income is invested at the date of charge in FOTRA securities and the securities qualify for the settled property FOTRA exemption (see **20.5** para (c)).

HMRC have stated that it is not necessary for trustees to keep highly detailed records of movements on income account. Unless a specific part of income has been distributed, HMRC will allow allocation of distributions to income received on a 'first in, first out' basis, so that to arrive at any balance to be treated as relevant property, trustees may take the balance on income account at the ten year anniversary date and deduct from it income that has arisen in the five preceding years (Trusts and Estates Newsletter August 2014).

Note that the above provisions effective from 6 April 2014 have no application to income which has been accumulated by trustees before the anniversary date. In that case the income becomes relevant property from the date of accumulation and there is no deeming it to have been such throughout the whole of the ten year period up to the next anniversary date.

In *Gilchrist v HMRC* [2014] UKUT 0169 (TCC) it was held that the proceeds of scrip dividend shares, treated as income for purposes of trust taxation due to the particular legislation now at ITTOIA 2005, s410(3), is trust capital for the purposes of IHT charges.

[*FA 2014, Sch 25 para 4; IHTA 1984, s 64 (1A), (1B), (1C); IHTA 1984, s 66(2A)*].

Related settlements

[43.5] These are brought into account when considering the rate at which tax is charged. Two settlements are related only if they have the same settlor and they commenced on the same day. If, however, the property in either settlement is held for charitable purposes only without limit of time (defined by date or otherwise) the settlements will not be related. [*IHTA 1984, s 62*]. The concept of related settlements is only relevant to settlements commencing after 26 March 1974.

Commencement of a settlement is the time when property first becomes comprised in the settlement. [*IHTA 1984, s 60*]. See Key Points in **41** SETTLEMENTS — GENERAL.

Property becoming comprised in a settlement in pursuance of a will or intestacy is treated for the purposes of the rules on settlements without interests in possession, *IHTA 1984, Pt III, Ch III*, as having become so comprised on the death of the testator or intestate. [*IHTA 1984, s 83*].

Ten-year anniversary charge

[43.6] A charge to tax arises if, immediately before the ten-year anniversary of a settlement, all or any part of the settled property is relevant property (see **43.3** above). Tax is calculated on the value of the relevant property at that time. See *Henderson & Henderson (Black's Trustees) v CIR*, Sp C November 2000, STC SCD 572 Sp C 263; *Rysaffe Trustee Co (CI) Ltd v CIR* [2001] STC SCD 225 Sp C 290; CA [2003] EWCA Civ 356. [*IHTA 1984, s 64*]. See **43.3** above for the treatment of income. All Trustees must sign Form IHT 101 'Account of a Chargeable Event' relating to the ten-year anniversary charge: note 10 of IHT 111.

Definition — 'Ten-year anniversary'

Ten-year anniversary is the tenth anniversary of the commencement of the settlement (see **43.3** above) and subsequent anniversaries at ten-yearly intervals but where a settlor or his spouse or civil partner, widow or widower or surviving civil partner is beneficially entitled to an interest in possession in property immediately after it becomes comprised in a settlement, and as a result of *IHTA 1984, s 80* (see **43.19** below) the property or part is treated as becoming comprised in a separate settlement at the time when neither of those persons are so entitled, the ten-year anniversaries are the dates that are (or would be apart from that section) the anniversaries of the original settlement. No date falling before 1 April 1983 could be a ten-year anniversary. The date when a settlement is made is in most cases when property first becomes comprised in it under *IHTA 1984, s 60*. This date of commencement is particularly important under the relevant property regime as this determines the when the ten year periodic charge is applied. See Key Points in **41** SETTLEMENTS — GENERAL. [*IHTA 1984, s 61*].

Rate of ten-year anniversary charge

[43.7] The rate at which the charge is levied depends upon whether a settlement commenced before, or on or after, 27 March 1974.

Where a settlement commenced before 27 March 1974, the rate is determined by reference to the settlement's cumulative transfers in the ten years preceding the anniversary.

Where a settlement commenced on or after 27 March 1974, the rate is determined by reference to the settlor's cumulative transfers in the seven years preceding the date on which the settlement commenced, as well as the settlement's cumulative transfers in the ten years preceding the anniversary.

Tax is calculated using lifetime Tables at the following rates:

(a) where the whole of the relevant property has been comprised in the settlement throughout the ten-year period ending immediately before the ten-year anniversary, at 30% of the effective rate (see **43.8** and **43.10** below);

(b) and where the whole or part of the relevant property was not relevant property or was not comprised in the settlement throughout the ten years ending immediately before the ten-year anniversary, at 30% of the effective rate reduced by one-fortieth for each successive 'quarter' in the ten-year period which expired before the property became, or last became, relevant property.

The '*effective rate*' is the rate found by expressing the tax chargeable as a percentage of the amount on which tax is charged on an assumed chargeable transfer by an assumed transferor. See **43.8** below. [*IHTA 1984, s 66(1)(2)*].

'*Quarter*' means a period of three months. [*IHTA 1984, s 63*].

Post-26 March 1974 settlements

[43.8] For ten-year charges arising up to the date of Royal Assent to *F (No 2) A 2015* (beyond which see below) the effective rate for post-26 March 1974 settlements is defined as the rate at which tax would be charged on:

(a) an *assumed chargeable transfer* equal to the aggregate of:
   (i) the value of the relevant property immediately before the ten-year anniversary (see **43.3** above for the treatment of income); and
   (ii) the value immediately after it became comprised in the settlement of any property which was not then relevant property and has not subsequently become relevant property while remaining in the settlement; and
   (iii) the value immediately after a related settlement (see **43.3** above) commenced of any property comprised in it,

(b) made immediately before the ten-year anniversary by an *assumed transferor* who, subject to the adjustment for added property and same-day additions etc. in **43.11** below, has made chargeable transfers in the preceding seven years equal to the aggregate of
   (i) the values of chargeable transfers made by the settlor in the seven years ending with the day on which the settlement commenced (but disregarding transfers made on that day or before 27 March 1974); and
   (ii) the amounts on which any proportionate charges (see **43.12** below) have been imposed in the ten years before the anniversary concerned; and
   (iii) in relation to the first ten-year anniversary of a settlement which commenced after 26 March 1974 and before 9 March 1982, the amounts of any distribution payments made in that period (or in some circumstances later) and within ten years before that anniversary.

[*IHTA 1984, s 66(3)–(6); FA 1986, Sch 19 para 16*].

For ten-year charges arising on or after the date of Royal Assent to *F(No 2)A 2015*, the rules are modified so that in broad terms only relevant property in the settlement or a related settlement is brought into the calculations. This is the culmination of the consultation on simplification of the rules and it should be noted that other proposals which were under consideration have not been continued with. Thus, for example, the settlor's cumulative total of chargeable transfers at commencement of the settlement remains part of the calculations. A further amendment ties in with the rules relating to same-day additions (see **43.11**).

Thus with these changes the effective rate for post-26 March 1974 settlements will be calculated as follows:

(a) an *assumed chargeable transfer* equal to the aggregate of:
  - (i) the value of the relevant property immediately before the ten-year anniversary (see **43.3** above for the treatment of income);
  - (ii) the value immediately after a related settlement (see **43.3** above) commenced of any relevant property then comprised in it; and
  - (iii) the value of any same-day addition to another settlement (see **43.11**) and where that other settlement is not a related settlement, the value of any relevant property in it at commencement.

The details at (b) above relating to the assumed transferor continue to be applicable.

Post-26 March 1974 settlements — Examples

Example 1

[43.9]

X, who is married to L (his second wife), dies on 12 January 2008 having already made gifts on 21 May 2005 of £281,000 utilising his available annual exemptions and nil rate band. By his will he left his assets valued at £500,000 to his second wife L in trust for life and then on her death on discretionary trusts for his son S, now aged 30, and X's grandchildren.

L dies on 8 January 2015 leaving her estate of £400,000 on life interest trusts for her son by her first marriage. The assets in X's will trust, now valued at £600,000, are to be held on relevant property trusts with overriding powers to apply capital and accumulated income to the beneficiary S. In consequence therefore the settlor of the discretionary trusts for S is L, by virtue of *IHTA 1984, s 80* and X's cumulative total of chargeable transfers on death is not relevant. The funds in L's will trust are a related property settlement as regards the funds in the settlement held for S. Notwithstanding this treatment, the first ten-year anniversary charge for X's settlement is on 12 January 2018.

The trustees made a capital advance of £200,000 (gross) to beneficiary S on 8 September 2015 of £180,000.

Assumed chargeable transfer	£
Value of settled property at commencement	600,000
Value of property in related settlements	400,000

Assumed chargeable transfer	£
	1,000,000
IHT at lifetime rates	£135,000
Effective rate	13.50%
Appropriate fraction:	
$^{3}/_{10}$ × 13.50% × 3/40ths = 0.3037%	
IHT charge on appointment: £180,000 × 0.3037%	£546.66

Notes to the example

(A) The first ten-year anniversary arises on the tenth anniversary when the settlement commenced, this being the date on which property first became comprised in the settlement. [*IHTA 1984, s 60*]. When property is left on will trust the date of death is the commencement of the settlement i.e. 12 January 2008. Even though the property is held on IIP settlement for the wife the actual date of the commencement is still taken as 12 January 2008 when calculating any subsequent ten-yearly charges appropriately apportioned for the number of quarters that have elapsed since X's death on 12 January 2008 to the ten-year anniversary on 12 January 2018, but not counting any quarter which expired before the settled property became relevant property, that is 8 January 2015.

(B) Under *IHTA 1984, s 80* the settlor of the discretionary trusts for X is L and thus the settlement made by her will is a related settlement. The funds in that settlement are therefore taken into account in calculating the charge on the appointment in favour of S on 8 September 2015. However under *F(No 2)A 2015* this will cease to be the case for appointments made after the date of Royal Assent to that Act.

(C) The exit charge before the first ten-year anniversary takes the effective rate payable on the value of the settled property when the settlement was made, treated for this purpose as being the death of L, plus the value of funds in a related settlement. From Royal Assent to *F(No 2)A 2015* only relevant property in a related settlement will be taken into account, and in this case there is no relevant property in L's will trust.

Example 2

On 22 May 2000, M, who had already used all available exemptions, settled property worth £56,000 on each of two settlements. One settlement is discretionary and the other is subject to a life interest. By 22 May 2010, the discretionary settlement is valued at £277,000, ignoring assets representing undistributed income.

Assuming no prior proportionate charge to tax or distribution payment, the first ten-year anniversary charge will be

Assumed chargeable transfer	£
Value of relevant property on 22.5.2010	277,000
Value of property in related settlement on 22.5.2000	56,000
	333,000
Assumed cumulative total	—
	£333,000
IHT at lifetime rates	£1,600

Assumed chargeable transfer	£
Effective rate $\frac{1{,}600}{333{,}000} = 0.48048\%$	
Rate of ten-year anniversary charge:	
$^3/_{10} \times 0.48048\% = 0.144144\%$	
Ten-year anniversary charge: 0.144144% × £277,000	£399

Example 3

Assume the same facts as in example 2 above except that the settlement subject to a life interest was made on 21 May 2000.

Assumed chargeable transfer	£
Value of relevant property on 22.5.2010	277,000
Assumed cumulative total	—
Value of chargeable transfers made by settlor in seven years to 22.5.2000	56,000
	£333,000
IHT at lifetime rates	£1,600
Effective rate $\frac{1{,}600}{277{,}000} = 0.57761\%$	
Rate of ten-year anniversary charge: $^3/_{10} \times 0.57761\% = 0.173283\%$	
Ten-year anniversary charge: 0.173283% × £277,000	£480

Example 4

Assume the facts in example 2 above except that the settlement subject to a life interest was made on 23 May 2000.

	£
Assumed chargeable transfer (as (2) above)	277,000
Assumed cumulative total	—
	277,000
IHT at lifetime rates	Nil
Ten-year anniversary charge	Nil

Example 5

On 22 May 2000, M's brother N, who had already used all available exemptions, settled £67,000. One half of the settlement was discretionary and the other half was subject to a life interest. On 22 May 2004, the life tenant dies and all the property of the trust becomes held on discretionary trusts. By 22 May 2010, the settlement is valued as follows.

Original discretionary fund, ignoring net assets representing undistributed income	£97,000
Funds previously subject to a life interest, ignoring net assets representing subsequent undistributed income	£238,000
The first ten-year anniversary charge will be:	
Assumed chargeable transfer	
Value of relevant property on 22.5.2010	335,000
Assumed cumulative total	—
	£335,000
IHT at lifetime rates	£2,000
Effective rate $\frac{2,000}{335,000} = 0.59701\%$	
Rate of ten-year anniversary charge: $\frac{3}{10} \times 0.59701\% = 0.179103\%$	
Ten-year anniversary charge:	
0.179103% × £97,000	174
$\frac{24}{40} \times 0.179103\% \times £238,000$	256
	£430

Pre-27 March 1974 settlements

[43.10] **The effective rate for pre-27 March 1974 settlements** is defined as the rate at which tax would be charged:

(a) on an *assumed chargeable transfer* equal to the value of the relevant property immediately before the ten-year anniversary;

(b) made immediately before that anniversary by an *assumed transferor* who, subject to the adjustments for added property etc. in **43.11** below, has made chargeable transfers in the preceding seven years equal to the aggregate of:

  (i) the amounts on which any proportionate charges (see **43.12** below) have been imposed in the ten years before the anniversary concerned; and

  (ii) in relation to the first ten-year anniversary, the amount of any distribution payment made out of the settled property before 9 March 1982 (or in some circumstances later) and within ten years before that anniversary.

[*IHTA 1984, s 66(3)–(6); FA 1986, Sch 19 para 16*].

See **43.3** above for the treatment of undistributed or unaccumulated income.

Example

On 1 June 1971 T settled property on discretionary trusts. The trustees made the following advances (gross) to beneficiaries:

1.1.74	H	£10,000
1.1.77	B	£20,000

1.1.82	C	£60,000
1.1.88	D	£40,000
1.1.94	E	£80,000

On 1 June 1991 the settled property was valued at £175,000 and on 1 June 2001 £180,000.

1 June 1991 Ten-year anniversary charge

Assumed chargeable transfer	£	£
Value of relevant property		£175,000
Assumed transferor's cumulative total		
(i) Aggregate of distribution payments made between 1 June 1981 and 8 March 1982	60,000	
(ii) Aggregate of amounts on which proportionate charge arises between 9 March 1982 and 1 June 1991	40,000	£100,000
	Gross	Tax
	£	£
Assumed cumulative total	100,000	—
Assumed chargeable transfer	175,000	27,000
	£275,000	£27,000

$$\text{Effective rate of tax} = \frac{27,000}{175,000} \times 100 = 15.429\%$$

Ten-year anniversary charge

The IHT payable is at 30% of the effective rate on the relevant property.

IHT payable = 30% × 15.429% × £175,000 = £8,100

1 June 2001 Ten-year anniversary charge

Assumed chargeable transfer		£180,000
Value of relevant property		
Assumed transferor's cumulative total		£80,000
Aggregate of amount on which proportionate charge arises between 1 June 1991 and 1 June 2001		
	Gross	Tax
	£	£
Assumed cumulative total	80,000	—
Assumed chargeable transfer	180,000	3,600
	£260,000	£3,600

$$\text{Effective rate of tax} = \frac{3,600}{180,000} \times 100 = 2\%$$

Ten-year anniversary charge

The IHT payable is at 30% of the effective rate on the relevant property.

IHT payable = 30% × 2% × £180,000 = £1,080

Adjustments for added property, etc.

[43.11] The previous chargeable transfers of the assumed transferor in **43.8**(b) and **43.10**(b) above are adjusted in the following circumstances.

(a) Where after the settlement commenced and after 8 March 1982, but before the ten-year anniversary concerned, the settlor makes a chargeable transfer which increases the *value* of the property in the settlement, the aggregate of the values of chargeable transfers made by the settlor in the seven years before the chargeable transfer in question is:
   (i) if the settlement commenced after 26 March 1974, substituted for **43.8**(b)(i) above if greater than that figure; and
   (ii) if the settlement commenced before 27 March 1974, added to the aggregate at **43.10**(b) above.

   For the purposes of both (i) and (ii) above, transfers made on the same day as the chargeable transfer in question are disregarded, but not transfers caught by the same-day additions rules (see **43.11**) and any values attributable to property brought into account under **43.8**(a) or **43.10**(a) above, and any amounts on which proportionate charges have been imposed and which are already taken into account in **43.8**(b)(ii) or **43.10**(b)(i) above are excluded. Where the settlor makes two or more such chargeable transfers in the period, the transfer which gives rise to the highest aggregate is used.

   At one time the scope of these provisions was open to doubt given the definition of settlement in *IHTA 1984, s 43(2)*, which includes 'any disposition'; thus arguably, an addition to an existing settlement is 'any disposition' and therefore forms a new and separate settlement. This view is not supported by the *dicta* of Park J in *Rysaffe Trustee Company (CI) Ltd v CIR* [2002] STC 872, and it is understood that HMRC accept that additions to existing settlements do not fall to be treated as new settlements, so that the provisions set out above apply.

   It is immaterial whether the *amount* as well as the *value* of the property in the settlement is increased as a result of the chargeable transfer. Where, however, the *amount* of the property is not increased, these provisions will not apply if the transfer was not primarily intended to increase the value of the settled property and it did not increase that value immediately after the transfer by more than 5% of its value immediately before the transfer.

   [*IHTA 1984, s 67(1)–(5); FA 1986, Sch 19 para 17*].

(b) Where property subject to the ten-year anniversary charge has previously, on ceasing to be relevant property within the preceding ten years, been subject to a proportionate charge (see **43.12** below), the aggregate of items at **43.8**(b) and **43.10**(b) above is reduced by the lesser of the amount subject to the proportionate charge *and* the value of the relevant property at the ten-year anniversary. Where only a part of the settled property was previously subject to the proportionate charge, the reduction is based on so much of the amounts mentioned above as is attributable to the part in question. If there were two or more occasions in the preceding ten years when the property was subject to a proportionate charge, the reduction above applies to each occasion. [*IHTA 1984, s 67(6)(7)*].

(c) *Same-day additions*. Before 6 April 2015 it was possible to reduce IHT charges on relevant property trusts by forming two or more pilot trusts with minimal capital on separate days and then subsequently transferring more substantial funds to each on the same day, or by will. By virtue of the charging structure on the trusts (see **43.8**), the settlements would not be related settlements and the additions would not be taken into account as a prior cumulative total of the settlor.

This planning is now obsolete for IHT charges on or after 6 April 2015, subject to the exceptions detailed below. The planning is blocked by legislation for 'same-day additions' to two or more settlements. Any such additions to other settlements are taken into account as part of the assumed chargeable transfer on the occasion of ten-year charge to IHT on a settlement (see **43.8** para (a)). They are also brought into account in relation to (a) interim charges before the first anniversary by treating the same-day addition as part of the assumed chargeable transfer (see **43.15** para (a)), (b) interim charges between ten-year anniversaries by treating the same-day addition as having been made immediately before that anniversary, and (c) and in relation to the charges on age 18–25 trusts (see **46.4**).

A *same-day addition* applies where there are transfers into two or more settlements on the same day, thereby increasing the value of the settlements and the same person is the settlor of each settlement. Each settlement must contain relevant property in the 'relevant period' which, for each settlement, is the period from its commencement to the time of the same-day addition. The provisions can apply to the initial transfer into the settlement concerned but not if they are related settlements. These provisions do not however apply in the following cases:

(a) where the settlements concerned are related settlements (see **43.5**);
(b) where the funds in the settlement concerned are held for charitable purposes only without any time limit;
(c) where the settlement concerned is a 'protected settlement', broadly defined as those which commenced before 10 December 2014 and to which no additions have been after that date apart from certain additions by will before 6 April 2016 (see further below);
(d) where the additions concerned are the payment of life insurance premiums on a policy or policies with premiums due regularly at one year or less throughout the term; and
(e) where a *de minimis* exception for additions of £5,000 or less applies, as detailed below.

A *protected settlement* is one which commenced before 10 December 2014 and where either condition A or condition B is met. Condition A is that there have been no transfers of value after that date by which the value of the settled property was increased. Condition B applies where property is added by will on a death before 6 April 2017 where the will is in substance the same as it was before 10 December 2014.

The *de minimis* exception referred to at (e) above is for lifetime settlements where additions are not made on death. If the additions to each settlement on the same day are £5,000 or less, then the new provisions do not apply. If there is more than one same-day addition to the settlements, then the value of the property in each settlement before the first such addition must be £5,000 or less than the value of the property in each settlement after the last such addition.

Example

Arthur creates two discretionary trusts with capital of £100 each for his two adult children, one dated 30 December 2013 and the other dated 31 December 2013. He dies on 5 May 2017 and by his will dated 1 January 2014 he leaves £500,000 to each trust.

£100,000 is released from the first trust to the beneficiary on 29 December 2018. The IHT charge on this is calculated as follows:

Assumed chargeable transfer	
Value of settlement at commencement	£100
Value of relevant property added after settlement commenced	£500,000
Value of 'same-day addition' to settlement dated 31 December 2013	£500,000
Initial value of settlement dated 31 December 2013	£100
Total assumed chargeable transfer	£1,000,200
IHT thereon at lifetime rate (20% × (£1,000,200 – £325,000)	£135,040
Effective rate	$\frac{135,040}{1,000,200} \times 100$
	$= 13.501\%$

Appropriate fraction: 3/10ths × 19/40ths = 57/400ths

Charge on funds released: £100,000 × 13.501% × 57/400 = £1,923.89

Note: if Arthur had died on 5 April 2017, the settlements would be protected settlements and no amounts would then be included above in relation to the settlement dated 31 December 2013.

Charge at other times (the proportionate charge)

[43.12] A charge to tax arises:

(a) where property comprised in a settlement, or any part, ceases to be relevant property (see **43.3** above) whether because it ceases to be comprised in the settlement or otherwise; and

(b) where (a) does not apply, where the trustees of the settlement make a disposition which reduces the value of the relevant property. '*Disposition*' includes an omission to exercise a right (unless not deliberate) which is treated as made at the latest time that the right could be exercised.

See **11.5** CLOSE COMPANIES for details of when a charge arises on a close company's transfer of value being apportioned to trustees.

Tax is charged on the amount by which the value of the relevant property is reduced as a result of the chargeable event (i.e. the loss to donor principle) grossed-up where the settlement pays the tax.

[*IHTA 1984, s 65(1)(2)(9)*].

Exceptions from charge

[43.13] No charge arises:

(i) if, under **43.12**(b) above, the trustees do not intend to confer gratuitous benefit and either the transaction is at arm's length between persons not connected with each other (see **12** CONNECTED PERSONS) or is such as might be expected in such a transaction (see **51.2**(a) TRANSFER OF VALUE); or

(ii) if, under **43.12**(b) above, the disposition is a grant of tenancy of agricultural property in the UK, Channel Islands or Isle of Man for use for agricultural purposes made for full consideration in money or money's worth; or

(iii) on the payment of costs or expenses so far as they are fairly attributable to relevant property; or

(iv) where any payment is, or will be, income for income tax purposes of any person (or, in the case of a person not resident in the UK, would be if he were so resident); or

(v) in respect of a liability to make a payment under (iii) or (iv) above; or

(vi) if the chargeable event occurs in the three month period beginning with either the day on which the settlement commenced or a ten-year anniversary (see **43.6** above); or

(vii) if the settlor was domiciled outside the UK at the time the settlement was made, and by virtue of *IHTA 1984, s 48(3)(a)* relevant property comprised in the settlement becomes excluded property by ceasing to be situated in the UK. At one time this relief did not expressly extend to circumstances where settled property becomes excluded property within *IHTA 1984, s 48(3)* — the purchase of units in an authorised unit trust or OEIC. However this omission is rectified by the *FA 2013, s 175* with full retrospective effect to 16 October 2002. See also **43.19** below where the settlor or his spouse or civil partner retains an interest in the settlement and **43.22** below where property moves between settlements; or

(viii) if the settlor was domiciled outside the UK at the time the settlement was made and property comprised in the settlement is invested in exempt Government securities and becomes excluded property by virtue of *IHTA 1984, s 48(4)(b)* because all known beneficiaries are of a description specified in the condition in question. The 'condition in question' is usually that referred to in *FA (No 2) 1931, s 22* and modified by *FA 1940, s 60* relating to questions of domicile and ordinary residence but is now purely to residence abroad. [*IHTA 1984, s 48(4); FA 1996, s 154, Sch 28 para 8*]. See **20.5** EXCLUDED PROPERTY. The special provisions relating to domicile in *IHTA 1984, s 267* (see **16.5** DOMICILE) are disregarded. But see **43.19** below where the settlor or his spouse or civil partner retain an interest in the settlement and **43.22** below where property moves between settlements; or

(ix) if the property becomes held for charitable purposes only without limit of time *or* the property of a qualifying political party *or* national body mentioned in *IHTA 1984, Sch 3; or* the subject of a gift for public benefit (see **21.4**, **21.6–21.8** EXEMPT TRANSFERS);

(x) if a reversionary interest, that is a future entitlement to trust assets currently subject to another interest e.g. a life interest in favour of someone else, where the property comprising in the trust is a holding in an authorised unit trust (AUT) and/or a share in an open-ended investment company (OEIC) where the reversioner to that property is non-UK domiciled. This assists, for instance, non-UK domiciled individuals who have a reversionary interest but die before that interest falls in and will no longer have the threat of an IHT charge in those particular circumstances. [*IHTA 1984, s 48(3A)(b) as inserted by FA 2003, s 186*];

(xi) where shares or securities of a company cease to be relevant property on becoming held on employee ownership trusts within *IHTA 1984, s 86(1)* if the company concerned meets the trading requirement of *TCGA 1992, s 236I*, the trusts are of a settlement which meets the all-employee benefit requirement of *TCGA 1992, s 236J*, and the settlement does not meet the controlling interest requirement of *TCGA 1992, s236M* immediately before the beginning of the tax year in which the shares or securities cease to be relevant property but does meet it at the end of that year. [*IHTA 1984, s75A* applicable from 6 April 2014].

[*IHTA 1984, ss 65(4)–(8), 76*].

Pre-ten-year anniversary charge

[43.14] **Rate of proportionate charge before** the first ten-year anniversary. On an occasion of charge before the first ten-year anniversary (see **43.6** above) the rate depends upon whether the settlement commenced before, or on or after, 27 March 1974.

Where a settlement commenced before 27 March 1974, the rate is calculated by reference to the settlement's own cumulative transfers in the preceding ten years.

Where a settlement commenced after 26 March 1974, the rate is determined by reference to the settlor's chargeable transfers in the seven years preceding the commencement of the settlement. [*IHTA 1984, ss 65(3), 68*].

Post-26 March 1974 settlements tax calculation

[43.15] The rate of tax for **post-26 March 1974 settlements** is the 'appropriate fraction' of the 'effective rate' at which tax would be charged using lifetime rates,

(a) on an *assumed chargeable transfer* equal to the aggregate of:
   (i) the value of property comprised in the settlement immediately after it commenced (see **43.3** above); and
   (ii) the value of any property comprised in a related settlement (see **43.3** above) immediately after its commencement; and

(iii) the value, immediately after it became comprised in a settlement, of any property which became so comprised after the settlement commenced and before the occasion of charge (whether or not it has remained so comprised);

(b) made at the time the proportionate charge arises by an *assumed transferor* who in the seven years ending with the day of the occasion to charge had aggregate chargeable transfers equal to those made by the settlor in the seven years ending with the day on which the settlement commenced (but, subject to the provisions relating to same-day additions (see **43.11**) excluding any transfers made on that day).

For ten-year charges arising on or after the date of Royal Assent to *F(No 2)A 2015*, the rules are modified so that in broad terms only relevant property in the settlement or a related settlement is brought into the calculations. Amendments are also made to tie in with the provisions relating to same-day additions (see **43.11**). Thus the assumed chargeable transfer will be:

(i) the value of relevant property comprised in the settlement immediately after it commenced (see **43.3** above);

(ii) the value of any relevant property comprised in a related settlement (see **43.3** above) immediately after its commencement;

(iii) the value, immediately after it became comprised in a settlement, of any relevant property which became so comprised after the settlement commenced and before the occasion of charge (whether or not it has remained so comprised);

(iv) the value at the time it became relevant property, of any property which became so comprised on or after the time the settlement commenced and before the occasion of charge and which was not relevant property at the outset. For this purpose it does not matter whether or not it has remained comprised in the settlement; and

(v) the value of any same-day addition to another settlement (see **43.11**) and where that other settlement is not a related settlement, the value of any relevant property in it at commencement.

Definitions

The '*effective rate*' is the rate found by expressing the tax chargeable as a percentage of the amount on which it is charged.

The '*appropriate fraction*' is three-tenths multiplied by so many fortieths as there are complete successive quarters in the period beginning with the day on which the settlement commenced and ending with the day before the occasion of charge. However, where the whole or part of the amount on which tax is charged was not relevant property or was not comprised in the settlement throughout that period, no quarter which expires before the day on which the property became, or last became, relevant property comprised in the settlement is counted except that if that day fell in the same quarter as that in which the period ends, that quarter is counted whether complete or not.

'*Quarter*' is a period of three months. [*IHTA 1984, ss 63, 68*].

See **43.3** above for the treatment of undistributed or unaccumulated income.

Example

On 19 May 1999, R settled £169,000 on discretionary trusts. He had previously made cumulative chargeable transfers of £167,000 in the previous seven years and had already used all available exemptions. On 18 July 2008, the trustees appoint £180,000 to beneficiaries absolutely (with the beneficiaries paying the IHT), and on 31 December 2008 appoint the remaining funds, then valued at £60,000 (ignoring assets representing undistributed income), to beneficiary C absolutely (who again pays the tax). The proportionate charges will be:

(a) 18 July 2008

	£
Assumed chargeable transfer	
Value of property in settlement at 19.5.99	169,000
Assumed cumulative total	
Aggregate chargeable transfers by settlor in seven years to 19.5.99	154,000
	£323,000
IHT at lifetime rates on £323,000	2,200
Deduct IHT at lifetime rates on £154,000	—
IHT on assumed chargeable transfer	£2,200

Effective rate $\frac{2,200}{169,000} = 1.30177\%$

No. of complete successive quarters between 19.5.99 and 17.7.08 = 36

Proportionate charge:

$1.30177\% \times {}^{3}/_{10} \times {}^{36}/_{40} \times £180,000$ — £633

(b) 31 December 2008

Effective rate (as above) = 1.30177%

No. of complete successive quarters between 19.5.99 and 30.12.08 = 38

Proportionate charge:

$1.30177\% \times {}^{3}/_{10} \times {}^{38}/_{40} \times £60,000$ — £223

See **43.17** below for occasion of charge arising following one or more ten-year anniversaries.

[43.16] The rate of tax for pre-27 March 1974 settlements is 30% of the 'effective rate' at which tax would be charged, using lifetime rates:

(a) on an *assumed chargeable transfer* equal to the amount on which the proportionate charge is calculated (see **43.12** above);

(b) which is made at the time of the proportionate charge by an *assumed transferor* who in the seven years ending with the day of the occasion of charge has made aggregate chargeable transfers equal to the aggregate of:
   (i) any amounts on which any proportionate charges have previously been imposed in the period of ten years ending with that day; and
   (ii) any distribution payments made out of the settled property after 26 March 1974 and before 9 March 1982 (or in some circumstances later), and within that ten-year period.

The '*effective rate*' is the rate found by expressing the tax chargeable as a percentage of the amount on which it is charged.

[*IHTA 1984, s 68; FA 1986, Sch 19 para 18*].

See **43.3** above for the treatment of undistributed or unaccumulated income.

Rate of the proportionate charge between ten-year anniversaries

[43.17] Where an occasion of charge arises following one or more ten-year anniversaries, tax is calculated as follows.

(a) The rate of tax is, subject to (b) below, the 'appropriate fraction' of the rate charged at the most recent ten-year anniversary ignoring any reduction made under **43.7**(b) above.

(b) If, at any time before the occasion of charge and on or after the most recent ten-year anniversary:
   (i) property becomes comprised in the settlement; or
   (ii) property which was comprised in the settlement immediately before that anniversary, but was not then relevant property (see **43.3** above) has become relevant property,

   then, whether or not the property has remained comprised in the settlement or has remained relevant property, the rate of tax is the appropriate fraction of the rate at which tax would have been charged at the most recent ten-year anniversary (see **43.7–43.11** above) if the property under (i) or (ii) above had then been relevant property comprised in the settlement. For these purposes, any property under (i) above which was relevant property immediately after it became comprised in the settlement or was not then, and has not subsequently become, relevant property while remaining comprised in the settlement, is included at its value immediately after becoming comprised in the settlement. All other property is included at its value when it became, or last became, relevant property.

For charges arising on or after the date of Royal Assent to *F(No 2)A 2015*, the rules are modified so that in broad terms only relevant property in the settlement or a related settlement is brought into the calculations. Amendments are also made to tie in with the provisions relating to same-day additions (see **43.11**).

The tax will be calculated as follows.

(a) The rate of tax is, subject to (b) below, the 'appropriate fraction' of the rate charged at the most recent ten-year anniversary ignoring any reduction made under **43.7**(b) above.

(b) If, at any time before the occasion of charge and on or after the most recent ten-year anniversary:
   (i) relevant property becomes comprised in the settlement; or
   (ii) property has become comprised in the settlement which was not relevant property at the outset but has since become relevant property, but was not then relevant property (see **43.3** above) has become relevant property; or

(iii) property was comprised in the settlement on the last anniversary date which was not relevant property at that time but has since become relevant property

then, whether or not the property has remained comprised in the settlement or has remained relevant property, the rate of tax is the appropriate fraction of the rate at which tax would have been charged at the most recent ten-year anniversary (see **43.7–43.11** above) if the property under (i), (ii) or (iii) above had then been relevant property comprised in the settlement. For these purposes, any property under (i) is included at its value immediately after becoming comprised in the settlement. All other property is included at its value when it became, or last became, relevant property. To tie in with the rules relating to same-day additions, any such addition made on or after the most recent ten-year anniversary is to be treated as made immediately before that anniversary.

The '*appropriate fraction*' is so many fortieths as there are complete successive quarters in the period beginning with the most recent ten-year anniversary and ending with the day before the occasion to charge. Where the whole or part of the property on which tax is charged was not relevant property, or was not comprised in the settlement, throughout that period, no quarter which expired before the day on which the property became or last became relevant property comprised in the settlement is counted except that if that day fell in the same quarter as that in which the period ends, that quarter is counted whether or not complete.

[*IHTA 1984, ss 68(3), 69*].

Where the most recent ten-year anniversary fell before 18 March 1986 the rate at which tax was charged must be recalculated for the purposes of the proportionate charge as if the amendments made by *FA 1986, Sch 19* had then been in force i.e. as if the provision outlined in **43.7** to **43.11** above applied at that time. [*FA 1986, Sch 19 para 43*].

See **43.3** above for the treatment of undistributed or unaccumulated income.

Reduction of rates

[43.18] For the purposes of (a) and (b) above, where there have been one or more substitutions of new Tables of rates between the most recent ten-year anniversary and the occasion of charge, the latest Table of rates is to be used in calculating the rate at which tax would have been charged at that most recent ten-year anniversary (and not the Table in force at the ten-year anniversary). [*IHTA 1984, Sch 2 para 3; FA 1986, Sch 19 para 37*].

Initial interest of settlor or spouse or civil partner

General

[43.19] Where a settlor, or his spouse or civil partner (including widow or widower or surviving civil partner), is beneficially entitled to an interest in possession in property immediately after it becomes comprised in a settlement (the 'first' settlement), then, if that event occurs after 27 March 1974, the property is treated as not having become comprised in the settlement on that occasion for the purposes of the rules on settlements without interests in possession in *IHTA 1984, Pt III, Ch III*. Instead, when the property or any part of it becomes held on trusts under which neither the settlor nor spouse (or civil partner) is beneficially entitled to an interest in possession, such property is treated as becoming comprised at that time in a separate settlement (the 'second' settlement) made by whichever of them last ceased to be so entitled. But the dates of the ten-year anniversaries of the deemed second settlement are those of the actual first settlement (see **43.6** above).

For a settlement made on or after 22 March 2006 this rule applies only where the interests in possession referred to are either IPDI or a disabled person's interest. If the initial interest in possession arose prior to that date and the spouse's interest arises after that date other than on the death of the first (so that it is not a transitional serial interest), the position is not adequately covered by the legislation. The second interest will be within the relevant property regime but no settlement is treated as subsisting for IHT until the death of that beneficiary and so no charge to IHT arises during the life of the second beneficiary or on his or her death. This anomaly has now been recognised by HMRC and with effect from Royal Assent to *F(No 2)A 2015* inheritance tax charges will apply. When a qualifying interest in possession (being one arising before 22 March 2006) in the settled property comes to an end in lifetime, and is followed by a non-qualifying interest to the spouse or civil partner, the settled property will become relevant property at that time. Where there is a subsisting interest in possession in place at the time of Royal Assent to *F(No 2)A 2015*, the settled property will not become relevant property until that subsisting interest terminates. A *subsisting interest in possession* is an interest in possession of the settlor, or spouse or civil partner of the settlor, where either of such interests has been in place throughout the period from the commencement of the settlement up to the date of Royal Assent.

Excluded property

[43.20] Property will only qualify as excluded property in the above circumstances for the purposes of the rules on settlements without interests in possession in *IHTA 1984, Pt III, Ch III* (but see application below) if it is situated outside the UK and the settlors of both the 'first' and 'second' settlements were domiciled outside the UK when their respective transfers were made. [*IHTA 1984, ss 48(3), 82(1)(3)*].

Where the property in the 'second' settlement is relevant property which becomes excluded property on being invested in Government securities within *IHTA 1984, s 48(4)(b)* (see **20.5**(c) EXCLUDED PROPERTY and **43.13**(viii) above) it will only be exempt from the proportionate charge on that occasion if both the settlor of the first settlement and the deemed settlor of the second settlement were domiciled outside the UK at their respective dates of settlement. For this purpose, where property became comprised in the settlement before 10 December 1974, the special provisions relating to domicile in *IHTA 1984, s 267* (see **16.5** DOMICILE) are disregarded. [*IHTA 1984, ss 65(8), 82(2)(3), 267(3)*].

Application

[43.21] The above applies to provisions on settlements without interests in possession in *IHTA 1984, Pt III, Ch III* except that the provisions on excluded property above do not apply to the rules relating to NATIONAL HERITAGE (33) property in *IHTA 1984, ss 78, 79, Ch III* includes both the general rules for settlements without interests in possession and also the provisions for various special trusts. See CHARITIES (10), NATIONAL HERITAGE (33) for settlements for heritage property and maintenance funds for historic buildings, SETTLEMENTS: ACCUMULATION AND MAINTENANCE TRUSTS (44), PROTECTIVE TRUSTS (45), TRUSTS FOR DISABLED PERSONS (47) and TRUSTS FOR EMPLOYEES (55).

Property moving between settlements

General

[43.22] For the purposes of the rules on settlements without interests in possession in *IHTA 1984, Pt III Ch III* where **after 9 December 1981** property ceases to be comprised in one settlement (the 'first settlement') and becomes comprised in another (the 'second settlement'), then, unless in the meantime any person becomes beneficially entitled to the property (and not merely to an interest in possession in it), it is treated as remaining comprised in the first settlement. For events *after 14 March 1983*, this does not apply where a reversionary interest in the property expectant on the termination of a qualifying interest in possession under the first settlement was settled in the second settlement before 10 December 1981. Where **after 26 March 1974 and before 10 December 1981** property ceased to be comprised in one settlement (the 'first settlement') and became comprised in another (the 'second settlement') by the same disposition, it is treated as remaining in the first settlement. [*IHTA 1984, s 81*].

Excluded property

[43.23] Where property in the second settlement is treated as remaining in the first settlement, it will only qualify as excluded property for the purposes of the rules on settlements without interests in possession in *IHTA 1984, Pt III Ch III* (but see application below) if it is situated outside the UK and the settlors of both the first and second settlements were domiciled outside the UK when their respective settlements were made but also see **43.13**(x) above. [*IHTA 1984, ss 48(3), 82(1)(3)*]. See also IR Tax Bulletin, February 1997, pages 398 and 399.

Where the property in the second settlement is relevant property which becomes excluded property on being invested in Government securities or and AUT or OEIC within *IHTA 1984, s 48(3A), (4)(b)* (see **20.5**(c) EXCLUDED PROPERTY and **43.13**(viii) above) it will only be exempt from the proportionate charge on that occasion if both settlors were domiciled outside the UK at the respective dates of settlement. For this purpose, where the property became comprised in the settlement before 10 December 1974, the special provisions relating to domicile in *IHTA 1984, s 267* (see **16.5** DOMICILE) are disregarded. [*IHTA 1984, ss 65(8), 82(2)(3), 267(3)*].

Application

[43.24] The above applies to the provisions on settlements without interests in possession in *IHTA 1984, Pt III Ch III* except that the provisions on excluded property above do not apply to the rules relating to NATIONAL HERITAGE (33) property in *IHTA 1984, ss 78, 79. Chapter III* includes both the general rules for settlements without interests in possession and also the provisions for various special trusts. See CHARITIES (10), NATIONAL HERITAGE (33) for settlements of heritage property and maintenance funds for historic buildings, SETTLEMENTS: ACCUMULATION AND MAINTENANCE TRUSTS (44), SETTLEMENTS: INTERESTS HELD ON PROTECTIVE TRUSTS (45), SETTLEMENTS: TRUSTS FOR DISABLED PERSONS (47) and TRUSTS FOR EMPLOYEES (55).

Offshore trusts

Non-resident trusts are within the charging provisions on relevant property. If the settlor was not domiciled or deemed domiciled in the UK when the settlement was made, foreign assets in the trust will be excluded property and therefore outside the scope of charge. HMRC take the view that this does not apply to additions to the settled property made at the time when the settlor has become domiciled or deemed domiciled in the UK (IHTM16162); additions made in these circumstances will remain relevant property.

Although there is no charge on the value of excluded property, it has to be taken into account in the calculation of ten yearly charges under *IHTA 1984, s 66(4)(b)*, as being property which was not relevant property when it became comprised in the settlement and has not subsequently become relevant property.

Credit for tax paid under the FA 1975 provisions

[43.25] Any tax charged on a foreign settlement under *FA 1975, Sch 5 para 12(2)* (annual charge of 3% under the periodic charge provisions was allowable as a credit against subsequent capital distributions made (but not later annual charges). Any excess could be carried forward against capital transfer tax chargeable on the settlement under the 1982 provisions. Any further excess is allowed as a credit against the tax chargeable under *IHTA 1984, Pt III, Ch III* (other than tax on NATIONAL HERITAGE (33) property under *IHTA 1984, s 79*) in respect of the settled property or part. [*IHTA 1984, s 85*].

Discretionary settlement excluding settlor and spouse or civil partner

[43.26] THIS DISCRETIONARY SETTLEMENT made on 2010

PARTIES

1. *Insert names* ("The Settlor")

2. *Insert names* ("The Original Trustees")

RECITALS
(Usual recitals)

NOW THIS DEED IRREVOCABLY WITNESSES:

1. DEFINITIONS

The following terms (where the context permits) shall have the following meanings:—

1.1 "the Beneficiaries" means

1.1.1 [the [grand]children and remoter issue of the Settlor]

1.1.2 the spouse's or civil partner's widows and widowers or surviving civil partners of persons within 1.2.1

1.2 "Excluded Person" means

1.2.1 the Settlor

1.2.2 any spouse or civil partner of the Settlor

1.3 "the Trust Fund" means

1.3.1 the sum specified in the First Schedule

1.3.2 any further money or property accepted by the Trustees as additions to the Trust Fund

1.3.3 all accumulated income

1.3.4 the assets from time to time representing such sum additions and accumulations

1.4 "the Trust Period" means the period beginning on the date of this Settlement and ending

1.4.1 125 years from that date (which period shall be the applicable perpetuity period) or

1.4.2 on such earlier date as the Trustees shall by deed prospectively specify

1.5 "the Trustees" means the Original Trustees or the other trustees or trustee for the time being of this Settlement

2. INCOME

THE Trustees shall

2.1 Have the power during the Trust Period to accumulate all or any part of the income of the Trust Fund as an accretion to it and to apply the whole or any part or parts of the accumulated income as if it were income arising in the then current year

2.2 otherwise during the Trust Period pay or apply the income of the Trust Fund to or for the benefit of such of the Beneficiaries who are living in such shares as the Trustees in their absolute discretion think fit

3. POWER OF APPOINTMENT

3.1 NOTWITHSTANDING the above trusts the Trustees shall hold the capital and income of the Trust Fund upon such trusts in favour or for the benefit of all or any one or more of the Beneficiaries exclusive of the other or others of them in such shares and with and subject to such powers and provisions for their respective maintenance education or other benefit or for the accumulation of income (including administrative powers and provisions and discretionary trusts and powers to be executed and exercised by any persons or person whether or not being or including the Trustees of any of them) as the Trustees in their absolute discretion think fit

3.2 The exercise of this power of appointment may be delegated to any extent and in such manner generally as the Trustees (subject to the application (if any) of the rule against perpetuities) by any deed or deeds revocable during the Trust Period or irrevocable and executed during the Trust Period shall with the written consent of the Settlor during his life but otherwise in their absolute discretion appoint

3.3 No exercise of this power shall invalidate any prior payment or application of all or any part or parts of the capital or income of the Trust Fund made under any other power or powers conferred by this Settlement or by law

4. ULTIMATE TRUSTS

SUBJECT to and in default of the above trusts powers and provisions the Trustees shall hold the capital and income of the Trust Fund upon trust for such charitable purposes as the Trustees in their absolute discretion select

Notes to the Precedent

(A) The provisions of *ss 31, 32,* powers, proper law, etc. plus full administrative provisions required to be added.

(B) The settlor and spouse or civil partner are excluded from this discretionary settlement extract.

Key points

[43.27] Points to consider are as follows.

- All trusts in existence now and set up in the future, with the exception of those listed below, will come within the relevant property regime. This has not changed its charging structure under the 2006 changes. The only lifetime settlement created by a settlor that is a PET will be a transfer into a disabled trust, which may be more common than one expects as the definition of disabled beneficiary includes a person in receipt of attendance allowance. With that exception, a transfer into a lifetime trust will be an immediately chargeable transfer at 20% subject to any available nil rate band of the settlor which will be deducted. Once a relevant property regime settlement is set up then the terms of the settlement can be altered as many times as the trustees think fit without any additional IHT consequences other than the ten-year anniversary charge and exit charges. An IHT charge arises when the outright capital distribution is made and on ten year anniversaries:
  (i) a qualifying IIP already in existence at 22 March 2006;
  (ii) an immediate post-death interest (IPDI);
  (iii) a transitional serial interest (TSI); or
  (iv) a disabled trust and certain other tax-favoured trusts (eg. Charitable trusts).

  There are likely to be less IIP trusts as time progresses as more and more interests fall within the relevant property regime. Once the trust falls into that regime the trustees have the option, where this is within the trust deed, to revoke interests in favour of other beneficiaries and incur no IHT charge. See further below.
- Protective trusts are sometimes set up in order to provide protection where a financially unastute beneficiary is 'vulnerable' and may become bankrupt through their actions. In such a case this principal beneficiary's interest ceases and their becomes a discretionary trust for that beneficiary and possibly other members of the family. [*Trustee Act 1925, s 33*]. A protective trust created by a person on death will be an IPDI or a disabled trust and will not be subject to the relevant property regime. However, such a trust created in lifetime of the settlor it would come within the relevant property regime with the consequence of ten-yearly and exit charges. See also 45 SETTLEMENTS: INTERESTS HELD ON PROTECTIVE TRUSTS.
- Care should be taken as to who is treated as the settlor of a trust where there has been a deed of variation (DoV). For example where H dies and leaves everything absolutely to W, W may decide to make a DoV putting assets into a discretionary trust, of which she is a beneficiary. She is treated as the settlor for income tax and capital gains tax purposes and the trust will be a '*settlor interested settlement*' for IT and CGT purposes. However, for

IHT purposes, H is treated as the settlor (at the date of death) and all IHT charges will be calculated on this basis. Consider also the effect of the related property rules where other Will Trusts are created by H.

- Where a trust has more than one settlor, this is treated as two (or more) separate trusts for IHT purposes, which can make relevant property calculations quite complex. By the same token it can offer a worthwhile reduction in IHT charges. In practice, the two funds of the settlement should be kept separate wherever possible, in order to ease the administrative burden. It may, in some cases, not be possible to determine which assets were initially provided by which settlor, particularly in cases where there have been a large number of transactions, such as where the trust fund consists only of a managed investment portfolio. In such cases, a practical approach would be to pro rata the current value of the trust fund (at the date of the IHT charge) in relation to the initial amounts settled by each settlor.
- Relevant property trusts can now be used quite advantageously in certain circumstances, for example, where the main (or only) trust asset is shares in a family trading company. The income from such a trust is likely to be dividend based and this impacts adversely on the overall income tax position since tax credits on the dividends are not allowed into the trustees' tax pool. It is now advisable to convert these type of trusts into relevant property IIPs — meaning that the treatment of the underlying capital remains within the IHT relevant property regime, yet one (or more) individuals have an interest in possession in the trust fund. For IT purposes, this alleviates the tax pool problem and allows the full dividend (less any trustees expenses) to be distributed to the beneficiaries.
- Relevant property trusts can be set up by will to contain any business or agricultural property qualifying for 100% relief. There will then be no IHT liability on the death and the trust assets will remain outside the estates of any of the beneficiaries. Where the spouse survives, consider whether to arrange that he or she purchases the trust assets so that they will qualify for relief a second time on his or her death. The purchase could be made by swap of other assets inherited on the death, where these did not benefit from any IHT reliefs, or by IOU given to the trustees by the spouse.
- Where an estate on death will in any event bear full IHT liability, for example where the spouse does not survive and no other reliefs are in point, consider whether it would be more appropriate for the assets to be left on discretionary trusts rather than to be given to legatees absolutely. This will prevent their falling into the estate of any legatee and the prospective charges under the relevant property regime may lower than a full 40% charge on the death of a legatee.
- Trusts set up by non-domiciled settlors should take steps to ensure that only excluded property is held on ten year anniversary dates. Moveable property such as works of art may be taken out of the

country before the anniversary date. Immoveable UK assets could be sheltered by new borrowings secured on them with the borrowed money being distributed out of the trust. However the GAAR guidance examples indicate that if the distribution is subsequently resettled into the trust by the settlor, this will be regarded as an abusive arrangement subject to counteraction under the GAAR provisions. Following Royal Assent to *FA 2013*, it is no longer possible to reduce IHT liability by depositing the borrowed funds overseas as the liability will not be deductible from the UK asset.

- The rule set out at **43.22** above as regards property moving between settlements means that any appointment of funds across to a new settlement does not alter the anniversary date in relation to the appointed funds. Nor is there an exit charge in relation to the appointment, unless the funds become subject to a disabled person's trust with interest in possession. If there is no exit charge there will be no capital gains tax hold over relief under *TCGA 1992, s 260*.

44

Settlements: Accumulation and Maintenance Trusts

Cross-references. 43 SETTLEMENTS: DISCRETIONARY TRUSTS AND OTHER TRUSTS OF RELEVANT PROPERTY; 46 SETTLEMENTS: TRUSTS FOR BEREAVED MINORS.

Other Sources. Tolley's Tax Planning 2010–11; Foster, Parts E5 and M8.04; IHTM16000.

Simon's Taxes. See **I5.5**, **I5.601–I5.613**.

Introduction

The accumulation and maintenance trust regime

[44.1] A tax-favoured regime for accumulation and maintenance trusts dates back to the introduction of Capital Transfer Tax by *FA 1975*, when *Sch 5, para 15* of that Act, headed 'Accumulation and maintenance settlements', introduced certain exclusions from the capital transfer tax charges for such trusts. Being a form of children's trust, they became immensely popular, particularly after the introduction of inheritance tax and the potentially exempt transfer provisions, although in many cases the funds settled were relatively modest so that an ordinary family discretionary trust might have suited almost as well. Following the 2006 changes to the settled property provisions for IHT, the regime has been brought to an end and although in theory trusts of this type can still be formed, there is no further point in doing so, since a widely drafted discretionary trust will have identical tax treatment and will give more flexibility than the erstwhile accumulation and maintenance trust.

Transfers into accumulation and maintenance trusts

[44.2] After 17 March 1986 but before 22 March 2006, a gift by an individual into an accumulation and maintenance trust, by virtue of which property becomes comprised in the trust, was a potentially exempt transfer. After 21 March 2006, a gift by an individual into an accumulation and maintenance trust, is no longer treated as a PET. See **38** POTENTIALLY EXEMPT TRANSFERS for further details. Accumulation and maintenance settlements that were reviewed before 6 April 2008 to ensure that the beneficiaries become absolutely entitled on or before the age of 18 remained settlements to which *IHTA 1984, s 71* applied otherwise they now come within the charging provisions of 'age 18–25 trusts' (see **46.3** SETTLEMENTS: TRUSTS FOR BEREAVED MINORS) or within the relevant property taxing regime. [*IHTA 1984, ss 58, 71, 71E–F*].

In addition, with respect to transfers of value made, and other events occurring, after 16 March 1987 but before 22 March 2006, a potentially exempt transfer also occurs where an individual disposed of or terminated his beneficial interest in possession in settled property by gift and on that event the property became settled on accumulation and maintenance trusts. Provided the transferor survives seven years or more from the date of the gift, the gift is exempt for inheritance tax purposes. Where an individual has a beneficial interest in possession in settled property which was in existence at 22 March 2006 and it terminates before 6 April 2008 and on that event the property is settled on accumulation and maintenance trusts then the new interest will come within the old taxing regime. See 3.2 below and **27** INTEREST IN POSSESSION.

See **38** POTENTIALLY EXEMPT TRANSFERS for further details. Also see **52.15** TRANSFERS ON DEATH for variation to create a trust. [*IHTA 1984, s 3A; FA 1986, Sch 19 para 1; F(No 2)A 1987, s 96; FA 2006, Sch 20 para 9*].

Case law — Pre-22 March 2006 transfers

In the recent case of *Marquess of Linlithgow v HMRC (and related appeals)* [2010] CSIH 19 in the Court of Sessions (CS) a Scottish landowner made two dispositions of land to an accumulation and maintenance trust. The dispositions were executed on 15 March 2006 i.e. before 22 March 2006. One of the dispositions was recorded in the Register of Sasines on 10 October 2006 and the other on 16 November 2006, so both were after 21 March 2006. HMRC issued a notice determining that the time of the disposition was the date when each disposition was recorded in the Register of Sasines (so that the dispositions were subject to the anti-avoidance provisions of *FA 2006*). The landowner and the trustees appealed, contending that so that the dispositions had taken place when they were *executed*, so that the anti-avoidance provisions of FA 2006 did not apply and the transfers were potentially exempt. The CS unanimously accepted this contention and allowed the appeals, applying the principles laid down in the estate duty case of *Thomas v Lord* CS [1953] SC 151.

Transfers out of accumulation and maintenance trusts

[44.3] Until property settled on accumulation and maintenance trusts vests, there will be no interest in possession so that, in the absence of special provisions, such settlements would be liable to tax under the provisions relating to **43** SETTLEMENTS: DISCRETIONARY TRUSTS AND OTHER TRUSTS OF RELEVANT PROPERTY. Where, however, a settlement qualifies as an accumulation and maintenance trust, its liability to tax is limited to the circumstances mentioned in **44.8**.

Qualification as accumulation and maintenance trust

Settlements created before 22 March 2006

[44.4] To qualify as an accumulation and maintenance settlement prior to 22 March 2006, the following conditions must have been satisfied.

(a) One or more 'persons' (beneficiaries) will on or before attaining a specified age, not exceeding 25, become beneficially entitled to, or to an interest in possession in, the settled property (see Example 4 below).
(b) No interest in possession subsists in the settled property and the income from it is to be accumulated so far as not applied for the maintenance, education or benefit of a beneficiary.
(c) Either:
  (i) not more than 25 years have elapsed since the commencement of the settlement or, if it was later, since the time (or latest time) when the conditions stated in (a) and (b) above became satisfied with respect to the property; or
  (ii) all the persons who are or have been beneficiaries are or were either grandchildren of a common grandparent *or* 'children', widows or widowers or surviving civil partners of such grandchildren who were themselves beneficiaries but died before the time when, had they survived, they would have become entitled as mentioned in (a) above.

Accumulation and maintenance settlements created prior to 22 March 2006 continued to be treated under the old regime but only until 6 April 2008. From that date onwards any existing accumulation and maintenance settlement have to conform to the new rules so that the beneficiary or beneficiaries must obtain a right to *capital* on or before the age of eighteen and not as in (a) above at age 25 to continue to attract the taxing benefits of the old regime of *IHTA 1984, s 71*. This may be achieved by the existing terms of the settlement which already allow the beneficiary or beneficiaries to obtain a right to capital at eighteen or the terms of trust powers of appointment providing for such entitlement. See example in **44.8** below. All such existing accumulation and maintenance settlements will have ceased to exist by 22 March 2024. All other existing accumulation and maintenance settlements formed prior to 22 March 2006 will otherwise from 6 April 2008 become subject to the '18–25 trusts' taxing regime or they may in other circumstances become subject to the relevant property trust regime. See Example 1 below, **43** SETTLEMENTS: DISCRETIONARY TRUSTS AND OTHER TRUSTS OF RELEVANT PROPERTY and **46.3** SETTLEMENTS: TRUSTS FOR BEREAVED MINORS. [*IHTA 1984, ss 71, 71D; FA 2006, Sch 20 paras 1, 2, 3; Sch 26 Pt 6*]. The mere existence of a power to appoint, as opposed to actual exercise, does not take a trust outside the common grandparent category. See HMRC Tax Bulletin, Issue 55.

'*Persons*' includes unborn persons; but the conditions in (a) and (b) above are not satisfied unless there is or has been a living beneficiary. A person's '*children*' include his illegitimate children, his adopted children and his stepchildren. [*IHTA 1984, s 71(1)(2)(7)(8)*].

There is no statutory definition of 'interest in possession' and the term has been the subject of judicial interpretation. See **27** INTEREST IN POSSESSION.

Settlements created after 21 March 2006

[44.5] New trusts from 22 March 2006 will not qualify as an accumulation and maintenance settlement under the old *IHTA 1984, s 71* regime but alternative trusts designated 'bereaved minors' (see **46** SETTLEMENTS: TRUSTS FOR BEREAVED MINORS) may attract similar taxing benefits, although these cannot apply to lifetime settlements. In order to qualify as a trust for 'bereaved minors' one of the following conditions must be satisfied:

(a) One or more 'persons' (beneficiaries) will, on or before attaining a specified age, not exceeding 18, become beneficially entitled to the settled property. See (b) below.

(b) Settled property is held on statutory trust for the benefit of a 'bereaved minor' where the trust is established under either the will of a deceased parent or under intestacy under *Administration of Estates Act 1925, ss 46, 47(1)*. But see also (c) below. The bereaved minor must, prior to or upon the attainment of the age of 18 years, be absolutely entitled to the settled property, any income arising therefrom and any income that has arisen but been accumulated in respect of the property held on trust. Whilst the beneficiary is under the age of 18 if any of the settled property is applied it must be applied for the benefit of the bereaved minor. If the trust property is not so applied then whilst the bereaved minor is under the age of 18 years the income arising, if any, must be a full entitlement or the income must not be applied for the benefit of any other person. In connection with the above, 'statutory trust' shall not be treated as failing the requirements of entitlement due to age, property, income or accumulations because of the requirements of the *Trustee Act 1925, s 32* or *Trustee Act (Northern Ireland) 1958, s 33*. See **46** SETTLEMENTS: TRUSTS FOR BEREAVED MINORS.

(c) Settled property is held on statutory trust for the benefit of a 'bereaved minor' as a result of payments from the Criminal Injuries Compensation schemes. Any such payments must be made for the benefit of the minor as a result of:
    (i) the scheme being established by arrangements under the *Criminal Injuries Compensation Act 1995*;
    (ii) arrangements made by the Secretary of State for compensation for criminal injuries which were in operation before commencement of those Criminal Injuries Compensation schemes;
    (iii) the scheme being established by arrangements under the *Criminal Injuries Compensation (Northern Ireland) Order 2002*.

[*IHTA 1984, ss 71, 71A, 71B, 71C; FA 2006, Sch 20 paras 1, 2, 3*].

'*Bereaved Minor*' means a person who has not yet attained the age of eighteen years and at least one of whose parents has died. For these purposes 'B' or 'bereaved minor' includes all beneficiaries within a relevant class provided they are alive and are under the specified age of 18. See CIOT/STEP clarification dated 29 June 2007. [*IHTA 1984, s 71C inserted by FA 2006, Sch 20 para 1*].

'*Parent*' for these purposes also means step-parent or person with 'parental responsibility' within the *Children Act 1989, s 3*. See **46** SETTLEMENTS: TRUSTS FOR BEREAVED MINORS. [*IHTA 1984, s 71H inserted by FA 2006, Sch 20 para 1*].

Meaning of 'will' in 'will become entitled to'

[44.6] The requirement in (a) above is regarded as being satisfied even if no age is specified in the trust instrument, provided that it is clear that a beneficiary will in fact become entitled to the settled property (or an interest in possession in it) by the age of 25 or, as the case may be, 18. See *Crawford Settlement Trustees v HMRC* [2005] STC SCD 457. (See F8 at **23** HMRC EXTRA-STATUTORY CONCESSIONS.) Where the trustees of a settlement exercise their powers of investment so that there is no certainty that anyone will be entitled to any income at any age (e.g. where all the investment by them is in non-income producing assets) this will not prevent a settlement from qualifying under (a) above provided the powers in the settlement deed are limited by a clause to the effect that none of the powers will ever be used so as to breach the provisions of *IHTA 1984, s 71* above (Tolley's Practical Tax 1990 p 159).

The existence of a power of revocation, which may be exercised for the benefit of other persons at ages exceeding 25 or, as the case may be, 18 is sufficient to prevent a settlement from qualifying under (a) above. The word 'will' implies a degree of certainty inconsistent with such a power (*Inglewood and Another v CIR*) CA 1982, [1983] STC 133. However, the word 'will' does not require absolute certainty. Some qualification is required. See *Maitland's Trustees v Lord Advocate* CS 1982, [1982] SLT 483 for the distinction drawn between a present contingency and a future or supervening contingency.

Powers of appointment and revocation limited to the class of beneficiaries. Where there is a trust for accumulation and maintenance of a class of persons who become entitled to the property (or to an interest in possession in it) at a specified age not exceeding 25 or, as the case may be, 18 it would not be disqualified under (a) above by the existence of a power to vary or determine the respective shares of members of the class (even to the extent of excluding some members altogether) provided the power is exercisable only in favour of a person under 25 or, as the case may be, 18 who is a member of the class. See HMRC Press Release 19 January 1976. (**25.E1** HMRC STATEMENTS OF PRACTICE).

Settlements created before 15 April 1976

[44.7] There are transitional provisions for settlements in existence on 15 April 1976 when the restrictions under (c) above became effective. Where such settlements (and the property comprised therein at that date) satisfied the conditions in (a) and (b) above on 15 April 1976:

(i) the 25 years referred to in (c)(i) above run from 15 April 1976 (i.e. to 14 April 2001) and not from the commencement of the settlement; and

(ii) the condition in (c)(ii) above is treated as satisfied if:
   (a) it is satisfied in respect of the period beginning with 15 April 1976; or
   (b) it is satisfied in respect of the period beginning with 1 April 1977 and either there was no beneficiary living on 15 April 1976 or the beneficiaries on 1 April 1977 included a living beneficiary; or
   (c) there is no power under the terms of the settlement whereby it could have become satisfied during the period beginning with 1 April 1977, and the settlement has not been varied after 15 April 1976.

[*IHTA 1984, s 71(6)*].

Taxation of settlements from 22 March 2006

[44.8] From 22 March 2006 new taxing rules apply with regard to accumulation and maintenance trusts in existence such that where one or more 'persons' (the beneficiaries) fail to, on or before attaining a specified age not exceeding 18, become beneficially entitled to the settled property that trust will come within the '18–25 trusts' or relevant property trust regime and be subject to an initial proportionate ten-yearly charge and charges on exit of funds from the trust. The *maximum* charge within the '18–25 trusts' will be 4.2% on, broadly, the value of the trusts fund over the period of the life of the trust if the beneficiary takes capital, income and accumulated income at the age of 25. If this event is deferred until the beneficiary is beyond that age before they take the capital then the maximum charge that will apply is 6%, the relevant property rules applying (see Table below and Example 2 below). Otherwise property leaving such trusts will be subject to a charge under *IHTA 1984, s 70*. [*IHTA 1984, ss 58, 71, 71D–G; FA 2006, Sch 20 paras 1, 2, 3*].

0.15% for each	1	quarter	1 quarter	0.15%
0.15% for each of the next	4	quarters	1 year	0.6%
0.15% for each of the next	28	quarters	7 years	4.2%
0.15% for each of the next	40	quarters	10 years	6.0%

See also **43.6** SETTLEMENTS: DISCRETIONARY TRUSTS AND OTHER TRUSTS OF RELEVANT PROPERTY.

Example 1

On 6 April 1983 G settled £50,000 on trust equally for his grandchildren. The beneficiaries were to take absolute entitlements at age 25, income being accumulated for minor beneficiaries as detailed within the accumulation and maintenance trust deed below. By 2007 G had three grandchildren; Alex, who becomes 25 on 28 February 2008, and Stephanie, born 27 September 1994, and Roger, born 25 July 1996, who are 13 and 11 years old respectively.

On 28 February 2008 Alex became entitled to an interest in possession in one-third on reaching age 25. There was no charge on the distribution of capital entitlement under the old rules on Alex attaining the age of 25. The remaining two-thirds continues to be held equally for Stephanie and Roger but is not subject to an interest in possession. On 6 April 2008, 25 years had elapsed since the date of the settlement but the settlement would not have ceased to qualify as an accumulation and maintenance trust as a result since all of the remaining beneficiaries have a common grandparent. The settlement does, however, cease to be an accumulation and maintenance settlement from that date because the remaining beneficiaries do not become entitled to settled property on or before attaining age 18 as required from that date by *IHTA 1984, s 71* as amended by *FA 2006, Sch 20 paras 2, 3*.

As this was an existing accumulation and maintenance settlement the existing pre-22 March 2006 rules for accumulation and maintenance trusts continued until 5 April 2008 so that if the beneficiaries will become absolutely entitled no later than age 18, the settlement will remain within *IHTA 1984, s 71*. Otherwise the settlement will fall within the '18–25 trust' regime from 6 April 2008 within *IHTA 1984, s 71D(3)(4)* but in this case applying from each of their eighteenth birthdays. [*IHTA 1984, s 71F(1)(2)(a)*]. Consequently there would have been no 'exit' tax charge on 6 April 2008 when the accumulation and maintenance settlement failed to qualify under the new rules under *IHTA 1984, s 71(1)(a)*. Also, there will have been no entry charge when it failed and became a '18–25 trust' with effect from 6 April 2008 but a charge will commence from the date of each of their birthdays at 18. From that point onwards the exit charges will apply to distributions of capital entitlement on or before Stephanie and Roger becoming aged 25. The value of the remaining settlement is £600,000 and the IHT threshold is, say, £455,000 on 26 September 2019, Stephanie's birthday at 25 years, when the Trustees decide to distribute the respective capital entitlements to Stephanie of £325,000 and Roger of £275,000.

27 September 2019 distribution charge within IHTA 1984, s 71F

Assumed chargeable transfer (as above)	600,000
Assumed cumulative total	—
Deduct Nil rate band, say,	(455,000)
	£145,000
IHT at lifetime rates	£29,000

Effective rate $\frac{29,000}{600,000} = 4.83\%$

Stephanie's exit charge: 27 September 2012 to 27 September 2019 = 7 years i.e. 28 complete quarters

Rate of Stephanie's exit charge:

$^{28}/_{40} \times 4.83\% = 3.381\%$

Exit charge: $^{3}/_{10} \times 3.381\% \times £325,000$	£3,296

Roger's exit charge: 25 July 2014 to 27 September 2019 = 5 years i.e. 20 complete quarters

Rate of Roger's exit charge:

$^{20}/_{40} \times 4.83\% = 2.415\%$

Exit charge: $^{3}/_{10} \times 2.415\% \times £275,000$	£1,992

Notes to the example

(A) There was no charge to IHT on Alex becoming entitled to his one-third absolute interest on his 25th birthday in February 2008 but his brother and sister who are beneficiaries of the remainder of the trust will effectively suffer an exit charge when they take their benefit at the appropriate time but see (C) below.

(B) As Stephanie and Roger are minors they may not be regarded as mature enough to receive distributions from the settlement at the age of 18. Therefore from 6 April 2008 the settlement can come within an '18–25 trust' within *IHTA 1984, s 71D(3)(4)* but the exit charge under *IHTA 1984, s 71F(5)* does not commence until each of them attain their 18th birthdays and ending on the day before the occasion of charge, e.g. their attaining age 25 or receiving capital entitlement or advance. One option may be to instead retain the trust assets on bare trusts for Stephanie and Roger and only inform them that they are objects when considering the appropriateness of any individual appointments to them. However, where individuals such as Stephanie and Roger have become aware of the existence of such a trust and that they are the objects of such power they may require that the trustees consider exercising the power from time to time. HMRC have confirmed that an absolute trust such as a bare trust is not a settlement for IHT purposes and therefore the trust property will form part of the beneficiary's estate and not be subject to the *FA 2006* rules. See CIOT Press Release, 23 March 2007.

(C) In order to ensure that this existing pre-22 March 2006 accumulation and maintenance settlement continues to benefit from IHT exemption after 6 April 2008 the assets in the trust must go to the beneficiaries absolutely on or before their attainment of the age of 18 years. Therefore Trustees must have modified the terms of the settlement prior to 6 April 2008 under a suitable power of appointment, (see 3.1.1 of the Settlement Deed below), so that the beneficiaries will be fully entitled to the assets and accumulations on or before the age of 18. HMRC have confirmed that the inclusion of the statutory power of advancement, or a wider power of similar effect, in the trust deed does not cause the trust to fail the requirements of *s 71A* or *s 71D, IHTA 1984*, even though such powers can be used to create continuing trusts for the beneficiary. Also, it was queried with HMRC whether the legislation should be interpreted as no longer permitting the pooling of the trust funds after 6 April 2008 so that separate trusts must exist for the beneficiaries who then become the sole beneficiary of that fund. HMRC, in published replies to submissions jointly by the CIOT and STEP, confirmed that pooling remains permissible for bereaved minors trusts and age 18–25 trusts.

(D) The question trustees may ask is whether by using their administrative powers to ensure that the beneficiaries benefit absolutely in the assets and accumulated income at aged 18 years constitutes tax avoidance. This is unlikely to be a cause for concern here because *FA 2006, Sch 20* approves such alteration but the case of *Richards v Mackay* [1990] 1 OTPR regarding tax avoidance is interesting because Millett J contrasts situations to distinguish cases where the courts are satisfied proposed arrangements which include tax avoidance are not so inappropriate that no reasonable trustee would entertain them.

Example 2

On 31 December 2000 G, who had made no cumulative chargeable transfers within the previous 7 years, settled £150,000 on accumulation and maintenance settlement for his son GS born on that date. The trust is contingent on GS attaining the age of 25 years subject thereto to G's nephew N, aged 21 at 22 March 2006, attaining the age of 26, subject thereto for H absolutely with *Trustee Act 1925, s 31* being applicable. GS died on 6 April 2009 at the age of 9 years.

The settlement is valued at £640,000 on 30 December 2010. The property in the settlement is valued at £700,000 at 21 March 2012, the day before N attains his 26th birthday when the funds are released to him.

As the settlement was an accumulation and maintenance settlement prior to 22 March 2006 it continued to be so until 6 April 2008 when it ceased to be subject to *IHTA 1984, s 71* when there was no charge. *IHTA 1984, s 71D(3)(4)* '18–25 trust' subsequently applies by reason particularly of *s 71D(3)(a)*. Unfortunately, GS died on 6 April 2009 and *s 71D* ceases to apply by reason of *s 71D(6)(c)* which, at that point, does not give rise to a charge. N, although entitled to income, does not yet have an interest in possession within *IHTA 1984, s 49(1A)* and therefore the relevant property trust regime will commence resulting in a 10-year anniversary charge on 31 December 2010 and an exit charge on 22 March 2012 when N reaches his birthday at 26 within the terms of the settlement.

	£
Ten-year anniversary charge 31 December 2010	
Value of relevant property on 31.12.2010	640,000
Less nil rate band £325,000	325,000
IHT at lifetime rates on £315,000 @ 20%	£63,000
Effective rate $\frac{63,000}{640,000} = 9.84375\%$	
Rate of charge for period 6.4.2009 to 31.12.2010:	
$^{3}/_{10} \times 9.84375\% = 2.953125\% \times {}^{6}/_{40} \times £640,000$	
Ten-year anniversary charge:	£1,019
Exit charge on N becoming absolutely entitled at 22 March 2012	
Effective rate (as above) = 9.84375%	
No. of complete successive quarters between 31.12.2010 to 22.3.2012 = 4	
Proportionate charge:	
$9.84375\% \times {}^{3}/_{10} \times {}^{4}/_{40} \times £700,000$	£2,067

Notes to the example

The settlement qualifies as an accumulation and maintenance settlement until 6 April 2008 when it then fails to qualify as an accumulation and maintenance settlement under *IHTA 1984, s 71* but the settlement now qualifies within the '18–25 trust' provisions under *IHTA 1984, s 71D(3)(4)*. From 6 April 2009 the settlement will come within the relevant property charging regime as it no longer qualifies as an original accumulation and maintenance trust or an 'age 18–25 trust'.

In cases where an accumulation and maintenance settlement is replaced with a life interest in favour of a beneficiary prior to 22 March 2006 that beneficiary is treated as beneficially entitled to the property in which the interest subsists, i.e. he is treated as owning it absolutely. There is an IHT charge based on the value of the settled property in which his interest subsists when a beneficiary disposes of his interest or it otherwise comes to an end, i.e. either as a transfer on death or as a PET where the termination of the interest occurs during the lifetime of the tenant, for example where there is an exercise of a power of appointment. [*IHTA 1984, ss 49(1), 51(1), 51A, 52(1); FA 2006, Sch 20 paras 11–13*]. From 22 March 2006 newly created IIP settlements will be treated under the relevant property taxing regime unless the interest is an immediate post-death interest (IPDI) or a transitional serial interest (TSI) or a disabled person's interest. See **42** SETTLEMENTS WITH INTERESTS IN POSSESSION.

Example 3

On 6 June 1989 G settled shares on trust equally for his three grandchildren on an accumulation and maintenance settlement. He had made no cumulative chargeable transfers within the previous seven years. He settled shares in a property investment company that he had set up many years before on an accumulation and maintenance settlement for his grandchildren. The trust is contingent on the grandchildren attaining 25 years when they would receive life interests. The first born grandchild, Graham, attained the age of 25 years on 28 February 2006, while Stephanie, who was born 27 September 1994, and Roger, born 25 July 1996, are 14 and 12 years old respectively.

The settlement is comprised of 1,000 shares in the company which were valued at £100 per share but are valued at £6,000 per share on 6 June 2009. The property in the settlement is valued at £7,000 per share at 6 June 2019.

As the settlement is an accumulation and maintenance settlement prior to 22 March 2006 it continued to be so until 6 April 2008 when it ceased to be subject to *IHTA 1984, s 71,* at which point there is no charge. Unfortunately, from 6 April 2008 it becomes a relevant property trust which, from that point, becomes subject to ten-yearly charges because the settlement is within *IHTA 1984, s 58*. The settlement will also suffer exit charges. The first charge arising after 6 April 2008 will be on 6 June 2009 and this is the first ten-yearly charge which will be appropriately apportioned. The next charge will be either a ten-yearly charge on 6 June 2019 or an exit charge prior to that date depending on the Trustees decisions.

		£
Ten-year anniversary charge 6 June 2009		
Value of relevant property on 6 June 2009 (see note A)		4,002,000
Value of other property (see note B)		33,333
Less nil rate band £325,000		325,000
IHT at lifetime rates on £3,710,333 @ 20%		£742,067
Effective rate	$\frac{742,067}{4,002,000} = 18.5424\%$	
Rate of charge for period 6.4.2008 to 6.6.2009:		
$^{3}/_{10} \times 18.5424\% = 5.56272\% \times {}^{4}/_{40} \times £4,002,000$		
First ten-year anniversary charge		£22,262
Ten-year anniversary charge 6 June 2019		
Value of relevant property on 6 June 2019 (see note A)		4,669,000
Value of other property (see note B)		33,333
Less nil rate band, say, £425,000		425,000
IHT at lifetime rates on £4,277,333 @ 20%		£855,467
Effective rate	$\frac{855,467}{4,669,000} = 18.32227\%$	
Rate of charge for period 7.6.2009 to 6.6.2019:		
$^{3}/_{10} \times 18.32227\% = 5.496681\% \times {}^{40}/_{40} \times £4,669,000$		
Second ten-year anniversary charge		£256,640

Notes to the example

(A) The value of the remaining 667 shares after deducting Graham's share which he had an interest in possession at 22 March 2006 is £6,000 per share. The ten-yearly charge then applies from 6 April 2008 when the new relevant property rules apply up to the date of the first ten-yearly anniversary date of the setting up of the settlement. This conveniently turns out to be only four quarters after the new rules come into force and the charge is a comparatively small £22,340. However, the Trustees will find it difficult to meet this liability if the company does not pay a dividend which is the case in many family grown businesses. Other options might be to sell back shares to the other existing shareholders/Directors, to borrow to settle the liability in the interim or sell to a third party individual; none of which are ideal. Action should be taken before 6 April 2008 to ensure that the beneficiaries either qualify within the '18–25 trust' provisions under *IHTA 1984, s 71D(3)(4)* or receive an absolute interest in their entitlement as soon as possible. This latter option may be inappropriate bearing in mind the value of the fund and age of the grandchildren. A bare trust may be set up or the funds may be transferred to a discretionary trust for the two younger grandchildren, but this depends on whether the terms of the settlement allow such conversions. See Notes B and C in Example 1 above.

(B) Graham's one-third portion must still be brought into account as other property in the trust which was never relevant property and which has not subsequently become relevant property: see *IHTA 1984, s 66(4)(b)*, i.e. £100,000 × 33.3%.

Treatment of payments, etc. out of accumulation and maintenance trusts prior to 6 April 2008

[44.9] A charge to tax arose:

(a) where settled property ceased to be property which satisfied the necessary conditions in **44.4** above (but see also **21.4, 21.6–21.8** EXEMPT TRANSFERS for certain situations where there is no charge when property becomes held for charitable purposes only without limit of time *or* that of a qualifying political party *or* a national body mentioned in *IHTA 1984, Sch 3, or,* under certain conditions, a body not established or conducted for profit); or

(b) if the trustees made a 'disposition' which reduced the value of the settled property. '*Disposition*' includes an omission to exercise a right, unless not deliberate, which is treated as made at the latest time the right could have been exercised. [*IHTA 1984, s 70(10), s 71(3)(5), s 76*].

No charge arose:

(i) on a beneficiary's becoming beneficially entitled to, or to an interest in possession in, settled property on or before attaining the specified age; or

(ii) on the death of a beneficiary before attaining the specified age; or

(iii) if, under (b) above the trustees did not intend to confer a gratuitous benefit and either the transaction was at arm's length between persons not connected with each other (see **12** CONNECTED PERSONS) or is such as might be expected in such a transaction (but see **51.2** TRANSFER OF VALUE for unquoted securities in such a transaction); or

(iv) if, under (b) above, the disposition was a grant of a tenancy of agricultural property in the UK, Channel Islands or Isle of Man, for use for agricultural purposes and is made for full consideration in money or money's worth; or

(v) on the 'payment' of costs or expenses attributable to the property; or

(vi) where any payment was, or will be, income for income tax purposes of any person (or, in the case of a non-resident, would be if he were so resident); or

(vii) in respect of a liability to make a payment under (v) or (vi) above.

'*Payment*' includes the transfer of assets other than money. [*IHTA 1984, ss 63, 70(3)(4), 71(4)(5)*].

Tax is charged on the amount

This is the amount by which the trust property is less immediately after the event (e.g. distribution of trust assets to a beneficiary) giving rise to the charge than it would have been but for the event (i.e. the loss to donor principle), grossed-up where the settlement pays the tax.

The rate at which tax is charged is the aggregate of the following percentages for each complete successive 'quarter' in the 'relevant period'.

	Cumulative Total
0.25% for each of the first 40 quarters	10%
0.20% for each of the next 40 quarters	8%
0.15% for each of the next 40 quarters	6%
0.10% for each of the next 40 quarters	4%
0.05% for each of the next 40 quarters	2%
Maximum rate chargeable after 50 years	30%

The rate charged may be reduced if any of the property is, or was, 20 EXCLUDED PROPERTY. See **44.9** below.

'*Relevant period*' is the period beginning with the day on which the property became (or last became) held on accumulation and maintenance trusts, or 13 March 1975 if later, and ending on the day before the chargeable event.

'*Quarter*' is a period of three months. [*IHTA 1984, ss 63, 70(5)(6)(8), 71(5)*].

Example 4

On 1 January 1982 G settled £50,000 on trust equally for his great nephews and nieces born before 1 January 2003. The beneficiaries were to take life interests at age 18, income being accumulated for minor beneficiaries. By 2003 G had three great nephews and nieces, A (his brother's grandson) born in 1979 and B and C (his sister's grandsons) born in 1993 and 1998 respectively. The settlement was valued at £150,000 on 1 January 2007.

On 1 January 2007 the settlement failed to qualify as an accumulation and maintenance settlement as more than 25 years have elapsed since the date of settlement and the beneficiaries do not have a common grandparent. A has an interest in possession in one-third as he is over 18, but the remaining two-thirds which is held equally for B and C is not yet subject to an interest in possession. There would have been a charge to IHT on two-thirds of the value of the settlement on 1 January 2007.

The rate of tax is the aggregate of:

0.25% for each of the first	40	quarters	10%
0.20% for each of the next	40	quarters	8%
0.15% for each of the next	20	quarters	3%
	100		21%

The IHT charge is 21% × ²⁄₃ × £150,000 = £21,000

Note to the example

(A) There was no charge to IHT on A becoming entitled to an interest in possession in one-third on his eighteenth birthday in 1997 (see (i) above).

(B) Where an accumulation and maintenance settlement was established before 15 April 1976 (see above) its qualification as an A&M settlement would have expired in 2001. However, the settlement may not have originally commenced as an A&M settlement as there may have been an intervening life interest or it may have commenced as a discretionary trust so that the expiration period could now be imminent. [*IHTA 1984, s 71(1)(2b)(5)*].

Excluded property

[44.10] Where the whole or part of the amount on which tax is charged is attributable to property which was 20 EXCLUDED PROPERTY at any time during the relevant period, then, in determining the rate at which tax is charged in respect of that amount or part, no quarter throughout which the property was excluded property is to be counted. [*IHTA 1984, ss 70(7), 71(5)*].

Key points

[44.11] Points to consider are as follows.

- It is no longer possible to set up an A&M settlement as from 22 March 2006 by which date there were three options:
  (a) to wind up the trust on or before 5 April 2008 or the date on which the beneficiaries attain the age of 18 years if sooner;
  (b) to have changed the terms of the trust on or before 5 April 2008 to ensure that income and capital vest absolutely at or before the beneficiary's eighteenth birthday; or,
  (c) to leave the trust unaltered so that it falls within the relevant property regime.

  See 43 SETTLEMENTS: DISCRETIONARY TRUSTS AND OTHER TRUSTS OF RELEVANT PROPERTY. A number of attractions in this latter option gave the trustees control and flexibility especially over shares which the options at (a) and (b) would not and also in the case of beneficiaries within the '18–25 trust' provisions under *IHTA 1984, s 71D(3)(4)*. Conversion of an A&M settlement into a discretionary trust incurs no IHT charge at the time of creation but the use of *Trustee Act 1925, s 32* to facilitate this but should vest for the benefit of the beneficiaries.
- Another alternative to the A&M settlement is the setting up of a bare trust which is not a settlement for IHT purposes within *IHTA 1984, s 43(2)(a)* and is a potentially exempt transfer. Such trusts may be ideal for grandparents or other relatives but if a parent sets up a bare trust for their child any income arising from that trust in excess of £100 is assessed on the parent/settlor under *ITTOIA 2005, ss 629–632*. The difficulty is that under a bare trust the beneficiary has an immediate and absolute entitlement to the income and capital. The inclusion of *Trustee Act 1925, s 31* which allows trustees to withhold income or distribute it at their discretion will not bring the bare trust within the definition of a

settlement as above but notwithstanding this the trustees may retain income and distribute it on the child becoming 18 years old. Further advantages arise with a bare trust in relation to CGT where the minor would be entitled to the annual CGT allowance of £10,100 and no disposal for CGT purposes when the trustees pass the assets on to the beneficiary at 18 years old.

- Extreme care should be taken when dealing with any trusts that were created as A&M trusts that are still in existence, as the beneficiaries may be treated differently for inheritance tax purposes. For example, take the case of two beneficiaries of an A&M trust that was created to give an interest in possession at age 25 and absolute entitlement to capital at age 50. The first beneficiary turned 25 in 2005 and has a qualifying interest in possession — that is to say, the assets effectively form part of his estate for inheritance tax purposes. The second beneficiary turned 25 in 2007 (i.e. after 22 March 2006) and so his interest in possession falls within the relevant property regime and will suffer ten yearly charges and exit charges whenever capital leaves the trust, including on his absolute entitlement. Where the trust contains illiquid assets, such as shares in a family company, periodic charges to inheritance tax can be difficult to fund due to a lack of cash within the trust.
- Where a bare trust is set up with transfer of business property that has the benefit of BPR then holdover relief under *TCGA 1992, s 165* will be available but other assets transferred do not attract holdover relief when transferred into a bare trust.
- If a minor under the age of 18 years who is the beneficiary of a bare trust dies then the intestacy rules will apply and the assets will be subject to distribution under those rules in **52.21** TRANSFERS ON DEATH. This may have the unfortunate result of placing assets that comprise a business in the hands of an inappropriate beneficiary under those rules. Also, notwithstanding the application of the intestacy rules on the death of a minor their estate will still be valued for IHT purposes and tax charged accordingly after the nil rate band has been applied. A personal representative needs to account for the value of the beneficiary's estate, including their stake in the bare trust, on form IHT400.

45

Settlements: Interests held on Protective Trusts

Cross-reference. See also **43** SETTLEMENTS: DISCRETIONARY TRUSTS AND OTHER TRUSTS OF RELEVANT PROPERTY.

Simon's Taxes. See I5.6.

Other Sources. HMRC Customer Guide to Inheritance Tax; Foster, Part E6.

Introduction

[45.1] 'Protective trust' is defined by the *Trustee Act 1925, s 33* and, broadly, is a trust under which a person ('the principal beneficiary') is entitled to an interest in possession in the settled property for the trust period unless he forfeits his interest e.g. by attempting to assign his interest or by becoming bankrupt. Usually, if the interest of the principal beneficiary is forfeited, the trust property is held on discretionary trusts for a class of beneficiaries. The class includes the principal beneficiary and his spouse and his children or more remoter issue or, in the absence of spouse and issue, the principal beneficiary and the persons who would be entitled to the trust fund or the income thereof on his death. Where property is held on trusts to the like effect as those specified in *Trustee Act 1925, s 33(1)*, special provisions apply. Trusts of 'like effect' to those defined in the *Trustee Act* are those that are not materially different in their tax consequences i.e. where there are only minor variations or additional administrative powers or duties. A 'minor variation' does not include the extension *ab initio* of the class of beneficiaries to brothers and sisters (although it is appreciated that so long as the principal beneficiary has no spouse or issue the statutory trusts extend to the next of kin for the time being who might well be brothers and sisters) (see E7 at **25** HMRC STATEMENTS OF PRACTICE with additions derived from the original source which was a former Inland Revenue letter published in the Law Society's Gazette of 3 March 1976 and reprinted in British Tax Review 1976, p 421). A protective trust of income for the benefit of the settlor is a trust of 'like effect' (*Thomas & Thomas v CIR* Ch D 1981, [1981] STC 382).

Forfeiture before 12 April 1978

[45.2] The following provisions apply where the principal beneficiary's interest in possession came to an end before 12 April 1978.

There is a charge to tax:

(a) where the settled property ceases to be held on discretionary trusts similar to those specified in *Trustee Act 1925, s 33(1)(ii)* (see **45.1** above) otherwise than by being applied for the principal beneficiary (but see also **21.4** EXEMPT TRANSFERS for certain situations where there is no charge when property becomes held for charitable purposes only without limit of time or that of a qualifying political party *or* a national body mentioned in *IHTA 1984, Sch 3* or, under certain conditions, a body not established or conducted for profit), or

(b) if the trustees make a 'disposition' otherwise than by way of payment for the benefit of the principal beneficiary which reduces the value of the settled property. '*Disposition*' includes an omission to exercise a right, unless not deliberate, which is treated as made at the latest time that the right could have been exercised.

[*IHTA 1984, ss 70(10), 73(1)(2), 76*].

No charge arises:

(i) if, under (b) above, the trustees do not intend to confer a gratuitous benefit and either the transaction is at arm's length between persons not connected with each other (see **12** CONNECTED PERSONS) or is such as might be expected in such a transaction; or

(ii) if, under (b) above, the disposition is a grant of a tenancy of agricultural property in the UK, Channel Islands or Isle of Man, for use for agricultural purposes and is made for full consideration in money or money's worth; or

(iii) on the 'payment' of costs or expenses attributable to the property; or

(iv) where any payment is, or will be, income for income tax purposes of any person (or, in the case of a non-resident, would be if he were so resident), or

(v) in respect of a liability to make a payment under (iii) or (iv) above.

'*Payment*' includes the transfer of assets other than money. [*IHTA 1984, ss 63, 70(3)(4), 73(3)*].

Tax is charged on the amount by which the trust property is less immediately after the event giving rise to the charge that it would have been but for the event (i.e. the loss to the donor principle), grossed-up where the settlement pays the tax.

The rate at which tax is charged is the aggregate of the following percentages for each complete successive 'quarter' in 'the relevant period':

	Cumulative Total
0.25% for each of the first 40 quarters	10%
0.20% for each of the next 40 quarters	8%
0.15% for each of the next 40 quarters	6%
0.10% for each of the next 40 quarters	4%
0.05% for each of the next 40 quarters	2%
Maximum rate chargeable after 50 years	30%

'*Relevant period*' is the period beginning with the day on which the property became (or last became) held on the discretionary trusts, or 13 March 1975 if later, and ending on the day before the chargeable event.

'*Quarter*' means any period of three months. [*IHTA 1984, ss 63, 70(5)(6)(8), 73(3)*].

Excluded property

[45.3] Where the whole or part of the amount on which tax is charged as in **45.2** above is attributable to property which was EXCLUDED PROPERTY (**20**) at any time during the relevant period, then, in determining the rate at which tax is charged in respect of that amount or part, no quarter throughout which the property was excluded property is to be counted. [*IHTA 1984, ss 70(7), 73(3)*].

See also the provisions under **43.19** and **43.22** SETTLEMENTS: DISCRETIONARY TRUSTS AND OTHER TRUSTS OF RELEVANT PROPERTY which also apply to property settled or appointed on protective trusts.

Example

In 1951 X left his estate on protective trusts for his son Z. On 1 January 1978 Z attempted to assign his interest and the protective trusts were accordingly determined. On 1 May 1983 the trustees advanced £25,000 to Z to enable him to purchase a flat. At the same time, they also advanced £10,000 (net) to his granddaughter D. On 1 May 2010 Z died and the trust fund, valued at £200,000, passed equally to his grandchildren absolutely.

1 May 1983

There is no charge to IHT on the payment to Z, but a charge arises on the payment to D.

The relevant period is the period from the determination of the protective trusts (1 January 1978) to 1 May 1983, i.e. 21 complete quarters.

The rate of tax is 0.25% for each of 21 quarters *5.25%*.

IHT payable is:

$$\frac{5.25}{100 - 5.25} \times £10{,}000 = \mathit{£554}$$

The gross payment is £10,554.

1 May 2010

There is a charge to IHT when the trust vests on the death of Z. 129 complete quarters have elapsed since the protective trusts determined.

The rate of tax is:

	%
0.25% for each of the first 40 quarters	10.00
0.20% for each of the next 40 quarters	8.00
0.15% for the next 40 quarters	6.00
0.10% for the next 9 quarter	0.90
	24.90%

IHT payable is 24.90% × £200,000 = £49,800

Forfeiture after 11 April 1978

[45.4] Where the principal beneficiary's interest in possession comes to an end after 11 April 1978, the 'failure or determination' of such trusts before the end of the trust period will be disregarded for the purposes of inheritance tax and the principal beneficiary will continue to be treated as beneficially entitled to an interest in possession while discretionary trusts similar to those in *Trustee Act 1925, s 33(1)(ii)* (see **45.1** above) continue to apply under the *Trustee Act*. The effect is that any distribution to the principal beneficiary is not chargeable (because he is treated as having an interest in possession) but distributions to any other beneficiary will be chargeable. Also, the value of the principal beneficiary's deemed interest will form part of his estate on his death. [*IHTA 1984, s 88*]. For a consideration of the meaning of '*failure or determination*' see *Cholmondeley and Another v CIR* Ch D, [1986] STC 384.

Forfeiture on or after 22 March 2006

[45.5] Where protective trusts are created by the forfeiting of a beneficiary's interest, e.g. when he tries to sell the interest on or after 22 March 2006, then *IHTA 1984, s 88(3)* treats forfeiture out of a protective trust interest in possession created on or before that date as if it had happened on or before that date. The effect is that the deemed interest in possession arising on forfeiture is treated as created before 22 March 2006 and therefore the *FA 2006* rules do not apply and **45.4** above applies. In circumstances where a protective trust is created under *Trustee Act 1925 s 33(1)(i)* after 21 March 2006 the beneficiary has an interest in possession to which the new rules apply then the interest of the principal beneficiary is forfeited and the trust property is held on discretionary trusts for a class of beneficiaries. The class includes the principal beneficiary and his spouse and his children or more remoter issue or, in the absence of spouse and issue, the principal beneficiary and the persons who would be entitled to the trust fund or the income thereof on his death. However, the transitional rules apply to attract continuing favourable treatment in circumstances where the underlying interest of the principal beneficiary is either an 'immediate post-death interest' (IPDI) (see Key Points below), a disabled person's interest within *IHTA 1984, s 89B(1)(c)(d)* or a 'transitional serial interest' (TSI). See SETTLEMENTS WITH INTERESTS IN POSSESSION (42) and TRUSTS FOR THE DISABLED (47). [*IHTA 1984, s 88(3)–(6) as inserted by FA 2006, Sch 20 para 24*].

Key points

[45.6] Points to consider are as follows.

- Where a protective trust is created during the lifetime of a settlor then it does not receive any special treatment and it will be subject to the relevant property regime with an appropriate chargeable disposal by the settlor on creation and then subsequent ten-yearly charges and exit charges.
- A protective trust set up by reason of a will secures treatment as an immediate post death interest for the principal beneficiary. The result of this is that on termination of the principal beneficiary's interest e.g. bankruptcy then as an immediate post death interest held by the principal beneficiary there are no ten-yearly, proportionate or exit charges as with relevant property trusts. However, on the principal beneficiary's death as an immediate post death interest the value of the trust at that time is treated as part of the principal beneficiary's estate for IHT purposes. There are however no special income tax or CGT advantages of such trusts other than the automatic uplift for CGT purposes on the creation of the immediate post death interest by the testator.
- Protective trusts are heavily dependant on the wording in *Trustee Act 1925, s 33*. In the case of *Dennis's Settlement Trusts Re* [1942] 1 All ER 520 a deed varying the terms of the protective trust resulted in a protective discretionary trust arising. *Section 33(1)(i)* provides that advances to the principal beneficiary under any statutory or express power will not impose a protective discretionary trust regime as follows:

  > 'Upon trust for the principal beneficiary during the trust period or until he, whether before or after the termination of any prior interest, does or attempts to do or suffers any act or thing, or until any event happens, other than an advance under any statutory or express power, whereby, if the said income were payable during the trust period to the principal beneficiary absolutely during that period, he would be deprived of the right to receive the same or any part thereof, in any of which cases, as well as on the termination of the trust period, whichever first happens, this trust of the said income shall fail or determine'

As a protective measure to prevent discretionary trusts arising when, say, the principal beneficiary tries to sell their interest it may be safe to provide that the beneficiary's interest can be terminated at the discretion of the trustees.

46

Settlements: Trusts for Bereaved Minors and 'Age 18–25 trusts'

Cross-references. 44 SETTLEMENTS: ACCUMULATION AND MAINTENANCE TRUSTS; 43 SETTLEMENTS: DISCRETIONARY TRUSTS AND OTHER TRUSTS OF RELEVANT PROPERTY.

Other Sources. HMRC Customer Guide to Inheritance Tax; Tolley's UK Taxation of Trusts; Foster, Part E1.02.

Introduction — Transfers into trusts for bereaved minors

[46.1] A trust created under the terms of someone's will or intestacy will not come within the relevant property trust regime if it is a trust for a bereaved minor. A 'trust for a bereaved minor' is a trust for the benefit of a person under the age of 18, at least one of whose parents, or as the case may be step-parent or person having parental responsibility e.g. legal guardian, has died and the trust arises in any one of the following circumstances:

(a) Statutory trusts arising on an intestacy under *Administration of Estates Act 1925, ss 46, 47(1)* where such terms of statutory trust are invariable so that any trust adhering to that act will qualify; or

(b) Settled property is held on statutory trusts for the benefit of a 'bereaved minor' where the trust is established under the will of a deceased parent or, as the case may be, step-parent; or

(c) Settled property is held on statutory trust for the benefit of a 'bereaved minor' as a result of payments from the Criminal Injuries Compensation Scheme such that payments have been made for the benefit of the minor as a result of:
   - (i) the scheme being established by arrangements under the *Criminal Injuries Compensation Act 1995*;
   - (ii) arrangements made by the Secretary of State for compensation for criminal injuries which were in operation before commencement of those Criminal Injuries Compensation schemes;
   - (iii) the scheme being established by arrangements under the *Criminal Injuries Compensation (Northern Ireland) Order 2002*.

[*IHTA 1984, ss 71, 71A, 71B, 71C, 71H; FA 2006, Sch 20 paras 1, 2, 3*].

In relation to (b) and (c) the bereaved minor must, prior to or upon the attainment of the age of 18 years, be absolutely entitled to the settled property and also absolutely entitled to any income arising therefrom and any income that has been accumulated. Whilst the beneficiary is under the age of 18 if any of the capital of the settled property is applied it must be applied for the benefit of the bereaved minor only. In relation to income whilst the beneficiary is under the age of 18, he or she must either be entitled to such income or alternatively none of the income may be applied for the benefit of any other person.

Trusts are not treated as failing the above conditions by virtue of trustee powers of advancement, whether under the *Trustee Act 1925, s 32* or *Trustee Act (Northern Ireland) 1958, s 33* or where trustees have similar powers but unrestricted. [*IHTA 1984, s 71A(4); FA 2006, Sch 20 para 1*]. For bereaved minors trusts set up on or after 8 April 2013, including those set up under a Will executed before that date, the trustees may have powers to apply sums, whether capital or income, for the benefit of someone other than the bereaved minor, but only up to an annual limit. This limit is the lower of either £3,000 or 3% of the amount that is the maximum value of the settled property in the period in question. The limit applies for each tax year. Where an amount is paid out in excess of the annual limit otherwise than for the benefit of the bereaved minor, and other exemptions do not apply, there is a tax charge under *IHTA 1984, s 71B* on that excess: *IHTA 1984, ss 71A (4)(za), 4A, 4B, and 4C*.

For these purposes 'parent' includes step-parent or 'guardian' who has parental responsibility for the minor as defined within the *Children Act 1989, s 3* or where applicable the *Children Act (Scotland) Act 1995, s 1(3)* or the *Children (Northern Ireland) Order 1995*. [*IHTA 1984, s 71H; FA 2006, Sch 20 para 1*].

Example 1

Mr and Mrs A both die in a boating accident on 12 July 2010 whilst on holiday and it is not known who survived the other and neither has made a will but Mr A is the elder of the two. They have two children who are aged four years and are twins and both the deceased have parents still living. Their estates are valued at £325,000 and £335,000 for Mr and Mrs A respectively. As there is no will or survivorship provision made by either there is the possibility that the parents of either Mr A or Mrs A may wish to prove their son/daughter survived the spouse and thereby share in both estates, however, under the *Law Reform (Succession) Act 1995, s 1* in the case of intestate spouses each estate passes as though the other had predeceased i.e. the estates pass as though each died as widow and widower. Note that there is a different treatment for IHT purposes where there is intestacy and deaths have occurred in *commorientes* circumstances. See Example 2 below.

The *Administration of Estates Act 1925, s 46(2A)* has the effect in Mr A's and Mrs A's case of their assets passing to their issue (applicable in this case to be held on statutory trusts as they are minors) so that no class of beneficiaries can participate unless all those in a prior class have predeceased. The parents of Mr and Mrs A will not therefore benefit from their children's intestate estates. The parents of Mrs A have agreed to act as guardians to the two children as the parents of Mr A are living abroad. Statutory trusts for the children due to their minority therefore arise on an intestacy and come within (a) above. However, see

Example 2 below regarding the situation where settled property on bereaved minors trusts ceases to be property which satisfies the necessary conditions of *IHTA 1984, s 71B(2)(3) as inserted by FA 2006, Sch 20 para 1.*

Notes to the example

(A) There will probably need to be a clause in the statutory trust that enables funds to be paid to the legal guardians of the two children so that income can be applied for their benefit. Trustees may pay funds to a guardian that belong to the child and the trust deed can be worded to incorporate this as seen below. A minor cannot give good receipt for trust income unless he/she is married and that is not the case in this situation. [*Law of Property Act 1925, s 21*].

> 'Where the Trustees may apply the income for the benefit of a minor, they may do so by paying the income to the minor's guardian on behalf of the minor, or to minor if he has attained the age of 16. The Trustees are under no duty to enquire into the use of the income unless they have knowledge of circumstances which call for enquiry.'

(B) In many cases where the bereaved minor's trust has been set up the funds pertaining to that trust will have been subject to death rates of IHT where the estate is in excess of the appropriate nil rate band.

(C) Provided the grandparents secure parental responsibility for the minors within the meaning of the *Children Act 1989, s 3* then provided the requirements within (a)–(c) are met above on the death of one of the grandparents any trust set up in favour of the children under 18 will also become a trust for a bereaved minor thereby enabling capital to skip a generation. [*IHTA 1984, 71H; FA 2006, Sch 20 para 1*].

Definitions

'*Bereaved Minor*' means a person who has not yet attained the age of 18 years and at least one of whose parents, or, as the case may be, step-parent has died. For these purposes '*bereaved minor*' includes all beneficiaries within a relevant class provided they are alive and are under the specified age of 18. See CIOT/STEP clarification dated 29 June 2007. [*IHTA 1984, s 71C inserted by FA 2006, Sch 20 para 1*].

'*Parent*' for these purposes also means step-parent or person with 'parental responsibility' within the *Children Act 1989, s 3*. [*IHTA 1984, s 71H inserted by FA 2006, Sch 20 para 1*].

Note that unlike accumulation and maintenance settlements where no interest in possession subsists in the settled property and the income from that settled property is to be accumulated so far as not applied for the maintenance, education or benefit of a beneficiary the new '*bereaved minor*' can be given an interest in possession at the outset. Therefore there are varying possibilities in the drafting of the trust deed for the '*bereaved minor*' which will need to address the fact whether a discretionary or interest in possession subsists. For income tax purposesit might be preferable to ensure that an interest in possession trust is formed. See SETTLEMENTS WITH INTERESTS IN POSSESSION (**42**).

Treatment of payments, etc. out of trusts for bereaved minors

[46.2] A charge to tax arises:

(a) where settled property on bereaved minors trusts ceases to be property which satisfies the necessary conditions of *IHTA 1984, s 71A* as detailed in **46.1** at (a)–(c) above; or
(b) if the trustees make a 'disposition' which reduces the value of the settled property. '*Disposition*' includes an omission to exercise a right, unless not deliberate, which is treated as made at the latest time the right could have been exercised. [*IHTA 1984, ss 70(10), 71B(1)(3)*].

The rate is determined by reference to the settlor's cumulative transfers in the seven years preceding the date on which the settlement commenced, as well as the settlement's cumulative transfers in the ten years preceding the anniversary.

Tax calculation

Tax is calculated using lifetime Tables (see **40** RATES OF TAX) at the following rates:

(1) where the whole of the relevant property has been comprised in the settlement throughout the ten-year period ending immediately before the ten-year anniversary, at 30% of the effective rate;
(2) and where the whole or part of the relevant property was not relevant property or was not comprised in the settlement throughout the ten years ending immediately before the ten-year anniversary, at 30% of the effective rate reduced by one-fortieth for each successive 'quarter' in the ten-year period which expired before the property became, or last became, relevant property.

The '*effective rate*' is the rate found by expressing the tax chargeable as a percentage of the amount on which tax is charged on an assumed chargeable transfer by an assumed transferor. [*IHTA 1984, s 66(1)(2)*].

Circumstances of no charge

No charge arises:

(i) on a beneficiary's becoming absolutely entitled to the settled property (not necessarily in fixed shares) on or before attaining the specified age of 18 years; or
(ii) on the death of a beneficiary before attaining the specified age of 18 years (but see temporary charitable exit rules below); or
(iii) on being paid or applied for the advancement or benefit of the bereaved minor(s); or
(iv) on the '*payment*' of costs or expenses attributable to the property; or
(v) where any payment is, or will be, income for income tax purposes of any person (or, in the case of a non-resident, would be if he were so resident).

[*IHTA 1984, ss 70(3)(8)(10), 71B(2)(3); FA 2006, Sch 20 para 1*].

'*Payment*' includes the transfer of assets other than money. [*IHTA 1984, ss 63, 70(3)(4), 71(4)(5)*].

Tax charging provisions

Tax is charged on the amount by which the trust property is less immediately after the event giving rise to the charge than it would have been but for the event (i.e. the loss to donor principle), grossed-up where the settlement pays the tax. [*IHTA 1984, s 71B(3); FA 2006, Sch 20 para 1*].

The rate at which tax is charged is the aggregate of the following percentages for each complete successive 'quarter' in the 'relevant period'. [*IHTA 1984, ss 70(7); 71B(3); FA 2006, Sch 20 para 1*].

'*Quarter*' is a period of three months. [*IHTA 1984, ss 63, 70(5)(6)(8), 71(5)*].

'*Relevant period*' is the period beginning with the day on which the property became (or last became) held on bereaved minors trusts, or which immediately before it became property held on bereaved minors trusts was property held on accumulation and maintenance trusts but which had ceased to be so held on or after 22 March 2006, and ending on the day before the chargeable event. [*IHTA 1984, ss 70(3)–(8)(10), 71B(3); FA 2006, Sch 20 paras 1, 2*].

Where *s 71A* ceases to apply as in (a) above then the rate of charge will be that given at *IHTA 1984, s 70(6)* i.e., the temporary charitable exit rules. Potential circumstances are a trust for a bereaved minor is established but the minor dies, for instance, before the age 18 and the trust continues after the death of the minor. See also Example 2 below. In such circumstances the temporary charitable trust rules would apply with a maximum rate of 30% after 50 years have elapsed. See table below. A charge does not arise where settled property held on trusts for bereaved minors ceases to be so because the bereaved minor becomes absolutely entitled on or before the age of 18 or dies under the age of 18 or the property is applied or advanced to the bereaved minor before the age of 18. [*IHTA 1984, ss 70(6); 71B(2)(3); FA 2006, Sch 20 paras 1, 2*].

	Cumulative Total
0.25% for each of the first 40 quarters	10%
0.20% for each of the next 40 quarters	8%
0.15% for each of the next 40 quarters	6%
0.10% for each of the next 40 quarters	4%
0.05% for each of the next 40 quarters	2%
Maximum rate chargeable after 50 years	30%

The rate charged may be reduced if any of the property is, or was, EXCLUDED PROPERTY (20).

Example 2

Following on from the example above the deceased's wills are located on 31 July 2021 as a result of which each of the deceased's assets are found to have been left in entirety to each other then to Mr and Mrs A's parents separately. The beneficiaries were, on or before attaining a specified age, not exceeding 18, to become beneficially entitled to the settled property under statutory trusts and therefore had qualified as bereaved minors for these purposes.

On 31 July 2021 as a result of the located wills the settlement fails to qualify as a bereaved minors trust and the clawback provisions apply. The settlement was valued at £594,000 on 12 July 2010 (see Note A) and at £750,000 on 31 July 2021. There will be a charge to IHT on the whole of the value of the settlement on 31 July 2021. The period from 12 July 2010 to 31 July 2021 is 44 complete quarters charged at the *IHTA 1984, s 70(6)* rate:

0.25% for each of the first	40	quarters	10%
0.20% for each of the next	4	quarters	0.8%
	44		10.8%

The IHT charge is 10.8% × £750,000 = £81,000

Notes to the example

(A) There would also have been a charge to IHT originally in respect of Mrs A's estate. See IHTM12197. In this case there are wills and by virtue of *IHTA 1984, s 4(2)* if it is not known which of the two survived the other then in assessing their respective estates neither is deemed to have survived the other. However, Mr A's estate devolves to Mrs A as he is the elder but his estate enjoys the benefit of the spouse exemption and in assessing Mrs A's estate no account is to be taken of Mr A's estate being passed on under the inter-spousal exemption. Therefore Mr A's estate is not taxable at all and Mrs A's estate is taxable on £4,000 (i.e. £335,000 – £325,000 × 40%). However, Mrs A's personal representatives may make a claim for Mr A's unused nil rate band under *IHTA 1984, s 8A* (or part thereof) to ensure that there is no IHT liability in the circumstances. See Example 1 at **52.2** TRANSFER ON DEATH.

(B) In the circumstances above or if trust for a bereaved minor continues after the death of that minor before his or her attaining the age of 18 years then the temporary charitable trust exit rules apply with a potential maximum rate of 30%. [*IHTA 1984, ss 70(6), 71B(3); FA 2006, Sch 20 paras 1, 2*].

Age 18–25 trusts

[46.3] Existing accumulation and maintenance settlements that satisfy the requirements detailed below by 6 April 2008 and newly created 'age 18–25 trusts' under the terms of a will or established under the Criminal Injuries Compensation Scheme will not come within the relevant property trust regime. [*IHTA 1984, s 71D(1)–(4) as inserted by FA 2006, Sch 20 para 1*]. Any such 'trust for a bereaved minor' detailed at **46.1** above or an existing accumulation and maintenance trust to which *s 71* ceased to have effect in the period 22 March 2006 to 6 April 2008, will be within the IHT regime detailed below.

'Age 18–25 trust' requirements

In order for the trusts to qualify as an 'age 18–25 trust' the following requirements and conditions will necessarily apply:

(a) The person for whom the trusts are held must, prior to or upon the attainment of the age of 25 years, be absolutely entitled to the settled property, and also absolutely entitled to any income arising therefrom together with any income that has arisen from the property but that has been accumulated; and

(b) Whilst the beneficiary 'B' is living and under the age of 25 any settled property must be applied solely for 'B's benefit, but see relaxation of this rule under FA 2013, as detailed below. For these purposes 'B' or '*bereaved minor*' includes all beneficiaries within a relevant class provided they are alive and are under the specified age of 18. See CIOT/STEP clarification dated 29 June 2007; and

(c) Whilst the beneficiary 'B' is living and under the age of 25 any income arising from the settled property is applied solely for 'B's benefit or, if not applied, it is not applied for anyone else's benefit, but also subject to the relaxation of this rule under *FA 2013*, as detailed below.

The trust will be established by the will of a deceased parent for the benefit of a beneficiary or beneficiaries not having yet attained the age of 25, or as a result payments from the Criminal Injuries Compensation schemes within **46.1**(c) above. Note however that if the will gives the beneficiary an immediate interest in possession, the interest will not fall under the provisions for Age 18–25 trusts but instead it will be treated as an immediate post death interest (see **42.2** SETTLEMENTS WITH INTEREST IN POSSESSION). [*IHTA 1984, s 71D(1)–(2)*].

Alternatively, it must be settled property to which *IHTA 1984, s 71* ceases to have effect in the period 22 March 2006 to 6 April 2008 but that settled property may then be treated as an 'age 18–25 trust' if it continues to be held on trusts for a person who has not yet attained the age of 25 years and the trusts satisfy the conditions in (a)–(c) above. [*IHTA 1984, s 71D(3)–(4)*]. See Example 2 at **44.8** SETTLEMENTS: ACCUMULATION AND MAINTENANCE SETTLEMENTS.

In relation to (a) to (c) above, whilst the beneficiary is living and under the age of 25 if any of the capital of the settled property is applied it must be applied for the benefit of the beneficiary only. If the trust property is not so applied then whilst the beneficiary is under the age of 25 years the income arising therefrom, if any, must be a full entitlement or the income must not be applied for the benefit of any other person. [*IHTA 1984, s 71D(6)*].

Trusts are not treated as failing the above conditions by virtue of trustee powers of advancement, whether under the *Trustee Act 1925, s 32* or the *Trustee Act (Northern Ireland) 1958, s 33* or where trustees have similar powers but unrestricted [*IHTA 1984, s 71D(7)*].

[*IHTA 1984, s 71D as inserted by FA 2006, Sch 20 para 1*].

For trusts set up on or after 8 April 2013, including those set up under a Will executed before that date, the trustees may have powers to apply sums, whether capital or income, for the benefit of someone other than the bereaved minor, but only up to an annual limit. This limit is the lower of either £3,000 or 3% of the amount that is the maximum value of the settled property in the period in question. The limit applies for each tax year. Where an amount is paid out in excess of the annual limit otherwise than for the benefit of the bereaved minor, and other exemptions do not apply, there is a tax charge under

IHTA 1984 s 71E on that excess: *IHTA 1984, s 71D(7A), (7B) and (7C)*. With effect from the same date, it is also provided that protective trusts within *Trustee Act 1925, s 33* may fall within the age 18–25 provisions where the other conditions set out above are satisfied. [*IHTA 1984 s 71D(6A)*].

Treatment of payments, etc. out of age 18–25 trusts

[46.4] A charge to tax arises:

(a) where 'B' becomes absolutely entitled the settled property, any income arising from it and any income that has arisen and been accumulated; on the death of 'B'; when the property settled is paid or applied for the advancement or benefit of 'B'; or
(b) if the trustees make a 'disposition' which reduces the value of the settled property. '*Disposition*' includes an omission to exercise a right, unless not deliberate, which is treated as made at the latest time the right could have been exercised.

[*IHTA 1984, ss 71E(1)(5), 71F(2) as inserted by FA 2006, Sch 20 para 1*].

Circumstances of no charge

No charge to tax arises:

(i) on a beneficiary at or under the age of 18 becoming absolutely entitled to, or to an interest in possession in, settled property on or before attaining the specified age of 25 years, or
(ii) on the death of a beneficiary before attaining the specified age of 18 years (but see temporary charitable exit rules below), or
(iii) on settled property becoming whilst the beneficiary is living and under the age of 18 property held under trust for a bereaved minor, or
(iv) on settled property being paid or applied for the advancement or benefit of the beneficiary before attaining the age of 18 but whilst still living or on attaining the age of 18, or
(v) on the 'payment' of costs or expenses attributable to the property, or
(vi) where any payment is, or will be, income for income tax purposes of any person (or, in the case of a non-resident, would be if he were so resident).

[*IHTA 1984, s 71E(2)(3); FA 2006, Sch 20 para 1*].

'*Payment*' includes the transfer of assets other than money. [*IHTA 1984, ss 63, 70(3)(4), 71(4)(5)*].

Tax calculation

Where tax is charged in accordance with an event arising under (a) or (b) above and it occurs after the beneficiary has attained the age of 18 years then the amount of the tax is calculated as follows:

Chargeable amount × *Relevant fraction* × *Settlement rate* = *Tax due*

- *Chargeable amount* is the amount by which the value of the property in the settlement has been decreased by following the event that gave rise to the charge or where the amount by which the value of the property in the settlement is reduced as a result of the chargeable event (i.e. the loss to donor principle) grossed-up where the settlement pays the tax;
- *Relevant fraction* is three-tenths multiplied by so many fortieths in the period beginning with the day on which the beneficiary attained 18 years or, if later, on the day when the property became subject to an '18–25 trust' and ending on the day prior to the occasion of the charge. For these purposes one fortieth is a complete three-month period;
- *Settlement rate* is the effective rate at which tax would be charged on the value transferred by a chargeable transfer where the value transferred is equal to the aggregate of the value of:
    - the settlement immediately after commencement; and
    - any related settlement on creation; and
    - any other property which became comprised in the settlement but before the charge arising under (a) or (b) above.

    With effect for charges on or after the date of Royal Assent to *F(No 2)A 2015*, only the value of property to which *IHTA 1984, s 71D* applies is counted in a related settlement.

[*IHTA 1984, s 71F; FA 2006, Sch 20 para 1*].

Example 3

X, a widower, dies on 29 August 2010 and by his will leaves all his assets in trust for his daughter Emily, aged 20 on 20 September 2010. The initial capital in the bereaved minor's trust amounts to £640,000 after IHT deductions. Emily will become absolutely entitled to capital and income by the age of 25 and whilst she is living before that date the trustees will only apply the settled property for her benefit within the terms of the trust. On her birthday on 20 September 2015 at age 25 the trustees appoint the capital and any accumulated income to her. The capital and remainder of accumulated income amounts to £640,000 on that date. X had made no previous transfers in the seven years prior to his death.

Assumed chargeable transfer 20 September 2015:	£
Value of relevant property on 20.9.2010	640,000
Less nil rate band, £325,000	325,000
	£315,000
IHT at lifetime rates on £315,000 @ 20%	£63,000

Effective rate $\frac{63,000}{640,000} = 9.843\%$

Rate of charge for period 29.8.2010 to 20.9.2015 (i.e. 20 complete quarters):

$\frac{3}{10} \times 9.843\% = 2.953\% \times \frac{20}{40} \times £640,000$

Exit charge on Emily becoming 25 payable by Emily:	£9,450

Notes to the example

(A) If between the ages of 18 and 25, the beneficiary becomes absolutely entitled or property is paid or applied out of the trust fund by the trustees for the beneficiary, or, the beneficiary dies, there will be a rateable apportionment of the non-IIP rate. See SETTLEMENTS: DISCRETIONARY TRUSTS AND OTHER TRUSTS OF RELEVANT PROPERTY (43).

(B) A clawback charge, a rare situation in the circumstances, similar to that shown in Example 2 above will apply where assets leave an 18–25 trust where *s 71D* above ceases to apply. In those unusual circumstances above then the rate of charge will be that given at *IHTA 1984, s 70(6)* i.e., the temporary charitable exit rules. [*IHTA 1984, ss 70(6)–(8), 71G; FA 2006, Sch 20 para 1*].

Key points

[46.5] Points to consider are:

- Under a bereaved minor's trust, the income arising may subject to either trusts for accumulation or alternatively may be payable for the benefit of the minor on interest in possession trusts. When the child attains the age of 18, the funds become payable to him or her absolutely, with no IHT exit charge applying. Capital gains tax hold over relief is also available. The trusts may contain a power of advancement, and this may give the opportunity, if the trustees think fit, to resettle the funds on new trusts for the bereaved minor, for example to delay absolute entitlement until a later age than age 18. Any such continuing trusts will be within the relevant property trust regime with ten yearly charges applying, notwithstanding any interest in possession given to the beneficiary. In this respect therefore, bereaved minors trusts have an advantage over an absolute gift on bare trusts, payable at the age of 18.
- Under an Age 18-25 trust, an IHT exit charge applies where absolute entitlement is conferred after the beneficiary attains the age of 18, although often the amounts involved will not be substantial and the tax liability will be justified by enabling the trustees to have continuing control of the trust fund until the beneficiary is more mature. Capital gains tax hold over relief is also available.
- Where funds are left by will on age 18-25 trusts for the children of the deceased, it may be preferable to have trusts for accumulation of income up to the age of entitlement so as to ensure that the same tax treatment applies to all beneficiaries. Without such a provision, beneficiaries over the age of 18 at the date of death will have immediate post death interests and, although there will as a result be no IHT exit charge on their becoming absolutely entitled, capital gains tax hold over relief will not be available at that time. Note that the *Perpetuities and Accumulations Act 2009*

came into force on 6th April 2010 and all new trusts created on, or after, that date have a trust period of 125 years from the date of creation, regardless of what the trust document states. In addition, all such trusts can accumulate income for the entire trust period unless the trust document states otherwise. However the provisions of that Act apply only to wills executed on or after 6 April 2010 and hence older wills must be re-executed in order to benefit from the newly extended accumulation period.

47

Settlements: Trusts for Disabled Persons

Cross-reference. 43 SETTLEMENTS: DISCRETIONARY TRUSTS AND OTHER TRUSTS OF RELEVANT PROPERTY.

Simon's Taxes. See **I5.207**.

Other Sources. HMRC Customer Guide to Inheritance Tax; Foster, Part E6.26–6.28; IHTM04102.

Introduction

[47.1] Special provisions in the IHT legislation apply to trusts for disabled persons. The purpose of the provisions is to enable trusts to be set up in lifetime for the benefit of those within various categories of disability without a charge to IHT arising. The transfer into the trust will be potentially exempt and the trust assets will be in the estate of the beneficiary for IHT purposes.

Definitions

'Disabled person's interest'

For IHT purposes there are four categories of disabled person's interests. In broad terms they cover a discretionary settlement made for the benefit of a disabled person (as defined), a settlement made by a person ahead of impending disabilities, and an interest in possession trust made after 22 March 2006 for a disabled person, whether by a third party or by the disabled person as settlor. In more detail, a disabled person's interest for IHT purposes means:

(i) a deemed interest in possession to which a person is beneficially entitled under *IHTA 1984, s 89(2)* (discretionary trusts for disabled persons); or

(ii) an interest in possession to which a person is beneficially entitled under *IHTA 1984, s 89A(4)* (self-settlement by person expected to become disabled); or

(iii) any other interest in possession to which the disabled person is beneficially entitled where the property of the settlement was transferred into settlement on or after 22 March 2006 (see also note below concerning impact of *FA 2013*); or

(iv) an interest in possession in settled property, other than in (i) and (ii) above, to which 'A' is beneficially entitled where A is the settlor and was entitled to the property immediately before its settlement on or after 22 March 2006 and satisfies the Commissioners of HMRC that he had a condition at the time which it was reasonable to expect that it would lead to him becoming a disabled person within any of the catagories (i) (ii) or (iii) listed under the definition of disabled person below.

[*IHTA 1984, ss 89, 89A, 89B; FA 2006, Sch 20 para 6; FA 2013, Sch 44 para 10*].

For property transferred into trust on or after 17 July 2013 the definition at (iii) above is amended so that if any settled property is applied during the beneficiary's life for the benefit of a beneficiary, the amount must be applied for the benefit of the disabled person, save for an amount of £3,000 or 3% of the maximum value of the settled property in the tax year concerned, whichever is the lower. Unrestricted powers of advancement are also permissible. [*FA 2013, Sch 44 para 10*].

Definition of a 'Disabled person'

A '*disabled person*' is one who, when property was transferred into settlement, was:

(i) incapable by reason of mental disorder within the meaning of the *Mental Health Act 1983* (but amended by the *Mental Health Act 2007* from 19 July 2007 and reference is made to any disorder or disability of the mind) of administering his property or managing his affairs, or
(ii) in receipt of an attendance allowance under *Social Security Contributions and Benefits Act 1992, s 64* or *Social Security Contributions and Benefits (Northern Ireland) Act 1992, s 64*, or
(iii) in receipt of a disability living allowance under *Social Security Contributions and Benefits Act 1992, s 71* or *Social Security Contributions and Benefits (Northern Ireland) Act 1992, s 71* by virtue of entitlement to the care component at the highest or middle rate. See also Taxation Magazine, 27 July 2006, p 468.

With effect on or after 8 April 2013, a uniform definition of 'disabled person' applies across various taxes including inheritance tax. The definition is in *FA 2005, Sch 1A* and this includes the circumstances at (i), (ii) and (iii) set out above, and in addition:

(iv) a person in receipt of personal independence payment by virtue of entitlement to the daily living component;
(v) a person in receipt of constant attendance allowance;
(vi) a person in receipt of Armed Forces independence payment; or
(vii) a person in receipt of increased disablement pension.

The reference to disabled persons in *IHTA 1984, s 89(1)* from 22 March 2006 ignores the disallowance provisions relating to (ii) and (iii) above where the disabled person is in paid-for accommodation e.g. hospitalisation due to renal failure, or where the person is living outside the UK and would fail (ii) and (iii) above. [*IHTA 1984, s 89* as amended by *FA 2006, Sch 20, para 6(2)*].

Discretionary trusts for a disabled person

[47.2]

Where property is transferred prior to 8 April 2013 into settlement under which, during the life of a 'disabled person', no interest in possession subsists, and which secures that not less than half of the settled property which is applied during his life is applied for his benefit, then the disabled person is treated as beneficially entitled to an interest in possession in the property. [*IHTA 1984, s 89*]. With effect for trusts created on and after 8 April 2013, this 50 per cent rule no longer applies and it is required that all income must be applicable for the disabled person, subject powers to apply sums, whether capital or income, for the benefit of someone other than the disabled person up to an annual limit, which is the lower of £3,000 and 3% of the maximum value of the settled property in the period in question. This is an annual limit applicable for each tax year.

A settlement will not fall outside these provisions by reason only of the trustees' power of advancement contained in *Trustee Act 1925, s 32* or *Trustee Act (Northern Ireland) 1958, s 33*. With effect for trusts created on or after 8 April 2013, it will be permissible to extend the *Trustee Act 1925, s 32* power of advancement beyond 50 per cent of the fund without infringing the rules for disabled persons trusts. [*FA 2013, Sch 42 para 6*].

Example 1

On 1 July 2002 Q settled £50,000 in trust mainly for his disabled son P, but with power to apply property to his daughter S as follows:

1.1 I give to my Trustees on the trusts set out hereinafter the sum of £50,000.
  1.1.1 'the Trust Fund' means the assets at a particular time held by my Trustees on the trusts set out in . . . .
  1.1.2 'my other Beneficiaries' means: my children other than . . . . [P's name]. . . . .
1.2 My Trustees shall hold the Trust Fund on the following trusts:
  1.2.1 During the lifetime of . . . . [P's name]. . . . .
    (a) to apply the capital of the Trust Fund for the benefit of . . . . [P's name]. . . . . and my other Beneficiaries as my Trustees think fit so long as not less than half of any capital applied is for the benefit of. . . . . [P's name]. . . . . ;
    (b) to have the power to accumulate the whole of any part of the income arising from the Trust Fund and to apply any income not accumulated solely for the benefit of . . . . [P's name]. . . . .
  1.2.2 After the death of . . . . [P's name]. . . . . :
    (a) to apply the capital of the Trust Fund for the benefit of such of my other Beneficiaries as my Trustees think fit;
    (b) to apply the income of the Trust Fund for the benefit of such of my other Beneficiaries as my Trustees think fit or to accumulate the whole or any part of it;
    (c) within . . . . [Year(s)]. . . . . of . . . . [P's name]. . . . . death to end these trusts by distributing the Trust Fund among such Beneficiaries as my Trustees think fit.
1.3 My Trustees shall have the following powers: . . . ' *Details of Trustees' powers continue*

On 1 January 2011 the trustees advanced £5,000 gross to S on her marriage.

IIP treatment

If the trust secures that not less than half the settled property which is applied during P's life is applied for his benefit, then P is treated as beneficially entitled to an interest in possession in the settled property. The transfer to S is a potentially exempt transfer which may become chargeable in the event of P's death within seven years of the transfer. The gift in consideration of marriage exemption applies (£1,000 on a gift from brother to sister) subject to the required notice. See **42.9** SETTLEMENTS WITH INTERESTS IN POSSESSION for an example of a notice under *IHTA 1984, s 57(3)* and the deed of release.

Otherwise, the trust is discretionary and the IHT liability, if any, would be calculated under the rules applying to settlements without interests in possession.

Property settled after 21 March 2006

[47.3] From 22 March 2006 where a person (designated 'A' in the legislation) transfers property into a settlement and that person was beneficially entitled to the property immediately before transferring it and satisfies the Commissioners of HMRC that he had a condition at the time which it was reasonable to expect that it would lead to him becoming a disabled person as defined for the purposes of *IHTA 1984, s 89* (see above) and the property is held on trusts that do not give 'A' during his lifetime an interest in possession then 'A' is treated as beneficially entitled to an interest in possession. Assumptions as to entitlement to state benefits may be made as detailed in *IHTA 1984, s 89A(5)*. Certain protective trusts may also qualify.

In addition, two conditions must apply:

- the requirement that if any of the settled property is applied during A's lifetime for the benefit of a beneficiary, it is applied for the benefit of A; and
- any power to terminate the trusts during the lifetime of A or another person is such that A or another person will have an absolute entitlement to, or a *disabled person's interest* subsisting in, the settled property. See also Fosters Inheritance Tax, para E6.29.

With effect for trusts created on and after 8 April 2013, it is required that all income must be applicable for the disabled person, subject powers to apply sums, whether capital or income, for the benefit of someone other than the disabled person up to an annual limit, which is the lower of £3,000 and 3% of the maximum value of the settled property in the period in question. This is an annual limit applicable for each tax year.

A settlement will not fall outside these provisions by reason only of the trustees' power of advancement contained in the *Trustee Act 1925, s 32* or *Trustee Act (Northern Ireland) 1958, s 33*. With effect for trusts created on or after 8 April 2013, it will be permissible to extend the *Trustee Act 1925, s 32* power of advancement beyond 50 per cent of the fund without infringing the rules for disabled persons trusts: [*FA 2013, Sch 42 para 6. IHTA 1984, s 89A*].

Mental Capacity Act 2005

The *Mental Capacity Act 2005* was brought into effect from April 2007 to protect those who lack mental capacity and introduces Lasting Powers of Attorney which replace the current Enduring Powers of Attorney and will cover financial decisions. Under *Mental Capacity Act 2005, s 18* there is a list of the actions that the appointed 'deputy' can take with regard to the subject of the Lasting Power of Attorney's financial affairs which include drawing up a will, carrying on a trade, discharging debts, contractual matters, etc. There are certain stipulations regarding the suitability of the person (referred to as the 'donee') acting on the individual's behalf such that the individual (or Trust Corporation) must be 18 years or over, not a bankrupt and cannot appoint a successor.

Example 2

On 31 July 2010 X who is British and is physically disabled but currently resides in Ireland settles £360,000 from liability insurance payments into a disabled trust for his benefit in the future. X who intends to return to the UK would have qualified for receipt of a disability living allowance under *Social Security Contributions and Benefits Act 1992, s 71* by virtue of entitlement to the care component at the highest rate (see Note D below) due to severe disability. Despite not qualifying for disability benefit because of not being resident for the relevant period X is still able to set up a trust and benefit from both the CGT and IHT advantages attaching to such settlements of property so that after seven years the £360,000 will effectively drop out of account for cumulation purposes. See (C) below.

Notes to the example

(A) Prior to 22 March 2006 the transfer into trust would not have qualified as a trust for disabled persons within *IHTA 1984, s 89* but following the amendments in *FA 2006, Sch 20 para 6(2)* the residence conditions of *Social Security Contributions and Benefits Act 1992, s 71(6)* are treated as if they were fulfilled.

(B) Similarly, if a disabled person's entitlement to attendance allowance is restricted because of *Social Security Contributions and Benefits Act 1992, s 64(1)* requirements of residence but the person would have qualified for attendance allowance then from 22 March 2006 the settlement may notwithstanding this be allowed as a trust for disabled person.

(C) The IHT advantages are that the gift into the disabled trust is treated as a PET but the disabled beneficiary is deemed to have an interest in possession so that on death of the disabled person the funds in the disabled trust will be amalgamated with the free estate for IHT purposes. The *FA 2006, Sch 20* amendments merely ensure that the beneficial treatment of IIP designation continues. See below for the position after 21 March 2006. [*IHTA 1984, ss 3A, 3B; FA 2006, Sch 20 paras 6, 9*].

(D) The highest rate applies where the individual is so physically or mentally disabled that he/she requires:

  (1) frequent attention throughout the day in connection with bodily functions, or continual supervision throughout the day to avoid substantial danger to them or others; and

  (2) prolonged or repeated attention at night in connection with bodily functions, or in order to avoid substantial danger to themselves or

others he/she requires another person to be awake at night for a prolonged period or at frequent intervals to watch them; or

(3) he/she is terminally ill.

Example 3

On 31 July 2010 X, who is in the early stages of dementia and currently resides in a care home, settles £300,000 into discretionary trust for his benefit in the future. X has been assessed by the care home at which he is registered to attend as Elderly Mentally Incapable (EMI). The trust qualifies as a settlement under *s 89A* because X's present condition advancing from dementia to Alzheimer's satisfies the criteria of the definition of a disabled person within *IHTA 1984, s 89(4)* that is required. The trust has been set up by X in conjunction with MENCAP. See *Mental Health Act 2007,* and also Note (A) below. See also *Masterman-Lister v Brutton & Co*, CA [2003] WTLR 259; CA [2003] All ER (D) 59 (Jan). See **58** TAX CASES.

X is treated as beneficially entitled to an interest in possession in the settled property. The transfer into settlement of the property would be a potentially exempt transfer which may become chargeable in the event of the donor's death within seven years of the transfer, but as it is X himself making the transfer it is not chargeable for IHT purposes. See (A) below and **42.9** SETTLEMENTS WITH INTERESTS IN POSSESSION for an example of a notice under *IHTA 1984, s 57(3)* and the deed of release.

Notes to the example

(A) In certain cases such as the example above it is often difficult to ensure that relatives or acquaintances have sufficient knowledge or time to act as trustees to the disabled trust. In these cases it is often possible to obtain independent trusteeship from a commercial organisation and one such as the Mencap Trust Company Ltd may be chosen. See http://www.mencap.org.uk. There is some dispute as to whether a transfer into a trust for a disabled person is a PET, a non-chargeable transfer or an exempt transfer. See *Taxation* magazine, 30 September 2004 and also *Foster's Inheritance Tax*, para E6.29. HMRC have confirmed in a letter that:

> 'Lifetime transfers into settlements for the disabled, that satisfy the conditions laid down in section 89, Inheritance Tax Act 1984, are indeed covered by the provisions of section 11, Inheritance Tax Act 1984. Accordingly such dispositions are not transfers of value if these conditions – depending on which apply – are satisfied. It follows that such dispositions do not require to be reported, at any time, to any office of Capital Taxes.'

HMRC reiterate that the provision must be 'reasonable provision for his care or maintenance' within *IHTA 1984, s 11(3)* and of course this is a subjective matter.

(B) Under *TCGA 1992, Sch 1 para 1* (see quotation below) the settlement will qualify for a CGT annual exemption of half the annual amount but settlements for disabled beneficiaries take the full allowance.

(C) Where the disabled person's disability may fluctuate so that entitlement to the disability living allowance changes between the lower and middle care component entitlement above then provided the beneficiary qualifies at the time at which the funds are given into trust then a subsequent reduced entitlement to the disability living allowance will not change the status of the trust. For instance, in the case of the example above medication may result in a marked improvement in a disabled beneficiary's mental health.

Capital gains implications

In respect of the counter measures within *TCGA 1992, s 226A* to prevent exploitation of the interaction between private residence relief and gifts relief for CGT these measures do not apply in the case of beneficiaries of trusts for disabled persons as *IHTA 1984, s 89* provides that a beneficiary of such a settlement has an interest in possession in the settled property. As a consequence of this, any transfer to such a trust is a potentially exempt transfer for IHT purposes and does not fall within *TCGA 1992, s 260* gifts holdover relief. [*TCGA 1992, s 226A inserted by FA 2004, Sch 22 para 6*].

Transfers into trusts for disabled persons

[47.4] In relation to transfers of value made, and other events occurring, after 17 March 1986, a gift by an individual into a trust for a disabled person, is a potentially exempt transfer subject to the transfer not being primarily exempt under *IHTA 1984, s 11* i.e. dispositions for family maintenance. In addition, in relation to transfers of value made, and other events occurring, after 16 March 1987, a potentially exempt transfer occurs where an individual disposes of or terminates his beneficial interest in settled property by gift and on that event the property is settled on disabled trusts. Provided the transferor survives seven years or more from the date of the original gift, the gift is exempt for inheritance tax purposes. See **38** POTENTIALLY EXEMPT TRANSFERS for further details. [*IHTA 1984, ss 3A, 3B; FA 1986, Sch 19 para 1; F(No 2)A 1987, s 96; FA 2006, Sch 20 para 9*].

Property settled before 10 March 1981

[47.5] Where property was transferred into a settlement before 10 March 1981 and is held on trusts under which there is no interest in possession but the property is to be applied only or mainly for the benefit of a disabled person within **47.1**(i)–(iii) above during his life, then there is a charge to tax

(a) where it ceases to be settled property otherwise than by being applied for the benefit of the disabled person (but see also **21.4, 21.6–21.8** EXEMPT TRANSFERS for certain situations where there is no charge when property becomes held for charitable purposes only without limit of time or the property of a qualifying political party or a national body mentioned in *IHTA 1984, Sch 3* or, under certain conditions, a body not established or conducted for profit), or

(b) if the trustees make a 'disposition' otherwise than for the benefit of the disabled person which reduces the value of the settled property. *Disposition* includes an omission to exercise a right (unless not deliberate), which is treated as made at the latest time that the right could be exercised.

Where no charge arises

No charge arises:

(i) if, under (b) above, the trustees do not intend to confer gratuitous benefit and either the transaction is at arm's length between persons not connected with each other (see **12** CONNECTED PERSONS) or is such as might be expected in such a transaction; or

(ii) if, under (b) above, the disposition is a grant of tenancy of agricultural property in the UK, Channel Islands or Isle of Man, for use for agricultural purposes and is made for full consideration in money or money's worth; or

(iii) on the payment of costs or expenses attributable to the property; or

(iv) where any payment is, or will be, income for income tax purposes of any person (or, in the case of a person not resident in the UK, would be if he were so resident); or

(v) in respect of a liability to make a payment under (iii) or (iv) above.

'*Payment*' includes the transfer of assets other than money.

[*IHTA 1984, ss 63, 70(3)(4), 74(3)*].

Amount on which tax is charged

Tax is charged on the amount by which the trust property is less immediately after the event giving rise to the charge than it would have been but for the event (i.e. the loss to the donor principle), grossed-up where the settlement pays the tax.

The rate at which tax is charged is the aggregate of the following percentages for each complete successive quarter in 'the relevant period':

	Cumulative Total
0.25% for each of the first 40 quarters	10%
0.20% for each of the next 40 quarters	8%
0.15% for each of the next 40 quarters	6%
0.10% for each of the next 40 quarters	4%
0.05% for each of the next 40 quarters	2%
Maximum rate chargeable after 50 years	30%

The rate charged may be reduced if any of the property is, or was, EXCLUDED PROPERTY (20), see **47.5** below.

Definitions

'*Relevant period*' is the period beginning with the day on which the property became (or last became) held on trusts for disabled persons or 13 March 1975 if later, and ending on the day before the chargeable event.

'*Quarter*' means any period of three months.

[*IHTA 1984, ss 63, 70(5)(6)(8), 74(3)*].

Excluded property

[47.6] Where the whole or part of the amount on which tax is charged as in 47.5 above is attributable to property which was EXCLUDED PROPERTY (20) at any time during the relevant period, then, in determining the rate at which tax is charged in respect of that amount or part, no quarter throughout which the property was excluded property is to be counted. [*IHTA 1984, ss 70(7), 74(3)*].

[*IHTA 1984, ss 74(1)(2)(4), 76*].

Example 4

In 1968 Q settled £50,000 in trust mainly for his disabled son P, but with power to apply property to his daughter S. On 1 January 2011 the trustees advanced £5,000 gross to S on her marriage.

There will be a charge to IHT on the payment to S

The relevant period is the period from settlement of the funds or, if later, 13 March 1975, to 1 January 2010, i.e. 139 complete quarters.

The rate of IHT is the aggregate of:

0.25% for each of the first	40	quarters	10.00%
0.20% for each of the next	40	quarters	8.00%
0.15% for each of the next	40	quarters	6.00%
0.10% for each of the next	23	quarters	2.30%
	143		26.30%

IHT payable is £5,000 × 26.30% = £1,315

Key points

[47.7] Points to consider are as follows.

- Disabled trusts are not simply for those who one might commonly regard as disabled, for example those with mobility difficulties. The trusts apply equally to anyone in receipt of attendance allowance, a Social Security benefit available to persons who are usually elderly but not necessarily having apparent disabled status. For such persons therefore old style interest in possession trusts may still be created, and the various IHT planning techniques available with such trusts may still be entered into.

  Where a person knows he/she will become disabled he/she may set up a settlement for themselves and as a consequence of this there will be no ten-yearly charge, exit charge, etc. but the assets will be treated as an aggregation with their other assets for IHT purposes. In order to qualify as a self-settlement the following must apply:

  (i) during the life of that disabled person there must not be an IIP in the settled property;

(ii) if trust property is applied for anyone's benefit it must be for the disabled person only;

(iii) if there is a power to terminate the trusts during the life of the disabled person then the disabled person (or another) will be absolutely entitled to the assets and *IHTA 1984, s 89B(1)(a)* or (c) arises. *Section 89B(1)(a)* states 'an interest in possession to which a person is under *s 89(2)* above treated as beneficially entitled' and (c) states 'an interest in possession in settled property (other than an interest within paragraph (a). . .'.

- There are a number of occasions where vulnerable persons who are not within the definition of *incapable by reason of mental disorder* within the meaning of the *Mental Health Act 1983* (but amended by the *Mental Health Act 2007* to any disorder or disability of the mind) of administering his property or managing his affairs but are vulnerable and different trusts may be considered as follows.

(i) Persons with irrational or compulsive behaviour who may be prone to irrational behaviour particularly with large sums of inherited money would be better suited to a life interest trust, preferably an IPDI or a discretionary trust. See **27** INTEREST IN POSSESSION and **42** SETTLEMENTS WITH INTERESTS IN POSSESSION.

(ii) Persons who have received large amounts of compensation may also be vulnerable to a variety of 'unscrupulous' offers of advice and again a self-settled life interest or discretionary trust would be appropriate. See **41** SETTLEMENTS WITH INTEREST IN POSSESSION and **42** SETTLEMENTS WITH INTERESTS IN POSSESSION. Or:

(iii) Persons whose concerns for heirs who are financially vulnerable or are disabled but not within *Mental Health Act 1983, s 1* and in receipt of Government funded means benefits which would be restricted should they receive a lump sum then a discretionary trust would be appropriate. See **42** SETTLEMENTS WITH INTERESTS IN POSSESSION.

48

Shares and Securities

Cross-reference. See **11** CLOSE COMPANIES.

Simon's Taxes. See **D6.617, I7.102, I7.103.**

Other Sources. HMRC Customer Guide to Inheritance Tax; SVD 1 'Shares Valuation Division'; Foster, Part H3; IHTM18000.

Definitions

[48.1] In relation to transfers of value made, and other events occurring, after 16 March 1987, '*quoted*' in relation to any shares or securities, means quoted on a recognised stock exchange. Up to 1996 it also included shares quoted on the erstwhile Unlisted Securities Market. '*Unquoted*', in relation to any shares or securities, means neither so quoted nor so dealt in. Shares on the London Alternative Investment Market (AIM) are unquoted for this purpose but if shares dealt in on AIM are also listed on a recognised stock exchange overseas, they will not be 'unquoted' and will not qualify for business property relief. Therefore a check should be made that AIM-listed shares are not listed elsewhere but also see **48.5** below. [*IHTA 1984, s 272; FA 1987, s 58(2), Sch 8 para 17*]. As from 1 April 1996 the word '*quoted*' on a recognised stock exchange is substituted by the word '*listed*'. [*FA 1996, Sch 38 para 2*]. In IHT 110 the definition of '*quoted*' and '*unquoted*' respectively are as follows:

> 'This means a company that is listed on a recognised stock exchange. This includes shares traded on the American NASDAQ and European EASDAQ for chargeable events after 9 March 1992.'

and

> 'This means a company that is not listed on a recognised stock exchange. Some companies although they are listed in the Stock Exchange Daily Official List are still "unquoted" for business relief.

This includes shares

- shares listed on the Alternative Investment Market (AIM)
- shares listed on the Unlisted Securities Market (USM), there are some complicated rules that apply to chargeable events before 10 March 1992. You should telephone our Helpline if the transferor owned shares listed on the USM and the date of the chargeable event, is before 10 March 1992.'

The above definition applies for all IHT purposes except that, in relation to transfers of value made, and other events occurring, after 9 March 1992, an alternative definition, whereby Unlisted Securities Market shares and securities are treated as unquoted, applies for the purposes of defining relevant business property (see **6.4** BUSINESS PROPERTY) and payment by instalments (see **35.5** PAYMENT OF TAX).

In relation to transfers of value made, and other events occurring, before 17 March 1987, shares and securities in companies dealt in on the Unlisted Securities Market were not treated as 'quoted on a recognised stock exchange' for all IHT purposes (Inland Revenue Statement of Practice SP 18/80, 23 December 1980). For amendment to the term 'recognised stock exchange' see **6.4** BUSINESS PROPERTY. Whilst *FA 2007* inserted new definitions of 'recognised stock exchange' for the purposes of income tax and capital gains tax the change did not include inheritance tax. However, it may be that in the future the inheritance tax definition will fall into line with the *FA 2007* changes. [*ITA 2007, s 1005; FA 2007, s 109, Sch 26 paras 1, 3, 4*].

See also **56.24** VALUATION.

Agricultural and business property reliefs

[48.2] Controlling shares in agricultural companies may attract AGRICULTURAL PROPERTY (4) relief.

Shares and securities in companies carrying on a business may attract BUSINESS PROPERTY (6) relief.

Payment of tax by instalments

[48.3] Under certain conditions, inheritance tax on shares and securities transferred may be paid by annual instalments over ten years, see **35.5–35.9** PAYMENT OF TAX for details.

Related property

[48.4] See **56.21** VALUATION.

Sales within one year after death

[48.5] Special provisions apply, see 56.26 VALUATION. Also, investments on the stock exchanges described in the list at IHTM34140 as qualifying investments for the purposes of loss on sale of shares relief.

Transfers within seven years before death

[48.6] See 53 TRANSFERS WITHIN SEVEN YEARS BEFORE DEATH for special provisions.

Trading companies

[48.7] Controlling shares or securities or a minority holding of unquoted shares may attract BUSINESS PROPERTY (6) relief.

Valuation

[48.8] See 56.24 VALUATION for valuation of quoted and unquoted shares and securities. See also http://www.voa.gov.uk.

Purchase by company of own shares

[48.9] A payment by an *unquoted trading* company (or *holding company* of a trading group) on the purchase, redemption or repayment of its own shares is not treated as a distribution if the price received from the company is used to meet the recipient's inheritance tax liability on a death. Substantially the whole of the payment (apart from any sum applied in paying capital gains tax on the purchase etc.) must be used for this purpose within two years of the death. The IHT liability must be one which could not be met without undue hardship otherwise than by means of such purchase etc. [*ICTA 1988, s 219*].

An *unquoted company* is one which has none of its shares listed in the official list of a stock exchange and which is not a 51% subsidiary of a company so listed.

A *trading company* is one whose business consists wholly or mainly of the carrying on of a trade or trades, excluding dealing in shares, securities, land or futures.

A *holding company* is one whose business, disregarding any trade carried on by it, consists wholly or mainly in the holding of shares or securities of one or more companies which are its 75% subsidiaries. [*ICTA 1988, s 229*].

Certain changes in company law have enabled listed companies to acquire their own shares as well as hold or dispose of them. *FA 2003, s 195* treats own shares held without cancellation as if they were cancelled for tax purposes. Up until the change in the treatment of listed companies in the *FA 2003* concerning the purchase by a company of its own shares the relieving provisions of *ICTA 1988, s 219* did not apply to listed companies. However, the change now secures equal treatment so that a payment by a *listed* company on the purchase, redemption or repayment of its own shares is not treated as a distribution if the price received from the company is used to meet the recipient's inheritance tax liability on a death. [*ICTA 1988, s 219; FA 2003, s 195*].

HMRC have refused to confirm that either a purchase etc. of a company's own shares or the alteration to any Articles of Association to enable it to make such a purchase etc. will not give rise to a transfer of value under *IHTA 1984, s 94* (tax charge on close company participators—see **11.8** CLOSE COMPANIES). (CCAB Memorandum, 22 June 1982).

49

Situs

Cross-reference. See **20** EXCLUDED PROPERTY.

Simon's Taxes. See **I9.329, I9.4**.

Introduction

[49.1] As the inheritance tax legislation contains no specific rules for determining whether property is or is not situated in the UK, the general law situs rules apply. It is important to note that the *Finance (No 2) Act 2005* included new rules for the determination of situs relevant for CGT purposes and whilst the new provisions do not affect the position for IHT it may be a precursor for future changes regarding non-domiciliaries and the situs of their assets. [*F(No 2)A 2005, s 34, Sch 4*].

Assets	**Location/situs**
Registered shares and securities.	Situated where they are registered unless transferable in more than one country when they are situated in the one in which they would be likely to be dealt with in the ordinary course of affairs. (*Standard Chartered Bank Ltd v CIR* Ch D, [1978] STC 272; *Treasurer for Ontario v Aberdein* PC 1946, [1947] AC 24; *R v Williams and Another* PC, [1942] 22 All ER 95).
Renounceable letters of allotment.	Shares in UK private companies have been held to be situated in the UK. (*Young and Another v Phillips* Ch D 1984, 58 TC 232).

Bearer shares and securities.	Situated in the country in which the certificate of title is kept. (*Winans and Another v A-G (No 2)* HL 1909, [1910] AC 27).

Interests in land and chattels

[49.2] Situs depends upon actual physical situation. However, *ships* are situated where registered unless within UK territorial or national waters when this is displaced by the actual situs. (*The Trustees Executors and Agency Co Ltd v CIR* Ch D 1972, [1973] 1 All ER 563). Agricultural land and woodland situated within the European Economic Area (EEA) from 22 April 2009 onwards qualifies now for existing reliefs. [*FA 2009, s 122(4); Interpretation Act 1978, Sch 1*].

For IHT purposes the application of extra-statutory concession F7 'Foreign owned works of art' ensures that even though a work of art is in the UK temporarily for cleaning or restoration or for a loan to a public exhibition by a non-UK domicile and a chargeable event arises then no charge to tax arises. This concession on the usual situs rules is perhaps designed to ensure that those owners of art works that are domiciled abroad do not remove valuable works of art from this country in fear of a tax charge arising out of the temporary situs in the UK of the work of art at a time of a chargeable event. See HMRC EXTRA-STATUTORY CONCESSIONS (23).

Debts

[49.3] Generally, a simple contract debt is situated where the debtor resides (*Kwok Chi Leung Karl v Commissioner of Estate Duty* PC, [1988] STC 728). However, if there is more than one country of residence the terms of the contract may serve to localise the debt. (*New York Life Insurance Co Ltd v Public Trustee* CA, [1924] 2 Ch 101). A specialty debt has been regarded as situated where the bond or specialty is kept. (*Royal Trust Co v A-G for Alberta* PC 1929, [1930] AC 144), but on 23 January 2013 HMRC published an amendment to para 27079 of its IHT Manual to state that they now regard a specialty debt as situate where the debtor resides. A debt owed by a bank (e.g. bank account) is situated at the branch where it is primarily recoverable. (*R v Lovitt*, [1912] AC 212). A judgment debt is situated where the judgment is recorded.

Other assets

[49.4] See also 20.6 EXCLUDED PROPERTY for foreign pensions and 35.24 PAYMENT OF TAX for foreign-owned works of art temporarily in the UK.

Double taxation agreements

[49.5] A double taxation agreement may determine where property is to be treated as situated for IHT purposes. [*IHTA 1984, s 158(1)*].

Inter-American development bank

[49.6] Securities issued by this Bank are treated as situated outside the UK. [*FA 1976, s 131*].

International organisations

[49.7] Securities issued by certain international organisations may be designated by the Treasury as being situated outside the UK for IHT purposes. The Asian Development Bank, the African Development Bank, the three European Communities and the European Investment Bank have been so designated. [*ICTA 1988, s 324 now repealed and replaced by ITTOIA 2005, s 774; FA 1985, s 96; SI 1984/1215; SI 1984/1634; SI 1985/1172*].

Key points

[49.8] Points to consider are as follows.

- The location of assets is key after establishing situs for IHT purposes. Worldwide assets situs is relevant for UK domiciled individuals and only UK situated assets held by non-UK domiciled individuals come within chargeability (and overseas assets are excluded). Table of asset locations:

Asset	Location/situs
Land, buildings and leases including any share in land or a building.	Where the land is physically situated.
Registered shares and securities (but see Government stocks above).	Where the shares or securities are registered or traded.
An interest in an unincorporated business or an interest in a partnership.	Where the business is carried out.
Chattels and personal possessions.	Where the item is situated at the time of the transfer or at the date of death.
Debts owed to the deceased.	Where the debtor lives at the time of transfer or on death.
Bank accounts.	Where the bank or branch holding the account is situated.

- As stated above situs depends upon actual physical situation. However, *ships* are situated where registered unless within UK territorial or national waters when this is displaced by the actual situs. In this latter case ownership and therefore as a consequence situs may change due to a declaration of trust which may be created orally as well as by deed. Because of an express declaration of trust a boat's situs may change due to the fact that actual situs i.e. in UK, is displaced by a declaration of trust to whereby a non-domiciled individual obtains ownership and the boat is re-registered abroad thereby effecting a change in situs and chargeability to IHT. See also *Rowe v Prance* [1999] 2 FLR 787.

50

Time Limits

In some cases the periods can be extended at the discretion of HMRC. See HMRC Customer Guide to Inheritance Tax; IHTM30151–30159.

Simon's Taxes. See **I11.2, I11.3, I11.4.**

Time limits of one year or less

[50.1] Time limits of one year or less are treated as follows:

(a) **30 days**
- (i) Appeal against a notice of determination. See **14.3** DETERMINATIONS AND APPEALS. From 1 April 2009 onwards where HMRC offer a review under the rules of the new Tax Chamber of the First-tier Tribunal, the taxpayer has 30 days in which to accept the offer. See **14.13** DETERMINATIONS AND APPEALS.
- (ii) Stated case from Special Commissioners, request. See **14.8** DETERMINATIONS AND APPEALS. For the position from 1 April 2009 regarding Tax Chamber First-tier Tribunal rules see **14.13** DETERMINATIONS AND APPEALS.
- (iii) Information must be furnished if requested by the Board. See **2.17** ACCOUNTS AND RETURNS.
- (iv) Appeal against an information notice issued by HMRC. See **2.17** ACCOUNTS AND RETURNS.

(b) **Three months**
- (i) Return to be made, in certain circumstances, by professional advisers acting for settlors. See **2.16** ACCOUNTS AND RETURNS.

(c) **Six months**
- (i) With effect from 6 April 2014, accounts to be delivered for charges in relation to relevant property trusts. Also, accounts to be delivered after ending of conditional exemption for works of art, historic buildings etc. and disposal of woodlands. See **2.14** ACCOUNTS AND RETURNS.
- (ii) Board may call for an account following an 'excepted termination'. See **2.11** ACCOUNTS AND RETURNS.

(iii) Corrective and supplementary accounts to be delivered after discovery of defect. See **2.15** ACCOUNTS AND RETURNS. This limit applies also in cases of innocent reporting errors where the CTO do not seek a penalty.

(iv) Payment of tax. Normal due date after end of month in which chargeable transfer occurs. See **35.1** PAYMENT OF TAX.

(v) A scheme administrator of an Alternatively Secured Pension (ASP) has six months from the end of the month in which he becomes aware or discovers the scheme member's death to pay IHT due. See **37.2** PENSION SCHEMES.

(d) **Twelve months**

(i) Delivery of accounts after lifetime transfers, transfers on death and transfers by trustees of settlements. See **2.14** ACCOUNTS AND RETURNS. A consultation document issued by HMRC on 6 June 2014 contains proposals to introduce new time limits with effect from 5 April 2015 in relation to relevant property trusts.

(ii) Valuation reduced for certain quoted shares if sold for less within twelve months after death. See **56.26** VALUATION.

(iii) Waiver of dividends within previous twelve months before any right accrues is not a transfer of value. See **51.1** TRANSFER OF VALUE.

(iv) Unused portion of annual exemption can be utilised against transfers during following twelve months. See **21.13** EXEMPT TRANSFERS.

(v) In relation to transfers of value made, and other events occurring, before 30 November 1993, property which is the subject of a lifetime transfer for which agricultural or business property relief is claimed but which is subsequently disposed of by the transferee, must be replaced by similar property within twelve months of the disposal. See **4.5** AGRICULTURAL PROPERTY and **6.11** BUSINESS PROPERTY.

(vi) A scheme administrator of an ASP has twelve months from the end of the month in which he becomes aware or discovers the scheme member's death to file a return. See **37.2** PENSION SCHEMES.

Two-year time limits

[50.2] Two-year time limits are treated as follows:

(a) Variations and disclaimers of dispositions on death are valid if made within two years after death. See **13** DEEDS OF VARIATION AND DISCLAIMERS.

(b) Woodlands. Election after a death to defer tax on trees and underwood. However, woodlands relief from 22 April 2009 onwards applying to property in the European Economic Area (EEA) and any IHT due from 23 April 2003 will become eligible for relief by claim from 21 April 2010. See **57.1** WOODLANDS.

(c) Scottish executors may elect to pay tax, ignoring legitim. See **52.19** TRANSFERS ON DEATH.

(d) Heritage property. A claim for conditional exemption on or after 17 March 1998 relating to death or other transfers and heritage property held in a discretionary trust. See **33.3** NATIONAL HERITAGE.
(e) Heritage property. A claim for exemption for transfers into maintenance funds for historic buildings, etc. See **33.3** NATIONAL HERITAGE and **8.5** CAPITAL GAINS TAX.
(f) Claims for the transfer of the nil rate band from the end of the month in which the survivor dies or (if it ends later) three months beginning with the date on which the personal representatives begin to act. See **21.10** EXEMPT TRANSFERS.

Three-year time limits

[50.3] Three-year time limits are treated as follows:

(a) Penalties. No proceedings by Board after notification of tax payable. See **36.9** PENALTIES.
(b) Valuation reduced for land or 'related property' sold for less within three years (four years in certain cases) after death. See **56.9** and **56.22** VALUATION.
(c) Woodlands. Expenses of replanting trees and underwood within three years after disposal are deductible. See **57.4** WOODLANDS.
(d) In relation to transfers of value made, and other events occurring, after 29 November 1993, property which is the subject of a lifetime transfer for which agricultural or business property relief is claimed but which is subsequently disposed of by the transferee, must be replaced by similar property within three years of the disposal. See **4.5** AGRICULTURAL PROPERTY and **6.11** BUSINESS PROPERTY.

Four-year time limit

[50.4] A four-year time limit is treated as follows:

(a) Repayment of tax overpaid claimable. See **35.20** PAYMENT OF TAX.
(b) Claims. Normal limit where not otherwise specified.

Five-year time limit

[50.5] A five-year time limit is treated as follows:

(a) Quick succession relief is available. See **39.1** QUICK SUCCESSION RELIEF.

Twenty-five year time limit

[50.6] A twenty-five year time limit is treated as follows:

(a) Interests in certain accumulation and maintenance trusts [now age 18–25 trusts] must vest within twenty-five years of creation of settlement. See **44.4**(c) SETTLEMENTS: ACCUMULATION AND MAINTENANCE TRUSTS.

Sunset time limits

[50.7] Sunset time limits are treated as follows:

(a) Election by the former owner of a pre-owned asset(s) for the asset(s) to be treated for IHT purposes as if it were a gift with reservation under existing rules is on or before 'the relevant filing date'. The relevant filing date means 31 January in the year of assessment that immediately follows the initial year but following *FA 2007, s 66* the filing date may be later if in a particular case the officer of Revenue and Customs allows. In most cases this will be 31 January 2007, but HMRC do give examples of circumstances where the late election option may be appropriate at http://www.hmrc.gov.uk/poa/late-election-guidance.htm. [*FA 2004, Sch 15 para 23*]. See **22.1** GIFTS WITH RESERVATION.

(b) Non-disclosure in connection with undeclared funds in estate returns incurring no additional IHT penalties was 30 September 2003. See also **36.11** PENALTIES.

(c) The New Disclosure Opportunity (NDO) and Liechtenstein Disclosure Facility (LDF) follow the previous Offshore Disclosure Facility on 2007 and can apply for IHT purposes. The NDO facility notification period was extended to 31 January 2010 for all paper and before 12 March 2010 for online notifications. The deadline for the LDF is 31 March 2015. See also **5.7** ANTI-AVOIDANCE.

51

Transfer of Value

Cross-references. See **9** CHARGEABLE TRANSFER; **19** ESTATE; **21** EXEMPT TRANSFERS.

Simon's Taxes. See **I3.1, I3.342, I4.151.**

Other Sources. HMRC Customer Guide to Inheritance Tax; Foster, Part C1; IHTM04000.

Introduction

[51.1] A transfer of value is any disposition (see **51.2** below) made by a *person* ('the transferor') as a result of which the value of his estate immediately after the disposition is less than it would be but for the disposition; and the amount by which it is less is the value transferred by the transfer. No account is taken of the value of EXCLUDED PROPERTY (**20**), which ceases to form part of a person's estate as a result of a disposition. References in *IHTA 1984* to a transfer of value made include references to events on the happening of which tax is chargeable *as if* a transfer of value had been made. [*IHTA 1984, s 3(1)(2)(4)*].

In *CIR v Eversden* [2003] STC 822 the Court of Appeal held that 'rightly or wrongly . . . . the draftsmen clearly did find it possible to equate a disposal by way of gift with a transfer of value'. This suggests that the two terms have a similar meaning.

The reduction in the transferor's estate will include any inheritance tax (but no other tax or duty or expenses of sale) borne by him on the value transferred. [*IHTA 1984, s 5(4)*]. For individuals, the 'net' value transferred, i.e. after taking account of any EXEMPT TRANSFERS (**21**), is grossed-up at the appropriate tax rate (see **7** CALCULATION OF TAX and **40** RATES OF TAX) when the transferor bears the tax (but not when the transferee pays it) in order to obtain the CHARGEABLE TRANSFER (**9**). If the transferee bears any related capital gains tax or incidental expenses (e.g. professional fees, stamp duties etc.) relating to the transfer, the value transferred is reduced by those charges. The reduction for capital gains tax applies to settled property only if the tax on the gain accruing to the trustees is borne by a person who becomes absolutely entitled to the settled property concerned. [*IHTA 1984, ss 164, 165*].

No transfer of value in the following circumstances

The following circumstances result in no transfer of value for IHT purposes:

(a) **Grant of agricultural tenancies.** See **4.15** AGRICULTURAL PROPERTY. See also **4.17** for the transfer of Scottish agricultural leases.

(b) **Waiver of remuneration** (including the repayment of remuneration already received) if such remuneration would otherwise have been subject to income tax as employment income [formerly Schedule E] and is not allowable as a deduction to the employer for purposes of income tax and corporation tax. [*IHTA 1984, s 14; ITEPA 2003, s 7*]. The employment income assessment must not have become final, the remuneration must be formally waived (usually by deed) and the employer's profits or allowable losses must be adjusted accordingly. (Inland Revenue Press Release 11 November 1975).

(c) **Waiver of dividends** by any person provided the waiver is within twelve months *before* any right to the dividend has accrued does not by itself make a transfer of value. [*IHTA 1984, s 15*]. See IHTM04052 regarding the use of the word 'person'.

Disposition

[51.2] Disposition is not defined in absolute terms but is thought to include payments of money, transfers of assets wholly or partly by way of gift, and any disposals of assets generally. It includes the following.

(i) A disposition effected by associated operations. See **5.5** ANTI-AVOIDANCE. [*IHTA 1984, s 272*].

(ii) An omission to exercise a right (unless shown not to be deliberate) by a person which diminishes his estate and increases the estate of another person or the value of a discretionary trust. The time of the disposition is the time or latest time when the right could be exercised. [*IHTA 1984, s 3(3)*].

(iii) Certain arrangements involving life insurance in conjunction with an annuity (a 'back to back' arrangement). [*IHTA 1984, s 263*]. See **31** LIFE ASSURANCE POLICIES AND ANNUITIES.

(iv) Certain loans of money or property for a fixed or minimum period granted for inadequate consideration. See **51.3** below.

(v) A disposition effected on the death of a registered scheme member on or after the age of 75 where funds are held in an alternatively secured pension (ASP) within *FA 2004, s 165*. The disposition on which a tax charge is imposed is the relevant amount of the ASP within *IHTA 1984, s 151A(2)(3)*. See **37.2** PENSION SCHEMES.

Dispositions not a transfer of value

Certain dispositions are not transfers of value as follows:

(a) it is shown that it was not intended, and was not made in a transaction (or series of transactions or by associated transactions) intended, to confer any gratuitous benefit on any person and either:

(i) it was made in a transaction at arm's length between persons not connected with each other; or

(ii) it was such as might be expected to be made in a transaction at arm's length between persons not connected with each other.

The above exception does not apply to a disposition whereby a person entitled to an interest (whether in possession or not) in any settled property acquires a reversionary interest expectant (whether immediately or not) on the interest. It also does not apply to a sale of unquoted shares or debentures (in relation to transfers of value made, and other events occurring, before 17 March 1987, shares or debentures not quoted on a recognised stock exchange) unless it is shown that it was at a price freely negotiated at the time of the sale or at a price such as might be expected to have been freely negotiated at that time. [*IHTA 1984, ss 10, 55; FA 1986, Sch 19 para 15; FA 1987, s 58, Sch 8 para 1*]. See also 5 ANTI-AVOIDANCE.

It is not sufficient, for example, that the shares were sold at a price which had been fixed under a provision of the company's articles of association (Originally in former Inland Revenue Booklet IHT 1 (1991) para 8.10).

The question of whether a disposition is excepted from being a transfer of value in the circumstances of (ii) above is one of fact although the burden of proof is on the taxpayer (*CIR v Spencer-Nairn* CS 1990, [1991] STC 60). (The facts were special in that a seller of land did not realise, at the time of sale, he was connected with the purchaser, and it was later found the advice he had received in connection with the sale, to the effect that he was liable under statute to incur expenditure to improve the land, was erroneous, with the effect that the sale was carried out at an apparent undervalue.)

The relevance of associated operations was considered in *CIR v Macpherson and Another* HL, [1988] STC 362. See **5.5** ANTI-AVOIDANCE.

(b) It is a disposition for family maintenance etc. see **21.15** EXEMPT TRANSFERS.

(c) It is allowable for income tax or corporation tax. [*IHTA 1984, s 12(1)*].

(d) It is a contribution to an approved retirement benefit scheme (occupational pension scheme) or is to provide retirement benefit for employees and their dependants or is a contribution under approved pension arrangements or, from 6 April 2006, a registered pension scheme (or *ICTA 1988, s 615(3)* scheme) entered into by an employee of the person making the disposition. [*IHTA 1984, s 12(2)–(5); F(No 2)A 1987, s 98(2)(3); FA 2004, s 203(2); FA 2006, Sch 22 para 2*]. See **21.19** EXEMPT TRANSFERS and **37.2** PENSIONS SCHEMES.

(e) It is by a close company to trustees for benefit of employees. [*IHTA 1984, ss 13, 13A*]. See **55** TRUSTS FOR EMPLOYEES.

(f) It is a capital gains tax liability of a close relative paid by an individual which has previously been postponed under *FA 1984, Sch 14*. [*IHTA 1984, s 163(5)*]. See **56.18** VALUATION.

(g) The disposition falls within the provisions relating to GIFTS WITH RESERVATION (**22**).

Loans, etc.

[51.3] A loan for a fixed or minimum period granted for inadequate consideration may be a transfer of value under the rules in *IHTA 1984, ss 3, 10*, see **51.1** and **51.2**(a) above. The value transferred is the difference between the amount or value of the property lent and the value of:

(a) the right to receive repayment or the return of the property when the loan has expired, plus

(b) the right to receive any interest or other consideration agreed between the parties.

See IHTM19010.

Example 1

David lends Albert £100,000 to buy a house but is unsure of the potential IHT implications. He might lend the money (a) interest free and repayable after a set period of time, say ten years time, or (b) repayable on demand with no interest.

The IHT treatment of the situation in (a) is that the repayment of the capital in ten years time is worth less than the current value of £100,000. If the value in ten years time is, say, £80,000 then David has made a PET of £20,000 at the time of the loan to Albert.

The IHT treatment in (b) is that David is entitled to receive repayment of the £100,000 loan on demand and so long as Albert is solvent, has not given anything away and his estate includes the amount of the loan. If David releases the loan by way of deed then his estate is diminished by that amount for IHT purposes and it is a PET.

In addition, HMRC consider that the foregone interest by David is treated as 'a clear intention to confer bounty' and 'the property disposed of is the interest foregone'. See IHTM14317. However, this view is not generally agreed; nothing is foregone with a cash loan since cash itself produces no income.

In the case of a lease, it is the difference between the value of the lessor's interest before the lease was granted and the value of his interest subject to the lease. The values are those at the time the loan is made. See **19.1** ESTATE for a deed of loan waiver.

Modification of exemptions for loans

[51.4] The exemptions that apply to outright gifts (see **21** EXEMPT TRANSFERS) apply, with appropriate modifications, to loans as follows.

(i) In the case of loans etc. to political parties (see **21.7**) the exemption limit in respect of transfer of value made within a year of death (which applied for transfers before 15 March 1988) does not apply.

(ii) For the purposes of loans etc. to charities (**21.2**), registered housing associations (to which only loans of land made after 13 March 1989 can be exempt) (**21.5**), political parties (**21.7**) or used for national purposes (see **21.6**) or public benefit (see **21.8**) the funds or property lent must be used solely for charitable purposes or the purposes of the appropriate political party or body. The value transferred is then treated as attributable to the property the borrower is allowed to use and the property is treated as having been given to, or having become the property of, the borrower. In addition, the exceptions to the exemptions in each of those paragraphs do not apply.

(iii) For the purposes of loans etc. between spouses or civil partners (see **21.10**) the borrower's estate is treated as increased by the amount of the value transferred but see *Phizackerley* below.

(iv) For the purposes of the small gifts exemption (see **21.13**(b)) and gifts in consideration of marriage (see **21.14**) the transfer of value is treated as made by outright gift.

(v) The normal expenditure out of income exemption (see **21.16**) applies if the transfer is a normal one on the part of the transferor and, after allowing for all transfers of value forming part of his normal expenditure, he is left with sufficient income to maintain his usual standard of living.

[*IHTA 1984, ss 29, 56(6); FA 1988, Sch 14*].

Repayment of certain debts during lifetime

[51.5] Under *FA 1986, s 103* certain debts may not be deducted from the value of a deceased's estate if owed to a person who has received property from the deceased, see **52.9** TRANSFERS ON DEATH. Where a debt incurred after 17 March 1986 which would have been disallowed under those provisions is repaid by the donor in whole or in part during lifetime, he is treated as having made a transfer of value at the time of the payment equal to the money or money's worth paid or applied by him and such transfer is treated as a POTENTIALLY EXEMPT TRANSFER (**38**). [*FA 1986, s 103(5)(6)*]. The effect of this is that the repayment (or part repayment) of a gift loaned back to the donor, although reducing the amount disallowed on death, is treated as a potentially exempt transfer and may be subject to tax if the donor dies within seven years of the repayment.

Example 2

Bernard gives his son Andrew shares worth £200,000. Some time thereafter Andrew, who is wealthy, lends his father £250,000 at a time when the shares have dropped in value to £170,000. Bernard dies and a deduction is claimed of the £250,000 owing by the Executors to Andrew.

In such a situation it is open to the parties to claim that the whole of the loan is to be allowed on the grounds that the gift was not made to facilitate the loan (see *IHTA 1984, s 103(2)(b)*). If the parties cannot establish this to the satisfaction of HMRC then the 'realisable value' at the time the debt was created will be in point and not £250,000, that is to say £80,000 (i.e. £250,000 – £170,000 shares). *IHTA 1984, s 103(2)* permits the deduction to the extent that the value of the consideration for the debt is shown by the parties to have exceeded the amount available by the application of all the property derived by the creditor from the deceased.

Estate

[51.6] A person's estate is the aggregate of all the property to which he is beneficially entitled, except that the estate of a person immediately before his death does not include EXCLUDED PROPERTY (20). It includes the value of any settled property in which the person has a beneficial INTEREST IN POSSESSION (27) except that it does not include property to which *IHTA 1984, ss 71A, 71D* (i.e. bereaved minor's trust and an 18 to 25 trust) apply nor does it include from 22 March 2006 an IPDI, a TSI, a disabled person's trust. These trusts will be charged to IHT under the relevant taxing regimes applicable depending on whichever trust is in point. [*IHTA 1984, ss 5(1), 49(1); FA 2006, Sch 20 paras 4, 10*]. See **19** ESTATE for full details of meaning of estate.

52

Transfers on Death

Cross-references. See **2.8** ACCOUNTS AND RETURNS; **7** CALCULATION OF TAX; **13** DEEDS OF VARIATION AND DISCLAIMERS; **19** ESTATE; **21.23** EXEMPT TRANSFERS; **35** PAYMENT OF TAX; **39** QUICK SUCCESSION RELIEF; **53** TRANSFERS WITHIN SEVEN YEARS BEFORE DEATH; **54** TRANSITIONAL PROVISIONS; **56** VALUATION.

Simon's Taxes. See **Part I4**.

Other Sources. Mellows, Chapter 5; Foster, Part D; HMRC Customer Guide to Inheritance Tax; IHTM05000.

Introduction

[52.1] On the death of any person after 17 March 1986, inheritance tax is chargeable as if he had made a transfer of value of his 'estate' immediately before his death. [*IHTA 1984, s 4(1)*]. The rate of tax applicable to the chargeable estate on death and to gifts which are chargeable transfers made within the seven years previously is 40%, but see **52.14** below for the 36% rate applicable where there are charitable gifts amounting to more than 10% or more of any component of the estate.

Where the chargeable estate on death includes the free estate and a pre-22 March 2006 life interest in settled property, the tax payable is calculated by aggregating all chargeable amounts including the settled property, after deduction from each of any reliefs due. The available nil rate band is then deducted from the total and the tax calculated on the net figure. The tax is then divided between the free estate and the settled fund by reference to the chargeable amounts of each.

Definition — 'Estate'

'*Estate*' of a deceased person is the aggregate of all the property to which he was beneficially entitled immediately before death, but not including EXCLUDED PROPERTY (**20**). [*IHTA 1984, s 5(1) as amended by FA 2006, Sch 20 para 10*]. See **19** ESTATE for details, and in particular for the extended IHT meaning of 'beneficially entitled'.

For a summary of the rules applying on intestacy see **52.22** below.

Transferable nil rate band

See **21.11** EXEMPT TRANSFERS for the provisions relating the transfer of unused nil rate bands between spouses or civil partners.

Valuation of estate on death

[52.2] The value transferred on death is the total value of all the property in the deceased's estate (see above) at a price which the property might reasonably be expected to fetch if sold in the open market at that time, less liabilities (see **52.10** below). [*IHTA 1984, ss 5(3), 160*]. See **56** VALUATION.

Mutual building societies

Where an investor in a mutual building society dies after the issue of the relevant Transfer Document or Prospectus and before vesting day, there may be IHT consequences in respect of their entitlement to receive either free shares or a cash bonus on de-mutualisation. Following the death others may become entitled to any free shares or cash bonus due in respect of the account held by the deceased. The precise consequences depend on a number of factors, including the rules of the particular society, the terms of the Transfer Document covering the de-mutualisation and whether the deceased was the sole or first-named holder of the account.

Accrued income scheme (AIS)

Since 6 April 1996, a person's death has not been an occasion of charge under the accrued income scheme (AIS) and valuations of holdings of AIS stocks have included gross interest and IHT has been charged on that gross interest.

However, this has led to a double charge to tax: that is, IHT is charged on the gross interest to the date of death and when the next interest payment is made a further charge arises on the personal representatives on the whole payment of interest including that accruing up to the date of death. The personal representatives have had no recourse to a deduction of the deceased's element of the accrued interest. HMRC Inheritance Tax have now confirmed that interest on AIS securities quoted 'cum-dividend' should be included net of tax at basic rate in the valuation. Similarly, where the securities are 'ex-dividend' at the date of death the allowance for interest accruing after death should be net of tax to the personal representatives. See http://www.hmrc.gov.uk/cto/newsletter.htm, May Special Edition 2003.

The only exception to the general valuation rule applies in certain cases involving the valuation of development sites or where building work is incomplete. The CTO will normally ask the DV to value the property at the relevant date as if the work had been completed. The CTO will then deduct the cost of completion as a charge against the deceased's estate. (VOA IHT manual, section 7, para 7.13 a).

Changes in the value of the estate

Any change in the value of the estate by reason of the death (e.g. life assurance monies receivable or loss of goodwill) are included as if occurring before death except:

(a) the termination on the death of any interest; or
(b) the passing of any interest by survivorship; or
(c) a decrease in value resulting from an alteration of a close company's unquoted share or loan capital or any rights attached thereto, see **11.8** CLOSE COMPANIES.

See IHTM04046 for further examples of changes in value deemed to occur before death.

[*IHTA 1984, s 171*].

Claims for reduction in value

Claims for a reduction in value of the estate may be made where:

(A) quoted shares are sold at a loss within one year of death (Form IHT35), see example below and **56.26** VALUATION;
(B) land is sold at a loss within three years (four years in certain cases) of death (Form IHT38), see **56.9** VALUATION; or
(C) 'related property' is sold at less value within three years of death, see **56.22** VALUATION.

[*IHTA 1984, ss 176, 179, 191; FA 2009, Sch 51 para 10*].

> ***Example 1***
>
> When Bill Blogs died on 15 December 2010 his estate included a portfolio of quoted and unquoted investments. The PRs are considering selling certain investments within twelve months of death. The realisations likely to be made are as follows.

	Probate Value	Gross Sales
	£	£
Share A plc	66,000	57,000
Share B plc	104,000	80,000
Share C plc	57,000	60,000
Share D Ltd (unquoted)	(25,000)	N/A
Incidental costs of sale of **A, B, C plc** only	Notes (A) & (E)	N/A
Net proceeds of sale	£ 227,000	£197,000

Loss on D Ltd unquoted shares not allowed.

The PRs have therefore potential losses on sale of qualifying investments of £10,000 making a total reduction in IHT of £4,000 (i.e. £10,000 × 40%) available to be claimed by Bill's personal representatives on his death.

Notes to the example

(A) No costs of selling investments may be deducted from the sale proceeds. Note 5 on IHT35.

(B) The cancelled shares are treated as sold for £1 immediately before cancellation. The suspended shares are treated as sold on the first anniversary of death at their value at that time (provided that value is less than their value on death). [*IHTA 1984, ss 186A, 186B; FA 1993, s 198*].

(C) The purchase is taken into account as it is made during the period beginning on date of death and ending two months after the end of the last sale taken into account (including deemed sales as in (B) above).

(D) The probate value of each of the investments sold will be adjusted, both for CGT and IHT purposes.

(E) Although excluded from computation of the loss on sale for inheritance tax purposes, incidental costs of sale and deductible from proceeds in calculating CGT. For deaths after 5 April 2004 see Inland Revenue Statement of Practice SP2/04.

Settled property

[52.3] Where the deceased was entitled to an interest in possession which terminated on his death, the value of the settled property would normally be included in his estate. See **19** ESTATE and Form IHT418 below. However, where such settled property:

(I) reverts to the settlor who is still living and neither the settlor (nor his spouse after 11 April 1978) had acquired the reversionary interest for money or money's worth, or

(II) reverts to the settlor's spouse or civil partner who is domiciled in the UK at the time of death and neither the settlor nor his spouse (or civil partner as the case may be) had acquired a reversionary interest for money or money's worth,

the value of the settled property is left out of account in determining the deceased's estate. The exemption also applies as under (II) where the reversion is to the widow or widower or surviving civil partner of the settlor where the settlor died less than two years before the deceased. Relief under these provisions does not apply to a reversionary interest transferred into a settlement after 9 March 1981. Where more than one person is the settlor in relation to such a settlement and the circumstances so require these provisions apply as if the settled property were comprised in separate settlements.

Post-21 March 2006 IIPs

From 22 March 2006 where a person becomes beneficially entitled to an interest in possession then it is included as part of his estate unless it is a disabled person's trust or a TSI. The exemption also applies as under (II) where the reversion is an IPDI to the widow or widower or surviving civil partner of the beneficiary where the settlor has died less than two years before the deceased beneficiary the value of the settled property is left out of account in determining the deceased's estate. See SETTLEMENTS WITH INTERESTS IN POSSESSION (**42**). [*IHTA 1984, ss 44(2), 54; FA 2006, Sch 20 para 15*].

HMRC are somewhat limited in the advice given and state; 'Sometimes, a trust will give trustees a choice about who can benefit under the trust. These trusts are called "discretionary trusts". As no one has a *right* to benefit from a discretionary trust, you should not fill in Form IHT418 for such a trust, even if the deceased has been receiving some benefit.'

Surviving spouse exemption

[52.4] Where a surviving spouse has received a life interest in property under the will of the deceased spouse who died before 13 November 1974, no inheritance tax will arise on that interest when the surviving spouse dies (because estate duty was or would have been payable on the first death). [*IHTA 1984, Sch 6 para 2*]. See **54.3** TRANSITIONAL PROVISIONS.

Survivorship clauses

[52.5] Where under the terms of a will, or otherwise, property is held for a person if he survives another for a specified period of six months or less, the subsequent dispositions at the end of that period (or on the person's earlier death) are treated as having had effect from the beginning of the period. This does not affect any distributions or applications of property occurring before those dispositions take effect. [*IHTA 1984, s 92*]. The *Law Reform (Succession) Act 1995, s 1* inserting a new *subsection 2A to section 46* in the *Administration of Estates Act 1925* applying to all deaths after 1 January 1996 states that a survivorship provision of at least 28 days where a husband or wife dies intestate; this will prevent problems where the intestate's assets are inherited by the spouse or civil partner where in most circumstances either, or both, would not wish this to occur on such deaths in quick succession.

Example 2

Mr and Mrs A both die in a boating accident on 12 July 2010 whilst on holiday but neither has made a will. They do not have any children but both have parents still living. The estates are valued at £325,000 and £335,000 for Mr and Mrs A respectively. As there is no will or survivorship provision made by either there is the possibility that the parents of either Mr A or Mrs A may wish to prove their son/daughter survived the spouse and thereby share in both estates as well as the claiming of the transferability of the nil rate band under *IHTA 1984, s 8A*. See also HMRC Inheritance Tax manual IHTM43040.

The *Administration of Estates Act 1925, s 46(2A)* has the effect of ensuring that where such deaths occur the survivorship of the one spouse over the other must be at least 28 days. In comparison *IHTA 1984, s 92* provides that the 'dispositions taking effect' under a survivorship clause will be treated as having 'had effect from the beginning of the period'. Therefore, if the survival of either Mr A or Mrs A did not exceed 6 months *IHTA 1984, s 92(1)* then *AEA 1925, s 46(2A)* has the effect in Mr A's and Mrs A's case of their assets passing to their issue (not applicable in this case) which enables them in this case utility of the £325,000 nil rate band. However, a surviving spouse or civil partner to whom *subsection (2A)* applies and whose estate is less than £325,000 will be able to use a proportion of the nil rate band up to that limit as the predeceased's assets will pass directly to their issue, in this case the parents under the intestacy rules.

Notes to the example

(1) It may be appropriate for interests on intestacy to be reallocated by the use of a deed of variation so that the unutilised nil rate band of up to £325,000 might be utilised. See *Daffodil (Daffodil's Administrator) v CIR* [2002] STC SCD 224 Sp C 311 and also the Precedent in **13** DEEDS OF VARIATION AND DISCLAIMERS.

(2) The *Law of Property Act 1925, s 184* provides for the younger to have survived the elder in cases of disaster and where it is not known which of them died first. Section 184 may be overridden where a clause is inserted in the will which states 'provided that [. . .] survives me for a period of twenty-eight days' so that the normal distribution is in accordance with testator's wishes. The twenty-eight day clause insertion in a will under the *Law Reform (Succession) Act 1995, s 1* results in each estate passing as though the other had predeceased and for IHT purposes this will mean that, for instance, couples in partnerships may in such circumstances wish their estate to go to their own family members so utilising their relevant nil rate bands.

(3) In the case of spouses or civil partners who die in *commorientes* circumstances (see paragraph **52.13** below) then the situation is complicated further by the inter-spouse/civil partner exemption under *IHTA 1984, s 18*; as there is an exempt transfer on the death under section 18(1) then the transfer to the younger spouse or civil partner is not a chargeable transfer. However, the younger of the spouses/civil partners is deemed to have inherited the elder spouse's/civil partner's estate under the *Law of Property Act 1925, s 184*, but for the purposes of IHT under *IHTA 1984, s 4(2)* eliminates mutual gifts between individuals in such circumstances and there is no transfer of value to the younger spouse/civil partner on which inheritance tax can be charged. There is a view therefore that the elder's estate escapes inheritance tax completely and therefore a survivorship condition, which is normally desirable, is deliberately excluded in the event of the spouses/civil partners dying simultaneously. In the case of civil partnerships this may not be desirable for the reasons as noted above, but in a case where a married couple's children benefit from their parents' estates then, depending on the size of the elder parent's estate, there could be a substantial saving in IHT. This view is not universally accepted but see the HMRC's IHT manual at IHTM12197 for text and a useful

example, which supports the view above that the elder spouse's estate is not subject to IHT at all. With the transferability of the nil rate band afforded by *IHTA 1984, s 8A* the personal representatives of the younger spouse/civil partner will be able to claim the full nil rate band of £325,000 notwithstanding the elder spouse's estate is not subject to IHT at all under *IHTA 1984, s 4(2)*. See also HMRC Inheritance Tax manual IHTM43040. See also Key Points below.

Non-residents' bank accounts

[52.6] On the death prior to 6 April 2013 of a person not domiciled, resident or ordinarily resident in the UK immediately before his death, the balance on any 'qualifying foreign currency account' is not included in the value of his estate immediately before his death. This also applies to such an account held by trustees of settled property in which the deceased held a beneficial interest in possession unless the settlor was domiciled in the UK at the time he made the settlement or the trustees are domiciled, resident and ordinarily resident there at the time of the beneficiary's death. Residence and ordinary residence are determined as for income tax purposes. The trustees of a settlement, however, were for these purposes regarded as not resident or ordinarily resident in the UK unless the general administration was ordinarily carried on there and the trustees or a majority of them (and where there is more than one class of trustees, a majority of each class) were resident and ordinarily resident in the UK. '*Qualifying foreign currency account*' means any foreign currency account with a bank or the Post Office. [*IHTA 1984, s 157; FA 1996, Sch 37 para 12(1), Sch 41 Pt VIII*].

For these purposes 'bank' has the same meaning as that given by *ITA 2007, s 991* (formerly *ICTA 1988, s 840A*). [*FA 1996, Sch 37 para 12(2)*].

With effect for deaths on or after 6 April 2013, this exemption continues to apply but is modified to delete the requirements relating to ordinary residence outside the UK. The conditions for exemption of a foreign currency bank account held by a person at the time of death are therefore that he is not domiciled and not resident in the UK immediately before his death. In relation to the trustee exemption, the requirement for the trustees is that a majority of them are not resident in the UK and that they are not domiciled in the UK. As to residence for tax purposes see the Statutory Residence Test in *FA 2013, Sch 45*.

Works of art temporarily in the UK

[52.7] Where the person beneficially entitled to foreign-owned work of art is not domiciled in the United Kingdom and on his or her death the work of art is situated in the United Kingdom for one or more of the purposes of public display (but not with a view to sale), cleaning and restoration (and for no other purpose), the item concerned is not to be included in that person's chargeable estate for IHT purposes. [*Enactment of Extra-Statutory Concessions Order 2009, Art 13*].

Compensation claims outstanding at death

[52.8] The right to pursue a claim for compensation is an item of property and therefore an asset of the estate. The open market value of the right at the date of death depends on several factors, but is fundamentally down to what was known, or capable of being known, at the date of death about:

(a) the amount of compensation that might be reasonably anticipated based on the information available;
(b) the likelihood of the claim being successful;
(c) the likely costs that would be expected to be incurred in obtaining a successful outcome; and
(d) the time delay between the date of death and the date when the compensation might reasonably be expected to be made.

The right to pursue a claim can be valuable whether or not the individual entitled to make the claim was aware of this right, provided that the information was capable of being known at the relevant date.

The open market value of the right to pursue the claim becomes more valuable as the outcome becomes more certain, so particular events can trigger a substantial increase in value.

Where personal representatives are aware of a potential claim at the date of death, they should record the existence of the claim on form IHT400 and provide as much information about the claim as they can. They should include a reasoned estimate of the open market value of the right to pursue the compensation where they are able to do so.

(Source: HMRC Trust and Estates Newsletter August 2013).

NHS Continuing Care Scheme payments

[52.9] Payments under the NHS Continuing Care Scheme whereby a right exists to make a reimbursement claim is to be treated as an asset of the deceased's estate. Where a claim is underway at the date of death and an offer has been made by the Strategic Health Authority/ Primary Care Trust then that offer should be included as an asset on Form IHT400. If the claim has not been quantified or is not known about at the time of death a corrective account should be submitted to HMRC Inheritance Tax as soon as possible. A discounted valuation should be applied to the expected/actual payment and this discount is dependent on the date of death as detailed below and in the December 2005 issue of the IHT Newsletter at http://www.hmrc.gov.uk/cto/newsletter.htm. [*IHTA 1984, s 160*]. The discount reflects the potential uncertainty of success in a claim for reimbursement and arises from the Coughlan case and subsequent reports by the Health Service Ombudsman. See also *R v North East Devon Health Authority, ex p Coughlan (Secretary of State for Health and another intervening* [2000] 3 All ER 850.

Date of death	Discount
Prior to 17/7/99	100%
17/7/99–13/2/03	75%
14/2/03–16/12/04	40%
On or after 17/12/04	10%

Liabilities deductible

[52.10] In determining the value of a person's estate his liabilities at that time must be taken into account except as otherwise provided by *IHTA 1984*. Except in the case of a liability imposed by the law, a liability incurred by the transferor may be taken into account only to the extent that it was incurred for a consideration in money or money's worth. [*IHTA 1984, s 5(3)(5)*]. By concession, income tax in Canada charged on deemed gains immediately before death will be allowed as a deductible liability. A deceased's worldwide estate of which the Canadian tax on deemed gains comprises a liability may be set-off against the value of UK assets where it exceeds assets (liable or not to IHT) held outside the UK. (ESC F18, now considered by HMRC to be an interpretation of the law and not strictly a concession so F18 is to be withdrawn). *IHTA 1984, s 5(3)* provides that 'in determining the value of a person's estate at any time his liabilities at that time shall be taken into account, except as otherwise provided by this Act . . . ' and in *Robertson v HMRC* [2005] STC SCD 723 Sp C 494 lump sum maintenance payments made to an ex-wife, which were not sanctioned under the maintenance agreement or by the court, were not to be treated as a liability to be returned to him and should be treated as part of the deceased ex-wife's estate for IHT purposes on her death.

A liability which is an encumbrance on any property shall, so far as possible, be taken to reduce the value of that property (*IHTA 1984, s 162(4)*) but see the provisions of *IHTA 1984, s 162A* which override this rule with effect for transfers of value made on or after 17 July 2013 in the case of liabilities incurred at any time which are attributable to financing excluded property, or if incurred after 5 April 2013 and which are attributable to property qualifying for business or agricultural reliefs or, in respect of woodlands, deferral of charge. These disallowances are extended to any liabilities attributable to financing non-residents' foreign currency accounts, with effect for transfers of value made on or after 17 July 2014. These provisions are explained at **56.20**.

Liabilities not discharged after death

The position of liabilities owing at the date of death, but which were not paid thereafter has historically been rather unclear. If the liability is released without payment during the executorship period, it will be appropriate to notify HMRC by way of a corrective IHT account. If however the liability is left unpaid and is not released during the administration period, the view might be taken that it remains deductible as a debt due at the time of death. It may however be released at some later time. Such circumstances might in particular arise in relation to loans made by employee benefit trusts.

With effect from 17 July 2013, it is now provided that a liability due from a person's estate on death may only be taken into account to the extent that it is discharged on or after the death out of the estate, or from excluded property owned by the person immediately before death, in money or monies worth, subject always to any other specific provision in the IHT legislation preventing the liability from being taken into account (for example, *FA 1986, s 103*, see below). For this purpose, the estate refers to the person's estate for IHT purposes immediately before death, and therefore includes IPDI property, pre-22 March 2006 life interest property and gift with reservation property.

Where the liability is not discharged out of the estate, it may be taken into account only if there is a real commercial reason for it not being discharged, wholly or in part, and the non-payment is not part of arrangements having a main purpose of securing a tax advantage. This is once again subject to any overriding provisions in the IHT legislation preventing deductibility. For these purposes, there is a real commercial reason for liability not being discharged, wholly or partly, where it is shown that either it is to a person dealing at arm's length, or if it were to such a person, that person would not require the liability to be discharged. If the debt is secured on an asset passing to the surviving spouse, and the debt is disallowed, the spouse exemption nevertheless applies to the full unencumbered value of the asset.

Example 3

David had a mortgage of £300,000 on a property in his name. He leaves the property to his son Edward, subject to the debt, and also takes out a life policy written in trust for Edward to provide a sum of £300,000 payable on David's death. If following David's death Edward uses to policy proceeds to pay off the mortgage, the debt will not be deductible for IHT purposes in David's estate because the liability is not discharged out of the estate after the death. If on the other hand Edward lends the policy proceeds to the executors so that they then pay off the mortgage, the debt will be deductible even though Edward may subsequently waive repayment of the debt due to him.

See also *Taxation* 31 October 2013 pp 15–16: where executors take out a new mortgage to repay one owing at death and then convey the property to a beneficiary subject to the new borrowing, a charge to stamp duty land tax arises. There is no such charge where the property is conveyed subject to a liability incurred by the deceased, but non-payment of that liability out of the estate could cause it to be disallowed as a deduction on the death, unless the commercial reason test is satisfied. See example in HMRC's inheritance tax manual at IHTM28029 where the test is considered to be satisfied in the case of a commercial mortgage.

These provisions are tied in with the rules relating to liabilities to finance excluded property or relievable property detailed at **56.19**. Where a liability is only partly paid off after the date of death, and it partly relates to a loan to finance excluded property, then that part is taken to be discharged first. After that, any part which was incurred to finance property qualifying for business property relief, agricultural property relief or woodlands is then to be taken as discharged and any remainder after the foregoing is to be treated as a general liability of the estate. [*IHTA 1984, s 175A*].

Specific liabilities deductible

Liabilities deductible (apart from normal debts) include the following.

(i) Reasonable funeral expenses (including a reasonable amount for mourning for the family and servants, see F1 at **23** HMRC EXTRA-STATUTORY CONCESSIONS and the cost of a tombstone or gravestone, see Inland Revenue Statement of Practice SP7/87, 15 July 1987 and IHT400 at Box 81). The word 'reasonable' depends upon the standard of living of the deceased so that in a case similar to the funeral of the Duke of Athol in 1996, where the expense of his private army acting as an honour guard would have been allowed, any expenses that are reasonable for the attendance of family and servants will be allowed as a funeral expense. For deaths abroad embalming and transport costs will be allowed as an expense (see also Foster Inheritance Tax, para D1.42).

(ii) Inheritance tax or capital transfer tax liabilities outstanding from a previous transfer, but if the tax is not eventually paid out of the estate, an adjustment must be made.

(iii) Expenses in administering or realising property situated outside the UK, up to 5% of the property's value where the expenses are shown to be attributable to the situation of the property. (The allowance is intended to cover the costs (in excess of the normal costs) of resealing a grant of probate etc. and obtaining the relevant tax clearance and not substantive expenses e.g. tax liabilities.) A separate note of charges should be kept to justify the claim. (Tolley's Practical Tax 1981, p 151).

(iv) Liabilities for future payments or transfer of assets taxable under *IHTA 1984, s 262*, see **7.10** CALCULATION OF TAX. Such liabilities are to be valued by reducing the amount of the further payments or assets by the chargeable portion.

(v) Income tax liabilities arising on deemed disposals on death in respect of offshore income gains under the provisions in *ICTA 1988, ss 757–764, 27, Sch 28* as amended by *FA 2004, Sch 26* and deep discount securities under the provisions in the former *ICTA 1988, s 57* as amended by *FA 1996, Sch 15*.

[*IHTA 1984, ss 172–175; FA 1996, Sch 13 para 4, Sch 14 para 2*].

Treatment of certain debts and encumbrances

[52.11] Certain liabilities may not be deducted if owed to a person who has received property from the deceased. Specifically, subject to below, where a debt incurred or encumbrance created by the deceased after 17 March 1986 would otherwise be taken into account in valuing his estate immediately before death, that liability is subject to abatement proportionate to the value of any consideration given for the debt etc. which consisted of:

(a) 'property derived from the deceased'; or
(b) consideration (not within (a) above) given by any person who was at any time entitled to, or amongst whose resources there was at any time included, any property derived from the deceased.

The abatement under (b) above does not apply to the extent it can be shown that the donee's loan etc. to the deceased was greater than the gifts received from the donor or was not made out of property derived from the deceased or that the deceased's gift was not made to facilitate the loan.

'*Property derived from the deceased*' means any property which was the subject matter of a disposition by the deceased (alone or with any other person) or which represented any of the subject matter of such a disposition (directly or indirectly) by one or more intermediate dispositions. If, however, the disposition by the deceased was neither:

(A) a transfer of value; nor
(B) part of associated operations which included a disposition *by the deceased* (with or without another person) otherwise than for full consideration in money or money's worth to the deceased for his own use or benefit or a disposition *by any other person* which reduced the value of the deceased's property

it is left out of account. [*FA 1986, s 103(1)–(4)(6)*].

Case law

A married woman died in 2000 and by her will she left an amount equal to the IHT nil rate band to a discretionary trust for her husband (P) and their children, and the residue to P. P agreed to pay £150,000 plus indexation to the discretionary trust in return for his wife's half-share in the matrimonial home, this purchase price being left outstanding as a loan. P had previously provided all the finance to purchase the property. He died in 2002, and HMRC issued a notice of determination charging IHT on his estate. His personal representative appealed, contending that the £153,222 which P owed to the discretionary trust should be deducted from the value of his estate. The Special Commissioner rejected this contention and dismissed his appeal, holding that the effect of *FA 1986, s 103* was that the debt was not deductible. The estate of his late wife included property derived from P and so the debt due to her estate was not deductible. It was argued that the section was prevented from applying because P's transfer of the property to his wife was not a transfer of value by virtue of *IHTA 1984, s 11* (providing that a 'disposition for maintenance' is not a 'transfer of value') but it was held that *s 11* did not apply to a situation 'when a husband puts a house in joint names of himself and his wife during their marriage'. Note that if the residue of the wife's estate had been left on interest in possession trusts for P, and the trustees of residue had purchased the share in the property from the nil rate band trustees on the same basis as above, this loan would have been deductible on P's death as the liability would not have been incurred by P. Alternatively, the executors could have charged the property with the sum due to the discretionary trust before transferring it to P. See also **5** ANTI-AVOIDANCE; **42.1** SETTLEMENTS WITH INTERESTS IN POSSESSION. See also Tax Adviser, June 2007 and *Phizackerley (Personal Representative of Dr PJR Phizackerley) v HMRC* [2007] STC SCD 328 Sp C 591 at tax cases (58).

Double charge relief

Double charges — liabilities subject to abatement and death. Relief from double charge to tax is given where, after 17 March 1986, a transfer of value which is or proves to be a chargeable transfer ('the transfer') is made by an individual ('the deceased') by virtue of which the estate of the transferee is increased or by virtue of which property becomes comprised in a settlement of which the transferee is a trustee *and* at any time before his death the deceased incurs a liability to the transferee ('the liability') which is subject to abatement under the provisions above.

Two separate calculations of tax payable as a result of death are made. In the first, the amount of the transfer of value is reduced by the amount of the debt which is disallowed or abated and, in the second, the amount of the transfer of value and of the debt are both taken into account. The higher amount of total tax is payable and, subject to below, relief is given, as the case may be, by either reducing the value of the transfer of value or by allowing the debt and charging the transfer of value in full.

Where the first calculation gives the higher amount:

(1) credit is available for any tax which became payable before the death of the deceased as is attributable to the amount of the reduction in that calculation (but not exceeding the difference between the amount of tax under the first calculation and the amount of tax which would have been paid under the second calculation if the liability had been taken into account); and

(2) the reduction applies for all IHT purposes other than a ten-year anniversary charge or a proportionate charge to tax on a discretionary settlement arising before the death of the deceased if the transfer of value was a chargeable transfer when it was made.

Where the total tax chargeable under the first and second calculations is the same, the first calculation is treated as producing the higher amount of tax.

Where there are a number of transfers by the deceased before his death which are relevant to the abated liability on death, the above provisions are applied to those transfers in reverse order i.e. latest first. [*FA 1986, s 104(1)(c); SI 1987/1130, Regs 6, 8*]. See also **22.13** GIFTS WITH RESERVATION regarding double charges relief in connection with pre-owned assets.

Example 4

A makes a potentially exempt transfer to B of £203,000 on 1 May 2003 and a further such transfer to him of £40,000 on 1 January 2004. On 1 July 2004 A makes a gift into a discretionary trust of £160,000 on which the trustees pay tax of £Nil. He makes a further potentially exempt transfer to B of £30,000 on 1 January 2005 but on 1 July 2005 B makes a loan to A of £100,000. No annual exemptions are available.

A dies on 1 December 2007 with a death estate of £200,000 against which a deduction is claimed for the debt of £100,000 due to B.

First calculation: disallow the debt and ignore corresponding amounts of potentially exempt transfers from A to B, starting with the latest

	IHT payable £
1 May 2003	
Potentially exempt transfer now reduced to £173,000*	—
1 January 2004	
Potentially exempt transfer now reduced to nil	—
1 July 2004	
Gift into trust £160,000 as top slice of £333,000	
Tax £13,200 less Nil already paid	13,200
1 January 2005	
Potentially exempt transfer now reduced to nil	—
1 December 2007	
Death estate £200,000 as top slice of £533,000	80,000
Total tax due as result of A's death	£93,200

* See note (C) below.

Second calculation: allow the debt and charge the potentially exempt transfers in full

	IHT payable £
1 May 2003	
Potentially exempt transfer £203,000	—
1 January 2004	
Potentially exempt transfer £40,000 as top slice of £243,000	—
1 July 2004	
Gift into trust £160,000 as top slice of £403,000	
Tax £41,200 less Nil already paid	41,200
1 January 2005	
Potentially exempt transfer £30,000 as top slice of £433,000	12,000
1 December 2007	
Death estate £100,000 as top slice of £533,000	40,000
Total tax due as a result of A's death	£93,200

Notes to the example

(A) If the two calculations above result in the same tax chargeable, as in this case, the first of the calculations is taken by reason of *Inheritance Tax (Double Charges Relief) Regulations 1987, SI 1987/1130, Reg 8* but no such provision applies in respect of *Inheritance Tax (Double Charges Relief) Regulations 2005, SI 2005/3441.*

(B) For examples where the calculation gives a marginal difference see 1996/97 edition and earlier.

(C) In the first calculation the debt of £100,000 is disallowed from B to A less the corresponding amounts of potentially exempt transfers from A to B which are ignored, starting with the latest i.e. (£30,000 + £40,000 + £203,000) = £173,000 balance.

Life insurance policies

[52.12] In determining the value of a person's estate immediately before death, no account is to be taken of any liability arising under or in connection with life insurance made after 30 June 1986 unless the whole of the sums assured under the policy form part of that person's estate immediately before his death. [*FA 1986, s 103(7)*]. See also April/May 2002, p 2 IHT Newsletter.

Reduced rate for certain estates with 10% gifts to charities

[52.13] For deaths on or after 6 April 2012 inheritance tax will be charged on the net chargeable value of any component of the estate at a rate of 36% where 10% or more of that component has been left to charity.

Where the estate comprises only the deceased's 'free estate' without any joint property passing by survivorship, the value of the estate on which the 10% threshold will be based (the 'baseline amount') will be the value of the net estate charged to IHT after deducting all available reliefs, exemptions and available nil rate band, but adding back the charitable legacy itself. So for example the amount of exempt gifts to the spouse and the value of assets qualifying for 100% business property relief are deducted from the total value of the estate to find the baseline amount, but charitable gifts are not. If the gifts to charities total 10% or more of the baseline amount, then the rate of tax applicable to the chargeable estate will be 36%.

In cases in which the estate for IHT purposes includes assets additional to those in the 'free estate', the 10% test will be applied to each category of assets, described as a 'component', that makes up the aggregate estate. The components are:

(a) the 'general component' being the free estate passing under the terms of the will. This excludes other components listed below and also gifts with reservation of benefit chargeable on the death;

(b) the 'survivorship component' being jointly owned assets passing by survivorship (in England, Wales and Northern Ireland), or under a special destination in Scotland, or under corresponding provisions of any applicable foreign law;

(c) the 'settled property component', being settled property comprised in the estate by virtue of an interest in possession to which the deceased was beneficially entitled.

If the assets passing to charity from one component exceed 10% of its baseline amount, other components may be merged with it to give an aggregate baseline amount for all of them. This merging of components will require an election to be made by all those who are 'appropriate persons' for each of the components involved; the appropriate persons are the personal representatives in relation to the general component, the settlement trustees in relation to the settled component and the surviving joint owner or owners in relation to the survivorship component. It should be noted that because gifts with reservation of benefit which form part of the chargeable estate on the death do not themselves comprise any component of the estate, they can only be brought within the scope of the reduced rate charge by election to merge them with one of the three components at (a), (b) or (c) above. If survivorship component relates an asset held jointly with the spouse, that component will not usually be relevant for the purposes of this relief because it is exempt, except where the limitation on the exemption applies owing to the deceased being UK domiciled and the spouse non-domiciled for IHT purposes.

The value of the assets passing to charity from a particular component will be compared to the baseline amount for that component. The baseline amount is calculated after deducting from that component all available reliefs, exemptions and the appropriate proportion of the available nil rate band, as increased by the transfer of nil rate band provisions. To find the appropriate proportion of the available nil band, deduct first the amounts of any chargeable transfers in the seven years ending with the date of death, as the nil band is allocated primarily to these, then find the percentage of the total chargeable transfers on the death which is represented by the value of component concerned. That percentage of the available nil band is the appropriate proportion of it to be deducted from the component. If the 10% test for a component is passed, IHT will be charged on that particular component at 36%.

Where the grossing up rules apply to gifts under a will (see **7.6** CALCULATION OF TAX), for the purpose of calculating the baseline amount the rate to be used for grossing up is 36%.

The reduced rate of IHT will apply automatically if the estate or component passes the 10% test. If it does not, IHT will be charged at the full rate. However, personal representatives and other relevant persons may elect for the reduced rate not to apply if, for example, the benefit obtained from applying the reduced rate is likely to be minimal and they do not wish to incur additional costs of valuing items left to charity. Elections must be made in writing to HMRC and no later than two years and one month after the date of death of the deceased. HMRC have discretion to extend this deadline.

The new provisions will apply equally to charitable legacies made by will or by an Instrument of Variation. The conditions for an Instrument of Variation to be taken into account for these purposes require that the charity has been notified that the devolution of the estate has been varied in its favour.

Example 5

The estate of Percival who died on 30 April 2012 is valued at £425,000, comprising quoted investments and cash. He leaves a legacy of £10,000 to the National Trust and the residue of £415,000 less IHT passes to his children. The IHT payable will be £90,000 at 36% – £32,400 because 10% of the estate after deduction of the nil-band is left to charity. So the gift to the charity reduces the residue by only £2,400 (£10,000 gift less IHT reduction £40,000 – £32,400).

Example 6

The estate of Albert, a widower, who died on 30 April 2012 is valued at £1,630,000, including a trust fund in which he has had an interest in possession since 2000 worth £500,000. He inherited the whole of his late wife's estate some years previously and neither had ever made any lifetime gifts within seven years of death. He leaves a legacy of £100,000 to the NSPCC and the residue of £1,030,000 along with the trust fund pass to his children after payment of IHT. The IHT payable by the free estate at the rate of 36% because 10% of the estate after deduction of the appropriate fraction of the nil-band is left to charity. The appropriate fraction is:

$£650,000 \times 1,030,000/1,530,000 = 437,581$

The chargeable estate is therefore £1030,000 – £437,582 = £592,419. To test whether the 10% threshold is satisfied, add back the amount of the charitable gifts (£100,000), The baseline amount is therefore £692,419 and the estate therefore qualifies for the 36% rate of IHT.

The trustees of the late wife's trust fund may elect to merge the settled property component with the general component (that is, the residue of the free estate) as the baseline amount for the merged components will be:

General component		£692,419
Settled component	£500,000	
less balance of nil band	£212,419	£287,581
Baseline amount of merged components		£980,000

The charitable gift under the will exceeds 10% of the merged components and so an election will enable both the free estate and the trust fund to bear IHT at the rate of 36%.

Quick successive relief: Where assets in the estate qualify for quick succession relief (see **39** QUICK SUCCESSION RELIEF), and it is necessary to apportion that relief between assets in different components of the estate, the apportionment is to be made by reference to the tax payable by each component and not the capital value of each component.

Conditionally exempt property: where a chargeable event arises in respect of heritage property which was allowed conditional exemption on the death of the owner (see **33.10** NATIONAL HERITAGE), the lower 36% rate of IHT cannot be claimed on that event even if the remaining estate had satisfied the conditions for that rate.

Woodlands: equally deferred charges in respect of woodlands (see 57.3 WOODLANDS) cannot benefit from the lower 36% rate of IHT even if the estate had satisfied the conditions for that rate.

[*FA 2012, s 207, Sch 32*].

Commorientes

[52.14] For the purposes of establishing if there has been a transfer on death, where it cannot be known which of two or more persons died first they are assumed to have died at the same instant (i.e. the rule in the *Law of Property Act 1925, s 184* that the elder is deemed to have died first does not apply for these purposes). [*IHTA 1984, s 4(2)*].

Example 7

If father and son die in the same accident, any property bequeathed by the father to the son passes to the son's estate (since the father is deemed under the rule quoted above to have died first) and then to the beneficiaries under the son's will, but inheritance tax is chargeable only on the transfer of the property to the son's estate and not again on the transfer of it to the beneficiaries of the son's estate.

In the case of spouses or civil partners who die in *commorientes* circumstances then the situation is complicated further by the inter-spouse/civil partner exemption under *IHTA 1984, s 18 as amended by The Tax and Civil Partnership Regulations 2005, SI 2005/3229, Reg 7*; as there is an exempt transfer on the death under *section 18(1)* then the transfer to the younger spouse or civil partner is not a chargeable transfer. However, the younger of the spouses/civil partners is deemed to have inherited the elder spouse's/civil partner's estate under the *Law of Property Act 1925, s 184* but for the purposes of Inheritance Tax under *IHTA 1984, s 4(2)* eliminates mutual gifts between individuals in such circumstances and there is no transfer of value to the younger spouse/civil partner on which inheritance tax can be charged. There is a view therefore that the elder's estate escapes inheritance tax completely and therefore a survivorship condition, which is normally desirable, is deliberately excluded in the event of the spouses/civil partners dying simultaneously (see Taxation magazine 24 September 1992 p 649 and 6 July 1995 p 362). This view is not universally accepted (see British Tax Review 1995 p 390). See also 52.2 above. See IHTM12197 for text and a useful example, which supports the view above that the elder spouse's estate is not subject to IHT at all.

See also 52.2 above regarding survivorship clauses, Key Points below and 39 QUICK SUCCESSION RELIEF.

Transferability of nil rate bands

[52.15] From 9 October 2007 on the death of the survivor of a married couple or civil partnership a claim may be made for the nil rate band to be increased by reference to any unused proportion of the nil rate band which there was on the death of the spouse or civil partner who pre-deceased. This provision described as the 'transfer of unused nil rate band between spouses and civil partners' is available to the widow, widower or surviving civil partner irrespective of when the original spouse or civil partner died. [*IHTA 1984, s 8A as inserted by FA 2008, s 10, Sch 4 para 2*]. Note that it is not available for chargeable transfers made in the lifetime of the survivor, except those within seven years of death. The size of the estate of the first to die is not relevant as such, and so for example, if he or she had no assets at all, a full additional nil rate band will be available on the death of the survivor. Also the domicile status of either spouses or civil partners is not relevant, except that where after 9 March 1982 the spouse or civil partner who predeceased was UK domiciled but at that time the survivor was not, bequests to a value in excess of £55,000 to the survivor will have been within the nil rate band. Prior to 9 March 1982, lower limits applied from the introduction of capital transfer tax. Gifts of excluded property do not impact on the nil rate band.

The parties must have been spouses or civil partners at the time of the death of the one who predeceased, and divorce prior to that time will prevent any claim. Equally, the relief will not apply in cases of couples living together. See *Burden & Burden v United Kingdom* [2006] ECHR Case 13378/05; [2007] STC 252, in which two elderly sisters lived together in a jointly-owned house on land which they had inherited from their parents. They lodged a complaint with the ECHR, contending that the provisions of *IHTA 1984, s 18* (as amended by the Tax and Civil Partnership Regulations 2005) were a breach of Article 14 of the European Convention on Human Rights, because when one of them died, the survivor would be required to pay IHT on her sister's share of their home, whereas no IHT would have been charged if they had lived together as a registered lesbian civil partnership. The ECHR rejected their application holding that 'the inheritance tax exemption for married and civil partnership couples . . . pursues a legitimate aim, namely to promote stable, committed heterosexual and homosexual relationships by providing the survivor with a measure of financial security after the death of the spouse or partner'. See also *Courten v United Kingdom* [2008] ECHR 1546.

Those in gay or lesbian relationships living together who do not have a civil partnership document within *CPA 2004, s 2(1)* but have a relationship was recognised under overseas law before the UK Act came into force are to be treated as having formed a civil partnership recognised in the UK on the date the Act came into force. In such cases the survivor's personal representatives will be able to claim the unused nil rate band of the predeceased but only in cases where the first death was after CPA 2004 coming into force, i.e. 5 December 2005. See HMRC Inheritance Tax manual IHTM43001.

See also Example 7 for the transferability of the unused nil rate band in cases of alternatively secured pensions in pension schemes (**37**). See also HMRC Inheritance Tax manual IHTM43001–IHTM43035.

To calculate the increased amount available on the death of the survivor, it is first necessary to find the nil rate band maximum at the time of the death of the spouse or civil partner who predeceased. For deaths after the introduction of capital transfer tax on 13 March 1975 the current nil band provisions and spouse exemption (although with certain alterations to the limited amount available between spouses of mixed domicile) have been in operation; a table of nil bands from 26 March 1974 is set out below. It is then necessary to establish what amount of that nil rate maximum was not utilised on the death of the first to die. The unutilised amount is then converted to a percentage of nil rate band maximum. That percentage of the nil rate band in force on the death of the survivor can then be claimed as an additional nil rate band on that death.

CAPITAL TRANSFER TAX AND INHERITANCE TAX NIL RATE BANDS

From	To	Nil rate band
13 March 1975	26 October 1977	£15,000
27 October 1977	25 March 1980	£25,000
26 March 1980	08 March 1982	£50,000
09 March 1982	14 March 1983	£55,000
15 March 1983	12 March 1984	£60,000
13 March 1984	05 April 1985	£64,000
06 April 1985	17 March 1986	£67,000
18 March 1986	16 March 1987	£71,000
17 March 1987	14 March 1988	£90,000
15 March 1988	05 April 1989	£110,000
06 April 1989	05 April 1990	£118,000
06 April 1990	05 April 1991	£128,000
06 April 1991	09 March 1992	£140,000
10 March 1992	05 April 1995	£150,000
06 April 1995	05 April 1996	£154,000
06 April 1996	05 April 1997	£200,000
06 April 1997	05 April 1998	£215,000
06 April 1998	05 April 1999	£223,000
06 April 1999	05 April 2000	£231,000
06 April 2000	05 April 2001	£234,000
06 April 2001	05 April 2002	£242,000
06 April 2002	05 April 2003	£250,000
06 April 2003	05 April 2004	£255,000
06 April 2004	05 April 2005	£263,000
06 April 2005	05 April 2006	£275,000
06 April 2006	05 April 2007	£285,000
06 April 2007	05 April 2008	£300,000
06 April 2008	05 April 2009	£312,000
06 April 2009	onwards	£325,000

When Estate Duty applied, there was no spouse exemption prior to 21 March 1972 and therefore any amounts transferred to a spouse were deducted from the tax free band that existed at that time — any balance of that tax free band will comprise the proportion of the unused nil rate band to be transferred. See Example 2 below.

Where a surviving spouse or civil partner was married to, or was in a civil partnership with, someone who (a) had survived an earlier marriage or civil partnership and (b) was entitled to transfer an unused nil rate band from that earlier death, the amount of any nil rate band available for transfer on the death of the survivor is first calculated by reference to the actual nil rate band that was appropriate on the intervening death, including the transferred element of nil rate band. Any chargeable transfers and bequests on taken into account on the intervening death are then primarily treated as deducted from that transferred element and only the excess is deducted from ordinary nil band available on that death. See example at IHTM43032.

A claim for transferability of the nil rate band must be made on form IHT402 on the death of the surviving spouse or civil partner by their personal representatives or accountable persons to obtain the use of the unused nil rate band of the predeceased spouse or civil partner. [*IHTA 1984, s 8B as inserted by FA 2008, Sch 4 para* 2]. A claim must be made in the permitted period, which is two years from the end of the month in which the survivor dies, or if later, three months beginning with the date on which the personal representatives act as such. HMRC have discretion to allow late claims — see IHTM43009 for circumstances in which late claims may be accepted. Claims can be withdrawn within one month after the end of the permitted period. Form IHT402 asks for the gifting history of the predeceased spouse or civil partner and once completed it is sent to HMRC Inheritance Tax with documentation such as the death certificate, marriage certificate and the will.

Where a person survives more than one spouse or civil partner who predeceased, claims can be made in relation to the unused nil bands of either or both of them, but the maximum claim on the death of the survivor is capped at the maximum nil rate band available on the survivor's death; thus at the present time the maximum claim under these provisions is £325,000. [*IHTA 1984, s 8A(5) as inserted by FA 2008, Sch 4 para* 2]. In the case of deferred charges regarding heritage property and woodlands which affect the calculation of the transferable nil rate band, see **33.10** NATIONAL HERITAGE and **57.6** WOODLANDS. [*IHTA 1984, s 8C as inserted by FA 2008, Sch 4 para* 2].

Claim to transfer unused nil rate band [Form IHT402]

HM Revenue & Customs

Claim to transfer unused nil rate band

Schedule IHT402

When to use this form

Fill in this form if:

- the deceased died on or after 9 October 2007, and
- their spouse or civil partner died before them, and
- when the spouse or civil partner died their estate did not use up all of the nil rate band available to it, and
- you want to transfer the unused amount to the deceased's estate.

Filling in this form

You will need to find out who was the executor or administrator of the spouse or civil partner's estate as you will need information from them to complete this form.

Make full enquiries so that the figures you give and the statements you make are correct.

Information you will need

You will need to know:

- who benefited under the Will or intestacy of the spouse or civil partner and what the beneficiaries were entitled to receive
- whether any assets, such as jointly owned assets or assets in trust were part of the estate of the spouse or civil partner, and
- whether the spouse or civil partner had made any gifts or other transfers within seven years before the date of their death that were chargeable on their death *(see note 5 on page 4)*.

The executor or administrator of the spouse or civil partner should be able to help you find out this information.

You should obtain copies of the documents listed aside and use them alongside any records that exist about the spouse or civil partner's estate.

If there are no records, you should try and find out the information about the spouse or civil partner's estate from others who might know, for example, the solicitor who acted for the estate, the executors or administrators, other family members, close friends.

Name of deceased (person who has died now)

[ ]

Date of death *DD MM YYYY*

[ ][ ] [ ][ ] [ ][ ][ ][ ]

IHT reference number (if known)

[ ]

Documents to be sent with this form

You must send photocopies of the following documents with this form:

- copy of the grant of representation (Confirmation in Scotland) to the estate of the spouse or civil partner (if no grant has been taken out, please provide a copy of the death certificate - see the note on page 4 about obtaining copies of certificates)
- if the spouse or civil partner left a Will, a copy of it
- if a Deed of Variation or other similar document was executed to change the people who inherited the estate of the spouse or civil partner, a copy of it.

Deadline

You must send this form to us no later than 24 months after the end of the month in which the deceased died.
For example, if the spouse or civil partner died on 15 May 2006, and the deceased died on 10 October 2007, you would need to send this form to us by 31 October 2009.

Help

For more information or help:

- go to **www.hmrc.gov.uk/inheritancetax/**
- phone our helpline on **0845 30 20 900**
  – if calling from outside the UK, phone **+44 115 974 3009.**

Spouse or civil partner's details

Fill in this section with details of the spouse or civil partner who died first.

1 Spouse or civil partner's name

Title - enter MR, MRS, MISS, MS or other title

[ ]

Surname or family name

[ ]

First name(s)

[ ]

[ ]

2 Date of death *DD MM YYYY*

[ ][ ] [ ][ ] [ ][ ][ ][ ]

3 Last known permanent address

[ ]

[ ]

[ ]

Postcode

4 Date of marriage or civil partnership *DD MM YYYY*

[ ][ ] [ ][ ] [ ][ ][ ][ ]

5 Place of marriage or civil partnership *(see note 6, page 4)*

[ ]

[ ]

IHT402 (Substitute) (LexisNexis) (Version 05/2011) Page 1 L11/08

Spouse or civil partner's details continued

6 **Did the spouse or civil partner who died first leave a Will?**

Yes ☐ *enclose a copy of the Will and any codicils, instruments of variation or disclaimers*

No ☐

7 **What was the net value of the spouse or civil partner's estate passing under their Will or intestacy?** *(see note 1 on page 4)*

£

8 **Was a grant of representation (Confirmation in Scotland) obtained for the estate of the spouse or civil partner who died first?**

Yes ☐ *enclose a copy of the grant or confirmation*

No ☐ *enclose a copy of the death certificate*

Spouse or civil partner's nil rate band

Fill in this section to work out the available nil rate band for the estate of the spouse or civil partner who died first.

9 **Inheritance Tax, Capital Transfer Tax or Estate Duty nil rate band in force at the date of death** *(see note 2 on page 4)* £

10 **Total chargeable value of gifts and other transfers of value made in the seven years before the date of death** *(see notes 3 and 5 on page 4)* £

11 **Nil rate band available against the estate of the spouse or civil partner who died first** *(box 9 minus box 10)* £

Spouse or civil partner's estate

Fill in this section with details of the estate of the spouse or civil partner who died first. Enter the value of the assets at their date of death after deduction of exemptions or reliefs.

12 **Legacies and assets passing under Will or intestacy of the spouse or civil partner who died first. Do not include legacies and assets that passed to the deceased who has died now** *(see note 3 on page 4)*

Legacy/asset	Value £
Continue on a separate sheet if necessary	£

13 **Share of assets jointly owned by the spouse or civil partner who died first, excluding assets that passed to the deceased who has died now** *(see note 3 on page 4)* £

14 **Assets held in trust to which the spouse or civil partner who died first was entitled to benefit** *(see note 3 on page 4)* £

15 **Gifts with reservation made by the spouse or civil partner who died first** *(see note 3 on page 4)* £

16 **Total chargeable estate of the spouse or civil partner** *(box 12 + box 13 + box 14 + box 15)* £

IHT402 Page 2

Transferable nil rate band

17 **Nil rate band available for transfer** *(box 11 minus box 16)* £

18 **Percentage by which to increase the nil rate band available on the deceased's death** *(box 17 divided by box 9 and multiplied by 100). Use four decimal places,* ***do not*** *round up* . %

19 **Nil rate band at the date of the deceased's death (the person who has died now)** - *see IHT400 Rates and tables* £

20 **Transferable nil rate band** *(box 19 multiplied by the box 18 percentage)* *Round up to the nearest £* £

Example

- If the percentage in box 18 is 66.6666%, and
- the nil rate band in box 19 is £300,000
- then the figure to enter in box 20 would be £300,000 x 66.6666%

(or £300,000 x 66.6666 ÷ 100) = £200,000 rounded up to the nearest £

Exemptions and reliefs

21 **List any exemptions or reliefs, other than spouse or civil partner exemption, taken into account in arriving at the values in boxes 10, 12, 13, 14 or 15** *(see note 4 on page 4)*

Box number	Exemptions or relief taken into account - *state amount and type* *(For example, box 14 Charity exemption £3,000)*

Pensions

Only answer question 22 where the spouse or civil partner who died first died on or after 6 April 2006 and before 6 April 2011.

22 **Was the spouse or civil partner in receipt of a pension from:**

- an Alternatively Secured Pension, or
- a pension scheme or annuity from which unauthorised payments were made after their death? No ☐ Yes ☐

If you have answered Yes, the calculation of the percentage to increase the deceased's nil rate band is complex. You may use the figure you worked out in box 20 provisionally. We will recalculate the percentage once you have sent us the form IHT400 for the deceased's estate.

If the spouse or civil partner was domiciled in Scotland at the date of death

Only answer question 23 where the spouse or civil partner who died first was domiciled in Scotland.

23 **Was there anyone who was entitled to claim the legitim fund?** No ☐ Yes ☐

If you have answered Yes, the calculation of the percentage to increase the deceased's nil rate band will depend on whether a claim for legitim is made. You may use the figure you worked out in box 20 provisionally. We will discuss the percentage once you have sent us the form IHT400 for the deceased's estate.

IHT402 Page 3

Notes

Your claim to transfer unused Inheritance Tax nil rate band
Where most or all of an estate passes to someone's surviving spouse or civil partner, those assets are generally exempt from Inheritance Tax. This means that most or all of the nil rate band available on the first death is not used.

The amount of the unused nil rate band can be transferred to the survivor of the marriage or civil partnership to increase the value of the nil rate band available on their death.

Since the transfer does not happen automatically, you must fill in this form and make a claim to transfer it. The claim must be made when the second spouse or civil partner dies.

How the transfer works
On the deceased's death, the nil rate band that is available to their estate is increased by the percentage of the nil rate band that was unused when their spouse or civil partner died.

For example:

- A spouse or civil partner died and the nil rate band was £250,000.
- They left legacies totalling £125,000 to their children with the remainder to the surviving spouse or civil partner. The legacies to the children would use up half of the nil rate band, leaving the other half (50%) unused.
- In our example, on the deceased's death, the nil rate band is £300,000. So, their nil rate band would be increased by 50% to £450,000.
- If the deceased's estate did not exceed £450,000 there would be no Inheritance Tax to pay on their death. If it did, there would be Inheritance Tax to pay on the value above that figure.

Obtaining copies of grants of representation and Wills

- England and Wales – phone **020 7947 6983**,
- Scotland – phone **0131 247 2850**
- Northern Ireland – phone **028 9023 5111**

Copies of death, marriage and/or civil partnership certificates are available from the General Register Office

- in England and Wales go to **www.gro.gov.uk**
- in Scotland go to **www.gro-scotland.gov.uk**
- in Northern Ireland go to **www.groni.gov.uk**

Spouse or civil partner's estate – notes to help you fill in this form

1 You can find the net value of the estate passing under the will or intestacy on the copy of the grant of representation* (if one was taken out) or by adding together all the assets in the estate and deducting any liabilities.

2 For the IHT nil rate band in force at the date the spouse or civil partner died, please refer to form IHT400 Rates and tables. If it does not go back far enough, the rates for earlier years are available from:

- **www.hmrc.gov.uk/inheritancetax/** or
- the Probate and Inheritance Tax Helpline on **0845 30 20 900**
  – if calling from outside the UK, phone **+44 115 974 3009**.

3 When filling in box 10 and boxes 12 to 15, you should include the value that was chargeable to tax. That is, the value after the deduction of exemptions and reliefs.

Spouse exemption where the first spouse died before 22 March 1972
Under Estate Duty there was no spouse exemption. All legacies and assets passing under Will or intestacy or by survivorship, irrespective of the recipient and value should be included in box 12.

Spouse exemption where the first spouse died between 22 March 1972 and 12 November 1974 inclusive
During this period spouse exemption was limited to £15,000 so all legacies and assets passing under Will or intestacy or by survivorship, that passed to the deceased in excess of £15,000 should be included in box 12.

Spouse exemption after 12 November 1974
After that date there is no limit to spouse exemption unless the deceased was domiciled in the UK and the surviving spouse was not domiciled in the UK, when it is limited to £55,000. If that is the case, legacies and assets that passed to the deceased in excess of £55,000 should be included in box 12.

4 List any exemptions or reliefs (other than spouse or civil partner exemption) you have taken into account in box 21. If you have been unable to find out whether or not any exemptions or relief applied when the spouse or civil partner died, leave this box blank.

For more information about the exemptions and reliefs that apply to Inheritance Tax, refer to IHT400 Notes.

If you are including assets which might qualify for an exemption or relief on this form, but are not sure whether the exemption or relief would have applied, tell us. We will discuss with you whether or not the exemption or relief might have applied.

5 For deaths between 27 July 1981 and 17 March 1986 you will need to know whether the spouse or civil partner had made any gifts or other transfers within **ten** years before the date of their death that were chargeable on their death.

6 Name of building, church or register office and locality.

**Please note that if the grant shows tax or duty as having been paid there will be no nil rate band available for transfer.*

Your rights and obligations

Your Charter explains what you can expect from us and what we expect from you. For more information go to **www.hmrc.gov.uk/charter**

We have a range of services for people with disabilities, including guidance in Braille, audio and large print. Most of our forms are also available in large print. Please contact us on any of our phone Helplines if you need these services.

IHT402 Page 4

Where a widow or widower has been previously married on more than one occasion, then on their death the availability of unused nil rate bands of their previous spouses may be aggregated with their own by their personal representatives but the aggregate of the predeceased spouses' unused nil rate bands should not exceed the nil rate band pertaining at the date of death of the widow or widower. See Example 2 and RATES OF TAX (40). See IHTM 43030. A similar situation will also apply in cases of civil partnerships for civil marriages that took place from 5 December 2005. [*IHTA 1984, s 8A(5)(6) as inserted by FA 2008, Sch 4 para 2*].

Example 1

John dies on 25 August 2008 with an estate of £300,000 and he leaves by his will £50,000 to each of his two grandchildren on discretionary trusts and the balance is left to his widow, Jean. Jean dies in October 2010 when the nil rate band at that time is £325,000. John's balance of nil rate band available to pass on to his wife is 66.66666% (i.e. (£300,000 – £100,000) ÷ £300,000 × 100%) and therefore when Jean dies her personal representatives can claim an unused nil rate band applicable to John of £216,667 (i.e. 66.66666% × £325,000). This is added to Jean's unused nil rate band at her date of death also of £325,000 to make a total of £541,667 which is within the maximum of £650,000 (i.e. £325,000 × 2).

Notes to the example

(A) The up rating of the predeceased's nil rate band on the death of the survivor spouse's or civil partner's death is calculated by applying the unused nil rate band (i.e. M > VT) under *IHTA 1984, s 8A(2)(4)* as follows:

$$\text{Percentage} = \frac{E}{NRBMD} \times 100$$

where:

M = maximum amount that could be transferred on the predeceased person's death where it is chargeable at the nil rate band at that time;
VT = value actually transferred by the chargeable transfer or nil if applicable;
E = the amount by which M above is greater than VT above;
NRBMD = the nil rate band maximum applying at the time of the deceased spouse's or civil partner's death.

(B) The claim for the unused nil rate band by Jean's personal representatives must be made within two years from the end of the month in which the survivor spouse or civil partner dies or, if later, the period three months after the personal representatives first begin to act. HMRC Commissioners may specify a longer period in certain circumstances. [*IHTA 1984, s 8B*].

(C) Under Scottish law, children (or remoter issue) have the right to share in the movable estate of a deceased parent. This is called legitim. In Scotland, a claim for legitim (see also **52.19** below) may result in a delay in claim due to the child's age which then has a knock on effect with regard to the transferability of the nil rate band to the survivor spouse or civil partner who will have predeceased the minor. If a claim is made then the nil rate band claimed by the personal representatives of the survivor spouse or civil partner will have to be amended to take into account the legitim. The child may renounce his claim to legitim by his twentieth birthday (or longer if the Board permit). [*IHTA 1984, s 147(10) as inserted by FA 2008, Sch 4 para 3*]. See also HMRC Inheritance Tax manual IHTM43041.

Example 2

Betty has been married and widowed twice before. Her first husband died in October 1974 when estate duty applied and **54** TRANSITIONAL PROVISIONS applied. He left all his assets in his will to Betty and this was within the £15,000 spouse's exemption applying at that time so that none of his tax free band was utilised in 1974. Betty's second husband Jack died three years ago on 18 June 2005 and left his assets to Betty excepting a £165,000 gift he made to his daughter in 2003. Jack therefore had used 60% of his £275,000 nil rate band at his death and a further 40% is available to transfer on to Betty on her death.

Say Betty dies in December 2009 the personal representatives would be entitled to claim 100% of her first husband's nil rate band (i.e. £325,000 × 100%) and also 40% of Jack's nil rate band (i.e. £325,000 × 40% = £130,000) as well as her own unused nil rate band of up to £325,000. This makes a total of £780,000 but is restricted to £650,000 (i.e. £325,000 × 2).

Notes to the example

(A) In such similar situations where the aggregate unused nil rate bands of previous deceased spouses or civil partners add up to more than the current amount pertaining at the date of death of the survivor a proportion will be wasted. It is, in this case, too late to effect a deed of variation within *IHTA 1984, s 142* as more than two years have elapsed since Jack's death. See Example 4 at **13** DEEDS OF VARIATION AND DISCLAIMERS.

(B) It may be appropriate in such circumstances to effect a deed of variation on the death of the second spouse, Jack in this example, to ensure that assets are passed on to the children to utilise the wasted portion of the nil rate band. The use of a nil rate band discretionary trust would achieve this or amending the will by codicil as follows:

I bequeath a legacy to [daughter] of the maximum amount to which I can bequeath without attracting inheritance tax on my death.

(C) Betty in fact will also be entitled to the War Pensions Agency (WPA) allowance of £20,000 exemption on her death. As Betty is intending to leave her substantial estate including her lottery winnings to charities the aggregate nil rate band available will be wasted but up to £670,000 (i.e. £325,000 × 2 + £20,000 WPA exemption) could be utilised by gifts to Jack's daughter or by increasing the gifts to the poorest villagers above the amount already contributed from her lottery win.

Example 3

Jeffrey, who is married to Margaret, dies on 2 January 2009 and leaves £450,000. A sum of £100,000 is left on trust for life for his ex-wife Pat and £50,000 legacies to each of his two sons by his first marriage with the balance of his estate going to his second wife, Margaret. Margaret dies on 6 April 2010 and leaves to her four children her estate valued at that date including the assets derived from Jeffrey's estate which are valued at £480,000.

Jeffrey's available nil rate band at death was £300,000 but £200,000 has been utilised in respect of the trusts in favour of his ex-wife and legacies to his two sons. Therefore, on Margaret's death her estate will benefit from 33.3333% of the nil rate band unutilised by Jeffrey. This amount of £108,333 is added to her available nil rate band of £325,000 making a total of £433,333 and gives a taxable estate of £46,667.

Notes to the example

(A) A number of issues arise in this example. This is a second marriage and the children of Jeffrey's first marriage, it could be said, are disadvantaged by the rules that give Margaret's estate the benefit of the unused nil rate band. Jeffrey could have amended his will to ensure that on his death some or all of his assets are left on trust to Margaret with the remainder going to his sons. This would constitute an immediate post death interest and as such there would be no IHT payable on Jeffrey's death but on the death of Margaret the trust assets would form part of her estate and be covered by a proportion of aggregate nil rate band and ensure that Jeffrey's sons inherit his relevant proportion. See Note A in Example 1 at **42.1** SETTLEMENTS WITH INTERESTS IN POSSESSION.

(B) A deed of variation may be appropriate but all the beneficiaries must agree to the variation. It should also be remembered that where any potential beneficiaries are minors, or are otherwise *sui juris*, it will be necessary for any variation to be approved on their behalf by the courts. This could include unborn children if the wording of the will is wide-ranging. Even though HMRC will normally accept that a woman who is aged over 55 is past child bearing age this is not necessarily true in practice. [*Variation of Trusts Act 1958; Trusts (Scotland) Act 1961*].

Relief for closely inherited main residence

[52.16] With effect for deaths on or after 6 April 2017 a *residence nil rate amount* is to be available for transfers on death where the deceased's interest in a qualifying residential interest, which has been their residence at some point and is included in their estate, is inherited by one or more direct descendants on death, whether by will or on intestacy. The nil rate amount will not be available where the property is left on trust unless the trust gives an immediate post-death interest in possession to a direct descendant, or alternatively the trust is a bereaved minor's trust or age 18–25 trusts for a direct descendant.

A direct descendant is defined as a child of the deceased, including a step-child, adopted child, foster child, and an infant subject to guardianship arrangement or a special guardianship order under the *Children Act 1989* or corresponding laws. Also included are the lineal descendants of any of these.

This additional nil amount will be available only against transfers on death, and not against lifetime transfers that are chargeable on death. However where there was a lifetime gift of the property in which there was a reservation of benefit retained by the donor, such that the property forms part of the donor's estate on death, the donee is treated as inheriting it on the death. Thus the nil rate amount may then be claimed against the amount chargeable under *FA 2006, s 102(3)*.

Any unused excess of the nil rate amount on the death of one spouse or civil partner will be available to transfer to a surviving spouse or civil partner. The *default allowance* comprises the total of the main residence nil amount for the year in which the death occurs, as set out below, plus any brought amount. The table of reliefs to commence with effect from 6 April 2017 is as follows.

- £100,000 for 2017/2018
- £125,000 for 2018/2019
- £150,000 for 2019/2020
- £175,000 for 2020/2021

The relief will be subject to tapering in larger estates. The taper will apply to give an *adjusted allowance* where the net value of the estate before reliefs and exemptions exceeds £2 million. In such cases the additional nil amount will be reduced by £1 for every £2 of the excess over £2 million. Where the value of the residence inherited by direct descendants exceeds or is equal to the adjusted allowance, none of the nil rate amount is available for transfer to a surviving spouse or civil partner, but if that value is below the adjusted allowance, the unused excess may be transferred.

The main residence nil amount will increase in line with the Consumer Price Index for years after 2020/2021.

The value of the main residence nil rate amount for an estate will be the lower of the net value of the interest in the residential property inherited by direct descendants (after deducting any liabilities secured on it and any agricultural or business property reliefs) or the default allowance, as reduced where applicable to the amount of the adjusted allowance.

A *qualifying residential interest* is a dwelling house which has been the person's residence at any time whilst it formed part of his or her estate. No minimum period for use as a residence is specified but it is thought likely that the interpretation adopted for capital gains tax main residence relief will apply, so that the usage must have been with some degree of permanence. The property need not be in the UK. The reference to dwelling house includes its garden or grounds, but not woodlands left out of account on the death under *IHTA 1984, s 125*. The relief is limited to one residential property but personal representatives will be able to nominate which residential property should qualify if there is more than one in the estate. A property which was never a residence of the deceased, because for example it was always let, will not qualify, but if the non-occupation of a home was due to the person residing in job-related accommodation (within *TCGA 1992, s 222(8A–8D)*), that home may be treated as occupied as a residence during the time that the deceased lived at the job-related accommodation.

On the death of a person's surviving spouse or civil partner after 5 April 2017, it will be possible to make a claim to transfer any unused proportion of the additional nil rate amount unused by the spouse or civil partner who predeceased, in the same way that the existing nil rate amount can be transferred. This applies irrespective of when the first of the couple died.

If the first death was before 6 April 2017, the brought forward amount is £100,000 but subject to tapering where the net value of the estate before reliefs and exemptions was in excess of £2 million. In such cases the additional nil amount will be reduced by £1 for every £2 of the excess over £2 million.

Example 6

Mavis died on 1 January 2014 leaving an estate of £2,100,000, including a half share in the home worth £450,000. She left her estate to her husband Jack.

Jack dies on 5 May 2017 leaving an estate of £2,200,000 after liabilities. He leaves gifts to charities of £100,000 and the residue to their two children.

The IHT on Jack's death will be calculated as follows:

Estate			£2,200,000
Nil band			(£325,000)
Transferred nil band			(£325,000)
Main residence nil amount: default allowance:			
		£100,000	
Brought forward amount:	$\frac{£2.1m - £2m}{2}$	£50,000	
		£150,000	
Adjusted allowance:			
Default allowance		£150,000	
Less	$\frac{£2.2m - £2m}{2}$	(£100,000)	
Nil amount available for claim		£50,000	(£50,000)
Charitable exemption			(£100,000)
IHT payable on			£1,400,000
IHT payable at 40%			£560,000

Note: the main residence nil amount cannot exceed the value of the interest inherited by direct descendants but this restriction does not apply in this example.

If the first death is on or after 6 April 2017, and that person's estate is below the £2 million threshold, the carry forward amount is the unused nil rate amount on the first death, expressed as a percentage of the full nil rate amount applicable at the time. That percentage of the nil rate amount applying on the death of the survivor will be added to the amount available on the survivor's death.

If the first death is on or after 6 April 2017, and that person's estate is above the £2 million threshold, the carry forward amount is the unused adjusted nil rate amount on that death (see above), expressed as a percentage of the full nil rate amount applicable at the time. That percentage of the nil rate amount applying on the death of the survivor will be added to the amount available on the survivor's death.

Claims must be made either by the person's personal representatives within the permitted period, or by any other person liable to the tax chargeable on the person's death within such later period as HMRC may in the particular case allow. The *permitted period* is either (*a*) the period of two years from the end of the month in which the person dies or (if it ends later) the period of three months beginning with the date on which the personal representatives first act as such, or (*b*) such longer period as HMRC may in the particular case allow. Claims may be withdrawn no later than one month after the end of the permitted period. A further provision allows a late claim in situations where there is a series of deaths and on one of the earlier deaths no claim was made for a transfer of unused allowance. If this affects the IHT liability in the latest estate, a claim may be made for a brought forward allowance within the same period detailed above for that estate.

Provision is made for cases where a residence left to direct descendants qualifies for conditional exemption. To the extent that a residence is conditionally exempt, it is treated as not closely inherited so that the appropriate proportion of the residence nil rate band is available to carry forward. The residence nil band may apply to charges which arise when conditional exemption ceases to apply (that is, if the undertakings to secure the conditional exemption are not kept, the owner dies, or the property is sold, given away or disposed of). Where the deceased's surviving spouse or civil partner dies before the charge arises and the residence nil rate band, or part of it, is transferred to that surviving spouse or partner, the residence nil rate band available against the charge is reduced by the amount so transferred. Similarly where the charge arises before death of the surviving spouse or partner, the amount of residence nil rate band available for transfer is recalculated to take account of the amount (if any) of the residence nil rate band that was used by the charge when conditional exemption ceases to apply.

In addition to the foregoing, legislation in Finance Bill 2016 will provide that where part of the main residence nil rate amount might be lost because the deceased had downsized to a less valuable residence or had ceased to own a residence on or after 8 July 2015, that part will still be available provided the deceased left that smaller residence, or assets of equivalent value, to direct descendants.

However, the total amount available will not exceed the maximum available residence nil rate amount. The technical details of how the additional nil rate amount will be enhanced to support those who have downsized or ceased to own their home will be the subject of a consultation to be published in September 2015 ahead of the draft Finance Bill 2016.

[*IHTA 1984, ss 8D–M*].

Alterations of dispositions on death

[52.17] Dispositions under a will or on an intestacy may be varied or disclaimed by an instrument in writing made by the persons who benefit or would benefit under the dispositions. Such variation or disclaimer may not be a transfer of value and may be treated as if effected by the deceased. For full details see **13** DEEDS OF VARIATION AND DISCLAIMERS.

Where a surviving spouse/civil partner elects under the *Administration of Estates Act 1925, s 47A* that his life interest in residuary estate be redeemed by the personal representatives by payment of its capital value, the redemption is not a transfer of value and the surviving spouse/civil partner is treated as having been entitled to that capital value instead of the life interest. [*IHTA 1984, ss 17(c), 145 as amended by The Tax and Civil Partnership Regulations 2005, SI 2005/3229, Regs 6, 31*].

Two year discretionary will trusts

Where property is settled by a person's will and, within two years after his death and before any IPDI or disabled person's interest has subsisted in the property, an event occurs (for example an appointment in favour of a beneficiary) on which tax would otherwise be chargeable under the provisions for SETTLEMENTS: DISCRETIONARY TRUSTS AND OTHER TRUSTS OF RELEVANT PROPERTY (**43**) (except in relation to a ten-year anniversary charge), no tax is chargeable and for IHT purposes the will is to be deemed to have provided that the assets concerned should be held as they are held as a result of the event. Equally, where the event within two years of death is one on which tax would be chargeable but for *IHTA 1984, ss 75, 76, Sch 4 para 16(1)* (property becoming subject to employee trusts or held for charitable purposes, national purposes, public benefit or a qualifying political party or comprised in a maintenance fund for historic buildings) then the will is deemed to have provided that the property should be held on the testator's death as it is after the event (i.e. the subsequent distribution to the employee trust etc.).

This provision applies to all appointments, including those which are outright or on trust, except those on IPDI, bereaved minors or age 18-25 trusts; these are subject to a separate provision (see below). Where a testator died before 22 March 2006 the requirement was that no interest in possession has subsisted in the settled property concerned. [*IHTA 1984, s 144(1), (1A) and (2)*].

Because a proportionate charge (as in **43.12** SETTLEMENTS: DISCRETIONARY TRUSTS AND OTHER TRUSTS OF RELEVANT PROPERTY) would not arise on a distribution from a discretionary settlement where made within three months of the settlement's creation, in the past it was important not to make a distribution under the above provisions within three months of the death (see *Frankland v CIR* CA [1997] STC 1450). However this anomaly will be corrected by *F(No 2)A 2015* in relation to appointments to the surviving spouse or civil partner where the death occurs on or after 10 December 2014 so that for such cases it is not necessary to wait until the three-month period has elapsed. See also *Harding and Leigh v CIR* where a testator expressed a wish that property bequeathed by his will should be transferred by the legatee to other persons and the legatee transfers any of the property in accordance with that wish within two years after the testator's death, then the transfer is not a transfer of value (i.e. not liable to inheritance tax) and it is treated as if the property had been bequeathed by the will to the transferee. [*IHTA 1984, ss 17(b), 143*]. However, in the case of *Harding and Leigh v CIR* [1997] STC SCD 321 Sp C 140 the Trustees could not be treated as legatees because the Trustees in this case exercised fiduciary powers and were not beneficially entitled. The Capital Taxes Sub-Committee asked HMRC's views on the interaction between *s 142* and *s 144* in relation to intestacy; HMRC replied that in their view an event under *s 144(1)* could follow a variation satisfying *s 142(1)*. Accordingly, it would be inconsistent to distinguish between testate and intestate estates when, all other things being equal, the ability to vary the disposition is the same. This is subject to the caveat that the tax position will depend on the facts as they are at the relevant time. See Taxation Practitioner, June 1999 p 9.

As a separate provision, where a testator dies after 21 March 2006 and his estate is held on discretionary trusts, if within two years after the death an appointment is made on trusts which would have qualified as IPDI or under *IHTA 1984, ss 71A, 71D* (i.e. bereaved minor's trusts and 18–25 trusts) then providing no IPDI or disabled person's interest has previously subsisted in the property concerned, no tax is chargeable and the event is treated as if the will had provided for it. In this case it is not necessary to ensure that the appointment is made more than three months from the death. [*IHTA 1984, s 144(3), (4)*]. A late amendment to the Finance Bill was made to ensure that trusts for a bereaved minor, an 18–25 trusts and an IPDI created under *s 144* write back into the will of a deceased within two years of death will be treated as if established by the will regardless of whether before or after 22 March 2006. HMRC accept that an appointment under these provisions to existing pilot trusts in which the spouse has an interest in possession can qualify as an appointment on IPDI trusts. [*IHTA 1984, s 144; FA 2006, Sch 20 para 27*]. See also 5 ANTI-AVOIDANCE.

Where a person disclaims his entitlement to an interest in settled property, then providing the disclaimer is not made for a consideration in money or money's worth, he is treated as not having become entitled to the interest. [*IHTA 1984, s 93*].

See **52.17** below for orders made under *Inheritance (Provision for Family and Dependants) Act 1975* and **52.19** below for legitim. See also **33.26** NATIONAL HERITAGE where, for deaths after 16 March 1987, settled property is exempt from IHT on the death of a person who has an interest in possession in the property if the terms on which the property is held are altered after his death so that it goes into a heritage maintenance fund within two years particularly with regard to the position after 21 March 2006. [*IHTA 1984, s 57A; FA 1987, s 59, Sch 9 paras 1, 4; FA 2006, Sch 20 para 17*].

Inheritance (Provision for Family and Dependants) Act 1975

[52.18] Under the above Act, as amended by the *Law Reform (Successors) Act 1995* and *Civil Partnership Act 2004, Sch 4 paras 15–27*, a court may order financial provision for family, civil partners and dependants of a deceased person out of his net estate. If the deceased died on or after 1 January 1996 a new category of applicant is defined as a person who 'during the whole of the period of two years ending immediately before the date when the deceased died' was living (a) in the same household as the deceased, and (b) as the husband or wife of the deceased. However, in (a) above 'living in the same household as the deceased' could also mean a period of temporary separation due to prevailing circumstances at the time. See *Gully v Dix; In re Dix deceased* CA [2004] TLR 28 January 2004. See TAX CASES (58).

Where an order is made under these provisions in relation to any property forming part of the estate of a deceased person, the estate is treated as devolving on death in accordance with the terms of the order. [*IHTA 1984, s146(1)*]. From 26 July 1989 it is not possible to circumvent this treatment where the estate is left to a surviving spouse and the claim is made by a non-exempt beneficiary. Before that date, it was possible for the surviving spouse to settle the claim out of her own resources as a transfer without gratuitous intent, leaving the IHT exemption for the estate unaffected, but this arrangement is now blocked by *IHTA 1984, s 29A*: see further details at **21.23** EXEMPT TRANSFERS.

Originating summons by a widow for leave to apply out of time and for reasonable provision

[52.19] IN THE HIGH COURT OF JUSTICE

2010 . . . B. No. . . . [Chancery or Family] Division

In the Matter of the Estate of B.B. deceased

Between

	A.B.	. . . .	Claimant
	And		
(1)	C.D.		
(2)	D.D.		
(3)	J.K.		
(4)	L.M. (a minor)	. . . .	Defendants

LET C.D. of (*address*), D.D. of (*address*), J.K. of (*address*) and L.M. of (*address*) attend before [*in the Chancery Division:* Master . . . . at Chancery Chambers, Room No . . . . . . , Thomas More Building, Royal Courts of Justice, Strand, London WC2A 2LL, *or in the Family Division:* District Judge . . . . in chambers at Somerset House, Strand, London WC2R 1LP, *or in a district registry:* the District Judge in chambers at the district registry of the High Court of Justice at (*address*)] on [[Mon]day the . . . . . . day of . . . . 2010 at . . . . o'clock in the [fore]noon *or* a day to be fixed] on the hearing of an application by the Claimant A.B. of (*address*):

(1) For an order that she be granted permission to make an application under the Inheritance (Provision for Family and Dependants) Act 1975 notwithstanding that a period of 6 months from the date on which representation in regard to the estate of the above-mentioned B. B, was first taken out has ended;

(2) For an order that such reasonable financial provision as this Honourable Court thinks fit to be made for the Claimant out of the net estate of the above mentioned B. B.;

(3) For such further or other relief as shall be just;

(4) For an order that the costs of this application be paid out of the said estate.

This application is made under the Inheritance (Provision for Family and Dependants) Act 1975.

AND let the defendant within [14] days after service of this summons on him counting the day of service, return the accompanying Acknowledgement of Service to the appropriate Court Office.

DATED the . . . . . . day of . . . . 2010.

[This provision is subject to the Court taking into account the co-habitee's age, the length of the relationship with the deceased and the contribution made by the co-habitee to the welfare of the deceased's family. [*Inheritance (Provision for Family and Dependants) Act 1975, s 1(1A)* as inserted by *Law Reform (Succession) Act 1995, s 2*]. Where such an order is made under *section 2* of the *Act* in relation to any property in the estate, the property is treated for purposes of inheritance tax as having devolved on his death subject to the provisions of the order. [*IHTA 1984, s 146(1)*].]

Between	A.B.	. . . .	Claimant
	And		
	C.D.	. . . .	Defendant

UPON THE APPLICATION of the Claimant by originating summons AND UPON HEARING Counsel for the Claimant and for the Defendant AND UPON READING the documents recorded in the court file as having been read.

[AND the Claimant and the Defendant by their Counsel consenting to this Order]

IT IS ORDERED pursuant to the provisions of Section 2 (1) of the Inheritance (Provision for Family and Dependants) Act 1975 that a sum of £ . . . . be paid to the Claimant out of the capital of the Testator's estate on . . . . 2010 together with interest at the rate of . . . . per cent per annum as from the date of the death of the Testator namely . . . . 2010.

AND IT IS ORDERED that there be taxed

(1) on the indemnity basis the costs of and incidental to the said application of the Defendant as Executrix of the said will

(2) on the [standard] basis the costs of the Claimant of the said application and

(3) on the [standard] basis the costs to which the Legal Aid Act 1988 applies incurred on behalf of the Claimant

AND IT IS ORDERED that the costs first and secondly herein before directed to be taxed be paid when taxed out of the residuary estate of the testator

Etc.

Case law — mutual wills

In the case of *Goodchild and another v Goodchild* [1997] 3 All ER 63 mutual wills were drawn up by Mr Goodchild and his wife as follows:

> 1. I REVOKE all former Wills and Codicils made by me. 2. IF my wife [. . . . .] survives me for the space of twenty-eight days then I DEVISE AND BEQUEATH all my real and personal estate to her absolutely and appoint her to be the sole Executrix of this my Will. 3. IF my said wife does not survive me for the period aforesaid then I APPOINT my son [. . . . .] and my daughter [. . . . .] to be the Executors and Trustees of this my Will and I DECLARE that the following clauses shall take effect . . . CLAUSE 5. UPON TRUST for my said son [. . . . .] if he survives me for the space of twenty-eight days and if he does not so survive me then UPON TRUST for . . .

The Goodchilds' wills did not contain the legal words 'mutually agreed' and the subsequent alteration of his will after Mrs Goodchild's death in favour of his new wife was a moral obligation that overcame the lack of the legal obligation. In consequence the sum awarded to the son under *section 2* for reasonable financial provision was not overturned. A further interesting point to arise out of the was the opportunity given to the parties by Carnwath J in an earlier judgment for the parties 'to arrive at a sensible financial arrangement, which meets as far as possible their respective requirements and is tax effective'. No agreement could be reached and in February 1996 it was too late; the only way of achieving a similar result would be for an order to be made under *Inheritance (Provision for Family and Dependants) Act 1975, s 2* as amended by *IHTA 1984, s 146* of which the relevant part at subsection (b) states ' . . . an order for the payment to the applicant out of that estate of a lump sum of such amount as may be so specified . . . '. *Section 2 (4) of the Inheritance (Provision for Family and Dependants) Act 1975* follows on to say that the court may order consequential and supplemental provisions to ' . . . vary the disposition of the deceased's estate effected by the will . . . in such a manner as the court thinks fair and reasonable having regard to the provisions of the order and all the circumstances of the case . . . '. However, Morritt LJ stated that where the effect of the order is to confer substantial advantage on the parties at the expense of HMRC the court should be satisfied that the order is not only within its jurisdiction but is also one which may properly be made. He went on to say ' . . . I think that it is important for the future that if an order such as this is to be made the grounds on which it is thought to be authorised by subsection (4) should be clearly demonstrated, for the consent and wishes of the parties is not enough'.

Where during his lifetime the deceased made a disposition of property, without full consideration, with the object of defeating an application under the Act, the court may order (under *s 10* of the Act) the donee to refund any money or property required for the deceased's family or dependants. In addition, if a subsequent windfall arises to the estate and a hearing decides that provision, whether or not a moral obligation, is required then the windfall may be deemed to make any previous provision unreasonable. *Snapes v Aram and others* [1998] TLR, 8 May 1998. If the disposition was a chargeable transfer, the *personal representatives* may claim the inheritance tax or capital transfer tax paid on that transfer be repaid to them (whether or not they paid the tax in the first instance) with interest from the date of claim. A reduction in the total of lifetime chargeable transfers by the deceased is made equal to the value of the transfer refunded. Any claim under *s 146(2)(a)* must be made not more than four years after the date on which the order (see above) is made. (*Note.*

This reduction will affect the tax rate applicable to the deceased's estate but not the rate on the other chargeable lifetime transfers). [*IHTA 1984, ss 146(2)(3), 236(3); FA 1989, s 179(1); FA 2009, Sch 53 para 8*].

The court may make orders for financial provision out of the net estate which is deemed to include property held by persons as a result of:

(i) *donatio mortis causa*;
(ii) any sums nominated by the deceased under any statute; and
(iii) the deceased's severable share of property held in joint tenancy.

Any such property on which inheritance tax is payable is treated as part of the net estate after deduction of the tax and for this purpose the amount of tax deducted is not affected by any court order. Any repayment of that tax is made to the personal representatives and not to the person holding the property. [*IHTA 1984, s 146(4)*].

Treatment of tax refunds

Any tax refund (including any interest thereon) to the personal representatives or property recovered is treated as part of the deceased's estate for the purposes of transfer of value made by him on his death. In the case of an amount which is repayable on a claim under *s 146(2)*, the repayment interest start date is from the date the order is made and not before. [*IHTA 1984, s 146(2)(5)(7); FA 2009, Sch 54 para 11*].

The court may also order financial provision out of settled property, or for property to be settled on variation of a settlement. In this case there is no charge to tax under *IHTA 1984, s 52(1)* (deemed transfer of value on termination of a life interest in settled property). Anything done in compliance with such a court order is not an occasion for charge under the provisions relating to SETTLEMENTS: DISCRETIONARY TRUSTS AND OTHER TRUSTS OF RELEVANT PROPERTY (**43**). [*IHTA 1984, s 146(6)*].

Northern Ireland. Corresponding provisions are applied by *SI 1979/924* and *927*.

Legitim

[52.20] Under Scottish law children (or remoter issue) have the right to share in one-third of the movable estate of a deceased parent but also see Key Points below. This is called legitim. Where a testator dies after 12 November 1974 bequeathing property to the surviving spouse/civil partner and leaving insufficient property in the estate to satisfy entitlement to legitim of a minor by their eighteenth birthday, inheritance tax is charged as if legitim had been satisfied (i.e. the spouse/civil partner exemption will not apply to that much of the property) but this may be varied as follows.

(a) The executors or judicial factor of the testator may elect in writing (within two years of the death or longer if the Board permit) that tax be charged as if the gift to the surviving spouse/civil partner took effect in full (so obtaining benefit of the spouse/civil partner exemption and the transferability of the nil rate band within *IHTA 1984, s 8A*). If the minor subsequently claims his legal rights by their eighteenth birthday or has not renounced his rights by his twentieth birthday (or longer if the Board permit), the spouse/civil partner exemption is lost to that extent and tax becomes payable (by the child) on the scale applicable at the date of death with interest from the original due date (i.e. six months after the end of the month in which death occurred). In the case of an amount which is payable under *IHTA 1984, s 147(4)*, the late payment interest start date is the day after the end of the period of six months beginning with the date of the testator's death. In the case of a renouncement of a claim to legitim an amount which is repayable under *IHTA 1984, s 147(2)*, the repayment interest start date is the date on which the tax was paid. If the child claiming legitim does not pay the tax, see points (b)–(d) at **30.5** LIABILITY FOR TAX for persons with secondary liability.

(b) The child may renounce his claim to legitim by his twentieth birthday (or longer if the Board permit) and tax will be repayable (because of the spouse/civil partner exemption or transferability of the nil rate band between spouses) with interest (which shall not constitute income for any tax purposes) from the date on which the tax was originally paid. Such a renunciation is not a transfer of value. See also HMRC Inheritance Tax manual IHTM43041.

(c) Where a child dies before renouncing his claim under (b) above, his executors may renounce his claim within two years of his death, and his legal rights to legitim will not form part of his estate on his death.

[*IHTA 1984, ss 17(d), 147, 209(2)(3), 236(4); FA 1989, s 179(1)(3); The Tax and Civil Partnership Regulations 2005, SI 2005/3229, Regs 6, 32; FA 2008, Sch 4 para 3; FA 2009, Sch 53 para 9, Sch 54 para 12*].

Scottish agricultural leases

[52.21] See **4.17** AGRICULTURAL PROPERTY for special rules regarding such leases passing on death.

Intestacy

The Distribution of Intestate Estates

[52.22] For deaths on or after 1 February 2008 under the *Administration of Estates Act 1925, s 49(1)(a)*; not applicable in Scotland. See also Key Points below. [*Intestate Succession (Interest and Capitalisation) Order 1977, SI 1977/1491* as amended by *Intestate Succession (Interest and Capitalisation (Amendment) Order 2008, SI 2008/3162*].

With effect from 1 February 2009, the amount of the statutory legacy will increase in line with Family Provision (Intestate Succession) Order 2009, *SI 2009/135*. [*Family Provision (Intestate Succession) Order 2009, SI 2009 No 135*].

The *Inheritance and Trustees Powers Act 2014* received Royal Assent on 14 May 2014 and came into force on 1 October 2014. It makes significant changes to the rules on intestacy in relation to the entitlements of the surviving spouse on a death occurring on or after that date. Under this Act the statutory legacy remains the same as before, that is £250,000 but a provision is introduced for it to be regularly increased in line with the consumer prices index. Interest on this legacy is to be paid at the Bank of England rate applying at the end of the month in which the death occurred.

Spouse and issue survive

Note. For these purposes spouse should also mean '*civil partner*'.

Spouse receives	*Issue receive*
All personal chattels; £250,000 absolutely (or the entire estate where this is less); for deaths up to 30 September 2014, a life interest in one half of residue (if any). For deaths on or after 1 October 2014, a one half of residue absolutely.	One half of residue (if any) on statutory trusts *plus*, for deaths up to 30 September 2014, the other half of residue on statutory trusts upon the death of the spouse.

Spouse survives without issue

Spouse receives	*For deaths up to 30 September 2014, remainder distributable to*
All personal chattels; plus, for deaths up to 30 September 2014 £400,000 absolutely (or the entire estate where this is less); plus one half share of residue (if any) absolutely. For deaths on or after 1 October 2014, the residue is held for the surviving spouse absolutely.	(a) The deceased's parents. If no parent survives: (b) on trust for the deceased's brother and sisters of the whole blood and the issue of any such deceased brother or sister.

Spouse survives but no issue, parents, brothers or sisters or their issue

Whole estate to surviving spouse.

No spouse survives

Estate held for the following in the order given with no class of beneficiaries participating unless all those in a prior class have predeceased. Statutory trusts may apply except under (b) and (e).

(a) Issue of the deceased.
(b) Parents.
(c) Brothers and sisters and the issue of a deceased brother or sister.
(d) Half-brothers and half-sisters and the issue of any deceased half-brother or half-sister.

(e) Grandparents.
(f) Uncles and aunts and the issue of any deceased uncle or aunt.
(g) Half-brothers and half-sisters of the deceased's parents and the issue of any deceased half-uncle or half-aunt.
(h) The Crown, the Duchy of Lancaster or the Duchy or Cornwall.

Notes

(A) See IHTM12177, IHTM35161 and IHTM35165 for disclaimer of absolute benefits under intestacy, election by spouse/civil partner of intestate and the treatment of settled property with regard to competency to dispose.
(B) In this context 'Spouse' means a person to whom the deceased was married at the date of death even where there is a separation or estrangement applicable. 'Spouse' does not mean cohabiter, who has no rights of benefit under the rules of intestacy or a divorced ex-spouse.
(C) 'Child' means an adopted child and an illegitimate child but excludes a stepchild or the child of a co-habitee.
(D) Note that the *Civil Partnership Act 2004, Sch 4 paras 7–12* amends the *Administration of Estates Act 1925* to ensure that the remaining surviving partner in a civil partnership will effectively acquire the same rights as a spouse in a case of intestacy.
(E) The above Table applies to England and Wales only. In Northern Ireland the statutory legacy rules are different and in Scotland the 'Prior rights' and *The Family Law (Scotland) Act 2006* limits vary markedly from the England and Wales statutory legacy rules.

Key points

[52.23] Points to consider are as follows.

- The new 36% rate for estates where more than 10% of any component is left to charity can be secured by deed of variation where necessary, and in certain circumstances can be achieved at no cost to the beneficiaries of the estate. For example if there is a gift of £25,000 to charity and apart from that the residue of £275,000 (all chargeable) is left to children, the IHT payable will be £110,000. The children will therefore receive £165,000. If however they enter into a deed of variation to increase the charitable gift to £30,000, the IHT payable will be 36% of £270,000, amount due £97,200. The children then receive £172,800, an increase of £7,800, whilst the charity receives £5000 more.
- When drafting a will consideration should be given to the situation where individuals die in *commorientes* circumstances (see **52.13** above) and there is a survivorship clause (see **52.5** above) in place. For instance, in the following cases such an event might require the survivorship clause to disapply where:

(i) one spouse has assets in excess of the nil rate band and the other does not. In such circumstances, a survivorship clause may ensure that the estate of the richer spouse passes to the poorer but because the survivorship clause applies the estate passes to, say, the child of both and the estate of the poorer to which the survivorship provisions apply passes independently to the child as well. The unutilised nil rate band of the poorer will not be able to be utilised whereas if the survivorship clause was disapplied the nil rate bands of both would be fully utilised. Ideally this would not apply if the estates were equalised;

(ii) the spouses/civil partners die in *commorientes* circumstances and there is the opportunity to take advantage of the exempt transfer on the death under *s 18(1)* then the transfer to the younger spouse or civil partner is not a chargeable transfer. However, the younger of the spouse/civil partner is deemed to have inherited the elder spouse's/civil partner's estate under the *Law of Property Act 1925, s 184* but for the purposes of IHT under *IHTA 1984, s 4(2)* eliminates mutual gifts between individuals in such circumstances and there is no transfer of value to the younger spouse/civil partner on which inheritance tax can be charged. See 52.5 above;

(iii) where children are to benefit and the survivorship clause is disapplied so that in *commorientes* circumstances the estate of the elder spouse passes to the younger and the younger spouse's will passes the estate into a trust that would an IPDI. As mentioned in the point above the application of *IHTA 1984, s 4(2)* the elder spouses estate is exempt from IHT in the estate of the younger and the younger's estate creates the IPDI. However, if the children are young and it is better that discretionary trusts are set up on death then *IHTA 1984, s 92* would not be met as the requirement of that section is that there is not '*property held for any person*' but it is held on discretion of the trustees. So if this was a requirement by the spouses to effect discretionary trusts a survivorship clause for a period, say, 28 days this would negate the creation of a discretionary settlement — a mere survivorship without a limiting period would not.

- Property owned jointly will pass to the surviving joint owner notwithstanding anything in the will of the deceased joint owner. In a case where there is a survivorship clause the jointly owned property is not affected by the survivorship clause and passes to the surviving joint owner. See page 5 of IHT404. In *commorientes* circumstances assets owned jointly pass to the younger joint owner of the property and onward under their will or by intestacy. In IHT400 schedule IHT404 jointly owned assets need to be detailed in the account. In the IHT account IHT400 on page 6 the jointly owned assets from IHT404 are entered showing the share the deceased had and this is normally presumed to be an equal share but in cases of bank accounts, life assurance policies, etc. it may be different depending on the circumstances.

- In connection with the above if the property is jointly owned with someone who is not the deceased person's spouse or civil partner, the value of the deceased person's fractional share can be subject to discount of between 10 and 15%. This does apply to property jointly held by husband and wife or by civil partners because of the related property rules. See **56.8** VALUATION.
- Wills in England (see point below re Scotland) are signed on the last page and witnessed by *two* individuals to be a validly executed document. The *Wills Act 1837, s 9* sets out the requirements. On the signing of the will by the testator the witnesses must see the signing or executing of the will. If one of the witnesses does not see the actual signing of the will by the testator then the will is not valid. Therefore, it is important for the witnesses to see the testator signing the will. In addition, having attested to and witnessed the signing of the will, the witnesses must attest the will by signing and acknowledging his signature in the presence of the testator. However *s 9(c)* states 'the signature is made or *acknowledged* by the testator in the presence of two or more witnesses present at the same time' so the will may have been signed at an earlier date.
- In contrast, in Scotland, every page of the will must be signed by the testator and the (one) witness signs the last page attesting to the signature. Also, co-habitees have certain legal rights if there is no valid will under the *Family Law (Scotland) Act 2006*. As application of the intestacy rules and co-habitee's legal rights may not be what the testator required a valid will should be executed at the outset.
- In connection with the above point, in Scotland the spouse and/or children have certain prior rights which entitle them to benefit from the deceased's moveable estate (not land and buildings) and therefore benefit, unless there is no moveable property, unlike the situation in England where a spouse and/or minor can be disinherited.

Assets held in trust [Form IHT418]

HM Revenue & Customs

Assets held in trust

Schedule IHT418

When to use this form

Fill in this form if the deceased had the right to benefit from a trust created by a deed or under someone's Will or intestacy.

If the deceased had the right to benefit from more than one trust, you should complete a separate form for each trust.

Help

Please read the guidance notes for form IHT418 in the IHT400 Notes before filling in this form.

For more information or help or another copy of this form:

- go to **www.hmrc.gov.uk/inheritancetax**
- phone our Helpline on **0845 30 20 900**
  – if calling from outside the UK, phone **+44 115 974 3009**.

Name of deceased

Date of death *DD MM YYYY*

IHT reference number (if known)

Deceased's interest in possession

Please read the IHT400 Notes about the definitions of an 'interest in possession' and the types of interests listed below, before completing this section.

1 Did the deceased have an interest in possession which was one of the following interests?

An interest in possession that started before 22 March 2006 and remained in existence until the date of death	No ☐	Yes ☐
An immediate post-death interest	No ☐	Yes ☐
A disabled person's interest	No ☐	Yes ☐
A transitional serial interest	No ☐	Yes ☐

- If you answered Yes to any of the above questions, go to box 2.
- If you answered No to all the above questions, go to box 19.

About the trust

2 Name of the person who created the trust either during their lifetime, or by their Will or intestacy

3 Name of the trust

4 Unique Taxpayer Reference of the trust

5 Date the trust was created *DD MM YYYY*

6 Do you have details of all the assets in the trust and their values? *The trustees may only give you a 'total value' figure for the trust fund*

No ☐ Yes ☐

If you answered No to question 6, complete only the 'total' boxes at 12 and 17 on pages 2 and 3.

If you answered Yes, complete all of pages 2 and 3.

7 Name(s) and address(es) of the trustees or the solicitors acting for the trust

Continue on page 4 if necessary

Assets in the trust

This page should only contain details of assets in trust consisting of:

- houses, land and buildings
- businesses or interests in businesses, and
- shares and securities which gave the deceased control of the company.

8 Details of the assets in the trust

Description of assets	Value at the date of death £
Total of assets	£

9 Mortgages, secured loans and other debts payable out of the assets shown in box 8

Description of liabilities	Amount £
Total of liabilities	£

10 Net assets (box 8 *minus* box 9). If a *minus* amount, write '0' £

11 Details of exemptions and reliefs to be deducted from the trust assets listed in box 8 (for example, business relief)

Description of exemptions and reliefs *If you are deducting charity exemption, enter the full name of the charity, the country of establishment and the HMRC charities reference, if available.*	Amount £
Total of exemptions and reliefs	£

12 Total (box 10 *minus* box 11) £

If the trustees want to pay the tax on these assets now, copy the amount in box 12 to form IHT400, box 99.
If not, copy the amount to box 18 of this form.

IHT418 Page 2

Other assets in the trust

This page should contain details of all the other assets in the trust not listed in box 8. For example, bank accounts and quoted shares, where the deceased did not have control of the company.

13 Details of all the other assets in the trust

Description of assets	Value at the date of death £
Total of assets	£

14 Details of liabilities to be deducted from assets listed in box 13

Description of liabilities	Amount £
Total of liabilities	£

15 Net assets (box 13 *minus* box 14). If a *minus* amount, write '0' £

16 Details of exemptions and reliefs to be deducted from the trust assets listed in box 13 (for example, charity exemption)

Description of exemptions and reliefs *If you are deducting charity exemption, enter the full name of the charity, the country of establishment and the HMRC charities reference, if available.*	Amount £
Total of exemptions and reliefs	£

17 Total (box 15 *minus* box 16) £

If the trustees want to pay the tax on these assets now, copy the amount in box 17 to form IHT400, box 100.
If not, copy the amount to box 18 of this form.

18 Total of assets in the trust on which the trustees do not wish to pay the tax now (box 12 + box 17) £

Copy this amount to form IHT400, box 105

IHT418 Page 3

Future right to assets in a trust

19 Did the deceased have the right to receive the assets in a trust at some future date? *For example, someone other than the deceased was receiving the dividends from stocks and shares or had the right to live in a house rent free. The deceased's estate will not receive the assets until the other person receiving the benefit has also died.*

No ☐ *You have finished this form*

Yes ☐ *Go to box 20*

20 Did any of the following apply to the deceased's future right:

- It had been purchased or exchanged.
- It arose under a settlement made by the deceased or the deceased's spouse or civil partner.
- It involved a lease of a property for life that is treated as a settlement for Inheritance Tax purposes.

No ☐ *The value does not need to be included*

Yes ☐ *Go to box 21*

21 What do you estimate was the value of these assets at the date of death?

£

Include this amount in form IHT400, box 76

22 What is the name of the person who set up the trust and either their date of death or the date of the settlement?

23 What is the name and age of the person who is receiving the benefit?

Any other information

Please use this box if there is not enough space for your answers on pages 1 to 4.

IHT418 Page 4

53

Transfers Within Seven Years Before Death

Cross-references. See 7 CALCULATION OF TAX; 40 RATES OF TAX; 52 TRANSFERS ON DEATH.

Simon's Taxes. See I3.361–I3.364, I3.511.

Other Sources. HMRC Customer Guide to Inheritance Tax.

Introduction

[53.1] HMRC states

> 'Some gifts are exempt from Inheritance Tax – especially any gifts made more than seven years before the deceased died. However, not all gifts are exempt. To find out more, follow the link below to find out more about gifts that are exempt from Inheritance Tax. If the deceased didn't leave a list of all of the gifts they made before they died, you should make a list of them and determine which are exempt and which aren't. You can try asking close friends and family if they know about any gifts or look through paperwork or bank statements that the deceased left.'

See http://www.hmrc.gov.uk/inheritancetax/how-to-value-estate/gifts.htm. However, page 5 of schedule IHT403 requires details name/relationship of the donee, description of assets (for their valuation purposes), value ascribed to the gifted assets and any exemptions available. This entails a great deal of retrospective investigation work for the executors to complete the page satisfactorily!

Taper relief

Where a chargeable lifetime transfer is made, tax on the value transferred is initially charged at one half of the death rates. Where a transferor then dies within seven years of the transfer, the tax is recomputed at the death rates but the tax rates (but not the value of the lifetime chargeable transfer) are subject to below, tapered as follows.

Years between transfer and death	Percentage of full tax rate
Not more than 3	100%
More than 3 but not more than 4	80%
More than 4 but not more than 5	60%
More than 5 but not more than 6	40%
More than 6 but not more than 7	20%

Where, between the chargeable transfer and the date of death, tax rates are reduced by the substitution of a new table of rates, the additional tax is charged as if the new table applicable on death had applied to the transfer.

The tapering provisions above do not apply where the tapered tax as calculated would be less than the tax which would have been chargeable using half death rates if the transferor had not died within seven years of the transfer i.e. the tax payable cannot be reduced below that originally chargeable at half death rates. [*IHTA 1984, s 7(2)(4)(5), Sch 2 para 2; FA 1986, Sch 19 paras 2, 37*].

Treatment of PETs

Where POTENTIALLY EXEMPT TRANSFERS (38) are made within seven years of death, no tax would have been payable at the time of the transfer. On death, tax is calculated at the full death rates applying at the time of death, subject to the tapering of tax rates (but not of values) above. (There is no lower limit on the tax, as no tax was chargeable when the transfer was made.) [*IHTA 1984, s 7(4)(5), Sch 2 para 1A; FA 1986, Sch 19 paras 2, 37*].

If no tax is actually due on a death in relation to a lifetime chargeable transfer or potentially exempt transfer which proves to be a chargeable transfer (e.g. because the value concerned falls within the nil rate band), the above relief can have no effect.

See 30.7 LIABILITY FOR TAX for the persons liable for the additional tax.

Transitional provisions

[53.2] Where a death occurs on or after 18 March 1986, the above provisions do not affect the tax chargeable on a transfer of value occurring before that date. [*FA 1986, Sch 19 para 40*]. The tax on such a chargeable transfer will continue only to be recomputed at the higher death rates if the transferor dies within three years of the transfer.

Relief

[53.3] Where tax or additional tax becomes payable because of the transferor's death within seven years of a transfer, relief is available where all or part of the value transferred is attributable to the value of property which:

(a) at the date of death is the property of the transferee or his spouse or civil partner; or

(b) before that date has been sold by the transferee or his spouse or civil partner by a '*qualifying sale*'

unless the property is tangible movable property that is a wasting asset (i.e. if, immediately before the transfer, it had a predictable useful life not exceeding 50 years, having regard to the purposes for which it was held by the transferor; and always treating plant and machinery as wasting).

Definitions

A '*qualifying sale*' is a sale at arm's length for a price freely negotiated at the time of sale where no person concerned as vendor (or any person having an interest in the proceeds) is connected with the purchaser (or any person having an interest in the purchase). No provision must be made in connection with the sale for the vendor etc. to have any right to acquire any part of the property sold or any interest in or created out of it.

Where the above conditions are satisfied, then on a claim by a person liable to pay the whole or part of the tax or additional tax payable as a result of the transferor's death within seven years of the transfer, the tax is calculated on the market value of the property at the 'relevant date' if lower than at the time of the chargeable transfer. The claim for relief under this section must be made not more than four years after the death of the transferor. [*IHTA 1984, ss 131, 132; FA 1986, Sch 19 para 23; The Tax and Civil Partnership Regulations 2005, SI 2005/3229, Reg 25; FA 2009, Sch 51 para 6*].

The '*relevant date*' is the date of death under (a) above or qualifying sale under (b) above.

Example

A makes transfers on 21 September 2006 to B of properties valued at that date at £490,000 and to C of cash of £240,116 on the same day. A died on 28 April 2010 when the properties gifted to B were valued at £390,000.

		Gross	Tax
		£	£
Value of properties to B	£490,000		
Less annual exemption (apportioned) Note B	£4,027	485,973	107,143
Cash to C	£240,116		
Less annual exemption (apportioned) Note B	£1,973	238,143	52,503
		724,116	
Less nil rate band		325,000	
		£399,116	£159,646

Recalculate the tax on the gifts to take into account the 20% taper relief as gifts were made between three and four years before death and in the case of B there has also been a fall in value of £100,000 in the properties since the gift of them by A to B and the executors have completed form IHT 38. With regard to the completion of form IHT 38 by the executors or personal representatives see **56.8** VALUATION.

Tax payable on PETs that have become chargeable because of A's death within seven years.

Value of properties	£490,000	
Less annual exemption	4,027	
	485,973	
Less fall in value	100,000	
	385,973	
Value of cash	238,143	
	624,116	
Less nil rate band	325,000	
	£299,116	@ 40% = £119,646

Apportionment of tax:

Gift to B

$$£119,646 \times \frac{385,973}{624,116} \times 80\ \% = £59,194$$

Gift to C

$$£159,646 \times \frac{238,143}{724,116} \times 80\ \% = £42,003$$

Notes to the example

(A) *Section 131* relief only reduces the value of a transfer for the purpose of calculating the tax on that transfer (i.e. B's gift) and it does *not* affect its value for cumulation purposes (i.e. C's gift).

(B) A's gifts to B and C were made on the same day so the annual exemption for 2006/07 and the unutilised annual exemption for 2005/06 are apportioned between B and C's gifts respectively.

(C) Tapering relief applies as the gifts were made between three and four years before death of A therefore 80% applies.

(D) The claim should be signed by one or more of the persons liable and should:
- identify the transfer and transferred property;
- confirm the property is retained (or sold by a qualifying sale in which case provide details);
- confirm that the property is the same at the date of death (or sale) as it was at the date of transfer (or give details of any changes).

(See IHTM14627).

Market value

[53.4] For these purposes, market value is the price which the property might reasonably be expected to fetch if sold in the open market but that price must not be assumed to be reduced on the ground that the whole property is on the market at one and the same time. In determining the price of unquoted shares (in relation to transfers of value made, and other events occurring, before 17 March 1987, shares not quoted on a recognised stock exchange), it is assumed that there is available to any prospective purchaser all the information which such a person might reasonably require if he were proposing to purchase them from a willing vendor by private treaty and at arm's length.

Where the property transferred is subject to AGRICULTURAL PROPERTY (4) or BUSINESS PROPERTY (6) relief, the market value at any time is calculated as reduced by the appropriate percentage under those provisions. [*IHTA 1984, ss 131(2A), 140(2); FA 1986, Sch 19 para 23*].

Special provisions

Special provisions apply to ascertaining the market value of specified property at the relevant date as follows:

(a) *Shares — capital receipts.* Any capital payment (i.e. any money or money's worth which is not income for the purposes of income tax), including the sale of a provisional allotment of shares, received by the transferee or his spouse or civil partner before the relevant date in respect of shares transferred is added to the market value of the shares unless already reflecting the right to the payment. See note 7 of form IHT 35.

(b) *Payments of calls* made by the transferee or his spouse or civil partner before the relevant date on the shares transferred reduce the market value unless already reflecting the liability.

(c) *Reorganisation of share capital etc.* A new holding received for the original shares transferred is treated as the same property, but where the transferee or his spouse or civil partner gives any consideration for the new holding before the relevant date, the market value is reduced accordingly unless already reflecting the liability.

Consideration for the new holding does not include any surrender, cancellation or other alteration of any of the original shares or rights attached thereto *or* any consideration consisting of the application, in paying up the new holding or any part of it, of assets of the company concerned or any dividend or other distribution declared out of those assets but not made.

(d) *Transactions of close companies.* Where the transferred property consists of shares in a close company and at any time after the chargeable transfer and before the relevant date, there is a '*relevant transaction*' in relation to the shares the market value of the property transferred on the relevant date is increased by the difference between:

   (i) the market value of the transferred property at the time of the chargeable transfer; and

   (ii) what that value would have been if the relevant transaction had occurred before rather than after that time.

Where the relevant transaction increases the estate of the transferor or his UK-domiciled spouse or civil partner, the increase to the market value of the property on the relevant date is reduced by that amount.

'*Relevant transactions*' is a transfer of value by the company or an alteration in the company's share or loan capital not consisting of quoted shares (in relation to transfers of value made, and other events occurring, before 17 March 1987, shares quoted on a recognised stock exchange) or in any rights attaching to unquoted shares or debentures in the company (in relation to transfers of value made, and other events occurring, before 17 March 1987, shares or debentures in the company not quoted on a recognised stock exchange). See Note below.

(e) *Interests in land*. Where there has been a change in the 'interest in land' or its state between the date of transfer and the relevant date, the difference between the market value at the date of transfer and what would have been the market value if the change had prevailed at that date is added to the market value at the relevant date. Any statutory compensation received is also added. '*Interest in land*' does not include any estate, interest or right by way of mortgage or other security. See Note below.

(f) *Leases*. Where the transferred property is a lease with less than fifty years to run at the time of the chargeable transfer, the market value on the relevant date is increased by the fraction:

$$\frac{P(1) - P(2)}{[P(1)]}$$

where

P(1) = the appropriate percentage from the table for depreciation of leases contained in *TCGA 1992, Sch 8 para 1* for the duration of the lease at the time of the chargeable transfer; and

P(2) = the appropriate percentage for the duration of the lease on the relevant date.

(g) *Other property*. Where the property at the relevant date is not the same in all respects as the property transferred, the difference between the value transferred and what that value would have been if the change in the property had prevailed at the time of the transfer, is added to the market value at the relevant date. Where, between the time of the chargeable transfer and the relevant date, any benefits in money or money's worth are derived from the property which exceed a reasonable return on its market value at the time of transfer, the excess is added to the market value at the relevant date. See Note below.

Note. In (d), (e) and (g) above, if the market value at the date of transfer is less than it would have been if a change had prevailed at that date, the market value at the relevant date is reduced to what it would have been if the change had not occurred. [*IHTA 1984, ss 133–140; FA 1987, s 58; Sch 8 paras 10, 11; The Tax and Civil Partnership Regulations 2005, SI 2005/3229, Regs 26–30*].

See **48.1** SHARES AND SECURITIES for the definition of 'quoted' or 'listed' and 'unquoted' in relation to shares and securities.

Gifts and other transfers of value [Form IHT 403]

HM Revenue & Customs

Gifts and other transfers of value

Schedule IHT403

When to use this form

Fill in this form to tell us about any gifts the deceased made on or after 18 March 1986.

Do not tell us about any gifts where the total value was £3,000 or less in any tax year, small amounts of £250 or less or if the gifts were made to a spouse or civil partner.

To work out the total value of the estate (on which tax is charged) we may need to add the value of these gifts to the value of the estate at the date of death.

Name of deceased

Date of death *DD MM YYYY*

IHT reference number (if known)

Help

Please read the guidance notes for form IHT403 in the IHT400 Notes before filling in this form. For more information or help or another copy of this form:

- go to **www.hmrc.gov.uk/inheritancetax/**
- phone our Helpline on **0845 30 20 900**
  – if calling from outside the UK, phone **+44 115 974 3009**.

Taper relief

Taper relief is available on gifts that exceed the Inheritance Tax nil rate band and which were made between three and seven years before the date of death.

The relief reduces the amount of tax paid on the gift, not the value of the gift itself. For more information about taper relief go to the customer guide at: **www.hmrc.gov.uk/inheritancetax/**

Gifts made within the seven years before death

1 Did the deceased make any gifts or transfer assets to or for the benefit of another person?

No ☐ Yes ☐

2 Did the deceased create a trust or settlement?

No ☐ Yes ☐

3 Did the deceased transfer additional assets into an existing trust or settlement?

No ☐ Yes ☐

4 Did the deceased pay any premium on a life assurance policy for the benefit of anyone (other than themselves) who was not their spouse or civil partner?

No ☐ Yes ☐

5 Was the deceased entitled to benefit from any assets held in trust or in a settlement which, during their lifetime, came to an end (either in whole or in part)?

No ☐ Yes ☐

6 Are you claiming that gifts should be treated as exempt as 'gifts out of income'?

No ☐ Yes ☐

ⓘ If you answered Yes to any of these questions, give full details on pages 2 to 5.
If you answered Yes to question 6, give full details on pages 2 to 6.

Gifts made within the seven years before death continued

- If you answered Yes to any of the questions on page 1, please give full details below.
- If you are deducting charity exemption enter the full name of the charity, the country of establishment and the HMRC charities reference, if available, in **column B**.

7

Date of gift	Name and relationship of person who received the gift *(For example, son, daughter, business partner)*	Description of assets given away *(For example, cash, the address of a house, the number of shares in a particular company, the premium paid on an insurance policy)* £	**A** Value at date of gift £	**B** If exemptions or reliefs deducted, state amount and type *(For example, annual, £3,000)* £	**C** Net value after exemptions and reliefs **A** minus **B** £
				Total net value after exemptions or reliefs **7**	£

Total of column above - copy this amount to form IHT400 Calculation, box 4

IHT403 Page 2

Gifts with reservation of benefit

- Please answer the following questions about gifts made by the deceased on or after 18 March 1986.
- If you are deducting charity exemption enter the full name of the charity, the country of establishment and the HMRC charities reference, if available, in **column B**.

8 Did the deceased transfer any assets to any individual, trust, company or other organisation during their lifetime where the person or organisation receiving the assets did not take full possession of them? No ☐ *Go to box 13* Yes ☐

If the gift was a house or land

9 Did the deceased (or their spouse or civil partner) continue to have a significant right or interest in the house or land, which enabled them to occupy or have some benefit from it? No ☐ Yes ☐

10 Was the deceased (or their spouse or civil partner) party to a significant arrangement such as a lease or trust which let them occupy or have some benefit from it? No ☐ Yes ☐

If the gift was *not* a house or land

11 Did the deceased continue to have some right to benefit from all or part of the asset? No ☐ Yes ☐

12 If you answered Yes to any of the above questions, please give full details below

Date of gift	Name and relationship of person who received the gift *(For example, son, daughter, business partner)*	Description of assets given away *(For example, cash, the address of a house, the number of shares in a particular company, the premium paid on an insurance policy)*	**A** Value at date of death £	**B** If exemptions or reliefs deducted, state amount and type *(For example, agricultural relief, £10,000)* £	**C** Net value after exemptions and reliefs **A** *minus* **B** £
				Total net value after exemptions or reliefs 12	£

IHT403 Page 3

Pre-owned assets (POA)

- If you are deducting charity exemption enter the full name of the charity, the country of establishment and the HMRC charities reference, if available, in **column B**.

13 Did the deceased receive any benefit from pre-owned assets and pay Income Tax on the benefit? No ☐ Yes ☐

14 Did the deceased receive any benefit from pre-owned assets and elect to pay the Inheritance Tax charge under the reservation of benefit rules? No ☐ Yes ☐ *If Yes, fill in the table at box 16*

15 Did the deceased contribute to the purchase of any assets by another person from which the deceased received a benefit? No ☐ Yes ☐ *If Yes, fill in the table at box 16*

16 If you answered Yes to questions 14 or 15, please give full details below

Date of transfer or purchase	Date of election shown on form IHT500	Description of assets transferred or purchased *if the asset was a house or land, give the address*	POA reference number (see IHT400 Notes)	**A** Value at date of death £	**B** If exemptions or reliefs deducted, type and amount *(For example, business relief, £20,000)* £	**C** Net value after exemptions and reliefs **A** *minus* **B** £

Total net value after exemptions or reliefs **16** £

Total of gifts with reservation and pre-owned assets (box 12 total + box 16 total) **17** £

Copy this amount to form IHT400, box 104

IHT403 Page 4

Earlier transfers

- If you are deducting charity exemption enter the full name of the charity, the country of establishment and the HMRC charities reference, if available, in column B.

18 Did the deceased make any chargeable transfers during the seven years before the earliest date of the gifts shown at box 7?

No ☐ *If you answered Yes to question 6 on page 1, go to box 20. If you answered No to question 6, you have finished this form*

Yes ☐ *Go to box 19*

19 If you answered Yes, please provide full details below. **Do not include** the value in any of the tax calculations

Date of gift	Name and relationship of person who received the gift *(For example, son, daughter, spouse or civil partner)*	Description of assets given away *(For example, cash, the address of a house, the number of shares in a particular company, the premium paid on an insurance policy)*	**A** Value at the date of gift £	**B** If exemptions or reliefs deducted, state amount and type *for example, annual £3,000* £	**C** Net value after exemptions and reliefs **A** *minus* **B** £

IHT403 Page 5

Gifts made as part of normal expenditure out of income

Only fill in this page if you have ticked Yes to box 6 on page 1. This is a guide to the type of income and expenditure the deceased may have had so that you can show that gifts made were part of the deceased's normal expenditure out of their income. Give details of the deceased's income and expenditure for each of the years in which the gifts were made.

20	**Income**							
	Tax year in which gifts made *(for example, 6 Apr 2005 to 5 Apr 2006)*							
	Salary							
	Pensions							
	Interest (including PEPs and ISAs)							
	Investments							
	Rents							
	Annuities (income element)							
	Other							
	Minus Income Tax paid							
	Net Income							
21	**Expenditure**							
	Mortgages							
	Insurance							
	Household bills							
	Council Tax							
	Travelling costs							
	Entertainment							
	Holidays							
	Nursing home fees							
	Other							
	Total Expenditure							
22	**Surplus (deficit) income for the year** (Net Income *minus* Total Expenditure)							
	Gifts made							

IHT403 Page 6

54

Transitional Provisions

Simon's Taxes. See **I1.207**, **I1.401**.

Estate duty

Nature and abolition of estate duty

[54.1] Estate duty was introduced by the *Finance Act 1894*. It levied a duty on all property passing on deaths after 1 August 1894, with certain exceptions and reliefs. The chargeable property was aggregated and the duty applied on successive slices at increasing rates. Gifts during the life of the donor were not subject to the duty unless they were made within seven years of the death (four years in Northern Ireland) and reduced rates applied if the death was during the fifth, sixth or seventh year (third and fourth in Northern Ireland).

Estate duty was abolished for property passing on deaths after 12 March 1975. [*FA 1975, s 49(1)*].

Estate and death duties

[54.2] Any reference (in whatever terms) to estate duty or death duties in any document (whenever executed) is to have effect as if it included a reference to CTT and IHT. See example below in **54.5**. [*IHTA 1984, Sch 6 para 1; FA 1986, s 100(1)(b)*].

Surviving spouse exemption

[54.3] Where a person's spouse (or former spouse) died before 13 November 1974 and left an interest in possession in property to the surviving spouse, estate duty would have been chargeable on that death. To avoid a double charge to tax, there is no charge to CTT or IHT on either the subsequent death of the surviving spouse, or on the lifetime termination of the interest provided that there would have been no charge on death. See also **21.10** EXEMPT

TRANSFERS where the personal nil rate band maximum of the deceased is the amount shown in the appropriate Table depending on the date of death as stipulated in *FA 2008, Sch 4 para 10*. [*FA 1894, s 5(2); IHTA 1984, Sch 6 para 2; FA 1986, s 100(1)(b)*].

Sales and mortgages of reversionary interests

[54.4] The CTT or IHT payable by a purchaser or mortgagee when a reversionary interest purchased or mortgaged for full consideration before 27 March 1974 falls into possession is not to exceed the estate duty which would have been charged before the introduction of CTT. This limitation does not apply if the interest was sold or mortgaged to a close company of which the seller or mortgagor was a participator except to the extent that other persons had rights or interests in the company. [*IHTA 1984, Sch 6 para 3; FA 1986, s 100(1)(b)*].

National heritage objects

[54.5] Where there is a chargeable event in relation to objects of national etc. interest which were conditionally exempt for estate duty purposes, there may be a charge to estate duty rather than CTT or IHT in certain circumstances. [*IHTA 1984, Sch 6 para 4; FA 1986, s 100(1)(b)*].

Example 1

Lord Alan died in 1952 leaving Netherington Hall in Wiltshire together with all its contents to his son Bertie. In the past public access by members of the general public has been allowed to the Hall. The contents of the Hall include a paintings by Whistler of Netherington Hall and also a rare painting of Mary Queen of Scots alongside Lord Bothwell her second husband. The pictures were exempted from estate duty which, at the time Lord Alan died, was applied at a marginal rate of 80%. Unfortunately, the son, Lord Bertie, dies in a hunting accident on Boxing Day 2000 and the Hall together with contents passed to his son, now Lord Charles. The Board considered the painting by Whistler of the Hall to be pre-eminent as it has a special close association with its historical setting, i.e. Netherington Hall. The painting was accepted as pre-eminent and is re-exempted on the death of Lord Bertie, subject to a contingent liability to IHT on any breach of undertaking or subsequent disposal by sale when the rate of IHT would be 40%. The Board did *not* consider the painting of Mary Queen of Scots, now valued at £5 million, to be pre-eminent in this context.

As the Mary Queen of Scots painting fails the pre-eminence test, IHT of £2 million (£5 million × 40%) is due and paid by the estate. Lord Charles decides to sell the painting for £8 million (net of expenses and CGT) thereby breaking the estate duty undertaking.

In view of the Board's decision there will be a tax charge in respect of the Mary Queen of Scots painting calculated as follows:

	£
Estate duty at 80% on £8 million	6,400,000
Less credit for IHT paid on Lord Bertie's death	2,000,000
Estate duty payable on sale	£4,400,000

Notes to the example

(A) Reference to 'estate duty exemption' means estate duty exemption obtained on a death on or after August 1930 (*Finance Act 1930, s 40*).

(B) The conferring of an exemption on death deferred the liability to estate duty, but with the possibility of triggering the charge later whether this was by way of sale (*FA 1930, s 40(2)*), breach of undertaking (*FA 1950, s 48(1)(3)* or otherwise *FA 1965, s 31(7)*).

Capital transfer tax

[54.6] Capital transfer tax was introduced by the *Finance Act 1975* and charged on lifetime transfers made after 26 March 1974 and on transfers on deaths occurring after 12 March 1975 when it replaced estate duty. Following the *Finance Act 1975* there were substantial alterations to the legislation including the reduction of the open-ended cumulation period to one of ten years and the introduction of a new regime for the taxation of discretionary trusts. The legislation was consolidated in *Capital Transfer Tax Act 1984* which came into force on 1 January 1985.

CTT was effectively replaced by the revised provisions relating to inheritance tax for events occurring after 17 March 1986.

The *Capital Transfer Act 1984* may be cited as the *Inheritance Tax Act 1984*. Any reference to CTT in the *1984 Act* or any other *Act* passed before or executed, made, served or issued on or before 25 July 1986 has effect as a reference to inheritance tax unless relating to a liability arising before that date. [*FA 1986, s 100*].

Transfers before 18 March 1986

[54.7] Although the provisions relating to IHT apply to events occurring on or after 18 March 1986, where a death or other event occurs on or after that date, the amendments to the CTT legislation in *FA 1986, Sch 19, Pt I* do not affect the tax chargeable on a transfer of value occurring before that date. [*FA 1986, Sch 19 para 40(1)*]. The effect of this provision is that any additional tax payable on a chargeable lifetime transfer made before 18 March 1986 as a result of the transferor's death after 17 March 1986 is calculated under the CTT rules. The tax is, however, calculated using the rates in force at the time of death. [*FA 1986, Sch 19 para 44*]. It should be noted that the rate of tax on a chargeable transfer (whether a lifetime chargeable transfer, a deemed transfer on death or a potentially exempt transfer proving to be a chargeable transfer) made after 17 March 1986 (i.e. when IHT rules apply) will depend on the cumulative value of previous chargeable transfers made within the seven-year period ending with the date of the transfer (including, where applicable, chargeable transfers made before 18 March 1986 when CTT rules applied). See **1.5** INTRODUCTION AND BASIC PRINCIPLES.

The above provision does not authorise the making of a claim under the rules relating to DOUBLE CHARGES RELIEF (**17**) where the donee's transfer occurs after 17 March 1986. [*FA 1986, Sch 19 para 40(2)*].

55

Trusts for Employees

Cross-reference. See also 43 SETTLEMENTS: DISCRETIONARY TRUSTS AND OTHER TRUSTS OF RELEVANT PROPERTY.

Simon's Taxes. See **I3.156, I4.223, I5.631, I5.648**.

Other Sources. HMRC Customer Guide to Inheritance Tax; Foster, Part E6.31; IHTM04100.

Introduction

[55.1] Subject to conditions, trusts for the benefit of employees of a company are exempt from inheritance tax liability on the ten-year anniversary charge (see 43 SETTLEMENTS: DISCRETIONARY TRUSTS AND OTHER TRUSTS OF RELEVANT PROPERTY). Also, transfers to such trusts may be made by individuals, close companies and settlements without interests in possession without liability to inheritance tax.

From 6 April 2014, the reliefs apply under two separate headings: (i) employee trusts within *IHTA 1984, s 86*, and (ii) employee ownership trusts for which wide-ranging reliefs were introduced by *FA 2014, Sch 37*.

Conditions for the trust

Employee trusts

[55.2] The conditions are that the settled property is held on trusts which, either indefinitely or until the end of a period (whether defined by a date or in some other way) do not permit that property to be applied otherwise than for the benefit of:

(a) persons employed in a particular trade or profession, or
(b) employees, or office holders, of a body carrying on a trade, profession or undertaking, or
(c) spouses, civil partners, relatives or dependants or partners of (a) or (b) above. See April 2006 at http://www.hmrc.gov.uk/cto/newsletter.htm.

For the settled property to qualify under (b), either all or most of the employees or office holders must be included as beneficiaries or the trust must be an approved profit sharing scheme under formerly *ICTA 1988, Sch 9* (now repealed by *ITEPA 2003, s 722, Sch 6* but see *ITEPA 2003, s 723, Sch 7*) or an employee share ownership plan approved under *FA 2000, Sch 8*. Where there are beneficiaries falling within (a), (b) or (c) above, the trusts are not disqualified by reason only that they also permit settled property to be applied for charitable purposes. [*IHTA 1984, s 86(1)–(3) as amended by FA 2000, s 138(4); Sch 8; The Tax and Civil Partnership Regulations 2005, SI 2005/3229, Reg 18*]. See **55.9** below regarding newspaper trusts.

The settled property:

(i) is treated as comprised in one settlement;
(ii) may contain an interest in possession (e.g. a right by a beneficiary to an annuity) of less than 5% of the whole. Such interests are disregarded for IHT purposes, with the exception of those in *IHTA 1984, s 55* relating to the acquisition by a person of a reversionary interest expectant on an interest to which he is already entitled; and
(iii) may cease to be comprised in one settlement and, if within one month it becomes wholly comprised in another settlement satisfying the above conditions, it is treated as if it had remained comprised in the first settlement.

[*IHTA 1984, s 86(4)(5)*].

Employee ownership trusts

Under the reliefs for employee ownership trusts the following three tests must be satisfied:

(a) the company must meet 'the trading requirement';
(b) the trusts must meet 'the all-employee benefit requirement'; and
(c) the settlement must not meet 'the controlling interest requirement' immediately before the beginning of the tax year in which the disposition of property occurs but does meet it at the end of that year.

The definitions of these requirements are as follows:

The trading requirement

The company meets the trading requirement if it is:

(a) a trading company which is not a member of a group, or
(b) the principal company of a trading group.

'Trading company' means a company carrying on activities in the course of, or for the purposes of, a trade being carried on by it, and whose activities do not include to a substantial extent activities other than trading activities.

'Trading group' means a group one or more of whose members carry on trading group activities, and the activities of whose members, taken together, do not include to a substantial extent activities other than trading group activities. 'Trading group activities' means activities carried on by a member of the group in the course of, or for the purposes of, a trade being carried on by any member of the group. The activities of the members of a group are to be treated as one business (with the result that activities are disregarded to the extent that they are intra-group activities), but a business carried on by a company in partnership with one or more other persons is to be treated as not being a trading activity or a trading group activity.

The all-employee benefit requirement

A settlement meets the all-employee benefit requirement if the trusts of the settlement do not permit any of the settled property to be applied, at any time, otherwise than for the benefit of all the eligible employees on the same terms, and do not permit the trustees at any time to apply any of the settled property by creating a trust, or by transferring property to the trustees of any settlement other than by an authorised transfer. In addition, the settlement must not permit the trustees at any time to make loans to beneficiaries of the trust, and must not permit the trustees or any other person at any time to amend the trusts in a way such that the amended trusts would not comply with the foregoing requirements. Benefits may be provided to a surviving spouse or civil partner of a deceased employee for up to 12 months. There are other detailed rules relating to employees or office-holders who may be excluded as well as transitional provisions for certain existing settlements.

An 'eligible employee' is any individual who is employed by or is an officeholder of the company or, if appropriate, of a relevant group company, but does not include an 'excluded participator'. 'Excluded participator' means:

(a) a person who is a participator in the company, or, where appropriate, in any relevant group company;
(b) any other person who is a participator in any close company that has made a disposition by which property became comprised in the same settlement, being a disposition which but for *IHTA 1984, s 13 or 13A* would have been a transfer of value for the purposes of inheritance tax;
(c) any other person who has been a participator in any company mentioned in paragraph (a) or (b) at any time on or after the look-back date, this being 10 years ending with the later of 10 December 2013 or, if later, the date on which the settlement was first funded;
(d) any person who is connected with any person within paragraph (a), (b) or (c).

However, a participator entitled to, or holding rights to acquire, less than 5 per cent of any class of the company's shares, and less than 5 per cent of the assets on a winding up is not excluded.

An 'authorised transfer' means a transfer of property consisting of or including any ordinary share capital of a company where that company meets the trading requirement, and the transfer is made to the trustees of a settlement which (i) meets the controlling interest requirement with respect to that company immediately after the transfer, and (ii) meets the all-employee benefit requirement with respect to the company.

The controlling interest requirement

A settlement meets the controlling interest requirement if:

(a) the trustees hold more than 50% of the ordinary share capital of the relevant company and have powers of voting on all questions affecting it as a whole which, if exercised, would yield a majority of the votes capable of being exercised on them;
(b) the trustees are entitled to more than 50% of the profits available for distribution to the equity holders of the company;
(c) the trustees would be entitled, on a winding up of the company, to more than 50% of the assets of C available for distribution to equity holders; and
(d) there are no provisions in any agreement or instrument affecting the company's constitution or management or its shares or securities whereby the condition in paragraph (a), (b) or (c) can cease to be satisfied without the consent of the trustees.

[*FA 2014, Sch 37*].

Creation of the trust

[55.3] Separate provisions apply to the creation of employee trusts by individuals (see 55.4 below) and close companies (see 55.5 below) and to property transferred from discretionary trusts (see 55.6 below).

Individual transferor

[55.4] A transfer to a trust as described in 55.2 above, by an individual who is beneficially entitled to shares in a company, is an exempt transfer if the value transferred is attributable to shares in or securities of the company and the conditions below are satisfied.

For a transfer to *employee trusts* the conditions are:

(a) the beneficiaries of the trust include all or most of the persons employed by or holding office with the company;
(b) within one year of the transfer:
    (i) the trustees hold more than one half of the ordinary shares of the company, and have majority voting powers on all questions affecting the company as a whole (but ignoring powers of any class of shares or securities limited to questions of winding up the company or primarily affecting that class); *and*
    (ii) there are no provisions or agreements which can affect (i) above without the trustees' consent;
(c) the trust does not permit *any* of the settled property (i.e. not only the shares or securities) *at any time* to be applied (except payments which are income of the recipient for income tax purposes, or would be if he were resident in the UK) for the benefit of:

(i) a participator in the company; or

(ii) any other person who is a participator in any close company that has made a disposition under *IHTA 1984, s 13* whereby property became comprised in the same settlement, see 55.5 below; or

(iii) any other person who has been a participator as mentioned in (i) or (ii) above at any time after, or during the ten years before, the transfer now being made; or

(iv) any person connected with the persons in (i) to (iii) above.

For these purposes, a participator mentioned above does not include any participator in a company who is not beneficially entitled to, or to rights entitling him to acquire, 5% or more of, or of any class of shares comprised in, its issued share capital and would not, on a winding up of the company, be entitled to 5% or more of its assets. Also participator includes, in the case of a company which is not a close company, a person who would be a participator in the company if it were a close company.

[*IHTA 1984, ss 13(5), 28*].

For a transfer to *employee ownership trusts* the relief applies where:

(a) the company meets 'the trading requirement'; and

(b) the trusts of the settlement meet 'the all-employee benefit requirement'; and

(c) the settlement does not meet 'the controlling interest requirement' immediately before the beginning of the tax year in which the shares leave the relevant property trust, but does meet it at the end of that year.

See 55.2 for the definitions of these three 'requirements'.

[*IHTA 1984, ss 13(5), 28A*].

See **21.23** EXEMPT TRANSFERS for abatement of the exemption.

Close company transferor

[55.5] A close company may transfer property to a trust as described in 55.2 above without it being a transfer of value.

For *employee trusts* the relief applies where:

(a) the beneficiaries of the trust include all or most of either:
   (i) the persons employed by or holding office with the same company; or
   (ii) the persons employed by or holding office with the company or any of its subsidiaries (but persons with a holding company may be excluded if they are in the minority, **25.E11** HMRC STATEMENTS OF PRACTICE); and

(b) the trust does not permit *any* property at *any time* to be applied to any of the persons mentioned in **55.4**(c) above except as payments which are income of the recipient for the purposes of income tax (or would be if he were resident in the UK), or as an appropriation of shares from a profit sharing scheme under formerly *ICTA 1988, Sch 9* (now repealed by *ITEPA 2003, s 722, Sch 6* but see *ITEPA 2003, s 723, Sch 7*); or

(c) the trust is an employee ownership share plan approved under *FA 2000, Sch 8*.

[*IHTA 1984, s 13 as amended by FA 2000, s 138(2) and Sch 8*].

For *employee ownership trusts* the relief applies where:

(a) the company meets 'the trading requirement'; and
(b) the trusts of the settlement meet 'the all-employee benefit requirement'; and
(c) the settlement does not meet 'the controlling interest requirement' immediately before the beginning of the tax year in which the shares leave the relevant property trust, but does meet it at the end of that year.

See **55.2** for the definitions of these three 'requirements'.

[*IHTA 1984, ss 13A*].

A close company with five or fewer participators may become subject to an *ICTA 1988, s 419(1)* (loans to participators incurring an income tax charge of 25% of the loan into the trust). In order to avoid this charge the loan into the trust might be conditional on, say, distribution amongst the beneficiaries on exit or repayable on substitution by third party funding within nine months of the end of the accounting period in which the loan was made or it is an outright gift to the trust. Note that now the *Companies Act 2006, ss 197–200* requires approval by a resolution by the members for loans to directors as from October 2007. See Taxation magazine 18 June 2009, page 610.

Property transferred from a discretionary trust etc.

[55.6] SETTLEMENTS: DISCRETIONARY TRUSTS AND OTHER TRUSTS OF RELEVANT PROPERTY (**43**) may transfer shares or securities in a company to trusts as described in **55.2** above without a proportionate charge to tax, provided:

For *employee trusts*:

(a) the beneficiaries of the trust include all or most of the persons employed by or holding office with the company; and
(b) without taking account of shares etc. held on other trusts, both conditions in **55.4**(b) above are satisfied at the date when the shares etc. cease to be comprised in the original settlement or within one year of that time; and
(c) the trust does not permit *any* property at *any time* to be applied:
    (i) to any of the persons mentioned in **55.4**(c) above except as payments which are regarded as the income of the recipient for the purposes of income tax (or would be if he were resident in the UK); or
    (ii) for the benefit of the settlor; or
    (iii) for the benefit of any person connected with the settlor. [*IHTA 1984, s 75*].

For *employee ownership trusts*:

(a) the company meets 'the trading requirement'; and

(b) the trusts of the settlement meet 'the all-employee benefit requirement'; and
(c) the settlement does not meet 'the controlling interest requirement' immediately before the beginning of the tax year in which the shares leave the relevant property trust, but does meet it at the end of that year.

See **55.2** for the definitions of these three 'requirements'.

[*IHTA 1984, ss 75A*].

See also the provisions of **43.19** and **43.22** SETTLEMENTS: DISCRETIONARY TRUSTS AND OTHER TRUSTS OF RELEVANT PROPERTY which also apply to property settled or appointed on trust for employees.

Position of the trust

[55.7] Settled property held on the conditions in **55.2** above for either employee trusts or employee ownership trusts is not subject to the principal charge to tax at the ten-year anniversary or the proportionate charge to tax under *IHTA 1984, ss 64, 65* but where the property is held in a SETTLEMENTS: DISCRETIONARY TRUSTS AND OTHER TRUSTS OF RELEVANT PROPERTY (**43**), the trust is subject to a charge when:

(a) the property ceases to be held on qualifying employee trusts otherwise than by virtue of a payment out of the settled property (but see also **21.4, 21.6–21.8** EXEMPT TRANSFERS for certain situations where there is no charge when property becomes held for charitable purposes only without limit of time or the property of a qualifying political party *or* a national body mentioned in *IHTA 1984, Sch 3* or, under certain conditions, a body not established or conducted for profit); or
(b) a payment is made for the benefit of a person who is, or is connected with:
    (i) a person who has directly or indirectly provided any of the settled property by amounts over £1,000 in any tax year; or
    (ii) where the employment in question is by a close company, a participator of that company who *either* is beneficially entitled to, or to rights entitling him to acquire, 5% or more of, or of any class of shares comprised in, its issued share capital, *or* would, on a winding up of the company be entitled to 5% or more of its assets (but this does not apply to any appropriation of shares under a profit sharing scheme approved under formerly *ICTA 1988, Sch 9* now repealed by *ITEPA 2003, s 722, Sch 6* but see *ITEPA 2003, s 723, Sch 7*); or
    (iii) a person who has acquired an interest in the employee trust for money or money's worth or as a result of transactions which include a disposition for such consideration (whether to him or another) of that interest or of other property, or
(c) the trustees make a 'disposition' (otherwise than by virtue of a payment out of the settled property) which reduces the value of the settled property.

'*Disposition*' includes an omission to exercise a right, unless not deliberate, which is treated as made at the latest time that the right could be exercised.

[*IHTA 1984, ss 70(10), 72, 76*].

No charge arises:

(i) if, under (c) above, the trustees do not intend to confer gratuitous benefit and either the transaction is at arm's length between persons not connected with each other (see **12** CONNECTED PERSONS) or is such as might be expected in such a transaction; or
(ii) if, under (c) above, the disposition is a grant of tenancy of agricultural property in the UK, Channel Islands, Isle of Man or EEA state for use for agricultural purposes and is made for full consideration in money or money's worth; or
(iii) on the payment of costs or expenses attributable to the property; or
(iv) where any payment is, or will be, income for income tax purposes of any person (or, in the case of a person not resident in the UK, would be if he was so resident); or
(v) in respect of a liability to make a payment under (iii) and (iv) above; or
(vi) on an appropriation of shares to an individual under an employee share ownership plan if the trusts are approved under *TA 1988, Sch 9* or *ITEPA 2003, Sch 2*; or
(vii) where a trust ceases to meet the requirements for employee ownership plans (see **55.2**) because either or both of the trading requirement or the controlling interest requirement is no longer met with respect to the company concerned.

'*Payment*' includes the transfer of assets other than money.

[*IHTA 1984, ss 63, 70(3)(4), 72(5); FA 2000, s 138(3)(b), Sch 8*].

Tax is charged on the amount by which the trust property is less immediately after the event giving rise to the charge than it would have been but for the event (i.e. the loss to the donor principle), grossed-up where the settlement pays the tax.

The rate at which tax is charged is the aggregate of the following percentages for each complete successive quarter in 'the relevant period'.

	Cumulative Total
0.25% for each of the first 40 quarters	10%
0.20% for each of the next 40 quarters	8%
0.15% for each of the next 40 quarters	6%
0.10% for each of the next 40 quarters	4%
0.05% for each of the next 40 quarters	2%
Maximum rate chargeable after 50 years	30%

The rate charged may be reduced if any of the property is, or was, EXCLUDED PROPERTY (**20**), see **55.8** below.

'*Relevant period*' is the period beginning with the day on which the property became (or last became) held on employee trusts, or 13 March 1975 if later, and ending on the day before the chargeable event. Where property in respect of which tax is chargeable was relevant property (see **43.3** SETTLEMENTS: DISCRETIONARY TRUSTS AND OTHER TRUSTS OF RELEVANT PROPERTY) immediately before 10 December 1981 (e.g. in a discretionary trust) and became (or last became) comprised in an employee trust after 9 December 1981 and before 9 March 1982, the relevant period begins with the day on which the property became (or last became) relevant property before 10 December 1981, or 13 March 1975 if later.

'*Quarter*' means a period of three months.

[*IHTA 1984, ss 63, 70(5)(6)(8)(9), 72(5)*].

Example

A qualifying trust for employees of a close company was created on 1 July 1983. On 4 May 1993, £15,000 is paid to a beneficiary who is a participator in the close company and holds 15% of the issued ordinary shares. On 4 August 2010, the whole of the remaining fund of £200,000 ceases to be held on qualifying trusts.

4 May 1993

There is a charge to IHT. The relevant period is the period from 1 July 1983 to 4 May 1993, i.e. 39 complete quarters.

The rate of tax is

0.25% for 39 quarters = 9.75%

IHT payable is

$$\frac{9.75}{100 - 9.75} \times £15,000 = £1,620$$

1 July 1993 and 1 July 2003

There is no liability at the ten-year anniversaries.

4 August 2010

The relevant period is the period from 1 July 1983 to 4 August 2010, i.e. 108 complete quarters.

The rate of tax is:

0.25% for 40 quarters =	10.00
0.20% for 40 quarters =	8.00
0.15% for 28 quarters =	4.20
	22.20%

IHT payable is £200,000 × 22.2% = £44,400

Excluded property

[55.8] Where the whole or part of the amount on which tax is charged as in 55.7 above is attributable to property which was EXCLUDED PROPERTY (20) at any time during the relevant period, then, in determining the rate at which tax is charged in respect of that amount or part, no quarter throughout which the property was excluded property is to be counted. [*IHTA 1984, s 70(7)*].

Newspaper trusts

[55.9] Newspaper publishing companies (i.e. companies whose businesses consist wholly or mainly in the publication of newspapers in the UK) are included among the persons within 55.2(a) to (c) above as permissible beneficiaries. The only or principal property comprised in a newspaper trust must be shares in a newspaper publishing company or a newspaper holding company (i.e. a company which has as its only or principal asset shares in a newspaper publishing company and has majority voting powers on all or most questions affecting the publishing company as a whole). Shares are treated as the principal property in a settlement or the principal asset of a company if the remaining property in the settlement or assets of the company are such as may be reasonably required to enable the trustees or the company to secure the operation of the newspaper publishing company concerned. [*IHTA 1984, s 87*].

Key points

[55.10] Points to consider are as follows.

- The transfer of the shares into an EBT is an exempt transfer if the value transferred is attributable to shares or securities in the company provided:
  - (i) the beneficiaries of the trust include all *or most* of the person's employed by holding office with the company;
  - (ii) within one year the trustees hold more than half of the ordinary shares of the company having majority voting powers (there being no provision or agreement affecting this without the trustees consent);
  - (iii) the trust does not permit any of the settled property to be applied for the benefit of a participator in the company or a participator in another close company that has benefited the same trust or any person connected with the previously mentioned.
- In order to qualify for favoured treatment an employee trust must satisfy the conditions set out in *IHTA 1984, s 86* and the necessity that all or most of the employees must be within a class of

potential beneficiaries (see below). If the trust falls outside *IHTA 1984, s 28* (or *ss 13, 86)* then contributions to the trust may be a transfer of value. If *IHTA 1984, s 86* does not apply then the trust will be subject to a ten-year anniversary charge and an exit charge when capital is distributed. An exit charge will in certain circumstances arise under *IHTA 1984, s 72*.

- Sometimes the employee trust does not hold more than 50% of the shares in the employing company and therefore the exemption will not apply. [*IHTA 1984, s 28(2)*]. However, there are a number of options in that within the year the trustees may be able to acquire the sufficient quantity of shares from retiring directors, former employees, etc. Whether these parties are going to agree to this is probably dependent on a number of factors.
- The settled property is held on trusts for the benefit of the persons employed in the company and spouses or civil partners or relatives of the employees using a settlement along these lines:

THIS SETTLEMENT is made the . . . . day of . . . .
BETWEEN (1) [Settlor] of [address] ('the Settlor') and (2) [trustees] of [addresses] ('the Original Trustees')

WHEREAS

The Settlor wishes to make provision for the employees of [..........] and companies in the same group (if applicable) and has transferred into the names of the Original Trustees the investments specified in the first schedule ('the Investments') to be held by the Original Trustees and their successors as trustees for the time being of this settlement on and with and subject to the following trust powers and provisions

NOW THIS DEED WITNESSES as follows:

1. Definitions and interpretation

 1.1 In this settlement unless the context otherwise requires the following expressions shall have the following meanings

  1.1.1 'the Trustees' means the Original Trustees . . . *continues*

  1.1.2 'the Trust Fund' means the Investments . . . *continues*

  1.1.3 'the Beneficiaries' means such of the following persons (not being an Excepted Person) as shall for the time being during such period of 125 years be in existence namely:

   1.1.3.1 persons for the time being and from time to time employed by or holding office with a Group Company and any wife husband widow widower or child or other issue or dependant of any such employee or officer or of any deceased employee or officer

   1.1.3.2 any person who at any time has been or shall have been employed by or has held or shall have held office with a Group Company and any wife husband widow widower or child or other issue or dependant of any such past employee or officer and 'Beneficiary' means any one of the 'Beneficiaries

The Precedent continues

- There are a number of important uses of an employee trust; the trust offers a non-quoted company the opportunity of creating a market for the sale and purchase of shares. These trusts can also be used to build up large shareholdings in sympathetic control so that the company will be protected against unwanted takeovers and outside interference. The employee trust will also build up good relations between staff and the employer. The trust provides for protection of workers and ex-workers in times of hardship or ill health. Even though the trust deed specifically excludes participators from benefiting i.e. clause specifically excluding participators, if a participator benefits by reason of a loan or assignment of funds to a sub-trust then a charge will arise. [*IHTA 1984, s 13(1)*].

56

Valuation

Cross-references. See **5.5** ANTI-AVOIDANCE; **33.14** NATIONAL HERITAGE; **42.5** and **42.9** SETTLEMENTS WITH INTERESTS IN POSSESSION; **53** TRANSFERS WITHIN SEVEN YEARS BEFORE DEATH.

Simon's Taxes. See **C2.121, I3.252, I3.611, I4.301–I4.309, I4.311–I4.319, Part I8.**

Other Sources. VOA IHT manual; HMRC Customer Guide to Inheritance Tax; Foster, Part H; IHTM09000.

Introduction

[56.1] The general valuation rule is that the value at any time of any property for the purposes of inheritance tax is the price which the property might reasonably be expected to fetch if sold in the open market at that time; but that price shall not be assumed to be reduced on the ground that the whole property is to be placed on the market at one and the same time. [*IHTA 1984, s 160*]. The valuation of particular property or in particular circumstances is dealt with below and under appropriate headings elsewhere in this book. See also the Valuation Office Agency website on www.voa.gov.uk/.

See Form IHT407 below.

'Open market value' has to be interpreted in the light of cases concerning other taxes, chiefly estate duty and capital gains tax, which have or had a similar valuation rule. HMRC have stated:

> 'A valuation for a "forced sale" is not acceptable. A "valuation for insurance", although a good place to start, may be the cost to replace the items and not necessarily a realistic price for which the item might be sold. As a rough guide, it might be worth having any individual items specifically mentioned in the Will and any other items that individually are thought to be worth more than £500 valued.'

Case law

In particular see *CIR v Clay* CA 1914, [1914–15] All ER 882 for position where special circumstances would affect the market price, and *Duke of Buccleuch and Another v CIR* HL 1966, [1967] 1 AC 506 for the need to assume property would be sold in 'natural units'. The decision in this last case was applied in *Gray (Executor of Lady Fox) v CIR* CA, [1994] STC 360, where the deceased was a freeholder of farm land and one of three partners in a partnership which farmed the land under an agricultural tenancy. It was held that a unit of property for the purposes of *IHTA 1984, s 160* above could comprise two or more component parts where at least one of those parts was 'land' and at least one of those parts was not 'land', and in this respect, although the question did not arise, the interest in the partnership included 'land'. See IR Tax Bulletin, August 1996, p 337. The freehold reversionary interest in the land and the 92.5% interest in the partnership held by the deceased at the time of death did, on the facts, form a unit of property to which the *Buccleuch* principle, as a matter of law, applied. The decision in the Lands Tribunal case of *Walton (Executor of Walton deceased) v CIR*, [1996] STC 68 diverged from the Capital Taxes Office [now HMRC Inheritance Tax] approach to a farm tenancy valuation. In this case the actual circumstances and intentions of co-owners of a tenancy were properly brought into account in assessing the value of the share in the tenancy of the outgoing interest. This case shows that the facts as to whether the landlord was in the market to buy in a tenant and, if the landlord was not, the only value is likely to be the capitalisation of the difference between the rent actually charged and the full market rental. See Taxation Vol 134, No 3492 pp 486–487 and Taxation Practitioner February 1995 pp 7–10).

Interests in land

For the valuation of an interest in land taking into account the liability to repay a discount allowed to a purchaser under the 'right to buy' provisions of *Housing Act 1980*, see *Alexander v CIR* CA, [1991] STC 112. The appeal concerned the valuation of a flat for Capital Transfer Tax purposes which had recently been acquired from the Local Authority under the right to buy. The difficulty was that the lease, and the *Housing Act 1980*, required the discount to be repaid on a sliding scale if it was resold within five years.

The death of the deceased did not trigger this clause but if the flat was sold at the date of death, as this was within one year of the original purchase, the full amount of the discount would have been repayable.

The Lands Tribunal had determined the value, without deduction for this obligation at £63,000. The parties successfully argued at an earlier hearing before the Special Commissioners that this value should be reduced by the discount of £24,600. HMRC contended for the DV's valuation of £50,000, being what someone would pay on the footing that if they then resold within the relevant period the discount (or part of it) would be payable, but not otherwise, and no further deduction.

Ralph Gibson LJ said:

> 'The essential question may be described thus: is the value of the lease to be taken as the value which the lease would have, if transferred, on the basis that the transferee must pay the relevant percentage of repayable premium, or is the lease to be valued as in the hands of the deceased immediately before her death when nothing had happened to cause any proportion of premium to be repayable?'

Gibson LJ concluded that the principles stated in *Inland Revenue Commissioners v Crossman and Others* HL, [1936] 1 All ER 762 are applicable.

The DV is reminded that the use of 'hindsight' is to be avoided whenever possible when considering evidence and the valuation should be based upon such knowledge as would be available on the particular date of the valuation. (VOA IHT manual, section 7, para 7.15). Also, in this connection, see *Tapp (Atkinson's Administratix) v Ryder* [2008] Lands Tribunal 5 September 2008 unreported at 58 TAX CASES.

District Valuer's considerations

The DV should have regard to the following when considering the effect on value of a restriction:

(a) the amount of the potential liability;
(b) the effective duration of the restriction;
(c) how onerous it is to comply with any restriction;
(d) the type of property;
(e) the state of the property market at the valuation date.

(VOA IHT manual, section 17, para 17.23).

The Royal Institute of Chartered Surveyors (RICS) published a new Guidance Note, GN 21, effective from 1 August 2003, which gives advice to members of RICS on the meaning of 'market value' for CGT and Inheritance Tax purposes.

Further guidance on property valuations for CGT, IHT and other taxes, together with a full explanation of the 'market value' basis of valuation can be found in the VOA's CGT and IHT Manuals which can be viewed on their website www.voa.gov.uk/ under 'Publications'.

For the purposes of the pre-owned assets anti-avoidance legislation the valuation of any property is the price which the property might reasonably be expected to fetch if sold in the open market at that time, but with the price not being reduced because the whole of the property is being placed on the market at one and the same time. See **56.24** below. [*FA 2004, Sch 15 para 15*].

Where there is a disagreement with a land valuation by the Valuation Office the matter may be negotiated with HMRC Inheritance Tax or, if that is not possible, then it can be referred to the Lands Tribunal. Any complaint regarding delay, mistake or poor handling by the Valuation Office must initially be made to the individual at the VO, their manager or Group Customer Service Manager. If still dissatisfied then contact should be made with:

The Chief Executive's Office
Valuation Office Agency
New Court
Carey Street
London WC2A 2JE

A customer service leaflet 'Putting Things Right' is available on the VO's website www.voa.gov.uk/. Tel: 020 7506 1801. Fax: 020 7506 1996. See www.hmrc.gov.uk/cto/newsletter.htm, April 2004.

Inspection of property

[56.2] The powers within *Finance Act 2008, Sch 36* are extended so that a HM Revenue & Customs officer or person accompanying the HMRC officer in assistance can enter and inspect premises and any other property on those premises in connection with checking a person's position with regard to inheritance tax. The valuation, measurement or determination of the premises or property must be *reasonably* required by HM Revenue & Customs. There are a number of inspection procedures that must be met before the Tribunal approves the inspection of the property or premises and these are set out at *Sch 36, para 12B*. [*FA 2008, Sch 36 paras 12A, 12B as inserted by FA 2009, Sch 48 para 5*]. Previously, if the Board authorised any person to inspect any property to ascertain its value for IHT purposes, the person having custody or possession of that property had to permit him to inspect it at such reasonable time as the Board considered necessary. Any person who wilfully delaying or obstructing a person acting under those powers was liable on summary conviction to a fine not exceeding level 1 on the standard scale within the meaning of *Criminal Justice Act 1982, s 75*. [*IHTA 1984, s 220 now repealed*].

Land registry and e-conveyancing

[56.3] With the advent of e-conveyancing many estates which are not registered are going to encounter problems and time delays with regard to valuations. This will particularly impact upon the period for which interest on overdue tax is due on an estate on a chargeable transfer where there are timing delays trying to ascertain boundaries, etc. It is estimated that at least 60% of the country is not registered with the Land Registry Office and in order to assist in complying with registration for e-conveyancing the Land Registry is recommending voluntary registration. See www.landregistry.gov.uk.

For large estates in excess of £1 million the fee for a 'Registered Title' will be £525 and the estate is then on the registry with all formalities completed. This will enable Executors or Trustees to obtain valuations quickly which in turn will reduce the prospect of interest on overdue IHT.

Agricultural property

[56.4] See **4.4**, **4.15** and **4.17** AGRICULTURAL PROPERTY for agricultural value, etc. See *Willett and Another v CIR Lands Tribunal*, [1982] 264 EG 257 and *Gray (Executor of Lady Fox) v CIR* (see **56.1** above) for valuation of a freehold interest in tenanted agricultural property. See *Baird's Exors v CIR Lands Tribunal for Scotland 1990*, [1991] 09 EG, 10 EG 153 for valuation of the tenant's interest in an agricultural lease containing a standard prohibition on assignation. Where there is an agricultural tie to a property it has been assumed that there should be a discount in the market value of that property, Traditionally this has been taken to be a one-third reduction, however, *IHTA 1984, s 115(3)* does not require the exclusive occupation of the property and this is a factor that should be borne in mind when assuming such discounts. Currently, many farming properties are being marketed with agricultural ties on the basis that they provide a tax shelter even with an agricultural tie. A discount in these circumstances would be inappropriate. In addition, in some cases there has been a breach of the agricultural tie for more than ten years and the legal protection for the tenant has expired so negating any perceived depression in the market value because of the agricultural tie. HMRC have had discussions with the Central Association of Agricultural Valuers on this matter. See Taxation Magazine, 3 April 2003, p 14.

The Lands Tribunal in *Lloyds TSB plc (Antrobus' Personal Representative) v Twiddy* [2004] DET/47/2004 reviewed and rejected the contention that the market value of a farmhouse represented the agricultural value, holding that the open market value of the farmhouse should be discounted by 30% to arrive at its 'agricultural value'. HMRC Inheritance Tax IHT manual sets down eight considerations as to 'character appropriateness' of a farmhouse which should be reviewed when considering a claim for relief under *IHTA 1984, s 115(2)*. See www.hmrc.gov.uk/manuals/ihtmanual/IHTM24036.htm.

Valuation based on local knowledge

Where land is situated in the United Kingdom, HMRC rely on professional advice from the Valuation Office Agency (VOA), or the Valuation and Lands Agency (VLA) in Northern Ireland, in arriving at a valuation unless specifically stated otherwise. Although most land in the UK which is chargeable to tax on the death is referred to the VOA there are some exceptions such as land subject to a binding contract for sale at the date of death. The role of the District Valuer (DV) is to agree the agricultural value and in cases where, the property has value for development or value for other non-agricultural uses or there is an imposing farmhouse in a location that would appeal to non-farming purchasers e.g. 'lifestyle farmers' the DV will also agree an open market value for the property. The DV bases his valuation at inspection on local knowledge, or on the basis of information provided by the parties and the inspection itself. If the DV has doubts as to whether or not part, or the whole, of the property was occupied for the purposes of agriculture he will let HMRC know and await further instructions from HMRC. This often occurs in the context of barns and other farm buildings, where the information provided by the parties suggests that there has been an agricultural element to the occupation but inspection suggests no recent such use.

Development, amenity or mineral value

The open market value of agricultural property may exceed its agricultural value where the land has planning permission or there is development or amenity value, or mineral value (such as gravel or sand extraction potential). A difference between the open market value and the agricultural value often occurs on farms where there are ranges of traditional buildings suitable for conversion into residential or commercial use; in many areas these can have significant excess value. Agricultural relief will not be available in respect of the excess value but business relief may be available as an alternative. Care should be taken to confirm that the parts of the farm with excess value for non-agricultural use are actually used as an asset of a qualifying business if business relief is to be claimed. Problems frequently arise with traditional buildings suitable for development that are obsolete for modern farming methods and have not been used for the business for some considerable time and do not qualify for 100% BPR or APR.

Example

Victor Acre died on 30 June 2010. He has been working as a full time farmer of Lower Meadow farm for the last 40 years after inheriting the farm from his father. The farm is a working farm and comprises of 1,000 acres of land, a farmhouse and barns. He has by his will left his whole farm to his son Bert who has worked with him on the farm since he was a boy. The farm had previously been the subject of planning order on 25 acres in conjunction with a local mineral extraction company and was subject of planning consent at the time of the death valuation. At the time of the District Valuer's visit a public enquiry was under review by the Secretary of State. The District Valuer had valued the 25 acres at £1,250 an acre and a premium of £50,750 due to the hope value of the potential mineral extractions over the next 20 years by the company. Since Victor Acre's death local objections have been raised and in the appeal to the Secretary of State the rights to mine the minerals at Lower Meadow have been upheld after a hearing and the rights of the gravel extraction company should be dismissed hence resulting in the lower market valuation of £1,250 compared the hope value at the time of the inspection by the District Valuer. For special valuation matters concerning minerals see IHTM23197.

Valuations for IHT purposes		£
1,000 acres at £1,250 per acre		1,250,000
Farmhouse (see above)		234,000
Development value		1,268,750
Total value		2,752,750
The transfers subject to tax on D's death:		
(i) Agricultural value of land		
1,000 acres × £1,250	1,250,000	
Less agricultural property relief at 100%	(1,250,000)	—
(ii) Farmhouse	234,000	
	(234,000)	—
(iii) Hope value of mineral workings not attracting BPR		2,752,750
		2,752,750
Deduct Nil rate band 2010/11		325,000
Chargeable at 40% on death of D		£2,427,750
IHT payable		971,100
Payable by ten-yearly instalments (*IHTA 1984, s 227*) of		147,800

Notes to the example

(A) Where qualifying agricultural property has an open market value in excess of its agricultural value under *IHTA 1984, s 115(3)* where for example the whole or part of it has hope value arising out of development potential or change of use then such excess value will not attract agricultural relief. As the excess value may attract business relief but a claim for business relief on the value of agricultural property on the excess over its agricultural value – e.g. farmland with planning permission, development value or mineral value (such as gravel and sand) is dependent on it being 'relevant business property'.

(B) The hope value by reference to the potential development is liable to tax and will include quarries, sand and gravel pits and the extraction of the stone, sand and gravel, etc. which is or is likely to be carried on by a company or business in which the deceased was interested.

(C) It would be advantageous for the son to receive the development land at a high value for CGT purposes for any future disposal but this is only of benefit where the land is covered by the APR or BPR 100% exemptions. If the land does not qualify then the high hope value placed on the land by the District Valuer at the date of death will be disadvantageous because of the 40% IHT charge on the balance over £325,000. HMRC are reviewing cases where APR and BPR are claimed to ensure that all the requirements of the 'relevant property' requirements apply. The drop in the value of the 25 acres where the planning permission has been rescinded post death on appeal may in certain circumstances require a third party sale or transfer into a settlement to ensure that the correct value is substituted within the four year period.

(D) In *Tapp v HMRC* [2008] EW Lands TMA/284/2008 a Lands Tribunal case shows the necessity of documentation, including photographs, regarding the state of repair of property at the time of death but a subsequent visit by the District Valuer at a later date may indicate a higher value which was not reflected at the time of death. See IHTM23203. Where property is damaged or defective, commonly from subsidence or damage from fire or storms, the personal representatives should assume the deceased's role and may be able to make a claim under an insurance policy or against a third party, for example a neighbour or negligent surveyor. If no insurance policy or right of action exists the Valuation Officer is instructed by HMRC to value the property in its defective or damaged state.

(E) The District Valuer may have been misinformed on the locale when undertaking his valuation and the market value and planning considerations were not reasonable. Special factors, little known about, may come relevant such as the *School Sites Act 1841, s 2* and the *Reverter of Sites Act 1987* each of which could affect the valuation of land value but may have been overlooked and an appeal may be warranted.

Creditors' rights

[56.5] In determining the value of a right to receive a sum it must be assumed that amounts receivable under any obligation will be received in full unless recovery of the sum is impossible or not reasonably practicable and has not become so by any act or omission of the person to whom the sum is due. [*IHTA 1984, s 166*]. However, for deaths on or after 5 July 2010, the right to receive compensation in respect of Bradford & Bingley (B&B) shares may be included at a nil value as agreed by HMRC. For deaths occurring before 5 July 2010, where the holding is of 1,000 B&B shares or less, the right to receive compensation in respect of those shares may be included at a nil value. Also, for deaths occurring before 5 July 2010, where the holding of B&B is of more than 1,000 shares, executors or others liable for IHT should contact the Shares and Assets Valuation Helpline on 0115 974 2222 for advice on the appropriate value to be included for IHT purposes.

See Form IHT416 below.

Death

[56.6] See above and 52.2 TRANSFERS ON DEATH for the valuation of a deceased person's estate generally and also below for certain sales after death.

Capital gains tax

[56.7] Where, on the death of any person, inheritance tax (or, when extant, capital transfer tax or estate duty) is chargeable on the value of his estate immediately before his death and the value of an asset forming part of his estate has been ascertained for those purposes, that value is to be taken as the market value at the date of death for capital gains tax purposes. However, in calculating the amount of nil rate band available for transfer under *IHTA 1984, s 8A* the value ascertained for that purpose shall not be adopted as the value for capital gains tax purposes. [*TCGA 1992, s 274, Sch 11 para 9; FA 2008, Sch 4 para 8*]. Because of the existence for inheritance tax of such factors as the spouse/civil partner exemption and 100% business and agricultural property relief, it is unclear whether in an appropriate case inheritance tax is 'chargeable' and a value has been 'ascertained'. In such cases, and where no IHT is payable on the deceased's estate, the value of an asset is not ascertained for IHT purposes and therefore no IHT value is available, then the normal rules of *TCGA 1992, s 272* are applied to determine the capital gains tax acquisition of the beneficiary (see HMRC Capital Gains Tax Manual paras 32222 and 32230).

A danger lies in cases where agricultural property comprises part of an estate and is expected to attract the 100% relief under *IHTA 1984, s 116* and a nominal or ill-considered valuation is made rather than a professional valuation. Subsequently, if relief is not due for any reason then the value of the asset will not have been 'ascertained' for the purposes of *TCGA 1992, s 274*. In such a case where there is an uplift in the value to the open market value then a penalty may be applicable. See **36.7** PENALTIES and at www.hmrc.gov.uk/cto/newsletter.htm, April 2004.

See **56.24** below in the case of quoted shares and securities.

Joint property

[56.8] The value of a half share of land owned by joint tenants or tenants in common is half vacant possession value less a discount to reflect the restricted demand for this type of interest. An appropriate discount has been held to be 15%. (*Wight and Moss v CIR Lands Tribunal*, [1982] 264 EG 935; *Barrett (Barrett's Personal Representatives) v HMRC Lands Tribunal*, 23 November 2005 unreported). It should be borne in mind that interests of joint owners will be 'related property' if they are spouses or civil partners, and in that event the valuation discount does not apply; see **56.21** below and **58** TAX CASES.

Where at the valuation date a co-owner remains in occupation the normal approach is for the DV to take half the freehold vacant possession value and deduct 15%. In cases where the co-owner has rights to occupy but does not and the purpose behind the trust for sale still exists then the discount would normally be 15% and 10% in other cases. A half share without rights of occupation will obtain a 10% deduction from the value. See paras 18.5 and 18.6 of section 18 in VOA IHT manual at www.voa.gov.uk/. The example in the VOA manual shows circumstances where the 10% and 15% discounts are appropriate as follows:

Example

Mr and Mrs A bought a house as tenants in common for their joint occupation. When Mr A died he left his one-half share to his son Mr B who lives elsewhere. Mrs A has now died and it is therefore necessary to value her one half-share.

When Mrs A dies the other co-owner is Mr B. Mr B is not in occupation and the house was not purchased for his occupation. When valuing Mrs A's one-half share a 10% discount should be applied.

If Mr B had died before Mrs A then, at the date of Mr B's death, the other co-owner, Mrs A, would still have been in occupation and the purpose behind the trust would still have existed. When valuing Mr B's one-half share a 15% discount should be applied.

Notes to the example

(A) The example in the VOA IHT manual shows in the first two paragraphs that a 10% discount would be due because the original purpose behind the trust for sale (be it a 'financial' trust for sale or an 'occupation' trust for sale) still exists on the death of the wife in occupation or the son not in occupation. However, in the third paragraph where Mr B dies first his estate would be entitled to the higher 15% discount because Mrs A is still in occupation of the property.

(B) Where an 'interest in land' in a deceased person's estate is sold within three years after the death by the '*appropriate person*', a claim (on Form IHT38) may be made by that person for the 'sale value' to be substituted for the value on death of *every* interest in land owned by the deceased and sold within three years of death by the same 'appropriate person' for which such a claim would be available. See **56.9** below. However, in cases where a discount of 10% has been claimed and then the interest is sold and a claim is made under *IHTA 1984, s 191* the 10% discount for joint ownership is not allowed as a further deduction from the sale proceeds. This may have the effect of HMRC assessing a higher than expected figure than was the case intended by the appropriate person.

(C) This (point B above) of course places the estate in a disadvantageous position and, as in many cases of HMRC elections which, once made, cannot be withdrawn, HMRC are instructed to ensure that they consider any disadvantageous elections under Form IHT38, see IHT manual extract at IHTM33182 where the claim is reviewed to 'help prevent the taxpayer making a disadvantageous claim'. See also Fosters at D3.12. However, HMRC confirm that such an instruction will not be binding where the IHT38 has been made on a commercially supplied copy of the form and submitted unsolicited to HMRC under *IHTA 1984, s 191*.

See also *St Clair-Ford (Youlden's Executor) v Ryder*, [2006] Lands Tribunal 22 June 2006 unreported. When dealing with minority shares in property which is vacant, or commercially let, it is necessary to consider the purpose behind the trust for sale and if it exists and can be fulfilled then the discount may be increased. (VOA IHT manual, section 18, paras 18.3–18.7). In *HSBC Trusts Co (UK) Ltd (Farmbrough's Executor) v Twiddy*, [2006] Lands Tribunal 24 August 2006 unreported, a woman had held a 16.25% interest in two large buildings comprising 28 flats and 9 shops. The Lands Tribunal held that since this was a minority interest, it should be valued on an income basis, declining to follow the earlier decision in *Charkham v CIR*, Lands Tribunal 1996, [2000] RVR 7.

For varying treatment of accounts held in joint names see *Anand v CIR* [1997] STC SCD 58 Sp C 107 and *O'Neill and others v CIR* [1998] STC SCD 110 Sp C 154. See also *Sillars and another v CIR* [2004] STC SCD 180 Sp C 401 and *Ms S Taylor (Executrix for Mrs K Boland) v HMRC* [2008] STC SCD 1159 Sp C 704.

See Form IHT404 below.

Partnership interests

The partners are collectively entitled to each and every asset of the partnership, in which each of them therefore has an undivided share. Consequently the valuation of an interest in a business carried on as a partnership should be by reference to the appropriate share of each asset, including any goodwill (except for farming where goodwill does not apply), less a deduction for a corresponding share of partnership liabilities. Reference must be made to the partnership deed to ascertain what that share is. If there is no deed or agreement, the provisions of the *Partnership Act 1890* will govern the position.

Partnership agreements may contain provisions to the effect that in the event of the death or retirement of a partner any interest in partnership property is taken over by the other partners with specific terms as to what consideration, if any, is to be payable. If the consideration is not to be full market value, the agreement will fall to be treated as a restriction on the freedom to dispose of property. Any such restriction is taken into account only to the extent that consideration was given for it in money or money's worth when it was created [*IHTA 1984, s 163*]. Often such terms can be construed as being for the mutual benefit of all the partners with no intended gratuitous transfers. However HMRC will review the full facts in the case of family partnerships to establish whether and to what extent *IHTA 1984, s 163* applies.

The VOA accept that it will normally be necessary to make some discount from the appropriate arithmetical share of the full partnership value in order to reflect the fact that the hypothetical purchaser of the partner's share will have to take steps to dissolve the partnership or negotiate a sale to the other partners. The discount will not normally exceed 10%. Following *Walton v CIR* [1996] STC 68, [1996] 1 EGLR 159, CA no discount is applied to the value of agricultural tenancies valued by capitalising profit rent. See VOA IHT manual, para 19.8 and 19.9.

Scottish law

Under Scots Law the 'survivorship destination' does not by itself pass the ownership of the funds in a joint account to the survivor. An account with a bank or building society is not a document of title as it is not a Deed of Trust in terms of the *Bank Bonds and Trusts Act 1696*. Instead, it is a contract between the bank and the customer which regulates the conditions on which the account is to be operated and is for administrative convenience only. See *Cairns v Davidson* [1913] SC 1054. If under the terms of the Will/Intestacy the funds in the account do not pass wholly to the surviving spouse then inheritance tax will be payable as appropriate. If under the terms of the Will/Intestacy the funds in the joint account pass to the spouse, then the spouse exemption should be claimed on page 4 of the IHT400 under the head 'Exemptions and Reliefs' on page 9. This applies to all bank/building society accounts governed by Scots Law so this is a point which practitioners should bear in mind when administering an estate subject to Scots Law.

Land sold within three years (four years in some cases) of death

Claim

[56.9] Where an 'interest in land' in a deceased person's estate is sold within three years after the death by the '*appropriate person*', a claim (on Form IHT38) may be made by that person for the 'sale value' to be substituted for the value on death of *every* interest in land owned by the deceased and sold within three years of death by the same 'appropriate person' for which such a claim would be available. In the case of a death after 15 March 1990, a sale in the fourth year after death is treated as having occurred within three years of death unless *either* **56.13** below applies *or* the 'sale value' would exceed the value on death. The claim for relief under *IHTA 1984, s 191* must be made not more than four years from the date of death of the person where the interest in land was comprised in that deceased person's estate. [*IHTA 1984, s 191(1A); FA 2009, s 99, Sch 51 para 10*].

Definitions

'*Interest in land*' does not include any estate, interest or right by way of mortgage or other security.

'*Appropriate person*' is the person liable for the tax or, if there is more than one such person and one of them is paying the tax, that person. For instance, if personal representatives pay the tax on the estate and then assent shares or land to a beneficiary who sells them at a loss, within the respective time limits, then no relief will be due as the beneficiary is not an 'appropriate person' under *IHTA 1984, ss 179(1), 191(1)*. In cases where 100% business or agricultural property relief is available then a substitution claim under *IHTA 1984, s 191* would not apply because there would not be an '*appropriate person*' who could make a claim. This may have a knock-on effect with regard to the capital gains tax position. See *Stoner and Another (Executors of Dickinson deceased) v CIR* [2001] STC SCD 199 Sp C 288 which underlines the fact that a claim can only be made where an IHT issue (not a CGT saving issue) is at stake. This would also exclude cases where the value was covered by business property relief, the spouse/civil partner exemption and the nil-rate. See **58** TAX CASES.

'*Sale value*' is the 'sale price' as adjusted by the provisions in **56.11** to **56.16** below. Note that an abortive contract is not a sale and the sale price cannot be the said to be the price stated in the contract. (*Jones and Another (Balls' Administrators) v CIR*, Ch D [1997] STC 359).

'*Sale price*' is the price for which the land is sold or, if greater, the best consideration that could reasonably have been obtained at the time of sale, ignoring incidental expenses of commission, stamp duty or otherwise. [*IHTA 1984, ss 190, 191(1), 197A(1)(2); FA 1993, s 199*].

No claim is available if in respect of the interest in land giving rise to the claim:

(a) the sale value differs from the value on death by less than the lower of £1,000 and 5% of the value on death (see note 7 on IHT38); or
(b) the sale is by a personal representative or trustee to:
  (i) a person who, at any time between death and the sale, has been beneficially entitled to, or to an interest in possession in, property comprising the interest sold; or
  (ii) the spouse, civil partner, child or remoter descendant of a person within (i) above; or
  (iii) a trustee of a settlement under which a person within (i) or (ii) above has an interest in possession in property comprising the interest sold, or
(c) the vendor or any person within (b) above obtains a right in connection with the sale to acquire the interest sold or any other interest in the same land.

For the above purposes, a person shall be treated as having the same rights in the property in an unadministered estate as he would have if the administration of the estate had been completed. In the case of (b)(ii) and (iii) above the restriction will not apply to a parent or sibling of the beneficiary or to the trustees of a discretionary settlement in which he is a potential object.

[*IHTA 1984, s 191(2)(3)*].

Further purchases of land

Because of the possibility of further purchases (see **56.15** below), the above loss on sale relief cannot be formally granted until four months have elapsed from the date of the last sale of an interest in land (see note 4 on IHT38). In many estates there is one interest in land and it has to be sold to give effect to the terms of the deceased's will so that there is no prospect of further purchases. In such circumstances, the HMRC Inheritance Tax will accept a loss on sale relief claim in advance of the statutory time limit and make a provisional repayment of tax accordingly. However, formal clearance by way of certificate of discharge (see **35.15** PAYMENT OF TAX) must await the personal representatives' confirmation (subsequent to the expiry of the four-month statutory time limit) that no changes have taken place since the claim was made (CTO Practice Note published in Taxation Practitioner August 1994 p 6).

Date applicable

[56.10] Date of sale or purchase of land by the 'appropriate person' is the date of the contract. If the transaction results from the exercise (by him or any other person) of an option granted not more than six months earlier, then the date of the transaction is the date on which the option is granted.

Where an interest in land is acquired in pursuance of a notice to treat served by an authority possessing powers of compulsory purchase, the date of sale is whichever is the earlier of:

(a) the date when the compensation is agreed or otherwise determined (any variation on appeal being disregarded), and
(b) the date when the authority enters on the land in pursuance of their powers.

If an interest in land is acquired from the 'appropriate person' by a general vesting declaration under the *Compulsory Purchase (Vesting Declarations) Act 1981* or, in Scotland, the *Town and Country Planning (Scotland) Act 1972, Sch 24* or, in NI, by a vesting order, the date of sale is the last day of the period specified in the declaration (in NI, the date on which the vesting order becomes operative). [*IHTA 1984, s 198*].

Adjustments

[56.11] Sales to beneficiaries etc. and exchanges require adjustment where the person making the claim, acting in the same capacity as that in which he makes the claim:

(a) sells land (or an interest in land) within three years after the death (a sale within four years after death which is treated as within three years under **56.9** above being ignored for this purpose) to any person within **56.9**(b) or (c) above; or
(b) within three years after the death exchanges (with or without payment) any interest in land which was comprised in the deceased's estate,

and the sale price (or market value in the case of an exchange) exceeds its value on death. In such a case an addition is made to the sale price of any interest to which the claim relates. If the claim relates to one interest only, the addition is the amount of the excess. If there is more than one interest, the addition is that part of the excess given by the fraction:

$$\frac{A}{B}$$

where:

A = the difference between the value on death of that interest and its sale price (as adjusted under **56.12** to **56.14** below); and
B = the aggregate of that difference and the corresponding differences for all other interests to which the claim relates, calculated without regard to which is the greater, in the case of any particular interest, of its value on death and its sale price. [*IHTA 1984, ss 196, 197A(4); FA 1993, s 199*].

Example

A (a bachelor) died on 1 May 2007 owning four areas of land, as follows.

(a) 10 acres valued at death £20,000
(b) 15 acres valued at death £30,000

(c) 20 acres valued at death £30,000
(d) 30 acres valued at death £40,000

He also owned a freehold house valued at death at £50,000.

In the four years following A's death, his executors made the following sales.

(i) Freehold house sold 15.11.07, proceeds £53,000, expenses £2,000
(ii) Land area (c) sold 1.6.09, proceeds £29,500, expenses £1,500
(iii) Land area (b) sold 8.8.10, proceeds £27,000, expenses £1,000
(iv) Land area (d) sold 19.9.10, proceeds £42,000, expenses £3,000

The following revisions must be calculated on a claim under *IHTA 1984, Pt VI, Chapter IV*

	£	
Gross sale proceeds of house	53,000	
Deduct probate value	50,000	£3,000
Gross sale proceeds of land area (b)	27,000	
Deduct probate value	30,000	£(3,000)
Gross sale proceeds of land area (c)	29,500	
Deduct probate value	30,000	£(500)

Notes to the example

(A) The sale of area (c) is disregarded as the loss on sale (before allowing for expenses) is less than 5% of £30,000 (£1,500) and is also lower than £1,000. [*IHTA 1984, s 191*]. Note 7 on IHT38.

(B) The overall allowable reduction on all sales is therefore nil even though there is a loss after expenses.

(C) For deaths after 15 March 1990, a sale *for less than the value at death* which is made in the fourth year after death is treated as having been made in the three years after death. [*IHTA 1984, s 197A; FA 1993, s 199*].

(D) Note that if the gross sale proceeds of the house of £53,000 had been incorrectly discounted by 10% to take account of a joint ownership at the date of death then the calculation would be recomputed to preclude the discount and a revised figure of £52,500 taken into account. This would result in a further *increase* in the value of the taxable estate thereby imposing a further IHT charge on the personal representatives which may also incur interest. See implications regarding an erroneous submission of IHT38 in the example in **56.8** above.

Changes between death and sale

[56.12] Where there has been a change between the date of death and the date of sale so that the interest is not the same in all respects and with the same incidents and the land in which the interest subsists is not in the same state and with the same incidents, the sale price is adjusted by the difference between the value on death and what that value would have been if the changed circumstances had prevailed at the time of death. The difference is added to the sale price if the original value on death was more than the new valuation and deducted if less. See also example at **56.9** above.

If compensation under any Act has been received by the 'appropriate person' (or any other person liable to tax on the interest in the land) between the death and the sale because of a restriction on the use or development of the land or because its value has been reduced for any other reason, such restriction or reduction is ignored for the adjustment of the sale price mentioned above but the sale price is increased by the amount of the compensation. [*IHTA 1984, s 193*]. See question 7 on form IHT38.

Compulsory acquisition more than three years after death

[56.13] Where an authority possessing powers of compulsory acquisition has served notice to treat before the death or within the following three years and has acquired the land *after* those three years from the 'appropriate person', the acquisition is treated in the same way as a sale during the three years. This provision is ignored if the sale value exceeds the value on death. [*IHTA 1984, s 197(1)(2)*].

Other interests in same or other land

[56.14] If in determining the value at death of any interest to which the claim relates, any other interests, whether in the same or other land, were taken into account, an addition must be made to the sale price of the interest equal to the difference between the value on death of the interest and the value which would have been the value on death if no other interests had been taken into account. [*IHTA 1984, s 195*].

Subsequent purchases

[56.15] **Further purchases** of any interests in land by the person making the claim as above in the same capacity during the period beginning with the death and ending four months after the date of the last sale may reduce the relief claimable on the sales. For this purpose any sale in the fourth year after death and taken into account under **56.9** above and any compulsory acquisition more than three years after death and taken into account under **56.13** above are ignored, and if the claim relates only to such sales, the following provisions are ignored.

The relief is lost if the aggregate of the purchase prices of all the interests purchased equals or exceeds the aggregate of the sale prices (as adjusted by **56.12** and **56.14** above and **56.16** below). Otherwise an addition is made to the sale price of every interest to which the claim relates given by the formula:

$$(V - S) \times \frac{A}{B}$$

where:

V = value on death of the interest;
S = sales price (as adjusted by **56.11, 56.12** and **56.14** above and **56.16** below as appropriate);

A = aggregate of the purchase prices; and
B = aggregate of the sales prices.

Where the value on death of an interest is less than its sale price as adjusted above, the sale price is reduced by the amount calculated from the above formula. [*IHTA 1984, ss 192, 197(3), 197A(3); FA 1993, s 199*].

Example

B died on 30 June 2010 owning a house and a seaside flat.

At death the valuations were

	£
House	50,000
Flat	30,000
	£80,000
Sales by the executors realised (gross)	
House proceeds 1.7.2011	42,000
Flat proceeds 1.12.2011	33,000
	£75,000

On 1 May 2011, the executors bought a town house for the deceased's daughter for £40,000 (excluding costs).

Initially relief is due of £(80,000 – 75,000) = £5,000

Recomputation of relief

$$\text{Appropriate fraction} = \frac{\text{Purchase price}}{\text{Selling price}} = \frac{40{,}000}{75{,}000} = \frac{8}{15}$$

		House		**Seaside Flat**
	£	£	£	£
Value on death		50,000		30,000
Sale price	42,000			
Add (£50,000 – £42,000) × 8/15	4,267			
Revised value for IHT		46,267		
Sale price			33,000	
Deduct (£33,000 – £30,000) × 8/15			1,600	
Revised value for IHT				31,400
Revised relief		£3,733		£(1,400)
Total			£2,333	

Note to the example

(A) The purchase is taken into account because it is made within the period 30 June 2010 (date of death) and 1 April 2012 (four months after the last of the sales affected by the claim). [*IHTA 1984, s 192(1)*]. If a sale made in the fourth year after death was affected by the claim (under *IHTA*

1984, s 197A), it would *not* be taken into account in determining the above-mentioned period. [*IHTA 1984, s 197A(3); FA 1993, s 199*].

Leases

[56.16] Where a claim relates to an interest in a lease of under 50 years duration at the date of death, the sale price is increased by the proportion of the amount of the value on death given by the fraction:

$$\frac{P(1) - P(2)}{P(2)}$$

where:

P(1) = the appropriate percentage from the table for depreciation of leases contained in *TCGA 1992, Sch 8 para 1* (see 8 CAPITAL GAINS TAX) for the duration of the lease at the date of death; and
P(2) = the appropriate percentage for the duration of the lease at the date of sale.

Note that on form IHT38 the unexpired term of the lease at the date of death must be entered on the form under the heading 'Tenure'.

[*IHTA 1984, s 194*].

Leased property

[56.17] If full consideration originally passed for the lease then the market value of the lease is taken when it is later transferred. Where a lessee's interest is for life or otherwise determinable by reference to a death, it may be treated as a settlement (see **41.6** SETTLEMENTS — GENERAL) and the value is calculated as the full value of the property less the value of the lessor's interest. The value of the lessor's interest is the proportion of the value of the property given by the fraction:

$$\frac{A}{B}$$

where:

A = the value of the consideration given by the lessee at the time the lease was granted; and B
B = the value of a full consideration in money or money's worth of the lease at that time.

[*IHTA 1984, ss 50(6), 170*].

Liabilities

[56.18] In determining the value of a person's estate at any time his liabilities at that time must be taken into account, except as otherwise provided by *IHTA 1984*. Except in the case of a liability imposed by the law, a liability incurred by the transferor may be taken into account only to the extent that it was incurred for a consideration in money or money's worth. [*IHTA 1984, s 5(3)(5)*].

The following rules apply for determining the amount or value of the liability.

(a) A liability in respect of which there is a right to reimbursement is taken into account only to the extent that reimbursement cannot reasonably be expected to be obtained.

(b) Subject to (c) below, where a liability falls to be discharged after the time at which it is to be taken into account, it must be valued at the time of being taken into account (i.e. at its discounted value).

(c) In determining the value of the transferor's estate immediately after the transfer, his liability for inheritance tax is computed:
  (i) without making any allowance for the fact that the tax will not be due immediately; and
  (ii) as if any tax recovered otherwise than from the transferor (or, under certain circumstances, the transferor's spouse or civil partner, see **30.2** LIABILITY FOR TAX) were paid in discharge of a liability in respect of which the transferor had a right to reimbursement.

(d) A liability which is an encumbrance on any property must, as far as possible, be taken to reduce the value of that property. However with effect from 17 July 2013 (the date of Royal Assent to the *Finance Act 2013*), any liability incurred on or after 6 April 2013 which financed excluded property or 'relievable property' is primarily deducted from the value of that property, notwithstanding the fact that it may be secured on other property. See details at **56.19** below.

(e) A liability due to a person resident outside the UK which neither falls to be discharged in the UK nor is an encumbrance on UK property must, as far as possible, be taken to reduce the value of non-UK property. [*IHTA 1984, s 162*]. See *Whittaker v CIR*, [2001] STC SCD 61 Sp C 272.

Where an individual receives a capital payment from a non-UK resident trust and, under the provisions in *FA 1984, Sch 14* that payment crystallises a previously deferred capital gains tax liability of a close relative of his, the payment by the individual of the capital gains tax is treated for inheritance tax purposes as made in satisfaction of a liability of his. [*IHTA 1984, s 165(3)*].

See also **52** TRANSFERS ON DEATH.

The value transferred is also reduced by:

(i) any capital gains tax (or income tax on a development gain) borne by the donee. In the case of settled property the reduction applies only if the tax on the gain accruing to the trustees is borne by a person who becomes absolutely entitled to the settled property concerned;

(ii) any incidental expenses incurred by the transferor in making the transfer but borne by the transferee. If borne by the transferor they are left out of account i.e. they do not have to be added to the amount of the gift.

[*IHTA 1984, ss 164, 165*].

See now form IHT419 below and **56.5** VALUATION.

Liabilities to finance excluded property or relievable property

[56.19] For transfers of value made or treated as made on or after 17 July 2013, it is no longer possible to reduce the value of an asset for IHT purposes by securing a loan on it where the loan is used to acquire or maintain (directly or indirectly) another asset which qualifies for certain IHT reliefs. Instead the loan will be primarily deductible from the asset qualifying for relief. These rules have equal effect for charges on settlements holding relevant property within *IHTA 1984, s 58*.

In the case of (ii) and (iii) below, this rule applies to any liability incurred on or after 6 April 2013. In the case of (i) and (v) below the rule applies to liabilities whenever incurred, but (i) has effect for transfers of value made or treated as made on or after 17 July 2013, whereas (v) effect for transfers of value made or treated as made on or after 17 July 2014. The provisions apply to liabilities incurred to acquire, finance, maintain or enhance the value of:

(i) excluded property (see **20** EXCLUDED PROPERTY);
(ii) property qualifying for business property relief (see **6** BUSINESS PROPERTY);
(iii) property qualifying for agricultural property relief (see **4** AGRICULTURAL PROPERTY);
(iv) woodlands where the value of them is to be left out of account on a person's death (see **57.1**(c)).
(v) a balance on any foreign currency account which is to be left out of account of a person's estate on death under the relief in *IHTA 1984, s 157* (NON-RESIDENTS' BANK ACCOUNTS) (see **21.22**).

In the case of a liability incurred in respect of excluded property, as above, the loan is not to be taken into account for IHT purposes. However, if the excluded property is subsequently disposed of for full consideration, the liability may then be deductible for IHT purposes to the extent that the proceeds of the disposal are not used to acquire or maintain other excluded property, or to pay off another loan which cannot not to be taken into account by virtue of this provision. A liability may be taken into account to the extent that it exceeds the value of any of the excluded property not disposed of, but not where this excess is attributable to arrangements to secure a tax advantage, an increase in the amount of the liability, or a disposal of any of the excluded property. For example, if a loan is taken out to buy shares in a foreign incorporated company, and arrangements are then made for tax reasons to reduce the value of those shares, the loan will remain non-deductible.

In the case of a liability which was incurred wholly or partly to finance the balance on a foreign currency account within (v) above, the loan may be deducted from the estate of the borrower to the extent that it exceeds the balance on the account so long as this excess does not arise either as a result of arrangements to secure a tax advantage or to increase the amount of the liability (e.g. by accruing interest on the loan).

In the case of a liability incurred in respect of business or agricultural property, or woodlands, as detailed above, the loan is to be primarily deducted from the value of that property before the any applicable reliefs for such property are given. If the business or agricultural property is gifted during lifetime, the loan is to be deducted only from the value of that property if the lifetime gift is or becomes a chargeable transfer, so that the liability cannot also be deducted from the estate on death. But if the lifetime gift is a PET and the donor survives for seven years, retaining liability for the loan, it may then be deducted from the estate on death.

A loan is considered by HMRC to indirectly finance an asset where it is initially used to buy asset 1 which is later sold and the proceeds reinvested in asset 2. The loan then indirectly finances asset 2 (see HMRC IHT Manual para IHTM28018). On this view it is not possible to circumvent the disallowance by first acquiring UK property with a loan, subsequently selling that property and then acquiring excluded property with the proceeds. Equally where a loan is taken out to buy a UK asset, say a painting, and that asset becomes excluded property, for example by being removed from the UK, the loan is deductible only to the extent that it exceeds the value of that asset and subject also to there being no arrangements to secure a tax advantage.

Where a liability is incurred partly for relievable property, as described above, and partly for other assets not qualifying for the reliefs, any part repayments of a liability are to be attributed first to the proportion of it incurred for the non-relievable property. If a loan is incurred partly in relation to assets within any of (ii), (iii) or (iv) above and partly in relation to assets within (i) above, part repayments are to be attributed primarily to the part relating to the assets within (ii), (iii) or (iv). For HMRC's view on apportionments of liabilities between relievable and non-relievable property, see IHT Manual para 28021. [*IHTA 1984, ss 162A and 162B*].

Life assurance policies and annuities

[56.20] See **31** LIFE ASSURANCE POLICIES AND ANNUITIES for the valuation of policies and contracts and **42.5** SETTLEMENTS WITH INTERESTS IN POSSESSION for annuities which are interests in possession.

HMRC have stated:

> 'Life insurance policies taken out on one person's life may be held in trust for the benefit of others. Parents and grandparents may often take out a life insurance policy but put it in trust for their children or grandchildren. Business partners or the directors of a company also take out insurance on their lives but for the benefit of

> their partners and co–directors. So, if the deceased died whilst still working, or they died before their parent(s), there is a possibility that they may have a right to benefit under a policy held in trust. If the deceased had a right to benefit under a life insurance policy held in trust, that right may be settled property.'

See Form IHT410 below. Note that reserved rights to a life annuity where there is a projected life expectancy can result in a discount in the valuation of the policy at death. In *CJ Bower & DN Chesterfield (Mrs ME Bower's Executors) v HMRC* [2008] STC SCD 582 Sp C 665; Ch D [2009] STC 510 there was a deduction of £4,200 allowed representing the deceased's reserved rights to the life annuity. HMRC appealed to the Ch D against this decision. The appeal in Chancery Division was allowed. For HMRC's practice, see HMRC Brief 23/08, issued on 11 April 2008. New cases regarding the discounted gift will continue to be dealt with in accordance with the May 2007 Technical Note www.hmrc.gov.uk/cto/dgs-tech-note.pdf.

Related property

[56.21] The value of any property in a person's estate is found by taking related property into account if by so doing a higher value for all or part of the property in his estate would be obtained. Property is related to the property in a person's estate if:

(a) it is in the estate of his spouse/civil partner, or

(b) it is, or was during the preceding five years, the property of a charity, charitable trust, qualifying political party (see **21.7** EXEMPT TRANSFERS), specified national body (see **33.29** NATIONAL HERITAGE), non-profit making body (see **21.8** EXEMPT TRANSFERS) or registered housing association (see **21.5** EXEMPT TRANSFERS), and became so as the result of a transfer of value made by him or his spouse or civil partner after 15 April 1976 and was exempt to the extent that the value transferred was attributable to the property.

The value of the estate property and the related property taken together is then apportioned to the estate property in the proportion that its value on its own bears to the sum of the separate values. See *Arkwright and Another (Williams' Personal Representatives) v CIR* Ch D [2004] STC 1323, Sp C 392. [*IHTA 1984, s 161(1)–(3); FA 1989, s 171(4)*].

Example 1

Husband owns a property worth £150,000 and his wife owns adjoining land worth £250,000. The combined value is £800,000.

The proportioned value of the husband's land is:

$$\frac{150{,}000}{150{,}000+250{,}000}\times £800{,}000 = £300{,}000$$

In the above example if the properties were each owned in equal shares and, say, the house was encumbered by mortgage of £60,000 in the husband's name sole then the value of the house is divisible in equal shares after the deduction of the mortgage even though this is in the husband's sole name in the sum of £45,000 (i.e. £150,000 – £60,000 ÷ 2).

In the case of shares etc. of the same class or similar units of property, the proportion is that which the number of shares in the estate bears to the total number of those and the related shares. Shares are of the same class if they are, or would be, so treated by the practice of a recognised stock exchange. [*IHTA 1984, s 161(4)(5)*].

The DV should value both interests together and make no reduction in the aggregate value because the related property is owned by the spouse/civil partner and not by the transferor. If vacant possession would become available on the merging of the interests the property should be valued with vacant possession. The aggregate value should reflect the full enhancement attributable to the merging of the transferor's property with the related property and no deduction should be made because more than one ownership is involved. (VOA IHT manual, section 15, para 15.5).

Example 2

On the death of a husband on 31 October 2010, the share capital of a private company was held as follows

	Shares	
Issued capital	10,000	
Husband	4,000	40%
Wife	4,000	40%
Others (employees)	2,000	20%
	10,000	100%

The value of an 80% holding is £80,000, while the value of a 40% holding is £24,000. In his will, the husband left his 4,000 shares to his daughter.

The related property rules apply to aggregate the shares of:

Husband	4,000	
Wife	4,000	
Related property	8,000	shares
Chargeable transfer on legacy to daughter		
IHT value of 8,000 shares (80%)		£80,000
IHT value attributed to legacy of husband's shares (4,000)		£40,000

(Subject to 100% business property relief if conditions satisfied.)

Sale within three years after death

[56.22] If property was valued on a death by reference to related property as in 56.21 above and is sold within the following three years at less than that valuation (allowing for any difference in circumstances between the times of death and sale), a claim may be made to revert to the value of that property at death without reference to the related property. The sale must qualify under the following conditions, namely that:

(a) the vendors are the persons in whom the property vested immediately after death or are the deceased's personal representatives; and
(b) the sale is at arm's length for a price freely negotiated at the time of the sale and is not made in conjunction with a sale of any of the related property; and
(c) no vendor (or any person having an interest in the sale proceeds) is, or is connected with, any purchaser (or any person having an interest in the purchase); and
(d) neither the vendors nor any other person having an interest in the sale proceeds obtain in connection with the sale a right to acquire the property sold or any interest in or created out of it.

Where the property is shares or securities of a close company, the above relief does not apply if between the death and sale the value is reduced by more than 5% as a result of an alteration in the company's share or loan capital or rights attaching thereto.

The above rules also apply where the property was valued at death in conjunction with other property which did not devolve on the vendors e.g. property in a trust of which the deceased was life tenant. [*IHTA 1984, s 176*].

Restriction on freedom to dispose

[56.23] If the right to dispose of any property has been excluded or restricted by a contract made at any time, then, on the next chargeable transfer of the property, the exclusion or restriction will be taken into account only to the extent that consideration in money or money's worth was given for it. If the contract was before 27 March 1974, this provision applies only if the next chargeable transfer is a transfer made on death.

If the contract was itself a chargeable transfer (including part of an associated operation), an allowance is made for so much of the value transferred thereby (ignoring tax) as is attributable to the exclusion or restriction. [*IHTA 1984, s 163*].

Shares and securities

[56.24] **Unquoted shares and securities** are valued at what they might reasonably be expected to fetch if sold in the open market on the assumption that there is available to any prospective purchaser all the information which a prudent prospective purchaser might reasonably require if he were proposing to purchase them from a willing vendor by private treaty and at arm's length. [*IHTA 1984, s 168; FA 1987, s 58, Sch 8 para 12*]. See also *CIR v Crossman and Others* HL, [1936] 1 All ER 762; *In re Lynall (decd.)* HL 1971, 47 TC 375; *Battle and Another v CIR* Ch D 1979, [1980] STC 86.

In a capital transfer tax case, both earlier arm's length transactions in the shares in question and previous agreements with HMRC were held to be admissible evidence for valuation purposes (*CIR v Stenhouse's Trustees* CS 1991, [1992] STC 103).

In order to ensure uniformity of approach, the DV should, unless otherwise instructed by Shares and Assets Valuation (SAV), value the underlying company property or assets on the basis of the statutory definition in *IHTA 1984, s 160* of 'open market value' disregarding any 'flooding of the market' effect and apply any relevant legal principles which have evolved over the years when the courts have ruled on the meaning of the similar definition for ED purposes contained in *FA 1894, s 7(5)* (VOA IHT manual, section 16, para 16.8). For these purposes the costs of sale are ignored.

The address of Shares and Assets Valuation is HMRC, Shares and Assets Valuation, Fitz Roy House, PO Box 46, Castle Meadow Road, Nottingham NG2 1BD. Tel: 0115-974 2222. Fax: 0115-974 2197. DX 701203 Nottingham 4. The address in Scotland is HMRC Inheritance Tax, Meldrum House, 15 Drumsheugh Gardens, Edinburgh EH3 7UH. Tel: 0131 777 4180. Fax. 0131 777 4220. DX 542002, Edinburgh 14.

Where it is evident that any possible variation in the value of shares in an unquoted company shown in the HMRC Account will still leave the total value of an estate below the IHT threshold, it is not necessary to ascertain the value of those shares. Where the total value of an estate is close to the IHT threshold, values may be considered but not necessarily 'ascertained'. For example, where SAV regard the value of such shares to be too high it is unlikely to negotiate an ascertained value for IHT when no tax is at stake. However, if the value of the shares seems too low, SAV may negotiate an ascertained value if the likely amount of IHT at stake warrants this (HMRC Tax Bulletin April 1995, pp 209, 210). See also *IC Mc Arthur's Executors v HMRC* [2008] STC SCD 1100 Sp C 700 and **58** TAX CASES.

Quoted shares and securities are in practice, unless there are special circumstances, valued (as for capital gains tax), at the lower of:

(a) the lower of the two prices quoted in the Stock Exchange Daily Official List for the relevant date, plus a quarter of the difference between those prices ('*the quarter-up rule*'), and
(b) the average of the highest and lowest prices for normal bargains recorded on that date, if any.

If there was no trading on the relevant date, the prices are to be taken by reference to the latest previous date or to the earliest subsequent date, whichever produces the lower figure.

The London Stock Exchange offers an historic price service for which there is a charge which is currently £5 plus VAT. To access this service go to www.londonstockexchange.com/hps.

Shares in unit trusts, subject as above, are valued at the lower of the two prices published by the managers on the relevant date or, if no price is published at that time, on the latest date before the relevant date. [*TCGA 1992, s 272(3)(4)*].

Note that in the case of sales of shares there is no *de minimis* amount applicable as applies to land and there is no restriction with regard to whom the sale is made.

Definitions

[56.25] In relation to transfers of value made, and other events occurring, after 16 March 1987, '*quoted*', in relation to any shares or securities, means quoted on a recognised stock exchange or dealt in on the Unlisted Securities Market (see Alternative Investment Market under 35.8), and '*unquoted*', in relation to any shares or securities, means neither so quoted nor so dealt in. [*IHTA 1984, s 272; FA 1987, s 58(2), Sch 8 para 17*]. This applies for all IHT purposes except that, in relation to transfers of value made, and other events occurring, after 9 March 1992, an alternative definition whereby Unlisted Securities Market (and AIM) shares and securities are treated as unquoted, applies for the purposes of defining relevant business property (see **6.4** BUSINESS PROPERTY) and payment by instalments (see **35.5** PAYMENT OF TAX). As from 1 April 1996 the word '*quoted*' is substituted by the word '*listed*'. [*FA 1996, Sch 38 para 2*]. In relation to transfers of value made, and other events occurring, before 17 March 1987, shares and securities in companies dealt in on the Unlisted Securities Market were not treated as 'quoted' or 'listed' on a recognised stock exchange for all IHT purposes where those terms were used in tax provisions. The shares or securities did, however, satisfy the tests of being 'authorised to be dealt in' and 'dealt in (regularly or from time to time)' on a recognised stock exchange (HMRC Statement of Practice SP 18/80, 23 December 1980).

Quoted shares sold within twelve months after death

[56.26] Where 'qualifying investments' comprised in a deceased person's estate are sold within twelve months for less than their value on death the 'appropriate person' may claim (specifying the capacity in which he makes the claim and using form IHT35) a reduction in the estate values equal to the amount by which the aggregate of the value of *all* the qualifying investments included in the estate which are sold in the twelve-month period exceeds the aggregate of the 'sale values' of those investments (i.e. the loss on sale). See *Lee & Lee (Lee's Executors) v CIR* [2003] STC SCD 41 Sp C 349 for strict adherence to the twelve-month time limit. For this purpose, if death occurred after 15 March 1992:

(a) qualifying investments which are 'cancelled' (this term is not defined but may cover the final act of a company liquidation; if so, any 'capital payments' received during the liquidation will presumably be dealt with as below) within the twelve-month period without being replaced by other shares etc. are treated as having been sold immediately before cancellation for a nominal sum of £1, and

(b) qualifying investments of which the listing is suspended at the end of the twelve-month period are treated as having been sold immediately before the end of that period at their value at that time (if this is lower than their value at death).

Where an individual died in the period 22 February 2007 to 21 February 2008 (inclusive) owning shares in Northern Rock, and the shares were subsequently taken into temporary public ownership before they were either sold by the personal representatives or transferred to the person(s) entitled under the deceased's will or intestacy, then for the purposes only of *IHTA 1984, s 186A* the shares will be treated as if they had been cancelled as at 22 February 2008. Provided the other conditions of *s 186A* are met, a claim to relief under those provisions may be made by the appropriate person. See IHT and Trusts Newsletter dated August 2008 at www.hmrc.gov.uk/cto/newsletter.htm. [*IHTA 1984, ss 178(1), 179, 186A(1), 186B(1)(2); FA 1993, s 198; FA 1996, Sch 38 para 4(1)(2)*].

Definitions

'*Qualifying investments*' are shares or securities which at the date of the death in question are quoted (in relation to transfers of value made, and other events occurring, before 17 March 1987, quoted on a recognised stock exchange), holdings in an authorised unit trust and shares in any common investment fund established under the *Administration of Justice Act 1965, s 1* (i.e. certain funds managed by the Public Trustee and held in court on behalf of the persons entitled). Where a listing on a recognised stock exchange or, in relation to transfers of value made, and other events occurring, after 16 March 1987, dealing on the Unlisted Securities Market (see Alternative Investment Market under **35.8** PAYMENT OF TAX) is suspended at the date of death, the investments are qualifying investments if they are again so listed or dealt in at the time of sale or exchange under **56.29** below. Where an individual died in the period 29 September 2007 to 28 September 2008 (inclusive) owning shares in Bradford & Bingley, and the shares were subsequently taken into public ownership before they were either sold by the personal representatives or transferred to the person(s) entitled under the deceased's will or intestacy, then for the purposes only of *IHTA 1984, s 186A* the shares will be treated as if they had been cancelled as at 29 September 2008. Providing the other conditions of *s 186A* are met, a claim to relief under those provisions may be made by the appropriate person i.e. personal representatives or executor on Form IHT35. Currently for the purposes of completing Inheritance Tax accounts HMRC is now prepared to accept, on a without prejudice basis, that the right to receive compensation in respect of Bradford & Bingley shares may be included at a nil value where the holding is of 1,000 shares or less. This position by HMRC will remain the valuation basis until the Independent Valuer is in a position to provide any further information about the amount of likely compensation or of the likely timescale for payment. At that point, HMRC will consider whether any further or amended guidance is necessary. [*IHTA 1984, s 178(1)(2); FA 1987, s 58, Sch 8 para 13; FA 1996, Sch 38 para 4(1)(3)*].

The '*appropriate person*' is the person liable for the tax attributable to the value of the investment concerned or, if there is more than one such person and one of them is paying the tax, that person. Note 2 of Form IHT35 states that the 'capacity' of the claimant (i.e. executor, administrator, trustee or donor) must be indicated but this must not include an agent. See **56.9** above.

'*Sale value*' of qualifying investments means the price for which they were sold or (except in the case of (a) or (b) above), if greater, the best consideration which could reasonably have been obtained for them at the time of the sale (ignoring incidental expenses of commission, stamp duty or otherwise). Any 'capital payment' (whether during or after the twelve months following the death) as is attributable to the investments comprised in the estate and sold by the appropriate person is added to the sale value. '*Capital payment*' includes consideration received for the disposal of a provisional allotment of shares or debentures and any money or money's worth which does not constitute income for income tax purposes. It does not include the price paid on the sale of the investment. [*IHTA 1984, ss 178(1)(5), 179(1), 181, 186A(2), 186B(3); FA 1993, s 198*].

Date of sale or purchase of investments by the 'appropriate person' is the date of the contract. If the transaction results from the exercise (by him or any other person) of an option, then the date of the transaction is the date on which the option was granted. [*IHTA 1984, s 189*].

Value at death of qualifying investments includes any calls on them paid by the 'appropriate person' during or after the twelve months following the death. [*IHTA 1984, s 182*]. Where part only of a holding of qualifying investments is comprised in a person's estate (e.g. if he is a joint tenant of settled property) and a claim is made as above, the whole of the holding is included in the calculation and the loss on sale is reduced by the proportion which the value of that part of the investments included in the estate bears to the entire value of those investments. [*IHTA 1984, s 186*].

Further qualifying investments

[56.27] Further purchases of qualifying investments by the 'appropriate person', in the same capacity in which he made the claim above, during the period beginning with the death and ending two months after the date of the last sale will reduce the 'loss on sale' by the proportion which the total of the purchase prices (ignoring incidental expenses) bears to the total of the sales values in the claim. If the aggregate purchase prices equals or exceeds the sales values, the loss is extinguished. [*IHTA 1984, s 180(1)*]. See form IHT35, p 3.

If a person makes a claim other than as personal representative or trustee, any purchase as above is ignored unless it is of qualifying investments of *the same description* (i.e. they are not separately listed on a recognised stock exchange nor, in relation to transfers of value made, and other events occurring, after 16 March 1987, separately dealt in on the Unlisted Securities Market (or AIM) nor in a different unit trust or common investment fund) as included in the claim and the purchase is made otherwise than in the capacity of personal representative or trustee. [*IHTA 1984, s 180(2)(3); FA 1987, s 58, Sch 8 para 14; FA 1996, Sch 38 para 3*].

Changes in holdings

[56.28] On any change within the period of twelve months following death due to a reorganisation, conversion, exchange, amalgamation or reconstruction to which *TCGA 1992, s 127* applies (or such a change in unit trust holding to which *TCGA 1992, s 127* is applied by virtue of *TCGA 1992, s 99*), the new holding is treated as the same as the original holding.

If within the twelve-month period the appropriate person sells any investment comprised in the new holding, the value on death of those investments are determined by the formula:

$$\frac{Vs}{Vs + Vr} \times (H - S)$$

where:

Vs = sales value of the investment;
Vr = market value at the time of sale of any investment remaining in the new holding after the sale;
H = value on death of the new holding; and
S = value on death of any investments which were originally comprised in the new holding but have been sold on a previous occasion or occasions.

The value on death of the new holding is the same as the value on death of the original holding increased by any consideration which the appropriate person gives, or becomes liable to give, as part of or in connection with the transaction by which he acquires the new holding. For this purpose, 'consideration' excludes any surrender, cancellation or other alteration of the investments comprised in the original holding or rights attached thereto. It also excludes any application, in paying up the new holding or part of it, of assets of the company concerned or any dividend or other distribution declared out of those assets but not made. [*IHTA 1984, s 183*].

Exchange of qualifying investments

[56.29] If, apart from 56.28 above, an 'appropriate person' exchanges qualifying investments within twelve months of the death for other property of any kind (with or without any payment by way of equality of exchange) and the market value of the investments at the date of exchange is *greater* than their value at the date of death, they are treated as having been sold at their market value at the date of exchange. [*IHTA 1984, s 184*].

Identification

[56.30] Where an 'appropriate person' has, in the same capacity, (i) investments comprised in the deceased's estate at death and (ii) investments of the same description subsequently acquired in some other way (but not under 56.28 above), any part of such investments sold within the twelve months after death is apportioned between (i) and (ii) in the same proportions as they bore to each other immediately before the sale. [*IHTA 1984, s 185*].

Attribution of specific values

[56.31] It is necessary (for the purposes of both inheritance tax and capital gains tax) to attribute values to specific investments included in a claim as under **56.26** above. Generally, the value of a specific investment is its sale value. Where the loss on sale is reduced by further purchases (see **56.27** above), that reduction is apportioned over all the investments sold in proportion to the differences between their sale values and their values at death.

Where a call has been paid, the sale value of that investment is reduced by the amount of the call.

Where under a reorganisation etc. under **56.28** above, consideration has been paid for the new holding, the sale value of any specific investment comprised in the new holding is reduced by an amount which bears to that consideration the like proportion as the value on death of the specific investment sold bears to the value on death of the whole of the new holding.

In no case can the value of an investment be reduced to a minus quantity. [*IHTA 1984, ss 187, 188*].

Example

An individual died on 30 June 2010 and included in his estate was a portfolio of quoted investments. The executors sold certain investments within twelve months of death. The realisations were as follows.

	Probate Value	Gross Sales
	£	£
Share A	7,700	7,200
Share B	400	600
Share C	2,800	2,900
Share D	13,600	11,600
Share E	2,300	2,300
Share F	5,700	5,100
Share G	19,400	17,450
Share H	8,500	8,600
	£60,400	55,750
Incidental costs of sale		2,750
Net proceeds of sale		£53,000

On 1 September 2010, share J, having a probate value of £200 and still held by the executors was cancelled.

On 1 December 2010, share K, having a probate value of £1,000 has its stock exchange quotation suspended. On 30 June 2011, the investment is still held by the executors, its estimated value is £49 and the quotation remains suspended.

On 30 April 2011, the executors purchased a new holding for £1,750.

The executors would initially be able to claim a reduction of

(£60,400 – £55,750) + (£200 – £1) + (£1,000 – £49) = £5,800

After the purchase, the reduction is restricted as follows:

$$\text{Relevant proportion} = \frac{\text{Reinvestment}}{\text{Total sales}} = \frac{1{,}750}{\pounds 55{,}750 + \pounds 1 + \pounds 49} = \frac{1{,}750}{55{,}800}$$

Original relief restricted by:

$$\frac{1{,}750}{55{,}800} \times \pounds 5{,}800 = \pounds 182$$

Total relief £5,800 less £182 = £5,618

Notes to the example

(A) No costs of selling investments may be deducted from the sale proceeds. Note 5 on IHT35.

(B) The cancelled shares are treated as sold for £1 immediately before cancellation. The suspended shares are treated as sold on the first anniversary of death at their value at that time (provided that value is less than their value on death). [*IHTA 1984, ss 186A, 186B; FA 1993, s 198*].

(C) The purchase is taken into account as it is made during the period beginning on date of death and ending two months after the end of the last sale taken into account (including deemed sales as in (B) above).

(D) The probate value of each of the investments sold will be adjusted, both for CGT and IHT purposes, to the gross sale proceeds plus the relevant proportion of the fall in value. Thus the probate value of share A will be revised from £7,700 to:

$$\pounds 7{,}200 + \left(\frac{1{,}750}{55{,}800} \times (7{,}700 - 7{,}200)\right) = \pounds 7{,}216$$

and in the case of share B where the sales price exceeds the probate value (i.e. profit on sale) the revised value will be:

$$\pounds 600 - \left(\frac{1{,}750}{55{,}800} \times \pounds 200\right) = \pounds 594$$

(i.e. £600 – £6) = £594

(E) Although excluded from computation of the loss on sale for inheritance tax purposes, incidental costs of sale and deductible from proceeds in calculating CGT. For deaths after 5 April 2004 see Inland Revenue Statement of Practice SP2/04.

Unincorporated business

[56.32] See 6.4 BUSINESS PROPERTY.

Demutualisations

Valuing the estate

[56.33] The valuation of the deceased's share, or other interest, in a building society or mutual insurance company is not directly concerned with the actual amount of cash received or the value of free shares received by their successors on or after vesting day. Rather, it is a matter of determining the value by reference only to the information that was available at the date of death. This is generally the information provided for the qualifying members in the Transfer Document or Prospectus.

Each Transfer Document or Prospectus provides:

- an anticipated price per share of the free share, or
- details of the proposed cash bonuses,

calculated by reference to the amounts involved.

These anticipated prices, or proposed amounts, are the starting point for determining the gross value of the qualifying member's share or other interest at the relevant time. A discount is then applied to reflect any uncertainty or delay. For example, if a qualifying member died after the issue of the Transfer Document but before the extraordinary general meeting at which the demutualisation was formally approved by the voting members, the discount would be greater than if the member died after the extraordinary general meeting but before vesting day.

In the interests of consistency, a Valuation Table is provided to help calculate the open market value of the deceased member's share, or other interest, in a mutual society where he or she died before vesting day. As explained below, this value is also relevant for capital gains tax purposes and local Tax Offices and Tax Enquiry Centres have also been provided with a similar Table.

Most societies making special provisions in their Transfer Documents to preserve the entitlement of those qualifying members who die before vesting day. Under those special provisions, the qualifying member's personal representatives, as the qualifying successors, generally receive the free shares or cash bonus in that capacity for the benefit of the estate. See *Ward and Others (Executors of Cook deceased) v IRC* [1999] STC SCD 1 Sp C 175.

For inheritance tax purposes, a person's estate is the aggregate of all the property to which that person is beneficially entitled. [*IHTA 1984, s 5(1)*]. The value of that property is the price which it might reasonably be expected to fetch if sold on the open market at that time. [*IHTA 1984, s 160*].

Society	*Vesting day*	*Date of death between*	*Percentage discount*	*Anticipated share price – Cash bonus*
Cheltenham & Gloucester	1.8.1995	10.8.1994–31.3.1995 1.4.1995–31.7.1995	32%–25% 10%–0%	Cash bonus £500 +13.3%
National & Provincial	6.8.1996	28.2.1996–11.4.1996 12.4.1996–5.8.1996	27.5%–25% 10%–0%	£500 in Abbey National shares

Society	*Vesting day*	*Date of death between*	*Percentage discount*	*Anticipated share price – Cash bonus*
Alliance & Leicester	22.4.1997	28.10.1996–10.12.1996 11.12.1996–21.4.1997	27.5%–25% 10%–0%	£3.97 per share
Halifax	3.6.1997	11.1.1996–24.12.1996 25.12.1996–2.6.1997	30%–25% 7.5%–0%	11.1.1997–28.4.1997 £4.05 per share 29.4.1997–2.6.1997 £5.30 per share
Woolwich	8.7.1997	6.1.1997–11.2.1997 12.2.1997–7.7.1997	27.5%–25% 12.5%–0%	£1.81 per share
Northern Rock	2.10.1997	17.2.1997–15.4.1997 16.4.1997–1.10.1997	27.5%–25% 12.5%–0%	£2.68 per share
Bristol & West	26.8.1997	27.2.1997–15.4.1997 16.4.1997–25.8.1997	30%–25% 10%–0%	Cash bonus 6.5% or £250 in Bank of Ireland shares
Greenwich	30.7.1997	13.5.1997–17.6.1997 18.6.1997–29.7.1997	27.5%–25% 5%–0%	Cash bonus 5%
Norwich Union	16.6.1997	18.4.1997–15.6.1997	5%–0%	£2.31 per share
Scottish Amicable	30.9.1997	27.5.1997–26.6.1997 27.6.1997–29.9.1997	27.5%–25% 7.5%–0%	Cash payment £550; immediate bonus £430; bonus on maturity £450
Colonial Mutual	23.5.1997	24.9.1996–10.11.1996 11.11.1996–22.5.1997	28%–25% 17.5%–0%	£1.30 per share

IR Tax Bulletin 1998, p 523.

Notes to the Valuation Table

(A) The discount rates offered are not intended to be prescriptive but are a guide to an acceptable valuation for the qualifying member's share, or interest, in the society at the date of death. The amount of any discount will be lower the closer that the date of death is to vesting day.

Example

An individual who is a UK policy holder of AMP, the Australian insurer which undertook demutualisation, died on 1 May 1998 a few days before the prospectus was published on 6 May 1998. The estimated share price was between A$12.50–16.00 per share when trading commenced on the Australian and New Zealand stock exchange on 15 June 1998.

As the individual died before the issue of the transfer document/prospectus, the value of the individual's qualifying member's share has increased but a discount is given of approximately 25–30%. However, if the individual had died after the prospectus issue then the discount may have been between 0–10%. The personal representative's valuation of the right to the shares owned by the deceased at the date of death can be valued as:

Value of shares at vesting day, say,	£3,700
Less: 25%, discount prior to vesting	(925)
Executor's value for estate	£2,775

If the shares are disposed of within twelve months of the death for, say, £4,200 then where this comprises part of the aggregate sale values under *IHTA 1984, s 179(1)* the increase of £1,425 (i.e. £4,200 – £2,775) will serve to reduce any overall loss on sale.

Note to the example

(A) In view of the effective loss of 'discount' where shares are sold within twelve months of the death and comprise part of a claim under *IHTA 1984, s 179* it is perhaps better to defer the disposal until a later date.

Household and personal goods [Form IHT407]

HM Revenue & Customs

Household and personal goods

Schedule IHT407

When to use this form

Fill in this form to tell us about the deceased's household and personal goods.

Do not include details of household or personal goods owned **jointly**. You should include details of **jointly** owned assets on form IHT404 *Jointly owned assets* and not on this form.

Help

Please read the guidance notes for form IHT407 in the IHT400 Notes before filling in this form. For more information or help or another copy of this form:

go to **www.hmrc.gov.uk/inheritancetax/**

phone our Helpline on **0845 30 20 900**

– if calling from outside the UK, phone **+44 115 974 3009**.

Name of deceased

Date of death *DD MM YYYY*

IHT reference number (if known)

Jewellery

Please enter details of any individual items of jewellery valued at £500 or more in the box below. If you have a professional valuation, enclose a copy.

1

Description of item	If the item has been sold, give the date of sale and gross sale proceeds	Open market value at date of death £
	Total 1	£ 0.00

IHT407 **(Substitute)(LexisNexis)** Page 1 HMRC Approval ref: L11/08

Vehicles, boats and aircraft

Please enter details of:

- cars, including vintage and classic
- motorcycles and other vehicles
- boats
- aircraft.

If you have a professional valuation, enclose a copy.

2

Manufacturer	Model	Year of manufacture or first registration	Registration number, where appropriate	Condition at the date of death and mileage for cars	If the item has been sold, enter the date of the sale and gross sale proceeds	Open market value at date of death £
					Total 2	£ 0.00

IHT407 Page 2

Antiques, works of art or collections

Please enter details of any antiques, works of art or collections. For example, antique furniture, paintings, sculptures and porcelain, collections of books, stamps, coins, medals and wines. If you have a professional valuation, enclose a copy.

3	Description of item	If the item has been sold, give the date of sale and gross sale proceeds	Open market value at date of death £
		Total 3	£ 0.00

IHT407 Page 3

Other household and personal goods

Please enter the total value of all other household and personal goods not already listed in boxes 1, 2 or 3. For example, items of jewellery valued at less than £500, furniture and other domestic items. You do not need to list these items here.

4 Total value of other household and personal goods £

5 Were any of the items included in box 4 individually listed on the deceased's household insurance policy?

Yes ☐ *include a copy of the policy (and schedule, if appropriate)*

No ☐

Summary of household and personal goods

6 Total value of all household and personal goods (total of boxes 1, 2, 3 and 4) £ *Include this amount on form IHT400, box 55*

Jointly owned assets [Form IHT404]

HM Revenue
& Customs

Jointly owned assets

Schedule IHT404

When to use this form

Fill in this form to give details of any assets that were owned jointly by the deceased and any other person(s).

Do not include the following:

- jointly owned assets outside the UK. These assets should be included on form IHT417 *Foreign assets*
- assets owned jointly by a business or partnership. These assets should be included on form IHT413 *Business and partnership interests and assets.*

Jointly owned assets where all the money was provided by the deceased
Sometimes assets may be owned jointly with another person, but one person provided all the money, either in an account or to buy an asset. For example, an elderly person who has difficulty getting out, may add the name of a relative to an account for convenience so the relative may draw out money on the elderly person's behalf.

If the person who provided all the money dies, then their share of this account will be the whole. But if the other joint owner has withdrawn money for their own use, those withdrawals may be gifts and you may need to include them on form IHT403 *Gifts and other transfers of value.*

It follows that if someone died with their name on a joint account but they did not provide any of the funds, no part of the account need be included in the estate unless the other joint owner intended to make a gift to the deceased.

If there is not enough space on pages 2 to 6 to include all of the details, please fill in another copy of this form.

Assets jointly owned with a surviving spouse or civil partner
If the other joint owner was the deceased's spouse or civil partner, at boxes 1 and 6 you only need to fill in columns A, B, F and G.

Name of deceased

Date of death *DD MM YYYY*

IHT reference number (if known)

Help

Please read the guidance notes for form IHT404 in the IHT400 Notes before filling in this form. For more information or help or another copy of this form:

- go to **www.hmrc.gov.uk/inheritancetax/**
- phone our Helpline on **0845 30 20 900**
- – if calling from outside the UK, phone **+44 115 974 3009**.

IHT404 **(Substitute)(LexisNexis)** Page 1 HMRC Approval ref: L11/08

Jointly owned assets

This page should only contain details of jointly owned:

houses, buildings and land, and

shares and securities which gave the deceased control of the company.

If there are none, write '0' in box 1.

1

Number each item *(1, 2, 3)*	**A** Description of asset *If the asset is the deceased's house (shown on form IHT400, box 11) write 'deceased's house' here and say whether it is freehold or leasehold*	**B** Names of other joint owners and relationship to the deceased	**C** Date joint ownership started	**D** Contribution by each joint owner *show as fractions or monetary values*	**E** Share of income received by each joint owner (if any)	**F** Value of the whole item at the date of death £	**G** Value of the deceased's share at the date of death £
						Total value of the deceased's share 1	£ 0.00

IHT404 Page 2

Liabilities for the jointly owned assets shown in box 1

Give details of any mortgages or loans secured against the jointly owned assets shown in box 1. If there are none, write '0' in box 2.
Do not enter household bills here. Give details of joint household bills in box 7 on page 5 of this form instead.

2

Item number *shown in box 1*	Description of the liability	Name of creditor	Total amount outstanding at the date of death £	Deceased's share of the amount outstanding £
			Total amount of the deceased's share 2	£ 0.00
			Net assets (box 1 *minus* box 2) 3	£ 0.00

Exemptions and reliefs for the jointly owned assets shown in box 1

Give details of any exemptions or reliefs claimed on the jointly owned assets shown in box 1. If there are none, write '0' in box 4.

4

Item number *shown in box 1*	Details of relief or exemption deducted *for example, if the jointly owned assets shown in box 1 are passing to the deceased's spouse or civil partner or to a charity, you should deduct spouse or civil partner or charity exemption here*	Amount of exemption or relief £
	Total amount of exemptions and reliefs 4	£ 0.00
	Net total of jointly owned assets (box 3 *minus* box 4) 5	£ 0.00 *Copy this amount to form IHT400, box 49*

IHT404 Page 3

Other jointly owned assets

Give details of other jointly owned assets which were **not** listed in box 1, for example, bank accounts, household and personal goods. If there are none, write '0' in the box 6.

6

Number each item *(1, 2, 3)*	A Description of asset *include account number for bank accounts*	B Names of other joint owners and relationship to the deceased	C Date joint ownership started	D Contribution by each joint owner *show as fractions or monetary values*	E Share of income received by each joint owner (if any)	F Value of the whole item at the date of death £	G Value of the deceased's share at the date of death £
						Total value of the deceased's share 6	£ 0.00

IHT404 Page 4

Liabilities for the other jointly owned assets shown in box 6

Give details of any liabilities to be deducted from the other jointly owned assets shown in box 6. If there are none, write '0' in box 7.

7

Item number *shown in box 6*	Description of the liability *for example, an overdrawn joint bank account or joint household bills such as unpaid council tax*	Name of creditor	Total amount outstanding at the date of death £	Deceased's share of the amount outstanding £
			Total amount of the deceased's share	7 £ 0.00
			Net assets (box 6 *minus* box 7)	8 £ 0.00

Exemptions and reliefs for the other jointly owned assets shown in box 6

Give details of any exemptions or reliefs claimed on the other jointly owned assets shown in box 6. If there are none, write '0' in box 9.

9

Item number *shown in box 6*	Details of relief or exemption deducted *for example, if the jointly owned assets shown in box 6 are passing to the deceased's spouse or civil partner or to a charity, you should deduct spouse or civil partner or charity exemption here*	Amount of exemption or relief £
	Total amount of exemptions and reliefs	9 £ 0.00
	Net total of other jointly owned assets (box 8 *minus* box 9)	10 £ 0.00 *Copy this amount to form IHT400, box 50*

IHT404 Page 5

Survivorship assets

On the death of one of the joint owners some joint assets pass by survivorship to the remaining joint owner(s). Assets which pass by survivorship do not pass under the terms of a person's Will or, if they did not make a Will, by the rules of intestacy.

We need to know which assets pass by survivorship because although they are included in the deceased's estate for Inheritance Tax purposes they are not included in the value of the estate for probate or Confirmation purposes. The rules are different for assets in England and Wales or Northern Ireland (English law) and Scotland.

English law
If all the joint owners of an asset intended that when one of them died their share would pass to the other joint owner(s), then this is a survivorship asset. This type of asset is always owned equally and the deceased's share of the asset passes to the other joint owner(s) by survivorship.

Joint bank and building society accounts are usually held in this way. Jointly owned houses or land can be held in this way or as 'tenants-in-common' where each joint owner owns a distinct share of the property and can pass their own share by Will to anyone they choose. To find out whether a jointly owned house or land is a survivorship asset you will need to check the conveyancing documents.

Scottish law
If assets are owned in the names of the joint owners 'and the survivor' (this is called special or survivorship destination), or if there is any mention of survivorship in the deeds to heritable property, the share of the first to die will normally pass by survivorship to the other joint owner(s).

Survivorship destinations in joint bank and building society accounts do not by themselves pass ownership of the funds to the survivor on the death of the first joint owner. The ownership remains with the provider unless there has been some further act of transfer, for example, a deed of gift. In the absence of any other act on the death of the provider, the whole account will pass under the terms of their Will or, if they did not make a Will, by the rules of intestacy.

Joint life and survivor policies
If the deceased was entitled to benefit from a joint life and survivor policy, the policy is more likely to pass by survivorship than by Will, but this is a complex area. You should also fill in form IHT410 *Life assurance and annuities.* You can find out more about life assurance policies at:
www.hmrc.gov.uk/inheritancetax/

11 Did any of the assets listed in box 1 or box 6 of this form pass to the other joint owner(s) by survivorship?

No ☐ *You have finished this form*

Yes ☐ *List the assets which passed by survivorship below*

Box number (1 or 6)	Item number	Value of the deceased's share after deduction of liabilities and exemptions £
	Total 11	£ 0.00

Copy this amount to form IHT421, box 2

IHT404 Page 6

Debts due to the estate [Form IHT416]

HM Revenue
& Customs

Debts due to the estate

Schedule IHT416

When to use this form

Fill in this form to tell us about any debts owed to the deceased's estate at the date of their death.

Use a separate form for each debt. If the money owed to the deceased was a director's loan account or a current account with a company or business, answer box 3 and box 9 only.

If the debt is not straightforward and you need to explain the circumstances surrounding the debt, please give full details on the 'Additional information' boxes, pages 15 and 16 on form IHT400.

Name of deceased

Date of death *DD MM YYYY*

IHT reference number (if known)

Help

For information or help or another copy of this form:

- go to **www.hmrc.gov.uk/inheritancetax/**
- phone our Helpline on **0845 30 20 900**
  – if calling from outside the UK, phone **+44 115 974 3009.**

Details of debt

If the deceased was owed some money when they died, you must assume that the debt will be repaid in full.
You should include the full value of the capital and interest outstanding at the date of death. If it is impossible or not reasonably possible for the money to be repaid you may include a reduced figure on form IHT400 and give details at box 9 on this form.

1 Date the original loan was made *DD MM YYYY*

2 Original value of the loan

£

3 Amount of the loan, including interest, outstanding at the date of death

Capital

£

Interest

£

Total (Capital + Interest)

3 £ 0.00

Copy to form IHT400, box 73

4 Was the loan secured by mortgage?

No Yes

5 Give the name of the borrower(s) and describe their relationship to the deceased

6 Enter the amount of interest charged on the loan, the rate(s) at which it was charged and the period over which it was charged

7 Enter details of capital repayments made on the loan

8 What evidence is there to support the existence of the loan?
You must provide copies of written evidence such as a letter or mortgage deed. A number of insurance linked products include a loan from the deceased to the trustees of a settlement or policy. If the loan is to be repaid by the trustees of such a scheme, provide a copy of the loan agreement and any settlement or policy document

9 If you wish to include a figure for the loan which is different from the total amount outstanding at box 3, please explain why here. Provide any evidence you have and show how you have worked out the figure

IHT416 Page 2

Debts owed by the deceased [Form IHT419]

HM Revenue & Customs

Debts owed by the deceased

Schedule IHT419

Name of deceased

Date of death *DD MM YYYY*

IHT reference number (if known)

When to use this form

Fill in this form if you wish to deduct any of the following from the value of the estate on form IHT400:

- money that was spent on behalf of the deceased and which has not been repaid
- loans or overdrafts
- liabilities related to a life assurance policy where the sum assured is not fully reflected in the IHT400
- debts that the deceased guaranteed on behalf ofanother person.

Include these debts on form IHT400, at box 80 or box 82, as appropriate.

If the deceased died on or after 17 July 2013 there are some conditions that must be met before a liability can be deducted. The conditions are to do with:

- what the borrowed money was used for, and
- whether the money is actually repaid from the estate.

If the liability does not meet the conditions, it may not be deducted from the estate.

The deduction cannot be allowed if:

- the money was borrowed to acquire, maintain or enhance excluded property. This applies whether the debt is actually repaid or not.
- the money is not repaid from the estate.

There are exceptions to this which are:

- if the excluded property has since been sold and the money received is now liable to tax, or if the excluded property itself has become liable to tax
- there is a real commercial reason for not repaying the debt, and not repaying the debt does not give rise to a tax advantage.

If any of these exceptions apply please say why you think so on this form at box 6 on page 4 or in the additional information boxes on pages 15 and 16 of the IHT400.

If a liability that can be allowed as a deduction was used to acquire, enhance or maintain property that qualifies for:

- Agricultural Relief
- Business Relief, or
- Woodlands Relief

and was incurred on or after 6 April 2013, you must deduct that liability from the property concerned before working out the amount of relief that is due.

For more information about liabilities please read the *IHT400 notes* page 49.

Gifts to, and loans from, the same person

In some cases, special rules apply where the deceased has both borrowed money from someone and made a gift to that same person. These types of debts owed by the deceased are generally not allowed as deductions for Inheritance Tax purposes.

For more information, phone our helpline on **0845 30 20 900**.

Help

For information or help or another copy of this form:

- go to www.hmrc.gov.uk/inheritancetax/
- phone our helpline on **0845 30 20 900**
  – if calling from outside the UK, phone **+44 115 974 3009**.

IHT419 Substitute (LexisNexis) (08/13) Page 1 HMRC Approval Reference L65/13

Money spent on the deceased's behalf

1 Did any person spend money on the deceased's behalf, which is now being claimed as a deduction from the estate? For example, paying domestic bills.

No ☐ Yes ☐ *If Yes, provide the following information about the money spent*

Name of the person who spent the money	Relationship to the deceased	What was the money spent on?	Explain why the deceased's own money was not used	Explain why the money wasn't repaid during the deceased's lifetime	Amount spent £

Loans and liabilities

2 Did the deceased have any outstanding loans, including loans from close friends and relatives?

No ☐ Yes ☐ *If Yes, provide the following information about loans and liabilities. Please provide copies of any written evidence of the loan(s)*

Name of lender	Relationship to the deceased	Date of loan DD MM YYYY	State the purpose of the loan and where the money is reflected in the value of the estate	Was the loan secured on any property?	Original amount of the loan £	Amount outstanding at the date of death £

Liabilities related to an insurance policy

3 Are there any liabilities claimed that are related to a life assurance policy and/or an investment bond, where the value of the policy or bond is not fully reflected elsewhere in the IHT400?

No ☐ Yes ☐ *If Yes, provide the following information. You must also provide a copy of the policy documents and any relevant trust or loan documents*

Name of insurance company	Amount owed £	Amount of sum assured, shown in the deceased's estate (if none, write 'Nil') £

Guaranteed debts

4 Did the deceased guarantee any debts on behalf of another person?

No ☐ Yes ☐ *If Yes, provide the following details. Please provide a copy of any written evidence*

Name of the person whose debts were guaranteed	Relationship to the deceased	Was the deceased called upon to repay the loan?	If No, explain why you think the loan should be deducted from the estate	Amount of debt guaranteed £

Gifts to and loans from the same person

5 Did the deceased make a gift to someone after 18 March 1986, and at any time after that gift, borrow money from that same person?

No ☐ Yes ☐ *If Yes, provide the following details.*

Gifts If the gift has already been described on form IHT403 *Gifts and other transfers of value,* you need only give us enough information to identify the gift concerned

Date of gift	Name of person to whom the gift was made	Description of the assets comprised in the gift	Assets value at gift date £

Loans Please provide copies of any written evidence of the loan(s). If the loan has already been described at box 2 of this form, you need only give us enough information to identify the gift concerned

Date of loan	Amount of loan £	Amounts and dates of any payments	What did the deceased use the money for and where is it reflected in the estate?

Additional information

6 Please give us any other information that you think we need to know

IHT419 Page 4

Life assurance and annuities [Form IHT410]

HM Revenue & Customs

Life assurance and annuities

Schedule IHT410

When to use this form

Fill in this form if the deceased was paying regular monthly or lump sum premiums on any:

- life assurance policies, or if any sums are payable by insurance companies to the estate as a result of the deceased's death. (It does not matter if the policies were on the deceased's life or someone else's life or whether the policies were for the deceased's benefit)
- unit-linked investment bonds with insurance companies or other financial service providers that pay 101% of the value of the units to the estate
- investment or reinvestment plans, bonds or contracts with financial service providers that pay out to the estate on death
- insurance policies and unit-linked investment bonds that are payable to the beneficiaries under a trust and do not form part of the estate
- joint life assurance policies under which the deceased was one of the lives assured but which remain in force after the date of death.

When not to use this form

Do not use this form to tell us about pension annuities. Use form IHT409 *Pensions* instead.

Mortgage protection policies

If the policy is a mortgage protection policy, you should include the property, the mortgage and the policy as separate items, as follows:

- If the deceased owned the property in their own name, you should include the policy details in question 2 below.
- If the deceased owned the property jointly, you should include the policy along with the property and the mortgage details on form IHT404 *Jointly owned assets*.

Name of deceased

Date of death *DD MM YYYY*

IHT reference number (if known)

Help

The notes to help you fill in this form are included on the form. For more information or help or another copy of this form:

- go to **www.hmrc.gov.uk/inheritancetax**
- phone our Helpline on **0845 30 20 900**
  – if calling from outside the UK, phone **+44 115 974 3009**

Your rights and obligations

To find out what you can expect from us and what we expect from you go to **www.hmrc.gov.uk/charter** and have a look at *Your Charter*.

We have a range of services for people with disabilities, including guidance in Braille, audio and large print. Most of our forms are also available in large print. Please contact us on any of our phone Helplines if you need these services.

Life assurance policies

1 **Were any sums payable by insurance companies to the estate as a result of the deceased's death?**

No ☐ *Go to* ***question 3*** Yes ☐ *Go to* ***question 2***

2 **Details of sums payable by insurance companies** *(In Scotland the policies will be listed on form C1 the Inventory: you do not need to list them again on this form, but please include their total here.)*

Name of insurance company	Policy number	Amount payable, including bonuses £
	Total 2	0.00

IHT410 (Substitute)(LexisNexis) Page 1 L3/00

3 **Was the deceased's life assured under a jointly owned assurance policy which continues after death?**

No ☐ *Go to **question 4***

Yes ☐ *Give details of the policy and its value on form IHT404 Jointly owned assets and not on this form. Go to **question 4***

4 **Was the deceased entitled to benefit from a life assurance policy on the life of another person where the policy continues after death?**

No ☐ *Go to **question 6***

Yes ☐ *Go to **question 5***

5 **Give details of life assurance policies. Please provide a copy of each policy**

Name of insurance company	Policy number	Name of person whose life is assured	Value of policy provided by insurance company at the date of death £
		Total 5	

6 **Total value of life assurance policies (box 2 + box 5)**
*Copy this amount to form IHT400, **Box 57***

IHT410 Page 2

Payments made after the deceased's death

Purchased life annuities

Payments made under a purchased life annuity have an income element and a capital element. You will find information about the two different elements on letters from the insurance company making the payments. Payments under an annuity purchased by the deceased to provide a pension will only consist of income. Give information here about purchased life annuities only. Pension annuities should be shown on schedule IHT409 *Pensions* instead.

7 **Did any payments that were made under a purchased life annuity continue after the deceased's death?**

No ☐ *Go to* ***question 10***

Yes ☐ *Go to* ***question 8***

8 **Give details of purchased life annuity payments**

You can find a guaranteed annuities calculator on our website to help you value the right to receive the remainder of the payments. Go to ***www.hmrc.gov.uk/inheritancetax***

Name of the company that sold the policy	How often were repayments made? *For example, weekly, monthly*	Details of increases in the payments during the remaining guaranteed period, if any	Date of final guaranteed payment	Value of the right to receive the remainder of the payments £
			Total 8	

Include this amount in the figure on form IHT400, Box 76

9 **What is the gross annual amount payable under the annuity?** ☐

What part of that amount is considered capital? ☐

What part of that amount is considered income? ☐

You may need to refer to letters from the insurance company for these figures

Lump sum payment made on the deceased's death

10 **Was a lump sum payable under a purchased life annuity as a result of the deceased's death?**

No ☐ *Go to **question 12***

Yes ☐ *Go to **question 11***

11 **Give details of lump sum payable**

Name of the company that sold the policy	Explain when and how the deceased disposed of the right to receive the lump sum, if not payable to the estate	Value of the lump sum payable £
	Total value 11	

Include this amount in the figure on form IHT400, Box 76

12 **Did the deceased, within seven years of their death, pay any premium on a life assurance policy for the benefit of someone else, other than the deceased's spouse or civil partner?**

No ☐ *Go to **question 14***

Yes ☐ *Provide details on form IHT403 Gifts and other transfers of value*

13 **Was an annuity purchased at any time?** *(The deceased may have purchased an annuity as well as paying the premiums on a life assurance policy for the benefit of someone else.)*

No ☐

Yes ☐ *Provide a copy of the policy schedule and provisions*

14 **Did the deceased have a right to benefit from a life assurance policy taken out on another person's life and held in trust for the benefit of the deceased (and others)?**

No ☐

Yes ☐

Life assurance policies taken out on one person's life may be held in a trust for the benefit of others. Parents may often take out a life assurance policy but put it in trust for their children. Business partners or the directors of a company may also take out insurance on their lives but for the benefit of their partners or co-directors.

If the deceased died whilst they were still working, or before their parent(s), there is a possibility that the deceased may have a right to benefit under a policy held in trust.

If the deceased had the right to benefit under a life assurance policy held in trust, you will need to fill in the form IHT418 *Assets held in trust. See IHT400 Notes.*

IHT410 Page 4

Listed stocks and shares [Form IHT411]

HM Revenue & Customs

Listed stocks and shares

Schedule IHT411

When to use this form

Fill in this form to tell us about the listed stocks, UK Government and municipal securities and shares owned by the deceased. We give details of how to value stocks and shares in the IHT400 Notes.

Do not include any shares or securities:

- listed on the Alternative Investment Market (AIM) or traded on OFEX
- in a Private Limited Company, Business Expansion Scheme (BES) or Business Start-up Scheme (BSS)
- listed on a recognised stock exchange, where the deceased had control of the company.

These should be listed on Schedule IHT412 *Unlisted stocks, shares and control holdings.*

If you have a stockbroker's valuation or if you have filled in Inventory form C1 (Scotland only) you need only copy the totals for each category of share to the form and enclose a copy of the valuation.

You need to tell us about any dividends and interest on the stocks and shares that were due at the date of death but have not yet been paid. In the IHT400 Notes we explain the different types of dividends, and what to include.

Name of deceased

Date of death *DD MM YYYY*

IHT reference number (if known)

Help

Please read the guidance notes for form IHT408 in the IHT400 Notes before filling in this form. For more information or help or another copy of this form:

- go to **www.hmrc.gov.uk/inheritancetax/**
- phone our Helpline on **0845 30 20 900**
  - if calling from outside the UK, phone **+44 115 974 3009**.

UK Government and municipal securities

List here any UK Government securities that the deceased held. For example, Treasury Stock, Exchequer Stock, War Loan and any other stock held on the Bank of England register. Also include any municipal securities, mortgages, debentures and stock held in countries, cities and towns, docks, harbours and water boards. Any Northern Ireland municipal stock should also be listed here.

1

Description of stock (For example, 3.5% War Loan)	Amount of stock held	Market price per unit at date of death £	Total value of stock at date of death £	Interest due to date of death £
		Totals 1	£ 0.00	£ 0.00
			Total of column above - *copy this amount to form IHT400, box 62*	Total of column above - *include this amount on form IHT400, box 64*

Listed stocks, shares and investments that did *not* give the deceased control of the company

List here any holdings of stocks, shares, debentures or other securities that are listed on the Stock Exchange Daily Official List. Include any:

- Personal Equity Plans (PEPs), (include a figure for any uninvested cash)
- shares held in an Individual Savings Account (ISA), (include a figure for any uninvested cash but not for any other cash or insurance policies)
- unit trusts (give the full name, for example, Axa Equity and Law Unit Trust Managers, Pacific Basin Trust Accumulation Units)
- investment trusts
- holdings in Open-Ended Investment Companies (OEICs)
- foreign shares, but only if they are listed on the London Stock Exchange.

If the deceased owned any of these types of shares that gave them control of the company you should list them at box 4 on Schedule IHT412 *Unlisted stocks, shares and contol holdings*, instead of here. This will be extremely rare.

2

Name of the company and type of shares or stock, or full name of unit trust and type of unit	Amount of stock held	Market price per unit at date of death £	Total value of stock at date of death £	Dividend or interest due to date of death £
		Totals 2	£ 0.00	£ 0.00
			Total of column above - copy this amount to form IHT400, box 63	*Total of column above - include this amount on form IHT400, box 64*

IHT411 Page 2

57

Woodlands

Cross-references. See also 4 AGRICULTURAL PROPERTY; 6 BUSINESS PROPERTY.

Simon's Taxes. See **I7.302, I7.4.**

Other Sources. Foster, Parts G3 and 4; HMRC Customer Guide to Inheritance Tax; HMRC IHT manual IHTM24000.

Introduction

[57.1] For IHT purposes, three main reliefs can be available in respect of woodlands:

(a) woodlands managed as a commercial business with a view to realisation of profits, and not held wholly or mainly as an investment, will qualify for 100% business property relief so long as the other requirements for that relief are satisfied (e.g. the two year period of ownership requirement): see 6 BUSINESS PROPERTY;

(b) woodlands occupied with agricultural land or pasture, and the occupation being ancillary to that of the agricultural land or pasture, will qualify for agricultural property relief: see 4 AGRICULTURAL PROPERTY;

(c) **On a person's death** an election may be made within two years (or such longer time as the Board allow *IHTA 1984, s 125(3)*) for the value of any trees or underwood on any land in the UK or another state which is an EEA state at the time of the person's death not being AGRICULTURAL PROPERTY (4) for the purposes of agricultural property relief to be left out of account in determining the value transferred on death. The value of the land cannot be excluded. The claim must be made by a person liable for the whole or part of the tax. This a deferral relief and the tax becomes chargeable on a later disposal. [*IHTA 1984, ss 125, 125(1A) as inserted by FA 2009, s 122(5)(6); Interpretation Act 1978, Sch 1*].

Deferral Relief

The District Valuer (DV) will advise HMRC Inheritance Tax if woodlands should be excluded from the relief because these are agricultural property as defined in *IHTA 1984, s 115(2)*. Land dedicated under the *Forestry Act 1967* is unlikely to be agricultural property. In woodlands relief cases the DV should value the underlying land leaving out the trees or underwood growing on it. (VOA IHT manual, section 10, paras 10.7 and 10.9). Note, however, this woodlands relief is uncommon due to the existence of 100% business relief (see Inspector's manual, para 3260 issue 12/94 'woodlands' does not include orchards or nurseries). For the treatment of orchards see *Dixon v CIR* [2002] STC SCD 53 Sp C 297.

Pro-forma woodlands election

HMRC Inheritance Tax

IHT reference

Date of death:. . . . .

<u>A B deceased</u>

1. Attached to this election are:

   1.1 Schedule 1 being details of the land on which the trees and underwood are growing and to which the election is to apply.

   1.2 Ordnance survey map of the area of trees and underwood to which the election is to apply with relevant areas boundaried in red. [*Note 1:10,000 or in Scotland 1:50,000 will normally suffice*].

   1.3 Copy of the deceased's will pertaining to the land to which this election is to apply.

2. The deceased AB was:

   2.1 beneficially entitled to the land on which the trees and underwood grow [for the five years immediately preceding AB's death]* [by entitlement otherwise than for money or money's worth].*

* *Delete as appropriate*

3. We, being the parties making the election, elect pursuant to section 125, Inheritance Tax Act 1984 shall apply to such woods and underwood referred to at 1 above.

Signed:. . . . . Capacity. . . . .

Address:. . . . .

Date:. . . . .

Signed:. . . . . Capacity. . . . .

Address:. . . . .

Date:. . . . .

Schedule 1

[*Full description including the precise location of the land to be included at Schedule 1*].

Notes to the election

(A) Normally it will be appropriate to pay the tax at the date of death where the trees are very young and in such a case the election would not be appropriate.

(B) This relief is also available where the deceased had an interest in possession in woodlands under a trust *IHTA 1984, ss 5(1), 49(1), 125(1)*.

Condition

[57.2] A condition for the election is that the deceased either was beneficially entitled to the land for the five years immediately preceding his death or became beneficially entitled to it otherwise than for money or money's worth. [*IHTA 1984, s 125(1)*]. A life tenant in possession under a settlement is treated as beneficially entitled but not a shareholder in a company owning woodlands. If a retrospective claim for relief is being made in respect of woodlands relief under the new EEA arrangements then a claim under *IHTA 1984, s 125* is to be made in writing quoting the Inheritance Tax file reference, name and date of death of the deceased and headed 'Retrospective claim for APR and/or WR for land in EEA'.

Tax charge

[57.3] Tax becomes chargeable on any disposal (other than between spouses or civil partners) of the trees or underwood (whether with or apart from the land on which they grow) before another death (which would be either another chargeable occasion itself or another occasion for an election). The liability for the tax is on the person who is entitled to the proceeds of sale or would be so entitled if the disposal were a sale. Where tax has been charged on a disposal under these provisions, it cannot be charged in relation to the same death on a further disposal of the same trees or underwood. [*IHTA 1984, ss 126, 208; The Tax and Civil Partnership Regulations 2005, SI 2005/3229, Reg 24*]. An account (Form C–5 (Timber)) must be delivered by the person liable within six months of the end of the month in which the disposal occurs. [*IHTA 1984, s 216(7)*]. Where the disposal is a chargeable transfer (e.g. by gift into a discretionary trust), tax will become chargeable both in respect of the previous death and on the later transfer, in which case the later value transferred is that value less the tax charged by reference to the previous death under **57.4** below. [*IHTA 1984, s 129*]. The deferred tax is payable in one sum but the tax on the lifetime transfer may be paid by instalments over ten years at the option of either the transferor or the transferee (see **35.5** PAYMENT OF TAX) and payment by instalments does not cease if the timber is later sold.

Woodlands in the European Economic Area (EEA)

The *Finance Act 2009* introduced legislation to retrospectively extend inheritance tax relief for woodlands from 22 April 2009 onwards for woodlands in the European Economic Area (EEA). In cases where tax is due or has been paid on or after 23 April 2003 in respect of woodlands situated in the EEA under the old rules then, by way of claim, a deferral or cancellation of the tax will apply. Where the claim results in a refund of tax this will be repaid with repayment supplement. For 2003/04 the claim must have been made by 31 January 2010. This extended woodlands relief applies to property placed into trust which then suffers periodic or exit charges and to such charges where IHT was paid or due on or after 22 April 2009. Similarly, where property was gifted and has become a PET within *IHTA 1984, s 3A* and the tax was due or paid because it 'failed' then the relief will apply retrospectively. Similarly, where tax has been paid from 23 April 2003 in connection with qualifying woodlands to HMRC under previous rules then it will be repaid with supplement where a claim may be made either by the date determined *IHTA 1984, s 241(1)* (four years), or before 22 April 2010. Any late payment interest at the start date for each instalment is also payable from the date on which that instalment is to be paid (see **35.8** PAYMENT OF TAX). [*IHTA 1984, ss 125, 229; FA 2009, s 122(6)(7), Sch 51, para 13, Sch 53 paras 7(2)*].

IHT 100 completion

A new account on Form IHT 100 (old forms IHT 100 and IHT 101 have been replaced as from April 2003) is required when there is a chargeable event described below:

- Assets ceasing to benefit from conditional exemption and being subject to a recapture charge (supplementary event form IHT 100f) e.g. sale of trees, timber or underwood.

Form D36, part of IHT 100, should be filled in to give details of land, buildings, timber and underwood included in the chargeable event. In box F4 of IHT 100 the value of any timber and woodland included in the chargeable event valued at the date of the chargeable event should be inserted which is not part of a farm. Most farms have coppices, small woods and belts of trees that shelter the land and these are to be valued separately and included in a separate box (F2) on the IHT 100. See LIFETIME TRANSFERS (**32**).

Tax rate

[57.4] The tax rate is what would have applied to the value of the deceased's (i.e. the last person to die) estate if the trees or underwood had been included at the highest part and is charged:

(a) if the disposal is a sale for full consideration in money or money's worth, on the 'net proceeds' of the sale; and
(b) in any other case, on the 'net value', at the time of disposal, of the trees or underwood.

The availability of the 36% rate of tax where 10% or more of the relevant component of the estate was given to charity is disregarded for this purpose. For deaths on or after 6 April 2012 therefore the tax rate must be calculated assuming that the chargeable estate was liable at 40%, even though in fact all or part may have been liable at 36%.

Definitions

'*Net proceeds*' or '*net value*' mean the proceeds of sale or value after any deduction of any of the following expenses so far as not allowed for income tax.

(a) if the disposal is a sale for full consideration in money or money's worth, on the '*net proceeds*' of the sale; and
(b) in any other case, on the '*net value*', at the time of disposal, of the trees or underwood.

'*Net proceeds*' or '*net value*' mean the proceeds of sale or value after any deduction of any of the following expenses so far as not allowed for income tax.

(i) The expenses incurred in disposing of the trees or underwood.
(ii) The expenses incurred in replanting, within three years of a disposal (or such longer time as the Board may allow), to replace the trees or underwood disposed of.
(iii) The expenses incurred in replanting to replace trees or underwood previously disposed of, so far as not allowed on the previous disposal.

Where, if the value of the trees or underwood had not been left out of account in determining the value of the deceased person's estate, BUSINESS PROPERTY (6) relief would have been available at a rate less than the current 100% rate the amount on which tax is charged is reduced by 50%. This relief relates to cases where the death was before 10 March 1992; from that date the rate of business property relief was increased to 100% and thus in such cases deferral relief would not be appropriate.

Deferred tax which becomes chargeable after tax has been reduced by the substitution of a new table of rates will be calculated on the new scale, even though the death occurred when the old scale applied. [*IHTA 1984, ss 9, 127, 128, 130, Sch 2 para 4; FA 1986, Sch 19 para 45*]. See also **57.6**(b) below.

'Net value'

In arriving at the 'net value' the DV's valuation should ignore any allowable expenses as well as any obligations to replant. The value will be the higher of (i) the value of the trees for sale for felling including any underwood, or (ii) the value of the standing trees or underwood as part of the transferor's estate. The DV's valuation will always exclude the value of the underlying land. The valuation on basis (ii) will probably only apply when immature woodland or growing timber of high amenity value is involved. (VOA IHT manual, section 10, para 10.16).

Example 1

A died owning woodlands valued at £275,000 being land valued at £200,000 and trees growing on the land valued at £75,000. The woodlands passed to his son D. The marginal IHT rate applicable was 40% but the executors elected to exclude the value of the trees from the taxable estate on A's death. D died six years later leaving the woodlands to trustees for his grandchildren. They were then valued at £400,000 being land at £250,000 and trees at £150,000. The rate of tax which would have applied to the value of trees on D's death was 40%, but once again the executors elected to exclude the value of the trees from his estate.

The trustees sold the woodlands for £500,000, including trees valued at £180,000, four years later.

The IHT on the trees is payable when the trees are sold. The trustees of the settlement pay IHT at what would have been the marginal rate on D's death had the tax scale at the time of the sale applied on D's death, e.g. 40% on £180,000 (the proceeds of sale) = £72,000.

Note to the example

(A) If D had gifted the land (with the trees) just before his death, the IHT would have become payable on the trees at what would have been the marginal rate on A's death had the scale at the time of the gift applied on A's death, on the value of the trees at the date of the gift. IHT would also have been payable on D's lifetime transfer (this being a PET but becoming chargeable by virtue of D's death shortly afterwards) but the value transferred by this transfer would have been reduced by the deferred IHT charge. See Example 2 below.

Example 2

B died in 1984 leaving woodlands, including growing timber valued at £100,000, to his daughter C. The executors elected to exclude the value of the timber from the taxable estate on B's death. B had made prior transfers of £50,000 and his taxable estate (excluding the growing timber) was valued at £210,000.

On 1 February 2005 C gave the woodlands to her nephew N, when the land was valued at £355,000 and the growing timber at £125,000. N agreed to pay any IHT on the gift. C died in January 2011, and had made no prior transfers other than to use her annual exemptions each year.

IHT on B's death

No IHT is payable on the growing timber until C's disposal when tax is charged on the net value at that time. The rates are those which would have applied (using the death scale applying on 1 February 2005) if that value had formed the highest part of B's estate on death. The tax was payable on 1 September 2004.

Deferred IHT payable £125,000 at 40% =	£50,000

IHT on C's lifetime transfer

IHT is payable on C's gift to N as C died within seven years of the gift. The deferred IHT is deducted from the value transferred.

			£
Value of land and timber			480,000
Deduct deferred IHT			50,000
Chargeable transfer			£430,000
IHT at death rates			
On first	£325,000		Nil
On next	£105,000	at 40%	42,000
	£430,000		£42,000

IHT payable at 40% of full rates (death between 5 and 6 years after gift)	£16,800
Total IHT payable	
Deferred IHT	50,000
Lifetime transfer	16,800
	£66,800

Note to the example

(A) In the above calculations it has been assumed that the woodlands were not run as a business either at the time of B's death or at the time of C's gift. If B had been running the woodlands as a business, such that business property relief would have been available on his death, the amount chargeable on C's disposal would have been reduced by 50%, i.e. to £62,500, on which IHT payable would have been £25,000. [*IHTA 1984, s 127(2)*]. If C ran the woodlands as a business (whether or not B had done so), business property relief would be available on her gift to N provided N also ran the woodlands as a business, but would be given after the credit for the deferred IHT. (With business property relief now usually at 100%, the order of set-off is not so relevant.)

	£
Value of land and timber	480,000
Deduct deferred IHT say	25,000
	455,000
Deduct business property relief at, say, 100%	455,000
Chargeable transfer	Nil

Liabilities to acquire woodlands

[57.5] For transfers of value made or treated as made on or after 17 July 2013, it is no longer possible to reduce the value of an asset for IHT purposes by securing a loan on it where the loan is used to acquire or maintain (directly or indirectly) another asset which qualifies for certain IHT reliefs, including woodlands where the value of them is to be left out of account on a person's death (see **57.1**(c)). Instead the loan will be primarily deductible from the value of the woodlands. These rules have equal effect for charges on settlements holding relevant property within *IHTA 1984, s 58*, and apply to loans incurred on or after 6 April 2013. See further commentary at **56.19**.

Estate duty

[57.6] *F(1909–10)A 1910, s 61(5)* is an estate duty provision and still applicable for deaths before 13 March 1975. It provides for the value of timber etc. to be left out of account on the deceased's death but with estate duty charged at the estate rate on subsequent net moneys (less outgoings since death) received from time to time in respect of cut or felled timber etc. sales in the period from the death until the underlying land, on the death of some other person, again became or would, but for the provision itself, have become liable to estate duty. However, if at any time the timber etc. is sold, with or without the underlying land, the amount of estate duty on its principal value which, apart from the provision itself, would have been payable on the death of the deceased, after deducting any amount of estate duty already paid as above on previous timber sales since death, becomes payable. For the purposes of inheritance tax it is provided that where estate duty is payable under *F(1909–10)A 1910, s 61(5)* on the net moneys received from the sale of timber etc. when felled or cut during the period referred to in that provision, that period ends immediately after the first transfer of value made in which the value transferred is, or is determined by reference to, the value of the land concerned, other than an exempt transfer between spouses or civil partners. [*FA 1975, s 49(4)*]. Where the first transfer of value including such woodlands is after 30 June 1986, that transfer cannot be a POTENTIALLY EXEMPT TRANSFER (**38**) (even if it would otherwise qualify). [*FA 1986, Sch 19 para 46*]. Although *FA 1986, Sch 19 para 46* denies treatment as a potentially exempt transfer to all property comprised in a single transfer of value any part of which, however small, is woodlands subject to a deferred estate duty charge, by concession after 4 December 1990 it will be restricted in its scope to that part of a transfer of value which is attributable to such woodlands (see former Inland Revenue Pamphlet IR1 (1996) F15).

Other reliefs

[57.7] Other reliefs are as follows:

(a) AGRICULTURAL PROPERTY (**4**) relief applies instead of the above if the woodlands are occupied and the occupation is ancillary to that of agricultural land or pasture. [*IHTA 1984, ss 115(2), 125(1)*].

(b) NATIONAL HERITAGE (**33**) property. Conditional exemption on a transfer may apply in certain circumstances.

(c) EXEMPT TRANSFERS **21.10** and the transferable nil rate band. From 9 October 2007 married couples and those in civil partnerships will be allowed to transfer any unused nil rate band on their death to the surviving spouse or civil partner (referred to in the legislation respectively as the 'deceased' and the 'survivor'). In addition, the transferable unused nil rate band will be available to the widow, widower or surviving civil partner irrespective of when the original spouse or civil partner died. [*IHTA 1984, s 8A* as inserted by *FA 2008, Sch 4 para 2*]. This may have been during the period when Capital Transfer Tax operated or when Estate Duty applied in which cases the new provisions are adapted to those situations. The personal nil rate band maximum of the deceased is the amount shown in the appropriate Table depending on the date of death as stipulated in *FA 2008, Sch 4 para 11*. [*IHTA 1984, s 8C as adapted by FA 2008, Sch 4 para 11*]. In cases where there has been a deferred charge such as in *IHTA 1984,* *s 126* and there is unused nil rate band available to the surviving spouse or civil partner and there is a deferred charge on woodlands before the transfer of the nil rate band is effected then that charge is taken into account before calculating the unused nil rate band of the surviving spouse or civil partner. See Example 3 below. If there is more than one deferred charge before the transfer of the nil rate band to the spouse or civil partner these deferred charges similarly reduce the nil rate band that may be claimed. See Example 4. Further, if there is a deferred charge after the nil rate band of the deceased has been claimed by the surviving spouse's personal representatives then any available nil rate band will be reduced by the amount claimed by the survivor's personal representatives. See Example 3 below. [*IHTA 1984, ss 8A, 8C* as inserted by *FA 2008, Sch 4 para 2*]. See HMRC Inheritance Tax manual IHTM04121, IHTM43044–IHTM43046.

Example 3

Chargeable event during lifetime of 'survivor' spouse or civil partner

C, who died in August 2002, had made previous lifetime chargeable transfers of £62,500, leaves his long-term ownership of woodlands to his brother, B. An election under *IHTA 1984, s 125* was made. His wife, D, received his remaining assets. In October 2008, the woodland trees are sold by B for £176,000 with deductible expenses of regarding sale and replanting £20,000. D dies in February 2011.

The claim for C's unused nil rate band by D's personal representatives must be calculated after taking into account the proportion of the current transferable nil rate band on D's death, i.e. £325,000 that has been reduced by the chargeable event under *IHTA 1984, s 126* by reference to the proportion of the nil rate band used at the time of the chargeable event, i.e. £312,000. C had used ¼ of his nil rate band on his death and therefore ¾ was unused (i.e. (£250,000 – £62,500) ÷ £250,000 × 100%) so at the time of the chargeable event when B sold the woodlands in October 2008 the nil rate band at that time is £312,000. As the amount on which tax is chargeable is £156,000 (see below) this is the amount referred to as TA below and NRBME is the nil rate band at the date of sale of the woodlands (i.e. (£156,000 ÷ £312,000 × 100% = ½). Therefore, the remaining available nil rate band on C's death, i.e. ¾– ½= ¼, i.e. 25%. At the time of D's death the nil rate band has increased to £325,000 and the remaining portion of C's nil rate band available to D's personal representatives at that time is £81,250 (i.e. £325,000 × ¼). [*IHTA 1984, s 8C(2)* as inserted by *FA 2008, Sch 4 para 2*].

Notes to the example

(A) The transferable amount of the unused nil rate band of the predeceased C to D in this example is calculated by applying the unused nil rate band under *IHTA 1984, s 8A(2)(4)* as follows:

$$\text{Percentage} = \left(\frac{E}{NRBMD} - \frac{TA}{NRBME}\right) \times 100$$

where

M = maximum amount that could be transferred on the predeceased person's death where it is chargeable at the nil rate band at that time, i.e. £250,000;
VT = value actually transferred by the chargeable transfer or nil if applicable, i.e £62,500;
E = the amount by which M above is greater than VT above, i.e. £187,500;
NRBMD = the nil rate band maximum applying at the time of the deceased spouse's or civil partner's death, i.e. £250,000;
TA = the amount on which tax is charged, i.e. £156,000;
NRBME = the nil rate band maximum at the time of the event giving rise to the deferred charge, i.e. £312,000.

(B) The expenses of sale and replanting of the trees would be allowed as a deduction. C's estate at death will be increased to take account of the chargeable event to determine the rates applicable to any later chargeable event as in Example 4 below. [*IHTA 1984, s 126; FA 1985, Sch 26 para 5*].

		£
Cumulative total of previous chargeable transfers of relevant person, i.e. VT above		62,500
Sale proceeds of woodlands	176,000	
Deduct allowable costs	(20,000)	
Balance, i.e. TA above		156,000
Revised cumulative total for relevant person, i.e. C above		£218,500

Example 4

Two or more chargeable events during lifetime of surviving spouse or civil partner

C, who died in August 2002, had made previous chargeable transfers of £125,000, left by will two separate woodlands to his brother, B. An election under *IHTA 1984, s 125* was made. His wife, D, received his remaining assets. In October 2008 and December 2008, the two areas of woodlands are sold for £63,415 each with expenses of sale of £11,415. D dies in February 2011.

The claim for the unused nil rate band by D's personal representatives must be calculated after taking into account the proportion of the current transferable nil rate band on D's death, i.e. £325,000 that has been reduced by the two chargeable events under *IHTA 1984, s 126* by reference to the proportion of the nil rate band used at the time of the chargeable events, i.e. £312,000. C had used ½ of his nil rate band on his death (i.e. (£250,000 – £125,000) ÷ £250,000 × 100%) so at the time of the chargeable events in October and December 2008 one half of the nil rate band at that time is £312,000 which is available. As the amount on which tax is chargeable after expenses is £52,000 on each chargeable event (see below) these are the amounts referred to as TA below and NRBME is the nil rate band at the date of sale of each of the woodlands (£52,000 ÷ £312,000 × 100% = $^1/_6$). Therefore, the remaining available nil rate band on C's death is $^1/_2$ – ($^1/_6$ + $^1/_6$) = 16.66667%. At the time of D's death, when the nil rate band has increased to £325,000, the portion of C's nil rate band available to the personal representatives at that time is therefore £54,167 (i.e. £325,000 ×

16.66667%), which together with her unused nil rate band of up to £325,000 makes a total of £379,167. [*IHTA 1984, s 8C(2)(3)* as inserted by *FA 2008, Sch 4 para* 2].

Note to the example

(A) The transferable amount of the unused nil rate band of the predeceased C to D in this example is calculated by applying the unused nil rate band under *IHTA 1984, s 8A(2)(4)* as follows:

$$\text{Percentage} = \frac{E}{NRBMD} - \left(\frac{TA}{NRBME} + \frac{TA}{NRBME}\right) \times 100$$

where:

M = maximum amount that could be transferred on the predeceased person's death where it is chargeable at the nil rate band at that time, i.e. £250,000;
VT = value actually transferred by the chargeable transfer or nil if applicable, i.e. £125,000;
E = the amount by which M above is greater than VT above, i.e. £125,000;
NRBMD = the nil rate band maximum applying at the time of the deceased spouse's or civil partner's death, i.e. £250,000;
TA = the amount on which tax is charged i.e. the sales in October and December 2008, i.e. £104,000;
NRBME = the nil rate band maximum at the time of the event giving rise to the deferred charge, i.e. £312,000, but if the second sale had been in December 2010 this figure would have been £325,000 not £312,000.

		£
Cumulative total of previous chargeable transfers of relevant person C		125,000
Net sale proceeds of woodlands in October 2008	63,415	
Deduct allowable expenses	(11,415)	52,000
Sale proceeds of conditionally exempt property December 2008	63,415	
Deduct allowable expenses	(11,415)	
Chargeable transfer		52,000
Revised cumulative total for relevant person of C		£229,000

Example 5

Chargeable event after the death of the surviving spouse or civil partner

C, who died in August 2002, had made previous chargeable transfers of £125,000, left by will woodlands to his brother, B. An election under *IHTA 1984, s 125* was made. His wife, D, received his remaining assets. D dies in February 2011 with an estate of £350,000. In October 2012, the woodland is sold by B for £300,000 and allowable expenses of £54,000 are paid.

The claim for the unused nil rate band by D's personal representatives on form IHT 402 (previously IHT 216) has already been made by the time the woodland is sold and becomes chargeable. C had used half of his 50% nil rate band on his death (i.e. (£250,000 – £125,000) ÷ £250,000 × 100%) so D's personal representatives are entitled to claim ½ × £325,000, i.e. the rate applicable at D's death. D's nil rate band of £325,000 added to the predeceased C's available nil rate band of £162,500 (i.e. (£250,000 – £125,000) = ½ × £325,000) makes a total of £487,500 of which £350,000 is used to cover the estate of D. Of this amount £25,000 is part of C's original nil rate band. In October 2012 the woodland is sold for £300,000, less expenses of £52,000, making net proceeds of £248,000 chargeable. Therefore the unused proportion of C's nil rate band of £200,000 (i.e. (£125,000 + £25,000) – £350,000), which is available to set against the net sale proceeds of the woodland to compute the tax payable by B. [*IHTA 1984, s 8C(4)(5) as inserted by FA 2008, Sch 4 para 2*].

Notes to the example

(A) In a case of breach of undertaking or death the person who is liable to pay the tax is the person who, if the property were sold at that time, would be entitled to receive (whether for his benefit or not) the proceeds of sale or any income arising from them, i.e. B. [*IHTA 1984, s 208*]. The tax is due six months after the end of the month in which the disposal took place. [*IHTA 1984, s 226(4)*].

(B) The personal nil rate band used is the one that is in force at the date of the breach which is October 2012, i.e. £325,000. This figure is 'appropriately reduced' by the amount of C's unused nil rate band used on the death of the survivor, D, i.e. £25,000. From this revised figure is deducted the chargeable transfers of the deceased (C) added to the net sale proceeds of the woodland and IHT charged accordingly. See below.

		£
Cumulative total of previous chargeable transfers of relevant person C		125,000
Value of woodland at date of breach in October 2012	300,000	
Deduct allowable expenses	(52,000)	
Chargeable transfer		248,000
Revised cumulative total for relevant person		£373,000

Inheritance tax payable after deducting the available nil rate band (by reference to death rates in February 2011), i.e. £325,000 – £150,000 (£125,000 + £25,000) = £175,000 – £248,000

£73,000 at 40% = £29,200 payable by B

58

Tax Cases

[58.1] This chapter includes summaries not only of IHT/CTT cases but also a number of other, mainly estate duty and anti-avoidance, where the principles established are relevant to IHT. Some of the legislation interpreted in the earlier cases has been amended, repealed or replaced. Nevertheless, the cumulative nature of IHT means that knowledge of the law in earlier years will continue to be necessary for some time to come. Where the CIR (or, in Scotland, the Lord Advocate) are a party, the case is listed under the name of the other party only. Judicial review cases are listed under the name of the applicant and the person who is the subject of the review but again excluding the CIR etc.

Legislative references marked with an asterisk (*) are to legislation which has replaced, or is substantially similar to, that involved in the case summarised.

A Beneficiary v CIR

Japanese citizen avoiding liability to taxation.

A woman (B) was born in the UK, of an English father and a Japanese mother. In 1991/92 B's maternal grandfather (G), who was a Japanese citizen, transferred a large sum of money to the UK for the purpose of benefiting B. On the advice of a solicitor, and in order to avoid liability to IHT, G subsequently (in June 1992) established a discretionary settlement in Jersey and transferred the money from the UK to this settlement. G informed the trustee of the settlement that he wished B to be the principal beneficiary (and did not want the money to be used to benefit B's mother). G died in Japan two years later. The Revenue issued a 1992/93 assessment charging tax on B under *Sec 740*. B appealed, contending that *Sec 740* did not apply, since 'the purpose of avoiding liability to taxation was not the purpose or one of the purposes for which the transfer or associated operations . . . were effected'. The Special Commissioners accepted this contention and allowed B's appeal. Applying *dicta* of Lord Templeman in *New Zealand Commr of Inland Revenue v Challenge Corporation Ltd*, G's motives in transferring the money from the UK to Jersey were tax mitigation rather than tax avoidance. The Commissioners observed that, by virtue of *IHTA, s 157(1)*, if G had arranged for the funds to be left in the UK in the form of foreign currency, no IHT would have been payable. By virtue of *IHTA, s 6(1)*, property situated outside the UK was excluded property if the person beneficially entitled to it was domiciled outside the UK. The Commissioners held that there was no 'difference in principle between an action designed to take advantage of the provisions of *s 157* as against actions designed to take advantage of the provisions of *s 6*'. On the evidence, the Commissioners found that, although UK tax was 'a consideration of (G's) advisers . . . the tax implications of siting the trust in Jersey were a matter of indifference to (G)'. [1999] STC SCD 134 Sp C 190.

Alexander v CIR

Valuation of leasehold flat.

In March 1983 A acquired a leasehold flat for £35,400 under the provisions of the *Housing Act 1980*. The market value of the lease was taken to be £60,000, and the lease contained a covenant requiring A to pay the landlords a percentage of the difference of £24,600 if she should dispose of the flat within five years. A died in 1984. However, her death did not constitute a disposal under the terms of the covenant. The

Revenue issued a determination on the basis that the value of the lease for CTT purposes was £52,000 (after taking into account the potential obligation to make a payment to the landlords if the flat were sold before March 1988). A's executor appealed to the Lands Tribunal, which determined the open market value of the lease at A's death as £63,000, and held that it had no jurisdiction to allow any deduction in respect of the potential obligation to make a payment to the landlords, considering that this was not a question of land valuation. The Revenue appealed to the CA, which remitted the case to the Tribunal. The liability to make a repayment of the discount allowed on the purchase of the flat was an encumbrance on the property and therefore a question as to the value of land, to be decided by the Tribunal. Applying the principles in *CIR v Crossman*, the Tribunal was required to determine the amount which, on a hypothetical sale, a purchaser would be willing to pay to acquire the lease subject to the obligation which would fall on the hypothetical purchaser to make a repayment to the landlords in the event of a disposal, but on the basis that the hypothetical sale did not itself give rise to such a disposal. CA 1991, 64 TC 59; [1991] STC 112; [1991] 26 EG 141.

Alford v Department for the Environment, Food and Rural Affairs

Restoring derelict farmland to previous levels of agricultural production did not involve using the land for intensive agricultural purposes – Environmental Impact Assessment (Uncultivated Land and Semi-Natural Areas)(England)Regs 2001.

The defendant owned land at Vixen Tor Farm, Merrivale, Dartmoor and undertook projects that involved the application of farmyard manures and calcified seaweed to four fields that had been left in their natural state for many years. The boundary walls and fences had fallen into disrepair and livestock from common land had relatively unrestricted access to the farm. On 10 June 2004 the defendant faced four charges of carrying out projects on land she owned without obtaining a screening decision or the grant of consent by the Secretary of State for the Environment, Food and Rural Affairs contrary to *Environmental Impact Assessment (Uncultivated Land and Semi-Natural Areas)(England) Regs 2001, SI 2001/3966, s 19*. In the case stated the deputy district judge found that from 1966 to 2002 the tenant farmers appeared to have abandoned the farm. There was no evidence of cultivation and nothing had been applied to the fields in terms of fertilizer or additives and it was kept as grazing moorland. The land was kept in its natural state. The land was then taken in hand by the defendant and the manures and seaweed applied to make the grass palatable for the cattle. Also boundary walls and fences were repaired to make the fields stock proof resulting in the charge that the unauthorised increase in productivity, or the intensification of the use to which the land had been put fell foul of the environmental protection law such that under *Environmental Impact Assessment (Uncultivated Land and Semi-Natural Areas)(England) Regs 2001, SI 2001/3966, s 2(1)* the projects constituted a) the execution of construction works or other installations or schemes; or b) other interventions in the natural surroundings and landscape, involving the use of uncultivated land or semi-natural areas for intensive agricultural purposes.

The question for the High Court was what was meant by the phrase 'intensive agricultural purposes' in regulation 2(1)? The circumstances of this case were such that the projects were not capable of being described as an intervention for intensive agricultural purposes, and although EEC Council Directive (97/11/EC) (OJ 1997 No L73/5) had a wide scope and a broad purpose, the framers of the legislation did not intend it to catch a project that was concerned only to bring land back to a normal level of agricultural productivity. The project did not amount to an intervention in the natural surroundings and landscape involving the use of uncultivated land or semi-natural areas for intensive agricultural purposes. [2005] TLR 30 May 2005.

Anand v CIR

Beneficial ownership of bank accounts

An individual (J), who had been born in India, died in 1988 domiciled and resident in Iran, with substantial funds in a number of UK bank accounts. The Revenue issued a notice of determination charging IHT on the basis that J was the beneficial owner of these funds. His executors appealed, contending that much of the money belonged to a family partnership which had been established in Iran, and that the partnership had transferred the money to London because of the political situation in Iran. The Special Commissioner accepted the executors' evidence and allowed their appeal, holding that the funds were 'partnership funds in origin and remained such. Placing them in an account in the deceased's sole name did not make him the sole beneficial owner.' J had been a 'trustee or nominee' of the funds, which 'belonged beneficially to the deceased and his three sons in equal shares'. [1997] STC SCD 58 Sp C 107.

Anderson (Anderson's Executor) v CIR

Scotsman resident in England at time of death – whether English domicile acquired.

An individual (A) was born in Scotland in 1909. He lived in Scotland until 1974, when he sold his property in Scotland and moved to Cornwall. A few months after moving, he suffered a serious heart attack. He died in 1982, having lived in Cornwall for eight years and leaving his widow as his executrix. Following her subsequent death, the Revenue considered that A had acquired a domicile of choice in England. Her executor (who was A's son) appealed contending that A had retained his domicile of origin in Scotland. The Special Commissioner accepted this contention and allowed the appeal, observing that there was 'an inherent improbability in a 65-year old Scotsman, who lived in Scotland all his life, abandoning his roots and intending to acquire a domicile of choice in England'. There was 'nothing inconsistent with an elderly Scottish gentleman acquiring a residence in the south of England at his retirement without having any intention to acquire a domicile in England'. It was significant that A had no English will or English Solicitor and the scattering of his ashes near his former home in Scotland were inferences that he had not intended his final resting place to be Cornwall. [1998] STC SCD 43 Sp C 147.

Arkwright and Another (Williams' Personal Representatives) v CIR

Related property under IHTA 1984, s 161.

A married couple owned a freehold property as tenants in common. The husband (W) died in 2001. By his will, he gave his widow a life interest in his 50% share of the property, with the remainder to his daughters. In January 2002 his widow and the daughters executed a deed of variation so that W's interest in the property vested in his daughters. The Inland Revenue issued a notice of determination that IHT was due on £275,000 (being 50% of the agreed open market value of the property). W's daughters (as his personal representatives) appealed to the Special Commissioners, contending that W's interest should be valued at less than 50% of the vacant possession value, because his widow had the right to occupy the property and not have it sold without her consent. The Commissioner accepted this contention and allowed the appeal in principle, holding that the value of W's interest should be determined in accordance with *IHTA 1984, s 161(3)*, and making various observations concerning the effect of *s 161(3)*. The Inland Revenue appealed to the Ch D, contending that the Commissioner had exceeded her jurisdiction and that the case should be referred to the Lands Tribunal. The Ch D accepted this contention. Gloster J held that 'the Special Commissioner was clearly entitled to conclude that, because *s 161(4)* did not apply, the value of the deceased's interest in the property was not inevitably a mathematical one-half of the vacant possession value'. However, she had exceeded her authority in purporting to determine 'that, as matter of fact, the value of his interest was indeed less than a mathematical one-half of the vacant possession value. That was properly an issue that should have been referred to the Lands Tribunal for determination by it.' Ch D [2004] STC 1323.

Arnander, Lloyd & Villiers (McKenna's Executors) v HMRC

Farmhouse and adjoining buildings – whether qualified for agricultural property relief – not main dwelling from which the agricultural operations over the land were conducted and managed.

A married couple had owned a small country estate comprising a large house with six acres of gardens and some domestic outbuildings, and 187 acres of land, most of which was farmland. They both died in 2003. HMRC issued notices of determination charging IHT on the house (while accepting that 110 acres of land and a farm outbuilding qualified for agricultural property relief). The executors appealed, contending that the house was a farmhouse which also qualified for agricultural property relief, as did 11 more outbuildings on the estate. The Special Commissioner reviewed the evidence in detail and held that three of the outbuildings qualified for relief but that the main house and eight of the outbuildings did not. The Commissioner observed that the farming activities were carried on by contractors who were managed by a land agent in a nearby town. The house which the couple lived in was not 'the main dwelling from which the agricultural operations over the land were conducted and managed'. [2006] STC SCD 800 Sp C 565.

Ashcroft v Barnsdale & Others

Rectification of deeds

A married woman's will left £10,000 plus some farmland to her husband, with the residue passing to her children. The executors of the will varied it by a deed of family arrangement giving £410,000 to the children and treating the husband as the residuary beneficiary. This deed had the unintended effect that the husband (as residuary beneficiary) became liable to additional inheritance tax. He applied to the Ch D for a deed of rectification. Judge Hodge granted the application, holding that there was an established distinction 'between a mistake as to the meaning or effect of a document (which may be amenable to rectification) and one as to its consequences (which is not)' and that 'the fact that the parties intended to use a particular form of words in the mistaken belief that it was achieving their common intention does not prevent the court from giving effect to their true intention'. On the evidence, he held that 'this is not a case where the parties merely proceeded under a misapprehension as to the true fiscal consequences of the deed of variation as actually drafted. Rather, the claimant has demonstrated a specific common intention as to how the parties' fiscal objectives were to be achieved; and he has established that, owing to a mistake in the way in which that intention was expressed in the deed of variation, effect has not been given to that intention. Underlying the parties' adoption of the deed of variation was the common intention, unarticulated and unexpressed, that the claimant should receive his entitlement under his late wife's will, as varied, free from all liability for inheritance tax, thereby replicating the position under the will as executed. There was never any intention to vary the burden of, or the incidence of the parties' liability for, inheritance tax. To the extent that the deed of variation had this effect, then it was executed under a relevant mistake, because it failed to give effect to the parties' true intention.' Ch D [2010] EWHC 1948 (Ch).

Aspden v Hildesley

Transfer of assets under Court Order on divorce.

The taxpayer and his wife had jointly owned certain property, not the private residence of either. They had been separated since 1970 and were divorced by decree nisi on 12 February 1976. The Court Order (by consent) provided, *inter alia*, for the taxpayer's half share of the property to be transferred to his wife, while she undertook to give an irrevocable order to her personal representatives that, should she die before 10 December 1984 and before her husband, a sum equal to half the equity in the property was to be paid to him out of her estate. The taxpayer was assessed on the footing that he had disposed of his share in the property on 12 February 1976, and that by virtue of *CGTA 1979, s 19(3)(a)** and *TCGA 1992, ss 18, 286** the consideration was to be taken as the market value. The Ch D upheld the assessment, reversing the decision of the Commissioners. On the facts, the taxpayer's interest in the property was transferred at the time of the decree nisi, the consent order being an unconditional contract for the transfer. As the decree was not then absolute, the parties were still married and *CGTA 1979, s 19(3)(a)** applied by virtue of *TCGA 1992, ss 18(2)*, 286(2)**. (Note. *CGTA 1979, s 19(3)* was repealed by *FA 1981* and replaced by what is now *TCGA 1992, s 17*.) Ch D 1981, 55 TC 609; [1982] STC 206; [1982] 1 WLR 264; [1982] 2 All ER 53.

Atkinson & Smith (WM Atkinson's Executors) v HMRC

IHTA 1984, s 117 – whether property occupied for agricultural purposes.

In 1957 a farmer (W) purchased some farmland. Initially he farmed it himself, but in 1980 he let it to a family farming partnership of which he was a member. W lived in a bungalow on the farm from 1966 until 2002, when he became ill. After leaving hospital he moved to a care home where he died in 2006. His bungalow remained unoccupied during his illness, although he occasionally visited it. His executors claimed that the bungalow qualified for agricultural property relief. HMRC rejected the claim on the basis that the bungalow had not been occupied for the purposes of agriculture throughout the seven years ending with W's death. The executors appealed. The First-Tier Tribunal allowed their appeal, on the basis that 'occupation by the partnership continued until (W's) death, and it was occupation for the purposes of agriculture in the relevant sense because the bungalow was still used to accommodate the diminishing needs of the senior partner. However, this decision was reversed on appeal by HMRC. The Upper Tribunal held that because there was little or no actual use of the property up to the date of death it was not possible to regard the property as continuing to be occupied for the purposes of agriculture. No relief was therefore available. First Tier Tribunal decision FTT [2010] UKFTT 108 (TC), TC00420 [2012] STC 289 (Upper Tax Tribunal decision).

A-G v Boden and Another

Valuation – partnership goodwill – whether transfer for full consideration.

A father in partnership with his two sons was not required to devote as much time to the business as his sons. On his death his share accrued equally to his sons, subject to their paying his estate the value of his share exclusive of any amount of goodwill. The obligations of the sons under the partnership deed were held to constitute full consideration for the deceased's share of the goodwill. KB 1911, [1912] 1 KB 539; 105 LT 247.

A-G v Farrell

Gifts with reservation – settlements.

A reservation of benefit arises where a settlor is included as a potential beneficiary under a discretionary trust. [1931] 1 KB 81.

A-G v Heywood

Gifts with reservation – settlements.

A reservation of benefit arises where a settlor is included as a potential beneficiary under a discretionary trust. QB, [1887] 19 QBD 326.

A-G v Ralli

Valuation – partnership reserves – whether transfer for full consideration.

The deceased was a partner in a partnership of bankers which held large reserves for the partnership business. The partnership deed provided that each partner's share in the reserves accrued on his death or retirement to the remaining partners. The court held that ED was not payable on the deceased's interest in the reserves. There was no gift but merely an ordinary commercial transaction for full consideration. KB 1936, 15 ATC 523.

A-G v Seccombe

Gifts with reservation – exclusion of donor from enjoyment.

The KB held that a donor may remain a guest in a house he has given away without tax being attracted provided that there was no agreement to this effect and it was a *bona fide* gift. KB, [1911] 2 KB 688. (Note. This proposition is, however, open to question following *Chick v Commrs of Stamp Duties of New South Wales* PC, [1958] AC 435; [1958] 2 All ER 623; [1958] 3 WLR 93.)

A-G v Worrall

Gifts with reservation – exclusion of donor from any benefit.

A collated annuity to the donor secured by personal covenant was held to be a benefit. QB [1895], 1 QB 99; [1891–94] All ER 861.

Bailhache Labesse Trustees Ltd & Others v HMRC

Charitable donation – whether IHTA 1984, s 23 applicable.

In 1985 an individual (K), who was domiciled in the UK, established a Jersey settlement, of which he was the life tenant. He died in 2001. Within twelve months of his death, the trustees of the settlement appointed 25% of the trust property to each of two charities. They appealed against a determination charging IHT on K's death, contending that the appointments should be treated as exempt transfers under *IHTA 1984, s 23* with effect from the date of K's death. The Special Commissioner rejected this contention and dismissed the appeals, holding that the settled property had to be treated as passing from K to the trustees on his death. The subsequent appointment to the charities could not 'turn what would otherwise be chargeable transfers of value into exempt transfers'. [2008] STC SCD 869 Sp C 688.

Baird's Executors v CIR

Valuation – renunciation of agricultural tenancy – valuation of interest transferred.

A father (B) and son were joint tenants of a farm in Scotland. In September 1977 the son was killed in a car accident. In December 1977 B renounced his tenancy in favour of his daughter-in-law and his grandson. This transfer was accepted by the landlord, and thereafter the land was farmed by the transferees in partnership with B until his death in 1985. The Revenue took the view that B had made a chargeable transfer of the tenancy, the value of which the District Valuer determined as £138,000 (being 25% of the agreed vacant possession value). B's executors appealed, contending that the tenancy had no value because it could not have been transferred without the landlord's consent, and that B's interest was in only a half share of the tenancy. The Lands Tribunal allowed the appeal in part, holding that the Revenue's valuation of the tenancy was correct, but that the chargeable transfer was of a half share in the tenancy, the half share previously held by B's son having passed to his widow rather than reverting to B. The Tribunal therefore determined that the amount of the chargeable transfer was £69,000. Lands Tribunal 1990, SVC 188.

Barclays Bank Trust Co Ltd v IRC

Business property relief regarding whether cash held by a company an excepted asset. IHTA 1984, s 112.

A married woman (W) died in 1990. Her estate included a 50% shareholding in a family company, which held cash of about £450,000 at her death. The Revenue issued a notice of determination, accepting in principle that the shares qualified for business property relief, but computed on the basis that the company only required cash of some £150,000 for the purposes of its business, and that the balance of £300,000 was an 'excepted asset', within *IHTA, s 112(2)*, and did not qualify for relief. W's executor appealed, contending that the company had held the cash 'as a contingency measure' in case 'an appropriate business opportunity should arise', so that the cash was 'required . . . for future use', within *IHTA, s 112(2)(b)*. The Special Commissioner rejected this contention and dismissed the appeal, holding on the evidence that the £300,000 was not 'required'. The Commissioner held that, for the purposes of *s 112*, 'required' did not include 'the possibility that the money might be required should an opportunity arise to make use of the money in two, three or seven years' time . . . The word "required" implies some imperative that the money will fall to be used upon a given project or for some palpable business purpose'. [1998] STC SCD 125 Sp C 22.

Barlow Clowes International Ltd (in liquidation) and Others v Henwood

Abandonment of domicile of choice – automatic reversion to domicile of origin

Mr Henwood had a domicile of origin in England which he then renounced in favour of a domicile of choice in the Isle of Man. At the time of a bankruptcy petition (see Barlow Clowes International Ltd (in liquidation) [2007] EWHC 1579 (Ch) it was held that Mr Henwood was not domiciled in England and Wales but had a domicile of choice in Mauritius (not the Isle of Man) because his case was abandonment of one domicile of choice by acquisition of a domicile of choice in Mauritius. The weight of evidence he had to prove that he had acquired another domicile of choice was no greater than that to show a domicile of choice had superseded another. Where a person maintains homes in two countries the question had to be decided by reference to the quality of residence in one of those countries to ascertain in which country he had an intention to permanently reside. Lord Justice Waller stated that the original Judge was in error in thinking that a domicile of choice could be lost only by the acquisition of another domicile of choice. A domicile of choice could be abandoned and, if abandoned, the domicile of origin revived. The evidence had not established that after abandoning a domicile of choice in the Isle of Man Mr Henwood had established the requisite intention to establish a domicile of choice elsewhere. Therefore the domicile of origin of Mr Henwood had revived in England. CA [2008] TLR.

Barrett (Barrett's Personal Representatives) v HMRC

Lands Tribunal decision – 15% discount for joint ownership

An individual (B) was joint owner of a semi-detached house built in the 1930s. He died in 2002. HMRC determined the value of his interest in the property as £144,500. His personal representative (who was the other joint-owner) appealed, contending that the house should be valued at £288,000, and that with a 15% discount for the joint ownership, the value of B's interest should be taken as £122,400. The Lands Tribunal reviewed the evidence in detail and held that the house should be valued at £315,000, so that with a 15% discount for joint ownership, the value of B's interest was £133,875. Lands Tribunal 23 November 2005 unreported.

Battle and Another v CIR

Valuation – value of unquoted shares – minority shareholding.

An ED avoidance case is of interest because the principles to be considered in establishing the discount on the asset value of a minority shareholding were discussed. The precise amount of the discount was not material to the outcome of the case but, on the facts, the stockbroker giving evidence for the Revenue suggested the discount should be in the region of 10 to 15% while the Capital Taxes Office [now HMRC Inheritance Tax] broadly concurred with a figure of 15%. Although the chief valuation witness for the taxpayers argued that other considerations should be taken into account in this particular case, he did, in general, accept the valuation principles indicated by the Revenue witnesses. Ch D 1979, [1980] STC 86.

Baylis v Gregory

Avoidance schemes – the Ramsay principle.

The managing director of a company (PGI) controlled the company through his own and trustee shareholdings. Another company, C, entered into negotiations to acquire PGI, and the taxpayer and his associates set up a Manx company to exchange their shares in PGI with shares in the Manx company. However, C ended the negotiations. Nevertheless the share exchange was proceeded with and completed in March 1974. No further steps were taken to sell PGI until May 1975 when a third company, H, became interested in it. Eventually, the Manx company sold the PGI shares to H. The Special Commissioners allowed the taxpayer's appeals and their decision was upheld by the Ch D, the CA, and the HL. The transactions were not a 'pre-ordained series of transactions'. HL 1988, 62 TC 1; [1988] STC 476; [1988] 3 WLR 423; [1988] 3 All ER 495.

Beckman v IRC

Relevant business property – IHTA, s 105(1).

A woman (H) and her daughter (B) had carried on business in partnership for many years until H retired in 1993. B then continued the business as sole proprietor. H died in 1997, having retained an interest in the business through her capital account. The Revenue issued a notice of determination charging IHT on the amounts owed by B to H at H's death. B appealed, contending that the amounts in question were 'relevant business property' within *IHTA, s 105(1)*. The Special Commissioner rejected this contention and dismissed the appeal. For the purposes of *IHTA, s 105*, H's interest in the business 'ceased when she retired from the partnership'. Following H's retirement from the business, her rights 'were simply those of a creditor of the business'. [2000] STC SCD 59 Sp C 226.

Begg-McBrearty v Stilwell (Trustee of the GE Coke Settlement)

Exercise of power of appointment in favour of grandchildren of settlor – whether grandchildren acquiring an interest in possession at age of 18 or 21.

In 1975 the trustees of a settlement made in 1959 exercised their power of appointment in favour of the settlor's three grandchildren, and thereafter held the trust fund contingently for the grandchildren contingently on their reaching the age of 21. The eldest grandchild became 21 in 1990, and thus became absolutely entitled to a one-third share of the settled property. The Revenue issued a 1990/91 assessment on one of the trustees, charging CGT on the deemed disposal to the grandchild in accordance with *TCGA 1992, s 71**. The trustee appealed, contending that the gain should be held over by virtue of an election made under *TCGA 1992, s 260(2)(d)**. The Ch D rejected this contention and upheld the assessment. The disposal could not be held over under *TCGA 1992, s 260(2)(d)** because the grandchild had become entitled to an interest in possession in her share of the settled property in 1987, when she reached the age of 18. Before the exercise of the power of appointment, the grandchild had had only a revocable interest in the trust property. Her relevant interest arose from the power of appointment. Since this had been exercised in 1975, it fell within the provisions of *Family Law Reform Act 1969* (which had reduced the age of majority to 18 with effect from 1 January 1970), even though the original settlement had been made before the date on which that act took effect. Ch D 1996, TL 3473; [1996] STC 413; [1996] 1 WLR 951; [1996] 4 All ER 205.

Benham's Will Trusts re (Lockhart v Harker & Others)

IHTA 1984, s 41 – allocation of exemptions.

A testatrix bequeathed her residuary estate between some charitable beneficiaries and some non-charitable beneficiaries. The executor issued an originating summons seeking the opinion of the court as to whether the non-charitable beneficiaries should receive their shares subject to IHT (as the charitable beneficiaries contended) or whether their shares should be grossed up (as the non-charitable beneficiaries themselves contended). The Ch D upheld the contention of the non-charitable beneficiaries, holding that the plain intention of the executrix was that each beneficiary in the list should receive the same amount, that this was not inconsistent with the provisions of *IHTA 1984, s 41*, and accordingly that the non-charitable beneficiaries should receive grossed-up shares. Ch D 1994, [1995] STC 210.

Bennett & Others v CIR

Gifts to sons – whether exempt from IHT as 'normal expenditure of the transferor' – IHTA 1984, s 21.

Under a will, the shares in a family company were held on trust, with the income from the shares and the residuary estate being paid to the testator's widow for her life and thereafter to the testator's three sons. The trustees sold the shares in 1987, as a result of which the income of the trust was greatly increased. The testator's widow was 87 years of age and had a settled lifestyle. She authorised the trustees to distribute equally between her three sons such of the trust income for each accounting year as was surplus to her financial requirements. In February 1989 the trustees paid £9,300 to each of the sons, and on 5 February 1990 they paid £60,000 to each of the sons. The widow died suddenly on 20 February 1990. The Revenue issued determinations that the payments to the sons were chargeable to IHT. The sons appealed, contending that the gifts were exempt from IHT under *IHTA 1984, s 21(1)* as 'part of the normal expenditure of the transferor'. The QB accepted this contention and allowed the appeals. Lightman J held that ' "normal expenditure" connotes expenditure which at the time it took place accorded with the settled pattern of expenditure adopted by the transferor . . . For an expenditure to be "normal" there is no fixed minimum period during which the expenditure shall have occurred. All that is necessary is that on the totality of evidence the pattern of actual or intended payments shall have been established and that the item in question conforms with that pattern . . . The pattern need not be immutable; it must however be established that the pattern was intended to remain in place for more than a nominal period and indeed for a sufficient period (barring unforeseen circumstances) fairly to be regarded as a regular feature of the transferor's annual expenditure. Thus a "death bed" resolution to make periodic payments "for life" and a payment made in accordance with such a determination will not suffice . . . The fact that the objective behind the expenditure is tax planning, e.g. to prevent an accumulation of income in the hands of the transferor liable to inheritance tax on his death, is no impediment.' On the evidence, the widow had adopted 'a pattern of expenditure in respect of the surplus, and the payments to the sons were made in accordance with this pattern'. Ch D 1994, [1995] STC 54.

Best (Exor of Buller deceased) v HMRC

Company holding business park – whether business property relief to be allowed – whether a business of mainly holding investments

A company held and managed a business centre comprising approximately 10% offices, and the balance being two thirds warehousing used by retailers or wholesalers and one third light industrial use. In total there were approximately 400 people in or around the Centre on a typical working day. The deceased spent considerable time each week at the Business Centre dealing with the everyday matters that might arise with occupiers. On his death the company employed a full time replacement as a site administrator. Units were occupied under licence agreements not conferring exclusive possession of a unit. Twenty-four hour security was provided along with a receptionist, forklift driver, maintenance person, office facilities, meeting rooms, central telephone switchboard and various other business facilities. Nevertheless it was held that the investment activity of letting the units was the predominant activity and the company was therefore mainly an investment company. The claim to business property relief on the shares was therefore refused. [2014] UKFTT 077 (TC).

Bower & Chesterfield (Mrs ME Bower's Executors) v HMRC

Valuation of reserved rights to life annuity.

In 2002 a 90-year-old woman (B) paid £73,000 for a life annuity policy, issued to a trust she had created, with reserved rights to a 5% life annuity. She died five months later. HMRC issued a determination that the £73,000 was chargeable to IHT. B's executors appealed, contending that there should be a deduction of £7,800 representing B's reserved rights to the life annuity, so that only £65,200 was chargeable to IHT. The Special Commissioner allowed the appeal in part, holding that in view of B's projected life expectancy, there should be a deduction of £4,200. The appeal in Chancery Division was allowed. [2008] STC SCD 582 Sp C 665; ChD [2009] STC 510. (*Note*. For HMRC's practice pending the hearing of the appeal, see HMRC Brief 23/08, issued on 11 April 2008. New cases will continue to be dealt with in accordance with the May 2007 Technical Note http://www.hmrc.gov.uk/cto/dgs-tech-note.pdf.)

Brander (Earl of Balfour's Personal Representative) v HMRC

Application of IHTA 1984, s 107 regarding replacement property vis BPR.

In 1968 the Earl of Balfour inherited a liferent interest in a family estate, much of which was used for farming. In November 2002 he entered into a farming partnership with his nephew (who was his heir and intended successor). In June 2003 he died. HMRC issued a ruling that business property relief (BPR) was not due. The Earl's personal representative appealed, contending that the effect of the 'replacement property' provisions in *IHTA 1984, s 107* was that the estate qualified for BPR. The First-tier Tribunal accepted this contention and allowed the appeal, finding that the Earl had 'appeared to manage the estate in a way that was characteristic of his generation' and 'dominated and in practice controlled the running of the estate'. On the evidence, the Earl's interest in the partnership which subsisted immediately before his death replaced the business which he had previously carried on. The tribunal also held that *IHTA 1984, s 105(3)* did not apply, since the management of the estate comprised far more than simply 'the making or holding of investment', and had been 'mainly a trading activity' in which 'the letting side was ancillary to the farming, forestry, woodland and sporting activities. The farming activities, albeit they included agricultural tenancies, occupied by far the greater area of the estate.' Accordingly, the Earl's interest in the partnership was 'relevant business property' which qualified for relief. The Upper Tribunal upheld this decision as one of fact, holding inter alia that the fact that the Earl 'as liferenter did not have a direct interest in the capital realisations of timber from the woodlands' did not prevent the woodlands from constituting 'business property' which qualified for relief. HMRC v AM Brander (Earl of Balfour's Personal Representative), CA 1991, 64 TC 59; FTT [2009] UKFTT 101 (TC), TC00069; FTT [2009] UKFTT 101 (TC), TC00069; UT [2010] UKUT 300 (TC).

Brown's Executors v CIR

IHTA 1984, s 105 – Proceeds of sale of a nightclub held on deposit to be reinvested – allowed.

An individual (B), who owned a 99% shareholding in an unquoted UK company, died in 1986. The company had operated a nightclub, but had sold this in 1985. The proceeds of the sale were held on short-term deposit pending re-investment in similar premises, but no such premises had been acquired at the time of B's death. The executors claimed that B's shareholding qualified for business property relief. The Revenue rejected the claim on the basis that the company's business consisted 'wholly or mainly . . . of making or holding investments'. The executors appealed, contending that until B's death, the company had been actively seeking alternative sites to open a new nightclub, and accordingly should not be treated as an investment-holding company. The Special Commissioner accepted the executors' evidence and allowed the appeal. [1996] STC SCD 277 Sp C 83.

Buccleuch (Duke of) & Another v CIR

Valuation – division of estate into units.

In an ED case the Revenue valued a substantial estate by dividing it into 532 'natural units' for valuation purposes. The trustees appealed, accepting that 46 of the units could be sold individually but contending that the remaining 486 could only be sold within a reasonable time if they were sold as a whole to an investor or speculator, and that the price payable by such a buyer would be some 20% less than the total valuation of the individual units. Their appeal was dismissed by the Land Tribunal, the CA and the HL. The HL held that the open market value was to be determined by reference to the aggregate of the proceeds of sale in a hypothetical market of each individual unit. The fact that it would have taken a long time to sell individual units separately, and that delay would have been caused by the need to avoid flooding the market, were held to be irrelevant. HL 1966, [1967] 1 All ER 129; [1967] 1 AC 506.

Bullock, CIR v

Domicile.

A Canadian married a woman of English parentage in 1946 and came to live in the UK. By 1966, he had given up any idea of returning to Canada during his wife's lifetime. He was held not to have acquired an English domicile of choice for the relevant years (1971–72 and 1972–73). CA 1976, 51 TC 522; [1976] STC 409; [1976] 1 WLR 1178; [1976] 3 All ER 353.

Burden & Burden v United Kingdom

IHTA 1984, s 18 – whether any breach of European Convention on Human Rights.

Two elderly sisters lived together in a jointly-owned house on land which they had inherited from their parents. They lodged a complaint with the ECHR, contending that the provisions of *IHTA 1984, s 18* (as amended by the *Tax and Civil Partnership Regulations 2005*) were a breach of *Article 14* of the *European Convention on Human Rights*, because when one of them died, the survivor would be required to pay IHT on her sister's share of their home, whereas no IHT would have been charged if they had lived together as a registered lesbian civil partnership. The case was referred to the Fourth Section of the ECHR, which rejected their application (by a 4-3 majority), holding that 'the inheritance tax exemption for married and civil partnership couples . . . pursues a legitimate aim, namely to promote stable, committed heterosexual and homosexual relationships by providing the survivor with a measure of financial security after the death of the spouse or partner'. The United Kingdom's decision 'to treat differently for tax purposes those who were married or who were parties to a civil partnership from other persons living together, even in a long-term settled relationship' was within the 'margin of appreciation' available to national authorities. The Grand Chamber upheld this decision (by a 15-2 majority), holding that 'the relationship between siblings is qualitatively of a different nature to that between married couples and homosexual civil partners . . . The fact that the applicants have chosen to live together all their adult lives, as do many married and *Civil Partnership Act* couples, does not alter this essential difference between the two types of relationship.' The absence of 'a legally binding agreement between the applicants' rendered 'their relationship of co-habitation, despite its long duration, fundamentally different to that of a married or civil partnership couple'. Accordingly, 'the applicants, as co-habiting sisters, cannot be compared for the purposes of *Article 14* to a married or *Civil Partnership Act* couple. It follows that there has been no discrimination and, therefore, no violation of *Article 14*'. [2008] ECHR Case 13378/05 unreported.

Burkinyoung (Burkinyoung's Executor) v CIR

Business property relief – deeds of variation.

Martin & Horsfall v CIR was applied in a similar case where the deceased had let four flats on shorthold tenancies. The Commissioner held that the letting of the flats was a business which was 'wholly one of making or holding investments', so that the effect of *IHTA 1984, s 105(3)* was that business property relief was not due. [1995] STC SCD 29 Sp C 3.

Burmah Oil Co Ltd, CIR v

Avoidance schemes – the Ramsay principle.

A company (H), which was a member of a group, was dormant but owned stock with a market value substantially less than its acquisition cost. Its parent company (B) carried out a series of transactions including a capital reorganisation and the loan of £160 million to H via another company in the same group. At the end of these transactions, B held the stock previously held by H, which had been put into liquidation. B claimed that it had made a loss of £160 million on the disposal of its shareholding in H. The HL rejected the claim (reversing the decision of the CS). The whole and only purpose of the scheme had been the avoidance of tax. Applying *WT Ramsay Ltd*, the transactions had 'no commercial purpose apart from the avoidance of a liability to tax', and should be disregarded. HL 1981, 54 TC 200; [1982] STC 30.

Bushell v Faith

Company law – special voting rights attached to shares.

The share capital of a company comprised 300 shares of £1 each which were held as to 100 each by F and his two sisters. By Article 9 of the articles of association 'in the event of a resolution being proposed at any general meeting of the company for the removal from office of any director, any shares held by that director shall on a poll in respect of such resolution carry the right to three votes per share'. The HL upheld the effectiveness of the article. The weighting of votes on the particular resolution does not infringe CA 1985, s 303*. [1970] AC 1099.

Buswell v CIR

Domicile.

A South African who married an Englishwoman, and who in the relevant years lived in the UK, was held not to have acquired an English domicile of choice. (In so deciding, the CA reversed the decisions of the Special Commissioners and the Ch D.) CA 1974, 49 TC 334; [1974] STC 266; [1974] 1 WLR 1631; [1974] 2 All ER 520.

Buzzoni and others v IRC

Mrs K held a lease for 100 years less one day commencing on 25 March 1994 in respect of a residential property. On 21 November 1997 she granted an underlease commencing on 24 November 1997 to a nominee company. The underlease was then transferred to a trust for her sons. The superior landland consented to the grant of the underlease on condition that the underlease contained the usual covenants on the part of the underlessee. The covenants which were contained in the underlease mirrored many of those contained in the headlease, e.g. payment of the service charges and an undertaking to keep the property in good repair, these all taking effect on the date when the underlease fell into possession. Although rent was payable under the headlease, there was however no rent payable under the terms of the underlease. Mrs K died on 2 May 2008 and HMRC contended that the covenants in the underlease fell to be treated as benefits reserved by her from the gift of it to the trust. For the executors it was argued that there was no benefit, but simply reimbursement of equivalent sums payable to the superior landlord. Both the First Tier Tax Tribunal and the Upper Tribunal held that the covenants were a clear benefit reserved to the headlessee out of the gift of the underlease. Accordingly on the death of Mrs K the value of underlease formed part of her estate by virtue of *FA 1986, s 102*. These decisions were reversed by the Court of Appeal in December 2013. The central point is whether or not the donee's enjoyment of the property gifted is to the exclusion of any benefit to the donor. The focus is not primarily on the question whether the donor has obtained a benefit from the gifted property but whether the donee's enjoyment of that property remains exclusive. In this case any benefit to the donor did not have any impact on the donee's enjoyment of the property and therefore the reservation of benefit rules were not in point. [2013] EWCA Civ 1684.

Cairns (VDE Webb's Personal Representative) v HMRC

IHTA 1984, s 249 HMRC seeking to impose penalty.

A former Inland Revenue employee died in October 2004. He owned a house in Midlothian, which was in poor condition. The solicitor who acted as his personal representative submitted a form IHT200 in which he valued the house at £400,000. HMRC subsequently formed the opinion that this valuation was too low. They laid an information before the Special Commissioners with a summons seeking to impose a penalty of more than £33,000 on the solicitor. The Special Commissioner signed the summons in accordance with *IHTA 1984, s 249(4)*, and the solicitor appealed. The appeal was heard by a different Special Commissioner (Mr Reid, who is now a Tribunal judge but was a Special Commissioner at the time of the hearing), who dismissed the summons, holding that it was 'wholly lacking specification'. Mr Reid held that 'the initiating document, be it summons, summary complaint or indictment must be set out the parameters of the enquiry, and the essential facts and basis in law upon which the public authority relies. If it does not do so, there is bound to be significant prejudice or the risk of such prejudice'. The solicitor was 'entitled to fair notice of the allegations being made against him and a reasonable opportunity to respond to them. Something more than bare words of the relevant statute are required to ensure that fair notice is given.' Mr Reid observed that when the previous Commissioner had issued the summons, that was 'a purely administrative act by which the summons reflects the material contained in the information'. It was not the responsibility of the Commissioner who signed the summons 'to make substantial revisions to the material produced and by a process of drafting create a relevant and specific summons. It might have been better in this case if the Special Commissioners had simply refused to issue a summons in terms of the draft presented to them on the grounds that the information which was reflected in the draft presented to them was a wholly inadequate basis upon which to commence proceedings, particularly as those proceedings appeared to involve bare allegations of fraud or negligence'. With regard to the merits of the case, Mr Reid held that the form IHT200 should have specifically declared that the valuation of the house was 'a provisional estimate.' Accordingly 'there had been a narrow, technical failure to comply with the provisions' of *s 247(1)*. However, the penalty should have been reduced to 'a nominal amount'. FTT May 2009 (TC00008).

Cancer Research Campaign and others v Ernest Brown & Co

Duty to exercise reasonable care in advising a deceased's beneficiary of the possibility of executing a deed of variation – IHTA 1984, s 142.

N died on 11 December 1986 leaving a will dated 21 December 1985 giving his residuary estate to his sister who then died on 28 May 1988. Seven charities named as residuary beneficiaries under the testatrix's will dated 14 September 1987, brought an action for damages for negligence against the defendant firm of solicitors. The plaintiffs claimed that by reason of the solicitors' negligence they were unable to take advantage of a deed of variation under *IHTA 1984, s 142* at a cost to them of some £200,000 of unnecessarily paid IHT on N's estate because the statutory election period had expired on 10 December 1988. The plaintiffs contended that the solicitors were in breach of their duty of care during the testatrix's lifetime in failing to advise her of the possibility of executing a deed of variation of N's bequests. In addition, a breach of duty of their care had arisen, following the testatrix's death, in the administration of the estate in failing to notify them of their prospective legacies.

The court could not accept that there was a duty to advise an intended testator/testatrix about the tax avoidance schemes of another estate. The executor's duty was to collect the assets and he was under no obligation to inform the beneficiaries of the contents of the will as well as owing no duty to inform a legatee that there was a prospective legacy. The action was dismissed. [1997] STC 1425.

Chadwick & Hobart (Hobart's Executors) v HMRC

Valuation of semi-detached house

In October 2002 an individual (H) purchased a semi-detached house for £268,450. H died in December 2005. His executors valued the house at £250,000. HMRC considered that this valuation was too low, and issued a notice of determination valuing the house at £275,000. The executors appealed. The Upper Tribunal reviewed the evidence and allowed the appeal, observing that the property had a 'relatively unattractive appearance' which would 'have resulted in reduced interest from potential purchasers'. KB 1911, [1912] 1 KB 539; UT [2010] UKUT 82 (LC).

Challenge Corporation Ltd, New Zealand CIR v

Tax avoidance – distinction between avoidance and mitigation.

In a New Zealand case heard by the PC and relating to NZ legislation which has no counterpart in UK legislation, Lord Templeman discussed the distinction between 'tax avoidance' and 'tax mitigation'. Tax mitigation occurs where a taxpayer obtains a tax advantage by reducing his income or by incurring expenditure in circumstances in which the taxing statutes afford a reduction in tax liability. Tax avoidance takes place where a taxpayer seeks to avoid a liability to tax by entering into an arrangement without actually incurring the expenditure or loss which would permit the desired reduction in liability. PC [1986] STC 548; [1987] 2 WLR 24; [1987] AC 155.

Charkham v IRC

Valuation of a joint owners minority interest in undivided shares in property secured varying discounts of 15%, 20% and 22.5%-LPA 1925, s 30 and TLATA 1996, s 14.

A joint owner's interest in *investment* properties are routinely discounted by between 10%–15% but in this case the taxpayer's valuer chose to adopt an income approach in arguing that a minority owner could not obtain an order for sale. A multiple was calculated by the valuer derived from the investment market. In its considerations the Tribunal chose to exercise its discretion on the basis of the likelihood of a holder of the percentage obtaining an order for sale from the court. In this connection the holder as a purchaser would be aware of the uncertainty of a *LPA 1925, s 30* application and therefore discount the open market value. Also, there should be a single discount notwithstanding the difference in the IHT values of 24.04% to 6.04%. In applying this the Tribunal held for discounts of 15% on certain properties (Tottenham Court Road) and 20% and 22.5% on other properties (Alderney Street). *Charkham v IRC* Lands Tribunal 1997.

Chick v Commrs of Stamp Duties of New South Wales

Gifts with reservation – exclusion of donor from enjoyment.

See under *A-G v Seccombe* above. PC, [1958] AC 435; [1958] 2 All ER 623; [1958] 3 WLR 93.

Cholmondeley & Another v CIR

Protective trust – failure or determination.

By a deed of appointment dated 11 June 1979, the trustees of a settlement appointed seven farms to be held on protective trusts for M for life. By a deed of advancement dated the following day, three of the seven farms were advanced to M's eldest son, to be held in trust for him absolutely. The Revenue charged CTT on the basis that the deed of advancement ended M's protected life interest in the three farms. The trustees appealed, contending that the trust had been determined within *IHTA 1984, s 88(2)**, so that no CTT was chargeable. The Ch D dismissed the appeal, holding that *IHTA 1984, s 88(2)** only applied where there was a failure or determination of the protected life interest as such, rather than in relation to any particular assets. Since the protected life interest continued in relation to the other four farms, *IHTA 1984, s 88(2)** did not apply. Furthermore, the deed of appointment and the deed of advancement should be read together, so that the 'trust period' expired when the deed of advancement came into effect. Ch D 1986, CTTL 29; [1986] STC 384.

Civil Engineer v CIR

Taxpayer setting up trusts in Guernsey and Jersey – Guernsey trust was discretionary in form and the Jersey trust was established under Jersey law to pay income and capital for such charitable objects as trustees thought fit – Trustees of the Jersey trust resident outside the UK. Whether chargeable transfers for IHT purposes – Whether Jersey trust charitable under UK law – Whether Guernsey trust discretionary.

The taxpayer was born in England and he was English domicile. He worked in England as a consulting civil engineer in 1949. In 1960 he moved to Hong Kong and took up a permanent and pensionable post with the Hong Kong government. In 1967 he also became a partner in a London firm of consulting engineers. He and his wife were also shareholders of a Dutch company, HBV. He left Hong Kong in September 1989. Whilst in Hong Kong he rented accommodation but from 1960 to 1976 he owned property in the United Kingdom. Following changes in the Finance Act 1974 he closed his London office and ceased to own any property. His visits to the United Kingdom varied between zero and 36 days in a tax year between 1980 and 1988. He left Hong Kong in September 1989 severing his business and social connections with Hong Kong in November 1990. His P86 recorded that he had left for Jersey 31 January 1990 and returned to the UK permanently on 23 April 1990. On 22 March 1990 he created the S Foundation, a charity, under Jersey law (£75,000) and A Trust in Guernsey on 27 March 1990 (£375,000). All the Trustees were resident in Jersey and A Trust was discretionary naming only the Red Cross of Geneva as beneficiary but with the power to add other beneficiaries.

The Inland Revenue took the view that the transfers on 23 April 1990 were chargeable transfers and IHT was payable. The taxpayer appealed stating that he had acquired a domicile of choice of Hong Kong and that A Trust and S Foundation were not properly constituted or alternatively that A Trust was a life interest Trust and S Foundation a charity. Leaving Hong Kong with the intention of not returning revived the UK domicile of origin and therefore at the time of the transfers to the Trust and Foundation he was within the UK for IHT purposes. A Trust and S Foundation were valid trusts and A was a discretionary trust. S Foundation was not governed by the law of part of the UK and not subject to the jurisdiction of the UK courts. See *Camille and Henry Dreyfus Foundation Inc v CIR* [1955} All ER 97.

A letter of wishes signed by the taxpayer and his wife that was inconsistent with it being a interest in possession trust. The Trustees had wide discretionary powers and these included fixed monthly payments to the taxpayer and his wife. There was nothing to show that it was not a valid trust. The foundation is not subject to the jurisdiction of the UK courts and therefore not charitable for UK tax purposes. The appeal was dismissed. [2002] STC SCD 72.

Clark & Southern (Clark's Executors) v HMRC

Company's business consisted 'mainly of holding investments'.

A woman owned a number of shares in a company which owned more than 100 different properties from which it received rents, and also managed 141 dwellings owned by members of the family for which it charged 7.5% of the rent. The company had its own workforce for carrying out building work, maintenance and refurbishment of all properties. More than half the income was from the company's own properties. Her executors claimed business property relief. The Revenue rejected the claim on the basis that the shares were not 'relevant business property', because the company's business consisted mainly of 'making or holding investments', within *IHTA 1984, s 105(3)*. The executors appealed, contending that because the company carried out maintenance work on the properties itself, it should not be treated as falling within *s 105(3)*. The Special Commissioner rejected this contention and dismissed the executors' appeal, holding that 'the company's maintenance activity is not the separate provision of services; it is inherent in property ownership'. On the evidence, the company's business consisted 'mainly of holding investments'. [2005] STC SCD 823 Sp C 502.

Clay, CIR v

Valuation – definition of open market value.

Special circumstances existed which meant that one potential purchaser would have been prepared to give more for a house than what would otherwise have been the market price. Knowledge of local conditions and requirements, including the existence of such a purchaser, were held to be factors to be taken into account in establishing the open market value of the house. CA 1914, [1914–15] All ER 882; [1914] 3 KB 466.

Clore (deceased), Re (CIR v Stype Investments (Jersey) Ltd)

Jurisdiction – intermeddling – executor de son tort.

In May 1979 C, a wealthy man who had recently left the UK and was in poor health, transferred valuable land in England to S, a Jersey company, as his nominee. Two days later, S contracted to sell the land for more than £20 million. C died in July 1979. The sale was completed in September 1979, the sale proceeds being paid in Jersey. At the request of the Revenue, the QB granted injunctions ordering C's executors (none of whom were UK-resident) and S not to remove any of C's or

S's assets from English jurisdiction. Meanwhile, the Family Division granted letters of administration of the estate to the Official Solicitor. The CA upheld the injunctions and the letters of administration, holding that the cause of action arose in England, so that the English courts had jurisdiction. S's acts in procuring payment outside England constituted an intermeddling with C's English estate within *IHTA 1984, ss 199(4), 200(4)* and rendered S liable to pay CTT in England as an executor *de son tort*. The letters of administration had been properly granted to the Official Solicitor. Templeman LJ commented that the conduct of S and the executors 'may have been the product of a criminal conspiracy to defraud the Revenue'. CA 1982, CTTL 15; [1982] STC 625; [1982] 3 WLR 228; [1982] 3 All ER 419.

Clore (deceased) (No 2), Re (Official Solicitor v Clore and Others)

Domicile.

Sir Charles Clore died in London on 26 July 1979, an immensely wealthy man. The Revenue claim to CTT on his free estate outside the UK, and on the assets of a Jersey settlement he had made on 20 February 1979, depended on whether, as considered by the Revenue, he was domiciled in England when he made the settlement and at his death. Towards the end of his life he spent part of each year abroad for tax reasons, and had been provisionally accepted by the Revenue as not resident or ordinarily resident in the UK since February 1977. He had taken steps to be associated with Monaco, as an acceptable 'tax haven', but there was no convincing evidence that he had formed a settled intention to reside permanently in Monaco. The Ch D held that, on the evidence, his father was domiciled in England when Sir Charles was born. His domicile of origin was therefore England and he had not abandoned this domicile at his death. Ch D, [1984] STC 609.

Clore (deceased) (No 3), Re (CIR v Stype Trustees (Jersey) Ltd and Others)

Delivery of accounts.

Foreign trustees contended that their admitted liability to pay CTT did not mean that they were liable to deliver accounts of the trust property under *IHTA 1984, s 216**. The Ch D rejected the trustees' argument that there was a territorial limitation to the section and held that their liability to pay tax meant that they were liable to comply with the administrative machinery of delivering accounts which normally precedes payment of tax. On a separate point, a former trustee was required to deliver an account giving details of settlement property 'to the best of his knowledge and belief'. 'Knowledge' was held to extend to the contents of documents in his possession, custody or power, but no further. He was not required to act as an information gatherer. Ch D, [1985] STC 394; [1985] 1 WLR 1290; [1985] 2 All ER 819.

Coates v Arndale Properties Ltd

Avoidance schemes – transfers within a group of companies.

Three companies, members of the same group, entered into transactions, not disputed to be genuine, but admittedly to secure expected favourable tax consequences. One company, SPI, had acquired and developed at a cost of £5,313,822 property the market value of which had fallen by March 1973 to £3,100,000. On 30 March 1973 it assigned the property to a property dealing company, A, for a consideration of £3,090,000. On the same day, A assigned the property for £3,100,000 to an investment company, APT. No cash passed, the matter being dealt with by book entries. A then purported to make an election under *TCGA 1992, s 161(3)**; the consequence would be that, by virtue of *TCGA 1992, s 171(1)**, the transfer from SPI to A would give rise to no loss or gain for CGT purposes, and in computing A's Case I profits it could treat the cost of the property as its market value plus the CGT loss which would have accrued under *TCGA 1992, s 161(1)** if the election had not been made. The Revenue assessed A under Case I on the footing that the election was invalid, contending that A had not acquired the property as trading stock within the meaning of *TCGA 1992, s 173(1)**. The HL upheld the assessment, holding that A never did decide to acquire, and never did acquire, the lease as trading stock. The transfer of the lease from SPI to A and from A to APT was procured with the object of obtaining group relief without in fact changing the lease from a capital asset to a trading asset. A lent its name to the transaction but it did not trade and never had any intention of trading with the lease. In these circumstances it was unnecessary to consider the principles enunciated in *CIR v Burmah Oil Co* and *Furniss v Dawson* or the dividend-stripping cases which had been considered in the courts below. HL 1984, 59 TC 516; [1984] STC 637; [1984] 1 WLR 1328; [1985] 1 All ER 15.

Cohen, CIR v

Domicile.

A taxpayer born in England, but who had spent a great deal of his life in Australia and who had in the relevant years had no permanent residence in the UK, was held to have retained his English domicile of origin. KB 1937, 21 TC 301.

Cook & Daw (Watkins' Executors) v CIR

Property division – Interest in possession.

A married woman (W) died in December 1999, having owned a house in Cardiff, which was divided into two flats. She had let the ground floor flat to tenants, and had lived in the first floor flat with her husband. By her will, she gave the house to trustees (her children by a previous marriage), but gave her husband the right to live in it 'and use it as his principal place of residence'. However, following her death, her husband stayed with his daughter for just over three weeks, before being admitted to hospital, where he died two months later. The Revenue issued a notice of determination to W's executors, ruling that her husband had not acquired an interest in possession in the house. They appealed. The Special Commissioner reviewed the evidence in detail and allowed the appeal in part, holding that the husband had acquired an interest in possession in the first floor flat but not in the ground-floor flat. [2002] STC SCD 318 Sp C 319.

Courten v United Kingdom

IHTA 1984, s 18 – whether any breach of European Convention on Human Rights.

In 1984 two homosexuals (C and S) purchased a property as joint tenants. They lived there until S died in January 2005. HMRC issued a determination that IHT was chargeable on S's share of the property. C applied to the ECHR for a ruling that the provisions of IHTA 1984, s 18 (prior to their amendment by the Tax and Civil Partnership Regulations 2005) were a breach of Article 14 of the European Convention on Human Rights. The ECHR rejected the application, holding that 'notwithstanding social changes, marriage remains an institution that is widely accepted as conferring a particular status on those who enter it' and that 'the promotion of marriage, by way of limited benefits for surviving spouses, cannot be said to exceed the margin of appreciation afforded to the respondent Government'.ECHR Case 4479/06; [2008] ECHR 1546.

Craven v White

Avoidance schemes – the Ramsay principle.

Three members of a family owned all the shares in a UK company (Q), which owned a number of shops. From 1973 they conducted negotiations with various other companies with a view to selling Q or merging it with a similar business. In July 1976, at a time when they were negotiating with two unconnected companies, they exchanged their shares for shares in an Isle of Man company (M). Nineteen days later M sold the shares in Q to one of the two companies with which negotiations had been in progress at the time of the share exchange. The sale proceeds were paid by M to the shareholders over a period of five years. The Revenue issued CGT assessments for 1976–77 on the basis that, applying the *Ramsay* principle, the disposal of the shares to M and their subsequent sale by M should be treated as a single composite transaction and that the transfer of the shares to M was a fiscal nullity. The Special Commissioners reduced the assessments, holding that the transfer could not be treated as a fiscal nullity but that the shareholders were assessable on the amounts they had received from M at the time of receipt. The Revenue's appeals against this decision were dismissed by the Ch D, the CA, and (by a 3–2 majority) the HL. In giving the leading judgment for the majority, Lord Oliver indicated the limitations of the principle adopted in *CIR v Ramsay*, as defined by Lord Brightman in *Furniss v Dawson*. The principle in question—that the Commissioners are not bound to consider individually each step in a composite transaction intended to be carried through as a whole—applied only where there was a 'pre-ordained series of transactions' or 'one single composite transaction' and where steps were inserted which had no commercial purpose apart from the avoidance of a liability to tax. Although the decision in *Furniss v Dawson* extended the *Ramsay* principle, by applying it to a linear transaction as opposed to a circular self-cancelling one, it did no more than apply that principle to different events. It did not lay down any proposition that a transaction entered into with the motive of minimising tax was to be ignored or struck down. In the *Ramsay* case, Lord Wilberforce had emphasised the continuing validity and application of the principle enunciated by Lord Tomlin in *Duke of Westminster v CIR* Lord Fraser had echoed this view, as had Lord Bridge in *Furniss v Dawson*. (The speech of Lord Roskill in that case, which implied the contrary, did not appear to represent the view of the majority.) The criteria by reference to which the *Ramsay* principle applied were not logically capable of expansion so as to apply to any similar case except one in which, when the intermediate transaction or transactions took place, the end result which in fact occurred was so certain of fulfilment that it was intellectually and practically possible to conclude that there had indeed taken place one single and indivisible process. For the principle to apply, the intermediate steps had to serve no purpose other than that of saving tax; all stages of the composite transaction had to be pre-ordained with a degree of certainty with the taxpayer having control over the end result at the time when the intermediate steps were taken; and there should be no interruption between the intermediate transaction and the disposal to the ultimate purchaser. In this case, however, the transactions that the Crown sought to reconstruct into a single direct disposal were not contemporaneous. Nor were they pre-ordained since, at the time of the share exchange, it was not certain what the ultimate destination of the property would be. Lord Jauncey considered that 'a step in a linear transaction which has no business purpose apart from the avoidance or deferment of tax liability will be treated as forming part of a pre-ordained series of transactions or of a composite transaction if it was taken at a time when negotiations or arrangements for the carrying through as a continuous process of a subsequent transaction which actually takes place had reached a stage when there was no real likelihood that such subsequent transaction would not take place and if thereafter such negotiations or arrangements were carried through to completion without genuine interruption'. Lord Oliver concurred with this definition. HL 1988, 62 TC 1; [1988] STC 476; [1988] 3 WLR 423; [1988] 3 All ER 495.

Crawford Settlement Trustees v HMRC

Assignation of interest in trust fund – whether IHTA 1984, s 71(3) applicable.

An individual (B) was born in 1969. He was due to become entitled to an interest in a trust fund, created under a 1954 settlement, on reaching the age of 21. In 1989, when he was 19 years old, he assigned the whole of his prospective interest to the trustees of a discretionary trust in which there was no interest in possession. The Revenue issued a notice of determination on the basis that the assignation of B's interest gave rise to a charge to IHT under *IHTA 1984, s 71(3)*. The trustees of the 1954 settlement appealed. The Special Commissioner allowed the appeal, holding that *IHTA 1984, s 71(3)* did not apply because 'immediately after the assignation, the trust comprised exactly the same property as immediately before the assignation; and viewing matters as at the date the assignation took effect, one or more persons "will" on or before attaining the age of 21 become beneficially entitled to an interest in possession in it. The conditions set forth in *s 71(1)* were met immediately after the assignation took effect in the same way they were met immediately before the assignation took effect. It cannot therefore be said that settled property ceased to be property to which *s 71* applied by virtue of the effect of the assignation. It follows that the assignation did not give rise to a charge to tax under *s 71(3)*.' [2005] STC SCD 457 Sp C 473.

Crossman and Others, CIR v

Valuation – value of unquoted shares subject to restrictions on transfers.

The open market value of unquoted shares had to be established for ED purposes. The articles of association imposed restrictions on transfer including a right of pre-emption in favour of existing shareholders. The value was not limited to that fixed by the pre-emption clause, but was estimated at the price obtainable in a hypothetical open market on the terms that the purchaser was registered as holder of the shares and held them subject to the same restrictions as his predecessor. HL 1936, 15 ATC 94; [1936] 1 All ER 762; [1937] AC 26.

Curnock (Curnock's Personal Representatives) v CIR

Cheque clearance after date of death but gift made before treated as part of deceased's estate.

A pensioner (P) had granted a power of attorney to his father (C). On 21 December 2001 C issued a cheque for £6,000 on behalf of P. On 22 December 2001 P died. The cheque was not cleared until 27 December. The Revenue issued a Notice of Determination on the basis that the £6,000 was part of P's estate. C (who was P's personal representative) appealed, contending that the £6,000 did not form part of P's estate, since he had disposed of the money on the day before he died. The Special Commissioner rejected this contention and dismissed C's appeal. Applying *dicta* of Pollock MR in *Re Swinburne*, CA [1926] Ch 38, a cheque was 'nothing more than an order to obtain a certain sum of money . . . and if the order is not acted upon in the lifetime of the person who gives it, it is worth nothing'. Accordingly, the £6,000 was part of P's estate when he died. [2003] STC SCD 283 Sp C 365.

Daffodil (Daffodil's Administrators) v CIR

Right under Administration of Estates Act 1925 – whether 'property' within IHTA 1984, s 272.

A married couple owned a bungalow as tenants in common. In 1994 the husband died intestate. His widow was entitled to apply for a grant of letters of administration of his estate, but did not do so, and continued to live in the bungalow. She died in 2000, leaving the couple's son (D) as administrator of her estate. He was advised by his solicitor that, in order to sell the bungalow, he would need letters of administration of his father's estate, which he duly obtained. The Revenue issued a notice of administration on the basis that, when D's mother died, the bungalow which she occupied formed part of her estate. D appealed, contending that because his mother had not obtained letters of administration of her husband's estate, his estate (including his 50% share of the bungalow) did not form part of her estate. The

Special Commissioner rejected this contention and dismissed D's appeal. Under *Administration of Estates Act 1925*, D's mother had had the right to require the whole of her husband's estate to be transferred to her. The effect of *IHTA 1984, s 272* was that this right formed part of her estate. [2002] STC SCD 224 Sp C 311.

Delamere's Settlement Trusts, Re (Kenny and Others v Cunningham-Reid and Others)

Interest in possession – effect of Trustee Act 1925, s 31.

An appointment in 1980 by trustees of a settlement which partly revoked the trusts of a 1971 appointment of income was expressed to have effect only if no interest in possession already subsisted in the relevant property for CTT purposes. The question before the CA was to what extent the *Trustee Act 1925, s 31* applied to the 1971 appointment. If it applied, a minor beneficiary's share of the accumulated income would fall back into the general capital of the trust in the event of his death before attaining 18 or marrying, and his interest in the accumulations would although vested, be defeasible. If *s 31(2)* did not apply, the accumulated income vested in the minor beneficiary as it accrued and was held by the trustees for him indefeasibly. The CA held that *s 31(2)* did not apply. The use of the word 'absolutely' and the fact that no time limit was placed on the duration of the income interests appointed, indicated the intention that the interests should not be defeasible in any circumstances during the subsistence of the 1971 appointment. CA 1983, [1984] 1 WLR 813; [1984] 1 All ER 584.

Dextra Accessories Ltd and others v MacDonald

Payments to employee benefit trust – whether FA 1989, s 43(11) applicable.

Six associated companies claimed deductions for payments which they made to an employee benefit trust. The Inland Revenue rejected the claims, considering that the payments were 'potential emoluments' within *FA 1989, s 43(11)* so that no deduction was allowable until the relevant employees were taxed on the fund as an emolument. The companies appealed, contending that the payments should not be treated as 'potential emoluments' within *s 43(11)*. The House of Lords unanimously rejected this contention and dismissed the companies' appeals. Lord Hoffmann held that 'in the ordinary use of language, the whole of the funds were potential emoluments. They could be used to pay emoluments.' He observed that this was 'the result of an arrangement into which the taxpayers have chosen to enter. Any untoward consequences can be avoided by segregating the funds held on trust to pay emoluments from funds held to benefit employees in other ways.' See also now *FA 2003, Sch 24*. This was intended to provide, with effect from 27 November 2002, that any contributions into an employee benefit trust will only attract corporation tax relief for the sponsoring company when payments subject to income tax and NICs have been made to the underlying employees. See Inland Revenue Budget Notice BN27, reproduced at SWTI 2003, pp 737–738. HL [2005] UKHL 47.

Dixon v CIR

Garden and orchard – whether 'agricultural property' for the purposes of Agricultural Property Relief under IHTA 1984, ss 115(2), 117(a).

A woman (B) died in 1998, owning 60% interest in a property consisting of a cottage, garden and orchard, with a total area of 0.6 acres. B had sometimes allowed a neighbouring farmer to graze sheep on the land, and had sometimes sold damsons from the orchard. The Inland Revenue issued a notice of determination charging IHT. B's executor appealed, contending that the property qualified for agricultural property relief. The Special Commissioner rejected this contention and dismissed the appeal, finding on the evidence that the property was not 'agricultural land or pasture' but was occupied as a private residence. [2002] STC SCD 53 Sp C 297.

Dreyfus (Camille & Henry) Foundation Inc v CIR

Charities – overseas trusts.

A foundation for the advancement of chemistry, etc. incorporated in the USA claimed exemption under *ICTA 1988, s 505(1)(c)** in respect of royalties. The claim was refused. The relief is limited to bodies and trusts subject to the jurisdiction of the courts of the UK. (The question of whether the foundation was established for charitable purposes was not considered.) HL 1955, 36 TC 126; [1956] AC 39; [1955] 3 All ER 97.

Dunstan v Young Austen Young Ltd

Avoidance schemes – whether issue of new shares not acquired at arm's length constituted a capital reorganisation.

The taxpayer company (Y) carried on business as a mechanical engineering contractor. In 1977 it acquired for £16,100 the 1,000 issued £1 shares of a company (J) in the same line of business. Shortly afterwards it joined a large group; one of the shares in J was registered in the name of a fellow-subsidiary (T), the remainder being registered in its own name. J was not trading profitably. By March 1979 it had incurred debts of £200,911 to other companies in the group, mainly to Y, and it was decided to sell it. An arm's length purchaser was found, and J issued a further 200,000 £1 shares on 12 June 1979. These were allotted to Y for £200,000 cash, which was promptly repaid to Y to clear its indebtedness. On 29 June an agreement was completed between Y, T and the purchaser for the sale of the 201,000 shares for £38,000. The appeal was against an assessment for the year to September 1979. The profits were agreed at nil and the substantive issue was whether Y had incurred a capital loss on its disposal of the shares in J and, if so, of what amount. It was common ground that Y acquired the additional 200,000 shares 'otherwise than by a bargain made at arm's length' and by virtue of *CGTA 1979, s 19(3)** the consideration for them should be taken to be their market value, which the Special Commissioner found to be nil 'or so near to it as to make no matter'. However, Y contended that the issue of the further 200,000 shares constituted a reorganisation of J's capital within *TCGA 1992, ss 126, 128**, with the consequence that the new shares would not be treated as a separate acquisition and that the £200,000 would be treated as having been given for the original 1,000 shares, making their cost £216,100 and the loss £178,100. This contention was upheld by the CA, reversing the decision of the Ch D and restoring that of the Special Commissioner. Properly construed, the phrase 'reorganisation of a company's share capital' in *TCGA 1992, s 126** included an increase in a company's share capital and the allotment of the new shares to its parent company for cash. (*Note. CGTA 1979, s 19(3)* was repealed by *FA 1981*. See now *TCGA 1992, s 128(2)* as regards reorganisations on or after 10 March 1981.) CA 1988, 61 TC 448; [1989] STC 69.

DWC Piercy's Executors v HMRC

IHTA 1984, s 105(3) – business of 'making or holding investments'.

A property development company (T) owned some land in Islington, on which it had erected some workshops which it let out. T's major shareholder died in 1999. His executors claimed business property relief. HMRC rejected the claim on the grounds that because T received significant rental income, its business consisted mainly of 'making or holding investments', within *IHTA 1984, s 105(3)*. The executors appealed, contending that it still wished to develop the land in Islington for residential purposes but had been unable to do so because of uncertainty about proposals for a new railway line. The Special Commissioner accepted this evidence and allowed the appeal, finding that the company continued to hold its land as trading stock, and holding that it was not an 'investment company' for the purposes of *IHTA 1984, s 105*. The Commissioner also held that 'the only type of land-dealing company whose shares fail to qualify for the relief is . . . some sort of dealing or speculative trader that does not actively develop or actually build on land'. [2008] STC SCD 858 Sp C 687.

Edwards v Bairstow & Harrison

Appeals – distinction between fact and law.

Two individuals were assessed under Case I on the profits from the sale in five lots of cotton spinning plant purchased for resale. The General Commissioners allowed their appeals, holding that there was no trade or adventure in the nature of trade. The HL allowed the Revenue's appeal and restored the assessments, holding that the only reasonable conclusion on the evidence before the Commissioners was that there had been an adventure in the nature of trade. (A leading case establishing the principle that the courts will not disturb a Commissioners' conclusion on a question of fact if it was one to which they were entitled to come, notwithstanding that the court or another body of Commissioners might have reached a different conclusion on the same evidence. This was approved and restated by Lord Brightman in *Furniss v Dawson*, to the effect that 'an appellate court . . . can and should interfere with an inference of fact drawn by the fact-finding tribunal which cannot be justified by the primary facts'. But 'if the primary facts justify alternative inferences of fact' the court should not 'substitute its own preferred inference for the inference drawn by the fact-finding tribunal'.) HL 1955, 36 TC 207; [1956] AC 14; [1955] 3 All ER 48.

Eilbeck v Rawling

Avoidance schemes – the Ramsay principle.

A taxpayer made a chargeable gain of £355,094 in 1974–75 as to which there was no dispute. Later in the same year he entered into a chain of transactions with the object of creating a commensurate allowable loss, at a cost to him of only £370 apart from the fees, etc. paid for the scheme, which was an 'off the peg' avoidance device obtained from a Jersey company. The central feature of the scheme involved his acquiring reversionary interests in two trust funds, one held by Jersey trustees and the other by Gibraltar trustees. Under a special power of appointment, the Gibraltar trustees advanced £315,000 to the Jersey trustees to be held on the trusts of the Jersey settlement. The taxpayer then sold both reversionary interests, making a gain on the sale of his interest under the Jersey settlement (claimed to be exempt under *TCGA 1992, s 76(1)**) and a matching loss of £312,470 on the sale of his interest under the Gibraltar settlement (claimed as an allowable loss). The CA refused the claim on the ground, *inter alia*, that the exercise of the power of appointment did not take the £315,000 outside the Gibraltar settlement; hence the sale of his reversionary interest in the £315,000 was a part sale of his interest under the Gibraltar settlement. The taxpayer appealed to the HL. The appeal was considered with *W T Ramsay Ltd*, and dismissed for the same general reason that, on the facts, the scheme was to be looked at as a composite transaction under which there was neither gain nor loss apart from the £370. Furthermore, the HL upheld the CA decision that the sale of the reversionary interest in the £315,000 was a sale of part of the taxpayer's reversionary interest in the Gibraltar settlement. (*Note*. The device would also now be caught by the value shifting provisions of *TCGA 1992, s 30*.) HL 1981, 54 TC 101; [1981] STC 174; [1981] 2 WLR 449; [1981] 1 All ER 865.

Essex & another (executors of Somerset deceased) v CIR

Relevant date for the purposes of FA 1986, s 102(5).

In 1988 a married woman (S) settled a 95% interest in a house on trust, to pay the income to her husband for life, and after his death to hold the capital and income on discretionary trusts for a class of beneficiaries that included herself and her children.

S's husband died in 1992 and she died in 1998. The Inland Revenue issued a notice of determination on the basis that, at her death, the property held by the settlement fell to be treated as her property by reason of *FA 1986, s 102*. Her executors appealed, contending that the effect of *FA 1986, s 102(5)* was that no IHT was due, since the settlement had taken advantage of the exemption under *IHTA 1984, s 18* for transfers between spouses. The Special Commissioners accepted this contention and allowed the appeal, holding that the creation of the settlement involved a single gift to S's husband. This was an exempt transfer between spouses to which *s 102(5)* applied. For the purposes of *s 102(5)*, the relevant date was the date of the settlement, rather than the date of S's death. [2002] STC SCD 39 Sp C 296.

Eversden and Another, CIR v

Relevant date for the purposes of FA 1986, s 102(5).

In 1988 a married woman (S) settled a 95% interest in a house on trust, to pay the income to her husband for life, and after his death to hold the capital and income on discretionary trusts for a class of beneficiaries which included herself and her children. S's husband died in 1992 and she died in 1998. The Revenue issued a notice of determination on the basis that, at her death, the property held by the settlement fell to be treated as her property by virtue of *FA 1986, s 102*. Her executors appealed, contending that the effect of *FA 1986, s 102(5)* was that no IHT was due, since the settlement had taken advantage of the exemption under *IHTA 1984, s 18* for transfers between spouses. The Special Commissioner accepted this contention and allowed the appeal, holding that, for the purposes of *FA 1986, s 102(5)*, the relevant date was the date of the settlement, rather than the date of S's death. The Ch D and CA upheld this decision. Carnwath LJ held that 'the "disposal of the property by way of gift" was the transfer of the property in 1988'. This was accepted as an exempt transfer under *IHTA 1984, s 18*. It was, therefore, outside the scope of *FA 1986, s 102*. He also observed that the effect of *IHTA 1984, s 49* was that 'in the present case, the estate of the settlor's husband is taxed on the property, but that of the settlor is not. There is nothing in *s 102* to modify that . . . If that is of concern to the Revenue, they must look for correction to Parliament, not to the Courts.' (*aka Essex & Essex (Somerset's Executors) v CIR*), CA [2003] STC 822; [2003] EWCA Civ 668. (*Note*. On 20 June 2003 the Government tabled an amendment to the 2003 Finance Bill (resulting in *FA 2003, s 185*) to amend *FA 1986, s 102* to reverse the effect of this decision. See the Inland Revenue Press Release issued on 20 June 2003.)

Farmer and another (Executors of Farmer deceased) v CIR

Relevant business property – deceased carrying on business of farming and letting some buildings and land on the farm – whether BPR excluded as consisting mainly of making or holding investments.

An individual (F), who owned a farm comprising 449 acres, died in 1997. Several of the properties at the farm were surplus to the requirements of the farm, and he had let these to tenants. The farm had an agreed probate value of £3,500,000. It was accepted that £2,250,000 of this related to the farmhouse, farm buildings and farmland, and qualified for 100% agricultural property relief. The balance of £1,250,000 related to the properties that had been let. F's executors claimed business property relief on the basis that there was a single business which qualified for relief (accepting that, by virtue of *IHTA 1984, s 114(1)*, the business property relief was restricted to the £1,250,000 which did not qualify for agricultural property relief). The Revenue rejected the claim and issued a notice of determination that the farm business consisted mainly of making or holding investments, within *IHTA 1984, s 105(3)*, and therefore was not 'relevant business property'. The executors appealed, accepting that the letting of property was 'making or holding investments' but contending that F's business had consisted mainly of farming. The Special Commissioner accepted this contention and allowed the appeal, holding on the evidence that 'the overall context of the business, the capital employed, the time spent by the employees and consultants, and the levels of turnover, all support the conclusion that the business consisted mainly of farming'. The fact that the lettings were more profitable than the rest of the business was not conclusive. See [1999] STC SCD 321 Sp C 216.

Faulkner (Adams' Trustee) v CIR

Licence to occupy property given to third party – whether interest in possession within IHTA 1984, s 49(1) – present right to present enjoyment of the property even though not occupied by the deceased.

In 1980 a widower (R), with no children, made a will allowing a friend (H) and his wife 'or the survivor of them for the time being still living' to live in his house 'and have the use of the furniture as long as he she or they so wish'. R died in 1981 and the couple duly moved into the house. H died in 1998 (having outlived his wife) and the house was sold later that year. The Revenue issued a notice of determination to R's surviving trustee, on the basis that H's right of occupation had been an interest in possession in settled property, within *IHTA 1984, s 49(1)*. The trustee appealed, contending firstly that R's will had given H a licence to use the house but had not conferred an interest in possession, and alternatively that if H had had an interest in possession, he should be deemed to have shared it with the three residuary beneficiaries under R's will. The Special Commissioner rejected these contentions and dismissed the appeal, holding that H had had a 'present right to the present enjoyment of the house'. This was an interest in possession in the whole of the house. [2001] STC SCD 112 Sp C 278.

Faye v CIR

Domicile.

An Australian woman, after 30 years in Australia, married a Frenchman, who acquired a domicile of choice in England. The marriage was dissolved and she remained in England and was held to be domiciled in the UK for the relevant years. Ch D 1961, 40 TC 103.

Fetherstonhaugh & Others v CIR

Business property relief – death of life tenant using settled property for business purposes.

In 1977 the life tenant of settled land, who had used that land in his farming and forestry business, died. The trustees claimed that the value of the settled land qualified for business property relief. The Revenue rejected the claim but the CA allowed the trustees' appeal. Although the land itself was not relevant business property, the life interest in the land was an asset used in the business. For CTT purposes the asset had to be valued as if the deceased was beneficially entitled to the land itself. 50% business property relief was therefore due. (*Note.* The relief would now be 100%—see *IHTA 1984, s 104* as amended by *F(No 2)A 1992, 13 Sch 1.*) CA 1984, CTTL 21; [1984] STC 261; [1984] 3 WLR 212.

Fielden v CIR

Domicile.

A taxpayer born in England, but who had spent part of his life in the USA and married a US citizen, was held to be domiciled in the UK in the relevant years. (He had obtained a domicile of choice in the USA at one time, but had since lost it.) Ch D 1965, 42 TC 501.

Fitzwilliam (Countess) & Others v CIR

Discretionary trust – mutual transfers of value – whether Ramsay principle applicable.

Trustees, appointed under a will, had discretion to appoint the residue among a class of beneficiaries during a period of 23 months from the testator's death. The main beneficiaries were the testator's widow (F), who was aged 81 and in poor health, and her daughter (H). There was a potentially heavy liability to CTT and the trustees undertook a number of transactions to mitigate the tax liability. On 20 December 1979, they declared that £4m should be held in trust as to both capital and income for F absolutely. On 9 January 1980 F made a gift to H of £2m net of CTT. On 14 January 1980 the trustees appointed £3.8m to be held on trust, subject to the income being paid to F until 15 February 1980 or her death, one half for H absolutely (the vested half) and the other half for a contingent interest. On 31 January 1980 F assigned to H, for £2m, her beneficial interest in the income of the contingent half. On 5 February 1980 H settled £1,000 on trust to pay the income to F until 15 March 1980 or her death, whichever was the earlier, and subject thereto in trust absolutely for herself. On 7 February 1980 H assigned to the trustees of her settlement her beneficial interest in the vested half of the trust established on 14 January 1980, to be accrued to the £1,000 as one fund. The Revenue served a notice of determination on the trustees, charging CTT on the basis that £4m and £3.8m had been appointed absolutely to F and H respectively. The trustees appealed, contending that the £4m was within what is now *IHTA 1984, s 144** and that the gift of £2m was exempt under *FA 1976, ss 86, 87*. The Ch D allowed the trustees' appeals and the HL upheld this decision (Lord Templeman dissenting). The Revenue's contention that the steps amounted to a single composite transaction within the *Ramsay* principle and that the original testator, rather than H, should be deemed to be the settlor of the settlement of the vested half made on 5 February were rejected. The steps taken in January and February 1980 could not be treated as a 'single and indivisible whole in which one or more of the steps was simply an element without independent effect'. The fact that they formed part of a 'pre-planned tax avoidance scheme' was not sufficient in itself 'to negative the application of an exemption from liability to tax which the series of transactions (was) intended to create', unless the series was 'capable of being construed in a manner inconsistent with the application of the exemption'. The series of transactions here could not be construed in such a way. *Craven v White* applied; *Furniss v Dawson* distinguished. With regard to the Revenue's alternative contention, the fact that the settled funds were historically derived from the original testator did not mean that he could reasonably be regarded as having provided property for the settlement made on 5 February 1980. HL, [1993] STC 502; 1 WLR 1189; [1993] 3 All ER 184.

Floor v Davis

Arrangements to reduce liability – interpretation of TCGA 1992, s 29(2) – exercise of control over shares.

It had been arranged that, subject to contract, the share capital of a company (IDM) would be sold (at a substantial profit to the shareholders) to another company (KDI). F and his two sons-in-law, who together controlled IDM, carried out a scheme under which the following transactions took place shortly after each other. They transferred their IDM shares to FNW, a company set up for the purpose, for preferred shares in FNW; FNW sold the IDM shares to KDI for cash; a Cayman Islands company, D, acquired a relatively insignificant holding of preferred shares in FNW; following a rights issue open to all preferred shareholders but accepted only by D, D became the sole ordinary shareholder in FNW; FNW went into liquidation and because of the differing rights attached to the two classes of shares, D, as the ordinary shareholder, became entitled to six-sevenths of the assets of FNW. The upshot was that the greater part of the proceeds of sale of the IDM shares reached D. The CA held (Eveleigh LJ dissenting), that F had disposed of his IDM shares to FNW (and not, as contended by the Revenue, to KDI) with the consequence that under *TCGA 1992, s 135** his FNW shares were treated as the IDM shares he originally held. However, the CA unanimously held that value had passed out of the FNW shares within the meaning of *TCGA 1992, s 29(2)** and F was assessable accordingly, on the grounds that (i) 'person' in *TCGA 1992, s 29(2)** includes the plural by virtue of *Interpretation Act 1889, s 1(1)(b)* and the definition of 'control' (see *TCGA 1992, s 288(1)**) and (ii) F and his sons-in-law had exercised their control, notwithstanding that two of them had not voted on the resolution to wind up FNW. The HL rejected F's appeal on this point. (The Revenue's contention that F had disposed of the shares to KDI was therefore not argued in the HL. See now as to this *Furniss v Dawson*, in which the dissenting judgment of Eveleigh LJ, who upheld the Revenue's contention that the shares had been disposed of to KDI, was approved.) (*Notes.* (1) The relevant transactions took place in 1969. See now for value-shifting transactions after 13 March 1989, *TCGA 1992, ss 30–34*. (2) The *Interpretation Act 1889* has since been repealed. See now *Interpretation Act 1978, s 6(c)*.) HL 1979, 52 TC 609; [1979] STC 379; [1979] 2 WLR 830; [1979] 2 All ER 677.

Fox (Lady), Gray (Executor of) v CIR

Valuation of related property.

Duke of Buccleuch was applied in a case where the freeholder of a large estate had, at the time of her death, held a 92.5% interest in a partnership which farmed the land. The Revenue issued a Notice of Determination claiming IHT on the combined value of the deceased's freehold reversion and her interest in the partnership. The CA upheld the Notice of Determination (reversing the decision of the Lands Tribunal). Hoffman LJ held that the hypothetical sale had to be supposed to have taken the course which would get the largest price provided that it did not entail 'undue expenditure of time and effort'. The freehold reversion and the partnership should be valued as one unit of property. CA [1994] STC 360.

Frankland v CIR

Distribution from property settled by will – whether IHTA 1984, s 144 applicable.

A married woman died on 26 September 1987, leaving property on discretionary trusts for the benefit of her husband and children. On 22 December 1987 the property was transferred to a trust, the income from which was to be paid to the deceased's husband for the duration of his life. The object of the transfer was to secure the benefit of the spouse exemption of *IHTA 1984, s 18(1)* in respect of the charge to tax otherwise payable in respect of the death. The Revenue issued a notice of determination on the basis that the spouse exemption did not apply since the transfer had not been made by the deceased. The trustee appealed, contending that the effect of *IHTA 1984, s 144* was that the husband's interest in possession should be treated as having arisen under the deceased's will. The Ch D rejected this contention and dismissed the appeal, holding that *IHTA 1984, s 144* did not apply. The effect of *IHTA 1984, s 65(4)* was that, since the December transfer had taken place within three months of the death, that transfer itself was not an event giving rise to a charge to tax. *IHTA 1984, s 144* only applied where there was an event on which tax would otherwise be chargeable. The wording of *IHTA 1984, s 144* was unambiguous. Accordingly the transfer could not be treated as having been made by the deceased, and the spouse exemption did not apply. The Court of Appeal reaffirmed the decision. CA [1997] STC 1450. See now draft legislation published in December 2014 to appear in the Finance Bill 2015 in order to correct the anomalous result of this decision, so that the spouse exemption will apply in such circumstances where the death was on or after 10 December 2014.

Friends' Provident Life Office v British Railways Board

Lease – variation of lease.

A variation of a lease may, depending upon the facts, constitute a deemed surrender and re-grant. [1996] 1 All ER 336.

Fryer, DM & Others (Personal Representatives of Ms P Arnold) v HMRC

Deferment of pension benefits – whether IHTA 1984, s 10 applicable.

A woman was born in 1942. In 1995 she set up a discretionary trust. Later that year she took out a pension plan. It was agreed that if she died before taking her retirement benefits, then the value of those benefits would pass to her discretionary trust. In 2002, shortly before her 60th birthday, she was diagnosed as suffering with terminal cancer. She died in 2003 without having taken the available benefits. HMRC issued a determination charging IHT on the basis that, by failing to take her retirement benefits when she reached the age of 60 in 2002, she had made a disposition of value for the purposes of *IHTA 1984, s 3(3)*. Her personal representatives appealed, contending firstly that she should not be treated as having made any such disposition, and alternatively that if she had made such a disposition, it was not 'intended to confer a gratuitous benefit', so that *IHTA 1984, s 10(3)* applied. The First-Tier Tribunal rejected these contentions and dismissed the appeal in principle, subject to a reduction in HMRC's valuation of the disposition. Clark J upheld HMRC's contention that 'the concept of a "disposition" was widened by *s 3(3)* to include passive dispositions, meaning omissions which resulted in the enhancement of another person's estate or of settled property in which no interest in possession subsisted'. He rejected HMRC's contention that the deemed disposition should be treated as having taken place on her 60th birthday (which was her normal retirement date under her pension policy), holding that the disposition should be treated as having taken place on the date of her death. Her omission to exercise her rights had increased the value of the settled property, and the evidence showed that this had been intentional. Accordingly *IHTA 1984, s 10* did not apply. With regard to the appropriate valuation, Clark J reviewed the evidence in detail and found that the total benefits amounted to £119,800. He directed that this should be discounted by 25%, resulting in a chargeable consideration of £89,950. FTT [2010] UKFTT 87 (TC), TC00398.

(Notes. (1) The determinations had been made in the name of the Commissioners of Her Majesty's Revenue & Customs. Clark J observed that the Commissioners' statutory title was 'the Commissioners *for* Her Majesty's Revenue & Customs' (see *CRCA 2005, s 1*), and commented that 'to avoid any possible suggestion that Notices of Determination (or any other documents issued by HMRC) are invalid, it is strongly desirable for the correct title to be used'. (2) The appellants were represented by an 'independent financial adviser', rather than by a lawyer. Clark J observed that it would have been better for the appellants 'to be represented by counsel, or by someone else equally experienced in representing parties before the Tribunal'.)

Fuller v Evans and Others

Accumulation and maintenance settlement – settlor divorced and beneficiaries were the children of the settlor – whether Trustees could exercise their discretion in the payment of school fees thereby relieving the settlor of financial responsibility for same.

A settlement that created an accumulation and maintenance trust for the benefit of the present and future children of the settlor. On the divorce between the settlor and his wife, a consent order was made which included provision for the settlor to make periodical payments to the mother of his children for general maintenance and for school fees inclusive of reasonable extras. The Clause 12 of the trust deed provided, inter alia, that no part of the capital or income of the trust fund be applied either directly or indirectly for the benefit of the settlor. The question raised was whether clause 12 precluded the trustees from exercising the power where the interests of the beneficiaries required its exercise if such exercise might incidentally benefit the settlor, and in particular might relieve the settlor from the actual or perceived need because of some legal or moral obligation, in this case an obligation arising under the consent order. Despite the breadth of the clause 12 Justice Lightman in the Chancery Division found it very difficult to read the settlement as paralysing the trustees in this situation. Clause 12 did little if anything more than vigorously reaffirm the duty of the trustees to have regard exclusively to the best interests of the beneficiaries and ignore those of the settlor. Therefore clause 12 did not preclude the trustees from exercising the power conferred upon them by reason of any incidental and unintended conferment of relief on the settlor.

Furniss v Dawson (and related appeals)

Avoidance schemes – the Ramsay principle.

The shareholders in two family companies wished to dispose of their shares, and found an unconnected company (W) willing to acquire the shares at an agreed price. Before disposing of the shares, they exchanged them for shares in a Manx company which in turn sold them to W. The Revenue issued assessments on the basis that the shares should be treated as having been disposed of directly to W, since the interposition of the Manx company had been designed solely to take advantage of the law then in force with regard to company reconstructions and amalgamations. The HL unanimously upheld the assessments (reversing the decision of the CA). Applying *WT Ramsay Ltd*, the transactions should be regarded as a single composite transaction. Lord Bridge of Harwich observed that 'the distinction between form and substance . . . can usefully be drawn in determining the tax consequences of composite transactions'. Lord Brightman held that the *Ramsay* principle applied in cases where there was a 'pre-ordained series of transactions; or . . . one single composite transaction' and steps were 'inserted which have no commercial (business) purpose apart from the avoidance of a liability to tax—not "no business effect". If these two ingredients exist, the inserted steps are to be disregarded for fiscal purposes. The court must look at the end result.' *Furniss v Dawson* HL 1984, 55 TC 324; [1984] STC 153; [1984] 2 WLR 226; [1984] 1 All ER 530. (Notes. (1) See also *TCGA 1992, s 137*. (2) Although the decision was unanimous, there was implicit disagreement as to the continuing validity of the Duke of Westminster principle. Lords Bridge and Scarman indicated that the principle still applied, but Lord Roskill specifically refrained from endorsing the Westminster decision. For subsequent developments, see the judgment of Lord Templeman in *Ensign Tankers (Leasing) Ltd v Stokes*, and that of Lord Keith in *Countess Fitzwilliam v CIR*.)

Furse (deceased), In re, Furse v CIR

Domicile.

A US citizen came to England as a boy in 1887. After completing his education in England he took up employment in America, where he married an American. In 1923, originally on medical advice, he came with his family to England, where his wife purchased a farm which remained the matrimonial home until he died in 1963, aged 80. From 1950 onwards he said that he would remain at the farm so long as he was able to do physical work there; he remained so able until his death. In an application by his executor for a declaration of his domicile for estate duty purposes, he was held to have acquired an English domicile of choice, distinguishing *CIR v Bullock*. Ch D, [1980] STC 597; [1980] 3 All ER 838.

Gaines-Cooper v IRC

Domicile.

Mr G-C, who was born in England, had a house and 27 acres in Henley-on-Thames, Oxfordshire, where he kept a collection of paintings, classic cars and guns, but claimed that his chief residence since 1976 had been on the Seychelles where he expressed the wish to spend his last days and have his ashes scattered there. His second wife had however taken up residence at the UK home together with his son who went to an English school. In 2002 Mr G-C had his will was drawn up under English law. HMRC had rejected his claim that he was not domiciled in the UK and he therefore appealed. A succession of eminent witnesses had told the Special Commissioners that he had 'fallen in love' with the Seychelles and wished to 'stay there forever' but it was nevertheless held that he remained domiciled in the UK. The High Court confirmed this decision, holding that the taxpayer, because the taxpayer had maintained a presence in England, the Commissioners simply did not accept his plea that he made his home on the Seychelles his chief residence in 1976, [2008] STC 1665.

Gartside v CIR

Meaning of interest in possession.

In an ED case which received much consideration in *Pearson and Others v CIR* the HL held that the objects of a discretionary trust, who were not entitled either individually or collectively to receive any part of the trust income in any year, did not have interests or interests in possession in the trust fund within the meaning of the relevant ED provisions. Per Lord Reid, an interest in possession must mean an interest which enables a person to claim now whatever may be the subject of his interest. HL 1967, [1968] 2 WLR 277; [1968] 1 All ER 121; [1968] AC 553.

George and Another, CIR v

Business Property Relief claim regarding caravans – provision of services not the holding of investments.

A widow (S) had owned 85% of the shares in a company which operated a residential caravan park, comprising 167 mobile homes, and a country club with a licensed bar. The Revenue issued a notice of determination on the basis that her shares in the company were not 'relevant business property', because the company's business consisted mainly of 'making or holding investments'. S's executors appealed. The Special Commissioner reviewed the evidence in detail and allowed the appeal, observing that the company had several full-time employees and was classed as a trading company for corporation tax purposes, and finding that '72% of the site fees goes in overheads (*sic*) . . . most of which relate to the provision of upkeep of the common parts'. On the evidence, the Commissioner held that the company's business was 'the provision of services and not the business of holding investments'. The Ch D upheld the notice. Laddie J held that the business of receiving site fees from the owners of the mobile homes in return for the right to use the company's land, and the receipt of fees for the storage of caravans, constituted the exploitation of the proprietary rights in the land and amounted to the holding of an investment. Accordingly the shares in the company failed to qualify for business property relief. [2002] STC SCD 358 Sp C 323; Ch D [2003] All ER (D) 376 (Feb); Ch D 2003, TL 3683; [2003] STC 468; [2003] EWHC 318.

George & Loochin (Stedman's Executors) v CIR

The holding of property as an investment was only one component of the business, and did not prevent the company from qualifying for business property relief.

A woman (S) had owned 85% of the shares in a company which operated a residential caravan park, comprising 167 mobile homes, and a country club with a licensed bar. The Revenue issued a notice of determination on the basis that her shares in the company were not 'relevant business property', because the company's business consisted mainly of 'making or holding investments'. S's executors appealed. The Special Commissioner reviewed the evidence in detail and allowed the appeal, observing that the company had several full-time employees and was classed as a trading company for corporation tax purposes, and finding that '72% of the site fees goes in overheads . . . most of which relate to the provision of upkeep of the common parts'. On the evidence, the Commissioner held that the company's business was 'the provision of services and not the business of holding investments'. The Ch D reversed this decision but the CA restored it. Carnwath LJ held that, on the evidence, the holding of property as an investment was only one component of the business, and did not prevent the company from qualifying for business property relief. CA [2003] EWCA Civ 1763; [2004] STC 147.

Gilchrist (as trustee of the J P Gilchrist 1993 Settlement) v HMRC

Proceeds of scrip dividend shares – whether trust capital for the purposes of the IHT 10 yearly charge on a discretionary trust.

Trustees of a relevant property had entered into a scrip dividend scheme to reduce the tax liability on a sale of the shareholdings in the company concerned. They contended that the proceeds of the scrip shares were income for the purposes of trust law and not therefore part of the capital of the settlement, liable to IHT under *IHTA 1984, s 64* on the next 10 yearly charge date. Certain aspects of the income tax treatment of scrip dividend schemes had been considered by the Court of Appeal, in *Howell v Trippier* [2004] STC 1245. The Tribunal noted that at no point in that appeal was there any suggestion that scrip dividends were income for purposes of trust law although the point would have been relevant. In the subsequent case of *Pierce v Wood* [2009] EWHC 3225 (Ch) the High Court, Chancery Division, did however expressly state that the decision in *Howell v Trippier* meant that a scrip dividend received by trustees was income in their hands for all purposes. The trustees relied on that decision. However the Upper Tribunal held that it was not bound by a decision of the High Court if it was satisfied that the decision in question was wrong. The Tribunal was satisfied that the decision in *Pierce v Wood* was wrong and so declined to follow it. Therefore the scrip dividend shares and their proceeds of sale were trust capital, both for general trust purposes and for the purposes of IHT, the trustees' appeal was accordingly dismissed. [2014] UKUT 0169 (TCC).

Gladstone v Bower

Agricultural holding – agreement to let land for a fixed period.

A landlord let a farm to a tenant for a fixed term of 18 months. He gave no notice to quit but at the end of the term brought an action for possession of the farm. The tenant contended that the letting took effect as a tenancy from year to year and could only be terminated by notice to quit. The CA held that, since the letting for 18 months created an interest greater than a tenancy from year to year at common law which could be terminated at the end of the first year, the landlord was entitled to possession. CA [1960] 3 All ER 353.

Glowacki's Personal Representatives v HMRC

IHTA 1984, s 142 – whether deed of variation effective.

A woman (G) died in 2004. Under her will, she left most of her estate to her husband. He died three months later. G's personal representatives purported to execute a deed of variation giving most of her estate (including her house) to her sister and the remainder to her nieces and nephew. HMRC issued a notice of determination, accepting that the deed was effective but holding that its effect was that the benefit of the nil rate of IHT was to be set first against G's house rather than against the pecuniary legacies. The personal representatives appealed, contending that the deed should be construed as meaning that the house was excluded from IHT and that the nil rate band was available to be set against the pecuniary legacies. The Special Commissioner reviewed the evidence in detail and rejected this contention, holding that the first part of the deed of variation was ineffective. The Commissioner held that *IHTA 1984, s 142* 'cannot operate to remove property from a person's estate so that it is no longer part of the estate subject to the deemed transfer of value on death under *s 4*. What *s 142* must vary is the destination of the estate on its deemed transfer under *s 4*.' In this case, the deed had purported 'to negate any disposition of the house as part of (G's) estate immediately before her death by pretending that she had transferred it immediately before the deemed *s 4* transfer of value'. However, 'nothing in *s 142* suggests that the variation that it permits should be other than a variation of the disposition on death effected by the deceased as part of the deemed transfer under *s 4* immediately before the death'. The Commissioner also held that HMRC's notice of determination had been issued on an incorrect basis, observing that HMRC appeared 'to have put the cart before the horse in terms of claiming to give effect to the deed and then considering its tax consequences'. The Commissioner concluded that 'the "variation" purported to be made by Clause 1 of the deed was not a variation capable of taking effect under *s 142* and, as a result of the proviso, did not therefore take effect at all'. [2007] STC SCD 188 Sp C 631.

Goodchild and Another v Goodchild

Husband and wife with wills drawn up under identical terms – whether mutually binding and failure to make reasonable provision for adult son. Inheritance (Provision for Family and Dependants) Act 1975.

A testator and his wife executed identical wills in favour of the survivor and then each in favour of their son. The wife died and the testator received all her estate. The testator then remarried and made a new will leaving all his estate to his new wife. The testator died and proceedings were brought against the inheriting wife by the testator's son seeking a declaration that the new wife held the testator's estate on trust for the son and to give effect to the provisions set out in the mutual wills and for reasonable financial provision to be made to the son. The mistaken belief held by the testator's first wife that the wills were mutually binding imposed a moral obligation on the testator which constituted special circumstances justifying the son's claim under the *Inheritance (Provision for Family and Dependants) Act 1975*. The sum of £185,000 was awarded to the son. An appeal against the decision was made and also a cross appeal by the son stating that the wills should have been deemed to be mutually binding. In the Court of Appeal the appeal and cross appeal were dismissed but comments by the Judges with regard to the case in matters of tax efficiency are relevant. See *Re Sainsbury's Settlement, Sainsbury v First C B Trustee Ltd* [1967] 1 All ER 878, [1967] 1 WLR 476. [1996] 1 All ER 670, CA [1997] 3 All ER 63.

Goulding and Another v James and Another

Variation of Trusts Act 1958, s 1. Application to vary contrary to testatrix's intentions – use in planning.

In 1994 the testatrix revoked her will made two years earlier and replaced it with a new will providing for the creation of a will trust under which the daughter J had a life interest in possession subject to the grandson, M, taking an absolute interest on his attaining the age of 40. J and M applied to the Court for a variation under the *Variation of Trusts Act 1958, s 1(1)(c)* so that the residuary estate would be held as to 45% for J absolutely, 45% for M absolutely and the remaining 10% held on the trusts of a grandchildren's trust fund. Since J and M were *sui juris* and legally entitled to do what they want and having also actuarially valued the contingent interest of the future children of M under the existing will at only 1.85% there was no reason for the beneficiaries not to exercise their proprietary rights to overbear and defeat the intention of the testatrix. Incidentally, the fund would also be taken offshore and, according to the proposed variation, be managed by professional trustees. The Court of Appeal allowed the appeal and consented to the variation. CA [1997] 2 All ER 239.

Green v HMRC

Furnished holiday letting business – whether eligible for business property relief.

The taxpayer held a number of units at a house and in its grounds which were let as self-catering holiday accommodation, producing income of around £87,000 per annum. The business was liable to business rates and VAT registered. All normal facilities for a holiday let were supplied, including furniture, household goods, linen and towels, plus wi-fi and a caretaker. Guests did their own laundry and had to leave the premises clean and tidy. Evidence was given that the properties would generate income of around £35,000 if let on assured shorthold tenancies, so that it was argued that the services element of the business therefore commanded the additional annual sum of £52,000. HMRC rejected this contention, saying that the additional rent was due to the scenic location of the properties. The Tribunal rejected the claim for relief on the basis that the services element of the business was insufficient to make the business one which was not mainly the holding of investments. [2015] UKFTT 0236 (TC).

Grey (Earl) v A-G

Gifts with reservation – exclusion of the donor from any benefit.

A covenant by the donee to pay the donor's debts and funeral expenses is a benefit. [1900] AC 124; [1900–1903] All ER 268.

Grey and Another v CIR

Time of disposition – disposition of equitable interest in settled property.

In a stamp duty case, an oral direction that an equitable interest in property be held on the trusts of a settlement was held not to be a valid disposition as it was not in writing. HL, [1959] 3 All ER 603; [1960] AC 1.

Grimwood-Taylor & Mallender (Mallender's Executors) v CIR

IHTA 1984, s 103 (3) – business 'carried on otherwise than for gain'.

An individual (M) died in 1986, owning substantial shareholdings in two companies. Each of the companies had purchased property, which was occupied by shareholders. The Revenue issued notices of determination charging IHT on the value of shares in the companies. M's executors appealed, contending that the shares qualified for business property relief. The Special Commissioner rejected this contention and dismissed the appeal, holding that the effect of *IHTA, s 103(3)* was that the shares did not qualify for relief, because the companies had used their funds to purchase land for occupation by their shareholders, so that their businesses had been carried on 'otherwise than for gain'. [2000] STC SCD 39 Sp C 223.

Guild v CIR

Bequest for sporting purposes – whether within IHTA 1984, s 23.

A testator left the residue of his estate to the town council of North Berwick for use in connection with the North Berwick sports centre or for 'some purpose in connection with sport'. The Revenue issued a determination to capital transfer tax, against which the executor appealed, contending that the bequest was charitable under the *Recreational Charities Act 1958, s 1*, and was therefore exempt from CTT by virtue of what is now *IHTA 1984, s 23(1)*. The HL allowed the executor's appeal (reversing the decision of the CS). The facilities at the sports centre were provided with the object of improving the conditions of life of the community generally. The phrase 'some similar purpose in connection with sport' implied a bequest which would display the leading characteristics of the sports centre, which lay in the nature of the facilities provided there and the fact that they were available to the public at large. *Dicta* of Bridge LJ in *CIR v McMullen & Others* approved and applied; *dicta* of Walton J in the same case disapproved. HL, [1992] STC 162; [1992] 2 WLR 397; [1992] 2 All ER 10.

Gully v Dix; In re Dix, deceased

Inheritance (Provision for family and Dependants) Act 1975 – whether temporary separation still within s 1 of the Act re living together in the same household definition.

A woman (W) living with her husband (H) had to leave the household due to H's continual drunkenness and antisocial behaviour which had caused her to leave the home she had shared with H over 27 years. After leaving the home in August 2001 H was found dead in the garden in October 2001. *Section 1* of the *Inheritance (Provision for Family and Dependants) Act 1975* required the claimant to be living in the same household and to be maintained by the deceased 'immediately' before the death of H. The issue was whether the claimant's leaving and living apart from the deceased during the last three months of his life had the consequence that W could not show their living in the same household during the whole of the period of two years ending immediately before the death, nor that, immediately before his death, she was being maintained by him. It was found that the claimant could still have been living with the deceased in the same household at the moment of his death even if they had been living separately at the moment in time. This would be substantiated if they were tied by their relationship, manifested by various elements, not simply living under the same roof; the public and private acknowledgement of the mutual society, protection and support that bound them together. Was there an acceptance or recognition that their relationship was in truth at an end? The claimant did not consider this to be the case. She still entertained the hope that, with the modification of the deceased's drinking, it would have been possible for her to return to H. Therefore a claim for financial provision by a woman who had lived with the deceased for 27 years succeeded despite her living elsewhere at the time of the deceased's death. CA [2004] TLR 28 January 2004.

Hall v Hall (Hall's Executors) v CIR

Making or holding investments – BPR

A widow (H) had owned a caravan park. The caravans were let from March to October each year. The park also contained 11 chalets which were let on 45 year leases. H's executors appealed against a notice of determination, contending that the park qualified for business property relief. The Special Commissioners rejected this contention and dismissed the appeal. On the evidence, almost 84% of H's income from the park consisted of rent and standing charges. It followed that H's business consisted 'mainly of making or holding investments' within IHTA 1984, s 105(3). [1997] STC SCD 126 Sp C 114.

Hanson v HMRC

A farmhouse was owned by a settlement in which the deceased had an interest in possession. The house had been jointly occupied by him and his son up to the date of his death. The son ran his own farming business from the property on land which he owned personally. Originally the business was conducted in partnership with the deceased but on dissolution of the partnership the son continued the business as a sole trader. The trustee of the settlement claimed agricultural property relief in respect of the farmhouse as it was occupied for agricultural purposes. HMRC refused the claim, citing the decision in *Rosser v CIR* [2003] STC SCD 311 Sp C 368 as authority for the proposition that the house and applicable farmland must be in both common occupation and common ownership ownership. The First Tier Tax Tribunal allowed the trustee's appeal on the basis that a test of common occupation of farmhouse and farmland, without any additional requirement of common ownership, fits the scheme of the IHT legislation best. The trustee's appeal was therefore allowed.

A subsidiary point concerned improvements to the property at a cost of approximately £175,000 which had been carried out by the trustee in a personal capacity as he also lived at the property. The trustee claimed that he had acquired an equitable interest in the property as a result of this expenditure, under a constructive trust in his favour, and thus the full value of the property should not be attributed to the life interest trust. This contention failed at the Tribunal on the reasoning that a constructive trust arises only where there is a common intention between two parties which has formed the basis of their mutual expectations and dealings. It could not be shown that there as any such mutual understanding in the present case. [2012] UKFTT 95.

Hardcastle & Hardcastle (Vernede's Executors) v CIR

Lloyd's Underwriter owing money on accounts open at date of death – whether 'liabilities incurred for the purpose of the business' – IHTA 1984, s 110(b).

A Lloyd's underwriter (V) died in 1994. It was accepted that his underwriting activities constituted a business, within *IHTA 1984, s 105(1)(a)*, qualifying for business property relief. The Revenue issued a determination charging IHT on the basis that, when computing the net value of V's business for the purposes of business property relief, the amounts owing on accounts open at the date of his death constituted 'liabilities incurred for the purposes of the business', and should be deducted from the value of the assets used in V's business. His executors appealed, contending that the amounts owing were not 'liabilities incurred for the purposes of the business', and should therefore be deducted from the value of his other estate. The Special Commissioner accepted this contention and allowed the appeal. Applying the principles in *Van den Berghs v Clark*, the insurance contracts in question were 'ordinary commercial contracts made in the course of carrying on the trade' and were not 'assets used in the business' for the purposes of *IHTA 1984, s 110*. Accordingly, the money owing on open accounts 'was not a liability incurred for the purposes within the meaning of *s 110(b)*'. [2000] STC SCD 532 Sp C 259.

Harding & Leigh v CIR

Appointment by Trustees in favour of testator's widow – whether IHTA 1984, s 143 applicable.

A married man died on 14 November 1993, leaving property on discretionary trust for the benefit of his wife and children. On 25 January 1994 the executors executed a deed of appointment, giving the deceased's widow a life interest in residue. The Revenue issued a notice of determination on the basis that the spouse exemption in *IHTA 1984, s 18* did not apply, since the appointment had not been made by the deceased, and that *IHTA 1984, s 144* did not apply for the reasons set out in *Frankland v CIR*. The executors appealed, contending that the appointment should be treated as a transfer made by the deceased by virtue of *IHTA 1984,s 143*. The Special Commissioner rejected this contention and dismissed the appeal, holding that *s 143* did not apply. Firstly, while 'in some contexts a legatee may include a trustee', the trustees here could not be treated as legatees for the purposes of *s 143*. Secondly, an appointment of property was not the same as a transfer of property. Thirdly, the Commissioner found that 'the evidence falls short of showing that the appointment was made in accordance with the deceased's wishes'. [1997] STC SCD 321 Sp C 140.

Hatton v CIR (and related appeals)

Two settlements executed on successive days – whether a preordained series of transactions – whether Ramsay principle applicable.

In August 1978 C, who was terminally ill, granted a power of attorney to her daughter (H) and her solicitor. The solicitor executed a settlement which provided that a fund was to be held on trust and that the income from the fund should be paid to C until midnight on the following day or until her death, whichever was the shorter period, and that subsequently the fund was to be held for the absolute benefit of H. On the following day a settlement was executed whereby H assigned her interest under the previous settlement to trustees to pay the income to C until midnight on the following day or until C's death, whichever occurred first, and subsequently to hold the fund for the absolute benefit of H. C died nine days later. The Revenue issued notices of determination on the basis that C had effected a chargeable transfer. H appealed, contending that what is now *IHTA 1984, s 53(3)** applied, and that no CTT was due since the property in question had reverted to her as settlor. The Special Commissioners upheld the notices of determination, holding that the creation of the two settlements was a 'preordained series of transactions' within the principle laid down in *W T Ramsay Ltd v CIR*. Accordingly C was to be treated as the settlor of both settlements and *IHTA 1984, s 53(3)** did not apply. The Ch D upheld the Commissioners' decision. The conditions laid down by Lord Oliver in *Craven v White* were satisfied. The transactions constituted a single composite transaction whereby C had created a settlement under which she was entitled to a beneficial interest in possession in the settled property at midnight two days after the creation of the settlement. As she was then living, tax was chargeable as if she had effected a chargeable transfer at that time. (Chadwick J commented that, even if the *Ramsay* principle had not applied, C would still fall to be treated as a joint settlor of the second settlement.) Ch D, [1992] STC 140.

Hatton LS (Hatton's Executor) v HMRC

Valuation of terraced house

The owner of a terraced house in Ealing died in September 2005. Her executor sold the house for £650,000 in November 2007. However, on the form IHT400, she declared the value of the house at the date of death as only £400,000. HMRC issued a determination valuing the house at £475,000. The Upper Tribunal upheld the determination and dismissed the executor's appeal, finding that the executor's evidence 'was misleading'. UT 23 June 2010 unreported.

Heirs of Van-Hilten Van der Heijden v Inspecteur van der Belastingdienst/Partculieren/Ondernemingen buitenland te Heerlen

Netherlands Law of Succession that levied inheritance tax on the estate of a person who resided in the Netherlands at the time of death – died within ten years of moving from the Netherlands. National had continued to reside in that member state.

The Netherlands Law of Succession that levied inheritance tax on the estate of a person who resided in the Netherlands at the time of death, and provided that a

Netherlands national who died within ten years of ceasing to reside in the Netherlands was deemed to be resident in the country at the time of death. A double-taxation law provided that the estate of a person so deemed was amenable to relief from tax to allow for tax charged in another state. Mrs V, a Netherlands national who had lived in the Netherlands and subsequently in Belgium then Switzerland, died within ten years of moving from the Netherlands, leaving an estate with assets in the Netherlands.

The ECJ ruled that Article 73B of the EC Treaty (prohibition of restrictions on the movement of capital) did not preclude legislation of a member state by which the estate of a national of that member state who died within ten years of ceasing to reside in that member state was to be taxed as if that national had continued to reside in that member state, while enjoying relief in respect of inheritance taxes levied by other states. [2006] (Case: C-513/03); [2006] WTLR 919; ECJ [2008] STC 1245.

Henderson & Henderson (Black's Trustees) v CIR

IHTA 1984, s 64 – charge at ten-year anniversary of settlement without interest in possession.

The Revenue issued a notice of determination under *IHTA 1984, s 64*, on the ten-year anniversary of a settlement without interest in possession. Following the determination, the trustees of the settlement appealed, and provided more information concerning the value of the property comprised in the settlement, which the Revenue accepted. The Commissioner upheld the determination in principle and confirmed it in the amended amount. [2000] STC SCD 572 Sp C 263.

Higginson's Executors v CIR

IHTA 1984, s 115(2) re large hunting lodge in 134 acres not a farmhouse.

In 1954 H purchased an estate comprising 134 acres and including a large hunting lodge, built in the early nineteenth century. He farmed the estate until 1985, from when he let the farmland but continued to live in the lodge. He died in 2000, and the property was sold in 2001 for £1,150,000. The Inland Revenue accepted that the land and agricultural outbuildings qualified for agricultural property relief, but issued a ruling that the lodge was not 'of a character appropriate to the property' for the purposes of *IHTA 1984, s 115(2)*, and thus did not qualify for agricultural property relief. H's executors appealed. The Special Commissioner dismissed the appeal, holding that 'for the purposes of *s 115(2)* the unit must be an agricultural unit: that is to say that within the unit, the land must predominate . . . (and) any qualifying cottages, farm buildings or farmhouses must be ancillary to the land'. However, in view of the price paid for the property, it was clear that 'within this particular unit it is the house which predominates, and that what we have here is a house with farmland going with it (and not vice versa)'. Accordingly, the lodge was not a 'farmhouse' for the purposes of *s 115(2)*. [2002] STC SCD 483 Sp C 337.

Holland (Holland's Executor) v CIR

IHTA 1984, s 18 – whether exemption for transfers between spouses applicable to transfers to common law wife.

An individual (H) separated from his wife in 1965 (and subsequently divorced). In 1968 he began living with another woman (K). They did not marry, but had two children together, and continued to live together until his death in 2000. H left his entire estate to K. The Inland Revenue issued a notice of determination charging IHT. K appealed, contending that she should be entitled to the inter-spouse exemption of *IHTA 1984, s 18*. The Special Commissioners rejected this contention and dismissed her appeal, holding that 'the word "spouse" in (*IHTA 1984, s 18*) means a person who is legally married and does not include a person who has lived with another as husband and wife'. [2003] STC SCD 43 Sp C 350. (*Note*. The Commissioners also held that this did not contravene the *Human Rights Act 1998*.)

Holmes & Another v McMullen & Others (re Ratcliffe (deceased))

IHTA 1984, s 41 – allocation of exemption.

The decision in *Lockhart v Harker & Others (re Benham's Will Trusts)*, see above, was not followed (and was implicitly disapproved) in this subsequent case in which the testatrix had left half her estate to two relatives and the other half to be held on trust for four charities. The executors issued a summons seeking the court's declaration as to the correct method of administering the net residuary estate. The Chancery Division held that the half shares were to be calculated before the payment of inheritance tax due in respect of the relatives' shares (so that the net amount received by the relatives would be less than the net amount received by the charities). Blackburne J held that an equal division of disposable residue between the relatives and charities inevitably meant that the inheritance tax attributable to the relatives' share had to be borne by that share, since to subject the charities' share to any part of that burden was prohibited by *IHTA 1984, s 41(b)*. [1999] STC SCD 262.

Howarth's Executors v CIR

IHTA 1984, s 221 – Notices of Determination.

A woman died in 1985. There were three executors. The Revenue issued Notices of Determination under *IHTA 1984, s 221* on each of the executors. They appealed. The Special Commissioner upheld the Notices and dismissed the appeals, observing that the fact that one of the executors had subsequently been made bankrupt, and that another was suffering from ill-health, did not provide any defence to the Notices. Applying *dicta* of Scott J in *CIR v Stannard*; 'the liability in respect of capital transfer tax for which a personal representative becomes liable . . . is necessarily an original liability which is in terms imposed on the personal representative'. [1997] STC SCD 162 Sp C 119.

HSBC Trusts Co (UK) Ltd (Farmbrough's Executor) v Twiddy

Valuation of a minority interest in property.

A woman (F) had held a 16.25% interest in two large buildings comprising 28 flats and 9 shops. The Lands Tribunal held that since this was a minority interest, it should be valued on an income basis, declining to follow the earlier decision in *Charkham v CIR*, Lands Tribunal 1996, [2000] RVR 7. The Tribunal assumed a net yield of 6.5% and therefore multiplied the net income of £170,000 by 15.38 to give a figure of £2,614,600 for the whole property and £425,000 (rounded to the nearest £1,000) for F's share. Lands Tribunal 24 August 2006 unreported.

Inglewood and Another v CIR

Accumulation and maintenance settlements – power of revocation.

By a 1964 appointment property was held on trust for the children of B who attained 21 or married under that age, subject to powers of revocation and reappointment and with interim powers of accumulation and maintenance. On 5 May 1975 B's eldest child became 21 and on 29 March 1976 the trustees released their power of revocation. The Revenue argued that a CTT charge arose on the former event under *FA 1975, 5 Sch 6(2)*, and on the latter under *FA 1975, 5 Sch 15(3)*. The trustees contended that the exemption for accumulation and maintenance settlements provided by *FA 1975, 5 Sch 15(1)(2)* applied so that no CTT was chargeable by reference to either event. The CA dismissed the trustees' appeal holding that the provisions of *para 15(1)(a)* were not satisfied by a trust subject to a power of revocation and reappointment under which the beneficiary's interest could be destroyed at the absolute discretion of the trustees and reappointed solely for the benefit of third parties at ages exceeding 25. The word 'will' in 'will . . . become entitled to' implied a degree of certainty inconsistent with such a power. CA 1982,

CTTL 16; [1983] STC 133; [1983] 1 WLR 366. (*Note. FA 1975, 5 Sch 15* was replaced by *IHTA 1984, s 71** for events after 8 March 1982 or, in some instances, 31 March 1983 or 31 March 1984.)

Ingram and Another v CIR

Transfer of freehold interest in property to family trust – equitable leasehold interest retained by transferor – whether a gift with reservation.

In 1987 a widow transferred a property which she owned to her solicitor, who executed declarations that he held the property as her nominee. The solicitor executed two leases purporting to give the widow a rent-free leasehold interest on the estate for 20 years, and the land subject to the leases was transferred to a family trust. The widow continued to live at the property until her death in 1989. The Revenue treated the transfer as a gift with reservation, within *FA 1986, s 102*, and issued a notice of determination accordingly. The House of Lords allowed the executors' appeal. Lord Hoffman held that 'although (*s 102*) does not allow a donor to have his cake and eat it, there is nothing to stop him from carefully dividing up the cake, eating part and having the rest. If the benefits which the donor continues to enjoy are by virtue of property which was never comprised in the gift, he has not reserved any benefit out of the property of which he disposed.' For these purposes, 'property' was 'not something which has physical existence like a house but a specific interest in that property, a legal construct, which can co-exist with other interests in the same physical object. *Section 102* does not therefore prevent people from deriving benefit from the object in which they have given away an interest. It applies only when they derive the benefit from that interest.' The policy of *s 102* was to require people to 'define precisely the interests which they are giving away and the interests, if any, which they are retaining'. The interest, which the widow retained, was 'a proprietary interest, defined with the necessary precision'. The gift was 'a gift of the capital value in the land after deduction of her leasehold interest in the same way as a gift of the capital value of the fund after deduction of an annuity'. *Munro v Commrs of Stamp Duties of New South Wales*, and *dicta* of Lord Simonds in *St Aubyn v Attorney-General*, HL 1951, [1952] AC 15; [1951] 2 All ER 473 applied. Furthermore, the leases were valid in law. Applying *Rye v Rye*, HL [1962] AC 496; [1962] 1 All ER 146, an owner of freehold property could not grant a lease to himself. However, a 'trustee in English law is not an agent for his beneficiary'. (The House of Lords declined to follow the Scottish stamp duty case of *Kildrummy (Jersey) Ltd v CIR*, CS [1990] STC 657, where the Court of Sessions held that the lease granted by a landowner to a nominee acting on his behalf was equivalent to the grant of a lease to himself.) *Dicta* of Goff J in *Nichols v CIR*, see below, disapproved. HL [1999] STC 37; [1999] 1 All ER 297.

Iveagh (Earl of) v Revenue Commissioners

Domicile – jurisdiction of Courts in relation to determination of domicile.

In an Irish case, the High Court reversed a decision by the Special Commissioners that the taxpayer had not given up his domicile of origin. The Supreme Court held that domicile is a question of fact and the Commissioners' decision, if one of fact, could not be reviewed by the Courts. However, in this case the Special Commissioners had approached the question as one of law and had misconstrued the law. The case was remitted to them to determine the question of domicile as one of fact. SC(I) 1930, 1 ITC 316; [1930] IR 431.

Jacques v HMRC

TMA 1970, s 31A – whether notice of appeal must specify grounds of appeal.

An accountant sent a notice of appeal against a penalty notice to the Special Commissioners, stating that 'due to the conduct of HMRC Officers we will not disclose the reasons for appeal'. HMRC applied for a ruling that the notice of appeal was invalid, as it had failed to state the grounds of appeal, as required by *TMA 1970, s 31A(5)*. The Commissioner accepted this contention, holding that the purported notice of appeal was invalid. [2006] STC SCD 40 Sp C 513.

Jones & Another (Ball's Administrators) v CIR

Uncompleted contract for sale of land – whether relief under IHTA 1984, s 191 available.

A farmer (B) died on 26 June 1988. On 25 June 1991 his administrators entered into a contract to sell the farm for £300,150. However, the contract was not completed and the farm was eventually sold for £400,000 under another contract in 1992. The probate value of the farm was agreed at £447,000, but the administrators claimed relief under *IHTA 1984, s 191*, contending that for IHT purposes the farm should be valued at £300,150 (the price payable under the 1991 contract). The Revenue rejected the claim and the Ch D dismissed the administrators' appeal. An abortive contract was not a sale, and the farm had not been sold within three years of B's death. Accordingly IHTA 1984, s 191 was not applicable and the farm had to be valued at its probate value of £447,000. Ch D 14 February 1997, [1997] STC 358.

Judge & Judge (Walden's Personal Representatives) v HMRC

Testator's widow continuing to occupy property at trustees' discretion – whether testator's will conferred interest in possession.

A woman (W) was widowed in 2000. Her husband's will gave his house to trustees, with a declaration that they should allow W to occupy the house 'for such period or periods as they shall in their absolute discretion think fit'. W continued to occupy the house until her death in 2003. The Revenue issued a notice of determination on the basis that her husband's will had given her an interest in possession in the house. Her personal representatives appealed. The Special Commissioner allowed their appeal, holding that the effect of W's husband's will was that she 'had no right to occupy the property but the trustees were given a discretion (but not a duty) to allow her to occupy'. Accordingly W did not have an interest in possession in the property. [2005] STC SCD 863 Sp C 506.

Kempe and Roberts (personal representatives of Lyon, deceased) v CIR

Life policy designation – whether deceased beneficially entitled to sum assured by reason of having a general power to dispose as he thought fit under IHTA 1984, s 5(2).

A company insured the life of one of its employees (L). Under the policy, L was allowed to designate the beneficiaries who would benefit on his demise and he nominated his two sisters as the beneficiaries in the event of his death. L died in 2001. The Inland Revenue issued a notice of determination charging IHT on the basis that the death benefits payable under the policy formed part of L's estate. His sisters (who were his personal representatives) appealed contending that the policy was not part of the estate of the deceased as it was for the benefit of the next of kin and to treat it as part of the estate of the deceased was to defeat the primary purpose of the policy. The Special Commissioner dismissed their appeal, holding that 'the deceased had a general power under (*IHTA 1984, s 5(2)*) which enabled him to dispose of the sum assured under the policy as he thought fit. That means that he was beneficially entitled to the sum assured and so it formed part of his estate and accordingly is chargeable to tax.' [2004] STC SCD 467 Sp C 424.

Kwok Chi Leung Karl (Executor of Lamson Kwok) v Commissioner of Estate Duty

Situation of property – contract debt.

New York Life Insurance Co Ltd was followed in a Hong Kong case where the testator had, on the day before his death, transferred assets to a Liberian company for a non-negotiable promissory note. The Privy Council, reversing the decision of the Hong Kong Court of Appeal, held that the fact that the document recording the debt was located in Hong Kong did not alter the principle that the debt was located where the debtor, rather than the creditor, resided. There was no suggestion by the Hong Kong Commissioner at any state of the proceedings that the transactions carried out so close to the testator's death were a sham. The Privy Council therefore had to treat them as genuine arm's length transactions. Per Lord Oliver, 'it would be unwise to assume that the genuineness of similar transactions in the future will necessarily be beyond challenge'. PC [1988] STC 728.

Lake v Lake & Others

Rectification of deeds.

A testator died in November 1986, and a Deed of Variation was executed three months later by his widow and the trustees. However, the solicitors drew up the Deed incorrectly, resulting in an increased inheritance tax liability. A second Deed was subsequently executed to correct the error, but following the decision in *Russell & Another v CIR*, the liability was nevertheless determined in accordance with the original Deed. The widow sought an Order for the rectification of the original Deed in accordance with the intentions, which the Ch D granted. On the facts, there was no doubt that the original Deed did not carry out the intentions of the parties, and the fact that there was no issue before the court did not present an obstacle to rectification. Ch D [1989] STC 865.

Lau (W Lau's Executor) v HMRC

IHTA 1984, s 142 – Whether deed of variation effective.

An individual (L) died in October 2004. His widow (M) acted as his executrix. L left specific legacies of £665,000 to each of his two daughters and to his stepson (H), who was M's only child from a previous marriage. M was the residuary beneficiary. In July 2005 L's two daughters and H executed deeds of variation renouncing their legacies. In October 2005 M paid each of them £1,000,000. HMRC formed the opinion that this payment represented consideration for the recipients having renounced their legacies under L's will, so that the effect of *IHTA 1984, s 142(3)* was that the deed of variation was ineffective. They issued a notice of determination accordingly. M appealed, accepting that the deed was ineffective with regard to L's two daughters, but contending that she had given H the £1,000,000 so that he could start a business, and that her gift to H was not connected with his renunciation of his legacy. The Special Commissioner reviewed the evidence in detail, rejected this contention and dismissed M's appeal, finding that H 'was entirely dependent upon the appellant for financial support. He had been out of work for most of his adult life, and at the time of his renunciation owned no assets of significant value.' On the evidence, 'the correspondence from the Appellant's solicitors and the circumstances of the payment demonstrated a direct connection between the £1,000,000 payment and (H's) renunciation of the bequest of £665,000. The appellant's evidence denying the existence of a connection was unconvincing and utterly unpersuasive.' Accordingly, the renunciation did not meet the requirements of *IHTA 1984, s 142(1)*, and 'was of no legal effect'. [2009] STC SCD 352 Sp C 740.

Lawton, In re

Domicile – whether English domicile of origin abandoned.

In an estate duty case, a testator who had been born in 1871 with an English domicile, but who from about 1890 onwards had lived abroad, was held, on the facts, to have been domiciled in France on his death in 1955, notwithstanding a declaration in his will made in 1948 that he had not abandoned his English domicile of origin. Ch D 1958, 37 ATC 216.

Lee & Lee (Lee's Executors) v CIR

IHTA, s 179(1) – application of twelve-month time limit.

An individual died in November 2000. In February 2002 his executors discovered that he had some investments in a unit trust, which had declined in value. They claimed relief under *IHTA 1984, s 178*. The Revenue rejected the claim, as it had been made outside the twelve-month time limit of *IHTA 1984, s 179(1)*. The Special Commissioner dismissed the executors' appeal. [2002] STC SCD 41 Sp C 349.

Lloyds Private Banking Ltd v CIR

Life interest in matrimonial home given to husband, daughter absolutely entitled on death of her father – whether an interest in possession conferred by the wife on husband. IHTA 1984, s 43(2).

A married couple lived together as tenants in common. The wife died in 1989. By her will, she appointed a trustee and bequeathed her 50% share in the matrimonial home to the trustee, directing that her husband should be permitted to continue to live there until his death, and that her share should then pass to her daughter. The husband continued to live in the property until his death in 1993. The Revenue issued a notice of determination, charging IHT on the basis that the deemed transfer of value on the husband's death included the entire interest in the property, on the basis that his wife's will had given him an interest in possession in her 50% share of the property. The trustee appealed, contending that the will did not confer an interest in possession, and that the will had conferred no new rights on the husband, who was entitled to the use and enjoyment of the property as a co-owner. The Special Commissioner accepted this contention and allowed the appeal. On the wife's death, the husband had continued to enjoy the right to reside in the property and that right could only have been terminated by the husband's volition or by a court order under Law of Property Act 1925, s 30. The effect of the wife's will was that there had been an absolute gift of her 50% share in the property to her daughter, subject to a direction to the trustee to postpone sale. The case was taken on appeal to the Chancery Division and in a reserved judgment Lightman J allowed the appeal brought by originating summons by the Inland Revenue. Lightman J stated that the critical issue was whether clause 3 was dispositive or merely laid down administrative directions to the Trustee. Clause 3 was dispositive and conferred on Mr Evans a determinable life interest in the half share although it was dressed up as a set of administrative instructions. See also dicta of Wood VC in *Maddison v Chapman*, 1859, 4 K & J 709, and Farwell J in *Re Shuckburgh's Settlement*, Ch D [1901] 2 Ch 794, applied. [1997] STC SCD 259 Sp C 133; [1998] STC 559.

Lloyds TSB plc (Antrobus' Personal Representatives) v CIR

Farmhouse set in 132 acres was 'a farmhouse with a farm and definitely not a house with land'.

A deceased estate included a six-bedroomed house, part of which had been built in the sixteenth century, and a number of agricultural buildings, set in about 132 acres of agricultural land. The site had been used as a farm by the same family for more than 90 years. The Revenue issued a notice of determination that the house was not 'of a character appropriate to the property' for the purposes of *IHTA 1984, s 115(2)*, and thus did not qualify for agricultural property relief. The company which acted as the deceased's personal representative appealed. The Special Commissioner allowed the appeal, finding that the property 'was in a poor state of repair and maintenance. The result was that, even if the dwelling-house had at one time been a family home of some distinction, it had, both in appearance and in use, become a farmhouse on a working farm.' On the evidence, the house was 'a farmhouse with a farm and definitely not a house with land'. It was 'of a character appropriate to the property' for the purposes of *s 115(2)*. [2002] STC SCD 468 Sp C 336.

Lloyds TSB plc (Antrobus' Personal Representative) v Twiddy

Lands Tribunal decision – 30% discount for farmhouse to reflect agricultural value.

HMRC issued a notice of determination that the farmhouse (see case report above) in question had a market value in excess of its value as agricultural property, so that IHT was payable on the amount by which the market value exceeded the agricultural value. The personal representatives appealed, contending that the agricultural value was the same as the market value. The Lands Tribunal reviewed the evidence in detail, rejected this contention and dismissed the appeal, holding that the open market value of the farmhouse should be discounted by 30% to arrive at its 'agricultural value'. [2004] DET/47/2004.

Lynall (deceased), In re

The amount or value of the consideration for an asset – value of unquoted shares while public flotation under consideration.

In an estate duty case the question at issue was the price which certain unquoted shares 'would fetch if sold in the open market at the time of the death of the deceased'. At the time of the death, the directors were considering public flotation and favourable confidential reports had been made to them for that purpose by a firm of accountants and a firm of stockbrokers. The HL held, *inter alia*, that although no general rule could be laid down as to the information a hypothetical purchaser in an open market may be deemed to have, the board could not be deemed to disclose confidential information. HL 1971, 47 TC 375; [1972] AC 680; [1971] 3 All ER 904. (*Note*. See now *TCGA 1992, s 273*, deriving from *FA 1973*. The substantive decision here is therefore no longer applicable, but the judgments include a useful review of estate duty cases dealing with the valuation of unquoted shares. See also *Battle v CIR* and *CIR v Crossman, Caton's Administrators v Couch* and *Clark (Clark's Executor) v CIR*.)

Lyon's Personal Representatives v HMRC; Trustees of the Alloro Trust v HMRC

FA 1986, s 102(1) – settlor retaining powers of revocation over discretionary trust – whether a gift with reservation.

In 1999 a settlor (L) gave £2,700,000 to the trustees of a discretionary trust. Under the trust deed, L retained the power of revocation, and was also a potential beneficiary of the trust. During his lifetime, L received distributions totalling £15,965 from the trust. L died in 2004. Following his death, HMRC issued a notice of determination on the basis that his transfer of the £2,700,000 to the trust was a 'gift with reservation', within *FA 1986, s 102*. The trustees, and L's personal representatives, appealed. The Special Commissioner dismissed the appeals, holding that there had been a 'reservation of benefit', within *s 102(1)(b)*. Furthermore, the manner in which the trust had been operated meant that the 'possession and enjoyment of the property' had not been 'bona fide assumed by the donee at the beginning of the relevant period', within *s 102(1)(a)* [2007] Sp C 616.

MacArthur's Executors v HMRC

Value of unquoted shares including loans with conversion rights.

A solicitor (M) died in 1994. He held shares in three family investment companies, and had made loans to two of the companies. HMRC issued notices of determination on the basis that these loans had given M options to acquire further shares in the companies, and were of the nature of convertible unsecured loan stock. HMRC's determination valued the shareholdings on an assets basis. For two of the companies, where M had a majority shareholding, HMRC allowed a discount of 12.5% to take account of lack of marketability. For the third company, where the shareholding was a minority one, HMRC allowed a discount of 45%. M's executors appealed, contending that the conversion rights had little or no value. The Special Commissioner reviewed the evidence in detail, rejected this contention, and upheld HMRC's determinations. The Commissioner observed that there was 'more than sufficient evidence in the form of writs of the debtor to prove the existence of the loans and conversion rights . . . the unit of valuation is the shares in each company plus the relevant conversion rights or options which must be regarded as valid, subsisting and enforceable'. [2008] STC SCD 1100 Sp C 700.

Macaulay & Another v Premium Life Assurance Co Ltd

Unsuccessful CTT avoidance scheme – action alleging negligence by promoters of scheme.

In 1984 an individual (M) undertook a scheme marketed by a life assurance company, which the company claimed would avoid liability to capital transfer tax (subsequently renamed inheritance tax). However, the scheme failed to take account of *IHTA, s 3(3)**, so that the whole of M's free estate became liable to IHT on her death (on 4 March 1991). On 3 March 1997 M's executors issued a writ against the life assurance company, alleging that it owed a duty of care to ensure that its brochure was accurate and pointed out any CTT risks inherent in the scheme. The company defended the action, contending that the writ had been issued outside the six-year time limit laid down by *Limitation Act 1980*. The Ch D rejected this contention and held that the writ had been issued within the six-year period. The cause of action had accrued when M died. Her executors were not suing in respect of a lost opportunity suffered by M in her lifetime; they were suing in respect of the IHT liability which arose on her death, and which did not exist until she died. Liability for IHT was payable by M's estate, and was not imposed on the deceased. M's executors were suing for a loss or damage which did not exist until M's death. Ch D 29 April 1999 unreported.

McCall & Keenan (Personal Representatives of Mrs E McClean) v HMRC

IHTA 1984, s 105(3) – business of 'making or holding investments'.

In 1983 a widow (M) inherited 33 acres of farmland on the death of her husband. She did not farm the land herself, but let it to local farmers under conacre or agistment agreements. She died in 1999. The Revenue issued a notice of determination charging IHT on her estate. Her personal representatives appealed, contending that the farmland qualified for business property relief. The Special Commissioner rejected this contention and dismissed the appeal, holding that although M was carrying on a business on the land, that business consisted mainly of making or holding investments, within *IHTA 1984, s 105(3)*, so that the land was not 'relevant business property'. The Commissioner observed that 'the activities of the business consisted of the making available of its major asset to other persons for payment without the separate provision of any substantial other goods or services'. The Court of Appeal (Northern Ireland) unanimously upheld this decision. Girvan LJ held that 'the use by the graziers was sufficiently exclusive for the land to be shown to be used as an investment. The agisting farmer had exclusive rights of grazing; he was entitled to exclude other graziers including the deceased; the deceased could not use the land for any purpose that interfered with the grazing and the letting for grazing was the way in which the deceased decided that the grasslands could be used and exploited as uncultivated grassland short of the creation of a lease. The deceased's business consisted of earning a return from grassland whose real and effective value lay in its grazing potential.' [2008] STC SCD 757 Sp C 678; CA(NI) [2009] NICA 12.

McDowall & Others (McDowall's Executors) v CIR (and related appeal)

Power of attorney – gifts out of deceased estate – whether valid.

In 1993 an elderly man (M) granted a deed conferring a power of attorney on his wife, and providing that if she predeceased him, the power should pass to his son-in-law. M's wife died in 1996. M's son-in-law used the power of attorney to make substantial gifts out of M's estate. M died in April 1998. His solicitors submitted an inventory to the Capital Taxes Office [now HMRC Inheritance Tax], accepting that gifts of £604,000 were chargeable transfers on which IHT was due, but treating gifts totalling £147,800 as exempt transfers. The Revenue issued notices of determination to M's executors, determining that these gifts were not allowable as deductions from M's estate in determining the IHT liability. The executors appealed. The Special Commissioners reviewed the evidence in detail and dismissed the appeals, holding that on a proper construction of the power of attorney, M's son-in-law had no authority to make the gifts. Applying *dicta* of Russell J in *Re Reckitt*, CA [1928] 2 KB 244, 'the primary object of a power of attorney is to enable the attorney to act in the management of his principal's affairs. An attorney cannot, in the absence of a clear power to do so, make presents to himself or to others of his principal's property.' The gifts which M's son-in-law had purported to make were *ultra vires*, and M's executors were entitled to recover them. Therefore the amounts in question formed part of M's estate at the time of his death, and were chargeable to IHT accordingly. [2004] STC SCD 22 Sp C 382.

McKelvey (personal representative of DV McKelvey) v HMRC

Dispositions for maintenance of family within IHTA 1984, s 11.

A spinster (D) lived with her widowed mother (M), who was 85-years-old, blind and in poor health. D, who owned two houses, was told that she was suffering from terminal cancer. In early 2003, D gave the houses to M. D died in 2005 and M died in 2007. HMRC issued a notice of determination, charging IHT on D's gift of the houses to M (the combined value of the houses being agreed as £169,000). D's executor appealed, contending that D had given the houses to M so that they could be sold in order to pay for nursing care, so that they were exempt transfers within *IHTA 1984, s 11(3)*. The Special Commissioner reviewed the evidence in detail and allowed the appeal in part, finding that it had been reasonable for D to have assumed that M 'would require nursing care in a residential setting'. The Commissioner held that, in order to determine what amount had been 'reasonably required' for M's care, 'the approach adopted in personal injury cases is appropriate'. On the evidence, he held that it would be reasonable to have assumed that M would have required paid nursing care for five and a half years, and that this care would have cost £21,000 pa, leading to a basic sum of £115,500. He also held that a further £25,000 should be made added 'to cover the contingency of (M's) admission to a home', so that 'reasonable provision at the time the transfers were made amounted in all to £140,500'. The Commissioner concluded that £140,500 of the transfers qualified as exempt within *IHTA 1984, s 11*, while the balance of £28,500 was a chargeable transfer within *IHTA 1984, s 3A(4)*. [2008] STC SCD Sp C 694.

MacNiven v Westmoreland Investments Ltd

Anti-avoidance – payments of money borrowed from the pension fund constituted payments of interest for the purposes of s 338 – meaning of 'paid'.

A property-holding company (W) suffered financial difficulties and was loaned substantial sums of money by its major shareholder (a pension fund). Subsequently it obtained further interest-free loans from the same source and paid accrued interest on the earlier loans. It claimed that these payments should be treated as charges on income. The Revenue rejected the claim, considering firstly that W did not qualify as an investment company, secondly that the accrued interest had not been paid for the purposes of *s 338*, and alternatively that even if the interest were held to have been paid, the payment was not wholly and exclusively for the purpose of W's business. The Special Commissioners allowed W's appeal, holding that W was an investment company within *s 130* and that the payments of interest were genuine, had been made for the purpose of W's business, and were effective for the purpose of *s 338*. The HL upheld the Commissioners' decision. The payments of money borrowed from the pension fund constituted payments of interest for the purposes of *s 338*, and the Commissioners were entitled to find that they had been made wholly and exclusively for the purpose of W's business. Lord Nicholls observed that 'the source from which a debtor obtains the money he uses in paying his debt is immaterial for the purpose of *s 338*'. Lord Hoffmann observed that 'the only apparent reason for the insistence on payment of yearly interest is that payment gives rise to an obligation to deduct tax. In the present case, (W) complied with that obligation. The Crown's real complaint is that the scheme, as an exempt fund, was able to reclaim the tax. But this cannot be remedied by giving the word "paid" a different meaning in the case of a payment to an exempt lender. The word must mean the same, whatever the status of the lender.' Lord Hutton observed that 'the obligation undertaken by (W) to pay interest on the sums it had been lent by the scheme trustees was a genuine one which existed in the real world'. Furthermore, the anti-avoidance provisions of *s 787* did not apply. HL 2001, TL 3631; [2001] STC 237; [2001] 2 WLR 377; [2001] 1 All ER 865.

Macpherson & Another v CIR

Associated operations.

On 29 March 1977, trustees of a discretionary settlement entered into an agreement with D which meant, in effect that D would have custody of some valuable trust paintings for 14 years. Although the agreement was on commercial terms, it reduced the value of the trustees' interest in the paintings. On the following day, the trustees appointed a protected life interest in the paintings, subject to the agreement, to D's son. The Revenue charged CTT on the reduction in value, and the trustees appealed, contending that *IHTA 1984, s 10** applied since the transactions had not been intended to confer gratuitous benefit. The HL rejected this contention and upheld the charge to CTT. The agreement and appointment were associated operations, and together constituted a transaction intended to confer gratuitous benefit on D's son. HL [1988] STC 362; [1988] 2 WLR 1261; [1988] 2 All ER 753.

Magnavox Electronics Co Ltd (in liquidation) v Hall

Date of disposal.

In September 1978 a company (M) exchanged contracts for the sale of a factory to another company (J) for £1,400,000. Completion was arranged for February 1979, but for financial reasons J was unable to complete the purchase, and forfeited its deposit. Meanwhile, M had gone into voluntary liquidation in December 1978. The liquidator did not rescind the contract of sale, but arranged for M to acquire an 'off-the-shelf' company (S), to which it assigned its beneficial interest under the contract on 6 July 1979. Three days later certain variations in the contract were agreed, including a reduction of the purchase price to £1,150,000 and a new completion date of 9 October 1979. On the same day S exchanged contracts with a fourth company (B) for the sale of the factory on terms practically identical with those in the original contract as varied. B duly completed. The Revenue issued an assessment on the basis that the disposal had taken place after M had gone into liquidation. M appealed, contending that the disposal had taken place in September 1978 (so that trading losses of that accounting period could be set against the gain). The Special Commissioners dismissed M's appeal, and the Ch D and CA upheld their decision. The disposal to B was not under the 1978 contract, but under a new contract made in July 1979. Furthermore, the interposition of S was part of an artificial avoidance scheme which could be disregarded, applying *Furniss v Dawson*. CA 1986, 59 TC 610; [1986] STC 561.

Maitland's Trustees v Lord Advocate

Deed of appointment executed by trustees – whether accumulation and maintenance settlement established.

The trustees of a discretionary settlement executed a deed of appointment with the intention of establishing a discretionary and maintenance settlement. The appointment was declared to be conditional on the power of accumulation being valid under the *Trusts (Scotland) Act 1961*, and provided that if the accumulations were contrary to law, the appointment should be void. The Revenue refused to accept the deed as establishing an accumulation and maintenance settlement, considering that *IHTA 1984, s 71(1)(a)** was not satisfied. The CS allowed the trustees appeal. The word 'will' in *IHTA 1984, s 71(1)(a)* did not require absolute certainty. Both the Revenue and the trustees agreed that there was no illegality, and the fact that a third party might question this in future did not prevent *IHTA 1984, s 71(1)(a)* being satisfied. The deed was not *ultra vires*, and the fact that the trustees might not safely make any distribution to the primary beneficiaries until the doubt as to the law was resolved did not affect the position. CS, [1982] SLT 483.

Mallender & Others (Drury-Lowe's Executors) v CIR

IHTA 1984, s 110(b) – Lloyd's underwriter – commercial property charged to bank – whether 'assets used in the business'.

A Lloyd's underwriter (D) died in 1993. His underwriting business was supported by several bank guarantees. In consideration for the guarantees, D had indemnified the bank against all liabilities and had secured this liability by a charge over some commercial property which D owned. The Revenue issued notices of determination on the basis that the commercial property did not qualify for business property relief. D's executors appealed, contending that the effect of the charge over the commercial property was that it was within the definition of 'assets used in the business', within *IHTA 1984, s 110(b)*. The Ch D rejected this contention and upheld the notices (reversing the decision of the Special Commissioner). Jacob J held that an asset used as a security for a guarantee was not 'relevant business property' within *IHTA 1984, s 105(1)(a)*. The property was not itself used in the business, and did not qualify for relief. STC SCD 574 Sp C 264; Ch D [2001] STC 514.

Mark v Mark

Person habitually resident and having a domicile of choice in England and Wales even though presence in the United Kingdom was a criminal offence – residence/domicile a question of fact not necessarily lawful.

Section 5(2) of the *Domicile and Matrimonial Proceedings Act 1973* provides for the following: '(2) The Court shall have jurisdiction to entertain proceedings for divorce or judicial separation if (but only if) either of the parties to the marriage (a) is domiciled in England and Wales on the date when proceedings are begun; or (b) was habitually resident in England and Wales throughout the period of one year ending with that date'. In an appeal from a decision by the Court of Appeal the House of Lords decided that Mrs Mark, a party to divorce proceedings, who was habitually resident and having a domicile of choice in England and Wales was domiciled here even though her presence in the United Kingdom was a criminal offence. There was no reason why, in principle, a person whose presence here, although unlawful under the *Immigration Act 1971*, could not acquire a domicile of choice in England and Wales. Either a person had acquired a domicile of choice in England and Wales or they had not. If having done so, that person was not to be denied it because the court considered the case unmeritorious or tainted with moral or legal turpitude. If that person had not done so, they were not to be granted it because the court considered them to be virtuous. The matter lay with the facts of the case whether the person had the required intention at the relevant time. HL [2005] UKHL 42.

Martin & Horsfall (Moore's Executors) v CIR

Business property relief – relevant business property – IHTA 1984, s 105(3).

A widow owned a number of industrial units. On her death, the Revenue issued a notice of determination. Her executors appealed, contending that the industrial units qualified for business property relief. The Special Commissioner dismissed the appeal, holding that the effect of *IHTA, s 105(3)* was that the property was not 'relevant business property', since the widow's business consisted 'wholly or mainly . . . of making or holding investments'. The Commissioner noted that *s 105(3)* derived from *FA 1976*, and that, during the relevant Finance Bill Debates, the Chief Secretary of the Treasury had stated that the letting of land did not qualify for business property relief. [1995] STC SCD 5 Sp C 2.

Marquess of Linlithgow v HMRC (and related appeal)

Disposition of interest in property

A Scottish landowner made two dispositions of land to an accumulation and maintenance trust. The dispositions were executed on 15 March 2006. One of the dispositions was recorded in the Register of Sasines on 10 October 2006 and the other on 16 November 2006. HMRC issued a notice determining that the time of the disposition was the date when each disposition was recorded in the Register of Sasines (so that the dispositions were subject to the anti-avoidance provisions of *FA 2006*). The landowner and the trustees appealed, contending that so that the dispositions had taken place when they were executed, so that the anti-avoidance provisions of *FA 2006* did not apply and the transfers were potentially exempt. The CS unanimously accepted this contention and allowed the appeals, applying the principles laid down in the estate duty case of *Thomas v Lord Advocate*. CS [2010] CSIH 19.

Masterman-Lister v Jewell and another; Masterman-Lister v Brutton and Co

Practice and procedure – Parties – Capacity to litigate and compromise – Claimant suffering brain damage as result of road traffic accident – Claimant issuing proceedings arising out of accident – Claimant agreeing to settle claim – Claimant alleging he was a patient at time of settlement – Burden of proof – Test to be applied – RSC Ord 80, rr 1, 10 – CPR Pt 21.

The claimant was born in 1963. In 1980, he was involved in a serious road traffic accident with a milk float driven by J, who was employed by the second defendant. As a result, the claimant suffered severe brain damage. The claimant instructed B and Co, who were the defendants to the second action, to issue a claim against J and HCD. In 1987, the claimant accepted an offer from HCD to compromise the action on the basis of £76,000 and costs. He returned to work some nine months after the accident, but was only able to perform menial tasks. He resigned in 1989, and had not worked since. He lived with his parents until 1992, when he purchased his own house. In 1993, he issued proceedings against the first defendant in relation to their conduct of that litigation. In 1997, the claimant was advised by a consultant in neuropsychiatric rehabilitation that he was, and had been since the accident, a patient within the meaning of *s 94(2)a* of the *Mental Health Act 1983*. The claimant sought to reopen the settlement of his personal injury action on the basis that it never received the approval of the court, as would have been required at the relevant time pursuant to RSC Ord 80 r 10b. RSC Ord 80 r 1c, which defined 'patient', was replaced by CPR 21.1(2)(b)d. The issue of whether the claimant was a patient within the 1983 Act was tried as a preliminary issue. The judge ruled that the court should only take over the individual's function of decision making when it was shown on the balance of probabilities that such person did not have the capacity sufficiently to understand, absorb and retain information, including advice, relevant to the matters in question sufficiently to enable him or her to make decisions based upon such information. He then considered the evidence and concluded that since 1983 at the latest, the claimant had been fully capable of managing and administering his property and affairs and therefore was not a 'patient' for the purposes of either the 1983 Act, RSC Ord 80 or CPR Pt 21. The claimant appealed. On appeal issues arose as to the burden of proof and the test for determining capacity to litigate and compromise.

The appeal would be dismissed.

(1) The burden of proof rested on those asserting incapacity. The fact that there was evidence that as a result of a head injury sustained in an accident it was agreed that the claimant was incapable of managing his property and affairs did not mean that he could rely on the presumption of continuance, although if there was clear evidence of incapacity for a considerable period then the burden of proof might be more easily discharged. There was no requirement that a judicial officer had to consider medical evidence or be satisfied as to incapacity before a person could be treated as a patient. However, following the implementation of the *Human Rights Act 1998* in order that a party was not deprived of his civil rights by being treated as a patient, the court should always, as a matter of practice, at the first convenient opportunity, investigate the question of capacity whenever there was any reason to suspect that it might be absent. That meant that, even where the issue did not seem to be contentious, a district judge who was responsible for case management would almost certainly require the assistance of a medical report before being able to be satisfied that incapacity existed.

(2) For the purposes of RSC Ord 80 and CPR Pt 21, the test to be applied was whether the party to legal proceedings was capable of understanding, with the assistance of such proper explanation from legal advisers and experts in other disciplines as the case might require, the issues on which his consent or decision was likely to be necessary in the course of those proceedings. If the party had capacity to understand that which he needed to understand in order to pursue or defend a claim, there was not reason why the law, whether substantive or procedural, should require the interposition of a next friend or a litigation friend. Moreover, a person should not be held unable to understand the information relevant to a decision if he could understand an explanation of that information in broad terms and simple language. Further, he should not be regarded as unable to make a rational decision merely because the decision which he did, in fact, make was a decision which would not be made by a person of ordinary prudence; *White v Fell* (12 November 1987, unreported, QBD) considered [2002] All ER (D) 297 (Dec); CA [2003] All ER (D) 59 (Jan).

Matthews v Martin & Others

Rectification of deed of family arrangement.

A widow agreed with her children that her late husband's estate should be distributed in a manner different from that laid down in the *Intestacy Rules*. The deed was executed within two years of the deceased's death as required by *IHTA 1984*, *s 182*, but it contained errors of which the parties only became aware after the expiry of the two-year period. The Ch D granted the widow's application for retrospective rectification of the deed. The deed was clearly defective and did not reflect the proper agreement of the parties. The fact that the sole purpose of seeking rectification was the obtaining of a fiscal advantage was not a bar to granting the relief sought. *Lake v Lake & Others* and *Seymour & Another v Seymour* applied. Ch D 1990, [1991] BTC 8048.

Mawson v Barclays Mercantile Business Finance Ltd (aka ABC Ltd v M)

General anti-avoidance – capital allowances.

A UK finance company (B) agreed to purchase a pipeline, which was accepted as plant and machinery, from the Irish Gas Board for £91,000,000 and to lease the pipeline back to the Board for 31 years. The Board in turn subleased the pipeline to a UK subsidiary company (G). Arrangements were agreed whereby the whole of the purchase price paid by B was deposited with a Jersey company (D), so that it was not available for immediate use by the Board, but was ultimately paid by D to B's holding company. B claimed capital allowances on the £91,000,000. The Revenue rejected the claim on the basis that the money was not expenditure incurred on the acquisition of plant or machinery, within *CAA 2001, s 11**. The CA allowed the company's appeal and the HL unanimously upheld this decision, observing that 'the object of granting the allowance is . . . to provide a tax equivalent to the normal accounting deduction from profits for the depreciation of machinery and plant used for the purposes of a trade. . . . When the trade is finance leasing, this means that the capital expenditure should have been incurred to acquire the machinery or plant for the purpose of leasing it in the course of the trade.' These requirements were 'in the case of a finance lease concerned entirely with the acts and purposes of the lessor'. On the evidence, the purchase and leaseback were part of B's 'ordinary trade of finance leasing'. What subsequently happened to the purchase price did 'not affect the reality of the expenditure by (B) and its acquisition of the pipeline for the purposes of its finance leasing trade'. *Mawson v Barclays Mercantile Business Finance Ltd (aka ABC Ltd v M)*, HL 2004, 76 TC 446; [2005] STC 1; [2004] UKHL 51; [2005] 1 All ER 97. (*Note.* See now, however, *CAA 2001, ss 221–228*, largely deriving from *F(No 2) A 1997, s 46.*)

Melville and Others v CIR

IHTA, s 272 – definition of 'property'.

In 1993 a settlor (M) made a discretionary settlement under terms which conferred on him a general power to direct the trustees to exercise a power of apportionment, and included the power to direct the trustees to transfer the whole of the trust fund to him absolutely. In 1999 the Revenue issued a notice of determination on the trustees. They appealed, contending that M's right to require them to revest all or part of the settled property on him was part of the 'rights and interests of any description' which, by virtue of *IHTA, s 272*, formed part of M's estate immediately after the settlement. The Ch D accepted this contention and allowed the appeal. Lightman J noted that the settlement had been intended 'to create a situation in which the settlor is able to make a substantial transfer of assets into a settlement which gives rise to a charge to inheritance tax in respect of the entire disposal, while at the same time ensuring that the amount of inheritance tax actually payable is negligible'. However, he held that not to treat the general power of appointment as 'property' within *s 272* would open the way 'to the artificial diminution of settlors' estates by the purchase of valuable consideration of enduring general powers of appointment under unconnected settlements'. A general power of appointment was 'something of very real value vested in the appointor'. [2000] STC 628; Ch D [2000] All ER(D) 832; CA [2001] STC 1271. The Court of Appeal upheld this decision. (*Note.* See now *FA 2002, s 119*. This is intended to ensure that, with effect from 17 April 2002, 'powers over trust property are to be disregarded for IHT purposes . . . except where doing so would create new scope for tax avoidance'.).

Miller & Others v CIR

Interest in possession – power to appropriate revenue to meet depreciation of capital value of assets – whether administrative or dispositive.

Property was held in trust to pay the whole of the free annual income to the wife for life but with the trustees having power, before striking the free income from any year, to appropriate such portion of the revenue as they thought proper to meet depreciation of the capital value of any asset or for any other reason they deemed advisable in their sole discretion. On the death of the wife, survived by her husband and children, the husband was entitled to one-third of the free income and the remainder was held for the maintenance and education of the children, also subject to the trustees' power to appropriate revenue to meet depreciation of assets etc. Following *Pearson and Others v CIR*, the CS held that, on the facts, the powers given to the trustees were administrative and not dispositive and that the wife had an interest in possession in the whole fund. On her death, therefore, a liability to CTT arose, subject to the exemption to the extent of the one-third interest passing to the husband, under the provisions of *CGTA 1984, ss 4(1), 5(1), 49(1)**. CS 1986, [1987] STC 108.

Millington v Secretary of State for the Environment

Wine making can be agriculture. Section 55, Town and Country Planning Act 1990.

Land was used for the creation of a new product from produce grown on that land, the land was still capable of being used for the purpose of agriculture and therefore was exempt from planning control. Mr Millington owned a site of nine hectares which included part of an old Roman city and this was turned over to vine growing, wine making and visits to the Roman site. The planning authority served Mr Millington with an enforcement notice relating to that part of the site on which a building stood which stored wine, wine making equipment and retail area. Mr Millington appealed to the Secretary of State who dismissed the appeal but granted planning permission for an existing building to provide facilities for the making of wine but selling the wine from the premises was disallowed. The Millingtons appealed and Judge Rich, QC, after due consideration remitted the case back to the Secretary of State. The Court of Appeal held that the making and selling of wine made from grapes grown on the land was capable of being an agricultural use. [1999] TLR 29 June 1999.

Moggs (Moggs' Executor) v CIR

Informal gift of 50% interest in property before the formal transfer – whether value of deceased's estate immediately before death included entirety of house with vacant possession.

In 1996 a woman (G), who was separated from her husband, moved into a house owned and occupied by her uncle (M). In August 2000 M, who had been diagnosed as having prostate cancer, formally transferred a 50% interest in the property to G. M died in April 2001. His executor appealed against a subsequent Notice of Determination, contending that M had made an informal gift of the 50% interest in the property before the formal transfer. The Special Commissioner rejected this contention and dismissed the executor's appeal. [2005] STC SCD 394 Sp C 464.

Montagu Trust Co (Jersey) Ltd and Others v CIR

Excluded property – trust fund invested in government securities – beneficiaries domiciled abroad.

The trust fund of a settlement made by K in 1970 was invested in a single holding of

1976 Treasury Loan Stock. This stock was exempt from taxation so long as it was in the beneficial ownership of persons neither domiciled nor ordinarily resident in the UK. K's daughter, W, made a similar settlement in 1976. The settlor, trustees and beneficiaries were all domiciled outside the UK but the trust was to be governed by English law. The trustees of the two settlements transferred the 1970 settlement trust fund to themselves as trustees of the 1976 settlement, to be held on trusts for the exclusive benefit of W's four children and their issue. On the following day the trustees executed a deed of appointment whereby each child became entitled to an interest in possession of one quarter of the trust fund. The Revenue raised assessments on the ground that the making of the appointment constituted a deemed capital distribution. The trustees'appeals were dismissed by the Ch D. There was a possibility that the fund might benefit people domiciled in the UK. On the facts, the trusts of the 1976 settlement were not exclusively for the benefit of W's four children, but might also benefit W's grandchildren. Accordingly there were resulting trusts to persons who might be resident in the UK and thus the trust fund was not excluded property. Ch D, [1989] STC 477.

Moodie v CIR & Sinnett

Tax avoidance schemes.

Under a tax avoidance scheme similar to that considered in *CIR v Plummer*, two taxpayers received sums from a registered charity in return for making five 'annual payments' to the charity. The taxpayers claimed to deduct the amounts of the payments in computing their income for tax purposes. The Revenue raised assessments on the basis that the payments were not deductible as 'annual payments', since the scheme should be treated as a fiscal nullity under the principles laid down in *W T Ramsay Ltd v CIR*. The HL upheld the assessments (reversing the decision of the CA and restoring that of the Special Commissioners). The taxpayers had not made annual payments within the meaning of *ICTA*, because the steps taken under the scheme were self-cancelling. The schemes had no object or effect other than the manufacture of claims that the taxpayers had reduced their income. The taxpayers had not reduced their actual income and had not been put to any capital expense other than the cost of the scheme. The decisions in *Plummer* and *Ramsay* were inconsistent. The decision in *Plummer* had been made on the assumption that payments had been made in implementation of each of the steps which constituted the scheme, and the fact that the scheme was self-cancelling had not been considered. In the subsequent case of *Ramsay*, however, the HL had held that schemes whereby an alleged loss was manufactured by a pre-arranged series of self-cancelling transactions were to be considered as a whole, and treated as fiscally ineffective. If this principle had been applied to the facts in *Plummer*, the decision in *Plummer* would have been different. Therefore the decision in *Ramsay* should be followed and the inconsistent decision in *Plummer* should be ignored. HL 1993, 65 TC 610; [1993] STC 188; [1993] 1 WLR 266; [1993] 2 All ER 49.

Moore and Osborne v CIR, In re Trafford's Settlements

Interest in possession – sole object of discretionary trust.

A settlor directed that income from certain trust funds was to be held upon protective trusts during his life, and that the trustees were to pay or apply the income to himself or to any wife or children he might have as they in their discretion saw fit. When he died in 1978 he was unmarried and childless, and the question arose as to whether or not he was beneficially entitled to an interest in possession in the trust funds immediately before his death. The Ch D upheld the trustees' contention that he was not so entitled. On the true construction of the relevant clause, the settlement had created an immediate discretionary trust rather than (as the Revenue argued) a protected life interest. The fact that the settlor was the sole existing object of the discretionary trust did not give him an interest in possession. The possibility, although remote, that another discretionary beneficiary might come into existence was sufficient to prevent him from having the necessary immediate entitlement to trust income as it arose. Ch D 1984, CTTL 20; [1984] STC 236; [1984] 3 WLR 341; [1984] 1 All ER 1108.

Moore's Executors v CIR

Domicile

A US citizen (M), born in Missouri, moved to the UK in 1991 and acquired a property in London. He lived in the UK until his death in 1997, although he continued to use a US passport. He left two wills, a US will leaving his US assets to two individual beneficiaries, and an English will, disposing of his non-US assets to a wide range of beneficiaries. The Inland Revenue issued a notice of determination that he had acquired a domicile of choice in England. The executors of his English will appealed. The Special Commissioners allowed the appeal, observing that M had remained a US citizen and taxpayer, and holding on the evidence that 'his living solely in London had been determined more by ill-health than by a desire to make England his permanent home'. [2002] STC SCD 463 Sp C 335.

Munro v Commrs of Stamp Duties of New South Wales

Gifts with reservation – exclusion of the donor from any benefit.

Arrangements between the donee and a third party to give the donor benefit is within the provisions but retention of rights under a contract made prior to the gift and quite separate from it is not. The gift of land already subject to a lease to the donor is not a gift with reservation as the lease is not part of the gift. PC [1934] AC 61; [1933] All ER 185.

Nadin v CIR

Irregular payments to close relatives – whether exempt from IHT as 'normal expenditure of the transferor' – IHTA 1984, s 21.

An elderly spinster (P) died in 1995. During the years before her death, she had made a number of irregular payments to close relatives. The Revenue issued a notice of determination charging IHT on the basis that the gifts made in the seven years before P's death were transfers of value. Her executor appealed, contending that the gifts were exempt from IHT under IHTA 1984, s 21 as 'part of the normal expenditure of the transferor'. The Special Commissioner rejected this contention and dismissed the appeal. On the evidence, the payments in question were abnormal expenditure rather than normal expenditure, and thus failed to qualify for exemption. Dicta of Lightman J in *Bennett & Others* applied. [1997] STC SCD 107 Sp C 112.

Nelson Dance Family Settlement Trustees v HMRC

Transfer of farmland with development value.

In 2002 a farmer transferred some farmland, which had development value, to the trustees of a family settlement. HMRC issued a ruling that 'none of the value transferred was attributable to the value of relevant business property'. The trustees appealed. The Special Commissioner allowed the appeal, specifically disapproving passages in Dymond's Capital Taxes and Foster's Inheritance Tax which suggested that the transfer of business assets (as distinct from the transfer of a business itself) would not qualify for relief. The Commissioner (Dr. Avery Jones) held that 'everything turns on the loss in value to the donor's estate, rather than what is given or how the loss to the estate arises, except where the identity of the recipient is crucial to a particular exemption'. He held that business property relief was 'much more concerned with values than property. Although the attribution is to the net value of the business as a whole, this does not imply that the value transferred must relate to the whole business. Indeed the exclusion for value attributed to excepted assets in *s 112* shows that the value transferred may need to be attributed to the value of particular business assets (although that would equally be the case if the relief were restricted to transfers of the whole business). Presumably the attribution to the net value of the business is to put a ceiling on the relief to prevent a transferor giving away the total assets of the business, claiming business relief for them, while retaining the liabilities and paying them out of other assets (although that seems to be possible for agricultural relief as the relief is given in terms of attribution to the agricultural value of agricultural property).' *IHTA 1984, s 104* should be construed as meaning that 'all that is required is that the value transferred by the transfer of value is attributable to the net value of the business'. Accordingly, the transfer of the farmland qualified for 100% business property relief. The Ch D upheld this decision. Sales J held that 'the general principle governing the operation of the *IHTA* is the loss to donor principle, which directs attention to changes in the value of the transferor's estate rather than in that of the transferee', and that 'any charge to tax does not turn upon what happens to property transferred when it is in the hands of the transferee'. [2008] STC SCD 792 Sp C 682; Ch D [2009] EWHC 71 (Ch).

New South Wales Commrs of Stamp Duties v Permanent Trustee Co of New South Wales Ltd

Gifts with reservation – exclusion of donor from enjoyment.

The PC held that this condition is not fulfilled if at some later date after the gift the property or income therefrom is voluntarily applied by the donee to the donor, even if the latter is under an obligation to repay sums used by him. PC [1956] AC 512; [1956] 2 All ER 512; [1956] 3 WLR 152.

New South Wales Commrs of Stamp Duties v Perpetual Trustee Co Ltd

Gifts with reservation – settlements.

A settlement of shares in favour of an infant child with absolute gift provided he reached the age of 21 but with a resulting trust to the donor if the child failed to reach that age was not a gift with reservation as the property comprised in the gift was the equitable interest which the donor had created in the shares. PC, [1943] AC 425; [1943] 1 All ER 525.

New York Life Insurance Co Ltd v Public Trustee

Situation of property – simple contract debt.

A simple contract debt is situate in the country in which the debtor resides. If there is more than one country of residence the terms of the contract may serve to localise the debt. CA 1924, 40 TLR 430; [1924] 2 Ch 101.

Nichols v CIR

Gifts with reservation – exclusion of the donor from any benefit.

A gift of land subject to an agreement to a lease-back created at the same or a later time is the grant of the whole with something reserved out of it and not a gift of a partial interest leaving something in the hands of the grantor which he has not given away. CA, [1975] STC 278; [1975] 2 All ER 120; [1975] 1 WLR 534.

Ninth Marquess of Hertford and others (Executors of Eighth Marquess of Hertford deceased) v CIR

IHTA, s 110(b) – historic house used for business purposes and as private residence – whether 'assets used in the business'.

Part of a historic house was open to the public, while part was used as a private residence and not open to the public. The freeholder died in 1997. The Inland Revenue issued a notice of determination charging IHT on 22% of the value of the house, on the basis that only 78% of the house was open to the public and thus only 78% of the house qualified for business property relief. The freeholder's executors appealed, contending that the house was a single asset and that the effect of *IHTA 1984, s 110(b)* was that the whole of the house qualified for business property relief even though 22% of the house was not open to the public. The Special Commissioner accepted this contention and allowed the appeal, observing that *s 110* made no provision for apportionment, and holding that 'it is natural to consider a single building as a single asset where the unencumbered freehold is in single ownership'. The house was 'plainly important as a single structure and the whole building is a vital backdrop to the business carried on. The whole of the exterior is essential to the business.' [2005] STC SCD 177 Sp C 44.

Oakes v Commrs of Stamp Duties of New South Wales

Gifts with reservation – exclusion of the donor from any benefit.

Remuneration paid to the settlor as trustee, but not money spent on the maintenance and education of the donor's children, is a benefit. PC [1954] AC 57; [1953] 2 All ER 1563; [1953] 3 WLR 1127.

Oakley & Hutson (Jossaume's Personal Representatives) v CIR

Testator's will giving company right to occupy property – whether testator's widow had interest in possession.

A company director (J) died in 1993. Under his will, as modified by a deed of family arrangement, he gave his shares in the company to his son, and two freehold properties to trustees, with directions to pay the trust income to his widow for her lifetime and thereafter to his three children in equal shares. One of the freehold properties was occupied by the company, and J directed that the trustees of his will should not require the company to pay any rent. J's executors treated the property as having been transferred to his widow, and as qualifying for the exemption for transfers between spouses. J's widow died in 2000, and the Inland Revenue issued a notice of determination that IHT was chargeable on her interest in possession in the premises which were occupied by the company. Her personal representatives appealed, contending that the executors had made an error in treating the interest in the premises as having been transferred to J's widow, that J's will had conferred an interest in possession on the company, and that his widow did not have an interest in possession. The Special Commissioner accepted this contention and allowed the appeal, holding that J had intended that his will should 'protect the position of the company and . . . preserve its use and occupancy' of the premises. The will gave the company a right to occupy the premises, and that right arose 'solely under the will'. The right in question was 'a present right to present enjoyment of property' and was an 'interest in possession' within *IHTA 1984, s 49(1)*. (The Commissioner observed that the effect of this decision was that IHT 'will have become due in respect of the transfer of the yard at his death . . . (but) that a lower amount of inheritance tax will be payable than would have been the case' if IHT had been charged on the death of J's widow.) [2005] STC SCD 343 Sp C 460.

Ogden & Hutchinson (Griffiths' Executors) v Trustees of the RHS Griffiths 2003 Settlement & Others

Application for transfers of assets into settlements to be set aside.

In April 2003 an individual (G) granted a deferred lease of his property to a settlement, and transferred his shares in a company to a short-term discretionary trust. In February 2004 he transferred his reversionary interest in the shares to a third settlement. Later that year he was diagnosed as suffering from cancer. He died in April 2005, so that the transfers became chargeable to IHT. His executors applied to the Chancery Division (Ch D) for the transfers to be set aside. The Ch D granted the application in part. Lewison J declined to set aside the April 2003 transfers, as medical evidence indicated that it was 'extremely unlikely' that G had been suffering from cancer at that time. Applying the principles laid down in *Ogilvie v Allen*, HL 1899, 15 TLR 294, 'a donor can only obtain back property which he has given away by showing that he was under some mistake of so serious a character as to render it unjust on the part of the donee to retain the property given to him'. However, the evidence suggested that G had already been suffering from cancer in February 2004, so that his chances of surviving for three years were very remote. If G had been aware of this, he would not have transferred his reversionary interest in the shares. It would be 'unjust for the donees to retain the gift in circumstances which impose upon the donor an unintended liability to a very substantial amount of inheritance tax'. Accordingly, the Ch D exercised its discretion to set aside the February 2004 transfer. Ch D [2008] EWHC 118 (Ch); STC 776.

O'Neill and others v IRC

Deposit account in joint names of deceased and daughter – whether general power to dispose of the whole account. IHTA 1984, s 5.

An individual (O) died in 1992. In 1980 and 1984 he had opened deposit accounts in an Isle of Man bank, in the joint names of O and his daughter. He had deposited substantial sums in the accounts. The Revenue issued a notice of determination charging IHT on the basis that the whole of the amounts in the deposit accounts formed part of O's estate. O's daughter and executors appealed, contending that only 50% of the sums in the accounts should be treated as part of O's estate. The Special Commissioner rejected this contention and dismissed the appeals, holding on the evidence that O 'enjoyed the entire beneficial interest in the accounts during his lifetime'. O's daughter had not known that the accounts existed until after her father's death. The fact that O's daughter was never informed of the accounts in her father's lifetime rebutted the presumption of advancement except to the extent that it applied to the right of survivorship. While she had a beneficial right of survivorship, she did not have 'a present beneficial interest in the accounts during her father's lifetime'. Only O had been able to operate the accounts, and this *de facto* control of the accounts was 'a clear pointer to the conclusion' that he had not made a lifetime gift of an immediate interest in the accounts to his daughter. [1998] STC SCD 110 Sp C 154.

Ontario (Treasurer for) v Aberdein

Situation of property – registered shares.

In a Canadian case the PC held that registered shares which could be dealt with in two countries were situate in the one in which in the ordinary course of affairs the shares would be dealt with by the registered owner. PC 1946, [1947] AC 24.

Oughtred v CIR

Time of disposition – disposition of equitable interest in settled property.

An oral agreement was not effective to transfer an equitable reversionary interest. Such a transfer could only be effected in writing. HL, [1959] 3 All ER 623.

Owen, Re, Owen v CIR

Time of disposition – time of gift by cheque.

More than three years before his death O gave a cheque to each of three relatives. However the cheques were not presented for payment until within the three year period before O's death. The gifts were held to have been made when the cheques cleared into each donee's own account and were therefore liable to ED as being gifts made within three years of the donor's death. Ch D, [1949] 1 All ER 901.

Parry and others as Personal representatives of R F Staveley deceased v HMRC

transfer of value for IHT purposes – IHTA 1984, s 12.

Mrs R F Staveley had been diagnosed with terminal cancer early in 2006. Subsequent to that she transferred the funds in a section 32 pension plan into a personal pension plan, the terms of which would allow the entire fund to be paid to her estate or to other beneficiaries. She was keen to ensure that her ex-husband could not benefit from the fund. She took no benefits from the policy prior to her death in December 2006 and nominated her two sons as the beneficiaries to receive the death benefits from the fund.

HMRC considered that the transfer of funds from the section 32 policy was a transfer of value for IHT purposes but her executors argued that it was exempt as being made without gratuitous intent – the purpose was to ensure the fund could not benefit the ex-husband. The Tribunal accepted that the exemption applied in relation to the transfer of the funds.

HMRC also considered that the failure to take pension benefits was an omission to exercise a right which caused an increase in the sons' estates. The decision on this point involved extensive analysis of *IHTA 1984, s 12* as it stood before the repeal of *FA 2011, ss 2A- 2E*. The Tribunal found for HMRC on this issue. [2014] UKFTT 419 (TC).

Patch's Executors v HMRC

IHTA 1984, s 52(1) – effect of deed of partition.

A testator (P) left his widow a life interest in his residuary estate, with the remainder passing to his two children (by a previous marriage). In July 2000 the trustees executed a deed of partition under which the widow assigned two-thirds of the trust fund under P's estate to the reversioners, and received an absolute interest in the remainder. In December 2000 the widow died. HMRC issued a notice of determination on the basis that the deed of partition had resulted in a transfer of value under *IHTA 1984, s 52(1)*. The executors appealed, contending that the deed of partition should not be treated as giving rise to a transfer of value. The Special Commissioner rejected this contention and dismissed the appeal. [2007] STC SCD 453 Sp C 600.

Pawson deceased (personal representatives of) v HMRC

A seaside bungalow was let on a weekly basis as holiday accommodation. It was a standard holiday let business, in that the property was fully furnished and equipped, and it was cleaned between lets and freshly laundered bedding provided on each occasion, but no supplementary services were provided. The appellant claimed that the property qualified for IHT business property relief, but the claim was refused by HMRC on the grounds that the business was mainly one of holding the property as an investment for rental income. The appeal was allowed on the basis that significant services were provided, such that 'an intelligent businessman would not regard the ownership of a holiday letting property as an investment and would regard it as involving far too active an operation for it to come under that heading'. On the appeal by HMRC to the Upper Tax Tribunal, the decision was reversed. The Upper Tribunal held that the only conclusion which it was reasonably open to draw from the facts was that the property was held as an investment. It was a typical example of a property letting business and the services did not preponderate to such an extent that the investment nature of the business was not the main element. *Pawson deceased v HMRC* [2013] UKUT 50(TCC).

Pearson and Others v CIR

Meaning of interest in possession.

Subject to the trustees' overriding power of appointment, to their power to accumulate income and to the possibility of partial defeasance on the birth of further children to the settlor, property in a 1964 settlement was held upon trust in equal shares absolutely for the three daughters of the settlor upon their attaining the age of 21. They were all 21 by the end of February 1974. On 20 March 1976 the trustees appointed the income of £16,000 to one of the daughters, F. The Revenue determined that F had become entitled to an interest in possession in the £16,000 at a time when no such interest subsisted in that part of the trust fund and that accordingly CTT became payable by virtue of *FA 1975, 5 Sch 6(2)*. By a three to two majority, and reversing the unanimous decision of the CA in favour of the trustees, the HL upheld the Revenue's determination. The trustees' power of accumulation prevented the interests the daughters obtained upon reaching 21 from being interests in possession. For there to be an interest in possession there must be a present right to the present enjoyment of something and the power of accumulation prevented the daughters from having an immediate right to anything. A distinction was drawn by Viscount Dilhorne between trustees' administrative powers, such as those to pay duties, taxes etc., and their dispositive power to dispose of the net income of the trust fund. A mere administrative power will not prevent an interest from being in possession. HL 1980, CTTL 5; [1980] STC 318; [1980] 2 All ER 479; [1980] 2 WLR 872.

Pemsel v Special Commissioners

The meaning of 'charitable purposes'.

Lands were vested in trustees to apply the rents in maintaining (i) certain missionary establishments, (ii) a school for the children of ministers and missionaries, and (iii) certain other religious establishments. The trustees were held to be entitled to exemption under *ICTA 1988, s 505(1)(a)**. (This is the leading case on the meaning of 'charitable purposes' in *ICTA 1988, s 505*. The Revenue's argument, based on an 1888 decision of the Court of Session (*Baird's Trustees v Lord Advocate* CS 1888, 25 SLR 533), was that 'charity' should be given its popular meaning of the relief of poverty, and not the wider technical meaning evolved over the years in English courts; that technical meaning differed from the technical meaning under Scottish law, and in an Act applying to both countries it should have the same meaning. In a series of judgments containing a comprehensive review of the relevant law, the HL by a majority held that 'charity' should be given its technical meaning under English law and comprises (per Lord Macnaghten) 'four principal divisions; trusts for the relief of poverty, trusts for the advancement of education, trusts for the advancement of religion, and trusts beneficial to the community and not falling under any of the preceding heads. The trusts last referred to are not the less charitable . . . because incidentally they benefit the rich as well as the poor.' These rules have been extensively applied in subsequent charity cases.) HL 1891, 3 TC 53; [1891] AC 531.

Pepper v Hart

Concessionary fees for sons of staff at public school – Parliamentary history of legislation.

Nine schoolmasters and the bursar of a public school had their sons educated at concessionary reduced fees of approximately one-fifth of the standard fees. The reduced fees covered the direct costs attributable to each boy, but did not include any indirect costs. The boys occupied surplus places at the school and their education there was at the discretion of the school, rather than an entitlement. The Revenue raised assessments on the basis that, in computing the cash equivalent of the benefits for the purpose of *ICTA 1988, s 156**, the overall running costs of the whole school should be apportioned pro rata to the concessionary places. The taxpayers appealed, contending that only the marginal costs should be assessed. The HL allowed the taxpayers' appeals against the assessments (reversing the decision of the CA and restoring that of the Special Commissioner). The wording of *ICTA 1988, s 156** was ambiguous. It derived from *FA 1976*, and, during the Parliamentary debates which preceded its enactment, the then Financial Secretary had clearly stated that the intention of the legislation was to assess such in-house benefits on the marginal cost to the employer, rather than on the average cost. Hansard could be used as an aid to interpretation where 'legislation is ambiguous or obscure, or leads to an absurdity; the material relied upon consists of one or more statements by a Minister or other promoter of the Bill together if necessary with such other Parliamentary material as is necessary to understand such statements and their effect; and the statements relied upon are clear'. In the light of these statements, the ambiguity should be resolved by construing the relevant legislation in such a way as to give effect to the intentions of Parliament. HL 1992, 65 TC 421; [1992] STC 898; [1992] 3 WLR 1032; [1993] 1 All ER 42.

Perry v CIR

IHTA 1984, s 200(1) – transfer on death – person liable.

A property dealer (K) had a joint bank account with a young woman (P), who lived in a property which K owned. K died in 1989, at which time there was more than £1,000,000 in the account. K's executors (a solicitor and an accountant) provided the Revenue with details of his estate, but made no reference to this bank account. In 1991 P replaced the accountant as K's personal representative. In 1995 the personal representatives (P and the solicitor) presented a bankruptcy petition, declaring that the estate was insolvent. The Revenue subsequently ascertained details of the bank account, and in 1997 they issued a notice of determination that P was liable to IHT in respect of half of the money in the account at K's death. The Special Commissioner upheld the determination and dismissed P's appeal, holding on the evidence that 'the joint account constituted a gift from (K) to the appellant of the balance for the time being in the account'. The effect of *IHTA 1984, s 200(1)(c)* was that P was liable to account for tax on the money in question. (The Commissioner also upheld a further notice of determination, holding that in 1984 K had given P 'an irrevocable licence to occupy rent-free . . . for life' the property in which she lived.) [2005] STC SCD 474 Sp C 474.

Phillips and Others (Phillips' Executor) v HMRC

Business property relief – activities of a money-lender who lent money to family companies qualified for business property relief.

A widow held a majority shareholding in a company (P) which lent money to related family companies. Her executors claimed business property relief. The Revenue rejected the claim on the basis that the shares were not 'relevant business property', because P's business consisted mainly of 'making or holding investments', within *IHTA 1984, s 105(3)*. The Special Commissioner allowed the executors' appeal, finding that P was 'a banking arm for in-house transactions' and holding that 'few would regard the activities of a money-lender as investment'. On the evidence, P 'was in the business of making loans and not in the business of investing in loans . . . . the loans were not investments for their own sake but the provision of a finance facility to the other companies'. Accordingly, the shares in P qualified for business property relief. [2006] STC SCD 639 Sp C 555.

Phizackerley (Personal Representative of Dr PJR Phizackerley) v HMRC

FA 1986, s 103 – treatment of certain debts.

A married woman died in 2000. Her will left an amount equal to the IHT nil rate band to a discretionary trust for her husband (P) and their children, and the residue to P. He agreed to pay £150,000 plus indexation to the discretionary trust in return for his wife's half-share in the matrimonial home. P died in 2002, and HMRC issued a notice of determination charging IHT on his estate. His personal representative appealed, contending that the £153,222 which P owed to the discretionary trust should be deducted from the value of his estate. The Special Commissioner rejected this contention and dismissed his appeal, holding that the effect of *FA 1986, s 103* was that the debt was not deductible. The Commissioner also held that *IHTA 1984, s 11* (providing that a 'disposition for maintenance' is not a 'transfer of value') did not apply to a situation 'when a husband puts a house in joint names of himself and his wife during their marriage'. [2007] STC SCD 328 Sp C 591.

Plummer v CIR

Domicile – whether foreign domicile of choice acquired.

A taxpayer aged 18 at the beginning of the relevant years, whose domicile of origin was English, claimed that she was domiciled in Guernsey for the purpose of a claim under *ICTA 1988, s 65(4)**. She was born in London of English parents. When she was aged 15, her mother and a sister went to take up residence in Guernsey with her grandmother. From then the taxpayer divided her residence between England and Guernsey, generally continuing her education and training in England (where she was reading for a degree at London University in the relevant years) and living with her father there during the week, and going with him to Guernsey for the week-end. She gave evidence before the Special Commissioners of her attachment to Guernsey and her intention to live and work there. The Commissioners held that she had not become an 'inhabitant' of Guernsey in the years of claim and therefore could not be said to have acquired a domicile of choice in Guernsey. Hoffmann J upheld their decision. A person who kept a residence in his domicile of origin could only acquire a domicile of choice in another country if the residence established there was his chief residence. On the facts the Commissioners were entitled to conclude that the taxpayer had not yet settled in Guernsey and therefore had not acquired a domicile of choice there. Ch D 1987, 60 TC 452; [1987] STC 698; [1988] 1 WLR 292; [1988] 1 All ER 97.

Portland, Duchess of, CIR v

Domicile – domicile acquired on marriage – effect of Matrimonial Proceedings Act 1973.

The taxpayer's domicile of origin was Canada. She acquired her husband's English domicile by dependence on her marriage. She lived in England with her husband but had a house in Canada which she visited annually and where she intended to live on her husband's retirement or death. The Ch D, reversing the decision of the Special Commissioners, held that by virtue of the *Matrimonial Proceedings Act 1973, s 1(2)* she retained her English domicile as a deemed domicile of choice, and her visits to Canada did not amount to an abandonment of that domicile. Ch D 1981, 54 TC 648; [1982] STC 149; [1982] 2 WLR 367; [1982] 1 All ER 784.

Postlethwaite's Executors v HMRC

Payment by close company to FURBS for controlling shareholder – whether IHTA 1984, s 10 applicable.*

A motor racing engineer (P) incorporated a Jersey company (L) in 1990. In 1991 L agreed to provide P's services to an Italian company (G) for £600,000 pa, and also agreed to employ P at a salary of £75,000 pa. In 1993 L paid £700,000 to a funded unapproved retirement benefits scheme for P. P died in 1999, aged 55. Subsequently the Inland Revenue issued a notice of determination that the payment of £700,000 was a transfer of value within *IHTA 1984, s 94*. P's executors appealed, contending that the payment was a disposition not intended to confer gratuitous benefit, within *IHTA*

1984, s 10. The Special Commissioners reviewed the evidence in detail, accepted this contention and allowed the appeal. The Commissioners observed that the fees paid by G to L were 'in line with the cost of the services of comparable motor racing engineers'. By contrast, 'the basic salary paid by (L) to (P) was very low for a person of his standing'. The payment of £700,000 was not unreasonable or gratuitous, since 'if (P) had contributed at the maximum allowable level to an approved UK scheme until he was 60 and his salary of £75,000 had increased with inflation, the pension which he would have obtained was about the same as that which the £700,000 would secure'. Furthermore, 'the fact that on legal analysis the payment was for past consideration does not mean that it was made with the intention of conferring a gratuitous benefit'. [2008] STC SCD 83 Sp C 571.

Powell & Halfhide, executor of G E Pearce v CIR

IHTA 1984, s 105(3). Business of managing a caravan park – making or holding investments.

The deceased and her daughter ran a caravan park where 23 of the 33 caravans were privately owned. The deceased or her representative needed to be in attendance at the site at all times. The profits of the business were assessed to tax under Schedule D, Case I. On death the personal representatives claimed relief under *s 105(3)* and this was refused by the Inspector who argued the 'making or holding investments' applied in this instance. The activities undertaken in the caravan park were either required under the terms of the lettings or the terms of the site licence which governed the lettings, or consisted of activities such as the social visits and organised medical visits, for which no charge was made, and so accordingly fell to be in the ambit of 'making and holding investments'. On the facts of the case it was determined that there was little difference in principle between, say, the owner of a portfolio of long leases receiving ground rents and the instant case where the main source of income was derived from pitch fees from long-term residents who owned their own caravans. The case has been withdrawn from application to be heard in the High Court by the taxpayers. [1997] STC SCD 181 Sp C 120.

Powell-Cotton v CIR

Interest in possession – life interest in settlement sold in consideration for shares in close company – subsequent transfer of shares by way of gift – whether a disposal of interest in possession in settled property.

In 1941 the taxpayer sold to a close company his life interest under a settlement for £25,000, to be paid by 25,000 £1 shares in the company. In 1964 he reacquired from the company his life interest in part of the settled property. His interest in the remainder of the settled property continued to be vested in the company. In 1982 the taxpayer transferred 2,999 of his shares to a charity by way of gift. Immediately before the transfer, he had held 8,993 of the 46,000 shares in the company. Accordingly, by virtue of what is now *IHTA 1984, s 101(1)* he fell to be treated as having been entitled to a part (8,993/46,000) of the interest in possession in the part of the settled property retained by the company. Following the transfer, he fell to be treated as being entitled to 5,994/46,000 of the interest in possession in question. The Revenue issued a notice of determination on the basis that he had made a transfer of value equal to (2,999/8,993 × 8993/46,000) of the settled property vested in the company. The taxpayer appealed, contending firstly that no part of the interest in possession had come to an end within *s 52(1)*, so that he had not made a disposal within *s 51(1)*, and alternatively that any transfer of value was exempt since it was attributable to property given to a charity within the meaning of what is now *IHTA 1984, s 23(1)*. The Ch D dismissed his appeal. The provisions of what is now *IHTA 1984, s 101(1)* required the interest in possession held by the close company to be treated as vested in the participators in that company. Accordingly, on the disposal of the shares, part of the taxpayer's interest in possession had come to an end within *IHTA 1984, s 52(1)*. The corollary of *IHTA 1984, s 101(1)* was that the company could not be treated as having an interest in possession in the settled property, since that would be inconsistent with the beneficial ownership attributed to the participator, and the company's right to the income of the retained part therefore had to be disregarded. Additionally, the effect of *IHTA 1984, s 56(3)* was that the deemed transfer of part of the settled property was not exempted by *IHTA 1984, s 23(1)*; Ch D, [1992] STC 625.

Price AL (Executor of Mrs RHP Price) v HMRC

Related property – IHTA 1984 s 161.

A married couple owned a freehold property as tenants in common. The wife (P) died in 1999. By her will, she left her share of the property to her children. It was agreed that if the property were to be sold as a whole, it would be valued at £1,500,000. HMRC issued a notice of determination charging IHT on this basis. P's husband (who was also her executor) appealed, contending inter alia that the effect of *IHTA 1984, s 161(1)* was there should be a substantial reduction in the valuation of P's half share of the property, to take account that of the fact that the property could not be sold with vacant possession. The First-Tier Tribunal rejected this contention and dismissed the appeal in principle, applying the principles laid down by the CA in *Gray & Others (Lady Fox's Executors) v CIR*, see above, and holding that for the purposes of *IHTA, s 161*, the 'value of the aggregate' should be taken to be 'the price which the two items of property would fetch in the open market if offered for sale at the same time'. The tribunal directed that, if the parties were unable to agree the valuation in the light of this decision, any further points of dispute should be heard by the Lands Chamber of the Upper Tribunal. 2010 UKFTT 474, TC00736.

Prosser (Jempson's Personal Representatives) v CIR

Interest charge under IHTA 1984, s 233(1)(b).

A personal representative failed to pay IHT of £8,000. The Revenue imposed an interest charge under *IHTA 1984, s 233(1)(b)*. The Special Commissioner upheld the charge to interest and dismissed the personal representative's appeal. [2003] STC SCD 250 Sp C 362.

R v Brentford Commissioners (ex p Chan & Others)

Application for judicial review.

A partnership had been under investigation for ten years, and negotiations with their accountant, a sole practitioner (G), were still in progress. At the request of the inspector, the clerk to the General Commissioners arranged a special meeting on 10 August 1983 to dispose of the matter. Notice of the meeting reached G's office on 18 July when he was on holiday. The inspector was also on holiday, returning on 8 August. G had a previous appointment on 10 August, and on 9 August he asked the inspector to agree to an adjournment, but the inspector refused. Accordingly the partners were represented at the meeting by W, an employee of G, who was qualified but who had had insufficient time to prepare his case. The Commissioners refused his request for an adjournment and determined the appeal against the partners. W expressed dissatisfaction and the Commissioners duly stated a case. The partners sought leave to apply for judicial review. The QB rejected the application, observing that *TMA 1970, s 56* gave the High Court the widest possible powers to remit the case to the Commissioners, and holding that the appeal, already under way, should proceed by way of Case Stated. QB 1985, 57 TC 651; [1986] STC 65.

R v CIR (ex p Goldberg)

Revenue information powers – legal professional privilege.

A barrister was served with a notice under *TMA 1970, s 20(3)*, requiring him to deliver or make available to the Revenue certain copies of documents in his possession which had been sent to him by a US attorney for legal advice. He refused to comply with the notice and the Revenue began penalty proceedings. His application for judicial review was granted, and a declaration made that the documents were subject to legal professional privilege and so excluded by *TMA 1970, s 20B(8)* from the application of *TMA 1970, s 20(3);* QB, 1988, 61 TC 403; [1988] STC 524. (Note. The decision was disapproved by the CA in *Dubai Bank Ltd v Galadari CA*, [1989] 3 WLR 1044; [1989] 3 All ER 769.)

R v CIR (ex p Kaye)

Application for judicial review by shareholders selling shares before publication of Statement of Practice.

In January 1989 a married couple sold shares to a German company. Four months later, the Inland Revenue published SP 5/89, stating that where, after 31 March 1982, a taxpayer acquired shares by a no gain/no loss transfer from someone who held them on that date, those shares would, together with any shares held by the taxpayer in the same company on 31 March 1982, be treated as a single holding acquired at market value on that date. The husband realised that, if his wife had transferred her shares to him before selling them, they could have been treated as a single holding, with a higher market value at 31 March 1982. He applied by way of judicial review for a declaration that the shares should be valued as if his wife had transferred them to him. The QB dismissed the application. There had not been an inter-spouse transfer of the shares, and the Revenue had a duty to demand the tax actually due. QB 1992, 65 TC 82; [1992] STC 581.

R v CIR (ex p Matrix Securities Ltd)

Application for judicial review – withdrawal of assurance given by Inspector – assurances based on inadequate disclosure of information by applicant.

A company sponsored a scheme which was designed to take advantage of the availability of industrial buildings allowances (at the rate of 100%) in designated enterprise zones. Under the scheme, 67.5% of the price payable by potential investors would be covered by loans from a merchant bank, so that the investors would make no net contribution. The loans themselves would be repaid under special 'exit arrangements', so that the investors would assume no significant risk. In July 1993 the company's solicitors submitted a letter giving some details of the scheme to an inspector of taxes, who agreed that the payments would qualify for industrial buildings allowances. Subsequently the Revenue received further information concerning the scheme, and in October 1993 the Revenue Financial Institutions Division wrote to the company informing it that the assurances made by the inspector had been wrongly given, and that it was not bound by them. The company applied for judicial review, seeking a declaration that the withdrawal was unfair and amounted to an abuse of power. The application was dismissed by the QB, the CA and the HL. The information submitted by the company had been 'inaccurate and misleading'. The Revenue were therefore entitled to withdraw the clearance. Lord Browne-Wilkinson and Lord Griffiths observed that the applicant had been aware that the Revenue required applications for clearance to be made to its Financial Institutions Division, so that a clearance by a local inspector was not to be treated as binding. HL 1994, TL 3396; [1994] STC 272; [1994] 1 WLR 334; [1994] 1 All ER 769.

R v CIR (ex p MFK Underwriting Agencies Ltd & Others)

Application for judicial review where taxpayers allegedly misled by informal statements by Revenue officers.

Between April 1986 and October 1988, there were more than 60 issues of index-linked bonds which were denominated in Canadian and US dollars. Various approaches were made to the Revenue, both by those considering issuing such bonds and by those considering them as an investment, to clarify whether the indexation uplift, reflected in the sale price or redemption values of the securities, would be taxed as capital or as income. In three cases inspectors informed the enquirers that they would be taxed as capital, and the Revenue proceeded accordingly. However, in several other cases the Revenue did not give an unequivocal reply until October 1988 when it issued a circular declaring that the indexation uplift was assessable as income. Five applicants (all Lloyd's underwriting syndicates or managing agents) sought judicial review of the Revenue's decision. The QB refused the applications. The Revenue could not be held to be bound by anything less than a clear, unambiguous and unqualified representation. In the five cases in question, the Revenue had neither promised nor indicated that it would follow a particular course and accordingly there had been no abuse of power. QB 1989, 62 TC 607; [1989] STC 873; [1990] 1 All ER 91; [1990] 1 WLR 1545.

R v CIR (ex p National Federation of Self-Employed and Small Businesses Ltd)

Tax amnesty – whether subject to judicial review.

In 1978, the Revenue offered an amnesty, on certain conditions, to casual workers in the newspaper industry who had been evading tax by using fictitious names. A federation of small businessmen, with a membership of 50,000, applied by way of judicial review for a declaration that the amnesty was unlawful and for a *mandamus* to the Revenue to collect the tax evaded. The HL, unanimously reversing the majority decision of the CA, held that the federation did not have a sufficient interest in the matter to support the application. The action taken by the Revenue had been 'genuinely in the care and management of the taxes, under the powers entrusted to them'. The HL opinions are a comprehensive and extensive discussion of the scope of judicial review in relation to a statutory body such as the CIR. HL 1981, 55 TC 133; [1981] STC 260; [1981] 2 WLR 722; [1981] 2 All ER 93.

R v CIR (ex p Rothschild (J) Holdings plc) (No 1) (and cross-appeal)

Application for discovery of Revenue documents in judicial review proceedings.

In a stamp duty case, a company sought discovery of documents relating to the Revenue practice in applying *FA 1973, 19 Sch 10* to share exchange transactions. Simon Brown J made an order limited to internal Revenue documents of a general nature, but excluding documents relating to individual and particular cases. Both sides appealed to the CA, the Revenue contending that the judge should not have made an order for discovery, and the company contending that the order should be varied to include, *inter alia*, copies of certain documents relating to successful applications under the relevant legislation. The CA dismissed both the appeal and the cross-appeal. CA 1987, 61 TC 178; [1987] STC 163.

R v CIR (ex p Taylor)

Application for order of discovery.

The taxpayer, a solicitor, was required by a notice under *TMA 1970, s 20*, to deliver certain documents to an inspector. He applied for an order of *certiorari* to quash the notice. He also applied to the QB for an order of discovery of a submission and report made to the Board of Inland Revenue by the inspector examining his affairs prior to the issue of the notice. His application for discovery was refused. The submission was subject to legal professional privilege, and he had not produced evidence suggesting that the decision to issue a notice was unreasonable. CA 1988, 62 TC 562; [1988] STC 832; [1989] 1 All ER 906.

R v HMIT (ex p Brumfield and Others)

Judicial review – interest paid by partnership on money lent by it to a partner.

A family partnership borrowed £120,558 from a bank at interest. It lent this amount to one of the partners interest-free. That partner used the loan to buy land in his name. The partnership claimed that the bank interest paid was deductible in computing its profits. The Revenue refused the claim. Twenty-six months later the partnership applied for judicial review. Peter Gibson J refused the application. SP 4/85, on which the partnership relied, did not apply in cases where a loan was made to a partnership and the money then made available to one of the partners. Furthermore, although it was strictly unnecessary to consider the point, the delay of 26 months in making the application was inexcusable. QB 1988, 61 TC 589; [1989] STC 151.

R v HMIT (ex p Fulford-Dobson)

Gift by wife to husband about to become non-resident – application of extra-statutory concession D2.

On 18 August 1980 the taxpayer entered into a contract of employment in Germany. He was required to begin work on 15 September and he left the UK for this purpose on 29 August 1980. From that date he became resident in Germany, having previously been resident and ordinarily resident in the UK. Acting on professional advice, and admittedly to take advantage of ESC D2, his wife by deed of gift transferred to him on 29 August a farm she had inherited in 1977 and had been considering selling in 1980. The farm was in fact sold by auction on 17 September. In due course the husband was assessed to CGT for 1980–81 on the substantial gain on the sale. It was common ground that apart from ESC D2 he was chargeable, but under the concession he would not be chargeable on gains accruing to him in the part of the year during which he was not resident in the UK. The Revenue refused to apply the concession, pointing out that, as is stated inside the front cover of the pamphlet IR1 listing the extra-statutory concessions in operation, a 'concession will not be given in any case where an attempt is made to use it for tax avoidance'. The taxpayer thereupon applied by way of judicial review for an order to quash the assessment. McNeill J refused the application, holding, after an extensive review of decisions in which the courts have considered the Revenue practice of making extra-statutory concessions, that they are lawful and within the proper exercise of managerial discretion. QB 1987, 60 TC 168; [1987] STC 344; [1987] 3 WLR 277.

R v HMIT (ex p Kissane and Another)

Whether ICTA 1988, s 776(8) assessments made for the purposes authorised by statute.*

The applicants were partners of a firm of solicitors and directors of a UK company (S), a subsidiary of a Jersey company (N). In 1981, N purchased land in the UK for £325,000 which it later sold to S for £1,125,000. S then resold the land to an independent purchaser for £1,150,000. The applicants were assessed under *ICTA 1988, s 776(8)**, on the basis that they had directly or indirectly provided an opportunity for another person to realise a gain. They applied for judicial review to quash the assessments, contending that there was no evidence that the tax assessed was due from them and that the inspector had acted improperly, having made the assessments for the purpose of making enquiries about other individuals of a kind not authorised by the statutory powers of enquiry. Nolan J, applying *R v Special Commissioners (ex p. Stipplechoice Ltd) (No 1)*, granted leave. It was arguable that there had been a misunderstanding by the Revenue in relation to material facts and that the inspector had acted irrationally. Moreover, although the points advanced could equally well be taken before the Special Commissioners, the applicants, if successful, would be prejudiced in that they would not be able to recover their costs in the appeal. QB [1986] STC 152; [1986] 2 All ER 37.

R v HMIT and Others (ex p Lansing Bagnall Ltd)

Whether 'may' in FA 1972, 16 Sch 3(1) mandatory or permissive.

A close company had made covenanted donations to charities in its four accounting periods to 30 April 1982. In 1984 the inspector served notices on the company for the annual payments to be apportioned among the participators, pursuant to *FA 1972, 16 Sch 3(1)*. The company applied, by way of judicial review, for the notices to be quashed, contending that 'may' in *16 Sch 3(1)* was permissive and that the inspector should have taken into account the company's representations in the matter. The QB granted the application and the CA upheld this decision. On the evidence, the inspector responsible for the issue of the notices had refused to consider the company's representations, regarding it as her duty to issue the notices. The wording of the legislation, however, conferred a general discretion to apportion the income of a close company and did not impose on the Revenue a duty to exercise the powers of apportionment. CA 1986, 61 TC 112; [1986] STC 453. (*Note. FA 1972, 16 Sch 3* was subsequently amended by *F(No 2)A 1987, s 61*. This case was subsequently distinguished in *Baylis v Roberts*.)

R v Hudson

Taxpayer prosecuted for fraud – whether indictable.

A taxpayer had submitted false accounts and a false certificate of disclosure and as a consequence was convicted on charges of making false statements to the prejudice of the Crown and the public revenue with intent to defraud, and was fined. He appealed on the ground that the offence charged was not one known to the law. The CCA held that he had been rightly convicted because the facts disclosed a fraud on the Crown and on the public which was indictable as a criminal offence. CCA 1956, 36 TC 561; [1956] 2 QB 252; [1956] 1 All ER 814.

R v Special Commissioners (ex p Emery)

Prerogative orders – jurisdiction of Divisional Courts.

A taxpayer applied to the QB for an order of *mandamus* to the Special Commissioners to amend a Stated Case. In the event, the applicant and the Revenue reached an agreement which made remission to the Commissioners unnecessary. However, Donaldson LJ observed that applications should normally be made to the Ch D as the specialised court in tax matters. The QB has residual jurisdiction over the supervision of such matters as the validity of, or errors in, the proceedings. QB 1980, 53 TC 555; [1980] STC 549.

R v Special Commissioners (ex p Esslemont)

Application for judicial review.

A taxpayer, whose appeal against a Schedule E assessment had been dismissed by the Special Commissioners, objected to their wording of the Case Stated, and applied for judicial review of their refusal to amend it in accordance with his wishes. His application was dismissed by the QB and the CA. CA 1984 STI 312.

R v Special Commissioners (ex p Morey)

Prerogative order sought to quash assessments.

On appeal, Special Commissioners confirmed certain out-of-time assessments made by the inspector with the leave of a General Commissioner. The taxpayer applied for an order of *certiorari* to quash the assessments. The order was refused. Per

Widgery CJ, the Court will not normally interfere by way of prerogative order with the system of appeals under the Income Tax Acts. CA 1972, 49 TC 71.

R v Special Commissioner (ex p Stipplechoice Ltd) (No 1)

Leave given under TMA 1970, s 41 – application for judicial review.

A Special Commissioner granted the Revenue leave to make an out of time assessment on a company, which thereupon applied for a judicial review of the decision. The CA allowed the application. There was no special provision for an appeal against the decision, and the company had an arguable case that the Commissioner had exercised her powers in so unreasonable a manner that it became open to review. (The facts are complex.) CA, [1985] STC 248; [1985] 2 All ER 465.

R v Special Commissioners (ex p Stipplechoice Ltd) (No 3)

Application for judicial review.

An order of *certiorari* was granted, quashing the determination of an appeal by a Special Commissioner, in a case where the accounting period of the assessment under appeal had been amended by the inspector by virtue of *ICTA 1988, s 12(8)** without adequate notice or information having been given to the taxpayer prior to the hearing of the appeal. The QB held that a taxpayer must know the nature of the assessment being made on him, and if the nature of the assessment changes, the taxpayer must know of the change and of the reasons why it is made before it can be confirmed on appeal. QB 1988, 61 TC 391; [1989] STC 93.

R v Tavistock Commissioners (ex p Worth and Another)

Judicial review – effect of delay in claim for judicial review.

In February 1982, General Commissioners determined appeals against assessments on a married couple who traded in partnership. In June 1982 the couple engaged a new accountant, and in March 1984 they applied for judicial review of the Commissioners' decision. The QB dismissed the application, holding that there was no good reason for extending the time limit laid down by RSC Order 53, r 4(1); QB 1985, 59 TC 116; [1985] STC 564.

R v Walton Commissioners (ex p Wilson)

Judicial review.

A 'higher-paid' employee had the use of a company car. The amounts of the resultant taxable benefits were taken into account in his codings for 1978–79 to 1980–81, by deduction from his allowances. He appealed, contending that only monetary payments could be dealt with under PAYE. The General Commissioners dismissed his appeal, whereupon he applied by way of judicial review for orders quashing the decision and ordering the inspector not to make the deductions in his coding. The application was refused. The relevant notices of coding were spent; the amount of any conceivable claim to interest by the taxpayer would be very small. This disposed of the matter, but in any event the notices of coding were correct. 'Income' in *ICTA 1988, s 203** and the PAYE regulations is wide enough to cover all emoluments within Schedule E including benefits in kind. CA, [1983] STC 464.

R v Williams and Another

Situation of property – registered shares.

Per Lord Maugham, shares are situate where they can be effectively dealt with as between the shareholder and the company so that the transferee will become legally entitled to all the rights of a member. PC, [1942] 2 All ER 95; [1942] AC 541.

Ramsay (W T) Ltd v CIR

Artificial avoidance scheme – whether a nullity for tax purposes.

A company, having made a substantial gain on the sale of a farm, carried out a number of share and loan transactions with the object of creating a large allowable loss at little cost to itself. The loss emerged as one of about £175,000 on shares it subscribed for in a company formed for the scheme, the success of which depended on its establishing that a loan to the same company, sold at a profit of about £173,000, was not a debt on a security within *TCGA 1992, s 251(1)**. The acceptance of the offer of the loan was given orally, but evidenced by a statutory declaration (*vide Statutory Declarations Act 1835*) by a director of the borrowing company. The CA held that the loan, being evidenced by the statutory declaration, which represented a marketable security, was a debt on a security. The scheme therefore failed. The company appealed to the HL, where the appeal was considered with that in *Eilbeck v Rawling* and in both cases the Revenue advanced the new argument that the scheme should be treated as a fiscal nullity producing neither loss nor gain (other than a loss of £370 in *Eilbeck v Rawling*). The HL accepted this approach. Lord Wilberforce held that although the *Duke of Westminster* principle prevented a court from looking behind a genuine document or transaction to some supposed underlying substance, it did not compel the court to view a document or transaction in blinkers, isolated from its context. A finding that a document or transaction is genuine does not preclude the Commissioners from considering whether, on the facts, what is in issue is a composite transaction or a number of independent transactions. The Commissioners are not 'bound to consider individually each separate step in a composite transaction intended to be carried through as a whole'. The question of whether what is in issue is a composite transaction or a number of independent transactions is a matter of law, reviewable by the courts. Such an approach does not introduce a new principle when dealing with legal avoidance, but applies existing legislation to new and sophisticated legal devices; 'while the techniques of tax avoidance progress, the courts are not obliged to stand still'. Turning to the facts here, it was clear that the scheme was for tax avoidance with no commercial justification, and that it was the intention to proceed through all its stages to completion once set in motion. It would therefore be wrong to consider one step in isolation. The true view was that, regarding the scheme as a whole, there was neither gain nor loss. The company's appeal was dismissed. Furthermore, although this ended the appeal, the CA had been correct in holding that the relevant debt was a 'debt on a security'. HL 1981, 54 TC 101; [1981] STC 174; [1981] 2 WLR 449; [1981] 1 All ER 865.

Re Applications to Vary the Undertakings of 'A' and 'B'

IHTA 1984, s 35A – variation of undertakings.

The Inland Revenue had agreed that the owners of certain valuable works of art should have the benefit of 'conditional exemption' from IHT in respect of those items, in return for the owners having entered into undertakings, within *IHTA 1984, s 31*, that there would be 'reasonable access to the public'. The owners required members of the public who wished to view the items to make appointments before doing so. Subsequently the Inland Revenue made applications, under *IHTA 1984, s 35A*, to vary the undertakings so as to give wider publicity to the existence of the items, and wider access to them. The Special Commissioner reviewed the evidence in detail and dismissed the Inland Revenue's applications, holding that 'the accumulated burdens placed on the particular owner' would 'so outweigh the benefit to the public as to make it neither just nor reasonable for me to direct that the proposals take effect'. There would be 'a serious intrusion into the family lives of the owners', and 'the increased risks of theft and damage to the owners' possessions' would go 'beyond what Parliament had in mind when empowering the inclusion of extended access requirements and publication requirements'.[2005] STC SCD 103 Sp C 439.

Reed v Nova Securities Ltd

Avoidance scheme – whether TCGA 1992, s 173(1) applicable.

Transactions resembling those in *Coates v Arndale Properties Ltd* were considered in another case a few months later. The taxpayer company (N) had traded in shares and securities since 1955. In March 1973 it was acquired by the well-known Littlewoods group. On 17 August 1973 Littlewoods sold to it shares owned by Littlewoods in, and debts owing to Littlewoods by, certain foreign companies. The sale price for the assets was £30,000, their market value, but their capital gains cost to Littlewoods was nearly £4m. When offering the assets to N, Littlewoods' Board said that about £55,000 would be received in part repayment of the debts and N had received a payment of £35,447 in 1979. They were not part of Littlewoods' trading stock. N purported to make an election under *TCGA 1992, s 161(3)** in respect of the assets acquired, and the issue in the appeal was whether they were trading stock, as defined in *ICTA 1988, s 100(2)** (see *TCGA 1992, s 288**). The General Commissioners found that they were and their decision was upheld by the Ch D and the CA. The HL unanimously upheld the decision as regards the debts but reversed it as regards the shares. The Commissioners had determined the appeal on the basis of an agreed statement of facts, without recourse to oral evidence, and no reasonable body of Commissioners could have concluded that the company had acquired the shares as trading stock; its acquisition of shares that had no value was without commercial justification. HL 1985, 59 TC 516; [1985] STC 124; [1985] 1 WLR 193; [1985] 1 All ER 686.

Reynaud & Others v CIR

Settlement of shares in company followed by purchase of shares by company – whether IHTA, s 268 applicable.

Four brothers were negotiating to sell their shares in a family company (C). Before the sale took place, they each transferred some of their shares to a discretionary trust. On the following day C purchased the shares from the trustees, and the remaining shares in C were sold to an unrelated purchaser (M). The Revenue issued notices of determination charging IHT on the transfer, on the basis that the settlement of the shares in C, and the subsequent purchase of those shares by C, were 'associated operations' (so that, by virtue of *IHTA 1984, s 268(3)*, business property relief was not available on the transfer of the shares). The brothers appealed, contending that C's purchase of the shares 'was not a relevant associated operation because it did not contribute anything to the transfer of value', so that the transfer of the shares to the trusts qualified for business property relief. The Special Commissioners accepted this contention and allowed the appeal, finding that 'when the discretionary trusts were made, there was a real possibility that the sale to (M) would not proceed' and that 'the discretionary trusts had more than just a tax purpose' since they also had the purpose of 'benefiting the families of the settlors and charity'. Although the transfer of shares to the trusts, and C's subsequent purchase of those shares, were 'associated operations' within *IHTA 1984, s 268*, an associated operation was relevant to a disposition 'only if it is part of the scheme contributing to the reduction of the estate'. The value of the brothers' estates 'were diminished as a result of the gift into settlement alone. The purchase of own shares contributed nothing to the diminution which had already occurred and was not therefore a relevant associated operation.' [1999] STC SCD 185 Sp C 196. (*Note.* The Commissioners also held that the principles in *WT Ramsay Ltd v CIR*, did not apply, finding that 'completion of the sale took place after a day of negotiations with the purchaser and there must have been a reasonable likelihood that the negotiations would fail. Accordingly . . . the two transactions were not part of a single composite transaction for the purpose of the doctrine.' Furthermore, there was no 'inserted step which could be cut out in such a way so as to transform the gift of shares into a gift of cash'.)

Robertson v CIR

IHTA 1984, s 216(3A) – whether personal representatives made 'the fullest enquiries that are reasonably practicable'.

A woman (S) died in October 1999. She owned a house and its contents in Scotland, and a cottage in England. Her executors, one of whom was a solicitor, wished to sell the properties as soon as possible. In November the solicitor (R) submitted an inventory of S's estate to the Capital Taxes Office [now HMRC Inheritance Tax], showing the Scottish house at a value of £60,000; its contents at £5,000; and the English cottage at £50,000. Although R had instructed valuers to carry out valuations of the two properties, he had not received these valuations at the time of submitting the inventory. Later that month the contents of the Scottish house were valued at £24,845, and in December the house was sold for £82,000. In January 2000 the English cottage and its grounds were valued at £315,000. R submitted a corrective inventory to the Capital Taxes Office, and paid the additional IHT due. The CTO informed him that they considered that the executors had not made 'the fullest enquiries that are reasonably practicable', as required by *IHTA 1984, s 216(3A)*, and they proposed to charge a penalty of £9,000, under *IHTA, s 247*. The Special Commissioner reviewed the evidence and held that R was not liable to any penalty, since he had made the fullest enquiries that were reasonably practicable in the circumstances. On the evidence, R had made a thorough examination of S's home shortly after her death, had appreciated that a valuation of the contents would be required, and had instructed a valuation promptly. In the meantime, he had, in accordance with accepted practice, inserted estimated valuations in the inventory and had disclosed that they were estimates. He had followed what was acceptable practice in the legal profession, and had fulfilled his duties as an executor and as a solicitor. The Revenue were not justified in seeking to impose a penalty. [2002] STC SCD 182 Sp C 309.

Note. The Special Commissioner held that the Revenue were not justified in seeking to impose a penalty on a solicitor who had submitted an estimated valuation in his capacity as an executor. The solicitor subsequently applied for costs under *Special Commissioners (Jurisdiction and Procedure) Regulations 1994 (SI 1994 No 1811), Reg 21(1)*. The Commissioner awarded costs to the solicitor, holding on the evidence that the Revenue had acted 'wholly unreasonably in connection with the hearing'. [2002] STC SCD 242 Sp C 313.

Robertson v HMRC

Lump sum payments received from ex-husband.

A married couple divorced in 1987. The husband agreed to make monthly maintenance payments to the wife (M). In 2001 he also made a lump sum payment of £20,000, and in May 2002 he made a similar payment of £6,000. M died in October 2002. The Inland Revenue issued a Notice of Determination charging IHT on her estate. Her personal representative appealed, contending that the lump sum payments totalling £26,000, which M had received from her ex-husband, should be returned to him and should not be treated as part of her estate for IHT purposes. The Special Commissioner rejected this contention and dismissed the appeal. [2005] STC SCD 723 Sp C 494.

Rose v Director of Assets Recovery Agency

Trade of dealing in drugs – finding 'on the balance of probabilities' that R was not carrying on a trade.

The Director of the Assets Recovery Agency issued assessments on an individual (R), on the basis that he was carrying on a trade of dealing in drugs. R appealed, contending that he was not carrying on a trade of dealing in drugs. The

Special Commissioner allowed his appeal, finding 'on the balance of probabilities' that R was not carrying on a trade. [2006] STC SCD 472 Sp C 543.

Rose, Re, Rose and Others v CIR

Time of disposition – registered shares.

A transfer under seal in the form appropriate to the company's regulations, together with delivery of the transfer and share certificate to the transferee, was held sufficient to constitute the transferee the beneficial owner of the shares at that time, although the transferee did not register the shares until a later date. So far as lay in his power the transferor had done all that he could to divest himself of his interest in the shares. CA, [1952] 1 All ER 1217; [1952] Ch 499.

Rowley, Holmes & Co v Barber

Employee and personal representative the same person-power as a PR to contract with himself as an individual.

G, a solicitor in practice, employed B for many years. G died and appointed B as his sole executor and trustee and bequeathed to B his practice. As B was unqualified he could not run the practice and sold the goodwill of the practice to R, a qualified solicitor, and was employed by R until R made B redundant. The firm contended that G's death had broken the continuity of the employment and that B was entitled to £292.50 but B contended that the redundancy payment should reflect continuous employment since 1954. It was held that the office of personal representative was capable of giving power to the PR to contract in his representative capacity with himself as in his individual capacity and therefore the redundancy payment should rightly apply to the longer period. Reference was made to Halsbury's Laws of England (9 Halsbury's Laws (4 Edition) para 204) concerning the power of an individual to contract with himself and this applies also to a trustee, executor, administrator or agent. [1977] 1 All ER 801.

Rosser v CIR

'Farmhouse' for the purpose of IHTA 1984, s 115(2).

P and his wife owned a farm with 41 acres of land. In 1989 they gave 39 acres to their daughter (R), who was carrying on a farming business with her husband seven miles away. P and his wife retained the farmhouse and two acres of land. Following the transfer, R and her husband farmed all 41 acres of land, including the two acres which P and his wife continued to own. P died in April 2001, and his wife died seven weeks later. The Revenue issued a notice of determination charging IHT on the farmhouse and a barn. (The Revenue accepted that the two acres of land were 'agricultural property' within *IHTA 1984, s 115(2)*.) R appealed, contending that she was entitled to agricultural property relief. The Special Commissioner allowed the appeal in part, holding that by 2001 the house was not a 'farmhouse' for the purpose of *IHTA 1984, s 115(2)*, since its 'prime function' was 'as a retirement home'. However, the barn was 'a working farm building' and qualified for relief. [2003] STC SCD 311 Sp C 368.

Royal Trust Co v A-G for Alberta

Situation of property – specialty debt.

A specialty debt is situate where the bond or specialty is kept. PC 1929, 46 TLR 25; [1930] AC 144.

Russell & Another v CIR

Business property relief – deeds of variation.

A testator's residuary estate included a reserve fund at Lloyd's which qualified for business property relief. His executors entered into a Deed of Variation in 1983 and executed a further variation in 1985. The Revenue made a determination to the effect that business property relief was not available on the first variation. The Revenue also refused to accept that the second variation was within the scope of the relieving provisions in *FA 1978, s 68* (subsequently *IHTA 1984, s 142*). It was held that the second variation was not effective for capital transfer tax, as *FA 1978, s 68* did not apply to variations of dispositions previously varied under *FA 1978, s 68*. However, business property relief was held to be due in respect of the first variation because on the facts of the case the legacies in question could only be satisfied out of qualifying assets. (The rules on which the case was decided have been altered by *IHTA 1984, s 39A* with effect from 18 March 1986.) Ch D, [1988] STC 195; [1988] 1 WLR 834; [1988] 2 All ER 405.

Rye v Rye

Conveyance by persons to themselves.

Two brothers carried on a partnership business, the profits of which were divisible between them in unequal shares. They had purchased in equal shares the premises used for the business and in order to reconcile their inequality as partners with their equal ownership of the premises, they agreed orally to grant to the partnership a yearly tenancy of the premises. Following the death of one of the brothers, his son became one of the owners of the premises and, subsequently a partner in the business. When the partnership was subsequently dissolved, the son continued to occupy part of the premises for his own business use and the surviving brother brought an action claiming possession of the property as the surviving tenant under the yearly tenancy. The HL held that, on the fact, the inference that the partners purported to grant an annual tenancy to themselves was justified but such grant was ineffective for two reasons. First, a 'conveyance' only applies, unless the context of a particular enactment requires otherwise, to an instrument in writing as distinct from an oral disposition. Secondly, *Law of Property Act 1925, s 72(3)* does not enable an individual to grant a lease to himself, nor several persons to grant a lease to themselves. HL [1962] AC 496; 1962 All ER 146.

Rysaffe Trustee Co (CI) Ltd v CIR

Valuation of settled property which comprised five discretionary settlements comprising trust funds of £10 each by way of a cheque for £50 with property to be added at a later date – deferred shares in a private company of which the settlors were members and directors were subsequently transferred to the five settlements. Was each settlement for the purposes of the ten yearly tax charge to be taken as property comprised in one settlement – whether creation of five settlements and transfer of shares to trustee associated operations – whether five settlements comprised five dispositions of property resulting in one settlement. IHTA 1984, ss 43(2), 64, 268(1)(b) and 272.

A settlor executed five settlements within a period of 35 days, and transferred shares of equal value to each settlement. The Inland Revenue issued a notice of determination that the five holdings should be treated as a single settlement for the purposes of the charge to tax under *IHTA 1984, s 64*. The company which acted as the trustee of the settlements appealed. The Ch D allowed the appeal, holding that there were five separate settlements for the purposes of *s 64*. Park J held that 'it is up to the settlor who places property in trust to determine whether he wishes to create one trust or several trusts, or for that matter merely to add more property to a settlement which had already been created in the past'. Each settlement was created by a 'disposition' within *IHTA 1984, s 43*. The 'associated operations' provisions of *IHTA 1984, s 268* did not apply, since *s 268* was 'not an operative provision which of itself imposes inheritance tax liabilities. It is a definition of an expression (associated operations) which is used elsewhere. The definition only comes into effect in so far as the expression "associated operations" is used elsewhere, and then only if the expression in another provision is relevant to the way in which that other provision applies to the facts of the particular case.' The CA unanimously upheld this decision. Mummery LJ held that 'the inclusion of "associated operations" in the statutory description of "disposition" is not intended for cases, such as this, where there is no dispute that there was a "disposition" of property falling within *s 43(2)*. They are intended for cases where there is a dispute as to whether there was a relevant "disposition" at all.' In this case, the Revenue were 'not seeking to use the extended sense of "disposition" to determine what is to be taken as a settlement or what is the property comprised in a settlement. They are seeking to use it for the purpose of determining the different question of counting how many settlements there are in a given case. The provisions do not entitle the CIR, in the absence of clear language, to conduct the exercise of shrinking the number of settlements which satisfy the definition of a "settlement" in *s 43(2)*, or to aggregate the settled property comprised in each of the separate settlements, so as to treat, for inheritance tax purposes, property subject to discrete settlements as if it were comprised, along with other settled property, in a single settlement'. CA [2003] EWCA Civ 356; CA [2003] STC 536.

Scottish Provident Institution, CIR v

Taxation of financial instruments – qualifying contracts – FA 1994, s 147A.

In 1995 a bank (C) and a company (S) initiated a series of transactions, admittedly designed as a 'tax avoidance scheme', under which each party granted a call option to the other party. The scheme was designed to take advantage of the provisions of *FA 1994, ss 147A, 150A* and produce a deemed net loss of £20,000,000. The Revenue issued an assessment on the basis that the relevant transactions should be treated as a single composite transaction having no commercial purpose, and giving rise to no gain or loss. The HL unanimously upheld the assessment, observing that 'the purpose of the transaction was to create a tax loss, not a real loss or profit'. The Special Commissioners had found that 'there was an outside but commercially real possibility that circumstances might occur in which the two options would not be exercised so as to cancel each other out'. Nevertheless, this did not require the Commissioners to treat the options as separate transactions. The HL held that 'it would destroy the value of the *Ramsay* principle of construing provisions such as (*FA 1994, s 150A(1)*) as referring to the effect of composite transactions if their composite effect had to be disregarded simply because the parties had deliberately included a commercially irrelevant contingency, creating an acceptable risk that the scheme might not work as planned. We would be back in the world of artificial tax schemes, now equipped with anti-*Ramsay* devices. The composite effect of such a scheme should be considered as it was intended to operate and without regard to the possibility that, contrary to the intention and expectations of the parties, it might not work as planned.' The scheme was a 'single composite transaction' which 'created no entitlement to gilts', so that 'there was therefore no qualifying contract'. HL 2004, 76 TC 538; [2005] STC 15; [2004] UKHL 52; [2005] 1 All ER 325.

Scott v HMRC

Gift of paintings during the lifetime of the deceased – whether effective delivery had taken place.

The appellant claimed that his mother had given certain paintings to him during her lifetime. At the time of the gifts the family home where the paintings were displayed was also the appellant's home. On the advice of their solicitor the paintings were removed in turn from the walls, handed to the appellant and then on his instruction re-hung where they had previously been. HMRC contended that there had been no effective delivery of the paintings to the appellant. The Tribunal noted that to effect a gift there has to be intention and (in the absence of a Deed of Gift) delivery. The procedure followed was sufficient for an effective gift to have been made. Similar issues arose in relation to a gift of paintings by the appellant's great aunt and the same principles were applied. [2015] UKFTT 0266 (TC).

Seddon (Trustees of Mrs M Seddon's Second Discretionary Trust) v HMRC

Scrip dividend received by discretionary trustees and subsequently sold – whether the scrip dividend was capital to be taken into account under IHTA 1984, s 68(5)(c) in the calculation of a later IHT exit charge.

The trustees of a discretionary trust received a scrip dividend in January 2000 which was partly realised for cash two days later. In March 2009, shortly before the trust ten-year anniversary, the trustees made certain capital distributions. The trustees contended that the scrip dividend was income in their hands on the authority of the Court of Appeal decision in *Howell v Trippier* [2004] EWCA Civ 885, a case which related to the income tax treatment of the scrip shares. However that decision was held not to apply as regards trust law generally in *Gilchrist v HMRC* [2014] UKUT 169 (TCC). The First Tier Tax Tribunal held that in case of conflict it was bound to follow the later authority where it had fully considered earlier authorities. On this basis the scrip dividend was received as capital in the settlement and was therefore to be taken into account in the calculation of IHT exit charges. [2015] UKFTT 0140 (TC).

Shepherd v HMRC

Ordinary residence claim failed – not temporarily resident and therefore liable to UK income tax. ICTA 1988, s 334.

An airline pilot (S), who was born and domiciled in the UK, purchased a flat in Cyprus in October 1998. He claimed that he was not ordinarily resident in the UK for 1999/2000. The Revenue rejected the claim and S appealed. The Special Commissioner dismissed his appeal, finding that during 1999/2000 he had spent 80 days in the UK, 77 days in Cyprus, 180 days flying in the course of his employment, and 28 days holidaying elsewhere. While in the UK, he had stayed in the house which he shared with his wife. The Commissioner held that 'the absences of (S) after October 1998 were temporary absences from the United Kingdom as were his absences when flying in the course of his duties'. S's time in Cyprus was only 'occasional residence abroad', within *ICTA 1998, s 334(a)*. The Ch D upheld the Commissioner's decision. Ch D [2006] All ER(D) 191; [2006] STC 1821.

Shepherd v Lyntress Ltd; News International plc v Shepherd

Applicability of Ramsay principle where subsidiary company acquired with accumulated tax losses.

A major public company (N) had acquired shares in companies that had appreciated in value. It decided to acquire companies which had accumulated tax losses so that the gains on the holdings could be realised and the accrued losses could be set off against them. Accordingly, in 1979 N acquired the issued share capital of L, a company claiming to have £4m of accumulated tax losses available for set-off. In 1980 N sold part of its holding of appreciated assets to L, and a few days later L realised the gains by disposing of the assets on the Stock Exchange. The Revenue raised assessments on N on the basis that the *Ramsay* principle applied, and that the sale of the assets by N to L was to be ignored for fiscal purposes, so that the transactions would fall to be treated as disposals on the Stock Exchange by N, and on L on the basis that, again applying the *Ramsay* principle, the losses incurred within the company's former group were not available against gains accruing to a company outside that group. The Special Commissioners reduced the assessment on L, rejecting the Revenue's contention that the accumulated losses were not available for set-off.

However, they upheld the assessment on N. Both sides appealed to the Ch D. Vinelott J allowed N's appeal and upheld the Commissioners' decision with regard to the assessment on L. On the facts, the Commissioners were clearly correct in rejecting the Revenue's contention that L's losses were not available for set-off. The real question in the case was whether the Commissioners were justified in concluding that the transfer and sale of the assets were part of a single composite transaction. Following *Craven v White*, this could not be held to be the case here, because no arrangements to sell the shares on the Stock Exchange had been made at the time when they were transferred from N to L. It was therefore impossible to conclude that the transfer of the shares to L, and their subsequent sale by L, was a single composite transaction within the *Ramsay* principle. L had an allowable loss at the time when its share capital was acquired by N. That loss remained an allowable loss after N had acquired L's share capital, and the gains which were realised when the transferred assets were sold on the Stock Exchange were gains realised by L at a time when it was a member of the same group of companies as N. Ch D 1989, 62 TC 495; [1989] STC 617.

Silber v HMRC

Various claims by personal representative of deceased, who failed to appear at the Tribunal hearing, dismissed

The personal representative of a deceased claimed that an amount paid by the deceased to a company was a gift, and not a loan as shown in the company accounts, and that two payments made after the death, one to a person who challenged the validity of the will and the other allegedly charitable, were deductible for IHT purposes. The First Tier Tax Tribunal found that there was no substance to any of the claims and the appeal was dismissed. [2012] UKFTT 700 (TC).

Sillars and Another v CIR

The effect of IHTA 1984, s 5(2) was that the whole of a joint building society account formed part of the deceased's estate.

In 1995 a woman (S) transferred her building society account into the names of herself and her two daughters. On her death her personal representatives treated her as having owned only one-third of the balance in the account. The Revenue issued a notice of determination that IHT was due on the whole balance in the account. The personal representatives appealed. The Special Commissioner dismissed the appeal, holding on the evidence that S retained power over the account. She was able to dispose of the balance as she thought fit, and withdrawals were made for her benefit. The effect of *IHTA 1984, s 5(2)* was that the whole of the account formed part of her estate. [2004] STC SCD 180 Sp C 401.

Smith v HMRC (and related appeals)

IHTA 1984, s 200(1)—transfer on death—person liable.

A woman (J) died in March 2003. She appointed one of her two sons (M) and his wife (S) as her executors and trustees. She left specific legacies of £5,000 each to six named grandchildren and great-grandchildren, and left the residue of her estate to be divided equally between her two sons (M and K). M and S distributed the estate, submitted an IHT return, and paid the IHT due. However the IHT return which they submitted failed to include a building society account in the joint names of J and M. The executors' solicitors disclosed this to HMRC in June 2004. HMRC issued Notices of Determination to M, K and S, charging IHT on the amount held in the building society account. All three appealed. The Special Commissioner reviewed the evidence in detail and partly allowed the appeals by S and K, but dismissed the appeal by M. The Commissioner observed that the executors had not divided the amount held in the building society account between M and K as if it had been formed part of J's residuary estate. Instead, M had retained the whole of the amount in question. On the evidence, it appeared that both J and M had 'considered that the interest earned in respect of the account belonged without question to the deceased whilst she was alive', and that the capital would pass to M on her death. It followed that the account been 'settled property', within *IHTA 1984, s 200(1)(d)*. Since the amount was settled property, 'the person liable for the tax attributable to it' was M 'in his capacity both as trustee and recipient of it'. The tax attributable to it was not the liability of the executors and S had no liability for it. However, 'the existence of the account will make the executors in their capacity as such to be liable for additional tax because the tax attributable to the property that was not settled increases as a result of including the value of the account in the deceased's estate for inheritance tax purposes but they do not have a liability for the tax attributable to the value of the settled property in their capacity as such'. With regard to K, the Commissioner observed that the fact that the value of the account had formed part of J's estate for IHT purposes 'will have given rise to a tax liability attributable to the property received by (K) that was not wholly discharged by the executors and he remains liable for tax to that extent'. [2009] Sp C 742.

Smith v HMRC (and related appeals)

IHTA 1984, s 263 – annuity purchased in conjunction with life policy.

In October 1996 a married couple took out three life assurance policies coupled with three annuities, and executed three 'declarations of trust' in favour of their children. The wife died in 2000 and the husband died in February 2003. HMRC issued notices of determination that the vesting of the life assurance policies under the terms of the 'declarations of trust' was a transfer of value under *IHTA 1984, s 263*. The executors and the beneficiaries appealed, contending that the purchase of the annuities and the making of the life assurance policies should not be treated as 'associated operations' by virtue of Revenue Statement of Practice E4. The Special Commissioner rejected this contention and dismissed the appeals, and the Ch D upheld this decision. Lightman J observed that the purpose of Statement of Practice E4 was to provide 'an effective means of protecting the Revenue from efforts made to avoid payment of inheritance tax by means of associated transactions in the form of life assurance policies and annuities. This is achieved by requiring that the life policy must be issued on the basis of the provision to the insurer of full medical evidence of the assured's health.' The information which the husband had given to the life assurance company did not constitute the 'full medical evidence' required by Statement of Practice E4. Ch D [2007] EWHC 2304; STC 1649 Sp C 605.

Snapes v Aram and others

Wind fall estate changes disinheritance position under Inheritance (Provision for Family and Dependants) Act 1975.

The father made his last will on 18 February 1980 and the estate comprised of a house and a plot of land. He made no financial provision for his daughter due to lack of funds. The land was used in the family business which was run by the sons and one daughter in the family. There was a specific provision in the deceased's will that if his wife predeceased him the remainder of the estate would be divided between the plaintiff, his other daughter and his seven grandchildren. In 1989 there was a change in the value of the land when Tesco bought the plot for £13 million. The widow died after the sale to Tesco and by her will she left the plaintiff a legacy of £1,000. The plaintiff did not make any application in respect of the mother's estate.

The main issues that arose on appeal were whether the father had made reasonable financial provision for the daughter and whether a subsequent windfall to the estate should change the original lack of financial provision to the daughter. From the will it was clear that the deceased was well disposed to the plaintiff and recognised that some provision ought, if resources permitted, to be made for her. That was a factor which it was to be taken into account under *s 3(1)(g)* and for the court to give such weight to. The judge was not obliged to find a special circumstance, such as moral obligation and was entitled to look at all the relevant matters under *s 3*. The Court of Appeal held that a subsequent windfall to the estate changed the position and an award was made to the plaintiff in respect of maintenance of £3,000 per annum. *TLR 8 May 1998.*

Soutter's Executry v CIR

IHTA 1984, s 142 – whether deed of variation effective.

A woman (S) died in November 1999. The value of her estate was less than the IHT threshold. She owned a house, in which she lived with a friend (G). Under her will, she gave G the right to live in the house, rent-free. G died in November 2000. In an attempt to reduce the IHT due on G's death, S's executors and G's executors purported to execute a deed of variation of S's estate, under *IHTA 1984, s 142*, removing the provision whereby G could live in the house rent-free. The Revenue issued a notice of determination that the purported deed of variation was ineffective. S's executors appealed. The Special Commissioner dismissed the appeal, observing that 'the executors of a liferentrix have nothing they can vary'. G's executors 'had neither right, title or interest to any liferent'. They 'could not have continued to receive the liferent so they had nothing to give up or vary. The liferent was not and could not be assigned to them . . . a purported assignation of an expired liferent has no reality'. [2002] STC SCD 385 Sp C 325.

Spencer-Nairn v CIR

Sale of property at undervalue – whether any gratuitous benefit.

In 1976 a landowner sold a farm, several buildings on which were in need of repair and replacement, to a Jersey company for £101,350. His son was a major shareholder in the company, which was, therefore, connected with him for the purposes of both CGT and IHT. The Revenue took the view that the sale had been at undervalue, and the Lands Tribunal subsequently valued the property (for CGT purposes) at £199,000. The Revenue issued a determination on the basis that the disposition of the farm was within *IHTA 1984, s 3(1)**, and constituted a chargeable transfer of value. The landowner appealed, contending that he had not known that the purchasing company was connected with him for IHT purposes, and that he had had no intention of conferring a gratuitous benefit on the company. The Special Commissioner allowed his appeal and the CS upheld this decision. On the evidence, the tenant of the farm had not wished to purchase it and the farm was unlikely to have been of interest to institutional investors. Accordingly it was reasonable to conclude that the sale had not been intended to confer a gratuitous benefit on the Jersey company, and was a disposition which 'might be expected to be made in a transaction at arm's length'. The transaction was within *IHTA 1984, s 10(1)(b)** and there was no chargeable transfer of value. CS 1990, [1991] STC 60.

Standard Chartered Bank Ltd v CIR

Situation of property – registered shares.

Following *R v Williams and Treasurer for Ontario v Aberdein*, it was held that registered shares transferable in either England or South Africa were situate in South Africa because in the ordinary course of affairs that country was the one in which the deceased owner would have been likely to deal with those shares. CIR Ch D, [1978] STC 272; [1978] 1 WLR 1160.

Stannard, CIR v

Jurisdiction – personal liability of executor.

The Jersey resident executor of a testator who died resident and domiciled in

England claimed that his Jersey residence made him immune from suit in England for unpaid CTT, and that he was liable for unpaid CTT only in a representative rather than in a personal capacity. The CA held, following *CIR v Stype Investments (Jersey) Ltd Re Clore (deceased)*, that the High Court has jurisdiction to deal with a claim for CTT arising on the death of a person resident and domiciled in England, and that the CTT liability arising on death could not be a liability of the deceased but was an original, personal liability of the personal representative. Ch D 1984, CTTL 22; [1984] STC 245; [1984] 2 All ER 105; [1984] 1 WLR 1039.

Starke & Another (Brown's Executors) v CIR

Agricultural property relief – definition of 'agricultural property'.

A deceased's estate included a 2.5 acre site containing a substantial six-bedroomed farmhouse and a number of outbuildings. The site was used as part of a moderately-sized farm. The Revenue issued a notice of determination under *IHTA 1984, s 221* that the transfer of the site was not a transfer of 'agricultural property' within *IHTA 1984, s 115(2)*, and thus did not qualify for agricultural property relief. The executors applied by way of an originating summons for leave to appeal and for a declaration that the determination was wrong. The Ch D dismissed the appeal and refused the declaration, holding that the site was not 'agricultural property', since it was not 'agricultural land or pasture'. The CA upheld this decision and dismissed the executor's appeal. CA [1995] STC 689; [1995] 1 WLR 1439; [1996] 1 All ER 622.

St Clair-Ford (Youlden's Executor) v Ryder

Joint owner of a retail shop – discount should be 15% rather than 10%. Lands Tribunal held that the discount should be 10%.

An individual (Y) was joint owner of a retail shop. He died in 2003. The Revenue determined the value of his interest in the shop as £175,000 (applying a 10% discount for joint ownership). Y's executor appealed, contending *inter alia* that the discount should be 15% rather than 10%. The Lands Tribunal rejected this contention and upheld the Revenue's determination, applying the decision in *Cust v CIR*, KB 1917, 91 EG 11 and holding that the discount should be 10%. *Lands Tribunal 22 June 2006 unreported.*

St Dunstan's v Major

Variation of will by sole legatee?tax repaid to charity, IHT on estate reduced. Whether 'qualifying donation' within FA 1990, s 25.

The sole legatee under a will entered into a Deed of Variation, whereby £20,000 was bequeathed to a charity. The legatee claimed relief under *FA 1990, s 25* and signed a form R190(SD) certifying that he had paid £26,666 (i.e. £20,000 grossed-up at 25%) to the charity. The charity claimed a repayment of £6,666, which the Revenue made. Subsequently the Revenue formed the opinion that the donation of £20,000 did not satisfy the requirements of *FA 1990, s 25(2)(e)* and thus was not a 'qualifying donation', since the legatee had saved inheritance tax of £8,000, and had therefore received a benefit in consequence of making it, so that the charity should not have received any repayment. They issued an assessment to recover £6,666. The charity appealed, contending that the inheritance tax saving should not be treated as a benefit within *s 25(2)(e)*. The Special Commissioner rejected this contention and dismissed the appeal, holding that since the legatee was the 'sole or residuary beneficiary of the estate, he ultimately benefited from the inheritance tax saving'. Accordingly, the donation was not a qualifying donation within FA 1990, s 25. [1997] STC SCD 212 Sp C 127.

Steiner v CIR

Domicile – whether English domicile of choice acquired.

A Jew, born in Czechoslovakia, who acquired a domicile of origin in Germany but came to England in 1939 to escape Nazi persecution and obtained British naturalisation, was held to have acquired an English domicile of choice. CA 1973, 49 TC 13; [1973] STC 547.

Stenhouse's Trustees v Lord Advocate

Time of capital distribution – trustees in breach of trust.

On 8 April 1975, trustees of a discretionary trust appointed shares in the trust fund to the three daughters of the settlor. As the trustees only had power to make such an appointment to each daughter on her attaining the age of 22, and as the youngest was not yet 22, the trustees were in breach of trust. They therefore resolved that payment would not be made until all three had signed an indemnity. The question before the court was whether the three became entitled to interests in possession on 8 April 1975 (as opposed to the date the indemnities were signed or the date the youngest became 22). The CS held that the interests of the daughters were severable, and that the two who were already 22 became entitled to interests in possession on 8 April 1975. However, the youngest daughter did not, as it would have been *ultra vires* the trustees to confer an absolute entitlement on her on that date. CS 1983, [1984] STC 195.

Stoner and another (executors of Dickinson deceased) v CIR

Valuation – sale of land from deceased's estate – residuary estate to charity included freehold property which was sold by executors at prices exceeding probate values – executors made claim that sale prices values for IHT purposes – whether appropriate persons for IHTA 1984, ss 190, 191.

The deceased's will left the residue of her estate exceeding the nil rate band to charities. There was therefore no IHT payable. Freehold properties in the estate were valued at £582,000. Some of these properties were sold and the CTO was informed of the amount £918,457. The executors were informed that confirmation by the CTO was not necessary as the since charity relief was applicable. In 1998 the executors made a formal claim under *IHTA 1984, s 191*. Reference in that section to 'appropriate person' making the claim was important to the executors as they wished the uplift in the values of the properties for CGT purposes. The IR issued a notice of determination in April 2001 that in relation to the deemed disposal for the purposes of *s 190(1)* there was no appropriate person to make the claim. The executors appealed contending that they were the appropriate person because they would have been liable for the tax if the residuary beneficiaries had not all been charities or if the value of the part estate not passing to the residuary beneficiaries had exceeded the nil rate band. The Special Commissioner noted the *s 191* was to grant relief where there was a fall in the value of the land after death. The section did not state that it should not apply to increases in values but did refer to 'appropriate person' who was defined as the person liable to IHT. Gifts to charities were exempt transfers and so no tax was chargeable. It followed that *s 190(1)* 'the person liable for inheritance tax' meant the person who either had paid the tax or had obligation to pay it. There was no person liable to pay IHT if there was no tax to pay. Therefore as there was no appropriate person under *s 191* the executors' appeal would be dismissed. [2001] STC SCD 199 Sp C 288.

Stow & Others v Stow & Others

Application for declaration of beneficial ownership of settlement.

The Revenue had issued substantial income tax assessments on an individual (S) who had business interests in Nigeria. He was also a trustee of several settlements. S died in 2005. His widow made claims against the trustees of six of the settlements under *Inheritance (Provision for Family and Dependants) Act 1975, s 10*, claiming that S had been the beneficial owner of the assets held by the settlements, and that she was therefore entitled to a substantial share of the settlement assets. In 2006, HMRC issued notices of determination charging IHT on the basis that S had been the settlor of each settlement, within *IHTA 1984, s 44*. The trustees of the six settlements took proceedings in the Chancery Division (Ch D), seeking a declaration that S had not been the beneficial owner of the assets transferred into these settlements, and that the assets had been beneficially owned by a Nigerian (K), who had had business connections with S. HMRC applied for the proceedings to be struck out on the grounds that the beneficial ownership of the settlements was a matter to be determined by the Special Commissioners under the normal statutory appeal procedure, applying the principles laid down in the 1964 case of *Argosam Finance Co Ltd v Oxby & CIR*. The Ch D dismissed HMRC's application. Warren J declined to follow the *Argosam* decision on the grounds that the 'beneficial ownership issue goes not only to the trustees' liabilities to inheritance tax but also to whether HMRC can obtain effective enforcement for a completely different liability – the liability of (S) and his estate for income tax – which has nothing at all to do with the possible inheritance tax liability of the trustees. . . . If a dispute or potential dispute arises between a person and HMRC which is independent of the tax appeal under consideration, the exclusive jurisdiction principle does not render that dispute or potential dispute non-justiciable in the High Court simply because the same, or a very similar, issue will be relevant to, or perhaps even determinative of, both that dispute and the tax appeal.' Ch D [2008] EWHC 495 (Ch).

Surveyor v CIR

IHTA 1984, s 6(1) re Hong Kong domicile of choice.

A surveyor had been born in England in 1958. He moved to Hong Kong in 1986, and married in 1990. In 1997 he and his wife received a 'right of permanent abode' in Hong Kong. In 1999 he established a discretionary trust in Jersey, for the benefit of his wife and children. He transferred £247,500 to the trustees. The Revenue issued a notice of determination that this was a chargeable transfer. He appealed, contending that he had lost his English domicile of origin and acquired a domicile of choice in Hong Kong (so that the money transferred to the trust was excluded property within *IHTA 1984, s 6(1)*). The Special Commissioner accepted this contention and allowed his appeal, finding that at the date of the transfer, he 'had the intention to reside permanently in Hong Kong'. [2002] STC SCD 501 Sp C 339.

Swales and Others v CIR

Interest in possession – effect of Trustee Act 1925, s 31.

In 1970 trustees appointed income from a trust fund to R absolutely, although the (complex) provisions of the trust prevented R's right to the income from vesting until one of her children became 21 in 1976 (the vesting date). The trustees disagreed with the Revenue as to whether an interest in possession was created in 1970 or in 1976. The interest in possession was held to have arisen in 1970. The 1970 appointment was a contingent appointment of income which was intended to carry the intermediate income of the fund before the vesting date, and *Trustee Act 1925, s 31(1)(ii)* applied so that R had a present right to that income as it arose and as such to an interest in possession in the trust fund. Ch D 1984, CTTL 24; [1984] STC 413; [1984] 1 All ER 16.

Tapp (Atkinsion's Administratix) v Ryder

Valuation of semi-detached house.

The owner of a semi-detached house in Bexley died in 2006. HMRC issued a determination that the house should be valued at £230,000. The administratix appealed, contending that the house should be valued at £195,000. The Lands Tribunal rejected this contention and upheld HMRC's valuation, observing that 'at the relevant date, the property market was extremely buoyant'. [2008] Lands EW Lands TMA/284/2008.

Taylor (Executrix Mrs K Boland) v HMRC

Beneficial ownership of bank accounts.

In 1996 a widow (B) inherited two building society accounts from her husband. She subsequently put the accounts into the joint names of herself and her brother-in-law (P). B died in 2004. HMRC issued a notice of determination that B had been beneficially entitled to the whole of the money in these accounts. B's Executrix appealed, contending that the money in the accounts should be treated as having belonged to P, and that B had simply held the accounts as a trustee. The Special Commissioner rejected this contention and dismissed the appeal, holding that B had not held the accounts as a trustee and that B had 'a general power which enabled her to dispose of the whole of the accounts'. Accordingly she had to be treated as beneficially entitled to the whole of the money in the accounts at the date of her death. [2008] STC SCD 1159 Sp C 704.

Thomas & Thomas v CIR

Protective trust – forfeiture before 12 April 1978.

In June 1976 a CTT avoidance scheme was used to take advantage of a loophole in the rules for protective trusts in *FA 1975, 5 Sch 18(2)* (subsequently *IHTA 1984, s 88(2)*). The Ch D rejected the Revenue's argument that a protective trust of income for the benefit of the settlor was not a trust 'to the like effect' as those in *Trustee Act 1925, s 33(1)*. Ch D 1981, CTTL 8; [1981] STC 382. (*Note*. The loophole was removed for forfeitures after 11 April 1978. *IHTA 1984, s 73** subsequently operated instead of *IHTA 1984, s 88(2)** where forfeiture was before 12 April 1978.)

Thomson (Thomson's Executor) v CIR

Determination under IHTA 1984, s 221 charging value on house bequeathed to daughter but non-evidence of transfer documents.

A widow died in 1971 and bequeathed her house to her daughter (J). J died in 2002. The Inland Revenue issued a Notice of Determination under *IHTA 1984, s 221*, charging IHT on the value of the house. J's executor appealed, contending that despite the terms of her mother's will, J should not be treated as having been the sole owner of the house, because she had never 'signed any document accepting the title to the house'. The Special Commissioner reviewed the evidence and dismissed the appeal, finding that J was the sole owner of the house, which accordingly formed part of her estate for IHT purposes. [2004] STC SCD 520 Sp C 429.

Thorogood v CIR

IHTA 1984, s 225 – right of appeal to High Court.

An individual (T) had been the executor of his deceased son's estate, but was declared bankrupt. A solicitor was appointed as the trustee of the estate. The Inland Revenue issued a Notice of Determination in respect of certain shares. The solicitor appealed. T applied under *Special Commissioners (Jurisdiction and Procedure) Regulations 1994, SI 1994/1811)* to be joined as a party to the appeal. The Special Commissioner dismissed this application, and T appealed to the Chancery Division. The Chancery Division dismissed T's appeal. Laddie J held that *IHTA 1984, s 225* provided that only a 'party to an appeal' had the right of appeal against a Special Commissioner's decision. T was not a party to the appeal. (*Note*. The appellant appeared in person.) [2005] All ER (D) 201; STC 897.

Trustees Executors and Agency Co Ltd and Others v CIR

Situation of property – ships.

The artificial situs abroad of a ship registered abroad was displaced by the actual situs when within English territorial or national waters. Ch D 1972, [1973] 1 All ER 563; [1973] Ch 254.

Trustees of the Douglas Trust (for Mrs I Fairbairn) v HMRC

Whether 'inter vivos' trust conferred interest in possession.

In a Scottish case, an individual (D) transferred certain securities and investments to trustees in 1962. The income arising from the trust was treated for tax purposes as income of the settlor under *FA 1958, s 22* (now *ITTOIA 2005, ss 624–628*). D died in 1981 and then his wife died in 2002. HMRC issued a notice of determination on the basis that she had enjoyed an interest in possession in the settled property. The trustees appealed. The Special Commissioner dismissed the appeal, finding that D's widow had effectively enjoyed 'a power of veto: the whole of the free annual income of the trust fund had to be paid or applied to her or for her benefit from year to year unless or until she should concur with a consideration by the trustees that it was proper and expedient for a lesser amount to be so paid or applied'. Accordingly the trust deed had conferred an interest in possession. [2007] STC SCD 338 Sp C 593.

Trustees of the David Zetland Settlement v HMRC

Business property relief claim in respect of tenanted building and associated shareholding.

Trustees held a commercial building divided into small office units let to tenants for periods normally ranging between one and five years, although these terms were operated on a flexible basis so that they might be terminated earlier. The senior trustee was engaged for much of his time on strategy and management in relation to the premises. There was also a team of staff, including a receptionist, cleaner, handyman and porters, each employed by the trustees. On the premises were a café, operated with the trustees support, and other facilities such as bicycle park and meeting rooms available for hire on a daily or hourly basis. The trustees also carried out conversion work to suit the tenants and dilapidations work on termination of each tenancy, some of which produced profits for the trust. Although it was accepted that most of the trust income was in the form of the rents receivable, it was contended that the business was eligible for business property relief in view of the fact that most of the daily work of the trustee and the staff involved providing their services to the tenants. HMRC denied the claim on the basis that the business was wholly or mainly one of holding an investment. The trustees also held 50% of the shares in a company which owned the freehold for the office building. It was held by the First-tier Tribunal that the business in the round was not eligible for business property relief. Although it was actively managed the services provided which were not investment related were not sufficient to tip the balance in favour of obtaining business property relief. (TC02690).

Two Settlors v CIR

Notices of Determination under IHTA 1984, s 221.

Two settlors transferred certain shares in the same company to two settlements. The Revenue issued purported Notices of Determination under *IHTA 1984, s 221* to the effect that there had been no loss to the transferors' estates. The settlors appealed, contending as a preliminary point that the Notices were premature and inappropriate, and that the Special Commissioner had no jurisdiction to decide whether there had been a transfer of a value, which was a matter to be decided in a future capital gains tax appeal. The Special Commissioner accepted this contention and held that the purported Notices of Determination were not within *IHTA 1984, s 221* and were not appropriate. The substantive issue of whether there had been any transfer of value 'will have to be determined in any subsequent capital gains tax appeal'. [2004] STC SCD 45 Sp C 385.

Vinton & Green (Mrs M Dugan-Chapman's Executors) v HMRC

IHTA 1984, s 107(4) – identification of shares.

In December 2002 a widow (D), who was in poor health, was allotted one million shares in a family company (W). She died two days later. HMRC issued a determination charging IHT. D's executors appealed, contending that she had been allotted the shares as part of a reorganisation of W's share capital, within *TCGA 1992, s 126*, so that the effect of *IHTA 1984, s 107(4)* was that the shares should be identified with shares which she already held and qualified for business property relief. The Special Commissioner rejected this contention and dismissed the appeal, holding that there had not been a reorganisation of W's share capital within *TCGA 1992, s 126*. Accordingly the provisions of *s 107(4)* did not apply and the shares did not qualify for business property relief. [2008] STC SCD 592 Sp C 666.

Von Ernst & Cie SA and Others v CIR

Discretionary settlement – whether capital distribution – whether excluded property – jurisdiction of High Court.

On 25 March 1976 the trustees of a discretionary settlement appointed property consisting of exempt government securities to the two children of the settlor. Neither was resident nor domiciled in the UK. On the failure of the trusts to the children the property would have been held on constructive discretionary trusts for two UK charities. The Board determined that the appointment was to be treated as giving rise to a capital distribution under *FA 1975, 5 Sch 6(2)*. The trustees appealed direct to the High Court, contending that para 6(2) did not apply because the property was excluded property as soon as there were interests in possession in it. After losing in the Ch D, the trustees adduced two new arguments before the CA. The CA held that (i) the question of whether settled property was excluded property for the purposes of *para 6(2)* depended on the state of affairs which existed immediately before the appointment; (ii) exemption from CTT depends on CTT legislation, not on *F(No 2)A 1931*; (iii) the exempt securities were excluded property before the appointment by virtue of *IHTA 1984, s 48(4)(b)** since the charities were not 'known persons' who might 'benefit' or become 'beneficially entitled' within the meaning of that provision. The appeal was therefore allowed. The Ch D had held that where a CTT appeal is taken direct to the High Court, the latter has the same power to quash etc. a determination of the Board as the Special Commissioners would have had if the appeal had gone first to them. (This was not contested in the CA.) CA 1979, CTTL 6; [1980] STC 111; [1980] 1 WLR 468; [1980] 1 All ER 677.

Walding & Others (Walding's Executors) v CIR

IHTA 1984, s 269(1) – whether deceased had control of company.

A woman held 45 of the 100 shares in a company at the time of her death. Of the remaining 55 shares, 24 were in the name of her four-year-old grandson. Her executors claimed that, since the grandson was not in a position to exercise the voting rights attached to his 24 shares, the deceased had had control of the company so that her shareholding qualified for business property relief. The Revenue rejected the claim and the Ch D dismissed the executors' appeal. *IHTA 1984, s 269(1)* dealt with the ambit of the powers of voting, not the capabilities of the shareholders in whose names the shares were registered. Ch D 1995 [1996] STC 13. (*Note*. See also *Hepworth v Smith* Ch D 1981, 54 TC 396; [1981] STC 354, a capital gains tax case, in which shares were taken into account for the purposes of *TCGA, s 163** although the relevant voting rights had never been exercised.)

Walker's Executors v CIR

Business property relief – casting vote gave control over the company IHTA 1984, s 269(1) – entitlement to BPR on land from which the company traded.

A married couple had formed a company to operate a road haulage business and petrol station. The husband died in 1983 and the wife died in 1996. At the time of her death, she was chairman of the company and held 50% of the shares in it, with a casting vote at general meetings. She also owned the land from which the company traded. The Revenue issued a determination charging IHT on the land. Her executors appealed, contending that she had control of the company by virtue of her casting vote, so that the land qualified for business property relief under *IHTA, s 105(1)(d)*. The Special Commissioner accepted this contention and allowed the appeal, holding that the casting vote had given her control of the company, within *IHTA 1984, s 269(1)*. *Dicta* of Rowlatt J in *CIR v BW Noble Ltd* applied. [2001] STC SCD 86 Sp C 275.

Wallach (deceased), In re

Domicile – husband's domicile retained on widowhood.

A widow had acquired her late husband's domicile on marriage. It was held, in an intestacy case, that she retained this until her death, not having changed it; her domicile of origin had not revived on her husband's death. HC 1949, 28 ATC 486; [1950] 1 All ER 199.

Walton (Walton's Executor) v CIR

Valuation of partnership interest in non-assignable agricultural tenancy.

The freehold of a farm was held by a father and his two sons as tenants in common in equal shares. The farm was let to a partnership comprising the father and one of the sons. In August 1984 the father died. It was agreed that the vacant possession premium (i.e. the difference between the open market value of the freehold interest in the farm with vacant possession and that when subject to the tenancy) was £200,000. The value of tenant-right and tenants' improvements, less dilapidations, was £40,000. The Revenue issued a notice of determination to CTT, valuing the tenancy at half the vacant possession premium with a 10% discount to reflect the part interest (i.e. at £90,000), plus the net value of tenant-right and tenants' improvements, thereby arriving at a value of £130,000. The father's half-share was, therefore, valued at £65,000. The executor appealed against the valuation, contending that it was excessive, since it assumed an immediate purchase by the freeholders, whereas in fact the freeholders would not have been interested in securing the surrender of the tenancy and did not have the financial resources for such a purchase. The Lands Tribunal accepted this evidence and allowed the appeal, holding on the evidence that the realisation of the vacant possession premium was 'so far from any market expectation as to make a valuation by reference to an apportionment of the vacant possession premium wholly inappropriate'. The property which was required to be valued in accordance with what is now *IHTA 1984, s 94* was an undivided beneficial interest in the joint tenancy as a partnership asset. The tenancy could only be sold and its value realised if the terms of the partnership agreement permitted it, which they did not. The sole value of the tenancy, as a partnership asset, rested upon the extent to which its terms enhanced the partnership profits by enabling the partners to exploit the partnership assets without paying a full market rent for the farm. The tribunal reviewed the evidence in detail and held that the value of the entire tenancy, on the basis of a valuation of profit rental and on the assumption that the landlords could not be regarded as a hypothetical purchaser, was approximately £12,600, so that the value of the deceased's share was £6,300. The Revenue appealed to the CA, which upheld the Tribunal decision as one of fact. The Tribunal had been entitled to conclude that the landlords were not to be regarded as a hypothetical purchaser, and it was for the tribunal to consider what premium (if any) any special purchaser would be prepared to pay. CA 1995, [1996] STC 68.

Ward and Others (Executors of Cook deceased) v IRC

Valuation of a deceased's interest in building society shares prior to conversion – whether deceased's interest in those shares to be valued at nil for IHT purposes.

The deceased, Cook, had a number of accounts with the Woolwich Building Society. The Society announced its proposed conversion into a public limited company subject to a number of conditions being met. In January 1997 the Woolwich sent out a copy of the transfer document. On 11 February at a special general meeting the members voted and the resolution to convert was carried. On 10 May 1997 Cook died. On 7 July 1997 the flotation took place. Under the transfer document the deceased was entitled to 450 free shares in Woolwich plc and an additional variable distribution. The first named executor was entitled to the shares as part of Cook's estate. The Revenue determined that on 10 May 1997 the anticipated benefit of the conversion enhanced the deceased's Woolwich holdings. The executors appealed saying that the deceased had merely a hope that she would receive the shares. Also, other arguments were advanced why the conversion might not have gone ahead. The Special Commissioners decided that the deceased held rights under the transfer document which transcended the mere hope that Cook would obtain shares in Woolwich plc. The rights conferred by the transfer document were part of Cook's property to which she was entitled and therefore held to be valued in calculating the extent of her estate and as such became part of her estate that Cook was deemed to have made immediately before her death. Therefore, the executors' valuation of nil would be rejected and the Revenue's valuation would be accepted. The executors' appeal was dismissed. [1999] STC SCD 1 Sp C 175.

Westminster (Duke of) v CIR

A taxpayer covenanted to make certain annual payments to a number of his domestic employees. The payments, having regard to the surrounding circumstances, were, in substance but not in form, remuneration. The HL held (Lord Atkin dissenting) that the payments were annual payments from which tax was deductible and were allowable deductions in arriving at the taxpayer's income for surtax. HL 1935, 19 TC 490. (*Notes*. (1) The covenants would now be 'caught'—see *ICTA 1988, ss 683, 684**. The case remains of importance in relation to the meaning of 'annual payment' and in illustrating whether the courts will look at substance rather than form. (2) Lord Tomlin's judgment includes the celebrated dictum that 'every man is entitled if he can to order his affairs so that the tax attaching under the appropriate Acts is less than it otherwise would be'. This *dictum* has frequently been discussed in subsequent cases, particularly in the light of the *Ramsay* principle. It was applied by Lord Oliver in the 1988 case of *Craven v White*. However, in the 1992 case of *Ensign Tankers (Leasing) Ltd v Stokes*, Lord Templeman stated that 'subsequent events have shown that though this *dictum* is accurate as far as tax mitigation is concerned it does not apply to tax avoidance'. For the distinction between tax mitigation and tax avoidance, see *New Zealand Commissioner of Inland Revenue v Challenge Corporation*. In *Ensign Tankers*, Lord Templeman also specifically approved Lord Atkin's dissenting judgment in the *Duke of Westminster* case.)

Westminster's (4th Duke of) Executors v Ministry of Defence (aka Barty-King v Ministry of Defence)

Death on active service – cause of death.

The Duke of Westminster, who was wounded in action in 1944, died of cancer in

1967. The septicaemia caused by his war wound was noted on the death certificate as a significant condition contributing to the death 'but not related to the disease or condition causing it'. Exemption from estate duty was provided by *FA 1952, s 71* for the estate of any person who was certified by the Defence Council to have 'died from a wound inflicted . . . when . . . the deceased was a member of the armed forces of the Crown . . . on active service against an enemy'. The Defence Council turned down the executors' application for a certificate. The QB held that the executors were entitled to a declaration that they ought to have been granted a certificate. Although a wound had to be a cause of death, it did not have to be the direct or only cause. QB 1978, CTTL 2; [1979] STC 218; [1979] 2 All ER 80. (*Note.* The equivalent IHT exemption is provided by *IHTA 1984, s 154.*)

Weston (Weston's Executor) v CIR

Inheritance tax – exempt transfers and reliefs – business property – relevant business property – business of managing caravan park – whether business excluded from business property relief as consisting wholly or mainly of making or holding investments – IHTA 1984, s 105(3).

At the deceased's death in 1993 her estate included shares in a company. The business of the company, which was a single business, included the purchase and sale of caravans, the sale of caravans for commission on behalf of owners, and the grant of the right to pitch caravans on the caravan park run by the company for a consideration consisting of the pitch fees. The business also included the maintenance and administration of the park and the provision of facilities, and the supply for a consideration of electricity and bottled gas used by the pitch holders at the park. The park was situated near the M25 motorway, and was not a holiday park. It was entirely residential, and residents had to be over 50. It did not accommodate touring caravans or caravan rallies. The appearance of the park was that of a suburban residential development in miniature and the appearance of the caravans was that of small neat bungalows. The park had no shop or social club, but each caravan owner had the use of a brick built laundry and storeroom. The caravans were owned by their occupiers. Residents were obliged to purchase a caravan from the company or another resident, usually through the company, which took a commission on sales between residents. The number of sales of caravans was not large. The company's three employees spent a total of 111 hours per week on park maintenance and 37 hours per week on sales activities. The company's accounts, which were drawn up in accordance with normal accounting practice as laid down by the Companies Acts, showed that pitch fees exceeded in amount the sums realised by caravan sales in four out of the six years from 1989 to 1994. Also, the profits from pitch fees exceeded the profits from caravan sales in every year from 1988 to 1994, with the exception of 1989, and that from 1988 to 1994 there was a substantial excess of pitch fees, and bank interest produced by a considerable cash reserve, over caravan sales. Following the deceased's death the Revenue issued a determination, in relation to the deemed disposal for the purposes of inheritance tax on her death and her holding of shares in the company which formed part of her estate at her death, that that holding was not relevant business property for the purposes of relief from inheritance tax, on the ground that it was excluded from the category of relevant business property by *IHTA 1984, s 105(3)* because the business of the company consisted wholly or mainly in the making or holding of investments. The executor appealed.

The Commissioner concluded that, standing back and looking at the matter in the round in the light of relevant decisions of the Special Commissioners, the pitch fees were not ancillary to caravan sales; the caravan sales were ancillary to pitch fees at the park. The company operated a caravan park, and was not a dealer selling caravans. Accordingly, the business of the company consisted mainly in making or holding investments. The notice of determination would therefore be upheld. [2000] STC SCD 30 Sp C 222.

Subsequently W's executor appealed. The Special Commissioner dismissed the appeal, applying *Hall & Hall (Hall's Executors) v CIR*, and distinguishing *Furness v CIR*. The Ch D upheld this decision as one of fact. [2000] STC 1064; Ch D [2000] All ER (D) 1870.

Wheatley and another (Executors of Wheatley deceased) v CIR

Grazing of horses on pasture-whether meadow qualified for APR within provisions of IHTA 1984, s 117.

An individual (W) owned a meadow, which he let to a women who owned some horses. She used the meadow for grazing her horses, paying rent to W. W died in 1997 and the Revenue issued notices of determination charging inheritance tax. W's executors appealed, contending that the meadow qualified for agricultural property relief. The Special Commissioner rejected this contention and dismissed the appeal, holding that, although the meadow constituted 'pasture' within *IHTA 1984, s 115 (2)*, it was not 'occupied for the purposes of agriculture', as required by *IHTA 1984, s 117*. On the evidence, the horses which grazed the meadow 'were not connected with agriculture' but were used by their owner for 'leisure pursuits'. Horses were not 'livestock' and grazing by horses would only fall within the provisions of *s 117* if the horses were connected with agriculture, which was not the case here. [1998] STC SCD 60 Sp C 149.

Whittaker v CIR

IHT liabilities – IHTA 1984, s 162 – foreign tax payable.

In a Scottish case where the facts are not fully set out in the decision, the Revenue issued a notice of determination in respect of a chargeable transfer of £334,771. The deceased's executor appealed, contending that the determination did not take account of a sum owed to the Italian tax authorities. The Special Commissioner dismissed the appeal, holding that the appellant had not shown that any further Italian tax was payable (and observing that, if any such tax were found to be due, double taxation relief would apply). [2001] STC SCD 61 Sp C 272. (*Note*. The appellant appeared in person.)

Wight and Moss v CIR

Valuation – joint property – value of half share.

Two women lived in a house which they owned as tenants in common in equal shares. When one of them died the value of her half share in the house had to be ascertained for CTT purposes. It was agreed that the other co-owner would be the most likely purchaser and that this was a relevant factor in the valuation. The Lands Tribunal held that the value was half vacant possession value less a discount to reflect the restricted demand for this type of interest. It was held that it was not likely that an outside purchaser would be able to obtain an order for sale under *Law of Property Act 1925, s 30* and, reflecting this, that the discount should be 15% rather than the 10% which had become customary following the earlier decision in *Cust v CIR* (1917) 91 EG 11. Lands Tribunal, [1982] 264 EG 935.

Williams (Williams' Personal Representative) v HMRC

'Broiler houses' used for intensive rearing of poultry – whether 'agricultural property' within IHTA 1984, s 115(2).

A farm occupied 7.41 acres of land. Part of the land was used for three 'broiler houses', which were used for the intensive rearing of poultry. In April 2000 the owner of the farm (W) let the broiler houses, and 2.59 acres of the land, to a company (S). W died in 2001. The Inland Revenue issued a ruling that the broiler houses, and the 2.59 acres of land which had been let to S, did not qualify as 'agricultural property' within *IHTA 1984, s 115(2)*. W's personal representative appealed. The Special Commissioner reviewed the evidence in detail and allowed the appeal in part, holding that the effect of *s 115(2)* was that the broiler houses could only qualify for relief if they had been 'a subsidiary part of the purpose of an overall agricultural activity carried out on the land'. Since they had been let to a separate company, this was not the case. Accordingly, the broiler houses had not been 'ancillary' to the farm, within *s 115(2)*, and did not qualify for relief. However, on the evidence, the broiler houses only occupied 0.68 acres of land. The Commissioner held that the remaining 1.91 acres of land which had been let to S was within the definition of 'agricultural property' and did qualify for relief. [2005] STC SCD 782 Sp C 500.

Willett and another (Mrs Benson's Executors) v CIR

Valuation – value of freehold interest in tenanted agricultural property.

The owner of a freehold interest in tenanted agricultural land died in 1977. The Revenue valued the interest for CTT purposes at £45,000. The executors appealed, contending that the valuation should be £28,000. The Lands Tribunal reviewed the evidence in detail and held that the valuation should be £39,000. The Tribunal reaffirmed the principle that a valuation must assume property is suitably lotted if it would fetch a better price if sold in that way, applying *Earl of Ellesmere v CIR* [1918] 2 KB 735. Although the length of time the tenant would continue in occupation was a relevant factor in the executors' valuation, the Tribunal rejected a strict life expectancy approach in favour of the Revenue's method of using the number of years before his probable retirement at the age of 75. In one of the two methods of valuation used by the Revenue, the vacant possession value had been taken at £70,000, and an allowance of £25,000 had been deducted from this, being an estimate of the amount a prospective purchaser would consider appropriate to cover deferment and obtain possession. The Tribunal held that the estimate was too low in view of the fact that the purchaser would be taking a considerable risk as to whether the tenant would vacate for £25,000, and bearing in mind a purchaser's requirement for profit. The Revenue's alternative method was to divide the vacant possession value between the 'pure investment value' (taking the reversion in perpetuity) and the 'vacant possession element' and to add 40% of the latter to the former, 40% being assumed to be what the tenant would pay to obtain the freehold interest. The Land Tribunal upheld this method in principle but held that the addition should be 33% rather than 40%. *Lands Tribunal 1982, 264 EG 257.*

Wills v Gibbs and Others

Rectification of deed of variation.

A farmer died in 2005, leaving most of his interest in the farm to his cousin (W). W wished to redirect some of his entitlement to his son by way of a deed of variation under *IHTA 1984, s 142(1)*. The farmer's solicitors prepared a deed of variation, but failed to include the statutory statement required to bring the deed within *s 142*. The solicitors subsequently noticed the omission, and W's son applied to the Ch D for rectification of the deed. The Ch D granted the application, applying the principles laid down in *Racal Group Services Ltd v Ashmore & Others*. Ch D [2008] STC 808.

Winans and Another v A-G (No 2)

Situation of property – bearer securities.

Bearer securities transferable by delivery are situate in the UK if the certificate of title is in the UK. HL 1909, [1910] AC 27.

Wolff & Wolff v Wolff and Others

IHT avoidance scheme – whether transaction may be set aside. Scheme set aside by use of Civil Procedure Rules.

A married couple owned a freehold property. They sought advice from a solicitor with a view to avoiding inheritance tax. On the solicitor's advice, in 1997 they entered into a reversionary lease of the property in favour of their daughters, to begin in 2017. Subsequently they became aware that the effect of the lease was that they would have no right to remain in the property after 2017. They applied to the Ch D to set aside the reversionary lease under the *Civil Procedure Rules 1998, SI 1998/3132 Part 8*. The Ch D granted their application. Mann J observed that the relevant deed was 'manifestly defective as a piece of drafting' and that the solicitor 'did not fully understand the implications of what he had brought about'. On the evidence, the couple 'did not know that the effect of the lease was to deprive them of their right to occupy the property in 2017'. Applying *dicta* of Millett J in *Gibbon v Mitchell*, Ch D [1990] 3 All ER 338, 'wherever there is a voluntary transaction by which one party intends to confer a bounty on another, the deed will be set aside if the court is satisfied that the disponor did not intend the transaction to have the effect which it did'. Ch D [2004] STC 1633.

Woodhall (Woodhall's Personal Representatives) v CIR

IHTA 1984, s 50(5) – interest in part of property.

An individual (GW) died in 1957, leaving three children. Under his will, he left his house to his two sons as trustees, and directed that it should not be sold as long as any of his three children was living in it. One of his sons (EW) had already moved out when GW died, and his daughter moved out the following year. However, his other son (AW) continued to live in the house until he died in 1997. The Revenue issued a notice of determination on the basis that, when AW died, he had a beneficial interest in the whole of the house. His personal representative appealed, accepting that the house was settled property but contending firstly that AW was not beneficially entitled to an interest in possession, and alternatively that he only had such an interest in one half of the house, as his brother (EW) had a beneficial entitlement to the other half. (Their sister had died in 1971.) The Special Commissioner accepted this contention and allowed the appeal in part, holding that the effect of GW's will was that, in 1997, both AW and EW 'had the right to claim to occupy the house jointly with the other'. Accordingly, when AW died, he was beneficially entitled to an interest in possession in the house within the meaning of *IHTA 1984, s 49(1)*, but that his interest subsisted in only half of the house, within *IHTA 1984, s 50(5)*. [2000] STC SCD 558 Sp C 261.

Young and Another v Phillips

Situs – location of letters of allotment.

Two brothers resident and ordinarily resident in the UK, but domiciled in South Africa, owned equally the ordinary shares of three associated UK companies, each with substantial sums to the credit of its profit and loss account. On professional advice, during 1978–79 they implemented a pre-arranged scheme with the aim of 'exporting' the shares outside the UK (and so taking them outside the scope of CTT) without incurring any CGT liability. In brief, each company created new preferred ordinary shares, ranking pari passu with the existing ordinary shares save for priority in a capital repayment on a winding up; capitalised the amounts credited to profit and loss; appropriated these amounts to the taxpayers and used them in paying up, in full, new preferred ordinary shares issued to them, in respect of which the company issued to them renounceable letters of allotment. Shortly afterwards two Channel Island companies, set up for the purpose, issued to the taxpayers shares at a premium of £1,364,216 and resolved to buy from them (by now directors of the Channel Island companies) their preferred ordinary shares in the UK companies for £1,364,216. The taxpayers then went to Sark with their letters of allotment and the scheme was completed by, *inter alia*, letters of renunciation in favour of the Channel Island companies. CGT assessments were made on the basis that there had been a disposal of assets situated in the UK. The Special Commissioners dismissed the taxpayers' appeals, and the Ch D upheld their decision. Nicholls J held that there had been a disposal of rights against the UK companies, and that these were situated in the UK irrespective of where the letters of allotment happened to be. Further, even had he held that there had been a disposal of assets outside the UK, *W T Ramsay Ltd* and *Furniss v Dawson*, would have applied, and he would have accepted an alternative Revenue contention that *TCGA 1992, s 29(2)** applied, the relieving provisions of *TCGA 1992, ss 127, 135** being curtailed by *TCGA 1992, s 137(1)** because one of the main purposes of the issuing of the shares in the UK companies was the avoidance of liability to tax. Ch D 1984, 58 TC 232; [1984] STC 520.

59

Finance Act 2015

Summary of IHT provisions

[59.1] The main changes applicable to inheritance tax in the *Finance Act 2015 (FA 2015)* are in sections 74 and 75 but there are also important changes to the penalty regime in Schedule 20.

Changes relating to the calculation of charges on relevant property trusts were expected to be included in this Finance Act, but due to the announcement of the General Election, these were deferred to the Summer 2015 Finance Bill which is to be enacted in October 2015.

Exemption for decorations and other awards

[59.2] A new exemption from IHT is made available by *FA 2015, s 74* with effect for transfers of value made on or after 3 December 2014. The exemption broadly applies to decorations or awards for valour or gallant conduct within the armed forces or the emergency services personnel.

Exemption on death of emergency service personnel and police service personnel

[59.3] The inheritance tax provisions, and before them the legislation relating to death duties, contain an exemption from liability where death occurs due to active war service, or due to a major health issue which arose during such service. This exemption is now extended in relation to deaths occurring on or after 19 March 2014 to emergency personnel, such as fire or ambulance staff, who die of an injury, accident or disease which arose due to their work. A similar exemption is provided for those in the police service who die of health issues sustained in the duties of their job.

Penalties

[59.4] The income tax and capital gains tax legislation has in recent years included provisions for higher penalties to apply where there are failures in relation to offshore matters. These higher penalties have not so far applied to inheritance tax but this is now set to change with effect from April 2016. Where an inaccuracy in an IHT return relates to an 'offshore transfer' or an 'offshore matter', higher penalties will apply depending on the overseas territory concerned. Territories will be sorted into different categories according to the level of disclosure of information which they supply to HMRC.

In addition, with effect from 27 March 2015 a new penalty applies where an asset is moved from a 'specified territory' to a 'non-specified territory' with a view to avoiding detection by HMRC of liability to IHT in respect of the asset. These provisions are in Schedule 21 to the Act and they apply an additional 50% of any earlier penalty for deliberate error, where an asset move of this type has been made between countries overseas.

60 Table of Statutes

L

V

W

61 Table of Statutory Instruments

62 Table of Cases

Note that a number of key cases are summarised at CHAPTER 58.

C

D

E

F

G

H

I

J

K

L

M

N

O

P

R

S

T

V

W

Y

Z

[illegible]

63 Index

This index is referenced to chapter and paragraph number.

C

E

F

G

H

J

L

T

U